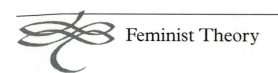

Feminist Theory

FEMINIST THEORY

A Reader

Wendy K. Kolmar

Drew University

Frances Bartkowski

Rutgers University

Mayfield Publishing Company
Mountain View, California
London • Toronto

Library of Congress Cataloging-in-Publication Data
Feminist theory : a reader / [compiled by] Wendy K. Kolmar, Frances
   Bartkowski.
      p.   cm.
   Includes bibliographical references.
   ISBN 1-55934-925-5
   1. Feminist theory. 2. Women—Social conditions. I. Kolmar,
Wendy K., 1950– . II. Bartkowski, Frances, 1948–
HQ1190.F4633   1999
305.42'01—dc21
                                     99-22903
                                       CIP

Manufactured in the United States of America
10   9   8   7   6   5   4

Mayfield Publishing Company
1280 Villa Street
Mountain View, California 94041

Sponsoring editor, Franklin C. Graham; production, Michael Bass & Associates; manuscript editor, Helen Walden; design manager, Jean Mailander; text and cover designer, Joan Greenfield; manufacturing manager, Randy Hurst. The text was set in 9.5/12 Plantin Light by Thompson Type and printed on 45# Custom LG by The Banta Book Group.

Cover art: Judy Dunworth, collage, *indeterminate space #8*, 36" × 22"

Text credits continue at the back of the book on pages 524–526, which constitute an extension of the copyright page.

Contents

Preface

This reader emerged from our need for a fairly comprehensive theory text for our own feminist theory courses, a text that would represent the history, intellectual breadth, and theoretical diversity of Anglo-American feminist writing. As women's studies faculty members, we have both taught feminist theory courses for more than a decade, but neither of us has found wholly satisfactory texts for those courses. Like many other faculty, we have pieced together syllabi by ordering one or two of the available texts and supplementing them with articles selected from a wide range of journals, anthologies, and books. Whatever choices we've made, we've found the various permutations and combinations inadequate to cover the field as we would wish.

As the field of feminist theory has grown and more and more anthologies have become available, we've tried many of them in our courses. All these anthologies have contributed in some way to the development of our courses, but they remain, for the most part, too narrowly focused to work well in core undergraduate courses. In general, we've faced three major frustrations with them. First, most texts and readers are organized around the categories of traditional political theory; that is, liberal, Marxist/socialist, radical, or by way of disciplines—psychoanalytic or sociological, for example. Neither mode of organization seems to us quite sufficient as a representation of the breadth of feminist theory. Second, the emphasis in these texts is most often on theory as exclusively the product of contemporary feminism. Third, few texts offer students a sense of the historical context or of the development of the arguments that now constitute contemporary feminist theories.

In compiling this book, we set out to produce a collection that would be useful within a number of different course organizations and that would clearly historicize feminist thought. For it, we have selected readings that present feminist thought as the province of women of different races, classes, nationalities, sexualities, etc., from its inception, readings that suggest a strong sense of continuity in the discussions taken up by feminist theory in spite of historical ruptures, silences, and amnesia.

In selecting writings for this collection, we have chosen largely from feminist theory written in Britain and the United States, both because of our own location and because of the development of academic women's studies within U.S. colleges and universities. Those continental texts included have been chosen because of their importance as spurs to complicating the debates within Anglo-American theory. For each period, we have selected texts produced inside and outside the academy. Though academic texts dominate in the later sections, we have, through the inclusion of manifestos, the founding statements of organizations, and the Beijing Platform for Action, indicated the ways in which feminist theorizing continues outside the academy.

To represent the breadth and variety of the feminist theoretical conversations in each period as well as the continuities between periods, we have often had to choose one or two voices to exemplify a more extended conversation. Although we have included here major pieces that women's studies teachers and students would expect to find in such a collection, we have sometimes also chosen pieces because they elaborate a particular discussion or because they present other important aspects of a writer's work.

We have sought to create a flexible resource that supports many different approaches to organizing feminist theory courses. A semester course might be organized chronologically or by simply using the ten debates framed in the lexicon, by selecting several of these debates to be explored in greater depth or by pairing early theorists with contemporary texts. We have, however, also provided in the first two sections approaches and strategies for reading feminist theory and some contexts for grappling with the specialized discourse of the field.

The choices we have made in compiling this reader grow out of our separate experiences of teaching women's studies courses and administering women's studies programs in two very different kinds of institutions in northern New Jersey. One of us teaches undergraduate and graduate students in a small, residential, private liberal arts university; the other teaches undergraduate and graduate students in a somewhat larger, urban, public state university with a study body made up primarily of commuters. Based on our own experiences and ongoing conversations with women's studies faculty in other institutions, we believe that this collection can be tailored to suit the needs of students of differing interests, abilities, and objectives in feminist theory courses in most institutions whether public or private, large or small.

The existence of this text depends on the work of so many other teachers, scholars, and students of feminist theory that it would be impossible to list or name everyone here. Every sentence we've written has been informed by what we've learned by teaching and reading the theorists whose work is included here or mentioned in a lexicon or cited in a bibliography. Those sentences also depend on insights we've gained from conversations with our students in our feminist theory courses and with many of our colleagues at our own and other institutions, in corridors, at lunch, and in conference sessions and meetings.

In particular, however, we would like to thank: Mary Margaret Fonow (Ohio State University), Kate Hausbeck (University of Nevada, Las Vegas), Angela E. Hubler (Kansas State University), Jeanne Kohl (University of Washington), and Sally McNall, (California State University at Chico) for their helpful reading of the preliminary manuscript; Dean Paolo Cucchi (Drew University), Dean David Hosford (Rutgers University-Newark), and Associate Dean Virginia Tiger (Rutgers University-Newark) for resources to support this project; Deborah Williams and Lisa Tomaszewski, our student assistants; Terri Green, Kristen Anderson (Drew), Renae Bredin (California

State University, Fullerton), Claire Buck (Brandeis), Jody Caldwell (Drew), Judy Gerson (Rutgers), Dorene Isenberg (Drew), Sandra Jamieson (Drew), Paula Krebs (Wheaton), Nadine Ollman (Drew), Traci West (Drew), and Bonnie Zimmerman (San Diego State), colleagues at our own and other institutions who recommended readings, read sections of the text, and offered support through the process; the National Women's Studies Association, where this project began and which provided a forum for discussing the book as it evolved; Frank Graham, April Wells-Hayes, and Marty Granahan at Mayfield Publishing Company and Tobi Giannone at Michael Bass & Associates for their encouragement, guidance, and patience; Jules Bartkowski and Anna Rachel Kolmar Muldoon, our children, for their tolerance; and finally, again, the engaged and enthusiastic students from many years of feminist theory classes, who are, after all, the reason for this book.

PART I

What Is Feminist Theory?
What Is Feminism?

Reading Feminist Theory

"I came to theory desperate, wanting to comprehend—to grasp what was happening around and within me"—bell hooks

This book is a collection of readings loosely grouped under the rubric "feminist theory." As you begin to read, you may be nervous, unsure of what you will find here, and perhaps a little put off, because of both the "feminist" part of its title and the "theory" part. Unfortunately, for many students the word "feminist" conjures up scary man-haters, and the word "theory" suggests equally scary and totally unintelligible texts written in unfamiliar language. We trust you will come to realize that neither of those preconceived notions adequately describes the variety of views, voices, and writings included in this book.

Put most simply, feminist theory is a body of writing that attempts to describe, explain, and analyze the conditions of women's lives. According to Charlotte Bunch, feminist theory is "a way of viewing the world"; it "provides a basis for understanding every area of our lives" (Bunch, "Not by Degrees," 250). According to bell hooks, it is a way "to grasp what is happening around and within" us (hooks, "Theory as Liberatory Practice," 59). Feminist theory also proposes strategies for activism and action to ameliorate the conditions in which women live and work.

The basic issue that has concerned feminist theory is, depending on the terms one prefers, women's inequality, subordination, or domination by men. At the root of these is the issue of gender asymmetry—the designation of women and things associated with women as different from, inferior to, of lesser value than men and things associated with men. Feminist theories examine and try to explain the causes and conditions in which men are more powerful and men's production, ideas, and activities are seen as having greater value and higher status than women's. For many feminist theorists this comes to mean examining and explaining all structures of domination, whether based on gender, race, class, age, sexuality, nation, or some other difference.

How any feminist theory explains and proposes to address gender asymmetry depends on the assumptions forming the basis of that theory. For example, psychoanalytic feminist theories locate the sources of gender asymmetry in the familial and psychosexual processes that form individual psyches. Materialist feminist theories pay more attention to the ways that concrete economic and social conditions contribute to gender inequality. Feminist theorists of color ground their theory in the assumption that the women's lives cannot be understood without also understanding the role of race/ethnicity in shaping their experience. As a reader of feminist theory, you will learn to tease out the assumptions that underpin each theory and to understand how they affect the theory's explanation of women's situation and the solutions proposed to ameliorate the conditions of women's lives.

Through the choices we made in putting this book together, we want to suggest several things about feminist theory. First, theorizing has been done by many women in many different situations and from many perspectives. Second, feminist theories have a history but not one that is unilinear or monocausal. Third, our reading of contemporary theory needs to be grounded in this history of debates and conversations.

Over its history, feminist theorizing has been an activity engaged in by many women in many different situations. We have tried to suggest this variety by including a range of writing from manifestos to scholarly essays. Among these are readings by political and social activists, scholars and academics, poor women, working-class women, and priviliged women. Women of different sexual orientations and racial and ethnic backgrounds are included, as well as women writing out of different national backgrounds and religious traditions. For example, in the 1792–1920 section an excerpt from Mary Wollstonecraft's *Vindication of the Rights of Women* immediately follows an early Navajo origin myth in order to suggest that feminist theory has many points of origin and lines of development. Wollstonecraft's liberal humanist argument for the rights of women is one origin point often cited in the history of feminist thought; we suggest that the Navajo myth's attempt to understand the place of woman in creation is another among many possible points of origin. The writers we include here have not always named their writing "feminist," nor have they always named it "theory." They are included because their writing engages in the activities and thought we describe as feminist theorizing; that is, they attempt to explain women's situation, to understand gender asymmetry, or to understand unequal distributions of privilege and power using gender as one element of their analysis.

Although thinking that meets our definition of feminist theory has probably been done in most cultures and nations, we do not attempt to represent that kind of breadth here. This reader centers on U.S. feminist theory produced in the last two hundred years. It includes some British, French, and Third World theorists who have been particularly important to the development of feminist theory in the United States, but the history it represents is largely that which grounds contemporary feminist theory in the United States.

However, in the choices we have made here, we are not trying to delineate, even for the United States, what Rosalind Delmar calls "a progressive and cumulative history of feminism." Rather we want to provide a body of material that allows us to study, as Delmar suggests we should, the "dynamics of persistence and change within feminism" (Delmar, "What Is Feminism?" 18). In other words, we want to suggest that certain ideas, issues, and themes are discussed and debated throughout the history of feminism and feminist theory, although theorists' approaches to those issues depend on each writer's perspective and historical and social location. For example, you will find writings in every time period discussing the sexual division of labor and power in one way or another, although how those divisions between the sexes are understood may vary. On the other hand, new insights and perspectives do emerge within feminism. Some of these are triggered by dialogue with other intellectual and social movements, some by the evolution of thinking within women's movements, and still others as a result of historical, political, and social developments and crises.

CONTENTS AND ORGANIZATION OF THE READER

We believe that the organization of this reader, with the majority of the readings in chronological order, allows you best to explore this multifaceted history of persistence and change within feminist theory. This organization is flexible, so that the readings can be approached in a variety of ways. At the same time, the reader provides various tools for contextualizing the selections and grappling with the sometimes difficult language and thought you will encounter while reading these examples of feminist theory.

The readings in the first section give you some preliminary definitions of feminism and of feminist theory. To work effectively with feminist theory, you will need to pay close attention to the language and terminology utilized by different theorists and to notice when theorists share terms, redefine terms, or use terms in very different ways. We have tried to suggest the importance of close attention to words and definitions by beginning our first section with multiple definitions of "feminist" and "feminism" taken from *The Feminist Dictionary* and by creating the "Lexicon" entries, which will help you associate some of the major debates in feminist theory with key words and terms.

The "Lexicon of the Debates," which follows the introductory section of readings, identifies 10 debates that are central to contemporary feminist theory. Most, but not all of these debates, surface in some way in the feminist theorizing done in earlier periods. Each lexicon entry attempts to trace both the persistence of and the changes in each thread of debate, using as examples selections from this reader. It would be possible to organize your reading of most, if not all, of the material by following the multiple threads of thought identified in the lexicon. In addition, the lexicon entries will familiarize you with important words and terms associated with each debate.

After these initial sections, the readings are organized into five chronological periods:

II	1792–1920
III	1920–1963
IV	1963–1975
V	1975–1985
VI	1985–1995

The boundaries of these periods are to some extent arbitrary, but the dates seem to us to mark, in broad terms, significant historical and epistemological shifts in women's movements and thought over the past three centuries. Our understanding of those shifts is sketched briefly here; each section introduction provides further historical context.

The reader begins with Mary Wollstonecraft's *Vindication of the Rights of Woman,* published in England in 1792. We begin at this point because Wollstonecraft's text is arguably one of the first in the Anglo-American tradition that attempts overtly to theorize the position of women within the dominant political and social discourses of its moment. Although issues of concern to later feminist theory are certainly raised by earlier writers (for example, Christine de Pisan, Sor Juana, Julian of Norwich), we chose Wollstonecraft's text as our starting point for its attempt at comprehensive analysis and because it has been viewed as a significant origin text by later feminist theorists.

Part II of the book ends with 1920, the year in which women in the United States were granted the right to vote. We chose the date of suffrage as our first division because, before its achievement, the demand for women's enfranchisement in politics and other areas dominated much of the thinking about women, even by those who felt that centering suffrage as THE issue for women was a mistake. The achievement of suffrage, a crucial moment of democratic, political victory for women, brought feminist concerns into public culture and discourse. After that moment, however, conversations about women and feminism were necessarily redirected and refocused.

Part III begins with 1920 and ends with 1963, the date of the publication of *The Feminine Mystique,* the text most historians identify as giving birth to the second wave of the U.S. women's movement. This period between the achievement of the vote and the 1960s is often viewed as an era of diminished feminist activity. The only text from this second period usually included in feminist theory anthologies and courses is Simone de Beauvior's *The Second Sex.* However, writing and thinking about women continued throughout this period and across a variety of disciplines and areas, as the material we have included here demonstrates.

Unlike Parts II and III of the reader, the latter parts are defined not so much by specific historical events or publication dates, as they are by shifts in the prevailing discourse and concerns of feminist theory. These shifts are gradual and evolve over a number of years through the impact of a variety of conversations and challenges, but they seem to us to bear fruit in changes that are roughly marked by the years 1975 and 1985.

The period 1963 through 1975, covered in Part IV of the reader, is defined largely by theorizing done as a part of the activism of the women's movement. In contrast, the period 1975 through 1985, comprising Part V, is characterized by theory produced primarily and for the first time by academic women associated with the new field of women's studies. This latter period is characterized by institution building within women's studies (founding of women's studies programs, campus women's centers, curriculum transformation projects, and the formation of the National Women's Studies Association); feminist canon formation and the continuing rediscovery of women's lives, texts, and practices; and efforts to disseminate this expanding body of knowledge and methods across the disciplines.

Between 1985 and 1995, covered by Part VI, the development of feminist theory shifts in response both to multiple challenges from within and to intellectual and global change outside its borders. Internal critiques come from groups who have felt excluded from feminism as an academic discourse, among them women of color, Third World women, poor and working-class women, grass-roots activists, older women, and women with disabilities. External intellectual influences on feminist inquiry come from postmodernism, cultural studies, queer theory, gay and lesbian studies, postcolonial theory, global feminist movements, ethnic studies, and the biological and information sciences, as well as from massive shifts in global power relations, social arrangements, reproductive technologies, and the global rise of fundamentalism. Although in some quarters feminism and feminists beat a hasty retreat in the face of backlash and an expanding conservative climate. At its best, feminist work and thinkers have shown their perennial willingness to respond to change in a dialectical manner, as the pieces included here demonstrate.

The reader ends around 1995, the year in which some 40,000 women gathered in Beijing and Huairou for the Fourth U.N. Conference on Women to attempt to articulate a common global agenda for change in women's lives. And it also seems to us that another sea change in feminist theory is inevitable and already underway.

Throughout much of the history we have traced here, the phrases "women's thinking" or "feminist theory" were considered oxymorons. For most of the history of Western culture, and certainly since the seventeenth-century philosopher Descartes theorized a split between the mind and the body, women have been associated with nature, the body, the concrete conditions of life, whereas men have been associated with culture, the mind and intellect, and abstract philosophizing. Throughout much of this period, women have had little access to higher education and intellectual culture, and still today women have differential access to educational, intellectual, and cultural resources. Yet as the selections in this reader profoundly demonstrate, women have thought in thorough and complex ways about their own condition, their bodies and their lives, social, political, and cultural institutions, creativity and science, justice and liberty. Like bell hooks, they have found in the activity of theorizing many ways "to grasp what was happening around and within" them, to comprehend it and to change it.

1

Feminism

PAULA TREICHLER and
CHERIS KRAMARAE

FEMINISM

(See all entries above and below)

A movement with a long history. Three basic positions of feminism during 1400–1789: (1) a conscious stand in opposition to male defamation and mistreatment of women; a dialectical opposition to misogyny. (2) a belief that the sexes are culturally, and not just biologically, formed; a belief that women were a social group shaped to fit male notions about a defective sex. (3) an outlook that transcended the accepted value systems of the time by exposing and opposing the prejudice and narrowness; a desire for a truly general conception of humanity. (Joan Kelly 1982, 6–7)

Has as its goal to give every woman "the opportunity of becoming the best that her natural faculties make her capable of." (Millicent Garrett Fawcett 1878, 357)

Has as a goal: The liberation of women for women. "We don't have to have anything to do with men at all. They've taken excellent care of themselves." (Jill Johnston 1973, 91)

"May be defined as a movement seeking the reorganization of the world upon a basis of sex-equality in all human relations; a movement which would reject every differentiation between individuals upon the ground of sex, would abolish all sex privileges and sex burdens, and would strive to set up the recognition of the common humanity of woman and man as the foundation of law and custom." (Teresa Billington-Greig 1911, 694, 703)

". . . has as yet no defined creed. . . . [Is] the articulate consciousness of mind in women . . . in its different forms of expression." ("The Freewoman" 1911, *Votes for Women,* 17 November, 103)

Is that part of the progress of democratic freedom which applies to women. (Beatrice Forbes-Robertson Hale 1914, 3)

"A many-headed monster which cannot be destroyed by singular decapitation. We spread and grow in ways that are incomprehensible to a hierarchical mentality." (Peggy Kornegger 1979, 243)

"Feminism at heart is a massive complaint. Lesbianism is the solution. . . . Until all women are lesbians there will be no true political revolution. No feminist per se has advanced a solution outside of accommodation to the man." (Jill Johnston 1973a, 166)

"An integration of various here-to-fore incompatible elements built on a collective base of thought–action–feeling. Feminism integrates the subjective and objective, the rational and the intuitive, the mystical and the scientific, the abstract and concrete aspects of the universe and considers them harmonious parts of a whole rather than in opposition to one another." (Anne Kent Rush and Anica Vesel Mander 1974, 14–15)

"Begins but cannot end with the discovery by an individual of her self-consciousness as a woman. It is not, finally, even the recognition of her reasons for anger, or the decision to change her life, to go back to school, to leave a marriage. . . . Feminism means finally that we renounce our obedience to the fathers and recognize that the world they have described is not the whole world. . . . Feminism implies that we recognize fully the inadequacy for us, the distortion, of male-created ideologies, and that we proceed to think, and act, out of that recognition." (Adrienne Rich 1976; rpt. 1979, 207)

"A method of analysis as well as a discovery of new material. It asks new questions as well as coming up with new answers. Its central concern is with the social distinction between men and women, with the fact of this distinction, with its meanings, and with its causes and consequences." (Juliet Mitchell and Ann Oakley 1976, 14)

"We are actively committed to struggling against racial, sexual, heterosexual, and class oppression and see as our particular task the development of integrated analysis and practice based upon the fact that the major systems of oppression are interlocking. The synthesis of these oppressions creates the conditions of our lives. As Black women we see Black feminism as the logical political movement to combat the manifold and simultaneous oppressions that all women of color face." (Combahee River Collective 1977; rpt. in Cherríe Moraga and Gloria Anzaldúa eds 1981, 210)

Women uniting as women to generate "a force which presses society to accept and accommodate femaleness as equal, even if different, in its attributes." (Devaki Jain 1978, 9)

"Potentially the most threatening of movements to Black and other Third World people because it makes it absolutely essential that we examine the way we live, how we treat each other, and what we believe. It calls into question the most basic assumptions about our existence and this is the idea that biological, i.e., sexual identity, determines all, that it is the rationale for power relationships as well as for all levels of human identity and action." (Barbara Smith 1983, xxv–xxvi)

"Is a mode of analysis, a method of approaching life and politics, a way of asking questions and searching for answers, rather than a set of political conclusions about the oppression of women." (Nancy Hartsock 1979, 58–59)

"Feminism is the political theory and practice to free all women: women of color, working-class women, poor women, physically challenged women, lesbians, old women, as well as white economically privileged heterosexual women. Anything less than this is not feminism, but merely female self-aggrandizement." (Barbara Smith 1979; quoted in Cherríe Moraga and Gloria Anzaldúa eds 1981, 61)

(See BLACK FEMINISM)

Woman responding to question, "As an Asian American woman, do you consider yourself a feminist?": "There is feminism where all the problems of women in society are seen as caused by men. I don't believe in that. I don't believe men are the creators of the problems in society. . . . I do believe that men and women have to work together to solve the problems in society." (In Susie Ling's dissertation; quoted by Lucie Cheng 1984, 11)

"Feminism means you have to read a lot, to understand a lot, to feel a lot, and to be honest." "To me, real feminism means being revolutionary. To be revolutionary means that one examines the problems of women from all aspects: historically, sociologically, economically, and psychologically. . . . And as a radical feminist, I think you should oppose imperialism, Zionism, feudalism, and inequality between nations, sexes, and classes." (Nawal el Saadawi 1980, 3)

A philosophy "based on the recognition that we live in a male dominated culture in which women remain unacknowledged, and where women are forced into sex roles which demand that they be dependent, passive, nurturant, etc. Men too must assume sex roles [but these] are not nearly as crippling as women's." (*Banshee: Journal of Irishwomen United* 1981, 8:10)

"Is a commitment to eradicating the ideology of domination that permeates Western culture on various levels—sex, race, and class, to name a few—and a commitment to reorganizing U.S. society, so that the self-development of people can take precedence over imperialism, economic expansion, and material desires." (bell hooks 1981, 194–195)

"Means to me the movement towards creating a society where women can live a full, self-determined life. This may seem a bland statement but in terms of the changes we need to achieve this, it is revolutionary." (Mary MacNamara c. 1982, 6)

Is "the desire and struggle for freedom," which is the same for each of us—Black, Latina, Native American, etc.—"even though our methods may differ." (Deborah Aslan Jamieson 1982, 6)

"Is an entire world view or *gestalt*, not just a laundry list of 'women's issues.' Feminist theory provides a basis for understanding every area of our lives, and a feminist perspective can affect the world politically, culturally, economically, and spiritually." (Charlotte Bunch 1983, 250)

"Two elements constitute the discipline of feminism: political, ideological, and strategic confrontation with the sex–class system—with sex hierarchy and sex segregation—and a single standard of human dignity. Abandon either element and the sex–class system is unbreachable, indestructible; feminism loses its rigor, the toughness of its visionary heart. . . . One other discipline is essential both to the practice of feminism and to its theoretical integrity: the firm, unsentimental, continuous recognition that women are a class having a common condition." (Andrea Dworkin 1983, 200)

"Is a theory that calls for women's attainment of social, economic, and political rights and opportunities equal to those possessed by men. Feminism is also a model for a social state—an ideal, or a desired standard of perfection not yet attained in the world." (Rebecca Lewin 1983, 17)

Is the fairy godmother. "Do you remember the story of Cinderella? She is sitting at home rather pissed off, wanting to go to the ball, and not having a thing to wear, when the fairy godmother whizzes in and puts it all right. One of the most important things about the fairy godmother is that she transforms all the old stuff around Cinderella into new and useful equipment: the rags, the pumpkin, the rats, and so forth. This little girl's fairy godmother turned out to be called Feminism. As well as cheering the little girl up no end Feminism also transformed all the old things around her." (Sara Maitland 1983, 18)

"Third World feminism is about feeding people in all their hungers." (Cherríe Moraga 1983, 132) "[It] is bringing the strains together." (Barbara Smith; quoted in Cherríe Moraga 1983, 133)

Is a powerful homeopathic remedy which goes beyond the symptoms to the deeper causes of our troubles: the imbalance between masculine and feminine energies, manifested in the ills of patriarchy. (Jill Raymond and Janice Wilson 1983, 59)

Is neither original nor radical; women's ideas about the relationship of women and men are either coopted or lost by men and have to be recreated every fifty years or so. (Dale Spender 1982)

A set of beliefs and "theoretical constructions about the nature of women's oppression and the part that this oppression plays within social reality more generally." (Liz Stanley and Sue Wise 1983, 55)

With a capital 'F' it is a theory, a position. With small 'f' it is an organic conviction based on experience. (Osha Davidson 1984, 11A)

• • •

FEMINIST

"I myself have never been able to find out precisely what feminism is: I only know that people call me a feminist whenever I express sentiments that differentiate me from a doormat . . ." (Rebecca West 1913, *The Clarion*, Nov. 14)

"Mother, what is a Feminist?"

"A Feminist, my daughter,
Is any woman now who cares
To think about her own affairs
    As men don't think she oughter"
    (Alice Duer Miller 1915; in Redstockings eds 1975, 52)

"Feminist is formed with the word 'femme,' 'woman,' and means: someone who fights for women. For many of us this means someone who fights for women as a class and for the disappearance of this class. For many others it means someone who fights for woman and her defense—for the myth, then, and its reinforcement." (Monique Wittig 1981, 50)

A person who knows that we hold up half the sky and who is going to make everyone else notice it. (Dawn Russell 1979, 75)

What is unique about the feminist mode of analysis: "(1) The focus on everyday life and experience makes action a necessity, not a moral choice or an option. We are not fighting other people's battles but our own. (2) The nature of our understanding of theory is altered and theory is brought into an integral and everyday relation with practice. (3) Theory leads directly to a transformation of social relations both in consciousness and in reality because of its close connection to real needs." (Nancy Hartsock 1979, 64)

A word that frightens some people. "For the feminist [literary] critic, however, it is less a bogey or a bugaboo than a badge of honor. . . . It refers to the conviction that our production of culture and meaning, like our consumption of culture and meaning, influences our sex/gender systems. In turn, our sex/gender systems influence our production and consumption of culture and meaning." (Catharine Stimpson 1981, 59)

"From the early generalizations about 'all women,' feminists are recognizing the need to understand the specific nature and conditions of women's oppression in differing cultures, societies, and economies." (Jill Lewis 1981; in Gloria I. Joseph and Jill Lewis 1981, 67)

"To be a feminist means recognizing that one is associated with all women not as an act of choice but as a matter of fact. . . . Feminists do not create this common condition by making alliances; feminists recognize this common condition because it exists as an intrinsic part of sex oppression. . . . What is that common condition? Subordination to men, sexually colonized in a sexual system of dominance and submission, denied rights on the basis of sex, historically chattel, generally considered biologically inferior, confined to sex and reproduction; this is the general description of the social environment in which all women live." (Andrea Dworkin 1983, 221)

"Well, I'm convinced that many frustrated and crabby women are merely feminists in restraints." (Diane F. Germain 1983, 154)

"A person, female or male, whose worldview places the female in the center of life and society, and/or who is not prejudiced based on gender or sexual preference. Also, anyone in a male-dominated or patriarchal society who works toward the political, economic, spiritual, sexual, and social equality of women." (*The Wise Woman* 1982, 4:2 [June 21], 7)

When used by a man to refer to himself it is a "male appropriation of language no less stupidly defensive than a white man imagining myself a black radical." Profeminist is a term used to describe the male who works towards feminist goals. (Irving Weinman 1983, 133–134)

(See WOMANIST)

FEMINIST DICTIONARY

A word book which calls into question the androcentric nature of much "standard language usage" and problematizes many words and phrases in the light of feminist perspectives and commentary. *This feminist dictionary* (1) recognizes women as linguistically creative speakers, (2) explicitly acknowledges the socio-political aspects of dictionary-making, (3) draws heavily on excerpted material from feminist publications, (4) does not generally specify "parts of speech" (noun, verb, etc.) or linguistic status (coinage, obsolete, etc.) but rather provides commentary on the general cultural knowledge that the reader brings to this book, (5) assumes that a book about words is inevitably a book about the world as well, (6) emphasizes definitions by feminists without making continual reference to male authorities, (7) sometimes offers "contradictions" without resolving them. That this book is incomplete goes without saying. It is not intended to be the last word. We urge readers to make their own contributions using the blank pages at the back of the book and send them to us for the next edition.

[1985]

REFERENCES

Billington-Greig, Teresa. 1911. "Feminism and Politics." *The Contemporary Review*, November, 693–703.

Bunch, Charlotte. 1983. "Not by Degrees: Feminist Theory and Education." In *Learning Our Way*. Ed. Charlotte Bunch and Sandra Pollack. Trumansburg, New York: The Crossing Press, 248–260.

Cheng, Lucie. 1984. "Asian American Women and Feminism." *Sojourner*, October, 11.

Combahee River Collective. 1977. "A Black Feminist Statement." Rpt. in *This Bridge Called My Back: Writings by Radical Women of Color*. Ed. Cherríe Moraga and Gloria Anzaldúa. Watertown, Massachusetts: Persephone Press, 1981, 210–218.

Davidson, Osha. 1984. "How feminism rescued desperate single father." *Des Moines Register*, 16 November, 11A.

Dworkin, Andrea. 1983. *Right-wing Women*. New York: Perigree Books.

Fawcett, Millicent Garrett. 1878. "The Future of Englishwomen: A Reply." *Nineteenth Century*, 4, 347–357.

Germain, Diane F. 1983. "Feminist Art and Education at Califia: My Personal Experience." In *Learning Our Way*. Ed. Charlotte Bunch and Sandra Pollack. Trumansburg, New York: The Crossing Press, 154–159.

Hale, Beatrice Forbes-Robertson. 1914. *What Women Want: An Interpretation of The Feminist Movement*. New York: Frederick A. Stokes.

Hartsock, Nancy. 1979. "Feminist Theory and the Development of Revolutionary Strategy." In *Capitalist Patriarchy and the Case for Socialist Feminism*. Ed. Zillah Eisenstein. New York and London: Monthly Review Press, 56–82.

hooks, bell. 1981. *Ain't I A Woman: Black Women and Feminism*. Boston: South End Press.

Jain, Devaki. 1978. "Can Feminism Be a Global Ideology?" *Quest: A Feminist Quarterly*, 4:2 (Winter), 9–15.

Jamieson, Deborah Aslan. 1982. Review of *This Bridge Called My Back: Writings by Radical Women of Color*, ed. Cherríe Moraga and Gloria Anzaldúa. *off our backs*, April, 6, 11.

Johnston, Jill. 1973. *Lesbian Nation: The Feminist Solution*. New York: Simon & Schuster.

Joseph, Gloria I. and Jill Lewis. 1981. *Common Differences: Conflicts in Black and White Feminist Perspectives*. Garden City, New York: Anchor/Doubleday.

Kelly, Joan. 1982. "Early Feminist Theory and the *Querelle des Femmes*, 1400–1789." *Signs*, 8:1 (Autumn), 4–28.

Kornegger, Peggy. 1979. "Anarchism: The Feminist Connection." In *Reinventing Anarchy*. Ed. Howard J. Ehrlich, Carol Ehrlich, David DeLeon, and Glenda Morris. London: Routledge & Kegan Paul, 237–249.

Lewin, Rebecca. 1983. "Truth-Telling Through Feminist Fiction." *Womanews*, 4:9 (October), 17.

MacNamara, Mary, c. 1982. "What Is Feminism? Another View . . ." *Wicca: 'Wise Woman' Irish Feminist Magazine*, 12, 6–7.

Maitland, Sara. 1983. "A Feminist Writer's Progress." In *On Gender and Writing*. Ed. Michelene Wandor. London: Pandora Press, 17–23.

Mitchell, Juliet and Ann Oakley, eds. 1976. *The Rights and Wrongs of Women*. Harmondsworth, Middlesex: Penguin Books.

Moraga, Cherríe. 1983. *Loving in the War Years*. Boston: South End Press.

Moraga, Cherríe and Gloria Anzaldúa, eds. 1981. *This Bridge Called My Back: Writings by Radical Women of Color*. Watertown, Massachusetts: Persephone Press.

Raymond, Jill and Janice Wilson. 1983. "Feminism—Healing the Patriarchal Disease." In *Reclaim the Earth: Women Speak Out for Life on Earth*. Ed. Léonie Caldecott and Stephanie Leland. London: The Women's Press, 59–65.

Redstockings of the Women's Liberation Movement, eds. 1975. *Feminist Revolution*. New York: Random House.

Rich, Adrienne. 1976. *Of Woman Born: Motherhood as Experience and Institution*. New York: W. W. Norton.

Rush, Anne Kent and Anica Vesel Mander. 1974. *Feminism as Therapy*. New York: Random House.

Russell, Dawn. 1979. "Black Women and Work: My Experiences." *Heresies*, 2:4 (Issue 8), 72–75.

Saadawi, Nawal el. 1980. Interview. *Newsfront International*, October. Excerpted in *Connexions*, 1 May, 1981, 3.

Smith, Barbara. 1979a. "Notes for Yet Another Paper on Black Feminism, Or Will the Real Enemy Please Stand Up?" *Conditions: 5 The Black Women's Issue*, 2:2 (Autumn), 123–132.

Smith, Barbara. 1983. Introduction to *Home Girls: A Black Feminist Anthology*. Ed. Barbara Smith. New York: Kitchen Table: Women of Color Press, xix–lvi.

Spender, Dale. 1982. *Women of Ideas and What Men Have Done to Them: From Aphra Behn to Adrienne Rich*. London: Routledge & Kegan Paul.

Stanley, Liz and Sue Wise. 1983. *Breaking Out: Feminist Consciousness and Feminist Research*. London: Routledge & Kegan Paul.

Stimpson, Catharine. 1981. "Feminist Criticism and Feminist Critics." In *Feminist Literary Criticism*. Research Triangle Park, North Carolina: National Humanities Center, 57–63.

Weinman, Irving. 1983. "On the Edge." In *On Gender and Writing*. Ed. Michelene Wandor. London: Pandora Press, 133–140.

West, Rebecca. 1911–17. Selections of Rebecca West's Writings. In *The Young Rebecca*. Ed. Jane Marcus. London: Macmillan, 1982.

Wittig, Monique. 1981. "One Is Not Born a Woman." *Feminist Issues*, 1:2 (Winter), 47–54.

 2

Womanist

ALICE WALKER

1.   From *womanish*. (Opp. of "girlish," i.e., frivolous, irresponsible, not serious.) A black feminist or feminist of color. From the black folk expression of mothers to female children, "You acting womanish," i.e., like a woman. Usually referring to outrageous, audacious, courageous or *willful* behavior. Wanting to know more and in greater depth than is considered "good" for one. Interested in grown-up doings. Acting grown up. Being grown up. Interchangeable with another black folk expression: "You trying to be grown." Responsible. In charge. *Serious*.

2.   *Also:* A woman who loves other women, sexually and/or nonsexually. Appreciates and prefers women's culture, women's emotional flexibility (values tears as natural counterbalance of laughter), and women's strength. Sometimes loves individual men, sexually and/or nonsexually. Committed to survival and wholeness of entire people, male *and* female. Not a separatist, except periodically, for health. Traditionally universalist, as in: "Mama, why are we brown, pink, and yellow, and our cousins are white, beige, and black?" Ans.: "Well, you know the colored race is just like a flower garden, with every color flower represented." Traditionally capable, as in: "Mama, I'm walking to Canada and I'm taking you and a bunch of other slaves with me." Reply: "It wouldn't be the first time."

3.   Loves music. Loves dance. Loves the moon. *Loves* the Spirit. Loves love and food and roundness. Loves struggle. *Loves* the Folk. Loves herself. *Regardless*.

4.   Womanist is to feminist as purple to lavender.

[1983]

 3

Not by Degrees: Feminist Theory and Education

CHARLOTTE BUNCH

The development of feminist theory and rigorous analysis of society are more important for us today than ever before. Feminists need to understand the forces working against us, as well as to analyze our experiences as a movement, if we are to survive the anti-woman backlash and keep our visions alive. When feminists despair, burn out, or give up, it is often because the forces against us are strong and because our theoretical framework does not give us a sense of how individual activities contribute to significant victories in the future. A solid feminist theory would help us understand present events in a way that would enable us to develop the visions and plans for change that sustain people engaged in day-to-day political activity.

When I left the university to do full-time work in "the movement" in the 1960s, it didn't occur to me that I would return one day to teach or write feminist theory. Like many others who chose to become movement activists then, I felt that I was leaving behind not only the academic world, but also what I saw as irrelevant theorizing. However, as I experienced the problems of movement organizing when an overall analysis was lacking, felt the frustration of conflicts where issues were not clear, and observed people dropping out of political activity, I became aware of the critical role of theory in the movement. I began to see feminist theory not as academic, but as a process based on understanding and advancing the activist movement.

While my growing sense of the importance of theory applied to all my feminist work, the urgency that I felt about it became clearest during my involvement with lesbian-feminism. When the lesbian issue became a major controversy in the women's movement in the early 1970s, I realized that in order for lesbians to function openly, we would have to understand *why* there was so much resistance to this issue. It was not enough to document discrimination against homosexuals or to appeal to fairness. We had to figure out why lesbianism was taboo, why it was a threat to feminists, and then devise strategies accordingly. I saw that my life as a lesbian in the movement depended on, among other things, the development of a theory that would explain our immediate conflicts in the context of a long-term view of feminism. This theoretical perspective developed along with our activism, but it required us to consciously ask certain questions, to look at our experiences in and out of the movement, and to consider existing feminist theory in new ways. Through this process, new interpretations of the relationship between lesbianism and feminism, and new strategies for ending lesbian oppression emerged.

For example, as we examined feminists' fear of being called lesbians, we were able to confront directly the role that such name calling played in the oppression of all women. Having a theory about lesbian oppression did not tell us what to do tactically, but it did provide a framework for understanding situations, for placing them in a broader context, and for evaluating possible courses of action. This experience showed me that theory was not simply intellectually interesting, but was crucial to the survival of feminism.

THE FUNCTIONS OF FEMINIST THEORY

Theory enables us to see immediate needs in terms of long-range goals and an overall perspective on the world.[1] It thus gives us a framework for evaluating various strategies in both the long and the short run, and for seeing the types of changes that they are likely to produce. Theory is not just a body of facts or a set of personal opinions. It involves explanations and hypotheses that are based on available knowledge and experience. It is also dependent on conjecture and insight about how to interpret those facts and experiences and their significance.

No theory is totally "objective," since it reflects the interests, values, and assumptions of those who created it. Feminist theory relies on the underlying assumption that it will aid the liberation of women. Feminist theory, therefore, is not an unengaged study of women. It is an effort to bring insights from the movement and from various female experiences together with research and data gathering to produce new approaches to understanding and ending female oppression.

While feminist theory begins with the immediate need to end women's oppression, it is also a way of viewing the world. Feminism is an entire world view or *gestalt*, not just a laundry list of "women's issues." Feminist theory provides a basis for understanding every area of our lives, and a feminist perspective can affect the world politically, culturally, economically, and spiritually. The initial tenets of feminism have already been established—the idea that power is based on gender differences and that men's illegitimate power over women taints all aspects of society, for instance. But now we face the arduous task of systematically working through these ideas, fleshing them out and discovering new ones.

When the development of feminist theory seems too slow for the changes that we seek, feminists are tempted to submerge our insights into one of the century's two dominant progressive theories of reality and change: democratic liberalism or Marxist socialism.[2] However, the limitations of both of these systems are increasingly obvious. While feminism can learn from both of them, it must not be tied to either because its greatest strength lies in providing an alternative view of the world.

The full implications of feminism will evolve over time, as we organize, experiment, think, analyze, and revise our ideas and strategies in light of our experiences. No theory emerges in full detail overnight; the dominant theories of our day have expanded and changed over many decades. That it will take time should not discourage us. That we might fail to pursue our ideas—given the enormous need for them in society today—is unconscionable.

Because feminist theory is still emerging and does not have agreed upon answers (or even approaches to many questions), it is difficult to work out strategies based on that theory. This difficulty can lead feminists to rely on the other theories of change or to fall into the "any action/no action" bind. When caught in this bind, one may go ahead with action—any action—for its own sake, or be paralyzed, taking no action for lack of a sense of what is "right." To escape this bind, we must remember that we do not need, and indeed never will have, all the answers before we act, and that it is often only through taking action that we can discover some of them. The purpose of theory, then, is not to provide a pat set of answers about what to do, but to guide us in sorting out options, and to keep us out of the "any action/no action" bind. Theory also keeps us aware of the questions that need to be asked, so that what we learn in each activity will lead to more effective strategies in the future. Theory thus both grows out of and guides activism in a continuous, spiraling process.

In pursuing feminist theory as an activist, I have become increasingly aware of the need to demystify it. Theory is not something set apart from our lives. Our assumptions about reality and change influence our actions constantly. The question is not whether we have a theory, but how aware we are of the assumptions behind our actions, and how conscious we are of the choices we make—daily—among different theories. For example, when we decide whether to put our energies into a rape crisis center or into efforts to change rape laws, we are acting according to certain theories about how service projects and legislation affect change. These theories may be implicit or explicit, but they are always there.

A MODEL FOR THEORY

Theory doesn't necessarily progress in a linear fashion, but examining its components is useful in understanding existing political theory as well as in developing new insights. In the model I have developed, I divide theory into four interrelated parts: description, analysis, vision, and strategy.

1. Description: *Describing what exists* may sound simple, but the choices that we make about interpreting and naming reality provide the basis for the rest of our theory. Changing people's perceptions of the world through new descriptions of reality is usually a prerequisite for altering that reality. For example, fifteen years ago, few people would say that women in the U.S. were oppressed. Today, the oppression of women is acknowledged by a large number of people, primarily because of feminist work which described that oppression in a number of ways. This work has involved consciousness raising, as well as gathering and interpreting facts about women in order to substantiate our assertions. Description is necessary for all theory; unfortunately for feminism, much of our work has not yet gone beyond this point.

2. Analysis: *Analyzing why that reality exists* involves determining its origins and the reasons for its perpetuation. This is perhaps the most complex task of theory and is often seen as its entire function. In seeking to understand the sources of women's oppression and why it is perpetuated, we have to examine biology, economics, psychology, sexuality, and so on. We must also look at what groups and institutions benefit from oppression, and why they will, therefore, strive to maintain it. Analyzing why women are oppressed involves such things as sorting out how the forms of oppression change over time while the basic fact of oppression remains, or probing how the forms of oppression vary in different cultures while there are cross-cultural similarities.

Analysis of why something happens sometimes gets short-circuited by the temptation to ascribe everything to one single factor, such as capitalism or motherhood. In developing an analysis, I find that it is useful to focus initially on a phenomenon in a limited context and consider a wide range of factors that may affect it. Then, as that context is understood, the analysis can be expanded. Above all, we need not feel that we must answer the "why" of everything all at once with a single explanation.

3. Vision: *Determining what should exist* requires establishing principles (or values) and setting goals. In taking action to bring about change, we operate consciously or unconsciously out of certain assumptions about what is right or what we value (principles), and out of our sense of what society ought to be (goals). This aspect of theory involves making a conscious choice about those principles in order to make our visions and goals concrete. We must look at our basic assumptions about such things as "human nature" and how it can be changed, about the relationships of individuals to groups, about whether men and women are essentially different, for example. We may choose not to address some of these issues yet, but since every action carries implicit assumptions, we must be conscious of them so that we do not operate out of old theoretical frameworks by default. The clearer we are about our principles—for example, whether we think that women should gain as much power as possible in every area, or believe, instead, that power itself should be eliminated—the more easily we can set our long-term goals. Immediate goals can then be based on an assessment of what can be accomplished that may be short of our long-term vision, but moves toward, not away, from it. Visions, principles, and goals will change with experience, but the more explicit we make them, the more our actions can be directed toward creating the society we want, as well as reacting to what we don't like.

4. Strategy: *Hypothesizing how to change what is to what should be* moves directly into questions of changing reality. Some people see strategy not as part of theory, but rather as a planning process based on theory. But I include strategy here in its broadest sense—the overall approach one takes to how to accomplish one's goals. The descriptive and analytic process of theory help develop a more systematic understanding of the way things work, but they usually do not make obvious what one should do. Developing a strategy requires that we draw out the consequences of our theory and suggest general directions for change.

Like the other aspects of theory, this involves a combination of information gathering and creative speculation. It entails making judgments about what will lead to change—judgments that are based both on description and analysis of reality, and on visions, principles, and goals. Developing a strategy also involves examining various tools for change—legislative, military, spiritual—and determining which are most effective in what situations. There are many questions to consider, such as what sectors of society can best be mobilized to carry out which types of action. And in working out which strategies will be most effective, the interaction between developing theory and actively experimenting with it becomes most clear. For in all aspects of theory development, theory and activism continually inform and alter each other.

USING THE MODEL

This four-part model for theory can be used in many ways. In my feminist theory classes, we have tried to understand different theories by outlining how various authors address each of its developmental parts. For example, we take Shulamith Firestone's *Dialectic of Sex* and discuss her approach to description, analysis, vision, and strategy. Then we compare her ideas in each area with those of other radical feminists, in an effort to see the common tenets of radical feminism, the important areas of disagreement, and the strategy implications of those differences. We then take the same approach to socialist-feminist authors, compare them to each other and to radical feminist works, etc.

Another way to use this approach to theory is to examine possible ways of addressing a specific issue in terms of these processes. For example, on the issue of reproductive freedom, we can use theoretical work to understand the implications behind various strategies. Considerable work has been done detailing the variety of ways in which women lack control over reproduction, from forced sterilization to negligence in the development of contraceptives. Several analyses of why women do not have control over our bodies have been suggested. These range from the idea that men fear women's powers to create life and therefore compensate by controlling reproduction, to the proposition that capitalism is the primary cause because it must control the number of workers produced, to the view that the Catholic Church is the dominant perpetuator of this situation because its control over reproduction and matters of family life is central to its power. Most analyses also look at which institutions are most influential and which are most vulnerable to change, and the relations between them—e.g., how the Catholic Church affects hospital and government policies.

There are considerable differences of opinion about how reproduction should be treated. Some feminists argue that women should have absolute control over our bodies and reproduction at all times and in all circumstances. Others contend that there can be some legitimate limits on an individual woman's control; in the case of abortion, for example, limiting a woman's right to abortion on demand to the first trimester. Some argue that the state should prescribe standards of control that "protect" women such as the requirement of a thirty-day waiting period of any sterilization; and still others hold that a woman's control must be subordinate to the obligation of government to supervise overall population growth.

The practical consequences of these differences in theory become clear when strategies for gaining women's reproductive rights are discussed. Even among those who agree that women's lack of control over reproduction is central to our oppression, there are differences in strategy based on differences in analysis and vision. Those who think that the Catholic Church is the primary enemy of women's reproductive rights may focus on efforts to remove Church influence on the state, the fight against religious tax exemptions, and so on, while those who see multinational corporations as the primary controller of population issues would focus on them. The controversy among feminists over whether having the government require a thirty-day waiting period for all sterilizations would protect women or further abridge our rights to control our bodies illustrates how disagreement over vision and goals leads to different strategies and often to conflict over what we will demand.

This example, though simplified here, illustrates how the four-part model in particular, and theory in general, can be used to clarify practical political problems. When we understand the basis of our disagreements and the nature of the forces against us,

we are better equipped to come to some agreement or to realize when compromise may not be possible. Theory helps clarify how things work and what our choices are, and thus aids in determining where to put our energies and how to challenge the sources of our oppression most effectively.

Theory is also a tool for passing on the knowledge we have gained from our life experiences and movement projects. Feminists need to analyze personal experiences as well as political developments—to sort out our initial assumptions about goals and analysis, to look at the strategies we used and why, and to evaluate the results in terms of what could be learned for the future. Making such feminist analysis accessible to others usually involves writing it down, which brings us to feminist education.

· · ·

[1979]

NOTES

1. There are many approaches to theory, and those, interested in exploring more about how theory is constructed should look at the literature of political philosophy. A model for feminist theory similar to the one that I discuss in this paper was developed by Judy Smith of the Women's Resource Center, in Missoula, Montana.
2. For more discussion of this problem and of nonaligned feminism as a response to it, see Charlotte Bunch, "Beyond Either/Or: Feminist Options," *Quest: A Feminist Quarterly,* vol. 3, no. 1 (Summer 1976), pp. 2–17.

 4

Poetry Is Not a Luxury

AUDRE LORDE

The quality of light by which we scrutinize our lives has direct bearing upon the product which we live, and upon the changes which we hope to bring about through those lives. It is within this light that we form those ideas by which we pursue our magic and make it realized. This is poetry as illumination, for it is through poetry that we give name to those ideas which are—until the poem—nameless and formless, about to be birthed, but already felt. That distillation of experience from which true poetry springs births thought as dream births concept, as feeling births idea, as knowledge births (precedes) understanding.

As we learn to bear the intimacy of scrutiny and to flourish within it, as we learn to use the products of that scrutiny for power within our living, those fears which rule our lives and form our silences begin to lose their control over us.

For each of us as women, there is a dark place within, where hidden and growing our true spirit rises, "beautiful/and tough as chestnut/stanchions against (y)our nightmare of weakness/"[1] and of impotence.

These places of possibility within ourselves are dark because they are ancient and hidden; they have survived and grown strong through that darkness. Within these deep places, each one of us holds an incredible reserve of creativity and power, of unexamined and unrecorded emotion and feeling. The woman's place of power within each of us is neither white nor surface; it is dark, it is ancient, and it is deep.

When we view living in the european mode only as a problem to be solved, we rely solely upon our ideas to make us free, for these were what the white fathers told us were precious.

But as we come more into touch with our own ancient, noneuropean consciousness of living as a situation to be experienced and interacted with, we learn more and more to cherish our feelings, and to respect those hidden sources of our power from where true knowledge and, therefore, lasting action comes.

At this point in time, I believe that women carry within ourselves the possibility for fusion of these two approaches so necessary for survival, and we come closest to this combination in our poetry. I speak here of poetry as a revelatory distillation of experience, not the sterile word play that, too often, the white fathers distorted the word *poetry* to mean— in order to cover a desperate wish for imagination without insight.

For women, then, poetry is not a luxury. It is a vital necessity of our existence. It forms the quality of the light within which we predicate our hopes and dreams toward survival and change, first made into language, then into idea, then into more tangible action. Poetry is the way we help give name to the nameless so it can be thought. The farthest horizons of our hopes and fears are cobbled by our poems, carved from the rock experiences of our daily lives.

As they become known to and accepted by us, our feelings and the honest exploration of them become sanctuaries and spawning grounds for the most radical and daring of ideas. They become a safe-house for that difference so necessary to change and the conceptualization of any meaningful action. Right now, I could name at least ten ideas I would have found intolerable or incomprehensible and frightening, except as they came after dreams and poems. This is not idle fantasy, but a disciplined attention to the true meaning of "it feels right to me." We can train ourselves to respect our feelings and to transpose them into a language so they can be shared. And where that language does not yet exist, it is our poetry which helps to fashion it. Poetry is not only dream and vision; it is the skeleton architecture of our lives. It lays the foundations for a future of change, a bridge across our fears of what has never been before.

Possibility is neither forever nor instant. It is not easy to sustain belief in its efficacy. We can sometimes work long and hard to establish one beachhead of real resistance to the deaths we are expected to live, only to have that beachhead assaulted or threatened by those canards we have been socialized to fear, or by the withdrawal of those approvals that we have been warned to seek for safety. Women see ourselves diminished or softened by the falsely benign accusations of childishness, of nonuniversality, of changeability, of sensuality. And who asks the question: Am I altering your aura, your ideas, your dreams, or am I merely moving you to temporary and reactive action? And even though the latter is no mean task, it is one that must be seen within the context of a need for true alteration of the very foundations of our lives.

The white fathers told us: I think, therefore I am. The Black mother within each of us—the poet— whispers in our dreams: I feel, therefore I can be free. Poetry coins the language to express and charter this revolutionary demand, the implementation of that freedom.

However, experience has taught us that action in the now is also necessary, always. Our children cannot dream unless they live, they cannot live unless they are nourished, and who else will feed them the real food without which their dreams will be no different from ours? "If you want us to change the world someday, we at least have to live long enough to grow up!" shouts the child.

Sometimes we drug ourselves with dreams of new ideas. The head will save us. The brain alone will set us free. But there are no new ideas still waiting in the wings to save us as women, as human. There are only old and forgotten ones, new combinations, extrapolations and recognitions from within ourselves—along with the renewed courage to try them out. And we must constantly encourage ourselves and each other to attempt the heretical actions that our dreams imply, and so many of our old ideas disparage. In the forefront of our move toward change, there is only poetry to hint at possibility made real. Our poems formulate the implications of ourselves, what we feel within and dare make real (or bring action into accordance with), our fears, our hopes, our most cherished terrors.

For within living structures defined by profit, by linear power, by institutional dehumanization, our feelings were not meant to survive. Kept around as unavoidable adjuncts or pleasant pastimes, feelings were expected to kneel to thought as women were expected to kneel to men. But women have survived. As poets. And there are no new pains. We have felt them all already. We have hidden that fact in the same place where we have hidden our power. They surface in our dreams, and it is our dreams that point the way to freedom. Those dreams are made realizable through our poems that give us the strength and courage to see, to feel, to speak, and to dare.

If what we need to dream, to move our spirits most deeply and directly toward and through promise, is discounted as a luxury, then we give up the core—the fountain—of our power, our womanness; we give up the future of our worlds.

For there are no new ideas. There are only new ways of making them felt—of examining what those ideas feel like being lived on Sunday morning at 7 A.M., after brunch, during wild love, making war, giving birth, mourning our dead—while we suffer the old longings, battle the old warnings and fears of being silent and impotent and alone, while we taste new possibilities and strengths.

[1977]

NOTE

1. From "Black Mother Woman," first published in *From a Land Where Other People Live* (Broadside Press, Detroit, 1973), and collected in *Chosen Poems: Old and New* (W. W. Norton and Company, New York, 1982) p. 53.

 5

Have We Got a Theory for You! Feminist Theory, Cultural Imperialism and the Demand for "The Woman's Voice"

MARIA C. LUGONES and
ELIZABETH V. SPELMAN

PROLOGUE

(*In a Hispana voice*) A veces quisiera mezclar en una voz el sonido canyenge, tristón y urbano del porteñismo que llevo adentro con la cadencia apacible, serrana y llena de corage de la hispana nuevo mejicana. Contrastar y unir

el piolín y la cuerda
el traé y el pepéname
el camión y la troca
la lluvia y el llanto

Pero este querer se me va cuando veo que he confundido la solidaridad con la falta de diferencia. La solidaridad requiere el reconocer, comprender, respetar y amar lo que nos lleva a llorar en distintas cadencias. El imperialismo cultural desea lo contrario, por eso necesitamos muchas voces. Porque una sola voz nos mata a las dos.

No quiero hablar por ti sino contigo. Pero si no aprendo tus modos y tu los mios la conversación es sólo aparente. Y la apariencia se levanta como una barrera sin sentido entre las dos. Sin sentido y sin sentimiento. Por eso no me debes dejar que te dicte tu ser y no me dictes el mio. Porque entonces ya no dialogamos. El diálogo entre nosotras requiere dos voces y no una.

Tal vez un día jugaremos juntas y nos hablaremos no en una lengua universal sino que vos me hablarás mi voz y yo la tuya.

PREFACE

This paper is the result of our dialogue, of our thinking together about differences among women and how these differences are silenced. (Think, for example, of all the silences there are connected with the fact that this paper is in English—for that is a borrowed tongue for one of us.) In the process of our talking and writing together, we saw that the differences between us did not permit our speaking in one voice. For example, when we agreed we expressed the thought differently; there were some things that both of us thought were true but could not express as true of each of us; sometimes we could not say "we"; and sometimes one of us could not express the thought in the first person singular, and to express it in the third person would be to present an outsider's and not an insider's perspective. Thus the use of two voices is central both to the process of constructing this paper and to the substance of it. We are both the authors of this paper and not just sections of it but we write together without presupposing unity of expression or of experience. So when we speak in unison it means just that—there are two voices and not just one.

INTRODUCTION

(*In the voice of a white/Anglo woman who has been teaching and writing about feminist theory*) Feminism is, among other things, a response to the fact that women either have been left out of, or included in demeaning and disfiguring ways in what has been an almost exclusively male account of the world. And so while part of what feminists want and demand for women is the right to move and to act in accordance with our own wills and not against them, another part is the desire and insistence that we give our *own* accounts of these movements and actions. For it matters to us what is said about us, who says it, and to whom it is said: having the opportunity to talk about one's life, to give an account of it, to interpret it, is integral to leading that life rather than being led through it; hence our distrust of the male monopoly over accounts of women's lives. To put the same point slightly differently, part of human life, human living, is talking about it, and we can be sure that being silenced in one's own account of one's life is a kind of amputation that signals oppres-sion. Another reason for not divorcing life from the telling of it or talking about it is that as humans our experiences are deeply influenced by what is said about them, by ourselves or powerful (as opposed to significant) others. Indeed, the phenomenon of internalized oppression is only possible because this is so: one experiences her life in terms of the impoverished and degrading concepts others have found it convenient to use to describe her. We can't separate lives from the accounts given of them; the articulation of our experience is part of our experience.

Sometimes feminists have made even stronger claims about the importance of speaking about our own lives and the destructiveness of others presuming to speak about us or for us. First of all, the claim has been made that on the whole men's accounts of women's lives have been at best false, a function of ignorance; and at worst malicious lies, a function of a knowledgeable desire to exploit and oppress. Since it matters to us that falsehood and lies not be told about us, we demand, of those who have been responsible for those falsehoods and lies, or those who continue to transmit them, not just that we speak but that they learn to be able to hear us. It has also been claimed that talking about one's life, telling one's story, in the company of those doing the same (as in consciousness-raising sessions), is constitutive of feminist method.[1]

And so the demand that the woman's voice be heard and attended to has been made for a variety of reasons: not just so as to greatly increase the chances that true accounts of women's lives will be given, but also because the articulation of experience (in myriad ways) is among the hallmarks of a self-determining individual or community. There are not just epistemological, but moral and political reasons for demanding that the woman's voice be heard, after centuries of androcentric din.

But what more exactly is the feminist demand that the woman's voice be heard? There are several crucial notes to make about it. First of all, the demand grows out of a complaint, and in order to understand the scope and focus of the demand we have to look at the scope and focus of the complaint. The complaint does not specify *which* women have been silenced, and in one way this is appropriate to the conditions it is a complaint about: virtually no women have had a voice, whatever their race, class, ethnicity, religion, sexual alliance, whatever place and period in history they lived. And if it is as women that women have been silenced, then of course the demand must be that women as women have a voice. But in another way the complaint is very misleading, insofar as it suggests that it is women as women who have been silenced, and that whether a woman is rich or poor, Black, brown or white, etc., is irrelevant to what it means for her to be a woman. For the demand thus simply made ignores at least two related points: (1) it is only possible for a woman who does not feel highly vulnerable with respect to other parts of her identity, e.g., race, class, ethnicity, religion, sexual alliance, etc., to conceive of her voice simply or essentially as a "woman's voice"; (2) just because not all women are equally vulnerable with respect to race, class, etc., some women's voices are more likely to be heard than others by those who have heretofore been giving—or silencing—the accounts of women's lives. For all these reasons, the women's voices most likely to come forth and the women's voices most likely to be heard are, in the United States anyway, those of white, middle-class, heterosexual Christian (or anyway not self-identified non-Christian) women. Indeed, many Hispanas, Black women, Jewish women—to name a few groups—have felt it an invitation to silence rather than speech to be requested—if they are requested at all—to speak about being "women" (with the plain wrapper—as if there were one) in distinction from speaking about being Hispana, Black, Jewish, working-class, etc., women.

The demand that the "woman's voice" be heard, and the search for the "woman's voice" as central to feminist methodology, reflects nascent feminist theory. It reflects nascent empirical theory insofar as it presupposes that the silencing of women is systematic, shows up in regular, patterned ways, and that there are discoverable causes of this widespread observable phenomenon; the demand reflects nascent political theory insofar as it presupposes that the silencing of women reveals a systematic pattern of power and authority; and it reflects nascent moral theory insofar as it presupposes that the silencing is unjust and that there are particular ways of remedying this injustice. Indeed, whatever else we know feminism to include—e.g., concrete direct political action—theorizing is integral to it: theories about the nature of oppression, the causes of it, the relation of the oppression of women to other forms of oppression. And certainly the concept of the woman's voice is itself a theoretical concept, in the sense that it presupposes a theory according to which our identities as human beings are actually compound identities, a kind of fusion or confusion of our otherwise separate identities as women or men, as Black or brown or white, etc. That is no less a theoretical stance than Plato's division of the person into soul and body or Aristotle's parcelling of the soul into various functions.

The demand that the "woman's voice" be heard also invites some further directions in the exploration of women's lives and discourages or excludes others. For reasons mentioned above, systematic, sustained reflection on being a woman—the kind of contemplation that "doing theory" requires—is most likely to be done by women who vis-a-vis other women enjoy a certain amount of political, social and economic privilege because of their skin color, class membership, ethnic identity. There is a relationship between the content of our contemplation and the fact that we have the time to engage in it at some length—otherwise we shall have to say that it is a mere accident of history that white middle-class women in the United States have in the main developed "feminist theory" (as opposed to "Black feminist theory," "Chicana feminist theory," etc.) and that so much of the theory has failed to be relevant to the lives of women who are not white or middle class. Feminist theory—of all kinds—is to be based on, or anyway touch base with, the variety of real life stories women provide about themselves. But in fact, because, among other things, of the structural political and social and economic inequalities among women, the tail has been wagging the dog: feminist theory has not for the most part arisen out of a medley of women's voices; instead, the theory has arisen out of the voices, the experiences, of a fairly small handful of women, and if other women's voices do not sing in harmony with the theory, they aren't counted as women's voices—rather, they are the voices of the woman as Hispana, Black, Jew, etc. There is another sense in which the tail is wagging the dog, too: it is presumed to be the case that those who do the theory know more about those who are theorized than vice versa; hence it ought to be the case that if it is white/Anglo women who write for and about all other women, the white/Anglo women must know more about all other women than other women know about them. But in fact just in order to survive, brown and Black women have to know a lot more about white/Anglo women—not through the sustained contemplation theory requires, but through the sharp observation stark exigency demands.

(*In an Hispana voice*) I think it necessary to explain why in so many cases when women of color appear in front of white/Anglo women to talk about feminism and women of color, we mainly raise a complaint: the complaint of exclusion, of silencing, of being included in a universe we have not chosen. We usually raise the complaint with a certain amount of disguised or undisguised anger. I can only attempt to explain this phenomenon from a Hispanic viewpoint and a fairly narrow one at that: the viewpoint of an Argentinian woman who has lived in the U.S. for 16 years, who has attempted to come to terms with the devaluation of things Hispanic and Hispanic people in "America" and who is most familiar with Hispano life in the Southwest of the U.S. I am quite unfamiliar with daily Hispano life in the urban centers, though not with some of the themes and some of the salient experiences of urban Hispano life.

When I say "we,"[2] I am referring to Hispanas. I am accustomed to use the "we" in this way. I am also pained by the tenuousness of this "we" given that I am not a native of the United States. Through the years I have come to be recognized and I have come to recognize myself more and more firmly as part of this "we." I also have a profound yearning for this firmness since I am a displaced person and I am conscious of not being of and I am unwilling to make myself of—even if this were possible—the white/Anglo community.

When I say "you" I mean not the non-Hispanic but the white/Anglo women that I address. "We" and "you" do not capture my relation to other non-white women. The complexity of that relation is not addressed here, but it is vivid to me as I write down my thoughts on the subject at hand.

I see two related reasons for our complaint-full discourse with white/Anglo women. Both of these reasons plague our world, they contaminate it through and through. It takes some hardening of oneself, some self-acceptance of our own anger to face them, for to face them is to decide that maybe we can change our situation in self-constructive ways and we know fully well that the possibilities are minimal. We know that we cannot rest from facing these reasons, that the tenderness towards others in us undermines our possibilities, that we have to fight our own niceness because it clouds our minds and hearts. Yet we know that a thoroughgoing hardening would dehumanize us. So, we have to walk through our days in a peculiarly fragile psychic state, one that we have to struggle to maintain, one that we do not often succeed in maintaining.

We and you do not talk the same language. When we talk to you we use your language: the language of your experience and of your theories. We try to use it to communicate our world of experience. But since your language and your theories are inadequate in expressing our experiences, we only succeed in communicating our experience of exclusion. We cannot talk to you in our language because you do not understand it. So the brute facts that we understand your language and that the place where most theorizing about women is taking place is your place, both combine to require that we either use your language and distort our experience not just in the speaking about it, but in the living of it, or that we remain silent. Complaining about exclusion is a way of remaining silent.

You are ill at ease in our world. You are ill at ease in our world in a very different way than we are ill at ease in yours. You are not of our world and again, you are not of our world in a very different way than we are not of yours. In the intimacy of a personal relationship we appear to you many times to be wholly there, to have broken through or to have dissipated the barriers that separate us because you are Anglo and we are raza. When we let go of the psychic state that I referred to above in the direction of sympathy, we appear to ourselves equally whole in your presence but our intimacy is thoroughly incomplete. When we are in your world many times you remake us in your own image, although sometimes you clearly and explicitly acknowledge that we are not wholly there in our being with you. When we are in your world we ourselves feel the discomfort of having our own being Hispanas disfigured or not understood. And yet, we have had to be in your world and learn its ways. We have to participate in it, make a living in it, live in it, be mistreated in it, be ignored in it, and rarely, be appreciated in it. In learning to do these things or in learning to suffer them or in learning to enjoy what is to be enjoyed or in learning to understand your conception of us, we have had to learn your culture and thus your language and self-conceptions. But there is nothing that necessitates that you understand our world: understand, that is, not as an observer understands things, but as a participant, as someone who has a stake in them understands them. So your being ill at ease in our world lacks the features of our being ill at ease in yours precisely because you can leave and you can always tell yourselves that you will be soon out of there and because the wholeness of your selves is never touched by us, we have no tendency to remake you in our image.

But you theorize about women and we are women, so you understand yourselves to be theorizing about us, and we understand you to be theorizing about us. Yet none of the feminist theories developed so far seems to me to help Hispanas in the articulation of our experience. We have a sense that in using them we are distorting our experiences. Most Hispanas cannot even understand the language used in these theories—and only in some cases the reason is that the Hispana cannot understand English. We do not recognize ourselves in these theories. They create in us a schizophrenic split between our concern for ourselves as women and ourselves as Hispanas, one that we do not feel otherwise. Thus they seem to us to force us to assimilate to some version of Anglo culture, however revised that version may be. They seem to ask that we leave our communities or that we become alienated so completely in them that we feel hollow. When we see that you feel alienated in your own communities, this confuses us because we think that maybe every feminist has to suffer this alienation. But we see that recognition of your alienation leads many of you to be empowered into the remaking of your culture, while we are paralyzed into a state of displacement with no place to go.

So I think that we need to think carefully about the relation between the articulation of our own experience, the interpretation of our own experience, and theory making by us and other non-Hispanic women about themselves and other "women."

The only motive that makes sense to me for your joining us in this investigation is the motive of friendship, out of friendship. A non-imperialist feminism requires that you make a real space for our articulating, interpreting, theorizing and reflecting about the connections among them—a real space must be a non-coerced space—and/or that you follow us into our world out of friendship. I see the "out of friendship" as the only sensical motivation for this following because the task at hand for you is one of extraordinary difficulty. It requires that you be willing to devote a great part of your life to it and that you be willing to suffer alientation and self-disruption. Self-interest has been proposed as a possible motive for entering this task. But self-interest does not seem to me to be a realistic motive, since whatever the benefits you may accrue from such a journey, they cannot be concrete enough for you at this time and they may not be worth your while. I do not think that you have any obligation to understand us. You do have an obligation to abandon your imperialism, your universal claims, your reduction of us to your selves simply because they seriously harm us.

I think that the fact that we are so ill at ease with your theorizing in the ways indicated above does indicate that there is something wrong with these theories. But what is it that is wrong? Is it simply that the theories are flawed if meant to be universal but accurate so long as they are confined to your particular group(s)? Is it that the theories are not really flawed but need to be translated? Can they be translated? Is it something about the process of theorizing that is flawed? How do the two reasons for our complaint-full discourse affect the validity of your theories? Where do *we* begin? To what extent are our experience and its articulation affected by our being a colonized people, and this by your culture, theories and conceptions? Should we theorize in community and thus as part of community life and outside the academy and other intellectual circles? What is the point of making theory? Is theory making a good thing for us to do at this time? When are we making theory and when are we just articulating and/or interpreting our experiences?

SOME QUESTIONABLE ASSUMPTIONS ABOUT FEMINIST THEORIZING

(*Unproblematically in Vicky's and Maria's voice*) Feminist theories aren't just about what happens to the female population in any given society or across all societies; they are about the meaning of those experiences in the lives of women. They are about beings who give their own accounts of what is happening to them or of what they are doing, who have culturally constructed ways of reflecting on their lives. But how can the theorizer get at the meaning of those experiences? What should the relation be between a woman's own account of her experiences and the theorizer's account of it?

Let us describe two different ways of arriving at an account of another woman's experience. It is one thing for both me and you to observe you and come up with our different accounts of what you are doing; it is quite another for me to observe myself and others much like me culturally and in other ways and to develop an account of myself and then use that account to give an account of you. In the first case you are the "insider" and I am the "outsider." When the outsider makes clear that she is an outsider and that this is an outsider's account of your behavior, there is a touch of honesty about what she is doing. Most of the time the "interpretation by an outsider" is left understood and most of the time the distance of outsidedness is understood to mark objectivity in the interpretation. But why is the outsider as an outsider interpreting your behavior? Is she doing it so that you can understand how she sees you? Is she doing it so that other outsiders will understand how you *are*? Is she doing it so that *you* will understand how you are? It would seem that if the outsider wants you to understand how she sees you and you have given your account of how you see yourself to her, there is a possibility of genuine dialogue between the two. It also seems that the lack of reciprocity could bar genuine dialogue. For why should you engage in such a one-sided dialogue? As soon as we ask this question, a host of other conditions for the possibility of a genuine dialogue between us arise: conditions having to do with your position relative to me in the various social, political

and economic structures in which we might come across each other or in which you may run face to face with my account of you and my use of your account of yourself. Is this kind of dialogue necessary for me to get at the meaning of your experiences? That is, is this kind of dialogue necessary for feminist theorizing that is not seriously flawed?

Obviously the most dangerous of the understanding of what I—an outsider—am doing in giving an account of your experience is the one that describes what I'm doing as giving an account of who and how you are whether it be given to you or to other outsiders. Why should you or anyone else believe me; that is, why should you or anyone else believe that you are as I say you are? Could I be right? What conditions would have to obtain for my being right? That many women are put in the position of not knowing whether or not to believe outsiders' accounts of their experiences is clear. The pressures to believe these accounts are enormous even when the woman in question does not see herself in the account. She is thus led to doubt her own judgment and to doubt all interpretation of her experience. This leads her to experience her life differently. Since the consequences of outsiders' accounts can be so significant, it is crucial that we reflect on whether or not this type of account can ever be right and if so, under what conditions.

The last point leads us to the second way of arriving at an account of another woman's experience, viz., the case in which I observe myself and others like me culturally and in other ways and use that account to give an account of you. In doing this, I remake you in my own image. Feminist theorizing approaches this remaking insofar as it depends on the concept of women as women. For it has not arrived at this concept as a consequence of dialogue with many women who are culturally different, or by any other kind of investigation of cultural differences which may include different conceptions of what it is to be a woman: it has simply presupposed this concept.

Our suggestion in this paper, and at this time it is no more than a suggestion, is that only when genuine and reciprocal dialogue takes place between "outsiders" and "insiders" can we trust the outsider's account. At first sight it may appear that the insider/outsider distinction disappears in the dialogue, but it is important to notice that all that happens is that we are now both outsider and insider with respect to each other. The dialogue puts us both in position to give a better account of each other's and our own experience. Here we should again note that white/Anglo women are much less prepared for this dialogue with women of color than women of color are for dialogue with them in that women of color have had to learn white/Anglo ways, self-conceptions, and conceptions of them.

But both the possibility and the desirability of this dialogue are very much in question. We need to think about the possible motivations for engaging in this dialogue, whether doing theory jointly would be a good thing, in what ways and for whom, and whether doing theory is in itself a good thing at this time for women of color or white/Anglo women. In motivating the last question let us remember the hierarchical distinctions between theorizers and those theorized about and between theorizers and doers. These distinctions are endorsed by the same views and institutions which endorse and support hierarchical distinctions between men/women, master race/inferior race, intellectuals/manual workers. Of what use is the activity of theorizing to those of us who are women of color engaged day in and day out in the task of empowering women and men of color face to face with them? Should we be articulating and interpreting their experience for them with the aid of theories? Whose theories?

WAYS OF TALKING OR BEING TALKED ABOUT THAT ARE HELPFUL, ILLUMINATING, EMPOWERING, RESPECTFUL

(*Unproblematically in Maria's and Vicky's voice*) Feminists have been quite diligent about pointing out ways in which empirical, philosophical and moral theories have been androcentric. They have thought it crucial to ask, with respect to such theories: who makes them? for whom do they make them? about what or whom are the theories? why? how are theories tested? what are the criteria for such tests and where did the criteria come from? Without posing such questions and trying to answer them, we'd never have been able to begin to mount evidence for our claims that particular theories are androcentric, sexist, biased, paternalistic, etc. Cer-

tain philosophers have become fond of—indeed, have made their careers on—pointing out that characterizing a statement as true or false is only one of many ways possible of characterizing it; it might also be, oh, rude, funny, disarming, etc.; it may be intended to soothe or to hurt; or it may have the effect, intended or not, of soothing or hurting. Similarly, theories appear to be the kinds of things that are true or false; but they also are the kinds of things that can be, e.g., useless, arrogant, disrespectful, ignorant, ethnocentric, imperialistic. The immediate point is that feminist theory is no less immune to such characterizations than, say, Plato's political theory, or Freud's theory of female psychosexual development. Of course this is not to say that if feminist theory manages to be respectful or helpful it will follow that it must be true. But if, say, an empirical theory is purported to be about "women" and in fact is only about certain women, it is certainly false, probably ethnocentric, and of dubious usefulness except to those whose position in the world it strengthens (and theories, as we know, don't have to be true in order to be used to strengthen people's positions in the world).

Many reasons can be and have been given for the production of accounts of people's lives that plainly have nothing to do with illuminating those lives for the benefit of those living them. It is likely that both the method of investigation and the content of many accounts would be different if illuminating the lives of the people the accounts are about were the aim of the studies. Though we cannot say ahead of time how feminist theory making would be different if all (or many more) of those people it is meant to be about were more intimately part of the theory-making process, we do suggest some specific ways being talked about can be helpful:

1. The theory or account can be helpful if it enables one to see how parts of one's life fit together, for example, to see connections among parts of one's life one hasn't seen before. No account can do this if it doesn't get the parts right to begin with, and this cannot happen if the concepts used to describe a life are utterly foreign.

2. A useful theory will help one locate oneself concretely in the world, rather than add to the mystification of the world and one's location in it. New

concepts may be of significance here, but they will not be useful if there is no way they can be translated into already existing concepts. Suppose a theory locates you in the home, because you are a woman, but you know full well that is not where you spend most of your time? Or suppose you can't locate yourself easily in any particular class as defined by some version of Marxist theory?

3. A theory or account not only ought to accurately locate one in the world but also enable one to think about the extent to which one is responsible or not for being in that location. Otherwise, for those whose location is as oppressed peoples, it usually occurs that the oppressed have no way to see themselves as in any way self-determining, as having any sense of being worthwhile or having grounds for pride, and paradoxically at the same time feeling at fault for the position they are in. A useful theory will help people work out just what is and is not due to themselves and their own activities as opposed to those who have power over them.

It may seem odd to make these criteria of a useful theory, if the usefulness is not to be at odds with the issue of the truth of the theory; for the focus on feeling worthwhile or having pride seems to rule out the possibility that the truth might just be that such-and-such a group of people has been under the control of others for centuries and that the only explanation of that is that they are worthless and weak people, and will never be able to change that. Feminist theorizing seems implicitly if not explicitly committed to the moral view that women *are* worthwhile beings, and the metaphysical theory that we are beings capable of bringing about a change in our situations. Does this mean feminist theory is "biased"? Not any more than any other theory, e.g., psychoanalytic theory. What is odd here is not the feminist presupposition that women are worthwhile but rather that feminist theory (and other theory) often has the effect of empowering one group and demoralizing another.

Aspects of feminist theory are as unabashedly value-laden as other political and moral theories. It is not just an examination of women's positions, for it includes, indeed begins with, moral and political judgments about the injustice (or, where relevant, justice) of them. This means that there are implicit or explicit judgments also about what kind of changes constitute a better or worse situation for women.

4. In this connection a theory that is useful will provide criteria for change and make suggestions for modes of resistance that don't merely reflect the situation and values of the theorizer. A theory that is respectful of those about whom it is a theory will not assume that changes that are perceived as making life better for some women are changes that will make, and will be perceived as making, life better for other women. This is *not* to say that if some women do not find a situation oppressive, other women ought never to suggest to the contrary that there might be very good reasons to think that the situation nevertheless *is* oppressive. But it is to say that, e.g., the prescription that life for women will be better when we're in the workforce rather than at home, when we are completely free of religious beliefs with patriarchal origins, when we live in complete separation from men, etc., are seen as slaps in the face to women whose life would be better if they could spend more time at home, whose identity is inseparable from their religious beliefs and cultural practices (which is not to say those beliefs and practices are to remain completely uncriticized and unchanged), who have ties to men—whether erotic or not—such that to have them severed in the name of some vision of what is "better" is, at that time and for those women, absurd. Our visions of what is better are always informed by our perception of what is bad about our present situation. Surely we've learned enough from the history of clumsy missionaries, and the white suffragists of the 19th century (who couldn't imagine why Black women "couldn't see" how crucial getting the vote for "women" was) to know that we can clobber people to destruction with our visions, our versions, of what is better. *But:* this does not mean women are not to offer supportive and tentative criticism of one another. But there is a very important difference between (a) developing ideas together, in a "pre-theoretical" stage, engaged as equals in joint enquiry, and (b) one group developing, on the basis of their own experience, a set of criteria for good change for women—and then reluctantly making revisions in the criteria at the insistence of women to whom such criteria seem ethnocentric and arrogant. The deck is stacked when one group takes it upon itself to develop the

theory and then have others criticize it. Categories are quick to congeal, and the experiences of women whose lives do not fit the categories will appear as anomalous when in fact the theory should have grown out of them as much as others from the beginning. This, of course, is why any organization or conference having to do with "women"—with no qualification—that seriously does not want to be "solipsistic" will from the beginning be multi-cultural or state the appropriate qualifications. How we think and what we think about does depend in large part on who is there—not to mention who is expected or encouraged to speak. (Recall the boys in the *Symposium* sending the flute girls out.) Conversations and criticism take place in particular circumstances. Turf matters. So does the fact of who if anyone already has set up the terms of the conversations.

5. Theory cannot be useful to anyone interested in resistance and change unless there is reason to believe that knowing what a theory means and believing it to be true have some connection to resistance and change. As we make theory and offer it up to others, what do we assume is the connection between theory and consciousness? Do we expect others to read theory, understand it, believe it, and have their consciousnesses and lives thereby transformed? If we really want theory to make a difference to people's lives, how ought we to present it? Do we think people come to consciousness by reading? only by reading? Speaking to people through theory (orally or in writing) is a *very* specific context-dependent activity. That is, theory makers and their methods and concepts constitute a community of people and of shared meanings. Their language can be just as opaque and foreign to those not in the community as a foreign tongue or dialect.[3] Why do we engage in *this* activity and what effect do we think it ought to have? As Helen Longino has asked: "Is 'doing theory' just a bonding ritual for academic or educationally privileged feminist women?" Again, whom does our theory making serve?

SOME SUGGESTIONS ABOUT HOW TO DO THEORY THAT IS NOT IMPERIALISTIC, ETHNOCENTRIC, DISRESPECTFUL

(*Problematically in the voice of a woman of color*)
What are the things we need to know about others,

and about ourselves, in order to speak intelligently, intelligibly, sensitively, and helpfully about their lives? We can show respect, or lack of it, in writing theoretically about others no less than in talking directly with them. This is not to say that here we have a well-worked out concept of respect, but only to suggest that together all of us consider what it would mean to theorize in a respectful way.

When we speak, write, and publish our theories, to whom do we think we are accountable? Are the concerns we have in being accountable to "the profession" at odds with the concerns we have in being accountable to those about whom we theorize? Do commitments to "the profession," method, getting something published, getting tenure, lead us to talk and act in ways at odds with what we ourselves (let alone others) would regard as ordinary, decent behavior? To what extent do we presuppose that really understanding another person or culture requires our behaving in ways that are disrespectful, even violent? That is, to what extent do we presuppose that getting and/or publishing the requisite information requires or may require disregarding the wishes of others, lying to them, wresting information from them against their wills? Why and how do we think theorizing about others provides *understanding* of them? Is there any sense in which theorizing about others is a short-cut to understanding them?

Finally, if we think doing theory is an important activity, and we think that some conditions lead to better theorizing than others, what are we going to do about creating those conditions? If we think it not just desirable but necessary for women of different racial and ethnic identities to create feminist theory jointly, how shall that be arranged for? It may be the case that at this particular point we ought not even try to do that—that feminist theory by and for Hispanas needs to be done separately from feminist theory by and for Black women, white women, etc. But it must be recognized that white/Anglo women have more power and privilege than Hispanas, Black women, etc., and at the very least they can use such advantage to provide space and time for other women to speak (with the above caveats about implicit restrictions on what counts as "the woman's voice"). And once again it is important to remember that the power of white/Anglo women vis-a-vis

Hispanas and Black women is in inverse proportion to their working knowledge of each other.

This asymmetry is a crucial fact about the background of possible relationships between white women and women of color, whether as political co-workers, professional colleagues, or friends.

If white/Anglo women and women of color are to do theory jointly, in helpful, respectful, illuminating and empowering ways, the task ahead of white/Anglo women because of this asymmetry, is a very hard task. The task is a very complex one. In part, to make an analogy, the task can be compared to learning a text without the aid of teachers. We all know the lack of contact felt when we want to discuss a particular issue that requires knowledge of a text with someone who does not know the text at all. Or the discomfort and impatience that arise in us when we are discussing an issue that presupposes a text and someone walks into the conversation who does not know the text. That person is either left out or will impose herself on us and either try to engage in the discussion or try to change the subject. Women of color are put in these situations by white/Anglo women and men constantly. Now imagine yourself simply left out but wanting to do theory with us. The first thing to recognize and accept is that you disturb our own dialogues by putting yourself in the left-out position and not leaving us in some meaningful sense to ourselves.

You must also recognize and accept that you must learn the text. But the text is an extraordinarily complex one: viz., our many different cultures. You are asking us to make ourselves more vulnerable to you than we already are before we have any reason to trust that you will not take advantage of this vulnerability. So you need to learn to become unintrusive, unimportant, patient to the point of tears, while at the same time open to learning any possible lessons. You will also have to come to terms with the sense of alienation, of not belonging, of having your world thoroughly disrupted, having it criticized and scrutinized from the point of view of those who have been harmed by it, having important concepts central to it dismissed, being viewed with mistrust, being seen as of no consequence except as an object of mistrust.

Why would any white/Anglo woman engage in this task? Out of self-interest? What in engaging in this task would be, not just in her interest, but perceived as such by her before the task is completed or well underway? Why should we want you to come into our world out of self-interest? Two points need to be made here. The task as described could be entered into with the intention of finding out as much as possible about us so as to better dominate us. The person engaged in this task would act as a spy. The motivation is not unfamiliar to us. We have heard it said that now that Third World countries are more powerful as a bloc, westerners need to learn more about them, that it is in their self-interest to do so. Obviously there is no reason why people of color should welcome white/Anglo women into their world for the carrying out of this intention. It is also obvious that white/Anglo feminists should not engage in this task under this description since the task under this description would not lead to joint theorizing of the desired sort: respectful, illuminating, helpful and empowering. It would be helpful and empowering only in a one-sided way.

Self-interest is also mentioned as a possible motive in another way. White/Anglo women sometimes say that the task of understanding women of color would entail self-growth or self-expansion. If the task is conceived as described here, then one should doubt that growth or expansion will be the result. The severe self-disruption that the task entails should place a doubt in anyone who takes the task seriously about her possibilities of coming out of the task whole, with a self that is not as fragile as the selves of those who have been the victims of racism. But also, why should women of color embrace white/Anglo women's self-betterment without reciprocity? At this time women of color cannot afford this generous affirmation of white/Anglo women.

Another possible motive for engaging in this task is the motive of duty, "out of obligation," because white/Anglos have done people of color wrong. Here again two considerations: coming into Hispano, Black, Native American worlds out of obligation puts white/Anglos in a morally self-righteous position that is inappropriate. You are active, we are passive. We become the vehicles of your own redemption. Secondly, we couldn't want you to come into our worlds "out of obligation." That is like wanting someone to make love to you out of obligation. So, whether or not you have an obligation to do this (and we would deny that you do), or whether this task could even be done out of obligation, this is an inappropriate motive.

Out of obligation you should stay out of our way, respect us and our distance, and forego the use of whatever power you have over us—for example, the power to use your language in our meetings, the power to overwhelm us with your education, the power to intrude in our communities in order to research us and to record the supposed dying of our cultures, the power to engrain in us a sense that we are members of dying cultures and are doomed to assimilate, the power to keep us in a defensive posture with respect to our own cultures.

So the motive of friendship remains as both the only appropriate and understandable motive for white/Anglo feminists engaging in the task as described above. If you enter the task out of friendship with us, then you will be moved to attain the appropriate reciprocity of care for your and our well-being as whole beings, you will have a stake in us and in our world, you will be moved to satisfy the need for reciprocity of understanding that will enable you to follow us in our experiences as we are able to follow you in yours.

We are not suggesting that if the learning of the text is to be done out of friendship, you must enter into a friendship with a whole community and for the purpose of making theory. In order to understand what it is that we are suggesting, it is important to remember that during the description of her experience of exclusion, the Hispana voice said that Hispanas experience the intimacy of friendship with white/Anglo women friends as thoroughly incomplete. It is not until this fact is acknowledged by our white/Anglo women friends and felt as a profound lack in our experience of each other that white/Anglo women can begin to see us. Seeing us in our communities will make clear and concrete to you how incomplete we really are in our relationships with you. It is this beginning that forms the proper background for the yearning to understand the text of our cultures that can lead to joint theory making.

Thus, the suggestion made here is that if white/Anglo women are to understand our voices, they must understand our communities and us in them. Again, this is not to suggest that you set out to make friends with our communities, though you may become friends with some of the members, nor is it to suggest that you should try to befriend us for the purpose of making theory with us. The latter would be a perversion of friendship. Rather, from within friendship you may be moved by friendship to undergo the very difficult task of understanding the text of our cultures by understanding our lives in our communities. This learning calls for circumspection, for questioning of yourselves and your roles in your own culture. It necessitates a striving to understand while in the comfortable position of not having an official calling card (as "scientific" observers of our communities have); it demands recognition that you do not have the authority of knowledge; it requires coming to the task without ready-made theories to frame our lives. This learning is then extremely hard because it requires openness (including openness to severe criticism of the white/Anglo world), sensitivity, concentration, self-questioning, circumspection. It should be clear that it does not consist in a passive immersion in our cultures, but in a striving to understand what it is that our voices are saying. Only then can we engage in a mutual dialogue that does not reduce each one of us to instances of the abstraction called "woman."

[1983]

NOTES

1. For a recent example, see MacKinnon, Catharine. 1982. Feminism, Marxism, method and the state: An agenda for theory. *Signs* 7 (3): 515–544.
2. I must note that when I think this "we," I think it in Spanish—and in Spanish this "we" is gendered, "nosotras." I also use "nosotros" lovingly and with ease and in it I include all members of "La raza cosmica" (Spanish-speaking people of the Americas, la gente de colores: people of many colors). In the U.S., I use "we" contextually with varying degrees of discomfort: "we" in the house, "we" in the department, "we" in the classroom, "we" in the meeting. The discomfort springs from the sense of community in the "we" and the varying degrees of lack of community in the context in which the "we" is used.
3. See Bernstein, Basil. 1972. Social class, language, and socialization. In Giglioli, Pier Paolo, ed., *Language and Social Context,* pp. 157–178. Penguin, Harmondsworth, Middlesex. Bernstein would probably, and we think wrongly, insist that theoretical terms and statements have meanings *not* "tied to a local relationship and to a local social structure," unlike the vocabulary of, e.g., working-class children.

6

Theory as Liberatory Practice

bell hooks

I came to theory because I was hurting—the pain within me was so intense that I could not go on living. I came to theory desperate, wanting to comprehend—to grasp what was happening around and within me. Most importantly, I wanted to make the hurt go away. I saw in theory then a location for healing.

I came to theory young, when I was still a child. In *The Significance of Theory* Terry Eagleton says:

> Children make the best theorists, since they have not yet been educated into accepting our routine social practices as "natural," and so insist on posing to those practices the most embarrassingly general and fundamental questions, regarding them with a wondering estrangement which we adults have long forgotten. Since they do not yet grasp our social practices as inevitable, they do not see why we might not do things differently.

Whenever I tried in childhood to compel folks around me to do things differently, to look at the world differently, using theory as intervention, as a way to challenge the status quo, I was punished. I remember trying to explain at a very young age to Mama why I thought it was highly inappropriate for Daddy, this man who hardly spoke to me, to have the right to discipline me, to punish me physically with whippings. Her response was to suggest I was losing my mind and in need of more frequent punishment.

Imagine if you will this young black couple struggling first and foremost to realize the patriarchal norm (that is of the woman staying home, taking care of the household and children while the man worked) even though such an arrangement meant that economically, they would always be living with less. Try to imagine what it must have been like for them, each of them working hard all day, struggling to maintain a family of seven children, then having to cope with one bright-eyed child relentlessly ques-

tioning, daring to challenge male authority, rebelling against the very patriarchal norm they were trying so hard to institutionalize.

It must have seemed to them that some monster had appeared in their midst in the shape and body of a child—a demonic little figure who threatened to subvert and undermine all that they were seeking to build. No wonder then that their response was to repress, contain, punish. No wonder that Mama would say to me, now and then, exasperated, frustrated, "I don't know where I got you from, but I sure wish I could give you back."

Imagine then if you will, my childhood pain. I did not feel truly connected to these strange people, to these familial folks who could not only fail to grasp my worldview but who just simply did not want to hear it. As a child, I didn't know where I had come from. And when I was not desperately seeking to belong to this family community that never seemed to accept or want me, I was desperately trying to discover the place of my belonging. I was desperately trying to find my way home. How I envied Dorothy her journey in *The Wizard of Oz*, that she could travel to her worst fears and nightmares only to find at the end that "there is no place like home." Living in childhood without a sense of home, I found a place of sanctuary in "theorizing," in making sense out of what was happening. I found a place where I could imagine possible futures, a place where life could be lived differently. This "lived" experience of critical thinking, of reflection and analysis, became a place where I worked at explaining the hurt and making it go away. Fundamentally, I learned from this experience that theory could be a healing place.

Psychoanalyst Alice Miller lets you know in her introduction to the book *Prisoners of Childhood* that it was her own personal struggle to recover from the wounds of childhood that led her to rethink and theorize anew prevailing social and critical thought about the meaning of childhood pain, of child abuse. In her adult life, through her practice, she experienced theory as a healing place. Significantly, she had to imagine herself in the space of childhood, to look again from that perspective, to remember "crucial information, answers to questions which had gone unanswered throughout [her] study of philosophy and psychoanalysis." When our lived experience of theorizing is fundamentally linked to processes of self-recovery, of collective liberation, no gap exists between theory and practice. Indeed, what such experience makes more evident is the bond between the two—that ultimately reciprocal process wherein one enables the other.

Theory is not inherently healing, liberatory, or revolutionary. It fulfills this function only when we ask that it do so and direct our theorizing towards this end. When I was a child, I certainly did not describe the processes of thought and critique I engaged in as "theorizing." Yet, as I suggested in *Feminist Theory: From Margin to Center,* the possession of a term does not bring a process or practice into being; concurrently one may practice theorizing without ever knowing/possessing the term, just as we can live and act in feminist resistance without ever using the word "feminism."

Often individuals who employ certain terms freely—terms like "theory" or "feminism"—are not necessarily practitioners whose habits of being and living most embody the action, the practice of theorizing or engaging in feminist struggle. Indeed, the privileged act of naming often affords those in power access to modes of communication and enables them to project an interpretation, a definition, a description of their work and actions, that may not be accurate, that may obscure what is really taking place. Katie King's essay "Producing Sex, Theory, and Culture: Gay/Straight Re-Mappings in Contemporary Feminism" (in *Conflicts in Feminism*) offers a very useful discussion of the way in which academic production of feminist theory formulated in hierarchical settings often enables women, particularly white women, with high status and visibility to draw upon the works of feminist scholars who may have less or no status, less or no visibility, without giving recognition to these sources. King discusses the way work is appropriated and the way readers will often attribute ideas to a well-known scholar/feminist thinker, even if that individual has cited in her work that she is building on ideas gleaned from less well-known sources. Focusing particularly on the work of Chicana theorist Chela Sandoval, King states, "Sandoval has been published only sporadically and eccentrically, yet her circulating unpublished manuscripts are much more cited and often appropriated, even while the range of

her influence is rarely understood." Though King risks positioning herself in a caretaker role as she rhetorically assumes the posture of feminist authority, determining the range and scope of Sandoval's influence, the critical point she works to emphasize is that the production of feminist theory is complex, that it is an individual practice less often than we think and usually emerges from engagement with collective sources. Echoing feminist theorists, especially women of color who have worked consistently to resist the construction of restrictive critical boundaries within feminist thought, King encourages us to have an expansive perspective on the theorizing process.

Critical reflection on contemporary production of feminist theory makes it apparent that the shift from early conceptualizations of feminist theory (which insisted that it was most vital when it encouraged and enabled feminist practice) begins to occur or at least becomes most obvious with the segregation and institutionalization of the feminist theorizing process in the academy, with the privileging of written feminist thought/theory over oral narratives. Concurrently, the efforts of black women and women of color to challenge and deconstruct the category "woman"—the insistence on recognition that gender is not the sole factor determining constructions of femaleness—was a critical intervention, one which led to a profound revolution in feminist thought and truly interrogated and disrupted the hegemonic feminist theory produced primarily by academic women, most of whom were white.

In the wake of this disruption, the assault on white supremacy made manifest in alliances between white women academics and white male peers seems to have been formed and nurtured around common efforts to formulate and impose standards of critical evaluation that would be used to define what is theoretical and what is not. These standards often led to appropriation and/or devaluation of work that did not "fit," that was suddenly deemed not theoretical—or not theoretical enough. In some circles, there seems to be a direct connection between white feminist scholars turning towards critical work and theory by white men, and the turning away of white feminist scholars from fully respecting and valuing the critical insights and theoretical offerings of black women or women of color.

Work by women of color and marginalized groups of white women (for example, lesbians, sex radicals), especially if written in a manner that renders it accessible to a broad reading public, is often de-legitimized in academic settings, even if that work enables and promotes feminist practice. Though such work is often appropriated by the very individuals setting restrictive critical standards, it is this work that they most often claim is not really theory. Clearly, one of the uses these individuals make of theory is instrumental. They use it to set up unnecessary and competing hierarchies of thought which reinscribe the politics of domination by designating work as either inferior, superior, or more or less worthy of attention. King emphasizes that "theory finds different uses in different locations." It is evident that one of the many uses of theory in academic locations is in the production of an intellectual class hierarchy where the only work deemed truly theoretical is work that is highly abstract, jargonistic, difficult to read, and containing obscure references. In Childers and hooks's "A Conversation about Race and Class" (also in *Conflicts in Feminism*) literary critic Mary Childers declares that it is highly ironic that "a certain kind of theoretical performance which only a small cadre of people can possibly understand" has come to be seen as representative of any production of critical thought that will be given recognition within many academic circles as "theory." It is especially ironic when this is the case with feminist theory. And, it is easy to imagine different locations, spaces outside academic exchange, where such theory would not only be seen as useless, but as politically nonprogressive, a kind of narcissistic, self-indulgent practice that most seeks to create a gap between theory and practice so as to perpetuate class elitism. There are so many settings in this country where the written word has only slight visual meaning, where individuals who cannot read or write can find no use for a published theory however lucid or opaque. Hence, any theory that cannot be shared in everyday conversation cannot be used to educate the public.

Imagine what a change has come about within feminist movements when students, most of whom are female, come to Women's Studies classes and read what they are told is feminist theory only to feel that what they are reading has no meaning, cannot be understood, or when understood in no way connects to "lived" realities beyond the classroom. As feminist activists we might ask ourselves, of what use is feminist theory that assaults the fragile psyches of women struggling to throw off patriarchy's oppressive yoke? We might ask ourselves, of what use is feminist theory that literally beats them down, leaves them stumbling bleary-eyed from classroom settings feeling humiliated, feeling as though they could easily be standing in a living room or bedroom somewhere naked with someone who has seduced them or is going to, who also subjects them to a process of interaction that humiliates, that strips them of their sense of value? Clearly, a feminist theory that can do this may function to legitimize Women's Studies and feminist scholarship in the eyes of the ruling patriarchy, but it undermines and subverts feminist movements. Perhaps it is the existence of this most highly visible feminist theory that compels us to talk about the gap between theory and practice. For it is indeed the purpose of such theory to divide, separate, exclude, keep at a distance. And because this theory continues to be used to silence, censor, and devalue various feminist theoretical voices, we cannot simply ignore it. Yet, despite its uses as an instrument of domination, it may also contain important ideas, thoughts, visions, that could, if used differently, serve a healing, liberatory function. However, we cannot ignore the dangers it poses to feminist struggle which must be rooted in a theory that informs, shapes, and makes feminist practice possible.

Within feminist circles, many women have responded to hegemonic feminist theory that does not speak clearly to us by trashing theory, and, as a consequence, further promoting the false dichotomy between theory and practice. Hence, they collude with those whom they would oppose. By internalizing the false assumption that theory is not a social practice, they promote the formation within feminist circles of a potentially oppressive hierarchy where all concrete action is viewed as more important than any theory written or spoken. Recently, I went to a gathering of predominantly black women where we discussed whether or not black male leaders, such as Martin Luther King and Malcolm X, should be subjected to feminist critiques that pose hard questions about their stance on gender issues. The entire discussion was less than two hours. As it drew to a close, a black woman who had been particularly silent, said that she was not interested in all this theory and rhetoric, all this talk, that she was more interested in action, in doing something, that she was "tired" of all the talk.

This woman's response disturbed me: it is a familiar reaction. Perhaps in her daily life she inhabits a world different from mine. In the world I live in daily, there are few occasions when black women or women-of-color thinkers come together to debate rigorously issues of race, gender, class, and sexuality. Therefore, I did not know where she was coming from when she suggested that the discussion we were having was common, so common as to be something we could dispense with or do without. I felt that we were engaged in a process of critical dialogue and theorizing that has long been taboo. Hence, from my perspective we were charting new journeys, claiming for ourselves as black women an intellectual terrain where we could begin the collective construction of feminist theory.

In many black settings, I have witnessed the dismissal of intellectuals, the putting down of theory, and remained silent. I have come to see that silence is an act of complicity, one that helps perpetuate the idea that we can engage in revolutionary black liberation and feminist struggle without theory. Like many insurgent black intellectuals, whose intellectual work and teaching is often done in predominantly white settings, I am often so pleased to be engaged with a collective group of black folks that I do not want to make waves, or make myself an outsider by disagreeing with the group. In such settings, when the work of intellectuals is devalued, I have in the past rarely contested prevailing assumptions, or have spoken affirmatively or ecstatically about intellectual process. I was afraid that if I took a stance that insisted on the importance of intellectual work, particularly theorizing, or if I just simply stated that I thought it was important to read widely, I would risk being seen as uppity, or as lording it over. I have often remained silent.

These risks to one's sense of self now seem trite when considered in relation to the crises we are facing as African Americans, to our desperate need to rekindle and sustain the flame of black liberation struggle. At the gathering I mentioned, I dared to speak, saying in response to the suggestion that we were just wasting our time talking, that I saw our words as an action, that our collective struggle to discuss issues of gender and blackness without censorship was subversive practice. Many of the issues that we continue to confront as black people—low self-esteem, intensified nihilism and despair, repressed rage and violence that destroys our physical and psychological well-being—cannot be addressed by survival strategies that have worked in the past. I insisted that we needed new theories rooted in an attempt to understand both the nature of our contemporary predicament and the means by which we might collectively engage in resistance that would transform our current reality. I was, however, not as rigorous and relentless as I would have been in a different setting in my efforts to emphasize the importance of intellectual work, the production of theory as a social practice that can be liberatory. Though not afraid to speak, I did not want to be seen as the one who "spoiled" the good time, the collective sense of sweet solidarity in blackness. This fear reminded me of what it was like more than ten years ago to be in feminist settings, posing questions about theory and practice, particularly about issues of race and racism that were seen as potentially disruptive of sisterhood and solidarity.

It seemed ironic that at a gathering called to honor Martin Luther King, Jr., who had often dared to speak and act in resistance to the status quo, black women were still negating our right to engage in oppositional political dialogue and debate, especially since this is not a common occurrence in black communities. Why did the black women there feel the need to police one another, to deny one another a space within blackness where we could talk theory without being self-conscious? Why, when we could celebrate together the power of a black male critical thinker who dared to stand apart, was there this eagerness to repress any viewpoint that would suggest we might collectively learn from the ideas and visions of insurgent black female intellectuals/theorists, who by the nature of the work they do are necessarily breaking with the stereotype that would have us believe the "real" black woman is always the one who speaks from the gut, who righteously praises the concrete over the abstract, the material over the theoretical?

Again and again, black women find our efforts to speak, to break silence and engage in radical progressive political debates, opposed. There is a link between the silencing we experience, the censoring, the anti-intellectualism in predominantly black settings that are supposedly supportive (like all-black woman space), and that silencing that takes place in institutions wherein black women and women of color are told that we cannot be fully heard or listened to because our work is not theoretical enough. In "Travelling Theory: Cultural Politics of Race and Representation," cultural critic Kobena Mercer reminds us that blackness is complex and multifaceted and that black people can be interpolated into reactionary and antidemocratic politics. Just as some elite academics who construct theories of "blackness" in ways that make it a critical terrain which only the chosen few can enter—using theoretical work on race to assert their authority over black experience, denying democratic access to the process of theory making—threaten collective black liberation struggle, so do those among us who react to this by promoting anti-intellectualism by declaring all theory as worthless. By reinforcing the idea that there is a split between theory and practice or by creating such a split, both groups deny the power of liberatory education for critical consciousness, thereby perpetuating conditions that reinforce our collective exploitation and repression.

I was reminded recently of this dangerous anti-intellectualism when I agreed to appear on a radio show with a group of black women and men to discuss Shahrazad Ali's *The Blackman's Guide to Understanding the Blackwoman*. I listened to speaker after speaker express contempt for intellectual work, and speak against any call for the production of theory. One black woman was vehement in her insistence that "we don't need no theory." Ali's book, though written in plain language, in a style that makes use of engaging black vernacular, has a theoretical foundation. It is rooted in theories of patriarchy (for example, the sexist, essentialist belief that male domination of females is "natural"), that misogyny is the only possible response black men can have to any attempt by women to be fully self-actualized. Many black nationalists will eagerly

embrace critical theory and thought as a necessary weapon in the struggle against white supremacy, but suddenly lose the insight that theory is important when it comes to questions of gender, of analyzing sexism and sexist oppression in the particular and specific ways it is manifest in black experience. The discussion of Ali's book is one of many possible examples illustrating the way contempt and disregard for theory undermines collective struggle to resist oppression and exploitation.

Within revolutionary feminist movements, within revolutionary black liberation struggles, we must continually claim theory as necessary practice within a holistic framework of liberatory activism. We must do more than call attention to ways theory is misused. We must do more than critique the conservative and at times reactionary uses some academic women make of feminist theory. We must actively work to call attention to the importance of creating a theory that can advance renewed feminist movements, particularly highlighting that theory which seeks to further feminist opposition to sexism, and sexist oppression. Doing this, we necessarily celebrate and value theory that can be and is shared in oral as well as written narrative.

. . .

I am grateful to the many women and men who dare to create theory from the location of pain and struggle, who courageously expose wounds to give us their experience to teach and guide, as a means to chart new theoretical journeys. Their work is liberatory. It not only enables us to remember and recover ourselves, it charges and challenges us to renew our commitment to an active, inclusive feminist struggle. We have still to collectively make feminist revolution. I am grateful that we are collectively searching as feminist thinkers/theorists for ways to make this movement happen. Our search leads us back to where it all began, to that moment when an individual woman or child, who may have thought she was all alone, began a feminist uprising, began to name her practice, indeed began to formulate theory from lived experience. Let us imagine that this woman or child was suffering the pain of sexism and sexist oppression, that she wanted to make the hurt go away. I am grateful that I can be a witness, testifying that we can create a feminist theory, a feminist practice, a revolutionary feminist movement that can speak directly to the pain that is within folks, and offer them healing words, healing strategies, healing theory. There is no one among us who has not felt the pain of sexism and sexist oppression, the anguish that male domination can create in daily life, the profound and unrelenting misery and sorrow.

Mari Matsuda has told us that "we are fed a lie that there is no pain in war," and that patriarchy makes this pain possible. Catharine MacKinnon reminds us that "we know things with our lives and we live that knowledge, beyond what any theory has yet theorized." Making this theory is the challenge before us. For in its production lies the hope of our liberation, in its production lies the possibility of naming all our pain—of making all our hurt go away. If we create feminist theory, feminist movements that address this pain, we will have no difficulty building a mass-based feminist resistance struggle. There will be no gap between feminist theory and feminist practice.

[1994]

Lexicon of the Debates

INTRODUCTION

This "Lexicon" has two purposes. Its first purpose is to familiarize you with some of the keywords of feminist theory and to put that vocabulary in context. The terms with which we have named these short essays come, for the most part, from the language of contemporary feminist theory. Nevertheless, they point to debates that have, in one way or another, contributed to shaping feminist theories throughout their history. Although "intersections of race, class and gender" or "essentialism," for example, were not the terms in which Sojourner Truth or Simone de Beauvoir cast their arguments specifically, the understanding and issues that these terms bring into focus were very much a part of their thinking about women. A few of the terms, most particularly "psychoanalysis" and "Third World women," emerged from specific historical moments along with new questions for theory and the need for new frameworks.

The second purpose of the "Lexicon" is to define some threads of debate that run through the readings collected here. Clearly these debates are not the only ones that a reader might identify. Nevertheless, those we have named do seem to us to raise major questions that have been of concern to feminist theory throughout the two-hundred-year history covered by this volume. The ten debates identified by the lexicon entries are, of course, interconnected and intersecting. Short bibliographies at the end of each lexicon entry suggest readings inside the reader that extrapolate the debates and arguments we have briefly outlined in each short essay.

These essays are meant to be starting places for thinking and reading. They attempt to raise very briefly some of the variety of perspectives that have, in different periods, shaped these debates in feminist theory and to help students connect these debates with the words and terms most frequently used to articulate them. We recommend that students pursue a thorough understanding of the debates through the reading recommended in the bibliographies. In addition, we suggest using some of the excellent references available on the language of feminist theory for more specific definitions of terms you encounter here and throughout the readings in this volume:

Sonya Andermahr, Terry Lovell, and Carol Walkowitz. (1997). *A Glossary of Feminist Theory.* London: Edward Arnold.
Janet Boles. (1996). *Historical Dictionary of Feminism.* Lanham, MD: Scarecrow.
Maggie Humm. (1995). *A Dictionary of Feminist Theory,* Second Edition. Columbus, OH: Ohio State University Press.
Cheris Kramarae and Paula Treichler. (1985). *A Feminist Dictionary.* Boston: Pandora.

BODIES

In Western thought (Euro/North American), bodies have historically been distinct from minds; the **mind** is privileged ("I think therefore I am") and the province of men/rational beings, whereas bodies are denigrated and associated with women. Because women have been linked with the **material** world through their bodies, they have become objects, property, and valuable for their exchangeability among men. Because they have been identified through their bodies with nature, they have become in Judeo–Christian discourse part of that over which "man" has dominion (Ortner, Plaskow). Because of the construction of their genitalia, their lack of a penis or phallus, psychology after Freud has viewed women as inferior to men in their mental and moral development. Because of their reproductive capacities, their pregnant bodies and monthly cycles, culture marks women as mysterious, taboo, or dangerous (Douglass), thus societies assign them to the **private sphere**, denying them access to employment, education, and civic life. Such assumptions about unambiguous anatomical and physiological distinctions—of **sexual difference**—have grounded both historical and contemporary discussions of "men" and "women."

Women's bodies are continually reshaped, covered, and uncovered according to prevailing ideology through fashion, corsets, diets, exercise programs, foot binding, or veiling, among other things. As material objects, women's bodies are "to be looked at" (Mulvey, Kaplan). They are displayed in art, film, advertising, and pornography. Bodily intactness, women's virginity, is protected in order to ensure marriageability and determination of paternity and inheritance. **Race and class** also determine the use of women's bodies—one body for leisure, decoration, and protection (the middle-upper-class woman's body) and another body for labor and exploitation (the working-class/woman of color's body).

Varied conceptions of women's bodies were central to many nineteenth century-feminists' campaigns. In the 1848 "Declaration of Sentiments," U.S. suffragists sought to end husbands' absolute power over their wives and their right of "chastisement" of their wives' bodies. The campaigns against the **trafficking in women** and the Contagious Diseases Acts condemned the sexual double standard, which ignored men's sexual promiscuity but permitted the sale and sexual exploitation of women's bodies in prostitution. (Butler; Goldman) Advocates of birth control see a woman's ability "to determine whether she will be a mother" (Sanger) as the basis of all other freedoms. The issue of women's difference, particularly based on their motherhood, also divided feminists in the nineteenth and early twentieth centuries. Labor advocates often used women's bodily differences and their role as child-bearers to argue for **protective** measures that would shorten their hours and improve their working conditions (Jones). Others, like Alice Paul and the Women's Party campaigners for an Equal Rights Amendment, saw such arguments for protection based on bodily difference as dooming women to continued second-class status. (See Cott, 1990.)

The struggle for women's right to control their bodies underlies much of second-wave feminist activism in the movement for reproductive rights and choice, the women's health movement, and the lesbian rights movement. Second-wave feminists analyzed the exploitation of women's bodies in advertising, pornography, film, art, and other visual media (e.g., Kate Millett, *Sexual Politics*; Susan Griffin, *Pornography and Silence*), and protested the violation of women's bodies through battering, rape (Brownmiller), and forced sterilization. In the United States, such efforts are rooted for the most part in **radical** and **cultural feminism, which** take women's differences, and motherhood in particular, to be resources for feminism that they must wrest from **patriarchal** control. So, for example, Adrienne Rich in *Of Woman Born* analyzed the history of male control of childbirth and argued that women must see motherhood as a resource and a power and take back control of that process. Influenced by French feminists Hélène Cixous and Luce Irigaray, who upended Lacan's consignment of women to prelinguistic immanence, feminist writers and critics have seen the body as a creative resource and speak of **"writing the body"** and of writing in the "white ink" of mother's milk.

More recently, feminist activists have analyzed the impact of cultural ideology on the bodies of girls, by examining the pervasiveness of anorexia nervosa, bulimia, and negative body image. They have continued to struggle for reproductive rights in the United States, looking now also at the proliferation of new reproductive technologies and joining the international struggle of women against coercive family planning policies and female genital mutilation, against the continued use of rape as a tool of war, and against environmental degradation and its particular impact on women's and children's health. Feminists, in this and other generations, have also recognized in myriad ways that just as the body is the basis for subjection and oppression, it is also there that resistance is first enacted—through talking back, marching, and fighting back.

Contemporary feminists also theorize the body not as the **essential** ground of women's difference, but as the site on which gender is constructed, inscribed, reinscribed, and through which gender is performed (Butler). Donna Haraway's "A Cyborg Manifesto" explores the body as a contested site overdetermined by science, technology, and culture. Haraway proposes the cyborg, "a hybrid of machine and organism," as a way out of the dilemmas of the Western construction of the body, "a way out of the maze of dualisms in which we have explained our bodies and our tools to ourselves" (Haraway).

FURTHER READING

In the Reader:

Sojourner Truth, "Ain't I a Woman?" (1851)
Josephine Butler, "Letter to My Countrywomen, Dwelling in the Farmsteads and Cottages of England" (1871)
Emma Goldman, "The Traffic in Women" (1911)
Margaret Sanger, from *Woman and the New Race* (1920)
Kate Millett, from *Sexual Politics* (1969)
Sherry B. Ortner, "Is Female to Male as Nature Is to Culture?" (1974)
Susan Brownmiller, from *Against Our Will: Men, Women and Rape* (1975)
Hélène Cixous, "The Laugh of the Medusa" (1975)
Luce Irigaray, from *This Sex Which Is Not One* (1977)
Donna Haraway, "A Cyborg Manifesto: Science, Technology and Socialist-Feminism in the Late Twentieth Century" (1985)
Angela Y. Davis, "Outcast Mothers and Surrogates: Racism and Reproductive Politics in the Nineties" (1991)
Judith Butler, from *Gender Trouble: Feminism and the Subversion of Identity* (1990)

EPISTEMOLOGIES

If "knowledge is power," it is not surprising that **epistemologies,** theories of **knowledge** and **knowledge production,** have been and are central to feminist theory. Knowledge is that body of information, facts, and theories through which a society or culture defines what is true and important, what constitutes its past, and how it understands the complexities of the natural and social worlds. To be excluded from these bodies of knowledge and the sites and processes of knowledge production, as women and other marginalized groups have been, is to live in a "reality" not of one's own making.

One project of feminist epistemology is therefore to critique this "partial knowledge" (Minnich) and to understand how it perpetuates hierarchy and domination. Creating an inclusive curriculum in all disciplines, expanding the canon in literature, music, art, and philosophy, as well as women's studies and feminist theory themselves—all represent such strategies. Another project of feminist epistemology is to ask how **social location**—gender, as well as race, class, sexuality, age, and ability—affects knowing and the processes of knowledge production. Are there **"women's ways of knowing"** and "women's knowledge"? How does the knowledge women produce about themselves differ from that produced by patriarchy and the dominant culture? Is the margin occupied by women and people of color a better location for knowledge production than the center? Do they, in other words, occupy a site of **epistemological privilege?**

In nineteenth-century and early twentieth-century feminist thought, the first of these feminist projects is most evident in the analysis of the exclusion of women from sites of knowledge production—education, government, the church, arts and letters, and the professions—and the omission of women from the knowledge produced and the denial to women, no matter their race or class, of authority as knowers. Thus Virginia Woolf found in the British Library catalogue only a distorted history of women written by men and Elizabeth Cady Stanton grappled with equally skewed interpretations of women in the Bible. Stanton's *Women's Bible* also engaged in the second project of feminist epistemology in that it attempted to replace patriarchal readings of biblical texts with feminist readings. Nineteenth-century women's public telling of their own experiences of sexuality (Butler), marriage (Cobbe), and racism and sexism (Cooper) were all attempts to produce new knowledge—women's knowledge—about women's lives. Many nineteenth-century arguments for women's political and professional enfranchisement assumed that women would bring to public life special kinds of knowledge acquired through lives of nurturance and care. Such arguments are not unlike the arguments made by **cultural feminists** in the 1970s and early 1980s.

Second-wave feminism developed its own epistemology in the process of **consciousness raising,** a model for generating knowledge from the **authority of** individual women's **experience.** At the same time, academic women's studies and feminist scholarship in the disciplines began to transform both the knowledge base and the theoretical and critical methodologies of academic research. In the 1980s, work by Carol Gilligan in *In a Different Voice,* by Blanche Clinchy and colleagues in *Women's Ways of Knowing,* and by Sara Ruddick in "Maternal Think-ing" suggested that women employed alternative processes of thought, moral deci-sion making, and theorizing. Simultaneously, French feminists and others influenced by postmodernism critiqued the **dualisms** inherent in **hegemonic** Western thought and sought sources of knowledge that would rupture, subvert, and free them from the control of being the devalued term "woman" in the equation (Cixous, Wittig). At the same time, and sometimes in response to these theories, feminists of color (hooks, Collins) and Third World feminists (Minh Ha, Chow) argued that the mar-ginal positions they occupy confer a certain **epistemological privilege** as locations for knowledge production and from which to analyze the structure of oppression and domination that constitute patriarchal Western thought. Gloria Anzaldúa, for exam-ple, suggested that a **mestiza consciousness,** a consciousness that comes from in-habiting contradictory locations simultaneously, can be a particularly productive location for knowledge production because it challenges dualism and is flexible and tolerant of ambiguity.

Feminist debates about epistemology have also focused particularly on what Sandra Harding called "the science question in feminism." Theorists have closely scrutinized Western enlightenment models of knowledge seeking, specifically **objec-tivity, empiricism, and positivism,** methods that supposedly guarantee neutrality and prevent the knower from "biasing," the knowledge "he" produces. These mod-els, characterized as "the Archimedean perspective" (Jehlen), "the view from no-where" (Harding, Minnich), and the "God's eye trick" (Haraway), deny the relevance of the identity and social location of knowers, so that they fail to notice how they perpetuate the world view of privileged, included groups and how they exclude the knowledge, experience, and questions of women and other marginalized groups. With Audre Lorde, who asserts that "the master's tools will never dismantle the mas-ter's house," some feminists have rejected positivism and empiricism entirely and the methodologies they have produced, and have argued instead that knowledge must always be produced out of women's **experience** and tested against it. Others have argued that empiricism, the scientific method, and quantitative analysis are neutral tools that have been deployed in biased research but that can, with care and close scrutiny, be used to advance feminist research as well. In either case, articulation of the position or **social location** of the researchers thus becomes a crucial component of research. Concepts such as **feminist standpoint** (Harding, Hartsock, Smith) and **situated knowledge** (Haraway) have been proposed by feminist theorists as models of knowing that can replace "the view from nowhere" with the "view from women's lives" (Harding, "Reinventing" 269). They may also provide feminism with episte-mologies and methodologies that can be used in the cause of liberation rather than of domination.

FURTHER READING

In the Reader:

Mary Wollstonecraft, from *Vindication of the Rights of Woman* (1792)
Elizabeth Cady Stanton, from *The Woman's Bible* (1895)
Monique Wittig, "The Straight Mind" (1978)
Carol Gilligan, from *In a Different Voice* (1982)

Maria C. Lugones and Elizabeth V. Spelman, "Have We Got a Theory for You! Feminist Theory, Cultural Imperialism and the Demand for 'The Woman's Voice'" (1983)

Donna Haraway, "A Cyborg Manifesto: Science, Technology, and Socialist-Feminism in the Late Twentieth Century" (1985)

Sandra Harding, from *The Science Question in Feminism* (1986)

Gloria Anzaldúa, "La Conciencia de la Mestiza: Towards a New Consciousness" (1987)

Elizabeth Minnich, from *Transforming Knowledge* (1989)

Patricia Hill Collins, from *Black Feminist Thought: Knowledge, Consciousness and the Politics of Empowerment* (1990)

Evelyn Fox Keller, "Making Gender Visible in the Pursuit of Nature's Secrets" (1993)

ESSENTIALISM/SOCIAL CONSTRUCTION/DIFFERENCE

One of the defining conversations in feminist theory has been that between an **essentialist** position—the belief that there is an immutable, eternal, and transhistorical essence of femaleness and maleness—and a **social constructionist** position, in which women and men are seen as produced through a "complex system of cultural, social, psychical and historical differences" (Fuss, xii). For the essentialist, **sexual difference** is innate, natural, inborn, and persistent, whereas the social constructionist would argue, with Simone de Beauvoir, Monique Wittig, and others, that "one is not born a woman" but becomes one through social and cultural processes.

Essentialism is exemplified by arguments invoking **sisterhood** or a unitary female culture or voice (Gilligan), by radical feminist assertions of the universal oppression/subordination of women (Daly), by psychological theories that assume that female genitalia or a single developmental pattern adequately explain all women (Freud), and by the assertion that "the" women's movement could speak with one voice for all women (NOW). Social constructionists, on the other hand, root their arguments in understandings of differences between and among women. Following on Margaret Mead's work in *Sex and Temperament,* they argue that there is a distinction between biological **sex** and **gender** that is socially produced. Therefore, to study women and sexual difference—the social constructionist would argue—one must specify and particularize the different social, cultural, and historical situations by which they are produced.

Though **"essentialism"** and **"social construction"** are twentieth-century terms, the issues to which they point were also concerns of nineteenth-century feminists. For example, both Mary Wollstonecraft in the eighteenth century and Florence Nightingale in the nineteenth century saw the socially prescribed frivolity and aimlessness of middle-class women's lives rather than any innate inferiority, as the roots of sexual difference. Women's contributions to public life and thought have been limited, not because they have different capacities or natures but because they live in different social circumstances. Sojourner Truth's question, "Ain't I a Woman?" challenged any concept of an essential "woman's nature" that is generalized from a white, middle-class idea of femininity. However, many nineteenth-century feminists based their arguments in an essentialist view of women. John Stuart Mill argued for women's right to exercise their talents in all facets of public and private life, yet he believed that they might naturally prefer motherhood and childrearing to public life. Some suffrage campaigners and social reformers made distinctly essentialist arguments, which, like the arguments of twentieth-century cultural feminists, valorized women's difference. They believed that women should have the vote and be involved in the formation of public and social policy *because* their moral natures were inherently different and superior to those of men.

Pointing out that the **essential woman** who became the subject of second-wave feminism was in fact white, middle-class and heterosexual, twentieth-century feminists of color, lesbian feminists, and postcolonial feminists have called for anti-essentialist feminist theory based on confronting and examining differences of race, class, gender, sexual orientation, age, ability, and nationality. "Women," said bell hooks in *Feminist Theory: From Margin to Center* "do not need to eradicate difference, to feel solidarity. We do not need to share common oppression to fight equally to end oppression" (65). As hooks' comment suggests, questions of essentialism have been central to recent discussions of **identity** and **identity politics.** Is a sense of gender, race, or sexual orientation as innate and inborn, or at least unitary and persistent, the only possible basis for resisting domination and oppression? Or can such a politics be rooted in an identity defined as "an active construction and a discursively mediated interpretation of one's history" (de Lauretis, 263)? Some, like Gayatri Spivak, have argued that a feminist politics can be rooted in a **"strategic essentialism,"** constructed by a subordinate group as a ground for organizing and resistance.

In the 1990s, feminist theorists, among them Ruth Hubbard, Diana Fuss, Teresa de Lauretis, and Linda Alcoff, began to resist the rigid opposition of the essentialist and social constructionist positions and to see them as unhelpful and reductionist ways to characterize feminist thought. Hubbard, for example, argued that biological and social determinants of gender are continually interacting and mutually constituting effects rather than opposing forces. Others articulated theoretical understandings that reconcile the two positions (Alcoff) or see how fully implicated in each other they are (Fuss); they argued in concert with Teresa de Lauretis that the subject of feminism is not "Woman" but rather the "female-embodied social subject" (267).

FURTHER READING
In the Reader:

Mary Wollstonecraft, from *A Vindication of the Rights of Woman* (1792)
Sojourner Truth, "Ain't I a Woman?" (1851)
John Stuart Mill and Harriet Taylor, from *The Subjection of Women* (1870)
Stella Browne, "Studies in Feminine Inversion" (1923)
Margaret Mead, from *Sex and Temperament in the Three Primitive Societies* (1935)
Simone de Beauvoir, from *The Second Sex* (1949)
Shulamith Firestone, from *The Dialectic of Sex* (1970)
Sherry B. Ortner, "Is Female to Male as Nature Is to Culture?" (1974)
Sara Ruddick, from *Maternal Thinking: Toward a Politics of Peace* (1980)
Linda Alcoff, "Cultural Feminism Versus Post-Structuralism: The Identity Crisis in Feminist Theory" (1988)
Joan W. Scott, "Deconstructing Equality Versus Difference" (1988)
Diana Fuss, from *Essentially Speaking* (1989)

INTERSECTIONS OF RACE, CLASS, AND GENDER

The phrase **"the intersections of race, class, and gender"** is one contemporary naming of the understanding that women's lives are not shaped by gender alone but rather that individuals are multiply constituted by gender, race, class, sexuality, nationality, age, ability, and other social experiences, identities, and phenomena that we live simultaneously rather than separately. Other phrases like bell hooks' **"interlocking systems of domination"** and Deborah King's **"multiple jeopardy"** also express this understanding. An intersections analysis allows us to understand "our capacity as women and men to be either dominated or dominating [as] a point of connection, or commonality" (hooks).

This paradigm is posed against **a hierarchy of oppression** in which one oppressive structure—racism, classism, sexism, heterosexism—is seen as the first, deepest, or most pervasive oppression. Examples of such thinking are found in the oppositions posed at some points in the nineteenth century between the cause of the abolition of slavery and the cause of women's suffrage or, in the 1960s, between civil rights and women's rights. Women working in labor and leftist movements have been urged to work for a revolution that will overthrow capitalist class oppression and, allegedly in the process, end gender oppression (Hartmann). Women of color and poor and working-class women have been urged by the women's movement to join in **sisterhood** with white women to struggle against sexism, and to give that work priority over struggling with men of color against racism or with poor and working-class men against class oppression. Black women "are made to feel disloyal to racial interests if they insist on women's rights" (Murray). An intersections analysis would propose that we understand all of these causes as interlocking pieces of a structure of domination that must be dismantled in toto.

Nineteenth-century women in the United States, black and white, did attempt to analyze the relationship between race and gender. Angelina Grimké speaks of the particularities of the sexual exploitation of female slaves and of the complicity and degradation of white women who witness this exploitation and do nothing. Anna Julia Cooper, Mary Church Terrell, and others see "the colored woman" as confronting both a "woman question" and "a race problem" (Cooper). For the most part, however, the white women's movement in the first and second waves failed to incorporate such an understanding and was critiqued by women of color, beginning with Sojourner Truth at the Seneca Falls women's suffrage convention. The work of feminist scholars of color, along with lesbian and socialist/working-class scholars, in the 1970s and 1980s (Audre Lorde, Gloria Anzaldúa, Barbara Smith, bell hooks, Charlotte Bunch, Marilyn Frye) in particular, extends this critique and attempts to insist on **difference** as a resource for feminist thinking and organizing. "It is not those differences between us that are separating us," writes Audre Lorde. "It is rather our refusal to recognize those differences, and to examine the distortions that result from our misnaming them and their effects upon human behavior and expectation" ("Age, Race, Sex, and Class"). Academic feminists must "recognize difference as a crucial strength. . . . In our world, divide and conquer must become define and empower" ("The Master's Tools . . .").

FURTHER READING

In the Reader:
Sojourner Truth, "Ain't I a Woman?" (1851)

Anna Julia Cooper, from *A Voice of the South* (1892)
Florynce Kennedy, "A Comparative Study: Accentuating the Similarities in the Social Positions of Women and Negroes" (1946)
Pauli Murray, "The Liberation of Black Women" (1970)
Combahee River Collective, "A Black Feminist Statement" (1977)
Audre Lorde, "Age, Race, Sex, and Class" (1978)
Mitsuye Yamada, "Asian Pacific American Women and Feminism" (1981)
Heidi Hartmann, "The Unhappy Marriage of Marxism and Feminism: Toward a More Progressive Union" (1981)
Maria C. Lugones and Elizabeth V. Spelman, "Have We Got a Theory for You! Feminist Theory, Cultural Imperialism and the Demand for 'The Woman's Voice'" (1983)
bell hooks, "Feminism: A Transformational Politic" (1989)
Emma Pérez, "Speaking from the Margin: Uninvited Discourse on Sexuality and Power" (1993)

LANGUAGE

"The words we use daily reflect our cultural understandings and at the same time transmit them to the next generation through an agency that subserves the culture's needs" (Miller and Swift). Language constructs assumptions about gender along with other cultural understandings. Therefore, critiques of language use have been central to feminist analysis: the most basic objections about forms of address, formal ("Miss," "Mrs.," "Ms.") and informal ("baby," "chick," "bitch," "honey"); the use of the generic "man"; challenges to religious systems in which "God the Father" is the primary way of designating the sacred. Women writers have questioned the possibility of writing in language, forms, or genres so burdened with patriarchal cultural assumptions that they may be unusable to express women's knowledge or experience.

"Finding one's voice," "naming oneself," reclaiming, reconstructing, and "stealing" the language are therefore essential activities and metaphors for feminist work and feminist theory. For some feminists, this means trying to rewrite the lexicon at the most basic level: by changing the titles of women who do certain jobs (as in actor not actress, flight attendant not stewardess); by reclaiming and redefining derogatory words like "dyke," "crone," and "bitch"; and by dictionary making, as in Treichler and Kramarae's *A Feminist Dictionary*, Mary Daly's *Intergalactic Wickedary*, and this lexicon itself. For others, this means recovering or transforming literary forms and genres or looking for sites of expression outside of language, in the nonverbal, in silence and in the body.

Nineteenth-century feminists grappled first with the assumption of women's public silence—their culture told them that the very acts of speaking and writing were unwomanly. In order to write novels or poetry or to speak or write publicly about politics, suffrage, or birth control, women had first to assert their right of access to language and then to claim for themselves the name of "author" or "citizen." The 1848 Seneca Falls Declaration of Sentiments, appropriating the language of the founding documents of the United States, was simultaneously engaged in asserting women's right to citizenship *and* women's right to the language of citizenship. Early in the twentieth century, Virginia Woolf attempted to imagine in *A Room of One's Own* how women may claim language and authorship for themselves and what their work and their words would look like undistorted by patriarchal culture.

Feminists of the second wave continue this project of giving public language to women's work and experience. The title that Betty Friedan gave to the first section of *The Feminine Mystique*—"The Problem That Has No Name"—points directly to the problem of language: women do not have the words to name their experiences. Among the activities of second-wave feminism was this activity of giving name and voice to women's experience through consciousness raising, through the recovery of women's writing, through attempts to reform the discourse of the church, the academy, the household and the workplace, and through cracking open generic concepts like "man" and "masculine" to reveal their asymmetry and women's invisibility in them (Miller and Swift).

French feminist theorists such as Cixous and Irigaray have approached these questions through Lacan's understanding of psychological development as the entry into language or the **symbolic order,** which he names **the Law of the father.** Women, in Lacan's understanding, are outside of language—they belong to the immanent, the prelinguistic moment when the child is not separate from the mother and therefore has no need of language. Cixous and Irigaray have suggested that this immanence, this association with the body and a location outside **phallogocentric** discourse, can be made a resource for speech and language—that women must **write the body** rather than the father's words.

Throughout the nineteenth and twentieth centuries, women writers have wrestled with these language questions. They have asked with Virginia Woolf whether there is a "female sentence," whether language is distinctly marked by gender. They have both transformed traditional forms and sought out the literary forms—letters, diaries, autobiographies, novels, memoirs—which seemed most apt for the expression of their lived experience. Latina, Asian, and Native American women writers and scholars (Anzaldúa, Gunn Allen) have produced bilingual texts that raise questions about translation and cultural identity and that explore the relationship between language, gender, and culture.

FURTHER READING

In the Reader:

Elizabeth Cady Stanton, from *The Woman's Bible* (1895)
Virginia Woolf, *A Room of One's Own* (1929)
Hélène Cixous, "The Laugh of the Medusa" (1975)
Casey Miller and Kate Swift, from *Words and Women* (1976)
Luce Irigaray, from *This Sex Which Is Not One* (1977)
Audre Lorde, "Poetry Is Not a Luxury" (1977)
Paula Treichler and Cheris Kramarae, from *The Feminist Dictionary* (1985)
Paula Gunn Allen, "Kochinnenako in Academe" (1986)
Gloria Anzaldúa, "La Conciencia de la Mestiza: Towards a New Consciousness" (1987)

POWER

Power is one of the two primary divisions in social and economic life decided on the basis of gender; the division of labor is the other. Any analysis of women's situations and conditions is grounded in the assumption of power's **asymmetrical division,** that "woman [is] always and everywhere subject to *male* man" (Beard). Power has been and remains a complex and vexing question for feminist theory. Power as force exerted through **domination** and **exploitation** has been condemned and repudiated by most feminist theorists, whereas power embodied as **equality** in political, legal, and economic rights has been sought by many. As feminist theorists have critiqued abuses of public power in militarism, economic exploitation, colonialism, and private power in rape, battering, harassment, and incest, they have also asked how power can be redefined and whether women have any special or distinctive contribution to make to that redefinition. Feminists have fruitfully disentangled the questions of **power over,** as opposed to the **power to,** act, think, speak, and demand change (Starhawk). This principle of **empowerment** underlies feminist activism and theory.

Power is located "everywhere" as Michel Foucault would later point out, in all aspects of the public and private realm. Nineteenth-century feminists examined the effects of women's exclusion from public power as it emanates through laws, governments, and other social institutions. They sought women's enfranchisement in these institutions, primarily through admission to political suffrage but also through campaigns for women's admission to full professional participation in law, education, medicine, politics, and so on. But they also understood, as John Stuart Mill asserted, that "the family is a school for depotism," that the private was as much a site for the exercise and abuse of power as the public sphere (Cobbe). They also realized that women always have the power of even the most abject subjects—the power to resist their conditions and situations.

Like their nineteenth-century sisters, twentieth-century liberal feminists attempted to address the unequal distribution of power through reform of public legal and political institutions. On the other hand, second-wave radical feminists made central the theoretical insight that the **"personal is political,"** that power relations operate in personal as in public life. This is one of the many things meant by Kate Millett's notion of **"sexual politics"**—that male dominance suffuses our most local and intimate lives. Hence the focus in radical feminist analysis on rape, battering, pornography, and all forms of violence against women. However, the emergence of lesbian writings on sadomasochism (also in the 1980s) opened up discussions of women's own relations to power in the realm of sexuality, and certainly helped to demystify the assumption that women wanted nothing to do with power.

A suspicion of power led to feminist organizing that attempted to make decisions on the basis of consensus, by assuming that this was a more "feminist" approach to forms of governance—**"sisterhood is powerful."** Cultural feminism theorizes women's more benign use of power as an inherent inclination to peace and "preservative love" (Ruddick) rather than to war and domination. Such a notion of women's rejection of paradigms of domination and exploitation in relation to the earth has been particularly crucial to **ecofeminism.**

Most recently, feminist theory has found useful Michel Foucault's understanding of power as polymorphous and "located everywhere." He argues that power is exercised in twentieth-century societies less through monolithic state institutions than through pervasive regulatory mechanisms of self-surveillance and discipline. These notions have proved useful to feminist theory in understanding, for example, women's submission of their bodies to the disciplines of diet and fashion.

FURTHER READING

In the Reader:

Sojourner Truth, "Keeping the Thing Going While Things Are Stirring" (1867)
Anna Julia Cooper, from *A Voice of the South* (1892)
Mary Ritter Beard, from *Woman as a Force in History* (1946)
Valerie Solanas, *SCUM Manifesto* (1967)
Hélène Cixous, "The Laugh of the Medusa" (1975)
Marilyn Frye, "Some Reflections on Separatism and Power" (1978)
Ynestra King, "Feminism and the Revolt Against Nature" (1981)
Chandra Talpade Mohanty, "Under Western Eyes: Feminist Scholarship and Colonial Discourses" (1984/ 1991)
Catharine A. MacKinnon, "Sexuality, Pornography and Method: 'Pleasure Under Patriarchy' " (1989)

PSYCHOANALYSIS IN/AND FEMINISM

Psychoanalysis has been both a productive and a problematic framework for feminism and feminist theory. Psychoanalytic theory as developed by Sigmund Freud in the late nineteenth and early twentieth centuries locates the roots of adult identity and male/female difference in sexuality and psychosexual development. Feminists throughout the twentieth century have critiqued the **biological determinism** of Freud's assertion that women are inferior and that their development is troubled because of their deficient genitalia, their **lack of and envy of the penis.** However, feminists have also found useful analytical tools in such key Freudian concepts as the **unconscious** and such methods as the **talking cure.**

Women were important in the very early decades of the establishment of psychoanalysis as practitioners and as some of Freud's most written-about patients (Dora, Anna O.), whose analysis led to some of the grounding insights of this new field. Karen Horney, an early disciple of psychoanalysis, was also one of the early feminist critics of Freud, and argued that social process and social relations rather than differences in genitalia are the source of differences between the sexes. Horney asserted that it is men's greater social power and not their penises that women envy and desire. In *The Second Sex* (1949), Simone de Beauvoir continued this critique. Although de Beauvoir saw some of the methods and insights of psychoanalysis as an advance over earlier wholly biological explanations of difference, she saw as problematic for women Freud's construction of the male as human norm and the female as "mutilated male." Freud's description of women as deviations from the male was, for de Beauvoir, one example of the ways that culture constructs woman as man's **other,** rather than as an autonomous being.

Some of Freud's concepts were eagerly assimilated in America and Great Britain in what would come to be characterized as ego psychology and object relations theory, a school of thought most closely associated with Melanie Klein and her followers, such as D. W. Winnicott in Great Britain or Nancy Chodorow and Jessica Benjamin in the United States. However, Freud's work was attacked by second-wave feminists, including Betty Friedan, Shulamith Firestone, and Kate Millett, as hostile to women and a contributing factor in their continued subordination.

During the 1960s in Paris, psychoanalysis underwent a transformation through the work of Jacques Lacan, who meticulously reread Freud and reinterpreted his ideas. In Lacan's work, sexual difference is marked not by different genitalia but by different relationships with language. Males break away from prelinguistic connection with the mother to enter into language, **subjectivity,** and **the symbolic order;** females never do make this transition but remain tied to the mother and outside of language. Despite its continued reinforcement of a concept of sexual difference, Lacan's work has been of tremendous use to feminist theory. Feminist film theorists have deployed Lacanian psychoanalysis to discuss relations established between filmgoers and cinematic representations. French feminist theorists, Cixous and Irigaray in particular, have borrowed from Lacanian discussions their critique of what they named **phallogocentrism**—the rule of language, the law, and the phallus as **"transcendental signifier."** However, they have also found ways to reimagine Lacan's relegation of women to a place outside of language as a resource for a new and subversive feminist thinking and writing, **l'écriture féminine.**

By the mid-1970s in the United States, with the publication of Juliet Mitchell's *Psychoanalysis and Feminism,* a reconsideration of psychoanalysis began that has continued to produce rich and complex questions about both the intersubjective (relations between people) and the intrapsychic (our understanding of our selves). Mitchell argued that psychoanalysis provides feminism with important tools for understanding the history of the **subject** and that Freud's work is not misogynistic, describing what woman is or should be, but rather an attempt, valuable to feminism, to "set about enquiring how she comes into being" (Mitchell, 252). In the past two decades, psychoanalysis as practiced and theorized by feminists in Europe and the United States—Jane Flax, Jane Gallop, Teresa de Lauretis, Diana Fuss, and Judith Butler among them—has remained an important tool for understanding the interrelationships of gender, sexuality, and subjectivity. Although feminism's engagements with psychoanalysis have been among the most politically charged and epistemologically troubled dialectics, many would still argue that a thoroughgoing analysis of gender and sexuality cannot be achieved without a psychology or an operative sense of the unconscious.

FURTHER READING

In the Reader:

Stella Browne, "Studies in Feminine Inversion" (1923)
Karen Horney, "The Dread of Woman" (1932)
Simone de Beauvoir, from *The Second Sex* (1949)
Kate Millett, from *Sexual Politics* (1970)
Gayle Rubin, "The Traffic in Women" (1975)
Nancy Chodorow, from *The Reproduction of Mothering: Psychoanalysis and the Sociology of Gender* (1978)
Monique Wittig, "The Straight Mind" (1978)
Diana Fuss, from *Essentially Speaking* (1989)
Carol Gilligan, "Women's Psychological Development" (1982)

SEXUAL DIVISION OF LABOR

The **sexual division of labor,** the arrangement of work into clearly gendered **public and private spheres** or spheres of **production** and **reproduction,** has been theorized particularly by **Marxist, materialist,** and **socialist feminists** in the nineteenth and twentieth centuries. Their analysis is rooted in Frederick Engels' *The Origin of the Family, Private Property and the State* (1884) which added an understanding of the sphere of reproduction and women's work to Marx's largely gender-blind division of labor analysis. Recent work of feminist ethnographers has also suggested that virtually every known society exhibits such a gendered division of labor, although specifics may vary from culture to culture. So "women's work" is always devalued although the work itself may vary.

In *The Origin of the Family,* Engels argued that "the world-wide defeat of the female sex" occurs at the moment at which early societies were able to produce surplus value (i.e., more wealth than the community or family needs to subsist) consolidated as private property. The need to pass private property on through inheritance, then, necessitates the control of women's sexuality and thus the confinement of women in the family, the private sphere of reproduction. This division of labor serves the goals of industrial capitalism well as women's unpaid labor in the private sphere is exploited by capital to reproduce and sustain the workforce.

Nineteenth- and twentieth-century feminists extended this division of labor analysis as a primary tool for understanding the gendered division of the work of child-rearing as well as occupational segregation of the paid workforce and the division of psychological and emotional labor in the family and society. Olive Schreiner critiqued women's exclusion from productive work because of her role as "child-bearer," although she notes the class bias of this ideology that keeps middle-class women idle while not protecting working-class women from drudgery as servants in those women's houses. Later, Shulamith Firestone argued that the division of reproductive labor is the cornerstone of the **sex/gender system.** Other **radical feminists** and **cultural feminists** have suggested that women's separate sphere can be a retreat, a resource, a place of safety for women, an entirely separate culture (Smith-Rosenberg).

Engels' solution to women's oppression under capitalist patriarchy was both to bring women into the public sphere of labor and to abolish the family as primary economic unit. Socialist feminists in the twentieth century have offered similar solutions. Charlotte Perkins Gilman, for example, proposed turning all of women's **unwaged labor** into paid labor through communal nurseries, laundries and kitchens, whereas other socialist feminists have proposed that women be paid "wages for housework." Psychologists Nancy Chodorow and Dorothy Dinnerstein, who saw the roots of inequality in the sexual division of child-rearing labor, argued that moving men into the private sphere to share the work of parenting equally with women will ultimately end inequality.

Although women of color and Third World women have critiqued socialist feminist analysis as, in some ways, particular to the experience of **middle-class, white, Western capitalist patriarchy,** they have also found the division of labor analysis a powerful tool for understanding their own situations in so-called developing economies. More recently, they have used it to understand the situation of Third World workers and particularly Third World women workers on the global assemblyline (Ehrenreich, Perez).

FURTHER READING
In the Reader:
Mary Wollstonecraft, from *A Vindication of the Rights of Woman* (1792)

Frederick Engels, from *The Origin of the Family, Private Property and the State* (1884)
Charlotte Perkins Gilman, from *Women and Economics* (1898)
Olive Schreiner, from *Women and Labor* (1911)
Mary Ritter Beard, from *Woman as a Force in History: A Study in Traditions and Realities* (1946)
Shulamith Firestone, from *The Dialectic of Sex* (1970)
Caroll Smith-Rosenberg, "The Female World of Love and Ritual: Relations Between Women in Nineteenth-Century America" (1975)
Heidi Hartmann, "The Unhappy Marriage of Marxism and Feminism: Towards a More Progressive Union" (1981)
Emma Pérez, "Speaking from the Margin: Uninvited Discourse on Sexuality and Power" (1993)

SEXUALITIES

"Because sexuality is," according to Gayle Rubin, "the nexus of relationship between the genders, much of the oppression of women is borne by, mediated through, and constituted within, sexuality" ("Thinking Sex" 35). Our use of the plural "sexualities" suggests that contemporary feminists theorize multiple possibilities for sexual identity, sexual orientation, and sexual expression, which have been defined through feminist theory as well as through gay and lesbian theory and queer theory. Feminists have theorized sexuality as both a site of women's domination and a potential resource for resistance, self-definition, and subjectivity.

Nineteenth-century feminists' first project was to claim sexuality for women, because prevailing ideologies defined women's "virtue" traditionally as the absence of sexual expression and experience. Indicative of the assumption of women's virtual sexlessness was the view that even physical intimacies between women were not for the most part considered to be sex. Nineteenth-century feminists organized in resistance to government, legal, and medical attempts to define and regulate women's sexuality, particularly such legislation as the Contagious Diseases Acts, which attempted to regulate prostitution, and the Comstock Act, which regulated "obscene" material and thus prevented the distribution of information on birth control. In response to these acts, Josephine Butler, Margaret Sanger, Beatrice Webb, and others argued and organized for women's right to control their own bodies and sexuality and to be free from male sexual exploitation. Their analyses offered the first comprehensive feminist analysis of **the sexual double standard**—a standard that demanded female chastity while permitting and even admiring male promiscuity.

Freud and his followers introduced into Western theory the notion that sexuality is the key determinant of identity, declaring the superiority of the penis over the inferior clitoris and defining for women "normal" sexuality as vaginally oriented and determined by penile penetration with the objective of producing a male child. All other forms of sexual expression, lesbianism in particular, were viewed as regressive and as indicative of a failure to mature.

Loosening the grip of Freudian theory in defining female sexuality was a major project of 1960's and 1970's feminists. Though they shared a common critique of the biological determinism of Freudian theory and of the "myth of the vaginal orgasm" at its center, they took many different approaches to proposing alternative views and theories of women's sexuality. American second-wave feminists like Friedan and Millett rejected Freud and argued that the social circumstances of middle-class women's lives within patriarchy rather than their genitalia are the origins of their inequality and oppression. **Sexual liberation,** a rejection of the sexual double standard and sexual freedom for women equivalent to that of men, was proposed by some feminists. **Androgyny,** a breaking of the rigid dualism of male and female and an acceptance of mingling male and female characteristics in each individual, was proposed by others. Radical feminists like Shulamith Firestone foregrounded the linkage between women's sexuality and reproduction. Firestone proposed in *The Dialectic of Sex* (1970) that women's liberation would only be accomplished when the link between sexuality and reproduction was severed through the use of technologies. French feminists Luce Irigaray and Hélène Cixous also critiqued the phallocentricism of Western thought, particularly as expressed by neo-Freudian theorist Jacques Lacan. They defined a female sexual economy that is multiple and fluid as opposed to monofocal, unitary, and linear defined by relation to the singular phallus.

The work of **lesbian theorists** Charlotte Bunch, Marilyn Frye, Ti-Grace Atkinson, Andrea Dworkin, and Monique Wittig has been central to shaping feminist understandings of sexuality. They have argued from a variety of perspectives that lesbianism is the only sexual and political choice that could free women from the domination of patriarchal heterosexuality. Adrienne Rich's essay, "Compulsory Heterosexuality and Lesbian Existence," redirects this debate by arguing that heterosexuality is a political institution that deploys a vast ideological apparatus to enforce it as normative. The essay proposes the concept of a **lesbian continuum,** "a range—through each woman's life and throughout history—of woman-identified experience, not simply the fact that a woman has had or consciously desired genital sexual experience with another woman."

In the 1980s, feminists were bitterly divided over issues of sexuality, particularly pornography, prostitution, and the status of such sexual identities and practices as sadomasochism, transgender, transsexual. Organizing against pornography and the commercial sex industry, so-called "anti-sex" feminists saw the commercial sex industry and all graphic representations of sexuality as the source of women's oppression. At the same time, other so-called "pro-sex" feminists argued for women's sexual autonomy, sexual liberation, sexual pleasure, and sexual pluralism (Vance, Rubin, MacKinnon).

In the late 1980s and the 1990s, feminist discussion of sexuality expanded in a variety of directions. Arguing that sexual desire is not innate or natural but constituted through specific social and historical processes, Foucault's *History of Sexuality* has been an important influence on recent feminist discussions of sexuality. Global/ Third World feminism has focused attention on the impact that Western sexual values and policies have had on Third World women in terms of the commercial sex trade, AIDS, international health, and family planning policy. Queer theorists have pushed these arguments further by suggesting that both sex *and* gender do not exist except as fluid performances of arbitrary categories.

FURTHER READING

In the Reader:

Josephine Butler, "Letter to My Countrywomen, Dwelling in the Farmsteads and Cottages of England" (1871)
Margaret Sanger, from *Woman and the New Race* (1920)
Stella Browne, "Studies in Feminine Inversion" (1923)
Margaret Mead, from *Sex and Temperament in Three Primitive Societies* (1935)

Kate Millett, from *Sexual Politics* (1969)
Shulamith Firestone, from *The Dialectic of Sex* (1970)
Radicalesbians, "The Woman-Identified Woman" (1970)
Hélène Cixous, "The Laugh of the Medusa" (1975)
Adrienne Rich, "Compulsory Heterosexuality and Lesbian Existence" (1980)
Catharine A. MacKinnon, "Sexuality, Pornography and Method: 'Pleasure Under Patriarchy'" (1989)
Judith Butler, from *Gender Trouble: Feminism and the Subversion of Identity* (1990)
Emma Pérez, "Speaking from the Margin: Uninvited Discourse on Sexuality and Power" (1993)
Jeannine Delombard, "Femmenism" (1995)

"THIRD WORLD"/GLOBAL FEMINISM

The term "Third World women" is used variously to designate the majority of the world's women who live outside the industrialized West and sometimes also to include women of color within Western countries. The quotation marks indicate the need to problematize this term in several ways. First, the term lumps together in a single category a vast number of women whose experiences vary widely according to class, nation, culture, and sexuality. Whatever coherence might be claimed by "Third World women" as a group is political, coming not from an identity of experience but, as Chandra Mohanty suggested, from a common context of struggle. Second, the term "Third World" itself must be handled critically as it suggests a hierarchy between First and Third Worlds that is the legacy of colonialism and imperialism. Some have suggested that the term Two-Thirds World might more appropriately be used, as it indicates the reality that the majority of the world's people live outside Europe and the United States.

According to Mohanty in her introduction to *Third World Women and the Politics of Feminism,* "histories of third world women's engagement with feminism are in short supply" (4). Certainly, nineteenth-century colonialism left Third World women largely invisible or represented them as "the exotic other." To see that these Eurocentric views were very much a part of nineteenth-century women's writing one need only look at Charlotte Bronte's representation of Bertha Mason and her use of the image of the seraglio in *Jane Eyre*.

Discussion of "Third World women" entered Anglo-American scholarship in the twentieth century through the work of women anthropologists from Margaret Mead on, who began to describe and particularize the lives of women in their ethnographic work and through sociologists and economists discussions of **women and/in development.** While these discourses have been and must be extensively critiqued for the persistence of Eurocentrism and imperialism, they also bring into Western feminism some awareness of the lives of women who had previously been invisible. Feminists working in ethnography have also been at the forefront of discussions about feminist method, reflecting on problems of gender and cultural bias in the research of Western anthropologists studying Third World peoples.

With the 1975–1985 U.N. Decade on Women meetings in Mexico City, Copenhagen, and Nairobi, attempts began to forge a **global feminism,** which means, as Charlotte Bunch put it, "recognizing that the oppression of women in one part of the world is often affected by what happens in another, and that no woman is free until the conditions of oppression of women are eliminated everywhere." Global feminism, for Bunch and others, means making the global local and the local global, understanding the different experiences of women in different parts of the world, and working in coalitions with the struggles of other women without imposing Western agendas on them.

Some of the efforts of Western women to begin to talk about the situation of Third World women were heavily critiqued by Third World women for their attempts to export a Western feminist agenda around the world and the failure to recognize the resistance and liberation struggles already being undertaken by Third World women or even to name them as feminist. The complexities of the debate over female genital mutilation have been most emblematic of the difficulties of forging such global alliances. Yet, the development of a global economy and workforce, the international trafficking in women, as well as other refugee and human rights issues for women, have made it increasingly clear how necessary it is to forge such global feminist alliances. The 1995 U.N. Conference on Women in Beijing *Platform for Action* is one clear statement of these basic needs.

Along with the work of U.S. women of color, theory produced by Third World feminist scholars, among them Rey Chow, Chandra Mohanty, and Trinh T. Minh Ha, have made crucial methodological and epistemological contributions to Anglo-American feminism. They have challenged its Eurocentricism, "uprooting dualistic thinking," as Anzaldúa suggested in her essay on a mestiza consciousness, and have demanded "a plural consciousness" . . . that "requires understanding multiple, often opposing ideas and knowledges, and negotiating these knowledges" (Mohanty 36). Some of this recent theory, most particularly the work of Gayatri Spivak, intersects with **postcolonial theory.** This work, produced by Third World and Western scholars, is closely allied with postmodernism in its attack on the hegemonic discourses of the West, in this case particularly that of colonialism/imperialism. Postcolonial feminist theory thus seeks a space and discourse in which the knowledge, activism, and subjectivity of Third World women can be articulated.

FURTHER READING

In the Reader:

Margaret Mead, from *Sex and Temperament in Three Primitive Societies* (1935)
Fatima Mernissi, from *Beyond the Veil: Male-Female Dynamics in Modern Muslim Society* (1975)
Mitsuye Yamada, "Asian-Pacific American Women and Feminism" (1981)
Chandra Talpade Mohanty, "Under Western Eyes: Feminist Scholarship and Colonial Discourses" (1984/ 1991)
Paula Gunn Allen, "Kochinnenako in Academe" (1986)
Gloria Anzaldúa, "La Conciencia de la Mestiza: Towards a New Consciousness" (1987)
The Beijing Declaration and Platform for Action (1995)

PART II

1792–1920

1792–1920: Introduction

At the end of the eighteenth century, most women in the United States and Great Britain had no public legal existence. They were either daughters identified by their fathers' status or wives identified by their husbands'. During this period, feminist theory—though this term would not have been used—for the most part attempted to analyze the legal and social disabilities women faced and to argue for the most basic rights for women. The principles of enlightenment and liberal humanism—arguments for the "rights of man," which had supported the French and American revolutions of the end of the eighteenth century—provided a theoretical basis for much nineteenth-century feminist writing. Mary Wollstonecraft's *Vindication of the Rights of Woman* (1792, reading #8) and the Seneca Falls "Declaration of Sentiments" (1848, reading #10) attempted to bring the language of "rights" to bear on the situations of women and to include women among the "humans" and "citizens" on behalf of whom rights had been won.

The major women's rights struggle of the nineteenth century was the campaign for women's suffrage, which began in the United States with the 1848 Seneca Falls meeting and continued through 1920 when the ratification of the Nineteenth Amendment gave U.S. women the vote. Such liberal arguments for basic rights were used by women's advocates in other areas as well. They supported middle-class women's struggles for the right to own property, to have custody of their children, to sue for divorce, and to gain admission to higher education, professional training, and to the professions themselves. They also supported working class women's struggles for access to employment, decent housing, and adequate wages.

Many of the women who became involved in the suffrage struggle were already involved in progressive or radical politics, mainly in the abolition movement. One of the debates that divided the suffrage movement through much of its history was how much the cause of suffrage could or should be linked to radical movements for reform, the movement to abolish slavery in particular, or even other women's campaigns, such as those for sexual integrity, birth control, or protective legislation for women workers. These political disputes were grounded in a fundamental theoretical disagreement about women's sameness or difference from men and from each other. The proponents of liberal feminism argued for women's admission to the same legal rights as men. Others—looking at women's work, productive and reproductive, their sexuality, and their social and cultural assignments and trying to understand the nature of their subordination—examined women's difference, and argued that women's special roles and duties resulted in unique contributions but also required special protections.

Much of the writing about women's situation in the nineteenth century focuses on the ways in which it has been shaped by urbanization and industrialization. The development of a sizeable urban middle class, beginning in the late eighteenth century, had some advantages for women in the increased prosperity of their households and the availability of more household services. However, the concomitant ideology of separate spheres, which assigned middle-class women ever more determinedly to the private world of mothering and domesticity, also imposed severe limitations on women's access to the public world. John Stuart Mill, Harriet Taylor, and Frederick Engels attempted to analyze the "subjection of women" that resulted from this middle-class ideology. Late in the century, Charlotte Perkins Gilman, deploying the tools of socialist analysis, proposed moving women's work out of the household to end entirely the tyranny of separate spheres.

For working-class women, urbanization meant factory or service work at low wages and in poor conditions, as well as the need to feed and care for a family under these circumstances. Many working-class girls found employment, not just in mills and factories, but also in the growing service sector with jobs as household servants, and later as clerks, waitresses, and hospital aides. Mother Jones (reading #21) was one of many women who became active in labor organizing and in writing and thinking about industrial working conditions and their particular effects on women.

Many working-class women newly arrived in the cities found that the only work they could get was as prostitutes, a situation that precipitated much concern and debate in both the United States and Great Britain. During the 1860s, attempts in Great Britain to regulate prostitution through the Contagious Diseases Acts provoked feminists like Josephine Butler to critique publicly the sexual double standard that demanded sexual restraint from women but condoned promiscuity in men. Arguments that developed in these struggles were deployed later by activists fighting for women's access to birth control (Sanger, reading #24) and their right to make decisions about their own sexuality.

Whereas much nineteenth-century writing and thinking was directed at the lives of women in the new urban middle and working classes, through most of this period the majority of U.S. women—European American, Native American, African American, Asian American, and Latina—lived in rural settings and spent their lives in agricultural and household labor without wages. The circumstances of their lives varied greatly from the relatively privileged lives of wives and daughters on long-established farms in the East and Midwest, to those women in poor white southern sharecropping families and in families who moved west during the westward expansion, to the lives of Native American women driven with their tribes from traditional homelands to reservations, to the lives of African American women living as slaves in the South.

By 1920, suffrage had been achieved as well as many other rights for women. Some women were better educated and had achieved legal rights and professional access as no women ever had before. Those who had worked so hard to gain the franchise for women saw its achievement as an acknowledgment of women's status as full social and political participants in U.S. democracy. Whether, finally, this vision would be realized and whether, in fact, it was the vision most likely to change the lives of most women remained questions for the next decades.

7

The Changing Woman

(NAVAJO ORIGIN MYTH)

In the great desert of multicolored sand stood the Mountain - Around - Which - Moving - Was - Done, and at the foot of this great mountain was found a baby girl.

First Man and First Woman found the child when the earth was still unformed and incomplete. They took her home with them and raised her carefully, and the gods smiled on her and loved her. As she grew into womanhood, the world itself reached maturity as the mountains and valleys were all put into the proper places.

At last she was grown and the world was complete, and to celebrate her becoming a woman, the gods gave her a Blessing Way, Walking-into-Beauty. Songs and chants were sung to her, and her body was shaped with a sacred stick so that it would grow strong and beautiful. Each morning of the ceremony, she ran to greet the sun as it arose. The sacred ceremony was preserved and it is now given to all Navajo girls when they reach adulthood.

But the young girl did not stay the same. Each winter she became withered and white-haired, just as the earth became bare and snow-covered. But each spring as the colors of life grew back on the land, the colors of youth and beauty appeared in her cheeks and in her hair. So she is calling Changing Woman, or "A Woman She Becomes Time and Again."

The sun fell in love with Changing Woman, but she did not know what to do with him. So she went to First Woman for advice. On the advice of First Woman, she met the sun and he made love to her. Nine months later, twin sons were born to her and she raised them with love and care. For monsters had now appeared in the world, and the people were being destroyed. Changing Woman hoped her sons could save the world from the monsters.

When the twin boys were grown, Changing Woman sent them to the sun, their father, to get power from him so that they could fight the monsters. After undergoing severe tests by their father, the boys returned and destroyed all the monsters.

Now the world was complete and the monsters were dead. It was a perfect place for people, but there were very few left. Changing Woman pondered over this problem, and at last she took two baskets of corn. One was of white corn and one was of yellow corn. From the white cornmeal she shaped a man and from the yellow cornmeal she shaped a woman.

And so the earth was populated again, a changing world and a beautiful world—the world of Changing Woman.

 8

From A Vindication of the Rights of Woman

MARY WOLLSTONECRAFT

OF THE PERNICIOUS EFFECTS WHICH ARISE FROM THE UNNATURAL DISTINCTIONS ESTABLISHED IN SOCIETY

From the respect paid to property flow, as from a poisoned fountain, most of the evils and vices which render this world such a dreary scene to the contemplative mind. For it is in the most polished society that noisome reptiles and venomous serpents lurk under the rank herbage; and there is voluptuousness pampered by the still sultry air, which relaxes every good disposition before it ripens into virtue.

One class presses on another, for all are aiming to procure respect on account of their property; and property once gained will procure the respect due only to talents and virtue. Men neglect the duties incumbent on man, yet are treated like demigods. Religion is also separated from morality by a ceremonial veil, yet men wonder that the world is almost, literally speaking, a den of sharpers or oppressors.

There is a homely proverb, which speaks a shrewd truth, that whoever the devil finds idle he will employ. And what but habitual idleness can hereditary wealth and titles produce? For man is so constituted that he can only attain a proper use of his faculties by exercising them, and will not exercise them unless necessity of some kind first set the wheels in motion. Virtue likewise can only be acquired by the discharge of relative duties; but the importance of these sacred duties will scarcely be felt by the being who is cajoled out of his humanity by the flattery of sycophants. There must be more equality established in society, or morality will never gain ground, and this virtuous equality will not rest firmly even when founded on a rock, if one-half of mankind be chained to its bottom by fate, for they will be continually undermining it through ignorance or pride.

It is vain to expect virtue from women till they are in some degree independent of men; nay, it is vain to expect that strength of natural affection which would make them good wives and mothers. Whilst they are absolutely dependent on their husbands they will be cunning, mean, and selfish; and the men who can be gratified by the fawning fondness of spaniel-like affection have not much delicacy, for love is not to be bought; in any sense of the words, its silken wings are instantly shrivelled up when anything beside a return in kind is sought. Yet whilst wealth enervates men, and women live, as it were, by their personal charms, how can we expect them to discharge those ennobling duties which equally require exertion and self-denial? Hereditary property sophisticates the mind, and the unfortunate victims to it—if I may so express myself—swathed from their birth, seldom exert the locomotive faculty of body or mind, and thus viewing everything through one medium, and that a false one, they are unable to discern in what true merit and happiness consist. False, indeed, must be the light when the drapery of situation hides the man, and makes him stalk in masquerade, dragging from one scene of dissipation to another the nerveless limbs that hang with stupid listlessness, and rolling around the vacant eye, which plainly tells us that there is no mind at home.

. . .

To illustrate my opinion, I need only observe that when a woman is admired for her beauty, and suffers herself to be so far intoxicated by the admiration she receives as to neglect to discharge the indispensable duty of a mother, she sins against herself by neglecting to cultivate an affection that would equally tend to make her useful and happy. True happiness—I mean all the contentment and virtuous satisfaction that can be snatched in this imperfect state—must arise from well-regulated affections, and an affection includes a duty. Men are not aware of the misery they cause, and the vicious weakness they cherish, by only inciting women to render themselves pleasing; they do not consider that they thus make natural and artificial duties clash by sacrificing the comfort and respectability of a woman's life to voluptuous notions of beauty when in nature they all harmonize.

Cold would be the heart of a husband, were he not rendered unnatural by early debauchery, who did not feel more delight at seeing his child suckled by its mother than the most artful wanton tricks could ever raise, yet this natural way of cementing the matrimonial tie, and twisting esteem with fonder recollections, wealth leads women to spurn. To preserve their beauty, and wear the flowery crown of the day, which gives them a kind of right to reign for a short time over the sex, they neglect to stamp impressions on their husbands' hearts that would be remembered with more tenderness when the snow on the head began to chill the bosom than even their virgin charms. The maternal solicitude of a reasonable affectionate woman is very interesting, and the chastened dignity with which a mother returns the caresses that she and her child receive from a father who has been fulfilling the serious duties of his station is not only a respectable, but a beautiful sight. So singular, indeed, are my feelings—and I have endeavoured not to catch factitious ones—that after having been fatigued with the sight of insipid grandeur and the slavish ceremonies that with cumbrous pomp supplied the place of domestic affections, I have turned to some other scene to relieve my eye by resting it on the refreshing green everywhere scattered by Nature. I have then viewed with pleasure a woman nursing her children, and discharging the duties of her station with perhaps merely a servant-maid to take off her hands the servile part of the household business. I have seen her prepare herself and children, with only the luxury of cleanliness, to receive her husband, who, returning weary home in the evening, found smiling babes and a clean hearth. My heart has loitered in the midst of the group, and has even throbbed with sympathetic emotion when the scraping of the well-known foot has raised a pleasing tumult.

Whilst my benevolence has been gratified by contemplating this artless picture, I have thought that a couple of this description, equally necessary and independent of each other, because each fulfilled the respective duties of their station, possessed all that life could give. Raised sufficiently above abject poverty not to be obliged to weigh the consequence of every farthing they spend, and having sufficient to prevent their attending to a frigid system of economy which narrows both heart and mind, I declare, so vulgar are my conceptions, that I know not what is wanted to render this the happiest as well as the most respectable situation in the world, but a taste for literature, to throw a little variety and interest into social converse, and some superfluous money to give to the needy and to buy books. For it is not pleasant when the heart is opened by compassion, and the head active in arranging plans of usefulness, to have a prim urchin continually twitching back the elbow to prevent the hand from drawing out an almost empty purse, whispering at the same time some prudential maxim about the priority of justice.

Destructive, however, as riches and inherited honours are to the human character, women are more debased and cramped, if possible, by them than men, because men may still in some degree unfold their faculties by becoming soldiers and statesmen.

. . .

The preposterous distinctions of rank, which render civilization a curse, by dividing the world between voluptuous tyrants and cunning envious dependents, corrupt, almost equally, every class of people, because respectability is not attached to the discharge of the relative duties of life, but to the station, and when the duties are not fulfilled the affections cannot gain sufficient strength to fortify the virtue of which they are the natural reward. Still there are some loop-holes out of which a man may creep, and dare to think and act for himself; but for a woman it is an herculean task, because she has difficulties peculiar to her sex to overcome, which require almost superhuman powers.

A truly benevolent legislator always endeavours to make it the interest of each individual to be virtuous; and thus private virtue becoming the cement of public happiness, an orderly whole is consolidated by the tendency of all the parts towards a common centre. But the private or public virtue of woman is very problematical, for Rousseau, and a numerous list of male writers, insist that she should all her life be subjected to a severe restraint, that of propriety. Why subject her to propriety—blind propriety—if she be capable of acting from a nobler spring, if she be an heir of immortality? Is sugar always to be produced by vital blood? Is one half of the human species, like the poor African slaves, to be subjected to prejudices that brutalize them, when principles would be a surer guard, only to sweeten the cup of man? Is not this indirectly to deny woman reason? for a gift is a mockery, if it be unfit for use.

Women are, in common with men, rendered weak and luxurious by the relaxing pleasures which wealth procures; but added to this they are made slaves to their persons, and must render them alluring that man may lend them his reason to guide their tottering steps aright. Or should they be ambitious, they must govern their tyrants by sinister tricks, for without rights there cannot be any incumbent duties. The laws respecting woman, which I mean to discuss in a future part, make an absurd unit of a man and his wife; and then, by the easy transition of only considering him as responsible, she is reduced to a mere cipher.

The being who discharges the duties of its station is independent; and, speaking of women at large, their first duty is to themselves as rational creatures, and the next, in point of importance, as citizens, is that, which includes so many, of a mother. The rank in life which dispenses with their fulfilling this duty, necessarily degrades them by making them mere dolls. Or should they turn to something more important than merely fitting drapery upon a smooth block, their minds are only occupied by some soft platonic attachment; or the actual management of an intrigue may keep their thoughts in motion; for when they neglect domestic duties, they have it not in their power to take the field and march and counter-march like soldiers, or wrangle in the senate to keep their faculties from rusting.

I know that, as a proof of the inferiority of the sex, Rousseau has exultingly exclaimed, How can they leave the nursery for the camp! And the camp has by some moralists been proved the school of the most heroic virtues; though I think it would puzzle a keen casuist to prove the reasonableness of the greater number of wars that have dubbed heroes. I do not mean to consider this question critically; because, having frequently viewed these freaks of ambition as the first natural mode of civilization, when the ground must be torn up, and the woods cleared by fire and sword, I do not choose to call them pests; but surely the present system of war has little connection with virtue of any denomination, being rather the school of *finesse* and effeminacy than of fortitude.

Yet, if defensive war, the only justifiable war, in the present advanced state of society, where virtue can show its face and ripen amidst the rigours which purify the air on the mountain's top, were alone to be adopted as just and glorious, the true heroism of antiquity might again animate female bosoms. But fair and softly, gentle reader, male or female, do not alarm thyself, for though I have compared the character of a modern soldier with that of a civilized woman, I am not going to advise them to turn their distaff into a musket, though I sincerely wish to see the bayonet converted into a pruning-hook. I only re-created an imagination, fatigued by contemplating the vices and follies which all proceed from a feculent stream of wealth that has muddied the pure rills of natural affection, by supposing that society will some time or other be so constituted, that man must necessarily fulfil the duties of a citizen, or be despised, and that while he was employed in any of the departments of civil life, his wife, also an active citizen, should be equally intent to manage her family, educate her children, and assist her neighbours.

But to render her really virtuous and useful, she must not, if she discharge her civil duties, want individually the protection of civil laws; she must not be dependent on her husband's bounty for her subsistence during his life, or support after his death; for how can a being be generous who has nothing of its own? or virtuous who is not free? The wife, in the present state of things, who is faithful to her husband, and neither suckles nor educates her children, scarcely deserves the name of a wife, and has no right to that of a citizen. But take away natural rights, and duties become null.

Women then must be considered as only the wanton solace of men, when they become so weak in mind and body that they cannot exert themselves unless to pursue some frothy pleasure, or to invent some frivolous fashion. What can be a more melancholy sight to a thinking mind, than to look into the numerous carriages that drive helter-skelter about this metropolis in a morning full of pale-faced creatures who are flying from themselves! I have often wished, with Dr Johnson, to place some of them in a little shop with half a dozen children looking up to their languid countenances for support. I am much mistaken, if some latent vigour would not soon give health and spirit to their eyes, and some lines drawn by the exercise of reason on the blank cheeks, which before were only undulated by dimples, might restore lost dignity to the character, or rather enable it to attain the true dignity of its nature. Virtue is not to be acquired even by speculation, much less by the negative supineness that wealth naturally generates.

Besides, when poverty is more disgraceful than even vice, is not morality cut to the quick? Still to avoid misconstruction, though I consider that women in the common walks of life are called to fulfil the duties of wives and mothers, by religion and reason, I cannot help lamenting that women of a superior cast have not a road open by which they can pursue more extensive plans of usefulness and independence. I may excite laughter, by dropping a hint, which I mean to pursue, some future time, for I really think that women ought to have representatives, instead of being arbitrarily governed without having any direct share allowed them in the deliberations of government.

. . .

But what have women to do in society? I may be asked, but to loiter with easy grace; surely you would not condemn them all to suckle fools and chronicle small beer! No. Women might certainly study the art of healing and be physicians as well as nurses. And midwifery, decency seems to allot to them though I am afraid the word midwife, in our dictionaries, will soon give place to *accoucheur*, and one proof of the former delicacy of the sex be effaced from the language.

They might also study politics, and settle their benevolence on the broadest basis; for the reading of history will scarcely be more useful than the perusal of romances, if read as mere biography; if the character of the times, the political improvements, arts, etc., be not observed. In short, if it be not considered as the history of man; and not of particular men, who filled a niche in the temple of fame, and dropped into the black rolling stream of time, that silently sweeps all before it into the shapeless void called—eternity.—For shape, can it be called, 'that shape hath none'?

Business of various kinds, they might likewise pursue, if they were educated in a more orderly manner, which might save many from common and legal prostitution. Women would not then marry for a support, as men accept of places under Government, and neglect the implied duties; nor would an attempt to earn their own subsistence, a most laudable one! sink them almost to the level of those poor abandoned creatures who live by prostitution. For are not milliners and mantuamakers reckoned the next class? The few employments open to women, so far, from being liberal, are menial; and when a superior education enables them to take charge of the education of children as governesses, they are not treated like the tutors of sons, though even clerical tutors are not always treated in a manner calculated to render them respectable in the eyes of their pupils to say nothing of the private comfort of the individual. But as women educated like gentlewomen, are never designed for the humiliating situation which necessity sometimes forces them to fill; these situations are considered in the light of a degradation; and they know little of the human heart, who need to be told, that nothing so painfully sharpens sensibility as such a fall in life.

Some of these women might be restrained from marrying by a proper spirit of delicacy, and others may not have had it in their power to escape in this pitiful way from servitude; is not that Government then very defective, and very unmindful of the happiness of one-half of its members, that does not provide for honest, independent women, by encouraging them to fill respectable stations? But in order to render their private virtue a public benefit, they must have a civil existence in the State, married or single; else we shall continually see some worthy woman, whose sensibility has been rendered painfully acute by undeserved contempt, droop like 'the lily broken down by a plowshare'.

It is a melancholy truth; yet such is the blessed effect of civilization! the most respectable women are the most oppressed; and, unless they have understandings far superior to the common run of understandings, taking in both sexes, they must, from being treated like contemptible beings, become contemptible. How many women thus waste life away the prey of discontent, who might have practised as physicians, regulated a farm, managed a shop, and stood erect, supported by their own industry, instead of hanging their heads surcharged with the dew of sensibility, that consumes the beauty to which it at first gave lustre; nay, I doubt whether pity and love are so near akin as poets feign, for I have seldom seen much compassion excited by the helplessness of females, unless they were fair; then, perhaps, pity was the soft handmaid of love, or the harbinger of lust.

How much more respectable is the woman who earns her own bread by fulfilling any duty, than the most accomplished beauty!—beauty did I say!—so sensible am I of the beauty of moral loveliness, or the harmonious propriety that attunes the passions of a well-regulated mind, that I blush at making the comparison; yet I sigh to think how few women aim at attaining this respectability by withdrawing from the giddy whirl of pleasure, or the indolent calm that stupefies the good sort of women it sucks in.

Proud of their weakness, however, they must always be protected, guarded from care, and all the rough toils that dignify the mind. If this be the fiat of fate, if they will make themselves insignificant and contemptible, sweetly to waste 'life away', let them not expect to be valued when their beauty fades, for it is the fate of the fairest flowers to be admired and pulled to pieces by the careless hand that plucked them. In how many ways do I wish, from the purest benevolence, to impress this truth on my sex; yet I fear that they will not listen to a truth that dear bought experience has brought home to many an agitated bosom, nor willingly resign the privileges of rank and sex for the privileges of humanity, to which those have no claim who do not discharge its duties.

Those writers are particularly useful, in my opinion, who make man feel for man, independent of the station he fills, or the drapery of factitious sentiments. I then would fain convince reasonable men of the importance of some of my remarks; and prevail on them to weigh dispassionately the whole tenor of my observations. I appeal to their understandings; and, as a fellow-creature, claim, in the name of my sex, some interest in their hearts. I entreat them to assist to emancipate their companion, to make her a *helpmeet* for them.

Would men but generously snap our chains, and be content with rational fellowship instead of slavish obedience, they would find us more observant daughters, more affectionate sisters, more faithful wives, more reasonable mothers—in a word, better citizens. We should then love them with true affection, because we should learn to respect ourselves; and the peace of mind of a worthy man would not be interrupted by the idle vanity of his wife, nor the babes sent to nestle in a strange bosom, having never found a home in their mother's.

[1792]

 9

From Letters on the Equality of the Sexes and the Condition of Women

SARAH M. GRIMKÉ

LETTER VIII. ON THE CONDITION OF WOMEN IN THE UNITED STATES.

Brookline, 1837.

My dear sister,—I have now taken a brief survey of the condition of woman in various parts of the world. I regret that my time has been so much occupied by other things, that I have been unable to bestow that attention upon the subject which it merits, and that my constant change of place has prevented me from having access to books, which might probably have assisted me in this part of my work. I hope that the principles I have asserted will claim the attention of some of my sex, who may be able to bring into view, more thoroughly than I have done, the situation and degradation of woman. I shall now proceed to make a few remarks on the condition of women in my own country.

During the early part of my life, my lot was cast among the butterflies of the *fashionable* world; and

of this class of women, I am constrained to say, both from experience and observation, that their education is miserably deficient; that they are taught to regard marriage as the one thing needful, the only avenue to distinction; hence to attract the notice and win the attentions of men, by their external charms, is the chief business of fashionable girls. They seldom think that men will be allured by intellectual acquirements, because they find, that where any mental superiority exists, a woman is generally shunned and regarded as stepping out of her 'appropriate sphere,' which, in their view, is to dress, to dance, to set out to the best possible advantage her person, to read the novels which inundate the press, and which do more to destroy her character as a rational creature, than any thing else. Fashionable women regard themselves, and are regarded by men, as pretty toys or as mere instruments of pleasure; and the vacuity of mind, heartlessness, the frivolity which is the necessary result of this false and debasing estimate of women, can only be fully understood by those who have mingled in the folly and wickedness of fashionable life; and who have been called from such pursuits by the voice of the Lord Jesus, inviting their weary and heavy laden souls to come unto Him and learn of Him, that they may find something worthy of their immortal spirit, and their intellectual powers; that they may learn the high and holy purposes of their creation, and consecrate themselves unto the service of God; and not, as is now the case, to the pleasure of man.

There is another and much more numerous class in this country, who are withdrawn by education or circumstances from the circle of fashionable amusements, but who are brought up with the dangerous and absurd idea, that *marriage* is a kind of preferment; and that to be able to keep their husband's house, and render his situation comfortable, is the end of her being. Much that she does and says and thinks is done in reference to this situation; and to be married is too often held up to the view of girls as the sine qua non of human happiness and human existence. For this purpose more than for any other, I verily believe the majority of girls are trained. This is demonstrated by the imperfect education which is bestowed upon them, and the little pains taken to cultivate their minds, after they leave school, by the little time allowed them for reading, and by the idea being constantly inculcated, that although all household concerns should be attended to with scrupulous punctuality at particular seasons, the improvement of their intellectual capacities is only a secondary consideration, and may serve as an occupation to fill up the odds and ends of time. In most families, it is considered a matter of far more consequence to call a girl off from making a pie, or a pudding, than to interrupt her whilst engaged in her studies. This mode of training necessarily exalts, in their view, the animal above the intellectual and spiritual nature, and teaches women to regard themselves as a kind of machinery, necessary to keep the domestic engine in order, but of little value as the *intelligent* companions of men.

. . .

There is another way in which the general opinion, that women are inferior to men, is manifested, that bears with tremendous effect on the laboring class, and indeed on almost all who are obliged to earn a subsistence, whether it be by mental or physical exertion—I allude to the disproportionate value set on the time and labor of men and of women. A man who is engaged in teaching, can always, I believe, command a higher price for tuition than a woman—even when he teaches the same branches, and is not in any respect superior to the woman. This I know is the case in boarding and other schools with which I have been acquainted, and it is so in every occupation in which the sexes engage indiscriminately. As for example, in tailoring, a man has twice, or three times as much for making a waistcoat or pantaloons as a woman, although the work done by each may be equally good. In those employments which are peculiar to women, their time is estimated at only half the value of that of men. A woman who goes out to wash, works as hard in proportion as a wood sawyer, or a coal heaver, but she is not generally able to make more than half as much by a day's work. The low remuneration which women receive for their work, has claimed the attention of a few philanthropists, and I hope it will continue to do so until some remedy is applied for this enormous evil. I have known a widow, left with four or five children, to provide for, unable to leave home because her helpless babes demand her attention, compelled to earn a scanty subsistence,

by making coarse shirts at 12 1-2 cents a piece, or by taking in washing, for which she was paid by some wealthy persons 12 1-2 cents per dozen. All these things evince the low estimation in which woman is held. There is yet another and more disastrous consequence arising from this unscriptural notion—women being educated, from earliest childhood, to regard themselves as inferior creatures, have not that self-respect which conscious equality would engender, and hence when their virtue is assailed, they yield to temptation with facility, under the idea that it rather exalts than debases them, to be connected with a superior being.

There is another class of women in this country, to whom I cannot refer, without feelings of the deepest shame and sorrow. I allude to our female slaves. Our southern cities are whelmed beneath a tide of pollution; the virtue of female slaves is wholly at the mercy of irresponsible tyrants, and women are bought and sold in our slave markets, to gratify the brutal lust of those who bear the name of Christians. In our slave States, if amid all her degradation and ignorance, a woman desires to preserve her virtue unsullied, she is either bribed or whipped into compliance, or if she dares resist her seducer, her life by the laws of some of the slave States may be, and has actually been sacrificed to the fury of disappointed passion. Where such laws do not exist, the power which is necessarily vested in the master over his property, leaves the defenceless slave entirely at his mercy, and the sufferings of some females on this account, both physical and mental, are intense. Mr. Gholson, in the House of Delegates of Virginia, in 1832, said, 'He really had been under the impression that he owned his slaves. He had lately purchased four women and ten children, in whom he thought he had obtained a great bargain; for he supposed they were his own property, *as were his brood mares.*' But even if any laws existed in the United States, as in Athens formerly, for the protection of female slaves, they would be null and void, because the evidence of a colored person is not admitted against a white, in any of our Courts of Justice in the slave States. 'In Athens, if a female slave had cause to complain of any want of respect to the laws of modesty, she could seek the protection of the temple, and demand a change of owners; and such appeals were never discountenanced, or neglected by the magistrate.' In Christian America, the slave has no refuge from unbridled cruelty and lust.

· · ·

Nor does the colored woman suffer alone: the moral purity of the white woman is deeply contaminated. In the daily habit of seeing the virtue of her enslaved sister sacrificed without hesitancy or remorse, she looks upon the crimes of seduction and illicit intercourse without horror, and although not personally involved in the guilt, she loses that value for innocence in her own, as well as the other sex, which is one of the strongest safeguards to virtue. She lives in habitual intercourse with men, whom she knows to be polluted by licentiousness, and often is she compelled to witness in her own domestic circle, those disgusting and heart-sickening jealousies and strifes which disgraced and distracted the family of Abraham. In addition to all this, the female slaves suffer every species of degradation and cruelty, which the most wanton barbarity can inflict; they are indecently divested of their clothing, sometimes tied up and severely whipped, sometimes prostrated on the earth, while their naked bodies are torn by the scorpion lash.

'The whip on WOMAN's shrinking flesh!
Our soil yet reddening with the stains
Caught from her scourging warm and fresh.'

Can any American woman look at these scenes of shocking licentiousness and cruelty, and fold her hands in apathy, and say, 'I have nothing to do with slavery'? *She cannot and be guiltless.*

I cannot close this letter, without saying a few words on the benefits to be derived by men, as well as women, from the opinions I advocate relative to the equality of the sexes. Many women are now supported, in idleness and extravagance, by the industry of their husbands, fathers, or brothers, who are compelled to toil out their existence, at the counting house, or in the printing office, or some other laborious occupation, while the wife and daughters and sisters take no part in the support of the family, and appear to think that their sole business is to spend the hard bought earnings of their male friends. I deeply regret such a state of things, because I believe that if women felt their responsibility, for the support of themselves, or their families it would add strength and dignity to their characters, and teach them more true sympathy for their husbands, than is now generally manifested,—a sympathy which would be exhibited by actions as well as words. Our brethren may reject my doctrine, because it runs counter to common opinions, and because it wounds their pride; but I believe they would be 'partakers of the benefit' resulting from the Equality of the Sexes, and would find that woman, as their equal, was unspeakably more valuable than woman as their inferior, both as a moral and an intellectual being.

Thine in the bonds of womanhood,

Sarah M. Grimké.

[1838]

 10

Declaration of Sentiments

ELIZABETH CADY STANTON

When, in the course of human events, it becomes necessary for one portion of the family of man to assume among the people of the earth a position different from that which they have hitherto occupied, but one to which the laws of nature and of nature's God entitle them, a decent respect to the opinions of mankind requires that they should declare the causes that impel them to such a course.

We hold these truths to be self-evident: that all men and women are created equal; that they are endowed by their Creator with certain inalienable rights; that among these are life, liberty, and the pursuit of happiness; that to secure these rights governments are instituted, deriving their just powers from the consent of the governed. Whenever any form of government becomes destructive of these ends, it is the right of those who suffer from it to refuse allegiance to it, and to insist upon the institution of a new government, laying its foundation on such principles, and organizing its powers in such form, as to them shall seem most likely to effect their safety and happiness. Prudence, indeed, will dictate that governments long established should not be changed for light and transient causes; and accordingly all experience hath shown that mankind are more disposed to suffer, while evils are sufferable, than to right themselves by abolishing the forms to which they were accustomed. But when a long train of abuses and usurpations, pursuing invariably the same object evinces a design to reduce them under absolute despotism, it is their duty to throw off such government, and to provide new guards for their future security. Such has been the patient sufferance of the women under this government, and such is now the necessity which constrains them to demand the equal station to which they are entitled.

The history of mankind is a history of repeated injuries and usurpations on the part of man toward woman, having in direct object the establishment of an absolute tyranny over her. To prove this, let facts be submitted to a candid world.

He has never permitted her to exercise her inalienable right to the elective franchise.

He has compelled her to submit to laws, in the formation of which she had no voice.

He has withheld from her rights which are given to the most ignorant and degraded men—both natives and foreigners.

Having deprived her of this first right of a citizen, the elective franchise, thereby leaving her without representation in the halls of legislation, he has oppressed her on all sides.

He has made her, if married, in the eye of the law, civilly dead.

He has taken from her all right in property, even to the wages she earns.

He has made her, morally, an irresponsible being, as she can commit many crimes with impunity, provided they be done in the presence of her husband. In the covenant of marriage, she is compelled to promise obedience to her husband, he becoming, to all intents and purposes, her master—the law giving him power to deprive her of her liberty, and to administer chastisement.

He has so framed the laws of divorce, as to what shall be the proper causes, and in case of separation, to whom the guardianship of the children shall be given, as to be wholly regardless of the happiness of women—the law, in all cases, going upon a false supposition of the supremacy of man, and giving all power into his hands.

After depriving her of all rights as a married woman, if single, and the owner of property, he has taxed her to support a government which recognizes her only when her property can be made profitable to it.

He has monopolized nearly all the profitable employments, and from those she is permitted to follow, she receives but a scanty remuneration. He closes against her all the avenues to wealth and distinction which he considers most honorable to himself. As a teacher of theology, medicine, or law, she is not known.

He has denied her the facilities for obtaining a thorough education, all colleges being closed against her.

He allows her in Church, as well as State, but a subordinate position, claiming Apostolic authority for her exclusion from the ministry, and, with some exceptions, from any public participation in the affairs of the Church.

He has created a false public sentiment by giving to the world a different code of morals for men and women, by which moral delinquencies which exclude women from society, are not only tolerated, but deemed of little account in man.

He has usurped the prerogative of Jehovah himself, claiming it as his right to assign for her a sphere of action, when that belongs to her conscience and to her God.

He has endeavored, in every way that he could, to destroy her confidence in her own powers, to lessen her self-respect, and to make her willing to lead a dependent and abject life.

Now, in view of this entire disfranchisement of one-half the people of this country, their social and religious degradation—in view of the unjust laws above mentioned, and because women do feel themselves aggrieved, oppressed, and fraudulently deprived of their most sacred rights, we insist that they have immediate admission to all the rights and privileges which belong to them as citizens of the United States.

In entering upon the great work before us, we anticipate no small amount of misconception, misrepresentation, and ridicule; but we shall use every instrumentality within our power to effect our object. We shall employ agents, circulate tracts, petition the State and National legislatures, and endeavor to enlist the pulpit and the press in our behalf. We hope this Convention will be followed by a series of Conventions embracing every part of the country.

. . .

Whereas, the great precept of nature is conceded to be, that "man shall pursue his own true and substantial happiness." Blackstone in his Commentaries remarks, that this law of Nature being coeval with mankind, and dictated by God himself, is of course superior in obligation to any other. It is binding over all the globe, in all countries and at all times; no human laws are of any validity if contrary to this, and such of them as are valid, derive all their force, and all their validity, and all their authority, mediately and immediately, from this original; therefore,

Resolved, That such laws as conflict, in any way, with the true and substantial happiness of woman, are contrary to the great precept of nature and of no validity, for this is "superior in obligation to any other."

Resolved, That all laws which prevent woman from occupying such a station in society as her conscience shall dictate, or which place her in a position inferior to that of man, are contrary to the great precept of nature, and therefore of no force or authority.

Resolved, That woman is man's equal—was intended to be so by the Creator, and the highest good of the race demands that she should be recognized as such.

Resolved, That the women of this country ought to be enlightened in regard to the laws under which they live, that they may no longer publish their degradation by declaring themselves satisfied with their present position, nor their ignorance, by asserting that they have all the rights they want.

Resolved, That inasmuch as man, while claiming for himself intellectual superiority, does accord to woman moral superiority, it is pre-eminently his duty to encourage her to speak and teach, as she has an opportunity, in all religious assemblies.

Resolved, That the same amount of virtue, delicacy, and refinement of behavior that is required of woman in the social state, should also be required of man, and the same transgressions should be visited with equal severity on both man and woman.

Resolved, That the objection of indelicacy and impropriety, which is so often brought against woman when she addresses a public audience, comes with a very ill-grace from those who encourage, by their attendance, her appearance on the stage, in the concert, or in feats of the circus.

Resolved, That woman has too long rested satisfied in the circumscribed limits which corrupt customs and a perverted application of the Scriptures have marked out for her, and that it is time she should move in the enlarged sphere which her great Creator has assigned her.

Resolved, That it is the duty of the women of this country to secure to themselves their sacred right to the elective franchise.

Resolved, That the equality of human rights results necessarily from the fact of the identity of the race in capabilities and responsibilities.

Resolved, therefore, That, being invested by the Creator with the same capabilities, and the same consciousness of responsibility for their exercise, it is demonstrably the right and duty of woman, equally with man, to promote every righteous cause by every righteous means; and especially in regard to the great subjects of morals and religion, it is self-evidently her right to participate with her brother in teaching them, both in private and in public, by writing and by speaking, by any instrumentalities proper to be used, and in any assemblies proper to be held; and this being a self-evident truth growing out of the divinely implanted principles of human nature, any custom or authority adverse to it, whether modern or wearing the hoary sanction of antiquity, is to be regarded as a self-evident falsehood, and at war with mankind.

. . .

Resolved, That the speedy success of our cause depends upon the zealous and untiring efforts of both men and women, for the overthrow of the monopoly of the pulpit, and for the securing to woman an equal participation with men in the various trades, professions, and commerce.

. . .

[1848]

❦ 11

Ain't I a Woman?

SOJOURNER TRUTH

Well, children, where there is so much racket there must be something out of kilter. I think that 'twixt the negroes of the South and the women at the North, all talking about rights, the white men will be in a fix pretty soon. But what's all this here talking about?

That man over there says that women need to be helped into carriages, and lifted over ditches, and to have the best place everywhere. Nobody ever helps me into carriages, or over mud-puddles, or gives me any best place! And ain't I a woman? Look at me! Look at my arm! I have ploughed and planted, and gathered into barns, and no man could head me! And ain't I a woman? I could work as much and eat as much as a man—when I could get it—and bear the lash as well! And ain't I a woman? I have borne thirteen children, and seen them most all sold off to slavery, and when I cried out with my mother's grief, none but Jesus heard me! And ain't I a woman?

Then they talk about this thing in the head; what's this they call it? [Intellect, someone whispers.] That's it, honey. What's that got to do with women's rights or negro's rights? If my cup won't hold but a pint, and yours holds a quart, wouldn't you be mean not to let me have my little half-measure full?

Then that little man in black there, he says women can't have as much rights as men, 'cause Christ wasn't a woman! Where did your Christ come from? Where did your Christ come from? From God and a woman! Man had nothing to do with Him.

If the first woman God ever made was strong enough to turn the world upside down all alone, these women together ought to be able to turn it back, and get it right side up again! And now they is asking to do it, the men better let them.

Obliged to you for hearing me, and now old Sojourner ain't got nothing more to say.

[1851]

Keeping the Thing Going While Things Are Stirring

SOJOURNER TRUTH

My friends, I am rejoiced that you are glad, but I don't know how you will feel when I get through. I come from another field—the country of the slave. They have got their liberty—so much good luck to have slavery partly destroyed; not entirely. I want it root and branch destroyed. Then we will all be free indeed. I feel that if I have to answer for the deeds done in my body just as much as a man, I have a right to have just as much as a man. There is a great stir about colored men getting their rights, but not a word about the colored women; and if colored men get their rights, and not colored women theirs, you see the colored men will be masters over the women, and it will be just as bad as it was before. So I am for keeping the thing going while things are stirring; because if we wait till it is still, it will take a great while to get it going again. White women are a great deal smarter, and know more than colored women, while colored women do not know scarcely anything. They go out washing, which is about as high as a colored woman gets, and their men go about idle, strutting up and down; and when the women come home, they ask for their money and take it all, and then scold because there is no food. I want you to consider on that, chil'n. I call you chil'n; you are somebody's chil'n, and I am old enough to be mother of all that is here. I want women to have their rights. In the courts women have no right, no voice; nobody speaks for them. I wish woman to have her voice there among the pettifoggers. If it is not a fit place for women, it is unfit for men to be there.

I am above eighty years old; it is about time for me to be going. I have been forty years a slave and forty years free, and would be here forty years more to have equal rights for all. I suppose I am kept here because something remains for me to do; I suppose I am yet to help to break the chain. I have done a great deal of work; as much as a man, but did not get so much pay. I used to work in the field and bind grain, keeping up with the cradler, but men doing no more, got twice as much pay; so with the

German women. They work in the field and do as much work, but do not get the pay. We do as much, we eat as much, we want as much. I suppose I am about the only colored woman that goes about to speak for the rights of the colored women. I want to keep the thing stirring, now that the ice is cracked. What we want is a little money. You men know that you get as much again as women when you write, or for what you do. When we get our rights we shall not have to come to you for money, for then we shall have money enough in our own pockets; and may be you will ask us for money. But help us now until we get it. It is a good consolation to know that when we have got this battle once fought we shall not be coming to you any more. You have been having our rights so long, that you think, like a slaveholder, that you own us. I know that it is hard for one who has held the reins for so long to give up; it cuts like a knife. It will feel all the better when it closes up again. I have been in Washington about three years, seeing about these colored people. Now colored men have the right to vote. There ought to be equal rights now more than ever, since colored people have got their freedom. I am going to talk several times while I am here; so now I will do a little singing. I have not heard any singing since I came here.

[1867]

❧ 12

From The Subjection of Women

JOHN STUART MILL
and HARRIET TAYLOR

2

It will be well to commence the detailed discussion of the subject by the particular branch of it to which the course of our observations has led us: the conditions which the laws of this and all other countries annex to the marriage contract. Marriage being the destination appointed by society for women, the prospect they are brought up to, and the object which it is intended should be sought by all of them, except those who are too little attractive to be chosen by any man as his companion; one might have supposed that everything would have been done to make this condition as eligible to them as possible, that they might have no cause to regret being denied the option of any other. Society, however, both in this, and, at first, in all other cases, has preferred to attain its object by foul rather than fair means: but this is the only case in which it has substantially persisted in them even to the present day. Originally women were taken by force, or regularly sold by their father to the husband. Until a late period in European history, the father had the power to dispose of his daughter in marriage at his own will and pleasure, without any regard to hers. The Church, indeed, was so far faithful to a better morality as to require a formal "yes" from the woman at the marriage ceremony; but there was nothing to shew that the consent was other than compulsory; and it was practically impossible for the girl to refuse compliance if the father persevered, except perhaps when she might obtain the protection of religion by a determined resolution to take monastic vows. After marriage, the man had anciently (but this was anterior to Christianity) the power of life and death over his wife. She could invoke no law against him; he was her sole tribunal and law. For a long time he could repudiate her, but she had no corresponding power in regard to him. By the old laws of England, the husband was called the *lord* of the wife; he was literally regarded as her sovereign, inasmuch that the murder of a man by his wife was called treason (*petty* as distinguished from *high* treason), and was more cruelly avenged than was usually the case with high treason, for the penalty was burning to death. Because the various enormities have fallen into disuse (for most of them were never formally abolished, or not until they had long ceased to be practised) men suppose that all is now as it should be in regard to the marriage contract; and we are continually told that civilization and Christianity have restored to the woman her just rights. Meanwhile the wife is the actual bond-servant of her husband: no less so, as far as legal obligation goes, than slaves commonly so called. She vows a lifelong obedience to him at the altar, and is held to it all through her life by law. Casuists may say that the obligation of obedience stops short of participation in crime, but it certainly extends to everything else. She can do no act whatever but by his permission, at least tacit. She can acquire no property but for him; the instant it becomes hers, even if by inheritance, it becomes *ipso facto* his. In this respect the wife's position under the common law of England is worse than that of slaves in the laws of many countries: by the Roman law, for example, a slave might have his *peculium*, which to a certain extent the law guaranteed to him for his exclusive use. The higher classes in this country have given an analogous advantage to their women, through special contracts setting aside the law, by conditions of pin-money, etc.: since parental feeling being stronger with fathers than the class feeling of their own sex, a father generally prefers his own daughter to a son-in-law who is a stranger to him. By means of settlements, the rich usually contrive to withdraw the whole or part of the inherited property of the wife from the absolute control of the husband: but they do not succeed in keeping it under her own control; the utmost they can do only prevents the husband from squandering it, at the same time debarring the rightful owner from its use. The property itself is out of the reach of both; and as to the income derived from it, the form of settlement most favourable to the wife (that called "to her separate use") only precludes the husband from receiving it instead of her: it must pass through her hands, but if he takes it from her by personal violence as soon as she receives it, he can neither be punished, nor compelled to restitution. This is the amount of the protection which, under the laws of this country, the most powerful nobleman can give to his own daughter as respects her husband. In the immense majority of cases there is no settlement: and the absorption of all rights, all property, as well as all freedom of action, is complete. The two are called "one person in law," for the purpose of inferring that whatever is hers is his, but the parallel inference is never drawn that whatever is his is hers; the maxim is not applied against the man, except to make him responsible to third parties for her acts, as a master is for the acts of his slaves or of his cattle. I am far from pretending that wives are in general no better treated than slaves; but no slave is a slave to the same lengths, and in so full a sense of the word, as a wife is. Hardly any slave, except one immediately attached to the master's person, is a slave at all hours and all minutes; in general he has, like a soldier, his fixed task, and when it is done, or when he is off duty, he disposes, within certain limits, of his own time, and has a family life into which the master rarely intrudes. "Uncle Tom" under his first master had his own life in his "cabin," almost as much as any man whose work takes him away from home, is able to have in his own family. But it cannot be so with the wife. Above all, a female slave has (in Christian countries) an admitted right, and is considered under a moral obligation, to refuse to her master the last familiarity. Not so the wife: however brutal a tyrant she may unfortunately be chained to—though she may know that he hates her, though it may be his daily pleasure to torture her, and though she may feel it impossible not to loathe him—he can claim from her and enforce the lowest degradation of a human being, that of being made the instrument of an animal function contrary to her inclinations. While she is held in this worst description of slavery as to her own person, what is her position in regard to the children in whom she and her master have a joint interest? They are by law *his* children. He alone has any legal rights over them. Not one act can she do towards or in relation to them, except by delegation from him. Even after he is dead she is not their legal guardian, unless he by will has made her so. He could even send them away from her, and deprive her of the means of seeing or corresponding with them, until this power was in some degree restricted by Serjeant Talfourd's Act. This is her legal state. And from this state she has no means of withdrawing herself. If she leaves her husband, she can take nothing with her, neither her children nor anything which is rightfully her own. If he chooses, he can compel her to return, by law, or by physical force; or he may content himself with seizing for his own use any thing which she may earn, or which may be given to her by her relations. It is only legal separation by a decree of a court of justice, which entitles her to live apart, without being forced back into the custody of an exasperated jailer—or which empowers her to apply any earnings to her own use, without fear that a man whom perhaps she has not seen for twenty years will pounce upon her some day and carry all off. This legal separation, until lately, the courts of justice would only give at an expense which made it inaccessible to any one out of the higher ranks. Even now it is only given in cases of desertion, or of the extreme of cruelty; and yet complaints are made every day that it is granted too easily. Surely, if a woman is denied any lot in life but that of being the personal body-servant of a despot, and is dependent for everything upon the chance of finding one who may be disposed to make a favourite of her instead of merely a drudge, it is a very cruel aggravation of her fate that she should be allowed to try this chance only once. The natural sequel and corollary from this state of things would be, that since her all in life depends upon obtaining a good master, she should be allowed to change again and again until she finds one. I am not saying that she ought to be allowed this privilege. That is a totally different consideration. The question of divorce, in the sense involving liberty of remarriage, is one into which it is foreign to my purpose to enter. All I now say is, that to those to whom nothing but servitude is allowed, the free choice of servitude is the only, though a most insufficient, alleviation. Its refusal completes the assimilation of the wife to the slave—and the slave under not the mildest form of slavery: for in some slave codes the slave could, under certain circumstances of ill usage, legally compel the master to sell him. But no amount of ill usage, without adultery superadded, will in England free a wife from her tormentor.

I have no desire to exaggerate, nor does the case stand in any need of exaggeration. I have described the wife's legal position, not her actual treatment. The laws of most countries are far worse than the people who execute them, and many of them are only able to remain laws by being seldom or never carried into effect. If married life were all that it might be expected to be, looking to the laws alone, society would be a hell upon earth. Happily there are both feelings and interests which in many men exclude, and in most, greatly temper, the impulses and propensities which lead to tyranny: and of those feelings, the tie which connects a man with his wife affords, in a normal state of things, incomparably the strongest example. The only tie which at all approaches to it, that between him and his children, tends, in all save exceptional cases, to strengthen, instead of conflicting with, the first. Because this is true; because men in general do not inflict, nor

women suffer, all the misery which could be inflicted and suffered if the full power of tyranny with which the man is legally invested were acted on; the defenders of the existing form of the institution think that all its iniquity is justified, and that any complaint is merely quarrelling with the evil which is the price paid for every great good. . . . If an appeal be made to the intense attachments which exist between wives and their husbands, exactly as much may be said of domestic slavery. It was quite an ordinary fact in Greece and Rome for slaves to submit to death by torture rather than betray their masters. In the proscriptions of the Roman civil wars it was remarked that wives and slaves were heroically faithful, sons very commonly treacherous. Yet we know how cruelly many Romans treated their slaves. But in truth these intense individual feelings nowhere rise to such a luxuriant height as under the most atrocious institutions. It is part of the irony of life, that the strongest feelings of devoted gratitude of which human nature seems to be susceptible, are called forth in human beings towards those who, having the power entirely to crush their earthly existence, voluntarily refrain from using that power. How great a place in most men this sentiment fills, even in religious devotion, it would be cruel to inquire. We daily see how much their gratitude to Heaven appears to be stimulated by the contemplation of fellow-creatures to whom God has not been so merciful as he has to themselves.

Whether the institution to be defended is slavery, political absolution, or the absolutism of the head of a family, we are always expected to judge of it from its best instances; and we are presented with pictures of loving exercise of authority on one side, loving submission to it on the other—superior wisdom ordering all things for the greatest good of the dependents, and surrounded by their smiles and benedictions. All this would be very much to the purpose if any one pretended that there are no such things as good men. Who doubts that there may be great goodness, and great happiness, and great affection, under the absolute government of a good man? Meanwhile, laws and institutions require to be adapted, not to good men, but to bad. Marriage is not an institution designed for a select few. Men are not required, as a preliminary to the marriage ceremony, to prove by testimonials that they are fit to be trusted with the exercise of absolute power. The tie of affection and obligation to a wife and children is very strong with those whose general social feelings are strong, and with many who are little sensible to any other social ties; but there are all degrees of sensibility and insensibility to it, as there are all grades of goodness and wickedness in men, down to those whom no ties will bind, and on whom society has no action but through its *ultima ratio,* the penalties of the law. In every grade of this descending scale are men to whom are committed all the legal powers of a husband. The vilest malefactor has some wretched woman tied to him, against whom he can commit any atrocity except killing her, and, if tolerably cautious, can do that without much danger of the legal penalty. And how many thousands are there among the lowest classes in every country, who, without being in a legal sense malefactors in any other respect, because in every other quarter their aggressions meet with resistance, indulge the utmost habitual excesses of bodily violence towards the unhappy wife, who alone, at least of grown persons, can neither repel nor escape from their brutality; and towards whom the excess of dependence inspires their mean and savage natures, not with a generous forbearance, and a point of honour to behave well to one whose lot in life is trusted entirely to their kindness, but on the contrary with a notion that the law has delivered her to them as their thing, to be used at their pleasure, and that they are not expected to practise the consideration towards her which is required from them towards everybody else. The law, which till lately left even these atrocious extremes of domestic oppression practically unpunished, has within these few years made some feeble attempts to repress them. But its attempts have done little, and cannot be expected to do much, because it is contrary to reason and experience to suppose that there can be any real check to brutality, consistent with leaving the victim still in the power of the executioner. Until a conviction for personal violence, or at all events a repetition of it after a first conviction, entitles the woman *ipso facto* to a divorce, or at least to a judicial separation, the attempt to repress these "aggravated assaults" by legal penalties will break down for want of a prosecutor, or for want of a witness.

When we consider how vast is the number of men, in any great country, who are little higher than brutes, and that this never prevents them from being able, through the law of marriage, to obtain a victim, the breadth and depth of human misery caused in this shape alone by the abuse of the institution swells to something appalling. . . . It would be tiresome to repeat the commonplaces about the unfitness of men in general for power, which, after the political discussions of centuries, every one knows by heart, were it not that hardly any one thinks of applying these maxims to the case in which above all others they are applicable, that of power, not placed in the hands of a man here and there, but offered to every adult male, down to the basest and most ferocious. It is not because a man is not known to have broken any of the Ten Commandments, or because he maintains a respectable character in his dealings with those whom he cannot compel to have intercourse with him, or because he does not fly out into violent bursts of ill-temper against those who are not obliged to bear with him, that it is possible to surmise of what sort his conduct will be in the unrestraint of home. Even the commonest men reserve the violent, the sulky, the undisguisedly selfish side of their character for those who have no power to withstand it. The relation of superiors to dependents is the nursery of these vices of character, which, wherever else they exist, are an overflowing from that source. A man who is morose or violent to his equals, is sure to be one who has lived among inferiors, whom he could frighten or worry into submission. If the family in its best forms is, as it is often said to be, a school of sympathy, tenderness, and loving forgetfulness of self, it is still oftener, as respects its chief, a school of wilfulness, overbearingness, unbounded self-indulgence, and a double-dyed and idealized selfishness, of which sacrifice itself is only a particular form: the care for the wife and children being only care from them as parts of the man's own interests and belongings, and their individual happiness being immolated in every shape to his smallest preferences. What better is to be looked for under the existing form of the institution? . . . I grant that the wife, if she cannot effectually resist, can at least retaliate; she, too, can make the man's life extremely uncomfortable, and by that power is able to carry many points which she ought, and many which she ought not, to prevail in. But this instrument of self-protection—which may be called the power of the scold, or the shrewish sanction—has the fatal defect, that it avails most against the least tyrannical superiors, and in favour of the least deserving dependents. It is the weapon of irritable and self-willed women; of those who would make the worst use of power if they themselves had it, and who generally turn this power to a bad use. The amiable cannot use such an instrument, the highminded disdain it. And on the other hand, the husbands against whom it is used most effectively are the gentler and more inoffensive; those who cannot be induced, even by provocation, to resort to any very harsh exercise of authority. The wife's power of being disagreeable generally only establishes a counter-tyranny, and makes victims in their turn chiefly of those husbands who are least inclined to be tyrants.

· · ·

Her power often gives her what she has no right to, but does not enable her to assert her own rights. A Sultan's favourite slave has slaves under her, over whom she tyrannizes; but the desirable thing would be that she should neither have slaves nor be a slave. By entirely sinking her own existence in her husband; by having no will (or persuading him that she has no will) but his, in anything which regards their joint relation, and by making it the business of her life to work upon his sentiments, a wife may gratify herself by influencing, and very probably perverting, his conduct, in those of his external relations which she has never qualified herself to judge of, or in which she is herself wholly influenced by some personal or other partiality or prejudice. . . .

But how, it will be asked, can any society exist without government? In a family, as in a state, some one person must be the ultimate ruler. Who shall decide when married people differ in opinion? Both cannot have their way, yet a decision one way or the other must be come to.

It is not true that in all voluntary association between two people, one of them must be absolute master: still less that the law must determine which of them it shall be. The most frequent case of voluntary association, next to marriage, is partnership in business: and it is not found or thought necessary to enact that in every partnership, one partner shall have entire control over the concern, and the others shall be bound to obey his orders. . . .

It is quite true that things which have to be decided every day, and cannot adjust themselves gradually, or wait for a compromise, ought to depend on one will: one person must have their sole control. But it does not follow that this should always be the same person. The natural arrangement is a division of powers between the two; each being absolute in the executive branch of their own department, and any change of system and principle requiring the consent of both. The division neither can nor should be pre-established by the law, since it must depend on individual capacities and suitabilities. If the two persons chose, they might pre-appoint it by the marriage contract, as pecuniary arrangements are now often pre-appointed. There would seldom be any difficulty in deciding such things by mutual consent, unless the marriage was one of those unhappy ones in which all other things as well as this, become subjects of bickering and dispute. The division of rights would naturally follow the division of duties and functions; and that is already made by consent, or at all events not by law, but by general custom, modified and modifiable at the pleasure of the persons concerned.

· · ·

A pertinacious adversary, pushed to extremities, may say, that husbands indeed are willing to be reasonable, and to make fair concessions to their partners without being compelled to it, but that wives are not: that if allowed any rights of their own, they will acknowledge no rights at all in any one else, and never will yield in anything, unless they can be compelled, by the man's mere authority, to yield in everything. This would have been said by many persons some generations ago, when satires on women were in vogue, and men thought it a clever thing to insult women for being what men made them. But it will be said by no one now who is worth replying to. It is not the doctrine of the present day that women are less susceptible of good feeling, and consideration for those with whom they are united by the strongest ties, than men are. On the contrary, we are perpetually told that women are better than men, by those who are totally opposed to treating them as if they were as good; so that the saying has passed into a piece of tiresome cant, intended to put a complimentary face upon an injury, and resembling those celebrations of royal clemency which, according to Gulliver, the king of Lilliput always prefixed to his most sanguinary decrees. If women are better than men in anything, it surely is in individual self-sacrifice for those of their own family. But I lay little stress on this, so long as they are universally taught that they are born and created for self-sacrifice. I believe that equality of rights would abate the exaggerated self-abnegation which is the present artificial ideal of feminine character, and that a good woman would not be more self-sacrificing than the best man: but on the other hand, men would be much more unselfish and self-sacrificing than at present, because they would no longer be taught to worship their own will as such a grand thing that it is actually the law for another rational being. There is nothing which men so easily learn as this self-worship: all privileged persons, and all privileged classes, have had it. The more we descend in the scale of humanity, the intenser it is; and most of all in those who are not, and can never expect to be, raised above anyone except an unfortunate wife and children. . . .

There are, no doubt, women, as there are men, whom equality of consideration will not satisfy; with whom there is no peace while any will or wish is regarded but their own. Such persons are a proper subject for the law of divorce. They are only fit to live alone, and no human beings ought to be compelled to associate their lives with them. But the legal subordination tends to make such characters among women more, rather than less, frequent. If the man exerts his whole power, the woman is of course crushed: but if she is treated with indulgence, and permitted to assume power, there is no rule to set limits to her encroachments. The law, not determining her rights, but theoretically allowing her none at all, practically declares that the measure of what she has a right to, is what she can contrive to get.

The equality of married persons before the law, is not only the sole mode in which that particular relation can be made consistent with justice to both sides, and conducive to the happiness of both, but it is the only means of rendering the daily life of mankind, in any high sense, a school of moral cultivation. Though the truth may not be felt or generally acknowledged for generations to come, the only school of genuine moral sentiment is society between equals. The moral education of mankind has hitherto emanated chiefly from the law of force, and is adapted almost solely to the relations which force creates. In the less advanced states of society, people hardly recognise any relation with their equals. To be an equal is to be an enemy. Society, from its highest place to its lowest, is one long chain, or rather ladder, where every individual is either above or below his nearest neighbour, and wherever he does not command he must obey. Existing moralities accordingly, are mainly fitted to a relation of command and obedience. Yet command and obedience are but unfortunate necessities of human life: society in equality is its normal state. Already in modern life, and more and more as it progressively improves, command and obedience become exceptional facts in life, equal association its general rule. The morality of the first ages rested on the obligation to submit to power; that of the ages next following, on the right of the weak to the forbearance and protection of the strong. How much longer is one form of society and life to content itself with the morality made for another? We have had the morality of submission, and the morality of chivalry and generosity; the time is now come for the morality of justice. Whenever, in former ages, any approach has been made to society in equality, Justice has asserted its claims as the foundation of virtue. It was thus in the free republics of antiquity. But even in the best of these, the equals were limited to the free male citizens; slaves, women, and the unenfranchised residents were under the law of force. . . . But the true virtue of human beings is fitness to live together as equals; claiming nothing for themselves but what they as freely concede to every one else; regarding command of any kind as an exceptional necessity, and in all cases a temporary one; and preferring, whenever possible, the society of those with whom leading and following can be alternate and reciprocal. To these virtues, nothing in life as at present constituted gives cultivation by exercise. The family is a school of despotism, in which the virtues of despotism, but also its vices, are largely nourished. Citizenship, in free countries, is partly a school of society in equality; but citizenship fills only a small place in modern life, and does not come near the daily habits or inmost sentiments. The family, justly constituted, woud be the real school of the virtues of freedom. It is sure to be a sufficient one of everything else. It will always be a school of obedience for the children, of command for the parents. What is needed is, that it should be a school of sympathy in equality, of living together in love, without power on one side or obedience on the other. This it ought to be between the parents. It would then be an exercise of those virtues which each requires to fit them for all other association, and a model to the children of the feelings and conduct which their temporary training by means of obedience is designed to render habitual, and therefore natural, to them. The moral training of mankind will never be adapted to the conditions of the life for which all other human progress is a preparation, until they practise in the family the same moral rule which is adapted to the normal constitution of human society.

. . .

After what has been said respecting the obligation of obedience, it is almost superfluous to say anything concerning the more special point included in the general one—a woman's right to her own property; for I need not hope that this treatise can make any impression upon those who need anything to convince them that a woman's inheritance or gains ought to be as much her own after marriage as before. The rule is simple: whatever would be the husband's or wife's if they were not married, should be under their exclusive control during marriage; which need not interfere with the power to tie up property by settlement, in order to preserve it for children. Some people are sentimentally shocked at the idea of a separate interest in money matters, as inconsistent with the ideal fusion of two lives into one. For my own part, I am one of the strongest supporters of community of goods, when resulting from an entire unity of feeling in the owners, which makes all things common between them. But I have no relish for a community of goods resting on the doctrine, that what is mine is yours but what is yours is not mine; and I should prefer to decline entering into such a compact with any one, though I were myself the person to profit by it. . . .

When the support of the family depends, not on property, but on earnings, the common arrangement, by which the man earns the income and the wife superintends the domestic expenditure, seems to me in general the most suitable division of labour between the two persons. If, in addition to the physical suffering of bearing children, and the whole responsibility of their care and education in early years, the wife undertakes the careful and economical application of the husband's earnings to the general comfort of the family; she takes not only her fair share, but usually the larger share, of the bodily and mental exertion required by their joint existence. If she undertakes any additional portion, it seldom relieves her from this, but only prevents her from performing it properly. The care which she is herself disabled from taking of the children and the household, nobody else takes; those of the children who do not die, grow up as they best can, and the management of the household is likely to be so bad, as even in point of economy to be a great drawback from the value of the wife's earnings. In an otherwise just state of things, it is not, therefore, I think, a desirable custom, that the wife should contribute by her labour to the income of the family. In an unjust state of things, her doing so may be useful to her, by making her of more value in the eyes of the man who is legally her master; but, on the other hand, it enables him still farther to abuse his power, by forcing her to work, and leaving the support of the family to her exertions, while he spends most of his time in drinking and idleness. The *power* of earning is essential to the dignity of a woman, if she has not independent property. But if marriage were an equal contract, not implying the obligation of obedience; if the connexion were no longer enforced to the oppression of those to whom it is purely a mischief, but a separation, on just terms (I do not now speak of a divorce), could be obtained by any woman who was morally entitled to it; and if she would then find all honourable employments as freely open to her as to men; it would not be necessary for her protection, that during marriage she should make this particular use of her faculties. Like a man when he chooses a profession, so, when a woman marries, it may in general be understood that she makes choice of the management of a household, and the bringing up of a family, as the first call upon her exertions, during as many years of her life as may be required for the purpose; and that she renounces, not all other objects and occupations, but all which are not consistent with the requirements of this. . . .

4

There remains a question, not of less importance than those already discussed, and which will be asked the most importunately by those opponents whose conviction is somewhat shaken on the main point. What good are we to expect from the changes proposed in our customs and institutions? Would mankind be at all better off if women were free? If not, why disturb their minds, and attempt to make a social revolution in the name of an abstract right?

It is hardly to be expected that this question will be asked in respect to the change proposed in the condition of women in marriage. The sufferings, immoralities, evils of all sorts, produced in innumerable cases by the subjection of individual women to individual men, are far too terrible to be overlooked. Unthinking or uncandid persons, counting those cases alone which are extreme, or which attain publicity, may say that the evils are exceptional; but no one can be blind to their existence, nor, in many cases, to their intensity. And it is perfectly obvious that the abuse of the power cannot be very much checked while the power remains. It is a power given, or offered, not to good men, or to decently respectable men, but to all men; the most brutal, and the most criminal. There is no check but that of opinion, and such men are in general within the reach of no opinion but that of men like themselves. If such men did not brutally tyrannize over the one human being whom the law compels to bear everything from them, society must already have reached a paradisiacal state. There could be no need any longer to curb men's vicious propensities. Astræa must not only have returned to earth, but the heart of the worst man must have become her temple. The law of servitude in marriage is a monstrous contradiction to all the principles of the modern world, and to all the experience through which those principles have been slowly and painfully worked out. It is the sole case, now that negro slavery has been abolished, in which a human being in the plenitude of every faculty is delivered up to the tender mercies of another human being, in the hope forsooth that this other will use the power solely for the good of the person subjected to it. Marriage is the only actual bondage known to our law. There remain no legal slaves, except the mistress of every house.

. . .

Think what it is to a boy, to grow up to manhood in the belief that without any merit or any exertion of his own, though he may be the most frivolous and empty or the most ignorant and stolid of mankind, by the mere fact of being born a male he is by right the superior of all and every one of an entire half of the human race: including probably some whose real superiority to himself he has daily or hourly occasion to feel; but even if in his whole conduct he habitually follows a woman's guidance, still, if he is a fool, she thinks that of course she is not, and cannot be, equal in ability and judgment to himself; and if he is not a fool, he does worse—he sees that she is superior to him, and believes that, notwithstanding her superiority, he is entitled to command and she is bound to obey. What must be the effect on his character, of this lesson? And men of the cultivated classes are often not aware how deeply it sinks into the immense majority of male minds. For, among right-feeling and well-bred people, the inequality is kept as much as possible out of sight; above all, out of sight of the children. As much obedience is required from boys to their mother as to their father: they are not permitted to domineer over their sisters, nor are they accustomed to see these postponed to them, but the contrary; the compensations of the chivalrous feeling being made prominent, while the servitude which requires them is kept in the background. Well brought-up youths in the higher classes thus often escape the bad influences of the situation in their early years, and only experience them when, arrived at manhood, they fall under the dominion of facts as they really exist. Such people are little aware, when a boy is differently brought up, how early the notion of his inherent superiority to a girl arises in his mind; how it grows with his growth and strengthens with his strength; how it is inoculated by one schoolboy upon another; how early the youth thinks himself superior to his mother, owing her perhaps forbearance, but no real respect; and how sublime and sultan-like a sense of superiority he feels, above all, over the woman whom he honours by admitting her to a partnership of his life. Is it imagined that all this does not pervert the whole manner of existence of the man, both as an individual and as a social being? . . .

The example afforded, and the education given to the sentiments, by laying the foundation of domestic existence upon a relation contradictory to the first principles of social justice, must, from the very nature of man, have a perverting influence of such magnitude, that it is hardly possible with our present experience to raise our imaginations to the conception of so great a change for the better as would be made by its removal. All that education and civilization are doing to efface the influences on character of the law of force, and replace them by those of justice, remains merely on the surface, as long as the citadel of the enemy is not attacked. The principle of the modern movement in morals and politics, is that conduct, and conduct alone, entitles to respect: that not what men are, but what they do, constitutes their claim to deference; that, above all, merit, and not birth, is the only rightful claim to power and authority. If no authority, not in its nature temporary, were allowed to one human being over another, society would not be employed in building up propensities with one hand which it has to curb with the other. The child would really, for the first time in man's existence on earth, be trained in the way he should go, and when he was old there would be a chance that he would not depart from it. But so long as the right of the strong to power over the weak rules in the very heart of society, the attempt to make the equal right of the weak the principle of its outward actions will always be an uphill struggle; for the law of justice, which is also that of Christianity, will never get possession of men's inmost sentiments; they will be working against it, even when bending to it.

The second benefit to be expected from giving to women the free use of their faculties, by leaving them the free choice of their employments, and opening to them the same field of occupation and the same prizes and encouragements as to other human beings, would be that of doubling the mass of mental faculties available for the higher service of humanity. Where there is now one person qualified to benefit mankind and promote the general improvement, as a public teacher, or an administrator of some branch of public or social affairs, there would then be a chance of two. . . .

This great accession to the intellectual power of the species, and to the amount of intellect available for the good management of its affairs, would be obtained, partly, through the better and more complete intellectual education of women, which would then improve *pari passu* with that of men. Women in general would be brought up equally capable of understanding business, public affairs, and the higher matters of speculation, with men in the same class of society; and the select few of the one as well as of the other sex, who were qualified not only to comprehend what is done or thought by others, but

to think or do something considerable themselves, would meet with the same facilities for improving and training their capacities in the one sex as in the other. In this way, the widening of the sphere of action for women would operate for good, by raising their education to the level of that of men, and making the one participate in all improvements made in the other. But independently of this, the mere breaking down of the barrier would of itself have an educational virtue of the highest worth. The mere getting rid of the idea that all the wider subjects of thought and action, all the things which are of general and not solely of private interest, are men's business, from which women are to be warned off— positively interdicted from most of it, coldly tolerated in the little which is allowed them—the mere consciousness a woman would then have of being a human being like any other, entitled to choose her pursuits, urged or invited by the same inducements as any one else to interest herself in whatever is interesting to human beings, entitled to exert the share of influence on all human concerns which belongs to an individual opinion, whether she attempted actual participation in them or not—this alone would effect an immense expansion of the faculties of women, as well as enlargement of the range of their moral sentiments.

. . .

[1870]

 13

Letter to My Countrywomen, Dwelling in the Farmsteads and Cottages of England

JOSEPHINE BUTLER

I

My Dear Friends,
There is a law now in force in this country which concerns you all, and yet of which many among you have never even heard. I want you to listen to me for a little, whilst I try to explain it to you, and when

you have heard and understood, you will, I think, feel about it as I do.

I daresay you all know that there are women, alas, thousands of women, in England who live by sin. Sometimes, when you have been late at your market-town, you may have passed one such in the street, and have shrunk aside, feeling it shame even to touch her; or perhaps, instead of scorn, a deep pity has filled your heart, and you have longed to take her hand, and to lead her back to a better and happier life. Now, it is the pity and not the scorn which I would fain have you feel towards these poor women, and when you have read what I have to tell you about them, I think it will not be hard for you to be merciful to them in your thoughts.

In the first place, you must understand that very few ever begin to lead a bad life from choice. Thousands of the miserable creatures whom we call *fallen* have really not fallen at all, for they never stood upon any height of virtue or knowledge from which it was possible for them to descend, and if they love darkness, it is because no light ever shone upon them; no tender mother ever spoke to *them* of God or Christ; no kind father ever shielded *them* from temptation; no pure examples ever encouraged *them* to resist evil, and to seek after that which is good; rather, they have been sold —yes, sold— into their life of bondage by those who ought to have died to save them from such misery.

I daresay you will hardly believe it, yet it is but too true. It is said that there were in one large sea-port town, only a few years ago, 1500 prostitutes under fifteen years of age, some of them mere children of eleven or twelve; and of these many had been sent upon the streets by their own parents, who lived upon the wages of their sin and shame.

Again, many girls are led astray when very young—sometimes most shamefully deceived and betrayed—then, finding the doors of their relatives and friends shut against them, they are driven by despair into recklessness and vice.

A still larger number, in fact far more than half of all the women who live by prostitution, fall into it through lack of food, and clothes, and shelter. Are we sure, you and I, that, in like case, we should not have done the same? Hunger and cold are hard to bear; it needs the courage of a martyr to die rather than to sin—and not only a martyr's courage, but a martyr's faith also; and how should those who find

this world so cruel and so sad, place their trust in the God who made it?

To show you how much want has to do with prostitution, I will just mention here that a French doctor, who inquired carefully into the histories of 3,000 fallen women in Paris, found that of those 3,000 only thirty-five had had any chance of earning their bread honestly.

Now, if you were to add together all the women who are trained to sin from their cradle, all those who are betrayed into it by deceit, or driven into it by despair, and all those who sink into it through real starvation, you would find very few left whom you could justly call bad—doing evil because they love evil; very few, therefore, to whom you have any right to deny your pity and your help.

Perhaps you will say, 'if all that this lady tells us about these women is true, we are very sorry for them, but we don't see how we can help them; the Government to whom we pay so much money that it may take care of the people ought to do that. Surely it is trying to save some of the poor creatures.'

To this I answer: the Parliament and the Government of England have done nothing *for* these women, what it has done *against* them you now shall hear.

I have taken it for granted that you all know that there is such an evil as prostitution in the land; but perhaps some of you are not aware that those who lead vicious lives are liable to certain painful and dangerous diseases, called *contagious,* because it is supposed that one person can only take them from another by *contact,* or *touch.* A healthy man, by merely walking down a street where there is smallpox or fever, may sicken and die; but with these contagious diseases it is quite different, all men are safe from them so long as they live virtuous lives. Therefore, as I daresay you will think, every man can preserve himself from them if he chooses, and if he does not choose, he deserves to suffer, and ought not to be saved from suffering, because through it he may, perhaps, learn to be wiser and better.

But as regards certain men, at least—I mean soldiers and sailors—our Government judges otherwise.

You know it costs a great deal of money to train a man to be a soldier or sailor, and if he is often ill and unfit for service that money is as good as lost. Now, when the Government found that very many soldiers and sailors were constantly in hospital, owing to contagious disorders, they asked themselves what they could do to prevent such a waste of the public funds, and such a weakening of the forces on which the country has to depend for safety in time of war, which was quite right; but instead of teaching or helping them to lead pure lives, they resolved to protect them against contagious diseases—in other words, to make it safe for them to sin.

So they took counsel with doctors and officers high in the army, and high in the navy, and they drew up a Bill—that is to say the plan of a new law—and brought it to Parliament to pass, but this they did not do until the beginning of August, when the business of Parliament was supposed to be over for the year, and many members of the House of Commons had already left town and gone to Scotland or abroad. They called the Bill a Contagious Diseases Bill, and because the Bills about the Cattle Plague were also called Contagious Diseases Bills, some of these members who might have returned to speak and vote against it, mistook it for one of these and stayed away—for which they were afterwards sorry; and because the newspapers gave no account of the Bill, nor any proper report of the speeches made about it in Parliament, it became law without the knowledge and consent of the people.

The particular measure of which I am writing was passed in 1869. There had been laws to protect soldiers and sailors against contagious diseases since 1864, but as they were milder in their provisions, and their operations confined to a very few places, little had been thought or said about them.

Now, the men who drew up these different Acts say that they kept them so quiet because they thought the matter with which they had to do indecent and disgusting, and unfit to be talked of or read about. But when I have told you what was written in the Act of 1869—for which the Acts passed in 1864 and 1866 prepared the way—I think you will agree with me that they were afraid to let Englishmen and Englishwomen understand the new laws lest they should cry out against them.

The Contagious Diseases Act of 1869 provides that in fifteen towns where there are always many soldiers and sailors—such as Canterbury, Aldershot, Portsmouth, and Plymouth—there shall be surgeons appointed to examine with certain instruments the persons of all prostitutes, to see in what state they are, and those whom they find to be healthy they are to allow to go away, having given them a notice of when they are to come to be examined again, and so long as a woman appears on the stated days for examination, the police do not arrest or otherwise interfere with her; but those whom the surgeons find to be diseased, they are to send to what are called hospitals, but are really prisons, to be cured, and when they are well, they are dismissed to follow their former pursuits, their certificates of health being put into the hands of the police.

Further, this Act gives power to certain police inspectors, to watch all women and girls. The Act does not specify the age. As a matter of fact, girls of most tender years are brought under it, and the police-officers say that they especially watch seamstresses, labourers' daughters, and domestic servants, in those towns, and for fifteen miles round each, and if one of these paid spies—for since they wear plain clothes, so that people cannot tell they belong to the police-force, they are really spies—*suspects* any woman of being a prostitute, or of *intending* prostitution, he can go to her and say, 'Come to Mr So and So', naming the Examining Surgeon, 'and sign the paper'. Now this paper is called the Voluntary Submission, and by signing it a woman agrees to submit for a whole year (it might, under the Act, be a shorter time, but the police have *always* filled it up for a year) to be examined whenever she is called upon to be so, but it is so carefully worded that an ignorant girl might put her name to it without knowing that by so doing she was signing away her liberty for twelve months, her character for ever.

If, however, she does understand this, and refuses to go to the surgeon, then the police spy can take her before a single magistrate, and that one magistrate, on the oath of that one policeman, who only needs to swear that he *suspects*, not that he knows her to be leading a vicious life, may order her to submit to the examination, periodically for twelve months, and if she does not obey can send her to prison for three months, and when the first three months are over, if she still refuses to be examined by the surgeon, the magistrate can commit her for three more, and so on again and again.

So, if a woman is ignorant or frightened, and goes to the surgeon, she is put on the list of common women, and if she is well informed and brave, and goes before the magistrate, she may be imprisoned for life, without ever having been properly tried; and the examination to which she is ordered to submit is so cruel and indecent, that it is shameful even to speak of it; and those who have undergone it a few times, become so hardened and degraded, that almost all hope of saving them is lost. The object for which they are thus brutalised, is that the men who share their guilt and often tempt them to it, may go on sinning as much as they like, without any danger to their health; for in the eyes of *generals and admirals,* the souls of English women are of less consequence than the bodies of English men—if those bodies happen to be clothed in a red coat or a blue jacket.

Now, I beg you to think first with what awful dangers such a law surrounds innocent women. Remember, a policeman can accuse a girl, or even a child, of prostitution merely on suspicion, and there is no rule laid down to fix the signs which shall be held to give him a right to think evil of her. Each policeman is to judge of them for himself; and it is clear that they do not all agree, for of several witnesses who were examined on this point before a committee of the House of Commons, one said that the police suspected a woman who was seen 'larking' about the street, and talking to men; and that when the police saw a woman out late of an evening, they were very liable to jump to the conclusion that she was a prostitute. A surgeon under the Act said that the ground of suspicion was more a question as to mannerism than anything else. But if to be out of doors alone at night, or to be seen talking to men in the streets, is to be looked upon as a sign of a bad character, and to give a policeman the right to accuse a girl of prostitution, what woman will not fear to leave her house after dark, or to exchange a greeting with a friend?

And if the oath of one policeman is enough to condemn a girl, how will she be safe even in her own house? For supposing that a policeman has a spite against her, or any of her people, what is there to prevent his accusing her falsely, since he cannot be punished, even if the accusation be proved false, if he swears that he believed it to be true?

And the danger is not only from the paid spy; every man if he is angry with a woman, perhaps because he has tried to seduce her, and she has re-

sisted him, can write to the police, not even signing his name to the letter, since he will not be called upon to appear as a witness, saying—'such a person is a prostitute', and without even knowing who her accuser is, she can be brought before the examining surgeon, or the magistrate, and so may be doomed to sin and shame for life, because some wretch envied her her innocence. Think, too, how the threat of such a false accusation might be used to extort money from the timid and weak.

I do not say that women would often be falsely accused, nor yet that money would often be extorted from them by the threat of such false accusation; but I do assert that whilst the Contagious Diseases Acts continue the law of the land, such things might happen, and that no innocent woman, however poor or ignorant, ought for a single day to be exposed to so frightful a risk; and I want you also to understand that it is just the poor and ignorant who are endangered by these Acts, since no police spy, or any other man, would dare to accuse a woman of wealth and position, able to protect herself, or with friends strong enough to protect her, unless he had the most certain proofs of her guilt, and perhaps not even then.

I feel sure you will see directly how cruel these laws are to good women, but I want you to see, too, how unjust they are to sinful ones. For when a woman sins, does she sin alone? Rather for one sinful woman are there not fifty—ay, a hundred—sinful men? And which of them, the ignorant, half-starved prostitutes, or the men, often well-taught and well-fed, who consort with them, are they that carry disease to virtuous wives, and transmit it to unconscious infants? Surely the men. Then they are not only more guilty, but also more dangerous in their guilt. Yet the punishment of the sin of *two* is made by these laws to fall upon *one* alone, and that one the least to be blamed, and the most to be pitied.

But even if a woman be utterly vile—the tempter not the tempted—ought she to be deprived of all her rights and liberties? It has always been the boast of Englishmen that the law of England treats every accused person as innocent until he has been proved to be guilty. The burglar, the murderer is not asked to accuse himself; he is tried in open court, so that all his countrymen may know what has been said for and against him, and judge whether he has been fairly treated; he has lawyers to defend him, twelve men to listen to the evidence, and a judge to help them to understand the law, and to remind them that they must not condemn him upon suspicion, but only upon proof; and he cannot be found guilty unless the whole jury is convinced that he really is so. All these safeguards against injustice and oppression the Law of England gives to the man accused of the darkest crime, but for the last two years Parliament has denied every one of them to women only charged with sin, whose accomplices it not only does not punish, but even tries to protect against those penalties which God himself has attached to vice.

And this brings me to the third charge which I have to make against the Contagious Diseases Acts, namely, that they tend to encourage men in vicious habits.

This they do in two ways; directly, by affording them opportunities of sinning safely; appointing for them, as it were, cities of refuge, to which they can flee, and in which they can indulge their evil desires without fear; and, indirectly, by accustoming them to think that vice is so natural, so necessary, that no one expects them to be virtuous; for they must see that those who framed these Acts despaired of ever improving mankind, since if they had had any hope of being able to reform it, instead of building hospitals in which to cure prostitutes, so that there may be always healthy women for soldiers and sailors (and of course all other men living in or near the subjected towns), to consort with, they would surely have founded schools and reading rooms, and clubs, and workshops, and other like institutions, where they might spend their idle time in learning good, instead of in doing evil.

But we have other proof that the Contagious Diseases Acts are founded on the belief that human nature is hopelessly brutal. Many writers, in newspapers and elsewhere, openly say that this is why they were passed, and this is why they must be maintained, and some doctors—not all, many are virtuous themselves, and believe that others can be virtuous too—go so far as to tell their patients that vice is good for their health.

And that these Acts have really increased vice among men is proved by the fact that on the nights after the prostitutes have been examined by the surgeons, and when it is *supposed* that there is no danger in approaching them, since all who were found to be diseased had been sent to the hospitals, the bad houses in the fifteen towns are crowded, especially by young lads and married men.

Supposed, I say, for the promise of safety contained in the fact of a woman being at large just after having been examined, often proves false, in truth it has not been shown that contagious disorders have diminished in England among soldiers and sailors, since the Contagious Diseases Act became law; and in France, where like laws have been in force for many years past, they abound so frightfully that persons, capable of forming an opinion on the subject, believe that it is to them that the French owe the terrible defeats of the late war, for they could neither march nor fight like the healthier and more virtuous Germans; and if this opinion is correct, it deserves to be carefully considered, since it is for the avowed purpose of keeping the army and navy healthy that our Contagious Diseases Acts were framed and carried.

In speaking of the hospitals in which prostitutes are cured, I have called them prisons, and it is right, therefore, that I should prove to you that they deserve the name.

They are prisons; firstly, because a woman can be sent to them against her will, on the word and at the mere pleasure of an examining surgeon; secondly, because she can be kept there against her will, for any length of time, not exceeding nine months, on the word and at the mere pleasure of the house surgeon, whose interest it is not to let her go, till some other unfortunate comes to take her place, because the Government pays a large sum to the hospital funds for every bed that is full, but much less for the beds that are empty; thirdly, because once within their walls, she can be forced to do any work which the governor and nurses may think fit to demand of her; lastly, because whilst she remains in them, she cannot see any of her friends, or even the clergyman of her parish, or her own lawyer, without the permission of the said house surgeon, much of whose power over the women in his charge is given him, not by the Acts which have at least been passed by Parliament, and are therefore the law of the land until such time as they are altered or repealed, but by the Admiralty—that is to say, the board of gentlemen who are appointed to manage the affairs of the navy and of the navy only, and who, therefore, have no legal right to interfere with, or make rules for, any person who is not a sailor.

I believe some of the points I have mentioned are true only of the Royal Albert Hospital at Devonport, but all the others are real prisons, in so far as women are sent to them and confined in them against their will.

Now, I think, I have made you understand what the Contagious Diseases Acts are, and the purpose for which they were passed; and I hope I have succeeded in convicting you of their cruelty, injustice, and immorality. In a second letter I will tell you what has been done towards forcing Parliament to undo its evil work, and will show you how you too can help to rid the country of these bad laws. But before concluding this I must just point out that all these police spies, and examining surgeons, and hospitals for diseased women, who are to be cured, not that they may be saved from their vicious life, but that soldiers and sailors may share it without risk, cost a great deal of money, and that all that money comes out of the pockets of the people.

I am, my dear Friends,
Yours very faithfully,
An English Lady

· · ·

[PETITION TO PARLIAMENT]
Protest

We, the undersigned, enter our solemn protest against the Contagious Diseases Acts.

First, because involving as they do such a momentous change in the legal safeguards enjoyed by women in common with men, they have been passed, not only without the knowledge of the country, but unknown to Parliament itself; and we hold that neither the representatives of the people, nor the press, fulfil the duties which are expected of them, when they allow such legislation to take place without the fullest discussion.

Second, because so far as women are concerned, they remove every guarantee of personal security which the law has established and held sacred, and put their reputation, their freedom, and their persons absolutely in the power of the police.

Third, because the law is bound in any country, professing to give civil liberty to its subjects, to define clearly an offence which it punishes.

Fourth, because it is unjust to punish the sex who are the victims of a vice, and leave unpunished the sex who are the main cause both of the vice and its dreaded consequences; and we consider that liability to arrest, forced surgical examination, or (where this is resisted) imprisonment with hard labour, to which these Acts subject women, are punishments of the most degrading kind.

Fifth, because, by such a system, the path of evil is made more easy to our sons and to the whole of the youth of England; inasmuch as a moral restraint is withdrawn the moment the State recognises, and provides convenience for the practice of a vice which it thereby declares to be necessary and venial.

Sixth, because these measures are cruel to the women who come under their action—violating the feelings of those whose sense of shame is not wholly lost, and further brutalising even the most abandoned.

Seventh, because the disease which these Acts seek to remove has never been removed by any such legislation. The advocates of the system have utterly failed to show, by statistics or otherwise, that these regulations have in any case, after several years' trial, and when applied to one sex only, diminished disease, reclaimed the fallen, or improved the general morality of the country. We have, on the contrary, the strongest evidence to show that in Paris and other continental cities where women have long been outraged by this forced inspection, the public health and morals are worse than at home.

Eighth, because the conditions of this disease, in the first instance, are moral, not physical. The moral evil through which the disease makes its way separates the case entirely from that of the plague, or other scourges which have been placed under police control or sanitary care. We hold that we are bound, before rushing into the experiment of legalising a revolting vice, to try to deal with the *causes* of the evil and we dare to believe that with wiser teaching and more capable legislation, those causes would not be beyond control.

· · ·

[1871]

14

Wife-Torture in England

FRANCES POWER COBBE

. . .

How does it come to pass that while the better sort of Englishmen are thus exceptionally humane and considerate to women, the men of the lower class of the same nation are proverbial for their unparalleled brutality, till wife-beating, wife-torture, and wife-murder have become the opprobrium of the land? How does it happen (still more strange to note!) that the same generous-hearted gentlemen, who would themselves fly to render succour to a lady in distress, yet read of the beatings, burnings, kickings, and "cloggings" of *poor* women well-nigh every morning in their newspapers without once setting their teeth, and saying, "This must be stopped! We can stand it no longer"?

The paradox truly seems worthy of a little investigation. What reason can be alleged, in the first place, why the male of the human species, and particularly the male of the finest variety of that species, should be the only animal in creation which maltreats its mate, or any female of its own kind?[1]

. . .

Wife-beating exists in the upper and middle classes rather more, I fear, than is generally recognized; but it rarely extends to anything beyond an occasional blow or two of a not dangerous kind. In his apparently most ungovernable rage, the gentleman or tradesman somehow manages to bear in mind the disgrace he will incur if his outbreak be betrayed by his wife's black eye or broken arm, and he regulates his cuffs or kicks accordingly. The dangerous wife-beater belongs almost exclusively to the artisan and labouring classes. Colliers, "puddlers," and weavers have long earned for themselves in this matter a bad reputation, and among a long list of cases before me, I reckon shoemakers, stonemasons, butchers, smiths, tailors, a printer, a clerk, a bird-catcher, and a large number of labourers. In the worse districts of London (as I have been informed by one of the most experienced magistrates) four-fifths of the wife-beating cases are among the lowest class of Irish labourers—a fact worthy of more than passing notice, had we time to bestow upon it, seeing that in their own country Irishmen of all classes are proverbially kind and even chivalrous towards women.

There are also various degrees of wife-beating in the different localities. In London it seldom goes beyond a severe "thrashing" with the fist—a sufficiently dreadful punishment, it is true, when inflicted by a strong man on a woman; but mild in comparison of the kickings and tramplings and "purrings" with hob-nailed shoes and clogs of what we can scarcely, in this connection, call the "dark and true and *tender* North." As Mr. Serjeant Pulling remarks,[2] "Nowhere is the ill-usage of woman so systematic as in Liverpool, and so little hindered by the strong arm of the law; making the lot of a married woman, whose locality is the 'kicking district' of Liverpool, simply a duration of suffering and subjection to injury and savage treatment, far worse than that to which the wives of mere savages are used." It is in the centres of dense mercantile and manufacturing populations that this offence reaches its climax. . . .

They are lives out of which almost every softening and ennobling element has been withdrawn, and into which enter brutalizing influences almost unknown elsewhere. They are lives of hard, ugly, mechanical toil in dark pits and hideous factories, amid the grinding and clanging of engines and the fierce heat of furnaces, in that Black Country where the green sod of earth is replaced by mounds of slag and shale, where no flower grows, no fruit ripens, scarcely a bird sings; where the morning has no freshness, the evening no dews; where the spring sunshine cannot pierce the foul curtain of smoke which overhangs these modern Cities of the Plain, and where the very streams and rivers run discoloured and steaming with stench, like Styx and Phlegethon, through their banks of ashes. If "God made the country and man made the town," we might deem that Ahrimanes devised this Tartarus of toil, and that here we had at last found the spot where the Psalmist might seek in vain for the handiwork of the Lord.

. . .

These, then, are the localities wherein Wife-torture flourishes in England; where a dense population is crowded into a hideous manufacturing or mining or mercantile district. Wages are usually high though fluctuating. Facilities for drink and vice abound, but those for cleanliness and decency are scarcely attainable. The men are rude, coarse, and brutal in their manners and habits, and the women devoid, in an extraordinary degree, of all the higher natural attractions and influences of their sex. Poor drudges of the factory, or of the crowded and sordid lodging-house, they lose, before youth is past, the freshness, neatness, and gentleness, perhaps even the modesty of the woman, and present, when their miserable cases come up before the magistrate, an aspect so sordid and forbidding that it is no doubt with difficulty he affords his sympathy to them rather than to the husband chained to so wretched a consort. Throughout the whole of this inquiry I think it very necessary, in justice to all parties, and in mitigation of too vehement judgement of cases only known from printed reports, to bear in mind that the women of the class concerned are, some of them woefully unwomanly, slatternly, coarse, foul-mouthed—sometimes loose in behaviour, sometimes madly addicted to drink. There ought to be no idealizing of them, *as a class,* into refined and suffering angels if we wish to be just. The home of a Lancashire operative, alas! is not a garden wherein the plants of refinement or sensitiveness are very likely to spring up or thrive.

Given this direful *milieu,* and its population, male and female, we next ask, What are the immediate incitements to the men to maltreat the women? They are of two kinds, I think,—general and particular.

First, the whole relation between the sexes in the class we are considering is very little better than one of master and slave. I have always abjured the use of this familiar comparison in speaking generally of English husbands and wives, because as regards the upper orders of society it is ridiculously over-strained and untrue. But in the "kicking districts," among the lowest labouring classes, Legree himself might find a dozen prototypes, and the condition of the women be most accurately matched by that of the negroes on a Southern plantation before the war struck off their fetters.[3] To a certain extent this marital tyranny among the lower classes is beyond the reach of law, and can only be remedied by the slow elevation and civilization of both sexes. But it is also in an appreciable degree, I am convinced, enhanced

by the law even as it now stands, and was still more so by the law as it stood before the Married Women's Property Act put a stop to the chartered robbery by husbands of their wives' earnings. At the present time, though things are improving year by year, thanks to the generous and far-seeing statesmen who are contending for justice to women inside and out of the House of Commons, the position of a woman before the law as wife, mother, and citizen, remains so much below that of a man as husband, father, and citizen, that it is a matter of course that she must be regarded by him as an inferior, and fail to obtain from him such a modicum of respect as her mental and moral qualities might win did he see her placed by the State on an equal footing.

. . .

I consider that it is a very great misfortune to both sexes that women should be thus depreciated in the opinion of that very class of men whom it would be most desirable to impress with respect and tenderness for them; who are most prone to despise physical infirmity and to undervalue the moral qualities wherein women excel. All the softening and refining influences which women exert in happier conditions are thus lost to those who most need them,—to their husbands and still more emphatically to their children; and the women themselves are degraded and brutified in their own eyes by the contempt of their companions. When I read all the fine-sounding phrases perpetually repeated about the invaluable influence of a good mother over her son,—how the worst criminals are admitted to be reclaimable if they have ever enjoyed it,—and how the virtues of the best and noblest men are attributed to it, as a commonplace of biography,—I often ask myself, "Why, then, is not something done to lift and increase, instead of to depreciate and lower, that sacred influence? Why are not mothers allowed to respect themselves, that they may fitly claim the respect of their sons? How is a lad to learn to reverence a woman whom he sees daily scoffed at, beaten, and abused, and when he knows that the laws of his country forbid her, ever and under any circumstances, to exercise the rights of citizenship; nay, which deny to her the guardianship of *himself*— of the very child of her bosom—should her husband choose to hand him over to her rival out of the street?"

The general depreciation of women *as a sex* is bad enough, but in the matter we are considering, the special depreciation of *wives* is more directly responsible for the outrages they endure. The notion that a man's wife is his PROPERTY, in the sense in which a horse is his property (descended to us rather through the Roman law than through the customs of our Teuton ancestors), is the fatal root of incalculable evil and misery. Every brutal-minded man, and many a man who in other relations of life is not brutal, entertains more or less vaguely the notion that his wife is his *thing*, and is ready to ask with indignation (as we read again and again in the police reports), of any one who interferes with his treatment of her, "May I not do what I will *with my own*?" It is even sometimes pleaded on behalf of poor men, that they possess *nothing else* but their wives, and that, consequently, it seems doubly hard to meddle with the exercise of their power in that narrow sphere.[4]

I am not intending to discuss the question of the true relation between husbands and wives which we may hope to see realized when

"Springs the happier race of human kind"

from parents "equal and free"—any more than the political and social rights of women generally. But it is impossible, in treating of the typical case wherein the misuse of wives reaches its climax in Wife-beating and Wife-torture, to avoid marking out with a firm line where lies the underground spring of the mischief. As one of the many results of this *proton pseudos*, must be noted the fact (very important in its bearing on our subject) that not only is an offence against a wife condoned as of inferior guilt, but any offence of the wife against her husband is regarded as a sort of *Petty Treason*. For her, as for the poor ass in the fable, it is more heinous to nibble a blade of grass than for the wolf to devour both the lamb and the shepherd. Should she be guilty of "nagging" or scolding, or of being a slattern, or of getting intoxicated, she finds usually a short shrift and no favour— and even humane persons talk of her offence as constituting, if not a justification for her murder, yet an explanation of it. She is, in short, liable to capital punishment without judge or jury for transgression which in the case of a man would never be punished at all, or be expiated by a fine of five shillings.[5]

Nay, in her case there is a readiness even to pardon the omission of the ordinary forms of law as needlessly cumbersome. In no other instance save that of the Wife-beater is excuse made for a man taking the law into his own hands. We are accustomed to accept it as a principle that "lynching" cannot be authorized in a civilized country, and that the first lesson of orderly citizenship is that no man shall be judge, jury, and executioner in his own cause. But when a wife's offences are in question this salutary rule is overlooked, and men otherwise just-minded, refer cheerfully to the *circonstance atténuante* of the wife's drunkenness or bad language, as if it not only furnished an excuse for outrage upon her, but made it quite fit and proper for the Queen's peace to be broken and the woman's bones along with it.

This underlying public opinion is fortunately no new thing. On the contrary, it is an idea of immemorial antiquity which has been embodied in the laws of many nations, and notably, as derived from the old Roman *Patria Potestas,* in our own. It was only in 1829, in the 9th George IV., that the Act of Charles II., which embodied the old Common Law, and authorized a man "to chastise his wife with any reasonable instrument," was erased from our Statute-Book. Our position is not retrograde, but advancing, albeit too slowly. It is not as in the case of the Vivisection of Animals, that a new passion of cruelty is arising, but only that an old one, having its origin in the remotest epochs of barbarian wife-capture and polygamy, yet lingers in the dark places of the land. By degrees, if our statesmen will but bring the educational influence of law to bear upon the matter, it will surely die out and become a thing of the past, like cannibalism,—than which it is no better fitted for a Christian nation.

Of course the ideas of the suffering wives are cast in the same mould as those of their companions. They take it for granted that a Husband is a Beating Animal, and may be heard to remark when extraordinarily ill-treated by a stranger,—that they "never were so badly used, no not by their own 'usbands." Their wretched proverbial similarity to spaniels and walnut-trees, the readiness with which they sometimes turn round and snap at a bystander who has interfered on their behalf, of course affords to cowardly people a welcome excuse for the "policy of non-intervention," and forms the culminating proof of how far the iron of their fetters has eaten into their souls. A specially experienced gentleman writes from Liverpool: "The women of Lancashire are *awfully fond* of bad husbands. It has become quite a truism that our women are like dogs, the more you beat them the more they love you." Surely if a bruised and trampled woman be a pitiful object, a woman who has been brought down by fear, or by her own gross passions so low as to fawn on the beast who strikes her, is one to make angels weep?

To close this part of the subject, I conceive then, that the common idea of the inferiority of women, and the special notion of the rights of husbands, form the undercurrent of feeling which induces a man, when for any reason he is infuriated, to wreak his violence on his wife. She is, in his opinion, his natural *souffre-douleur*.

It remains to be noted what are the principal incitements to such outbursts of savage fury among the classes wherein Wife-beating prevails. They are not far to seek. The first is undoubtedly *Drink*—poisoned drink. The seas of brandy and gin, and the oceans of beer, imbibed annually in England, would be bad enough, if taken pure and simple, but it is the vile adulterations introduced into them which make them the infuriating poisons which they are—which literally *sting* the wretched drinkers into cruelty, perhaps quite foreign to their natural temperaments. As an experienced minister in these districts writes to me, "I have known men almost as bad as those you quote (a dozen wife-murderers) made into most kind and considerate husbands by total abstinence." If the English people will go on swallowing millions' worth yearly of brain poison, what can we expect but brutality the most hideous and grotesque? Assuredly the makers and vendors of these devil's philtres are responsible for an amount of crime and ruin which some of the worst tyrants in history might have trembled to bear on their consciences; nor can the national legislature be absolved for suffering the great Drink interest thus foully to tamper with the health—nay, with the very souls of our countrymen. What is the occult influence which prevents the Excise from performing its duty as regards these frauds on the revenue?

2. Next to drunkenness as a cause of violence to women, follows the other "great sin of great cities,"

of which it is unnecessary here to speak. The storms of jealousy thence arising, the hideous alternative *possession* of the man by the twin demons of cruelty and lust—one of whom is never very far from the other—are familiar elements in the police-court tragedies.

3. Another source of the evil may be found in that terrible, though little recognized passion, which rude men and savages share with many animals, and which is the precise converse of sympathy, for it consists in anger and cruelty, excited by the signs of pain; and impulse to hurt and destroy any suffering creature, rather than to relieve or help it. Of the widespread influence of this passion (which I have ventured elsewhere to name *Heteropathy*), a passion only slowly dying out as civilization advances, there can, I think, be no doubt at all. It is a hideous mystery of human nature that such feelings should lie latent in it, and that cruelty should grow by what it feeds on; that the more the tyrant causes the victim to suffer the more he hates him, and desires to heap on him fresh sufferings. Among the lower classes the emotion of Heteropathy unmistakably finds vent in the cruelty of parents and step-parents to unfortunate children who happen to be weaker or more stupid than others, or to have been once excessively punished, and whose joyless little faces and timid crouching demeanour, instead of appeals for pity, prove provocations to fresh outrage. The group of his shivering and starving children and weeping wife is the sad sight which, greeting the eyes of the husband and father reeling home from the gin-shop, somehow kindles his fury. If the baby cry in the cradle, he stamps on it. If his wife wring her hands in despair, he fells her to the ground.[6]

4. After these I should be inclined to reckon, as a cause of brutal outbreaks, the impatience and irritation which must often be caused in the homes of the working classes by sheer *friction*. While rich people, when they get tired of each other or feel irritable, are enabled to recover their tempers in the ample space afforded by a comfortable house, the poor are huddled together in such close quarters that the sweetest tempers and most tender affections must sometimes feel the trial. Many of us have shuddered at Miss Octavia Hill's all-too-graphic description of a hot, noisome couple in the heart of London on a fine summer evening, with men,

women, and children "pullulating," as the French say, on the steps, at the windows, on the pavement, all dirty, hot, and tired, and scarcely able to find standing or sitting room. It is true the poor are happily more gregarious than the rich. Paradoxical as it sounds, it takes a good deal of civilization to make a man love savage scenery, and a highly cultivated mind to find any "pleasure in the pathless woods" or "rapture in the lonely shore." Nevertheless, for moral health as much as for physical, a certain number of cubic inches of space are needed for every living being.

· · ·

Turn we now from the beaters to the beaten. I have already said that we must not idealize the women of the "kicking districts." They are mostly, poor souls, very coarse, very unwomanly. Some of them drink whenever they can procure drink. Some are bad and cruel mothers (we cannot forget the awful stories of the Burial Clubs); many are hopelessly depraved, and lead as loose lives as their male companions.

· · ·

But *all* women of the humblest class are not those terrible creatures, drunken, depraved, or ill-tempered; or even addicted to "nagging." On the contrary, I can affirm from my own experience, as well, I believe, as that of all who have had much to do with the poor of great cities, there are among them at least as many good women as bad—as many who are sober, honest, chaste, and industrious, as are the contrary. There is a type which every clergyman, and magistrate, and district visitor will recognize in a moment as very common: a woman generally small and slight of person, but alert, intelligent, active morning, noon, and night, doing the best her strength allows to keep her home tidy, and her children neat and well fed, and to supply her husband's wants. Her face was, perhaps, pretty at eighteen: by the time she is eight-and-twenty, toil and drudgery and many children have reduced her to a mere rag, and only her eyes retain a little pathetic relic of beauty. This woman expresses herself well and simply: it is a special "note" of her character that she uses no violent words, even in describing the worst injuries. There is nothing "loud" about her in voice, dress, or manners. She is emphatically a "*decent,*" respectable woman. Her only fault, if fault it be, is

that she will insist on obtaining food and clothing for her children, and that when she is refused them she becomes that depressed, broken-spirited creature whose mute, reproachful looks act as a goad, as I have said, to the passions of her oppressor. We shall see presently what part this class of woman plays in the horrible domestic tragedies of England.

We have now glanced at the conditions under which Wife-beating takes place, at the incentives immediately leading to it, the men who beat, and the women who are beaten. Turn we now to examine more closely the thing itself.

There are two kinds of Wife-beating which I am anxious the reader should keep clearly apart in his mind. There is what may be called *Wife-beating by Combat,* and there is Wife-beating properly so called, which is only wife, and not wife-and-husband beating. In the first, both parties have an equal share. Bad words are exchanged, then blows. The man hits, the woman perhaps scratches and tears. If the woman generally gets much the worst of it, it is simply because cats are weaker than dogs. The man cannot so justly be said to have "beaten" his wife as to have vanquished her in a boxing-match. Almost without exception in these cases it is mentioned that "both parties were the worse for liquor." It is in this way the drunken woman is beaten, *by the drunken man,* not by the ideal sober and industrious husband, who has a right to be disgusted by her intoxication. It is nearly exclusively, I think, in such drunken quarrels that the hateful virago gets beaten at all. As a general rule she commands too much fear, and is so ready to give back curse for curse and blow for blow, that, in cold blood, nobody meddles with her. Such a termagant is often the tyrant of her husband, nay, of the whole court or lane in which she lives; and the sentiments she excites are the reverse of those which bring down the fist and the clogs of the ruffian husband on the timid and meek-faced woman who tries, too often unsuccessfully, the supposed magic of a soft answer to turn away the wrath of such a wild beast as he.

One word, however, must be said, before we leave this revolting picture, even for that universally condemned creature, the drunken wife. Does any save one, the Great Judge above, ever count how many of such doubly-degraded beings have been *driven* to intemperance by sheer misery? How many have been lured to drink by companionship with their drunken husbands? How many have sunk into the habit because, worn out in body by toil and child-bearing, degraded in soul by contempt and abuse, they have not left in them one spark of that self-respect which enables a human being to resist the temptation to drown care and remembrance in the dread forgetfulness of strong drink?

The second kind of Wife-beating is when the man alone is the striker and the woman the stricken. These are the cases which specially challenge our attention, and for which it may be hoped some palliative may be found. In these, the husband usually comes home "the worse for liquor," and commences, sometimes without any provocation at all, to attack his wife, or drag her out of the bed where she is asleep, or has just been confined. . . . Sometimes there is preliminary altercation, the wife imploring him to give her some money to buy necessaries, or reproaching him for drinking all he has earned. In either case the wife is passive so far as blows are concerned, unless at the last, in self-defence, she lays her hand on some weapon to protect her life—a fact which is always cited against her as a terrible delinquency.[7]

Such are the two orders of Wife-beating with which a tolerably extensive study of the subject has made me familiar. It will be observed that neither includes that ideal Wife-beater of whom we hear so much, the sober, industrious man goaded to frenzy by his wife's temper or drunkenness. I will not venture to affirm that the Ideal Wife-beater is as mythical as the griffin or the sphinx, but I will affirm that in all my inquiries I have never yet come on his track.

· · ·

Regarding the extent of the evil it is difficult to arrive at a just calculation. Speaking of those cases only which come before the courts,—probably, of course, not a third of the whole number,—the elements for forming an opinion are the following:—

In the Judicial Statistics for England and Wales, issued in 1877 for 1876, we find that of Aggravated Assaults on Women and Children, of the class which since 1853 have been brought under Summary Jurisdiction there were reported,

In 1876 - - - - - 2,737
In 1875 - - - - - 3,106
In 1874 - - - - - 2,841

How many of these were assaults made by husbands on wives there is no means of distinguishing, but, judging from other sources,[8] I should imagine they formed about four-fifths of the whole.

· · ·

Let us now proceed from the number to the nature of the offences in question. I have called this paper English *Wife-torture* because I wish to impress my readers with the fact that the familiar term "wife-beating" conveys about as remote a notion of the extremity of the cruelty indicated as when candid and ingenuous vivisectors talk of "scratching a newt's tail" when they refer to burning alive, or dissecting out the nerves of living dogs, or torturing ninety cats in one series of experiments.

Wife-*beating* is the mere preliminary canter before the race,—the preface to the serious matter which is to follow. Sometimes, it is true, there are men of comparatively mild dispositions who are content to go on beating their wives year after year, giving them occasional black-eyes and bruises, or tearing out a few locks of their hair and spitting in their faces, or bestowing an ugly print of their iron fingers on the woman's soft arm, but not proceeding beyond these minor injuries to anything perilous. Among the lower classes, unhappily, this rude treatment is understood to mean very little more than that the man uses his weapon—the fists—as the woman uses hers—the tongue—and neither are very much hurt or offended by what is either done by one or said by the other. The whole state of manners is what is deplored, and our hope must be to change the bear-garden into the semblance of a civilized community, rather than by any direct effort to correct the special offence. Foul words, gross acts, drink, dirt, and vice, oaths, curses, and blows, it is all, alas! *in keeping*—nor can we hope to cure one evil without the rest. But the unendurable mischief, the discovery of which has driven me to try to call public attention to the whole matter, is this—Wife-*beating* in the process of time, and in numberless cases, advances to Wife-*torture*, and the Wife-torture usually ends in Wife-maiming, Wife-blinding, or Wife-murder. A man who has "thrashed" his wife with his fists half-a-dozen times, becomes satiated with such enjoyment as that performance brings, and next time he is angry he kicks her with his hob-nailed shoes. When he has kicked her a few times standing or sitting, he kicks her down and stamps on her stomach, her breast, or her face. If he does not wear clogs or hob-nailed shoes, he takes up some other weapon, a knife, a poker, a hammer, a bottle of vitriol, or a lighted lamp, and strikes her with it, or sets her on fire;—and then, and then only, the hapless creature's sufferings are at an end.

. . .

I think I may now safely ask the reader to draw breath after all these horrors, and agree with me that they cannot, *must* not, be allowed to go on unchecked, without some effort to stop them, and save these perishing and miserable creatures. Poor, stupid, ignorant women as most of them are, worn out with life-long drudgery, burdened with all the pangs and cares of many children, poorly fed and poorly clothed, with no pleasures and many pains, there is an enormous excuse to be made for them even if they do sometimes seek in drink the oblivion of their misery—a brief dream of unreal joy, where real natural happiness is so far away.[9] But for those who rise above these temptations, who are sober where intoxication holds out their only chance of pleasure; chaste in the midst of foulness; tender mothers when their devotion calls for toilsome days and sleepless nights,—for these good, industrious, struggling women who, I have shown, are the chief victims of all this cruelty,—is it to be borne that we should sit patiently by and allow their lives to be trampled out in agony?

What ought to be done?

. . .

The relief which I most earnestly desire to see extended to these women, and from which I would confidently hope for *some* alleviation of their wretched condition, though its entire cure is beyond hope, is of a very different sort. It is this. A Bill should, I think, be passed, *affording to these poor women, by means easily within their reach, the same redress which women of the richer classes obtain through the Divorce Court.* They should be enabled to obtain from the Court which sentences their husbands a Protection Order, which should in their case have the same validity as a judicial separation. In addition to this, the *Custody of the Children should be given to the wife,* and an order should be made for *the husband to pay to the wife such weekly sum for her own and her children's maintenance as the Court may see fit.*

. . .

[1878]

NOTES

1. With the exception, perhaps, of the Seal. Mr. Darwin gives a sad picture of amphibious conjugal life: "As soon as a female reaches the shore ('comes out,' as we should say in 'society'), the nearest male goes down to meet her, making meanwhile a noise like the clucking of a hen to her chickens. He bows to her and coaxes her, until he gets between her and the water so that she cannot escape him. Then his manner changes, and with a harsh growl he drives her to a place in his harem."—*Descent of Man,* vol. ii. p.269. What an "o'er true tale" is this of many a human wooing and of what comes later; the "bowing and coaxing" first, and the "harsh growl" afterwards! I am surprised Mr. Darwin did not derive from it an argument for the Descent of Man from the Seal. . . .

2. Transactions Social Science Association, 1876, p.345.

3. Let it be noted that while they *were* slaves, these negroes were daily subjected to outrages and cruelties of which it thrilled our blood to hear. Since they have been emancipated their white neighbours have learned at least so far to recognize them as human beings, that these *tortures* have become comparatively rare.

4. Stripped of the euphemisms of courtesy wherewith we generally wrap them up, it cannot be denied that the sentiments of a very large number of men towards women consist of a wretched alternation of exaggerated and silly homage, and of no less exaggerated and foolish contempt. One moment on a pedestal, the next in the mire; the woman is adored while she gives pleasure, despised the moment she cease to do so. . . . We laugh at the great engineer who gave as his opinion before a Royal Commission that rivers were created to feed navigable canals; and a farmer would certainly be treated as betraying the "bucolic mind" who avowed that he thought his horse was made to carry him to market, and his cat to eat his mice and spare his cheese; yet where women are concerned—beings who are understood to be at least *quasi*-rational, and to whom their religion promises an immortal life hereafter of good and glory—the notion that the Final Cause of Woman is Man seems never to strike them as supremely ridiculous.

5. Old English legislation embodied this view so far as to inflict the cruellest of all punishments—burning to death—on a woman guilty of *petty treason, i.e.,* the murder of her husband, while the husband was only liable to hanging for murdering his wife. A woman was burned to death under this atrocious law at Chester, in 1760, for poisoning her husband. The wretched creature was made to linger four months in jail under her awful sentence before it was executed.

6. Hopes of the Human Race, p.172 (the Evolution of the Social Sentiment). By Frances Power Cobbe. Williams and Norgate.

7. Such was the case of Susannah Palmer, a few years ago, whose husband had beaten her, and sold up her furniture again and again, blackened her eyes, and knocked out her five front teeth. At last on one occasion, with the knife with which she was cutting her children's supper, she somehow inflicted a slight cut on the man while he was knocking her about the head. He immediately summoned her for "cutting and wounding him," and she was sent to Newgate. I found her there, and afterwards received the very best possible character of her from several

respectable tradespeople in whose houses she had worked as a charwoman for years. Friends subscribed to help her, and the admirable chaplain of Newgate interested himself warmly in her case and placed her in safety.

8. *E.g.* the Report of the Society for the Protection of Women and Children, which has this significant passage: "Some of the cases of assaults were of a brutal and aggravated character, . . . thirty-three by husbands on wives, five by fathers, and four by mothers on their children."

9. Few people reflect how utterly devoid of pleasures are the lives of the women of the working classes. An excellent woman, living near Bristol, having opened a Mothers Meeting, was surprised to find that not more than one out of forty of her poor friends had ever seen the sea, and not more than three had travelled on the railway. Of course their fathers, husbands, brothers, and sons had all seen these wonders, but they never. That good woman accordingly took the whole party one summer's day to the beach at Weston-super-Mare, and the sight of their enjoyment drew the tears from her eyes,—and from mine when she described it.

 15

From *The Origin of the Family, Private Property and the State*

FREDERICK ENGELS

The family [says Morgan] represents an active principle. It is never stationary, but advances from a lower to a higher form as society advances from a lower to a higher condition. . . . Systems of consanguinity, on the contrary, are passive; recording the progress made by the family at long intervals apart, and only changing radically when the family has radically changed [1963: 444].

"And," adds Marx, "the same is true of the political, juridicial, religious, and philosophical systems in general." While the family undergoes living changes, the system of consanguinity ossifies; while the system survives by force of custom, the family outgrows it. But just as Cuvier could deduce from the marsupial bone of an animal skeleton found near Paris that it belonged to a marsupial animal and that extinct marsupial animals once lived there, so with the same certainty we can deduce from the historical survival of a system of consanguinity that an extinct form of family once existed which corresponded to it.

The systems of consanguinity and the forms of the family we have just mentioned differ from those of today in the fact that every child has more than one father and mother. In the American system of consanguinity, to which the Hawaiian family corresponds, brother and sister cannot be the father and mother of the same child; but the Hawaiian system of consanguinity, on the contrary, presupposes a family in which this was the rule. Here we find ourselves among forms of family which directly contradict those hitherto generally assumed to be alone valid. The traditional view recognizes only monogamy, with, in addition, polygamy on the part of individual men, and at the very most polyandry on the part of individual women; being the view of moralizing philistines, it conceals the fact that in practice these barriers raised by official society are quietly and calmly ignored. The study of primitive history, however, reveals conditions where the men live in polygamy and their wives in polyandry at the same time, and their common children are therefore considered common to them all—and these conditions in their turn undergo a long series of changes before they finally end in monogamy.

• • •

Thus the history of the family in primitive times consists in the progressive narrowing of the circle, originally embracing the whole tribe, within which the two sexes have a common conjugal relation. The continuous exclusion, first of nearer, then of more and more remote relatives, and at last even of relatives by marriage, ends by making any kind of group marriage practically impossible. Finally, there remains only the single, still loosely linked pair, the molecule with whose dissolution marriage itself ceases. This in itself shows what a small part individual sex love, in the modern sense of the word, played in the rise of monogamy. Yet stronger proof is afforded by the practice of all peoples at this stage of development. Whereas in the earlier forms of the family, men never lacked women but on the contrary, had too many rather than too few, women had now become scarce and highly sought after. Hence it is with the pairing marriage that there begins the capture and purchase of women—widespread *symptoms,* but no more than symptoms, of the much deeper change that had occurred. . . .

The pairing family, itself too weak and unstable to make an independent household necessary or even desirable, in no wise destroys the communistic household inherited from earlier times. Communistic housekeeping, however, means the supremacy of women in the house; just as the exclusive recognition of the female parent, owing to the impossibility of recognizing the male parent with certainty, means that the women—the mothers—are held in high respect. One of the most absurd notions taken over from 18th century enlightenment is that in the beginning of society woman was the slave of man. Among all savages and all barbarians of the lower and middle stages, and to a certain extent of the upper stage also, the position of women is not only free, but honorable. . . .

The communistic household, in which most or all of the women belong to one and the same gens, while the men come from various gentes, is the material foundation of that supremacy of the women which was general in primitive times.

· · ·

Only when the women had brought about the transition to pairing marriage were the men able to introduce strict monogamy—though indeed only for women.

The first beginnings of the pairing family appear on the dividing line between savagery and barbarism; they are generally to be found already at the upper stage of savagery, but occasionally not until the lower stage of barbarism. The pairing family is the form characteristic of barbarism, as group marriage is characteristic of savagery and monogamy of civilization. To develop it further, to strict monogamy, other causes were required than those we have found active hitherto. In the single pair the group was already reduced to its final unit, its two-atom molecule: one man and one woman. Natural selection, with its progressive exclusions from the marriage community, had accomplished its task; there was nothing more for it to do in this direction. Unless new, *social* forces came into play, there was no reason why a new form of family should arise from the single pair. But these new forces did come into play.

· · ·

[T]he domestication of animals and the breeding of herds had developed a hitherto unsuspected source of wealth and created entirely new social relations. Up to the lower stage of barbarism, permanent wealth had consisted almost solely of house, clothing, crude ornaments and the tools for obtaining and preparing food—boat, weapons, and domestic utensils of the simplest kind. Food had to be won afresh day by day. Now, with their herds of horses, camels, asses, cattle, sheep, goats, and pigs, the advancing pastoral peoples—the Semites on the Euphrates and the Tigris, and the Aryans in the Indian country of the Five Streams (Punjab), in the Ganges region, and in the steppes then much more abundantly watered by the Oxus and the Jaxartes—had acquired property which only needed supervision and the rudest care to reproduce itself in steadily increasing quantities and to supply the most abundant food in the form of milk and meat. All former means of procuring food now receded into the background; hunting, formerly a necessity, now became a luxury.

But to whom did this new wealth belong? Originally to the gens, without a doubt. Private property in herds must have already started at an early period, however. It is difficult to say whether the author of the so-called first book of Moses regarded the patriarch Abraham as the owner of his herds in his own right as head of a family community or by right of his position as actual hereditary head of a gens. What is certain is that we must not think of him as a property owner in the modern sense of the word. And it is also certain that at the threshold of authentic history we already find the herds everywhere separately owned by heads of families, as are the artistic products of barbarism (metal implements, luxury articles and, finally, the human cattle—the slaves).

For now slavery had also been invented. To the barbarian of the lower stage, a slave was valueless. Hence the treatment of defeated enemies by the American Indians was quite different from that at a higher stage. The men were killed or adopted as brothers into the tribe of the victors; the women were taken as wives or otherwise adopted with their surviving children. At this stage human labor power still does not produce any considerable surplus over and above its maintenance costs. That was no longer the case after the introduction of cattle breeding, metalworking, weaving and, lastly, agriculture. Just as the wives whom it had formerly been so easy to obtain had now acquired an exchange value and were bought, so also with labor power, particularly since the herds had definitely become family possessions. The family did not multiply so rapidly as the cattle. More people were needed to look after them; for this purpose use could be made of the enemies captured in war, who could also be bred just as easily as the cattle themselves.

Once it had passed into the private possession of families and there rapidly begun to augment, this wealth dealt a severe blow to the society founded on pairing marriage and the matriarchal gens. Pairing marriage had brought a new element into the family. By the side of the natural mother of the child it placed its natural and attested father with a better warrant of paternity, probably, than that of many a "father" today. According to the division of labor within the family at that time, it was the man's part to obtain food and the instruments of labor necessary for the purpose. He therefore also owned the instruments of labor, and in the event of husband and wife separating, he took them with him, just as she retained her household goods. Therefore, according to the social custom of the time, the man was also the owner of the new source of subsistence, the cattle, and later of the new instruments of labor, the slaves. But according to the custom of the same society, his children could not inherit from him. For as regards inheritance, the position was as follows:

At first, according to mother right—so long, therefore, as descent was reckoned only in the female line—and according to the original custom of inheritance within the gens, the gentile relatives inherited from a deceased fellow member of their gens. His property had to remain within the gens. His effects being insignificant, they probably always passed in practice to his nearest gentile relations— that is, to his blood relations on the mother's side. The children of the dead man, however, did not belong to his gens, but to that of their mother; it was from her that they inherited, at first conjointly with her other blood-relations, later perhaps with rights of priority; they could not inherit from their father because they did not belong to his gens within which

his property had to remain. When the owner of the herds died, therefore, his herds would go first to his brothers and sisters and to his sister's children, or to the issue of his mother's sisters. But his own children were disinherited.

Thus on the one hand, in proportion as wealth increased it made the man's position in the family more important than the woman's, and on the other hand created an impulse to exploit this strengthened position in order to overthrow, in favor of his children, the traditional order of inheritance. This, however, was impossible so long as descent was reckoned according to mother right. Mother right, therefore, had to be overthrown, and overthrown it was. This was by no means so difficult as it looks to us today. For this revolution—one of the most decisive ever experienced by humanity—could take place without disturbing a single one of the living members of a gens. All could remain as they were. A simple decree sufficed that in the future the offspring of the male members should remain within the gens, but that of the female should be excluded by being transferred to the gens of their father. The reckoning of descent in the female line and the matriarchal law of inheritance were thereby overthrown, and the male line of descent and the paternal law of inheritance were substituted for them. As to how and when this revolution took place among civilized peoples, we have no knowledge. It falls entirely within prehistoric times. But that it *did* take place is more than sufficiently proved by the abundant traces of mother right which have been collected.

. . .

The overthrow of mother right was the *world historical defeat of the female sex*. The man took command in the home also; the woman was degraded and reduced to servitude; she became the slave of his lust and a mere instrument for the production of children. This degraded position of the woman, especially conspicuous among the Greeks of the heroic and still more of the classical age, has gradually been palliated and glossed over, and sometimes clothed in a milder form; in no sense has it been abolished.

The establishment of the exclusive supremacy of the man shows its effects first in the patriarchal family, which now emerges as an intermediate form. Its essential characteristic is not polygyny, of which more later, but "the organization of a number of persons, bond and free, into a family under paternal power for the purpose of holding lands and for the care of flocks and herds, . . . (In the Semitic form) the chiefs, at least, lived in polygamy. . . . Those held to servitude and those employed as servants lived in the marriage relation" [Morgan, 1963: 474].

Its essential features are the incorporation of un-free persons and paternal power; hence the perfect type of this form of family is the Roman. The original meaning of the word "family" (*familia*) is not that compound of sentimentality and domestic strife which forms the ideal of the present-day philistine; among the Romans it did not at first even refer to the married pair and their children but only to the slaves. *Famulus* means domestic slave, and *familia* is the total number of slaves belonging to one man. As late as the time of Gaius, the *familia, id est patrimonium* (family, that is, the patrimony, the inheritance) was bequeathed by will. The term was invented by the Romans to denote a new social organism whose head ruled over wife and children and a number of slaves, and was invested under Roman paternal power with rights of life and death over them all.

. . .

Marx adds:

The modern family contains in germ not only slavery (*servitus*) but also serfdom, since from the beginning it is related to agricultural services. It contains *in miniature* all the contradictions which later extend throughout society and its state.

Such a form of family shows the transition of the pairing family to monogamy. In order to make certain of the wife's fidelity and therefore of the paternity of the children, she is delivered over unconditionally into the power of the husband; if he kills her, he is only exercising his rights.

. . .

Thus, wherever the monogamous family remains true to its historical origin and clearly reveals the antagonism between the man and the woman expressed in the man's exclusive supremacy, it exhibits in miniature the same oppositions and contradictions as those in which society has been moving, without power to resolve or overcome

them, ever since it split into classes at the beginning of civilization. . . .

[1884]

 16

From A Voice of the South: By a Black Woman of the South

ANNA JULIA COOPER

THE STATUS OF WOMAN IN AMERICA

To-day America counts her millionaires by the thousand; questions of tariff and questions of currency are the most vital ones agitating the public mind. In this period, when material prosperity and well-earned ease and luxury are assured facts from a national standpoint, woman's work and woman's influence are needed as never before; needed to bring a heart power into this money-getting, dollar-worshipping civilization; needed to bring a moral force into the utilitarian motives and interests of the time needed to stand for God and Home and Native Land *versus gain and greed and grasping selfishness.*

There can be no doubt that this fourth centenary of America's discovery which we celebrate at Chicago, strikes the keynote of another important transition in the history of this nation; and the prominence of woman in the management of its celebration is a fitting tribute to the part she is destined to play among the forces of the future. This is the first congressional recognition of woman in this country, and this Board of Lady Managers constitute the first women legally appointed by any government to act in a national capacity. This of itself marks the dawn of a new day.

Now the periods of discovery, of settlement, of developing resources and accumulating wealth have passed in rapid succession. Wealth in the nation as in the individual brings leisure, repose, reflection. The struggle with nature is over, the struggle with ideas begins. We stand then, it seems to me, in this last decade of the nineteenth century, just in the portals of a new and untried movement on a higher plain and in a grander strain than any the past has called forth. It does not require a prophet's eye to divine its trend and image its possibilities from the forces we see already at work around us; nor is it hard to guess what must be the status of woman's work under the new regime.

In the pioneer days her role was that of a camp-follower, an additional something to fight for and be burdened with, only repaying the anxiety and labor she called forth by her own incomparable gifts of sympathy and appreciative love; unable herself ordinarily to contend with the bear and the Indian, or to take active part in clearing the wilderness and constructing the home.

In the second or wealth-producing period her work is abreast of man's, complementing and supplementing; counteracting excessive tendencies, and mollifying over-rigorous proclivities.

In the era now about to dawn, her sentiments must strike the keynote and give the dominant tone. And this because of the nature of her contribution to the world.

Her kingdom is not over physical forces. Not by might, nor by power can she prevail. Her position must ever be inferior where strength of muscle creates leadership. If she follows the instincts of her nature, however, she must always stand for the conservation of those deeper moral forces which make for the happiness of homes and the righteousness of the country. In a reign of moral ideas she is easily queen.

There is to my mind no grander and surer prophecy of the new era and of woman's place in it, than the work already begun in the waning years of the nineteenth century by the WCTU [Women's Christian Temperance Union] in America, an organization which has even now reached not only national but international importance, and seems destined to permeate and purify the whole civilized world. It is the living embodiment of woman's activities and woman's ideas, and its extent and strength rightly prefigure her increasing power as a moral factor.

The colored woman of to-day occupies, one may say, a unique position in this country. In a period of itself transitional and unsettled, her status seems one of the least ascertainable and definitive of all the forces which make for our civilization. She is confronted by both a woman question and a race prob-lem, and is as yet an unknown or an unacknowledged factor in both. While the women of the white race can with calm assurance enter upon the work they feel by nature appointed to do, while their men give loyal support and appreciative countenance to their efforts, recognizing in most avenues of usefulness the propriety and the need of woman's distinctive cooperation, the colored woman too often finds herself hampered and shamed by a less liberal sentiment and a more conservative attitude on the part of those for whose opinion she cares most. That this is not universally true I am glad to admit. There are to be found both intensely conservative white men and exceedingly liberal colored men. But as far as my experience goes the average man of our race is less frequently ready to admit the actual need among the sturdier forces of the world for woman's help or influence. That great social and economic questions await her interference, that she could throw any light on problems of national import, that her intermeddling could improve the management of school systems, or elevate the tone of public institutions, or humanize and sanctify the far-reaching influence of prisons and reformatories and improve the treatment of lunatics and imbeciles—that she has a word worth hearing on mooted questions in political economy, that she could contribute a suggestion on the relations of labor and capital, or offer a thought on honest money and honorable trade, I fear the majority of "Americans of the colored variety" are not yet prepared to concede. It may be that they do not yet see these questions in their right perspective, being absorbed in the immediate needs of their own political complications. A good deal depends on where we put the emphasis in this world; and our men are not perhaps to blame if they see everything colored by the light of those agitations in the midst of which they live and move and have their being. The part they have had to play in American history during the last twenty-five or thirty years has tended rather to exaggerate the importance of mere political advantage, as well as to set a fictitious valuation on those able to secure such advantage. It is the astute politician, the manager who can gain preferment for himself and his favorites, the demagogue known to stand in with the powers at the White House and consulted on the bestowal of government plums, whom we set in high places and denominate great. It is they who receive the hosannas of the multitude and are regarded as leaders of the people. The thinker and the doer, the man who solves the problem by enriching his country with an invention worth thousands or by a thought inestimable and precious is given neither bread nor a stone. He is too often left to die in obscurity and neglect even if spared in his life the bitterness of fanatical jealousies and detraction.

And yet politics, and surely American politics, is hardly a school for great minds. Sharpening rather than deepening, it develops the faculty of taking advantage of present emergencies rather than the insight to distinguish between the true and the false, the lasting and the ephemeral advantage. Highly cultivated selfishness rather than consecrated benevolence is its passport to success. Its votaries are never seers. At best they are but manipulators—often only jugglers. It is conducive neither to profound statesmanship nor to the higher type of manhood. Altruism is its *mauvais succès* and naturally enough it is indifferent to any factor which cannot be worked into its own immediate aims and purposes. As woman's influence as a political element is as yet nil in most of the commonwealths of our republic, it is not surprising that with those who place the emphasis on mere political capital she may yet seem almost a nonentity so far as it concerns the solution of great national or even racial perplexities.

There are those, however, who value the calm elevation of the thoughtful spectator who stands aloof from the heated scramble; and, above the turmoil and din of corruption and selfishness, can listen to the teachings of eternal truth and righteousness. There are even those who feel that the black man's unjust and unlawful exclusion temporarily from participation in the elective franchise in certain states is after all but a lesson "in the desert" fitted to develop in him insight and discrimination against the day of his own appointed time. One needs occasionally to stand aside from the hum and rush of human interests and passions to hear the voices of God. And it not unfrequently happens that the All-loving gives a great push to certain souls to thrust them out, as it were, from the distracting current for awhile to promote their discipline and growth, or to enrich them by communion and reflection. And similarly it may be woman's privilege from her peculiar coigne of vantage as a quiet observer, to whisper just the needed suggestion or the almost forgotten truth. The colored woman, then, should not be ignored because her bark is resting in the silent waters of the sheltered cove. She is watching the movements of the contestants none the less and is all the better qualified, perhaps, to weigh and judge and advise because not herself in the excitement of the race. Her voice, too, has always been heard in clear, unfaltering tones, ringing the changes on those deeper interests which make for permanent good. She is always sound and orthodox on questions affecting the well-being of her race. You do not find the colored woman selling her birthright for a mess of pottage. Nay, even after reason has retired from the contest, she has been known to cling blindly with the instinct of a turtle dove to those principles and policies which to her mind promise hope and safety for children yet unborn. It is notorious that ignorant black women in the South have actually left their husbands' homes and repudiated their support for what was understood by the wife to be race disloyalty, or "voting away," as she expresses it, the privileges of herself and little ones.

It is largely our women in the South to-day who keep the black men solid in the Republican party. The latter as they increase in intelligence and power of discrimination would be more apt to divide on local issues at any rate. They begin to see that the Grand Old Party regards the Negro's cause as an outgrown issue, and on Southern soil at least finds a too intimate acquaintanceship with him a somewhat unsavory recommendation. Then, too, their political wits have been sharpened to appreciate the fact that it is good policy to cultivate one's neighbors and not depend too much on a distant friend to fight one's home battles. But the black woman can never forget—however lukewarm the party may to-day appear—that it was a Republican president who struck the manacles from her own wrists and gave the possibilities of manhood to her helpless little ones; and to her mind a Democratic Negro is a traitor and a time-server. Talk as much as you like of venality and manipulation in the South, there are not many men, I can tell you, who would dare face a wife quivering in every fiber with the consciousness that her husband is a coward who could be paid to desert her deepest and dearest interests.

Not unfelt, then, if unproclaimed has been the work and influence of the colored women of America. Our list of chieftains in the service, though not long, is not inferior in strength and excellence, I dare believe, to any similar list which this country can produce.

Among the pioneers, Frances Watkins Harper could sing with prophetic exaltation in the darkest days, when as yet there was not a rift in the clouds overhanging her people:

"Yes, Ethiopia shall stretch
Her bleeding hands abroad;
Her cry of agony shall reach the burning throne of
  God.
  Redeemed from dust and freed from chains,
    Her sons shall lift their eyes,
  From cloud-capt hills and verdant plains
    Shall shouts of triumph rise."

Among preachers of righteousness, an unanswerable silencer of cavilers and objectors, was Sojourner Truth, that unique and rugged genius who seemed carved out without hand or chisel from the solid mountain mass; and in pleasing contrast, Amanda Smith, sweetest of natural singers and pleaders in dulcet tones for the things of God and of His Christ.

Sarah Woodson Early and Martha Briggs, planting and watering in the school room, and giving off from their matchless and irresistible personality an impetus and inspiration which can never die so long as there lives and breathes a remote descendant of their disciples and friends.

Charlotte Forten Grimké, the gentle spirit whose verses and life link her so beautifully with America's great Quaker poet and loving reformer.

Hallie Quinn Brown, charming reader, earnest, effective lecturer and devoted worker of unflagging zeal and unquestioned power.

Fannie Jackson Coppin, the teacher and organizer, preeminent among women of whatever country or race in constructive and executive force.

These women represent all shades of belief and as many departments of activity; but they have one thing in common—their sympathy with the oppressed race in America and the consecration of their several talents in whatever line to the work of its deliverance and development.

Fifty years ago woman's activity according to orthodox definitions was on a pretty clearly cut "sphere," including primarily the kitchen and the nursery, and rescued from the barrenness of prison bars by the womanly mania for adorning every discoverable bit of china or canvass with forlorn looking cranes balanced idiotically on one foot. The woman of to-day finds herself in the presence of responsibilities which ramify through the profoundest and most varied interests of her country and race. Not one of the issues of this plodding, toiling, sinning, repenting, falling, aspiring humanity can afford to shut her out, or can deny the reality of her influence. No plan for renovating society, no scheme for purifying politics, no reform in church or in state, no moral, social, or economic question, no movement upward or downward in the human plane is lost on her. A man once said when told his house was afire: "Go tell my wife; I never meddle with household affairs." But no woman can possibly put herself or her sex outside any of the interests that affect humanity. All departments in the new era are to be hers, in the sense that her interests are in all and through all; and it is incumbent on her to keep intelligently and sympathetically *en rapport* with all the great movements of her time, that she may know on which side to throw the weight of her influence. She stands now at the gateway of this new era of American civilization. In her hands must be moulded the strength, the wit, the statesmanship, the morality, all the psychic force, the social and economic intercourse of that era. To be alive at such an epoch is a privilege, to be a woman then is sublime.

In this last decade of our century, changes of such moment are in progress, such new and alluring vistas are opening out before us, such original and radical suggestions for the adjustment of labor and capital, of government and the governed, of the family, the church, and the state, that to be a possible factor though an infinitesimal one in such a movement is pregnant with hope and weighty with responsibility. To be a woman in such an age carries with it a privilege and an opportunity never implied before. But to be a woman of the Negro race in America, and to be able to grasp the deep significance of the possibilities of the crisis, is to have a heritage, it seems to me, unique in the ages. In the first place, the race is young and full of the elasticity and hopefulness of youth. All its achievements are before it. It does not look on the masterly triumphs of nineteenth-century civilization with that *blasé* world-weary look which characterizes the old washed-out and worn-out races which have already, so to speak, seen their best days. . . .

[1892]

From The Woman's Bible

ELIZABETH CADY STANTON

INTRODUCTION

From the inauguration of the movement for woman's emancipation the Bible has been used to hold her in the "divinely ordained sphere," prescribed in the Old and New Testaments.

The canon and civil law; church and state; priests and legislators; all political parties and religious denominations have alike taught that woman was made after man, of man, and for man, an inferior being, subject to man. Creeds, codes, Scriptures and statutes, are all based on this idea. The fashions, forms, ceremonies and customs of society, church ordinances and discipline all grow out of this idea.

Of the old English common law, responsible for woman's civil and political status, Lord Brougham said, "it is a disgrace to the civilization and Christianity of the Nineteenth Century." Of the canon law, which is responsible for woman's status in the church, Charles Kingsley said, "this will never be a good world for women until the last remnant of the canon law is swept from the face of the earth."

The Bible teaches that woman brought sin and death into the world, that she precipitated the fall of the race, that she was arraigned before the judgment seat of Heaven, tried, condemned and sentenced. Marriage for her was to be a condition of bondage, maternity a period of suffering and anguish, and in silence and subjection, she was to play the role of a dependent on man's bounty for all her material

wants, and for all the information she might desire on the vital questions of the hour, she was commanded to ask her husband at home. Here is the Bible position of woman briefly summed up.

Those who have the divine insight to translate, transpose and transfigure this mournful object of pity into an exalted, dignified personage, worthy our worship as the mother of the race, are to be congratulated as having a share of the occult mystic power of the eastern Mahatmas.

The plain English to the ordinary mind admits of no such liberal interpretation. The unvarnished texts speak for themselves. The canon law, church ordinances and Scriptures, are homogeneous, and all reflect the same spirit and sentiments.

These familiar texts are quoted by clergymen in their pulpits, by statesmen in the halls of legislation, by lawyers in the courts, and are echoed by the press of all civilized nations, and accepted by woman herself as "The Word of God." So perverted is the religious element in her nature, that with faith and works she is the chief support of the church and clergy; the very powers that make her emancipation impossible. When, in the early part of the Nineteenth Century, women began to protest against their civil and political degradation, they were referred to the Bible for an answer. When they protested against their unequal position in the church, they were referred to the Bible for an answer.

This led to a general and critical study of the Scriptures. Some, having made a fetish of these books and believing them to be the veritable "Word of God," with liberal translations, interpretations, allegories and symbols, glossed over the most objectionable features of the various books and clung to them as divinely inspired. Others, seeing the family resemblance between the Mosaic code, the canon law, and the old English common law, came to the conclusion that all alike emanated from the same source; wholly human in their origin and inspired by the natural love of domination in the historians. Others, bewildered with their doubts and fears, came to no conclusion. While their clergymen told them on the one hand, that they owed all the blessings and freedom they enjoyed to the Bible, on the other, they said it clearly marked out their circumscribed sphere of action: that the demands for political and civil rights were irreligious, dangerous to the stability of the home, the state and the church. Clerical appeals were circulated from time to time conjuring members of their churches to take no part in the anti-slavery or woman suffrage movements, as they were infidel in their tendencies, undermining the very foundations of society. No wonder the majority of women stood still, and with bowed heads, accepted the situation.

Listening to the varied opinions of women, I have long thought it would be interesting and profitable to get them clearly stated in book form. To this end six years ago I proposed to a committee of women to issue a Woman's Bible, that we might have women's commentaries on women's position in the Old and New Testaments. It was agreed on by several leading women in England and America and the work was begun, but from various causes it has been delayed, until now the idea is received with renewed enthusiasm, and a large committee has been formed, and we hope to complete the work within a year.

. . .

THE BOOK OF GENESIS

Chapter I

Genesis i : 26, 27, 28.

26 ¶ And God said, Let us make man in our image, after our likeness: and let them have dominion over the fish of the sea, and over the fowl of the air, and over the cattle, and over all the earth, and over every creeping thing that creepeth upon the earth.

27 So God created man in his *own* image, in the image of God created he him; male and female created he them.

28 And God blessed them, and God said unto them, Be fruitful, and multiply, and replenish the earth, and subdue it; and have dominion over the fish of the sea, and over the fowl of the air, and over every living thing that moveth upon the earth.

Here is the sacred historian's first account of the advent of woman; a simultaneous creation of both sexes, in the image of God. It is evident from the language that there was consultation in the Godhead, and that the masculine and feminine elements were equally represented. Scott in his commentaries

says, "this consultation of the Gods is the origin of the doctrine of the trinity." But instead of three male personages, as generally represented, a Heavenly Father, Mother, and Son would seem more rational.

The first step in the elevation of woman to her true position, as an equal factor in human progress, is the cultivation of the religious sentiment in regard to her dignity and equality, the recognition by the rising generation of an ideal Heavenly Mother, to whom their prayers should be addressed, as well as to a Father.

If language has any meaning, we have in these texts a plain declaration of the existence of the feminine element in the Godhead, equal in power and glory with the masculine. The Heavenly Mother and Father! "God created man in his *own image, male and female.*" Thus Scripture, as well as science and philosophy, declares the eternity and equality of sex—the philosophical fact, without which there could have been no perpetuation of creation, no growth or development in the animal, vegetable, or mineral kingdoms, no awakening nor progressing in the world of thought. The masculine and feminine elements, exactly equal and balancing each other, are as essential to the maintenance of the equilibrium of the universe as positive and negative electricity, the centripetal and centrifugal forces, the laws of attraction which bind together all we know of this planet whereon we dwell and of the system in which we revolve.

In the great work of creation the crowning glory was realized, when man and woman were evolved on the sixth day, the masculine and feminine forces in the images of God, that must have existed eternally, in all forms of matter and mind. All the persons in the Godhead are represented in the Elohim the divine plurality taking counsel in regard to this last and highest form of life. Who were the members of this high council, and whether a duality or a trinity? Verse 27 declares the image of God male and female. How then is it possible to make woman an afterthought? We find in verses 5–16 the pronoun "he" used. Should it not in harmony with verse 26 be "they," a dual pronoun? We may attribute this to the same cause as the use of "his" in verse 11 instead of "it." The fruit tree yielding fruit after "his" kind instead of after "its" kind. The paucity of a language may give rise to many misunderstandings.

The above texts plainly show the simultaneous creation of man and woman, and their equal importance in the development of the race. All those theories based on the assumption that man was prior in the creation, have no foundation in Scripture.

As to woman's subjection, on which both the canon and the civil law delight to dwell, it is important to note that equal dominion is given to woman over every living thing, but not one word is said giving man dominion over woman.

Here is the first title deed to this green earth giving alike to the sons and daughters of God. No lesson of woman's subjection can be fairly drawn from the first chapter of the Old Testament.

[1895]

 18

From Women and Economics: A Study of the Economic Relation Between Men and Women as a Factor in Social Evolution

CHARLOTTE PERKINS GILMAN

. . .

The economic status of the human race in any nation, at any time, is governed mainly by the activities of the male: the female obtains her share in the racial advance only through him.

Studied individually, the facts are even more plainly visible, more open and familiar. From the day laborer to the millionnaire, the wife's worn dress or flashing jewels, her low roof or her lordly one, her weary feet or her rich equipage,—these speak of the economic ability of the husband. The comfort, the luxury, the necessities of life itself, which the woman receives, are obtained by the husband, and given her by him. And, when the woman, left alone with no man to "support" her, tries to meet her own economic necessities, the difficulties which confront her prove conclusively what the general economic status of the woman is. None can deny these patent facts,—that the economic status of women generally depends upon that of men generally, and that the economic status of women individually depends upon that of men individually, those men to whom they are related. But we are instantly confronted by the commonly received opinion that, although it must be admitted that men make and distribute the wealth of the world, yet women earn their share of it as wives. This assumes either that the husband is in the position of employer and the wife as employee, or that marriage is a "partnership," and the wife an equal factor with the husband in producing wealth.

Economic independence is a relative condition at best. In the broadest sense, all living things are economically dependent upon others,—the animals upon the vegetables, and man upon both. In a narrower sense, all social life is economically interdependent, man producing collectively what he could by no possibility produce separately. But, in the closest interpretation, individual economic independence among human beings means that the individual pays for what he gets, works for what he gets, gives to the other an equivalent for what the other gives him. I depend on the shoemaker for shoes, and the tailor for coats; but, if I give the shoemaker and the tailor enough of my own labor as a house-builder to pay for the shoes and coats they give me, I retain my personal independence. I have not taken of their product, and given nothing of mine. As long as what I get is obtained by what I give, I am economically independent.

Women consume economic goods. What economic product do they give in exchange for what they consume? The claim that marriage is a partnership, in which the two persons married produce wealth which neither of them, separately, could produce, will not bear examination. A man happy and comfortable can produce more than one unhappy and uncomfortable, but this is as true of a father or son as of a husband. To take from a man any of the conditions which make him happy and strong is to cripple his industry, generally speaking. But those relatives who make him happy are not therefore his business partners, and entitled to share his income.

Grateful return for happiness conferred is not the method of exchange in a partnership. The comfort a man takes with his wife is not in the nature of a business partnership, nor are her frugality and industry. A housekeeper, in her place, might be as frugal, as industrious, but would not therefore be a partner. Man and wife are partners truly in their mutual obligation to their children,—their common love, duty, and service. But a manufacturer who marries, or a doctor, or a lawyer, does not take a partner in his business, when he takes a partner in parenthood, unless his wife is also a manufacturer, a doctor, or a lawyer. In his business, she cannot even advise wisely without training and experience. To love her husband, the composer, does not enable her to compose; and the loss of a man's wife, though it may break his heart, does not cripple his business, unless his mind is affected by grief. She is in no sense a business partner, unless she contributes capital or experience or labor, as a man would in like relation. Most men would hesitate very seriously before entering a business partnership with any woman, wife or not.

If the wife is not, then, truly a business partner, in what way does she earn from her husband the food, clothing, and shelter she receives at his hands? By house service, it will be instantly replied. This is the general misty idea upon the subject,—that women earn all they get, and more, by house service. Here we come to a very practical and definite economic ground. Although not producers of wealth, women serve in the final processes of preparation and distribution. Their labor in the household has a genuine economic value.

For a certain percentage of persons to serve other persons, in order that the ones so served may produce more, is a contribution not to be overlooked. The labor of women in the house, certainly, enables men to produce more wealth than they otherwise could; and in this way women are economic factors in society. But so are horses. The labor of horses enables men to produce more wealth than they otherwise could. The horse is an economic factor in society. But the horse is not economically independent, nor is the woman. If a man plus a valet can perform more useful service than he could minus a valet, then the valet is performing useful service. But, if the valet is the property of the man, is obliged to perform this service, and is not paid for it, he is not economically independent.

The labor which the wife performs in the household is given as part of her functional duty, not as employment. The wife of the poor man, who works hard in a small house, doing all the work for the family, or the wife of the rich man, who wisely and gracefully manages a large house and administers its functions, each is entitled to fair pay for services rendered.

To take this ground and hold it honestly, wives, as earners through domestic service, are entitled to the wages of cooks, housemaids, nursemaids, seamstresses, or housekeepers, and to no more. This would of course reduce the spending money of the wives of the rich, and put it out of the power of the poor man to "support" a wife at all, unless, indeed, the poor man faced the situation fully, paid his wife her wages as house servant, and then she and he combined their funds in the support of their children. He would be keeping a servant: she would be helping keep the family. But nowhere on earth would there be "a rich woman" by these means. Even the highest class of private housekeeper, useful as her services are, does not accumulate a fortune. She does not buy diamonds and sables and keep a carriage. Things like these are not earned by house service.

But the salient fact in this discussion is that, whatever the economic value of the domestic industry of women is, they do not get it. The women who do the most work get the least money, and the women who have the most money do the least work. Their labor is neither given nor taken as a factor in economic exchange. It is held to be their duty as women to do this work; and their economic status bears no relation to their domestic labors, unless an inverse one. Moreover, if they were thus fairly paid,—given what they earned, and no more,—all women working in this way would be reduced to the economic status of the house servant. Few women—or men either—care to face this condition. The ground that women earn their living by domestic labor is instantly forsaken, and we are told that they obtain their livelihood as mothers. This is a peculiar position. We speak of it commonly enough, and often with deep feeling, but without due analysis.

In treating of an economic exchange, asking what return in goods or labor women make for the goods and labor given them,—either to the race collectively or to their husbands individually,—what payment women make for their clothes and shoes and furniture and food and shelter, we are told that the duties and services of the mother entitle her to support.

If this is so, if motherhood is an exchangeable commodity given by women in payment for clothes and food, then we must of course find some relation between the quantity or quality of the motherhood and the quantity and quality of the pay. This being true, then the women who are not mothers have no economic status at all; and the economic status of those who are must be shown to be relative to their motherhood. This is obviously absurd. The childless wife has as much money as the mother of many,—more; for the children of the latter consume what would otherwise be hers; and the inefficient mother is no less provided for than the efficient one. Visibly, and upon the face of it, women are not maintained in economic prosperity proportioned to their motherhood. Motherhood bears no relation to their economic status. Among primitive races, it is true,—in the patriarchal period, for instance,—there was some truth in this position. Women being of no value whatever save as bearers of children, their favor and indulgence did bear direct relation to maternity; and they had reason to exult on more grounds than one when they could boast a son. To-day, however, the maintenance of the woman is not conditioned upon this. A man is not allowed to discard his wife because she is barren. The claim of motherhood as a factor in economic exchange is false to-day. But suppose it were true. Are we willing to hold this ground, even in theory? Are we willing to consider motherhood as a business, a form of commercial exchange? Are the cares and duties of the mother, her travail and her love, commodities to be exchanged for bread?

It is revolting so to consider them; and, if we dare face our own thoughts, and force them to their logical conclusion, we shall see that nothing could be more repugnant to human feeling, or more socially and individually injurious, than to make motherhood a trade. Driven off these alleged grounds of women's economic independence; shown that women, as a class, neither produce nor distribute wealth; that women, as individuals, labor mainly as house servants, are not paid as such, and would not be satisfied with such an economic status if they were so paid; that wives are not business partners or co-producers of wealth with their husbands, unless they actually practise the same profession; that they are not salaried as mothers, and that it would be unspeakably degrading if they were,—what remains to those who deny that women are supported by men? This (and a most amusing position it is),—that the function of maternity unfits a woman for economic production, and, therefore, it is right that she should be supported by her husband.

· · ·

[1898]

 19

From The Progress of Colored Women

MARY CHURCH TERRELL

"I expected to see a dozen clever colored women, but instead of twelve I saw two hundred. It was simply an eye opener." This is the way one white woman expressed herself, after she had attended a convention of colored women held in Chicago about four years ago. This sentiment was echoed by many other white women who assisted at the deliberations of the colored women on that occasion. These Chicagoans were no more surprised at the intelligence, culture, and taste in dress which the colored women displayed than white people of other cities. When the National Association of Colored Women held its biennial two years ago in Buffalo, New York, the logic, earnestness and common sense of the delegates were quite as much a nine days' wonder as it was in Chicago. "I hold myself above the pettiness of race prejudice, of course," said one of the best women journalists in the country, "but for all my liberal mindedness the four days session of this federation of colored women's clubs has been a revelation. It has been my lot, first and last to attend a good many conventions of women—'Mothers, Daughters,' and what not, and of them all, the sanest, the liveliest, the most practical was that of the colored women." And so quotation after quotation might be cited to prove that even the white people who think they know all about colored people and are perfectly just in their estimate of them are surprised when they have an ocular demonstration of the rapidity with which a large number of colored women has advanced. When one considers the obstacles encountered by colored women in their effort to educate and cultivate themselves, since they became free, the work they have accomplished and the progress they have made will bear favorable comparisons at least with that of their more fortunate sisters, from whom the opportunity of acquiring knowledge and the means of self culture have never been entirely withheld. Not only are colored women with ambition and aspiration handicapped on account of their sex, but they are almost everywhere baffled and mocked because of their race. Not only because they are women, but because they are colored women are discouragement and disappointment meeting them at every turn. But in spite of the obstacles encountered, the progress made by colored women along many lines appears like a veritable miracle of modern times. Forty years ago for the great masses of colored women there was no such thing as home. To-day in each and every section of the country there are hundreds of homes among colored people, the mental and moral tone of which is as high and as pure as can be found among the best people of any land. To the women of the race may be attributed in large measure the refinement and purity of the colored home. The immorality of colored women is a theme upon which those who know little about them or those who maliciously misrepresent them love to descant. Foul aspersions upon the character of colored women are assiduously circulated by the press of certain sections and especially by the direct descendants of those who in years past were responsible for the moral degradation of their female slaves. And yet, in spite of the fateful heritage of slavery, even though the safe guards usually thrown around maidenly youth and innocence are in some sections entirely withheld from colored girls. Statistics compiled by men not inclined to falsify in favor of my race show that immorality among the colored women of the United States is not so great as among women with

similar environment and temptations in Italy, Germany, Sweden, and France.

Scandals in the best colored society are exceedingly rare, while the progressive game of divorce and remarriage is practically unknown.

The intellectual progress of colored women has been marvelous. So great has been their thirst for knowledge and so herculean their efforts to acquire it that there are few colleges, universities, high, and normal schools in the North, East, and West from which colored girls have not graduated with honor. In Wellesley, Vassar, Ann Arbor, Cornell, and in Oberlin, my dear alma mater, whose name will always be loved and whose praise will always be sung as the first college in the country broad, just, and generous enough to extend a cordial welcome to the Negro and to open its doors to women on an equal footing with the men, colored girls by their splendid records have forever settled the question of their capacity and worth. The instructors in these and other institutions cheerfully bear testimony to their intelligence, their diligence, and their success. As the brains of colored women expanded, their hearts began to grow. No sooner had the heads of a favored few been filled with knowledge than their hearts yearned to dispense blessings to the less fortunate of their race. With tireless energy and eager zeal colored women have worked in every conceivable way to elevate their race. Of the colored teachers engaged in instructing our youth it is probably no exaggeration to say that fully eighty percent are women. In the backwoods, remote from the civilization and comforts of the city and town colored women may be found courageously battling with those evils which such conditions always entail. Many a heroine of whom the world will never hear has thus sacrificed her life to her race amid surroundings and in the face of privations which only martyrs can bear.

Through the medium of their societies in the church, beneficial organizations out of it, and clubs of various kinds, colored women are doing a vast amount of good. It is almost impossible to ascertain exactly what the Negro is doing in any field, for the records are so poorly kept. This is particularly true in the case of the women of the race. During the past forty years there is no doubt that colored women in their poverty have contributed large sums of money to charitable and educational institutions as well as to the foreign and home missionary work. Within the twenty-five years in which the educational work of the African Methodist Episcopal church has been systematized, the women of that organization have contributed at least five hundred thousand dollars to the cause of education. Dotted all over the country are charitable institutions for the aged, orphaned, and poor which have been established by colored women, just how many it is difficult to state, owing to the lack of statistics bearing on the progress, possessions, and prowess of colored women. Among the charitable institutions either founded, conducted, or supported by colored women, may be mentioned the Hale Infirmary of Montgomery, Alabama, the Carrie Steele Orphanage of Atlanta, the Reed Orphan Home of Covington, and the Haines Industrial School of Augusta, all three in the state of Georgia; a home for the aged of both races in New Bedford and St. Monica's home of Boston, in Massachusetts; Old Folks Home of Memphis, Tennessee, and the Colored Orphan's Home of Lexington, Kentucky, together with others which lack of space forbids me to mention. Mt. Meigs Institute is an excellent example of a work originated and carried into successful execution by a colored woman. The school was established for the benefit of colored people on the plantations in the black belt of Alabama. In the township of Mt. Meigs the population is practically all colored. Instruction given in this school is of the kind best suited to the needs of the people for whom it was established. Along with some scholastic training, girls are taught everything pertaining to the management of the home, while boys are taught practical farming, wheelwrighting, blacksmithing, and have some military training. Having started with almost nothing, at the end of eight years the trustees of the school owned nine acres of land and five buildings in which several thousand pupils had received instructions, all through the energy, the courage, and the sacrifice of one little woman.

Up to date, politics have been religiously eschewed by colored women, although questions affecting our legal status as a race is sometimes agitated by the most progressive class. In Louisiana and Tennessee colored women have several times petitioned the legislatures of their respective states to repel the obnoxious Jim Crow Car Laws. Against the Convict Lease System, whose atrocities have been so frequently exposed of late, colored women here and there in the South are waging a ceaseless war. So long as hundreds of their brothers and sisters, many of whom have committed no crime or misdemeanor whatever, are thrown into cells, whose cubic contents are less than those of a good size grave, to be overworked, under-fed, and only partially covered with vermin-infested rags, and so long as children are born to the women in these camps who breathe the polluted atmosphere of these dens of horror and vice from the time they utter their first cry in the world till they are released from their suffering by death, colored women who are working for the emancipation and elevation of their race know where their duty lies. By constant agitation of this painful and hideous subject, they hope to touch the conscience of the country, so that this stain upon its escutcheon shall be forever wiped away.

Alarmed at the rapidity with which the Negro is losing ground in the world of trade, some of the far-sighted women are trying to solve the labor question, so far as it concerns the women at least, by urging the establishment of Schools of Domestic Science wherever means therefor can be secured. Those who are interested in this particular work hope and believe that if colored women and girls are thoroughly trained in domestic service, the boycott which has undoubtedly been placed upon them in many sections of the country will be removed. With so few vocations open to the Negro and with the labor organizations increasingly hostile to him, the future of the boys and girls of the race appears to some of our women very foreboding and dark.

The cause of temperance has been eloquently espoused by two women, each of whom has been appointed National Superintendent of work among colored people by the Woman's Christian Temperance Union. In business, colored women have had signal success. There is in Alabama a large milling and cotton business belonging to and controlled by a colored woman who has sometimes as many as seventy-five men in her employ. Until a few years ago the principal ice plant of Nova Scotia was owned and managed by a colored woman, who sold it for a large amount. In the professions there are dentists and doctors, whose practice is lucrative and large. Ever since a book was published in 1773 entitled "Poems on Various Subjects, Religious and Moral by Phyllis Wheatley, Negro Servant of Mr. John Wheatley," of Boston, colored women have given abundant evidence of literary ability. In sculpture we are represented by a woman upon whose chisel Italy has set her seal of approval; in painting by one of Bougoureau's pupils; and in music by young women holding diplomas from the best conservatories in the land.

In short, to use a thought of the illustrious Frederick Douglass, if judged by the depths from which they have come, rather than by the heights to which those blessed with centuries of opportunities have attained, colored women need not hang their heads in shame. They are slowly but surely making their way up to the heights, wherever they can be scaled. In spite of handicaps and discouragements they are not losing heart. In a variety of ways they are rendering valiant service to their race. Lifting as they climb, onward and upward they go, struggling and striving and hoping that the buds and blossoms of their desires may burst into glorious fruition ere long. Seeking no favors because of their color nor charity because of their needs, they knock at the door of Justice and ask for an equal chance.

[1898]

 20

The Traffic in Women

EMMA GOLDMAN

Our reformers have suddenly made a great discovery—the white slave traffic. The papers are full of these "unheard-of conditions," and lawmakers are already planning a new set of laws to check the horror.

It is significant that whenever the public mind is to be diverted from a great social wrong, a crusade is inaugurated against indecency, gambling, saloons, etc. And what is the result of such crusades? Gambling is increasing, saloons are doing a lively business through back entrances, prostitution is at its height, and the system of pimps and cadets is but aggravated.

How is it that an institution, known almost to every child, should have been discovered so suddenly? How is it that this evil, known to all sociologists, should now be made such an important issue?

To assume that the recent investigation of the white slave traffic (and, by the way, a very superficial investigation) has discovered anything new, is, to say the least, very foolish. Prostitution has been, and is, a widespread evil, yet mankind goes on its business, perfectly indifferent to the sufferings and distress of the victims of prostitution. As indifferent, indeed, as mankind has remained to our industrial system, or to economic prostitution.

. . .

What is really the cause of the trade in women? Not merely white women, but yellow and black women as well. Exploitation, of course; the merciless Moloch of capitalism that fattens on underpaid labor, thus driving thousands of women and girls into prostitution. With Mrs. Warren these girls feel, "Why waste your life working for a few shillings a week in a scullery, eighteen hours a day?"

Naturally our reformers say nothing about this cause. They know it well enough, but it doesn't pay to say anything about it. It is much more profitable to play the Pharisee, to pretend an outraged morality, than to go to the bottom of things.

. . .

Nowhere is woman treated according to the merit of her work, but rather as a sex. It is therefore almost inevitable that she should pay for her right to exist, to keep a position in whatever line, with sex favors. Thus it is merely a question of degree whether she sells herself to one man, in or out of marriage, or to many men. Whether our reformers admit it or not, the economic and social inferiority of woman is responsible for prostitution.

Just at present our good people are shocked by the disclosures that in New York City alone one out of every ten women works in a factory, that the average wage received by women is six dollars per week for forty-eight to sixty hours of work, and that the majority of female wage workers face many months of idleness which leaves the average wage about $280 a year. In view of these economic horrors, is it to be wondered at that prostitution and the white slave trade have become such dominant factors?

Lest the preceding figures be considered an exaggeration, it is well to examine what some authorities on prostitution have to say:

"A prolific cause of female depravity can be found in the several tables, showing the description of the employment pursued, and the wages received, by the women previous to their fall, and it will be a question for the political economist to decide how far mere business consideration should be an apology on the part of employers for a reduction in their rates of remuneration, and whether the savings of a small percentage on wages is not more than counterbalanced by the enormous amount of taxation enforced on the public at large to defray the expenses incurred on account of a system of vice, *which is the direct result, in many cases, of insufficient compensation of honest labor.*"[1]

Our present-day reformers would do well to look into Dr. Sanger's book. There they will find that out of 2,000 cases under his observation, but few came from the middle classes, from well-ordered conditions, or pleasant homes. By far the largest majority were working girls and working women; some driven into prostitution through sheer want, others because of a cruel, wretched life at home, others again because of thwarted and crippled physical natures (of which I shall speak later on). Also it will do the maintainers of purity and morality good to learn that out of two thousand cases, 490 were married women, women who lived with their husbands. Evidently there was not much of a guaranty for their "safety and purity" in the sanctity of marriage.[2]

Dr. Alfred Blaschko, in *Prostitution in the Nineteenth Century,* is even more emphatic in characterizing economic conditions as one of the most vital factors of prostitution.

"Although prostitution has existed in all ages, it was left to the nineteenth century to develop it into a gigantic social institution. The development of industry with vast masses of people in the competitive market, the growth and congestion of large cities, the insecurity and uncertainty of employment, has given prostitution an impetus never dreamed of at any period in human history."

And again Havelock Ellis, while not so absolute in dealing with the economic cause, is nevertheless compelled to admit that it is indirectly and directly the main cause. Thus he finds that a large percentage of prostitutes is recruited from the servant class, although the latter have less care and greater security. On the other hand, Mr. Ellis does not deny that the daily routine, the drudgery, the monotony of the servant girl's lot, and especially the fact that she may never partake of the companionship and joy of a home, is no mean factor in forcing her to seek recreation and forgetfulness in the gaiety and glimmer of prostitution. In other words, the servant girl, being treated as a drudge, never having the right to herself, and worn out by the caprices of her mistress, can find an outlet, like the factory or shopgirl, only in prostitution.

The most amusing side of the question now before the public is the indignation of our "good, respectable people," especially the various Christian gentlemen, who are always to be found in the front ranks of every crusade. Is it that they are absolutely ignorant of the history of religion, and especially of the Christian relgion? Or is it that they hope to blind the present generation to the part played in the past by the Church in relation to prostitution? Whatever their reason, they should be the last to cry out against the unfortunate victims of today, since it is known to every intelligent student that prostitution is of religious origin, maintained and fostered for many centuries, not as a shame, but as a virtue, hailed as such by the Gods themselves.

"It would seem that the origin of prostitution is to be found primarily in a religious custom, religion, the great conserver of social tradition, preserving in a transformed shape a primitive freedom that was passing out of the general social life. The typical example is that recorded by Herodotus, in the fifth century before Christ, at the Temple of Mylitta, the Babylonian Venus, where every woman, once in her life, had to come and give herself to the first stranger, who threw a coin in her lap, to worship the goddess. Very similar customs existed in other parts of western Asia, in North Africa, in Cyprus, and other islands of the eastern Mediterranean, and also in Greece, where the temple of Aphrodite on the fort at Corinth possessed over a thousand hierodules, dedicated to the service of the goddess.

"The theory that religious prostitution developed, as a general rule, out of the belief that the generative activity of human beings possessed a mysterious and sacred influence in promoting the fertility of Nature, is maintained by all authoritative writers on the subject. Gradually, however, and when prostitution became an organized institution under priestly influence, religious prostitution developed utilitarian sides, thus helping to increase public revenue.

"The rise of Christianity to political power produced little change in policy. The leading fathers of the Church tolerated prostitution. Brothels under municipal protection are found in the thirteenth century. They constituted a sort of public service, the directors of them being considered almost as public servants."[3]

To this must be added the following from Dr. Sanger's work:

"Pope Clement II. issued a bull that prostitutes would be tolerated if they pay a certain amount of their earnings to the Church.

"Pope Sixtus IV. was more practical; from one single brothel, which he himself had built, he received an income of 20,000 ducats."

In modern times the Church is a little more careful in that direction. At least she does not openly demand tribute from prostitutes. She finds it much more profitable to go in for real estate, like Trinity Church, for instance, to rent out death traps at an exorbitant price to those who live off and by prostitution.

. . .

It would be one-sided and extremely superficial to maintain that the economic factor is the only cause of prostitution. There are others no less important and vital. That, too, our reformers know, but dare discuss even less than the institution that saps the very life out of both men and women. I refer to the sex question, the very mention of which causes most people moral spasms.

It is a conceded fact that woman is being reared as a sex commodity, and yet she is kept in absolute ignorance of the meaning and importance of sex. Everything dealing with that subject is suppressed, and persons who attempt to bring light into this terrible darkness are persecuted and thrown into prison. Yet it is nevertheless true that so long as a girl is not to know how to take care of herself, not to know the function of the most important part of her life, we need not be surprised if she becomes an easy prey to prostitution, or to any other form of a relationship which degrades her to the position of an object for mere sex gratification.

It is due to this ignorance that the entire life and nature of the girl is thwarted and crippled. We have long ago taken it as a self-evident fact that the boy may follow the call of the wild; that is to say, that the boy may, as soon as his sex nature asserts itself, satisfy that nature; but our moralists are scandalized at the very thought that the nature of a girl should assert itself. To the moralist prostitution does not consist so much in the fact that the woman sells her body, but rather that she sells it out of wedlock. That this is no mere statement is proved by the fact that marriage for monetary considerations is perfectly legitimate, sanctified by law and public opinion, while any other union is condemned and repudiated. Yet a prostitute, if properly defined, means nothing else than "any person for whom sexual relationships are subordinated to gain."[4]

. . .

Of course, marriage is the goal of every girl, but as thousands of girls cannot marry, our stupid social customs condemn them either to a life of celibacy or prostitution. Human nature asserts itself regardless of all laws, nor is there any plausible reason why nature should adapt itself to a perverted conception of morality.

Society considers the sex experiences of a man as attributes of his general development, while similar experiences in the life of a woman are looked upon as a terrible calamity, a loss of honor and of all that is good and noble in a human being. This double standard of morality has played no little part in the creation and perpetuation of prostitution. It involves the keeping of the young in absolute ignorance on sex matters, which alleged "innocence," together with an overwrought and stifled sex nature, helps to bring about a state of affairs that our Puritans are so anxious to avoid or prevent.

Not that the gratification of sex must needs lead to prostitution; it is the cruel, heartless, criminal persecution of those who dare divert from the beaten track, which is responsible for it.

Girls, mere children, work in crowded, over-heated rooms ten to twelve hours daily at a machine, which tends to keep them in a constant over-excited sex state. Many of these girls have no home or comforts of any kind; therefore the street or some place of cheap amusement is the only means of forgetting their daily routine. This naturally brings them into close proximity with the other sex. It is hard to say which of the two factors brings the girl's over-sexed condition to a climax, but it is certainly the most natural thing that a climax should result. That is the first step toward prostitution. Nor is the girl to be held responsible for it. On the contrary, it is altogether the fault of society, the fault of our lack of understanding, of our lack of appreciation of life in the making; especially is it the criminal fault of our moralists, who condemn a girl for all eternity, because she has gone from the "path of virtue"; that is, because her first sex experience has taken place without the sanction of the Church.

The girl feels herself a complete outcast, with the doors of home and society closed in her face. Her entire training and tradition is such that the girl herself feels depraved and fallen, and therefore has no ground to stand upon, or any hold that will lift her up, instead of dragging her down. Thus society creates the victims that it afterwards vainly attempts to get rid of. The meanest, most depraved and decrepit man still considers himself too good to take as his wife the woman whose grace he was quite willing to buy, even though he might thereby save her from a life of horror. Nor can she turn to her own sister for help. In her stupidity the latter deems herself too pure and chaste, not realizing that her own position is in many respects even more deplorable than her sister's of the street.

• • •

Moralists are ever ready to sacrifice one-half of the human race for the sake of some miserable institution which they can not outgrow. As a matter of fact, prostitution is no more a safeguard for the purity of the home than rigid laws are a safeguard against prostitution. Fully fifty per cent of married men are patrons of brothels. It is through this virtuous element that the married women—nay, even the children—are infected with venereal diseases. Yet society has not a word of condemnation for the man, while no law is too monstrous to be set in mo-

tion against the helpless victim. She is not only preyed upon by those who use her, but she is also absolutely at the mercy of every policeman and miserable detective on the beat, the officials at the station house, the authorities in every prison.

• • •

Much stress is laid on white slaves being imported into America. How would America ever retain her virtue if Europe did not help her out? I will not deny that this may be the case in some instances, any more than I will deny that there are emissaries of Germany and other countries luring economic slaves into America; but I absolutely deny that prostitution is recruited to any appreciable extent from Europe. It may be true that the majority of prostitutes of New York City are foreigners, but that is because the majority of the population is foreign. The moment we go to any other American city, to Chicago or the Middle West, we shall find that the number of foreign prostitutes is by far a minority.

Equally exaggerated is the belief that the majority of street girls in this city were engaged in this business before they came to America. Most of the girls speak excellent English, are Americanized in habits and appearance,—a thing absolutely impossible unless they had lived in this country many years. That is, they were driven into prostitution by American conditions, by the thoroughly American custom for excessive display of finery and clothes, which, of course, necessitates money,—money that cannot be earned in shops or factories.

In other words, there is no reason to believe that any set of men would go to the risk and expense of getting foreign products, when American conditions are overflooding the market with thousands of girls. On the other hand, there is sufficient evidence to prove that the export of American girls for the purpose of prostitution is by no means a small factor.

• • •

In view of the above facts it is rather absurd to point to Europe as the swamp whence come all the social diseases of America. Just as absurd is it to proclaim the myth that the Jews furnish the largest contingent of willing prey. I am sure that no one will accuse me of nationalistic tendencies. I am glad to say that I have developed out of them, as out of many other prejudices. If, therefore, I resent the statement that Jewish prostitutes are imported, it is not because of any Judaistic sympathies, but because of the facts inherent in the lives of these people. No one but the most superficial will claim that Jewish girls migrate to strange lands, unless they have some tie or relation that brings them there. The Jewish girl is not adventurous. Until recent years she had never left home, not even so far as the next village or town, except it were to visit some relative. Is it then credible that Jewish girls would leave their parents or families, travel thousands of miles to strange lands, through the influence and promises of strange forces? Go to any of the large incoming steamers and see for yourself if these girls do not come either with their parents, brothers, aunts, or other kinsfolk. There may be exceptions, of course, but to state that large numbers of Jewish girls are imported for prostitution, or any other purpose, is simply not to know Jewish psychology.

Those who sit in a glass house do wrong to throw stones about them; besides, the American glass house is rather thin, it will break easily, and the interior is anything but a gainly sight.

· · ·

An educated public opinion, freed from the legal and moral hounding of the prostitute, can alone help to ameliorate present conditions. Wilful shutting of eyes and ignoring of the evil as a social factor of modern life, can but aggravate matters. We must rise above our foolish notions of "better than thou," and learn to recognize in the prostitute a product of social conditions. Such a realization will sweep away the attitude of hypocrisy, and insure a greater understanding and more humane treatment. As to a thorough eradication of prostitution, nothing can accomplish that save a complete transvaluation of all accepted values—especially the moral ones—coupled with the abolition of industrial slavery.

[1910]

NOTES

1. Dr. Sanger, *The History of Prostitution.*
2. It is a significant fact that Dr. Sanger's book has been excluded from the U. S. mails. Evidently the authorities are not anxious that the public be informed as to the true cause of prostitution.
3. Havelock Ellis, *Sex and Society.*
4. Guyot, *La Prostitution.*

 21

Girl Slaves of the Milwaukee Breweries

MOTHER (MARY) JONES

It is the same old story, as pitiful as old, as true as pitiful.

When the whistle blows in the morning it calls the girl slaves of the bottle-washing department of the breweries to don their wet shoes and rags and hustle to the bastile to serve out their sentences. It is indeed true, they are *sentenced* to hard, brutal labor—labor that gives no cheer, brings no recompense. Condemned for life, to slave daily in the wash room in wet shoes and wet clothes, surrounded with foul-mouthed, brutal foremen, whose orders and language would not look well in print and would surely shock over-sensitive ears or delicate nerves! And their crime? Involuntary poverty. It is hereditary. They are no more to blame for it than is a horse for having the glanders. It is the accident of birth. This accident that throws them into surging, seething mass known as the working class is what forces them out of the cradle into servitude, to be willing(?) slaves of the mill, factory, department store, hell, or bottling shop in Milwaukee's colossal breweries; to create wealth for the brewery barons, that they may own palaces, theaters, automobiles, blooded stock, farms, banks, and Heaven knows what all, while the poor girls slave on all day in the vile smell of sour beer, lifting cases of empty and full bottles weighing from 100 to 150 pounds, in their wet shoes and rags, for God knows they cannot buy clothes on the miserable pittance doled out to them by their soulless master class. The conscienceless rich see no reason why the slave should not be content on the crust of bread for its share of all the wealth created. That these slaves of the dampness should contract rheumatism is a foregone conclusion. Rheumatism is one of the chronic ailments, and is closely followed by consumption. Consumption is well known to be only a disease of poverty. The Milwaukee law makers, of course, enacted an antispit ordinance to protect the public health, and the brewers contributed to the Red Cross Society to make war on the shadow of tuberculosis, and all the while the big capitalists are setting out incubators to hatch out germs enough among the poor workers to destroy the nation. Should one of these poor girl slaves spit on the sidewalk, it would cost her more than she can make in two weeks' work. Such is the *fine* system of the present-day affairs. The foreman even regulates the time that they may stay in the toilet room, and in the event of overstaying it gives the foreman an opportunity he seems to be looking for to indulge in indecent and foul language. Should the patient slave forget herself and take offense, it will cost her the job in that prison. And after all, bad as it is, it is all that she knows how to do. To deprive her of the job means less crusts and worse rags in "the land of the free and the home of the brave." Many of the girls have no home nor parents and are forced to feed and clothe and shelter themselves, and all this on an average of $3.00 per week. Ye Gods! What a horrible nightmare! What hope is there for decency when unscrupulous wealth may exploit its producers so shamelessly?

No matter how cold, how stormy, how inclement the weather, many of these poor girl slaves must walk from their shacks to their work, for their miserable stipend precludes any possibility of squeezing a street car ride out of it. And this is due our much-vaunted greatness. Is this civilization? If so, what, please, is barbarism?

As an illustration of what these poor girls must submit to, one about to become a mother told me with tears in her eyes that every other day a depraved specimen of mankind took delight in measuring her girth and passing such comments as befits such humorous(?) occasion.

While the wage paid is 75 to 85 cents a day, the poor slaves are not permitted to work more than three or four days a week, and the continual threat of idle days makes the slave much more tractable and submissive than would otherwise obtain. Often when their day's work is done they are put to washing off the tables and lunch room floors and the other odd jobs, for which there is not even the suggestion of compensation. Of course, abuse always follows power, and nowhere is it more in evidence than in this miserable treatment the brewers and their hirelings accord their girl slaves.

The foreman also uses his influence, through certain living mediums near at hand, to neutralize any effort having in view the organization of these poor helpless victims of an unholy and brutal profit system, and threats of discharge were made, should these girls attend my meetings.

One of these foremen actually carried a union card, but the writer of this article reported him to the union and had him deprived of it for using such foul language to the girls under him. I learned of him venting his spite by discharging several girls, and I went to the superintendent and told him the character of the foreman. On the strength of my charges, he was called to the office and when he was informed of the nature of the visit, he patted the superintendent familiarly on the back and whined out how loyal he was to the superintendent, the whole performance taking on the character of servile lickspittle. As he fawns on his superior, so he expects to play autocrat with his menials and exact the same cringing from them under him. Such is the petty boss who holds the living of the working-class girls in his hands.

The brewers themselves were always courteous when I called on them, but their underlings were not so tactful, evidently working under instructions. The only brewer who treated me rudely or denied me admittance was Mr. Blatz, who brusquely told me his feelings in the following words: "The Brewers' Association of Milwaukee met when you first came to town and decided not to permit these girls to organize." This Brewers' Association is a strong union of all the brewery plutocrats, composed of Schlitz, Pabst, Miller, and Blatz breweries, who are the principal employers of women. And this union met and decided as above stated, that these women should not be permitted to organize! I then told Mr. Blatz that he could not shut me out of the halls of legislation, that as soon as the legislature assembles I shall appear there and put these conditions on record and demand an investigation and the drafting of suitable laws to protect the womanhood of the state.

Organized labor and humanity demand protection for these helpless victims of insatiable greed, in the interest of motherhood of our future state.

Will the people of this country at large, and the organized wage-workers in particular, tolerate and stand any longer for such conditions as existing in the bottling establishments of these Milwaukee breweries? I hope not! Therefore, I ask all fair-minded people to refrain from purchasing the product of these baron brewers until they will change things for the better for these poor girls working in their bottling establishments.

Exploited by the brewers! Insulted by the petty bosses! Deserted by the press, which completely ignored me and gave no helping hand to these poor girls' cause. Had they had a vote, however, their case would likely have attracted more attention from all sides. Poor peons of the brewers! Neglected by all the Gods! Deserted by all mankind. The present shorn of all that makes life worth living, the future hopeless, without a comforting star or glimmer. What avails our boasted greatness built upon such human wreckage? What is civilization and progress to them? What "message" bears the holy brotherhood in the gorgeous temples of modern worship? What terrors has the over-investigated white-slave traffic for her? What a prolific recruiting station for the red light district! For after all, the white slave *eats, drinks,* and wears good clothing, and to the hopeless this means living, if it only lasts a minute. What has the beer slave to—the petty boss will make her job cost her virtue anyhow. This has come to be a price of a job everywhere nowadays. Is it any wonder the white-slave traffic abounds on all sides? No wonder the working class has lost all faith in Gods. Hell itself has no terrors worse than a term in industrial slavery. I will give these brewery lords of Milwaukee notice that my two months' investigation and efforts to organize, in spite of all obstacles placed in my way, will bear fruit, and the sooner they realize their duty the better it will be for themselves. Will they do it?

Think of it, fathers and mothers. Think of it, men and women. When it is asked of thee, "What hast thou done for the economic redemption of the sisters of thy brother Abel?" what will thy answer be?

[1910]

 22

From Women and Labor

OLIVE SCHREINER

CHAPTER VI
CERTAIN OBJECTIONS

It has been stated sometimes, though more often implicitly than in any direct or logical form, (this statement being one it is not easy to make definitely without its reducing itself to nullity!) that woman should seek no fields of labor in the new world of social conditions that is arising about us, as she has her function as child-bearer: a labor which, by her own showing, is arduous and dangerous, though she may love it as a soldier loves his battle field; that woman should perform her sex functions only, allowing man or the state to support her, even when she is only potentially a child-bearer and bears no children.[1]

There is some difficulty in replying to a theorist so wholly delusive. Not only is he to be met by all the arguments against parasitism of class or race; but, at the present day, when probably much more than half the world's most laborious and ill-paid labor is still performed by women, from tea pickers and cocoa tenders in India and the islands, to the washerwomen, cooks, and drudging laboring men's wives, who, in addition to the sternest and most unending toil, throw in their child-bearing as a little addition: and when in some civilized countries women exceed the males in numbers by one million, so that there would still be one million females for whom there was no legitimate sexual outlet, though each male in the nation supported a female, it is somewhat difficult to reply with gravity to the assertion, "Let Woman be content to be the 'Divine Child-bearer,' and ask no more."

Were it worth replying gravely to so idle a theorist, we might answer:—Through all the ages of the past, when, with heavy womb and hard labor-worn hands, we physically toiled beside man, bearing up by the labor of our bodies the world about us, it was never suggested to us, "You, the child-bearers of the race, have in that one function a labor that equals all others combined; therefore, toil no more in other directions, we pray of you. Neither plant, nor build, nor bend over the grindstone, nor far into the night, while we sleep, sit weaving the clothing we and our children are to wear! Leave it to us, to plant, to reap, to weave, to work, to toil for you, O sacred child-bearer! Work no more; every man of the race will work for you!" This cry in all the grim ages of our past toil we never heard.

And to-day the lofty theorist, who to-night stands before the drawing-room fire in spotless shirt-front and perfectly fitting clothes, and declaims upon the amplitude of woman's work in life as child-bearer, and the mighty value of that labor which exceeds all other, making it unnecessary for her to share man's grosser and lower toils: does he always remember his theory? When waking to-morrow morning, he finds that the elderly house drudge, who rises at dawn while he yet sleeps, to make his tea and clean his boots, has brought his tea late, and polished his boots ill; may he not even sharply condemn her, and assure her she will have to leave unless she works harder and rises earlier? He does not exclaim to her, "Divine child-bearer! Potential mother of the race! Why should you clean my boots or bring up my tea, while I lie warm in bed? Is it not enough you should have the holy and mysterious power of bringing the race to life? Let that content you. Henceforth I shall get up at dawn and make my own tea and clean my own boots, and pay you just the same!" Nor, should his landlady, now about to give birth to her ninth child, send him up a poorly-cooked dinner or forget to bring up his scuttle of coal, does he send for her and thus apostrophize the astonished matron: "Child-bearer of the race! Producer of men! Cannot you be contented with so noble and lofty a function in life without toiling and moiling? Why carry up heavy coal-scuttles from the cellar and bend over hot fires, wearing out nerve and muscle that should be reserved for higher duties? We, we men of the race, will perform its mean, its sordid, its grinding toil! For woman is beauty, peace, repose! Your function is to give life, not to support it by labor. The Mother, the Mother! How wonderful it sounds! Toil no more! Rest is for you; labor and drudgery for us!" Would he not rather assure her that, unless she labored more assiduously and sternly, she would lose his custom and so be unable to pay her month's rent, and perhaps so, with children and an invalid or drunken husband whom she supports, be turned out into the streets? For it is remarkable, that, with theorists of this class, it is not toil, or the amount of toil, crushing alike to brain and body, which the female undertakes that he objects to; it is the form and the amount of the reward. It is not the hand-laboring woman, even in his own society, worn out and prematurely aged at forty with grinding domestic toil that has no beginning and knows no end—

"Man's work is from sun to sun,
But woman's work is never done"—

it is not the haggard, work-worn woman and mother who irons his shirts, or the potential mother who destroys health and youth in the sweater's den where she sews the garments in which he appears so radiantly in the drawing-room who disturbs him.

It is the thought of the woman-doctor with an income of some hundreds a year, who drives round in her carriage to see her patients, or receives them in her consulting-rooms, and who spends the evening smoking and reading before her study fire or receiving her guests; it is the thought of the woman who, as legislator, may loll for perhaps six hours on the padded seat of legislative bench, relieving the tedium now and then by a turn in the billiard- or refreshment-room, when she is not needed to vote or speak; it is the woman as Greek professor, with three or four hundred a year, who gives half a dozen lectures a week, and has leisure to enjoy the society of her husband and children, and to devote to her own study and life of thought; it is she who wrings his heart. It is not the woman, who, on hands and knees, at tenpence a day, scrubs the floors of the public buildings, or private dwellings, that fills him with anguish for womanhood: that somewhat quadrupedal posture is for him truly feminine, and does not interfere with the ideal of the mother and child-bearer. That, in some other man's house, or perhaps his own, while he and the wife he keeps for his pleasure are visiting concert or entertainment, some weary woman paces till far into the night bearing with aching back and tired head the fretful teething child he brought into the world, for a pittance of twenty or thirty pounds a year, does not distress him. But that the same woman by work in an office should earn one hundred and fifty pounds, be able to have a comfortable home of her own and her evening free for study or pleasure, distresses him deeply. It is not the labor, or the amount of labor, so much as the amount of reward that interferes with his ideal of the eternal womanly; he is as a rule contented that the women of the race should labor for him, whether as tea-pickers or washerwoman, or toilers for the children he brings into the world, provided the reward they receive is not large, nor in such fields as he might himself desire to enter.

. . .

As the women of old planted and reaped and ground the grain that the children they bore might eat, as the maidens of old spun that they might make linen for their households and obtain the right to bear men; so, though we bend no more over grindstones, or labor in the fields, or weave by hand, it is our intention to enter all the new fields of labor, that we also may have the power and right to bring men into the world. It is our faith that the day comes in which not only shall no man dare to say, "It is enough portion for a woman in life that she bear a child," but when it will rather be said, "What noble labor has that woman performed, that she should have the privilege of bringing a man or woman child into the world?"

But, it may be objected, "What if the female half of humanity, though able, in addition to the exercise of its reproductive functions, to bear its share in the new fields of social labor as it did in the old, be yet in certain directions a less productive laborer than the male? What if, in the main, the result of the labor of the two halves should not be found to be exactly equal?"

To this it may be answered that it is within the range of possibility that, mysteriously coordinated with the male reproductive function in the human, there may also be in many directions a tendency to possess gifts useful and beneficial to the race, in the stage of growth it has now reached, in excess of those possessed by the female. We see no reason why this should be so, and, in the present state of our knowledge, this is a point on which no sane person would dogmatize; but it is possible! It may, on the other hand, be that, taken in the bulk, when all the branches of productive labor be considered, the value of the labor of the two halves of humanity will be found so identical and so closely to balance that

no superiority can possibly be asserted of either, as the result of the closest analysis. This also is possible.

. . .

It is quite possible, in the new world which is arising about us, that the type of human most useful to society and best fitted for its future conditions, and who will excel in the most numerous forms of activity, will be, not the muscularly powerful and bulky, but the highly versatile, active, vital, adaptive, sensitive, physically fine-drawn type: and, as that type, though, like the muscularly heavy and powerful, by no means peculiar to and confined to one sex, is yet rather more commonly found in conjunction with a female organism, it is quite possible that, taken in the bulk and on the whole, the female half of humanity may, by virtue of its structural adaptations, be found most fitted for the bulk of human labors in the future!

As with individuals and races, so also with sexes, changed social conditions may render exactly those subtle qualities, which in one social state were a disadvantage, of the highest social advantage in another.

. . .

[1911]

NOTE

1. Such a scheme, as has before been stated, was actually put forward by a literary man in England some years ago: but he had the sense to state that it should apply only to women of the upper classes; the mass of laboring women, who form the vast bulk of the English women of the present day, being left to their ill-paid drudgery and their child-bearing as well!

 23

Now We Can Begin

CRYSTAL EASTMAN

Most women will agree that August 23, the day when the Tennessee legislature finally enacted the Federal suffrage amendment, is a day to begin with, not a day to end with. Men are saying perhaps "Thank God, this everlasting woman's fight is over!" But women, if I know them, are saying, "Now at last we can begin." In fighting for the right to vote most women have tried to be either non-committal or thoroughly respectable on every other subject. Now they can say what they are really after; and what they are after, in common with all the rest of the struggling world, is *freedom*.

Freedom is a large word.

Many feminists are socialists, many are communists, not a few are active leaders in these movements. But the true feminist, no matter how far to the left she may be in the revolutionary movement, sees the woman's battle as distinct in its objects and different in its methods from the workers' battle for industrial freedom. She knows, of course, that the vast majority of women as well as men are without property, and are of necessity bread and butter slaves under a system of society which allows the very sources of life to be privately owned by a few, and she counts herself a loyal soldier in the working-class army that is marching to overthrow that system. But as a feminist she also knows that the whole of woman's slavery is not summed up in the profit system, not her complete emancipation assured by the downfall of capitalism.

Woman's freedom, in the feminist sense, can be fought for and conceivably won before the gates open into industrial democracy. On the other hand, woman's freedom, in the feminist sense, is not inherent in the communist ideal. All feminists are familiar with the revolutionary leader who "can't see" the woman's movement. "What's the matter with the women? My wife's all right," he says. And his wife, one usually finds, is raising his children in a Bronx flat or a dreary suburb, to which he returns occasionally for food and sleep when all possible excitement and stimulus have been wrung from the fight. If we should graduate into communism tomorrow this man's attitude to his wife would not be changed. The proletarian dictatorship may or may not free women. We must begin now to enlighten the future dictators.

What, then, is "the matter with women"? What is the problem of women's freedom? It seems to me to be this: how to arrange the world so that women can be human beings, with a chance to exercise their infinitely varied gifts in infinitely varied ways, instead of being destined by the accident of their sex to one field of activity—housework and child-raising. And second, if and when they choose housework and child-raising to have that occupation recognized by the world as work, requiring a definite economic reward and not merely entitling the performer to be dependent on some man.

This is not the whole of feminism, of course, but it is enough to begin with. "Oh! don't begin with economics," my friends often protest, "Woman does not live by bread alone. What she needs first of all is a free soul." And I can agree that women will never be great until they achieve a certain emotional freedom, a strong healthy egotism, and some unpersonal sources of joy—that in this inner sense we cannot make woman free by changing her economic status. What we can do, however, is to create conditions of outward freedom in which a free woman's soul can be born and grow. It is these outward conditions with which an organized feminist movement must concern itself.

Freedom of choice in occupation and individual economic independence for women: How shall we approach this next feminist objective? First, by breaking down all remaining barriers, actual as well as legal, which make it difficult for women to enter or succeed in the various professions, to go into and get on in business, to learn trades and practice them, to join trades unions. Chief among these remaining barriers is inequality in pay. Here the ground is already broken. This is the easiest part of our program.

Second, we must institute a revolution in the early training and education of both boys and girls. It must be womanly as well as manly to earn your own living, to stand on your own feet. And it must be manly as well as womanly to know how to cook and sew and clean and take care of yourself in the ordinary exigencies of life. I need not add that the second part of this revolution will be more passionately resisted than the first. Men will not give up their privilege of helplessness without a struggle. The average man has a carefully cultivated ignorance about household matters—from what to do with the crumbs to the grocer's telephone number—a sort of cheerful inefficiency which protects him better than the reputation for having a violent temper. It was his mother's fault in the beginning, but even as a boy he was quick to see how a general reputation for being "no good around the house" would serve him throughout life, and half-consciously he began to cultivate that helplessness until to-day it is the despair of feminist wives.

A growing number of men admire the woman who has a job, and, especially since the cost of living doubled, rather like the idea of their own wives contributing to the family income by outside work. And of course for generations there have been whole towns full of wives who are forced by the bitterest necessity to spend the same hours at the factory that their husbands spend. But these bread-winning wives have not yet developed home-making husbands. When the two come home from the factory the man sits down while his wife gets supper, and he does so with exactly the same sense of fore-ordained right as if he were "supporting her." Higher up in the economic scale the same thing is true. The business or professional woman who is married, perhaps engages a cook, but the responsibility is not shifted, it is still hers. She "hires and fires," she orders meals, she does the buying, she meets and resolves all domestic crises, she takes charge of moving, furnishing, settling. She may be, like her husband, a busy executive at her office all day, but unlike him, she is also an executive in a small way every night and morning at home. Her noon hour is spent in planning, and too often her Sundays and holidays are spent in "catching up."

Two business women can "make a home" together without either one being over-burdened or over-bored. It is because they both know how and both feel responsible. But it is a rare man who can marry one of them and continue the home-making partnership. Yet if there are no children, there is nothing essentially different in the combination. Two self-supporting adults decide to make a home together: if both are women it is a pleasant partnership, more fun than work; if one is a man, it is almost never a partnership—the woman simply adds running the home to her regular outside job. Unless she is very strong, it is too much for her, she gets tired and bitter over it, and finally perhaps gives up her outside work and condemns herself to the tiresome half-job of housekeeping for two.

Cooperative schemes and electrical devices will simplify the business of home-making, but they will not get rid of it entirely. As far as we can see ahead people will always want homes, and a happy home cannot be had without a certain amount of rather monotonous work and responsibility. How can we change the nature of man so that he will honorably share the work and responsibility and thus make the home-making enterprise a song instead of a burden? Most assuredly not by laws or revolutionary decrees. Perhaps we must cultivate or simulate a little of that highly prized helplessness ourselves. But fundamentally it is a problem of education, of early training—we must bring up feminist sons.

Sons? Daughters? They are born of women—how can women be free to choose their occupation, at all times cherishing their economic independence, unless they stop having children? This is a further question for feminism. If the feminist program goes to pieces on the arrival of the first baby, it is false and useless. For ninety-nine out of every hundred women want children, and seventy-five out of every hundred want to take care of their own children, or at any rate so closely superintend their care as to make any other full-time occupation impossible for at least ten or fifteen years. Is there any such thing then as freedom of choice in occupation for women? And is not the family the inevitable economic unit and woman's individual economic independence, at least during that period, out of the question?

The feminist must have an answer to these questions, and she has. The immediate feminist program must include voluntary motherhood. Freedom of any kind for women is hardly worth considering unless it is assumed that they will know how to control the size of their families. "Birth control" is just as elementary an essential in our propaganda as "equal pay." Women are to have children when they want them, that's the first thing. That ensures some freedom of occupational choice; those who do not wish to be mothers will not have an undesired occupation thrust upon them by accident, and those who do wish to be mothers may choose in a general way how many years of their lives they will devote to the occupation of child-raising.

But is there any way of insuring a woman's economic independence while child-raising is her chosen occupation? Or must she sink into the dependent state from which, as we all know, it is so hard to rise again? That brings us to the fourth feature of our program—motherhood endowment. It seems that the only way we can keep mothers free, at least in a capitalist society, is by the establishment of a principle that the occupation of raising children is peculiarly and directly a service to society, and that the mother upon whom the necessity and privilege of performing this service naturally falls is entitled to an adequate economic reward from the political government. It is idle to talk of real economic independence for women unless this principle is accepted. But with a generous endowment of motherhood provided by legislation, with all laws against voluntary motherhood and education in its methods repealed, with the feminist ideal of education accepted in home and school, and with all special barriers removed in every field of human activity, there is no reason why woman should not become almost a human thing.

It will be time enough then to consider whether she has a soul.

[1919]

PART III

1920–1963

1920–1963: Introduction

It has become a truism of American women's history that the decades immediately after 1920 represented the "doldrums" of American feminism. That might appear to be the case, if one identifies the campaign for suffrage as the exclusive site of feminist thinking and activity. During this period, proponents of suffrage were disappointed to discover that the women's vote did not radically alter the outcome of elections, that women voted in relatively small numbers and, for the most part, with their husbands, fathers, and brothers. At the same time, suffrage organizations were disbanding and their members dispersing into a variety of organizations. The image of the "flapper" suggests a 1920's woman who is socially and sexually freer but is not a political activist in the way her suffragist foremothers might have hoped.

However, as Leila Rupp and Veta Taylor have documented in *Survival in the Doldrums,* feminist thinking and activity did continue. Women's political activity moved into organizations like the moderate League of Women Voters and the more radical Women's Party with its campaign to pass an Equal Rights Amendment to address forms of discrimination not ameliorated by achieving the vote. Black and white women and women from new immigrant populations were active in labor organizing, confronting both workplace discrimination (exacerbated by postwar and Depression female unemployment) and sexism within labor organizations themselves. Following World War I and throughout this period, women also became active in internationalist and peace movements through organizations like the Women's International League for Peace and Freedom (WILPF) and, during the 1950s, in opposition to nuclear testing. After World War II, working with such leaders as Eleanor Roosevelt, these women also worked to help found the League of Nations and the United Nations. African American women in this period also found outlets for social activism through the club movement and for creative and intellectual energy through the ferment of the Harlem Renaissance. And in the 1950s, African American women and a few white women became involved in the beginning of civil rights activism.

The readings included in this section clearly express the persistence of many nineteenth-century discussions into this period. The selections by Margaret Sanger, Stella Browne, and Jeannette Foster continue the discussion about women's right to sexual autonomy and sexual self-definition; the latter two articles are early attempts to grapple with issues of lesbian sexuality and identity. Readings by Virginia Woolf and Mary Ritter Beard continue attempts to understand women's erasure from literary and historical knowledge as well as from public intellectual and political life. Karen Horney's "The Dread of Woman" asks similar questions in the context of psychology.

In this period, with women entering higher education and the professions in unprecedented numbers, academically trained women working in specific fields were beginning to produce some substantial writing about women and feminism. The essays by Simone de Beauvoir, Margaret Mead, and Florynce Kennedy all fall into this category. Interestingly, these essays are related too in the perspectives they try to explore. All three, in attempting to understand women's subordination, examine it from the perspective of difference. Florynce Kennedy's essay looks at the parallels in subordination based on racial and sexual difference. Margaret Mead examines sex difference in three non-Western societies. Simone de Beauvoir expresses woman's difference—her otherness where man is the one, the subject, the norm—as a cultural construct layered on to the biological difference of the female body, observing that "one is not born but rather becomes a woman" (de Beauvoir).

Certainly, this middle period of the twentieth century demonstrates that culture and ideology make women what they are. When the United States needed women's labor in war industries during the early 1940s, Rosie the Riveter became the model of good womanhood. By the late 1940s, however, when men returning from the war needed jobs, the ideological representation of women placed the highest value on the homemaker and full-time mother. Though women of all classes continued to seek training and to enter the workforce during this period, many of them did so with the kinds of conflicts about roles and identity that Betty Friedan documents, at least among middle-class women. Friedan's *The Feminine Mystique* (1963) is often credited with launching the second wave of the women's movement.

24

From Woman and the New Race

MARGARET SANGER

BIRTH CONTROL—A PARENTS' PROBLEM OR WOMAN'S?

The problem of birth control has arisen directly from the effort of the feminine spirit to free itself from bondage. Woman herself has wrought that bondage through her reproductive powers and while enslaving herself has enslaved the world. The physical suffering to be relieved is chiefly woman's. Hers, too, is the love life that dies first under the blight of too prolific breeding. Within her is wrapped up the future of the race—it is hers to make or mar. All of these considerations point unmistakably to one fact—it is woman's duty as well as her privilege to lay hold of the means of freedom. Whatever men may do, she cannot escape the responsibility. For ages she has been deprived of the opportunity to meet this obligation. She is now emerging from her helplessness. Even as no one can share the suffering of the overburdened mother, so no one can do this work for her. Others may help, but she and she alone can free herself.

The basic freedom of the world is woman's freedom. A free race cannot be born out of slave mothers. A woman enchained cannot choose but give a measure of that bondage to her sons and daughters. No woman can call herself free who does not own and control her body. No woman can call herself free until she can choose consciously whether she will or will not be a mother.

It does not greatly alter the case that some women call themselves free because they earn their own livings, while others profess freedom because they defy the conventions of sex relationship. She who earns her own living gains a sort of freedom that is not to be undervalued, but in quality and in quantity it is of little account beside the untrammeled choice of mating or not mating, of being a mother or not being a mother. She gains food and clothing and shelter, at least, without submitting to the charity of her companion, but the earning of her own living does not give her the development of her inner sex urge, far deeper and more powerful in its outworkings than any of these externals. In order to have that development, she must still meet and solve the problem of motherhood.

With the so-called "free" woman, who chooses a mate in defiance of convention, freedom is largely a question of character and audacity. If she does attain to an unrestricted choice of a mate, she is still in a position to be enslaved through her reproductive powers. Indeed, the pressure of law and custom upon the woman not legally married is likely to make her more of a slave than the woman fortunate enough to marry the man of her choice.

Look at it from any standpoint you will, suggest any solution you will, conventional or unconventional, sanctioned by law or in defiance of law, woman is in the same position, fundamentally, until she is able to determine for herself whether she will be a mother and to fix the number of her offspring. This unavoidable situation is alone enough to make birth control, first of all, a woman's problem. On the very face of the matter, voluntary motherhood is chiefly the concern of the woman.

It is persistently urged, however, that since sex expression is the act of two, the responsibility of controlling the results should not be placed upon woman alone. Is it fair, it is asked, to give her, instead of the man, the task of protecting herself when she is, perhaps, less rugged in physique than her mate, and has, at all events, the normal, periodic inconveniences of her sex?

We must examine this phase of her problem in two lights—that of the ideal, and of the conditions working toward the ideal. In an ideal society, no doubt, birth control would become the concern of the man as well as the woman. The hard, inescapable fact which we encounter to-day is that man has not only refused any such responsibility, but has individually and collectively sought to prevent woman from obtaining knowledge by which she could assume this responsibility for herself. She is still in the position of a dependent to-day because her mate has refused to consider her as an individual apart from his needs. She is still bound because she has in the past left the solution of the problem to him. Having left it to him, she finds that instead of rights, she has only such privileges as she has gained by petitioning, coaxing and cozening. Having left it to him, she is exploited, driven and enslaved to his desires.

While it is true that he suffers many evils as the consequence of this situation, she suffers vastly more. While it is true that he should be awakened to the cause of these evils, we know that they come home to her with crushing force every day. It is she who has the long burden of carrying, bearing and rearing the unwanted children. . . . It is her heart that the sight of the deformed, the subnormal, the undernourished, the overworked child smites first and oftenest and hardest. It is *her* love life that dies first in the fear of undesired pregnancy. It is her opportunity for self expression that perishes first and most hopelessly because of it.

Conditions, rather than theories, facts, rather than dreams, govern the problem. They place it squarely upon the shoulders of woman. She has learned that whatever the moral responsibility of the man in this direction may be, he does not discharge it. She has learned that, lovable and considerate as the individual husband may be, she has nothing to expect from men in the mass, when they make laws and decree customs. She knows that regardless of what ought to be, the brutal, unavoidable fact is that she will never receive her freedom until she takes it for herself.

Having learned this much, she has yet something more to learn. Women are too much inclined to follow in the footsteps of men, to try to think as men think, to try to solve the general problems of life as men solve them. If after attaining their freedom, women accept conditions in the spheres of government, industry, art, morals and religion as they find them, they will be but taking a leaf out of man's book. The woman is not needed to do man's work. She is not needed to think man's thoughts. She need not fear that the masculine mind, almost universally dominant, will fail to take care of its own. Her mission is not to enhance the masculine spirit, but to express the feminine; hers is not to preserve a man-made world, but to create a human world by the infusion of the feminine element into all of its activities.

Woman must not accept; she must challenge. She must not be awed by that which has been built up around her; she must reverence that within her

which struggles for expression. Her eyes must be less upon what is and more clearly upon what should be. She must listen only with a frankly questioning attitude to the dogmatized opinions of man-made society. When she chooses her new, free course of action, it must be in the light of her own opinion—of her own intuition. Only so can she give play to the feminine spirit. Only thus can she free her mate from the bondage which he wrought for himself when he wrought hers. Only thus can she restore to him that of which he robbed himself in restricting her. Only thus can she remake the world. . . .

Woman must have her freedom—the fundamental freedom of choosing whether or not she shall be a mother and how many children she will have. Regardless of what man's attitude may be, that problem is hers—and before it can be his, it is hers alone.

She goes through the vale of death alone, each time a babe is born. As it is the right neither of man nor the state to coerce her into this ordeal, so it is her right to decide whether she will endure it. That right to decide imposes upon her the duty of clearing the way to knowledge by which she may make and carry out the decision.

Birth control is woman's problem. The quicker she accepts it as hers and hers alone, the quicker will society respect motherhood. The quicker, too, will the world be made a fit place for her children to live.

[1920]

25

Studies in Feminine Inversion

STELLA BROWNE

I must apologise for what I feel to be a misleading title chosen for reasons of brevity and economy of effort in the framing of notices; for, what I have to put before you today are only very fragmentary data, and suggestions of a peculiarly obscure subject. They have, however, this validity; that they are the result of close and careful observation, conducted so far as I am consciously aware, without any prejudice, though they would probably be much more illuminating had they been recorded by an observer who was herself entirely or predominantly homosexual. I hope that the endless omissions will be to some extent supplied by comment and criticism, from our members, in the course of debate.

My material would have been both less limited and much more definite and intimate had I been able to include cases which have been told me in confidence. Those, of course, I have omitted.

The cases which I will now briefly describe to you are all well-known to me; they are all innate, and very pronounced and deeply rooted, not episodical. At the same time though I am sure there has been, in some of them at least, no definite and conscious physical expression, they are absolutely distinguishable from affectionate friendship. They have all of them in varying degrees, the element of passion: and here I should like to quote a definition of passion by Desmond McCarthy, which seems to me very apt and very true:

> It differs from lust in the intensity with which the personality of the object is apprehended, and in being also an excitement of the whole being, and, therefore, not satisfied so simply: from other kinds of love, in that it is intensely sexual and not accompanied, necessarily, by any contemplation of the object as good, or any strong desire for his or her welfare apart from the satisfaction of itself.

Now for my cases, and then a few comments and conclusions.

Case A. Member of a small family, but numerous cousins on both sides. The mother's family is nervous, with a decided streak of eccentricity of varying kinds, and some of its members much above the average in intelligence. The father's family much more commonplace, but robust. She is of small-boned frame, but childish rather than feminine in appearance, the liberating and illuminating effect of some definite and direct physical sex-expression, have had, and still have, a disastrous effect on a nature which has much inherent force and many fine qualities. Her whole outlook on life is subtly distorted and dislocated, moral values are confused and a false standard of values is set up. The hardening and narrowing effect of her way of life is shown in a tremendous array of prejudices on every

conceivable topic: caste prejudices, race prejudices, down to prejudices founded on the slightest eccentricity of dress or unconventionality of behaviour; also in an immense intolerance of normal passion, even in its most legally sanctioned and certificated forms. As to unlegalised sex-relationships, they are of course considered the very depth alike of depravity and of crass folly. And all the while, her life revolves round a deep and ardent sex-passion, frustrated and exasperated through functional repression, but entirely justified in her own opinion as pure family affection and duty! Though the orthodox and conventional point of view she takes on sex-questions, generally, would logically condemn just *that* form of sex-passion, as peculiarly reprehensible.

Case B. Also the member of a small family though with numerous cousins, paternal and maternal. Family of marked ability—on both sides, especially the mother's. Of very graceful and attractive appearance, entirely feminine, beautiful eyes and classical features, but indifferent to her looks and abnormally lacking in vanity, self-confidence and animal vitality generally, though no one is quicker to appreciate any beauty or charm in other women. I think she is a pronounced psychic invert whose intuitive faculties and bent towards mysticism have never been cultivated. Keen instinctive delicacy and emotional depth, enthusiastically devoted and generous to friends; much personal pride (though no vanity) and reserve. Too amenable to group suggestions and the influences of tradition. Artistic and musical tastes and a faculty for literary criticism which has lain fallow for want of systematic exercise. Rather fond of animals and devoted to children, especially to young relatives and the children of friends. Has done good philanthropic work for children, but is essentially interested in *persons* rather than in theories, or institutions. Is a devout Christian and I think gets much support and comfort from her religious beliefs. A distaste, even positive disgust, for the physical side of sex, which is tending more and more to manifest itself in conventional moral attitudes and judgements. General social attitude towards men less definitely *hostile* than that of Case A, but absolutely aloof. Devoted to women friends and relatives, yet has had no full and satisfying expression of this devotion. This inhibition of a whole infinitely important set of feelings and activities has weakened her naturally very sound judgment, and also had a bad permanent effect on her bodily health.

Case C. The sixth, and second youngest of a large and very able and vigorous family. Tall, and of the typical Diana build; long limbs, broad shoulders, slight bust, narrow hips. Decidedly athletic. Voice agreeable in tone and quite deep, can whistle well. Extremely energetic and capable, any amount of initiative and enthusiasm, never afraid to assume responsibility; very dominating and managing, something of a tyrant in practice, though an extreme democrat in theory, and most intolerant towards different emotional temperaments. Scientific training, interested in politics and public affairs; logical and rationalistic bent of mind. Emotionally reserved, intense, jealous and monopolistic. Will always try to express all emotion in terms of reason and moral theory, and is thus capable of much mental dishonesty, while making a fetich of complete and meticulous truthfulness. An agnostic and quite militant and aggressive. The episode in her life which I observed fairly closely was a long and intimate friendship with a young girl—ten years her junior—of a very attractive and vivacious type, who roused the interest of both men and women keenly. Cleverness and physical charm in girls appealed to her, but she instinctively resented any independent divergent views or standard of values. For years she practically formed this girl's mental life, and they spent their holidays together. When the girl fell in love with and impulsively married a very masculine and brilliantly gifted man, who has since won great distinction in his special profession, C's agony of rage and desolation was terrible and pitiable, though here again, she tried to hide the real nature of her loss by misgivings as to the young man's 'type of ethical theory'—her own phrase! I cannot for a moment believe that she was ignorant of her own sex-nature, and I hope she has by now found free and full personal realisation with some beloved woman—though, unless the beloved woman is exceptionally understanding or exceptionally docile, it will be a stormy relationship. She is a very strong personality, and a born ruler. Her attitude towards men was one of perfectly unembarrassed and equal comradeship.

Case D. Is on a less evolved plane than the three aforementioned, being conspicuously lacking in refinement of feeling and, to some extent, of habit. But is well above the average in vigor, energy and efficiency. A decided turn for carpentry, mechanics and executive manual work. Not tall; slim, boyish figure; very hard, strong muscles, singularly impassive face, with big magnetic eyes. The dominating tendency is very strong here, and is not held in leash by a high standard of either delicacy or principle. Is professionally associated with children and young girls, and shows her innate homosexual tendency by excess of petting and spoiling, and intense jealousy of any other person's contact with, or interest in the children. I do not definitely know if there is any physical expression of her feelings, beyond the kissing and embracing which is normal, and even, in some cases conventional, between women or between women and children. But the *emotional tone* is quite unmistakable; will rave for hours over some 'lovely kiddy', and injure the children's own best interests, as well as the working of the establishment, by unreasonable and unfair indulgence.

Her sexual idiosyncracy in the post which she occupies is extremely harmful, and together with her jealous and domineering nature, leads to a general atmosphere of slackness and intrigue, and the children under her care, of course, take advantage of it. As she has had medical training, I cannot suppose she is ignorant on the subject of her own sex nature. Member of a large family, mostly brothers.

Case E. This was a case which at one time was fairly well-known to me, and is very well-marked. Two assistant mistresses at a girl's boarding-school were completely inseparable. They took all their walks together, and spent all their time when they were 'off duty' and not walking, in one another's rooms—they occupied adjoining rooms.

One of them was a slim, graceful, restless, neurotic girl with a distinct consumptive tendency; quick in perception and easy in manner, but it seemed to me then, and it seems still, decidedly superficial and shallow. The other partner was an invert of the most pronounced physical type. Her tall, stiff, rather heavily muscular figure, her voice, and her chubby, fresh-coloured face, which was curiously eighteenth-century in outline and expression, were so like those of a very young and very well-groomed youth, that all the staff of the school nicknamed her 'Boy', though I do not believe any of them clearly realised what this epithet—and her intimacy with a woman of such strongly contrasted type, implied. 'Boy' was extremely self-conscious and curiously inarticulate; she had musical tastes and played rather well—not in the colourless and amateurish style of the musical hack. I think music was an outlet for her. She was also fond of taking long walks, and of driving, and of dogs and horses. Beyond these matters I don't think I ever heard her express an opinion about anything. The intimacy with her restless, tricky adored one ran its course, unhindered either by circumstances, or by unconscious public opinion. There was some idealism in the relationship, at least on 'Boy's' side.

There was no community of intellectual interests—or rather there was community in the mutual absence of intellectual interests. I lost sight of them completely, but heard later that the friend had taken a post in South Africa, and 'Boy' was planning to join her there, but I do not know whether this plan materialised.

I have omitted from consideration that episodical homosexuality on the part of women who are normally much more attracted to men, of which every experienced observer must know instances.

I have also left out of consideration here, various instances known to me of passionate but unconscious inversion in girls whose sex-life is just beginning. All of these are important, and may throw helpful light not only on the problem [of] inversion, but on the sexual impulse of women generally.

There exists no document in modern English literature comparable in authenticity or artistic merit, as a study of the female homosexual or bi-sexual temperaments, with the hauntingly beautiful verse of Renee Vivien (Pauline Tarn) or the vivid autobiographical novels of Colette Willy (Gabrielle Gauthier Villars).

I know of two modern English novels in which the subject is touched on with a good deal of subtlety, and in both cases in association with school life. *Regiment of Women* by Clemence Dane—a brilliant piece of psychology, and a novel by an Australian writer, cruder and shorter, but unmistakably powerful, *The Getting of Wisdom* by Henry Handel Richardson. There is frank and brilliant description of the feminine intermediate and homosexual temperaments in *I, Mary MacLane,* (New York, Stokes & Co).

I would draw your attention to one quality which two of my cases have in common, and to a very marked degree: the maternal instinct. Two of the most intensely maternal women I know are cases A and B, both congenital inverts.

A friend has suggested to me that in such cases in the future, the resources of developed chemistry and biology will be made use of, in artificial fertilisation. And I now see in reading Dr Marie Stopes's interesting Essay 'Married Love', that she makes a similar suggestion, though not with reference to inversion.

This problem of feminine inversion is very pressing and immediate, taking into consideration the fact that in the near future, for at least a generation, the circumstances of women's lives and work will tend, even more than at present, to favour the frigid, and next to the frigid, the inverted types. Even at present, the social and affectional side of the invert's nature has often fuller opportunity of satisfaction than the heterosexual woman's, but often at the cost of adequate and definite physical expression. And how decisive for vigour, sanity and serenity of body and mind, for efficiency, for happiness, for the mastery of life, and the understanding of one's fellow-creatures—just this definite physical expression is! The lack of it, 'normal' and 'abnormal', is at the root of most of what is most trivial and unsatisfactory in women's intellectual output, as well as of their besetting vice of cruelty. How can anyone be finely or greatly creative, if one's supreme moral law is a negation! Not to *live,* not to *do,* not even to try to understand.

In the cases which I have called A and B, sexual experience along the lines of their own psychic idiosyncrasy would have revealed to them definitely where they stood, and as both are well above the average in intelligence, would have been a key to many mysteries of human conduct which are now judged with dainty shrinking from incomprehensible folly and perversity.

I am sure that much of the towering spiritual arrogance which is found, e.g., in many high places in the Suffrage movement, . . . is really unconscious inversion.

I think it is perhaps not wholly uncalled-for, to underline very strongly my opinion that the homosexual impulse *is not in any way superior* to the normal; it has a fully equal right to existence and expression, it is no worse, no lower; *but no better.*

By all means let the invert—let all of us—have as many and varied 'channels of sublimation' as possible; and far more than are at present available. But, to be honest, are we not too inclined to make 'sublimation' an excuse for refusing to tackle fundamentals? The tragedy of the repressed invert is apt to be not only one of emotional frustration, but complete dislocation of mental values.

Moreover, our present social arrangements, founded as they are on the repression and degradation of the normal erotic impulse, artificially stimulate inversion and have thus forfeited all right to condemn it. There is a huge, persistent, indirect pressure on women of strong passions and fine brains to find an emotional outlet with other women. A woman who is unwilling to accept either marriage—under present laws—or prostitution, and at the same time refuses to limit her sexual life to auto-erotic manifestations, will find she has to struggle against the whole social order for what is nevertheless her most precious personal right. The right sort of woman faces the struggle and counts the cost well worth while; but it is impossible to avoid seeing that she risks the most painful experiences, and spends an incalculable amount of time and energy on things that should be matters of course. Under these conditions, some women who *are not innately or predominantly homosexual* do form more or less explicitly erotic relations with other women, yet these are makeshifts and essentially substitutes, which cannot replace the vital contact, mental and bodily, with congenial men.

No one who has observed the repressed inverted impulse flaring into sex-antagonism, or masked as the devotion of daughter or cousin or the solicitude of teacher or nurse, or perverted into the cheap, malignant cant of conventional moral indignation, can deny its force. Let us recognise this force, as frankly as we recognise and reverence the love between men and women. When Paris was devouring and disputing over Willy and Colette Willy's wonderful Claudine stories, another gifted woman-writer, who had also touched on the subject of inversion, defended not only the artistic conception and treatment of the stories (they need no defence, and remain one of the joys and achievements of modern French writing),

but also their ethical content: Mme Rachilde wrote *'une amoureuse d'amour n'est pas une vicieuse'.*

After all: every strong passion, every deep affection, has its own endless possibilities, of pain, change, loss, incompatibility, satiety, jealousy, incompleteness: why add wholly extraneous difficulties and burdens? Harmony may be incompatible with freedom; we do not yet know, for few of us know either. But both truth and the most essential human dignity are incompatible with things as they are.

[1923]

 26

From A Room of One's Own

VIRGINIA WOOLF

CHAPTER FIVE

I had come at last, in the course of this rambling, to the shelves which hold books by the living; by women and by men; for there are almost as many books written by women now as by men. Or if that is not yet quite true, if the male is still the voluble sex, it is certainly true that women no longer write novels solely. There are Jane Harrison's books on Greek archaeology; Vernon Lee's books on aesthetics; Gertrude Bell's books on Persia. There are books on all sorts of subjects which a generation ago no woman could have touched. There are poems and plays and criticism; there are histories and biographies, books of travel and books of scholarship and research; there are even a few philosophies and books about science and economics. And though novels predominate, novels themselves may very well have changed from association with books of a different feather. The natural simplicity, the epic age of women's writing, may have gone. Reading and criticism may have given her a wider range, a greater subtlety. The impulse towards autobiography may be spent. She may be beginning to use writing as an art, not as a method of self-expression. Among these new novels one might find an answer to several such questions.

I took down one of them at random. It stood at the very end of the shelf, was called *Life's Adventure*, or some such title, by Mary Carmichael, and was published in this very month of October. It seems to be her first book, I said to myself, but one must read it as if it were the last volume in a fairly long series, continuing all those other books that I have been glancing at—Lady Winchilsea's poems and Aphra Behn's plays and the novels of the four great novelists. For books continue each other, in spite of our habit of judging them separately. And I must also consider her—this unknown woman—as the descendant of all those other women whose circumstances I have been glancing at and see what she inherits of their characteristics and restrictions. So, with a sigh, because novels so often provide an anodyne and not an antidote, glide one into torpid slumbers instead of rousing one with a burning brand, I settled down with a notebook and a pencil to make what I could of Mary Carmichael's first novel, *Life's Adventure*.

To begin with, I ran my eye up and down the page. I am going to get the hang of her sentences first, I said, before I load my memory with blue eyes and brown and the relationship that there may be between Chloe and Roger. There will be time for that when I have decided whether she has a pen in her hand or a pickaxe. So I tried a sentence or two on my tongue. Soon it was obvious that something was not quite in order. The smooth gliding of sentence after sentence was interrupted. Something tore, something scratched; a single word here and there flashed its torch in my eyes. She was "unhanding" herself as they say in the old plays. She is like a person striking a match that will not light, I thought. But why, I asked her as if she were present, are Jane Austen's sentences not of the right shape for you? Must they all be scrapped because Emma and Mr. Woodhouse are dead? Alas, I sighed, that it should be so. For while Jane Austen breaks from melody to melody as Mozart from song to song, to read this writing was like being out at sea in an open boat. Up one went, down one sank. This terseness, this short-windedness, might mean that she was afraid of something; afraid of being called "sentimental" perhaps; or she remembers that women's writing has been called flowery and so provides a superfluity of thorns; but until I have read a scene with some care,

I cannot be sure whether she is being herself or some one else. At any rate, she does not lower one's vitality, I thought, reading more carefully. But she is heaping up too many facts. She will not be able to use half of them in a book of this size. (It was about half the length of *Jane Eyre*.) However, by some means or other she succeeded in getting us all— Roger, Chloe, Olivia, Tony and Mr. Bigham—in a canoe up the river. Wait a moment, I said, leaning back in my chair, I must consider the whole thing more carefully before I go any further.

I am almost sure, I said to myself, that Mary Carmichael is playing a trick on us. For I feel as one feels on a switchback railway when the car, instead of sinking, as one has been led to expect, swerves up again. Mary is tampering with the expected sequence. First she broke the sentence; now she has broken the sequence. Very well, she has every right to do both these things if she does them not for the sake of breaking, but for the sake of creating. Which of the two it is I cannot be sure until she has faced herself with a situation. I will give her every liberty, I said, to choose what that situation shall be; she shall make it of tin cans and old kettles if she likes; but she must convince me that she believes it to be a situation; and then when she has made it she must face it. She must jump. And, determined to do my duty by her as reader if she would do her duty by me as writer, I turned the page and read . . . I am sorry to break off so abruptly. Are there no men present? Do you promise me that behind that red curtain over there the figure of Sir Chartres Biron is not concealed? We are all women, you assure me? Then I may tell you that the very next words I read were these—"Chloe liked Olivia . . ." Do not start. Do not blush. Let us admit in the privacy of our own society that these things sometimes happen. Sometimes women do like women.

"Chloe liked Olivia," I read. And then it struck me how immense a change was there. Chloe liked Olivia perhaps for the first time in literature. Cleopatra did not like Octavia. And how completely *Antony and Cleopatra* would have been altered had she done so! As it is, I thought, letting my mind, I am afraid, wander a little from *Life's Adventure*, the whole thing is simplified, conventionalised, if one dared say it, absurdly. Cleopatra's only feeling about Octavia is one of jealousy. Is she taller than I am?

How does she do her hair? The play, perhaps, required no more. But how interesting it would have been if the relationship between the two women had been more complicated. All these relationships between women, I thought, rapidly recalling the splendid gallery of fictitious women, are too simple. So much has been left out, unattempted. And I tried to remember any case in the course of my reading where two women are represented as friends. There is an attempt at it in *Diana of the Crossways*. They are confidantes, of course, in Racine and the Greek tragedies. They are now and then mothers and daughters. But almost without exception they are shown in their relation to men. It was strange to think that all the great women of fiction were, until Jane Austen's day, not only seen by the other sex, but seen only in relation to the other sex. And how small a part of a woman's life is that; and how little can a man know even of that when he observes it through the black or rosy spectacles which sex puts upon his nose. Hence, perhaps, the peculiar nature of woman in fiction; the astonishing extremes of her beauty and horror; her alternations between heavenly goodness and hellish depravity—for so a lover would see her as his love rose or sank, was prosperous or unhappy. This is not so true of the nineteenth-century novelists, of course. Woman becomes much more various and complicated there. Indeed it was the desire to write about women perhaps that led men by degrees to abandon the poetic drama which, with its violence, could make so little use of them, and to devise the novel as a more fitting receptacle. Even so it remains obvious, even in the writing of Proust, that a man is terribly hampered and partial in his knowledge of women, as a woman in her knowledge of men.

Also, I continued, looking down at the page again, it is becoming evident that women, like men, have other interests besides the perennial interests of domesticity. "Chloe liked Olivia. They shared a laboratory together. . . ." I read on and discovered that these two young women were engaged in mincing liver, which is, it seems, a cure for pernicious anaemia: although one of them was married and had—I think I am right in stating—two small children. Now all that, of course, has had to be left out, and thus the splendid portrait of the fictitious woman is much too simple and much too monotonous. Suppose, for instance, that men were only represented in literature as the lovers of women, and were never the friends of men, soldiers, thinkers, dreamers; how few parts in the plays of Shakespeare could be allotted to them; how literature would suffer! We might perhaps have most of Othello; and a good deal of Antony; but no Caesar, no Brutus, no Hamlet, no Lear, no Jaques—literature would be incredibly impoverished, as indeed literature is impoverished beyond our counting by the doors that have been shut upon women. Married against their will, kept in one room, and to one occupation, how could a dramatist give a full or interesting or truthful account of them? Love was the only possible interpreter. The poet was forced to be passionate or bitter, unless indeed he chose to "hate women," which meant more often than not that he was unattractive to them.

Now if Chloe likes Olivia and they share a laboratory, which of itself will make their friendship more varied and lasting because it will be less personal; if Mary Carmichael knows how to write, and I was beginning to enjoy some quality in her style; if she has a room to herself, of which I am not quite sure; if she has five hundred a year of her own—but that remains to be proved—then I think that something of great importance has happened.

· · ·

CHAPTER SIX

· · ·

Here I would stop, but the pressure of convention decrees that every speech must end with a peroration. And a peroration addressed to women should have something, you will agree, particularly exalting and ennobling about it. I should implore you to remember your responsibilities, to be higher, more spiritual; I should remind you how much depends upon you, and what an influence you can exert upon the future. But those exhortations can safely, I think, be left to the other sex, who will put them, and indeed have put them, with far greater eloquence than I can compass. When I rummage in my own mind I find no noble sentiments about being companions and equals and influencing the world to higher ends. I find myself saying briefly and prosaically that it is much more important to be oneself than anything else. Do not dream of influencing other people, I would say, if I knew how to make it sound exalted. Think of things in themselves.

And again I am reminded by dipping into newspapers and novels and biographies that when a woman speaks to women she should have something very unpleasant up her sleeve. Women are hard on women. Women dislike women. Women—but are you not sick to death of the word? I can assure you that I am. Let us agree, then, that a paper read by a woman to women should end with something particularly disagreeable.

But how does it go? What can I think of? The truth is, I often like women. I like their unconventionality. I like their subtlety. I like their anonymity. I like—but I must not run on in this way. That cupboard there,—you say it holds clean table-napkins only; but what if Sir Archibald Bodkin were concealed among them? Let me then adopt a sterner tone. Have I, in the preceding words, conveyed to you sufficiently the warnings and reprobation of mankind? I have told you the very low opinion in which you were held by Mr. Oscar Browning. I have indicated what Napoleon once thought of you and what Mussolini thinks now. Then, in case any of you aspire to fiction, I have copied out for your benefit the advice of the critic about courageously acknowledging the limitations of your sex. I have referred to Professor X and given prominence to his statement that women are intellectually, morally and physically inferior to men. I have handed on all that has come my way without going in search of it, and here is a final warning—from Mr. John Langdon Davies.[1] Mr. John Langdon Davies warns women "that when children cease to be altogether desirable, women cease to be altogether necessary." I hope you will make a note of it.

How can I further encourage you to go about the business of life? Young women, I would say, and please attend, for the peroration is beginning, you are, in my opinion, disgracefully ignorant. You have never made a discovery of any sort of importance. You have never shaken an empire or led an army into battle. The plays of Shakespeare are not by you, and you have never introduced a barbarous race to the blessings of civilisation. What is your excuse? It is all very well for you to say, pointing to the streets and squares and forests of the globe swarming with black and white and coffee-coloured inhabitants, all busily engaged in traffic and enterprise and love-making, we have had other work on our hands. Without our doing, those seas would be unsailed and those fertile lands a desert. We have borne and bred and washed and taught, perhaps to the age of six or seven years, the one thousand six hundred and twenty-three million human beings who are, according to statistics, at present in existence, and that, allowing that some had help, takes time.

There is truth in what you say—I will not deny it. But at the same time may I remind you that there have been at least two colleges for women in existence in England since the year 1866; that after the year 1880 a married woman was allowed by law to possess her own property; and that in 1919—which is a whole nine years ago—she was given a vote? May I also remind you that the most of the professions have been open to you for close on ten years now? When you reflect upon these immense privileges and the length of time time during which they have been enjoyed, and the fact that there must be at this moment some two thousand women capable of earning over five hundred a year in one way or another, you will agree that the excuse of lack of opportunity, training, encouragement, leisure and money no longer holds good. Moreover, the economists are telling us that Mrs. Seton has had too many children. You must, of course, go on bearing children, but, so they say, in twos and threes, not in tens and twelves.

Thus, with some time on your hands and with some book learning in your brains—you have had enough of the other kind, and are sent to college partly, I suspect, to be uneducated—surely you should embark upon another stage of your very long, very laborious and highly obscure career. A thousand pens are ready to suggest what you should do and what effect you will have. My own suggestion is a little fantastic, I admit; I prefer, therefore, to put it in the form of fiction.

I told you in the course of this paper that Shakespeare had a sister; but do not look for her in Sir Sidney Lee's life of the poet. She died young—alas, she never wrote a word. She lies buried where the omnibuses now stop, opposite the Elephant and Castle. Now my belief is that this poet who never wrote a word and was buried at the crossroads still lives. She lives in you and in me, and in many other women who are not here tonight, for they are washing up the dishes and putting the children to bed. But she lives; for great poets do not die; they are continuing presences; they need only the opportunity to walk among us in the flesh. This opportunity, as I think, it is now coming within your power to give her. For my belief is that if we live another century or so—I am talking of the common life which is the real life and not of the little separate lives which we live as individuals—and have five hundred a year each of us and rooms of our own; if we have the habit of freedom and the courage to write exactly what we think; if we escape a little from the common sitting-room and see human beings not always in their relation to each other but in relation to reality; and the sky, too, and the trees or whatever it may be in themselves; if we look past Milton's bogey, for no human being should shut out the view; if we face the fact, for it is a fact, that there is no arm to cling to, but that we go alone and that our relation is to the world of reality and not only to the world of men and women, then the opportunity will come and the dead poet who was Shakespeare's sister will put on the body which she has so often laid down. Drawing her life from the lives of the unknown who were her fore-runners, as her brother did before her, she will be born. As for her coming without that preparation, without that effort on our part, without that determination that when she is born again she shall find it possible to live and write her poetry, that we cannot expect, for that would be impossible. But I maintain that she would come if we worked for her, and that so to work, even in poverty and obscurity, is worth while.

[1929]

NOTE

1. *A Short History of Women,* by John Langdon Davies.

 27

The Dread of Woman

KAREN HORNEY

Observations on a Specific Difference in the Dread Felt by Men and by Women Respectively for the Opposite Sex

• • •

Is it not really remarkable . . . that so little recognition and attention are paid to the fact of men's secret dread of women? It is almost more remarkable that women themselves have so long been able to overlook it; I will discuss in detail elsewhere the reasons for their attitude in this connection (i.e., their own anxiety and the impairment of their self-respect). The man on his side has in the first place very obvious strategic reasons for keeping his dread quiet. But he also tries by every means to deny it even to himself. This is the purpose of the efforts to which we have alluded, to "objectify" it in artistic and scientific creative work. We may conjecture that even his glorification of women has its source not only in his cravings for love, but also in his desire to conceal his dread. A similar relief, however, is also sought and found in the disparagement of women that men often display ostentatiously in their attitudes. The attitude of love and adoration signifies: "There is no need for me to dread a being so wonderful, so beautiful, nay, so saintly." That of disparagement implies: "It would be too ridiculous to dread a creature who, if you take her all round, is such a poor thing."[1] This last way of allaying his anxiety has a special advantage for the man: It helps to support his masculine self-respect. The latter seems to feel itself far more threatened at its very core by the admission of a dread of women than by the admission of dread of a man (the father). The reason why the self-feeling of men is so peculiarly sensitive just in relation to women can only be understood by reference to their early development, to which I will return later.

In analysis this dread of women is revealed quite clearly. Male homosexuality has for its basis, in common indeed with all the other perversions, the desire to escape from the female genital, or to deny its very existence. Freud has shown that this is a fundamental trait in fetishism,[2] in particular; he believes it to be based, however, not on anxiety, but on a feeling of abhorrence due to the absence of the penis in women. I think, however, that even from his account we are absolutely forced to the conclusion that there is anxiety at work as well. What we actually see is dread of the vagina, thinly disguised under the abhorrence. Only *anxiety* is a strong enough motive to hold back from his goal a man whose libido is assuredly urging him on to union with the woman. But Freud's account fails to explain this anxiety. A boy's castration anxiety in relation to his father is not an adequate reason for his dread of a being to whom this punishment has already happened. Besides the dread of the father, there must be a further dread, the object of which is the woman or the female genital. Now this dread of the vagina itself appears unmistakably not only in homosexuals and perverts, but also in the dreams of male analysands. All analysts are familiar with dreams of this sort and I need only give the merest outline of them: e.g., a motorcar is rushing along and suddenly falls into a pit and is dashed to pieces; a boat is sailing in a narrow channel and is suddenly sucked into a whirlpool; there is a cellar with uncanny, blood-stained plants and animals; one is climbing a chimney and is in danger of falling and being killed.

* · · ·

From all this I think it probable that the masculine dread of the woman (the mother) or of the female genital is more deep-seated, weighs more heavily, and is usually more energetically repressed than the dread of the man (father), and that the endeavor to find the penis in women represents first and foremost a convulsive attempt to deny the existence of the sinister female genital.

* · · ·

When we endeavor to understand this anxiety in psychological and ontogenetic terms, we find ourselves rather at a loss if we take our stand on Freud's notion that what distinguishes infantile from adult sexuality is precisely that the vagina remains "undiscovered" for the child. According to that view, we cannot properly speak of a genital primacy; we must rather term it a primacy of the phallus. Hence it would be better to describe the period of infantile genital organization as the "phallic phase."[3] The many recorded remarks of boys at that period of life leave no doubt of the correctness of the observations on which Freud's theory is based. But if we look more closely at the essential characteristics of this phase, we cannot help asking whether his description really sums up infantile genitality as such, in its specific manifestation, or applies only to a relatively later phase of it. Freud states that it is characteristic that the boy's interest is concentrated in a markedly narcissistic manner on his own penis: "The driving force which this male portion of his body will gen-

erate later at puberty expresses itself in childhood essentially as an impulsion to inquire into things— as sexual curiosity." A very important part is played by questions as to the existence and size of the phallus in other living beings.

But surely the essence of the phallic impulses proper, starting as they do from organ sensations, is a desire to *penetrate*. That these impulses do exist can hardly be doubted; they manifest themselves too plainly in children's games and in the analysis of little children. Again, it would be difficult to say what the boy's sexual wishes in relation to his mother really consisted in if not in these very impulses; or why the object of his masturbation anxiety should be the father as the castrator, were it not that masturbation was largely the autoerotic expression of heterosexual phallic impulses.

In the phallic phase the boy's psychic orientation is predominantly narcissistic; hence the period in which his genital impulses are directed toward an object must be an earlier one. The possibility that they are not directed toward a female genital, of which he instinctively divines the existence, must certainly be considered. In dreams, both of earlier and later life, as well as in symptoms and particular modes of behavior, we find, it is true, representations of coitus that are oral, anal, or sadistic without specific localization. But we cannot take this as a proof of the primacy of corresponding impulses, for we are uncertain whether, or how far, these phenomena already express a displacement from the genital goal proper. At bottom, all that they amount to is to show that a given individual is influenced by specific oral, anal, or sadistic trends. Their evidential value is the less because these representations are always associated with certain affects directed against women, so that we cannot tell whether they may not be essentially the product or the expression of these affects. For instance, the tendency to debase women may express itself in anal representations of the female genital, while oral representations may express anxiety.

But besides all this, there are various reasons why it seems to me improbable that the existence of a specific female opening should remain "undiscovered." On the one hand, of course, a boy will automatically conclude that everyone else is made like himself; but on the other hand his phallic impulses surely bid him instinctively to search for the appropriate opening in the female body—an opening, moreover, that he himself lacks, for the one sex always seeks in the other that which is complementary to it or of a nature different from its own. If we seriously accept Freud's dictum that the sexual theories formed by children are modeled on their own sexual constitution, it must surely mean in the present connection that the boy, urged on by his impulses to penetrate, pictures in fantasy a complementary female organ. And this is just what we should infer from all the material I quoted at the outset in connection with the masculine dread of the female genital.

It is not at all probable that this anxiety dates only from puberty. At the beginning of that period the anxiety manifests itself quite clearly, if we look behind the often very exiguous façade of boyish pride that conceals it. At puberty a boy's task is obviously not merely to free himself from his incestuous attachment to his mother, but more generally, to master his dread of the whole female sex. His success is as a rule only gradual; first of all he turns his back on girls altogether, and only when his masculinity is fully awakened does it drive him over the threshold of anxiety. But we know that as a rule the conflicts of puberty do but revive, *mutatis mutandis,* conflicts belonging to the early ripening of infantile sexuality and that the course they take is often essentially a faithful copy of a series of earlier experiences. Moreover, the grotesque character of the anxiety, as we meet with it in the symbolism of dreams and literary productions, points unmistakably to the period of early infantile fantasy.

At puberty a normal boy has already acquired a conscious knowledge of the vagina, but what he fears in women is something uncanny, unfamiliar, and mysterious. If the grown man continues to regard woman as the great mystery, in whom is a secret he cannot divine, this feeling of his can only relate ultimately to one thing in her: the mystery of motherhood. Everything else is merely the residue of his dread of this.

What is the origin of this anxiety? What are its characteristics? And what are the factors that cloud the boy's early relations with his mother?

In an article on female sexuality[4] Freud has pointed out the most obvious of these factors: It is the mother who first forbids instinctual activities, because it is she who tends the child in its babyhood.

Secondly, the child evidently experiences sadistic impulses against its mother's body,[5] presumably connected with the rage evoked by her prohibitions, and according to the talion principle, this anger has left behind a residue of anxiety. Finally—and this is perhaps the principal point—the specific fate of the genital impulses itself constitutes another such factor. The anatomical differences between the sexes lead to a totally different situation in girls and in boys, and really to understand both their anxiety and the diversity of their anxiety we must take into account first of all *the children's real situation* in the period of their early sexuality. The girl's nature as biologically conditioned gives her the desire to receive, to take into herself;[6] she feels or knows that her genital is too small for her father's penis and this makes her react to her own genital wishes with direct anxiety; she dreads that if her wishes were fulfilled, she herself or her genital would be destroyed.[7]

The boy, on the other hand, feels or instinctively judges that his penis is much too small for his mother's genital and reacts with the dread of his own inadequacy, of being rejected and derided. Thus his anxiety is located in quite a different quarter from the girl's; his original dread of women is not castration anxiety at all, but a reaction to the menace to his self-respect.[8]

In order that there may be no misunderstanding, let me emphasize that I believe these processes take place purely instinctively on the basis of organ sensations and the tensions of organic needs; in other words, I hold that these reactions would occur even if the girl had never seen her father's penis or the boy his mother's genital, and neither had any sort of intellectual knowledge of the existence of these genitalia.

Because of this reaction on the part of the boy, he is affected in another way and more severely by his frustration at the hands of his mother than is the girl by her experience with her father. A blow is struck at the libidinal impulses in either case. But the girl has a certain consolation in her frustration— she preserves her physical integrity. But the boy is hit in a second sensitive spot—his sense of genital inadequacy, which has presumably accompanied his libidinal desires from the beginning. If we assume that the most general reason for violent anger is the foiling of impulses that at the moment are of vital importance, it follows that the boy's frustration by his mother must arouse a twofold fury in him: first through the thrusting back of his libido upon itself, and secondly, through the wounding of his masculine self-regard.

· · ·

[1932]

NOTES

1. I well remember how surprised I was myself the first time I heard the above ideas asserted—by a man—in the shape of a universal proposition. The speaker was Groddeck, who obviously felt that he was stating something quite self-evident when he remarked in conversation, "Of course men are afraid of women." In his writings Groddeck has repeatedly emphasized this fear.
2. Freud, "Fetishism," *Int. J. Psycho-Anal.*, Vol IX (1928).
3. Freud, "The Infantile Genital Organization of the Libido" (1923), *Collected Papers,* Vol. II.
4. *Int. J. Psycho-Anal.,* Vol. XI (1930), p. 281.
5. Cf. the work of Melanie Klein, quoted above, to which I think insufficient attention has been paid.
6. This is not to be equated with passivity.
7. In another paper I will discuss the girl's situation more fully.
8. I would refer here also to the points I raised in a paper entitled "Das Misstrauen zwischen den Geschlechtern," *Die psychoanalytische Bewegung* (1930).

 28

From Sex and Temperament in Three Primitive Societies

MARGARET MEAD

SEX AND TEMPERAMENT

This study is not concerned with whether there are or are not actual and universal differences between the sexes, either quantitative or qualitative. It is not concerned with whether women are more variable than men, which was claimed before the doctrine of evolution exalted variability, or less variable, which was claimed afterwards. It is not a treatise on the rights of women, nor an inquiry into the basis of feminism. It is, very simply, an account of how three primitive societies have grouped their social attitudes towards temperament about the very obvious facts of sex-difference. I studied this problem in simple societies because here we have the drama of civilization writ small, a social microcosm alike in kind, but different in size and magnitude, from the complex social structures of peoples who, like our own, depend upon a written tradition and upon the integration of a great number of conflicting historical traditions. Among the gentle mountain-dwelling Arapesh, the fierce cannibalistic Mundugumor, and the graceful head-hunters of Tchambuli, I studied this question. Each of these tribes had, as has every human society, the point of sex-difference to use as one theme in the plot of social life, and each of these three peoples has developed that theme differently. In comparing the way in which they have dramatized sex-difference, it is possible to gain a greater insight into what elements are social constructs, originally irrelevant to the biological facts of sex-gender.

· · ·

. . . We know that human cultures do not all fall into one side or the other of a single scale and that it is possible for one society to ignore completely an issue which two other societies have solved in contrasting ways. Because a people honour the old may mean that they hold children in slight esteem, but a people may also, like the Ba Thonga of South Africa, honour neither old people nor children; or, like the Plains Indians, dignify the little child and the grandfather; or, again, like the Manus and parts of modern America, regard children as the most important group in society. In expecting simple reversals—that if an aspect of social life is not specifically sacred, it must be specifically secular; that if men are strong, women must be weak—we ignore the fact that cultures exercise far greater licence than this in selecting the possible aspects of human life which they will minimize, overemphasize, or ignore. And while every culture has in some way institutionalized the roles of men and women, it has not necessarily been in terms of contrast between the prescribed personalities of the two sexes, nor in terms of dominance or submission. With the paucity of material for elaboration, no culture has failed to seize upon the conspicuous facts of age and sex in some way, whether it be the convention of one Philippine tribe that no man can keep a secret, the Manus assumption that only men enjoy playing with babies, the Toda prescription of almost all domestic work as too sacred for women, or the Arapesh insistence that women's heads are stronger than men's. In the division of labour, in dress, in manners, in social and religious functioning—sometimes in only a few of these respects, sometimes in all—men and women are socially differentiated, and each sex, as a sex, forced to conform to the role assigned to it. In some societies, these socially defined roles are mainly expressed in dress or occupation, with no insistence upon innate temperamental differences. Women wear long hair and men wear short hair, or men wear curls and women shave their heads; women wear skirts and men wear trousers, or women wear trousers, and men wear skirts. Women weave and men do not, or men weave and women do not. Such simple tie-ups as these between dress and occupation and sex are easily taught to every child and make no assumptions to which a given child cannot easily conform.

It is otherwise in societies that sharply differentiate the behaviour of men and of women in terms which assume a genuine difference in temperament. Among the Dakota Indians of the Plains, the importance of an ability to stand any degree of danger or hardship was frantically insisted upon as a masculine characteristic. From the time that a boy was five or six, all the conscious educational effort of the household was bent towards shaping him into an indubitable male. Every tear, every timidity, every clinging to a protective hand or desire to continue to play with younger children or with girls, was obsessively interpreted as proof that he was not going to develop into a real man. In such a society it is not surprising to find the *berdache,* the man who had voluntarily given up the struggle to conform to the masculine role and who wore female attire and followed the occupations of a woman. The institution of the *berdache* in turn served as a warning to every father; the fear that the son might become a *berdache* informed the parental efforts with an extra desperation, and the very pressure which helped to drive a boy to that choice was redoubled. The invert who lacks any discernible physical basis for his inversion has long puzzled students of sex, who when they can find no observable glandular abnormality turn to theories of early conditioning or identification with a parent of opposite sex. In the course of this investigation, we shall have occasion to examine the "masculine" woman and the "feminine" man as they occur in these different tribes, to inquire

whether it is always a woman of dominating nature who is conceived as masculine, or a man who is gentle, submissive, or fond of children or embroidery who is conceived as feminine.

. . . [W]e shall be concerned with the patterning of sex-behaviour from the standpoint of temperament, with the cultural assumptions that certain temperamental attitudes are "naturally" masculine and others "naturally" feminine. In this matter, primitive people seem to be, on the surface, more sophisticated than we are. Just as they know that the gods, the food habits, and the marriage customs of the next tribe differ from those of their own people, and do not insist that one form is true or natural while the other is false or unnatural, so they often know that the temperamental proclivities which they regard as natural for men or for women differ from the natural temperaments of the men and women among their neighbours. Nevertheless, within a narrower range and with less of a claim for the biological or divine validity of their social forms than we often advance, each tribe has certain definite attitudes towards temperament, a theory of what human beings, either men or women or both, are naturally like, a norm in terms of which to judge and condemn those individuals who deviate from it.

· · ·

The knowledge that the personalities of the two sexes are socially produced is congenial to every programme that looks forward towards a planned order of society. It is a two-edged sword that can be used to hew a more flexible, more varied society than the human race has ever built, or merely to cut a narrow path down which one sex or both sexes will be forced to march, regimented, looking neither to the right nor to the left. . . .

There are at least three courses open to a society that has realized the extent to which male and female personality are socially produced. Two of these courses have been tried before, over and over again, at different times in the long, irregular, repetitious history of the race. The first is to standardize the personality of men and women as clearly contrasting, complementary, and antithetical, and to make every institution in the society congruent with this standardization. If the society declared that women's sole function was motherhood and the teaching and care of young children, it could so arrange matters that every woman who was not physiologically debarred should become a mother and be supported in the exercise of this function. It could abolish the discrepancy between the doctrine that women's place is the home and the number of homes that were offered to them. It could abolish the discrepancy between training women for marriage and then forcing them to become the spinster supports of their parents.

Such a system would be wasteful of the gifts of many women who could exercise other functions far better than their ability to bear children in an already overpopulated world. It would be wasteful of the gifts of many men who could exercise their special personality gifts far better in the home than in the market-place. It would be wasteful, but it would be clear. It could attempt to guarantee to each individual the role for which society insisted upon training him or her, and such a system would penalize only those individuals who, in spite of all the training, did not display the approved personalities. There are millions of persons who would gladly return to such a standardized method of treating the relationship between the sexes, and we must bear in mind the possibility that the greater opportunities open in the twentieth century to women may be quite withdrawn, and that we may return to a strict regimentation of women.

The waste, if this occurs, will be not only of many women, but also of as many men, because regimentation of one sex carries with it, to greater or less degree, the regimentation of the other also. Every parental behest that defines a way of sitting, a response to a rebuke or a threat, a game, or an attempt to draw or sing or dance or paint, as feminine, is moulding the personality of each little girl's brother as well as moulding the personality of the sister. There can be no society which insists that women follow one special personality-pattern, defined as feminine, which does not do violence also to the individuality of many men.

Alternatively, society can take the course that has become especially associated with the plans of most radical groups: admit that men and women are capable of being moulded to a single pattern as easily as to a diverse one, and cease to make any distinction in the approved personality of both sexes. Girls can be trained exactly as boys are trained, taught the

same code, the same forms of expression, the same occupations. This course might seem to be the logic which follows from the conviction that the potentialities which different societies label as either masculine or feminine are really potentialities of some members of each sex, and not sex-linked at all. If this is accepted, is it not reasonable to abandon the kind of artificial standardizations of sex-differences that have been so long characteristic of European society, and admit that they are social fictions for which we have no longer any use? In the world today, contraceptives make it possible for women not to bear children against their will. The most conspicuous actual difference between the sexes, the difference in strength, is progressively less significant. Just as the difference in height between males is no longer a realistic issue, now that lawsuits have been substituted for hand-to-hand encounters, so the difference in strength between men and women is no longer worth elaboration in cultural institutions.

. . .

So in our own society. To insist that there are no sex-differences in a society that has always believed in them and depended upon them may be as subtle a form of standardizing personality as to insist that there are many sex-differences. This is particularly so in a changing tradition, when a group in control is attempting to develop a new social personality, as is the case today in many European countries. Take, for instance, the current assumption that women are more opposed to war than men, that any outspoken approval of war is more horrible, more revolting, in women than in men. Behind this assumption women can work for peace without encountering social criticism in communities that would immediately criticize their brothers or husbands if they took a similarly active part in peace propaganda. This belief that women are naturally more interested in peace is undoubtedly artificial, part of the whole mythology that considers women to be gentler than men. But in contrast let us consider the possibility of a powerful minority that wished to turn a whole society whole-heartedly towards war. One way of doing this would be to insist that women's motives, women's interests, were identical with men's, that women should take as bloodthirsty a delight in preparing for war as ever men do. The insistence upon the opposite point of view, that the woman as a mother prevails over the woman as a citizen at least puts a slight drag upon agitation for war, prevents a blanket enthusiasm for war from being thrust upon the entire younger generation. The same kind of result follows if the clergy are professionally committed to a belief in peace. The relative bellicosity of different individual clerics may be either offended or gratified by the prescribed pacific role, but a certain protest, a certain dissenting note, will be sounded in society. The dangerous standardization of attitudes that disallows every type of deviation is greatly reinforced if neither age nor sex nor religious belief is regarded as automatically predisposing certain individuals to hold minority attitudes. The removal of all legal and economic barriers against women's participating in the world on an equal footing with men may be in itself a standardizing move towards the wholesale stamping-out of the diversity of attitudes that is such a dearly bought product of civilization.

· · ·

Let us suppose that, instead of the classification laid down on the "natural" bases of sex and race, a society had classified personality on the basis of eye-colour. It had decreed that all blue-eyed people were gentle, submissive, and responsive to the needs of others, and all brown-eyed people were arrogant, dominating, self-centred, and purposive. In this case two complementary social themes would be woven together—the culture, in its art, its religion, its formal personal relations, would have two threads instead of one. There would be blue-eyed men, and blue-eyed women, which would mean that there were gentle, "maternal" women, and gentle, "maternal" men. A blue-eyed man might marry a woman who had been bred to the same personality as himself, or a brown-eyed woman who had been bred to the contrasting personality. One of the strong tendencies that makes for homosexuality, the tendency to love the similar rather than the antithetical persons, would be eliminated. Hostility between the two sexes as groups would be minimized, since the individual interests of members of each sex could be woven together in different ways, and marriages of similarity and friendships of contrast need carry no necessary handicap of possible psycho-sexual maladjustment. The individual would still suffer a mutilation of his temperamen-

tal preferences, for it would be the unrelated fact of eye-colour that would determine the attitudes which he was educated to show. Every blue-eyed person would be forced into submissiveness and declared maladjusted if he or she showed any traits that it had been decided were only appropriate to the brown-eyed. The greatest social loss, however, in the classification of personality on the basis of sex would not be present in this society which based its classification on eye-colour. Human relations, and especially those which involve sex, would not be artificially distorted.

But such a course, the substitution of eye-colour for sex as a basis upon which to educate children into groups showing contrasting personalities, while it would be a definite advance upon a classification by sex, remains a parody of all the attempts that society has made through history to define an individual's role in terms of sex, or colour, or date of birth, or shape of head.

However, the only solution of the problem does not lie between an acceptance of standardization of sex-differences with the resulting cost in individual happiness and adjustment, and the abolition of these differences with the consequent loss in social values. A civilization might take its cues not from such categories as age or sex, race or hereditary position in a family line, but instead of specializing personality along such simple lines recognize, train, and make a place for many and divergent temperamental endowments. It might build upon the different potentialities that it now attempts to extirpate artificially in some children and create artificially in others.

· · ·

To break down one line of division, that between the sexes, and substitute another, that between classes, is no real advance. It merely shifts the irrelevancy to a different point. And meanwhile, individuals born in the upper classes are shaped inexorably to one type of personality, to an arrogance that is again uncongenial to at least some of them, while the arrogant among the poor fret and fume beneath their training for submissiveness. At one end of the scale is the mild, unaggressive young son of wealthy parents who is forced to lead, at the other the aggressive, enterprising child of the slums who is condemned to a place in the ranks. If our aim is greater expression for each individual temperament, rather than any partisan interest in one sex or its fate, we must see these historical developments which have aided in freeing some women as nevertheless a kind of development that also involved major social losses.

The second way in which categories of sex-differences have become less rigid is through a recognition of genuine individual gifts as they occurred in either sex. Here a real distinction has been substituted for an artificial one, and the gains are tremendous for society and for the individual. Where writing is accepted as a profession that may be pursued by either sex with perfect suitability, individuals who have the ability to write need not be debarred from it by their sex, nor need they, if they do write, doubt their essential masculinity or femininity. An occupation that has no basis in sex-determined gifts can now recruit its ranks from twice as many potential artists. And it is here that we can find a ground-plan for building a society that would substitute real differences for arbitrary ones. We must recognize that beneath the superficial classifications of sex and race the same potentialities exist, recurring generation after generation, only to perish because society has no place for them. Just as society now permits the practice of an art to members of either sex, so it might also permit the development of many contrasting temperamental gifts in each sex. It might abandon its various attempts to make boys fight and to make girls remain passive, or to make all children fight, and instead shape our educational institutions to develop to the full the boy who shows a capacity for maternal behaviour, the girl who shows an opposite capacity that is stimulated by fighting against obstacles. No skill, no special aptitude, no vividness of imagination or precision of thinking would go unrecognized because the child who possessed it was of one sex rather than the other. No child would be relentlessly shaped to one pattern of behaviour, but instead there should be many patterns, in a world that had learned to allow to each individual the pattern which was most congenial to his gifts.

Such a civilization would not sacrifice the gains of thousands of years during which society has built up standards of diversity. The social gains would be conserved, and each child would be encouraged on the basis of his actual temperament. Where we now

have patterns of behaviour for women and patterns of behaviour for men, we would then have patterns of behaviour that expressed the interests of individuals with many kinds of endowment. There would be ethical codes and social symbolisms, an art and a way of life, congenial to each endowment.

Historically our own culture has relied for the creation of rich and contrasting values upon many artificial distinctions, the most striking of which is sex. It will not be by the mere abolition of these distinctions that society will develop patterns in which individual gifts are given place instead of being forced into an ill-fitting mould. If we are to achieve a richer culture, rich in contrasting values, we must recognize the whole gamut of human potentialities, and so weave a less arbitrary social fabric, one in which each diverse human gift will find a fitting place.

[1935]

 29

From Woman as a Force in History: A Study in Traditions and Realities

MARY RITTER BEARD

THE HAUNTING IDEA: ITS NATURE AND ORIGIN

There is no need for a Sherlock Holmes to serve as a detective in a search for the controlling or influential ideas employed in modern books, articles, reviews, and published addresses dealing with men and women. Even a novice can discover one obtruding conception that haunts thousands of printed pages. It is the image of woman throughout long ages of the past as a being always and everywhere subject to *male* man or as a ghostly creature too shadowy to be even that real.

As for centuries the Ptolemaic conception of the astrophysical universe dominated discussions and "reasonings" in astronomy, so the theory of woman's subjection to man, the obliteration of her personality from consideration, governs innumerable discussions and reasonings in relation to human affairs. Here, there, and almost everywhere, it gives animus, tendency, and opinionative assurance to the man-woman controversies of our day.

There came a time, however, when the Ptolemaic idea of the starry universe was tested by patient observation and study—with the aid of scientific instruments—and declared to be a myth—a false theory. When that decision was made on the basis of more knowledge than Ptolemy possessed, rapid progress in astrophysics occurred and the art of navigating uncharted seas was brought nearer to perfection.

Out of such experiences in the natural sciences has been developed the idea that advancement in other branches of learning can be best effected by the application of what John Morley calls "engines of criticism, skepticism, and verification" to popular theories, even those held by everybody, always, and everywhere. This has become a maxim of modern science and scholarship. So it seems fair to conclude that, if learning about man and woman is to be advanced, these engines of intellectual progress must be applied to the ideas of their relations which have come from times past and are still widely current.

The value of learning lies not in sheer erudition, if there at all. Learning can provide creative guidance for civilization.

In the very nature of things historical, at the beginning of an inquiry into the idea of woman's historic subjection, four questions arise: When did this idea originate? By whom was it originated? In what circumstances was it formulated? Why did it obtain such an empire over human minds? In short, what is its real nature and origin?

Blackstone Extinguished the Married Woman's Personality

It is difficult, admittedly, to trace all the mental processes which converged into the idea that women were a subject sex or nothing at all—in any past or the total past—until they began to win "emancipation" in our age of enlightenment. But, if one works backward in history hunting for the origin of this idea, one encounters, near the middle of the nineteenth century, two illuminating facts: (1) the idea was first given its most complete and categorical form by American women who were in rebellion

against what they regarded as restraints on their liberty; (2) the authority whom they most commonly cited in support of systematic presentations of the idea was Sir William Blackstone, author of *Commentaries on the Laws of England*—the laws of the mother country adopted in part by her offspring in the new world. . . . The first volume of this work appeared in 1765 and the passage from that volume which was used with unfailing reiteration by insurgent women in America was taken from Blackstone's chapter entitled "Of Husband and Wife."

That passage (7th edition, 1775) ran as follows: "By marriage, the husband and wife are one person in law; that is, the very being or legal existence of the woman is suspended during the marriage, or at least is incorporated and consolidated into that of the husband; under whose wing, protection, and *cover,* she performs every thing; . . . Upon this principle, of an union of person in husband and wife, depend almost all the legal rights, duties, and disabilities that either of them acquire by the marriage. . . . A man cannot grant any thing to his wife, or enter into covenant with her, for the grant would be to suppose her separate existence; . . . A woman indeed may be attorney for her husband; for that implies no separation from, but is rather a representation of her lord. And a husband may also bequeath any thing to his wife by will; for that cannot take effect till the coverture is determined by his death. The husband is bound to provide his wife with necessaries by law, as much as himself: and if she contracts debts for them, he is obliged to pay them; but for any thing besides necessaries, he is not chargeable. . . . If the wife be indebted before marriage, the husband is bound afterward to pay the debt; for he has adopted her and her circumstances together. . . .

"The husband also (by the old law) might give his wife moderate correction. For, as he is to answer for her misbehaviour, the law thought it reasonable to intrust him with this power of restraining her, by domestic chastisement. . . . But, with us, in the politer reign of Charles the second, this power of correction began to be doubted: and a wife may now have security of the peace against her husband; or, in return, a husband against his wife. . . .

"These are the chief legal effects of marriage during the coverture; upon which we may observe, that even the disabilities, which the wife lies under, are for the most part intended for her protection and benefit. So great a favourite is the female sex of the laws of England."

It is also a matter of historical record that for nearly a century or more Blackstone's *Commentaries* was a standard textbook for the training of lawyers, particularly in the United States. The work was written with such rhetorical persuasiveness and such display or semblance of learning, that it captivated innumerable students of law. Thomas Jefferson was scarcely exaggerating when he wrote long after the *Commentaries* appeared: "The opinion seems to be that Blackstone is to us what the Alcoran is to the Mahometans, that everything which is necessary is in him, and what is not in him is not necessary."

Whenever an American writer after 1783 was moved to instruct women on what he regarded as their rights and duties, he was almost certain to employ the authority of Blackstone, and likely to associate with the *Commentaries* expositions of divine law. For example, in 1845, eighty years after Blackstone's first volume was published, three years before the first "woman's rights" convention assembled at Seneca Falls in the state of New York, Edward D. Mansfield, A.M., "Late Professor of History in Cincinnati College, Author of the Political Grammar, and Corresponding Member of the National Institute," issued in Ohio a treatise bearing the following arresting title and descriptive subtitle: *"The Legal Rights, Liabilities and Duties of Women;* With an Introductory History of their Legal Condition in the Hebrew, Roman and Feudal Civil Systems. Including the law of marriage and divorce, the social relations of husband and wife, parent and child, of guardian and ward, and of employer and employed." In this work Professor Mansfield summarized his subject so concisely that none could miss his main points: namely, that women were subject to divine law and civil law: "The first great principle of Scripture, the unity of husband and wife, is repeated by the law. They are *in law, one person.* . . . Upon it, as observed by Blackstone, depend nearly all the legal rights, duties and disabilities acquired by marriage."

. . .

Mary Wollstonecraft Reinforces Blackstone

To the vogue of the Blackstonian doctrine, respecting the nothingness of women, Mary Wollstonecraft contributed, perhaps unwittingly. In the midst of the French upheaval, she issued in 1790 a reply to Edmund Burke's strictures—a volume which she entitled *A Vindication of the Rights of Men.* Two years later, in 1792, and twelve years after the death of Blackstone, while the strife over his legal conservatism was raging in England, when the "rights of man" was challenging all restrictions on human freedom, she published her *Vindication of the Rights of Woman.*

In arguing for the rights of woman she made use of the writings of philosophers, moralists, educators, and agitators rather than the works by lawyers. She depended most on Rousseau for the doctrine of "natural" rights. The objects of her special aspersions were customs and opinions, not specific provisions of law affecting women, married and single. She attacked the "*divine right* of husbands," and expressed the hope that it might be contested "without danger." Here she was not speaking of the dominion exercised by Blackstone's "lord" or "baron" over the *feme covert.* Rather she was dealing with mental and emotional attitudes. But in her portrayal of the alleged social tyranny exercised by man over woman, she helped to vitalize the doctrine that married women were civilly dead, members of a subject sex in effect, nothing in history save perhaps obsequious playthings or furtive intriguers trying to make their way out from under man's domination.

In the manipulation of this theory of life one fact is outstanding and immediately germane to all thought about the subject. This fact is that Rousseau who set the Western world aflame with the doctrine of equality and democracy for men also formulated and put into circulation a doctrine claiming that woman should be content to please man and get very little in return. "Woman," he declared in *Émile,* "is expressly formed to please the man: if the obligation be reciprocal also, and the man ought to please in his turn, it is not so immediately necessary: his great merit is in his power, and he pleases merely because he is strong. This, I must confess, is not one of the refined maxims of love; it is, however, one of the laws of nature, prior to love itself. If woman be formed to please and to be subjected to man, it is her place, doubtless, to render herself agreeable to him, instead of challenging his passion. The violence of his desires depends on her charms; it is by means of these she should urge him to the exertion of those powers which nature hath given him."

Yet Rousseau did not deny that woman had power and was a force in history. Nor did he reduce her qualities to those of mere futility. On the contrary, he ascribed to her extraordinary endowments for discernment and judgment. "A woman," he asserted, "who is naturally weak and does not carry her ideas to any great extent, knows how to judge and make a proper estimate of those movements which she set to work, in order to aid her weakness; and those movements are the passions of men. The mechanism she employs is much more powerful than ours, for all her levers move the human heart. She must have the skill to incline us to do everything which her sex will not enable her to do herself, and which is necessary or agreeable to her; therefore she ought to study the mind of man thoroughly, not the mind of man in general, abstractedly, but the dispositions of those men to whom she is subject either by the laws of her country or by the force of opinion. She should learn to penetrate into their real sentiments from their conversation, their actions, their looks and gestures. She should also have the art, by her own conversation, actions, looks, and gestures, to communicate those sentiments which are agreeable to them, without seeming to intend it. Men will argue more philosophically about the human heart; but women will read the heart of men better than they. . . . Women have the most wit, men have most genius; women observe, men reason. From the concurrence of both we derive the clearest light and the most perfect knowledge which the human mind is of itself capable of attaining. . . . The world is the book of woman."

Rousseau's doctrine that woman's duty is to please man fitted neatly, not only with Rousseau's personal egotism but also into the genteel theory respecting woman which was then spreading among the middle classes in England. In short form, this theory maintained that if woman would exercise the faculty of gratifying and deluding men, God or providence would assure to her a good father, a pro-

tective husband, economic security, and freedom from the responsibility of fending for herself in the struggle for existence. To attain this "fortunate" position, woman needs only to practice the arts of apparent submission and actual cunning, and to refrain from challenging man by a resort to learning, the acquisition of worldly knowledge, and the use of reason. If she should willfully leave the sphere thus assigned to her, she would fail to achieve the idea of irresponsible comfort so highly cherished in a bourgeois society.

It was this vision of modesty, or gentility, fortified by the pronouncement of Rousseau, that Mary Wollstonecraft assailed in her *Vindication of the Rights of Woman*. In contending for the rights of woman she appealed to reason, justice, and virtue. She did not inquire how far and in what respects the genteel theory conformed to innumerable known facts about women in contemporary society or in deeper history. Perhaps it never occurred to her to do that. At any rate Mary Wollstonecraft conceded the central point of the genteel theory with these words: "That woman is naturally weak, or degraded by a concurrence of circumstances, is, I think, clear." In effect she took over Rousseau's thesis, and phrased it in her fashion: Woman is everywhere in chains but I propose to show her the road to freedom.

In Wollstonecraft's view, the idea that woman was formed to please man and could govern him by the use of sex charms "is the philosophy of lasciviousness," an offense against virtue, reason, and respectability—against everything that gives dignity and value to human life. The educational ideal of the doctrine, she held, is to deprive girls of the physical exercise necessary to bodily strength, to restrain them in the use of the reason with which they are endowed, to deny them access to the knowledge which belongs of right to human beings and is indispensable to women in the discharge of the responsibilities that fall upon them in actual life. Law, custom, education, and opinion, she contended, sustain this false ideal for woman, force her to regard her subjection as her proper lot in life, and mold her in the image of the tradition. Thus not only is woman subjected to tyranny and degraded, but man is encouraged to cultivate his worst passions and prejudices, to grow in arrogance, and to applaud ignorance.

The genteel business, Wollstonecraft declared, flouts all the virtues that give worth to human character and works against civilization itself. Is not truth the same for men and women? Is not the exercise of reason by women as desirable as the exercise of reason by men? By what just and intelligible principle are women denied free access to knowledge? If freedom is a value, by what right are women deprived of it? "Women," she granted, ". . . may have different duties to fulfill; but they are *human* duties, and the principles that should regulate the discharge of them, I sturdily maintain, must be the same. To become respectable, the exercise of their understanding is necessary; there is no other foundation for independence of character; I mean explicitly to say that they must only bow to the authority of reason, instead of being the *modest* slaves of opinion."

That under the sway of the genteel impulse women could exercise great powers Wollstonecraft did not deny: "Women . . . sometimes boast of their weakness, cunningly obtaining power by playing on the *weakness* of men; and they may well glory in their illicit sway, for, like Turkish bashaws, they have more real power than their masters." But exercising power in this manner is an evidence of degradation: "Virtue is sacrificed to temporary gratifications, and the respectability of life to the triumph of an hour." Thus, in Wollstonecraft's theory, even the very power exercised by women in history—the force in history which she had readily conceded—symbolized their subjection, and it was only by breaking the tyranny of custom and opinion which degraded them that women could escape from the status so assigned to women in history.

Neither a trained psychologist nor a student of history, Mary Wollstonecraft speculated freely in thinking about the relation of men and women. One of the many loose generalizations which stand out conspicuously in her volume reads: "It is wandering from my present subject, perhaps, to make a political remark; but as it was produced naturally by the train of my reflections, I shall not pass it silently over. Standing armies can never consist of resolute robust men; they may be well-disciplined machines, but they will seldom contain men under the influence of strong passions, or with very vigorous faculties; and as for any depth of understanding, I will venture to affirm that it is as rarely to be found in the army as amongst women. And the cause, I maintain, is the same. It may be further observed that officers are also particularly attentive to their persons, fond of dancing, crowded rooms, adventures, and ridicule."

Then in a footnote she asked these questions: "Why should women be censured with petulant acrimony because they seem to have a passion for a scarlet coat? Has not education placed them more on a level with soldiers than any other class of men?"

Going back to the main identification of women with soldiers as "well-disciplined machines," Wollstonecraft averred that in the case of soldiers, "like the *fair* sex, the business of their lives is gallantry; they were taught to please, and they only live to please. Yet they do not lose their rank in the distinction of sexes, for they are still reckoned superior to women, though in what their superiority consists, beyond what I have just mentioned, it is difficult to discover."

Scattered through *Vindication of the Rights of Woman* were innumerable opinions equally preposterous. Yet the boldness of the book, like the experiments in living which the author undertook, attracted attention, friendly and adverse, to this ardent advocate of human "rights." Mary Wollstonecraft's unrepressed thrust at conventions was issued in an American edition at Boston the same year of its publication in England. Her name entered the stream of consciousness in which other names of social rebels floated near the surface or deeper in memory. To this day she is a near-saint of countless feminists, most of whom have probably never read a line of her pamphlet on women critically at least.

Liberals and Socialists Carry the Idea Through Universal History

Although Wollstonecraft's *Vindication* appeared in the United States shortly after publication in England, it attained no very great sale in this country, either then or later. After all, she had left her argument unfinished and had given to women no program of legislation guaranteed to bring about their "emancipation." However that may be, leaders of the woman movement in America formulated their own statement on the subjection of women at Seneca Falls in 1848, in terms more economic and political than Wollstonecraft's effusion and definitely in accord with Blackstone's legal thesis. Subsequent formulations at other women's conventions merely amplified and enlarged upon the Seneca Falls declaration of their historic servitude and their will to independence. And there is good reason for believing that American statements of this kind helped to crystallize insurgent opinion in England along similar lines and to bring the Blackstone creed forcibly to the attention of English feminists and their friends among men as the warrant for adopting the theory of total subjection on which to base a demand for freedom and equality.

At all events the following facts have a distinct bearing on the acceptance in England of the Blackstone formula of subjection as the starting point for the feminist argument. First, Blackstone never acquired in that country the tyranny over the legal mind which he exercised in America; from the very beginning powerful critics, led by Jeremy Bentham, assailed his underlying philosophy with devastating effect and English scholarship made inroads upon the soundness of his treatise in detail. Second, the first great textbook for the English feminist movement, written by John Stuart Mill, in cooperation with his wife, and published in 1869, was entitled *The Subjection of Women* and was based on the acceptance of the Blackstone formula as an irreducible datum applicable not only to married women but to all women. How did Mill happen to choose this title and take this line?

Some pertinent facts may provide the answer. Mill, the economist, political philosopher, and sometime Liberal member of the House of Commons, had long been associated with Harriet Taylor, whom he finally married in 1851. Under the influence of this friend, later his wife, his views on economics and social affairs in general were profoundly modified. As his autobiography discloses, it is also certain that Mrs. Mill was interested in the woman movement in the United States as well as in England; and it is said that the report of an American convention, held in Massachusetts in 1850 for the promotion of women's rights, published by the *New York Tribune* in 1851, "aroused her to active thought

on this question." That very year Mrs. Mill published in the *Westminster Review* a comprehensive article on the convention and on the general subject of women's social and political rights. It is also recorded that John Stuart Mill's *The Subjection of Women* was "thought out and partly written in collaboration with his wife."

In the call for the Massachusetts convention, reference was made to the theory of woman's annihilation and enslavement as Blackstone had expounded it, and it was declared that women were in the "condition of a disabled caste." In her article in the *Westminster Review,* Mrs. Mill declared that "there are indications that the example of America will be followed on this side of the Atlantic," Mr. and Mrs. Mill, in *The Subjection of Women,* certainly followed the American example in taking Blackstone's creed without qualifications and in making it a dogma of history to be accepted by everybody, everywhere, as if established by irrefutable knowledge.

In the first paragraph of the first chapter the premise stands stark: "The principle which regulates the existing social relations between the two sexes [is] the legal subjection of one sex to the other." From that position the argument proceeds: Laws "always begin by recognizing the relations they find already existing between individuals." And what are the real relations of men and women? "In early times the great majority of the male sex were slaves, as well as the whole of the female." In this summary fashion Mill, or the Mills, disposed of the beginnings of civilization. The contemporary subjection of women (in 1869), the argument continued, "is the primitive state of slavery lasting on, through successive mitigations and modifications occasioned by the same causes which have softened the general manners, and brought all human relations more under the control of justice and the influence of humanity." After these generalizations come detailed statements on the status of women in the very terms which Blackstone had employed in the eighteenth century.

Having historicized the Blackstone creed and stripped it of all its qualifications in law and equity, the Mills provided a moral antithesis in the form of women's revolt against their status. Then to perfect the argument the Mills set up the synthesis: The emancipation of women from the tyranny of history can only come by abolishing all the legal signs of this subjection and putting women on a legal equality with men in competition for place, security, and advancement in society.

The Mills conceded that practice did not exactly coincide with the legal theory which they accepted as if true: "I have described the wife's legal position, not her actual treatment. The laws of most countries are far worse than the people who execute them, and many of them are only able to remain laws by being seldom or never carried into effect. If married life were all that it might be expected to be, looking to the laws alone, society would be a hell on earth. Happily there are both feelings and interests which in many men exclude, and in most, greatly temper, the impulses and propensities which lead to tyranny; and of those feelings, the tie which connects a man with his wife affords, in a normal state of things, incomparably the strongest example. The only tie which at all approaches to it, that between him and his children, tends, in all save exceptional cases, to strengthen, instead of conflicting with, the first."

But for feminists of the middle class the Mills' treatise on subjection became the "authority" in respect of woman's status in law, history, and society as the nineteenth century passed its meridian. In the contest to free women from a long list of common-law disabilities and attain enfranchisement, feminists used *The Subjection of Women* as a veritable bible.

The Mills' references to the qualifications induced by practice were easily overlooked by those who read the book or readily forgotten in the urge for agitation and for simplified ideas to be used in popular propaganda. Had Mill not swept them aside himself when he declared that woman's subjection to man had been a fact even if ninety-nine marriages out of a hundred had not been hellish for women? He took E. E. Schwabach's position that the thesis of subjection was confirmed if the hundredth marriage "is a hell and is legalized as a hell." The severe simplification of woman's status into the dogma of her historic subjection was for innumerable feminists in England, the United States, Germany, and other countries a primary source of concepts about their sex in the past.

To the doctrines of Blackstone, American feminists, and the Mills, pertaining to woman in law and history, Marxian Socialists added a revised version near the middle of the nineteenth century. What Blackstone had done for British patricians in respect to law and order, what Wollstonecraft and the Mills had done for the bourgeoisie in respect of manners, law, and history, the Marxists did for the proletariat in their interpretation of woman, law, and history.

In two fundamental respects the Socialist thesis of woman's status differed from that of Wollstonecraft and the Mills. In primitive times, it asserted, women had not been subject to men: they had either governed the community or been equals of men in it. Once dominated or equal, women had been driven, however, into subjection by the appearance of private property and the beginning of capitalism. "The overthrow of mother-right," wrote Friedrich Engels, "was the world-historical downfall of the female sex." Since the subjection of woman has been due to the rise and tyranny of private property, not merely to man's lust of power over woman, it follows, the Socialist thesis concluded, that woman's emancipation lies not in the equal competition of women with men for wealth and employment but in the socialization of the instruments of production and in the provision of employment for all.

This version of woman's historical subjection to man was presented to the German public and indeed, through translations, to the whole modern world by many writers, but first in systematic form by August Bebel, a leader of the German Social Democrats from about 1865 until his death in 1913. Among Bebel's writings on this subject two became classics or bibles for socialists all over the world. The first, *Die Frau und der Sozialismus,* which appeared in 1879, was subsequently revised, republished in fifty-seven German editions by 1926, and translated into all leading languages. The second, *Die Frau in Vergangenheit, Gegenwart und Zukunft,* came out in 1883 and, although it did not have the popularity that marked the career of *Woman and Socialism,* also served to spread the doctrine of women's subjection far and wide among working women who might never have heard of it otherwise.

When the first of Bebel's works on women came out in 1879 bourgeois feminists were stirring in Germany. For their benefit *The Subjection of Women* by the Mills had been translated into German shortly after its publication in 1869 and had quickly gone into a second edition. The Communist Manifesto of 1848 on the contrary had declared: "Differences of age and sex have no longer any distinctive social validity for the working class. All are instruments of labor. . . . The bourgeois sees in his wife a mere instrument of production." The Manifesto had called upon the proletarians of the world to unite and win emancipation through a socialist revolution. It was Bebel's task to formulate the doctrine of subjection and emancipation in the effort to counteract the bourgeois appeal to women made in the name of laissez faire economy.

Bebel's socialistic creed for women employed without question the thesis of woman's historic subjection to man in all the ages since primitive times, ascribed the subjection mainly to the tyrannical features of capitalism, and offered complete emancipation through the overthrow of the capitalist system and the ushering in of the socialist society.

Bebel supported, it is true, the struggle of German women to win the legal and political rights which feminists in general demanded, but in his view woman's "spring into freedom" was to come only with the triumph of the working classes over capitalism. In anticipation of that triumph, he favored the march of women by the millions into industry. Thus, he maintained, women would be freed from the backwardness and submission of the historic, rural, patriarchal family, would become individualized and educated for the revolution, and would be prepared for the universal freedom to be achieved under socialism.

Under the stimulus of this doctrine, women's socialist societies for equal rights were formed in Germany, women were drawn in large numbers into the socialist movement, and publications to advance their interests were launched. As socialist and communist propaganda spread around the world, the doctrine of woman's subjection, her nothingness in history, also spread to the four corners of the earth, affecting the ideas and beliefs of the Orient and coming back in novel versions to the Occident. Thus this world-image of women throughout history became almost universal in its sweep.

Each construct or version of this doctrine fitted into the requirements of some political party or fac-

tion as a convenient instrument of agitation for the vindication of traditions or for the reform or overthrow of social and economic institutions. The doctrine in its totality or special phases of it were utilized in all media of literary expression—polite letters, historical treatises, sociological surveys, economic and political works, and educational philosophy, programs, and critiques. It haunted the dreams of Freudian disciples and incited women to brave police and prison in passionate struggles for equality with their historic "masters."

In the whole intellectual history of human beings there is surely nothing more extraordinary—and fateful—than this dogmatic summarizing of all women's history from antiquity to recent times under the head of "subjection."

[1946]

 30

A Comparative Study: Accentuating the Similarities of the Societal Position of Women and Negroes

FLORYNCE KENNEDY

The similarities of the societal positions of women and Negroes are fundamental rather than superficial. The obvious differences are accentuated by the fact that women are supposed to occupy a privileged position. No such pretense is usually made where the Negro is concerned, but a dispassionate consideration of the economic, sociological, historical, psychological, political, and even physiological aspects reveals some rather startling parallels.

The majority of both groups are generally dependent economically upon the dominant group. Great lengths are attained to insure these dependencies. The necessity for an F.E.P.C. (Fair Employment Practices Committee) in a "Democracy," and support clauses in divorce codes, which according to Hobhouse existed in pre-Christian societies, and which Monica Hunter, Naomi M. Griffen, Ruth Benedict, and Cora Du Bois refer to in their accounts of various primitive societies, may be accepted as proof of the excessive abuses prevalent.

More than any other aspect of culture, the economic factor determines cultural development and direction. The political and social implications of this fact are infinite. It is therefore of primary importance to examine carefully the means by which women as a group and Negroes as a group are rendered *hors de combat* by being deprived of economic equality and independence. The far-reaching effects of their economic incompetencies leave not the minutest detail of their lives unaffected.

Women and Negroes are less apt to be hired and more apt to be fired than a similarly equipped member of the currently dominant group. Exceptions are made for extraordinary competence or during emergencies such as wartime or political revolutions. Both women and Negroes command lower wages, and are usually confined to lower-bracket positions.

In times of economic stress working women and Negroes arouse the resentment of those of the dominant group who are unemployed. Thus a returned serviceman may be especially upset to find his job occupied by a woman or Negro. With entering into a which-came-first-the-chicken-or-the-egg argument, it seems sufficient to point out that rivalry for jobs provides a source of serious friction.

Industry frequently adds insult to injury by exploiting the subordinate group to lower wage scales or break strikes. A dual purpose is served, since this divide-and-rule technique further alienates society from those women or Negroes thus exploited. It goes without saying that the disdain is directed not at the employer but at the tool.

Both groups are barred from many specialized fields. Prestige of a position tends to decline upon their entrance. The withholding of training and education precludes development of potentialities. Exclusion from intimate situations where powerful combines are made places a definite barrier in their path. Even those women or Negroes who have attained some prominence in a preferential field are only tolerated in exclusive clubs, at banquets, or on golf courses with equally distinguished members of the dominant group. In the isolated instance where such chummy relationships prevail, the adoption of patronage and subtle condescension saves the day for the dominants.

The preeminence of those exceptional among the weaker group is paradoxically viewed. Many conflicting theories and realizations are encountered: "Determination will win" . . . "The majority (e.g., of women or Negroes) are inferior; these are the exceptions that prove the rule" . . . (bosh) . . . "This woman has a masculine mind" . . . or . . . "This Negro has white blood" . . . what "Negro" hasn't? . . . "Women are getting all the best jobs" . . . "Negroes are 'taking over' the theatre" . . .

This magnifying of hard-won advancement makes it seem that a weak gnarled tree that pushes through the concrete in Brooklyn is a threat to miles of centuries-old forests which have flourished in fertile lands where the best of expert care has been lavished.

How are subordinate groups kept in subordination? Is their suppression a reflection of the will of all of the dominants? Do those who are submerged struggle to reach the level of their "betters"? If not, why not? How, if at all, are the submerged groups rewarded? How punished? Why do not the "superiors" crush them entirely? Women are much loved; Negroes are generally ignored, distrusted, pitied, or even disliked; do not these differences make any attempt to draw parallels seem a bit ridiculous? . . .

The psychological implications are vastly important in any consideration of personal-social relationships. The geographical, temperamental, financial, political, social, psychological, physiological, and historical are but a few of the most abstract factors which enter into every formula. For example: a customer is asking for a pound of butter . . . Alabama or New York? . . . Humbly or peremptorily? . . . Mink coat or Union Square special? . . . New Deal and O.P.A. or Republicans and "free enterprise"? . . . Does the butcher read *P.M.* or the *Daily News*? Is he young or old? . . . a Coughlin-Bilbo fan or Henry Wallace devotee? . . . All generalizations ignore these variables. . . .

Social sanctions take many forms. There are written laws governing franchise, property, political participation, and legal articulation. Social legislation reflects the comparative insignificance of women and Negroes. Educational budgets and medical care for Negroes or women have long been unequal. In housing, Negro districts are invariably slumlike. The kitchen where the average housewife spends the majority of her time is often the least spacious, attractive, comfortable, or even practical room of the house. Overwork is the lot of most of the members of the subordinate groups. When their health suffers due to this insanitary environment, their poor health immediately becomes the "reason" for their exclusion from desirable endeavor or choice programs. . . .

The unwritten laws are often more convenient and certainly more difficult to combat. Some are rational; most are nonrational or irrational. Many paradoxes and inconsistencies exist. There are great discrepancies between theory and practice.

Nonsupport cases belie the exaltation of motherhood so often heard. Societal penalties and punishments are more severe for sex "transgressions" by women or Negroes. Both are regarded as evil and dangerous. The Christian and other religious influences, and the white southerner, are but two sources from which such ideas have come. Overemphasis of the potency of women and Negroes in personal-societal relations serves to place an almost insurmountable barrier between these groups whenever it is advantageous. Sex taboos do not prevent miscegenation, but usually guarantee secrecy and therefore minimize the possibilities for legalized union and familial solidarity. There's no denying that sex drives are frequently far more democratic than contemporary societal pretence.

Paradoxically, criminal action by women or Negroes may be approached with extraordinary leniency; depending upon the offense, a paternal we-don't-expect-much-of-you attitude is frequently encountered. A Negro who cohabits with a white southern woman is almost certainly doomed to die; a Negro who kills another Negro in a brawl may be rescued by his white employer. In rare conformance with the theory that they are the weaker sex, women may receive preferential treatment in criminal courts.

Indeed, so numerous are the devices employed to delineate and emphasize the desired role that it is difficult to account for the many digressions that exist. Fiction and nonfiction, movies (with silly Billy Burke and groveling Ingrid Bergman, shuffling Stepin Fetchit, and Mammy Louise Beavers as "typical" women and Negroes), radio, drama, myths and legends, gossip and rumor, implication and innuendo leave little to the average imagination as to what is acceptable to "society."

A passive woman or Negro is presented with a ready-made role. Choice may be made from a wide range of conceptualizations which are considered ideal and/or average. Individual distinctions are minimized. Accomplishment outside circumscribed areas is discouraged.

Clothing is designed to accentuate the societal roles which have been chosen for the weaker group. Any concerted attempted to emulate or imitate the dominant group in dress is frowned upon—or laughed at. Women in slacks or a well-dressed Negro in a small southern town may be subjected to numerous embarrassments.

Religious participation is encouraged. Futile, blind alley endeavor is sponsored. Docility, forbearance, reticence, faithfulness, blind loyalty, silent suffering, acceptance of the *status quo,* and recognition of the divine right of the dominants are dramatized and applauded by society. Eager for status, the subordinate group accepts the role assigned by the powers-that-be. *Hence comes the irony.*

The subordinates become the enthusiastic sponsors of the campaign for their own suppression!

Endless complexity results from the fact that the majority of a subordinate group, though rejecting the ignominious position, will accept and popularize the devices through which the suppression is maintained. . . .

Thus, the longer the history of an inferior position, the greater the necessity for a break with tradition. Little effort is required by either group to further the submergence of those chosen, once religion and the prescribed pattern are accepted. The program becomes self-perpetuating. The desire to be identified with the dominant group results in the least significant of the societal underlings becoming the unpaid guardians and champions of their exploiters' theories.

Rewards for conformance are spurious or superficial. Security and independence for the entire group are never expected or offered without a death struggle. The inevitability of the societal position is accepted by many of the most militant opposers to inequality.

Reforms are usually much too little and centuries too late. Reforms are at best not the result of intellectual conviction but of emotional effort. The recognitions of rights are considered concessions; sentimental reasons are offered to explain long-overdue justices. Progress results from struggle. Little fundamental change can be cited. Superficial progress has been merely a shifting of emphasis rather than an alteration of balance. Progress has seemed to some extent related to societal advancement.

Women and Negroes are but two of hundreds of groups within groups which occupy subordinate positions.

Foremost authorities to the contrary notwithstanding, I am convinced that the glorification—without qualification—of family life militates against the achievement of full equality for women. It would be interesting to see how many marriages would result without the church, *True Stories,* Myrna Loy, sex myths, and the *Ladies' Home Journal.* It would be more interesting to see how many monogamous marriages would endure if polygamy were legalized and popularized, and children's support were guaranteed by the states.

If women weren't coaxed and lured from industry and professions by societal cupids, those who are unsuited to marriage and breeding could direct their energies into other channels. Without pleading a case for a doctrine of individualism, it would seem that a recognition of the infinite variations among women and Negroes will lessen the occurrence of the every-girl-should-marry, women's-place-is-in-the-home philosophy as well as the more diabolical but no less effective keep-the-Negro-in-his-place attitude. Few societies at any cultural level provide for an acceptance of

an independent life for large numbers of unmarried women. Emancipation for women and Negroes would seem to be contingent upon the emancipation of societal thought. This is, of course, question-begging at its worst, since there remains to be solved the problem of how to revolutionize the theories and thinking of "civilized" society.

If a study of this type has any value, it lies in the possible counteraction to the divide-and-rule technique which minority dominants invariably employ. Recognition of the similarity of their position can hasten the formation of alliances to combat the forces which advocate the suppression of many for the aggrandizement of the few.

The continuation of conscious or unconscious subordination of one group by another will hasten the coarsening of the moral fibre of society. Psychological maladjustments result from the difficulty of reconciling pretense with practice. Personal-social behavior is cramped when societal sanctions and taboos are at too great variance with logic and humanitarian proclivities.

Societal impoverishment inevitably results from policies of discrimination, segregation, and limitation. That such policies are absolutely necessary disproves the much-publicized contention that women and/or Negroes are "naturally" inferior. Bitterness and societal unrest arise out of attempts to exclude women and Negroes from full participation in societal endeavor.

No amount of segregation separates one unit of society from society as a whole. Thus, general societal health is ever contingent upon the health of its least significant member.

Exclusivistic tendencies deprive society of innumerable skills and contributions. The dissatisfied minorities within the subordinate groups provide an ever-present threat to societal peace. Need it again be necessary to call the attention of those who defend the *status quo* to the fact that it has never been a question of whether or not a subordinate group is capable of self-rule and equal right, but rather whether or not any group is worthy of the right to dominance and autocracy?

[1946]

31

From The Second Sex

SIMONE DE BEAUVOIR

INTRODUCTION

For a long time I have hesitated to write a book on woman. The subject is irritating, especially to women; and it is not new. Enough ink has been spilled in the quarreling over feminism, now practically over, and perhaps we should say no more about it. It is still talked about, however, for the voluminous nonsense uttered during the last century seems to have done little to illuminate the problem. After all, is there a problem? And if so, what is it? Are there women, really? Most assuredly the theory of the eternal feminine still has its adherents who will whisper in your ear: "Even in Russia women still are *women*"; and other erudite persons—sometimes the very same—say with a sigh: "Woman is losing her way, woman is lost." One wonders if women still exist, if they will always exist, whether or not it is desirable that they should, what place they occupy in this world, what their place should be. "What has become of women?" was asked recently in an ephemeral magazine.[1]

But first we must ask: what is a woman? *"Tota mulier in utero,"* says one, "woman is a womb." But in speaking of certain women, connoisseurs declare that they are not women, although they are equipped with a uterus like the rest. All agree in recognizing the fact that females exist in the human species; today as always they make up about one half of humanity. And yet we are told that femininity is in danger; we are exhorted to be women, remain women, become women. It would appear, then, that every female human being is not necessarily a woman; to be so considered she must share in that mysterious and threatened reality known as femininity. Is this attribute something secreted by the ovaries? Or is it a Platonic essence, a product of the philosophic imagination? Is a rustling petticoat enough to bring it down to earth? Although some women try zealously to incarnate this essence, it is hardly patentable. It is frequently described in vague and dazzling terms that seem to have been borrowed from the vocabulary of the seers, and indeed in the times of St. Thomas it was considered an essence as certainly defined as the somniferous virtue of the poppy.

But conceptualism has lost ground. The biological and social sciences no longer admit the existence of unchangeably fixed entities that determine given characteristics, such as those ascribed to woman, the Jew, or the Negro. Science regards any characteristic as a reaction dependent in part upon a *situation.* If today femininity no longer exists, then it never existed. But does the word *woman,* then, have no specific content? This is stoutly affirmed by those who hold to the philosophy of the enlightenment, of rationalism, of nominalism; women, to them, are merely the human beings arbitrarily designated by the word *woman.* Many American women particularly are prepared to think that there is no longer any place for woman as such; if a backward individual still takes herself for a woman, her friends advise her to be psychoanalyzed and thus get rid of this obsession. In regard to a work, *Modern Woman: The Lost Sex,* which in other respects has its irritating features, Dorothy Parker has written: "I cannot be just to books which treat of woman as woman. . . . My idea is that all of us, men as well as women, should be regarded as human beings." But nominalism is a rather inadequate doctrine, and the antifeminists have had no trouble in showing that women simply *are not* men. Surely woman is, like man, a human being; but such a declaration is abstract. The fact is that every concrete human being is always a singular, separate individual. To decline to accept such notions as the eternal feminine, the black soul, the Jewish character, is not to deny that Jews, Negroes, women exist today—this denial does not represent a liberation for those concerned, but rather a flight from reality. Some years ago a well-known woman writer refused to permit her portrait to appear in a series of photographs especially devoted to women writers; she wished to be counted among the men. But in order to gain this privilege she made use of her husband's influence! Women who assert that they are men lay claim none the less to masculine consideration and respect. I recall also a young Trotskyite standing on a platform at a boisterous meeting and getting ready to use her fists, in spite of her evident fragility. She was denying her feminine weakness; but it was for love of a militant male whose equal she wished to be. The attitude of defiance of many American women proves that they are haunted by a sense of their femininity. In truth, to go for a walk with one's eyes open is enough to demonstrate that humanity is divided into two classes of individuals whose clothes, faces, bodies, smiles, gaits, interests, and occupations are manifestly different. Perhaps these differences are superficial, perhaps they are destined to disappear. What is certain is that right now they do most obviously exist.

If her functioning as a female is not enough to define woman, if we decline also to explain her through "the eternal feminine," and if nevertheless we admit, provisionally, that women do exist, then we must face the question: what is a woman?

To state the question is, to me, to suggest, at once, a preliminary answer. The fact that I ask it is in itself significant. A man would never get the notion of writing a book on the peculiar situation of the human male.[2] But if I wish to define myself, I must first of all say: "I am a woman"; on this truth must be based all further discussion. A man never begins by presenting himself as an individual of a certain sex; it goes without saying that he is a man. The terms *masculine* and *feminine* are used symmetrically only as a matter of form, as on legal papers. In actuality the relation of the two sexes is not quite like that of two electrical poles, for man represents both the positive and the neutral, as is indicated by the common use of *man* to designate human beings in general; whereas woman represents only the negative, defined by limiting criteria, without reciprocity. In the midst of an abstract discussion it is vexing to hear a man say: "You think thus and so because you are a woman"; but I know that my only defense is to reply: "I think thus and so because it is true," thereby removing my subjective self from the argument. It would be out of the question to reply: "And you think the contrary because you are a man," for it is understood that the fact of being a man is no peculiarity. A man is in the right in being a man; it is the woman who is in the wrong. It amounts to this: just as for the ancients there was an absolute vertical with reference to which the oblique was

defined, so there is an absolute human type, the masculine. Woman has ovaries, a uterus; these peculiarities imprison her in her subjectivity, circumscribe her within the limits of her own nature. It is often said that she thinks with her glands. Man superbly ignores the fact that his anatomy also includes glands, such as the testicles, and that they secrete hormones. He thinks of his body as a direct and normal connection with the world, which he believes he apprehends objectively, whereas he regards the body of woman as a hindrance, a prison, weighed down by everything peculiar to it. "The female is a female by virtue of a certain *lack* of qualities," said Aristotle; "we should regard the female nature as afflicted with a natural defectiveness." And St. Thomas for his part pronounced woman to be an "imperfect man," an "incidental" being. This is symbolized in Genesis where Eve is depicted as made from what Bossuet called "a supernumerary bone" of Adam.

Thus humanity is male and man defines woman not in herself but as relative to him; she is not regarded as an autonomous being. Michelet writes: "Woman, the relative being. . . ." And Benda is most positive in his *Rapport d' Uriel:* "The body of man makes sense in itself quite apart from that of woman, whereas the latter seems wanting in significance by itself. . . . Man can think of himself without woman. She cannot think of herself without man." And she is simply what man decrees; thus she is called "the sex," by which is meant that she appears essentially to the male as a sexual being. For him she is sex—absolute sex, no less. She is defined and differentiated with reference to man and not he with reference to her; she is the incidental, the inessential as opposed to the essential. He is the Subject, he is the Absolute—she is the Other.[3]

The category of the *Other* is as primordial as consciousness itself. In the most primitive societies, in the most ancient mythologies, one finds the expression of a duality—that of the Self and the Other. This duality was not originally attached to the division of the sexes; it was not dependent upon any empirical facts. It is revealed in such works as that of Granet on Chinese thought and those of Dumézil on the East Indies and Rome. The feminine element was at first no more involved in such pairs as Varuna-Mitra, Uranus-Zeus, Sun-Moon, and Day-

Night than it was in the contrasts between Good and Evil, lucky and unlucky auspices, right and left, God and Lucifer. Otherness is a fundamental category of human thought.

Thus it is that no group ever sets itself up as the One without at once setting up the Other over against itself. If three travelers chance to occupy the same compartment, that is enough to make vaguely hostile "others" out of all the rest of the passengers on the train. In small-town eyes all persons not belonging to the village are "strangers" and suspect; to the native of a country all who inhabit other countries are "foreigners"; Jews are "different" for the anti-Semite, Negroes are "inferior" for American racists, aborigines are "natives" for colonists, proletarians are the "lower class" for the privileged.

Lévi-Strauss, at the end of a profound work on the various forms of primitive societies, reaches the following conclusion: "Passage from the state of Nature to the state of Culture is marked by man's ability to view biological relations as a series of contrasts; duality, alternation, opposition, and symmetry, whether under definite or vague forms, constitute not so much phenomena to be explained as fundamental and immediately given data of social reality."[4] These phenomena would be incomprehensible if in fact human society were simply a *Mitsein* or fellowship based on solidarity and friendliness. Things become clear, on the contrary, if, following Hegel, we find in consciousness itself a fundamental hostility toward every other consciousness; the subject can be posed only in being opposed—he sets himself up as the essential, as opposed to the other, the inessential, the object.

But the other consciousness, the other ego, sets up a reciprocal claim. The native traveling abroad is shocked to find himself in turn regarded as a "stranger" by the natives of neighboring countries. As a matter of fact, wars, festivals, trading, treaties, and contests among tribes, nations, and classes tend to deprive the concept *Other* of its absolute sense and to make manifest its relativity; willy-nilly, individuals and groups are forced to realize the reciprocity of their relations. How is it, then, that this reciprocity has not been recognized between the sexes, that one of the contrasting terms is set up as the sole essential, denying any relativity in regard to its correlative and defining the latter as pure other-

ness? Why is it that women do not dispute male sovereignty? No subject will readily volunteer to become the object, the inessential; it is not the Other who, in defining himself as the Other, establishes the One. The Other is posed as such by the One in defining himself as the One. But if the Other is not to regain the status of being the One, he must be submissive enough to accept this alien point of view. Whence comes this submission in the case of woman?

There are, to be sure, other cases in which a certain category has been able to dominate another completely for a time. Very often this privilege depends upon inequality of numbers—the majority imposes its rule upon the minority or persecutes it. But women are not a minority, like the American Negroes or the Jews; there are as many women as men on earth. Again, the two groups concerned have often been originally independent; they may have been formerly unaware of each other's existence, or perhaps they recognized each other's autonomy. But a historical event has resulted in the subjugation of the weaker by the stronger. The scattering of the Jews, the introduction of slavery into America, the conquests of imperialism are examples in point. In these cases the oppressed retained at least the memory of former days; they possessed in common a past, a tradition, sometimes a religion or a culture.

The parallel drawn by Bebel between women and the proletariat is valid in that neither ever formed a minority or a separate collective unit of mankind. And instead of a single historical event it is in both cases a historical development that explains their status as a class and accounts for the membership of *particular individuals* in that class. But proletarians have not always existed, whereas there have always been women. They are women in virtue of their anatomy and physiology. Throughout history they have always been subordinated to men,[5] and hence their dependency is not the result of a historical event or a social change—it was not something that *occurred*. The reason why otherness in this case seems to be an absolute is in part that it lacks the contingent or incidental nature of historical facts. A condition brought about at a certain time can be abolished at some other time, as the Negroes of Haiti and others have proved; but it might seem that a natural condition is beyond the possibility of change. In truth, however, the nature of things is no more immutably given, once for all, than is historical reality. If woman seems to be the inessential which never becomes the essential, it is because she herself fails to bring about this change. Proletarians say "We"; Negroes also. Regarding themselves as subjects, they transform the bourgeois, the whites, into "others." But women do not say "We," except at some congress of feminists or similar formal demonstration; men say "women," and women use the same word in referring to themselves. They do not authentically assume a subjective attitude. The proletarians have accomplished the revolution in Russia, the Negroes in Haiti, the Indo-Chinese are battling for it in Indo-China; but the women's effort has never been anything more than a symbolic agitation. They have gained only what men have been willing to grant; they have taken nothing, they have only received.[6]

The reason for this is that women lack concrete means for organizing themselves into a unit which can stand face to face with the correlative unit. They have no past, no history, no religion of their own; and they have no such solidarity of work and interest as that of the proletariat. They are not even promiscuously herded together in the way that creates community feeling among the American Negroes, the ghetto Jews, the workers of Saint-Denis, or the factory hands of Renault. They live dispersed among the males, attached through residence, housework, economic condition, and social standing to certain men—fathers or husbands—more firmly than they are to other women. If they belong to the bourgeoisie, they feel solidarity with men of that class, not with proletarian women; if they are white, their allegiance is to white men, not to Negro women. The proletariat can propose to massacre the ruling class, and a sufficiently fanatical Jew or Negro might dream of getting sole possession of the atomic bomb and making humanity wholly Jewish or black; but woman cannot even dream of exterminating the males. The bond that unites her to her oppressors is not comparable to any other. The division of the sexes is a biological fact, not an event in human history. Male and female stand opposed within a primordial *Mitsein*, and woman has not broken it. The

couple is a fundamental unity with its two halves riveted together, and the cleavage of society along the line of sex is impossible. Here is to be found the basic trait of woman: she is the Other in a totality of which the two components are necessary to one another.

One could suppose that this reciprocity might have facilitated the liberation of woman. When Hercules sat at the feet of Omphale and helped with her spinning, his desire for her held him captive; but why did she fail to gain a lasting power? To revenge herself on Jason, Medea killed their children; and this grim legend would seem to suggest that she might have obtained a formidable influence over him through his love for his offspring. In *Lysistrata* Aristophanes gaily depicts a band of women who joined forces to gain social ends through the sexual needs of their men; but this is only a play. In the legend of the Sabine women, the latter soon abandoned their plan of remaining sterile to punish their ravishers. In truth woman has not been socially emancipated through man's need—sexual desire and the desire for offspring—which makes the male dependent for satisfaction upon the female.

Master and slave, also, are united by a reciprocal need, in this case economic, which does not liberate the slave. In the relation of master to slave the master does not make a point of the need that he has for the other; he has in his grasp the power of satisfying this need through his own action; whereas the slave, in his dependent condition, his hope and fear, is quite conscious of the need he has for his master. Even if the need is at bottom equally urgent for both, it always works in favor of the oppressor and against the oppressed. That is why the liberation of the working class, for example, has been slow.

Now, woman has always been man's dependent, if not his slave; the two sexes have never shared the world in equality. And even today woman is heavily handicapped, though her situation is beginning to change. Almost nowhere is her legal status the same as man's,[7] and frequently it is much to her disadvantage. Even when her rights are legally recognized in the abstract, long-standing custom prevents their full expression in the mores. In the economic sphere men and women can almost be said to make up two castes; other things being equal, the former hold the better jobs, get higher wages, and have more opportunity for success than their new competitors. In industry and politics men have a great many more positions and they monopolize the most important posts. In addition to all this, they enjoy a traditional prestige that the education of children tends in every way to support, for the present enshrines the past—and in the past all history has been made by men. At the present time, when women are beginning to take part in the affairs of the world, it is still a world that belongs to men—they have no doubt of it at all and women have scarcely any. To decline to be the Other, to refuse to be a party to the deal—this would be for women to renounce all the advantages conferred upon them by their alliance with the superior caste. Man-the-sovereign will provide woman-the-liege with material protection and will undertake the moral justification of her existence; thus she can evade at once both economic risk and the metaphysical risk of a liberty in which ends and aims must be contrived without assistance. Indeed, along with the ethical urge of each individual to affirm his subjective existence, there is also the temptation to forgo liberty and become a thing. This is an inauspicious road, for he who takes it—passive, lost, ruined—becomes henceforth the creature of another's will, frustrated in his transcendence and deprived of every value. But it is an easy road; on it one avoids the strain involved in undertaking an authentic existence. When man makes of woman the *Other,* he may, then, expect her to manifest deep-seated tendencies toward complicity. Thus, woman may fail to lay claim to the status of subject because she lacks definite resources, because she feels the necessary bond that ties her to man regardless of reciprocity, and because she is often very well pleased with her role as the *Other.*

But it will be asked at once: how did all this begin? It is easy to see that the duality of the sexes, like any duality, gives rise to conflict. And doubtless the winner will assume the status of absolute. But why should man have won from the start? It seems possible that women could have won the victory; or that the outcome of the conflict might never have been decided. How is it that this world has always belonged to the men and that things have begun to change only recently? Is this change a good thing?

Will it bring about an equal sharing of the world between men and women?

These questions are not new, and they have often been answered. But the very fact that woman *is the Other* tends to cast suspicion upon all the justifications that men have ever been able to provide for it. These have all too evidently been dictated by men's interest. A little-known feminist of the seventeenth century, Poulain de la Barre, put it this way: "All that has been written about women by men should be suspect, for the men are at once judge and party to the lawsuit." Everywhere, at all times, the males have displayed their satisfaction in feeling that they are the lords of creation. "Blessed be God . . . that He did not make me a woman," say the Jews in their morning prayers, while their wives pray a note of resignation: "Blessed be the Lord, who created me according to His will." The first among the blessings for which Plato thanked the gods was that he had been created free, not enslaved; the second, a man, not a woman. But the males could not enjoy this privilege fully unless they believed it to be founded on the absolute and the eternal; they sought to make the fact of their supremacy into a right. "Being men, those who have made and compiled the laws have favored their own sex, and jurists have elevated these laws into principles," to quote Poulain de la Barre once more.

Legislators, priests, philosophers, writers, and scientists have striven to show that the subordinate position of woman is willed in heaven and advantageous on earth. The religions invented by men reflect this wish for domination. In the legends of Eve and Pandora men have taken up arms against women. They have made use of philosophy and theology, as the quotations from Aristotle and St. Thomas have shown. Since ancient times satirists and moralists have delighted in showing up the weaknesses of women. We are familiar with the savage indictments hurled against women throughout French literature. Montherlant, for example, follows the tradition of Jean de Meung, though with less gusto. This hostility may at times be well founded, often it is gratuitous; but in truth it more or less successfully conceals a desire for self-justification. As Montaigne says, "It is easier to accuse one sex than to excuse the other." Sometimes what is going on is clear enough. For instance, the Roman law limiting the rights of woman cited "the imbecility, the instability of the sex" just when the weakening of family ties seemed to threaten the interests of male heirs. And in the effort to keep the married woman under guardianship, appeal was made in the sixteenth century to the authority of St. Augustine, who declared that "woman is a creature neither decisive nor constant," at a time when the single woman was thought capable of managing her property. Montaigne understood clearly how arbitrary and unjust was woman's appointed lot: "Women are not in the wrong when they decline to accept the rules laid down for them, since the men make these rules without consulting them. No wonder intrigue and strife abound." But he did not go so far as to champion their cause.

It was only later, in the eighteenth century, that genuinely democratic men began to view the matter objectively. Diderot, among others, strove to show that woman is, like man, a human being. Later John Stuart Mill came fervently to her defense. But these philosophers displayed unusual impartiality. In the nineteenth century the feminist quarrel became again a quarrel of partisans. One of the consequences of the industrial revolution was the entrance of women into productive labor, and it was just here that the claims of the feminists emerged from the realm of theory and acquired an economic basis, while their opponents became the more aggressive. Although landed property lost power to some extent, the bourgeoisie clung to the old morality that found the guarantee of private property in the solidity of the family. Woman was ordered back into the home the more harshly as her emanciaption became a real menace. Even within the working class the men endeavored to restrain woman's liberation, because they began to see the women as dangerous competitors—the more so because they were accustomed to work for lower wages.[8]

In proving woman's inferiority, the antifeminists then began to draw not only upon religion, philosophy, and theology, as before, but also upon science—biology, experimental psychology, etc. At most they were willing to grant "equality in difference" to the *other* sex. That profitable formula is most significant; it is precisely like the "equal but separate" formula of the Jim Crow laws aimed at the North American Negroes. As is well known, this so-called equalitarian segregation has resulted only in

the most extreme discrimination. The similarity just noted is in no way due to chance, for whether it is a race, a caste, a class, or a sex that is reduced to a position of inferiority, the methods of justification are the same. "The eternal feminine" corresponds to "the black soul" and to "the Jewish character." True, the Jewish problem is on the whole very different from the other two—to the anti-Semite the Jew is not so much an inferior as he is an enemy for whom there is to be granted no place on earth, for whom annihilation is the fate desired. But there are deep similarities between the situation of woman and that of the Negro. Both are being emancipated today from a like paternalism, and the former master class wishes to "keep them in their place"— that is, the place chosen for them. In both cases the former masters lavish more or less sincere eulogies, either on the virtues of "the good Negro" with his dormant, childish, merry soul—the submissive Negro—or on the merits of the woman who is "truly feminine"—that is, frivolous, infantile, irresponsible—the submissive woman. In both cases the dominant class bases its argument on a state of affairs that it has itself created. As George Bernard Shaw puts it, in substance, "The American white relegates the black to the rank of shoeshine boy; and he concludes from this that the black is good for nothing but shining shoes." This vicious circle is met with in all analogous circumstances; when an individual (or a group of individuals) is kept in a situation of inferiority, the fact is that he *is* inferior. But the significance of the verb *to be* must be rightly understood here; it is in bad faith to give it a static value when it really has the dynamic Hegelian sense of "to have become." Yes, women on the whole *are* today inferior to men; that is, their situation affords them fewer possibilities. The question is: should that state of affairs continue?

Many men hope that it will continue; not all have given up the battle. The conservative bourgeoisie still see in the emancipation of women a menace to their morality and their interests. Some men dread feminine competition. Recently a male student wrote in the *Hebdo-Latin:* "Every woman student who goes into medicine or law robs us of a job." He never questioned his rights in this world. And economic interests are not the only ones concerned. One of the benefits that oppression confers upon the oppressors is that the most humble among them is made to *feel* superior; thus, a "poor white" in the South can console himself with the thought that he is not a "dirty nigger"—and the more prosperous whites cleverly exploit this pride.

Similarly, the most mediocre of males feels himself a demigod as compared with women. It was much easier for M. de Montherlant to think himself a hero when he faced women (and women chosen for his purpose) than when he was obliged to act the man among men—something many women have done better than he, for that matter. And in September 1948, in one of his articles in the *Figaro littéraire*, Claude Mauriac—whose great originality is admired by all—could[9] write regarding woman: "*We* listen on a tone [*sic!*] of polite indifference . . . to the most brilliant among them, well knowing that her wit reflects more or less luminously ideas that come from *us*." Evidently the speaker referred to is not reflecting the ideas of Mauriac himself, for no one knows of his having any. It may be that she reflects ideas originating with men, but then, even among men there are those who have been known to appropriate ideas not their own; and one can well ask whether Claude Mauriac might not find more interesting a conversation reflecting Descartes, Marx, or Gide rather than himself. What is really remarkable is that by using the questionable *we* he identifies himself with St. Paul, Hegel, Lenin, and Nietzsche, and from the lofty eminence of their grandeur looks down disdainfully upon the bevy of women who make bold to converse with him on a footing of equality. In truth, I know of more than one woman who would refuse to suffer with patience Mauriac's "tone of polite indifference."

I have lingered on this example because the masculine attitude is here displayed with disarming ingenuousness. But men profit in many more subtle ways from the otherness, the alterity of woman. Here is miraculous balm for those afflicted with an inferiority complex, and indeed no one is more arrogant toward women, more aggressive or scornful, than the man who is anxious about his virility. Those who are not fear-ridden in the presence of their fellow men are much more disposed to recognize a fellow creature in woman; but even to these the myth of woman, the Other, is precious for many reasons.[10] They cannot be blamed for not cheerfully

relinquishing all the benefits they derive from the myth, for they realize what they would lose in relinquishing woman as they fancy her to be, while they fail to realize what they have to gain from the woman of tomorrow. Refusal to pose oneself as the Subject, unique and absolute, requires great self-denial. Furthermore, the vast majority of men make no such claim explicitly. They do not *postulate* woman as inferior, for today they are too thoroughly imbued with the ideal of democracy not to recognize all human beings as equals.

In the bosom of the family, woman seems in the eyes of childhood and youth to be clothed in the same social dignity as the adult males. Later on, the young man, desiring and loving, experiences the resistance, the independence of the woman desired and loved; in marriage, he respects woman as wife and mother, and in the concrete events of conjugal life she stands there before him as a free being. He can therefore feel that social subordination as between the sexes no longer exists and that on the whole, in spite of differences, woman is an equal. As, however, he observes some points of inferiority—the most important being unfitness for the professions—he attributes these to natural causes. When he is in a co-operative and benevolent relation with woman, his theme is the principle of abstract equality, and he does not base his attitude upon such inequality as may exist. But when he is in conflict with her, the situation is reversed: his theme will be the existing inequality, and he will even take it as justification for denying abstract equality.[11]

So it is that many men will affirm as if in good faith that women *are* the equals of man and that they have nothing to clamor for, while *at the same time* they will say that women can never be the equals of man and that their demands are in vain. It is, in point of fact, a difficult matter for man to realize the extreme importance of social discriminations which seem outwardly insignificant but which produce in woman moral and intellectual effects so profound that they appear to spring from her original nature.[12] The most sympathetic of men never fully comprehend woman's concrete situation. And there is no reason to put much trust in the men when they rush to the defense of privileges whose full extent they can hardly measure. We shall not, then, permit ourselves to be intimidated by the number and violence of the attacks launched against women, nor to be entrapped by the self-seeking eulogies bestowed on the "true woman," nor to profit by the enthusiasm for woman's destiny manifested by men who would not for the world have any part of it.

We should consider the arguments of the feminists with no less suspicion, however, for very often their controversial aim deprives them of all real value. If the "woman question" seems trivial, it is because masculine arrogance has made of it a "quarrel"; and when quarreling, one no longer reasons well. People have tirelessly sought to prove that woman is superior, inferior, or equal to man. Some say that, having been created after Adam, she is evidently a secondary being; others say on the contrary that Adam was only a rough draft and that God succeeded in producing the human being in perfection when He created Eve. Woman's brain is smaller; yes, but it is relatively larger. Christ was made a man; yes, but perhaps for his greater humility. Each argument at once suggests its opposite, and both are often fallacious. If we are to gain understanding, we must get out of these ruts; we must discard the vague notions of superiority, inferiority, equality which have hitherto corrupted every discussion of the subject and start afresh.

Very well, but just how shall we pose the question? And, to begin with, who are we to propound it at all? Man is at once judge and party to the case; but so is woman. What we need is an angel—neither man nor woman—but where shall we find one? Still, the angel would be poorly qualified to speak, for an angel is ignorant of all the basic facts involved in the problem. With a hermaphrodite we should be no better off, for here the situation is most peculiar; the hermaphrodite is not really the combination of a whole man and a whole woman, but consists of parts of each and thus is neither. It looks to me as if there are, after all, certain women who are best qualified to elucidate the situation of woman. Let us not be misled by the sophism that because Epimenides was a Cretan he was necessarily a liar; it is not a mysterious essence that compels men and women to act in good or in bad faith, it is their situation that inclines them more or less toward the search for truth. Many of today's women, fortunate in the restoration of all the privileges pertaining to the estate of the human being, can afford the luxury of impartiality—we even recognize its necessity. We are no longer like our partisan elders; by and large we have won the game. In recent debates on the status of women the United Nations has persistently maintained that the equality of the sexes is now becoming a reality, and already some of us have never had to sense in our femininity an inconvenience or an obstacle. Many problems appear to us to be more pressing than those which concern us in particular, and this detachment even allows us to hope that our attitude will be objective. Still, we know the feminine world more intimately than do the men because we have our roots in it, we grasp more immediately than do men what it means to a human being to be feminine; and we are more concerned with such knowledge. I have said that there are more pressing problems, but this does not prevent us from seeing some importance in asking how the fact of being women will affect our lives. What opportunities precisely have been given us and what withheld? What fate awaits our younger sisters, and what directions should they take? It is significant that books by women on women are in general animated in our day less by a wish to demand our rights than by an effort toward clarity and understanding. As we emerge from an era of excessive controversy, this book is offered as one attempt among others to confirm that statement.

But it is doubtless impossible to approach any human problem with a mind free from bias. The way in which questions are put, the points of view assumed, presuppose a relativity of interest; all characteristics imply values, and every objective description, so called, implies an ethical background. Rather than attempt to conceal principles more or less definitely implied, it is better to state them openly at the beginning. This will make it unnecessary to specify on every page in just what sense one uses such words as *superior, inferior, better, worse, progress, reaction,* and the like. If we survey some of the works on woman, we note that one of the points of view most frequently adopted is that of the public good, the general interest; and one always means by this the benefit of society as one wishes it to be maintained or established. For our part, we hold that the only public good is that which assures the private good of the citizens; we shall pass judgment on institutions according to their effectiveness in giving concrete opportunities to individuals. But we do not confuse the idea of private interest with that of happiness, although that is another common point of view. Are not women of the harem more happy than women voters? Is not the housekeeper happier than the workingwoman? It is not too clear just what the word *happy* really means and still less what true values it may mask. There is no possibility of measuring the happiness of others, and it is always easy to describe as happy the situation in which one wishes to place them.

In particular those who are condemned to stagnation are often pronounced happy on the pretext that happiness consists in being at rest. This notion we reject, for our perspective is that of existentialist ethics. Every subject plays his part as such specifically through exploits or projects that serve as a mode of transcendence; he achieves liberty only through a continual reaching out toward other liberties. There is no justification for present existence other than its expansion into an indefinitely open future. Every time transcendence falls back into immanence, stagnation, there is a degradation of existence into the *"en-soi"*—the brutish life of subjection to given conditions—and of liberty into constraint and contingence. This downfall represents a moral fault if the subject consents to it; if it is inflicted upon him, it spells frustration and oppression. In both cases it is an absolute evil. Every individual concerned to justify his existence feels that his existence involves an undefined need to transcend himself, to engage in freely chosen projects.

Now, what peculiarly signalizes the situation of woman is that she—a free and autonomous being like all human creatures—nevertheless finds herself living in a world where men compel her to assume the status of the Other. They propose to stabilize her as object and to doom her to immanence since her transcendence is to be overshadowed and forever transcended by another ego (*conscience*) which is essential and sovereign. The drama of woman lies in this conflict between the fundamental aspirations of every subject (ego)—who always regards the self as the essential—and the compulsions of a situation in which she is the inessential. How can a human being in woman's situation attain fulfillment? What roads are open to her? Which are blocked? How can independence be recovered in a state of dependency? What circumstances limit woman's liberty and how can they be overcome? These are the fundamental questions on which I would fain throw some light. This means that I am interested in the fortunes of the individual as defined not in terms of happiness but in terms of liberty.

Quite evidently this problem would be without significance if we were to believe that woman's destiny is inevitably determined by physiological, psychological, or economic forces. Hence I shall discuss first of all the light in which woman is viewed by biology, psychoanalysis, and historical materialism. Next I shall try to show exactly how the concept of the "truly feminine" has been fashioned—why woman has been defined as the Other—and what have been the consequences from man's point of view. Then from woman's point of view I shall describe the world in which women must live; and thus we shall be able to envisage the difficulties in their way as, endeavoring to make their escape from the sphere hitherto assigned them, they aspire to full membership in the human race.

FROM CHAPTER XXI "WOMAN'S SITUATION AND CHARACTER"

There are many aspects of feminine behavior that should be interpreted as forms of protest. We have seen that a woman often deceives her husband through defiance and not for pleasure; and she may be purposely careless and extravagant because he is methodical and economical. Misogynists who accuse woman of always being late think she lacks a sense of punctuality; but as we have seen, the fact is that she can adjust herself very well to the demands of time. When she is late, she has deliberately planned to be. Some coquettish women think they stimulate the man's desire in this way and make their presence the more highly appreciated; but in making the man wait a few minutes, the woman is above all protesting against that long wait: her life.

In a sense her whole existence is waiting, since she is confined in the limbo of immanence and contingence, and since her justification is always in the hands of others. She awaits the homage, the approval of men, she awaits love, she awaits the gratitude and praise of her husband or her lover. She awaits her support, which comes from man; whether she keeps the checkbook or merely gets a weekly or monthly allowance from her husband, it is necessary for him to have drawn his pay or obtained that raise if she is to be able to pay the grocer or buy a new dress. She waits for man to put in an appearance, since her economic dependence places her at his disposal; she is only one element in masculine life while man is her whole existence. The husband has his occupations outside the home, and the wife has to put up with his absence all day long; the lover—passionate as he may be—is the one who decides on their meetings and separations in accordance with his obligations. In bed, she awaits the male's desire, she awaits—sometimes anxiously— her own pleasure.

All she can do is arrive later at the rendezvous her lover has set, not be ready at the time designated by her husband; in that way she asserts the importance of her own occupations, she insists on her independence; and for the moment she becomes the essential subject to whose will the other passively submits. But these are timid attempts at revenge; however persistent she may be in keeping men waiting, she will never compensate for the interminable hours she has spent in watching and hoping, in awaiting the good pleasure of the male.

Woman is bound in a general way to contest foot by foot the rule of man, though recognizing his over-all supremacy and worshipping his idols. Hence that famous "contrariness" for which she has often been reproached. Having no independent domain, she cannot oppose positive truths and values of her own to those asserted and upheld by males; she can only deny them. Her negation is more or less thoroughgoing, according to the way respect and resentment are proportioned in her nature. But in fact she knows all the faults in the masculine system, and she has no hesitation in exposing them.

Women have no grasp on the world of men because their experience does not teach them to use logic and technique; inversely, masculine apparatus loses its power at the frontiers of the feminine realm. There is a whole region of human experience which the male deliberately chooses to ignore because he fails to *think* it: this experience woman *lives*. The engineer, so precise when he is laying out his diagrams, behaves at home like a minor god: a word, and behold, his meal is served, his shirts starched, his children quieted; procreation is an act as swift

as the wave of Moses' wand; he sees nothing astounding in these miracles. The concept of the miracle is different from the idea of magic: it presents, in the midst of a world of rational causation, the radical discontinuity of an event without cause, against which the weapons of thought are shattered; whereas magical phenomena are unified by hidden forces the continuity of which can be accepted— without being understood—by a docile mind. The newborn child is miraculous to the paternal minor god, magical for the mother who has experienced its coming to term within her womb. The experience of the man is intelligible but interrupted by blanks; that of the woman is, within its own limits, mysterious and obscure but complete. This obscurity makes her weighty; in his relations with her, the male seems light: he has the lightness of dictators, generals, judges, bureaucrats, codes of law, and abstract principles. This is doubtless what a housekeeper meant when she said, shrugging her shoulders: "Men, they don't think!" Women say, also: "Men, they don't know, they don't know life." To the myth of the praying mantis, women contrast the symbol of the frivolous and obstrusive drone bee.

It is understandable, in this perspective, that woman takes exception to masculine logic. Not only is it inapplicable to her experience, but in his hands, as she knows, masculine reasoning becomes an underhand form of force; men's undebatable pronouncements are intended to confuse her. The intention is to put her in a dilemma: either you agree or you do not. Out of respect for the whole system of accepted principles she should agree; if she refuses, she rejects the entire system. But she cannot venture to go so far; she lacks the means to reconstruct society in different form. Still, she does not accept it as it is. Halfway between revolt and slavery, she resigns herself reluctantly to masculine authority. On each occasion he has to force her to accept the consequences of her halfhearted yielding. Man pursues that chimera, a companion half slave, half free: in yielding to him, he would have her yield to the convincingness of an argument, but she knows that he has himself chosen the premises on which his rigorous deductions depend. As long as she avoids questioning them, he will easily reduce her to silence; nevertheless he will not convince her, for she senses his arbitrariness. And so, annoyed, he will accuse her of being obstinate and illogical; but she refuses to play the game because she knows the dice are loaded.

Woman does not entertain the positive belief that the truth is something *other* than men claim; she recognizes, rather, that there *is not* any fixed truth. It is not only the changing nature of life that makes her suspicious of the principle of constant identity, nor is it the magic phenomena with which she is surrounded that destroy the notion of causality. It is at the heart of the masculine world itself, it is in herself as belonging to this world that she comes upon the ambiguity of all principle, of all value, of everything that exists. She knows that masculine morality, as it concerns her, is a vast hoax. Man pompously thunders forth his code of virtue and honor; but in secret he invites her to disobey it, and he even counts on this disobedience; without it, all that splendid façade behind which he takes cover would collapse.

. . .

[1952]

NOTES

1. *Franchise,* dead today.
2. The Kinsey Report [Alfred C. Kinsey and others: *Sexual Behavior in the Human Male* (W. B. Saunders Co., 1948)] is no exception, for it is limited to describing the sexual characteristics of American men, which is quite a different matter.
3. E. Lévinas expresses this idea most explicitly in his essay *Temps et l'Autre.* "Is there not a case in which otherness, alterity [*altérité*], unquestionably marks the nature of a being, as its essence, an instance of otherness not consisting purely and simply in the opposition of two species of the same genus? I think that the feminine represents the contrary in its absolute sense, this contrariness being in no wise affected by any relation between it and its correlative and thus remaining absolutely other. Sex is not a certain specific difference . . . no more is the sexual difference a mere contradiction. . . . Nor does this difference lie in the duality of two complementary terms, for two complementary terms imply a pre-existing whole. . . . Otherness reaches its full flowering in the feminine, a term of the same rank as consciousness but of opposite meaning."

   I suppose that Lévinas does not forget that woman, too, is aware of her own consciousness, or ego. But it is striking that he deliberately takes a man's point of view, disregarding the reciprocity of subject and object. When he writes that woman is mystery, he implies that she is mystery for man. Thus his description, which is intended to be objective, is in fact an assertion of masculine privilege.
4. See C. Lévi-Strauss: *Les Structures élémentaires de la parenté.* My thanks are due to C. Lévi-Strauss for his kindness in furnishing me with the proofs of his work, which, among others, I have used liberally in Part II.

5. With rare exceptions, perhaps, like certain matriarchal rulers, queens, and the like—Tr.
6. See Part II, ch. viii.
7. At the moment in "equal rights" amendment to the Constitution of the United States is before Congress.—Tr.
8. See Part II, pp. 129–131.
9. Or at least he thought he could.
10. A significant article on this theme by Michel Carrouges appeared in No. 292 of the *Cahiers du Sud.* He writes indignantly: "Would that there were no woman-myth at all but only a cohort of cooks, matrons, prostitutes, and bluestockings serving functions of pleasure or usefulness!" That is to say, in his view woman has no existence in and for herself; he thinks only of her *function* in the male world. Her reason for existence lies in man. But then, in fact, her poetic "function" as a myth might be more valued than any other. The real problem is precisely to find out why woman should be defined with relation to man.
11. For example, a man will say that he considers his wife in no wise degraded because she has no gainful occupation. The profession of housewife is just as lofty, and so on. But when the first quarrel comes he will exclaim: "Why, you couldn't make your living without me!"
12. The specific purpose of Book II of this study is to describe this process.

 32

From Sex Variant Women in Literature

JEANETTE FOSTER

INTRODUCTION

. . .

First, what is meant by *sex variant*? The term was selected because it is not as yet rigidly defined nor charged with controversial overtones. Intrinsically, *variant* means no more than differing from a chosen standard, and in the field of sex experience the standard generally accepted is adequate heterosexual adjustment. . . .

Possible deviations from this standard are many, but the present study will stay within the limits set by a work of 1941 entitled *Sex Variants,*[1] which was devoted to persons having emotional experience with others of their own sex. Under this head the author included homosexuals, a term which he confined to those having only such experience; bisexuals, capable of enjoying relations with both sexes;

and narcissists, attracted to both but able to achieve satisfaction with neither.

. . .

Not all women recognize a sexual factor in their subjective emotional relations, particularly in the intrasexual field so heavily shadowed by social disapproval. Still they often exhibit indirect responses which have all the intensity of physical passion and which quite as basically affect the pattern of their lives. Hence this study includes not only women who are conscious of passion for their own sex, with or without overt expression, but also those who are merely obsessively attached to other women over a longer period or at a more mature age than is commonly expected. If "commonly expected" is another nebulous phrase, a species of pooled judgment is available to clarify it. During the past few decades— that is, since Freudian concepts have become a part of the common background—most works on sex guidance have taken some account of homosexuality. These agree in general that passionate attachments during puberty and early adolescence may lie within the norm, but if occurring later they constitute variance. Without here debating the absolute validity of this opinion, one may borrow it as a working criterion.

As to women who habitually wear men's clothing or even for a part of their lives pass for men, such transvestism is not in itself variant. To be sure, many psychoanalysts consider it indicative of latent homosexuality, but to bring a woman properly within the scope of this study her transvestism must be accompanied by some evidence of fondness for her own sex. And, of course, mere sex disguise arising from pressure of circumstance, a favorite device for plot complication from ballads to modern films, has no significance here.

With the meaning of *variance* clarified, the more familiar terms *homosexual* and *lesbian* need attention. In popular usage the latter implies overt sexual expression and so it will be used only where such implication is intended. *Homosexual* is more ambiguous, . . . but is more nearly synonymous with . . . *variant*.

. . .

CONCLUSION

. . .

Does sexual behavior, then, fall into patterns which might argue for some uniformities in endo-

crine balance? Again, it is impossible to classify the majority honestly, even by the simplest divisions into active and passive, homosexual and bisexual, and feel confident that the operative factors are innate. One may separate those whose passion is masculine in violence from the cool, the gentle, the maternally tender; but among the last may fall such conspicuously masculine figures as Stephen Gordon and Jan Morale. Or the aggressive Maupins or Leos may prove bisexual, the gentle Mettas and Miss Caffertys immutably set upon their own kind, and a petite and delicate Flordespine or Almond may be bold in her sexual advances. It is, however, possible to detect certain rough patterns not in physique or in sex behavior but in psychological attitude. There are masterful spirits who need to prove themselves the equal of any man, or to dominate rather than follow. There are rebels and lone wolves who defy authority or public opinion and are usually jealously possessive of the few they love. There are the more detached egotists and narcissists who see others only in terms of their own advantage and abandon themselves to no one. There are the shy and clinging who crave protection. And there are the maternal types, forgetful of self and eager to cherish and support.

If not heredity, what explanation does literature offer for these variants? Sometimes none. Lyric poets in particular simply register their sentiments and leave readers to search elsewhere for explanations of the enigma. In a different fashion the same is true in unsympathetic narratives, and those where interest lies in plot alone. In these cases, too, variants are presented, as it were, Minerva-born, but are assumed to be a recognized type sure to generate dramatic tensions. Usually, however, as in more conventional fiction, authors supply some personal history for main characters and often directly or implicitly hold it responsible for their anomalies. This last is, of course, especially noticeable in recent years since the spread of Freudian psychology. Even where no notion of causality seems to exist in the author's mind, the same sort of background may recur in more than one narrative. Thus it is possible to identify a number of conditions, some fairly universal, some characteristic of their period, which appear repeatedly as antecedents or accompaniments of variance.

Of the universal class the most prevalent factor is some degree of negative reaction to men. In psychiatric casebooks this is often the result of sexual violation in childhood or adolescence, or of the witnessing of intercourse at an early age, which is almost equally traumatic. But such experiences and their sequelae of neurotic antipathy are rare in fiction. There a less compulsive aversion may result from rough or undesired caresses, or from their antithesis, pointed physical repudiation. Or it may grow from social neglect or slighting by men, or from deliberate indoctrination by a puritanic guardian. It may also stem indirectly from conjugal discord at home or elsewhere, through observation of a hated man's unfaithfulness or cruelty, a beloved woman's frigidity or suffering.

The next most frequent causal factor comprises a large and varied constellation of troubled family relations. Among our hundreds of variant women, those who enjoyed the sort of family life that social psychologists now exhort all parents to provide could be counted on one hand. Even those living with both parents on any terms would not multiply the number many times. Most often, the mother is found wanting in some way; indeed, the percentage of outright motherless girls is impressive. But, it may well be asked, what about the number in ordinary fiction? In novels of psychological cast dealing with the vicissitudes of young unmarried women the count is certainly high. The margin in favor of variant novels is further narrowed when one considers that few of these are literary masterpieces, and that minor fiction has, from its beginnings, capitalized heavily on the orphaned or motherless heroine. The reasons are obvious: a girl thus deprived can be a sympathetic character despite unconventional conduct; this conduct affords the reader escape-through-identification; and the author is guilty of no profanation of the revered mother image. Nevertheless, after all these allowances are duly made, a lack of maternal tenderness and understanding bulks large among influences leading to variant behavior.

The comparable lack of a father is seldom stressed. Paternal harshness appears rather oftener than the same trait in the mother, and the father is also sometimes a party to general parental indifference or neglect, but by and large the variant girl

actively mistreated by either or both parents is fairly rare. A father fixation, on the other hand, though infrequent, is significant when it does occur, and Balzac's *Seraphita* bears witness that it is not confined to the Freudian twentieth century. The badgering of a lone girl by a parental surrogate—stepmother, relative or guardian—is featured now and then, as in *The Scorpion,* but this sympathy-begging device is less overworked in variant than in other minor fiction. The influence of siblings in producing either sexual fixation or aversion is negligible, unless their conspicuous absence is significant, for a considerable number of variant girls are presented as actually or virtually "only" children.

All this wide variety of subjective situations apparently contributes to the equally diverse range of variant experiences; yet none in the two lists is so consistently paired as to establish certainty of explicit cause and effect. In fact, more than one family factor and a measure of sex antagonism often occur simultaneously or successively in the same narrative.

In addition to subjective influences there remains the category of external circumstances which encourage variance. And while the psychological situations remain fairly constant from one period to another, environmental factors vary considerably with time. The more strictly convention limits a woman's activities, the more certain is her mere overstepping its bounds to produce significant results. From medieval times through the nineteenth century, to wear men's clothing was taboo. Therefore, when Clémentine or Fragoletta assumed man's dress, grave emotional consequences were inevitable. Today the donning of slacks or hunting costume produces little emotional impact. Similarly in nineteenth-century France or early twentieth-century England, when modesty forbade revealing the feminine body, a glimpse of uncovered breasts might stir a woman to passion, or Proust's Albertine and her friend might enjoy a half-hour's dalliance in a beach cabin because they had undressed together. Today, when beach, pool and gymnasium showers are communal affairs, their dressing-cubicles are unlikely to be the scene of tender passages. Furthermore, in days when woman's sphere was definitely the home, girls who claimed independence outside it exerted a strong imaginative appeal. Artists, actresses or mere bachelor girls attracted one another as strongly as they fascinated more sheltered women. But how many such "bohemians" have aroused general excitement since the 1920s? Few, certainly, in fiction.

One objective setting, however, has for decades remained basically constant as a hotbed of variance—those institutions which restrict young women to the company of their own sex. Until well into the nineteenth century, convents or convent schools were the segregating agency. After 1850, secular boarding schools took over the role, without the occasional compensating outlet of religious emotion. With the spread of higher education in our own times, women's colleges joined the list, and the latest additions have been reform schools, military barracks, sorority houses and metropolitan residence clubs. The results of a cloistered existence, then, might seem to argue for environment as a cause of variance just as strongly as recurrence of the "Maupin" type argued for heredity. But we have already seen that when many women wear men's clothes at one time or another, the effect of even the most boyish is less pronounced than it used to be. As for environment, excepting disciplinary and military quarters, twentieth-century cloisters allow their residents so much more freedom than their predecessors that variant or lesbian developments within them can no longer be laid wholly to pressure of circumstance.

Thus, it appears that literary testimony from a score of centuries confirms the current psychiatric verdict: variance is one possible solution of pressing emotional problems; but arrival at this particular solution depends upon so many variables that as yet no certain predictive formula has been derived.

An aspect of the current scene not yet duly recognized in literature is the relation of variant experience to gainful employment. In the heyday of feminism a good deal of concern was voiced by antifeminists lest women's financial and social independence might breed lesbianism on a grand scale. But a comparison of French fiction from 1870 to 1900, when women were still dependent, with the English and American record since World War I suggests that the fear was unjustified. The issue at stake in our own time is not the influence of earning upon variance but the reverse effect of variance on a woman's capacity to hold a paid position. Before 1900 it was normal for the unmarried girl or the estranged wife to be supported by her parents or her long-suffering husband. For the last fifty years more and more women have been obliged to earn their own livings in ordinary unromantic jobs, and to this trend fiction has not done full justice. To be sure, creative license has always allowed the freedom of an independent income to more persons than are so favored in everyday life. It is true also that in recent variant novels a good many occupations have at least made an appearance. We have met actresses, modiste's assistants, novelists, interior decorators, social workers, a number of teachers, a trio of nurses, a department store executive and a minor clerk, and several girls employed in business offices. But in general these positions have served only as realistic backdrops for action which did not impinge upon them. In less than half a dozen cases has variance interfered with earning capacity. It gravely affected the actresses in *Queer Patterns;* the schoolmistresses in *The Children's Hour;* a college instructor in *Diana;* and it constituted a serious risk for nurses in *Promise of Love* and government employees in *Either is Love.* This meagre proportion, especially at the level of mere risk, does not reflect "things as they are" according to factual evidence in psychiatric literature, and the failure of variant fiction to come to grips with this aspect of reality is a count against it. It is also a waste of one fertile potential source of dramatic tension.

There remains a final ticklish question which leads straight into controversial territory, but to which a wide range of possible answers must be considered: why are variant belles-lettres so generally ignored? When so much has been written on the theme, why has it been slighted in library collections, histories of literature, and bibliographic records? One immediate answer will be that it is generally inferior, which is to a certain extent true; but it is not inferior to a deal of ordinary literature which has not been so slighted, notably that by the same authors who have produced variant titles. According to their generation or to their more considered convictions, different persons will explain this comparative neglect by claiming that variance is immoral, or abnormal, or the concern of an eccentric few and of no importance or interest to humanity at large. None of these claims can be summarily dismissed as negligible.

. . .

Variant fiction is of course not alone among feminine efforts in being disparaged by the opposite sex. The battle over the quality of feminine writing is old; to do it full justice would require a small volume in itself. But a brief comment is required to conclude this long discussion. Male critics (who comprise better than nine-tenths of the whole) can be roughly divided into three schools of opinion. The least charitable maintain that women lack creative power in all artistic fields because nature has designated them for biological creation alone. (Otto Weininger[2] is the extreme example of this school, but he is not alone in his opinions.) The largest group make the point that women's artistic efforts are almost exclusively imitative rather than original, and, without investigating reasons, they argue that this fact demonstrates patent creative inferiority. A few—Nathaniel Hawthorne was among the first—feel that

> Generally women write like emasculated men and are only to be distinguished from men by greater feebleness and folly; but when they throw off [imitative] restraints . . . and come before the public stark naked as it were—then their books are sure to possess character and value.[3]

Hawthorne did not, however, live up to his convictions; he gave up writing fiction in the 1850s and fled the country because it was full of "damned scribbling females." The average quality of the scribbling perhaps justified his flight, but his apostasy was symbolic of his sex.

The women who began in the mid-nineteenth century to write like women are writing also largely *for* women, and on a level to be printed in newspapers and in the newly born "home" magazines. They wrote from the limited conventional experience that was known to them and their numerous audience; sentimental religious exaltation and dreams of romantic love supplied the only emotional color in their lives. The common lot of marriage brought mainly domestic drudgery and constant childbearing, with the loss of so many children that even the universal experience of the death of a child lost its keen edge. Had such lives been presented with the austere truth to experience demanded of good literature, the results would have been read no more widely than are starkly realistic novels at any time. And most of those women authors needed to earn money. Thus, feminine fiction concentrated upon blameless romantic passion, took wild liberties with reality, and was altogether unrelated to art. But it sold in the hundreds of thousands, and it set a style in popular feminine narrative which has altered in detail from decade to decade but has not yet gone out. Until well after 1900 few women authors rose above this level save those who more or less successfully imitated men, and chiefly such men as Dickens and Trollope. This sentimental tide has always been completely alien to men, both as individuals and as critics, and it has done much to solidify the majority male opinion that women are not creative artists. Even those men who achieve some intellectual appreciation of the best feminine writing find that, in general, they, like Hawthorne, cannot accept it completely. One might say that, beginning with Dorothy Richardson and Katherine Mansfield, women have attempted to raise essentially feminine writing to a level of absolute quality. No pretense will be made here to trace this growing trend, or to separate the more from the less "feminine" authors. The trend has run to more and more subjective content, as is evident in such current authors as Shirley Jackson and Jean Stafford.

Variance is, of course, more than any other subject, exclusively feminine. Had it not suffered the handicap of taboo, probably more literature of high quality would have grown up around it. Indeed, had such inhibited spirits as Emily Brontë, Emily Dickinson and Rose O'Neill, to mention only the most obvious, been less paralyzed emotionally, they might have had richer experience from which to write as well as more courage to write about it. This is not a plea for the cultivation of either homosexual experience or variant literature. It is simply a suggestion that if those women who are irremediably so constituted, and who happen also to be artists, were less shackled, the world's literature might be by that slight degree the richer. Before that comes to pass, of course, two changes must occur: public opinion in general must come closer to the most lenient psychiatric evaluation of variance. And men must become aware of the unconscious prejudice in their literary evaluation of all, and particularly of variant, feminine writing. If they cannot surmount this prejudice, they should leave the variant field to feminine critics. Also, more women should enter the field of literary criticism.

To conclude: we have seen that feminine variance has persisted in human experience since the beginning of literary records. It has repeatedly aroused sufficient interest to be the subject of literature, some of it good enough to have survived through many centuries against all odds. The odds have been of two very different sorts—religious taboo and masculine distaste. The first operated stringently from the beginning of the Christian era to the Renaissance, and is not yet dead. The second was apparent in classical times and has been especially evident whenever the neo-classical spirit prevailed, for that spirit exalts objective and intellectual experience, stresses the physical aspects of sex, and is contemptuous of subjective emotional preoccupation. In Romantic periods when emotion was glorified—that is, when essentially feminine values prevailed—variant literature has at least comparatively flourished. In our own day the ancient religious taboo has weakened and psychiatric values have to some extent been substituted. Now immaturity rather than sin is the socioethical argument against variance. To each age its own new wisdom seems a social panacea more cogent than all that have gone before but none has ushered in Utopia. Momentarily, however, we have attained—or at least it seems to us that we have attained—to somewhat more tolerance than the elder moralists. If variance is to be always with us, calm acceptance of that fact may become as prevalent as the recognition of human evolution has come to be. And since variant literary expression appears equally persistent, it may conceivably become a narrow but similarly recognized field, permitted to come to fruition according to its own laws, and to contribute the best of which it is capable to the total sum of world literature.

[1956]

NOTES

1. Ellis, Havelock. Studies in the psychology of sex. N.Y., Random, 7v. in 2, 1940.
2. Weininger, Otto. Sex and character. N.Y., Putnam, 1906.
3. Pattee, F. L. The feminine fifties. N.Y., Appleton, 1940.

PART IV

1963–1975

1963–1975: Introduction

The 1960s were a decade of social upheaval in the United States epitomized by the assassinations of President John Kennedy in 1963 and of Martin Luther King and Robert Kennedy in 1968. Movements for civil rights and gay rights and against the United State's escalating military involvement in Vietnam strengthened as the decade progressed. The anger and unrest of the period were epitomized by the riots and urban uprisings that foregrounded the poverty and racism of large northern cities (Detroit, Newark, and Los Angeles); by the 1968 Stonewall Rebellion, which founded the gay/lesbian rights movement; as well as by the bus boycotts, freedom rides, and sit-ins that were a direct response to southern segregation. Many of the women who became active in the women's movement in this decade learned political activism in these other social justice movements, where they also experienced sexism firsthand.

The so-called Second Wave of the women's movement was catalyzed by the 1963 publication of Betty Friedan's *The Feminine Mystique* (reading #33). Her book captured in its analysis of "the problem that has no name" the restlessness and discontent that predominated in the lives of many middle-class white college-educated women, trapped in domesticity by the conservative social values of the 1950s. Some of those women helped to found the National Organization of Women (reading #34). Many of their college-age daughters became involved in groups like Redstockings (reading #38) or a variety of feminist collectives. Many other women across the spectrum of middle-class American life joined consciousness-raising groups where they began to share their experiences of life as women. Much feminist activism in the period, influenced by NOW's basically liberal position, continued to focus on issues of access and equal opportunity for women in education, employment, athletics, and politics. Some successes in these areas prompted NOW to revive the campaign for the Equal Rights Amendment, which continued through the 1970s and finally ended in failure in 1982 with the amendment ratified by only 32 of the required 36 states.

For women of color (a designation that no one had yet learned), identification with feminist issues cut across and into their alliances with and allegiances to their racial and ethnic origins and struggles. Despite those strains and crosscurrents, women of color, trained in radical politics and organizing, in the civil rights movement wrote feminist theory (Weathers, reading #37) and worked in the feminist movement, both in separate organizations like the National Black Feminist Organization and in organizations with white women.

The work and activism of radical feminists and lesbian feminists was essential to development of feminist thought in this period. With their analysis of the sex/gender system, and particularly of sexuality and reproduction as the root causes of women's oppression, key texts like Shulamith Firestone's *The Dialectic of Sex* (1970, reading #40), Kate Millett's *Sexual Politics* (1970, reading #36) as well as lesbian theory by

Charlotte Bunch and Ti-Grace Atkinson, crystallized the notion that "the personal is political." These women articulated the necessity of radical transformations in sexuality and the patriarchal family and the value of separatism as a strategy of survival and resistance in women's lives, spaces, institutions, and organizations.

In the early 1970s, although U.S. national politics were in disarray with the end of the Vietnam War and the resignation of President Nixon, feminists were able to consolidate some gains and establish some institutions. The first women's studies programs were created in these years, as were rape crisis centers and hotlines, battered women's shelters, women's centers, and women's bookstores. Feminist activism in this period achieved perhaps its greatest victory in the 1973 Supreme Court decision of *Roe v. Wade,* which legalized women's access to abortion. This campaign for reproductive choice pulled together many of the strands of argument about birth control and women's sexuality that had run through the century. However, the climate in which this success occurred was heated from the start, and the scope of women's reproductive choice and freedom remained a flashpoint in national politics throughout the next two decades.

In the years between 1963 and 1975, one might say that a U.S. women's movement reemerged as a force for change in national politics, and thousands of women learned that "sisterhood is powerful" through work in liberal and radical organizations. The work of the next decade was to reexamine this sisterhood from the perspective and through the critiques of the women it excluded: women of color, poor and working-class women, Third World women. The 1975 World Conference on Women in Mexico City and the 1976 founding conference of the U.N. Decade for Women can perhaps be seen as preliminary markers of a feminism that thinks both locally and globally.

33

From The Feminine Mystique

BETTY FRIEDAN

THE PROBLEM THAT HAS NO NAME

The problem lay buried, unspoken, for many years in the minds of American women. It was a strange stirring, a sense of dissatisfaction, a yearning that women suffered in the middle of the twentieth century in the United States. Each suburban wife struggled with it alone. As she made the beds, shopped for groceries, matched slipcover material, ate peanut butter sandwiches with her children, chauffeured Cub Scouts and Brownies, lay beside her husband at night—she was afraid to ask even of herself the silent question—"Is this all?"

For over fifteen years there was no word of this yearning in the millions of words written about women, for women, in all the columns, books and articles by experts telling women their role was to seek fulfillment as wives and mothers. Over and over women heard in voices of tradition and of Freudian sophistication that they could desire no greater destiny than to glory in their own femininity. Experts told them how to catch a man and keep him, how to breastfeed children and handle their toilet training, how to cope with sibling rivalry and adolescent rebellion; how to buy a dishwasher, bake bread, cook gourmet snails, and build a swimming pool with their own hands; how to dress, look, and act more feminine and make marriage more exciting; how to keep their husbands from dying young and their sons from growing into delinquents. They were taught to pity the neurotic, unfeminine, unhappy women who wanted to be poets or physicists or presidents. They learned that truly feminine women do not want careers, higher education, political rights—the independence and the opportunities that the old-fashioned feminists fought for. Some women, in their forties and fifties, still remembered painfully giving up those dreams, but most of the younger women no longer even thought about them. A thousand expert voices applauded their femininity, their adjustment, their new maturity. All they had to do was devote their lives from earliest girlhood to finding a husband and bearing children.

By the end of the nineteen-fifties, the average marriage age of women in America dropped to 20, and was still dropping, into the teens. Fourteen million girls were engaged by 17. The proportion of women attending college in comparison with men dropped from 47 per cent in 1920 to 35 per cent in 1958. A century earlier, women had fought for higher education; now girls went to college to get a husband. By the mid-fifties, 60 per cent dropped out of college to marry, or because they were afraid too much education would be a marriage bar. Colleges built dormitories for "married students," but the students were almost always the husbands. A new degree was instituted for the wives—"Ph.T." (Putting Husband Through).

Then American girls began getting married in high school. And the women's magazines, deploring the unhappy statistics about these young marriages, urged that courses on marriage, and marriage counselors, be installed in the high schools. Girls started going steady at twelve and thirteen, in junior high. Manufacturers put out brassieres with false bosoms of foam rubber for little girls of ten. And an advertisement for a child's dress, sizes 3–6x, in the *New York Times* in the fall of 1960, said: "She Too Can Join the Man-Trap Set."

By the end of the fifties, the United States birthrate was overtaking India's. The birth-control movement, renamed Planned Parenthood, was asked to find a method whereby women who had been advised that a third or fourth baby would be born dead or defective might have it anyhow. Statisticians were especially astounded at the fantastic increase in the number of babies among college women. Where once they had two children, now they had four, five, six. Women who had once wanted careers were now making careers out of having babies. So rejoiced *Life* magazine in a 1956 paean to the movement of American women back to the home.

In a New York hospital, a woman had a nervous breakdown when she found she could not breastfeed her baby. In other hospitals, women dying of cancer refused a drug which research had proved might save their lives: its side effects were said to be unfeminine. "If I have only one life, let me live it as a blonde," a larger-than-life-sized picture of a pretty, vacuous woman proclaimed from newspaper, magazine, and drugstore ads. And across America, three out of every ten women dyed their hair blonde. They ate a chalk called Metrecal, instead of food, to shrink to the size of the thin young models. Department-store buyers reported that American women, since 1939, had become three and four sizes smaller. "Women are out to fit the clothes, instead of vice-versa," one buyer said.

Interior decorators were designing kitchens with mosaic murals and original paintings, for kitchens were once again the center of women's lives. Home sewing became a million-dollar industry. Many women no longer left their homes, except to shop, chauffeur their children, or attend a social engagement with their husbands. Girls were growing up in America without ever having jobs outside the home. In the late fifties, a sociological phenomenon was suddenly remarked: a third of American women now worked, but most were no longer young and very few were pursuing careers. They were married women who held part-time jobs, selling or secretarial, to put their husbands through school, their sons through college, or to help pay the mortgage. Or they were widows supporting families. Fewer and fewer women were entering professional work. The shortages in the nursing, social work, and teaching professions caused crises in almost every American city. Concerned over the Soviet Union's lead in the space race, scientists noted that America's greatest source of unused brain-power was women. But girls would not study physics: it was "unfeminine." A girl refused a science fellowship at Johns Hopkins to take a job in a real-estate office. All she wanted, she said, was what every other American girl wanted—to get married, have four children and live in a nice house in a nice suburb.

The suburban housewife—she was the dream image of the young American women and the envy, it was said, of women all over the world. The American housewife—freed by science and labor-saving appliances from the drudgery, the dangers of childbirth and the illnesses of her grandmother. She was healthy, beautiful, educated, concerned only about her husband, her children, her home. She had found true feminine fulfillment. As a housewife and mother, she was respected as a full and equal partner to man in

his world. She was free to choose automobiles, clothes, appliances, supermarkets; she had everything that women ever dreamed of.

In the fifteen years after World War II, this mystique of feminine fulfillment became the cherished and self-perpetuating core of contemporary American culture. Millions of women lived their lives in the image of those pretty pictures of the American suburban housewife, kissing their husbands goodbye in front of the picture window, depositing their stationwagonsful of children at school, and smiling as they ran the new electric waxer over the spotless kitchen floor. They baked their own bread, sewed their own and their children's clothes, kept their new washing machines and dryers running all day. They changed the sheets on the beds twice a week instead of once, took the rug-hooking class in adult education, and pitied their poor frustrated mothers, who had dreamed of having a career. Their only dream was to be perfect wives and mothers; their highest ambition to have five children and a beautiful house, their only fight to get and keep their husbands. They had no thought for the unfeminine problems of the world outside the home; they wanted the men to make the major decisions. They gloried in their role as women, and wrote proudly on the census blank: "Occupation: housewife."

For over fifteen years, the words written for women, and the words women used when they talked to each other, while their husbands sat on the other side of the room and talked shop or politics or septic tanks, were about problems with their children, or how to keep their husbands happy, or improve their children's school, or cook chicken, or make slipcovers. Nobody argued whether women were inferior or superior to men; they were simply different. Words like "emancipation" and "career" sounded strange and embarrassing; no one had used them for years. When a Frenchwoman named Simone de Beauvoir wrote a book called *The Second Sex,* an American critic commented that she obviously "didn't know what life was all about," and besides, she was talking about French women. The "woman problem" in America no longer existed.

If a woman had a problem in the 1950's and 1960's, she knew that something must be wrong with her marriage, or with herself. Other women were satisfied with their lives, she thought. What kind of a woman was she if she did not feel this mysterious fulfillment waxing the kitchen floor? She was so ashamed to admit her dissatisfaction that she never knew how many other women shared it. If she tried to tell her husband, he didn't understand what she was talking about. She did not really understand it herself. For other fifteen years women in America found it harder to talk about this problem than about sex. Even the psychoanalysts had no name for it. When a woman went to a psychiatrist for help, as many women did, she would say, "I'm so ashamed," or "I must be hopelessly neurotic." "I don't know what's wrong with women today," a suburban psychiatrist said uneasily. "I only know something is wrong because most of my patients happen to be women. And their problem isn't sexual." Most women with this problem did not go to see a psychoanalyst, however. "There's nothing wrong really," they kept telling themselves. "There isn't any problem."

But on an April morning in 1959, I heard a mother of four, having coffee with four other mothers in a suburban development fifteen miles from New York, say in a tone of quiet desperation, "the problem." And the others knew, without words, that she was not talking about a problem with her husband, or her children, or her home. Suddenly they realized they all shared the same problem, the problem that has no name. They began, hesitantly, to talk about it. Later, after they had picked up their children at nursery school and taken them home to nap, two of the women cried, in sheer relief, just to know they were not alone.

Gradually I came to realize that the problem that has no name was shared by countless women in America. As a magazine writer I often interviewed women about problems with their children, or their marriages, or their houses, or their communities. But after a while I began to recognize the telltale signs of this other problem. I saw the same signs in suburban ranch houses and split-levels on Long Island and in New Jersey and Westchester County; in colonial houses in a small Massachusetts town; on patios in Memphis; in suburban and city apartments; in living rooms in the Midwest. Sometimes I sensed the problem, not as a reporter, but as a suburban housewife, for during this time I was also bringing up my own three children in Rockland County, New York. I heard echoes of the problem in college dormitories and semi-private maternity wards, at PTA meetings and luncheons of the League of Women Voters, at suburban cocktail parties, in station wagons waiting for trains, and in snatches of conversation overheard at Schrafft's. The groping words I heard from other women, on quiet afternoons when children were at school or on quiet evenings when husbands worked late, I think I understood first as a woman long before I understood their larger social and psychological implications.

Just what was this problem that has no name? What were the words a woman used when they tried to express it? Sometimes women would say "I feel empty somehow . . . incomplete." Or she would say, "I feel as if I don't exist." Sometimes she blotted out the feeling with a tranquilizer. Sometimes she thought the problem was with her husband, or her children, or that what she really needed was to redecorate her house, or move to a better neighborhood, or have an affair, or another baby. Sometimes, she went to a doctor with symptoms she could hardly describe: "A tired feeling . . . I get so angry with the children it scares me . . . I feel like crying without any reason." (A Cleveland doctor called it "the housewife's syndrome.") A number of women told me about great bleeding blisters that break out on their hands and arms. "I call it the housewife's blight," said a family doctor in Pennsylvania. "I see it so often lately in these young women with four, five and six children who bury themselves in their dishpans. But it isn't caused by detergent and it isn't cured by cortisone."

Sometimes a woman would tell me that the feeling gets so strong she runs out of the house and walks through the streets. Or she stays inside her house and cries. Or her children tell her a joke, and she doesn't laugh because she doesn't hear it. I talked to women who had spent years on the analyst's couch, working out their "adjustment to the feminine role," their blocks to "fulfillment as a wife and mother." But the desperate tone in these women's voices, and the look in their eyes, was the same as the tone and the look of other women, who were sure they had no problem, even though they did have a strange feeling of desperation.

· · ·

And so she must accept the fact that "American women's unhappiness is merely the most recently won of women's rights," and adjust and say with the happy housewife found by *Newsweek:* "We ought to salute the wonderful freedom we all have and be proud of our lives today. I have had college and I've worked, but being a housewife is the most rewarding and satisfying role. . . . My mother was never included in my father's business affairs . . . she couldn't get out of the house and away from us children. But I am an equal to my husband; I can go along with him on business trips and to social business affairs."

The alternative offered was a choice that few women would contemplate. In the sympathetic words of the *New York Times:* "All admit to being deeply frustrated at times by the lack of privacy, the physical burden, the routine of family life, the confinement of it. However, none would give up her home and family if she had the choice to make again." *Redbook* commented: "Few women would want to thumb their noses at husbands, children and community and go off on their own. Those who do may be talented individuals, but they rarely are successful women."

The year American women's discontent boiled over, it was also reported (*Look*) that the more than 21,000,000 American women who are single, widowed, or divorced do not cease even after fifty their frenzied, desperate search for a man. And the search begins early—for seventy per cent of all American women now marry before they are twenty-four. A pretty twenty-five-year-old secretary took thirty-five different jobs in six months in the futile hope of finding a husband. Women were moving from one political club to another, taking evening courses in accounting or sailing, learning to play golf or ski, joining a number of churches in succession, going to bars alone, in their ceaseless search for a man.

Of the growing thousands of women currently getting private psychiatric help in the United States, the married ones were reported dissatisfied with their marriages, the unmarried ones suffering from anxiety and, finally, depression. Strangely, a number of psychiatrists stated that, in their experience, unmarried women patients were happier than married ones. So the doors of all those pretty suburban houses opened a crack to permit a glimpse of uncounted thousands of American housewives who suffered alone from a problem that suddenly everyone was talking about, and beginning to take for granted, as one of those unreal problems in American life that can never be solved—like the hydrogen bomb. By 1962 the plight of the trapped American housewife had become a national parlor game. Whole issues of magazines, newspaper columns, books learned and frivolous, educational conferences and television panels were devoted to the problem.

Even so, most men, and some women, still did not know that this problem was real. But those who had faced it honestly knew that all the superficial remedies, the sympathetic advice, the scolding words and the cheering words were somehow drowning the problem in unreality. A bitter laugh was beginning to be heard from American women. They were admired, envied, pitied, theorized over until they were sick of it, offered drastic solutions or silly choices that no one could take seriously. They got all kinds of advice from the growing armies of marriage and child-guidance counselors, psychotherapists, and armchair psychologists, on how to adjust to their role as housewives. No other road to fulfillment was offered to American women in the middle of the twentieth century. Most adjusted to their role and suffered or ignored the problem that has no name. It can be less painful for a woman, not to hear the strange, dissatisfied voice stirring within her.

It is no longer possible to ignore that voice, to dismiss the desperation of so many American women. This is not what being a woman means, no matter what the experts say. For human suffering there is a reason; perhaps the reason has not been found because the right questions have not been asked, or pressed far enough. I do not accept the answer that there is no problem because American women have luxuries that women in other times and lands never dreamed of; part of the strange newness of the problem is that it cannot be understood in terms of the age-old material problems of man: poverty, sickness, hunger, cold. The women who suffer this problem have a hunger that food cannot fill. It persists in women whose husbands are struggling internes and law clerks, or prosperous doctors and lawyers; in wives of workers and executives who make $5,000 a year or $50,000. It is not caused by lack of material advantages; it may not even be felt by women preoccupied with desperate problems of hunger, poverty or illness. And women who think it will be solved by more money, a bigger house, a second car, moving to a better suburb, often discover it gets worse.

It is no longer possible today to blame the problem on loss of femininity: to say that education and independence and equality with men have made American women unfeminine. I have heard so many women try to deny this dissatisfied voice within themselves because it does not fit the pretty picture of femininity the experts have given them. I think, in fact, that this is the first clue to the mystery: the problem cannot be understood in the generally accepted terms by which scientists have studied women, doctors have treated them, counselors have advised them, and writers have written about them. Women who suffer this problem, in whom this voice is stirring, have lived their whole lives in the pursuit of feminine fulfillment. They are not career women (although career women may have other problems); they are women whose greatest ambition has been marriage and children. For the oldest of these women, these daughters of the American middle class, no other dream was possible. The ones in their forties and fifties who once had other dreams gave them up and threw themselves joyously into life as housewives. For the youngest, the new wives and mothers, this was the only dream. They are the ones who quit high school and college to marry, or marked time in some job in which they had no real interest until they married. These women are very "feminine" in the usual sense, and yet they still suffer the problem.

· · ·

The fact is that no one today is muttering angrily about "women's rights," even though more and more women have gone to college. In a recent study of all the classes that have graduated from Barnard College,[1] a significant minority of earlier graduates blamed their education for making them want "rights," later classes blamed their education for giving them career dreams, but recent graduates blamed the college for making them feel it was not enough simply to be a housewife and mother; they did not want to feel guilty if they did not read books or take part in community activities. But if education is not the cause of the problem, the fact that education somehow festers in these women may be a clue.

· · ·

Can the problem that has no name be somehow related to the domestic routine of the housewife? When a woman tries to put the problem into words, she often merely describes the daily life she leads. What is there in this recital of comfortable domestic detail that could possibly cause such a feeling of desperation? Is she trapped simply by the enormous demands of her role as modern housewife: wife, mistress, mother, nurse, consumer, cook, chauffeur; expert on interior decoration, child care, appliance repair, furniture refinishing, nutrition, and education? Her day is fragmented as she rushes from dishwasher to washing machine to telephone to dryer to station wagon to supermarket, and delivers Johnny to the Little League field, takes Janey to dancing class, gets the lawnmower fixed and meets the 6:45. She can never spend more than 15 minutes on any one thing; she has no time to read books, only magazines; even if she had time, she has lost the power to concentrate. At the end of the day, she is so terribly tired that sometimes her husband has to take over and put the children to bed.

Thus terrible tiredness took so many women to doctors in the 1950's that one decided to investigate it. He found, surprisingly, that his patients suffering from "housewife's fatigue" slept more than an adult needed to sleep—as much as ten hours a day—and that the actual energy they expended on housework did not tax their capacity. The real problem must be something else, he decided—perhaps boredom. Some doctors told their women patients they must get out of the house for a day, treat themselves to a movie in town. Others prescribed tranquilizers. Many suburban housewives were taking tranquilizers like cough drops. "You wake up in the morning, and you feel as if there's no point in going on another day like this. So you take a tranquilizer because it makes you not care so much that it's pointless."

It is easy to see the concrete details that trap the suburban housewife, the continual demands on her time. But the chains that bind her in her trap are chains in her own mind and spirit. They are chains made up of mistaken ideas and misinterpreted facts, of incomplete truths and unreal choices. They are not easily seen and not easily shaken off.

How can any woman see the whole truth within the bounds of her own life? How can she believe that voice inside herself, when it denies the conventional, accepted truths by which she has been living? And yet the women I have talked to, who are finally listening to that inner voice, seem in some incredible way to be groping through to a truth that has defied the experts.

I think the experts in a great many fields have been holding pieces of that truth under their microscopes for a long time without realizing it. I found pieces of it in certain new research and theoretical developments in psychological, social and biological science whose implications for women seem never to have been examined. I found many clues by talking to suburban doctors, gynecologists, obstetricians, child-guidance clinicians, college professors, marriage counselors, psychiatrists and ministers—questioning them not on their theories, but on their actual experience in treating American women. I became aware of a growing body of evidence, much of which has not been reported publicly because it does not fit current modes of thought about women—evidence which throws into question the standards of feminine normality, feminine adjustment, feminine fulfillment, and feminine maturity by which most women are still trying to live.

I began to see in a strange new light the American return to early marriage and the large families that are causing the population explosion; the recent movement to natural childbirth and breastfeeding; suburban conformity, and the new neuroses, character pathologies and sexual problems being reported by the doctors. I began to see new dimensions to old problems that have long been taken for granted among women: menstrual difficulties, sexual frigidity, promiscuity, pregnancy fears, childbirth depression, the high incidence of emotional breakdown and suicide among women in their twenties and thirties, the menopause crises, the so-called passivity and immaturity of American men, the discrepancy between women's tested intel-

lecutal abilities in childhood and their adult achievement, the changing incidence of adult sexual orgasm in American women, and persistent problems in psychotherapy and in women's education.

If I am right, the problem that has no name stirring in the minds of so many American women today is not a matter of loss of femininity or too much education, or the demands of domesticity. It is far more important than anyone recognizes. It is the key to these other new and old problems which have been torturing women and their husbands and children, and puzzling their doctors and educators for years. It may well be the key to our future as a nation and a culture. We can no longer ignore that voice within women that says: "I want something more than my husband and my children and my home."

[1963]

NOTE

1. Marian Freda Poverman, "Alumnae on Parade," *Barnard Alumnae Magazine*, July, 1957.

 34

Statement of Purpose (1966)

NATIONAL ORGANIZATION FOR WOMEN

We, men and women who hereby constitute ourselves as the National Organization for Women, believe that the time has come for a new movement toward true equality for all women in America, and toward a fully equal partnership of the sexes, as part of the world-wide revolution of human rights now taking place within and beyond our national borders.

The purpose of NOW is to take action to bring women into full participation in the mainstream of American society now, exercising all the privileges and responsibilities thereof in truly equal partnership with men.

We believe the time has come to move beyond the abstract argument, discussion and symposia over the status and special nature of women which has raged in America in recent years; the time has come to confront, with concrete action, the conditions that now prevent women from enjoying the equality of opportunity and freedom of choice which is their right, as individual Americans, and as human beings.

NOW is dedicated to the proposition that women, first and foremost, are human beings, who, like all other people in our society, must have the chance to develop their fullest human potential. We believe that women can achieve such equality only by accepting to the full the challenges and responsibilities they share with all other people in our society, as part of the decision-making mainstream of American political, economic and social life.

We organize to initiate or support action, nationally, or in any part of this nation, by individuals or organizations, to break through the silken curtain of prejudice and discrimination against women in government, industry, the professions, the churches, the political parties, the judiciary, the labor unions, in education, science, medicine, law, religion and every other field of importance in American society.

Enormous changes taking place in our society make it both possible and urgently necessary to advance the unfinished revolution of women toward true equality, now. With a life span lengthened to nearly 75 years it is no longer either necessary or possible for women to devote the greater part of their lives to child-rearing; yet childbearing and rearing which continues to be a most important part of most women's lives—still is used to justify barring women from equal professional and economic participation and advance.

· · ·

There is no civil rights movement to speak for women, as there has been for Negroes and other victims of discrimination. The National Organization for Women must therefore begin to speak.

WE BELIEVE that the power of American law, and the protection guaranteed by the U.S. Constitution to the civil rights of all individuals, must be effectively applied and enforced to isolate and remove patterns of sex discrimination, to ensure equality of opportunity in employment and education, and equality of civil and political rights and responsibilities on behalf of women, as well as for Negroes and other deprived groups.

We realize that women's problems are linked to many broader questions of social justice; their solution will require concerted action by many groups. Therefore, convinced that human rights for all are indivisible, we expect to give active support to the common cause of equal rights for all those who suffer discrimination and deprivation, and we call upon other organizations committed to such goals to support our efforts toward equality for women.

WE DO NOT ACCEPT the token appointment of a few women to high-level positions in government and industry as a substitute for a serious continuing effort to recruit and advance women according to their individual abilities. To this end, we urge American government and industry to mobilize the same resources of ingenuity and command with which they have solved problems of far greater difficulty than those now impeding the progress of women.

WE BELIEVE that this nation has a capacity at least as great as other nations, to innovate new social institutions which will enable women to enjoy true equality of opportunity and responsibility in society, without conflict with their responsibilities as mothers and homemakers. In such innovations, America does not lead the Western world, but lags by decades behind many European countries. We do not accept the traditional assumption that a woman has to choose between marriage and motherhood, on the one hand, and serious participation in industry or the professions on the other. We question the present expectation that all normal women will retire from job or profession for 10 or 15 years, to devote their full time to raising children, only to reenter the job market at a relatively minor level. This, in itself, is a deterrent to the aspirations of women, to their acceptance into management or professional training courses, and to the very possibility of equality of opportunity or real choice, for all but a few women. Above all, we reject the assumption that these problems are the unique responsibility of each individual woman, rather than a basic social dilemma which society must solve. True equality of opportunity and freedom of choice for women requires such practical and possible innovations as a nationwide network of childcare centers, which will make it unnecessary for women to retire completely from society until their children are grown, and national programs to provide retraining for women who have chosen to care for their own children full-time.

WE BELIEVE that it is as essential for every girl to be educated to her full potential of human ability as it is for every boy—with the knowledge that such education is the key to effective participation in today's economy and that, for a girl as for a boy, education can only be serious where there is expectation that it will be used in society. We believe that American educators are capable of devising means of imparting such expectations to girl students. Moreover, we consider the decline in the proportion of women receiving higher and professional education to be evidence of discrimination. This discrimination may take the form of quotas against the admission of women to colleges, and professional schools; lack of encouragement by parents, counsellors and educators; denial of loans or fellowships; or the traditional or arbitrary procedures in graduate and professional training geared in terms of men, which inadvertently discriminate against women. We believe that the same serious attention must be given to high school dropouts who are girls as to boys.

WE REJECT the current assumptions that a man must carry the sole burden of supporting himself, his wife, and family, and that a woman is automatically entitled to lifelong support by a man upon her marriage, or that marriage, home and family are primarily woman's world and responsibility—hers, to dominate—his to support. We believe that a true partnership between the sexes demands a different concept of marriage, an equitable sharing of the responsibilities of home and children and of the economic burdens of their support. We believe that proper recognition should be given to the economic and social value of homemaking and child-care. To these ends, we will seek to open a reexamination of laws and mores governing marriage and divorce, for we believe that the current state of "half-equality" between the sexes discriminates against both men and women, and is the cause of much unnecessary hostility between the sexes.

WE BELIEVE that women must now exercise their political rights and responsibilities as Ameri-

can citizens. They must refuse to be segregated on the basis of sex into separate-and-not-equal ladies' auxiliaries in the political parties, and they must demand representation according to their numbers in the regularly constituted party committees—at local, state, and national levels—and in the informal power structure, participating fully in the selection of candidates and political decision-making, and running for office themselves.

IN THE INTERESTS OF THE HUMAN DIGNITY OF WOMEN, we will protest, and endeavor to change, the false image of women now prevalent in the mass media, and in the texts, ceremonies, laws, and practices of our major social institutions. Such images perpetuate contempt for women by society and by women for themselves. We are similarly opposed to all policies and practices—in church, state, college, factory, or office—which, in the guise of protectiveness, not only deny opportunities but also foster in women self-denigration, dependence, and evasion of responsibility, undermine their confidence in their own abilities and foster contempt for women.

NOW WILL HOLD ITSELF INDEPENDENT OF ANY POLITICAL PARTY in order to mobilize the political power of all women and men intent on our goals. We will strive to ensure that no party, candidate, president, senator, governor, congressman, or any public official who betrays or ignores the principle of full equality between the sexes is elected or appointed to office. If it is necessary to mobilize the votes of men and women who believe in our cause, in order to win for women the final right to be fully free and equal human beings, we so commit ourselves.

WE BELIEVE THAT women will do most to create a new image of women by *acting* now, and by speaking out in behalf of their own equality, freedom, and human dignity—not in pleas for special privilege, nor in enmity toward men, who are also victims of the current, half-equality between the sexes—but in an active, self-respecting partnership with men. By so doing, women will develop confidence in their own ability to determine actively, in partnership with men, the conditions of their life, their choices, their future and their society.

[1966]

35

SCUM Manifesto

VALERIE SOLANAS

Life in this society being, at best, an utter bore and no aspect of society being at all relevant to women, there remains to civic-minded, responsible, thrill-seeking females only to overthrow the government, eliminate the money system, institute complete automation, and destroy the male sex.

It is now technically possible to reproduce without the aid of males (or, for that matter, females) and to produce only females. We must begin immediately to do so. Retaining the male has not even the dubious purpose of reproduction. The male is a biological accident: the Y (male) gene is an incomplete X (female) gene, that is, has an incomplete set of chromosomes. In other words, the male is an incomplete female, a walking abortion, aborted at the gene stage. To be male is to be deficient, emotionally limited; maleness is a deficiency disease and males are emotional cripples.

. . .

But SCUM is impatient; SCUM is not consoled by the thought that future generations will thrive; SCUM wants to grab some thrilling living for itself. And, if a large majority of women were SCUM, they could acquire complete control of this country within a few weeks simply by withdrawing from the labor force, thereby paralyzing the entire nation. Additional measures, any one of which would be sufficient to completely disrupt the economy and everything else, would be for women to declare themselves off the money system, stop buying, just loot and simply refuse to obey all laws they don't care to obey. The police force, National Guard, Army, Navy, and Marines combined couldn't squelch a rebellion of over half the population, particularly when it's made up of people they are utterly helpless without.

If all women simply left men, refused to have anything to do with any of them—ever, all men, the government, and the national economy would collapse completely. Even without leaving men, women

who are aware of the extent of their superiority to and power over men, could acquire complete control over everything within a few weeks, could effect a total submission of males to females. In a sane society the male would trot along obediently after the female. The male is docile and easily led, easily subjected to the domination of any female who cares to dominate him. The male, in fact, wants desperately to be led by females, wants Mama in charge, wants to abandon himself to her care. But this is not a sane society, and most women are not even dimly aware of where they're at in relation to men.

The conflict, therefore, is not between females and males, but between SCUM—dominant, secure, self-confident, nasty, violent, selfish, independent, proud, thrill-seeking, free-wheeling, arrogant females, who consider themselves fit to rule the universe, who have freewheeled to the limits of this "society," and are ready to wheel on to something far beyond what it has to offer—and nice, passive, accepting, "cultivated," polite, dignified, subdued, dependent, scared, mindless, insecure, approval-seeking Daddy's Girls, who can't cope with the unknown; who want to continue to wallow in the sewer that is, at least, familiar, who want to hang back with the apes; who feel secure only with Big Daddy standing by, with a big, strong man to lean on and with a fat, hairy face in the White House; who are too cowardly to face up to the hideous reality of what a man is, what Daddy is; who have cast their lot with the swine, who have adapted themselves to animalism, feel superficially comfortable with it and know no other way of "life;" who have reduced their minds, thoughts and sights to the male level; who, lacking sense, imagination, and wit can have value only in a male "society;" who can have a place in the sun, or, rather, in the slime, only as soothers, ego-boosters, relaxers, and breeders; who are dismissed as inconsequents by other females, who project their deficiencies, their maleness, onto all females and see the female as a worm.

But SCUM is too impatient to hope and wait for the debrainwashing of millions of assholes. Why should the swinging females continue to plod dismally along with the dull male ones? Why should the fates of the groovy and the creepy be intertwined? Why should the active and imaginative consult the passive and dull on social policy? Why should the independent be confined to the sewer along with the dependent who need Daddy to cling to?

A small handful of SCUM can take over the country within a year by systematically fucking up the system, selectively destroying property, and murder:

• SCUM will become members of the unwork force, the fuck-up force; they will get jobs of various kinds and unwork. For example, SCUM sales-girls will not charge for merchandise; SCUM telephone operators will not charge for calls; SCUM office and factory workers, in addition to fucking up their work, will secretly destroy equipment.

• SCUM will unwork at a job until fired, then get a new job to unwork at.

• SCUM will forcibly relieve bus drivers, cab drivers, and subway-token sellers of their jobs and run buses and cabs and dispense free tokens to the public.

• SCUM will destroy all useless and harmful objects—cars, store windows, "Great Art," etc.

• Eventually SCUM will take over the air-waves—radio and TV networks—by forcibly relieving of their jobs all radio and TV employees who would impede SCUM's entry into the broadcasting studios.

• SCUM will couple-bust—barge into mixed (male-female) couples, wherever they are, and bust them up.

SCUM will kill all men who are not in the Men's Auxiliary of SCUM. Men in the Men's Auxiliary are those men who are working diligently to eliminate themselves, men who, regardless of their motives, do good, men who are playing ball with SCUM. A few examples of the men in the Men's Auxiliary are: men who kill men; biological scientists who are working on constructive programs, as opposed to biological warfare; journalists, writers, editors, publishers, and producers who disseminate and promote ideas that will lead to the achievement of SCUM's goals; faggots who, by their shimmering, flaming example, encourage other men to de-man themselves and thereby make themselves relatively inoffensive; men who consistently give things away—money, things, services; men who tell it like it is (so far not one ever has), who put women straight, who reveal the truth about themselves, who give the mindless male females correct sentences to parrot, who tell them a woman's primary goal in life should be to squash the male sex (to aid men in this endeavor SCUM will conduct Turd Sessions, at which every male present will give a speech beginning with the sentence: "I am a turd, a lowly, abject turd," then proceed to list all the ways in which he is. His reward for so doing will be the opportunity to fraternize after the session for a whole, solid hour with the SCUM who will be present. Nice, clean-living male women will be invited to the sessions to help clarify any doubts and misunderstandings they may have about the male sex); makers and promoters of sex books and movies, etc., who are hastening the day when all that will be shown on the screen will be Suck and Fuck (males, like the rats following the Pied Piper, will be lured by Pussy to their doom, will be overcome and submerged by and will eventually drown in the passive flesh that they are); drug pushers and advocates, who are hastening the dropping out of men.

. . .

It is most tempting to pick off the female "Great Artists," liars and phonies, etc., along with the men, but that would be inexpedient, as it would not be clear to most of the public that the female killed was a male. All women have a fink streak in them, to a greater or lesser degree, but it stems from a lifetime of living among men. Eliminate men and women will shape up. Women are improvable; men are not, although their behavior is. When SCUM gets hot on their asses it'll shape up fast.

Simultaneously with the fucking-up, looting, couple-busting, destroying, and killing, SCUM will recruit. SCUM, then, will consist of recruiters; the elite corps—the hard-core activists (the fuck-ups, looters and destroyers) and the elite of the elite—the killers.

Dropping out is not the answer; fucking-up is. Most women are already dropped out; they were never in. Dropping out gives control to those few who don't drop out; dropping out is exactly what the establishment leaders want; it plays into the hands of the enemy; it strengthens the system instead of undermining it, since it is based entirely on the nonparticipation, passivity, apathy, and noninvolvement of the mass of women. Dropping out, however, is an excellent policy for men, and SCUM will enthusiastically encourage it.

. . .

SCUM will keep on destroying, looting, fucking-up, and killing until the money-work system no longer exists and automation is completely instituted or until enough women cooperate with SCUM to make violence unnecessary to achieve these goals, that is, until enough women either unwork or quit work, start looting, leave men, and refuse to obey all laws inappropriate to a truly civilized society. Many women will fall into line; but many others, who surrendered long ago to the enemy, who are so adapted to animalism, to maleness, that they like restrictions and restraints, don't know what to do with freedom, will continue to be toadies and doormats, just as peasants in rice paddies remain peasants in rice paddies as one regime topples another. A few of the more volatile will whimper and sulk and throw their toys and dishrags on the floor, but SCUM will continue to steamroller over them.

A completely automated society can be accomplished very simply and quickly once there is a public demand for it. The blueprints for it are already in existence, and its construction will only take a few weeks with millions of people working at it. Even though off the money system, everyone will be most happy to pitch in and get the automated society built; it will mark the beginning of a fantastic new era, and there will be a celebration atmosphere accompanying the construction. The elimination of money and the complete institution of automation are basic to all other SCUM reforms; without these two the others can't take place; with them the others will take place very rapidly. The government will automatically collapse. With complete automation it will be possible for every woman to vote directly on every issue by means of an electronic voting machine in her house. Since the government is occupied almost entirely with regulating economic affairs and legislating against purely private matters, the elimination of money and with it the elimination of males who wish to legislate "morality" will mean that there will be practically no issues to vote on.

After the elimination of money there will be no further need to kill men; they will be stripped of the

only power they have over psychologically independent females. They will be able to impose themselves only on the doormats, who like to be imposed on. The rest of the women will be busy solving the few remaining unsolved problems before planning their agenda for eternity and Utopia—completely revamping educational programs so that millions of women can be trained within a few months for high-level intellectual work that now requires years of training (this can be done very easily once our educational goal is to educate and not to perpetuate an academic and intellectual elite); solving the problems of disease and old age and death and completely redesigning our cities and living quarters. Many women will for awhile continue to think they dig men, but as they become accustomed to female society and as they become absorbed in their projects, they will eventually come to see the utter uselessness and banality of the male.

. . .

[1967]

 36

Sexual Politics

KATE MILLETT

THEORY OF SEXUAL POLITICS

The three instances of sexual description we have examined so far were remarkable for the large part which notions of ascendancy and power played within them. Coitus can scarcely be said to take place in a vacuum; although of itself it appears a biological and physical activity, it is set so deeply within the larger context of human affairs that it serves as a charged microcosm of the variety of attitudes and values to which culture subscribes. Among other things, it may serve as a model of sexual politics on an individual or personal plane.

But of course the transition from such scenes of intimacy to a wider context of political reference is a great step indeed. In introducing the term "sexual politics," one must first answer the inevitable question "Can the relationship between the sexes be viewed in a political light at all?" The answer de-

MONey = Mj source of pwr for men

pends on how one defines politics.[1] This essay does not define the political as that relatively narrow and exclusive world of meetings, chairmen, and parties. The term "politics" shall refer to power-structured relationships, arrangements whereby one group of persons is controlled by another. By way of parenthesis one might add that although an ideal politics might simply be conceived of as the arrangement of human life on agreeable and rational principles from whence the entire notion of power *over* others should be banished, one must confess that this is not what constitutes the political as we know it, and it is to this that we must address ourselves.

The following sketch, which might be described as "notes toward a theory of patriarchy," will attempt to prove that sex is a status category with political implications. Something of a pioneering effort, it must perforce be both tentative and imperfect. Because the intention is to provide an overall description, statements must be generalized, exceptions neglected, and subheadings overlapping and, to some degree, arbitrary as well.

The word "politics" is enlisted here when speaking of the sexes primarily because such a word is eminently useful in outlining the real nature of their relative status, historically and at the present. It is opportune, perhaps today even mandatory, that we develop a more relevant psychology and philosophy of power relationships beyond the simple conceptual framework provided by our traditional formal politics. Indeed, it may be imperative that we give some attention to defining a theory of politics which treats of power relationships on grounds less conventional than those to which we are accustomed.[2] I have therefore found it pertinent to define them on grounds of personal contact and interaction between members of well-defined and coherent groups: races, castes, classes, and sexes. For it is precisely because certain groups have no representation in a number of recognized political structures that their position tends to be so stable, their oppression so continuous.

In America, recent events have forced us to acknowledge at last that the relationship between the races is indeed a political one which involves the general control of one collectivity, defined by birth, over another collectivity, also defined by birth. Groups who rule by birthright are fast disappearing,

yet there remains one ancient and universal scheme for the domination of one birth group by another—the scheme that prevails in the area of sex. The study of racism has convinced us that a truly political state of affairs operates between the races to perpetuate a series of oppressive circumstances. The subordinated group has inadequate redress through existing political institutions, and is deterred thereby from organizing into conventional political struggle and opposition.

Quite in the same manner, a disinterested examination of our system of sexual realtionship must point out that the situation between the sexes now, and throughout history, is a case of that phenomenon Max Weber defined as *herrschaft,* a relationship of dominance and subordinance.[3] What goes largely unexamined, often even unacknowledged (yet is institutionalized nonetheless) in our social order, is the birthright priority whereby males rule females. Through this system a most ingenious form of "interior colonization" has been achieved. It is one which tends moreover to be sturdier than any form of segregation, and more rigorous than class stratification, more uniform, certainly more enduring. However muted its present appearance may be, sexual dominion obtains nevertheless as perhaps the most pervasive ideology of our culture and provides its most fundamental concept of power.

This is so because our society, like all other historical civilizations, is a patriarchy.[4] The fact is evident at once if one recalls that the military, industry, technology, universities, science, political office, and finance—in short, every avenue of power within the society, including the coercive force of the police, is entirely in male hands. As the essence of politics is power, such realization cannot fail to carry impact. What lingers of supernatural authority, the Deity, "His" ministry, together with the ethics and values, the philosophy and art of our culture—its very civilization—as T. S. Eliot once observed, is of male manufacture.

If one takes patriarchal government to be the institution whereby that half of the populace which is female is controlled by that half which is male, the principles of patriarchy appear to be twofold: male shall dominate female, elder male shall dominate younger. However, just as with any human institution, there is frequently a distance between the real and the ideal; contradictions and exceptions do exist within the system. While patriarchy as an institution is a social constant so deeply entrenched as to run through all other political, social, or economic forms, whether of caste or class, feudality or bureaucracy, just as it pervades all major religions, it also exhibits great variety in history and locale. In democracies,[5] for example, females have often held no office or do so (as now) in such miniscule numbers as to be below even token representation. Aristocracy, on the other hand, with its emphasis upon the magic and dynastic properties of blood, may at times permit women to hold power. The principle of rule by elder males is violated even more frequently. Bearing in mind the variation and degree in patriarchy—as say between Saudi Arabia and Sweden, Indonesia and Red China—we also recognize our own form in the U.S. and Europe to be much altered and attenuated by the reforms described in the next chapter.

[1969]

NOTES

1. The American Heritage Dictionary's fourth definition is fairly approximate: "methods or tactics involved in managing a state or government." *American Heritage Dictionary* (New York: American Heritage and Houghton Mifflin, 1969). One might expand this to a set of stratagems designed to maintain a system. If one understands patriarchy to be an institution perpetuated by such techniques of control, one has a working definition of how politics is conceived in this essay.
2. I am indebted here to Ronald V. Samson's *The Psychology of Power* (New York: Random House, 1968) for his intelligent investigation of the connection between formal power structures and the family and for his analysis of how power corrupts basic human relationships.
3. "Domination in the quite general sense of power, i.e. the possibility of imposing one's will upon the behavior of other persons, can emerge in the most diverse forms." In this central passage of *Wirtschaft und Gesellschaft* Weber is particularly interested in two such forms: control through social authority ("patriarchal, magisterial, or princely") and control through economic force. In patriarchy as in other forms of domination "that control over economic goods, i.e. economic power, is a frequent, often purposively willed, consequence of domination as well as one of its most important instruments." Quoted from Max Rheinstein's and Edward Shil's translation of portions of *Wirtschaft und Gesellschaft* entitled *Max Weber on Law in Economy and Society* (New York: Simon and Schuster, 1967), pp. 323–24.
4. No matriarchal societies are known to exist at present. Matrilineality, which may be, as some anthropologists have held, a residue or a transitional stage of matriarchy,

does not constitute an exception to patriarchal rule, it simply channels the power held by males through female descent—e.g. the Avunculate.
5. Radical democracy would, of course, preclude patriarchy. One might find evidence of a general satisfaction with a less than perfect democracy in the fact that women have so rarely held power within modern "democracies."

 37

An Argument for Black Women's Liberation as a Revolutionary Force

MARY ANN WEATHERS

"Nobody can fight your battles for you; you have to do it yourself." This will be the premise used for the time being for stating the case for Black women's liberation, although certainly it is the least significant. Black women, at least the Black women I have come in contact with in the movement have been expounding all their energies in "liberating" Black men (if you yourself are not free, how can you "liberate" someone else?). Consequently, the movement has practically come to a standstill. Not entirely due however to wasted energies but, adhering to basic false concepts rather than revolutionary principles and at this stage of the game we should understand that if it is not revolutionary it is false.

We have found that Women's Liberation is an extremely emotional issue, as well as an explosive one. Black men are still parroting the master's prattle about male superiority. This now brings us to a very pertinent question: How can we seriously discuss reclaiming our African Heritage—cultural living modes which clearly refute not only patriarchy and matriarchy, but our entire family structure as we know it. African tribes live communally where households let alone heads of households are non-existent.

It is really disgusting to hear Black women talk about giving Black men their manhood—or allowing them to get it. This is degrading to other Black women and thoroughly insulting to Black men (or at least it should be). How can someone "give" one something as personal as one's adulthood? That's precisely like asking the beast for your freedom. We also chew the fat about standing behind our men. This forces me to the question: Are we women or leaning posts and props? It sounds as if we are saying if we come out from behind him, he'll fall down. To me, these are clearly maternal statements and should be closely examined.

Women's Liberation should be considered as a strategy for an eventual tie-up with the entire revolutionary movement consisting of women, men, and children. We are now speaking of real revolution (armed). If you can not accept this fact purely and without problems examine your reactions closely. We are playing to win and so are they. Viet Nam is simply a matter of time and geography.

Another matter to be discussed is the liberation of children from a sick slave culture. Although we don't like to see it, we are still operating within the confines of the slave culture. Black women use their children for their own selfish needs of worth and love. We try to live our lives which are too oppressing to bear through our children and thereby destroy them in the process. Obviously the much acclaimed plaudits of the love of the Black mother has some discrepancies. If we allow ourselves to run from the truth we run the risk of spending another 400 years in self-destruction. Assuming of course the beast would tolerate us that long, and we know he wouldn't.

Women have fought with men and we have died with men in every revolution, more timely in Cuba, Algeria, China, and now in Viet Nam. If you notice, it is a woman heading the "Peace Talks" in Paris for the NLF. What is wrong with Black women? We are clearly the most oppressed and degraded minority in the world, let alone the country. Why can't we rightfully claim our place in the world?

Realizing fully what is being said, you should be warned that the opposition for liberation will come from everyplace, particularly from other women and from Black men. Don't allow yourselves to be intimidated any longer with this nonsense about the "Matriarchy" of Black women. Black women are not matriarchs but we have been forced to live in abandonment and been used and abused. The myth of the matriarchy must stop and we must not allow ourselves to be sledgehammered by it any longer—

not if we are serious about change and ridding ourselves of the wickedness of this alien culture. Let it be clearly understood that Black women's liberation is not anti-male; any such sentiment or interpretation as such can not be tolerated. It must be taken clearly for what it is—pro-human for all peoples.

The potential for such a movement is boundless. Whereas in the past only certain type Black people have been attracted to the movement—younger people, radicals, and militants. The very poor, the middle class, older people and women have not become aware or have not been able to translate their awareness into action. Women's liberation offers such a channel for these energies.

Even though middle-class Black women may not have suffered the brutal suppression of poor Black people, they most certainly have felt the scourge of the male-superiority-oriented society as women, and would be more prone to help in alleviating some of the conditions of our more oppressed sisters by teaching, raising awareness and consciousness, verbalizing the ills of women and this society, helping to establish communes.

Older women have a wealth of information and experience to offer and would be instrumental in closing the communications gap between the generations. To be Black and to tolerate this jive about discounting people over 30 is madness.

Poor women have knowledge to teach us all. Who else in this society see more and are more realistic about ourselves and this society and about the faults that lie within our own people than our poor women? Who else could profit and benefit from a communal setting that could be established than these sisters? We must let the sisters know that we are capable and some of us already do love them. We women must begin to unabashedly learn to use the word "love" for one another. We must stop the petty jealousies, the violence that we Black women have for so long perpetrated on one another about fighting over this man or the other. (Black men should have better sense than to encourage this kind of destructive behavior.) We must turn to ourselves and one another for strength and solace. Just think for a moment what it would be like if we got together and internalized our own 24-hour-a-day communal centers knowing our children would be safe and loved constantly. Not to mention what it would do for everyone's egos, especially the children. Women should not have to be enslaved by this society's concept of motherhood through their children; and then the kids suffer through a mother's resentment of it by beatings, punishment, and rigid discipline. All one has to do is look at the statistics of Black women who are rapidly filling the beast's mental institutions to know that the time for innovation and change and creative thinking is here. We cannot sit on our behinds waiting for someone else to do it for us. We must save ourselves.

We do not have to look at ourselves as someone's personal sex objects, maids, baby sitters, domestics and the like in exchange for a man's attention. Men hold this power, along with that of the breadwinner, over our heads for these services and that's all it is—servitude. In return we torture him, and fill him with insecurities about his manhood, and literally force him to "cat" and "mess around" bringing in all sorts of conflicts. This is not the way really human people live. This is whitey's thing. And we play the game with as much proficiency as he does.

If we are going to bring about a better world, where best to begin than with our selves? We must rid ourselves of our own hang-ups, before we can begin to talk about the rest of the world and we mean the world and nothing short of just that. (Let's not kid ourselves.) We will be in a position soon of having to hook up with the rest of the oppressed peoples of the world who are involved in liberation just as we are, and we had better be ready to act. *All* women suffer oppression, even white women, particularly poor white women, and especially Indian, Mexican, Puerto Rican, Oriental and Black American women whose oppression is tripled by any of the above mentioned. But we do have female's oppression in common. This means that we can begin to talk to other women with this common factor and start building links with them and thereby build and transform the revolutionary force we are now beginning to amass. This is what Dr. King was doing. We can no longer allow ourselves to be duped by the guise of racism. Any time the White man admits to something you know he is trying to cover something else up. We are all being exploited, even the white middle class, by the few people in control of this entire world. And to keep the real issue

clouded, he keeps us at one another's throats with this racism jive. Although Whites are most certainly racist, we must understand that they have been programmed to think in these patterns to divert their attention. If they are busy fighting us, then they have no time to question the policies of the war being run by this government. With the way the elections went down it is clear that they are as powerless as the rest of us. Make no question about it, folks, this fool knows what he is doing. This man is playing the death game for money and power, not because he doesn't like us. He couldn't care less one way or the other. But think for a moment if we all got together and just walked on out. Who would fight his wars, who would run his police state, who would work his factories, who would buy his products?

We women must start this thing rolling.

[1969]

 38

Redstockings Manifesto

REDSTOCKINGS

I. After centuries of individual and preliminary political struggle, women are uniting to achieve their final liberation from male supremacy. Redstockings is dedicated to building this unity and winning our freedom.

II. Women are an oppressed class. Our oppression is total, affecting every facet of our lives. We are exploited as sex objects, breeders, domestic servants, and cheap labor. We are considered inferior beings, whose only purpose is to enhance men's lives. Our humanity is denied. Our prescribed behavior is enforced by the threat of physical violence.

Because we have lived so intimately with our oppressors, in isolation from each other, we have been kept from seeing our personal suffering as a political condition. This creates the illusion that a woman's relationship with her man is a matter of interplay between two unique personalities, and can be worked out individually. In reality, every such relationship is a *class* relationship, and the conflicts between individual men and women are *political* conflicts that can only be solved collectively.

III.   We identify the agents of our oppression as men. Male supremacy is the oldest, most basic form of domination. All other forms of exploitation and oppression (racism, capitalism, imperialism, etc.) are extensions of male supremacy: men dominate women, a few men dominate the rest. All power structures throughout history have been male-dominated and male-oriented. Men have controlled all political, economic and cultural institutions and backed up this control with physical force. They have used their power to keep women in an inferior position. *All men* receive economic, sexual, and psychological benefits from male supremacy. *All men* have oppressed women.

IV.   Attempts have been made to shift the burden of responsibility from men to institutions or to women themselves. We condemn these arguments as evasions. Institutions alone do not oppress; they are merely tools of the oppressor. To blame institutions implies that men and women are equally victimized, obscures the fact that men benefit from the subordination of women, and gives men the excuse that they are forced to be oppressors. On the contrary, any man is free to renounce his superior position provided that he is willing to be treated like a woman by other men.

We also reject the idea that women consent to or are to blame for their own oppression. Women's submission is not the result of brainwashing, stupidity, or mental illness but of continual, daily pressure from men. We do not need to change ourselves, but to change men.

The most slanderous evasion of all is that women can oppress men. The basis for this illusion is the isolation of individual relationships from their political context and the tendency of men to see any legitimate challenge to their privileges as persecution.

V.   We regard our personal experience, and our feelings about that experience, as the basis for an analysis of our common situation. We cannot rely on existing ideologies as they are all products of male supremacist culture. We question every generalization and accept none that are not confirmed by our experience.

Our chief task at present is to develop female class consciousness through sharing experience and publicly exposing the sexist foundation of all our institutions. Consciousness-raising is not "therapy," which implies the existence of individual solutions and falsely assumes that the male-female relationship is purely personal, but the only method by which we can ensure that our program for liberation is based on the concrete realities of our lives.

The first requirement for raising class consciousness is honesty, in private and in public, with ourselves and other women.

VI.   We identify with all women. We define our best interest as that of the poorest, most brutally exploited woman.

We repudiate all economic, racial, educational or status privileges that divide us from other women. We are determined to recognize and eliminate any prejudices we may hold against other women.

We are committed to achieving internal democracy. We will do whatever is necessary to ensure that every woman in our movement has an equal chance to participate, assume responsibility, and develop her political potential.

VII.   We call on all our sisters to unite with us in struggle.

We call on all men to give up their male privileges and support women's liberation in the interest of our humanity and their own.

In fighting for our liberation we will always take the side of women against their oppressors. We will not ask what is "revolutionary" or "reformist," only what is good for women.

The time for individual skirmishes has passed. This time we are going all the way.

July 7, 1969
[1969]

 39

From Patriarchal Attitudes

EVA FIGES

LEARNING TO BE A WOMAN

We have suggested earlier on in this book that a patriarchal society depends on sexual taboos, and that psychological taboos have to be enforced with the decline of direct physical control. We see a modern example of this principle at work in an area of learning which, perhaps more than any other, has profoundly influenced our attitudes to ourselves and each other today. I refer to the teachings of Sigmund Freud, which came to full flower just when the social and economic dependency of women was being vigorously challenged. As women demanded the right to learn and work, to share in the capitalist sytem which men had come to regard as a natural male prerogative, Freudian analysis appeared on the intellectual horizon to provide a subtle psychological taboo: the would-be emancipated woman froze in her tracks, stopped from going further by a magic formula more powerful than any fence, and the psychological taboo which forbade her from venturing to compete still operates now.

· · ·

Freud's whole theory of civilization is based on the narrow world he lived in, and ironically, sexual demands both provided the foundation stone and constantly threatened to undermine the whole structure. The whole purpose of a civilized form of life was a fair share-out of the available women (for which we could read monogamy, marriage as Freud understood it) but its continuation depended on a renunciation of instinctual demands. Not only must we not be too greedy, by encroaching on another male's preserves, but we must learn to postpone immediate gratification for work, replace the pleasure principle with the reality principle. This, in a new language, is a reflection of a nineteenth-century morality that extolled hard work and sexual restraint, and advised its ambitious young men to postpone marriage until they were sufficiently established in a profession or industry to bring up a family in middle-class comfort. Civilization is and must be repressive. 'Every individual is virtually an enemy of civilization,' Freud wrote in *The Future of an Illusion,* and:

> We know that a human child cannot successfully complete its development to the civilized stage without passing through a phase of neurosis sometimes of greater and sometimes of lesser distinctness. This is because so many instinctual demands which will later be unserviceable cannot be suppressed by the rational operation of the child's intellect but have to be tamed by acts of repression. . . .

But a large majority of people never become sufficiently repressed and/or civilized. The class distinctions made in that early letter to Martha Bernays are reiterated: 'It is just as impossible to do without control of the mass by a minority as it is to dispense with coercion in the work of civilization. For masses are lazy and unintelligent; they have no love for instinctual renunciation. . . . It is only through the influence of individuals who can set an example and whom masses recognize as their leaders that they can be induced to perform the work and undergo the renunciations on which the existence of civilization depends.'[1]

· · ·

In his biography of Freud, Ernest Jones wrote that he regarded women 'as having their main function to be ministering angels to the needs and comforts of men. His letters and love choice make it plain that he had only one type of sexual object in his mind, a gentle feminine one. While women might belong to the weaker sex, however, he regarded them as finer and ethically nobler than men'.[2] This is an attitude we have already analysed, it remained in force throughout the nineteenth century, but it does not augur well for the founder of psycho-analysis. And, indeed, Ernest Jones goes on: 'There is little double that Freud found the psychology of women more enigmatic than that of men. He said once to Marie Bonaparte: "The great question that has never been answered and which I have not yet been able to answer, despite my thirty years of research into the feminine soul, is *What does a woman want?*".'

Since he had never thought to ask her what she wanted, since his whole life and work had been devoted to telling her what she should want, the fact that woman should have remained an enigma is hardly surprising. And, of course, one of the results of the sexual role-playing which both Freud and society as a whole encouraged, is that most women, even if asked, would no longer really know what they wanted, or would want what they had been told to want. It is like the repressive parent who shouts at his child: 'Do not argue with me, do as you are told' and then, when the child becomes dull and sulky, silent and moody, shrugs his shoulders and complains to a neighbour: 'I don't know what's the matter with him. What does he want?' The more strongly patriarchal a society, the more there will be a tendency for a mystique of womanhood, for women to be regarded as something of an enigma. As late as 1933 Freud, pioneer explorer of the human mind, opened a lecture on 'Femininity' with the words:

> Throughout history people have knocked their heads against the riddle of the nature of femininity. . . . Nor will *you* have escaped worrying over this problem—those of you who are men; to those of you who are women this will not apply—you are yourselves the problem.

. . .

Once again one is faced with Freud's lack of a historical sense. In a society not sexually repressive little boys would be unlikely to develop castration fears; in a society where all the material rewards did not go to those endowed with penises there would be no natural envy of that regalia. We know why blacks try to whiten their skins. But more important, Freud himself is really convinced that women lack something, that there is something missing, rather like the psycho-analyst who reassures his patient with the words: 'Don't worry, you do not have an inferiority complex, you *are* inferior.' It is when a woman refuses to accept this state of affairs, rebels against her inevitable lot, that the trouble really starts. When men reach adult life, all that is left of the castration complex is 'a certain amount of disparagement in their attitude towards women, whom they regard as being castrated',[3] but: 'Quite different are the effects of the castration complex in the female. She acknowledges the fact of her castration, and with it, too, the superiority of the male and her own inferiority; but she rebels against this unwelcome state of affairs.'[4]

> The wish to get the longed-for penis eventually in spite of everything may contribute to the motives that drive a mature woman to analysis, and what she may reasonably expect from analysis—a capacity, for instance, to carry on an intellectual profession—may often be recognized as a sublimated modification of this repressed wish.[5]

In a paper highly praised by Freud, Karl Abraham puts forward the same view of female ambition as a manifestation of the castration complex. 'A considerable number of women', he writes, 'are unable to carry out a full psychical adaption to the female sexual role.' In this case the women may become homosexual, but:

> In some cases their homosexuality does not break through to consciousness; the repressed wish to be male is here found in a sublimated form in the shape of masculine pursuits of an intellectual and professional character and other allied interests. Such women do not, however, consciously deny their femininity, but usually proclaim that these interests are just as much feminine as masculine ones. They consider that the sex of a person has nothing to do with his or her capacities, especially in the mental field. This type of woman is well represented in the woman's movement of today.[6]

So homosexuality disguised as intellect is one consequence of the failure to take what Freud called the 'very circuitous path' to the 'normal female attitude'.[7] Another possible consequence was frigidity.

Now until very recently sexual frigidity in women was undoubtedly a very real problem, thanks to the unnatural restraints imposed upon them for so long. But when one reads Freud and, for that matter, Karl Abraham, one cannot help feeling that both analysts were more concerned with male discomfiture than with female unhappiness. 'Frigidity', wrote Abraham in the essay quoted above, 'is a form of aggression against the man by disappointing him', and anyone who has read Freud's 'The Taboo of Virginity'[8] cannot but be struck by the awful dangers that await the unfortunate male in the bedroom.

'Sexual thraldom' (meaning the psychological dependency which we associate with being in love) is necessary, says Freud in this essay, for the maintenance of civilized, monogamous marriage. It is far more common in women than in men and largely depends on the fact of a girl being a virgin at the time of her marriage. The thraldom is enforced by defloration. But the act of defloration can arouse a deep hostility in the woman towards her sexual partner, women have even been known to attack their husbands after coitus and this hostility can last as long as the marriage; which is why, says Freud, second marriages are often so much more successful.

True to his habit of ignoring historical and sociological factors, this hostility is not ascribed by Freud to a combination of male clumsiness on the one hand, and unnaturally prolonged ignorance and chastity on the other, but firstly to a continuation of 'immature sexuality', i.e. the father fixation ('A husband is, so to speak, never anything but a proxy') and secondly to a much more deep-seated hostility, the result of penis envy, the woman's refusal to fulfil her feminine function. When one imagines the orthodox disciple of Freud in his bedchamber, refusing to acknowledge the function, teleological or otherwise, of his wife's clitoris, one can understand the nervous preoccupation with frigidity. But Freudian feminine psychology, with its emphasis on female passivity in general and exclusively vaginal excitation in particular, must have caused more frigidity than it ever cured.

. . .

The cult of Freudian femininity is by no means dead—one might almost say that it is the last bastion of the institution of marriage. After all, if both partners in a marriage consider their own wishes and interests as equally important conflict is bound to arise. A study made in 1963[9] found that marital satisfaction was related to the wife's ability to perceive her husband's expectations. Their happiness was not correlated with the husband's perception of the wife's expectations, or with their agreement on various aspects of family living. In other words, someone has to be the boss, and it ought to be the man. So a woman's femininity is still defined in terms of her plasticity with regard to man. The predominant trait of the feminine woman, wrote Helene Deutsch, is eroticism.[10] Which is just another way of saying that she is primarily a sexual object. 'What is common to all these [feminine] types is facility in identifying with man in a manner that is most conducive to the happiness of both partners. . . . To the woman falls the larger share of the work of adjustment: she leaves the initiative to the man and out of her own need renounces originality.' For Helene Deutsch, a traditional Freudian, these are the 'good' women, what she calls 'ideal life companions for men'— 'They are the loveliest and most unaggressive of helpmates and they want to remain in that role; they do not insist on their rights—quite the contrary. They are easy to handle in every way—if one only

loves them.' The 'bad' women are people like George Sand, who, she said, 'led a very promiscuous life and ruined many men'. 'Each of George Sand's numerous love affairs terminated in literally the self-same catastrophe: the man was destroyed.'[11] Surely a gross distortion of the true facts. But it is really her intellectuality, which she calls 'a kind of refuge from disappointments in love' which Deutsch cannot forgive. Intellectual activity in woman is a sublimation of the masculinity complex, successful women in this field 'are not aware of the fact that they have paid a high price for it in their feminine values. Woman's intellectuality is to a large extent paid for by the loss of valuable feminine qualities: it feeds on the sap of the affective life and results in impoverishment of this life . . . intuition is God's gift to the feminine woman; everything relating to exploration and cognition, all the forms and kinds of human cultural aspiration that require a strictly objective approach, are with few exceptions, the domain of the masculine intellect, of man's spiritual power, against which woman can rarely compete. All observations point to the fact that the intellectual woman is masculinized; in her, warm intuitive knowledge has yielded to cold unproductive thinking'.[12] And she goes on to say that the masculinized woman does not really achieve anything original but simply exploits masculine achievement. 'She likes to show her identification with men, but unlike the feminine woman, she proposes to do so not by intuitive sympathy, but by a kind of shrewd grasp of masculine ideas and a flattering appreciation of them.' Familiar echoes of Rousseau. 'They can pick up a little of everything, I daresay,' said Mr. Stelling, when Tom Tulliver asked his tutor whether girls could do Euclid. 'They've a great deal of superficial cleverness; but they couldn't go far into anything. They're quick and shallow.' George Eliot was speaking ironically, since the heart of the tragedy in *The Mill on the Floss* is the fact that Maggie was deprived of an education that would have benefited her, an education that was quite unsuitable for her brother, whose real interests were practical. But Helene Deutsch is speaking in deadly earnest. Male dominance can only work with the connivance of the women of a society, and taboos must have their psychological effect on everyone in order to work; but the fact that women themselves (and educated specialists at that) should perpetuate the cult of the womanly woman to this extent is surely proof, not only of the powerful influence of Freud, but of the conformist tendencies which exist at an intellectual as well as a social level: reasoning is shaped by our attitudes, and not vice versa. The outlook is alarming when the conformist is a therapist. The power of such ideas is alarming because it affects both the sick and the healthy, it affects the way we educate people both at home and at school. The people who give marriage guidance are affected by it—I opened a book on one of the foremost marriage guidance services in this country and the first words that caught my eye was a description of one of the female clients: *Accepts femininity sexually, but tries to behave as a man in other respects.* What in god's name is this supposed to mean? The book was published in 1968.[13] That particular patient became increasingly depressed and eventually suicidal, according to the follow-up reports. A leucotomy was even considered. The patient had originally arrived with depression and a confused attitude to her own femininity, which the therapist was trying so unsuccessfully to stabilize. The victims of our social way of life are being treated with a double dose of the disease which originally struck them down—the inadequate brainwashing of childhood is reinforced with a course of therapy when those who break down come for help. There is always a price to be paid for social adjustment, but the price being paid for marital stability is often far too high. It is being paid for by both men and women but, since we live in a male-dominated society, women are by and large paying the higher price. We may become aware of it when there is unhappiness, neurosis and breakdown, but none of us will ever really know just how many corpses are walking about, people who are spiritually dead and defeated, people whose lives are one big might-have-been.

[1970]

NOTES

1. *The Future of an Illusion.*
2. Ernest Jones, *The Life and Work of Sigmund Freud,* p. 377.
3. 'Female Sexuality.'
4. Ibid.
5. 'Femininity.'
6. 'The Female Castration Complex' (1920) from *Selected Papers of Karl Abraham M.D.* (Hogarth Press, 1927).
7. 'Female Sexuality.'
8. *Collected Papers,* Vol. IV.
9. *The Development of Sex Differences,* edited by Eleanor E. Maccoby, pp. 211–12.
10. Helene Deutsch, *Psychology of Women,* Vol. I, p. 151.
11. Ibid., p. 235.
12. Ibid., pp. 229–30.
13. M. Courtenay, *Sexual Discord in Marriage* (Tavistock Publications, 1968).

 40

From The Dialectic of Sex

SHULAMITH FIRESTONE

Sex class is so deep as to be invisible. Or it may appear as a superficial inequality, one that can be solved by merely a few reforms, or perhaps by the full integration of women into the labor force. But the reaction of the common man, woman, and child—"*That?* Why you can't change *that!* You must be out of your mind!"—is the closest to the truth. We are talking about something every bit as deep as that. This gut reaction—the assumption that, even when they don't know it, feminists are talking about changing a fundamental biological condition—is an honest one. That so profound a change cannot be easily fit into traditional categories of thought, e.g., "political," is not because these categories do not apply but because they are not big enough: radical feminism bursts through them. If there were another word more all-embracing than *revolution,* I would use it.

Until a certain level of evolution had been reached and technology had achieved its present sophistication, to question fundamental biological conditions was insanity. Why should a woman give up her precious seat in the cattle car for a bloody struggle she could not hope to win? But, for the first time in some countries, the preconditions for feminist revolution exist—indeed, the situation is beginning to *demand* such a revolution.

The first women are fleeing the massacre, and, shaking and tottering, are beginning to find each other. Their first move is a careful joint observation, to resensitize a fractured consciousness. This is painful: No matter how many levels of consciousness one reaches, the problem always goes deeper. It is everywhere. The division Yin and Yang pervades all culture, history, economics, nature itself; modern Western versions of sex discrimination are only the most recent layer. To so heighten one's sensitivity to sexism presents problems far worse than the black militant's new awareness of racism: Feminists have to question, not just all of *Western* culture, but the organization of culture itself, and further, even the very organization of nature. Many women give up in despair: if *that's* how deep it goes they don't want to know. Others continue strengthening and enlarging the movement, their painful sensitivity to female oppression existing for a purpose: eventually to eliminate it.

Before we can act to change a situation, however, we must know how it has arisen and evolved, and through what institutions it now operates. Engels' "[We must] examine the historic succession of events from which the antagonism has sprung in order to discover in the conditions thus created the means of ending the conflict." For feminist revolution we shall need an analysis of the dynamics of sex war as comprehensive as the Marx-Engels analysis of class antagonism was for the economic revolution. More comprehensive. For we are dealing with a larger problem, with an oppression that goes back beyond recorded history to the animal kingdom itself.

In creating such an analysis we can learn a lot from Marx and Engels: Not their literal opinions about women—about the condition of women as an oppressed class they know next to nothing, recognizing it only where it overlaps with economics— but rather their analytic *method*.

Marx and Engels outdid their socialist forerunners in that they developed a method of analysis which was both *dialectical* and *materialistic*. The first in centuries to view history dialectically, they saw the world as process, a natural flux of action and reaction, of opposites yet inseparable and interpenetrating. Because they were able to perceive history as movie rather than as snapshot, they attempted to avoid falling into the stagnant "metaphysical" view that had trapped so many other great minds. (This sort of analysis itself may be a product of the sex division. . . . They combined this view of the dynamic interplay of historical forces with a material-

istic one, that is, they attempted for the first time to put historical and cultural change on a real basis, to trace the development of economic classes to organic causes. By understanding thoroughly the mechanics of history, they hoped to show men how to master it.

. . . Marx and Engels . . . attempted a scientific approach to history. They traced the class conflict to its real economic origins, projecting an economic solution based on objective economic preconditions already present: the seizure by the proletariat of the means of production would lead to a communism in which government had withered away, no longer needed to repress the lower class for the sake of the higher. In the classless society the interests of every individual would be synonymous with those of the larger society.

But the doctrine of historical materialism, much as it was a brilliant advance over previous historical analysis, was not the complete answer, as later events bore out. For though Marx and Engels grounded their theory in reality, it was only a *partial* reality. . . . It would be a mistake to attempt to explain the oppression of women according to this strictly economic interpretation. The class analysis is a beautiful piece of work, but limited: Although correct in a linear sense, it does not go deep enough. There is a whole sexual substratum of the historical dialectic that Engels at times dimly perceives, but because he can see sexuality only through an economic filter, reducing everything to that, he is unable to evaluate in its own right.

Engels did observe that the original division of labor was between man and woman for the purposes of childbreeding; that within the family the husband was the owner, the wife the means of production, the children the labor; and that reproduction of the human species was an important economic system distinct from the means of production.

But Engels has been given too much credit for these scattered recognitions of the oppression of women as a class. In fact he acknowledged the sexual class system only where it overlapped and illuminated his economic construct. Engels didn't do so well even in this respect. But Marx was worse: There is a growing recognition of Marx's bias against women (a cultural bias shared by Freud as well as all men of culture), dangerous if one attempts to squeeze feminism into an orthodox Marxist framework—freezing what were only incidental insights of Marx and Engels about sex class into dogma. Instead, we must enlarge historical materialism to *include* the strictly Marxian, in the same way that the physics of relativity did not invalidate Newtonian physics so much as it drew a circle around it, limiting its application—but only through comparison—to a smaller sphere. For an economic diagnosis traced to ownership of the means of production, even of the means of *re*production, does not explain everything. There is a level of reality that does not stem directly from economics.

The assumption that, beneath economics, reality is psychosexual is often rejected as ahistorical by those who accept a dialectical materialist view of history because it seems to land us back where Marx began: groping through a fog of utopian hypotheses, philosophical systems that might be right, that might be wrong (there is no way to tell), systems that explain concrete historical developments by *a priori* categories of thought; historical materialism, however, attempted to explain "knowing" by "being" and not vice versa.

But there is still an untried third alternative: We can attempt to develop a materialist view of history based on sex itself.

The early feminist theorists were to a materialist view of sex what Fourier, Bebel, and Owen were to a materialist view of class. By and large, feminist theory has been as inadequate as were the early feminist attempts to correct sexism. This was to be expected. The problem is so immense that, at first try, only the surface could be skimmed, the most blatant inequalities described. Simone de Beauvoir was the only one who came close to—who perhaps has done—the definitive analysis. Her profound work *The Second Sex*—which appeared as recently as the early fifties to a world convinced that feminism was dead—for the first time attempted to ground feminism in its historical base. Of all feminist theorists De Beauvoir is the most comprehensive and far-reaching, relating feminism to the best ideas in our culture.

It may be this virtue is also her one failing: she is almost too sophisticated, too knowledgeable. Where this becomes a weakness—and this is still certainly debatable—is in her rigidly existentialist interpretation of feminism (one wonders how much Sartre had to do with this). This in view of the fact that all cultural systems, including existentialism, are themselves determined by the sex dualism. She says:

> Man never thinks of himself without thinking of the Other; he views the world under the sign of duality *which is not in the first place sexual in character.* But being different from man, who sets himself up as the Same, it is naturally to the category of the Other that woman is consigned; the Other includes woman. [Italics mine.]

Perhaps she has overshot her mark: Why postulate a fundamental Hegelian concept of Otherness as the final explanation—and then carefully document the biological and historical circumstances that have pushed the class "women" into such a category—when one has never seriously considered the much simpler and more likely possibility that the fundamental dualism sprang from sex itself? To posit *a priori* categories of thought and existence—Otherness, Transcendence, Immanence—into which history then falls may not be necessary. Marx and Engels had discovered that these philosophical categories themselves grew out of history.

Before assuming such categories, let us first try to develop an analysis in which biology itself—procreation—is at the origin of the dualism. The immediate assumption of the layman that the unequal division of the sexes is "natural" may be well-founded. . . .

The *biological family*—the basic reproductive unit of male/female/infant, in whatever form of social organization—is characterized by these fundamental—if not immutable—facts:

1. That women throughout history before the advent of birth control were at the continual mercy of their biology—menstruation, menopause, and "female ills," constant painful childbirth, wetnursing and care of infants, all of which made them dependent on males (whether brother, father, husband, lover, or clan, government, community-at-large) for physical survival.

2. That human infants take an even longer time to grow up than animals, and thus are helpless and, for some short period at least, dependent on adults for physical survival.

3. That a basic mother/child interdependency has existed in some form in every society, past or present, and thus has shaped the psychology of every mature female and every infant.

4. That the natural reproductive difference between the sexes led directly to the first division of labor based on sex, which is at the origins of all further division into economic and cultural classes and is possibly even at the root of all caste (discrimination based on sex and other biologically determined characteristics such as race, age, etc.).

. . .The biological family that we have described has existed everywhere throughout time. Even in matriarchies where woman's fertility is worshipped, and the father's role is unknown or unimportant, though perhaps not the genetic father, there is still some dependence of the female and the infant on the male. And though it is true that the nuclear family is only a recent development, one which, as I shall attempt to show, only intensifies the psychological penalties of the biological family, though it is true that throughout history there have been many variations on this biological family, the contingencies I have described existed in all of them, causing specific psychosexual distortions in the human personality.

· · ·

Though the sex class system may have originated in fundamental biological conditions, this does not guarantee once the biological basis of their oppression has been swept away that women and children will be freed. On the contrary, the new technology, especially fertility control, may be used against them to reinforce the entrenched system of exploitation.

So that just as to assure elimination of economic classes requires the revolt of the underclass (the proletariat) and, in a temporary dictatorship, their seizure of the means of production, so to assure the elimination of sexual classes requires the revolt of the underclass (women) and the seizure of control of reproduction: the restoration to women of ownership of their own bodies, as well as feminine control of human fertility, including both the new technology and all the social institutions of childbearing and childrearing. And just as the end goal of socialist revolution was not only the elimination of the economic class *privilege* but of the economic class *distinction* itself, so the end goal of feminist revolution must be, unlike that of the first feminist movement, not just the elimination of male *privilege* but of the sex *distinction* itself: genital differences between human beings would no longer matter culturally. (A reversion to an unobstructed *pansexuality*—Freud's "polymorphous perversity"—would probably supersede hetero-, homo-, bisexuality.) The reproduction of the species by one sex for the benefit of both would be replaced by (at least the option of) artificial reproduction: children would be born to both sexes equally, or independently of either, however one chooses to look at it; the dependence of the child on the mother (and vice versa) would give way to a greatly shortened dependence on a small group of others in general, and any remaining inferiority to adults in physical strength would be compensated for culturally. The division of labor would be ended by the elimination of labor altogether (cybernation). The tyranny of the biological family would be broken.

And with it the psychology of power. As Engels claimed for strictly socialist revolution:

> The existence of not simply this or that ruling class but of any ruling class at all [will have] become an obsolete anachronism.

That socialism has never come near achieving this predicated goal is not only the result of unfulfilled or misfired economic preconditions, but also because the Marxian analysis itself was insufficient: it did not dig deep enough to the psychosexual roots of class. Marx was onto something more profound than he knew when he observed that the family contained within itself in miniature all the antagonisms that later develop on a wide scale within the society and the state. For unless revolution disturbs the basic social organization, the biological family—the vinculum through which the psychology of power can always be smuggled—the tapeworm of exploitation will never be annihilated. We shall need a sexual revolution much larger than—inclusive of—a socialist one to truly eradicate all class systems.

· · ·

[1970]

41

The Liberation of Black Women

PAULI MURRAY

Black women, historically, have been doubly victimized by the twin immoralities of Jim Crow and Jane Crow. Jane Crow refers to the entire range of assumptions, attitudes, stereotypes, customs, and arrangements which have robbed women of a positive self-concept and prevented them from participating fully in society as equals with men. Traditionally, racism and sexism in the United States have shared some common origins, displayed similar manifestations, reinforced one another, and are so deeply intertwined in the country's institutions that the successful outcome of the struggle against racism will depend in large part upon the simultaneous elimination of all discrimination based upon sex. Black women, faced with these dual barriers, have often found that sex bias is more formidable than racial bias. If anyone should ask a Negro woman in America what has been her greatest achievement, her honest answer would be, "I survived!"

Negro women have endured their double burden with remarkable strength and fortitude. With dignity they have shared with black men a partnership as members of an embattled group excluded from the normal protections of the society and engaged in a struggle for survival during nearly four centuries of a barbarous slave trade, two centuries of chattel slavery, and a century or more of illusive citizenship. Throughout this struggle, into which has been poured most of the resources and much of the genius of successive generations of American Negroes, these women have often carried a disproportionate share of responsibility for the black family as they strove to keep its integrity intact against a host of indignities to which it has been subjected. Black women have not only stood shoulder to shoulder with black men in every phase of the struggle, but they have often continued to stand firmly when their men were destroyed by it. Few Blacks are unfamiliar with that heroic, if formidable, figure exhorting her children and grandchildren to overcome every obstacle and humiliation and to "Be somebody!"

In the battle for survival, Negro women developed a tradition of independence and self-reliance, characteristics which according to the late Dr. E. Franklin Frazier, Negro sociologist, have "provided generally a pattern of equalitarian relationship between men and women in America." The historical factors which have fostered the black women's feeling of independence have been the economic necessity to earn a living to help support their families—if indeed they were not the sole breadwinners—and the need for the black community to draw heavily upon the resources of all of its members in order to survive.

Yet these survival values have often been distorted, and the qualities of strength and independence observable in many Negro women have been stereotyped as "female dominance" attributed to the "matriarchal" character of the Negro family developed during slavery and its aftermath. The popular conception is that because society has emasculated the black male, he has been unable to assume his economic role as head of the household and the black woman's earning power has placed her in a dominant position. The black militant's cry for the retrieval of black manhood suggests an acceptance of this stereotype, an association of masculinity with male dominance and a tendency to treat the values of self-reliance and independence as purely masculine traits. Thus, while Blacks generally have recognized the fusion of white supremacy and male dominance (note the popular expressions "The Man" and "Mr. Charlie"), male spokesmen for Negro rights have sometimes pandered to sexism in their fight against racism. When nationally known civil rights leader James Farmer ran for Congress against Mrs. Shirley Chisholm in 1968, his campaign literature stressed the need for a "strong male image" and a "man's voice" in Washington.

If idealized values of masculinity and femininity are used as criteria, it would be hard to say whether the experience of slavery subjected the black male to any greater loss of his manhood than the black female of her womanhood. The chasm between the slave woman and her white counterpart (whose own enslavement was masked by her position as a symbol of high virtue and an object of chivalry) was as impassable as the gulf between the male slave and his arrogant white master. If black males suffered from real and psychological castration, black females bore the burden of real or psychological rape. Both situations involved the negation of the individual's personal integrity and attacked the foundations of one's sense of personal worth.

The history of slavery suggests that black men and women shared a rough equality of hardship and degradation. While the black woman's position as sex object and breeder may have given her temporarily greater leverage in dealing with her white master than the black male enjoyed, in the long run it denied her a positive image of herself. On the other hand, the very nature of slavery foreclosed certain conditions experienced by white women. The black women had few expectations of economic dependence upon the male or of derivative status through marriage. She emerged from slavery without the illusions of a specially protected position as a woman or the possibilities of a parasitic existence as a woman. As Dr. Frazier observed, "Neither economic necessity nor tradition has instilled in her the spirit of subordination to masculine authority. Emancipation only tended to confirm in many cases the spirit of self-sufficiency which slavery had taught."

Throughout the history of Black America, its women have been in the forefront of the struggle for human rights. A century ago Harriet Tubman and Sojourner Truth were titans of the Abolitionist movement. In the 1890's Ida B. Wells-Barnett carried on a one-woman crusade against lynching. Mary McLeod Bethune and Mary Church Terrell symbolize the stalwart woman leaders of the first half of the twentieth century. At the age of ninety, Mrs. Terrell successfully challenged segregation in public places in the nation's capital through a Supreme Court decision in 1953.

In contemporary times we have Rosa Parks setting off the mass struggle for civil rights in the South by refusing to move to the back of the bus in Montgomery in 1955; Daisy Bates guiding the Little Rock Nine through a series of school desegregation crises in 1957–59; Gloria Richardson facing down the National Guard in Cambridge, Maryland, in the early sixties; or Coretta Scott King picking up the fallen standard of her slain husband to continue the fight. Not only these and many other women whose names are well known have given this great human effort its peculiar vitality, but also women in many communities whose name will never be known have revealed the courage and strength of the black woman in America. They are the mothers who stood in schoolyards of the South with their children, many times alone. One cannot help asking: "Would the black struggle have come this far without the indomitable determination of its women?"

Now that some attention is finally given to the place of the Negro in American history, how much do we hear of the role of the Negro woman? Of the many books published on the Negro experience and the Black Revolution in recent times, to date not one has concerned itself with the struggles of black women and their contributions to history. Of approximately 800 full-length articles published in the *Journal of Negro History* since its inception in 1916, only six have dealt directly with the Negro woman. Only two have considered Negro women as a group: Carter G. Woodson's "The Negro Washerwoman: A Vanishing Figure" (14 *JNH*, 1930) and Jessie W. Pankhurst's "The Role of the Black Mammy in the Plantation Household" (28 *JNH*, 1938).

This historical neglect continues into the present. A significant feature of the civil rights revolution of the 1950's and 1960's was its inclusiveness born of the broad participation of men, women, and children without regard to age and sex. As indicated, school children often led by their mothers in the 1950's won world-wide acclaim for their courage in desegregating the schools. A black child can have no finer heritage to give a sense of "somebodiness" than the knowledge of having personally been part of the great sweep of history. (An older generation, for example, takes pride in the use of the term "Negro," having been part of a seventy-five-year effort to dignify the term by capitalizing it. Now some black militants with a woeful lack of historical perspective have allied themselves symbolically with white racists by downgrading the term to lower case again.) Yet, despite the crucial role which Negro women have played in the struggle, in the great mass of magazine and newspaper print expended on the racial crisis, the aspirations of the black community have been articulated almost exclusively by black males. There has been very little public discussion of the problems, objectives, or concerns of black women.

Reading through much of the current literature on the Black Revolution, one is left with the impression that for all the rhetoric about self-determination, the main thrust of black militancy is a bid of black males to share power with white males in a continuing patriarchal society in which both black and white females are relegated to a secondary status. For example, *Ebony* magazine published a special issue on the Negro woman in 1966. Some of the articles attempted to delineate the contributions of Negro women as heroines in the civil rights battle in Dixie, in the building of the New South, in the arts and professions, and as intellectuals. The editors, however, felt it necessary to include a full-page editorial to counter the possible effect of the articles by women contributors. After paying tribute to the Negro woman's contributions in the past, the editorial reminded *Ebony*'s readers that "the past is behind us," that "the immediate goal of the Negro woman today should be the establishment of a strong family unit in which the father is the dominant person," and that the Negro woman would do well to follow the example of the Jewish mother "who pushed her husband to success, educated her male children first and engineered good marriages for her daughters." The editors also declared that the career woman "should be willing to postpone her aspirations until her children, too, are old enough to be on their own," and, as if the point had not been made clear enough, suggested that if "the woman should, by any chance, make more money than her husband, the marriage could be in real trouble."

While not as blatantly Victorian as *Ebony,* other writers on black militancy have shown only slightly less myopia. In *Black Power and Urban Crisis,* Dr. Nathan Wright, Chairman of the 1967 National Black Power Conference, made only three brief references to women: "the employment of female skills," "the beauty of black women," and housewives. His constant reference to Black Power was in terms of black males and black manhood. He appeared to be wholly unaware of the parallel struggles of women and youth for inclusion in decision-making, for when he dealt with the reallocation of power, he noted that "the churches and housewives of America" are the most readily influential groups which can aid in this process.

In *Black Rage,* psychiatrists Greer and Cobbs devote a chapter to achieving womanhood. While they sympathetically describe the traumatic experience of self-deprecation which a black woman undergoes in a society in which the dominant standard of beauty is "the blond, blue-eyed, white-skinned girl with regular features," and make a telling point about the burden of the stereotype that Negro women are available to white men, they do not get beyond a framework in which the Negro woman is seen as a sex object. Emphasizing her concern with "feminine narcissism" and the need to be "lovable" and "attractive," they conclude: "Under the sign of discouragement and rejection which governs so much of her physical operation, she is inclined to organize her personal ambitions in terms of her achievements serving to compensate for other losses and hurts." Nowhere do the authors suggest that Negro women, like women generally, might be motivated to achieve as *persons.* Implied throughout the discussion is the sexuality of Negro females.

The ultimate expression of this bias is the statement attributed to a black militant male leader: "The position of the black woman should be prone." Thus, there appears to be a distinctly conservative and backward-looking view in much of what black males write today about black women, and many black women have been led to believe that the restoration of the black male to his lost manhood must take precedence over the claims of black women to egalitarian status. Consequently, there has been a tendency to acquiesce without vigorous protest to policies which emphasize the "underemployment" of the black male in relation to the black female and which encourage the upgrading and education of black male youth while all but ignoring the educational and training needs of black female youth, although the highest rates of unemployment today are among black female teenagers. A parallel tendency to concentrate on career and training opportunities primarily for black males is evident in government and industry.

As this article goes to press, further confirmation of a patriarchal view on the part of organizations dominated by black males is found in the BLACK DECLARATION OF INDEPENDENCE published as a full-page advertisement in *The New York Times* on July 3, 1970. Signed by members of the National Committee of Black Churchmen and presuming to speak "By Order and on Behalf of Black People," this document ignores both the personhood and the contributions of black women to the cause of human rights. The drafters show a shocking insensitivity to the revitalized women's rights/women's liberation movement which is beginning to capture the front pages of national newspapers and the mass media. It evidences a parochialism which has hardly moved beyond the eighteenth century in its thinking about women. Not only does it paraphrase the 1776 Declaration about the equality of "all Men" with a noticeable lack of imagination, but it also declares itself "in the Name of our good People and our own Black Heroes." Then follows a list of black males prominent in the historical struggle for liberation. The names of Harriet Tubman, Sojourner Truth, Mary McLeod Bethune, or Daisy Bates, or any other black women are conspicuous by their absence. If black male leaders of the Christian faith—who concededly have suffered much through denigration of their personhood and who are committed to the equality of all in the eyes of God—are callous to the indivisibility of human rights, who is to remember?

In the larger society, of course, black and white women share the common burden of discrimination based upon sex. The parallels between racism and sexism have been distinctive features of American society, and the movements to eliminate these two evils have often been allied and sometimes had interchangeable leadership. The beginnings of a women's rights movement in this country is linked with the Abolitionist movement. In 1840, William Lloyd Garrison and Charles Remond, the latter a Negro, refused to be seated as delegates to the World Anti-Slavery Convention in London when they learned that women members of the American delegation had been excluded because of their sex and could sit only in the balcony and observe the proceedings. The seed of the Seneca Falls Convention of 1848, which marked the formal beginning of the women's rights struggle in the United States, was planted at that London conference. Frederick Douglass attended the Seneca Falls Convention and rigorously supported Elizabeth Cady Stanton's daring resolution on woman's suffrage. Except for a temporary defection during the controversy over adding "sex" to the Fifteenth Amendment, Douglass remained a staunch advocate of women's rights until his death in 1895. Sojourner Truth and other black women were also active in the movement for women's rights, as indicated earlier.

Despite the common interests of black and white women, however, the dichotomy of a racially segregated society which has become increasingly polarized has prevented them from cementing a natural alliance. Communication and the cooperation have been hesitant, limited, and formal. In the past Negro women have tended to identify discrimination against them as primarily racial and have accorded high priority to the struggle for Negro rights. They have had little time or energy for consideration of women's rights. And, until recent years, their egalitarian position in the struggle seemed to justify such preoccupation.

As the drive for black empowerment continues, however, black women are becoming increasingly aware of a new development which creates for them a dilemma of competing identities and priorities. On the one hand, as Dr. Jeanne Noble has observed, "establishing 'black manhood' became a prime goal of black revolution," and black women began to realize "that black men wanted to determine the policy and progress of black people without female participation in decisionmaking and leadership positions." On the other hand, a rising movement for women's liberation is challenging the concept of male dominance which the Black Revolution appears to have embraced. Confronted with the multiple barriers of poverty, race, and sex, the quandary of black women is how best to distribute their energies among these issues and what strategies to pursue which will minimize conflicting interests and objectives.

Cognizant of the similarities between paternalism and racial arrogance, black women are nevertheless handicapped by the continuing stereotype of the black "matriarchy" and the demand that black women now step back and push black men into positions of leadership. They are made to feel disloyal to racial interests if they insist upon women's rights.

Moreover, to the extent that racial polarization often accompanies the thrust for Black Power, black women find it increasingly difficult to make common cause with white women. These developments raise several questions. Are black women gaining or losing in the drive toward human rights? As the movement for women's liberation becomes increasingly a force to be reckoned with, are black women to take a backward step and sacrifice their egalitarian tradition? What are the alternatives to matriarchal dominance on the one hand or male supremacy on the other?

Much has been written in the past about the matriarchal character of Negro family life, the relatively favored position of Negro women, and the tensions and difficulties growing out of the assumptions that they are better educated and more able to obtain employment than Negro males. These assumptions require closer examination. It is true that according to reports of the Bureau of the Census, in March 1968 an estimated 278,000 nonwhite women had completed four or more years of college—86,000 more than male college graduates in the nonwhite population (Negro women constitute 93 per cent of all nonwhite women, and that in March 1966 the median years of school completed by Negro females (10.1) was slightly higher than that for Negro males (9.4). It should be borne in mind that this is not unique to the black community. In the white population as well, females exceed males in median years of school completed (12.2 to 12.0) and do not begin to lag behind males until the college years. The significant fact is that the percentage of both sexes in the Negro population eighteen years of age and over in 1966 who had completed four years of college was roughly equivalent (males: 2.2 per cent; females: 2.3 per cent). When graduate training is taken into account, the proportion of Negro males with five or more years of college training (3.3 per cent) moved ahead of the Negro females (3.2 per cent). Moreover, 1966 figures show that a larger proportion of Negro males (63 per cent) than Negro females (57 per cent) was enrolled in school and that this superiority continued into college enrollments (males: 5 per cent; females 4 per cent). These 1966 figures reflect a concerted effort to broaden educational opportunities for Negro males manifested in recruitment policies and scholarship programs made available primarily to Negro male students. Though later statistics are not now available, this trend appears to have accelerated each year.

The assumption that Negro women have more education than Negro men also overlooks the possibility that the greater number of college-trained Negro women may correspond to the larger number of Negro women in the population. Of enormous importance to a consideration of Negro family life and the relation between the sexes is the startling fact of the excess of females over males. The Bureau of the Census estimated that in July 1968 there were 688,000 more Negro females than Negro males. Although census officials attribute this disparity to errors in counting a "floating" Negro male population, this excess has appeared in steadily increasing numbers in every census since 1860, but has received little analysis beyond periodic comment. Over the past century the reported ratio of black males to black females has decreased. In 1966, there were less than 94 black males to every 100 females.

The numerical imbalance between the sexes in the black population is more dramatic than in any other group in the United States. Within the white population the excess of women shows up in the middle or later years. In the black population, however, the sex imbalance is present in every age group over fourteen and is greatest during the age when most marriages occur. In the twenty-five to forty-four age group, the percentage of males within the black population drops to 86.9 as compared to 96.9 for white males.

It is now generally known that females tend to be constitutionally stronger than males, that male babies are more fragile than female babies, that boys are harder to rear than girls, that the male death rate is slightly higher and life expectancy for males is shorter than that of females. Add to these general factors the special hardships to which the Negro minority is exposed—poverty, crowded living conditions, poor health, marginal jobs, and minimum protection against hazards of accident and illness—and it becomes apparent that there is much in the American environment that is particularly hostile to the survival of the black male. But even if we discount these factors and accept the theory that the sex ratio is the result of errors in census counting, it

is difficult to avoid the conclusion that a large number of black males have so few stable ties that they
are not included as functioning units of the society.
In either case formidable pressures are created for
black women.

The explosive social implications of an excess of
more than half a million black girls and women over
fourteen years of age are obvious in a society in
which the mass media intensify notions of glamour
and expectations of romantic love and marriage,
while at the same time there are many barriers
against interracial marriages. When such marriages
do take place they are more likely to involve black
males and white females, which tends to aggravate
the issue. (No value judgment about interracial
marriages is implied here. I am merely trying to describe a social dilemma.) The problem of an excess
female population is a familiar one in countries
which have experienced heavy male casualties during wars, but an excess female ethnic minority as an
enclave within a larger population raises important
social issues. To what extent are the tensions and
conflicts traditionally associated with the matriarchal framework of Negro family life in reality due to
this imbalance and the pressures it generates? Does
this excess explain the active competition between
Negro professional men and women seeking employment in markets which have limited or excluded
Negroes? And does this competition intensify the
stereotype of the matriarchal society and female
dominance? What relationship is there between the
high rate of illegitimacy among black women and
the population figures we have described?

These figures suggest that the Negro woman's
fate in the United States, while inextricably bound
with that of the Negro male in one sense, transcends
the issue of Negro rights. Equal opportunity for her
must mean equal opportunity to compete for jobs
and to find a mate in the total society. For as long as
she is confined to an area in which she must compete fiercely for a mate, she will remain the object of
sexual exploitation and the victim of all the social
evils which such exploitation involves.

When we compare the position of the black
woman to that of the white woman, we find that she
remains single more often, bears more children, is
in the labor market longer and in greater proportion,
has less education, earns less, is widowed earlier,

and carries a relatively heavier economic responsibility as family head than her white counterpart.

In 1966, black women represented one of every
seven women workers, although Negroes generally
constitute only 11 per cent of the total population in
the United States. Of the 3,105,000 black women
eighteen years of age and over who were in the labor
force, however, nearly half (48.2 per cent) were either
single, widowed, divorced, separated from their husbands, or their husbands were absent for other reasons, as compared with 31.8 per cent of white women
in similar circumstances. Moreover, six of every ten
black women were in household employment or other
service jobs. Conversely, while 58.8 per cent of all
women workers held white collar positions, only 23.2
per cent of black women held such jobs.

As working wives, black women contribute a
higher proportion to family income than do white
women. Among nonwhite wives in 1965, 58 per
cent contributed to 20 per cent or more of the total
family income, 43 per cent contributed 30 per cent
or more and 27 per cent contributed 40 per cent or
more. The comparable percentages for white wives
were 56 per cent, 40 per cent, and 24 per cent
respectively.

Black working mothers are more heavily represented in the labor force than white mothers. In
March 1966, nonwhite working mothers with children under eighteen years of age represented 48 per
cent of all nonwhite mothers with children this age
as compared with 35 per cent of white working
mothers. Nonwhite working mothers also represented four of every ten of all nonwhite mothers of
children under six years of age. Of the 12,300,000
children under fourteen years of age in February
1965 whose mothers worked, only 2 per cent were
provided group care in day-care centers. Adequate
child care is an urgent need for working mothers
generally, but it has particular significance for the
high proportion of black working mothers of young
children.

Black women also carry heavy responsibilities as
family heads. In 1966, one-fourth of all black families were headed by a woman as compared with less
than one-tenth of all white families. The economic
disabilities of women generally are aggravated in the
case of black women. Moreover, while all families
headed by women are more vulnerable to poverty

than husband–wife families, the black woman family head is doubly victimized. For example, the median wage or salary income of all women workers who were employed full time the year round in 1967 was only 58 per cent of that of all male workers, and the median earnings of white females was less than that of black males. The median wage of nonwhite women workers, however, was $3,268, or only 71 per cent of the median income of white women workers. In 1965, one-third of all families headed by women lived in poverty, but 62 per cent of the 1,132,000 nonwhite families with a female head were poor.

A significant factor in the low economic and social status of black women is their concentration at the bottom rung of the employment ladder. More than one-third of all nonwhite working women are employed as private household workers. The median wages of women private household workers who were employed full time the year round in 1968 was only $1,701. Furthermore, these workers are not covered by the Federal minimum wage and hours law and are generally excluded from state wage and hours laws, unemployment compensation, and workmen's compensation.

The black woman is triply handicapped. She is heavily represented in nonunion employment and thus has few of the benefits to be derived from labor organization or social legislation. She is further victimized by discrimination because of race and sex. Although she has made great strides in recent decades in closing the educational gap, she still suffers from inadequate education and training. In 1966, only 71.1 per cent of all Negro women had completed eight grades of elementary school compared to 88 per cent of all white women. Only one-third (33.2 per cent) of all Negro women had completed high school as compared with more than one-half of all white women (56.3). More than twice as many white women, proportionally, have completed college (7.2 per cent) as black women (3.2 per cent).

The notion of the favored economic position of the black female in relation to the black male is a myth. The 1966, median earnings of full-time year-round nonwhite female workers was only 65 per cent of that of nonwhite males. The unemployment rate for adult nonwhite women (6.6) was higher than for their male counterparts (4.9). Among non-

white teenagers, the unemployment rate for girls was 31.1 as compared with 21.2 for boys.

In the face of their multiple disadvantages, it seems clear that black women can neither postpone nor subordinate the fight against sex discrimination to the Black Revolution. Many of them must expect to be self-supporting and perhaps to support others for a considerable period or for life. In these circumstances, while efforts to raise educational and employment levels for black males will ease some of the economic and social burdens now carried by many black women, for a large and apparently growing minority these burdens will continue. As a matter of sheer survival black women have no alternative but to insist upon equal opportunities without regard to sex in training, education, and employment. Given their heavy family responsibilities, the outlook for their children will be bleak indeed unless they are encouraged in every way to develop their potential skills and earning power.

Because black women have an equal stake in women's liberation and black liberation, they are key figures at the juncture of these two movements. White women feminists are their natural allies in both causes. Their own liberation is linked with the issues which are stirring women today: adequate income maintenance and the elimination of poverty, repeal or reform of abortion laws, a national system of child-care centers, extension of labor standards to workers now excluded, cash maternity benefits as part of a system of social insurance, and the removal of all sex barriers to educational and employment opportunities at all levels. Black women have a special stake in the revolt against the treatment of women primarily as sex objects, for their own history has left them with the scars of the most brutal and degrading aspects of sexual exploitation.

The middle-class Negro woman is strategically placed by virtue of her tradition of independence and her long experience in civil rights and can play a creative role in strengthening the alliance between the Black Revolution and Women's Liberation. Her advantages of training and her values make it possible for her to communicate with her white counterparts, interpret the deepest feelings within the black community, and cooperate with white women on the basis of mutual concerns as women. The possibility of productive interchange between black and white women is greatly facilitated by the absence of power relationships which separate black and white males as antagonists. By asserting a leadership role in the growing feminist movement, the black woman can help to keep it allied to the objectives of black liberation while simultaneously advancing the interests of all women.

The lesson of history that all human rights are indivisible and that the failure to adhere to this principle jeopardizes the rights of all is particularly applicable here. A built-in hazard of an aggressive ethnocentric movement which disregards the interests of other disadvantaged groups is that it will become parochial and ultimately self-defeating in the face of hostile reactions, dwindling allies, and mounting frustrations. As Dr. Caroline F. Ware has pointed out, perhaps the most essential instrument for combating the divisive effects of a black-only movement is the voice of black women insisting upon the unity of civil rights of women and Negroes as well as other minorities and excluded groups. Only a broad movement for human rights can prevent the Black Revolution from becoming isolated and can insure its ultimate success.

Beyond all the present conflict lies the important task of reconciliation of the races in America on the basis of genuine equality and human dignity. A powerful force in bringing about this result can be generated through the process of black and white women working together to achieve their common humanity.

[1970]

 42

Why OWL (Older Women's Liberation)?

OLDER WOMEN'S LEAGUE

In general, the Women's Liberation Movement is a young movement. Statistics on age are not available but observation indicates the average age of women participating in the movement to be around 25. Older women in the movement are exceedingly

rare. OWL (women 30 and above), unlike the younger women's liberation groups, was consciously created by women who:

1. felt different from the main body of the movement because of age, life experiences, family commitments and goal orientations.

2. felt that we had experienced long years of personal oppression and participated in the events of life (child birth, child rearing, marriage, divorce, homemaking and careers) that many of the younger groups theorized about.

3. felt that our special skills and knowledge could be utilized for the benefit of the movement.

OWL addresses itself to problems that do not often arise at other meetings. *Problems* like:

1. How does one live equitably with a husband when the relationship is not egalitarian?

2. How does one bring up children in an oppressive society?

3. How does a mother relate to adolescent sons who are attempting to reach male maturity by emulating male stereotyped role models?

4. How does one raise a daughter?

5. Problems of rearing children when there is one parent.

6. Problems of alimony.

7. How to cope with aging and dependent parents.

8. How to pursue a job, career or *anything* while raising a family.

9. How to participate in the movement if one's husband objects.

10. How to change from 20 to 40 years of behavioral response.

We of OWL believe that we can speak to a broad segment of Amerikan women. Having shared the problems of housewives, of the poor, of the dependent, OWL is developing programs that will speak to all our needs. Programs like:

1. Pay for housewives, the housewives' bill of rights
2. Divorce referral service
3. Transitional communes
4. Job training, employment services
5. Child care, total health care

Sisters, join with us to create a new society.

[1970]

 43

The Woman Identified Woman

RADICALESBIANS

Our awareness is due to all women who have struggled and learned in consciousness raising groups, but particularly to gay women whose path has delineated and focused the women's movement on the nature and underlying causes of our oppression.

What is a lesbian? A lesbian is the rage of all women condensed to the point of explosion. She is the woman who, often beginning at an extremely early age, acts in accordance with her inner compulsion to be a more complete and freer human being than her society—perhaps then, but certainly later—cares to allow her. These needs and actions, over a period of years, bring her into painful conflict with people, situations, the accepted ways of thinking, feeling and behaving, until she is in a state of continual war with everything around her, and usually with her self. She may not be fully conscious of the political implications of what for her began as personal necessity, but on some level she has not been able to accept the limitations and oppression laid on her by the most basic role of her society—the female role. The turmoil she experiences tends to induce guilt proportional to the degree to which she feels she is not meeting social expectations and/or eventually drives her to question and analyze what the rest of her society more or less accepts. She is forced to evolve her own life pattern, often living much of her life alone, learning usually much earlier than her "straight" (heterosexual) sisters about the essential aloneness of life (which the myth of marriage obscures) and about the reality of illusions. To the extent that she cannot expel the heavy socialization that goes with being female, she can never truly find peace with herself. For she is caught somewhere between accepting society's view of her—in which

case she cannot accept herself—and coming to understand what this sexist society has done to her and why it is functional and necessary for it to do so. Those of us who work that through find ourselves on the other side of a tortuous journey through a night that may have been decades long. The perspective gained from that journey, the liberation of self, the inner peace, the real love of self and of all women, is something to be shared with all women—because we are all women.

It should first be understood that lesbianism, like male homosexuality, is a category of behavior possible only in a sexist society characterized by rigid sex roles and dominated by male supremacy. Those sex roles dehumanize women by defining us as a supportive/serving caste *in relation to* the master caste of men, and emotionally cripple men by demanding that they be alienated from their own bodies and emotions in order to perform their economic/political/military functions effectively. Homosexuality is a by-product of a particular way of setting up roles (or approved patterns of behavior) on the basis of sex; as such it is an inauthentic (not consonant with "reality") category. In a society in which men do not oppress women, and sexual expression is allowed to follow feelings, the categories of homosexuality and heterosexuality would disappear.

But lesbianism is also different from male homosexuality, and serves a different function in the society. "Dyke" is a different kind of put-down from "faggot," although both imply you are not playing your socially assigned sex role . . . are not therefore a "real woman" or a "real man." The grudging admiration felt for the tomboy, and the queasiness felt around a sissy boy point to the same thing: the contempt in which women—or those who play a female role—are held. And the investment in keeping women in that contemptuous role is very great. Lesbian is the word, the label, the condition that holds women in line. When a woman hears this word tossed her way, she knows she is stepping out of line. She knows that she has crossed the terrible boundary of her sex role. She recoils, she protests, she reshapes her actions to gain approval. Lesbian is a label invented by the Men to throw at any woman who dares to be his equal, who dares to challenge his prerogatives (including that of all women as part of the exchange medium among men), who dares to assert the primacy of her own needs. To have the label applied to people active in women's liberation is just the most recent instance of a long history; older women will recall that not so long ago, any woman who was successful, independent, not orienting her whole life about a man, would hear this word. For in this sexist society, for a woman to be independent means she *can't be* a woman—she must be a dyke. That in itself should tell us where women are at. It says as clearly as can be said: women and person are contradictory terms. For a lesbian is not considered a "real woman." And yet, in popular thinking, there is really only one essential difference between a lesbian and other women: that of sexual orientation—which is to say, when you strip off all the packaging, you must finally realize that the essence of being a "woman" is to get fucked by men.

"Lesbian" is one of the sexual categories by which men have divided up humanity. While all women are dehumanized as sex objects, as the objects of men they are given certain compensations: identification with his power, his ego, his status, his protection (from other males), feeling like a "real woman," finding social acceptance by adhering to her role, etc. Should a woman confront herself by confronting another woman, there are fewer rationalizations, fewer buffers by which to avoid the stark horror of her dehumanized condition. Herein we find the overriding fear of many women toward being used as a sexual object by a woman, which not only will bring her no male-connected compensations, but also will reveal the void which is woman's real situation. This dehumanization is expressed when a straight woman learns that a sister is a lesbian; she begins to relate to her lesbian sister as her potential sex object, laying a surrogate male role on the lesbian. This reveals her heterosexual conditioning to make herself into an object when sex is potentially involved in a relationship, and it denies the lesbian her full humanity. For women, especially those in the movement, to perceive their lesbian sisters through this male grid of role definitions is to accept this male cultural conditioning and to oppress their sisters much as they themselves have been oppressed by men. Are we going to continue the male classification system of defining all females in sexual relation to some other category of people?

Affixing the label lesbian not only to a woman who aspires to be a person, but also to any situation of real love, real solidarity, real primacy among women, is a primary form of divisiveness among women: it is the condition which keeps women within the confines of the feminine role, and it is the debunking/scare term that keeps women from forming any primary attachments, groups, or associations among ourselves.

Women in the movement have in most cases gone to great lengths to avoid discussion and confrontation with the issue of lesbianism. It puts people up-tight. They are hostile, evasive, or try to incorporate it into some "broader issue." They would rather not talk about it. If they have to, they try to dismiss it as a "lavender herring." But it is no side issue. It is absolutely essential to the success and fulfillment of the women's liberation movement that this issue be dealt with. As long as the label "dyke" can be used to frighten a woman into a less militant stand, keep her separate from her sisters, keep her from giving primacy to anything other than men and family—then to that extent she is controlled by the male culture. Until women see in each other the possibility of a primal commitment which includes sexual love, they will be denying themselves the love and value they readily accord to men, thus affirming their second class status. As long as male acceptability is primary—both to individual women and to the movement as a whole—the term lesbian will be used effectively against women. Insofar as women want only more privileges within the system, they do not want to antagonize male power. They instead seek acceptability for women's liberation, and the most crucial aspect of the acceptability is to deny lesbianism—i.e., to deny any fundamental challenge to the basis of the female. It should also be said that some younger, more radical women have honestly begun to discuss lesbianism, but so far it has been primarily as a sexual "alternative" to men. This, however, is still giving primacy to men, both because the idea of relating more completely to women occurs as a negative reaction to men, and because the lesbian relationship is being characterized simply by sex, which is divisive and sexist. On one level, which is both personal and political, women may withdraw emotional and sexual energies from men, and work out various alternatives for those energies in their own lives. On a different po-litical/psychological level, it must be understood that what is crucial is that women begin disengaging from male-defined response patterns. In the privacy of our own psyches, we must cut those cords to the core. For irrespective of where our love and sexual energies flow, if we are male-identified in our heads, we cannot realize our autonomy as human beings.

But why is it that women have related to and through men? By virtue of having been brought up in a male society, we have internalized the male culture's definition of ourselves. That definition consigns us to sexual and family functions, and excludes us from defining and shaping the terms of our lives. In exchange for our psychic servicing and for performing society's non-profitmaking func-tions, the man confers on us just one thing: the slave status which makes us legitimate in the eyes of the society in which we live. This is called "femininity" or "being a real woman" in our cultural lingo. We are authentic, legitimate, real to the extent that we are the property of some man whose name we bear. To be a woman who belongs to no man is to be invisible, pathetic, inauthentic, unreal. He confirms his image of us—of what we have to be in order to be acceptable by him—but not our real selves; he confirms our womanhood—as he defines it, in rela-tion to him—but cannot confirm our personhood, our own selves as absolutes. As long as we are de-pendent on the male culture for this definition, for this approval, we cannot be free.

The consequence of internalizing this role is an enormous reservoir of self-hate. This is not to say the self-hate is recognized or accepted as such; in-deed most women would deny it. It may be experi-enced as discomfort with her role, as feeling empty, as numbness, as restlessness, as a paralyzing anxiety at the center. Alternatively, it may be expressed in shrill defensiveness of the glory and destiny of her role. But it does exist, often beneath the edge of her consciousness, poisoning her existence, keeping her alienated from herself, her own needs, and render-ing her a stranger to other women. They try to escape by identifying with the oppressor, living through him, gaining status and identity from his ego, his power, his accomplishments. And by not identifying with other "empty vessels" like them-selves. Women resist relating on all levels to other women who will reflect their own oppression, their own secondary status, their own self-hate. For to confront another woman is finally to confront oneself—the self we have gone to such lengths to avoid. And in the mirror we know we cannot really respect and love that which we have been made to be.

As the source of self-hate and the lack of real self are rooted in our male-given identity, we must cre-ate a new sense of self. As long as we cling to the idea of "being a woman," we will sense some con-flict with that incipient self, that sense of I, that sense of a whole person. It is very difficult to realize and accept that being "feminine" and being a whole per-son are irreconcilable. Only women can give to each other a new sense of self. That identity we have to develop with reference to ourselves, and not in re-lation to men. This consciousness is the revolution-ary force from which all else will follow, for ours is an organic revolution. For this we must be available and supportive to one another, give our commit-ment and our love, give the emotional support nec-essary to sustain this movement. Our energies must flow toward our sisters, not backward toward our oppressors. As long as women's liberation tries to free women without facing the basic heterosexual structure that binds us in one-to-one-relationship with our oppressors, tremendous energies will con-tinue to flow into trying to straighten up each partic-ular relationship with a man, into finding how to get better sex, how to turn his head around—into trying to make the "new man" out of him, in the delusion that this will allow us to be the "new woman." This obviously splits our energies and commitments, leaving us unable to be committed to the construc-tion of the new patterns which will liberate us.

It is the primacy of women relating to women, of women creating a new consciousness of and with each other, which is at the heart of women's libera-tion, and the basis for the cultural revolution. To-gether we must find, reinforce, and validate our authentic selves. As we do this, we confirm in each other that struggling, incipient sense of pride and strength, the divisive barriers begin to melt, we feel this growing solidarity with our sisters. We see our-selves as prime, find our centers inside of ourselves. We find receding the sense of alienation, of being cut off, of being behind a locked window, of being unable to get out what we know is inside. We feel a real-ness, feel at last we are coinciding with our-selves. With that real self, with that consciousness, we begin a revolution to end the imposition of all coercive identifications, and to achieve maximum autonomy in human expression.

[1970]

 44

From Toward a Recognition of Androgyny

CAROLYN HEILBRUN

THE HIDDEN RIVER OF ANDROGYNY

An olive tree sprang from the earth, and in another spot water gushed forth. Frightened, the king sent to Delphi and inquired what this meant and what was to be done. The god replied that the olive tree meant Minerva and the water Neptune, and it was for the citizens to decide after which of the two deities they wished to name their city. Thereupon Cecrops called an assembly of the citizens, both men and women, for in those days the women also took part in public deliberations. The men voted for Nep-tune, the women for Minerva, and since there was one more woman, Minerva won out. Neptune was angry at this, and the sea flooded the entire Athenian territory. To appease the god's wrath, the citizens imposed a threefold punishment on their women: they should lose their right of suffrage, their children should no longer take the names of their mothers, and they themselves should no longer bear the title of Athenians.

— Saint Augustine, *The City of God*

We are accustomed to think of history as a contin-uous record of masculine social dominance. Yet beyond the Greece of Periclean Athens, beyond recorded history, the evidence of mythology and archaeology suggests a time when the feminine prin-ciple prevailed. On this evidence it seems likely that mankind's earliest gods were female, and that early societies were matriarchal. Jane Harrison, who has been called in some respects the most brilliant of the many brilliant scholars who in the early years of this century applied to classical studies the results of modern social anthropology, believed that Greek

religion showed the marks of a prehistoric trans-formation from female to male dominion that accompanied the overthrow of matriarchy. "Zeus the father will have no great Earth-goddess, Mother and Maid in one, in his man-fashioned Olympus, but her figure *is* from the beginning, so he remakes it; woman, who was the inspirer, becomes the temptress; she who made all things, gods and mortals alike, is become their plaything, their slave, dowered only with physical beauty, and with a slave's tricks and blandishments. To Zeus, the arch-patriarchal *bourgeois,* the birth of the first woman is but a huge Olympian jest."[1] "The memory of prim-itive matriarchal conditions often survives," Jane Harrison writes, "rather curiously in mythology."[2] Zeus, who established the new patriarchal hierar-chy, nonetheless retains in his "family" many mem-ories of the earlier, matriarchal time. Thus, as Gilbert Murray points out, Apollo has a mother but no father, and Hera is gradually transformed from the chief goddess in the myths of Jason and others to the shrew, the scold, the jealous wife in the *Illiad*.[3]

· · ·

Whether or not we accept the historicity of this shift—and today many scholars challenge the view of men like J. J. Bachofen that there existed an earlier matriarchy—we are left insofar as Greece is con-cerned with extraordinary literary evidence for the strength still remaining to the "feminine" impulse. By the time of the great writers of Periclean Athens, when women had on the whole become the sub-merged part of the human race, they still, as repre-sentatives of the "feminine" impulse, stood in again and again for mankind in the great tragedies. . . .

Kate Millett, who believes in the shift from the matriarchal to the patriarchal world, suggests that we can still observe that shift in the *Eumenides* of Aeschylus. When Orestes has murdered his mother, Clytemnestra, in revenge for her murder of his fa-ther, Agamemnon, the final decision to forgive this crime is a triumph for patriarchal justice.[4] Athena, who was born of a father without a mother, defends Orestes' claim that only the father is the parent of the child, the mother merely serving as some sort of incubator. Athena has the deciding vote and, like many women who can envisage themselves only as the defenders of besieged masculinity, she casts her vote for Orestes. As Millett phrases it, the *Eumenides* can be seen as a "confrontation drama between patriarchal or paternal authority and what appear to be the defeated claims of an earlier order, one which had placed emphasis upon maternal claims."[5]

The major argument against Millett's interpretation takes the form that since Athena's vote is cast for acquittal, what we have is a new, more forgiving reign of law which eschews simple revenge, and changes the Furies into protective, rather than ferocious, spirits. Yet the Furies themselves insist they are instruments of pity, because they protect the weak and the old and do not leave mother-murderers free to practice their violence.[6] Few critics before our age have seen the entire defeat of the female principle, for all its parade of law, to be in fact a celebration of the right of male violence and the depriving of the female forces of strength and power. The female forces, particularly as represented by the Furies and the raging Maenads of the *Bacchae,* are scarcely unbloody, gentle, or what we would today call "feminine." But their bloodiness and revenge were reserved only for those who denied the "feminine" powers. These raging females were not sackers of cities, nor despoilers for gain of others' homes or homelands. The Furies represented the strongest deterrent against the male usurpation of female rights and powers, and Aeschylus, in dramatizing their defeat, marked the beginning of rule by the "masculine" principle alone. Nor should it be lost on anyone that a female goddess created by a male god for his purposes should have betrayed the female forces in the end. That was perhaps the most prophetic note of all, and reminds us that the fact of being a woman does not guarantee the possession of "feminine" powers.

. . .

Today, even though we have emerged somewhat from the shadow of Victorianism and Freud's views on women, it is still commonly said that any woman acting apart from her "conventional" role is "masculine." Therefore, it is the more important to perceive that it is in those works where the roles of the male and female protagonist can be reversed without appearing ludicrous or perverted that the androgynous ideal is present. The early Greeks, not yet wholly cut off from their matriarchal origins, had many festivals in which boys dressed as girls and girls as boys during the major ceremonies of life. Such ceremonies are sharply distinguishable from the Arab and Hebrew laws which make the blurring of even the most superficial distinctions between the sexes a crime against God.

. . .

. . . Ignored as well have been the androgynous overtones of *Oedipus,* which suggest that the destiny of murdering one's father and marrying one's mother might perhaps refer to strong inner impulses toward the rediscovery of one's "feminine" self.[7] When Oedipus tears out his eyes rather than gaze on what he has done, he seems to accede in the patriarchal myth whereby father-murder and mother-marriage become symbolic not of renewal, but of all anti-paternal crime. Yet we notice that the only faithful children left to Oedipus are his daughters who will care for him and lead him to Colonus and redemption.

Noticing this, we begin to reinterpret the received or Freudian interpretation of Oedipus's self-blinding. This, of course, is the reading which equates eyeballs and "balls," thus finding the act of blinding himself to be, for Oedipus, an act of self-castration. True, Oedipus eschews "masculine" vision: for the Greeks, eyes and seeing generally are Olympian and "masculine"—the contrast is between Apollonian light and Dionysian darkness. But only for the Freudians is the turning from "masculine" seeing to "feminine" perception of the dark wisdom seen to be an anti-sexual or anti-genital act. The contrary is probably nearer to the truth, even if those devoted to worship of the male genitalia do not so perceive it. In the *Bacchae* and in other ancient sources, it is the male figure who stands for "reason," the female who stands for frenzy, orgy, and sexuality. The identification of sexuality and maleness is one of the many distortions which became acute in the nineteenth century. Teiresias himself is made androgynous when Hera takes away his "masculine" eyes; Zeus makes it up to him by giving him "feminine" powers of sight or, as we say, intuition. In the *Oedipus Rex,* it is Teiresias and Jocasta, both intuitive knowers, who see ahead of Oedipus and can only warn him. Having followed the truth of reason through to its end, he resigns himself, at the close of the play, to another way of knowing, a more "feminine" way. He deserts the proud knowledge of men, the "masculine" way of seeing. This rational route to wisdom has tempted him to flee the oracular prophecies. Now that such flight has been discovered to be impossible, he must try to recognize what he has "seen" in the light of a different sort of knowledge, the wisdom discoverable through another form of seeing.

· · ·

Euripides is so obvious a source for the androgynous vision, and for our understanding of the destruction which follows when we ignore justified feminine demands—in the *Medea* and *The Trojan Women,* to name only two of the plays—that there is no need to belabor the point. It is in the *Alcestis* that the androgynous ideal is most easily seen. Admetus, condemned to die, will be allowed to escape death if he can find another to die in his place. His aging father, loving life, refuses the privilege, and it is Admetus's wife, Alcestis, who agrees to die for her husband, and does so. The play, in fact, ends happily as Heracles, a *deus ex machina,* wrestles with death and restores Alcestis to Admetus. But the question the play raises and leaves unanswered for all its happy ending is: What is the quality of Admetus, who accepted this sacrifice? Much as we admire the noble and self-sacrificing Alcestis, Euripides does not rest on a patriarchal acceptance of feminine sacrifice as the evident female role. T. S. Eliot based *The Cocktail Party* on the *Alcestis,* and suggests in his play that there are three ways to seek or find grace, that of Celia (the Alcestis figure) being the noblest, or at least the most adventurous. But even if Celia dies crucified, she does not die for a husband but, woman though she is, enacts the most sacrificial destiny of which the human soul is capable. Freud, one feels, would not have agreed with Riley's suggestion of this destiny as the proper way for her in life: Freud or his followers would probably have urged her to assume her feminine role of wife and mother while denouncing her aspirations to worldly service as penis envy.

As for Aristophanes, it is probably true, as Gilbert Murray has said, that only his own age could really understand him.[8] *Lysistrata* reread today (in a translation which even in 1938 the editors listed as anonymous because of its bawdiness)[9] makes us wonder if an age which can appreciate Aristophanes will come round again. Everyone has heard that in the *Lysistrata* women (women of many nations) refuse to sleep with their husbands until wars cease, but few have observed that these women are not sneered at, or made to look like fools. Realizing that in the division of roles they have taken too little part in the prevention of war, the women of *Lysistrata* attempt to achieve peace. In an early play, the *Archarnians,* Aristophanes had allowed a character to remark: "She is a woman and not to blame for war,"[10] but in *Lysistrata* women realize that if they do not try to prevent war, they are, indeed, to blame for it; furthermore, if they allow the male principle total power in the world, they have acquiesced in the tone of exaggerated aggression which rules the state. Between Aristophanes and Shaw, there does not appear to have been a playwright who could make a revolutionary point in good humor, and Shaw with his Victorian roots was incapable of the good-natured bawdy which marks the work of Aristophanes. It is amusing to note that in the *Ecclesiazusae,* where the women take over the government, Athens accepts the proposal to entrust the state to women because, in Gilbert Norwood's words, "It was felt that here was the only device that had never been tried before."[11] This is remarkably close to Shaw's remarks on the same question.[12]

It is surely no coincidence that Aristophanes, who wrote three extant plays on the need to have women express themselves politically (if we may so put it), was also the one in whom Plato invests his theories of the eternal eggs seeking their other halves. It is Aristophanes in the *Symposium* who regrets that the word "androgynous" is now only a term of reproach.[13] The closeness of Aristophanes's *Ecclesiazusae* to the section of Plato's *Republic* where he speaks of the need for total equality for women has often been noticed. Socrates points out that if women would appear ridiculous joining with men in their activities, it was not so long ago that in other countries men appeared ridiculous in the same way. This is largely overlooked by those who think that in *Lysistrata* Aristophanes wishes merely to ridicule the idea of women participating in politics. On the contrary, Lysistrata herself is competent and not jested at. Furthermore, Aristophanes shows the relationship between the sexes to be one of mutual need.

Scholars are uncertain how Aristophanes's and Plato's ideas came to be so close, or which man originated them. Each man in his work seems to refer to the other, and the question of who influenced whom persists. Suffice it to say that not only had they talked together and exchanged ideas, but that for both the idea of the presence of the "feminine" principle in the governance of the ideal state had not yet wholly died.

. . .

[1973]

NOTES

1. Jane Harrison, *Prolegomena to the Study of Greek Religion* (1903; reprint ed., New York: Meridian Books, 1966), p. 285. The description of Jane Harrison is from Jessie G. Stewart, *Jane Ellen Harrison* (London: The Merlin Press, 1959), p. ix.
2. Jane Harrison, *Themis: A Study of the Social Origins of Greek Religion* (1912; reprint ed., New York: Meridian Books, 1962), p. 41.
3. Gilbert Murray, *Five Stages of Greek Religion* (1912, 1925; reprint ed., New York: Doubleday, Anchor Books, 1955), pp. 49, 55. See also pp. 10, 43, 56, 61, 67, 71.
4. Kate Millett, *Sexual Politics* (Garden City, N.Y.: Doubleday, 1970), p. 115. In this connection, see also George Thomson, *Aeschylus and Athens: A Study in the Social Origins of Drama* (London: Lawrence & Wishart, 1950). Thomson writes: "Apollo's reply . . . is not consistent, being an attempt at compromise between two incompatible principles. He uses the law of retribution to condemn Clytemnestra, the law of purification to protect Orestes; but if Clytemnestra forfeited her life by murdering her husband, then by murdering his mother Orestes had forfeited his own. Apollo's attitude is transitional. He has challenged the old order, but it is not for him to construct the new" (p. 281). Thomson's book, tiresome in its Marxist bias, is very interesting on the subject of the Greek attitudes toward women.
5. Millett, *Sexual Politics*, p. 112.
6. Gilbert Murray, *Aeschylus* (1940; reprint ed., Oxford: Clarendon Press, 1962), p. 197.
7. I owe this interpretation of Oedipus to Debby Whittle, a student in an honors seminar in comparative fiction at Swarthmore College, who offered it in a discussion of *Death in Venice*.
8. Gilbert Murray, *The Literature of Ancient Greece* (1897; reprint ed., Chicago: University of Chicago Press, Phoenix Books, 1956), p. 293.
9. Whitney J. Oates & Eugene O'Neill, *The Complete Greek Drama*, Vol. II. The *Lysistrata* has also been translated by Dudley Fitts. Fitts's attitude toward Aristophanes is typical of his time. In 1959, in an introduction to his translation of *Thesmophoriazusae*, which he translated skittishly as *Ladies' Day*, Fitts announces the play as "one of the three plays in which Aristophanes handles the idea of women interfering in men's affairs." Dudley Fitts, *Aristophanes's Ladies' Day* (New York: Harcourt, Brace and Company, 1959), p. vii.
10. Quoted in Gilbert Norwood, *Greek Comedy* (New York: Hill and Wang, 1963), p. 205.
11. *Ibid.,* p. 266.
12. For an excellent discussion of all of Shaw's attitudes toward women and androgyny, see Barbara Bellow Watson, *A Shavian Guide to the Intelligent Woman* (New York: W. W. Norton, 1964).
13. *The Dialogues of Plato,* Vol. I, p. 316.

 45

The Older Woman— A Stockpile of Losses

TI GRACE ATKINSON

It is appropriate that I make my first major statement in nearly a year at a conference for the liberation of older women. I have not spoken for a long time. About a year ago, I made a serious political mistake. I did not fight hard enough for what Joseph Colombo was about to prevent his near-fatal shooting.

I have had to rethink myself, to find out and correct in myself whatever made such a mistake possible. This conference will be the first group to enjoy the fruits of the new me, although some of you may see the "fruits" as more accurately described as "fallout."

I

OW (OLDER WOMEN) AS THE BÊTE NOIRE OF WM (THE WOMEN'S MOVEMENT)

I learned a year ago that there is at least one thing more brutal than the truth, and that is the consequence of saying less than the truth. One becomes an accessory to any facts one attempts—however much—to conceal.

The issue of the older woman is the strategic Achilles' heel of Women's Liberation. The definition of her problem was evaded from the beginning, its existence even denied at first. The definition of the "older woman" *is* "woman." This definition exposes the softness of the feminist analysis.

"Woman," bluntly put, means "garbage," waste. Woman is "potential." The older woman is "past potential." A contradiction in terms? Not if you understand the meaning of "potential."

"Potential" means "not actualized," "nonexistent." The non-older woman has "hope." She may still be used. The older woman is use-less, past the possibility of use. She is no longer in danger of, has lost the "opportunity" of, being politically raped by one man. The older woman is *guaranteed* ravagement by the whole fucking system.

The older woman no longer has potential. She's *had* it. Or rather she can no longer *have* it. The older woman has had it. She's been ejected from the system. She is a stockpile of losses, a walking history of lost potentials. She should, of course, have the good taste to lie down and die, like a lady. Be that as it may, for better or for worse, the "older woman" hangs in. And I say, "As long as we're gonna hang in, we might as well hang *out,* too."

II
HISTORY OF OW IN WM

In 1966, OW *was* WM, only OW wasn't *in* WM. I was *one* of the, if not *the,* youngest active members in N.O.W. (the OW of "Never"). But most of the women prefaced nearly all their major statements with: "It's too late for me. I'm fighting for my daughters." Charitable kamikazes have always seemed a dubious lot to me. These proved no exception.

The OW in WM didn't "care" enough for the future of their daughters to fight for it in the only way the future can ever be fought for—on the battleground of your own present. If OW isn't worth the fight, then neither are women as a class worth the fight. My thesis here is that the older woman is the conceptual nub of the class of women.

The conveners of the present two days have had the tenacity and, yes, the courage to hack out the area of "older women" as a special section within the Women's Movement. My question is: "Do you have the guts to take it over?" It is only when the OW becomes WM that we will have a Movement. It's only when you're all the way in the shit, that the shoveling is worth it in the long run.

Do older women care enough about all women to hammer home within the Movement that the truth about the older woman is the truth about *all* women?

I have heard for many years now, particularly from so-called "leaders" within the Women's Movement, that Simone de Beauvoir's work on old age gives the lie to her feminism. No feminist, the line goes, could be concerned with old age.

I am one of the few feminists I ever met who did not become aware of her feminism before the age of five years. I did not become a feminist until I was old enough (about 18) to fix my beady little eye on my prospects at age 70!

III
SIGNIFICANCE OF OW TO WM

I have already suggested the ideological significance of the "older woman" to Women's Liberation. Her *tactical* significance is no less important.

I used to say that, "Come the Revolution, I want one housewife for every ten Revolutionaries on *my* barricade, [since] the middle-aged housewife has no place to go but revenge." The OW of WM is liberated from any false hopes. And hope is always a political extravagance.

One can see the older woman as a reject. Or, one can see her as a true leader of women's liberation, because she is free of her womanhood.

I am aware that few older women, even women here, take that position of "liberation." Most, still, see their age as politically negative. *Outside* the Movement this negative view, as it affects their lives, may be valid. But *within* the Movement, this outside condition places the older woman in a natural position of leadership. *If,* that is, the Women's Movement wants radical, that is, sufficient, changes in society for *all* women.

The OW in WM has always interested me. I had thought my final realization of this issue had arrived last May. I was the keynote speaker at the New School's graduation exercises of their Continuing Education program. Elinor Guggenheimer opened with some bright and cheery remarks about the burgeoning possibilities of the After-Life.

My speech was entitled, "Where Can You Go When You've Been There?" I had studied the New School's Continuing Education program, the oldest in the country, with considerable care. I attempted to raise certain questions.

1. Why spend time and money on "diplomas" without academic value?

2. What kind of "education" prepares you to "assist" in a job you required *no* education to "boss" in? for example, that occupation of glorified mother's helper.

3. What kind of "education" led to, almost without exception, "volunteerism"? Jobs, with no loot.

All these seemed like sound questions, before I arrived at the auditorium. But it was immediately clear upon my arrival that the two years of "continuing education" had been spent on preparing physically for this event of presentation. Ladies in blue hair arose amidst much applause to accept diplomas in lavish leather folders, each of which had the name of the recipient embossed outside in gold. Several of the diplomas, as it happened, had their contents misplaced in the wrong folders. These "errors" were greeted with much high-pitched giggling.

Prior to my arrival, I had been looking forward to the presentation of my speech, as a kind of shared enlightenment. I began, instead, to cringe, at giving the death blow to cripples. To make matters worse, I tried in the end to soften the blows. This resulted, of course, in an agonizingly slow and painful death for all.

My speech was received first with shock, then stolid resentment. Needless to say, there was little applause.

Only months later did I get any feedback. The consensus appeared to be that I was not at all well, and obviously addicted to a mixture of speed and heroin. This puzzled me, at first, until I translated this ladylike curse properly. "Drop dead as fast as possible!"

I hope, today, that my remarks are received more happily. But I think it's appropriate here to repeat what I said earlier. I have spent the past year learning a bitter lesson. The consequences of the truth left unsaid are far more brutal than any facts stated, however raw. I fear such a year, as this past one, far more than the most negative temporary response of the combined energies of all those present here today.

I leave you on a note of optimism. You may or may not be familiar with the cliché of Women's Liberation that "all women are treated like a joke." I say,

"If women are to be a joke, let's make older women into a bloody riot!"

[1974]

 46

Is Female to Male as Nature Is to Culture?

SHERRY B. ORTNER

Much of the creativity of anthropology derives from the tension between two sets of demands: that we explain human universals, and that we explain cultural particulars. By this canon, woman provides us with one of the more challenging problems to be dealt with. The secondary status of woman in society is one of the true universals, a pan-cultural fact. Yet within that universal fact, the specific cultural conceptions and symbolizations of woman are extraordinarily diverse and even mutually contradictory. Further, the actual treatment of women and their relative power and contribution vary enormously from culture to culture, and over different periods in the history of particular cultural traditions. Both of these points—the universal fact and the cultural variation—constitute problems to be explained.

My interest in the problem is of course more than academic: I wish to see genuine change come about, the emergence of a social and cultural order in which as much of the range of human potential is open to women as is open to men. The universality of female subordination, the fact that it exists within every type of social and economic arrangement and in societies of every degree of complexity, indicates to me that we are up against something very profound, very stubborn, something we cannot rout out simply by rearranging a few tasks and roles in the social system, or even by reordering the whole economic structure. In this paper I try to expose the underlying logic of cultural thinking that assumes the inferiority of women; I try to show the highly persuasive nature of the logic, for if it were not so persuasive, people would not keep subscribing to it. But I also try to show the social and cultural sources of that logic, to indicate wherein lies the potential for change.

. . .

We may differentiate three levels of the problem:

1. The universal fact of culturally attributed second-class status of woman in every society. Two questions are important here. First, what do we mean by this; what is our evidence that this is a universal fact? And second, how are we to explain this fact, once having established it?

2. Specific ideologies, symbolizations, and socio-structural arrangements pertaining to women that vary widely from culture to culture. The problem at this level is to account for any particular cultural complex in terms of factors specific to that group—the standard level of anthropological analysis.

3. Observable on-the-ground details of women's activities, contributions, powers, influence, etc., often at variance with cultural ideology (although always constrained within the assumption that women may never be officially preeminent in the total system). This is the level of direct observation, often adopted now by feminist-oriented anthropologists.

This paper is primarily concerned with the first of these levels, the problem of the universal devaluation of women. The analysis thus depends not upon specific cultural data but rather upon an analysis of "culture" taken generically as a special sort of process in the world. A discussion of the second level, the problem of cross-cultural variation in conceptions and relative valuations of women, will entail a great deal of cross-cultural research and must be postponed to another time. As for the third level, it will be obvious from my approach that I would consider it a misguided endeavor to focus only upon women's actual though culturally unrecognized and unvalued powers in any given society, without first understanding the overarching ideology and deeper assumptions of the culture that render such powers trivial.

THE UNIVERSALITY OF FEMALE SUBORDINATION

. . .

On any or all of these counts, then, I would flatly assert that we find women subordinated to men in every known society. The search for a genuinely egalitarian, let alone matriarchal, culture has proved fruitless. An example from one society that has traditionally been on the credit side of this ledger will suffice. Among the matrilineal Crow, as Lowie (1956) points out, "Women . . . had highly honorific offices in the Sun Dance; they could become directors of the Tobacco Ceremony and played, if anything, a more conspicuous part in it than the men; they sometimes played the hostess in the Cooked Meat Festival; they were not debarred from sweating or doctoring or from seeking a vision" (p. 61). Nonetheless, "Women [during menstruation] formerly rode inferior horses and evidently this loomed as a source of contamination, for they were not allowed to approach either a wounded man or men starting on a war party. A taboo still lingers against their coming near sacred objects at these times" (p. 44). Further, just before enumerating women's rights of participation in the various rituals noted above, Lowie mentions one particular Sun Dance Doll bundle that was not supposed to be unwrapped by a woman (p. 60). Pursuing this trail we find: "According to all Lodge Grass informants and most others, the doll owned by Wrinkled-face took precedence not only of other dolls but of all other Crow medicines whatsoever. . . . This particular doll was not supposed to be handled by a woman" (p. 229).[1]

In sum, the Crow are probably a fairly typical case. Yes, women have certain powers and rights, in this case some that place them in fairly high positions. Yet ultimately the line is drawn: menstruation is a threat to warfare, one of the most valued institutions of the tribe, one that is central to their self-definition; and the most sacred object of the tribe is taboo to the direct sight and touch of women.

Similar examples could be multiplied ad infinitum, but I think the onus is no longer upon us to demonstrate that female subordination is a cultural universal; it is up to those who would argue against the point to bring forth counterexamples. I shall take the universal secondary status of women as a given, and proceed from there.

NATURE AND CULTURE

. . .

I translate the problem, in other words, into the following simple question. What could there be in the generalized structure and conditions of existence, common to every culture, that would lead every culture to place a lower value upon women? Specifically, my thesis is that woman is being identified with—or, if you will, seems to be a symbol of—something that every culture devalues, something that every culture defines as being of a lower order of existence than itself. Now it seems that there is only one thing that would fit that description, and that is "nature" in the most generalized sense. Every culture, or, generically, "culture," is engaged in the process of generating and sustaining systems of meaningful forms (symbols, artifacts, etc.) by means of which humanity transcends the givens of natural existence, bends them to its purposes, controls them in its interest. We may thus broadly equate culture with the notion of human consciousness, or with the products of human consciousness (i.e., systems of thought and technology), by means of which humanity attempts to assert control over nature.

Now the categories of "nature" and "culture" are of course conceptual categories—one can find no boundary out in the actual world between the two states or realms of being. And there is no question that some cultures articulate a much stronger opposition between the two categories than others—it has even been argued that primitive peoples (some or all) do not see or intuit any distinction between the human cultural state and the state of nature at all. Yet I would maintain that the universality of ritual betokens an assertion in all human cultures of the specifically human ability to act upon and regulate, rather than passively move with and be moved by, the givens of natural existence. In ritual, the purposive manipulation of given forms toward regulating and sustaining order, every culture asserts that proper relations between human existence and natural forces depend upon culture's employing its special powers to regulate the overall processes of the world and life.

One realm of cultural thought in which these points are often articulated is that of concepts of purity and pollution. Virtually every culture has some such beliefs, which seem in large part (though not, of course, entirely) to be concerned with the relationship between culture and nature (see Ortner, 1973, n.d.). A well-known aspect of purity/pollution beliefs cross-culturally is that of the natural "contagion" of pollution; left to its own devices, pollution (for these purposes grossly equated with the unregulated operation of natural energies) spreads and overpowers all that it comes in contact with. Thus a puzzle—if pollution is so strong, how can anything be purified? Why is the purifying agent not itself polluted? The answer, in keeping with the present line of argument, is that purification is effected in a ritual context; purification ritual, as a purposive activity that pits self-conscious (symbolic) action against natural energies, is more powerful than those energies.

In any case, my point is simply that every culture implicitly recognizes and asserts a distinction between the operation of nature and the operation of culture (human consciousness and its products); and further, that the distinctiveness of culture rests precisely on the fact that it can under most circumstances transcend natural conditions and turn them to its purposes. Thus culture (i.e. every culture) at some level of awareness asserts itself to be not only distinct from but superior to nature, and that sense of distinctiveness and superiority rests precisely on the ability to transform—to "socialize" and "culturalize"—nature.

Returning now to the issue of women, their pancultural second-class status could be accounted for, quite simply, by postulating that women are being identified or symbolically associated with nature, as opposed to men, who are identified with culture. Since it is always culture's project to subsume and transcend nature, if women were considered part of nature, then culture would find it "natural" to subordinate, not to say oppress, them. Yet although this argument can be shown to have considerable force, it seems to oversimplify the case. The formulation I would like to defend and elaborate on in the following section, then, is that women are seen "merely" as being *closer* to nature than men. That is, culture (still equated relatively unambiguously with men) recognizes that women are active participants in its special processes, but at the same time sees them as being more rooted in, or having more direct affinity with, nature.

· · ·

WHY IS WOMAN SEEN AS CLOSER TO NATURE?

It all begins of course with the body and the natural procreative functions specific to women alone. We can sort out for discussion three levels at which this absolute physiological fact has significance: (1) woman's *body and its functions,* more involved more of the time with "species life," seem to place her closer to nature, in contrast to man's physiology, which frees him more completely to take up the projects of culture; (2) woman's body and its functions place her in *social roles* that in turn are considered to be at a lower order of the cultural process than man's; and (3) woman's traditional social roles, imposed because of her body and its functions, in turn give her a different *psychic structure,* which, like her physiological nature and her social roles, is seen as being closer to nature. I shall discuss each of these points in turn, showing first how in each instance certain factors strongly tend to align woman with nature, then indicating other factors that demonstrate her full alignment with culture, the combined factors thus placing her in a problematic intermediate position. It will become clear in the course of the discussion why men seem by contrast less intermediate, more purely "cultural" than women. And I reiterate that I am dealing only at the level of cultural and human universals. These arguments are intended to apply to generalized humanity; they grow out of the human condition, as humanity has experienced and confronted it up to the present day.

1. Woman's physiology seen as closer to nature. This part of my argument has been anticipated, with subtlety, cogency, and a great deal of hard data, by de Beauvoir (1953). De Beauvoir reviews the physiological structure, development, and functions of the human female and concludes that "the female, to a greater extent than the male, is the prey of the species" (p. 60). She points out that many major areas and processes of the woman's body serve no apparent function for the health and stability of the individual; on the contrary, as they perform their specific organic functions, they are often sources of discomfort, pain, and danger. The breasts are irrelevant to personal health; they may be excised at any time of a woman's life. "Many of the ovarian secretions function for the benefit of the egg, promoting its maturation and adapting the uterus to its requirements; in respect to the organism as a whole, they make for disequilibrium rather than for regulation—the woman is adapted to the needs of the egg rather than to her own require-

ments" (p. 24). Menstruation is often uncomfortable, sometimes painful; it frequently has negative emotional correlates and in any case involves bothersome tasks of cleansing and waste disposal; and—a point that de Beauvoir does not mention—in many cultures it interrupts a woman's routine, putting her in a stigmatized state involving various restrictions on her activities and social contacts. In pregnancy many of the woman's vitamin and mineral resources are channeled into nourishing the fetus, depleting her own strength and energies. And finally, childbirth itself is painful and dangerous (pp. 24–27 *passim*). In sum, de Beauvoir concludes that the female "is more enslaved to the species than the male, her animality is more manifest" (p. 239).

· · ·

Thus if male is, as I am suggesting, everywhere (unconsciously) associated with culture and female seems closer to nature, the rationale for these associations is not very difficult to grasp, merely from considering the implications of the physiological contrast between male and female. At the same time, however, woman cannot be consigned fully to the category of nature, for it is perfectly obvious that she is a full-fledged human being endowed with human consciousness just as a man is; she is half of the human race, without whose cooperation the whole enterprise would collapse. She may seem more in the possession of nature than man, but having consciousness, she thinks and speaks; she generates, communicates, and manipulates symbols, categories, and values. She participates in human dialogues not only with other women but also with men. As Lévi-Strauss says, "Woman could never become just a sign and nothing more, since even in a man's world she is still a person, and since insofar as she is defined as a sign she must [still] be recognized as a generator of signs" (1969a: 496).

Indeed, the fact of woman's full human consciousness, her full involvement in and commitment to culture's project of transcendence over nature, may ironically explain another of the great puzzles of "the woman problem"—woman's nearly universal unquestioning acceptance of her own devaluation. For it would seem that, as a conscious human and member of culture, she has followed out the logic of culture's arguments and has reached culture's conclusions along with the men. As de Beau-voir puts it (p. 59):

> For she, too, is an existent, she feels the urge to surpass, and her project is not mere repetition but transcendence towards a different future—in her heart of hearts she finds confirmation of the masculine pretensions. She joins the men in the festivals that celebrate the successes and victories of the males. Her misfortune is to have been biologically destined for the repetition of Life, when even in her own view Life does not carry within itself its reasons for being, reasons that are more important than life itself.

In other words, woman's consciousness—her membership, as it were, in culture—is evidenced in part by the very fact that she accepts her own devaluation and takes culture's point of view.

I have tried here to show one part of the logic of that view, the part that grows directly from the physiological differences between men and women. Because of woman's greater bodily involvement with the natural functions surrounding reproduction, she is seen as more a part of nature than man is. Yet in part because of her consciousness and participation in human social dialogue, she is recognized as a participant in culture. Thus she appears as something intermediate between culture and nature, lower on the scale of transcendence than man.

2. Woman's social role seen as closer to nature. Woman's physiological functions, I have just argued, may tend in themselves to motivate[2] a view of woman as closer to nature, a view she herself, as an observer of herself and the world, would tend to agree with. Woman creates naturally from within her own being, whereas man is free to, or forced to, create artificially, that is, through cultural means, and in such a way as to sustain culture. In addition, I now wish to show how woman's physiological functions have tended universally to limit her social movement, and to confine her universally to certain social contexts which *in turn* are seen as closer to nature. That is, not only her bodily processes but the social situation in which her bodily processes locate her may carry this significance. And insofar as she is permanently associated (in the eyes of culture) with these social milieux, they add weight (perhaps the decisive part of the burden) to the view of woman as closer to nature. I refer here of course

to woman's confinement to the domestic family context, a confinement motivated, no doubt, by her lactation processes.

. . .

Woman's association with the domestic circle would contribute to the view of her as closer to nature in several ways. In the first place, the sheer fact of constant association with children plays a role in the issue; one can easily see how infants and children might themselves be considered part of nature. Infants are barely human and utterly unsocialized; like animals they are unable to walk upright, they excrete without control, they do not speak. Even slightly older children are clearly not yet fully under the sway of culture. They do not yet understand social duties, responsibilities, and morals; their vocabulary and their range of learned skills are small. One finds implicit recognition of an association between children and nature in many cultural practices. For example, most cultures have initiation rites for adolescents (primarily for boys; I shall return to this point below), the point of which is to move the child ritually from a less than fully human state into full participation in society and culture; many cultures do not hold funeral rites for children who die at early ages, explicitly because they are not yet fully social beings. Thus children are likely to be categorized with nature, and woman's close association with children may compound her potential for being seen as closer to nature herself. It is ironic that the rationale for boys' initiation rites in many cultures is that the boys must be purged of the defilement accrued from being around mother and other women so much of the time, when in fact much of the woman's defilement may derive from her being around children so much of the time.

. . .

Now, since women are associated with, and indeed are more or less confined to, the domestic context, they are identified with this lower order of social/cultural organization. What are the implications of this for the way they are viewed? First, if the specifically biological (reproductive) function of the family is stressed, as in Lévi-Strauss's formulation, then the family (and hence woman) is identified with nature pure and simple, as opposed to culture. But this is obviously too simple; the point seems more adequately formulated as follows: the family (and hence woman) represents lower-level, socially fragmenting, particularistic sort of concerns, as opposed to interfamilial relations representing higher-level, integrative, universalistic sorts of concerns. Since men lack a "natural" basis (nursing, generalized to child care) for a familial orientation, their sphere of activity is defined at the level of interfamilial relations. And hence, so the cultural reasoning seems to go, men are the "natural" proprietors of religion, ritual, politics, and other realms of cultural thought and action in which universalistic statements of spiritual and social synthesis are made. Thus men are identified not only with culture, in the sense of all human creativity, as opposed to nature; they are identified in particular with culture in the old-fashioned sense of the finer and higher aspects of human thought—art, religion, law, etc.

Here again, the logic of cultural reasoning aligning woman with a lower order of culture than man is clear and, on the surface, quite compelling. At the same time, woman cannot be fully consigned to nature, for there are aspects of her situation, even within the domestic context, that undeniably demonstrate her participation in the cultural process. It goes without saying, of course, that except for nursing newborn infants (and artificial nursing devices can cut even this biological tie), there is no reason why it has to be mother—as opposed to father, or anyone else—who remains identified with child care. But even assuming that other practical and emotional reasons conspire to keep woman in this sphere, it is possible to show that her activities in the domestic context could as logically put her squarely in the category of culture.

In the first place, one must point out that woman not only feeds and cleans up after children in a simple caretaker operation; she in fact is the primary agent of their early socialization. It is she who transforms newborn infants from mere organisms into cultured humans, teaching them manners and the proper ways to behave in order to become full-fledged members of the culture. On the basis of her socializing functions alone, she could not be more a representative of culture. Yet in virtually every society there is a point at which the socialization of boys is transferred to the hands of men. The boys are considered, in one set of terms or another, not yet "really" socialized; their entrée into the realm of

fully human (social, cultural) status can be accomplished only by men. We still see this in our own schools, where there is a gradual inversion in the proportion of female to male teachers up through the grades: most kindergarten teachers are female; most university professors are male.[3]

Or again, take cooking. In the overwhelming majority of societies cooking is the woman's work. No doubt this stems from practical considerations—since the woman has to stay home with the baby, it is convenient for her to perform the chores centered in the home. But if it is true, as Lévi-Strauss has argued (1969b), that transforming the raw into the cooked may represent, in many systems of thought, the transition from nature to culture, then here we have woman aligned with this important culturalizing process, which could easily place her in the category of culture, triumphing over nature. Yet it is also interesting to note that when a culture (e.g. France or China) develops a tradition of *haute cuisine*—"real" cooking, as opposed to trivial ordinary domestic cooking—the high chefs are almost always men. Thus the pattern replicates that in the area of socialization—women perform lower-level conversions from nature to culture, but when the culture distinguishes a higher level of the same functions, the higher level is restricted to men.

• • •

3. *Woman's psyche seen as closer to nature.* The suggestion that woman has not only a different body and a different social locus from man but also a different psychic structure is most controversial. I will argue that she probably *does* have a different psychic structure, but I will draw heavily on Chodorow's paper to establish first that her psychic structure need not be assumed to be innate; it can be accounted for, as Chodorow convincingly shows, by the facts of the probably universal female socialization experience. Nonetheless, if we grant the empirical near universality of a "feminine psyche" with certain specific characteristics, these characteristics would add weight to the cultural view of woman as closer to nature.

It is important to specify what we see as the dominant and universal aspects of the feminine psyche. If we postulate emotionality or irrationality, we are confronted with those traditions in various parts of the world in which women functionally are, and are seen as, more practical, pragmatic, and this-worldly than men. One relevant dimension that does seem pan-culturally applicable is that of relative concreteness vs. relative abstractness: the feminine personality tends to be involved with concrete feelings, things, and people, rather than with abstract entities; it tends toward personalism and particularism. A second, closely related, dimension seems to be that of relative subjectivity vs. relative objectivity: Chodorow cites Carlson's study (1971), which concludes that "males represent experiences of self, others, space, and time in individualistic, objective, and distant ways, while females represent experiences in relatively interpersonal, subjective, immediate ways" (quoting Carlson, p. 270). Although this and other studies were done in Western societies, Chodorow sees their findings on the differences between male and female personality—roughly, that men are more objective and inclined to relate in terms of relatively abstract categories, women more subjective and inclined to relate in terms of relatively concrete phenomena—as "general and nearly universal differences" (p. 43).

· · ·

It is thus not difficult to see how the feminine personality would lend weight to a view of women as being "closer to nature." Yet at the same time, the modes of relating characteristic of women undeniably play a powerful and important role in the cultural process. For just as relatively unmediated relating is in some sense at the lower end of the spectrum of human spiritual functions, embedded and particularizing rather than transcending and synthesizing, yet that mode of relating also stands at the upper end of that spectrum. Consider the mother-child relationship. Mothers tend to be committed to their children as individuals, regardless of sex, age, beauty, clan affiliation, or other categories in which the child might participate. Now any relationship with this quality—not just mother and child but any sort of highly personal, relatively unmediated commitment—may be seen as a challenge to culture and society "from below," insofar as it represents the fragmentary potential of individual loyalties vis-à-vis the solidarity of the group. But it may also be seen as embodying the synthesizing agent for culture and society "from above," in that it represents generalized human values above and beyond loyalties to particular social categories. Every society must have social categories that transcend personal loyalties, but every society must also generate a sense of ultimate moral unity for all its members above and beyond those social categories. Thus that psychic mode seemingly typical of women, which tends to disregard categories and to seek "communion" (Chodorow, p. 55, following Bakan, 1966) directly and personally with others, although it may appear infracultural from one point of view, is at the same time associated with the highest levels of the cultural process.

THE IMPLICATIONS OF INTERMEDIACY

My primary purpose in this paper has been to attempt to explain the universal secondary status of women. Intellectually and personally, I felt strongly challenged by this problem; I felt compelled to deal with it before undertaking an analysis of woman's position in any particular society. Local variables of economy, ecology, history, political and social structure, values, and world view—these could explain variations within this universal, but they could not explain the universal itself. And if we were not to accept the ideology of biological determinism, then explanation, it seemed to me, could only proceed by reference to other universals of the human cultural situation. Thus the general outlines of the approach—although not of course the particular solution offered—were determined by the problem itself, and not by any predilection on my part for global abstract structural analysis.

I argued that the universal devaluation of women could be explained by postulating that women are seen as closer to nature than men, men being seen as more unequivocally occupying the high ground of culture. The culture/nature distinction is itself a product of culture, culture being minimally defined as the transcendence, by means of systems of thought and technology, of the natural givens of existence. This of course is an analytic definition, but I argued that at some level every culture incorporates this notion in one form or other, if only through the performance of ritual as an assertion of the human ability to manipulate those givens. In any case, the core of the paper was concerned with showing why women might tend to be assumed, over and over, in the most diverse sorts of world views and in cultures of every degree of complexity, to be closer to nature than men. Woman's physiology, more involved more of the time with "species of life"; woman's association with the structurally subordinate domestic context, charged with the crucial function of transforming animal-like infants into cultured beings; "woman's psyche," appropriately molded to mothering functions by her own socialization and tending toward greater personalism and less mediated modes of relating—all these factors make woman appear to be rooted more directly and deeply in nature. At the same time, however, her "membership" and fully necessary participation in culture are recognized by culture and cannot be denied. Thus she is seen to occupy an intermediate position between culture and nature.

This intermediacy has several implications for analysis, depending upon how it is interpreted. First, of course, it answers my primary question of why woman is everywhere seen as lower than man, for even if she is not seen as nature pure and simple, she is still seen as achieving less transcendence of nature than man. Here intermediate simply means "middle status" on a hierarchy of being from culture to nature.

Second, intermediate may have the significance of "mediating," i.e. performing some sort of synthesizing or converting function between nature and culture, here seen (by culture) not as two ends of a continuum but as two radically different sorts of processes in the world. The domestic unit—and hence woman, who in virtually every case appears as its primary representative—is one of culture's crucial agencies for the conversion of nature into culture, especially with reference to the socialization of children. Any culture's continued viability depends upon properly socialized individuals who will see the world in that culture's terms and adhere more or less unquestioningly to its moral precepts. The functions of the domestic unit must be closely controlled in order to ensure this outcome; the stability of the domestic unit as an institution must be placed as far as possible beyond question. (We see some aspects of the protection of the integrity and stability of the domestic group in the powerful taboos against incest, matricide, patricide, and fratricide.[4]) Insofar as woman is universally the primary agent of early socialization and is seen as virtually the embodiment of the functions of the domestic

group, she will tend to come under the heavier restrictions and circumscriptions surrounding that unit. Her (culturally defined) intermediate position between nature and culture, here having the significance of her *mediation* (i.e. performing conversion functions) between nature and culture, would thus account not only for her lower status but for the greater restrictions placed upon her activities. In virtually every culture her permissible sexual activities are more closely circumscribed than man's, she is offered a much smaller range of role choices, and she is afforded direct access to a far more limited range of its social institutions. Further, she is almost universally socialized to have a narrower and generally more conservative set of attitudes and views than man, and the limited social contexts of her adult life reinforce this situation. This socially engendered conservatism and traditionalism of woman's thinking is another—perhaps the worst, certainly the most insidious—mode of social restriction, and would clearly be related to her traditional function of producing well-socialized members of the group.

Finally, woman's intermediate position may have the implication of greater symbolic ambiguity (see also Rosaldo). Shifting our image of the culture/nature relationship once again, we may envision culture in this case as a small clearing within the forest of the larger natural system. From this point of view, that which is intermediate between culture and nature is located on the continuous periphery of culture's clearing; and though it may thus appear to stand both above and below (and beside) culture, it is simply outside and around it. We can begin to understand then how a single system of cultural thought can often assign to woman completely polarized and apparently contradictory meanings, since extremes, as we say, meet. That she often represents both life and death is only the simplest example one could mention.

For another perspective on the same point, it will be recalled that the psychic mode associated with women seems to stand at both the bottom and the top of the scale of human modes of relating. The tendency in that mode is to get involved more directly with people as individuals and not as representatives of one social category or another; this mode can be seen as either "ignoring" (and thus subverting) or "transcending" (and thus achieving a higher synthesis of) those social categories, depending upon the cultural view for any given purpose. Thus we can account easily for both the subversive feminine symbols (witches, evil eye, menstrual pollution, castrating mothers) and the feminine symbols of transcendence (mother goddesses, merciful dispensers of salvation, female symbols of justice, and the strong presence of feminine symbolism in the realms of art, religion, ritual, and law). Feminine symbolism, far more often than masculine symbolism, manifests this propensity toward polarized ambiguity—sometimes utterly exalted, sometimes utterly debased, rarely within the normal range of human possibilities.

If woman's (culturally viewed) intermediacy between culture and nature has this implication of generalized ambiguity of meaning characteristic of marginal phenomena, then we are also in a better position to account for those cultural and historical "inversions" in which women are in some way or other symbolically aligned with culture and men with nature. A number of cases come to mind: the Sirionó of Brazil, among whom, according to Ingham (1971: 1098), "nature, the raw, and maleness" are opposed to "culture, the cooked, and femaleness";[5] Nazi Germany, in which women were said to be the guardians of culture and morals; European courtly love, in which man considered himself the beast and woman the pristine exalted object— a pattern of thinking that persists, for example, among modern Spanish peasants (see Pitt-Rivers, 1961; Rosaldo). And there are no doubt other cases of this sort, including some aspects of our own culture's view of women. Each such instance of an alignment of women with culture rather than nature requires detailed analysis of specific historical and ethnographic data. But in indicating how nature in general, and the feminine mode of interpersonal relations in particular, can appear from certain points of view to stand both under and over (but really simply outside of) the sphere of culture's hegemony, we have at least laid the groundwork for such analyses.

In short, the postulate that woman is viewed as closer to nature than man has several implications for further analysis, and can be interpreted in several different ways. If it is viewed simply as a *middle* position on a scale from culture down to nature, then it is still seen as lower than culture and thus accounts for the pan-cultural assumption that woman is lower than man in the order of things. If it is read as a *mediating* element in the culture-nature relationship, then it may account in part for the cultural tendency not merely to devalue woman but to circumscribe and restrict her functions, since culture must maintain control over its (pragmatic and symbolic) mechanisms for the conversion of nature into culture. And if it is read as an *ambiguous* status between culture and nature, it may help account for the fact that, in specific cultural ideologies and symbolizations, woman can occasionally be aligned with culture, and in any event is often assigned polarized and contradictory meanings within a single symbolic system. Middle status, mediating functions, ambiguous meaning—all are different readings, for different contextual purposes, of woman's being seen as intermediate between nature and culture.

CONCLUSIONS

Ultimately, it must be stressed again that the whole scheme is a construct of culture rather than a fact of nature. Woman is not "in reality" any closer to (or further from) nature than man—both have consciousness, both are mortal. But there are certainly reasons why she appears that way, which is what I have tried to show in this paper. The result is a (sadly) efficient feedback system: various aspects of woman's situation (physical, social, psychological) contribute to her being seen as closer to nature, while the view of her as closer to nature is in turn embodied in institutional forms that reproduce her situation. The implications for social change are similarly circular: a different cultural view can only grow out of a different social actuality; a different social actuality can only grow out of a different cultural view.

It is clear, then, that the situation must be attacked from both sides. Efforts directed solely at changing the social institutions—through setting quotas on hiring, for example, or through passing equal-pay-for-equal-work laws—cannot have far-reaching effects if cultural language and imagery continue to purvey a relatively devalued view of women. But at the same time efforts directed solely at changing cultural assumptions—through male and female consciousness-raising groups, for example, or through revision of educational materials and mass-media imagery—cannot be successful unless the institutional base of the society is changed to support and reinforce the changed cultural view. Ultimately, both men and women can and must be equally involved in projects of creativity and transcendence. Only then will women be seen as aligned with culture, in culture's ongoing dialectic with nature.

[1974]

REFERENCES

Bakan, David, 1966. The Duality of Human Existence. Boston.

Carlson, Rae. 1971. "Sex Differences in Ego Functioning: Exploratory Studies of Agency and Communion," *Journal of Consulting and Clinical Psychology*, 37: 267–77.

De Beauvoir, Simone. 1953. The Second Sex. New York. Originally published in French in 1949.

Ingham, John M. 1971. "Are the Sirionó Raw or Cooked?" *American Anthropologist*, 73: 1092–99.

Lévi-Strauss, Claude. 1969a. The Elementary Structures of Kinship. Trans. J. H. Bell and J. R. von Strumer; ed. R. Needham. Boston.

———— 1969b. The Raw and the Cooked. Trans. J. and D. Weightman. New York.

Lowie, Robert. 1956. The Crow Indians. New York. Originally published in 1935.

Ortner, Sherry B. 1973. "Sherpa Purity," *American Anthropologist*, 75: 49–63.

———— n.d. "Purification Beliefs and Practices," *Encyclopaedia Britannica*, forthcoming.

Pitt-Rivers, Julian. 1961. People of the Sierra. Chicago.

Siu, R. G. H. 1968. The Man of Many Qualities. Cambridge, Mass.

Ullman, Stephen. 1963. "Semantic Universals," in Joseph H. Greenberg, ed., Universals of Language. Cambridge, Mass.

NOTES

1. While we are on the subject of injustices of various kinds, we might note that Lowie secretly bought this doll, the most sacred object in the tribal repertoire, from its custodian, the widow of Wrinkled-face. She asked $400 for it, but this price was "far beyond [Lowie's] means," and he finally got it for $80 (p. 300).

2. Semantic theory uses the concept of motivation of meaning, which encompasses various ways in which a meaning may be assigned to a symbol because of certain objective properties of that symbol, rather than by arbitrary association. In a sense, this entire paper is an inquiry into the motivation of the meaning of woman as a symbol, asking why woman may be unconsciously assigned the significance of being closer to nature. For a concise statement on the various types of motivation of meaning, see Ullman (1963).

3. I remember having my first male teacher in the fifth grade, and I remember being excited about that—it was somehow more grown-up.

4. Nobody seems to care much about sororicide—a point that ought to be investigated.

5. Ingham's discussion is rather ambiguous itself, since women are also associated with animals: "The contrasts man/animal and man/woman are evidently similar . . . hunting is the means of acquiring women as well as animals" (p. 1095). A careful reading of the data suggests that both women and animals are mediators between nature and culture in this tradition.

 47

The Laugh of the Medusa

HÉLÈNE CIXOUS

I shall speak about women's writing: about *what it will do*. Woman must write her self: must write about women and bring women to writing, from which they have been driven away as violently as from their bodies—for the same reasons, by the same law, with the same fatal goal. Woman must put herself into the text—as into the world and into history—by her own movement.

The future must no longer be determined by the past. I do not deny that the effects of the past are still with us. But I refuse to strengthen them by repeating them, to confer upon them an irremovability the equivalent of destiny, to confuse the biological and the cultural. Anticipation is imperative.

Since these reflections are taking shape in an area just on the point of being discovered, they necessarily bear the mark of our time—a time during which the new breaks away from the old, and, more precisely, the (feminine) new from the old (*la nouvelle de l'ancien*). Thus, as there are no grounds for establishing a discourse, but rather an arid millennial ground to break, what I say has at least two sides and two aims: to break up, to destroy; and to foresee the unforeseeable, to project.

I write this as a woman, toward women. When I say "woman," I'm speaking of woman in her inevitable struggle against conventional man; and of a universal woman subject who must bring women to their senses and to their meaning in history. But first it must be said that in spite of the enormity of the repression that has kept them in the "dark"—that dark which people have been trying to make them accept as their attribute—there is, at this time, no general woman, no one typical woman. What they have *in common* I will say. But what strikes me is the infinite richness of their individual constitutions: you can't talk about *a* female sexuality, uniform, homogeneous, classifiable into codes—any more than you can talk about one unconscious resembling another. Women's imaginary is inexhaustible, like music, painting, writing: their stream of phantasms is incredible.

I have been amazed more than once by a description a woman gave me of a world all her own which she had been secretly haunting since early childhood. A world of searching, the elaboration of a knowledge, on the basis of a systematic experimentation with the bodily functions, a passionate and precise interrogation of her erotogeneity. This practice, extraordinarily rich and inventive, in particular as concerns masturbation, is prolonged or accompanied by a production of forms, a veritable aesthetic activity, each stage of rapture inscribing a resonant vision, a composition, something beautiful. Beauty will no longer be forbidden.

I wished that that woman would write and proclaim this unique empire so that other women, other unacknowledged sovereigns, might exclaim: I, too, overflow; my desires have invented new desires, my body knows unheard-of songs. Time and again I, too, have felt so full of luminous torrents that I could burst—burst with forms much more beautiful than those which are put up in frames and sold for a stinking fortune. And I, too, said nothing, showed nothing; I didn't open my mouth, I didn't repaint my half of the world. I was ashamed. I was afraid, and I swallowed my shame and my fear. I said to myself: You are mad! What's the meaning of these waves, these floods, these outbursts? Where is the ebullient, infinite woman who, immersed as she was in her naiveté, kept in the dark about herself, led into self-disdain by the great arm of parental-conjugal phallocentrism, hasn't been ashamed of her strength? Who, surprised and horrified by the fantastic tumult of her drives (for she was made to believe that a well-adjusted normal woman has a . . . divine composure), hasn't accused herself of being a monster? Who, feeling a funny desire stirring inside her (to sing, to write, to dare to speak, in short, to bring out something new), hasn't thought she was sick? Well, her shameful sickness is that she resists death, that she makes trouble.

And why don't you write? Write! Writing is for you, you are for you; your body is yours, take it. I know why you haven't written. (And why I didn't write before the age of twenty-seven.) Because writing is at once too high, too great for you, it's reserved for the great—that is for "great men"; and it's "silly." Besides, you've written a little, but in secret. And it wasn't good, because it was in secret, and because you punished yourself for writing, because you didn't go all the way, or because you wrote, irresistibly, as when we would masturbate in secret, not to go further, but to attenuate the tension a bit, just enough to take the edge off. And then as soon as we come, we go and make ourselves feel guilty—so as to be forgiven; or to forget, to bury it until the next time.

Write, let no one hold you back, let nothing stop you: not man; not the imbecilic capitalist machinery, in which publishing houses are the crafty, obsequious relayers of imperatives handed down by an economy that works against us and off our backs; and not *yourself*. Smug-faced readers, managing editors, and big bosses don't like the true texts of women—female-sexed tests. That kind scares them.

I write woman: woman must write woman. And man, man. So only an oblique consideration will be found here of man; it's up to him to say where his masculinity and femininity are at: this will concern us once men have opened their eyes and seen themselves clearly.[1]

Now women return from afar, from always: from "without," from the heath where witches are kept alive; from below, from beyond "culture"; from their childhood which men have been trying desperately to make them forget, condemning it to "eternal rest." The little girls and their "ill-mannered" bodies immured, well-preserved, intact unto themselves, in the mirror. Frigidified. But are they ever seething underneath! What an effort it takes—there's no end to it—for the sex cops to bar their threatening return. Such a display of forces on both sides that the struggle has for centuries been immobilized in the trembling equilibrium of a deadlock.

Here they are, returning, arriving over and again, because the unconscious is impregnable. They have wandered around in circles, confined to the narrow room in which they've been given a deadly brainwashing. You can incarcerate them, slow them down, get away with the old Apartheid routine, but for a time only. As soon as they begin to speak, at the same time as they're taught their name, they can be taught that their territory is black: because you are Africa, you are black. Your continent is dark. Dark is dangerous. You can't see anything in the dark, you're afraid. Don't move, you might fall. Most of all, don't go into the forest. And so we have internalized this horror of the dark.

Men have committed the greatest crime against women. Insidiously, violently, they have led them to hate women, to be their own enemies, to mobilize their immense strength against themselves, to be the executants of their virile needs. They have made for women an antinarcissism! A narcissism which loves itself only to be loved for what women haven't got! They have constructed the infamous logic of antilove.

We the precocious, we the repressed of culture, our lovely mouths gagged with pollen, our wind knocked out of us, we the labyrinths, the ladders, the trampled spaces, the bevies—we are black and we are beautiful.

We're stormy, and that which is ours breaks loose from us without our fearing any debilitation. Our glances, our smiles, are spent; laughs exude from all our mouths; our blood flows and we extend ourselves without ever reaching an end; we never hold back our thoughts, our signs, our writing; and we're not afraid of lacking.

What happiness for us who are omitted, brushed aside at the scene of inheritances; we inspire ourselves and we expire without running out of breath, we are everywhere!

· · ·

She must write her self, because this is the invention of a *new insurgent* writing which, when the moment of her liberation has come, will allow her to carry out the indispensable ruptures and transformations in her history, first at two levels that cannot be separated.

(a)   Individually. By writing her self, woman will return to the body which has been more than confiscated from her, which has been turned into the uncanny stranger on display—the ailing or dead figure, which so often turns out to be the nasty com-

panion, the cause and location of inhibitions. Censor the body and you censor breath and speech at the same time.

Write your self. Your body must be heard. Only then will the immense resources of the unconscious spring forth. Our naphtha will spread, throughout the world, without dollars—black or gold—non-assessed values that will change the rules of the old game.

To write. An act which will not only "realize" the decensored relation of woman to her sexuality, to her womanly being, giving her access to her native strength; it will give her back her goods, her pleasures, her organs, her immense bodily territories which have been kept under seal; it will tear her away from the superegoized structure in which she has always occupied the place reserved for the guilty (guilty of everything, guilty at every turn: for having desires, for not having any; for being frigid, for being "too hot"; for not being both at once; for being too motherly and not enough; for having children and for not having any; for nursing and for not nursing . . .)—tear her away by means of this research, this job of analysis and illumination, this emancipation of the marvelous text of her self that she must urgently learn to speak. A woman without a body, dumb, blind, can't possibly be a good fighter. She is reduced to being the servant of the militant male, his shadow. We must kill the false woman who is preventing the live one from breathing. Inscribe the breath of the whole woman.

(b)   An act that will also be marked by woman's *seizing* the occasion to *speak,* hence her shattering entry into history, which has always been based *on her suppression.* To write and thus to forge for herself the antilogos weapon. To become *at will* the taker and initiator, for her own right, in every symbolic system, in every political process.

· · ·

Because the "economy" of her drives is prodigious, she cannot fail, in seizing the occasion to speak, to transform directly and indirectly *all* systems of exchange based on masculine thrift. Her libido will produce far more radical effects of political and social change than some might like to think.

Because she arrives, vibrant, over and again, we are at the beginning of a new history, or rather of a process of becoming in which several histories intersect with one another. As subject for history, woman always occurs simultaneously in several places. Woman un-thinks[2] the unifying, regulating history that homogenizes and channels forces, herding contradictions into a single battlefield. In woman, personal history blends together with the history of all women, as well as national and world history. As a militant, she is an integral part of all liberations. She must be farsighted, not limited to a blow-by-blow interaction. She foresees that her liberation will do more than modify power relations or toss the ball over to the other camp; she will bring about a mutation in human relations, in thought, in all praxis: hers is not simply a class struggle, which she carries forward into a much vaster movement. Not that in order to be a woman-in-struggle(s) you have to leave the class struggle or repudiate it; but you have to split it open, spread it out, push it forward, fill it with the fundamental struggle so as to prevent the class struggle, or any other struggle for the liberation of a class or people, from operating as a form of repression, pretext for postponing the inevitable, the staggering alteration in power relations and in the production of individualities. This alteration is already upon us—in the United States, for example, where millions of night crawlers are in the process of undermining the family and distintegrating the whole of American sociality.

The new history is coming; it's not a dream, though it does extend beyond men's imagination, and for good reason. It's going to deprive them of their conceptual orthopedics, beginning with the destruction of their enticement machine.

It is impossible to *define* a feminine practice of writing, and this is an impossibility that will remain, for this practice can never be theorized, enclosed, coded—which doesn't mean that it doesn't exist. But it will always surpass the discourse that regulates the phallocentric system; it does and will take place in areas other than those subordinated to philosophico-theoretical domination. It will be conceived of only by subjects who are breakers of automatisms, by peripheral figures that no authority can ever subjugate.

Hence the necessity to affirm the flourishes of this writing, to give form to its movement, its near and distant byways. Bear in mind to begin with

(1) that sexual opposition, which has always worked for man's profit to the point of reducing writing, too, to his laws, is only a historico-cultural limit. There is, there will be more and more rapidly pervasive now, a fiction that produces irreducible effects of femininity. (2) That it is through ignorance that most readers, critics, and writers of both sexes hesitate to admit or deny outright the possibility or the pertinence of a distinction between feminine and masculine writing. It will usually be said, thus disposing of sexual difference: either that all writing, to the extent that it materializes, is feminine; or, inversely—but it comes to the same thing—that the act of writing is equivalent to masculine masturbation (and so the woman who writes cuts herself out a paper penis); or that writing is bisexual, hence neuter, which again does away with differentiation. To admit that writing is precisely working (in) the in-between, inspecting the process of the same and of the other without which nothing can live, undoing the work of death—to admit this is first to want the two, as well as both, the ensemble of the one and the other, not fixed in sequences of struggle and expulsion or some other form of death but infinitely dynamized by an incessant process of exchange from one subject to another. A process of different subjects knowing one another and beginning one another anew only from the living boundaries of the other: a multiple and inexhaustible course with millions of encounters and transformations of the same into the other and into the in-between, from which woman takes her forms (and man, in his turn; but that's his other history).

In saying "bisexual, hence neuter," I am referring to the classic conception of bisexuality, which, squashed under the emblem of castration fear and along with the fantasy of a "total" being (though composed of two halves), would do away with the difference experienced as an operation incurring loss, as the mark of dreaded sectility.

To this self-effacing, merger-type bisexuality, which would conjure away castration (the writer who puts up his sign: "bisexual written here, come and see," when the odds are good that it's neither one nor the other), I oppose the *other bisexuality* on which every subject not enclosed in the false theater of phallocentric representationalism has founded his/her erotic universe. Bisexuality: that is, each one's location in self (*repérage en soi*) of the presence—variously manifest and insistent according to each person, male or female—of both sexes, nonexclusion either of the difference or of one sex, and, from this "self-permission," multiplication of the effects of the inscription of desire, over all parts of my body and the other body.

Now it happens that at present, for historico-cultural reasons, it is women who are opening up to and benefiting from this vatic bisexuality which doesn't annul differences but stirs them up, pursues them, increases their number. In a certain way, "woman is bisexual"; man—it's a secret to no one—being poised to keep glorious phallic monosexuality in view. By virtue of affirming the primacy of the phallus and of bringing it into play, phallocratic ideology has claimed more than one victim. As a woman, I've been clouded over by the great shadow of the scepter and been told: idolize it, that which you cannot brandish. But at the same time, man has been handed that grotesque and scarcely enviable destiny (just imagine) of being reduced to a single idol with clay balls. And consumed, as Freud and his followers note, by a fear of being a woman! For, if psychoanalysis was constituted from woman, to repress femininity (and not so successful a repression at that—men have made it clear), its account of masculine sexuality is now hardly refutable; as with all the "human" sciences, it reproduces the masculine view, of which it is one of the effects.

Here we encounter the inevitable man-with-rock, standing erect in his old Freudian realm, in the way that, to take the figure back to the point where linguistics is conceptualizing it "anew," Lacan preserves it in the sanctuary of the phallos (ϕ) "sheltered" from *castration's lack!* Their "symbolic" exists, it holds power—we, the sowers of disorder, know it only too well. But we are in no way obliged to deposit our lives in their banks of lack, to consider the constitution of the subject in terms of a drama manglingly restaged, to reinstate again and again the religion of the father. Because we don't want that. We don't fawn around the supreme hole. We have no womanly reason to pledge allegiance to the negative. The feminine (as the poets suspected) affirms: ". . . And yes," says Molly, carrying *Ulysses* off beyond any book and toward the new writing; "I said yes, I will Yes."

The Dark Continent is neither dark nor unexplorable.—It is still unexplored only because we've been made to believe that it was too dark to be explorable. And because they want to make us believe that what interests us is the white continent, with its monuments to Lack. And we believed. They riveted us between two horrifying myths: between the Medusa and the abyss. That would be enough to set half the world laughing, except that it's still going on. For the phallologocentric sublation[3] is with us, and it's militant, regenerating the old patterns, anchored in the dogma of castration. They haven't changed a thing: they've theorized their desire for reality! Let the priests tremble, we're going to show them our sexts!

Too bad for them if they fall apart upon discovering that women aren't men, or that the mother doesn't have one. But isn't this fear convenient for them? Wouldn't the worst be, isn't the worst, in truth, that women aren't castrated, that they have only to stop listening to the Sirens (for the Sirens were men) for history to change its meaning? You only have to look at the Medusa straight on to see her. And she's not deadly. She's beautiful and she's laughing.

. . .

. . . Her libido is cosmic, just as her unconscious is worldwide. Her writing can only keep going, without ever inscribing or discerning contours, daring to make these vertiginous crossing of the other(s) ephemeral and passionate sojourns in him, her, them, whom she inhabits long enough to look at from the point closest to their unconscious from the moment they awaken, to love them at the point closest to their drives; and then further, impregnated through and through with these brief, identificatory embraces, she goes and passes into infinity. She alone dares and wishes to know from within, where she, the outcast, has never ceased to hear the resonance of fore-language. She lets the other language speak—the language of 1,000 tongues which knows neither enclosure nor death. To life she refuses nothing. Her language does not contain, it carries; it does not hold back, it makes possible. When id is ambiguously uttered—the wonder of being several—she doesn't defend herself against these unknown women whom she's surprised at becoming, but derives pleasure from this gift of alterability.

I am spacious, singing flesh, on which is grafted no one knows which I, more or less human, but alive because of transformation.

Write! and your self-seeking text will know itself better than flesh and blood, rising, insurrectionary dough kneading itself, with sonorous, perfumed ingredients, a lively combination of flying colors, leaves, and rivers plunging into the sea we feed. "Ah, there's her sea," he will say as he holds out to me a basin full of water from the little phallic mother from whom he's inseparable. But look, our seas are what we make of them, full of fish or not, opaque or transparent, red or black, high or smooth, narrow or bankless; and we are ourselves sea, sand, coral, seaweed, beaches, tides, swimmers, children, waves . . . More or less wavily sea, earth, sky—what matter would rebuff us? We know how to speak them all.

Heterogeneous, yes. For her joyous benefits she is erogenous; she is the erotogeneity of the heterogeneous: airborne swimmer, in flight, she does not cling to herself; she is dispersible, prodigious, stunning, desirous and capable of others, of the other woman that she will be, of the other woman she isn't, of him, of you.

. . .

The woman who still allows herself to be threatened by the big dick, who's still impressed by the commotion of the phallic stance, who still leads a loyal master to the beat of the drum: that's the woman of yesterday. They still exist, easy and numerous victims of the oldest of farces: either they're cast in the original silent versions in which, as titanesses lying under the mountains they make with their quivering, they never see erected that theoretic monument to the golden phallus looming, in the old manner, over their bodies. Or, coming today out of their *infans* period and into the second, "enlightened" version of their virtuous debasement, they see themselves suddenly assaulted by the builders of the analytic empire and, as soon as they've begun to formulate the new desire, naked, nameless, so happy at making an appearance, they're taken in their bath by the new old men, and then, whoops! Luring them with flashy signifiers, the demon of interpretation—oblique, decked out in modernity—sells them the same old handcuffs, baubles, and chains. Which castration do you prefer? Whose degrading do you like better, the father's or the

mother's? Oh, what pwetty eyes, you pwetty little girl. Here, buy my glasses and you'll see the Truth-Me-Myself tell you everything you should know. Put them on your nose and take a fetishist's look (you are me, the other analyst—that's what I'm telling you) at your body and the body of the other. You see? No? Wait, you'll have everything explained to you, and you'll know at last which sort of neurosis you're related to. Hold still, we're going to do your portrait, so that you can begin looking like it right away.

Yes, the naives to the first and second degree are still legion. If the New Women, arriving now, dare to create outside the theoretical, they're called in by the cops of the signifier, fingerprinted, remonstrated, and brought into the line of order that they are supposed to know; assigned by force of trickery to a precise place in the chain that's always formed for the benefit of a privileged signifier. We are pieced back to the string which leads back, if not to the Name-of-the-Father, then, for a new twist, to the place of the phallic-mother.

Beware, my friend, of the signifier that would take you back to the authority of a signified! Beware of diagnoses that would reduce your generative powers. "Common" nouns are also proper nouns that disparage your singularity by classifying it into species. Break out of the circles; don't remain within the psychoanalytic closure. Take a look around, then cut through!

And if we are legion, it's because the war of liberation has only made as yet a tiny breakthrough. But women are thronging to it. I've seen them, those who will be neither dupe nor domestic, those who will not fear the risk of being a woman; will not fear any risk, any desire, any space still unexplored in themselves, among themselves and others or anywhere else. They do not fetishize, they do not deny, they do not hate. They observe, they approach, they try to see the other woman, the child, the lover—not to strengthen their own narcissism or verify the solidity or weakness of the master, but to make love better, to invent.

Other love.—In the beginning are our differences. The new love dares for the other, wants the other, makes dizzying, precipitous flights between knowledge and invention. The woman arriving over and over again does not stand still; she's everywhere, she exchanges, she is the desire-that-gives. (Not enclosed in the paradox of the gift that takes nor under the illusion of unitary fusion. We're past that.) She comes in, comes-in-between herself me and you, between the other me where one is always infinitely more than one and more than me, without the fear of ever reaching a limit; she thrills in our becoming. And we'll keep on becoming! She cuts through defensive loves, motherages, and devourations: beyond selfish narcissism, in the moving, open, transitional space, she runs her risks. Beyond the struggle-to-the-death that's been removed to the bed, beyond the love-battle that claims to represent exchange, she scorns at an Eros dynamic that would be fed by hatred. Hatred: a heritage, again, a reminder, a duping subservience to the phallus. To love, to watch-think-seek the other in the other, to despecularize, to unhoard. Does this seem difficult? It's not impossible, and this is what nourishes life— a love that has no commerce with the apprehensive desire that provides against the lack and stultifies the strange; a love that rejoices in the exchange that multiplies. Wherever history still unfolds as the history of death, she does not tread. Opposition, hierarchizing exchange, the struggle for mastery which can end only in at least one death (one master—one slave, or two nonmasters ≠ two dead)—all that comes from a period in time governed by phallocentric values. The fact that this period extends into the present doesn't prevent woman from starting the history of life somewhere else. Elsewhere, she gives. She doesn't "know" what she's giving, she doesn't measure it; she gives, though, neither a counterfeit impression nor something she hasn't got. She gives more, with no assurance that she'll get back even some unexpected profit from what she puts out. She gives that there may be life, thought, transformation. This is an "economy" that can no longer be put in economic terms. Wherever she loves, all the old concepts of management are left behind. At the end of a more or less conscious computation, she finds not her sum but her differences. I am for you what you want me to be at the moment you look at me in a way you've never seen me before: at every instant. When I write, it's everything that we don't know we can be that is written out of me, without exclusions, without stipulation, and everything we will be calls us to the unflagging, intoxicating, un-

appeasable search for love. In one another we will never be lacking.

Translated by Keith Cohen and Paula Cohen
[1975]

NOTES

1. Men still have everything to say about their sexuality, and everything to write. For what they have said so far, for the most part, stems from the opposition activity/passivity from the power relation between a fantasized obligatory virility meant to invade, to colonize, and the consequential phantasm of woman as a "dark continent" to penetrate and to "pacify." (We know what "pacify" means in terms of scotomizing the other and misrecognizing the self.) Conquering her, they've made haste to depart from her borders, to get out of sight, out of body. The way man has of getting out of himself and into her whom he takes not for the other but for his own, deprives him, he knows, of his own bodily territory. One can understand how man, confusing himself with his penis and rushing in for the attack, might feel resentment and fear of being "taken" by the woman, of being lost in her, absorbed or alone.

2. *Dé-pense,* a neologism formed on the verb *penser,* hence "unthinks," but also "spends" (from *dépenser*).—Tr.

3. Standard English term for the Hegelian *Aufhebung,* the French *la relève.*

 48

From Beyond the Veil: Male-Female Dynamics in Modern Muslim Society

FATIMA MERNISSI

CONCLUSION
WOMEN'S LIBERATION IN MUSLIM COUNTRIES

People tend to perceive women's liberation as a spiritual and not a material problem. We have seen this to be true in the case of Islam, where changes in conditions for women were perceived by Muslim male literature as involving solely religious problems. Muslims argued that changes in women's conditions were a direct attack on Allah's realm and order. But changes in the twentieth century, mainly in socialist societies, have showed that the liberation of women is predominantly an economic issue. Liberation is a costly affair for any society, and women's liberation is primarily a question of the allocation of resources. A society that decides to liberate women not only has to provide them with jobs, but also has to take upon itself the responsibility for providing child care and food for all workers regardless of sex. A system of kindergartens and canteens is an indispensable investment promoting the liberation of women from traditional domestic chains.

The capacity to invest in women's liberation is not a function of a society's wealth, but of its goals and objectives. A society whose ultimate goal is profit rather than the development of human potential proves reluctant and finally unable to afford a state system of child-care centres and canteens. Mariarosa Della Costa explains how capitalism maintains, in the midst of its modern management of human resources and services, a pre-capitalist army of wageless workers—housewives—who provide unpaid child-care and domestic services.[1] Hence the paradox: the 'richest' nation in the world (the nation that controls most of the world's resources), the United States, is unable in spite of its much publicized abundance to afford a system of free kindergartens and canteens to promote women's humanhood.

Have Arab societies taken a stand on the question? Until now, they have had no effective systematic and coherent programme. In the absence of such programmes, and because it is too soon to judge the emerging trends concerning the liberation of women in independent Arab-Muslim states, I will limit myself to a few speculative remarks on the likely future of women in the Arab world. Before going any further, I want to draw attention to the inadequacy of the only two models for 'women's liberation' presently available in the Arab-Muslim world.

The scarcity of effective models for 'liberated women' might explain the particularly strong reaction that 'women's liberation' evokes from most Muslims. (By effective models I mean models which evoke images specific enough to stir people's emotions.) One of these is an intrinsic Arab model, that of pre-Islamic family and sexuality patterns, the other is exogenous, the Western model. The socialist models of sexuality and family patterns are hardly known and enjoy a carefully cultivated indifference, based more often on ignorance than on knowledgeable analysis. Both the pre-Islamic and

Western models provoke traumatizing images of sexuality, although for different reasons.

Pre-Islamic sexuality is described in Arab literature as a chaotic, all-embracing, rampant promiscuity whose essence is women's self-determination, freedom to choose and dismiss their sexual partner, or partners, and the utter unimportance of the biological father and paternal legitimacy. The idea of female sexual self-determination which is suggested by the term 'women's liberation' is likely to stir ancestral fears of this mythical (pre-civilized) *jahiliya* woman before whom the male is deprived of all his initiative, control, and privilege. The way to win over a 'liberated woman' is to please her and make her love you, not to coerce and threaten her. But Muslim society does not socialize men to win women through love; they are badly equipped to deal with a self-determined woman; hence the repulsion and fear that accompany the idea of women's liberation.

Confusing sexual self-determination of women with chaotic, lawless animalistic promiscuity is not exclusive to Muslim societies facing drastic changes in their family structure. This confusion existed and still exists in any society whose family system is based on the enslavement of the woman. Marx and Engels had to attack repeatedly the confusion of bourgeois writers which distorted their thinking about any family in which the woman was not reduced to an acquiescent slave.[2] They had to show again and again that a non-bourgeois sexuality based on equality of the sexes does not necessarily lead to promiscuity, and that the bourgeois family pattern was an unjustified dehumanization of half of society. The same argument holds for Muslim societies. Muslim marriage is based on the premises that social order can be maintained only if women's dangerous potential for chaos is restrained by a dominating non-loving husband who has, besides his wife, other females (concubines, co-wives, and prostitutes) available for his sexual pleasure under equally degrading conditions.[3] A new sexual order based on the absence of dehumanizing limitations of women's potential means the destruction of the traditional Muslim family. In this respect, fears associated with changes in the family and the condition of women are justified. These fears, embedded in the culture through centuries of women's oppression, are echoed and nourished by the vivid, equally degrading images of Western sexuality and its disintegrating family patterns portrayed on every imported television set.

It is understandable that Muslim fathers and husbands feel horrified at the idea of their own family and sexuality patterns being transformed into Western patterns. The striking characteristic of Western sexuality is the mutilation of the woman's integrity, her reduction to a few inches of nude flesh whose shades and forms are photographed *ad infinitum* with no goal other than profit. While Muslim exploitation of the female is cloaked under veils and hidden behind walls, Western exploitation has the bad taste of being bare and over-exposed.

It is worth noting that the fears of Muslim fathers and husbands are not totally unfounded; the nascent 'liberation' of Muslim women has indeed borrowed many characteristics of Western women's way of life. The first gesture of 'liberated' Arab women was to discard the veil for Western dress, which in the thirties, forties, and fifties was that of the wife of the colonizer. Speaking a foreign language was often a corollary to discarding the veil, the first 'liberated' women usually being members of the upper and middle classes. And here we touch upon another aspect of the difficulty Muslim societies have in adjusting to female self-determination. The Westernization of the first 'liberated' women was and still is part and parcel of the Westernization of the Arab-Muslim ruling classes. The fears awakened by the Westernization of women can be interpreted as simply another instance of Muslim society believing that males are able to select what is good in Western civilization and discard bad elements, while women are unable to choose correctly. This is concordant with the classical Muslim view of women as being unable to judge what is good and what is bad.

Another factor that helps in understanding men's fears of the changes now taking place is that Westernization of women has enhanced their seductive powers. We have seen that the Muslim ethic is against women's ornamenting themselves and exposing their charms; veil and walls were particularly effective anti-seduction devices. Westernization allowed ornamented and seductively clad female bodies to appear on the streets. It is interesting that while Western women's liberation movements had

to repudiate the body in pornographic mass media, Muslim women are likely to claim the right to their bodies as part of their liberation movement. Previously a Muslim woman's body belonged to the man who possessed her, father or husband. The mushrooming of beauty salons and ready-to-wear boutiques in Moroccan towns can be interpreted as a forerunner of women's urge to claim their own bodies, which will culminate in more radical claims, such as the claim to birth control and abortion.

Having described the available models and their negative reception, let me hazard a few speculations on the future of women's liberation in Muslim societies, based on a projection from the current situation.

It is hardly contestable that there have been substantial changes in Muslim women's condition. Women have gained many rights that were denied them before, such as the right to education, the right to vote and be elected, and the right to use non-domestic spaces. But an important characteristic of this nascent 'liberation' is that it is not the outcome of a careful plan of controlled nation-wide development. Neither is it the outcome of the massive involvement of women in labour markets, coupled with organized women's movements. The partial, fragmented acquisition of rights by women in Arab-Muslim countries is a random, non-planned, non-systematic phenomenon, due mainly to the disintegration of the traditional system under pressures from within and without. Muslim women's liberation is therefore likely to follow a *sui generis* pattern.

To the dismay of rigid conservatives desperately preoccupied with static tradition, change is shaking the foundations of the Muslim world. Change is multidimensional and hard to control, especially for those who deny it. Whether accepted or rejected, change gnaws continuously at the intricate mechanisms of social life, and the more it is thwarted, the deeper and more surprising are its implications. The heterosexual unit is not yet officially admitted by Muslim rulers to be a crucial focus of the process of national development. Development plans devote hundreds of pages to the mechanization of agriculture, mining, and banking, and only a few pages to the family and women's condition. I want to emphasize on the one hand the deep and far-reaching processes of change at work in the Muslim family, and on the other hand the decisive role of women and the family in any serious development plan in the Third World economy.

The Family and Women

As shown earlier, one of the distinctive characteristics of Muslim sexuality is its territoriality, which reflects a specific division of labour and a specific conception of society and power. The territoriality of Muslim sexuality sets patterns of ranks, tasks, and authority. Spatially confined, women were taken care of materially by the men who possessed them, in exchange for total obedience and sexual and reproductive services. The whole system was organized so that the Muslim *umma* was actually a society of male citizens who possessed, among other things, the female half of the population. In his introduction to *Women and Socialism,* George Tarabishi remarks that people generally say that there are one hundred million Arabs, but in fact there are only fifty million, the female population being prevented from taking part in social responsibilities.[4] Muslim men have always had many more rights and privileges than Muslim women, including even the right to kill their women. (The Moroccan penal code still shows a trace of this power in Article 418, which grants extenuating circumstances to a man who kills his adulterous wife.[5]) Men imposed on women an artificially narrow existence both physically and spiritually.

• • •

One of the results of the break-up of traditional family life is that, for the first time in the history of modern Morocco, the husband is facing his wife directly. Men and women live more closely and interact more than they ever did before, partly because of the decline of anti-heterosexual factors such as the mother-in-law's presence and sexual segregation. This direct confrontation between men and women brought up in sexually antagonistic traditions is likely to be laden with tensions and fears on both sides.

The future of male-female dynamics greatly depends on the way modern states handle the readjustment of sexual rights and the reassessment of sexual status. In Morocco the legislature has retained the traditional concept of marriage. The ancient definition of sex statuses based on division of labour according to sex was reenacted as the basis of family law: Article 35 defines the man as the sole provider for the family. He is responsible not only for himself but also for his able-bodied wife, who is consequently defined as economically dependent, her participation being limited to sexual services, reproduction, and housework.

To define masculinity as the capacity to earn a salary is to condemn those men suffering from unemployment (or the threat of it) to perceive economic problems as castration threats. Moreover, since the *Code* defines earning a salary as a man's role, a woman who earns a salary will be perceived as either masculine or castrating. If the privileges of men become more easily accessible to women, then men will be perceived as becoming more feminine.

• • •

The State as the Main Threat to Traditional Male Supremacy

In spite of its continuous support for traditional male rights, the state constitutes a threat and a mighty rival to the male as both father and husband. The state is taking over the traditional functions of the male head of the family, such as education and the provision of economic security for members of the household. By providing a nation-wide state school system and an individual salary for working wives, daughters, and sons, the state has destroyed two pillars of the father's authority. The increasingly preeminent role of the state has stripped the traditionally powerful family head of his privileges and placed him in a subordinate position with respect to the state not very different from the position of women in the traditional family. The head of the family is dependent on the state (the main employer) to provide for him just as women are dependent on their husbands in traditional settings. Economic support is given in exchange for obedience, and this tends to augment male-female solidarity as a defence against the state and its daily frustrations.

The word 'sexist' as it is currently employed in English has the connotation that males are favoured at the expense of females. It is my belief that, in spite of appearances, the Muslim system does not favour men; the self-fulfilment of men is just as impaired and limited as that of women. Though this equality of oppression is concealed by the world-renowned 'privileges' of the Muslim male, I have tried to illustrate it by showing how polygamy and repudiation are oppressive devices for both sexes. The Muslim theory of sexuality views women as fatally attractive and the source of many delights. Any restrictions on the man's right to such delights, even if they take the form of restrictions on women alone (seclusion, for example), are really attacks on the male's potential for sexual fulfilment.

It might well be argued that the Muslim system makes men pay a higher psychological price for the satisfaction of sexual needs than women, precisely because women are conditioned to accept sexual restrictions as 'natural', while men are encouraged to expect a thorough satisfaction of their sexual needs. Men and women are socialized to deal with sexual frustration differently. We know that an individual's discontent grows as his expectations rise. From the age of four or earlier, a woman in Moroccan society is made aware of the sexual restrictions she has to face. The difficulties a Moroccan male experiences in dealing with sexual frustration are almost unknown to the Moroccan woman, who is traumatized early enough to build adequate defences. In this sense also the Muslim order is not 'sexist'.

· · ·

Future Trends

· · ·

Islam's basically positive attitude toward sexuality is more conducive to healthy perspectives of a self-realizing sexuality, harmoniously integrated in social life, than the West's basically negative attitude toward sexuality. Serious changes in male-female conditioning in Western countries imply revolutionary changes in society which these reformist countries are determined to avoid at any cost. Muslim societies *cannot* afford to be reformist; they do not have sufficient resources to be able to offer palliatives. A superficial replastering of the system is not a possible solution for them.

At a deeper level than laws and official policy, the Muslim social order views the female as a potent aggressive individual whose power can, if not tamed and curbed, corrode the social order. It is very likely

that in the long run such a view will facilitate women's integration into the networks of decision-making and power. One of the main obstacles Western women have been dealing with is their society's view of women as passive inferior beings. The fact that generations of university-educated women in both Europe and America failed to win access to decision-making posts is due in part to this deeply ingrained image of women as inferior. The Muslim image of women as a source of power is likely to make Muslim women set higher and broader goals than just equality with men. The most recent studies on the aspirations of both men and women seem to come to the same conclusion: the goal is not to achieve equality with men. Women have seen that what men have is not worth getting. Women's goals are already being phrased in terms of a global rejection of established sexual patterns, frustrating for males and degrading for females. This implies a revolutionary reorganization of the entire society, starting from its economic structure and ending with its grammar. Jalal al-Azm excuses himself at the beginning of the book for using the term 'he' throughout the book while in fact he should be using a neutral term, because his findings are valid for both men and women.[6] As a social scientist he resents being a prisoner of Arabic grammar, which imposes a sex-defined pronoun.[7] But not many Arab males yet feel ill-at-ease with sex-biased Arabic grammar, though a majority already feel indisposed by the economic situation.

The holders of power in Arab countries, regardless of their political make-up, are condemned to promote change, and they are aware of this, no matter how loud their claim to uphold the 'prestigious past' as the path to modernity. Historians have interpreted the somewhat cyclical resurgence of traditional rhetoric as a reflex of ruling groups threatened by acute and deep processes of change.[8] The problem Arab societies face is not whether or not to change, but how fast to change. The link between women's liberation and economic development is shown by the similarities in the conditions of the two sexes in the Third World; both sexes suffer from exploitation and deprivation. Men do not have, as in the so-called abundant Western societies, glaring advantages over women. Illiteracy and unemployment are suffered by males as well as females. This similarity of men and women as equally deprived and exploited individuals assumes enormous importance in the likely evolution of Third World family structure. George Tarabishi has pointed out the absurdity of men who argue that women should not be encouraged to get jobs in Arab society, where men suffer from unemployment.[9] He argues that society should not waste human resources in unemployment, but systematically channel the wealth of resources into productive tasks. The female half of human resources is more than welcome in the Arab future.

One may speculate that women's liberation in an Arab context is likely to take a faster and more radical path than in Western countries. Women in Western liberal democracies are organizing themselves to claim their rights, but their oppressors are strong, wealthy, and reformist regimes. The dialogue takes place within the reformist framework characteristic of bourgeois democracies. In such situations, serious changes are likely to take a long time. American women will get the right to abortion but it will be a long time before they can prevent the female's body from being exploited as a marketable product. Muslim women, on the contrary, engage in a silent but explosive dialogue with a fragile ruling class whose major task is to secure economic growth and plan a future without exploitation and deprivation. The Arab ruling classes are beginning to realize that they are charged with building a sovereign future, which necessarily revolves around the location and adequate utilization of all human and natural resources for the benefit of the entire populations. The Arab woman is a central element in any sovereign future. Those who have not realized this fact are misleading themselves and their countries.

[1975]

NOTES

1. Mariarosa Della Costa, *Women and the Subversion of the Community,* Bristol 1972.
2. 'Communism in Marriage', article by David Riazanov, published in Moscow in 1926, reproduced in *al-Mar'a wa al-Ishtiraqiya* (Women and Socialism), translated and edited by George Tarabishi, Beirut 1974 (second edition), pp. 33–70.
3. Dr. Salwa Khammash, *al-Mar'a al-Arabiya wa'l-Mujtama al-Taqlidiya* (Arab Women and Traditional Society), Beirut 1973, particularly chapter V (the relation between the sexes) and chapter VII (the position of the wife).
4. George Tarabishi, in his introduction to *Women and Socialism,* p. 13.
5. The article states: 'Killing, wounding, and beating are excusable if they are committed by a husband against his wife and/or her accomplice at the moment that he surprises them *in flagrante delicto* committing adultery.'
6. Sadiq al-Azm, pp. 110–111.
7. Ibid., p. 28.
8. Abdallah Laroui, 'La Crise des Intellectuels Arabes', paper read at colloquium in Louvain, 1970, published in *La Crise des Intellectuels Arabes,* Paris 1974.
9. George Tarabishi, introduction to *Women and Socialism,* p. 13.

 49

From Words and Women

CASEY MILLER AND KATE SWIFT

SEMANTIC POLARIZATION

Two statements, one by a professor of linguistics and the other by a professor of psychiatry, explain rather neatly, when looked at together, the part words play in molding cultural assumptions. Dr. Calvert Watkins, the linguist, says, "The lexicon of a language remains the single most effective way of approaching and understanding the culture of its speakers."[1] Dr. Theodore Lidz, the psychiatrist, says, "The form and functions of the family evolve with the culture and subserve the needs of the society of which it is a subsystem. . . . Among the most crucial tasks performed by the family is the inculcation [in children] of a solid foundation in the language of the society."[2] Put together, the statements say: the words we use daily reflect our cultural understandings and at the same time transmit them to the next generation through an agency that subserves the culture's needs.

Dr. Lidz spells out the relationship of language to culture in more detail:

. . . Language is the means by which people internalize experience, think about it, try out alternatives, conceptualize a future and strive toward future goals. . . . Indeed, the capacity to direct the self into the future, which we shall term "ego functioning," depends upon a person's having verbal symbols with which to construct an internalized symbolic version of the world that can be manipulated in imaginative trial and error before committing himself or herself to irrevocable actions.

To understand the importance of language to ego functioning, we must appreciate that in order for anyone to understand, communicate, and think about the ceaseless flow of experiences, people must be able to divide their experiences into categories. . . . Each child must learn the culture's system of categorizing, not only in order to communicate with others in the society, but also in order to think coherently. Each culture is distinctive in the way in which its members categorize their experiences and its vocabulary is, in essence, the catalogue of the categories into which the culture divides its world and its experiences.[3]

This basic linguistic theory is borne out by anthropological studies of widely diverse cultures throughout the world. The recognition of the relationship of vocabulary to culture was what led to the realization that the way human beings view such things as time and space, color, family relationships, sex, and supernatural beings varies enormously from one society to another. Surprisingly, however, few studies of the dominant culture of present-day America have explored its "categories of experience" by looking at our common vocabulary—the ordinary words that ordinary people speak every day. These are the words of the mass media and popular literature, the currency of basic verbal exchange. They are the building blocks of the language we use continuously to structure thinking and to convey ideas and information. Inevitably, since they are accepted and used within the culture, these everyday words carry a burden of the culture's preconceptions and prejudices.

This is not to say that words themselves are pejorative or oppressive. When a social practice like prostitution exists, there can be no objection to giving it a name. But when such ordinary words for a female person as *woman* and *girl* acquire the additional commonly understood meanings of "mistress" and "prostitute," as Webster's unabridged dictionary attests has happened in English, an attitude toward women held by some members of society becomes part of the experience of all the society's members. When parents or teachers tell a boy not to cry because it isn't "manly" or praise a girl for her "feminine" way of dressing, they are using the words *manly* and *feminine* to reinforce the categories our culture has assigned to males and females. As Calvert Watkins says, language "is at once the expression of culture and a part of it."[4]

. . .

Webster's Third New International Dictionary (1986) defines *manly,* for example, as "having qualities appropriate to a man: not effeminate or timorous; bold, resolute, open in conduct or bearing." The definition goes on to include "belonging to or appropriate in character to a man" (illustrated by "manly sports" and "beer is a manly drink"), "of undaunted courage: gallant, brave." The same dictionary's definition of *womanly* is less specific, relying heavily on phrases like "marked by qualities characteristic of a woman"; "possessed of the character or behavior befitting a grown woman"; "characteristic of, belonging to, or suitable to women: conforming to or motivated by a woman's nature and attitudes rather than to a man's." Two of the examples provided are more informative: "convinced that drawing was a waste of time, if not downright womanly . . ." and "her usual womanly volubility."

In its definition of *manly* the Random House Dictionary of the English Language (1967) supplies the words "strong, brave, honorable, resolute, virile" as "qualities usually considered desirable in a man" and cites "feminine; weak, cowardly," as antonyms. Its definitions of *womanly* are "like or befitting a woman; feminine; not masculine or girlish" and "in the manner of, or befitting, a woman." The same dictionary's synonym essays for these words are worth quoting in full because of the contrasts they provide:

MANLY, MANFUL, MANNISH mean possessing the qualities of a man. MANLY implies possession of the most valuable or desirable qualities a man can have, as dignity, honesty, directness, etc., in opposition to servility, insincerity, underhandedness, etc.: *A manly foe is better than a weak friend.* It also connotes courage, strength, and fortitude: *manly determination to face what comes.* MANFUL stresses the reference to courage, strength, and industry: *manful resistance.* MANNISH applies to that which resembles man: *a boy with a mannish voice.* Applied to a woman, the term is derogatory, suggesting the aberrant possession of masculine characteristics: *a man-nish girl; a mannish stride.*

WOMANLY, WOMANLIKE, WOMANISH, mean resembling a woman. WOMANLY implies resemblance in appropriate, fitting ways: *womanly decorum, modesty.* WOMANLIKE, a neutral synonym, may suggest mild disapproval or, more rarely, disgust: *Womanlike, she (he) burst into tears.* WOMANISH usually implies an inappropriate resemblance and suggests weakness or effeminacy: *womanish petulance.*

What are these parallel essays saying? That we perceive males in terms of human qualities, females in terms of qualities—often negative—assigned to them as females. The qualities males possess may be good or bad, but those that come to mind when we consider what makes "a man" are positive. Women are defined circularly, through characteristics seen to be appropriate or inappropriate to women—not to human beings. In fact, when women exhibit positive attributes considered typical of men—dignity, honesty, courage, strength, or fortitude—they are thought of as aberrant. A person who is "womanlike" may (although the term is said to be "neutral") prompt a feeling of disgust.

The broad range of positive characteristics used to define males could be used to define females too, of course, but they are not. The characteristics of women—weakness is among the most frequently cited—are something apart. At its entry for *woman* Webster's Third provides this list of "qualities considered distinctive of womanhood": "Gentleness, affection, and domesticity or on the other hand fickleness, superficiality, and folly." Among the "qualities considered distinctive of manhood" listed in the entry for *man,* no negative attributes detract from the "courage, strength, and vigor" the definers associate with males. According to this dictionary, *womanish* means "unsuitable to a man or to a strong character of either sex."

Lexicographers do not make up definitions out of thin air. Their task is to record how words are used, it is not to say how they should be used. The examples they choose to illustrate meanings can therefore be especially revealing of cultural expectations. The American Heritage Dictionary (1969), which provides "manly courage" and "masculine charm," also gives us "Woman is fickle," "brought out the woman in him," "womanly virtue," "femi-

nine allure," "feminine wiles," and "womanish tears." The same dictionary defines *effeminate,* which comes from the Latin *effeminare,* meaning "to make a woman out of," as "having the qualities associated with women; not characteristic of a man; unmanly" and "characterized by softness, weakness, or lack of force; not dynamic or vigorous." For synonyms one is referred to *feminine.*

Masculine, manly, manlike, and other male-associated words used to compliment men are frequently also considered complimentary when applied to women: thus a woman may be said to have manly determination, to have a masculine mind, to take adversity like a man, or to struggle manfully against overwhelming odds. The one-male associated word sometimes used to insult her is *mannish,* which may suggest she is too strong or aggressive to be a true woman, or that she is homosexually oriented, in which case *mannish* can become a code word.

Female-associated words, on the other hand, must be hedged, as in "He has almost feminine intuition," if they are used to describe a man without insulting him. He may be praised for admirable qualities defined as peculiar to women, but he cannot be said to have womanly compassion or womanlike tenderness. In exceptions to this rule—for example, when a medic on the battlefield or a sports figure in some situation of unusual drama is said to be "as gentle as a woman"—the life-and-death quality of the circumstances makes its own ironic and terrible commentary on the standards of "masculinity" ordinarily expected of men.

• • •

If, as Theodore Lidz and others maintain, words are "carriers of categories developed by the culture" and language is the means by which we internalize our experience, the polarized meanings of the words we use to describe women and men cannot be ignored. By the age of five, children are already affected by the positive qualities culturally assigned to males and the almost complete absence of positive qualities attributed to females. Hartley cites several research studies of kindergarten children which show that "boys are aware of what is expected of them . . . and restrict their interests and activities to what is suitably 'masculine' in the kindergarten, while girls amble gradually in the direction of 'feminine' patterns for five more years. In other words, more stringent demands are made on boys than on girls and at an early age, when they are least able to understand either the reasons for or the nature of the demands." The reaction of young males is "anxiety which frequently expresses itself in over-straining to be masculine, in virtual panic at being caught doing anything traditionally defined as feminine, and in hostility toward anything even hinting at 'femininity' including females themselves."

No wonder. The women these boys are trying to escape were once little girls whose only challenge was to amble toward femininity. In tragic numbers they have either become ciphers or their rebellion against nonentity has turned them into the overdemanding, overpossessive moms of the caricatures. In some cases the dictionary examples are all too appropriate. For many women it has become natural to cry, to be petulant, to waste time, to be late, to accomplish things through deceitful stratagems, to be domineering, ill-tempered viragoes. No wonder little boys want to run from them and what they seem to stand for, even if doing so blocks their own wellsprings of tenderness and compassion.

And no wonder little girls grow aimlessly. "What woman needs," Margaret Fuller once said, "is not as a woman to act or rule, but as a nature to grow, as an intellect to discern, as a soul to live freely, and unimpeded to unfold such powers as were given her."[5] If she is thought of and defined only as a woman, not as a nature free to develop full human powers, she is doomed to revolve in that unreal circle of what is "characteristic of, belonging to, or suitable to a woman's nature."

· · ·

In general, such changes in the meanings of words according to their sex assignment follow a pattern that might be called semantic polarization. Having acquired a sense that is related more to one sex than the other, words tend to fit into and reinforce the male-positive-important and female-negative-trivial cultural categories. *Master* and *mistress* are striking examples. Both come from the Indo-European root form meaning "great" or "much," and in some contexts both retain a sense of authority over others (though today the others are more likely

to be pets than people). In their most common uses, however, *master* now denotes excellence in performance, and *mistress* labels the so-called kept woman. When titles for nobility are given extended applications, their meanings diverge in a similar way. *Queen, dame,* and *madam* have all acquired additional derogatory connotations without counterparts in *king, lord,* and *sir.* A teacher writes of trying to describe one of her most attractive and capable students: "I found myself saying 'She's really a prince.' Appalled as I was at my own pro-masculine description, I just couldn't say that she was a *princess* because *princess* connotes someone who is fussy and spoiled and accustomed to living in the lap of luxury."[6]

The devaluation of words has its uses, of course, and can easily be accomplished by tagging them with feminine-gender suffixes. When Ella Grasso was campaigning in 1974 for the chief executive office of Connecticut, some of her political rivals came up with the slogan "Connecticut doesn't need a governess." Seventy years earlier opponents of suffrage for women employed the ridiculing label "suffragette." The effect of "-ette" is so immediately belittling, in fact, that it is often invoked on the spot—as in *jockette* or *astronette*—to establish a female-negative-trivial category when male prerogatives are threatened.

Tomboy is one of the few words whose meaning was elevated rather than degraded when it came to be used of females only. According to the Oxford English Dictionary the word in its earliest uses meant "a rude, boisterous, or forward boy." An example, "whiskyng and ramping abroade like a Tom boy," dates from 1553. Since then the meaning has changed twice. The first change extended it to females in the sense of "a bold or immodest woman." The OED quotes from a sermon of 1579, "Sainte Paul meaneth that women must not be impudent, they must not be tomboyes, to be shorte, they must not bee unchaste." The quotation illustrates the first thing that customarily happens to a low-value word when it is switched from males to females: it acquires a sense of sexual promiscuity.

This meaning of *tomboy* did not persist, however. Perhaps the aura of full-blown adult female sexuality was incompatible with the sense of sexual inexperience or innocence brought to mind by the word *boy*. In any case, as the male meaning of *tomboy* disappeared and the female meaning dropped in age level, the word lost its connotation of sexiness and began to acquire some of the attractive qualities of *boy*. "What I mean by 'tomboyism,'" wrote the English novelist Charlotte Yonge in 1876, "is a wholesome delight in rushing around at full speed, playing at active games, climbing trees, rowing boats, making dirt-pies, and the like."[7]

That a girl could behave in such a fashion, especially with wholesome delight, was a shockingly new idea in the Anglo-American culture of Yonge's day. Clothes and manners were constricting, and active role models for young girls were almost nonexistent. So were active word models. When the early meaning of *virago* became obsolete and no alternative arose to take its place, the language lost a word that described heroic qualities in women. Even so, *virago* had never been a completely positive word, for in addition to meaning strong and courageous it also meant—as is clear from its derivation—manlike. In other words, a woman was not thought of as heroic in her own right; she had to be likened to a man.

Tomboy is similarly faulted as a word model, and because it is used of children, the psychic damage it inflicts is even greater. A tomboy is "a girl of boyish behavior," according to one dictionary, "a young girl who behaves like a lively, active boy," according to another. But why must a girl be defined in terms of something she is not—namely, a boy? Where is the word that would bring to mind a lively, spirited girl without the subliminal implication of imitation or penis envy? Most girls who like sports and the out-of-doors or who have intellectual or mechanical abilities are not trying to be boys. They are trying to be themselves. To call them tomboys, even with the intention of being complimentary, disparages them for being girls.

· · ·

Unfortunately, a cherished and semantically underlined precept of our culture seems to be that the sexes must be thought of as opposite. *Opposite* frequently means "set over against," hostile, opposed. It denies mutuality and equality. The ancient belief that contrasting female and male forces are at work in everything—the yin-yang of dark and light, of passive and active, of negative and positive in inanimate nature as well as in people—too easily becomes an adversary concept. The biological union of female and male is not.

Whether applied to living things or by analogy to objects, the adjectives *female* and *male* are culture-free and explicit. No one needs to consult a manual to find out how female and male electrical parts fit together to form a union, and one part is not considered better or stronger or more important than the other. They work together, and their use is limited to performing a particular function.

Masculine and *feminine* are very different from *male* and *female*. Instead of being specific they are vague and subjective and perhaps the most culturally biased words in the language. Rarely employed in a biological sense, they are used instead to describe what a group or society has decided female and male persons should (or should not) be. As Margaret Mead phrased it, "the potentialities which different societies label as either masculine or feminine are really potentialities of some members of each sex, and not sex-linked at all."[8]

To describe a woman or girl as feminine seems innocuous enough, yet no matter how well intended, it reinforces the demand being made on her to conform to whatever standard of "femininity" is culturally accepted. On a science field trip for inner-city school children, the teacher invited a group of sixth-graders to look for specimens in a small stream. Within moments the boys had run down the bank and were knee-deep in muddy water. The girls hung back, self-conscious and apparently resentful at missing the fun. When one of the boys shouted up to them, "Why aren't there any girls down here?" a girls answered, "Because we're *girls*, that's why." "Because," she might as well have said, "we don't want anyone to think we're not feminine."[9] Betty Friedan cites a similar attitude among college women in the 1950s. As one senior explained, "A girl who got serious about anything she studied—like, wanting to go on and do research—would be peculiar, unfeminine."[10]

· · ·

[1976]

NOTES

1. Calvert Watkins, "Indo-European and the Indo-Europeans," in the American Heritage Dictionary of the English Language, New York, American Heritage Publishing Company, 1969, p. 1498.
2. Theodore Lidz, *The Person: His Development throughout the Life Cycle,* New York, Basic Books, 1968, pp. 60, 62.
3. Theodore Lidz, *The Person: His and Her Development throughout the Life Cycle,* rev. ed., New York, Basic Books, 1983, p. 62. The use of gender-inclusive language in this passage contrasts significantly with the wording used in the 1968 edition of *The Person.* In the first edition, quoted in earlier printings of *Words and Women,* the passage read as follows:

    > Language is the means by which man internalizes his experience, thinks about it, tries out alternatives, conceptualizes a future and strives toward future goals. . . . Indeed, the capacity to direct the self into the future, which we shall term "ego functioning," depends upon a person having verbal symbols with which he constructs an internalized symbolic version of the world which he can manipulate in imaginative trial and error before committing himself to irrevocable actions *etc.* . . .

    In a 1989 article published in *The Journal of the American Medical Women's Association,* two psychiatrists discuss the implications of false generics in scientific and medical writing. They quote statements from Dr. Lidz's chapter "The Oedipal Period" as it read in the original edition of *The Person,* and they comment: "Here the author's use of 'he' to refer to a child of either sex sets the stage for a discussion of the oedipal rivalry from a boy's point of view only, and readers must extrapolate on their own to understand such rivalry from a girl's perspective." Referring to the revised edition, they note, "Here the explanation of similar material gains richness and accuracy with non-sexist phrasing and without false generics." Susan Schneider, M.D., and Ana Maria Soto, M.D., "Sexist Language: Should We Be Concerned?" JAMWA, Vol. 44, No. 3, May/June 1989.
4. Watkins, loc. cit.
5. Quoted by Betty Friedan, *The Feminine Mystique,* New York, Dell Publishing Company, 1970, p. 75. (First published in 1963.)
6. Alleen and Don Nilsen, "Ms. and Mr. Nilsen Debate Sexism in English," transcript of a presentation made at a National Council of Teachers of English meeting, November 23, 1973.
7. Oxford English Dictionary, under the entry *tomboy.*
8. Mead, *Sex and Temperament,* p. 286. For a helpful analysis of what the word *normal* has come to mean with reference to human females and males, see Ruth Herschberger, *Adam's Rib,* note 1 to Chapter 1 (pp. 203–12 in the paperback edition published by Harper & Row).
9. The incident described took place on October 18, 1973, on a field trip for New York City school children at the Croton River conducted by the Wave Hill Center for Environmental Studies.
10. Friedan, op. cit., p. 145.

 50

The Traffic in Women: Notes on the "Political Economy" of Sex

GAYLE RUBIN

The literature on women—both feminist and antifeminist—is a long rumination on the question of the nature and genesis of women's oppression and social subordination. The question is not a trivial one, since the answers given it determine our visions of the future, and our evaluation of whether or not it is realistic to hope for a sexually egalitarian society. More importantly, the analysis of the causes of women's oppression forms the basis for any assessment of just what would have to be changed in order to achieve a society without gender hierarchy. Thus, if innate male aggression and dominance are at the root of female oppression, then the feminist program would logically require either the extermination of the offending sex, or else a eugenics project to modify its character. If sexism is a by-product of capitalism's relentless appetite for profit, then sexism would wither away in the advent of a successful socialist revolution. . . .

     • • •

The purpose of this essay is to arrive at a more fully developed definition of the sex/gender system, by way of a somewhat idiosyncratic and exegetical reading of Lévi-Strauss and Freud. I use the word "exegetical" deliberately. The dictionary defines "exegesis" as a "critical explanation or analysis; especially, interpretation of the Scriptures." At times, my reading of Lévi-Strauss and Freud is freely interpretive, moving from the explicit content of a text to its presuppositions and implications. My reading of certain psychoanalytic texts is filtered through a lens provided by Jacques Lacan, whose own interpretation of the Freudian scripture has been heavily influenced by Lévi-Strauss.[1]

I will return later to a refinement of the definition of a sex/gender system. First, however, I will try to demonstrate the need for such a concept by discussing the failure of classical Marxism to fully express or conceptualize sex oppression. This failure results from the fact that Marxism, as a theory of social life, is relatively unconcerned with sex. In Marx's map of the social world, human beings are workers, peasants, or capitalists; that they are also men and women is not seen as very significant. By contrast, in the maps of social reality drawn by Freud and Lévi-Strauss, there is a deep recognition of the place of sexuality in society, and of the profound differences between the social experience of men and women.

MARX

There is no theory which accounts for the oppression of women—in its endless variety and monotonous similarity, cross-culturally and throughout history—with anything like the explanatory power of the Marxist theory of class oppression. Therefore, it is not surprising that there have been numerous attempts to apply Marxist analysis to the question of women. There are many ways of doing this. It has been argued that women are a reserve labor force for capitalism, that women's generally lower wages provide extra surplus to a capitalist employer, that women serve the ends of capitalist consumerism in their roles as administrators of family consumption, and so forth.

· · ·

Briefly, Marx argued that capitalism is distinguished from all other modes of production by its unique aim: the creation and expansion of capital. Whereas other modes of production might find their purpose in making useful things to satisfy human needs, or in producing a surplus for a ruling nobility, or in producing to insure sufficient sacrifice for the edification of the gods, capitalism produces capital. Capitalism is a set of social relations—forms of property, and so forth—in which production takes the form of turning money, things, and people into capital. And capital is a quantity of goods or money which, when exchanged for labor, reproduces and augments itself by extracting unpaid labor, or surplus value, from labor and into itself.

> The result of the capitalist production process is neither a mere produce (use-value) nor a *commodity,* that is, a use-value which has exchange value. Its result, its product, is the creation of *surplus-value* for capital, and consequently the actual *transfor-*

mation of money or commodity into capital. . . ." (Marx, 1969:399; italics in the original)

The exchange between capital and labor which produces surplus value, and hence capital, is highly specific. The worker gets a wage; the capitalist gets the things the worker has made during his or her time of employment. If the total value of the things the worker has made exceeds the value of his or her wage, the aim of capitalism has been achieved. The capitalist gets back the cost of the wage, plus an increment—surplus value. This can occur because the wage is determined not by the value of what the laborer makes, but by the value of what it takes to keep him or her going—to reproduce him or her from day to day, and to reproduce the entire work force from one generation to the next. Thus, surplus value is the difference between what the laboring class produces as a whole, and the amount of that total which is recycled into maintaining the laboring class.

· · ·

The amount of the difference between the reproduction of labor power and its products depends, therefore, on the determination of what it takes to reproduce that labor power. Marx tends to make that determination on the basis of the quantity of commodities—food, clothing, housing, fuel—which would be necessary to maintain the health, life, and strength of a worker. But these commodities must be consumed before they can be sustenance, and they are not immediately in consumable form when they are purchased by the wage. Additional labor must be performed upon these things before they can be turned into people. Food must be cooked, clothes cleaned, beds made, wood chopped, etc. Housework is therefore a key element in the process of the reproduction of the laborer from whom surplus value is taken. Since it is usually women who do housework, it has been observed that it is through the reproduction of labor power that women are articulated into the surplus value nexus which is the *sine qua non* of capitalism. . . .

· · ·

ENGELS

In *The Origin of the Family, Private Property, and the State,* Engels sees sex oppression as part of capitalism's heritage from prior social forms. Moreover,

Engels integrates sex and sexuality into his theory of society. . . . Nevertheless, it is a book whose considerable insight should not be overshadowed by its limitations. The idea that the "relations of sexuality" can and should be distinguished from the "relations of production" . . . indicates an important recognition—that a human group must do more than apply its activity to reshaping the natural world in order to clothe, feed, and warm itself. We usually call the system by which elements of the natural world are transformed into objects of human consumption the "economy." But the needs which are satisfied by economic activity even in the richest, Marxian sense, do not exhaust fundamental human requirements. A human group must also reproduce itself from generation to generation. The needs of sexuality and procreation must be satisfied as much as the need to eat. . . . Sex is sex, but what counts as sex is equally culturally determined and obtained. Every society also has a sex/gender system—a set of arrangements by which the biological raw material of human sex and procreation is shaped by human, social intervention and satisfied in a conventional manner, no matter how bizarre some of the conventions may be.

The realm of human sex, gender, and procreation has been subjected to, and changed by, relentless social activity for millennia. Sex as we know it—gender identity, sexual desire and fantasy, concepts of childhood—is itself a social product. We need to understand the relations of its production, and forget, for awhile, about food, clothing, automobiles, and transistor radios. In most Marxist tradition, and even in Engels' book, the concept of the "second aspect of material life" has tended to fade into the background, or to be incorporated into the usual notions of "material life." Engels' suggestion has never been followed up and subjected to the refinement which it needs. But he does indicate the existence and importance of the domain of social life which I want to call the sex/gender system.

· · ·

KINSHIP
(ON THE PART PLAYED BY SEXUALITY IN THE TRANSITION FROM APE TO "MAN")

To an anthropologist, a kinship system is not a list of biological relatives. It is a system of categories and statuses which often contradict actual genetic relationships. There are dozens of examples in which socially defined kinship statuses take precedence over biology. The Nuer custom of "woman marriage" is a case in point. The Nuer define the status of fatherhood as belonging to the person in whose name cattle bridewealth is given for the mother. Thus, a woman can be married to another woman, and be husband to the wife and father of her children, despite the fact that she is not the inseminator (Evans-Pritchard, 1951:107–109).

In pre-state societies, kinship is the idiom of social interaction, organizing economic, political, and ceremonial, as well as sexual, activity. One's duties, responsibilities, and privileges vis-à-vis others are defined in terms of mutual kinship or lack thereof. The exchange of goods and services, production and distribution, hostility and solidarity, ritual and ceremony, all take place within the organizational structure of kinship. The ubiquity and adaptive effectiveness of kinship has led many anthropologists to consider its invention, along with the invention of language, to have been the developments which decisively marked the discontinuity between semi-human hominids and human beings (Sahlins, 1960; Livingstone, 1969; Lévi-Strauss, 1969).

While the idea of the importance of kinship enjoys the status of a first principle in anthropology, the internal workings of kinship systems have long been a focus for intense controversy. Kinship systems vary wildly from one culture to the next. They contain all sorts of bewildering rules which govern whom one may or may not marry. Their internal complexity is dazzling. Kinship systems have for decades provoked the anthropological imagination into trying to explain incest taboos, cross-cousin marriage, terms of descent, relationships of avoidance or forced intimacy, clans and sections, taboos on names—the diverse array of items found in descriptions of actual kinship systems. In the nineteenth century, several thinkers attempted to write comprehensive accounts of the nature and history of human sexual systems (see Fee, 1973). One of these was *Ancient Society*, by Lewis Henry Morgan. It was this book which inspired Engels to write *The Origin of the Family, Private Property, and the State*. Engels' theory is based upon Morgan's account of kinship and marriage.

In taking up Engels' project of extracting a theory of sex oppression from the study of kinship, we have the advantage of the maturation of ethnology since the nineteenth century. We also have the advantage of a peculiar and particularly appropriate book, Lévi-Strauss' *The Elementary Structures of Kinship.* This is the boldest twentieth-century version of the nineteenth-century project to understand human marriage. It is a book in which kinship is explicitly conceived of as an imposition of cultural organization upon the facts of biological procreation. It is permeated with an awareness of the importance of sexuality in human society. It is a description of society which does not assume an abstract, genderless human subject. On the contrary, the human subject in Lévi-Strauss's work is always either male or female, and the divergent social destinies of the two sexes can therefore be traced. Since Lévi-Strauss sees the essence of kinship systems to lie in an exchange of women between men, he constructs an implicit theory of sex oppression. Aptly, the book is dedicated to the memory of Lewis Henry Morgan.

"VILE AND PRECIOUS MERCHANDISE"
—MONIQUE WITTIG

The Elementary Structures of Kinship is a grand statement on the origin and nature of human society. It is a treatise on the kinship systems of approximately one-third of the ethnographic globe. Most fundamentally, it is an attempt to discern the structural principles of kinship. Lévi-Strauss argues that the application of these principles (summarized in the last chapter of *Elementary Structures*) to kinship data reveals an intelligible logic to the taboos and marriage rules which have perplexed and mystified Western anthropologists. He constructs a chess game of such complexity that it cannot be recapitulated here. But two of his chess pieces are particularly relevant to women—the "gift" and the incest taboo, whose dual articulation adds up to his concept of the exchange of women.

The Elementary Structures is in part a radical gloss on another famous theory of primitive social organization, Mauss' *Essay on the Gift* (See also Sahlins, 1972:Chap. 4). It was Mauss who first theorized as to the significance of one of the most striking features of primitive societies: the extent to which giving, receiving, and reciprocating gifts dominates social intercourse. In such societies, all sorts of things circulate in exchange—food, spells, rituals, words, names, ornaments, tools, and powers.

• • •

Although both Mauss and Lévi-Strauss emphasize the solidary aspects of gift exchange, the other purposes served by gift giving only strengthen the point that it is an ubiquitous means of social commerce. Mauss proposed that gifts were the threads of social discourse, the means by which such societies were held together in the absence of specialized governmental institutions. "The gift is the primitive way of achieving the peace that in civil society is secured by the state. . . . Composing society, the gift was the liberation of culture" (Sahlins, 1972: 169, 175).

Lévi-Strauss adds to the theory of primitive reciprocity the idea that marriages are a most basic form of gift exchange, in which it is women who are the most precious of gifts. He argues that the incest taboo should best be understood as a mechanism to insure that such exchanges take place between families and between groups. Since the existence of incest taboos is universal, but the content of their prohibitions variable, they cannot be explained as having the aim of preventing the occurrence of genetically close matings. Rather, the incest taboo imposes the social aim of exogamy and alliance upon the biological events of sex and procreation. The incest taboo divides the universe of sexual choice into categories of permitted and prohibited sexual partners. Specifically, by forbidding unions within a group it enjoins marital exchange between groups.

> The prohibition on the sexual use of a daughter or a sister compels them to be given in marriage to another man, and at the same time it establishes a right to the daughter or sister of this other man. . . . The woman whom one does not take is, for that very reason, offered up. (Lévi-Strauss, 1969:51)

> The prohibition of incest is less a rule prohibiting marriage with the mother, sister, or daughter, than a rule obliging the mother, sister, or daughter to be given to others. It is the supreme rule of the gift. . . . (Ibid.:481)

The result of a gift of women is more profound than the result of other gift transactions, because the relationship thus established is not just one of reciprocity, but one of kinship. The exchange partners have become affines, and their descendents will be related by blood: "Two people may meet in friendship and exchange gifts and yet quarrel and fight in later times, but intermarriage connects them in a permanent manner" (Best, cited in Lévi-Strauss, 1969: 481). As is the case with other gift giving, marriages are not always so simply activities to make peace. Marriages may be highly competitive, and there are plenty of affines who fight each other. Nevertheless, in a general sense the argument is that the taboo on incest results in a wide network of relations, a set of people whose connections with one another are a kinship structure. All other levels, amounts, and directions of exchange—including hostile ones—are ordered by this structure. The marriage ceremonies recorded in the ethnographic literature are moments in a ceaseless and ordered procession in which women, children, shells, words, cattle names, fish, ancestors, whale's teeth, pigs, yams, spells, dances, mats, etc., pass from hand to hand, leaving as their tracks the ties that bind. Kinship is organization, and organization gives power. But who is organized?

If it is women who are being transacted, then it is the men who give and take them who are linked, the woman being a conduit of a relationship rather than a partner to it.[2] The exchange of women does not necessarily imply that women are objectified, in the modern sense, since objects in the primitive world are imbued with highly personal qualities. But it does imply a distinction between gift and giver. If women are the gifts, then it is men who are the exchange partners. And it is the partners, not the presents, upon whom reciprocal exchange confers its quasi-mystical power of social linkage. The relations of such a system are such that women are in no position to realize the benefits of their own circulation. As long as the relations specify that men exchange women, it is men who are the beneficiaries of the product of such exchanges—social organization.

The total relationship of exchange which constitutes marriage is not established between a man and a woman, but between two groups of men, and the woman figures only as one of the objects in the exchange, not as one of the partners. . . . This remains true even when the girl's feelings are taken into consideration, as, moreover, is usually the case.

In acquiescing to the proposed union, she precipitates or allows the exchange to take place, she cannot alter its nature. . . . (Lévi-Strauss in ibid.:115)[3]

To enter into a gift exchange as a partner, one must have something to give. If women are for men to dispose of, they are in no position to give themselves away.

"What woman," mused a young Northern Melpa man, is ever strong enough to get up and say, 'Let us make *moka*, let us find wives and pigs, let us give our daughters to men, let us wage war, let us kill our enemies!' No indeed not! . . . they are little rubbish things who stay at home simply, don't you see?" (Strathern, 1972:161)

What women indeed! The Melpa women of whom the young man spoke can't get wives, they *are* wives, and what they get are husbands, an entirely different matter. The Melpa women can't give their daughters to men, because they do not have the same rights in their daughters that their male kin have, rights of bestowal (although *not* of ownership).

The "exchange of women" is a seductive and powerful concept. It is attractive in that it places the oppression of women within social systems, rather than in biology. Moreover, it suggests that we look for the ultimate locus of women's oppression within the traffic in women, rather than within the traffic in merchandise. It is certainly not difficult to find ethnographic and historical examples of trafficking in women. Women are given in marriage, taken in battle, exchanged for favors, sent as tribute, traded, bought, and sold. Far from being confined to the "primitive" world, these practices seem only to become more pronounced and commercialized in more "civilized" societies. Men are of course also trafficked—but as slaves, hustlers, athletic stars, serfs, or as some other catastrophic social status, rather than as men. Women are transacted as slaves, serfs, and prostitutes, but also simply as women. And if men have been sexual subjects—exchangers—and women sexual semi-objects—gifts—for much of human history, then many customs, clichés, and personality traits seem to make a great deal of sense (among others, the curious custom by which a father gives away the bride).

The "exchange of women" is also a problematic concept. Since Lévi-Strauss argues that the incest taboo and the results of its application constitute the origin of culture, it can be deduced that the world historical defeat of women occurred with the origin of culture, and is a prerequisite of culture. If his analysis is adopted in its pure form, the feminist program must include a task even more onerous than the extermination of men; it must attempt to get rid of culture and substitute some entirely new phenomena on the face of the earth. However, it would be a dubious proposition at best to argue that if there were no exchange of women there would be no culture, if for no other reason than that culture is, by definition, inventive. It is even debatable that "exchange of women" adequately describes all of the empirical evidence of kinship systems. Some cultures, such as the Lele and the Luma, exchange women explicitly and overtly. In other cultures, the exchange of women can be inferred. In some—particularly those hunters and gatherers excluded from Lévi-Strauss's sample—the efficacy of the concept becomes altogether questionable. What are we to make of a concept which seems so useful and yet so difficult?

The "exchange of women" is neither a definition of culture nor a system in and of itself. The concept is an acute, but condensed, apprehension of certain aspects of the social relations of sex and gender. A kinship system is an imposition of social ends upon a part of the natural world. It is therefore "production" in the most general sense of the term: a molding, a transformation of objects (in this case, people) to and by a subjective purpose (for this sense of production, see Marx, 1971a:80–99). It has its own relations of production, distribution, and exchange, which include certain "property" forms in people. These forms are not exclusive, private property rights, but rather different sorts of rights that various people have in other people. Marriage transactions—the gifts and material which circulate in the ceremonies marking a marriage—are a rich source of data for determining exactly who has which rights in whom. It is not difficult to deduce from such transactions that in most cases women's rights are considerably more residual than those of men.

Kinship systems do not merely exchange women. They exchange sexual access, genealogical statuses, lineage names and ancestors, rights and *people*—

men, women, and children—in concrete systems of social relationships. These relationships always include certain rights for men, others for women. "Exchange of women" is a shorthand for expressing that the social relations of a kinship system specify that men have certain rights in their female kin, and that women do not have the same rights either to themselves or to their male kin. In this sense, the exchange of women is a profound perception of a system in which women do not have full rights to themselves. The exchange of women becomes an obfuscation if it is seen as a cultural necessity, and when it is used as the single tool with which an analysis of a particular kinship system is approached.

If Lévi-Strauss is correct in seeing the exchange of women as a fundamental principle of kinship, the subordination of women can be seen as a product of the relationships by which sex and gender are organized and produced. The economic oppression of women is derivative and secondary. But there is an "economics" of sex and gender, and what we need is a political economy of sexual systems. We need to study each society to determine the exact mechanisms by which particular conventions of sexuality are produced and maintained. The "exchange of women" is an initial step toward building an arsenal of concepts with which sexual systems can be described.

DEEPER INTO THE LABYRINTH

More concepts can be derived from an essay by Lévi-Strauss, "The Family," in which he introduces other considerations into his analysis of kinship. In *The Elementary Structures of Kinship*, he describes rules and systems of sexual combination. In "The Family," he raises the issue of the preconditions necessary for marriage systems to operate. He asks what sort of "people" are required by kinship systems, by way of an analysis of the sexual division of labor.

Although every society has some sort of division of tasks by sex, the assignment of any particular task to one sex or the other varies enormously. In some groups, agriculture is the work of women, in others, the work of men. Women carry the heavy burdens in some societies, men in others. There are even examples of female hunters and warriors, and of men performing child-care tasks. Lévi-Strauss concludes from a survey of the division of labor by sex that it is not a biological specialization, but must have some other purpose. This purpose, he argues, is to insure the union of men and women by making the smallest viable economic unit contain at least one man and one woman.

> The very fact that it [the sexual division of labor] varies endlessly according to the society selected for consideration shows that . . . it is the mere fact of its existence which is mysteriously required, the form under which it comes to exist being utterly irrelevant, at least from the point of view of any natural necessity . . . the sexual division of labor is nothing else than a device to institute a reciprocal state of dependency between the sexes. (Lévi-Strauss, 1971:347–348)

The division of labor by sex can therefore be seen as a "taboo": a taboo against the sameness of men and women, a taboo dividing the sexes into two mutually exclusive categories, a taboo which exacerbates the biological differences between the sexes and thereby *creates* gender. The division of labor can also be seen as a taboo against sexual arrangements other than those containing at least one man and one woman, thereby enjoining heterosexual marriage.

The argument in "The Family" displays a radical questioning of all human sexual arrangements, in which no aspect of sexuality is taken for granted as "natural" (Hertz, 1960, constructs a similar argument for a thoroughly cultural explanation of the denigration of left-handedness). Rather, all manifest forms of sex and gender are seen as being constituted by the imperatives of social systems. From such a perspective, even *The Elementary Structures of Kinship* can be seen to assume certain preconditions. In purely logical terms, a rule forbidding some marriages and commanding others presupposes a rule enjoining marriage. And marriage presupposes individuals who are disposed to marry.

It is of interest to carry this kind of deductive enterprise even further than Lévi-Strauss does, and to explicate the logical structure which underlies his entire analysis of kinship. At the most general level, the social organization of sex rests upon gender, obligatory heterosexuality, and the constraint of female sexuality.

Gender is a socially imposed division of the sexes. It is a product of the social relations of sexu-

ality. Kinship systems rest upon marriage. They therefore transform males and females into "men" and "women," each an incomplete half which can only find wholeness when united with the other. Men and women are, of course, different. But they are not as different as day and night, earth and sky, yin and yang, life and death. In fact, from the standpoint of nature, men and women are closer to each other than either is to anything else—for instance, mountains, kangaroos, or coconut palms. The idea that men and women are more different from one another than either is from anything else must come from somewhere other than nature. Furthermore, although there is an average difference between males and females on a variety of traits, the range of variation of those traits shows considerable overlap. There will always be some women who are taller than some men, for instance, even though men are on the average taller than women. But the idea that men and women are two mutually exclusive categories must arise out of something other than a nonexistent "natural" opposition.[4] Far from being an expression of natural differences, exclusive gender identity is the suppression of natural similarities. It requires repression: in men, of whatever is the local version of "feminine" traits; in women, of the local definition of "masculine" traits. The division of the sexes has the effect of repressing some of the personality characteristics of virtually everyone, men and women. The same social system which oppresses women in its relations of exchange, oppresses everyone in its insistence upon a rigid division of personality.

Furthermore, individuals are engendered in order that marriage be guaranteed. Lévi-Strauss comes dangerously close to saying that heterosexuality is an instituted process. If biological and hormonal imperatives were as overwhelming as popular mythology would have them, it would hardly be necessary to insure heterosexual unions by means of economic interdependency. Moreover, the incest taboo presupposes a prior, less articulate taboo on homosexuality. A prohibition against *some* heterosexual unions assumes a taboo against *non*-heterosexual unions. Gender is not only an identification with one sex; it also entails that sexual desire be directed toward the other sex. The sexual division of labor is implicated in both aspects of gender—male and female it creates them, and it creates them heterosexual. The suppression of the homosexual component of human sexuality, and by corollary, the oppression of homosexuals, is therefore a product of the same system whose rules and relations oppress women.

In fact, the situation is not so simple, as is obvious when we move from the level of generalities to the analysis of specific sexual systems. Kinship systems do not merely encourage heterosexuality to the detriment of homosexuality. In the first place, specific forms of heterosexuality may be required. For instance, some marriage systems have a rule of obligatory cross-cousin marriage. A person in such a system is not only heterosexual, but "cross-cousin-sexual." If the rule of marriage further specifies matrilateral cross-cousin marriage, then a man will be "mother's-brother's-daughter-sexual" and a woman will be "father's-sister's-son-sexual."

· · ·

[T]he rules of gender division and obligatory heterosexuality are present even in their transformations. These two rules apply equally to the constraint of both male and female behavior and personality. Kinship systems dictate some sculpting of the sexuality of both sexes. But it can be deduced from *The Elementary Structures of Kinship* that more constraint is applied to females when they are pressed into the service of kinship than to males. If women are exchanged, in whatever sense we take the term, marital debts are reckoned in female flesh. A woman must become the sexual partner of some man to whom she is owed as return on a previous marriage. If a girl is promised in infancy, her refusal to participate as an adult would disrupt the flow of debts and promises. It would be in the interests of the smooth and continuous operation of such a system if the woman in question did not have too many ideas of her own about whom she might want to sleep with. From the standpoint of the system, the preferred female sexuality would be one which responded to the desire of others, rather than one which actively desired and sought a response.

· · ·

One last generality could be predicted as a consequence of the exchange of women under a system in which rights to women are held by men. What would happen if our hypothetical woman not only refused the man to whom she was promised, but asked for a woman instead? If a single refusal were disruptive, a double refusal would be insurrection-

ary. If each woman is promised to some man, neither has a right to dispose of herself. If two women managed to extricate themselves from the debt nexus, two other women would have to be found to replace them. As long as men have rights in women which women do not have in themselves, it would be sensible to expect that homosexuality in women would be subject to more suppression than in men.

In summary, some basic generalities about the organization of human sexuality can be derived from an exegesis of Lévi-Strauss's theories of kinship. These are the incest taboo, obligatory heterosexuality, and an asymmetric division of the sexes. The asymmetry of gender—the difference between exchanger and exchanged—entails the constraint of female sexuality. Concrete kinship systems will have more specific conventions, and these conventions vary a great deal. While particular socio-sexual systems vary, each one is specific, and individuals within it will have to conform to a finite set of possibilities. Each new generation must learn and become its sexual destiny, each person must be encoded with its appropriate status within the system. It would be extraordinary for one of us to calmly assume that we would conventionally marry a mother's brother's daughter, or a father's sister's son. Yet there are groups in which such a marital future is taken for granted.

Anthropology, and descriptions of kinship systems, do not explain the mechanisms by which children are engraved with the conventions of sex and gender. Psychoanalysis, on the other hand, is a theory about the reproduction of kinship. Psychoanalysis describes the residue left within individuals by their confrontation with the rules and regulations of sexuality of the societies to which they are born.

· · ·

THE OEDIPUS HEX

· · ·

Freud was never as much of a biological determinist as some would have him. He repeatedly stressed that all adult sexuality resulted from psychic, not biologic, development. But his writing is often ambiguous, and his wording leaves plenty of room for the biological interpretations which have been so popular in American psychoanalysis. In France, on the other hand, the trend in psychoanalytic theory has been to de-biologize Freud, and to conceive of psychoanalysis as a theory of information rather than organs. Jacques Lacan, the instigator of this line of thinking, insists that Freud never meant to say anything about anatomy, and that Freud's theory was instead about language and the cultural meanings imposed upon anatomy. The debate over the "real" Freud is extremely interesting, but it is not my purpose here to contribute to it. Rather, I want to rephrase the classic theory of femininity in Lacan's terminology, after introducing some of the pieces on Lacan's conceptual chessboard.

KINSHIP, LACAN, AND THE PHALLUS

Lacan suggests that psychoanalysis is the study of the traces left in the psyches of individuals as a result of their conscription into systems of kinship.

> Isn't it striking that Lévi-Strauss, in suggesting that implication of the structures of language with that part of the social laws which regulate marriage ties and kinship, is already conquering the very terrain in which Freud situates the unconscious? (Lacan, 1968:48)

> For where on earth would one situate the determinations of the unconsciousness if it is not in those nominal cadres in which marriage ties and kinship are always grounded. . . . And how would one apprehend the analytical conflicts and their Oedipean prototype outside the engagements which have fixed, long before the subject came into the world, not only his destiny, but his identity itself? (Ibid.:126)

> This is precisely where the Oedipus complex . . . may be said, in this connection, to mark the limits which our discipline assigns to subjectivity: that is to say, what the subject can know of his unconscious participation in the movement of the complex structures of marriage ties, by verifying the symbolic effects in his individual existence of the tangential movement towards incest. . . . (Ibid.:40)

Kinship is the culturalization of biological sexuality on the societal level; psychoanalysis describes the transformation of the biological sexuality of individuals as they are enculturated.

Kinship terminology contains information about the system. Kin terms demarcate statuses, and indicate some of the attributes of those statuses. For instance, in the Trobriand Islands a man calls the women of his clan by the term for "sister." He calls the women of clans into which he can marry by a term indicating their marriageability. When the young Trobriand male learns these terms, he learns which women he can safely desire. In Lacan's scheme, the Oedipal crisis occurs when a child learns of the sexual rules embedded in the terms for family and relatives. The crisis begins when the child comprehends the system and his or her place in it; the crisis is resolved when the child accepts that place and accedes to it. Even if the child refuses its place, he or she cannot escape knowledge of it. Before the Oedipal phase, the sexuality of the child is labile and relatively unstructured. Each child contains all of the sexual possibilities available to human expression. But in any given society, only some of these possibilities will be expressed, while others will be constrained. When the child leaves the Oedipal phase, its libido and gender identity have been organized in conformity with the rules of the culture which is domesticating it.

The Oedipal complex is an apparatus for the production of sexual personality. It is a truism to say that societies will inculcate in their young the character traits appropriate to carrying on the business of society. For instance, E. P. Thompson (1963) speaks of the transformation of the personality structure of the English working class, as artisans were changed into good industrial workers. Just as the social forms of labor demand certain kinds of personality, the social forms of sex and gender demand certain kinds of people. In the most general terms, the Oedipal complex is a machine which fashions the appropriate forms of sexual individuals (see also the discussion of different forms of "historical individuality" in Althusser and Balibar, 1970: 112, 251–253).

In the Lacanian theory of psychoanalysis, it is the kin terms that indicate a structure of relationships which will determine the role of any individual or object within the Oedipal drama. For instance, Lacan makes a distinction between the "function of the father" and a particular father who embodies this function. In the same way, he makes a radical distinction between the penis and the "phallus," between organ and information. The phallus is a set of meanings conferred upon the penis. The differentiation between phallus and penis in contemporary French psychoanalytic terminology emphasizes the idea that the penis could not and does not play the role attributed to it in the classical terminology of the castration complex.[5]

In Freud's terminology, the Oedipal complex presents two alternatives to a child: to have a penis or to be castrated. In contrast, the Lacanian theory of the castration complex leaves behind all reference to anatomical reality:

> The theory of the castration complex amounts to having the male organ play a dominant role—this time as a symbol—*to the extent that its absence or presence transforms an anatomical difference into a major classification of humans, and to the extent that, for each subject, this presence or absence is not taken for granted, is not reduced purely and simply to a given, but is the problematical result of an intra- and intersubjective process* (the subject's assumption of his own sex). (Laplanche and Pontalis, in Mehlman, 1972: 198–199; my italics)

The alternative presented to the child may be rephrased as an alternative between having, or not having, the phallus. Castration is not having the (symbolic) phallus. Castration is not a real "lack," but a meaning conferred upon the genitals of a woman:

> Castration may derive support from . . . the apprehension in the Real of the absence of the penis in women—but even this supposes a symbolization of the object, since the Real is full, and "lacks" nothing. Insofar as one finds castration in the genesis of neurosis, it is never real but symbolic. . . . (Lacan, 1968:271)

The phallus is, as it were, a distinctive feature differentiating "castrated" and "noncastrated." The presence or absence of the phallus carries the differences between two sexual statuses, "man" and "woman" (see Jakobson and Halle, 1971, on distinctive features). Since these are not equal, the phallus also carries a meaning of the dominance of men over women, and it may be inferred that "penis envy" is a recognition thereof. Moreover, as long as men have rights in women which women do not have in themselves, the phallus also carries the meaning of the difference between "exchanger" and "exchanged," gift and giver. Ultimately, neither the classical Freudian nor the rephrased Lacanian theories of the Oedipal process make sense unless at

least this much of the paleolithic relations of sexuality are still with us. We still live in a "phallic" culture.

Lacan also speaks of the phallus as a symbolic object which is exchanged within and between families (see also Wilden, 1968:303–305). It is interesting to think about this observation in terms of primitive marriage transactions and exchange networks. In those transactions, the exchange of women is usually one of many cycles of exchange. Usually, there are other objects circulating as well as women. Women move in one direction, cattle, shells, or mats in the other. In one sense, the Oedipal complex is an expression of the circulation of the phallus in intrafamily exchange, an inversion of the circulation of women in interfamily exchange. In the cycle of exchange manifested by the Oedipal complex, the phallus passes through the medium of women from one man to another—from father to son, from mother's brother to sister's son, and so forth. In this family *Kula* ring, women go one way, the phallus the other. It is where we aren't. In this sense, the phallus is more than a feature which distinguishes the sexes: it is the embodiment of the male status, to which men accede, and in which certain rights inhere—among them, the right to a woman. It is an expression of the transmission of male dominance. It passes through women and settles upon men.[6] The tracks which it leaves include gender identity, the division of the sexes. But it leaves more than this. It leaves "penis envy," which acquires a rich meaning of the disquietude of women in a phallic culture.

OEDIPUS REVISITED

We return now to the two pre-Oedipal androgynes, sitting on the border between biology and culture. Lévi-Strauss places the incest taboo on that border, arguing that its initiation of the exchange of women constitutes the origin of society. In this sense, the incest taboo and the exchange of women are the content of the original social contract (see Sahlins, 1972: Chap. 4). For individuals, the Oedipal crisis occurs at the same divide, when the incest taboo initiates the exchange of the phallus.

The Oedipal crisis is precipitated by certain items of information. The children discover the differences between the sexes, and that each child must become one or the other gender. They also discover the incest taboo, and that some sexuality is prohibited—in this case, the mother is unavailable to either child because she "belongs" to the father. Lastly, they discover that the two genders do not have the same sexual "rights" or futures.

In the normal course of events, the boy renounces his mother for fear that otherwise his father would castrate him (refuse to give him the phallus and make him a girl). But by this act of renunciation, the boy affirms the relationships which have given mother to father and which will give him, if he becomes a man, a woman of his own. In exchange for the boy's affirmation of his father's right to his mother, the father affirms the phallus in his son (does not castrate him). The boy exchanges his mother for the phallus, the symbolic token which can later be exchanged for a woman. The only thing required of him is a little patience. He retains his initial libidinal organization and the sex of his original love object. The social contract to which he has agreed will eventually recognize his own rights and provide him with a woman of his own.

What happens to the girl is more complex. She, like the boy, discovers the taboo against incest and the division of the sexes. She also discovers some unpleasant information about the gender to which she is being assigned. For the boy, the taboo on incest is a taboo on certain women. For the girl, it is a taboo on all women. Since she is in a homosexual position vis-à-vis the mother, the rule of heterosexuality which dominates the scenario makes her position excruciatingly untenable. The mother, and all women by extension, can only be properly beloved by someone "with a penis" (phallus). Since the girl has no "phallus," she has no "right" to love her mother or another woman, since she is herself destined to some man. She does not have the symbolic token which can be exchanged for a woman.

If Freud's wording of this moment of the female Oedipal crisis is ambiguous, Lampl de Groot's formulation makes the context which confers meaning upon the genitals explicit:

> . . . *if the little girl comes to the conclusion that such an organ is really indispensable to the possession of the mother, she experiences* in addition to the narcissistic insults common to both sexes still another blow, namely *a feeling of inferiority about her genitals.* (Lampl de Groot, 1933:497; my italics)

The girl concludes that the "penis" is indispensable for the possession of the mother because only those who possess the phallus have a "right" to a woman, and the token of exchange. She does not come to her conclusion because of the natural superiority of the penis either in and of itself, or as an instrument for making love. The hierarchical arrangement of the male and female genitals is a result of the definitions of the situation—the rule of obligatory heterosexuality and the relegation of women (those without the phallus, castrated) to men (those with the phallus).

The girl then begins to turn away from the mother, and to the father.

> To the girl, it [castration] is an accomplished fact, which is irrevocable, but the recognition of which compels her finally to renounce her first love object and to taste to the full the bitterness of its loss . . . the father is chosen as a love-object, the enemy becomes the beloved. . . . (Lampl de Groot, 1948:213)

This recognition of "castration" forces the girl to redefine her relationship to herself, her mother, and her father.

She turns from the mother because she does not have the phallus to give her. She turns from the mother also in anger and disappointment, because the mother did not give her a "penis" (phallus). But the mother, a woman in a phallic culture, does not have the phallus to give away (having gone through the Oedipal crisis herself a generation earlier). The girl then turns to the father because only he can "give her the phallus," and it is only through him that she can enter into the symbolic exchange system in which the phallus circulates. But the father does not give her the phallus in the same way that he gives it to the boy. The phallus is affirmed in the boy, who then has it to give away. The girl never gets the phallus. It passes through her, and in its passage is transformed into a child. When she "recognizes her castration," she accedes to the place of a woman in a phallic exchange network. She can "get" the phallus—in intercourse, or as a child—

but only as a gift from a man. She never gets to give it away.

When she turns to the father, she also represses the "active" portions of her libido:

> The turning away from her mother is an extremely important step in the course of a little girl's development. It is more than a mere change of object . . . hand in hand with it there is to be observed a marked lowering of the active sexual impulses and a rise of the passive ones. . . . The transition to the father object is accomplished with the help of the passive trends in so far as they have escaped the catastrophe. The path to the development of femininity now lies open to the girl. (Freud, 1961b:239)

The ascendance of passivity in the girl is due to her recognition of the futility of realizing her active desire, and of the unequal terms of the struggle. Freud locates active desire in the clitoris and passive desire in the vagina, and thus describes the repression of active desire as the repression of clitoral eroticism in favor of passive vaginal eroticism. In this scheme, cultural stereotypes have been mapped onto the genitals. Since the work of Masters and Johnson, it is evident that this genital division is a false one. Any organ—penis, clitoris, vagina—can be the locus of either active or passive eroticism. What is important in Freud's scheme, however, is not the geography of desire, but its self-confidence. It is not an organ which is repressed, but a segment of erotic possibility. Freud notes that "more constraint has been applied to the libido when it is pressed into the service of the feminine function . . ." (Freud, 1965:131). The girl has been robbed.

If the Oedipal phase proceeds normally and the girl "accepts her castration," her libidinal structure and object choice are now congruent with the female gender role. She has become a little woman—feminine, passive, heterosexual. Actually, Freud suggests that there are three alternate routes out of the Oedipal catastrophe. The girl may simply freak out, repress sexuality altogether, and become asexual. She may protest, cling to her narcissism and desire, and become either "masculine" or homosexual. Or she may accept the situation, sign the social contract, and attain "normality."

Karen Horney is critical of the entire Freud/Lampl de Groot scheme. But in the course of her critique she articulates its implications:

> . . . when she [the girl] first turns to a man (the father), it is in the main only by way of the narrow bridge of resentment . . . we should feel it a contradiction if the relation of woman to man did not retain throughout life some tinge of this enforced substitute for that which was really desired. . . . The same character of something remote from instinct, secondary and substitutive, would, even in normal women, adhere to the wish for motherhood. . . . The special point about Freud's viewpoint is rather that it sees the wish for motherhood not as an innate formation, but as something that can be reduced psychologically to its ontogenetic elements and draws its energy originally from homosexual or phallic instinctual elements. . . . It would follow, finally, that women's whole reaction to life would be based on a strong subterranean resentment. (Horney, 1973:148–149)

Horney considers these implications to be so far-fetched that they challenge the validity of Freud's entire scheme. But it is certainly plausible to argue instead that the creation of "femininity" in women in the course of socialization is an act of psychic brutality, and that it leaves in women an immense resentment of the suppression to which they were subjected. It is also possible to argue that women have few means for realizing and expressing their residual anger. One can read Freud's essays on femininity as descriptions of how a group is prepared psychologically, at a tender age, to live with its oppression.

There is an additional element in the classic discussions of the attainment of womanhood. The girl first turns to the father because she must, because she is "castrated" (a woman, helpless, etc.). She then discovers that "castration" is a prerequisite to the father's love, that she must be a woman for him to love her. She therefore begins to desire "castration," and what had previously been a disaster becomes a wish.

> Analytic experience leaves no room for doubt that the little girl's first libidinal relation to her father is masochistic, and the masochistic wish in its earliest distinctively feminine phase is: "I want to be castrated by my father." (Deutsch, 1948a:228)

Deutsch argues that such masochism may conflict with the ego, causing some women to flee the entire situation in defense of their self-regard. Those women to whom the choice is "between finding bliss in suffering or peace in renunciation" (Ibid.:231) will have difficulty in attaining a healthy attitude to intercourse and motherhood. Why Deutsch appears to consider such women to be special cases, rather than the norm, is not clear from her discussion.

The psychoanalytic theory of femininity is one that sees female development based largely on pain and humiliation, and it takes some fancy footwork to explain why anyone ought to enjoy being a woman. At this point in the classic discussions biology makes a triumphant return. The fancy footwork consists in arguing that finding joy in pain is adaptive to the role of women in reproduction, since childbirth and defloration are "painful." Would it not make more sense to question the entire procedure? If women, in finding their place in a sexual system, are robbed of libido and forced into a masochistic eroticism, why did the analysts not argue for novel arrangements, instead of rationalizing the old ones?

Freud's theory of femininity has been subjected to feminist critique since it was first published. To the extent that it is a rationalization of female subordination, this critique has been justified. To the extent that it is a description of a process which subordinates women, this critique is a mistake. As a description of how phallic culture domesticates women, and the effects in women of their domestication, psychoanalytic theory has no parallel (see also Mitchell, 1971 and 1974; Lasch, 1974). And since psychoanalysis is a theory of gender, dismissing it would be suicidal for a political movement dedicated to eradicating gender hierarchy (or gender itself). We cannot dismantle something that we underestimate or do not understand. The oppression of women is deep; equal pay, equal work, and all of the female politicians in the world will not extirpate the roots of sexism. Lévi-Strauss and Freud elucidate what would otherwise be poorly perceived parts of the deep structures of sex oppression. They serve as reminders of the intractability and magnitude of what we fight, and their analyses provide preliminary charts of the social machinery we must rearrange.

WOMEN UNITE TO OFF THE OEDIPAL RESIDUE OF CULTURE
. . .

The organization of sex and gender once had functions other than itself—it organized society.

Now, it only organizes and reproduces itself. The kinds of relationships of sexuality established in the dim human past still dominate our sexual lives, our ideas about men and women, and the ways we raise our children. But they lack the functional load they once carried. One of the most conspicuous features of kinship is that it has been systematically stripped of its functions—political, economic, educational, and organizational. It has been reduced to its barest bones—*sex and gender.*

Human sexual life will always be subject to convention and human intervention. It will never be completely "natural," if only because our species is social, cultural, and articulate. The wild profusion of infantile sexuality will always be tamed. The confrontation between immature and helpless infants and the developed social life of their elders will probably always leave some residue of disturbance. But the mechanisms and aims of this process need not be largely independent of conscious choice. Cultural evolution provides us with the opportunity to seize control of the means of sexuality, reproduction, and socialization, and to make conscious decisions to liberate human sexual life from the archaic relationships which deform it. Ultimately, a thoroughgoing feminist revolution would liberate more than women. It would liberate forms of sexual expression, and it would liberate human personality from the straightjacket of gender.

"DADDY, DADDY, YOU BASTARD, I'M THROUGH."   —SYLVIA PLATH

In the course of this essay I have tried to construct a theory of women's oppression by borrowing concepts from anthropology and psychoanalysis. But Lévi-Strauss and Freud write within an intellectual tradition produced by a culture in which women are oppressed. The danger in my enterprise is that the sexism in the tradition of which they are a part tends to be dragged in with each borrowing. "We cannot utter a single destructive proposition which has not already slipped into the form, the logic, and the implicit postulations of precisely what it seeks to contest" (Derrida, 1972:250). And what slips in is formidable. Both psychoanalysis and structural anthropology are, in one sense, the most sophisticated ideologies of sexism around.[7]

For instance, Lévi-Strauss sees women as being like words, which are misused when they are not "communicated" and exchanged. On the last page of a very long book, he observes that this creates something of a contradiction in women, since women are at the same time "speakers" and "spoken." His only comment on this contradiction is this:

> But woman could never become just a sign and nothing more, since even in a man's world she is still a person, and since insofar as she is defined as a sign she must be recognized as a generator of signs. In the matrimonial dialogue of men, woman is never purely what is spoken about; for if women in general represent a certain category of signs, destined to a certain kind of communication, each woman preserves a particular value arising from her talent, before and after marriage, for taking her part in a duet. In contrast to words, which have wholly become signs, woman has remained at once a sign and a value. *This explains why the relations between the sexes have preserved that affective richness, ardour and mystery which doubtless originally permeated the entire universe of human communications.* (Lévi-Strauss, 1969:496; my italics)

This is an extraordinary statement. Why is he not, at this point, denouncing what kinship systems do to women, instead of presenting one of the greatest rip-offs of all time as the root of romance?

A similar insensitivity is revealed within psychoanalysis by the inconsistency with which it assimilates the critical implications of its own theory. For instance, Freud did not hesitate to recognize that his findings posed a challenge to conventional morality:

> We cannot avoid observing with critical eyes, and we have found that it is impossible to give our support to conventional sexual morality or to approve highly of the means by which society attempts to arrange the practical problems of sexuality in life. *We can demonstrate with ease that what the world calls its code of morals demands more sacrifices than it is worth,* and that its behavior is neither dictated by honesty nor instituted with wisdom. (Freud, 1943: 376–377; my emphasis)

Nevertheless, when psychoanalysis demonstrates with equal facility that the ordinary components of feminine personality are masochism, self-hatred, and passivity,[8] a similar judgment is *not* made. Instead, a double standard of interpretation is employed. Masochism is bad for men, essential to women. Adequate narcissism is necessary for men, impossible for women. Passivity is tragic in man, while lack of passivity is tragic in a woman.

It is this double standard which enables clinicians to try to accommodate women to a role whose destructiveness is so lucidly detailed in their own theories. It is the same inconsistent attitude which permits therapists to consider lesbianism as a problem to be cured, rather than as the resistance to a bad situation that their own theory suggests.[9]

There are points within the analytic discussions of femininity where one might say, "This is oppression of women," or "We can demonstrate with ease that what the world calls femininity demands more sacrifices than it is worth." It is precisely at such points that the implications of the theory are ignored, and are replaced with formulations whose purpose is to keep those implications firmly lodged in the theoretical unconscious. It is at these points that all sorts of mysterious chemical substances, joys in pain, and biological aims are substituted for a critical assessment of the costs of femininity. These substitutions are the symptoms of theoretical repression, in that they are not consistent with the usual canons of psychoanalytic argument. The extent to which these rationalizations of femininity go against the grain of psychoanalytic logic is strong evidence for the extent of the need to suppress the radical and feminist implications of the theory of femininity (Deutsch's discussions are excellent examples of this process of substitution and repression).

The argument which must be woven in order to assimilate Lévi-Strauss and Freud into feminist theory is somewhat tortuous. I have engaged it for several reasons. First, while neither Lévi-Strauss nor Freud questions the undoubted sexism endemic to the systems they describe, the questions which ought to be posed are blindingly obvious. Secondly, their work enables us to isolate sex and gender from "mode of production," and to counter a certain tendency to explain sex oppression as a reflex of economic forces. Their work provides a framework in which the full weight of sexuality and marriage can be incorporated into an analysis of sex oppression. It suggests a conception of the women's movement as analogous to, rather than isomorphic with, the working-class movement, each addressing a different source of human discontent. In Marx's vision, the working-class movement would do more than throw off the burden of its own exploitation. It also had the potential to change society, to liberate humanity, to create a classless society. Perhaps the women's movement has the task of effecting the same kind of social change for a system of which Marx had only an imperfect apperception. Something of this sort is implicit in Wittig (1973)—the dictatorship of the Amazon *guérillères* is a temporary means for achieving a genderless society.

The sex/gender system is not immutably oppressive and has lost much of its traditional function. Nevertheless, it will not wither away in the absence of opposition. It still carries the social burden of sex and gender, of socializing the young, and of providing ultimate propositions about the nature of human beings themselves. And it serves economic and political ends other than those it was originally designed to further (cf. Scott, 1965). The sex/gender system must be reorganized through political action.

Finally, the exegesis of Lévi-Strauss and Freud suggests a certain vision of feminist politics and the feminist utopia. It suggests that we should not aim for the elimination of men, but for the elimination of the social system which creates sexism and gender. I personally find a vision of an Amazon matriarchate, in which men are reduced to servitude or oblivion (depending on the possibilities for parthenogenetic reproduction), distasteful and inadequate. Such a vision maintains gender and the division of the sexes. It is a vision which simply inverts the arguments of those who base their case for inevitable male dominance or ineradicable and *significant* biological differences between the sexes. But we are not only oppressed *as* women, we are oppressed by having to *be* women, or men as the case may be. I personally feel that the feminist movement must dream of even more than the elimination of the oppression of women. It must dream of the elimination of obligatory sexualities and sex roles. The dream I find most compelling is one of an androgynous and genderless (though not sexless) society, in which one's sexual anatomy is irrele-vant to who one is, what one does, and with whom one makes love.

• • •

[1975]

REFERENCES

Althusser, Louis and Balibar, Etienne. 1970. *Reading Capital.* London: New Left Books.

Derrida, Jacques. 1972. "Structure, Sign, and Play in the Discourse of the Human Sciences." In *The Structuralist Controversy,* edited by R. Macksey and E. Donato. Baltimore: Johns Hopkins Press.

Deutsch, Helene. 1948. "The Significance of Masochism in the Mental Life of Women." In *The Psychoanalytic Reader,* edited by R. Fleiss. New York: International Universities Press.

Engels, Frederick. 1891. *The Origin of the Family, Private Property, and the State.* 4th ed. Moscow: Foreign Languages Publishing House.

Evans-Pritchard, E. E. 1951. *Kinship and Marriage Among the Nuer.* London: Oxford University Press.

Fee, Elizabeth. 1973. "The Sexual Politics of Victorian Social Anthropology." *Feminist Studies* (Winter/Spring): 23–29.

Freud, Sigmund. 1943. *A General Introduction to Psychoanalysis.* Garden City, N.Y.: Garden City Publishing Company.

———. 1961b. "Female Sexuality." In *The Complete Works of Sigmund Freud,* vol. 21, edited by J. Strachey. London: Hogarth.

———. 1965. "Feminity." In *New Introductory Lectures in Psychoanalysis,* edited by J. Strachey. New York: W. W. Norton.

Hertz, Robert. 1960. *Death and the Right Hand.* Glencoe: Free Press.

Horney, Karen. 1973. "The Denial of the Vagina." In Karen Horney, *Feminine Psychology,* edited by Harold Kelman. New York: W. W. Norton.

Jakobson, Roman, and Halle, Morris. 1971. *Fundamentals of Language.* The Hague: Mouton.

Lacan, Jacques. 1968. "The Function of Language in Psychoanalysis." In Anthony Wilden, *The Language of Self.*

Lampl de Groot, Jeanne. 1933. "Problems of Femininity." *Psychoanalytic Quarterly* 2: 489–518.

———. 1948. "The Evolution of the Oedipus Complex in Women." In *The Psychoanalytic Reader,* edited by R. Fleiss. New York: International Universities Press.

Lasch, Christopher. 1974. "Freud and Women." *New York Review of Books* 21, no. 15: 12–17.

Lévi-Strauss, Claude. 1969. *The Elementary Structures of Kinship.* Boston: Beacon Press.

———. 1971. "The Family." In *Man, Culture, and Society,* edited by H. Shapiro. London: Oxford University Press.

Livingstone, Frank. 1969. "Genetics, Ecology, and the Origins of Incest and Exogamy." *Current Anthropology* 10, no. 1: 45–49.

Marx, Karl. 1969. *Theories of Surplus Value,* Part I. Moscow: Progress Publishers.

———. 1971a. *Pre-Capitalist Economic Formations.* New York: International Publishers.

———. 1972. *Capital,* vol. 1. New York: International Publishers.

Mehlman, Jeffrey. 1972. *French Freud: Structural Studies in Psychoanalysis.* New Haven: Yale French Studies #48.

Mitchell, Juliet. 1974. *Psychoanalysis and Feminism.* New York: Pantheon.

Sahlins, Marshall. 1960*a*. "The Origin of Society." *Scientific American* 203, no. 3: 76–86.

———. 1960*b*. "Political Power and the Economy in Primitive Society." In *Essays in the Science of Culture,* edited by Robert Dole and Robert Carneiro. New York: Crowell.

———. 1972. *Stone Age Economics.* Chicago: Aldine-Atherton.

Scott, John Finley. 1965. "The Role of Collegiate Sororities in Maintaining Class and Ethnic Endogamy." *American Sociological Review* 30, no. 4: 415–26.

Strathern, Marilyn. 1972. *Women in Between.* New York: Seminar.

Thompson, E. P. 1963. *The Making of the English Working Class.* New York: Vintage.

Wilden, Anthony. 1968. *The Language of the Self.* Baltimore: Johns Hopkins Press.

Wittig,-Monique. 1973. *Les Guérillères.* New York: Avon.

NOTES

1. Moving between Marxism, structuralism, and psychoanalysis produces a certain clash of epistemologies. In particular, structuralism is a can from which worms crawl out all over the epistemological map. Rather than trying to cope with this problem, I have more or less ignored the fact that Lacan and Lévi-Strauss are among the foremost living ancestors of the contemporary French intellectual revolution (see Foucault, 1970). It would be fun, interesting, and, if this were France, essential, to start my argument from the center of the structuralist maze and work my way out from there, along the lines of a "dialectical theory of signifying practices" (see Hefner, 1974).

2. "What, would you like to marry your sister? What is the matter with you? Don't you want a brother-in-law? Don't you realize that if you marry another man's sister and another man marries your sister, you will have at least two brothers-in-law, while if you marry your own sister you will have none? With whom will you hunt, with whom will you garden, whom will you go visit?" (Arapesh, cited in Lévi-Strauss, 1969:485).

3. This analysis of society as based on bonds between men by means of women makes the separatist responses of the women's movement thoroughly intelligible. Separatism can be seen as a mutation in social structure, as an attempt to form social groups based on unmediated bonds between women. It can also be seen as a radical denial of men's "rights" in women, and as a claim by women of rights in themselves.

4. "The woman shall not wear that which pertaineth unto a man, neither shall a man put on a woman's garment: for all that do so *are* abomination unto the LORD thy God" (Deuteronomy, 22:5; emphasis not mine).

5. I have taken my position on Freud somewhere between the French structuralist interpretations and American biologistic ones, because I think that Freud's wording is similarly somewhere in the middle. He does talk about penises, about the "inferiority" of the clitoris, about the psychic consequences of anatomy. The Lacanians, on the other hand, argue from Freud's text that he is unintelligible if his words are taken literally, and that a thoroughly nonanatomical theory can be deduced as Freud's intention (see Althusser, 1969). I think that they are right; the penis is walking around too much for its role to be taken literally. The detachability of the penis, and its transformation in fantasy (e.g., penis = feces = child = gift), argue strongly for a symbolic interpretation. Nevertheless, I don't think that Freud was as consistent as either I or Lacan would like him to have been, and some gesture must be made to what he said, even as we play with what he must have meant.

6. The pre-Oedipal mother is the "phallic mother," e.g., she is believed to possess the phallus. The Oedipal-inducing information is that the mother does not possess the phallus. In other words, the crisis is precipitated by the "castration" of the mother, by the recognition that the phallus only passes through her, but does not settle on her. The "phallus" must pass through her, since the relationship of a male to every other male is defined through a woman. A man is linked to a son by a mother, to his nephew by virtue of a sister, etc. Every relationship between male kin is defined by the woman between them. If power is a male prerogative, and must be passed on, it must go through the woman-in-between. Marshall Sahlins (personal communication) once suggested that the reason women are so often defined as stupid, polluting, disorderly, silly, profane, or whatever, is that such categorizations define women as "incapable" of possessing the power which must be transferred through them.

7. Parts of Wittig's *Les Guérillères* (1973) appear to be tirades against Lévi-Strauss and Lacan. For instance:

   > Has he not indeed written, power and the possession of women, leisure and the enjoyment of women? He writes that you are currency, an item of exchange. He writes, barter, barter, possession and acquisition of women and merchandise. Better for you to see your guts in the sun and utter the death rattle than to live a life that anyone can appropriate. What belongs to you on this earth? Only death. No power on earth can take that away from you. And—consider explain tell yourself—if happiness consists in the possession of something, then hold fast to this sovereign happiness—to die. (Wittig, 1973:115–116; see also 106–107; 113–114; 134)

   The awareness of French feminists of Lévi-Strauss and Lacan is most clearly evident in a group called "Psychoanalyse et Politique" which defined its task as a feminist use and critique of Lacanian psychoanalysis.

8. "Every woman adores a fascist."—Sylvia Plath

9. One clinician, Charlotte Wolff (1971) has taken the psychoanalytic theory of womanhood to its logical extreme and proposed that lesbianism is a healthy response to female socialization.

   > Women who do not rebel against the status of object have declared themselves defeated as persons in their own right. (Wolff, 1971:65)

The lesbian girl is the one who, by all means at her disposal, will try to find a place of safety inside and outside the family, through her fight for equality with the male. She will not, like other women, play up to him: indeed, she despises the very idea of it. (Ibid.:59)

The lesbian was and is unquestionably in the avant-garde of the fight for equality of the sexes, and for the psychical liberation of women. (Ibid.:66)

It is revealing to compare Wolff's discussion with the articles on lesbianism in Marmor, 1965.

PART V

1975–1985

1975–1985: Introduction

The period from 1975 through 1985 is marked by conflicting political, social, and intellectual currents. In national politics, the war in Vietnam had ended in defeat for the United States. The Nixon presidency also ended, after the Watergate hearings, with Nixon's resignation, leaving a general sense of political disillusionment. At the same time, for women inside and outside the academy this was a period of excitement, of some fulfillment of earlier struggles, and of hope for future transformation. In colleges and universities, new women's studies programs were being founded every year and a large-scale effort, supported by prestigious funders like the Ford Foundation and FIPSE (the Fund for the Improvement of Post-Secondary Education), was mounted to transform the entrenched masculinist curriculum in every field. The campaign to ratify the Equal Rights Amendment was in full swing and the creation of women's organizations, businesses, and institutions continued. In 1975, the United Nations declared 1976–1985 the Decade for Women, and many women in the United States and around the world thought it could be. By 1982, however, Ronald Reagan had been elected and ratification of the ERA had failed. With hindsight we see that organizing in opposition to the ERA laid the groundwork intellectually and organizationally for full-scale backlash against feminist and other social activism in the latter part of the 1980s.

In terms of feminist theory, 1975 stands out as a year of significant publication. In 1975, Gayle Rubin published her landmark essay "The Traffic in Women" and, across the Atlantic, Hélène Cixous published "The Laugh of the Medusa." We could almost without exaggeration use these two essays to define the span of feminist thinking of the next decade—the one materialist and social, the other heavily invested in discourse and the symbolic. In this period the breadth of disciplines in which the work of feminist theory is being done becomes apparent, including philosophers (Frye), theologians (Pagels), poets (Lorde, Rich), anthropologists (Ortner), historians (Smith-Rosenberg) and psychoanalysts (Chodorow, Irigaray), all of whom attempt to understand from different perspectives the division of labor and power that undergird sexism and women's oppression.

Arguments for female difference, articulated in radical and cultural feminism, also shaped the development (or further development) in this period of ecofeminism, feminist spirituality, and a feminist peace politics. The work of ecofeminists, among them Susan Griffin and Ynestra King, suggested an analogy between man's domination of woman and his domination of nature, and the possibility of a different relationship between women and nature. Feminist spirituality found expression both in the critiques of such established religions as Christianity, Judaism, or Islam (Pagels, Plaskow, Mernissi), and in interest in exploring goddess religion and pre-Christian practice, to develop feminist or womanist theologies and liturgical practices. Feminist peace politics is perhaps best embodied in the Greenham Women's Peace Camp established in 1981 outside the gates of the U.S. missile base at Greenham Common in the United Kingdom. Analyses like Sara Ruddick's of "maternal thinking" and women's "preservative love" provide the theoretical grounding for this kind of peace activism.

Various rifts within feminism—focused around race, sexuality, and activism, and probably always there under the surface—became apparent in the latter part of this period. The publication of *This Bridge Called My Back* (1981) and *All the Women Are White, All the Blacks Are Men, But Some of Us Are Brave: Black Women's Studies* (1982) articulated a critique by women of color of the domination of both women's studies and women's movement by white women. These volumes also claimed attention for the growing body of creative and intellectual work being produced by women of color that should become a part of the knowledge base of feminist thought. Conflicts between lesbians and straight women over separatism, heterosexism, and the role of men in the feminist movement tore organizations apart. At the same time, a perhaps artificial divide between those still doing grassroots work and those now working primarily within academic institutions was perceived and described as a split between theory and practice.

The U.N. Decade for Women closed in 1985 with a conference in Nairobi, Kenya, which was for many women the beginning of attempts to understand what a truly global feminism might be. Published in 1984, Chandra Mohanty's essay on "Third World Women and the Politics of Feminism" is one attempt to provide a theoretical frame for this project.

51

The Female World of Love and Ritual: Relations Between Women in Nineteenth-Century America

CARROLL SMITH-ROSENBERG

The female friendship of the nineteenth century, the long-lived intimate, loving friendship between two women, is an excellent example of the type of historical phenomena which most historians know something about, which few have thought much about, and which virtually no one has written about.[1] It is one aspect of the female experience which consciously or unconsciously we have chosen to ignore. Yet an abundance of manuscript evidence suggests that eighteenth- and nineteenth-century women routinely formed emotional ties with other women. Such deeply felt, same-sex friendships were casually accepted in American society. Indeed, from at least the late eighteenth through the mid-nineteenth century, a female world of varied and yet highly structured relationships appears to have been an essential aspect of American society. These relationships ranged from the supportive love of sisters, through the enthusiasms of adolescent girls, to sensual avowals of love by mature women. It was a world in which men made but a shadowy appearance.[2]

Defining and analyzing same-sex relationships involves the historian in deeply problematical questions of method and interpretation. This is especially true since historians, influenced by Freud's libidinal theory, have discussed these relationships almost exclusively within the context of individual psychosexual developments or, to be more explicit, psychopathology.[3] Seeing same-sex relationships in terms of a dichotomy between normal and abnormal, they have sought the origins of such apparent deviance in childhood or adolescent trauma and detected the symptoms of "latent" homosexuality in the lives of both those who later became "overtly" homosexual and those who did not. Yet theories concerning the nature and origins of same-sex relationships are frequently contradictory or based on questionable or arbitrary data. In recent years such hypotheses have been subjected to criticism both from within and without the psychological professions. Historians who seek to work within a psychological framework, therefore, are faced with two hard questions: Do sound psychodynamic theories concerning the nature and origins of same-sex relationships exist? If so, does the historical datum exist which would permit the use of such dynamic models?

I would like to suggest an alternative approach to female friendships—one which would view them within a cultural and social setting rather than from an exclusively individual psychosexual perspective. Only by thus altering our approach will we be in the position to evaluate the appropriateness of particular dynamic interpretations. Intimate friendships between men and men and women and women existed in a larger world of social relations and social values. To interpret such friendships more fully they must be related to the structure of the American family and to the nature of sex-role divisions and of male-female relations both within the family and in society generally. The female friendship must not be seen in isolation; it must be analyzed as one aspect of women's overall relations with one another. The ties between mothers and daughters, sisters, female cousins and friends, at all stages of the female life cycle constitute the most suggestive framework for the historian to begin an analysis of intimacy and affection between women. Such an analysis would not only emphasize general cultural patterns rather than the internal dynamics of a particular family or childhood; it would shift the focus of the study from a concern with deviance to that of defining configurations of legitimate behavioral norms and options.

This analysis will be based upon the correspondence and diaries of women and men in thirty-five families between the 1760s and the 1880s. These families, though limited in number, represented a broad range of the American middle class, from hard-pressed pioneer families and orphaned girls to daughters of the intellectual and social elite. It includes families from most geographic regions, rural and urban, and a spectrum of Protestant denominations ranging from Mormon to orthodox Quaker. Although scarcely a comprehensive sample of America's increasingly heterogeneous population, it does, I believe, reflect accurately the literate middle class to which the historian working with letters and diaries is necessarily bound. It has involved an analysis of many thousands of letters written to women friends, kin, husbands, brothers, and children at every period of life from adolescence to old age. Some collections encompass virtually entire life spans; one contains over 100,000 letters as well as diaries and account books. It is my contention that an analysis of women's private letters and diaries which were never intended to be published permits the historian to explore a very private world of emotional realities central both to women's lives and to the middle-class family in nineteenth-century America.

The question of female friendships is peculiarly elusive; we know so little or perhaps have forgotten so much. An intriguing and almost alien form of human relationship, they flourished in a different social structure and amidst different sexual norms. Before attempting to reconstruct their social setting, therefore, it might be best first to describe two not atypical friendships. These two friendships, intense, loving, and openly avowed, began during the women's adolescence and, despite subsequent marriages and geographic separation, continued throughout their lives. For nearly half a century these women played a central emotional role in each other's lives, writing time and again of their love and of the pain of separation. Paradoxically to twentieth-century minds, their love appears to have been both sensual and platonic.

Sarah Butler Wister first met Jeannie Field Musgrove while vacationing with her family at Stockbridge, Massachusetts, in the summer of 1849.[4] Jeannie was then sixteen, Sarah fourteen. During two subsequent years spent together in boarding school, they formed a deep and intimate friendship. Sarah began to keep a bouquet of flowers before Jeannie's portrait and wrote complaining of the intensity and anguish of her affection.[5] Both young women assumed nom de plumes, Jeannie a female name, Sarah a male one; they would use these secret names into old age.[6] They frequently commented

on the nature of their affection: "If the day should come," Sarah wrote Jeannie in the spring of 1861, "when you failed me either through your fault or my own, I would forswear all human friendship, thenceforth." A few months later Jeannie commented: "Gratitude is a word I should never use toward you. It is perhaps a misfortune of such intimacy and love that it makes one regard all kindness as a matter of course, as one has always found it, as natural as the embrace in meeting."[7]

Sarah's marriage altered neither the frequency of their correspondence nor their desire to be together. In 1864, when twenty-nine, married, and a mother, Sarah wrote to Jeannie: "I shall be entirely alone [this coming week]. I can give you no idea how desperately I shall want you. . . ." After one such visit Jeannie, then a spinster in New York, echoed Sarah's longing: "Dear darling Sarah! How I love you & how happy I have been! You are the joy of my life. . . . I cannot tell you how much happiness you gave me, nor how constantly it is all in my thoughts. . . . My darling how I long for the time when I shall see you. . . ." After another visit Jeannie wrote: "I want you to tell me in your next letter, to assure me, that I am your dearest. . . . I do not doubt you, & I am not jealous but I long to hear you say it once more & it seems already a long time since your voice fell on my ear. So just fill a quarter page with caresses & expressions of endearment. Your silly Angelina." Jeannie ended one letter: "Goodbye my dearest, dearest lover—ever your own Angelina." And another, "I will go to bed . . . [though] I could write all night—A thousand kisses—I love you with my whole soul—your Angelina."

When Jeannie finally married in 1870 at the age of thirty-seven, Sarah underwent a period of extreme anxiety. Two days before Jeannie's marriage Sarah, then in London, wrote desperately: "Dearest darling—How incessantly have I thought of you these eight days—all today—the entire uncertainty, the distance, the long silence—are all new features in my separation from you, grevious to be borne. . . . Oh Jeannie. I have thought & thought & yearned over you these two days. Are you married I wonder? My dearest love to you wherever and *who*ever you are."[8] Like many other women in this collection of thirty-five families, marriage brought Sarah and Jeannie physical separation: it did not cause emotional distance. Although at first they may have wondered how marriage would affect their relationship, their affection remained unabated throughout their lives, underscored by their loneliness and their desire to be together.[9]

During the same years that Jeannie and Sarah wrote of their love and need for each other, two slightly younger women began a similar odyssey of love, dependence and—ultimately—physical, though not emotional, separation. Molly and Helena met in 1868 while both attended the Cooper Institute School of Design for Women in New York City. For several years these young women studied and explored the city together, visited each other's families, and formed part of a social network of other artistic young women. Gradually, over the years, their initial friendship deepened into a close intimate bond which continued throughout their lives. The tone in the letters which Molly wrote to Helena changed over these years from "My dear Helena," and signed "your attached friend," to "My dearest Helena," "My Dearest," "My Beloved," and signed "Thine always" or "thine Molly."[10]

The letters they wrote to each other during these first five years permit us to reconstruct something of their relationship together. As Molly wrote in one early letter:

> I have not said to you in so many or so few words that I was happy with you during those few so incredibly short weeks but surely you do not need words to tell you what you must know. Those two or three days so dark without, so bright with firelight and contentment within I shall always remember as proof that, for a time, at least—I fancy for quite a long time—we might be sufficient for each other. We know that we can amuse each other for many idle hours together and now we know that we can also work together. And that means much, don't you think so?

She ended: "I shall return in a few days. Imagine yourself kissed many times by one who loved you so dearly."

The intensity and even physical nature of Molly's love was echoed in many of the letters she wrote during the next few years, as, for instance in this short thank-you note for a small present: "Imagine yourself kissed a dozen times my darling. Perhaps it is well for you that we are far apart. You might find

my thanks so expressed rather overpowering. I have that delightful feeling that it doesn't matter much what I say or how I say it, since we shall meet so soon and forget in that moment that we were ever separated. . . . I shall see you soon and be content."[11]

At the end of the fifth year, however, several crises occurred. The relationship, at least in its intense form, ended, though Molly and Helena continued an intimate and complex relationship for the next half-century. The exact nature of these crises is not completely clear, but it seems to have involved Molly's decision not to live with Helena, as they had originally planned, but to remain at home because of parental insistence. Molly was now in her late twenties. Helena responded with anger and Molly became frantic at the thought that Helena would break off their relationship. Though she wrote distraught letters and made despairing attempts to see Helena, the relationship never regained its former ardor—possibly because Molly had a male suitor.[12] Within six months Helena had decided to marry a man who was, coincidentally, Molly's friend and publisher. Two years later Molly herself finally married. The letters toward the end of this period discuss the transition both women made to having male lovers—Molly spending much time reassuring Helena, who seemed depressed about the end of their relationship and with her forthcoming marriage.[13]

It is clearly difficult from a distance of 100 years and from a post-Freudian cultural perspective to decipher the complexities of Molly and Helena's relationship. Certainly Molly and Helena were lovers—emotionally if not physically. The emotional intensity and pathos of their love becomes apparent in several letters Molly wrote Helena during their crisis: "I wanted so to put my arms round my girl of all the girls in the world and tell her . . . I love her as wives do love their husbands, as *friends* who have taken each other for life—and believe in her as I believe in my God. . . . If I didn't love you do you suppose I'd care about anything or have ridiculous notions and panics and behave like an old fool who ought to know better. I'm going to hang on to your skirts. . . . You can't get away from [my] love." Or as she wrote after Helena's decision to marry: "You know dear Helena, I really was in love with you. It was a passion such as I had never known until I saw you. I don't think it was the noblest way to love you."

The theme of intense female love was one Molly again expressed in a letter she wrote to the man Helena was to marry: "Do you know sir, that until you came along I believe that she loved me almost as girls love their lovers. *I know I loved her so.* Don't you wonder that I can stand the sight of you." This was in a letter congratulating them on their forthcoming marriage.[14]

The essential question is not whether these women had genital contact and can therefore be defined as heterosexual or homosexual. The twentieth-century tendency to view human love and sexuality within a dichotomized universe of deviance and normality, genitality and platonic love, is alien to the emotions and attitudes of the nineteenth century and fundamentally distorts the nature of these women's emotional interaction. These letters are significant because they force us to place such female love in a particular historical context. There is every indication that these four women, their husbands and families—all eminently respectable and socially conservative—considered such love both socially acceptable and fully compatible with heterosexual marriage. Emotionally and cognitively, their heterosocial and their homosocial worlds were complementary.

One could argue, on the other hand, that these letters were but an example of the romantic rhetoric with which the nineteenth century surrounded the concept of friendship. Yet they possess an emotional intensity and a sensual and physical explicitness that is difficult to dismiss. Jeannie longed to hold Sarah in her arms; Molly mourned her physical isolation from Helena. Molly's love and devotion to Helena, the emotions that bound Jeannie and Sarah together, while perhaps a phenomenon of nineteenth-century society were not the less real for their Victorian origins. A survey of the correspondence and diaries of eighteenth- and nineteenth-century women indicates that Molly, Jeannie, and Sarah represented one very real behavioral and emotional option socially available to nineteenth-century women.

This is not to argue that individual needs, personalities, and family dynamics did not have a significant role in determining the nature of particular relationships. But the scholar must ask if it is historically possible and, if possible, important to study the intensely individual aspects of psychosexual dynamics. It is not the historian's first task to explore the social structure and the world view which made intense and sometimes sensual female love both a possible and an acceptable emotional option? From such a social perspective a new and quite different series of questions suggests itself. What emotional function did such female love serve? What was its place within the hetero- and homosocial worlds which women jointly inhabited? Did a spectrum of love-object choices exist in the nineteenth century across which some individuals, at least, were capable of moving? Without attempting to answer these questions it will be difficult to understand either nineteenth-century sexuality or the nineteenth-century family.

Several factors in American society between the mid-eighteenth and the mid-nineteenth centuries may well have permitted women to form a variety of close emotional relationships with other women. American society was characterized in large part by rigid gender-role differentiation within the family and within society as a whole, leading to the emotional segregation of women and men. The roles of daughter and mother shaded imperceptibly and ineluctably into each other, while the biological realities of frequent pregnancies, childbirth, nursing, and menopause bound women together in physical and emotional intimacy. It was within just such a social framework, I would argue, that a specifically female world did indeed develop, a world built around a generic and unself-conscious pattern of single-sex or homosocial networks. These supportive networks were institutionalized in social conventions or rituals which accompanied virtually every important event in a woman's life, from birth to death. Such female relationships were frequently supported and paralleled by severe social restrictions on intimacy between young men and women. Within such a world of emotional richness and complexity devotion to and love of other women became a plausible and socially accepted form of human interaction.

An abundance of printed and manuscript sources exists to support such a hypothesis. Etiquette books, advice books on child rearing, religious sermons, guides to young men and young women, medical texts, and school curricula all suggest that late eighteenth- and most nineteenth-century Americans assumed the existence of a world composed of distinctly male and female spheres, spheres determined by the immutable laws of God and nature. The unpublished letters and diaries of Americans during this same period concur, detailing the existence of sexually segregated worlds inhabited by human beings with different values, expectations, and personalities. Contacts between men and women frequently partook of a formality and stiffness quite alien to twentieth-century America and which today we tend to define as "Victorian." Women, however, did not form an isolated and oppressed subcategory in male society. Their letters and diaries indicate that women's sphere had an essential integrity and dignity that grew out of women's shared experiences and mutual affection and that, despite the profound changes which affected American social structure and institutions between the 1760s and the 1870s, retained a constancy and predictability. The ways in which women thought of and interacted with each other remained unchanged. Continuity, not discontinuity, characterized this female world. Molly Hallock's and Jeannie Fields's words, emotions, and experiences have direct parallels in the 1760s and the 1790s.[15] There are indications in contemporary sociological and psychological literature that female closeness and support networks have continued into the twentieth century—not only among ethnic and working-class groups but even among the middle class.[16]

Most eighteenth- and nineteenth-century women lived within a world bounded by home, church, and the institution of visiting—that endless trooping of women to each others' homes for social purposes. It was a world inhabited by children and by other women.[17] Women helped each other with domestic chores and in times of sickness, sorrow, or trouble. Entire days, even weeks, might be spent almost exclusively with other women.[18] Urban and town women could devote virtually every day to visits, teas, or shopping trips with other women. Rural women developed a pattern of more extended visits that lasted weeks and sometimes months, at times even dislodging husbands from their beds and bedrooms so that dear friends might spend every hour of every day together.[19] When husbands traveled, wives routinely moved in with other women, invited women friends to teas and suppers, sat together sharing and comparing the letters they had received from other close women friends. Secrets were exchanged and cherished, and the husband's return at times viewed with some ambivalence.[20]

· · ·

Friends did not form isolated dyads but were normally part of highly integrated networks. Knowing each other, perhaps related to each other, they played a central role in holding communities and kin systems together. Especially when families became geographically mobile women's long visits to each other and their frequent letters filled with discussions of marriages and births, illness and deaths, descriptions of growing children, and reminiscences of times and people past provided an important sense of continuity in a rapidly changing society.[21] Central to this female world was an inner core of kin. The ties between sisters, first cousins, aunts, and nieces provided the underlying structure upon which groups of friends and their network of female relatives clustered. Although most of the women within this sample would appear to be living within isolated nuclear families, the emotional ties between nonresidential kin were deep and binding and provided one of the fundamental existential realities of women's lives. . . .

· · ·

These female friendships served a number of emotional functions. Within this secure and empathetic world women could share sorrows, anxieties, and joys, confident that other women had experienced similar emotions. One mid-nineteenth-century rural matron in a letter to her daughter discussed this particular aspect of women's friendships: "To have such a friend as thyself to look to and sympathize with her—and enter into all her little needs and in whose bosom she could with freedom pour forth her joys and sorrows—such a friend would very much relieve the tedium of many a wearisome hour. . . ." A generation later Molly more informally underscored the importance of this same function in a letter to Helena: "Suppose I come down . . . [and] spend Sunday with you quietly," she wrote Helena ". . . that means talking all the time until you are relieved of all your latest troubles, and I of mine. . . ."[22] These were frequently troubles that apparently no man could understand. When Anne

Jefferis Sheppard was first married, she and her older sister Edith (who then lived with Anne) wrote in detail to their mother of the severe depression and anxiety which they experienced. Moses Sheppard, Anne's husband, added cheerful postscripts to the sisters' letters—which he had clearly not read—remarking on Anne's and Edith's contentment. Theirs was an emotional world to which he had little access.[23]

This was, as well, a female world in which hostility and criticism of other women were discouraged, and thus a milieu in which women could develop a sense of inner security and self-esteem. As one young woman wrote to her mother's longtime friend: "I cannot sufficiently thank you for the kind unvaried affection & indulgence you have ever shown and expressed both by words and actions for me. . . . Happy would it be did all the world view me as you do, through the medium of kindness and forbearance."[24] They valued each other. Women, who had little status or power in the larger world of male concerns, possessed status and power in the lives and worlds of other women.[25]

· · ·

Eighteenth- and nineteenth-century women thus lived in emotional proximity to each other. Friendships and intimacies followed the biological ebb and flow of women's lives. Marriage and pregnancy, childbirth and weaning, sickness and death involved physical and psychic trauma which comfort and sympathy made easier to bear. Intense bonds of love and intimacy bound together those women who, offering each other aid and sympathy, shared such stressful moments.

These bonds were often physical as well as emotional. An undeniably romantic and even sensual note frequently marked female relationships. This theme, significant throughout the stages of a woman's life, surfaced first during adolescence. As one teenager from a struggling pioneer family in the Ohio Valley wrote in her diary in 1808: "I laid with my dear R[ebecca] and a glorious good talk we had until about 4 [A.M.]—O how hard I do *love* her. . . ."[26] Only a few years later Bostonian Eunice Callender carved her initials and Sarah Ripley's into a favorite tree, along with a pledge of eternal love, and then waited breathlessly for Sarah to discover and respond to her declaration of affection. The re-

sponse appears to have been affirmative.[27] A half-century later urbane and sophisticated Katherine Wharton commented upon meeting an old school chum: "She was a great pet of mine at school & I thought as I watched her light figure how often I had held her in my arms—how dear she had once been to me." Katie maintained a long intimate friendship with another girl. When a young man began to court this friend seriously, Katie commented in her diary that she had never realized "how deeply I loved Eng and how fully." She wrote over and over again in that entry: "Indeed I love her!" and only with great reluctance left the city that summer since it meant also leaving Eng with Eng's new suitor.[28]

Peggy Emlen, a Quaker adolescent in Philadelphia in the 1760s, expressed similar feelings about her first cousin, Sally Logan. The girls sent love poems to each other (not unlike the ones Elizabeth Bordley wrote to Nellie Custis a generation later), took long solitary walks together, and even haunted the empty house of the other when one was out of town. Indeed Sally's absences from Philadelphia caused Peggy acute unhappiness. So strong were Peggy's feelings that her brothers began to tease her about her affection for Sally and threatened to steal Sally's letters, much to both girls' alarm. In one letter that Peggy wrote the absent Sally she elaborately described the depth and nature of her feelings: "I have not words to express my impatience to see My Dear Cousin, what would I not give just now for an hours sweet conversation with her, it seems as if I had a thousand things to say to thee, yet when I see thee, everything will be forgot thro' joy. . . . I have a very great friendship for several Girls yet it dont give me so much uneasiness at being absent from them as from thee. . . . [Let us] go and spend a day down at our place together and there unmolested enjoy each others company."[29]

Sarah Alden Ripley, a young, highly educated woman, formed a similar intense relationship, in this instance with a woman somewhat older than herself. The immediate bond of friendship rested on their atypically intense scholarly interests, but it soon involved strong emotions, at least on Sarah's part. "Friendship," she wrote Mary Emerson, "is fast twining about her willing captive the silken hands of dependence, a dependence so sweet who would renounce it for the apathy of self-sufficiency?"

Subsequent letters became far more emotional, almost conspiratorial. Mary visited Sarah secretly in her room, or the two women crept away from family and friends to meet in a nearby woods. Sarah became jealous of Mary's other young woman friends. Mary's trips away from Boston also thrust Sarah into periods of anguished depression. Interestingly, the letters detailing their love were not destroyed but were preserved and even reprinted in a eulogistic biography of Sarah Alden Ripley.[30]

Tender letters between adolescent women, confessions of loneliness and emotional dependency, were not peculiar to Sarah Alden, Peggy Emlen, or Katie Wharton. They are found throughout the letters of the thirty-five families studied. They have, of course, their parallel today in the musings of many female adolescents. Yet these eighteenth- and nineteenth-century friendships lasted with undiminished, indeed often increased, intensity throughout the women's lives. Sarah Alden Ripley's first child was named after Mary Emerson. Nelly Custis Lewis's love for and dependence on Elizabeth Bordley Gibson only increased after her marriage. Eunice Callender remained enamored of her cousin Sarah Ripley for years and rejected as impossible the suggestion by another woman that their love might some day fade away.[31] Sophie DuPont and her childhood friend, Clementina Smith, exchanged letters filled with love and dependency for forty years while another dear friend, Mary Black Couper, wrote of dreaming that she, Sophie, and her husband were all united in one marriage. Mary's letters to Sophie are filled with avowals of love and indications of ambivalence toward her own husband. Eliza Schlatter, another of Sophie's intimate friends, wrote to her at a time of crisis: "I wish I could be with you present in the body as well as the mind & heart—I would turn your *good husband out of bed*—and snuggle into you and we would have a long talk like old times in Pine St.—I want to tell you so many things that are not *writable....*"[32]

Such mutual dependency and deep affection is a central existential reality coloring the world of supportive networks and rituals. In the case of Katie, Sophie, or Eunice—as with Molly, Jeannie, and Sarah—their need for closeness and support merged with more intense demands for a love which was at the same time both emotional and sensual. Perhaps the most explicit statement concerning women's lifelong friendships appeared in the letter abolitionist and reformer Mary Grew wrote about the same time, referring to her own love for her dear friend and lifelong companion, Margaret Burleigh. Grew wrote, in response to a letter of condolence from another woman on Burleigh's death: "Your words respecting my beloved friend touch me deeply. Evidently . . . you comprehend and appreciate, as few persons do . . . the nature of the relation which existed, which exists, between her and myself. Her only surviving niece . . . also does. To me it seems to have been a closer union than that of most marriages. We know there have been other such between two men and also between two women. And why should there not be. Love is spiritual, only passion is sexual."[33]

How then can we ultimately interpret these long-lived intimate female relationships and integrate them into our understanding of Victorian sexuality? Their ambivalent and romantic rhetoric presents us with an ultimate puzzle: the relationship along the spectrum of human emotions between love, sensuality, and sexuality.

One is tempted, as I have remarked, to compare Molly, Peggy, or Sophie's relationships with the friendships adolescent girls in the twentieth century routinely form—close friendships of great emotional intensity. Helene Deutsch and Clara Thompson have both described these friendships as emotionally necessary to a girl's psychosexual development. But, they warn, such friendships might shade into adolescent and postadolescent homosexuality.[34]

It is possible to speculate that in the twentieth century a number of cultural taboos evolved to cut short the homosocial ties of girlhood and to impel the emerging women of thirteen or fourteen toward heterosexual relationships. In contrast, nineteenth-century American society did not taboo close female relationships but rather recognized them as a socially viable form of human contact—and, as such, acceptable throughout a woman's life. Indeed it was not these homosocial ties that were inhibited but rather heterosexual leanings. While closeness, freedom of emotional expression, and uninhibited physical contact characterized women's relationships with each other, the opposite was frequently true of male-female relationships. One could thus argue that within such a world of female support, intimacy, and ritual it was only to be expected that adult women would turn trustingly and lovingly to each other. It was a behavior they had observed and learned since childhood. A different type of emotional landscape existed in the nineteenth century, one in which Molly and Helena's love became a natural development.

Of perhaps equal significance are the implications we can garner from this framework for the understanding of heterosexual marriages in the nineteenth century. If men and women grew up as they did in relatively homogeneous and segregated sexual groups, then marriage represented a major problem in adjustment. From this perspective we could interpret much of the emotional stiffness and distance that we associate with Victorian marriage as a structural consequence of contemporary sex-role differentiation and gender-role socialization. With marriage both women and men had to adjust to life with a person who was, in essence, a member of an alien group.

I have thus far substituted a cultural or psycho-social for a psychosexual interpretation of women's emotional bonding. But there are psychosexual implications in this model which I think it only fair to make more explicit. Despite Sigmund Freud's insistence on the bisexuality of us all or the recent American Psychiatric Association decision on homosexuality, many psychiatrists today tend explicitly or implicitly to view homosexuality as a totally alien or pathological behavior—as totally unlike heterosexuality. I suspect that in essence they may have adopted an explanatory model similar to the one used in discussing schizophrenia. As a psychiatrist can speak of schizophrenia and of a borderline schizophrenic personality as both ultimately and fundamentally different from a normal or neurotic personality, so they also think of both homosexuality and latent homosexuality as states totally different from heterosexuality. With this rapidly dichotomous model of assumption, "latent homosexuality" becomes the indication of a disease in progress—seeds of a pathology which belie the reality of an individual's heterosexuality.

Yet at the same time we are all aware that cultural values can effect choices in the gender of a person's sexual partner. We, for instance, do not necessarily consider homosexual-object choice among men in prison, on shipboard or in boarding schools a necessary indication of pathology. I would urge that we expand this relativistic model and hypothesize that a number of cultures might well tolerate or even encourage diversity in sexual and nonsexual relations. Based on my research into this nineteenth-century world of female intimacy, I would further suggest that rather than seeing a gulf between the normal and the abnormal we view sexual and emotional impulses as a part of a continuum or spectrum of affect gradations strongly effected by cultural norms and arrangements, a continuum influenced in part by observed and thus learned behavior. At one end of the continuum lies committed heterosexuality, at the other uncompromising homosexuality; between, a wide latitude of emotions and sexual feelings. Certain cultures and environments permit individuals a great deal of freedom in moving across this spectrum. I would like to suggest that the nineteenth century was such a cultural environment. That is, the supposedly repressive and destructive Victorian sexual ethos, may have been more flexible and responsive to the needs of particular individuals than those of mid-twentieth century.

[1975]

NOTES

1. The most notable exception to this rule is now eleven years old: William R. Taylor and Christopher Lasch, "Two 'Kindred Spirits': Sorority and Family in New England, 1839–1846," *New England Quarterly* 36 (1963): 25–41. Taylor has made a valuable contribution to the history of women and the history of the family with his concept of "sororial" relations. I do not, however, accept the Taylor-Lasch thesis that female friendships developed in the mid-nineteenth century because of geographic mobility and the breakup of the colonial family. I have found these friendships as frequently in the eighteenth century as in the nineteenth and would hypothesize that the geographic mobility of the mid-nineteenth century eroded them as it did so many other traditional social institutions. Helen Vendler (*Review of Notable American Women, 1607–1950*, ed. Edward James and Janet James, *New York Times* [November 5, 1972]: sec 7) points out the significance of these friendships.

2. I do not wish to deny the importance of women's relations with particular men. Obviously, women were

close to brothers, husbands, fathers, and sons. However, there is evidence that despite such closeness relationships between men and women differed in both emotional texture and frequency from those between women. . . .

3. See Freud's classic paper on homosexuality, "Three Essays on the Theory of Sexuality," in *The Standard Edition of the Complete Psychological Works of Sigmund Freud,* trans. James Strachey (London: Hogarth Press, 1953), 7:135–172. . . .

4. Sarah Butler Wister was the daughter of Fanny Kemble and Pierce Butler. In 1859 she married a Philadelphia physician, Owen Wister. The novelist Owen Wister is her son. Jeannie Field Musgrove was the half-orphaned daughter of constitutional lawyer and New York Republican politician David Dudley Field. Their correspondence (1855–1898) is in the Sarah Butler Wister Papers, Wister Family Papers, Historical Society of Pennsylvania.

5. Sarah Butler, Butler Place, S.C., to Jeannie Field, New York, September 14, 1855.

6. See, e.g., Sarah Butler Wister, Germantown, Pa., to Jeannie Field, New York, September 25, 1862, October 21, 1863; or Jeannie Field, New York, to Sarah Butler Wister, Germantown, July 3, 1861, January 23 and July 12, 1863.

7. Sarah Butler Wister, Germantown, to Jeannie Field, New York, June 5, 1861, February 29, 1864; Jeannie Field to Sarah Butler Wister November 22, 1861, January 4 and June 14, 1863.

8. Sarah Butler Wister, London, to Jeannie Field Musgrove, New York, June 18 and August 3, 1870.

9. See, e.g., two of Sarah's letters to Jeannie: December 21, 1873, July 16, 1878.

10. This is the 1868–1920 correspondence between Mary Hallock Foote and Helena, a New York friend (the Mary Hallock Foote Papers are in the Manuscript Division, Stanford University). . . .

11. Mary Hallock [Foote] to Helena, n.d. [1869–1870], n.d. [1871–1872]. Folder 1, Mary Hallock Foote Letters, Manuscript Division, Stanford University.

12. Mary Hallock [Foote] to Helena, September 15 and 23, 1873, n.d. [October 1873]. October 12, 1873.

13. Mary Hallock [Foote] to Helena, n.d. [January 1874], n.d. [Spring 1874].

14. Mary Hallock [Foote] to Helena, September 23, 1873; Mary Hallock [Foote] to Richard, December 13, 1873. Molly's and Helena's relationship continued for the rest of their lives. . . .

15. See, e.g., the letters of Peggy Emlen to Sally Logan, 1768–1772, Wells Morris Collection, Box 1, Historical Society of Pennsylvania; and the Eleanor Parke Custis Lewis Letters, Historical Society of Pennsylvania.

16. See esp. Elizabeth Botts, *Family and Social Network* (London: Tavistock Publications, 1957); Michael Young and Peter Willmott, *Family and Kinship in East London,* rev. ed. (Baltimore: Penguin Books, 1964).

17. This pattern seemed to cross class barriers. A letter that an Irish domestic wrote in the 1830s contains seventeen separate references to women and but only seven to men, most of whom were relatives and two of whom were infant brothers living with her mother and mentioned in relation to her mother (Ann McGrann, Phila-

delphia, to Sophie M. DuPont, Philadelphia, July 3, 1834, Sophie Madeleine DuPont Letters, Eleutherian Mills Foundation).

18. Harriett Manigault Diary, June 28, 1814, and passim; Jeannie Field, New York, to Sarah Butler Wister, Germantown, April 19, 1863; Phoebe Bradford Diary, January 30, February 19, March 4, August 11, and October 14, 1832, Historical Society of Pennsylvania; Sophie M. DuPont, Brandywine, to Henry DuPont, Germantown, July 9, 1827, Eleutherian Mills Foundation.

19. Martha Jefferis to Anne Jefferis Sheppard, July 9, 1843; Anne Jefferis Sheppard to Martha Jefferis, June 28, 1846; Anne Sterling Biddle Papers, passim, Biddle Family Papers, Friends Historical Society, Swarthmore College; Eleanor Parke Custis Lewis, Virginia, to Elizabeth Bordley Gibson, Philadelphia, November 24 and December 4, 1820, November 6, 1821.

20. Phoebe Bradford Diary, January 13, November 16–19, 1832, April 26 and May 7, 1833; Abigail Brackett Lyman to Mrs. Catling, Litchfield, Conn., May 3, 1801, collection in private hands; Martha Jefferis to Anne Jefferis Sheppard, August 28, 1845.

21. For a prime example of this type of letter, see Eleanor Parke Custis Lewis to Elizabeth Bordley Gibson, passim, or Fanny Canby to Mary Canby, Philadelphia, May 27, 1801; or Sophie M. DuPont, Brandywine, to Henry DuPont, Germantown, February 4, 1832.

22. Martha Jefferis to Edith Jefferis, March 15, 1841; Mary Hallock Foote to Helena, n.d. [1874–1875?]; see also Jeannie Field, New York, to Sarah Butler Wister, Germantown, May 5, 1863, Emily Howland Diary, December 1879, Howland Family Papers.

23. Anne Jefferis Sheppard to Martha Jefferis, September 29, 1841.

24. Frances Parke Lewis to Elizabeth Bordley Gibson, April 29, 1821.

25. Mary Jane Burleigh, Mount Pleasant, S.C., to Emily Howland, Sherwood N.Y., March 27, 1872, Howland Family Papers; Emily Howland Diary, September 16, 1879, January 21 and 23, 1880; Mary Black Couper, New Castle, Del., to Sophie M. DuPont, Brandywine, April 7, 1834.

26. Sarah Foulke [Emlen] Diary, December 29, 1808.

27. Eunice Callender, Boston, to Sarah Ripley [Stearns] Greenfield, Mass., May 24, 1803.

28. Katherine Johnstone Brinley [Wharton] Journal, April 26, May 30, and May 29, 1856, Historical Society of Pennsylvania.

29. A series of roughly fourteen letters written by Peggy Emlen to Sally Logan (1768–1771) has been preserved in the Wells Morris Collection, Box 1, Historical Society of Pennsylvania (see esp. May 3 and July 4, 1769, January 8, 1768).

30. The Sarah Alden Ripley Collection, the Arthur M. Schlesinger, Sr., Library, Radcliffe College, contains a number of Sarah Alden Ripley's letters to Mary Emerson. Most of these are undated, but they extend over a number of years and contain letters written both before and after Sarah's marriage.

31. See Sarah Alden Ripley to Mary Emerson, November 19, 1823. Sarah Alden Ripley routinely, and one must assume ritualistically, read Mary Emerson's letters to her infant daughter, Mary. Eleanor Parke Custis Lewis reported doing the same with Elizabeth Bordley Gibson's

letters, passim. Eunice Callender, Boston, to Sarah Ripley [Stearns], October 19, 1808.

32. Mary Black Couper to Sophie M. DuPont, March 5, 1832. The Clementina Smith–Sophie DuPont correspondence of 1,678 letters is in the Sophie DuPont Correspondence. The quotation is from Eliza Schlatter, Mount Holly, N.J., to Sophie DuPont, Brandywine, August 24, 1834. I am indebted to Anthony Wallace for informing me about this collection.

33. Mary Grew, Providence, R.I., to Isabel Howland, Sherwood, N.Y., April 27, 1892, Howland Correspondence, Sophia Smith Collection, Smith College.

34. Helene Deutsch, *Psychology of Women* (New York: Grune & Stratton, 1944), vol. 1, chaps. 1–3; Clara Thompson, *On Women,* ed. Maurice Green (New York: New American Library, 1971).

 52

From Against Our Will: Men, Women and Rape

SUSAN BROWNMILLER

WOMEN FIGHT BACK

On the fourteenth of November, 1642, *a young Virgine, daughter to Mr. Adam Fisher,* was hurrying along a country road in Devonshire *so darke that she could scarce discerne her hand* when the figure of *a Gentleman, Mr. Ralph Ashley,* a debased Cavalier, approached on horseback. Inspired by the *Devill* himself, this gentleman told the trusting maiden that he knew her father well and would be pleased to escort her home in safety, for there were lustful soldiers in those parts.

And then, Dear Reader, as if you didn't know what next, he galloped her off to a deserted spot and *went about to ravish her* while she fervently prayed, *Help, Lord, or I perish.*

Just then a *fearefull Comet burst out in the ayre* and *strucke* the rapacious Cavalier with *a streame of fire* so that *he fell downe staggering.*

According to some shepherds folding their flock who had witnessed the *Blazing Starre* from a distance, Mr. Ashley expired within the night, ranting and raving in terrible blasphemy about *that Round-headed whore.* Adam Fisher's daughter, aroused

from a graceful faint, found her Virginity intact and thanked her lucky starres and God Almighty.

The original text of this Puritan fable, a seventeenth-century propaganda pamphlet aimed at "those Cavaliers which esteem murder and rapine the chiefe Principalls of their religion," is housed today in the British Museum.

Three eventful centuries have passed since that fateful autumn night when Mr. Ralph Ashley attempted to ravish Mr. Adam Fisher's nameless daughter and was struck in his tracks by a bolt from the sky. Fewer of us these days, we would all agree, are young Virgines. The automobile has replaced the horse and blazing comets have proved fairly unpredictable after all. But the problem of rape, and how to deal with it, remains.

To a woman the definition of rape is fairly simple. A sexual invasion of the body by force, an incursion into the private, personal inner space without consent—in short, an internal assault from one of several avenues and by one of several methods—constitutes a deliberate violation of emotional, physical and rational integrity and is a hostile, degrading act of violence that deserves the name of rape.

Yet by tracing man's concept of rape as he defined it in his earliest laws, we now know with certainty that the criminal act he viewed with horror, and the deadly punishments he saw fit to apply, had little to do with an actual act of sexual violence that a woman's body might sustain. True, the law has come some distance since its beginnings when rape meant simply and conclusively the theft of a father's daughter's virginity, a specialized crime that damaged valuable goods before they could reach the matrimonial market, but modern legal perceptions of rape are rooted still in ancient male concepts of property.

From the earliest times, when men of one tribe freely raped women of another tribe to secure new wives, the laws of marriage and the laws of rape have been philosophically entwined, and even today it is largely impossible to separate them out. Man's historic desire to maintain sole, total and complete access to woman's vagina, as codified by his earliest laws of marriage, sprang from his need to be the sole physical instrument governing impregnation, progeny and inheritance rights. As man understood his male reality, it was perfectly lawful to capture and rape some other tribe's women, for what better way for his own tribe to increase? But it was unlawful, he felt, for the insult to be returned. The criminal act he viewed with horror and punished as rape was not sexual assault *per se*, but an act of unlawful possession, a trespass against his tribal right to control vaginal access to all women who belonged to him and his kin.

Since marriage, by law, was consummated in one manner only, by defloration of virginity with attendant ceremonial tokens, the act man came to construe as criminal rape was the illegal destruction of virginity outside a marriage contract of his making. Later, when he came to see his own definition as too narrow for the times, he broadened his criminal concept to cover the ruination of his wife's chastity as well, thus extending the law's concern to nonvirgins too. Although these legal origins have been buried in the morass of forgotten history, as the laws of rape continued to evolve they never shook free of their initial concept—that the violation was first and foremost a violation of *male* rights of possession, based on *male* requirements of virginity, chastity and consent to private access as the female bargain in the marriage contract (the underpinnings, as he enforced them, of man's economic estate).

To our modern way of thinking, these theoretical origins are peculiar and difficult to fully grasp. A huge disparity in thought—male logic versus female logic—affects perception of rape to this very day, confounding the analytic processes of some of the best legal minds. Today's young rapist has no thought of capturing a wife or securing an inheritance or estate. His is an act of impermanent conquest, not a practical approach to ownership and control. The economic advantage of rape is a forgotten concept. What remains is the basic male-female struggle, a hit-and-run attack, a brief expression of physical power, a conscious process of intimidation, a blunt, ugly sexual invasion with possible lasting psychological effects on all women.

When rape is placed where it truly belongs, within the context of modern criminal violence and not within the purview of ancient masculine codes, the crime retains its unique dimensions, falling midway between robbery and assault. It is, in one act, both a blow to the body and a blow to the mind, and a "taking" of sex through the use or threat of force.

Yet the differences between rape and an assault or a robbery are as distinctive as the obvious similarities. In a prosecutable case of assault, bodily damage to the victim is clearly evident. In a case of rape, the threat of force does not secure a tangible commodity as we understand the term, although sex traditionally has been viewed by men as "the female treasure"; more precisely, in rape the threat of force obtains a highly valued sexual service through temporary access to the victim's intimate parts, and the intent is not merely to "take," but to humiliate and degrade.

This, then, is the modern reality of rape as it is defined by twentieth-century practice. It is not, however, the reality of rape as it is defined by twentieth-century law.

In order for a sexual assault to qualify as felonious rape in an American courtroom, there must be "forcible penetration of the vagina by the penis, however slight." In other words, rape is defined by law as a heterosexual offense that is characterized by genital copulation. It is with this hallowed, restrictive definition, the *sine qua non* of rape prosecutions, that our argument begins.

That forcible genital copulation is the "worst possible" sex assault a person can sustain, that it deserves by far the severest punishment, equated in some states with the penalties for murder, while all other manner of sexual assaults are lumped together under the label of sodomy and draw lesser penalties by law, can only be seen as an outdated masculine concept that no longer applies to modern crime.

Sexual assault in our day and age is hardly restricted to forced genital copulation, nor is it exclusively a male-on-female offense. Tradition and biologic opportunity have rendered vaginal rape a particular political crime with a particular political history, but the invasion may occur through the mouth or the rectum as well. And while the penis may remain the rapist's favorite weapon, his prime instrument of vengeance, his triumphant display of power, it is not in fact his only tool. Sticks, bottles and even fingers are often substituted for the "natural" thing. And as men may invade women through other orifices, so, too, do they invade other men. Who is to say that the sexual humiliation suffered through forced oral or rectal penetration is a lesser violation of the personal, private inner space, a lesser injury to mind, spirit and sense of self?

All acts of sex forced on unwilling victims deserve to be treated in concept as equally grave offenses in the eyes of the law, for the avenue of penetration is less significant than the intent to degrade. Similarly, the gravity of the offense ought not be bound by the victim's gender. That the law must move in this direction seems clear.

A gender-free, non-activity-specific law governing all manner of sexual assaults would be but the first step toward legal reform. The law must rid itself of other, outdated masculine concepts as well.

· · ·

In cases of rape within a marriage, the law must take a philosophic leap of the greatest magnitude, for while the ancient concept of conjugal rights (female rights as well as male) might continue to have some validity in annulments and contested divorces—civil procedures conducted in courts of law—it must not be used as a shield to cover acts of force perpetrated by husbands on the bodies of their wives. There are those who believe that the current laws governing assault and battery are sufficient to deal with the cases of forcible rape in marriage, and those who take the more liberal stand that a sexual assault law might be applicable only to those men legally separated from their wives who return to "claim" their marital "right," but either of these solutions fails to come to grips with the basic violation.

Since the beginning of written history, criminal rape has been bound up with the common law of consent in marriage, and it is time, once and for all, to make a clean break. A sexual assault is an invasion of bodily integrity and a violation of freedom and self-determination wherever it happens to take place, in or out of the marriage bed. I recognize that it is easier to write these words than to draw up a workable legal provision, and I recognize the difficulties that juries will have in their deliberations when faced with a wife who accuses her husband of forcing her into copulation against her will, but the principle of bodily self-determination must be established without qualification, I think, if it is to become an inviolable principle on any level. . . .

The concept of consent rears its formidable head in the much debated laws of statutory rape, but here consent is construed in the opposite sense—not as

something that cannot be retracted, as in marriage, but as something that cannot be given. Since the thirteenth-century Statutes of Westminster, the law has sought to fix an arbitrary age below which an act of sexual intercourse with a female, with or without the use of force, is deemed a criminal offense that deserves severe punishment because the female is too young to know her own mind. Coexistent with these statutory rape laws, and somewhat contradictory to them, have been the laws governing criminal incest, sexual victimization of a child by a blood relation, where the imposition of legal penalties has been charitably lenient, to say the least—yet another indication of the theoretical concept that the child "belongs" to the father's estate. Under current legislation, which is by no means uniform, a conviction for statutory rape may draw a life sentence in many jurisdictions, yet a conviction for incest rarely carries more than a ten-year sentence, approximately the same maximum penalty that is fixed by law for sodomy offenses.

If protection of the bodily integrity of all children is to be genuinely reflected in the law, and not simply the protection of patriarchal interests, then the current division of offenses (statutory rape for outsiders; incest for members of the victim's family) must be erased. Retaining a fixed age of consent seems a necessary and humane measure for the protection of young girls and young boys alike, although it must be understood that any arbitrary age limit is at best a judicious compromise since sexual maturity and wisdom are not automatically conferred with the passage of time. Feminists who have applied themselves to this difficult question are in agreement that all children below the age of twelve deserve unqualified protection by a statutory age provision in sexual assault legislation, since that age is reasonably linked with the onset of puberty and awareness of sex, its biologic functions and repercussions. In line with the tradition of current statutory rape legislation, offenses committed against children below the age of twelve should carry the maximum penalty, normalized to twenty years. Recognizing that young persons above twelve and below sixteen remain particularly vulnerable to sexual coercion by adults who use a position of authority, rather than physical force, to achieve their aim (within the household or within an institution or a medical facility, to give three all-too-common examples), the law ought to be flexible enough to allow prosecutorial discretion in the handling of these cases under a more limited concept of "statutory sexual assault," with corresponding lesser penalties as the outer age limits are reached.

"Consent" has yet another role to play in a case of sexual assault. In reviewing the act, in seeking to determine whether or not a crime was committed, the concept of consent that is debated in court hinges on whether or not the victim offered sufficient resistance to the attack, whether or not her will was truly overcome by the use of force or the threat of bodily harm. The peculiar nature of sexual crimes of violence, as much as man's peculiar historic perception of their meaning, has always clouded the law's perception of consent.

It is accepted without question that robbery victims need not prove they resisted the robber, and it is never inferred that by handing over their money, they "consented" to the act and therefore the act was no crime. Indeed, police usually advise law-abiding citizens not to resist a robbery, but rather to wait it out patiently, report the offense to the proper authorities, and put the entire matter in the hands of the law. As a matter of fact, successful resistance to a robbery these days is considered heroic.

· · ·

Currently employed standards of resistance or consent *vis-à-vis* force or the threat of force have never been able to accurately gauge a victim's terror, since terror is a psychological reaction and not an objective standard that can be read on a behavior meter six months later in court, as jury acquittal rates plainly show. For this reason, feminists have argued that the special burden of proof that devolves on a rape victim, that she resisted "within reason," that her eventual compliance was no indication of tacit "consent," is patently unfair, since such standards are not applied in court to the behavior of victims in other kinds of violent crime. A jury should be permitted to weigh the word of a victimized complainant at face value, that is what it boils down to—no more or less a right than is granted to other victims under the law.

Not only is the victim's response during the act measured and weighed, her past sexual history is scrutinized under the theory that it relates to her "tendency to consent," or that it reflects on her credibility, her veracity, her predisposition to tell the truth or to lie. Or so the law says. As it works out in practice, juries presented with evidence concerning a woman's past sexual history make use of such information to form a moral judgment on her character, and here all the old myths of rape are brought into play, for the feeling persists that a virtuous woman either cannot get raped or does not get into situations that leave her open to assault. Thus the questions in the jury room become "Was she or wasn't she asking for it?"; "If she had been a decent woman, wouldn't she have fought to the death to defend her 'treasure'?"; and "Is this bimbo worth the ruination of a man's career and reputation?"

The crime of rape must be totally separated from all traditional concepts of chastity, for the very meaning of chastity presupposes that it is a woman's duty (but not a man's) to refrain from sex outside the matrimonial union. That sexual activity renders a woman "unchaste" is a totally male view of the female as *his* pure vessel. The phrase "prior chastity" as well as the concept must be stricken from the legal lexicon, along with "prosecutrix," as inflammatory and prejudicial to a complainant's case.

A history of sexual activity with many partners may be indicative of a female's healthy interest in sex, or it may be indicative of a chronic history of victimization and exploitation in which she could not assert her own inclinations; it may be indicative of a spirit of adventure, a spirit of rebellion, a spirit of curiosity, a spirit of joy or a spirit of defeat. Whatever the reasons, and there are many, prior consensual intercourse between a rape complainant and other partners of her choosing should not be scrutinized as an indicator of purity or impurity of mind or body, not in this day and age at any rate, and it has no place in jury room deliberation as to whether or not, in the specific instance in question, an act of forcible sex took place. Prior consensual intercourse between the complainant and *the defendant* does have some relevance, and such information probably should not be barred.

An overhaul of present laws and a fresh approach to sexual assault legislation must go hand in hand with a fresh approach to enforcing the law. The question of who interprets and who enforces the statutes is as important as the contents of the law itself. At present, female victims of sexual crimes of violence who seek legal justice must rely on a series of male authority figures whose masculine orientation, values and fears place them securely in the offender's camp.

. . .

That women have been excluded by tradition and design from all significant areas of law enforcement, from the police precinct, from the prosecutor's office, from the jury box and from the judge's bench, up to and including the appellate and supreme court jurisdictions, has created a double handicap for rape victims seeking justice under the laws of man's devise. And so it is not enough that the face of the law be changed to reflect the reality; the faces of those charged with the awesome responsibility of enforcing the law and securing justice must change as well.

I am convinced that the battle to achieve parity with men in the critical area of law enforcement will be the ultimate testing ground on which full equality for women will be won or lost. Law enforcement means quite literally the use of force when necessary, to maintain the social order, and force since the days of the rudimentary *lex talionis* has been a male prerogative because of size, weight, strength, biologic construction and *deliberate training,* training from which women have been barred by custom as stern as the law itself.

If in the past women had no choice but to let men be our lawful protectors, leaving to them not only the law but its enforcement, it would now seem to be an urgent priority to correct the imbalance. For things have come full circle. The biologic possibility that allows the threat and use of rape still exists, but our social contract has reached a point of sophistication whereby brute force matters less to the maintenance of law and order, or so I believe. I am not unaware that members of the police force in various cities have shown considerable reluctance to admit that size and strength may not be the prime factor in the making of an effective police officer, and they may be temporarily pardoned for sticking to outdated male values. New studies show quite conclusively that women police officers are as effective as

men in calming a disturbance and in making an arrest, and they accomplish their work in potentially violent situations without resorting to the unnecessary force that deserves its label, "police brutality."

I am not one to throw the word "revolutionary" around lightly, but full integration of our cities' police departments, and by full I mean fifty-fifty, no less, is a revolutionary goal of the utmost importance to women's rights. And if we are to continue to have armies, as I suspect we will for some time to come, then they, too, must be fully integrated, as well as our national guard, our state troopers, our local sheriffs' offices, our district attorneys' offices, our state prosecuting attorneys' offices—in short, the nation's entire lawful *power* structure (and I mean power in the physical sense) must be stripped of male dominance and control—if women are to cease being a colonized protectorate of men.

A system of criminal justice and forceful authority that genuinely works for the protection of women's rights, and most specifically the right not to be sexually assaulted by men, can become an efficient mechanism in the control of rape insofar as it brings offenders speedily to trial, presents the case for the complainant in the best possible light, and applies just penalties upon conviction. While I would not underestimate the beneficial effects of workable sex assault laws to "hold the line" and provide a positive deterrent, what feminists (and all right-thinking people) must look toward is the total eradication of rape, and not just an effective policy of containment.

A new approach to the law and to law enforcement can take us only part of the way. Turning over to women 50 percent of the power to enforce the law and maintain the order will be a major step toward eliminating *machismo.* However, the ideology of rape is aided by more than a system of lenient laws that serve to protect offenders and is abetted by more than the fiat of total male control over the lawful use of power. The ideology of rape is fueled by cultural values that are perpetuated at every level of our society, and nothing less than a frontal attack is needed to repel this cultural assault.

The theory of aggressive male domination over women as a natural right is so deeply embedded in our cultural value system that all recent attempts to expose it—in movies, television commercials or even in children's textbooks—have barely managed to scratch the surface. As I see it, the problem is not that polarized role playing (man as doer; woman as bystander) and exaggerated portrayals of the female body as passive sex object are simply "demeaning" to women's dignity and self-conception, or that such portrayals fail to provide positive role models for young girls, but that cultural sexism is a conscious form of female degradation designed to boost the male ego by offering "proof" of his native superiority (and of female inferiority) everywhere he looks.

. . .

Once we accept as basic truth that rape is not a crime of irrational, impulsive, uncontrollable lust, but is a deliberate, hostile, violent act of degradation and possession on the part of a would-be conqueror, designed to intimidate and inspire fear, we must look toward those elements in our culture that promote and propagandize these attitudes, which offer men, and in particular, impressionable, adolescent males, who form the potential raping population, the ideology and psychologic encouragement to commit their acts of aggression *without awareness, for the most part, that they have committed a punishable crime,* let alone a moral wrong. The myth of the heroic rapist that permeates false notions of masculinity, from the successful seducer to the man who "takes what he wants when he wants it," is inculcated in young boys from the time they first become aware that being a male means access to certain mysterious rites and privileges, including the right to buy a woman's body. When young men learn that females may be bought for a price, and that acts of sex command set prices, then how should they not also conclude that that which may be bought may also be taken without the civility of a monetary exchange?

. . .

A law that reflects the female reality and a social system that no longer shuts women out of its enforcement and does not promote a masculine ideology of rape will go a long way toward the elimination of crimes of sexual violence, but the last line of defense shall always be our female bodies and our female minds. In making rape a *speakable* crime, not a matter of shame, the women's movement has already fired the first retaliatory shots in a war as ancient as civilization. When, just a few years ago, we began to hold our speak-outs on rape, our conferences, borrowing a church meeting hall for an afternoon, renting a high-school auditorium and some classrooms for a weekend of workshops and discussion, the world out there, the world outside of radical feminism, thought it was all very funny.

"You're talking about *rape?* Incredible! A *political* crime against women? How is a sex crime political? You're actually having women give testimony about their own rapes and what happened to them afterwards, the police, the hospitals, the courts? Far out!" And then the nervous giggles that betray confusion, fear and shame disappeared and in their place was the dim recognition that in daring to speak the unspoken, women had uncovered yet another part of our oppression, perhaps the central key: historic physical repression, a conscious process of intimidation, guilt and fear.

Within two years the world out there had stopped laughing, and the movement had progressed beyond the organizational forms of speak-outs and conferences, our internal consciousness-raising, to community outreach programs that were imaginative, original and unprecedented: rape crisis centers with a telephone hot line staffed twenty-four hours a day to provide counseling, procedural information and sisterly solidarity to recent rape victims and even to those whose assault had taken place years ago but who never had the chance to talk it out with other women and release their suppressed rage; rape legislation study groups to work up model codes based on a fresh approach to the law and to work with legislators to get new laws adopted; anti-rape projects in conjunction with the emergency ward of a city hospital, in close association with policewomen staffing newly formed sex crime analysis squads and investigative units. With pamphlets, newsletters, bumper stickers, "Wanted" posters, combative slogans—"STOP RAPE"; "WAR—WOMEN AGAINST RAPE"; "SMASH SEXISM, DISARM RAPISTS!"—and with classes in self-defense, women turned around and seized the offensive.

The wonder of all this female activity, decentralized grass-roots organizations and programs that sprung up independently in places like Seattle, Indianapolis, Ann Arbor, Toronto, and Boulder,

Colorado, is that none of it had been predicted, encouraged, or faintly suggested by men anywhere in their stern rules of caution, their friendly advice, their fatherly solicitude in more than five thousand years of written history. That women should *organize* to combat rape was a women's movement invention.

Men are not unmindful of the rape problem. To the contrary, their paternalistic codes reserved the harshest penalties for a violation of their property. But given an approach to rape that saw the crime as an illegal encroachment by an unlicensed intruder, a stranger come into their midst, the advice they gave (and still try to give) was all of one piece: a set of rules and regulations designed to keep their property penned in, much as a sheepherder might try to keep his flock protected from an outlaw rustler by taking precautions against their straying too far from the fold. By seeing the rapist always as a stranger, never as one of their own, and by viewing the female as a careless, dumb creature with an unfortunate tendency to stray, they exhorted, admonished and warned the female to hide herself from male eyes as much as possible. In short, they told her not to claim the privileges they reserved for themselves. Such advice—well intentioned, solicitous and genuinely concerned—succeeded only in further aggravating the problem, for the message they gave was to live a life of fear, and to it they appended the dire warning that the woman who did not follow the rules must be held responsible for her own violation.

. . .

A fairly decent article on rape in the March, 1974, issue of *The Reader's Digest* was written by two men who felt obliged to warn,

Don't broadcast the fact that you live alone or with another woman. List only your last name and initial on the mailbox and in the phone book. Before entering your car, check to see if anyone is hiding on the rear seat or on the rear floor. If you're alone in a car, keep the doors locked and the windows rolled up. If you think someone is following you . . . do not go directly home if there is no adult male there. Possible weapons are a hatpin, corkscrew, pen, keys, umbrella. If no weapons are available, fight back physically *only* if you feel you can do so with telling effect.

What immediately pops into mind after reading [this] advice is the old-time stand-up comedian's favorite figure of ridicule, the hysterical old maid armed with hatpin and umbrella who looks under the bed each night before retiring. Long a laughable stereotype of sexual repression, it now appears that the crazy old lady was a pioneer of sound mind after all.

But the negative value of this sort of advice, I'm afraid, far outweighs the positive. What it tells us, implicitly and explicitly, is:

1. A woman alone probably won't be able to defend herself. Another woman who might possibly come to her aid will be of no use whatsoever.

2. Despite the fact that it is men who are the rapists, a woman's ultimate security lies in being accompanied by men at all times.

3. A woman who claims to value her sexual integrity cannot expect the same amount of freedom and independence that men routinely enjoy. Even a small pleasure like taking a spin in an automobile with the windows open is dangerous, reckless behavior.

4. In the exercise of rational caution, a woman should engage in an amazing amount of pretense. She should pretend she has a male protector even if she hasn't. She should deny or obscure her personal identity, life-style and independence, and function on a sustained level of suspicion that approaches a clinical definition of paranoia.

Of course I think all people, female and male, child and adult, must be alert and on guard against the warning signs of criminal violence and should take care in potentially hazardous situations, such as a dark, unfamiliar street at night, or an unexpected knock on the door, but to impose a special burden of caution on women is no solution at all. There can be no private solutions to the problem of rape. A woman who follows this sort of special cautionary advice to the letter and thinks she is acting in society's interest—or even in her own personal interest—is deluding herself rather sadly. While the risk to one potential victim might be slightly diminished (and I even doubt this, since I have known of nuns who were raped within walled convents), not only does the number of potential rapists on the loose remain constant, but the ultimate effect of rape upon the woman's mental and emotional health has been accomplished *even without the act*. For to accept a special burden of self-protection is to reinforce the concept that women must live and move about in fear and can never expect to achieve the personal freedom, independence and self-assurance of men.

That's what rape is all about, isn't it? And a possible deep-down reason why even the best of our concerned, well-meaning men run to stereotypic warnings when they seek to grapple with the problem of rape deterrence is that they *prefer* to see rape as a woman's problem, rather than as a societal problem resulting from a distorted masculine philosophy of aggression. For when men raise the spectre of the unknown rapist, they refuse to take psychologic responsibility for the nature of his act.

We know, or at least the statistics tell us, that no more than half of all reported rapes are the work of strangers, and in the hidden statistics, those four out of five rapes that go unreported, the percent committed by total strangers is probably lower. The man who jumps out of the alley or crawls through the window is the man who, if caught, will be called "the rapist" by his fellow men. But the known man who presses his advantage, who uses his position of authority, who forces his attentions (fine Victorian phrase), who will not take "No" for an answer, who assumes that sexual access is his right-of-way and physical aggression his right-on expression of masculinity, conquest and power is no less of a rapist—yet the chance that this man will be brought to justice, even under the best of circumstances, is comparatively small.

I am of the opinion that the most perfect rape laws in the land, strictly enforced by the best concerned citizens, will not be enough to stop rape. Obvious offenders will be punished, and that in itself will be a significant change, but the huge gray area of sexual exploitation, of women who are psychologically coerced into acts of intercourse they do not desire because they do not have the wherewithal to physically, or even psychologically, resist, will remain a problem beyond any possible solution of criminal justice. It would be deceitful to claim that the murky gray area of male sexual aggression and female passivity and submission can ever be made

amenable to legal divination—nor should it be, in the final analysis. Nor should a feminist advocate to her sisters that the best option in a threatening, unpleasant situation is to endure the insult and later take her case to the courts.

• • •

Prohibitions against a fighting female go back to the Bible. In one of the more curious passages in Deuteronomy it is instructed that when two men are fighting and the wife of one seeks to come to his aid and "drag her husband clear of his opponent, if she puts out her hand and catches hold of the man's genitals, you shall cut off her hand and show her no mercy." When the patriarchs wrote the law, it would seem, they were painfully cognizant of woman's one natural advantage in combat and were determined to erase it from her memory.

Man's written law evolved from a rudimentary system of retaliatory force, a system to which women were not particularly well adapted to begin with, and from which women were deliberately excluded, ostensibly for our own protection, as time went by. Combat has been such a traditional, exclusionary province of man that the very idea of a fighting woman often brings laughter, distaste or disbelief and the opinion that it must be "unnatural." In a confusion partially of their own making, local police precincts put out contradictory messages: they "unfound" a rape case because, by the rule of their own male logic, the woman did not show normal resistance; they report on an especially brutal rape case and announce to the press that the multiple stab wounds were the work of an assailant who was enraged because the woman resisted.

Unthinkingly cruel, because it is deceptive, is the confidential advice given from men to women (it appears in *The Reader's Digest* article), or even from women to women in some feminist literature, that a sharp kick to the groin or a thumb in the eye will work miracles. Such advice is often accompanied by a diagram in which the vulnerable points of the human anatomy are clearly marked—as if the mere knowledge of these pressure spots can translate itself into devastating action. It is true that this knowledge has been deliberately obscured or withheld from us in the past, but mere knowledge is not enough. What women need is systematic training in self-defense that begins in childhood, so that the inhibition resulting from the prohibition may be overcome.

It would be decidedly less than honest if at this juncture I did not admit that my researches for this book included a three-month training program in ju-jitsu and karate, three nights a week, two and a half hours a night, that ended summarily one evening when I crashed to the mat and broke my collarbone. I lost one month of writing and the perfect symmetry of my clavicular structure, but I gained a new identification with the New York Mets' injury list, a recognition that age thirty-eight is not the most propitious time in life *to begin* to learn how to kick and hit and break a stranglehold, and a new and totally surprising awareness of my body's potential to inflict real damage. I learned I had natural weapons that I didn't know I possessed, like elbows and knees. I learned how to kick backward as well as forward. I learned how to fight dirty, and I learned that I loved it.

Most surprising to me, I think, was the recognition that these basic aggressive movements, the sudden twists, jabs and punches that were so foreign to my experience and ladylike existence, were the stuff that all little boys grow up learning, that boy kids are applauded for mastering while girl kids are put in fresh white pinafores and patent-leather Mary Janes and told not to muss them up. And did that early difference in rearing ever raise its draconic head! At the start of our lessons our Japanese instructor freely invited all the women in the class, one by one, to punch him in the chest. It was not a foolhardy invitation, for we discovered that the inhibition against hitting was so strong in each of us that on the first try none of us could make physical contact. Indeed, the inhibition against striking out proved to be a greater hindrance to our becoming fighting women than our pathetic underdeveloped muscles. (Improvement in both departments was amazingly swift.)

Not surprisingly, the men in our class did not share our inhibitions in the slightest. Aggressive physical grappling was part of their heritage, not ours. And yet, and yet . . . we women discovered in wonderment that as we learned to place our kicks and jabs with precision we were actually able to inspire fear in the men. We *could* hurt them, we learned to our astonishment, and hurt them hard at the core of their sexual being—if we broke that Biblical injunction.

Is it possible that there is some sort of metaphysical justice in the anatomical fact that the male sex organ, which has been misused from time immemorial as a weapon of terror against women, should have at its root an awkward place of painful vulnerability? Acutely conscious of their susceptibility to damage, men have protected their testicles throughout history with armor, supports and forbidding codes of "clean," above-the-belt fighting. A gentleman's agreement is understandable—among gentlemen. When women are threatened, as I learned in my self-defense class, "Kick him in the balls, it's your best maneuver." How strange it was to hear for the first time in my life that women could fight back, *should* fight back and make full use of a natural advantage; that it is *in our interest* to know how to do it. How strange it was to understand with the full force of unexpected revelation that male allusions to psychological defeat, particularly at the hands of a woman, were couched in phrases like emasculation, castration and ball-breaking because of that very special physical vulnerability.

Fighting back. On a multiplicity of levels, that is the activity we must engage in, together, if we—women—are to redress the imbalance and rid ourselves and men of the ideology of rape.

Rape can be eradicated, not merely controlled or avoided on an individual basis, but the approach must be long-range and cooperative, and must have the understanding and good will of many men as well as women.

My purpose in this book has been to give rape its history. Now we must deny it a future.

[1975]

 53

What Became of God the Mother? Conflicting Images of God in Early Christianity

ELAINE H. PAGELS

Unlike many of his contemporaries among the deities of the ancient Near East, the God of Israel shares his power with no female divinity, nor is he the divine Husband or Lover of any.[1] He scarcely can be characterized in any but masculine epithets:

King, Lord, Master, Judge, and Father.[2] Indeed, the absence of feminine symbolism of God marks Judaism, Christianity, and Islam in striking contrast to the world's other religious traditions, whether in Egypt, Babylonia, Greece, and Rome or Africa, Polynesia, India, and North America. Jewish, Christian, and Islamic theologians, however, are quick to point out that God is not to be considered in sexual terms at all. Yet the actual language they use daily in worship and prayer conveys a different message and gives the distinct impression that God is thought of in exclusively *masculine* terms. And while it is true that Catholics revere Mary as the mother of Jesus, she cannot be identified as divine in her own right: if she is "mother of God," she is not "God the Mother" on an equal footing with God the Father.

Christianity, of course, added the trinitarian terms to the Jewish description of God. And yet of the three divine "Persons," two—the Father and Son—are described in masculine terms, and the third—the Spirit—suggests the sexlessness of the Greek neuter term *pneuma*. This is not merely a subjective impression. Whoever investigates the early development of Christianity—the field called "patristics," that is, study of "the fathers of the church"—may not be surprised by the passage that concludes the recently discovered, secret *Gospel of Thomas:* "Simon Peter said to them [the disciples]: Let Mary be excluded from among us, for she is a woman, and not worthy of Life. Jesus said: Behold I will take Mary, and make her a male, so that she may become a living spirit, resembling you males. For I tell you truly, that every female who makes herself male will enter the Kingdom of Heaven."[3] Strange as it sounds, this only states explicitly what religious rhetoric often assumes: that the men form the legitimate body of the community, while women will be allowed to participate only insofar as their own identity is denied and assimilated to that of the men.

Further exploration of the texts which include this *Gospel*—written on papyrus, hidden in large clay jars nearly 1,600 years ago—has identified them as Jewish and Christian gnostic works which were attacked and condemned as "heretical" as early as A.D. 100–150. What distinguishes these "heterodox" texts from those that are called "orthodox" is at least partially clear: they abound in feminine symbolism that is applied, in particular, to

God. Although one might expect, then, that they would recall the archaic pagan traditions of the Mother Goddess, their language is to the contrary specifically Christian, unmistakably related to a Jewish heritage. Thus we can see that certain gnostic Christians diverged even more radically from the Jewish tradition than the early Christians who described God as the "three Persons" or the Trinity. For instead of a monistic and masculine God, certain of these texts describe God as a dyadic being, who consists of *both* masculine and feminine elements. One such group of texts, for example, claims to have received a secret tradition from Jesus through James, and significantly, through Mary Magdalene.[4] Members of this group offer prayer to *both* the divine Father and Mother: "From Thee, Father, and through Thee, Mother, the two immortal names, Parents of the divine being, and thou, dweller in heaven, mankind of the mighty name. . . ."[5] Other texts indicate that their authors had pondered the nature of the beings to whom a single, masculine God proposed, "Let us make mankind in our image, after our likeness" (Gen. 1:26). Since the Genesis account goes on to say that mankind was created "male and female" (1:27), some concluded, apparently, that the God in whose image we are created likewise must be both masculine and feminine—both Father and Mother.

The characterization of the divine Mother in these sources is not simple since the texts themselves are extraordinarily diverse. Nevertheless, three primary characterizations merge. First, a certain poet and teacher, Valentinus, begins with the premise that God is essentially indescribable. And yet he suggests that the divine can be imagined as a Dyad consisting of two elements: one he calls the Ineffable, the Source, the Primal Father; the other, the Silence, the Mother of all things.[6] Although we might question Valentinus's reasoning that Silence is the appropriate complement of what is Ineffable, his equation of the former with the feminine and the latter with the masculine may be traced to the grammatical gender of the Greek words. Followers of Valentinus invoke this feminine power, whom they also call "Grace" (in Greek, the feminine term *charis*), in their own private celebration of the Christian eucharist: they call her "divine, eternal Grace, She who is before all things."[7] At other times they pray to her for protection as the

Mother, "Thou enthroned with God, eternal, mystical Silence."[8] Marcus, a disciple of Valentinus, contends that "when Moses began his account of creation, he mentioned the Mother of all things at the very beginning, when he said, 'In the beginning God created the heavens and the earth,'"[9] for the word "beginning" (in Greek, the feminine *arche*) refers to the divine Mother, the source of the cosmic elements. When they describe God in this way different gnostic writers have different interpretations. Some maintain that the divine is to be considered masculo-feminine—the "great male-female power." Others insist that the terms are meant only as metaphors—for, in reality, the divine is *neither* masculine nor feminine. A third group suggests that one can describe the Source of all things in *either* masculine or feminine terms, depending on which aspect one intends to stress.[10] Proponents of these diverse views agree, however, that the divine is to be understood as consisting of a harmonious, dynamic relationship of opposites—a concept that may be akin to the eastern view of *yin* and *yang* but remains antithetical to orthodox Judaism and Christianity.

A second characterization of the divine Mother describes her as Holy Spirit. One source, the *Secret Book of John,* for example, relates how John, the brother of James, went out after the crucifixion with "great grief," and had a mystical vision of the Trinity: "As I was grieving . . . the heavens were opened, and the whole creation shone with an unearthly light, and the universe was shaken. I was afraid . . . and behold . . . a unity in three forms appeared to me, and I marvelled: how can a unity have three forms?" To John's question the vision answers: "It said to me, 'John, John, why do you doubt, or why do you fear? . . . I am the One who is with you always: I am the Father; I am the Mother; I am the Son.'"[11] John's interpretation of the Trinity—as Father, Mother, and Son—may not at first seem shocking but is perhaps the more natural and spontaneous interpretation. Where the Greek terminology for the Trinity, which includes the neuter term for spirit (*pneuma*), virtually requires that the third "Person" of the Trinity be asexual, the author of the *Secret Book* looks to the Hebrew term for spirit, *ruah*—a feminine word. He thus concludes, logically enough, that the feminine "Person" conjoined with Father and Son must be the Mother! Indeed,

the text goes on to describe the Spirit as Mother: ". . . the image of the invisible virginal perfect spirit. . . . She became the mother of the all, for she existed before them all, the mother-father [matropater]."[12] This same author, therefore, alters Genesis 1:2 ("the Spirit of God moved upon the face of the deep") to say "the Mother then was moved. . . ."[13] The secret *Gospel to the Hebrews* likewise has Jesus speak of "my Mother, the Spirit."[14] And in the *Gospel of Thomas,* Jesus contrasts his earthly parents, Mary and Joseph, with his divine Father—the Father of Truth—and his divine Mother, the Holy Spirit. The author interprets a puzzling saying of Jesus in the New Testament ("whoever does not hate his father and mother is not worthy of me") by adding: "Whoever does not love his father and mother in my way cannot be my disciple; for my [earthly] mother gave me death but my true Mother gave me the Life."[15] Another secret gnostic gospel, the *Gospel of Phillip,* declares that whoever becomes a Christian "gains both a father and a mother."[16] The author refers explicitly to the feminine Hebrew term to describe the Spirit as "Mother of many."[17]

If these sources suggest that the Spirit constitutes the maternal element of the Trinity, the *Gospel of Phillip* makes an equally radical suggestion concerning the doctrine that later developed as the virgin birth. Here again the Spirit is praised as both Mother and Virgin, the counterpart—and consort—of the Heavenly Father: "If I may utter a mystery, the Father and the all united with the Virgin who came down,"[18] that is, with the Holy Spirit. Yet because this process is to be understood symbolically, and not literally, the Spirit remains a virgin! The author explains that "for this reason, Christ was 'born of a virgin'"—that is, of the Spirit, his divine Mother. But the author ridicules those "literal-minded" Christians who mistakenly refer the virgin birth to Mary, Jesus' earthly mother, as if she conceived apart from Joseph: "Such persons do not know what they are saying; for when did a female ever impregnate a female?"[19] Instead, he argues, virgin birth refers to the mysterious union of the two divine powers, the Father of the All with the Holy Spirit.

Besides the eternal, mystical Silence, and besides the Holy Spirit, certain gnostics suggest a third characterization of the divine Mother as Wisdom.

Here again the Greek feminine term for wisdom, *sophia*, like the term for spirit, *ruah*, translates a Hebrew feminine term, *hokhmah*. Early interpreters had pondered the meaning of certain biblical passages, for example, Proverbs: "God made the world in Wisdom." And they wondered if Wisdom could be the feminine power in which God's creation is "conceived"? In such passages, at any rate, Wisdom bears two connotations: first, she bestows the Spirit that makes mankind wise; second, she is a creative power. One gnostic source calls her the "first universal creator";[20] another says that God the Father was speaking to her when he proposed to "make mankind in our image."[21] The *Great Announcement*, a mystical writing, explains the Genesis account in the following terms: ". . . One Power that is above and below, self-generating, self-discovering, its own mother; its own father; its own sister; its own son: Father, Mother, unity, Root of all things."[22] The same author explains the mystical meaning of the Garden of Eden as a symbol of the womb: "Scripture teaches us that this is what is meant when Isaiah says, 'I am he that formed thee in thy mother's womb' [Isaiah 44:2]. The Garden of Eden, then, is Moses' symbolic term for the womb, and Eden the placenta, and the river which comes out of Eden the navel, which nourishes the fetus. . . ."[23] This teacher claims that the Exodus, consequently, symbolizes the exodus from the womb, "and the crossing of the Red Sea, they say, refers to the blood." Evidence for this view, he adds, comes directly from "the cry of the newborn," a spontaneous cry of praise for "the glory of the primal being, in which all the powers above are in harmonious embrace."[24]

The introduction of such symbolism in gnostic texts clearly bears implications for the understanding of human nature. The *Great Announcement* for example, having described the Source as a masculo-feminine being, a "bisexual Power," goes on to say that "what came into being from the Power, that is, humanity, being one, is found to be two: a male-female being that bears the female within it."[25] This refers to the story of Eve's "birth" out of Adam's side (so that Adam, being one, is "discovered to be two," an androgyne who "bears the female within him"). Yet this reference to the creation story of Genesis 2—an account which inverts the biological birth process, and so effectively denies the creative

function of the female—proves to be unusual in gnostic sources. More often, such sources refer instead to the first creation account in Genesis 1:26–27. ("And God said, let us make mankind in Our image, after Our image and likeness . . . in the image of God he created him: male and female he created them"). Rabbis in Talmudic times knew a Greek version of the passage, one that suggested to Rabbi Samuel bar Nahman that "when the Holy One . . . first created mankind, he created him with two faces, two sets of genitals, four arms, and legs, back to back: Then he split Adam in two, and made two backs, one on each side."[26] Some Jewish teachers (perhaps influenced by the story in Plato's *Symposium*) had suggested that Genesis 1:26–27 narrates an androgynous creation—an idea that gnostics adopted and developed. Marcus (whose prayer to the Mother is given above) not only concludes from this account that God is dyadic ("Let *us* make mankind"), but also that "mankind, which was formed according to the image and likeness of God [Father and Mother] was masculo-feminine."[27] And his contemporary, Theodotus, explains, "the saying that Adam was created 'male and female' means that the male and female elements together constitute the finest production of the Mother, Wisdom."[28] We can see, then, that the gnostic sources which describe God in both masculine and feminine terms often give a similar description of human nature as a dyadic entity, consisting of two equal male and female components.

All the texts cited above—secret "gospels," revelations, mystical teachings—are among those rejected from the select list of twenty-six that comprise the "New Testament" collection. As these and other writings were sorted and judged by various Christian communities, every one of these texts which gnostic groups revered and shared was rejected from the canonical collection as "heterodox" by those who called themselves "orthodox" (literally, straight-thinking) Christians. By the time this process was concluded, probably as late as the year A.D. 200, virtually all the feminine imagery for God (along with any suggestion of an androgynous human creation) had disappeared from "orthodox" Christian tradition.

What is the reason for this wholesale rejection? The gnostics themselves asked this question of their "orthodox" attackers and pondered it among themselves. Some concluded that the God of Israel himself initiated the polemics against gnostic teaching which his followers carried out in his name. They argued that he was a derivative, merely instrumental power, whom the divine Mother had created to administer the universe, but who remained ignorant of the power of Wisdom, his own Mother: "They say that the creator believed that he created everything by himself, but that, in reality, he had made them because his Mother, Wisdom, infused him with energy, and had given him her ideas. But he was unaware that the ideas he used came from her: He was even ignorant of his own Mother."[29] Followers of Valentinus suggested that the Mother herself encouraged the God of Israel to think that he was acting autonomously in creating the world; but, as one teacher adds, "It was because he was foolish and ignorant of his Mother that he said, 'I am God; there is none beside me.'"[30] Others attribute to him the more sinister motive of jealousy, among them the *Secret Book of John*: "He said, 'I am a jealous God, and you shall have no other God before me,' already indicating that another god does exist. For if there were no other god, of whom would he be jealous? Then the Mother began to be distressed. . . ."[31] A third gnostic teacher describes the Lord's shock, terror, and anxiety "when he discovered that he was not the God of the universe." Gradually his shock and fear gave way to wonder, and finally he came to welcome the teaching of Wisdom. The gnostic teacher concluded: "This is the meaning of the saying, 'The fear of the Lord is the beginning of wisdom.'"[32]

All of these are, of course, mythical explanations. To look for the actual, historical reasons why these gnostic writings were suppressed is an extremely difficult proposition, for it raises the much larger question of how (i.e., by what means and what criteria) certain ideas, including those expressed in the texts cited above, came to be classified as heretical and others as orthodox by the beginning of the third century. Although the research is still in its early stages, and this question is far from being solved, we may find one clue if we ask whether these secret groups derived any practical, social consequences from their conception of God—and of mankind—that included the feminine element? Here again, the

answer is yes and can be found in the orthodox texts themselves. Irenaeus, an orthodox bishop, for example, notes with dismay that women in particular are attracted to heretical groups—especially to Marcus's circle, in which prayers are offered to the Mother in her aspects as Silence, Grace, and Wisdom; women priests serve the eucharist together with men; and women also speak as prophets, uttering to the whole community what "the Spirit" reveals to them.[33] Professing himself to be at a loss to understand the attraction that Marcus's group holds, he offers only one explanation: that Marcus himself is a diabolically successful seducer, a magician who compounds special aphrodisiacs to "deceive, victimize, and defile" these "many foolish women!" Whether his accusation has any factual basis is difficult, probably impossible, to ascertain. Nevertheless, the historian notes that accusations of sexual license are a stock-in-trade of polemical arguments.[34] The bishop refuses to admit the possibility that the group might attract Christians—especially women—for sound and comprehensible reasons. While expressing his own moral outrage, Tertullian, another "father of the church," reveals his fundamental desire to keep women out of religion: "These heretical women—how audacious they are! They have no modesty: they are bold enough to teach, to engage in argument, to enact exorcisms, to undertake cures, and, it may be, even to baptize!"[35] Tertullian directs yet another attack against "that viper"—a woman teacher who led a congregation in North Africa.[36] Marcion had, in fact, scandalized his "orthodox" contemporaries by appointing women on an equal basis with men as priests and bishops among his congregations.[37] The teacher Marcillina also traveled to Rome to represent the Carpocratian group, an esoteric circle that claimed to have received secret teaching from Mary, Salome, and Martha.[38] And among the Montanists, a radical prophetic circle, the prophet Philumene was reputed to have hired a male secretary to transcribe her inspired oracles.[39]

Other secret texts, such as the *Gospel of Mary Magdalene* and the *Wisdom of Faith,* suggest that the activity of such women leaders challenged and therefore was challenged by the orthodox communities who regarded Peter as their spokesman. The *Gospel of Mary* relates that Mary tried to encourage the disciples after the crucifixion and to tell them what the Lord had told her privately. Peter, furious at the suggestion, asks, "Did he then talk secretly with a woman, instead of to us? Are we to go and learn from *her* now? Did he love her more than us?" Distressed at his rage, Mary then asks Peter: "What do you think? Do you think I made this up in my heart? Do you think I am lying about the Lord?" Levi breaks in at this point to mediate the dispute: "Peter, you are always irascible. You object to the woman as our enemies do. Surely the Lord knew her very well, and indeed, he loved her more than us. . . ." Then he and the others invite Mary to teach them what she knows.[40] Another argument between Peter and Mary occurs in *Wisdom of Faith*. Peter complains that Mary is dominating the conversation, even to the point of displacing the rightful priority of Peter himself and his brethren; he urges Jesus to silence her—and is quickly rebuked. Later, however, Mary admits to Jesus that she hardly dares to speak freely with him, because "Peter makes me hesitate: I am afraid of him, because he hates the female race." Jesus replies, that whoever receives inspiration from the Spirit is divinely ordained to speak, whether man or woman.[41]

As these texts suggest, then, women were considered equal to men, they were revered as prophets, and they acted as teachers, traveling evangelists, healers, priests, and even bishops. In some of these groups they played leading roles and were *excluded* from them in the orthodox churches, at least by A.D. 150–200. Is it possible, then, that the recognition of the feminine element in God and the recognition of mankind as a male and female entity bore within it the explosive social possibility of women acting on an equal basis with men in positions of authority and leadership? If this were true it might lead to the conclusion that these gnostic groups, together with their conception of God and human nature, were suppressed only because of their positive attitude toward women. But such a conclusion would be a mistake—a hasty and simplistic reading of the evidence. In the first place, orthodox Christian doctrine is far from wholly negative in its attitude toward women. Second, many other elements of the gnostic sources diverge in fundamental ways from what came to be accepted as orthodox Christian

teaching. To examine this process in detail would require a much more extensive discussion than is possible here. Nevertheless the evidence does indicate that two very different patterns of sexual attitudes emerged in orthodox and gnostic circles. In simplest form, gnostic theologians correlate their description of God in both masculine and feminine terms with a complementary description of human nature. Most often they refer to the creation account of Genesis 1, which suggests an equal (or even androgynous) creation of mankind. This conception carries the principle of equality between men and women into the practical social and political structures of gnostic communities. The orthodox pattern is strikingly different: it describes God in exclusively masculine terms, and often uses Genesis 2 to describe how Eve was created from Adam and for his fulfillment. Like the gnostic view, the orthodox also translates into sociological practice: by the late second century, orthodox Christians came to accept the domination of men over women as the proper, God-given order—not only for the humam race, but also for the Christian churches. This correlation between theology, anthropology, and sociology is not lost on the apostle Paul. In his letter to the disorderly Corinthian community, he reminds them of a divinely ordained chain of authority: as God has authority over Christ, so the man has authority over the woman, argues Paul citing Genesis 2: "The man is the image and glory of God, but the woman is the glory of man. For man is not from woman, but woman from man; and besides, the man was not created for the woman's sake, but the woman for the sake of the man."[42] Here the three elements of the orthodox pattern are welded into one simple argument: the description of God corresponds to a description of human nature which authorizes the social pattern of male domination.

A striking exception to this orthodox pattern occurs in the writings of one revered "father of the church," Clement of Alexandria. Clement identifies himself as orthodox, although he knows members of gnostic groups and their writings well; some scholars suggest that he was himself a gnostic initiate. Yet his own works demonstrate how all three elements of what we have called the "gnostic pattern" could be worked into fully "orthodox" teaching. First, Clement characterizes God not only in masculine but also in feminine terms: "The Word is everything to the child, both father and mother, teacher and nurse. . . . The nutriment is the milk of the Father . . . and the Word alone supplies us children with the milk of love, and only those who suck at this breast are truly happy. . . . For this reason seeking is called sucking; to those infants who seek the Word, the Father's loving breasts supply milk."[43] Second, in describing human nature, he insists that "men and women share equally in perfection, and are to receive the same instruction and discipline. For the name 'humanity' is common to both men and women; and for us 'in Christ there is neither male nor female.'"[44] Even in considering the active participation of women with men in the Christian community Clement offers a list—unique in orthodox tradition—of women whose achievements he admires. They range from ancient examples, like Judith, the assassin who destroyed Israel's enemy, to Queen Esther, who rescued her people from genocide, as well as others who took radical political stands. He speaks of Arignole the historian, of Themisto the Epicurean philosopher, and of many other women philosophers including two who studied with Plato and one trained by Socrates. Indeed, he cannot contain his praise: "What shall I say? Did not Theano the Pythagoran make such progress in philosophy than when a man, staring at her, said, 'Your arm is beautiful,' she replied, 'Yes, but it is not on public display.'"[45] Clement concludes his list with famous women poets and painters.

If the work of Clement, who taught in Egypt before the lines of orthodoxy and heresy were rigidly drawn (ca. A.D. 160–180) demonstrates how gnostic principles could be incorporated even into orthodox Christian teaching, the majority of communities in the western empire headed by Rome did not follow his example. By the year A.D. 200, Roman Christians endorsed as "canonical" the pseudo-Pauline letter to Timothy, which interpreted Paul's views: "Let a woman learn in silence with full submissiveness. I do not allow any woman to teach or to exercise authority over a man; she is to remain silent, *for* [note Gen. 2!] Adam was formed first, then Eve and furthermore, Adam was not deceived, but the woman was utterly seduced

and came into sin. . . ."[46] How are we to account for this irreversible development? The question deserves investigation which this discussion can only initiate. For example, one would need to examine how (and for what reasons) the zealously patriarchal traditions of Israel were adopted by the Roman (and other) Christian communities. Further research might disclose how social and cultural forces converged to suppress feminine symbolism—and women's participation—from western Christian tradition. Given such research, the history of Christianity never could be told in the same way again.

[1976]

NOTES

1. Where the God of Israel is characterized as husband and lover in the Old Testament (OT), his spouse is described as the community of Israel (i.e., Isa. 50:1, 54:1–8; Jer. 2: 2–3, 20–25, 3:1–20; Hos. 1–4, 14) or as the land of Israel (cf. Isa. 62:1–5).
2. One may note several exceptions to this rule: Deut. 32: 11; Hos. 11:1; Isa. 66:12 ff; Num. 11:12.
3. *The Gospel according to Thomas* (hereafter cited as *ET*), ed. A. Guillaumount, H. Ch. Puech, G. Quispel, W. Till, Yassah 'Abd-al-Masih (London: Collins, 1959), logion 113–114.
4. Hippolytus, *Refutationis Omnium Haeresium* (hereafter cited as *Ref*), ed. L. Dunker, F. Schneidewin (Göttingen, 1859), 5.7.
5. *Ref*, 5.6.
6. Irenaeus, *Adversus Haereses* (hereafter cited as *AH*), ed. W. W. Harvey (Cambridge, 1857), 1.11.1.
7. Ibid., 1.13.2.
8. Ibid., 1.13.6.
9. Ibid., 1.18.2.
10. Ibid., 1.11.5.—21.1, 3; *Ref*, 6.29.
11. *Apocryphon Johannis* (hereafter cited as *AJ*), ed. S. Giversen (Copenhagen: Prostant Apud Munksgaard, 1963), 47.20–48.14.
12. *AJ*, 52.34–53.6.
13. Ibid., 61.13–14.
14. Origen, *Commentary on John*, 2.12; *Hom. on Jeremiah*, 15.4.
15. *ET*, 101. The text of this passage is badly damaged; I follow here the reconstruction of G. MacRae of the Harvard Divinity School.
16. *L'Evangile selon Phillipe* (hereafter cited as *EP*), ed. J. E. Ménard (Leiden: Brill, 1967), logion 6.
17. *EP*, logion 36.
18. Ibid., logion 82.
19. Ibid., logion 17.
20. *Extraits de Théodote* (hereafter cited as *Exc*), ed. F. Sagnard, Sources chrétiennes 23 (Paris: Sources chrétiennes, 1948).
21. *AH*, 1.30.6.
22. *Ref*, 6.17.
23. Ibid., 6.14.
24. *AH*, 1.14.7–8.

25. *Ref*, 6.18.
26. Genesis Rabba 8.1, also 17.6; cf. Levitius Rabba 14. For an excellent discussion of androgyny, see W. Meeks, "The Image of the Androgyne: Some Uses of a Symbol in Earliest Christianity," *History of Religions* 13 (1974): 165–208.
27. *AH*, 1.18.2.
28. *Exc*, 21.1.
29. *Ref*, 6.33.
30. *AH*, 1.5.4; *Ref*, 6.33.
31. *AJ*, 61.8–14.
32. *Ref*, 7.26.
33. *AH*, 1.13.7.
34. Ibid., 1.13.2–5.
35. Tertullian, *De Praescriptione Haereticorum* (hereafter cited as *DP*), ed. E. Oehler (Lipsius, 1853–54), p. 41.
36. *De Baptismo* 1. I am grateful to Cyril Richardson for calling my attention to this passage and to the three subsequent ones.
37. Epiphanes, *De Baptismo*, 42.5.
38. *AH*, 1.25.6.
39. *DP*, 6.30.
40. *The Gospel according to Mary*, Codex Berolinensis, *BG*, 8502,1.7.1–1.19.5, ed., intro., and trans. G. MacRae, unpublished manuscript.
41. *Pistis Sophia*, ed. Carl Schmidt (Berlin: Academie-Verlag, 1925), 36 (57), 71 (161).
42. 1 Cor. 11:7–9. For discussion, see R. Scroggs, "Paul and the Eschatological Woman," *Journal of the American Academy of Religion* 40 (1972): 283–303; R. Scroggs, "Paul and the Eschatological Woman: Revisited," *Journal of the American Academy of Religion* 42 (1974): 532–537; and E. Pagels, "Paul and Women: A Response to Recent Discussion," *Journal of the American Academy of Religion* 42 (1974): 538–549.
43. Clement Alexandrinus, *Paidegogos*, ed. O. Stählin (Leipzig, 1905), 1.6.
44. Ibid., 1.4.
45. Ibid., 1.19.
46. 2 Tim. 2:11–14.

 54

A Black Feminist Statement

COMBAHEE RIVER COLLECTIVE

We are a collective of Black feminists who have been meeting together since 1974.[1] During that time we have been involved in the process of defining and clarifying our politics, while at the same time doing political work within our own group and in coalition with other progressive organizations and movements. The most general statement of our politics at the present time would be that we are actively committed to struggling against racial, sexual, heterosexual, and class oppression and see as our particular task the development of integrated analysis and practice based upon the fact that the major systems of oppression are interlocking. The synthesis of these oppressions creates the conditions of our lives. As Black women we see Black feminism as the logical political movement to combat the manifold and simultaneous oppressions that all women of color face.

We will discuss four major topics in the paper that follows: (1) the genesis of contemporary Black feminism; (2) what we believe, i.e., the specific province of our politics; (3) the problems in organizing Black feminists, including a brief herstory of our collective; and (4) Black feminist issues and practice.

1. THE GENESIS OF CONTEMPORARY BLACK FEMINISM

Before looking at the recent development of Black feminism we would like to affirm that we find our origins in the historical reality of Afro-American women's continuous life-and-death struggle for survival and liberation. Black women's extremely negative relationship to the American political system (a system of white male rule) has always been determined by our membership in two oppressed racial and sexual castes. As Angela Davis points out in "Reflections on the Black Woman's Role in the Community of Slaves," Black women have always embodied, if only in their physical manifestation, an adversary stance to white male rule and have actively resisted its inroads upon them and their communities in both dramatic and subtle ways. There have always been Black women activists—some known, like Sojourner Truth, Harriet Tubman, Frances E. W. Harper, Ida B. Wells Barnett, and Mary Church Terrell, and thousands upon thousands unknown—who had a shared awareness of how their sexual identity combined with their racial identity to make their whole life situation and the focus of their political struggles unique. Contemporary Black feminism is the outgrowth of countless generations of personal sacrifice, militancy, and work by our mothers and sisters.

A Black feminist presence has evolved most obviously in connection with the second wave of the American women's movement beginning in the late 1960s. Black, other Third World, and working women have been involved in the feminist movement from its start, but both outside reactionary forces and racism and elitism within the movement itself have served to obscure our participation. In 1973 Black feminists, primarily located in New York, felt the necessity of forming a separate Black feminist group. This became the National Black Feminist Organization (NBFO).

Black feminist politics also have an obvious connection to movements for Black liberation, particularly those of the 1960s and 1970s. Many of us were active in those movements (civil rights, Black nationalism, the Black Panthers), and all of our lives were greatly affected and changed by their ideology, their goals, and the tactics used to achieve their goals. It was our experience and disillusionment within these liberation movements, as well as experience on the periphery of the white male left, that led to the need to develop a politics that was antiracist, unlike those of white women, and antisexist, unlike those of Black and white men.

There is also undeniably a personal genesis for Black feminism, that is, the political realization that comes from the seemingly personal experiences of individual Black women's lives. Black feminists and many more Black women who do not define themselves as feminists have all experienced sexual oppression as a constant factor in our day-to-day existence. As children we realized that we were different from boys and that we were treated differently. For example, we were told in the same breath to be quiet both for the sake of being "ladylike" and to make us less objectionable in the eyes of white people. As we grew older we became aware of the threat of physical and sexual abuse by men. However, we had no way of conceptualizing what was so apparent to us, what we *knew* was really happening.

Black feminists often talk about their feelings of craziness before becoming conscious of the concepts of sexual politics, patriarchal rule, and most importantly, feminism, the political analysis and practice that we women use to struggle against our oppression. The fact that racial politics and indeed racism are pervasive factors in our lives did not allow us, and still does not allow most Black women, to look more deeply into our own experiences and, from that sharing and growing consciousness, to build a politics that will change our lives and inevitably end our oppression. Our development must also be tied to the contemporary economic and political position of Black people. The post World War II generation of Black youth was the first to be able to minimally partake of certain educational and employment options, previously closed completely to Black people. Although our economic position is still at the very bottom of the American capitalistic economy, a handful of us have been able to gain certain tools as a result of tokenism in education and employment which potentially enable us to more effectively fight our oppression.

A combined antiracist and antisexist position drew us together initially, and as we developed politically we addressed ourselves to hetero-sexism and economic oppression under capitalism.

2. WHAT WE BELIEVE

Above all else, our politics initially sprang from the shared belief that Black women are inherently valuable, that our liberation is a necessity not as an adjunct to somebody else's but because of our need as human persons for autonomy. This may seem so obvious as to sound simplistic, but it is apparent that no other ostensibly progressive movement has ever considered our specific oppression as a priority or worked seriously for the ending of that oppression. Merely naming the pejorative stereotypes attributed to Black women (e.g. mammy, matriarch, Sapphire, whore, bulldagger), let alone cataloguing the cruel, often murderous, treatment we receive, indicates how little value has been placed upon our lives during four centuries of bondage in the Western hemisphere. We realize that the only people who care enough about us to work consistently for our liberation is us. Our politics evolve from a healthy love for ourselves, our sisters and our community which allows us to continue our struggle and work.

This focusing upon our own oppression is embodied in the concept of identity politics. We believe that the most profound and potentially the most radical politics come directly out of our own identity, as opposed to working to end somebody else's oppression. In the case of Black women this is a particularly repugnant, dangerous, threatening, and therefore revolutionary concept because it is obvious from looking at all the political movements that have preceded us that anyone is more worthy of liberation than ourselves. We reject pedestals, queenhood, and walking ten paces behind. To be recognized as human, levelly human, is enough.

We believe that sexual politics under patriarchy is as pervasive in Black women's lives as are the politics of class and race. We also often find it difficult to separate race from class from sex oppression because in our lives they are most often experienced simultaneously. We know that there is such a thing as racial-sexual oppression which is neither solely racial nor solely sexual, e.g., the history of rape of Black women by white men as a weapon of political repression.

Although we are feminists and lesbians, we feel solidarity with progressive Black men and do not advocate the fractionalization that white women who are separatists demand. Our situation as Black people necessitates that we have solidarity around the fact of race, which white women of course do not need to have with white men, unless it is their negative solidarity as racial oppressors. We struggle together with Black men against racism, while we also struggle with Black men about sexism.

We realize that the liberation of all oppressed peoples necessitates the destruction of the political-economic systems of capitalism and imperialism as well as patriarchy. We are socialists because we believe the work must be organized for the collective benefit of those who do the work and create the products, and not for the profit of the bosses. Material resources must be equally distributed among those who create these resources. We are not convinced, however, that a socialist revolution that is not also a feminist and antiracist revolution will guarantee our liberation. We have arrived at the necessity for developing an understanding of class relationships that takes into account the specific class position of Black women who are generally marginal in the labor force, while at this particular time some of us are temporarily viewed as doubly desirable tokens at white-collar and professional levels. We need to articulate the real class situation of persons who are not merely raceless, sexless workers, but for whom racial and sexual oppression are significant determinants in their working/economic lives. Although we are in essential agreement with Marx's theory as it applied to the very specific economic relationships he analyzed, we know that his analysis must be extended further in order for us to understand our specific economic situation as Black women.

A political contribution which we feel we have already made is the expansion of the feminist principle that the personal is political. In our consciousness-raising sessions, for example, we have in many ways gone beyond white women's revelations because we are dealing with the implications of race and class as well as sex. Even our Black women's style of talking/testifying in Black language about what we have experienced has a resonance that is both cultural and political. We have spent a great deal of energy delving into the cultural and experiential nature of our oppression out of necessity because none of these matters has ever been looked at before. No one before has ever examined the multilayered texture of Black women's lives. An example of this kind of revelation/conceptualization occurred at a meeting as we discussed the ways in which our early intellectual interests had been attacked by our peers, particularly Black males. We discovered that all of us, because we were "smart" had also been considered "ugly," *i.e.*, "smart-ugly." "Smart-ugly" crystallized the way in which most of us had been forced to develop our intellects at great cost to our "social" lives. The sanctions in the Black and white communities against Black women thinkers is comparatively much higher than for white women, particularly ones from the educated middle and upper classes.

As we have already stated, we reject the stance of lesbian separatism because it is not a viable political analysis or strategy for us. It leaves out far too much and far too many people, particularly Black men, women, and children. We have a great deal of criticism and loathing for what men have been socialized to be in this society: what they support, how they act, and how they oppress. But we do not have the misguided notion that it is their maleness, per se— *i.e.*, their biological maleness—that makes them what they are. As Black women we find any type of biological determinism a particularly dangerous and reactionary basis upon which to build a politic. We must also question whether lesbian separatism is an adequate and progressive political analysis and strategy, even for those who practice it, since it so completely denies any but the sexual sources of women's oppression, negating the facts of class and race.

3. PROBLEMS IN ORGANIZING BLACK FEMINISTS

During our years together as a Black feminist collective we have experienced success and defeat, joy and pain, victory and failure. We have found that it is very difficult to organize around Black feminist issues, difficult even to announce in certain contexts that we *are* Black feminists. We have tried to think about the reasons for our difficulties, particularly since the white women's movement continues to be strong and to grow in many directions. In this section we will discuss some of the general reasons for the organizing problems we face and also talk specifically about the stages in organizing our own collective.

The major source of difficulty in our political work is that we are not just trying to fight oppression on one front or even two, but instead to address a whole range of oppressions. We do not have racial, sexual, heterosexual, or class privilege to rely upon, nor do we have even the minimal access to resources and power that groups who possess any one of these types of privilege have.

The psychological toll of being a Black woman and the difficulties this presents in reaching political consciousness and doing political work can never be underestimated. There is a very low value placed upon Black women's psyches in this society, which is both racist and sexist. As an early group member once said, "We are all damaged people merely by virtue of being Black women." We are dispossessed psychologically and on every other level, and yet we feel the necessity to struggle to change the condition of all Black women. In "A Black Feminist's Search for Sisterhood," Michele Wallace arrives at this conclusion:

"We exist as women who are Black who are feminists, each stranded for the moment, working

independently because there is not yet an environment in this society remotely congenial to our struggle—because, being on the bottom, we would have to do what no one else has done: we would have to fight the world."[2]

Wallace is pessimistic but realistic in her assessment of Black feminists' position, particularly in her allusion to the nearly classic isolation most of us face. We might use our position at the bottom, however, to make a clear leap into revolutionary action. If Black women were free, it would mean that everyone else would have to be free since our freedom would necessitate the destruction of all the systems of oppression.

Feminism is, nevertheless, very threatening to the majority of Black people because it calls into question some of the most basic assumptions about our existence, i.e., that sex should be a determinant of power relationships. Here is the way male and female voices were defined in a Black nationalist pamphlet from the early 1970's.

> "We understand that it is and has been traditional that the man is the head of the house. He is the leader of the house/nation because his knowledge of the world is broader, his awareness is greater, his understanding is fuller and his application of this information is wiser . . . After all, it is only reasonable that the man be the head of the house because he is able to defend and protect the development of his home . . . Women cannot do the same things as men—they are made by nature to function differently. Equality of men and women is something that cannot happen even in the abstract world. Men are not equal to other men, i.e. ability, experience or even understanding. The value of men and women can be seen as in the value of gold and silver—they are not equal but both have great value. We must realize that men and women are a complement to each other because there is no house/family without a man and his wife. Both are essential to the development of any life."[3]

The material conditions of most Black women would hardly lead them to upset both economic and sexual arrangements that seem to represent some stability in their lives. Many Black women have a good understanding of both sexism and racism, but because of the everyday constrictions of their lives cannot risk struggling against them both.

The reaction of Black men to feminism has been notoriously negative. They are, of course, even more threatened than Black women by the possibility that Black feminists might organize around our own needs. They realize that they might not only lose valuable and hardworking allies in their struggles but that they might also be forced to change their habitually sexist ways of interacting with and oppressing Black women. Accusations that Black feminism divides the Black struggle are powerful deterrents to the growth of an autonomous Black women's movement.

Still, hundreds of women have been active at different times during the three-year existence of our group. And every Black woman who came, came out of a strongly-felt need for some level of possibility that did not previously exist in her life.

When we first started meeting early in 1974 after the NBFO first eastern regional conference, we did not have a strategy for organizing, or even a focus. We just wanted to see what we had. After a period of months of not meeting, we began to meet again late in the year and started doing an intense variety of consciousness-raising. The overwhelming feeling that we had is that after years and years we had finally found each other. Although we were not doing political work as a group, individuals continued their involvement in Lesbian politics, sterilization abuse and abortion rights work, Third World Women's International Women's Day activities, and support activity for the trials of Dr. Kenneth Edelin, Joan Little, and Inéz García. During our first summer, when membership had dropped off considerably, those of us remaining devoted serious discussion to the possibility of opening a refuge for battered women in a Black community. (There was no refuge in Boston at that time.) We also decided around that time to become an independent collective since we had serious disagreements with NBFO's bourgeois-feminist stance and their lack of a clear political focus.

We also were contacted at that time by socialist feminists, with whom we had worked on abortion rights activities, who wanted to encourage us to attend the National Socialist Feminist Conference in Yellow Springs. One of our members did attend and despite the narrowness of the ideology that was promoted at that particular conference, we became more aware of the need for us to understand our own economic situation and to make our own economic analysis.

In the fall, when some members returned, we experienced several months of comparative inactivity and internal disagreements which were first conceptualized as a Lesbian-straight split but which were also the result of class and political differences. During the summer those of us who were still meeting had determined the need to do political work and to move beyond consciousness-raising and serving exclusively as an emotional support group. At the beginning of 1976, when some of the women who had not wanted to do political work and who also had voiced disagreements stopped attending of their own accord, we again looked for a focus. We decided at that time, with the addition of new members, to become a study group. We had always shared our reading with each other, and some of us had written papers on Black feminism for group discussion a few months before this decision was made. We began functioning as a study group and also began discussing the possibility of starting a Black feminist publication. We had a retreat in the late spring which provided a time for both political discussion and working out interpersonal issues. Currently we are planning to gather together a collection of Black feminist writing. We feel that it is absolutely essential to demonstrate the reality of our politics to other Black women and believe that we can do this through writing and distributing our work. The fact that individual Black feminists are living in isolation all over the country, that our own numbers are small, and that we have some skills in writing, printing, and publishing makes us want to carry out these kinds of projects as a means of organizing Black feminists as we continue to do political work in coalition with other groups.

4. BLACK FEMINIST ISSUES AND PROJECTS

During our time together we have identified and worked on many issues of particular relevance to Black women. The inclusiveness of our politics makes us concerned with any situation that impinges upon the lives of women, Third World and working people. We are of course particularly committed to working on those struggles in which race, sex and class are simultaneous factors in oppression. We might, for example, become involved in workplace organizing at a factory that employs Third World women or picket a hospital that is cutting back on already inadequate health care to a Third World community, or set up a rape crisis center in a Black neighborhood. Organizing around welfare and daycare concerns might also be a focus. The work to be done and the countless issues that this work represents merely reflect the pervasiveness of our oppression.

Issues and projects that collective members have actually worked on are sterilization abuse, abortion rights, battered women, rape and health care. We have also done many workshops and educationals on Black feminism on college campuses, at women's conferences, and most recently for high school women.

One issue that is of major concern to us and that we have begun to publicly address is racism in the white women's movement. As Black feminists we are made constantly and painfully aware of how little effort white women have made to understand and combat their racism, which requires among other things that they have a more than superficial comprehension of race, color, and black history and culture. Eliminating racism in the white women's movement is by definition work for white women to do, but we will continue to speak to and demand accountability on this issue.

In the practice of our politics we do not believe that the end always justifies the means. Many reactionary and destructive acts have been done in the name of achieving "correct" political goals. As feminists we do not want to mess over people in the name of politics. We believe in collective process and a nonhierarchical distribution of power within our own group and in our vision of a revolutionary society. We are committed to a continual examination of our politics as they develop through criticism and self-criticism as an essential aspect of our practice. In her introduction to *Sisterhood is Powerful* Robin Morgan writes:

> "I haven't the faintest notion what possible revolutionary role white heterosexual men could fulfill, since they are the very embodiment of reactionary-vested-interest-power."

As Black feminists and Lesbians we know that we have a very definite revolutionary task to perform and we are ready for the lifetime of work and struggle before us.

[1977]

NOTES

The Combahee River Collective is a Black feminist group in Boston whose name comes from the guerrilla action conceptualized and led by Harriet Tubman on June 2, 1863, in the Port Royal region of South Carolina. This action freed more than 750 slaves and is the only military campaign in American history planned and led by a woman.
1. This statement is dated April 1977.
2. Michele Wallace, "A Black Feminist's Search for Sisterhood," The Village Voice, 28 July 1975, pp. 6–7.
3. Mumininas of Committee for Unified Newark, Mwanamke Mwananchi (The Nationalist Woman), Newark, N.J., © 1971, pp. 4–5.

 55

From This Sex Which Is Not One

LUCE IRIGARAY

Female sexuality has always been conceptualized on the basis of masculine parameters. Thus the opposition between "masculine" clitoral activity and "feminine" vaginal passivity, an opposition which Freud—and many others—saw as stages, or alternatives, in the development of a sexually "normal" woman, seems rather too clearly required by the practice of male sexuality. For the clitoris is conceived as a little penis pleasant to masturbate so long as castration anxiety does not exist (for the boy child), and the vagina is valued for the "lodging" it offers the male organ when the forbidden hand has to find a replacement for pleasure-giving.

In these terms, woman's erogenous zones never amount to anything but a clitoris-sex that is not comparable to the noble phallic organ, or a hole-envelope that serves to sheathe and massage the penis in intercourse: a non-sex, or a masculine organ turned back upon itself, self-embracing.

About woman and her pleasure, this view of the sexual relation has nothing to say. Her lot is that of "lack," "atrophy" (of the sexual organ), and "penis envy," the penis being the only sexual organ of recognized value. Thus she attempts by every means available to appropriate that organ for herself: through her somewhat servile love of the father-husband capable of giving her one, through her desire for a child-penis, preferably a boy, through access to the cultural values still reserved by right to males alone and therefore always masculine, and so on. Woman lives her own desire only as the expectation that she may at last come to possess an equivalent of the male organ.

Yet all this appears quite foreign to her own pleasure, unless it remains within the dominant phallic economy. Thus, for example, woman's autoeroticism is very different from man's. In order to touch himself, man needs an instrument: his hand, a woman's body, language . . . And this self-caressing requires at least a minimum of activity. As for woman, she touches herself in and of herself without any need for mediation, and before there is any way to distinguish activity from passivity. Woman "touches herself" all the time, and moreover no one can forbid her to do so, for her genitals are formed of two lips in continuous contact. Thus, within herself, she is already two—but not divisible into one(s)—that caress each other.

This autoeroticism is disrupted by a violent break-in: the brutal separation of the two lips by a violating penis, an intrusion that distracts and deflects the woman from this "self-caressing" she needs if she is not to incur the disappearance of her own pleasure in sexual relations. If the vagina is to serve *also*, but *not only*, to take over for the little boy's hand in order to assure an articulation between autoeroticism and hetero-eroticism in intercourse (the encounter with the totally other always signifying death), how, in the classic representation of sexuality, can the perpetuation of autoeroticism for woman be managed? Will woman not be left with the impossible alternative between a defensive virginity, fiercely turned in upon itself, and a body open to penetration that no longer knows, in this "hole" that constitutes its sex, the pleasure of its own touch? The more or less exclusive—and highly anxious—attention paid to erection in Western sexuality proves to what extent the imaginary that governs it is foreign to the feminine. For the most part, this sexuality offers nothing but imperatives dictated by male rivalry: the "strongest" being the one who has the best "hard-on," the longest, the biggest, the stiffest penis, or even the one who "pees the farthest" (as in little boys' contests). Or else one finds imperatives dictated by the enactment of sadomasochistic fantasies, these in turn governed by man's relation to his mother: the desire to force entry, to penetrate, to appropriate for himself the mystery of this womb where he has been conceived, the secret of his begetting, of his "origin." Desire/need, also to make blood flow again in order to revive a very old relationship—intrauterine, to be sure, but also prehistoric—to the maternal.

Woman, in this sexual imaginary, is only a more or less obliging prop for the enactment of man's fantasies. That she may find pleasure there in that role, by proxy, is possible, even certain. But such pleasure is above all a masochistic prostitution of her body to a desire that is not her own, and it leaves her in a familiar state of dependency upon man. Not knowing what she wants, ready for anything, even asking for more, so long as he will "take" her as his "object" when he seeks his own pleasure. Thus she will not say what she herself wants; moreover, she does not know, or no longer knows, what she wants. As Freud admits, the beginnings of the sexual life of a girl child are so "obscure," so "faded with time," that one would have to dig down very deep indeed to discover beneath the traces of this civilization, of this history, the vestiges of a more archaic civilization that might give some clue to woman's sexuality. That extremely ancient civilization would undoubtedly have a different alphabet, a different language . . . Woman's desire would not be expected to speak the same language as man's; woman's desire has doubtless been submerged by the logic that has dominated the West since the time of the Greeks.

Within this logic, the predominance of the visual, and of the discrimination and individualization of form, is particularly foreign to female eroticism. Woman takes pleasure more from touching than from looking, and her entry into a dominant scopic economy signifies, again, her consignment to pas-

sivity: she is to be the beautiful object of contemplation. While her body finds itself thus eroticized, and
called to a double movement of exhibition and of
chaste retreat in order to stimulate the drives of the
"subject," her sexual organ represents *the horror of
nothing to see*. A defect in this systematics of representation and desire. A "hole" in its scoptophilic lens. It
is already evident in Greek statuary that this nothing-
to-see has to be excluded, rejected, from such a scene
of representation. Woman's genitals are simply absent, masked, sewn back up inside their "crack."

This organ which has nothing to show for itself
also lacks a form of its own. And if woman takes
pleasure precisely from this incompleteness of form
which allows her organ to touch itself over and over
again, indefinitely, by itself, that pleasure is denied
by a civilization that privileges phallomorphism.
The value granted to the only definable form excludes the one that is in play in female autoeroticism. The *one* of form, of the individual, of the
(male) sexual organ, of the proper name, of the
proper meaning . . . supplants, while separating and
dividing, that contact of *at least two* (lips) which
keeps woman in touch with herself, but without any
possibility of distinguishing what is touching from
what is touched.

Whence the mystery that woman represents in a
culture claiming to count everything, to number
everything by units, to inventory everything as individualities. *She is neither one nor two.* Rigorously
speaking, she cannot be identified either as one person, or as two. She resists all adequate definition.
Further, she has no "proper" name. And her sexual
organ, which is not *one* organ, is counted as *none*.
The negative, the underside, the reverse of the only
visible and morphologically designatable organ
(even if the passage from erection to detumescence
does pose some problems): the penis.

But the "thickness" of that "form," the layering
of its volume, its expansions and contractions and
even the spacing of the moments in which it produces itself as form—all this the feminine keeps secret. Without knowing it. And if woman is asked to
sustain, to revive, man's desire, the request neglects
to spell out what it implies as to the value of her own
desire. A desire of which she is not aware, moreover,

at least not explicitly. But one whose force and continuity are capable of nurturing repeatedly and at
length all the masquerades of "feminity" that are
expected of her.

It is true that she still has the child, in relation to
whom her appetite for touch, for contact, has free
rein, unless it is already lost, alienated by the taboo
against touching of a highly obsessive civilization.
Otherwise her pleasure will find, in the child, compensations for and diversions from the frustrations
that she too often encounters in sexual relations per
se. Thus maternity fills the gaps in a repressed female sexuality. Perhaps man and woman no longer
caress each other except through that mediation between them that the child—preferably a boy—represents? Man, identified with his son, rediscovers
the pleasure of maternal fondling; woman touches
herself again by caressing that part of her body: her
baby-penis-clitoris.

What this entails for the amorous trio is well
known. But the Oedipal interdiction seems to be a
somewhat categorical and factitious law—although it
does provide the means for perpetuating the authoritarian discourse of fathers—when it is promulgated
in a culture in which sexual relations are impractica-
ble because man's desire and woman's are strangers
to each other. And in which the two desires have to
try to meet through indirect means, whether the archaic one of a sense-relation to the mother's body, or
the present one of active or passive extension of the
law of the father. These are regressive emotional behaviors, exchanges of words too detached from the
sexual arena not to constitute an exile with respect to
it: "mother" and "father" dominate the interactions
of the couple, but as social roles. The division of labor
prevents them from making love. They produce or
reproduce. Without quite knowing how to use their
leisure. Such little as they have, such little indeed as
they wish to have. For what are they to do with leisure? What substitute for amorous resource are they
to invent? Still . . .

Perhaps it is time to return to that repressed entity, the female imaginary. So woman does not have
a sex organ? She has at least two of them, but they
are not identifiable as ones. Indeed, she has many

more. Her sexuality, always at least double, goes even further: it is *plural*. Is this the way culture is seeking to characterize itself now? Is this the way texts write themselves / are written now? Without quite knowing what censorship they are evading? Indeed, woman's pleasure does not have to choose between clitoral activity and vaginal passivity, for example. The pleasure of the vaginal caress does not have to be substituted for that of the clitoral caress. They each contribute, irreplaceably, to woman's pleasure. Among other caresses . . . Fondling the breasts, touching the vulva, spreading the lips, stroking the posterior wall of the vagina, brushing against the mouth of the uterus, and so on. To evoke only a few of the most specifically female pleasures. Pleasures which are somewhat misunderstood in sexual difference as it is imagined—or not imagined, the other sex being only the indispensable complement to the only sex.

But *woman has sex organs more or less everywhere*. She finds pleasure almost anywhere. Even if we refrain from invoking the hystericization of her entire body, the geography of her pleasure is far more diversified, more multiple in its differences, more complex, more subtle, than is commonly imagined— in an imaginary rather too narrowly focused on sameness.

"She" is indefinitely other in herself. This is doubtless why she is said to be whimsical, incomprehensible, agitated, capricious . . . not to mention her language, in which "she" sets off in all directions leaving "him" unable to discern the coherence of any meaning. Hers are contradictory words, somewhat mad from the standpoint of reason, inaudible for whoever listens to them with ready-made grids, with a fully elaborated code in hand. For in what she says, too, at least when she dares, woman is constantly touching herself. She steps ever so slightly aside from herself with a murmur, an exclamation, a whisper, a sentence left unfinished . . . When she returns, it is to set off again from elsewhere. From another point of pleasure, or of pain. One would have to listen with another ear, as if hearing *an "other meaning" always in the process of weaving itself, of embracing itself with words, but also of getting rid of words in order not to become fixed, congealed in them*. For if "she" says something, it is not, it is already no

longer, identical with what she means. What she says is never identical with anything, moreover; rather, it is contiguous. *It touches (upon)*. And when it strays too far from that proximity, she breaks off and starts over at "zero": her body-sex.

It is useless, then, to trap women in the exact definition of what they mean, to make them repeat (themselves) so that it will be clear; they are already elsewhere in that discursive machinery where you expected to surprise them. They have returned within themselves. Which must not be understood in the same way as within yourself. They do not have the interiority that you have, the one you perhaps suppose they have. Within themselves means *within the intimacy of that silent, multiple, diffuse touch*. And if you ask them insistently what they are thinking about, they can only reply: Nothing. Everything.

Thus what they desire is precisely nothing, and at the same time everything. Always something more and something else besides that *one*—sexual organ, for example,—that you give them, attribute to them. Their desire is often interpreted, and feared, as a sort of insatiable hunger, a voracity that will swallow you whole. Whereas it really involves a different economy more than anything else, one that upsets the linearity of a project, undermines the goal-object of a desire, diffuses the polarization toward a single pleasure, disconcerts fidelity to a single discourse . . .

Must this multiplicity of female desire and female language be understood as shards, scattered remnants of a violated sexuality? A sexuality denied? The question has no simple answer. The rejection, the exclusion of a female imaginary certainly puts woman in the position of experiencing herself only fragmentarily, in the little-structured margins of a dominant ideology, as waste, or excess, what is left of a mirror invested by the (masculine) "subject" to reflect himself, to copy himself. Moreover, the role of "femininity" is prescribed by this masculine specula(riza)tion and corresponds scarcely at all to woman's desire, which may be recovered only in secret, in hiding, with anxiety and guilt.

But if the female imaginary were to deploy itself, if it could bring itself into play otherwise than as scraps, uncollected debris, would it represent itself, even so, in the form of *one* universe? Would it even be volume instead of surface? No. Not unless it were understood, yet again, as a privileging of the maternal over the feminine. Of a phallic maternal, at that. Closed in upon the jealous possession of its valued product. Rivaling man in his esteem for productive excess. In such a race for power, woman loses the uniqueness of her pleasure. By closing herself off as volume, she renounces the pleasure that she gets from the *nonsuture of her lips:* she is undoubtedly a mother, but a virgin mother; the role was assigned to her by mythologies long ago. Granting her a certain social power to the extent that she is reduced, with her own complicity, to sexual impotence.

(Re-)discovering herself, for a woman, thus could only signify the possibility of sacrificing no one of her pleasures to another, of identifying herself with none of them in particular, *of never being simply one*. A sort of expanding universe to which no limits could be fixed and which would not be incoherence nonetheless—nor that polymorphous perversion of the child in which the erogenous zones would lie waiting to be regrouped under the primacy of the phallus.

Woman always remains several, but she is kept from dispersion because the other is already within her and is autoerotically familiar to her. Which is not to say that she appropriates the other for herself, that she reduces it to her own property. Ownership and property are doubtless quite foreign to the feminine. At least sexually. But not *nearness*. Nearness so pronounced that it makes all discrimination of identity, and thus all forms of property, impossible. Woman derives pleasure from what is *so near that she cannot have it, nor have herself.* She herself enters into a ceaseless exchange of herself with the other without any possibility of identifying either. This puts into question all prevailing economies: their calculations are irremediably stymied by woman's pleasure, as it increases indefinitely from its passage in and through the other.

However, in order for woman to reach the place where she takes pleasure as woman, a long detour by way of the analysis of the various systems of oppression brought to bear upon her is assuredly necessary. And claiming to fall back on the single solution of pleasure risks making her miss the process of going back through a social practice that *her* enjoyment requires.

For woman is traditionally a use-value for man, an exchange value among men; in other words, a commodity. As such, she remains the guardian of material substance, whose price will be established, in terms of the standard of their work and of their need/desire, by "subjects": workers, merchants, consumers. Women are marked phallically by their fathers, husbands, procurers. And this branding determines their value in sexual commerce. Woman is never anything but the locus of a more or less competitive exchange between two men, including the competition for the possession of mother earth.

How can this object of transaction claim a right to pleasure without removing her/itself from established commerce? With respect to other merchandise in the marketplace, how could this commodity maintain a relationship other than one of aggressive jealousy? How could material substance enjoy her/itself without provoking the consumer's anxiety over the disappearance of his nurturing ground? How could that exchange—which can in no way be defined in terms "proper" to woman's desire—appear as anything but a pure mirage, mere foolishness, all too readily obscured by a more sensible discourse and by a system of apparently more tangible values?

A woman's development, however radical it may seek to be, would thus not suffice to liberate woman's desire. And to date no political theory or political practice has resolved, or sufficiently taken into consideration, this historical problem, even though Marxism has proclaimed its importance. But women do not constitute, strictly speaking, a class, and their dispersion among several classes makes their political struggle complex, their demands sometimes contradictory.

There remains, however, the condition of underdevelopment arising from women's submission by and to a culture that oppresses them, uses them, makes of them a medium of exchange, with very little profit to them. Except in the quasi monopolies of masochistic pleasure, the domestic labor force, and reproduction. The powers of slaves? Which are not negligible powers, moreover. For where pleasure is concerned, the master is not necessarily well served. Thus to reverse the relation, especially in the economy of sexuality, does not seem a desirable objective.

But if women are to preserve and expand their autoeroticism, their homo-sexuality, might not the renunciation of heterosexual pleasure correspond once again to that disconnection from power that is traditionally theirs? Would it not involve a new prison, a new cloister, built of their own accord? For women to undertake tactical strikes, to keep themselves apart from men long enough to learn to defend their desire, especially through speech, to discover the love of other women while sheltered from men's imperious choices that put them in the position of rival commodities, to forge for themselves a social status that compels recognition, to earn their living in order to escape from the condition of prostitute . . . these are certainly indispensable stages in the escape from their proletarization on the exchange market. But if their aim were simply to reverse the order of things, even supposing this to be possible, history would repeat itself in the long run, would revert to sameness: to phallocratism. It would leave room neither for women's sexuality, nor for women's imaginary, nor for women's language to take (their) place.

[1977]

 56

Some Reflections on Separatism and Power

MARILYN FRYE

I have been trying to write something about separatism almost since my first dawning of feminist consciousness, but it has always been for me somehow a mercurial topic which, when I tried to grasp it, would softly shatter into many other topics like sexuality, man-hating, so-called reverse discrimination, apocalyptic utopianism, and so on. What I have to share with you today is my latest attempt to get to the heart of the matter.

In my life, and within feminism as I understand it, separatism is not a theory or a doctrine, nor a demand for certain specific behaviors on the part of feminists, though it is undeniably connected with lesbianism. Feminism seems to me to be kaleidoscopic—something whose shapes, structures and patterns alter with every turn of feminist creativity; and one element which is present through all the changes in an element of separation. This element has different roles and relations in different turns of the glass—it assumes different meanings, is variously conspicuous, variously determined or determining, depending on how the pieces fall and who is the beholder. The theme of separation, in its multitude variations, is there in everything from divorce to exclusive lesbian separatist communities, from shelters for battered women to witch covens, from women's studies programs to women's bars, from expansion of daycare to abortion on demand. The presence of this theme is vigorously obscured, trivialized, mystified and outright denied by many feminist apologists, who seem to find it embarrassing, while it is embraced, explored, expanded and ramified by most of the more inspiring theorists and activists. The theme of separation is noticeably absent or heavily qualified in most of the things I take to be personal solutions and band-aid projects, like legalization of prostitution, liberal marriage contracts, improvement of the treatment of rape victims and affirmative action. It is clear to me, in my own case at least, that the contrariety of assimilation and separation is one of the main things that guides or determines assessments of various theories, actions and practices as reformist or radical, as going to the root of the thing or being relatively superficial. So my topical question comes to this: What is it about separation, in any or all of its many forms and degrees, that makes it so basic and so sinister, so exciting and so repellent?

Feminist separation is, of course, separation of various sorts or modes from men and from institutions, relationships, roles and activities which are male-defined, male-dominated and operating for the benefit of males and the maintenance of male privilege—this separation being initiated or maintained, at will, *by women*. (Masculist separatism is the partial segregation of women from men and male domains *at the will of men*. This difference is crucial.) The feminist separation can take many forms. Breaking up or avoiding close relationships or working relationships; forbidding someone to enter your house; excluding someone from your company, or from your meeting; withdrawal from participation in some activity or institution, or avoidance of participation; avoidance of communications and influence from certain quarters (not listening to music with sexist lyrics, not watching tv); withholding commitment or support; rejection of or rudeness toward obnoxious individuals.[1] Some separations are subtle realignments of identification, priorities and commitments, or working with agendas which only incidently coincide with the agendas of the institution one works in.[2] Ceasing to be loyal to something or someone is a separation; and ceasing to love. The feminist's separations are rarely if ever sought or maintained directly as ultimate personal or political ends. The closest we come to that, I think, is the separation which is the instinctive and self-preserving recoil from the systematic misogyny that surrounds us.[3] Generally, the separations are brought about and maintained for the sake of something else like independence, liberty, growth, invention, sisterhood, safety, health, or the practice of novel or heretical customs.[4] Often the separations in question evolve, unpremeditated, as one goes one's way and finds various persons, institutions or relationships useless, obstructive or noisome and leaves them aside or behind. Sometimes the separations are consciously planned and cultivated as necessary prerequisites or conditions for getting on with one's business. Sometimes the separations are accomplished or maintained easily, or with a sense of relief, or even joy; sometimes they are accomplished or maintained with difficulty, by dint of constant vigilance, or with anxiety, pain or grief.

Most feminists, probably all, practice some separation from males and male-dominated institutions. A separatist practices separation consciously, systematically, and probably more generally than the others, and advocates thorough and "broad-spectrum" separation as part of the conscious strategy of liberation. And, contrary to the image of the

separatist as a cowardly escapist,[5] hers is the life and program which inspires the greatest hostility, disparagement, insult and confrontation and generally she is the one against whom economic sanctions operate most conclusively. The penalty for refusing to work with or for men is usually starvation (or, at the very least, doing without medical insurance[6]); and if one's policy of noncooperation is more subtle, one's livelihood is still constantly on the line, since one is not a loyal partisan, a proper member of the team, or what have you. The penalties for being a lesbian are ostracism, harassment and job insecurity or joblessness. The penalty for rejecting men's sexual advances is often rape and, perhaps even more often, forfeit of such things as professional or job opportunities. And the separatist lives with the added burden of being assumed by many to be a morally depraved man-hating bigot. But there is a clue here: if you are doing something that is so strictly forbidden by the patriarchs, you must be doing something right.

There is an idea floating around in both feminist and antifeminist literature to the effect that females and males generally live in a relation of parasitism,[7] a parasitism of the male on the female . . . that it is, generally speaking, the strength, energy, inspiration and nurturance of women that keeps men going, and not the strength, aggression, spirituality and hunting of men that keeps women going.

It is sometimes said that the parasitism goes the other way around, that the female is the parasite. But one can conjure the appearance of the female as parasite only if one takes a very narrow view of human living—historically parochial, narrow with respect to class and race, and limited in conception of what are the necessary goods. Generally, the female's contribution to her material support is and always has been substantial; in many times and places it has been independently sufficient. One can and should distinguish between a partial and contingent material dependence created by a certain sort of money economy and class structure, and the nearly ubiquitous spiritual, emotional and material dependence of males on females. Males presently provide, off and on, a portion of the material support of women, within circumstances apparently designed to make it difficult for women to provide them for themselves. But females provide and generally have provided for males the energy and spirit for living; the males are nurtured by the females. And this the males apparently cannot do for themselves, even partially.

The parasitism of males on females is, as I see it, demonstrated by the panic, rage and hysteria generated in so many of them by the thought of being abandoned by women. But it is demonstrated in a way that is perhaps more generally persuasive by both literary and sociological evidence. Evidence cited in Jesse Bernard's work in *The Future of Marriage* and in George Gilder's *Sexual Suicide* and *Men Alone* convincingly shows that males tend in shockingly significant numbers and in alarming degree to fall into mental illness, petty crime, alcoholism, physical infirmity, chronic unemployment, drug addiction and neurosis when deprived of the care and companionship of a female mate, or keeper. (While on the other hand, women without male mates are significantly healthier and happier than women with male mates.) And masculist literature is abundant with indications of male cannibalism, of males deriving essential sustenance from females. Cannibalistic imagery, visual and verbal, is common in pornography: images likening women to food, and sex to eating. And, as documented in Millett's *Sexual Politics* and many other feminist analyses of masculist literature, the theme of men getting high off beating, raping or killing women (or merely bullying them) is common. These interactions with women, or rather, these actions upon women, make men feel good, walk tall, feel refreshed, invigorated. Men are drained and depleted by their living by themselves and with and among other men, and are revived and refreshed, re-created, by going home and being served dinner, changing to clean clothes, having sex with the wife; or by dropping by the apartment of a woman friend to be served coffee or a drink and stroked in one way or another; or by picking up a prostitute for a quicky or for a dip in favorite sexual escape fantasies; or by raping refugees from their wars (foreign and domestic). The ministrations of women, be they willing or unwilling, free or paid for, are what restore in men the strength, will and confidence to go on with what they call living.

If it is true that a fundamental aspect of the relations between the sexes is male parasitism, it might help to explain why certain issues are particularly exciting to patriarchal loyalists. For instance, in view of the obvious advantages of easy abortion to population control, to control of welfare rolls, and to ensuring sexual availability of women to men, it is a little surprising that the loyalists are so adamant and riled up in their objection to it. But look . . .

The fetus lives parasitically. It is a distinct animal surviving off the life (the blood) of another animal creature. It is incapable of surviving on its own resources, of independent nutrition; incapable even of symbiosis. If it is true that males live parasitically upon females, it seems reasonable to suppose that many of them and those loyal to them are in some way sensitive to the parallelism between their situation and that of the fetus. They could easily identify with the fetus. The woman who is free to see the fetus as a parasite[8] might be free to see the man as a parasite. The woman's willingness to cut off the life line to one parasite suggests a willingness to cut off the life line to another parasite. The woman who is capable (legally, psychologically, physically) of decisively, self-interestedly, independently rejecting the one parasite, is capable of rejecting, with the same decisiveness and independence, the like burden of the other parasite. In the eyes of the other parasite, the image of the wholly self-determined abortion, involving not even a ritual submission to male veto power, is the mirror image of death.

Another clue here is that one line of argument against free and easy abortion is the slippery slope argument that if fetuses are to be freely dispensed with, old people will be next. Old people? Why are old people next? And why the great concern for them? Most old people are women, indeed, and patriarchal loyalists are not generally so solicitous of the welfare of any women. Why old people? Because, I think, in the modern patriarchal divisions of labor, old people too are parasites on women. The anti-abortion folks seem not to worry about wife beating and wife murder—there is no broad or emotional popular support for stopping these violences. They do not worry about murder and involuntary sterilization in prisons, nor murder in war, nor murder by pollution and industrial accidents.

Either these are not real to them or they cannot identify with the victims; but anyway, killing in general is not what they oppose. They worry about the rejection *by women, at women's discretion,* of something which lives parasitically on women. I suspect that they fret not because old people are next, but because men are next.

There are other reasons, of course, why patriarchal loyalists should be disturbed about abortion on demand; a major one being that it would be a significant form of female control of reproduction, and at least from certain angles it looks like the progress of patriarchy *is* the progress toward male control of reproduction, starting with possession of wives and continuing through the invention of obstetrics and the technology of extrauterine gestation. Giving up that control would be giving up patriarchy. But such an objection to abortion is too abstract, and requires too historical a vision, to generate the hysteria there is now in the reaction against abortion. The hysteria is, I think, to be accounted for more in terms of a much more immediate and personal presentiment of ejection by the woman-womb.[9]

I discuss abortion here because it seems to me to be the most publicly emotional and most physically dramatic ground on which the theme of separation and male parasitism is presently being played out. But there are other locales for this play. For instance,[10] women with newly raised consciousnesses tend to leave marriages and families, either completely through divorce, or partially, through unavailability of their cooking, housekeeping and sexual services. And women academics tend to become alienated from their colleagues and male mentors and no longer serve as sounding board, ego booster, editor, mistress or proofreader. Many awakening women become celibate or lesbian, and the others become a very great deal more choosy about when, where and in what relationships they will have sex with men. And the men affected by these separations generally react with defensive hostility, anxiety and guilt-tripping, not to mention descents into illogical argument which match and exceed their own most fanciful images of female irrationality. My claim is that they are very afraid because they depend very heavily upon the goods they receive from women, and these separations cut them off from those goods.

Male parasitism means that males *must have access* to women; it is the Patriarchal Imperative. But feminist no-saying is more than a substantial removal (redirection, reallocation) of goods and services because Access is one of the faces of Power. Female denial of male access to females substantially cuts off a flow of benefits, but it has also the form and full portent of assumption of power.

Differences of power are always manifested in asymmetrical access. The President of the United States has access to almost everybody for almost anything he might want of them, and almost nobody has access to him. The super-rich have access to almost everybody; almost nobody has access to them. The resources of the employee are available to the boss as the resources of the boss are not to the employee. The parent has unconditional access to the child's room; the child does not have similar access to the parent's room. Students adjust to professors' office hours; professors do not adjust to students' conference hours. The child is required not to lie; the parent is free to close out the child with lies at her discretion. The slave is unconditionally accessible to the master. Total power is unconditional access; total powerlessness is being unconditionally accessible. The creation and manipulation of power is constituted of the manipulation and control of access.

All-woman groups, meetings, projects seem to be great things for causing controversy and confrontation. Many women are offended by them; many are afraid to be the one to announce the exclusion of men; it is seen as a device whose use needs much elaborate justification. I think this is because conscious and deliberate exclusion of men by women, from anything, is blatant insubordination, and generates in women fear of punishment and reprisal (fear which is often well-justified). Our own timidity and desire to avoid confrontations generally keep us from doing very much in the way of all-woman groups and meetings. But when we do, we invariably run into the male champion who challenges our right to do it. Only a small minority of men go crazy when an event is advertised to be for women only—just one man tried to crash our women-only Rape Speak-Out, and only a few hid under the auditorium seats to try to spy on a women-only meeting at a NOW convention in Philadelphia. But these few are onto something their less rabid com-patriots are missing. The woman-only meeting is a fundamental challenge to the structure of power. It is always the privilege of the master to enter the slave's hut. The slave who decides to exclude the master from her hut is declaring herself not a slave. The exclusion of men from the meeting not only deprives them of certain benefits (which they might survive without); it is a controlling of access, hence an assumption of power. It is not only mean, it is arrogant.

It becomes clearer now why there is always an off-putting aura of negativity about separatism— one which offends the feminine pollyanna in us and smacks of the purely defensive to the political theorist in us. It is this: First: When those who control access have made you totally accessible, your first act of taking control must be denying access, or must have denial of access as one of its aspects. This is not because you are charged up with (unfeminine or politically incorrect) negativity; it is because of the logic of the situation. When we start from a position of total accessibility there *must* be an aspect of no-saying (which is the beginning of control) in *every effective* act and strategy, the effective ones being precisely those which *shift power,* i.e., ones which involve manipulation and control of access. Second: Whether or not one says "no," or withholds or closes out or rejects, on this occasion or that, the capacity and ability to say "no" (with effect) is logically necessary to control. When we are in control of access to ourselves there will be some no-saying, and when we are more accustomed to it, when it is more common, an ordinary part of living, it will not seem so prominent, obvious, or strained . . . we will not strike ourselves or others as being particularly negative. In this aspect of ourselves and our lives, we will strike ourselves pleasingly as active beings with momentum of our own, with sufficient shape and structure— with sufficient integrity—to generate friction. Our experience of our no-saying will be an aspect of our experience of our definition.

When our feminist acts or practices have an aspect of separation, we are assuming power by controlling access and simultaneously by undertaking definition. The slave who excludes the master from her hut thereby declares herself *not a slave.* And *definition* is another face of power.

The powerful normally determine what is said and sayable. When the powerful label something or dub it or baptize it, the thing becomes what they call it. When the Secretary of Defense calls something a peace negotiation, for instance, then whatever it is that he called a peace negotiation is an instance of negotiating peace. If the activity in question is the working out of terms of a trade-off of nuclear reactors and territorial redistributions, complete with arrangements for the resulting refugees, that is peacemaking. People laud it, and the negotiators get Noble Piece Prizes for it. On the other hand, when I call a certain speech act a rape, my "calling" it does not make it so. At best, I have to explain and justify and make clear exactly what it is about this speech act which is assaultive in just what way, and then the others acquiesce in saying the act was *like* rape or could figuratively be called a rape. My counterassault will not be counted a simple case of self-defense. And what I called rejection of parasitism, they call the loss of the womanly virtues of compassion and "caring." And generally, when renegade women call something one thing and patriarchal loyalists call it another, the loyalists get their way.[11]

Women generally are not the people who do the defining, and we cannot from our isolation and powerlessness simply commence saying different things than others say and make it stick. There is a humpty-dumpty problem in that. But we are able to arrogate definition to ourselves when we repattern access. Assuming control of access, we draw new boundaries and create new roles and relationships. This, though it causes some strain, puzzlement and hostility, is to a fair extent within the scope of individuals and small gangs, as outright verbal redefinition is not, at least in the first instance.

One may see access as coming in two sorts, "natural" and humanly arranged. A grizzly bear has what you might call natural access to the picnic basket of the unarmed human. The access of the boss to the personal services of the secretary is humanly arranged access; the boss exercises institutional power. It looks to me, looking from a certain angle, like institutions *are* humanly designed patterns of access—access to persons and their services. But institutions are artifacts of definition. In the case of intentionally and formally designed institutions, this is very clear, for the relevant definitions are explicitly set forth in by-laws and constitutions, regulations and rules. When one defines the term "president," one defines presidents in terms of what they can do and what is owed them by other offices, and "what they can do" is a matter of their access to the services of others. Similarly, definitions of *dean, student, judge,* and *cop* set forth patterns of access, and definitions of *writer, child, owner,* and of course, *husband, wife,* and *man* and *girl.* When one changes the pattern of access, one forces new uses of words on those affected. The term 'man' has to shift in meaning when rape is no longer possible. When we take control of sexual access to us, of access to our nurturance and to our reproductive function, access to mothering and sistering, we redefine the word 'woman.' The shift of usage is pressed on others by a change in social reality; it does not await their recognition of our definitional authority.

When women separate (withdraw, break out, regroup, transcend, shove aside, step outside, migrate, say *no*), we are simultaneously controlling access and defining. We are doubly insubordinate, since neither of these is permitted. And access and definition are fundamental ingredients in the alchemy of power, so we are doubly, and radically, insubordinate.

If these, then, are some of the ways in which separation is at the heart of our struggle, it helps to explain why separation is such a hot topic. If there is one thing women are queasy about it is *actually taking power.* As long as one stops just short of that, the patriarchs will for the most part take an indulgent attitude. We are afraid of what will happen to us when we really frighten them. This is not an irrational fear. It is our experience in the movement generally that the defensiveness, nastiness, violence, hostility and irrationality of the reaction to feminism tends to correlate with the blatancy of the element of separation in the strategy or project which triggers the reaction.

The separations involved in women leaving homes, marriages and boyfriends, separations from fetuses, and the separation of lesbianism are all pretty dramatic. That is, they are dramatic and blatant when perceived from within the framework provided by the patriarchal world view and male parasitism. Matters pertaining to marriage and divorce, lesbianism and abortion touch individual men (and their sympathizers) because they can feel the relevance of these to themselves—they can feel the threat that they might be the next. Hence, heterosexuality, marriage and motherhood, which are the institutions which most obviously and individually maintain female accessibility to males, form the core triad of antifeminist ideology; and all-woman spaces, all-woman organizations, all-woman meetings, all-woman classes, are outlawed, suppressed, harassed, ridiculed and punished—in the name of that other fine and enduring patriarchal institution, Sex Equality.

To some of us these issues can seem almost foreign . . . strange ones to be occupying center stage. We are busily engaged in what seem to *us* our blatant insubordinations: living our own lives, taking care of ourselves and one another, doing our work, and in particular, telling it as we see it. Still, the original sin is the separation which these presuppose, and it is that, not our art or philosophy, not our speechmaking, nor our "sexual acts" (or abstinences), for which we will be persecuted, when worse comes to worst.

[1978]

NOTES

1. *Adrienne Rich: ". . . makes me question the whole idea of 'courtesy' or 'rudeness'—surely their constructs, since women become 'rude' when we ignore or reject male obnoxiousness, while male 'rudeness' is usually punctuated with the 'Haven't you a sense of humor' tactic."* Yes; me too. I embrace rudeness; our compulsive/compulsory politeness so often is what coerces us into their "fellowship."

2. Help from Claudia Card.

3. *Ti-Grace Atkinson: Should give more attention here to our vulnerability to assault and degradation, and to separation as protection.* Okay, but then we have to re-emphasize that it has to be separation at *our* behest—we've had enough of their imposed separation for our "protection." (There's no denying that in my real-life, protection and maintenance of places for healing are major motives for separation.)

4. Help from Chris Pierce and Sara Ann Ketchem. See "Separatism and Sexual Relationships," in *A Philosophical Approach to Women's Liberation,* eds. S. Hill and M. Weinzweig (Wadsworth, Belmont, California, 1978).

5. Answering Claudia Card.

6. Levity due to Carolyn Shafer.

7. I first noticed this when reading *Beyond God the Father,* by Mary Daly (Beacon Press, Boston, 1973). See also *Women's Evolution,* by Evelyn Reed (Pathfinder Press, New York, 1975) for rich hints about male cannibalism and male dependence.

8. *Caroline Whitbeck: Cross-cultural evidence suggests it's not the fetus that gets rejected in cultures where abortion is common, it is the role of motherhood, the burden, in particular, of "illegitimacy"; where the institution of illegitimacy does not exist, abortion rates are pretty low.* This suggests to me that the woman's rejection of the fetus is even more directly a rejection of the male and his world than I had thought.

9. Claudia Card.

10. The instances mentioned are selected for their relevance to the lives of the particular women addressed in this talk. There are many other sorts of instances to be drawn from other sorts of women's lives.

11. This paragraph and the succeeding one are the passage which has provoked the most substantial questions from women who read the paper. One thing that causes trouble here is that I am talking from a stance or position that is ambiguous—it is located in two different and non-communicating systems of thought-action. *Re* the patriarchy and the English language, there is general usage over which I/we do not have the control that elite males have (with the cooperation of all the ordinary patriarchal loyalists). *Re* the new being and meaning which are being created now by lesbian-feminists, we *do* have semantic authority and, collectively, can and do define with effect. I think it is only by maintaining our boundaries through controlling concrete access to us that we can enforce on those who are not-us our definitions of ourselves, hence force on them *the fact of our existence* and thence open up the *possibility* of our having semantic authority with them. (I wrote some stuff that's relevant to this in the last section of my paper "Male Chauvinism—A Conceptual Analysis"—see note 12.) Our unintelligibility to patriarchal loyalists is a source of pride and delight, in some contexts; but if we don't have an effect on their usage while we continue, willy nilly, to be subject to theirs, being totally unintelligible to them could be fatal. (A friend of mine had a dream where the women were meeting in a cabin at the edge of town, and they had a sort of inspiration through the vision of one of them that they should put a sign on the door which would connect with the patriarchs' meaning-system, for otherwise the men would be too curious/frightened about them and would break the door down to get in. They put a picture of a fish on the door.) Of course, you might say that *being* intelligible to them might be fatal. Well, perhaps it's best to be in a position to make tactical decisions about when and how to be intelligible and unintelligible.

12. In (improbably enough) *Philosophy and Sex,* edited by Robert Baker and Frederick Elliston (Prometheus Books, Buffalo, New York, 1976).

 57

Age, Race, Class, and Sex: Women Redefining Difference

AUDRE LORDE

Much of Western European history conditions us to see human differences in simplistic opposition to each other: dominant/subordinate, good/bad, up/down, superior/inferior. In a society where the good is defined in terms of profit rather than in terms of human need, there must always be some group of people who, through systematized oppression, can be made to feel surplus, to occupy the place of the dehumanized inferior. Within this society, that group is made up of Black and Third World people, working-class people, older people, and women.

As a forty-nine-year-old Black lesbian feminist socialist mother of two, including one boy, and a member of an interracial couple, I usually find myself a part of some group defined as other, deviant, inferior, or just plain wrong. Traditionally, in american society, it is the members of oppressed, objectified groups who are expected to stretch out and bridge the gap between the actualities of our lives and the consciousness of our oppressor. For in order to survive, those of us for whom oppression is as american as apple pie have always had to be watchers, to become familiar with the language and manners of the oppressor, even sometimes adopting them for some illusion of protection. Whenever the need for some pretense of communication arises, those who profit from our oppression call upon us to share our knowledge with them. In other words, it is the responsibility of the oppressed to teach the oppressors their mistakes. I am responsible for educating teachers who dismiss my children's culture in school. Black and Third World people are expected to educate white people as to our humanity. Women are expected to educate men. Lesbians and gay men are expected to educate the heterosexual world. The oppressors maintain their position and evade responsibility for their own actions. There is a constant drain of energy which might be better used in redefining ourselves and devising realistic scenarios for altering the present and constructing the future.

Institutionalized rejection of difference is an absolute necessity in a profit economy which needs outsiders as surplus people. As members of such an economy, we have *all* been programmed to respond to the human differences between us with fear and loathing and to handle that difference in one of three ways: ignore it, and if that is not possible, copy it if we think it is dominant, or destroy it if we think it is subordinate. But we have no patterns for relating across our human differences as equals. As a result, those differences have been misnamed and misused in the service of separation and confusion.

Certainly there are very real differences between us of race, age, and sex. But it is not those differences between us that are separating us. It is rather our refusal to recognize those differences, and to examine the distortions which result from our misnaming them and their effects upon human behavior and expectation.

Racism, the belief in the inherent superiority of one race over all others and thereby the right to dominance. Sexism, the belief in the inherent superiority of one sex over the other and thereby the right to dominance. Ageism. Heterosexism. Elitism. Classism.

It is a lifetime pursuit for each one of us to extract these distortions from our living at the same time as we recognize, reclaim, and define those differences upon which they are imposed. For we have all been raised in a society where those distortions were endemic within our living. Too often, we pour the energy needed for recognizing and exploring difference into pretending those differences are insurmountable barriers, or that they do not exist at all. This results in a voluntary isolation, or false and treacherous connections. Either way, we do not develop tools for using human difference as a springboard for creative change within our lives. We speak not of human difference, but of human deviance.

Somewhere, on the edge of consciousness, there is what I call a *mythical norm,* which each one of us within our hearts knows "that is not me." In america, this norm is usually defined as white, thin, male, young, heterosexual, christian, and financially secure. It is with this mythical norm that the trappings of power reside within this society. Those of us who

stand outside that power often identify one way in which we are different, and we assume that to be the primary cause of all oppression, forgetting other distortions around difference, some of which we ourselves may be practising. By and large within the women's movement today, white women focus upon their oppression as women and ignore differences of race, sexual preference, class, and age. There is a pretense to a homogeneity of experience covered by the word *sisterhood* that does not in fact exist.

Unacknowledged class differences rob women of each others' energy and creative insight. Recently a women's magazine collective made the decision for one issue to print only prose, saying poetry was a less "rigorous" or "serious" art form. Yet even the form our creativity takes is often a class issue. Of all the art forms, poetry is the most economical. It is the one which is the most secret, which requires the least physical labor, the least material, and the one which can be done between shifts, in the hospital pantry, on the subway, and on scraps of surplus paper. Over the last few years, writing a novel on tight finances, I came to appreciate the enormous differences in the material demands between poetry and prose. As we reclaim our literature, poetry has been the major voice of poor, working class, and Colored women. A room of one's own may be a necessity for writing prose, but so are reams of paper, a typewriter, and plenty of time. The actual requirements to produce the visual arts also help determine, along class lines, whose art is whose. In this day of inflated prices for material, who are our sculptors, our painters, our photographers? When we speak of a broadly based women's culture, we need to be aware of the effect of class and economic differences on the supplies available for producing art.

As we move toward creating a society within which we can each flourish, ageism is another distortion of relationship which interferes without vision. By ignoring the past, we are encouraged to repeat its mistakes. The "generation gap" is an important social tool for any repressive society. If the younger members of a community view the older members as contemptible or suspect or excess, they will never be able to join hands and examine the living memories of the community, nor ask the all important question, "Why?" This gives rise to a historical amnesia that keeps us working to invent the wheel every time we have to go to the store for bread.

We find ourselves having to repeat and relearn the same old lessons over and over that our mothers did because we do not pass on what we have learned, or because we are unable to listen. For instance, how many times has this all been said before? For another, who would have believed that once again our daughters are allowing their bodies to be hampered and purgatoried by girdles and high heels and hobble skirts?

Ignoring the differences of race between women and the implications of those differences presents the most serious threat to the mobilization of women's joint power.

As white women ignore their built-in privilege of whiteness and define *woman* in terms of their own experience alone, then women of Color become "other," the outsider whose experience and tradition is too "alien" to comprehend. An example of this is the signal absence of the experience of women of Color as a resource for women's studies courses. The literature of women of Color is seldom included in women's literature courses and almost never in other literature courses nor in women's studies as a whole. All too often, the excuse given is that the literatures of women of Color can only be taught by Colored women, or that they are too difficult to understand, or that classes cannot "get into" them because they come out of experiences that are "too different." I have heard this argument presented by white women of otherwise quite clear intelligence, women who seem to have no trouble at all teaching and reviewing work that comes out of the vastly different experiences of Shakespeare, Molière, Dostoyefsky, and Aristophanes. Surely there must be some other explanation.

This is a very complex question, but I believe one of the reasons white women have such difficulty reading Black women's work is because of their reluctance to see Black women as women and different from themselves. To examine Black women's literature effectively requires that we be seen as whole people in our actual complexities—as individuals, as women, as human—rather than as one of those problematic but familiar stereotypes provided in this society in place of genuine images of Black women. And I believe this holds true for the literatures of other women of Color who are not Black.

The literatures of all women of Color recreate the textures of our lives, and many white women are heavily invested in ignoring the real differences. For as long as any difference between us means one of us must be inferior, then the recognition of any difference must be fraught with guilt. To allow women of Color to step out of stereotypes is too guilt provoking, for it threatens the complacency of those women who view oppression only in terms of sex.

Refusing to recognize difference makes it impossible to see the different problems and pitfalls facing us as women.

Thus, in a patriarchal power system where white-skin privilege is a major prop, the entrapments used to neutralize Black women and white women are not the same. For example, it is easy for Black women to be used by the power structure against Black men, not because they are men, but because they are Black. Therefore, for Black women, it is necessary at all times to separate the needs of the oppressor from our own legitimate conflicts within our communities. This same problem does not exist for white women. Black women and men have shared racist oppression and still share it, although in different ways. Out of that shared oppression we have developed joint defenses and joint vulnerabilities to each other that are not duplicated in the white community, with the exception of the relationship between Jewish women and Jewish men.

On the other hand, white women face the pitfall of being seduced into joining the oppressor under the pretense of sharing power. This possibility does not exist in the same way for women of Color. The tokenism that is sometimes extended to us is not an invitation to join power; our racial "otherness" is a visible reality that makes that quite clear. For white women there is a wider range of pretended choices and rewards for identifying with patriarchal power and its tools.

Today, with the defeat of ERA, the tightening economy, and increased conservatism, it is easier once again for white women to believe the dangerous fantasy that if you are good enough, pretty enough, sweet enough, quiet enough, teach the children to behave, hate the right people, and marry the right men, then you will be allowed to co-exist with patriarchy in relative peace, at least until a man needs your job or the neighborhood rapist happens along. And true, unless one lives and loves in the trenches it is difficult to remember that the war against dehumanization is ceaseless.

But Black women and our children know the fabric of our lives is stitched with violence and with hatred, that there is no rest. We do not deal with it only on the picket lines, or in dark midnight alleys, or in the places where we dare to verbalize our resistance. For us, increasingly, violence weaves through the daily tissues of our living—in the supermarket, in the classroom, in the elevator, in the clinic and the schoolyard, from the plumber, the baker, the saleswoman, the bus driver, the bank teller, the waitress who does not serve us.

Some problems we share as women, some we do not. You fear your children will grow up to join the patriarchy and testify against you, we fear our children will be dragged from a car and shot down in the street, and you will turn your backs upon the reasons they are dying.

The threat of difference has been no less blinding to people of Color. Those of us who are Black must see that the reality of our lives and our struggle does not make us immune to the errors of ignoring and misnaming difference. Within Black communities where racism is a living reality, differences among us often seem dangerous and suspect. The need for unity is often misnamed as a need for homogeneity, and a Black feminist vision mistaken for betrayal of our common interests as a people. Because of a continuous battle against racial erasure that Black women and Black men share, some Black women still refuse to recognize that we are also oppressed as women, and that sexual hostility against Black women is practiced not only by the white racist society, but implemented within our Black communities as well. It is a disease striking the heart of Black nationhood, and silence will not make it disappear. Exacerbated by racism and the pressures of powerlessness, violence against Black women and children often becomes a standard within our communities, one by which manliness can be measured. But these woman-hating acts are rarely discussed as crimes against Black women.

As a group, women of Color are the lowest paid wage earners in america. We are the primary targets of abortion and sterilization abuse, here and abroad. In certain parts of Africa, small girls are still being sewed shut between their legs to keep them docile and for men's pleasure. This is known as female circumcision, and it is not a cultural affair as the late Jomo Kenyatta insisted, it is a crime against Black women.

Black women's literature is full of the pain of frequent assault, not only by a racist patriarchy, but also by Black men. Yet the necessity for and history of shared battle have made us, Black women, particularly vulnerable to the false accusation that anti-sexist is anti-Black. Meanwhile, womanhating as a recourse of the powerless is sapping strength from Black communities, and our very lives. Rape is on the increase, reported and unreported, and rape is not aggressive sexuality, it is sexualized aggression. As Kalamu ya Salaam, a Black male writer points out, "As long as male domination exists, rape will exist. Only women revolting and men made conscious of their responsibility to fight sexism can collectively stop rape."[1]

Differences between ourselves as Black women are also being misnamed and used to separate us from one another. As a Black lesbian feminist comfortable with the many different ingredients of my identity, and a woman committed to racial and sexual freedom from oppression, I find I am constantly being encouraged to pluck out some one aspect of myself and present this as the meaningful whole, eclipsing or denying the other parts of self. But this is a destructive and fragmenting way to live. My fullest concentration of energy is available to me only when I integrate all the parts of who I am, openly, allowing power from particular sources of my living to flow back and forth freely through all my different selves, without the restrictions of externally imposed definition. Only then can I bring myself and my energies as a whole to the service of those struggles which I embrace as part of my living.

A fear of lesbians, or of being accused of being a lesbian, has led many Black women into testifying against themselves. It has led some of us into destructive alliances, and others into despair and isolation. In the white women's communities, heterosexism is sometimes a result of identifying with the white patriarchy, a rejection of that interdependence between women-identified women which allows the self to be, rather than to be used in the service of men. Sometimes it reflects a die-hard belief in the protective coloration of heterosexual relationships, sometimes a self-hate which all women have to fight against, taught us from birth.

Although elements of these attitudes exist for all women, there are particular resonances of heterosexism and homophobia among Black women. Despite the fact that woman-bonding has a long and honorable history in the African and African-american communities, and despite the knowledge and accomplishments of many strong and creative women-identified Black women in the political, social and cultural fields, heterosexual Black women often tend to ignore or discount the existence and work of Black lesbians. Part of this attitude has come from an understandable terror of Black male attack within the close confines of Black society, where the punishment for any female self-assertion is still to be accused of being a lesbian and therefore unworthy of the attention or support of the scarce Black male. But part of this need to misname and ignore Black lesbians comes from a very real fear that openly women-identified Black women who are no longer dependent upon men for their self-definition may well reorder our whole concept of social relationships.

Black women who once insisted that lesbianism was a white woman's problem now insist that Black lesbians are a threat to Black nationhood, are consorting with the enemy, are basically un-Black. These accusations, coming from the very women to whom we look for deep and real understanding, have served to keep many Black lesbians in hiding, caught between the racism of white women and the homophobia of their sisters. Often, their work has been ignored, trivialized, or misnamed, as with the work of Angelina Grimke, Alice Dunbar-Nelson, Lorraine Hansberry. Yet women-bonded women have always been some part of the power of Black communities, from our unmarried aunts to the amazons of Dahomey.

And it is certainly not Black lesbians who are assaulting women and raping children and grandmothers on the streets of our communities.

Across this country, as in Boston during the spring of 1979 following the unsolved murders of twelve Black women, Black lesbians are spearheading movements against violence against Black women.

What are the particular details within each of our lives that can be scrutinized and altered to help bring about change? How do we redefine difference for all women? It is not our differences which separate women, but our reluctance to recognize those differences and to deal effectively with the distortions which have resulted from the ignoring and misnaming of those differences.

As a tool of social control, women have been encouraged to recognize only one area of human difference as legitimate, those differences which exist between women and men. And we have learned to deal across those differences with the urgency of all oppressed subordinates. All of us have had to learn to live or work or coexist with men, from our fathers on. We have recognized and negotiated these differences, even when this recognition only continued the old dominant/subordinate mode of human relationship, where the oppressed must recognize the masters' difference in order to survive.

But our future survival is predicated upon our ability to relate within equality. As women, we must root out internalized patterns of oppression within ourselves if we are to move beyond the most superficial aspects of social change. Now we must recognize differences among women who are our equals, neither inferior nor superior, and devise ways to use each others' difference to enrich our visions and our joint struggles.

The future of our earth may depend upon the ability of all women to identify and develop new definitions of power and new patterns of relating across difference. The old definitions have not served us, nor the earth that supports us. The old patterns, no matter how cleverly rearranged to imitate progress, still condemn us to cosmetically altered repetitions of the same old exchanges, the same old guilt, hatred, recrimination, lamentation, and suspicion.

For we have, built into all of us, old blueprints of expectation and response, old structures of oppression, and these must be altered at the same time as we alter the living conditions which are a result of those structures. For the master's tools will never dismantle the master's house.

As Paulo Freire shows so well in *The Pedagogy of the Oppressed*,[2] the true focus of revolutionary change is never merely the oppressive situations which we seek to escape, but that piece of the oppressor which is planted deep within each of us, and which knows only the oppressors' tactics, the oppressors' relationships.

Change means growth, and growth can be painful. But we sharpen self-definition by exposing the self in work and struggle together with those whom we define as different from ourselves, although sharing the same goals. For Black and white, old and young, lesbian and heterosexual women alike, this can mean new paths to our survival.

We have chosen each other
and the edge of each others battles
the war is the same
if we lose
someday women's blood will congeal
upon a dead planet
if we win
there is no telling
we seek beyond history
for a new and more possible meeting.[3]

[1984]

NOTES

1. From "Rape: A Radical Analysis, An African-American Perspective" by Kalamu ya Salaam in *Black Books Bulletin,* vol. 6, no. 4 (1980).
2. Seabury Press, New York, 1970.
3. From "Outlines," unpublished poem.

 58

From The Reproduction of Mothering: Psychoanalysis and the Sociology of Gender

NANCY CHODOROW

THE SEXUAL SOCIOLOGY OF ADULT LIFE

Hence, there is a typically asymmetrical relation of the marriage pair to the occupational structure.

This asymmetrical relation apparently both has exceedingly important positive functional significance and is *at the same time an important source of strain in relation to the patterning of sex roles.*

—Talcott Parsons,
"The Kinship System of the
Contemporary United States"

Girls and boys develop different relational capacities and senses of self as a result of growing up in a family in which women mother. These gender personalities are reinforced by differences in the identification processes of boys and girls that also result from women's mothering. Differing relational capacities and forms of identification prepare women and men to assume the adult gender roles which situate women primarily within the sphere of reproduction in a sexually unequal society.

Gender Identification and Gender Role Learning

All social scientists who have examined processes of gender role learning and the development of a sense of identification in boys and girls have argued that the asymmetrical organization of parenting in which women mother is the basic cause of significant contrasts between feminine and masculine identification processes.[1] Their discussions range from concern with the learning of appropriate gender role behavior—through imitation, explicit training and admonitions, and cognitive learning processes—to concern with the development of basic gender identity. The processes these people discuss seem to be universal, to the extent that all societies are constituted around a structural split, growing out of women's mothering, between the private, domestic world of women and the public, social world of men.[2] Because the first identification for children of both genders has always been with their mother, they argue, and because children are first around women, women's family roles and being feminine are more available and often more intelligible to growing children than masculine roles and being masculine. Hence, male development is more complicated than female because of the difficult shifts of identification which a boy must make to attain his expected gender identification and gender role assumption. Their view contrasts sharply to the psychoanalytic stress on the difficulties inherent in feminine development as girls make their convoluted way to heterosexual object choice.[3]

Because all children identify first with their mother, a girl's gender and gender role identification processes are continuous with her earliest identifications and a boy's are not. A girl's oedipal identification with her mother, for instance, is continuous with her earliest primary identification (and also in the context of her early dependence and attachment). The boy's oedipal crisis, however, is supposed to enable him to shift in favor of an identification with his father. He gives up, in addition to his oedipal and preoedipal attachment to his mother, his primary identification with her.

What is true specifically for oedipal identification is equally true for more general gender identification and gender role learning. A boy, in order to feel himself adequately masculine, must distinguish and differentiate himself from others in a way that a girl need not—must categorize himself as someone apart. Moreover, he defines masculinity negatively as that which is not feminine and/or connected to women, rather than positively.[4] This is another way boys come to deny and repress relation and connection in the process of growing up.

These distinctions remain even where much of a girl's and boy's socialization is the same, and where both go to school and can participate in adulthood in the labor force and other nonfamilial institutions. Because girls at the same time grow up in a family where mothers are the salient parent and caretaker, they also can begin to identify more directly and immediately with their mothers and their mothers' familial roles than can boys with their fathers and men. Insofar as a woman's identity remains primarily as a wife/mother, moreover, there is greater generational continuity in role and life-activity from mother to daughter than there can be from father to son. This identity may be less than totally appropriate, as girls must realistically expect to spend much of their life in the labor force, whereas their mothers were less likely to do so. Nevertheless, family organization and ideology still produce these gender differences, and generate expectations that women much more than men will find a primary identity in the family.

Permanent father-absence, and the "father absence" that is normal in our society, do not mean that boys do not learn masculine roles or proper masculine behavior, just as there is no evidence that homosexuality in women correlates with father absence.[5] What matters is the extent to which a child of either gender can form a personal relationship with their object of identification, and the differences in modes of identification that result from this. Mitscherlich, Slater, Winch, and Lynn all speak to these differences.[6] They suggest that girls in contemporary society develop a personal identification with their mother, and that a tie between affective processes and role learning—between libidinal and ego development—characterizes feminine development. By contrast, boys develop a positional identification with aspects of the masculine role. For them, the tie between affective processes and role learning is broken.

Personal identification, according to Slater and Winch, consists in diffuse identification with someone else's general personality, behavioral traits, values, and attitudes. Positional identification consists, by contrast, in identification with specific aspects of another's role and does not necessarily lead to the internalization of the values or attitudes of the person identified with. According to Slater, children preferentially choose personal identification because this grows out of a positive affective relationship to a person who is there. They resort to positional identification residually and reactively, and identify with the perceived role or situation of another when possibilities for personal identification are not available.

In our society, a girl's mother is present in a way that a boy's father, and other adult men, are not. A girl, then, can develop a personal identification with her mother, because she has a real relationship with her that grows out of their early primary tie. She learns what it is to be womanlike in the context of this personal identification with her mother and often with other female models (kin, teachers, mother's friends, mothers of friends). Feminine identification, then, can be based on the gradual learning of a way of being familiar in everyday life, exemplified by the relationship with the person with whom a girl has been most involved.

A boy must attempt to develop a masculine gender identification and learn the masculine role in the absence of a continuous and ongoing personal relationship to his father (and in the absence of a continuously available masculine role model). This positional identification occurs both psychologically and sociologically. Psychologically, as is clear from descriptions of the masculine oedipus complex, boys appropriate those specific components of the masculinity of their father that they fear will be otherwise used against them, but do not as much identify diffusely with him as a person. Sociologically, boys in father-absent and normally father-remote families develop a sense of what it is to be masculine through identification with cultural images of masculinity and men chosen as masculine models.

Boys are taught to be masculine more consciously than girls are taught to be feminine. When fathers or men are not present much, girls are taught the heterosexual components of their role, whereas boys are assumed to learn their heterosexual role without teaching, through interaction with their mothers.[7] By contrast, other components of masculinity must be more consciously imposed. Masculine identification, then, is predominantly a gender role identification. By contrast, feminine identification is predominantly *parental:* "Males tend to identify with a cultural stereotype of the masculine role; whereas females tend to identify with aspects of their own mother's role specifically."[8]

Girls' identification processes, then, are more continuously embedded in and mediated by their ongoing relationship with their mother. They develop through and stress particularistic and affective relationships to others. A boy's identification processes are not likely to be so embedded in or mediated by a real affective relation to his father. At the same time, he tends to deny identification with and relationship to his mother and reject what he takes to be the feminine world; masculinity is defined as much negatively as positively. Masculine identification processes stress differentiation from others, the denial of affective relation, and categorical universalistic components of the masculine role. Feminine identification processes are relational, whereas masculine identification processes tend to deny relationship.

These distinctions do not mean that the development of femininity is all sugar and spice for a girl, but that it poses different *kinds* of problems for her than the development of masculinity does for a boy.

The feminine identification that a girl attains and the masculine identification about which a boy remains uncertain are valued differently. In their unattainability, masculinity and the masculine role are fantasized and idealized by boys (and often by girls), whereas feminity and the feminine role remain for a girl all too real and concrete. The demands on women are often contradictory—for instance, to be passive and dependent in relation to men, and active and independently initiating toward children. In the context of the ego and object-relational issues I described in the preceding chapters, moreover, it is clear that mother-identification presents difficulties. A girl identifies with and is expected to identify with her mother in order to attain her adult feminine identification and learn her adult gender role. At the same time she must be sufficiently differentiated to grow up and experience herself as a separate individual—must overcome primary identification while maintaining and building a secondary identification.

Studies suggest that daughters in American society have problems with differentiation from and identification with their mothers.[9] Slater reports that all forms of personal parental identification (cross-gender and same-gender) correlate with freedom from psychosis or neurosis except personal identification of a daughter with her mother. Johnson reports that a boy's identification with his father relates to psychological adjustment, whereas a girl's with her mother does not. The implication in both accounts is that for a girl, just as for a boy, there can be too much of mother. It may be easy, but possibly too easy, for a girl to attain a feminine gender identification.

. . .

Even when men and women cross into the other's sphere, their roles remain different. Within the family, being a husband and father is different from being a wife and mother; as women have become more involved in the family, men have become less so. Parson's characterization of men's instrumental role in the family may be too extreme, but points us in the right direction. A father's first responsibility is to "provide" for his family monetarily. His emotional contribution is rarely seen as of equal importance. Men's work in the home, in all but a few households, is defined in gender-stereotyped ways. When men do "women's" chores—the dishes, shopping, putting children to bed—this activity is often organized and delegated by the wife/mother, who retains residual responsibility (men "babysit" their own children; women do not). Fathers, though they relate to their children, do so in order to create "independence."[10] This is facilitated by a father's own previous socialization for repression and denial of relation, and his current participation in the public nonrelational world. Just as children know their fathers "under the sway of the reality principle,"[11] so also do fathers know their children more as separate people than mothers do.

. . .

Mothering, Masculinity, and Capitalism

. . .

Masculinity is presented to a boy as less available and accessible than femininity, as represented by his mother. A boy's mother is his primary caretaker. At the same time, masculinity is idealized or accorded superiority, and thereby becomes even more desirable. Although fathers are not as salient as mothers in daily interaction, mothers and children often idealize them and give them ideological primacy, precisely because of their absence and seeming inaccessibility, and because of the organization and ideology of male dominance in the larger society.

Masculinity becomes an issue in a way that femininity does not. Masculinity does not become an issue because of some intrinsic male biology, nor because masculine roles are inherently more difficult than feminine roles, however. Masculinity becomes an issue as a direct result of a boy's experience of himself in his family—as a result of his being parented by a woman. For children of both genders, mothers represent regression and lack of autonomy. A boy associates these issues with his gender identification as well. Dependence on his mother, attachment to her, and identification with her represent that which is not masculine; a boy must reject dependence and deny attachment and identification. Masculine gender role training becomes much more rigid than feminine. A boy represses those qualities he takes to be feminine inside himself, and rejects and devalues women and whatever he considers to be feminine in the social world.

Thus, boys define and attempt to construct their sense of masculinity largely in negative terms. Given that masculinity is so elusive, it becomes important for masculine identity that certain social activities are defined as masculine and superior, and that women are believed unable to do many of the things defined as socially important. It becomes important to think that women's economic and social contribution cannot equal men's. The secure possession of certain realms, and the insistence that these realms are superior to the maternal world of youth, become crucial both to the definition of masculinity and to a particular boy's own masculine gender identification.[12]

Freud describes the genesis of this stance in the masculine oedipal crisis. A boy's struggle to free himself from his mother and become masculine generates "the contempt felt by men for a sex which is the lesser"[13]—"What we have come to consider the normal male contempt for women."[14]

Both sexes learn to feel negatively toward their mother during the oedipal period. A girl's negative feelings, however, are not so much contempt and devaluation as fear and hostility: "The little girl, incapable of such contempt because of her own identical nature, frees herself from the mother with a degree of hostility far greater than any comparable hostility in the boy."[15] A boy's contempt serves to free him not only from his mother but also from the femininity within himself. It therefore becomes entangled with the issue of masculinity and is generalized to all women. A girl's hostility remains tied more to her relationship to her mother (and/or becomes involved in self-depreciation).

A boy's oedipus complex is directly tied to issues of masculinity, and the devaluation of women is its "normal" outcome. A girl's devaluation of or hostility toward her mother may be a part of the process, but its "normal" outcome, by contrast, entails acceptance of her own femininity and identification with her mother. Whatever the individual resolution of the feminine oedipus complex, however, it does not become institutionalized in the same way.

. . .

Women's mothering produces a psychological and ideological complex in men concerning women's secondary valuation and sexual inequality. Because women are responsible for early child care and for most later socialization as well, because fathers are more absent from the home, and because men's activities generally have been removed from the home while women's have remained within it, boys have difficulty in attaining a stable masculine gender role identification. Boys fantasize about and idealize the masculine role and their fathers, and society defines it as desirable.

Given that men control not only major social institutions but the very definition and constitution of society and culture, they have the power and ideological means to enforce these perceptions as more general norms, and to hold each other accountable for their enforcement. (This is not solely a matter of force. Since these norms define men as superior, men gain something by maintaining them.[16]) The structure of parenting creates ideological and psychological modes which reproduce orientations to and structures of male dominance in individual men, and builds an assertion of male superiority into the definition of masculinity itself.

The same repressions, denials of affect and attachment, rejection of the world of women and things feminine, appropriation of the world of men and identification with the father that create a psychology of masculine superiority also condition men for participation in the capitalist work world. Both capitalist accumulation and proper work habits in workers have never been purely a matter of economics. Particular personality characteristics and behavioral codes facilitated the transition to capitalism. Capitalists developed inner direction, rational planning, and organization, and workers developed a willingness to come to work at certain hours and work steadily, whether or not they needed money that day.

Psychological qualities become perhaps even more important with the expansion of bureaucracy and hierarchy: In modern capitalism different personality traits are required at different levels of the bureaucratic hierarchy.[17] Lower level jobs are often directly and continuously supervised, and are best performed by someone willing to obey rules and conform to external authority. Moving up the hierarchy, jobs require greater dependability and predictability, the ability to act without direct and continuous supervision. In technical, professional, and managerial positions, workers must on their own initiative carry out the goals and values of the organization for which they work, making those goals and values their own. Often they must be able to draw on their interpersonal capacities as a skill. Parental child-rearing values and practices (insofar as these latter reflect parental values) reflect these differences: Working class parents are more likely to value obedience, conformity to external authority, neatness, and other "behavioral" characteristics in their children; middle-class parents emphasize more "internal" and interpersonal characteristics like responsibility, curiosity, self-motivation, self-control, and consideration.[18]

· · ·

In American families, Parsons argues, where mothers tend not to have other primary affective figures around, a mutual erotic investment between son[19] and mother develops—an investment the mother can then manipulate. She can love, reward, and frustrate him at appropriate moments in order to get him to delay gratification and sublimate or repress erotic needs. This close, exclusive, preoedipal mother-child relationship first develops dependency in a son, creating a motivational basis for early learning and a foundation for dependency on others. When a mother "rejects" her son or pushes him to be more independent, the son carries his still powerful dependence with him, creating in him both a general need to please and conform outside of the relationship to the mother herself and a strong assertion of independence. The isolated, husband-absent mother thus helps to create in her son a pseudo-independence masking real dependence, and a generalized sense that he ought to "do well" rather than an orientation to specific goals. This generalized sense can then be used to serve a variety of specific goals—goals not set by these men themselves. The oedipus complex in the contemporary family creates a "'dialectical' relationship between dependency, on the one hand, independence and achievement on the other."[20]

In an earlier period of capitalist development, individual goals were important for more men, and entrepreneurial achievement as well as worker discipline had to be based more on inner moral direction and repression. Earlier family arrangements, where dependency was not so salient nor the mother-child bond so exclusive, produced this greater inner direction. Today, with the exception of a very few, individual goals have become increasingly superseded by the goals of complex organizations: "Goals can no longer be directly the individual's responsibility and cannot be directly specified to him as a preparation for his role."[21] The contemporary family, with its manipulation of dependency in the mother-child relationship, and its production of generalized achievement orientation rather than inner goals and standards, produces personalities "that have become a fully fluid resource for societal functions."[22]

Slater extends Parsons's discussion. People who start life with only one or two emotional objects, he argues, develop a "willingness to put all [their] emotional eggs in one symbolic basket."[23] Boys who grow up in American middle-class nuclear families have this experience.[24] Because they received such a great amount of gratification from their mother relative to what they got from anyone else, and because their relationship to her was so exclusive, it is unlikely that they can repeat such a relationship. They relinquish their mother as an object of dependent attachment and deny their dependence on her, but, because she was so uniquely important, they retain her as an oedipally motivated object to win in fantasy—they retain an unconscious sense that there is one finally satisfying prize to be won. They turn their lives into a search for a success that will both prove their independence and win their mother. But because they have no inner sense of goals or real autonomy apart from this unconscious, unattainable goal from the past, and because success in the external world does not for the most part bring real satisfactions or real independence, their search is likely to be never-ending. They are likely to continue to work and to continue to accept the standards of the situation that confronts them.

This situation contrasts to that of people who have had a larger number of pleasurable relationships in early infancy. Such people are more likely to expect gratification in immediate relationships and maintain commitments to more people, and are less likely to deny themselves now on behalf of the future. They would not be the same kind of good worker, given that work is defined in individualist, noncooperative, outcome-oriented ways, as it is in our society.

. . .

Contemporary family structure produces not only malleability and lack of internalized standards, but often a search for manipulation. These character traits lend themselves to the manipulations of modern capitalism—to media and product consumerism, to the attempt to legitimate a polity that serves people unequally, and finally to work performance. The decline of the oedipal father creates an orientation to external authority and behavioral obedience. Exclusive maternal involvement and the extension of dependence create a generalized need to please and to "succeed," and a seeming independence. This need to succeed can help to make someone dependable and reliable. Because it is divorced from specific goals and real inner standards but has involved the maintenance of an internal dependent relationship, it can also facilitate the taking of others' goals as one's own, producing the pseudo-independent organization man.

An increasingly father-absent, mother-involved family produces in men a personality that both corresponds to masculinity and male dominance as these are currently constituted in the sex-gender system, and fits appropriately with participation in capitalist relations of production. Men continue to enforce the sexual division of spheres as a defense against powerlessness in the labor market. Male denial of dependence and of attachment to women helps to guarantee both masculinity and performance in the world of work. The relative unavailability of the father and overavailability of the mother create negative definitions of masculinity and men's fear and resentment of women, as well as the lack of inner autonomy in men that enables, depending on particular family constellation and class origin, either rule-following or the easy internalization of the values of the organization.

Thus, women's and men's personality traits and orientations mesh with the sexual and familial division of labor and unequal ideology of gender and shape their asymmetric location in a structure of production and reproduction in which women are in the first instance mothers and wives and men are workers. This structure of production and reproduction requires and presupposes those specific relational modes, between husband and wife, and mother and children, which form the center of the family in contemporary society. An examination of the way that gender personality is expressed in adulthood reveals how women and men create, and are often committed to creating, the interpersonal relationships which underlie and reproduce the family structure that produced them.

[1978]

NOTES

1. For a review of the literature which argues this, see Biller, 1971, *Father, Child.* See also Stoller, 1965, "The Sense of Maleness." For a useful recent formulation, see Johnson, 1975, "Fathers, Mothers."
2. See Mead, 1949, *Male and Female;* Michelle Z. Rosaldo, 1974, "Woman, Culture, and Society"; Nancy Chodorow, 1971, "Being and Doing," and 1974, "Family Structure and Feminine Personality," in Rosaldo and Lamphere, eds., *Woman, Culture and Society,* pp. 43–66; Beatrice Whiting, ed., 1963, *Six Cultures;* Beatrice B. Whiting and John W. M. Whiting, 1975, *Children of Six Cultures;* John Whiting, 1959, "Sorcery, Sin"; Burton and Whiting, 1961, "The Absent Father."
3. The extent of masculine difficulty varies, as does the extent to which identification processes for boys and girls differ. This variance depends on the extent of the public-domestic split in a subculture or society—the extent to which men, men's work, and masculine activities are removed from the home, and therefore masculinity and personal relations with adult men are hard to come by for a child.
4. See Richard T. Roessler, 1971, "Masculine Differentiation and Feminine Constancy," *Adolescence,* 6, #22, pp. 187–196; E. M. Bennett and L. R. Cohen, 1959, "Men and Women, Personality Patterns and Contrasts," *Genetic Psychology Monographs,* 59, pp. 101–155; Johnson, 1963, "Sex Role Learning," and 1975, "Fathers, Mothers"; Stoller, 1964, "A Contribution to the Study," 1965, "The Sense of Maleness," and 1968, "The Sense of Femaleness," *Psychoanalytic Quarterly,* 37, #1, pp. 42–55.
5. See Biller, 1971, *Father, Child.*
6. Mitscherlich, 1963, *Society Without the Father;* Philip E. Slater, 1961, "Toward a Dualistic Theory of Identification," *Merrill-Palmer Quarterly of Behavior and Development,* 7, #2, pp. 113–126; Robert F. Winch, 1962, *Identification and Its Familial Determinants;* David B. Lynn, 1959, "A Note on Sex Differences," and 1962, "Sex Role and Parent."
7. Johnson, 1975, "Fathers, Mothers," and Maccoby and Jacklin, 1974, *The Psychology of Sex Differences,* point this out.
8. D. B. Lynn, 1959, "A Note on Sex Differences," p. 130.
9. See Slater, 1961, "Toward a Dualistic Theory," and Johnson, 1975, "Fathers, Mothers."
10. See, for example, Johnson, 1975, "Fathers, Mothers"; Parsons and Bales, 1955, *Family, Socialization;* Deutsch, 1944, *Psychology of Women.*
11. Alice Balint, 1939, "Love for the Mother."

12. On these issues, see Lynn, 1959, "A Note on Sex Differences," and 1962, "Sex Role and Parent"; Parsons, 1942, "Age and Sex"; Mitscherlich, 1963, *Society Without the Father;* Slater, 1968, *The Glory of Hera;* Mead, 1949, *Male and Female.*
13. Freud, 1925, "Some Psychical Consequences," p. 253.
14. Brunswick, 1940, "The Preoedipal Phase," p. 246.
15. Ibid.
16. But for discussions of ways that this accountability is actively maintained, see Joseph H. Plock and Jack Sawyer, 1974. *Men and Masculinity,* and Marc F. Fasteau, 1974, *The Male Machine.*
17. It is certainly possible that these same characteristics apply in all extensively bureaucratic and hierarchical settings (in the U.S.S.R. and Eastern Europe, for instance); however, the work I am drawing on has investigated only the capitalist West, and especially the United States. My formulation of the personality requirements of the hierarchical firm follows Edwards, 1975, "The Social Relations of Production."
18. See Melvin L. Kohn, 1969, *Class and Conformity.*
19. Parsons and his colleagues talk of the "mother-child" relationship. However, they focus on erotic, oedipal attachment as motivating, and on the development of character traits which are appropriate to masculine work capacity and not to feminine expressive roles. It is safe to conclude, therefore, that the child they have in mind is male.
20. Talcott Parsons with Winston White, 1961, "The Link Between Character and Society," in *Social Structure and Personality,* p. 218.
21. Ibid., p. 203.
22. Ibid, p. 233.
23. Slater, 1974. *Earthwalk.* See also Slater, 1970. *The Pursuit of Loneliness.*
24. Again, girls do as well, and both genders transfer it to monogamic, jealous tendencies. But Slater is talking about the sexually toned oedipal/preoedipal relationship that is more specific to boys.

 59

The Straight Mind

MONIQUE WITTIG

In recent years in Paris, language as a phenomenon has dominated modern theoretical systems and the social sciences and has entered the political discussions of the lesbian and women's liberation movements. This is because it relates to an important political field where what is at play is power, or more than that, a network of powers, since there is a multiplicity of languages that constantly act upon the social reality. The importance of language as such as a political stake has only recently been perceived.[1] But the gigantic development of linguistics, the multiplication of schools of linguistics, the advent of the sciences of communication, and the technicality of the metalanguages that these sciences utilize, represent the symptoms of the importance of what is politically at stake. The science of language has invaded other sciences, such as anthropology through Lévi-Strauss, psychoanalysis through Lacan, and all the disciplines which have developed from the basis of structuralism.

The early semiology of Roland Barthes nearly escaped from linguistic domination to become a political analysis of the different systems of signs, to establish a relationship between this or that system of signs—for example, the myths of the petit bourgeois class—and the class struggle within capitalism that this system tends to conceal. We were almost saved, for political semiology is a weapon (a method) that we need to analyze what is called ideology. But the miracle did not last. Rather than introducing into semiology concepts which are foreign to it—in this case Marxist concepts—Barthes quickly stated that semiology was only a branch of linguistics and that language was its only object.

Thus, the entire world is only a great register where the most diverse languages come to have themselves recorded, such as the language of the Unconscious,[2] the language of fashion, the language of the exchange of women where human beings are literally the signs which are used to communicate. These languages, or rather these discourses, fit into one another, interpenetrate one another, support one another, reinforce one another, auto-engender, and engender one another. Linguistics engenders semiology and structural linguistics, structural linguistics engenders structuralism, which engenders the Structural Unconscious. The ensemble of these discourses produces a confusing static for the oppressed, which makes them lose sight of the material cause of their oppression and plunges them into a kind of ahistoric vacuum.

For they produce a scientific reading of the social reality in which human beings are given as invariants, untouched by history and unworked by class conflicts, with identical psyches because genetically programmed. This psyche, equally untouched by history and unworked by class conflicts, provides the specialists, from the beginning of the twentieth century, with a whole arsenal of invariants: the symbolic language which very advantageously functions with very few elements, since, like digits (0–9), the symbols "unconsciously" produced by the psyche are not very numerous. Therefore, these symbols are very easy to impose, through therapy and theorization, upon the collective and individual unconscious. . . .

• • •

The discourses which particularly oppress all of us, lesbians, women, and homosexual men, are those which take for granted that what founds society, any society, is heterosexuality.[3] These discourses speak about us and claim to say the truth in an apolitical field, as if anything of that which signifies could escape the political in this moment of history, and as if, in what concerns us, politically insignificant signs could exist. These discourses of heterosexuality oppress us in the sense that they prevent us from speaking unless we speak in their terms. Everything which puts them into question is at once disregarded as elementary. Our refusal of the totalizing interpretation of psychoanalysis makes the theoreticians say that we neglect the symbolic dimension. These discourses deny us every possibility of creating our own categories. But their most ferocious action is the unrelenting tyranny that they exert upon our physical and mental selves.

When we use the overgeneralizing term "ideology" to designate all the discourses of the dominating group, we relegate these discourses to the domain of Irreal Ideas; we forget the material (physical) violence that they directly do to the oppressed people, a violence produced by the abstract and "scientific" discourses as well as by the discourses of the mass media. I would like to insist on the material oppression of individuals by discourses, and I would like to underline its immediate effects through the example of pornography.

Pornographic images, films, magazine photos, publicity posters on the walls of the cities, constitute a discourse, and this discourse covers our world with its signs, and this discourse has a meaning: it signifies that women are dominated. Semioticians can interpret the system of this discourse, describe its disposition. What they read in that discourse are signs whose function is not to signify and which have no *raison d'être* except to be elements of a certain system or disposition. But for us this discourse is not divorced from the real as it is for semioticians. Not only does it maintain very close relations with the social reality which is our oppression (economically and politically), but also it is in itself real since it is one of the aspects of oppression, since it exerts a precise power over us. The pornographic discourse is one of the strategies of violence which are exercised upon us: it humiliates, it degrades, it is a crime against our "humanity." As a harassing tactic it has another function, that of a warning. It orders us to stay in line, and it keeps those who would tend to forget who they are in step; it calls upon fear. These same experts in semiotics, referred to earlier, reproach us for confusing, when we demonstrate against pornography, the discourses with the reality. They do not see that this discourse *is* reality for us, one of the facets of the reality of our oppression. They believe that we are mistaken in our level of analysis.

I have chosen pornography as an example because its discourse is the most symptomatic and the most demonstrative of the violence which is done to us through discourses, as well as in the society at large. There is nothing abstract about the power that sciences and theories have to act materially and actually upon our bodies and our minds, even if the discourse that produces it is abstract. It is one of the forms of domination, its very expression. I would say, rather, one of its exercises. All of the oppressed know this power and have had to deal with it. It is the one which says: you do not have the right to speech because your discourse is not scientific and not theoretical, you are on the wrong level of analysis, you are confusing discourse and reality, your discourse is naive, you misunderstand this or that science.

If the discourse of modern theoretical systems and social science exert a power upon us, it is because it works with concepts which closely touch us. In spite of the historic advent of the lesbian, feminist, and gay liberation movements, whose proceedings have already upset the philosophical and political categories of the discourses of the social sciences, their categories (thus brutally put into

question) are nevertheless utilized without examination by contemporary science. They function like primitive concepts in a conglomerate of all kinds of disciplines, theories, and current ideas that I will call the straight mind. (See *The Savage Mind* by Claude Lévi-Strauss.) They concern "woman," "man," "sex," "difference," and all of the series of concepts which bear this mark, including such concepts as "history," "culture," and the "real." And although it has been accepted in recent years that there is no such thing as nature, that everything is culture, there remains within that culture a core of nature which resists examination, a relationship excluded from the social in the analysis—a relationship whose characteristic is ineluctability in culture, as well as in nature, and which is the heterosexual relationship. I will call it the obligatory social relationship between "man" and "woman." (Here I refer to Ti-Grace Atkinson and her analysis of sexual intercourse as an institution.[4]) With its ineluctability as knowledge, as an obvious principle, as a given prior to any science, the straight mind develops a totalizing interpretation of history, social reality, culture, language, and all the subjective phenomena at the same time. I can only underline the oppressive character that the straight mind is clothed in in its tendency to immediately universalize its production of concepts into general laws which claim to hold true for all societies, all epochs, all individuals. Thus one speaks of *the* exchange of women, *the* difference between the sexes, *the* symbolic order, *the* Unconscious, Desire, *Jouissance*, Culture, History, giving an absolute meaning to these concepts when they are only categories founded upon heterosexuality, or thought which produces the difference between the sexes as a political and philosophical dogma.

The consequence of this tendency toward universality is that the straight mind cannot conceive of a culture, a society where heterosexuality would not order not only all human relationships but also its very production of concepts and all the processes which escape consciousness, as well. Additionally, these unconscious processes are historically more and more imperative in what they teach us about ourselves through the instrumentality of specialists. The rhetoric which expresses them (and whose seduction I do not underestimate) envelops itself in myths, resorts to enigma, proceeds by accumulating metaphors, and its function is to poeticize the obligatory character of the "you-will-be-straight-or-you-will-not-be."

In this thought, to reject the obligation of coitus and the institutions that this obligation has produced as necessary for the constitution of a society, is simply an impossibility, since to do this would mean to reject the possibility of the constitution of the other and to reject the "symbolic order," to make the constitution of meaning impossible, without which no one can maintain an internal coherence. Thus lesbianism, homosexuality, and the societies that we form cannot be thought of or spoken of, even though they have always existed. Thus, the straight mind continues to affirm that incest, and not homosexuality, represents its major interdiction. Thus, when thought by the straight mind, homosexuality is nothing but heterosexuality.

Yes, straight society is based on the necessity of the different/other at every level. It cannot work economically, symbolically, linguistically, or politically without this concept. This necessity of the different/other is an ontological one for the whole conglomerate of sciences and disciplines that I call the straight mind. But what is the different/other if not the dominated? For heterosexual society is the society which not only oppresses lesbians and gay men, it oppresses many different/others, it oppresses all women and many categories of men, all those who are in the position of the dominated. To constitute a difference and to control it is an "act of power, since it is essentially a normative act. Everybody tries to show the other as different. But not everybody succeeds in doing so. One has to be socially dominant to succeed in it."[5]

For example, the concept of difference between the sexes ontologically constitutes women into different/others. Men are not different, whites are not different, nor are the masters. But the blacks, as well as the slaves, are. This ontological characteristic of the difference between the sexes affects all the concepts which are part of the same conglomerate. But for us there is no such thing as being-woman or being-man. "Man" and "woman" are political concepts of opposition, and the copula which dialectically unites them is, at the same time, the one which abolishes them.[6] It is the class struggle between women and men which will abolish men and women.[7] The concept of difference has nothing ontological about it. It is only the way that the masters interpret a historical situation of domination. The function of difference is to mask at every level the conflicts of interest, including ideological ones.

In other words, for us, this means there cannot any longer be women and men, and that as classes and categories of thought or language they have to disappear, politically, economically, ideologically. If we, as lesbians and gay men, continue to speak of ourselves and to conceive of ourselves as women and as men, we are instrumental in maintaining heterosexuality. I am sure that an economic and political transformation will not dedramatize these categories of language. Can we redeem *slave*? Can we redeem *nigger, negress*? How is *woman* different? Will we continue to write *white, master, man*? The transformation of economic relationships will not suffice. We must produce a political transformation of the key concepts, that is of the concepts which are strategic for us. For there is another order of materiality, that of language, and language is worked upon from within by these strategic concepts. It is at the same time tightly connected to the political field, where everything that concerns language, science and thought refers to the person as subjectivity and to her/his relationship to society. And we cannot leave this within the power of the straight mind or the thought of domination.

If among all the productions of the straight mind I especially challenge the models of the Structural Unconscious, it is because: at the moment in history when the domination of social groups can no longer appear as a logical necessity to the dominated, because they revolt, because they question the differences, Lévi-Strauss, Lacan, and their epigones call upon necessities which escape the control of consciousness and therefore the responsibility of individuals.

They call upon unconscious processes, for example, which require the exchange of women as a necessary condition for every society. According to them, that is what the unconscious tells us with authority, and the symbolic order, without which there is no meaning, no language, no society, depends on it. But what does women being exchanged mean if not that they are dominated? No wonder then that there is only one Unconscious, and that it is heterosexual. It is an Unconscious which looks too consciously after the interests of the masters[8] in whom it lives for them to be dispossessed of their concepts so easily. Besides, domination is denied; there is no slavery of women, there is difference. To which I will answer with this statement made by a Rumanian peasant at a public meeting in 1848: "Why do the gentlemen say it was not slavery, for we know it to have been slavery, this sorrow that we have sorrowed." Yes, we know it, and this science of oppression cannot be taken away from us.

It is from this science that we must track down the "what-goes-without-saying" heterosexual, and (I paraphrase the early Roland Barthes) we must not bear "seeing Nature and History confused at every turn."[9] We must make it brutally apparent that psychoanalysis after Freud and particularly Lacan have rigidly turned their concepts into myths—Difference, Desire, the Name-of-the-father, etc. They have even "over-mythified" the myths, an operation that was necessary for them in order to systematically heterosexualize that personal dimension which suddenly emerged through the dominated individuals into the historical field, particularly through women, who started their struggle almost two centuries ago. And it has been done systematically, in a concert of interdisciplinarity, never more harmonious than since the heterosexual myths started to circulate with ease from one formal system to another, like sure values that can be invested in anthropology as well as in psychoanalysis and in all the social sciences.

This ensemble of heterosexual myths is a system of signs which uses figures of speech, and thus it can be politically studied from within the science of our oppression; "for-we-know-it-to-have-been-slavery" is the dynamic which introduces the diachronism of history into the fixed discourse of eternal essences. This undertaking should somehow be a political semiology, although with "this sorrow that we have sorrowed" we work also at the level of language/manifesto, of language/action, that which transforms, that which makes history.

In the meantime, in the systems that seemed so eternal and universal that laws could be extracted from them, laws that could be stuffed into computers, and in any case for the moment stuffed into the unconscious machinery, in these systems, thanks to our action and our language, shifts are happening. Such a model, as for example, the exchange of women, reengulfs history in so violent and brutal a way that the whole system, which was believed to be formal, topples over into another dimension of knowledge. This dimension of history belongs to us, since somehow we have been designated, and since, as Lévi-Strauss said, we talk, let us say that we break off the heterosexual contract.

So, this is what lesbians say everywhere in this country and in some others, if not with theories at least through their social practice, whose repercussions upon straight culture and society are still unenvisionable. An anthropologist might say that we have to wait for fifty years. Yes, if one wants to universalize the functioning of these societies and make their invariants appear. Meanwhile the straight concepts are undermined. What is woman? Panic, general alarm for an active defense. Frankly, it is a problem that the lesbians do not have because of a change of perspective, and it would be incorrect to say that lesbians associate, make love, live with women, for "woman" has meaning only in heterosexual systems of thought and heterosexual economic systems. Lesbians are not women.

[1978]

NOTES

1. However, the classical Greeks knew that there was no political power without mastery of the art of rhetoric, especially in a democracy.
2. Throughout this paper, when Lacan's use of the term "the Unconscious" is referred to it is capitalized, following his style.
3. Heterosexuality: a word which first appears in the French language in 1911.
4. Ti-Grace Atkinson, *Amazon Odyssey* (New York: Links Books, 1974), pp. 13–23.
5. Claude Faugeron and Philippe Robert, *La Justice et son public et les représentations sociales du système pénal* (Paris: Masson, 1978).
6. See, for her definition of "social sex," Nicole-Claude Mathieu, "Notes pour une définition sociologique des catégories de sexe," *Epistémologie Sociologique* 11 (1971). Translated as *Ignored by Some, Denied by Others: The Social Sex Category in Sociology* (pamphlet), Explorations in Feminism 2 (London: Women's Research and Resources Centre Publications, 1977), pp. 16–37.
7. In the same way that in every other class struggle the categories of opposition are "reconciled" by the struggle whose goal is to make them disappear.
8. Are the millions of dollars a year made by the psychoanalysts symbolic?
9. Roland Barthes, *Mythologies* (New York: Hill and Wang, 1972), p. 11.

❦ 60

Compulsory Heterosexuality and Lesbian Existence

ADRIENNE RICH

II

If women are the earliest sources of emotional caring and physical nurture for both female and male children, it would seem logical, from a feminist perspective at least, to pose the following questions: whether the search for love and tenderness in both sexes does not originally lead toward women; *why in fact women would ever redirect that search;* why species survival, the means of impregnation, and emotional/erotic relationships should ever have become so rigidly identified with each other; and why such violent strictures should be found necessary to enforce women's total emotional, erotic loyalty and subservience to men. I doubt that enough feminist scholars and theorists have taken the pains to acknowledge the societal forces which wrench women's emotional and erotic energies away from themselves and other women and from woman-identified values. These forces, as I shall try to show, range from literal physical enslavement to the disguising and distorting of possible options.

I do not assume that mothering by women is a "sufficient cause" of lesbian existence. But the issue of mothering by women has been much in the air of late, usually accompanied by the view that increased parenting by men would minimize antagonism between the sexes and equalize the sexual imbalance of power of males over females. These discussions are carried on without reference to compulsory heterosexuality as a phenomenon, let alone as an ideology. I do not wish to psychologize here, but rather to identify sources of male power. I believe large numbers of men could, in fact, undertake child care on a large scale without radically altering the balance of male power in a male-identified society.

In her essay "The Origin of the Family," Kathleen Gough lists eight characteristics of male power in archaic and contemporary societies which I would like to use as a framework: "men's ability to deny women sexuality or to force it upon them; to command or exploit their labor to control their produce; to control or rob them of their children; to confine them physically and prevent their movement; to use them as objects in male transactions; to cramp their creativeness; or to withhold from them large areas of the society's knowledge and cultural attainments."[1] (Gough does not perceive these power characteristics as specifically enforcing heterosexuality, only as producing sexual inequality.) Below, Gough's words appear in italics; the elaboration of each of her categories, in brackets, is my own.

Characteristics of male power include *the power of men*

1. *to deny women* [their own] *sexuality*—[by means of clitoridectomy and infibulation; chastity belts; punishment, including death, for female adultery; punishment, including death, for lesbian sexuality; psychoanalytic denial of the clitoris; strictures against masturbation; denial of maternal and post-menopausal sensuality; unnecessary hysterectomy; pseudolesbian images in the media and literature; closing of archives and destruction of documents relating to lesbian existence]

2. *or to force it* [male sexuality] *upon them*—[by means of rape (including marital rape) and wife beating; father-daughter, brother-sister incest; the socialization of women to feel that male sexual "drive" amounts to a right,[2] idealization of heterosexual romance in art, literature, the media, advertising, etc.; child marriage; arranged marriage; prostitution; the harem; psychoanalytic doctrines of frigidity and vaginal orgasm; pornographic depictions of women responding pleasurably to sexual violence and humiliation (a subliminal message being that sadistic heterosexuality is more "normal" than sensuality between women)]

3. *to command or exploit their labor to control their produce*—[by means of the institutions of marriage and motherhood as unpaid production; the horizontal segregation of women in paid employment; the decoy of the upwardly mobile token woman; male control of abortion, contraception, sterilization, and childbirth; pimping; female infanticide, which robs

8 Charac. of Male Power

mothers of daughters and contributes to generalized devaluation of women]

4. *to control or rob them of their children*—[by means of father right and "legal kidnaping";[3] enforced sterilization; systematized infanticide; seizure of children from lesbian mothers by the courts; the malpractice of male obstetrics; use of the mother as "token torturer"[4] in genital mutilation or in binding the daughter's feet (or mind) to fit her for marriage]

5. *to confine them physically and prevent their movement*—[by means of rape as terrorism, keeping women off the streets; purdah; foot binding; atrophying of women's athletic capabilities; high heels and "feminine" dress codes in fashion; the veil; sexual harassment on the streets; horizontal segregation of women in employment; prescriptions for "full-time" mothering at home; enforced economic dependence of wives]

6. *to use them as objects in male transactions*—[use of women as "gifts"; bride price; pimping; arranged marriage; use of women as entertainers to facilitate male deals—e.g., wife-hostess, cocktail waitress required to dress for male sexual titillation, call girls, "bunnies," geisha, *kisaeng* prostitutes, secretaries]

7. *to cramp their creativeness*—[witch persecutions as campaigns against midwives and female healers, and as pogrom against independent, "unassimilated" women;[5] definition of male pursuits as more valuable than female within any culture, so that cultural values become the embodiment of male subjectivity; restriction of female self-fulfillment to marriage and motherhood; sexual exploitation of women by male artists and teachers; the social and economic disruption of women's creative aspirations;[6] erasure of female tradition][7]

8. *to withhold from them large areas of the society's knowledge and cultural attainments*—[by means of noneducation of females; the "Great Silence" regarding women and particularly lesbian existence in history and culture;[8] sex-role tracking which deflects women from science, technology, and other "masculine" pursuits; male social/professional bonding which excludes women; discrimination against women in the professions]

These are some of the methods by which male power is manifested and maintained. Looking at the schema, what surely impresses itself is the fact that

we are confronting not a simple maintenance of inequality and property possession, but a pervasive cluster of forces, ranging from physical brutality to control of consciousness, which suggests that an enormous potential counterforce is having to be restrained.

· · ·

III

I have chosen to use the terms *lesbian existence* and *lesbian continuum* because the word *lesbianism* has a clinical and limiting ring. *Lesbian existence* suggests both the fact of the historical presence of lesbians and our continuing creation of the meaning of that existence. I mean the term *lesbian continuum* to include a range—through each woman's life and throughout history—of woman-identified experience, not simply the fact that a woman has had or consciously desired genital sexual experience with another woman. If we expand it to embrace many more forms of primary intensity between and among women, including the sharing of a rich inner life, the bonding against male tyranny, the giving and receiving of practical and political support, if we can also hear it in such associations as *marriage resistance* and the "haggard" behavior identified by Mary Daly (obsolete meanings: "intractable," "willful," "wanton," and "unchaste," "a woman reluctant to yield to wooing"),[9] we begin to grasp breadths of female history and psychology which have lain out of reach as a consequence of limited, mostly clinical, definitions of *lesbianism.*

Lesbian existence comprises both the breaking of a taboo and the rejection of a compulsory way of life. It is also a direct or indirect attack on male right of access to women. But it is more than these, although we may first begin to perceive it as a form of naysaying to patriarchy, an act of resistance. It has of course, included isolation, self-hatred, breakdown, alcoholism, suicide, and intrawoman violence; we romanticize at our peril what it means to love and act against the grain, and under heavy penalties; and lesbian existence has been lived (unlike, say, Jewish or Catholic existence) without access to any knowledge of a tradition, a continuity, a social underpinning. The destruction of records and memorabilia and letters documenting the realities of lesbian existence must be taken very seriously as a means of keeping heterosexuality compulsory for women, since what has been kept from our knowledge is joy, sensuality, courage, and community, as well as guilt, self-betrayal, and pain.[10]

Lesbians have historically been deprived of a political existence through "inclusion" as female versions of male homosexuality. To equate lesbian existence with male homosexuality because each is stigmatized is to erase female reality once again. Part of the history of lesbian existence is, obviously, to be found where lesbians, lacking a coherent female community, have shared a kind of social life and common cause with homosexual men. But there are differences: women's lack of economic and cultural privilege relative to men; qualitative differences in female and male relationships—for example, the patterns of anonymous sex among male homosexuals, and the pronounced ageism in male homosexual standards of sexual attractiveness. I perceive the lesbian experience as being, like motherhood, a profoundly *female* experience, with particular oppressions, meanings, and potentialities we cannot comprehend as long as we simply bracket it with other sexually stigmatized existences. Just as the term *parenting* serves to conceal the particular and significant reality of being a parent who is actually a mother, the term *gay* may serve the purpose of blurring the very outlines we need to discern, which are of crucial value for feminism and for the freedom of women as a group.[11]

As the term *lesbian* has been held to limiting, clinical associations in its patriarchal definition, female friendship and comradeship have been set apart from the erotic, thus limiting the erotic itself. But as we deepen and broaden the range of what we define as lesbian existence, as we delineate a lesbian continuum, we begin to discover the erotic in female terms: as that which is unconfined to any single part of the body or solely to the body itself; as an energy not only diffuse but, as Audre Lorde has described it, omnipresent in "the sharing of joy, whether physical, emotional, psychic," and in the sharing of work; as the empowering joy which "makes us less willing to accept powerlessness, or those other supplied states of being which are not native to me, such as resignation, despair, self-effacement, depression, self-denial."[12] In another context, writing of women

and work, I quoted the autobiographical passage in which the poet H.D. described how her friend Bryher supported her in persisting with the visionary experience which was to shape her mature work:

> I knew that this experience, this writing-on-the-wall before me, could not be shared with anyone except the girl who stood so bravely there beside me. This girl said without hesitation, "Go on." It was she really who had the detachment and integrity of the Pythoness of Delphi. But it was I, battered and dissociated . . . who was seeing the pictures, and who was reading the writing or granted the inner vision. Or perhaps, in some sense, we were "seeing" it together, for without her, admittedly, I could not have gone on.[13]

If we consider the possibility that all women—from the infant suckling at her mother's breast, to the grown woman experiencing orgasmic sensations while suckling her own child, perhaps recalling her mother's milk smell in her own, to two women, like Virginia Woolf's Chloe and Olivia, who share a laboratory,[14] to the woman dying at ninety, touched and handled by women—exist on a lesbian continuum, we can see ourselves as moving in and out of this continuum, whether we identify ourselves as lesbian or not.

We can then connect aspects of woman identification as diverse as the impudent, intimate girl friendships of eight or nine year olds and the banding together of those women of the twelfth and fifteenth centuries known as Beguines who "shared houses, rented to one another, bequeathed houses to their room-mates . . . in cheap subdivided houses in the artisans' area of town," who "practiced Christian virtue on their own, dressing and living simply and not associating with men," who earned their livings as spinsters, bakers, nurses, or ran schools for young girls, and who managed—until the Church forced them to disperse—to live independent both of marriage and of conventual restrictions.[15] It allows us to connect these women with the more celebrated "Lesbians" of the women's school around Sappho of the seventh century B.C., with the secret sororities and economic networks reported among African women, and with the Chinese marriage-resistance sisterhoods—communities of women who refused marriage or who, if married, often refused to consummate their marriages and soon left their husbands, the only women in China who were not footbound and who, Agnes Smedley tells us, welcomed the births of daughters and organized successful women's strikes in the silk mills.[16] It allows us to connect and compare disparate individual instances of marriage resistance: for example, the strategies available to Emily Dickinson, a nineteenth-century white woman genius, with the strategies available to Zora Neale Hurston, a twentieth-century Black woman genius. Dickinson never married, had tenuous intellectual friendships with men, lived self-convented in her genteel father's house in Amherst, and wrote a lifetime of passionate letters to her sister-in-law Sue Gilbert and a smaller group of such letters to her friend Kate Scott Anthon. Hurston married twice but soon left each husband, scrambled her way from Florida to Harlem to Columbia University to Haiti and finally back to Florida, moved in and out of white patronage and poverty, professional success, and failure; her survival relationships were all with women, beginning with her mother. Both of these women in their vastly different circumstances were marriage resisters, committed to their own work and selfhood, and were later characterized as "apolitical." Both were drawn to men of intellectual quality; for both of them women provided the ongoing fascination and sustenance of life.

If we think of heterosexuality as *the* natural emotional and sensual inclination for women, lives such as these are seen as deviant, as pathological, or as emotionally and sensually deprived. Or, in more recent and permissive jargon, they are banalized as "life styles." And the work of such women, whether merely the daily work of individual or collective survival and resistance or the work of the writer, the activist, the reformer, the anthropologist, or the artist—the work of self-creation—is undervalued, or seen as the bitter fruit of "penis envy" or the sublimation of repressed eroticism or the meaningless rant of a "man-hater." But when we turn the lens of vision and consider the degree to which and the methods whereby heterosexual "preference" has actually been imposed on women, not only can we understand differently the meaning of individual lives and work, but we can begin to recognize a cen-

tral fact of women's history: that women have always resisted male tyranny. A feminism of action, often though not always without a theory, has constantly re-emerged in every culture and in every period. We can then begin to study women's struggle against powerlessness, women's radical rebellion, not just in male-defined "concrete revolutionary situations"[17] but in all the situations male ideologies have not perceived as revolutionary—for example, the refusal of some women to produce children, aided at great risk by other women;[18] the refusal to produce a higher standard of living and leisure for men (Leghorn and Parker show how both are part of women's unacknowledged, unpaid, and ununionized economic contribution). We can no longer have patience with Dinnerstein's view that women have simply collaborated with men in the "sexual arrangements" of history. We begin to observe behavior, both in history and in individual biography, that has hitherto been invisible or misnamed, behavior which often constitutes, given the limits of the counterforce exerted in a given time and place, radical rebellion. And we can connect these rebellions and the necessity for them with the physical passion of woman for woman which is central to lesbian existence: the erotic sensuality which has been, precisely, the most violently erased fact of female experience.

Heterosexuality has been both forcibly and subliminally imposed on women. Yet everywhere women have resisted it, often at the cost of physical torture, imprisonment, psychosurgery, social ostracism, and extreme poverty. "Compulsory heterosexuality" was named as one of the "crimes against women" by the Brussels International Tribunal on Crimes against Women in 1976. Two pieces of testimony from two very different cultures reflect the degree to which persecution of lesbians is a global practice here and now. A report from Norway relates:

> A lesbian in Oslo was in a heterosexual marriage that didn't work, so she started taking tranquillizers and ended up at the health sanatorium for treatment and rehabilitation. . . . The moment she said in family group therapy that she believed she was a lesbian, the doctor told her she was not. He knew from "looking into her eyes," he said. She had the

eyes of a woman who wanted sexual intercourse with her husband. So she was subjected to so-called "couch therapy." She was put into a comfortably heated room, naked, on a bed, and for an hour her husband was to . . . try to excite her sexually. . . . The idea was that the touching was always to end with sexual intercourse. She felt stronger and stronger aversion. She threw up and sometimes ran out of the room to avoid this "treatment." The more strongly she asserted that she was a lesbian, the more violent the forced heterosexual intercourse became. This treatment went on for about six months. She escaped from the hospital, but she was brought back. Again she escaped. She has not been there since. In the end she realized that she had been subjected to forcible rape for six months.

And from Mozambique:

I am condemned to a life of exile because I will not deny that I am a lesbian, that my primary commitments are, and will always be to other women. In the new Mozambique, lesbianism is considered a left-over from colonialism and decadent Western civilization. Lesbians are sent to rehabilitation camps to learn through self-criticism the correct line about themselves. . . . If I am forced to denounce my own love for women, if I therefore denounce myself, I could go back to Mozambique and join forces in the exciting and hard struggle of rebuilding a nation, including the struggle for the emancipation of Mozambiquan women. As it is, I either risk the rehabilitation camps, or remain in exile.[19]

Nor can it be assumed that women like those in Carroll Smith-Rosenberg's study, who married, stayed married, yet dwelt in a profoundly female emotional and passional world, "preferred" or "chose" heterosexuality. Women have married because it was necessary, in order to survive economically, in order to have children who would not suffer economic deprivation or social ostracism, in order to remain respectable, in order to do what was expected of women, because coming out of "abnormal" childhoods they wanted to feel "normal" and because heterosexual romance has been represented as the great female adventure, duty, and fulfillment. We may faithfully or ambivalently have obeyed the institution, but our feelings—and our sensuality—have not been tamed or contained within it. There is no statistical documentation of the numbers of lesbians who have remained in heterosexual mar-

riages for most of their lives. But in a letter to the early lesbian publication *The Ladder,* the playwright Lorraine Hansberry had this to say:

I suspect that the problem of the married woman who would prefer emotional-physical relationships with other women is proportionally much higher than a similar statistic for men. (A statistic surely no one will ever really have.) This because the estate of woman being what it is, how could we ever begin to guess the numbers of women who are not prepared to risk a life alien to what they have been taught all their lives to believe was their "natural" destiny— AND—their only expectation for ECONOMIC security. It seems to be that this is why the question has an immensity that it does not have for male homosexuals. . . . A woman of strength and honesty may, if she chooses, sever her marriage and marry a new male mate and society will be upset that the divorce rate is rising so—but there are few places in the United States, in any event, where she will be anything remotely akin to an "outcast." Obviously this is not true for a woman who would end her marriage to take up life with another woman.[20]

This *double life*—this apparent acquiescence to an institution founded on male interest and prerogative—has been characteristic of female experience: in motherhood and in many kinds of heterosexual behavior, including the rituals of courtship; the pretense of asexuality by the nineteenth-century wife; the simulation of orgasm by the prostitute, the courtesan, the twentieth-century "sexually liberated" woman.

Meridel LeSueur's documentary novel of the depression, *The Girl,* is arresting as a study of female double life. The protagonist, a waitress in a St. Paul working-class speakeasy, feels herself passionately attracted to the young man Butch, but her survival relationships are with Clara, an older waitress and prostitute, with Belle, whose husband owns the bar, and with Amelia, a union activist. For Clara and Belle and the unnamed protagonist, sex with men is in one sense an escape from the bedrock misery of daily life, a flare of intensity in the gray, relentless, often brutal web of day-to-day existence:

It was like he was a magnet pulling me. It was exciting and powerful and frightening. He was after me too and when he found me I would run, or be petrified, just standing in front of him like a zany. And he told me not to be wandering with Clara to the Marigold where we danced with strangers. He said he would knock the shit out of me. Which made me shake and tremble, but it was better than being a husk full of suffering and not knowing why.[21]

Throughout the novel the theme of double life emerges; Belle reminisces about her marriage to the bootlegger Hoinck:

You know, when I had that black eye and said I hit it on the cupboard, well he did it the bastard, and then he says don't tell anybody. . . . He's nuts, that's what he is, nuts, and I don't see why I live with him, why I put up with him a minute on this earth. But listen kid, she said, I'm telling you something. She looked at me and her face was wonderful. She said, Jesus Christ, Goddam him I love him that's why I'm hooked like this all my life, Goddam him I love him.[22]

After the protagonist has her first sex with Butch, her women friends care for her bleeding, give her whiskey, and compare notes.

My luck, the first time and I got into trouble. He gave me a little money and I come to St. Paul where for ten bucks they'd stick a huge vet's needle into you and you start it and then you were on your own. . . . I never had no child. I've just had Hoinck to mother, and a hell of a child he is.[23]

Later they made me go back to Clara's room to lie down. . . . Clara lay down beside me and put her arms around me and wanted me to tell her about it but she wanted to tell about herself. She said she started it when she was twelve with a bunch of boys in an old shed. She said nobody had paid any attention to her before and she became very popular. . . . They like it so much, she said, why shouldn't you give it to them and get presents and attention? I never cared anything for it and neither did my mama. But it's the only thing you got that's valuable.[24]

Sex is thus equated with attention from the male, who is charismatic though brutal, infantile, or unreliable. Yet it is the women who make life endurable for each other, give physical affection without causing pain, share, advise, and stick by each other. (*I am trying to find my strength through women—without my friends, I could not survive.*) LeSueur's *The Girl* parallels Toni Morrison's remarkable *Sula*, another revelation of female double life:

Nel was the one person who had wanted nothing from her, who had accepted all aspects of her. . . .

Nel was one of the reasons Sula had drifted back to Medallion. . . . The men . . . had merged into one large personality: the same language of love, the same entertainments of love, the same cooling of love. Whenever she introduced her private thoughts into their rubbings and goings, they hooded their eyes. They taught her nothing but love tricks, shared nothing but worry, gave nothing but money. She had been looking all along for a friend, and it took her a while to discover that a lover was not a comrade and could never be—for a woman.

But Sula's last thought at the second of her death is "Wait'll I tell Nel." And after Sula's death, Nel looks back on her own life:

"All that time, all that time, I thought I was missing Jude." And the loss pressed down on her chest and came up into her throat. "We was girls together," she said as though explaining something. "O Lord, Sula," she cried, "Girl, girl, girlgirlgirl!" It was a fine cry—loud and long—but it had no bottom and it had no top, just circles and circles of sorrow.[25]

The Girl and *Sula* are both novels which examine what I am calling the lesbian continuum, in contrast to the shallow or sensational "lesbian scenes" in recent commercial fiction.[26] Each shows us woman identification untarnished (till the end of LeSueur's novel) by romanticism; each depicts the competition of heterosexual compulsion for women's attention, the diffusion and frustration of female bonding that might, in a more conscious form, reintegrate love and power.

IV

Woman identification is a source of energy, a potential springhead of female power, curtailed and contained under the institution of heterosexuality. The denial of reality and visibility to women's passion for women, women's choice of women as allies, life companions, and community, the forcing of such relationships into dissimulation and their disintegration under intense pressure have meant an incalculable loss to the power of all women *to change the social relations of the sexes, to liberate ourselves and each other.* The lie of compulsory female heterosexuality today afflicts not just feminist scholarship, but every profession, every reference work, every curriculum, every organizing attempt, every relationship or conversation over which it hovers. It creates, specifically, a profound falseness, hypocrisy, and hysteria in the heterosexual dialogue, for every heterosexual relationship is lived in the queasy strobe light of that lie. However we choose to identify ourselves, however we find ourselves labeled, it flickers across and distorts our lives.[27]

The lie keeps numberless women psychologically trapped, trying to fit mind, spirit, and sexuality into a prescribed script because they cannot look beyond the parameters of the acceptable. It pulls on the energy of such women even as it drains the energy of "closeted" lesbians—the energy exhausted in the double life. The lesbian trapped in the "closet," the woman imprisoned in prescriptive ideas of the "normal" share the pain of blocked options, broken connections, lost access to self-definition freely and powerfully assumed.

The lie is many-layered. In Western tradition, one layer—the romantic—asserts that women are inevitably, even if rashly and tragically, drawn to men; that even when that attraction is suicidal (e.g., *Tristan and Isolde*, Kate Chopin's *The Awakening*), it is still an organic imperative. In the tradition of the social sciences it asserts that primary love between the sexes is "normal"; that women *need* men as social and economic protectors, for adult sexuality, and for psychological completion; that the heterosexually constituted family is the basic social unit; that women who do not attach their primary intensity to men must be, in functional terms, condemned to an even more devastating outsiderhood than their outsiderhood as women. Small wonder that lesbians are reported to be a more hidden population than male homosexuals. The Black lesbian-feminist critic Lorraine Bethel, writing on Zora Neale Hurston, remarks that for a Black woman—already twice an outsider—to choose to assume still another "hated identity" is problematic indeed. Yet the lesbian continuum has been a life line for Black women both in Africa and the United States.

> Black women have a long tradition of bonding together . . . in a Black/women's community that has been a source of vital survival information, psychic and emotional support for us. We have a distinct Black woman-identified folk culture based on our experiences as Black women in this society; symbols, language and modes of expression that are specific to the realities of our lives. . . . Because

Black women were rarely among those Blacks and females who gained access to literary and other acknowledged forms of artistic expression, this Black female bonding and Black woman-identification has often been hidden and unrecorded except in the individual lives of Black women through our own memories of our particular Black female tradition.[28]

Another layer of the lie is the frequently encountered implication that women turn to women out of hatred for men. Profound skepticism, caution, and righteous paranoia about men may indeed be part of any healthy woman's response to the misogyny of male-dominated culture, to the forms assumed by "normal" male sexuality, and to *the failure even of "sensitive" or "political" men to perceive or find these troubling*. Lesbian existence is also represented as mere refuge from male abuses, rather than as an electric and empowering charge between women. One of the most frequently quoted literary passages on lesbian relationship is that in which Colette's Renée, in *The Vagabond*, describes "the melancholy and touching image of two weak creatures who have perhaps found shelter in each other's arms, there to sleep and weep, safe from man who is often cruel, and there to taste *better than any pleasure, the bitter happiness of feeling themselves akin, frail and forgotten* [emphasis added]."[29] Colette is often considered a lesbian writer. Her popular reputation has, I think, much to do with the fact that she writes about lesbian existence as if for a male audience; her earliest "lesbian" novels, the Claudine series, were written under compulsion for her husband and published under both their names. At all events, except for her writings on her mother, Colette is a less reliable source on the lesbian continuum than, I would think, Charlotte Brontë, who understood that while women may, indeed must, be one another's allies, mentors, and comforters in the female struggle for survival, there is quite extraneous delight in each other's company and attraction to each others' minds and character, which attend a recognition of each others' strengths.

By the same token, we can say that there is a *nascent* feminist political content in the act of choosing a woman lover or life partner in the face of institutionalized heterosexuality.[30] But for lesbian existence to realize this political content in an ultimately liberating form, the erotic choice must deepen and expand into conscious woman identification—into lesbian feminism.

The work that lies ahead, of unearthing and describing what I call here "lesbian existence," is potentially liberating for all women. It is work that must assuredly move beyond the limits of white and middle-class Western Women's Studies to examine women's lives, work, and groupings within every racial, ethnic, and political structure. There are differences, moreover, between "lesbian existence" and the "lesbian continuum," differences we can discern even in the movement of our own lives. The lesbian continuum, I suggest, needs delineation in light of the "double life" of women, not only women self-described as heterosexual but also of self-described lesbians. We need a far more exhaustive account of the forms the double life has assumed. Historians need to ask at every point how heterosexuality as institution has been organized and maintained through the female wage scale, the enforcement of middle-class women's "leisure," the glamorization of so-called sexual liberation, the withholding of education from women, the imagery of "high art" and popular culture, the mystification of the "personal" sphere, and much else. We need an economics which comprehends the institution of heterosexuality, with its doubled workload for women and its sexual divisions of labor, as the most idealized of economic relations.

The question inevitably will arise: Are we then to condemn all heterosexual relationships, including those which are least oppressive? I believe this question, though often heartfelt, is the wrong question here. We have been stalled in a maze of false dichotomies which prevents our apprehending the institution as a whole: "good" versus "bad" marriages; "marriage for love" versus arranged marriage; "liberated" sex versus prostitution; heterosexual intercourse versus rape; *Liebeschmerz* versus humiliation and dependency. Within the institution exist, of course, qualitative differences of experience; but the absence of choice remains the great unacknowledged reality, and in the absence of choice, women will remain dependent upon the chance or luck of particular relationships and will have no collective power to determine the meaning and place of sexuality in their lives. As we address the institution itself, moreover, we begin to perceive a history of

female resistance which has never fully understood itself because it has been so fragmented, miscalled, erased. It will require a courageous grasp of the politics and economics, as well as the cultural propaganda, of heterosexuality to carry us beyond individual cases or diversified group situations into the complex kind of overview needed to undo the power men everywhere wield over women, power which has become a model for every other form of exploitation and illegitimate control.

[1980]

NOTES

1. Kathleen Gough, "The Origin of the Family," in *Toward an Anthropology of Women,* ed. Rayna [Rapp] Reiter (New York: Monthly Review Press, 1975), pp. 69–70.
2. Kathleen Barry, *Female Sexual Slavery* (Englewood Cliffs, N.J.: Prentice-Hall, 1979), pp. 216–219.
3. Anna Demeter, *Legal Kidnapping* (Boston: Beacon, 1977), pp. xx, 126–128.
4. Mary Daly, *Gyn/Ecology: The Metaethics of Radical Feminism* (Boston: Beacon, 1978), pp. 139–141, 163–165.
5. Barbara Ehrenreich and Deirdre English, *Witches, Midwives and Nurses: A History of Women Healers* (Old Westbury, N.Y.: Feminist Press, 1973); Andrea Dworkin, *Woman Hating* (New York: Dutton, 1974), pp. 118–154; Daly, pp. 178–222.
6. See Virginia Woolf, *A Room of One's Own* (London: Hogarth, 1929), and *id., Three Guineas* (New York: Harcourt Brace, [1938] 1966); Tillie Olsen, *Silences* (Boston: Delacorte, 1978); Michelle Cliff, "The Resonance of Interruption," *Chrysalis: A Magazine of Women's Culture* 8 (1979): 29–37.
7. Mary Daly, *Beyond God the Father* (Boston: Beacon, 1973), pp. 347–351; Olsen, pp. 22–46.
8. Daly, *Beyond God the Father,* p. 93.
9. Daly, *Gyn/Ecology,* p. 15.
10. "In a hostile world in which women are not supposed to survive except in relation with and in service to men, entire communities of women were simply erased. History tends to bury what it seeks to reject" (Blanche W. Cook, " 'Women Alone Stir My Imagination': Lesbianism and the Cultural Tradition," *Signs: Journal of Women in Culture and Society* 4, no. 4 [Summer 1979]: 719–720). The Lesbian Herstory Archives in New York City is one attempt to preserve contemporary documents on lesbian existence—a project of enormous value and meaning, working against the continuing censorship and obliteration of relationships, networks, communities in other archives and elsewhere in the culture.
11. [A.R., 1986: The shared historical and spiritual "cross-over" functions of lesbians and gay men in cultures past and present are traced by Judy Grahn in *Another Mother Tongue: Gay Words, Gay Worlds* (Boston: Beacon, 1984). I now think we have much to learn both from the uniquely female aspects of lesbian existence and from the complex "gay" identity we share with gay men.]
12. Audre Lorde, "Uses of the Erotic: The Erotic as Power," in *Sister Outsider* (Trumansburg, N.Y.: Crossing Press, 1984).

13. Adrienne Rich, "Conditions for Work: The Common World of Women," in *On Lies, Secrets, and Silence,* p. 209; H.D., *Tribute to Freud* (Oxford: Carcanet, 1971), pp. 50–54.

14. Woolf, *A Room of One's Own,* p. 126.

15. Gracia Clark, "The Beguines: A Mediaeval Women's Community," *Quest: A Feminist Quarterly* 1, no. 4 (1975): 73–80.

16. See Denise Paulmé, ed., *Women of Tropical Africa* (Berkeley: University of California Press, 1963), pp. 7, 266–267. Some of these sororities are described as "a kind of defensive syndicate against the male element," their aims being "to offer concerted resistance to an oppressive patriarchate," "independence in relation to one's husband and with regard to motherhood, mutual aid, satisfaction of personal revenge." See also Audre Lorde, "Scratching the Surface: Some Notes on Barriers to Women and Loving," in *Sister Outsider,* pp. 45–52; Marjorie Topley, "Marriage Resistance in Rural Kwangtung," in *Women in Chinese Society,* ed. M. Wolf and R. Witke (Stanford, Calif.: Stanford University Press, 1978), pp. 67–89; Agnes Smedley, *Portraits of Chinese Women in Revolution,* ed. J. MacKinnon and S. MacKinnon (Old Westbury, N.Y.: Feminist Press, 1976), pp. 103–110.

17. See Rosalind Petchesky, "Dissolving the Hyphen: A Report on Marxist-Feminist Groups 1–5," in *Capitalist Patriarchy and the Case for Socialist Feminism,* ed. Zillah Eisenstein (New York: Monthly Review Press, 1979), p. 387.

18. [A.R., 1986: See Angela Davis, *Women, Race and Class* (New York: Random House, 1981), p. 102; Orlando Patterson, *Slavery and Social Death: A Comparative Study* (Cambridge: Harvard University Press, 1982), p. 133.]

19. Diana Russell and Nicole van de Ven, eds., *Proceedings of the International Tribunal of Crimes against Women* (Millbrae, Calif.: Les Femmes, 1976), pp. 42–43, 56–57.

20. I am indebted to Jonathan Katz's *Gay American History* (*op. cit.*) for bringing to my attention Hansberry's letters to *The Ladder* and to Barbara Grier for supplying me with copies of relevant pages from *The Ladder,* quoted here by permission of Barbara Grier. See also the reprinted series of *The Ladder,* ed. Jonathan Katz *et al.* (New York: Arno, 1975), and Deirdre Carmody, "Letters by Eleanor Roosevelt Detail Friendship with Lorena Hickok," *New York Times* (October 21, 1979).

21. Meridel LeSueur, *The Girl* (Cambridge, Mass.: West End Press, 1978), pp. 10–11. LeSueur describes, in an afterword, how this book was drawn from the writings and oral narrations of women in the Workers Alliance who met as a writers' group during the depression.

22. *Ibid.,* p. 20.

23. *Ibid.,* pp. 53–54.

24. *Ibid.,* p. 55.

25. Toni Morrison, *Sula* (New York: Bantam, 1973), pp. 103–104, 149. I am indebted to Lorraine Bethel's essay " 'This Infinity of Conscious Pain': Zora Neale Hurston and the Black Female Literary Tradition," in *All the Women Are White, All the Blacks Are Men, but Some of Us Are Brave: Black Women's Studies,* ed. Gloria T. Hull, Patricia Bell Scott, and Barbara Smith (Old Westbury, N.Y.: Feminist Press, 1982).

26. See Maureen Brady and Judith McDaniel, "Lesbians in the Mainstream: The Image of Lesbians in Recent Commercial Fiction," *Conditions* 6 (1979): 82–105.

27. See Russell and van de Ven, p. 40: "Few heterosexual women realize their lack of free choice about their sexuality, and few realize how and why compulsory heterosexuality is also a crime against them."

28. Bethel, " 'This Infinity of Conscious Pain,' " *op. cit.*

29. Dinnerstein, the most recent writer to quote this passage, adds ominously: "But what has to be added to her account is that these 'women enlaced' are sheltering each other not just from what men want to do to them, but also from what they want to do to each other" (Dorothy Dinnerstein, *The Mermaid and the Minotaur: Sexual Arrangements and the Human Malaise* (New York: Harper & Row, 1976), p. 103). The fact is, however, that woman-to-woman violence is a minute grain in the universe of male-against-female violence perpetuated and rationalized in every social institution.

30. Conversation with Blanche W. Cook, New York City, March 1979.

 61

Feminism and the Revolt of Nature

YNESTRA KING

Ecology is a feminist issue. But why? Is it because women are more a part of nature than men? Is it because women are morally superior to men? Is it because ecological feminists are satisfied with the traditional female stereotypes and wish to be limited to the traditional concerns of women? Is it because the domination of women and the domination of nature are connected?

The feminist debate over ecology has gone back and forth and is assuming major proportions in the movement; but there is a talking-past-each-other, not-getting-to-what's-really-going-on quality to it. The differences derive from unresolved questions in our political and theoretical history, so the connection of ecology to feminism has met with radically different responses from the various feminisms.

RADICAL FEMINISM AND ECOLOGY

Radical feminists of one genre deplore the development of connections between ecology and feminism and see it as a regression which is bound to reinforce sex-role stereotyping. Since the ecological issue has universal implications, so the argument goes, it should concern men and women alike. Ellen Willis, for instance, wrote recently:

> From a feminist perspective, the only good reason for women to organize separately from men is to fight sexism. Otherwise women's political organizations simply reinforce female segregation and further the idea that certain activities and interests are inherently feminine. All-female groups that work against consumer fraud, or for the improvement of schools, implicitly acquiesce in the notion that women have special responsibilities as housewives and mothers, that it is not men's job to worry about what goes on at the supermarket, or the conditions of their children's education. Similarly, groups like Women Strike for Peace, Women's International League for Peace and Freedom, and Another Mother for Peace perpetuate the idea that women have a specifically female interest in preventing war. . . . If feminism means anything, it's that women are capable of the full range of human emotions and behavior; politics based on received definitions of women's nature and role are oppressive, whether promoted by men or by my alleged sisters.[1]

Other radical feminists—most notably Mary Daly and Susan Griffin—have taken the opposite position. Daly believes that women should identify with nature against men, and that *whatever* we do, we should do it separately from men. For her, the oppression of women under patriarchy and the pillage of the natural environment are basically the same phenomenon.[2] Griffin's book is a long prose poem (actually the form defies precise description; it is truly original).[3] It is not intended to spell out a political philosophy, but to let us know and feel how the woman/nature connection has been played out historically in the victimization of women and nature. It suggests a powerful potential for a movement linking feminism and ecology.

So how do women who call themselves radical feminists come to such divergent positions? Radical feminism roots the oppression of women in biological difference. It sees patriarchy (the systematic dominance of men) preceding and laying the foundation for other forms of oppression and exploitation; it sees men hating and fearing women (misogyny) and identifying us with nature; it sees men seeking to enlist both women and nature in the service of male projects designed to protect men from feared nature and mortality. The notion of women being closer to nature is essential to such projects. If patriarchy is the archetypal form of human oppression, then radical feminists argue that getting rid of it will also cause other forms of oppression to crumble. But the essential difference between the two or more types of radical feminists is whether the woman/nature connection is potentially liberating or simply a rationale for the continued subordination of women.

Other questions follow from this theoretical disagreement: (1) Is there a separate female life experience in this society? If so, is there a separate female culture? (2) If there is, is a female culture merely a male-contrived ghetto constructed long ago by forcibly taking advantage of our physical vulnerability born of our child-bearing function and smaller stature? Or does it suggest a way of life providing a critical vantage point on male society? (3) What are the implications of gender difference? Do we want to do away with gender difference? (4) Can we recognize "difference" without shoring up dominance based on difference?

Rationalist radical feminists (Willis's position) and radical cultural feminists (Daly's and Griffin's position) offer opposite answers, just as they come to opposite conclusions on connecting feminism to ecology—and for the same reasons. The problem with both analyses, however, is that gender identity is neither fully natural nor fully cultural. And it is neither inherently oppressive nor inherently liberating. It depends on other historical factors, and how we consciously understand woman-identification and feminism.

SOCIALIST FEMINISM AND ECOLOGY

Socialist feminists[4] have for the most part yet to enter feminist debates on "the ecology question." They tend to be uneasy with ecological feminism, fearing that it is based on an ahistorical, anti-rational woman/nature identification; or they see the cultural emphasis in ecological feminism as "idealist" rather than "materialist." The Marxist side of their politics implies a primacy of material transformation (economic/structural transformation precedes changes in ideas/culture/consciousness). Cultural and material changes are not completely separate. There is a dialectical interaction between the two, but in the last instance the cultural is part of the superstructure and the material is the base.

Historically socialism and feminism have had a curious courtship[5] and a rather unhappy marriage,[6] characterized by a tug of war over which is the primary contradiction—sex or class. In an uneasy truce, socialist feminists try to overcome the contradictions, to show how the economic structure and the sex-gender system[7] are mutually reinforced in historically specific ways depending on material conditions, and to show their interdependence. They suggest the need for an "autonomous" (as opposed to a "separatist") women's movement, to maintain vigilance over women's concerns within the production and politics of a mixed society. They see patriarchy as different under feudalism, capitalism, and even under socialism without feminism.[8] And they hold that nobody is free until everybody is free.

Socialist feminists see themselves as integrating the best of Marxism and radical feminism. They have been weak on radical cultural critique and strong on helping us to understand how people's material situations condition their consciousnesses and their possibilities for social transformation. But adherence to Marxism with its economic orientation means opting for the rationalist severance of the woman/nature connection and advocating the integration of women into production. It does not challenge the culture-versus-nature formulation itself. Even where the issue of woman's oppression and its identification with that of nature has been taken up, the socialist feminist solution has been to align women with culture in culture's ongoing struggle with nature.[9]

HERE WE GO AGAIN; THIS ARGUMENT IS AT LEAST ONE HUNDRED YEARS OLD!

The radical feminist/socialist feminist debate does sometimes seem to be the romantic feminist/rationalist feminist debate of the late nineteenth century revisited.[10] We can imagine nineteenth-century women watching the development of robber-baron capitalism, "the demise of morality" and the rise of the liberal state which furthered capitalist interests while touting liberty, equality, and fraternity. Small wonder that they saw in the domestic sphere ves-

tiges of a more ethical way of life, and thought its values could be carried into the public sphere. This perspective romanticized women, although it is easy to sympathize with it and share the abhorrence of the pillage and plunder imposed by the masculinist mentality in modern industrial society. But what nineteenth-century women proclaiming the virtues of womanhood did not understand was that they were a repository of organic social values in an increasingly inorganic world. Women placed in male-identified power positions can be as warlike as men. The assimilation or neutralization of enfranchised women into the American political structure has a sad history.

Rationalist feminists in the nineteenth century, on the other hand, were concerned with acquiring power and representing women's interests. They opposed anything that reinforced the idea that women were "different" and wanted male prerogatives extended to women. They were contemptuous of romantic feminists and were themselves imbued with the modern ethic of progress. They opposed political activity by women over issues not seen as exclusively feminist for the same reasons rationalist radical feminists today oppose the feminism/ecology connection.

THE DIALECTIC OF MODERN FEMINISM

According to the false dichotomy between subjective and objective—one legacy of male Western philosophy to feminist thought—we must root our movement *either* in a rationalist-materialist humanism *or* in a metaphysical-feminist naturalism. This supposed choice is crucial as we approach the ecology issue. *Either* we take the anthropocentric position that nature exists solely to serve the needs of the male bourgeois who has crawled out of the slime to be lord and master of everything, *or* we take the naturalist position that nature has a purpose of its own apart from serving "man." We are *either* concerned with the "environment" because we are dependent on it, *or* we understand ourselves to be *of* it, with human oppression part and parcel of the domination of nature. For some radical feminists, only women are capable of full consciousness.[11] Socialist feminists tend to consider the naturalist position as historically regressive, antirational, and probably fascistic. This is the crux of the anthropocentric/

naturalist debate, which is emotionally loaded for both sides, but especially for those who equate progress and rationality.

However, we do not have to make such choices. Feminism is both the product and potentially the negation of the modern rationalist world view and capitalism. There was one benefit for women in the "disenchantment of the world,"[12] the process by which all magical and spiritual beliefs were denigrated as superstitious nonsense and the death of nature was accomplished in the minds of men.[13] This process tore asunder women's traditional sphere of influence, but it also undermined the ideology of "natural" social roles, opening a space for women to question what was "natural" for them to be and to do. In traditional Western societies, social and economic relationships were connected to a land-based way of life. One was assigned a special role based on one's sex, race, class, and place of birth. In the domestic sphere children were socialized, food prepared, and men sheltered from their public cares. But the nineteenth-century "home" also encompassed the production of what people ate, used, and wore. It included much more of human life and filled many more human needs than its modern corollary—the nuclear family—which purchases commodities to meet its needs. The importance of the domestic sphere, and hence women's influence, declined with the advent of market society.

Feminism also negates capitalist social relations by challenging the lopsided male-biased values of our culture. When coupled with an ecological perspective, it insists that we remember our origins in nature, our connections to one another as daughters, sisters, and mothers. It refuses any longer to be the unwitting powerless symbol of all the things men wish to deny in themselves and project onto us—the refusal to be the "other."[14] It can heal the splits in a world divided against itself and built on a fundamental lie: the defining of culture in opposition to nature.

The dialectic moves on. Now it is possible that a conscious visionary feminism could place our technology and productive apparatus in the service of a society based on ecological principles and values, with roots in traditional women's ways of being in the world. This in turn might make possible a total cultural critique. Women can remember what men have denied in themselves (nature), and women can know what men know (culture). Now we must develop a transformative feminism that sparks our utopian imaginations and embodies our deepest knowledge—a feminism that is an affirmation of our vision at the same time it is a negation of patriarchy. The skewed reasoning that opposes matter and spirit and refuses to concern itself with the objects and ends of life, which views internal nature and external nature as one big hunting ground to be quantified and conquered is, in the end, not only irrational but deadly. To fulfill its liberatory potential, feminism needs to pose a *rational reenchantment* that brings together spiritual and material, being and knowing. This is the promise of ecological feminism.

DIALECTICAL FEMINISM: TRANSCENDING THE RADICAL FEMINIST/SOCIALIST FEMINIST DEBATE

The domination of external nature has necessitated the domination of internal nature. Men have denied their own embodied naturalness, repressed memories of infantile pleasure and dependence on the mother and on nature.[15] Much of their denied self has been projected onto women. Objectification is forgetting. The ways in which women have been both included in and excluded from a culture based on gender differences provide a critical ledge from which to view the artificial chasm male culture has placed between itself and nature. Woman has stood with one foot on each side. She has been a bridge for men, back to the parts of themselves they have denied, despite their need of women to attend to the visceral chores they consider beneath them.

An ecological perspective offers the possibility of moving beyond the radical (cultural) feminist/socialist feminist impasse. But it necessitates a feminism that holds out for a separate cultural and political activity so that we can imagine, theorize or envision from the vantage point of *critical otherness*. The ecology question weights the historic feminist debate in the direction of traditional female values over the overly rationalized, combative male way of being in the world. Rationalist feminism is the Trojan horse of the women's movement. Its piece-of-the-action mentality conceals a capitulation to a culture bent on the betrayal of nature. In that sense it is unwittingly both misogynist and anti-ecological. Denying biology, espousing androgyny and valuing what men have done over what we have done are all forms of self-hatred which threaten to derail the teleology of the feminist challenge to this violent civilization.

The liberation of women is to be found neither in severing all connections that root us in nature nor in believing ourselves to be more natural than men. Both of these positions are unwittingly complicit with nature/culture dualism. Women's oppression is neither strictly historical nor strictly biological. It is both. Gender is a meaningful part of a person's identity. The facts of internal and external genitalia and women's ability to bear children will continue to have social meaning. But we needn't think the choices are external sexual warfare or a denatured (and boring) androgyny. It is possible to take up questions of spirituality and meaning without abandoning the important insights of materialism. We can use the insights of socialist feminism, with its debt to Marxism, to understand how the material conditions of our daily lives interact with our bodies and our psychological heritages. Materialist insights warn us not to assume an *innate* moral or biological superiority and not to depend on alternative culture alone to transform society. Yet a separate radical feminist culture within a patriarchal society is necessary so we can learn to speak our own bodies and our own experiences, so the male culture representing itself as the "universal" does not continue to speak for us.[16]

We have always thought our lives and works, our very beings, were trivial next to male accomplishments. Women's silence is deafening only to those who know it's there. The absence is only beginning to be a presence. Writers like Zora Neale Hurston, Tillie Olsen, Grace Paley, and Toni Morrison depict the beauty and dignity of ordinary women's lives and give us back part of ourselves. Women artists begin to suggest the meanings of female bodies and their relationships to nature.[17] Women musicians give us the sounds of loving ourselves.[18] The enormous and growing lesbian feminist community is an especially fertile ground for women's culture. Lesbians are pioneering in every field and building communities with ecological feminist consciousness. Third-World women are speaking the experience of multiple otherness—of race, sex, and (often) class oppression. We are learning how women's lives are the same and different across these divisions, and we are beginning to engage the complexities of racism in our culture, our movement, and our theory.

There is much that is redemptive for humanity as a whole in women's silent experience, and there are voices that have not yet been heard. Cultural feminism's concern with ecology takes the ideology of womanhood which has been a bludgeon of oppression—the woman/nature connection—and transforms it into a positive factor. If we proceed dialectically and recognize the contributions of both socialist feminism and radical cultural feminism, operating at both the structural and cultural levels, we will be neither materialists nor idealists. We will understand our position historically and attempt to realize the human future emerging in the *feminist present*. Once we have placed ourselves in history, we can move on to the interdependent issues of feminist social transformation and planetary survival.

TOWARD AN ECOLOGICAL CULTURE

Acting on our own consciousness of our own needs, we act in the interests of all. We stand on the biological dividing line. We are the less-rationalized side of humanity in an overly rationalized world, yet we can think as rationally as men and perhaps transform the idea of reason itself. As women, we are naturalized culture in a culture defined against nature. If nature/culture antagonism is the primary contradiction of our time, it is also what weds feminism and ecology and makes woman the historic subject. Without an ecological perspective which asserts the interdependence of living things, feminism is disembodied. Without a more sophisticated dialectical method which can transcend historic debates and offer a nondualistic theory of history, social transformation and nature/culture interaction, feminism will continue to be mired in the same old impasse. There is more at stake in feminist debates over "the ecology question" than whether feminists should organize against the draft, demonstrate at the Pentagon, or join mixed antinuke organizations. At stake is the range and potential of the feminist social movement.

Ecological feminism is about reconciliation and conscious mediation, about recognition of the underside of history and all the invisible voiceless activities of women over millennia. It is about connectedness and wholeness of theory and practice. It is the return of the repressed—all that has been denigrated and denied to build this hierarchal civilization with its multiple systems of dominance. It is the potential voice of the denied, the ugly, and the speechless—all those things called "feminine." So it is no wonder that the feminist movement rose again in the same decade as the ecological crisis. The implications of feminism extend to issues of the meaning, purpose, and survival of life.

Never to despise in myself what I have been taught
to despise. Not to despise the other.
Not to despise the *it*. To make this relation
with it: to know that I am it.
— Muriel Rukeyser, "Despisals"[19]
[1981]

NOTES

1. Ellen Willis, *Village Voice,* 23 June 1980. In the *Village Voice,* July 1980, Willis began with the question: "Is ecology a feminist issue?" and was more ambiguous than in her earlier column, although her theoretical position was the same.
2. Mary Daly, *Gyn/Ecology: The Meta-Ethics of Radical Feminism* (Boston: Beacon Press, 1978).
3. Susan Griffin, *Woman and Nature: The Roaring Inside Her* (New York: Harper and Row, 1979).
4. For an overview of socialist feminist theory, see Zillah Eisenstein, ed., *Capitalist Patriarchy and the Case for Socialist Feminism* (New York: Monthly Review Press, 1979).
5. See Batya Weinbaum, *The Curious Courtship of Women's Liberation and Socialism* (Boston: South End Press, 1978).
6. See Heidi Hartman, "The Unhappy Marriage of Marxism and Feminism: Towards a More Progressive Union," *Capital and Class* 8 (Summer 1979).
7. The notion of a "sex-gender system" was first developed by Gayle Rubin in "The Traffic in Women," in *Toward an Anthropology of Women,* ed. R. R. Reiter (New York: Monthly Review Press, 1975).
8. See Hilda Scott, *Does Socialism Liberate Women?* (Boston: Beacon Press, 1976).
9. See Sherry B. Ortner, "Is Female to Male as Nature Is to Culture?" in *Woman, Culture, and Society,* ed. M. Z. Rosaldo and L. Lamphere (Stanford, Calif.: Stanford University Press, 1974).
10. For a social history of the nineteenth-century romanticist/rationalist debate, see Barbara Ehrenreich and Dierdre English, *For Her Own Good* (New York: Doubleday, Anchor, 1979).
11. Mary Daly comes very close to this position. Other naturalist feminists have a less clear stance on *essential* differences between women and men.
12. The "disenchantment of the world" is another way of talking about the process of rationalization discussed above. The term was coined by Max Weber.
13. See Carolyn Merchant, *The Death of Nature: Women, Ecology and the Scientific Revolution* (San Francisco: Harper and Row, 1980).
14. For a full development of the idea of "woman as other," see Simone de Beauvoir, *The Second Sex* (New York: Modern Library, 1968).
15. Dorothy Dinnerstein in *The Mermaid and the Minotaur* (New York: Harper and Row, 1977) makes an important contribution to feminist understanding by showing that although woman is associated with nature because of her mothering role, this does not in itself explain misogyny and the hatred of nature.
16. See de Beauvoir, *Second Sex.*
17. See Lucy Lippard, "Quite Contrary: Body, Nature and Ritual in Women's Art," *Chrysalis* 1, no. 2 (1977): 31–47.
18. Alive, Sweet Honey in the Rock, Meg Christian, Holly Near, Margie Adam—the list is long and growing.
19. Muriel Rukeyser, *The Complete Poems of Muriel Rukeyser* (New York: McGraw-Hill, 1978).

 62

Asian Pacific American Women and Feminism

MITSUYE YAMADA

Most of the Asian Pacific American women I know agree that we need to make ourselves more visible by speaking out on the condition of our sex and race and on certain political issues which concern us. Some of us feel that visibility through the feminist perspective is the only logical step for us. However, this path is fraught with problems which we are unable to solve among us, because in order to do so, we need the help and cooperation of the white feminist leaders, the women who coordinate programs, direct women's buildings, and edit women's publications throughout the country. Women's organizations tell us they would like to have us "join" them and give them "input." These are the better ones; at least they know we exist and feel we might possibly have something to say of interest to them, but every time I read or speak to a group of people about the condition of my life as an Asian Pacific woman, it is as if I had never spoken before, as if I were speaking to a brand new audience of people who had never known an Asian Pacific woman who is other than the passive, sweet etc. stereotype of the "Oriental" woman.

When Third World women are asked to speak representing our racial or ethnic group, we are expected to move, charm or entertain, but not to educate in ways that are threatening to our audiences. We speak to audiences that sift out those parts of our speech (if what we say does not fit the image they have of us), come up to shake our hands with "That was lovely my dear, just lovely," and go home with the same mind set they come in with. No matter what we say or do, the stereotype still hangs on. I am weary of starting from scratch each time I speak or write, as if there were no history behind us, of hearing that among the women of color, Asian women are the least political, or the least oppressed, or the most polite. It is too bad not many people remember that one of the two persons in Seattle who stood up to contest the constitutionality of the Evacuation Order in 1942 was a young Japanese American woman. As individuals and in groups, we Asian Pacific women have been (more intensively than ever in the past few years) active in community affairs and speaking and writing about our activities. From the highly political writings published in *Asian Women* in 1971 (incisive and trenchant articles, poems and articles), to more recent voices from the Basement Workshop in New York to Unbound Feet in San Francisco, as well as those Asian Pacific women showcased at the Asian Pacific Women's Conferences in New York, Hawaii and California this year, these all tell us we *have* been active and vocal. And yet, we continue to hear, "Asian women are of course traditionally not attuned to being political," as if most other women are; or that Asian women are too happily bound to their traditional roles as mothers and wives, as if the same cannot be said of a great number of white American women among us.

When I read in *Plexus* recently that at a Workshop for Third World women in San Francisco, Cherríe Moraga exploded with "What each of us needs to do about what we don't know is to go look for it," I felt like standing up and cheering her. She was speaking at the Women's Building to a group of white sisters who were saying, in essence, "it is *your* responsibility as Third World women to teach *us*." If the majority culture know so little about us, it must be *our* problem, they seem to be telling us; the burden of teaching is on us. I do not want to be unfair; I know individual women and some women's groups that have taken on the responsibility of teaching themselves through reaching out to women of color, but such gestures by the majority of women's groups are still tentatively made because of the sometimes touchy reaction of women who are always being asked to be "tokens" at readings and workshops.

Earlier this year, when a group of Asian Pacific American women gathered together in San Francisco poet Nellie Wong's home to talk about feminism, I was struck by our general agreement on the subject of feminism *as an ideal*. We all believed in equality for women. We agreed that it is important for each of us to know what it means to be a woman in our society, to know the historical and psychological forces that have shaped and are shaping our thoughts which in turn determine the directions of our lives. We agreed that feminism means a commitment to making changes in our own lives and a conviction that as women we have the equipment to do so. One by one, as we sat around the table and talked (we women of all ages ranging from our early twenties to the mid-fifties, single and married, mothers and lovers, straight women and lesbians), we knew what it was we wanted out of feminism, and what it was supposed to mean to us. For women to achieve equality in our society, we agreed, we must continue to work for a common goal.

But there was a feeling of disappointment in that living room toward the women's movement as it stands today. One young woman said she had made an effort to join some women's groups with high expectations but came away disillusioned because these groups were not receptive to the issues that were important to her as an Asian woman. Women in these groups, were, she said "into pushing their own issues" and were no different from the other organizations that imposed opinions and goals on their members rather than having them shaped by the needs of the members in the organizations. Some of the other women present said that they felt the women's organizations with feminist goals are still "a middle-class women's thing." This pervasive feeling of mistrust toward the women in the movement is fairly representative of a large group of women who live in the psychological place we now call Asian Pacific America. A movement that fights sexism in the social structure must deal with racism, and we had hoped the leaders in the women's movement would be able to see the parallels in the lives of the women of color and themselves, and would "join" *us* in our struggle and give *us* "input."

It should not be difficult to see that Asian Pacific women need to affirm our own culture while working within it to change it. Many of the leaders in the women's organizations today had moved naturally from the civil rights politics of the 60's to sexual politics, while very few of the Asian Pacific women who were involved in radical politics during the same period have emerged as leaders in these same women's organizations. Instead they have become active in groups promoting ethnic identity, most notably ethnic studies in universities, ethnic theater groups or ethnic community agencies. This doesn't mean that we have placed our loyalties on the side of ethnicity over womanhood. The two are not at war with one another; we shouldn't have to sign a "loyalty oath" favoring one over the other. However, women of color are often made to feel that we must make a choice between the two.

If I have more recently put my energies into the Pacific Asian American Center (a job center for Asians established in 1975, the only one of its kind in Orange County, California) and the Asian Pacific Women's Conferences (the first of its kind in our history), it is because the needs in these areas are so great. I have thought of myself as a feminist first, but my ethnicity cannot be separated from my feminism.

Through the women's movement, I have come to truly appreciate the meaning of my mother's life and the lives of immigrant women like her. My mother, at nineteen years of age, uprooted from her large extended family, was brought to this country to bear and raise four children alone. Once here, she found that her new husband who had been here as a student for several years prior to their marriage was a bachelor-at-heart and had no intention of changing his lifestyle. Stripped of the protection and support of her family, she found the responsibilities of raising us alone in a strange country almost intolerable during those early years. I thought for many years that my mother did not love us because she often spoke of suicide as an easy way out of her miseries. I know now that for her to have survived "just for the sake" of her children took great strength and determination.

If I digress it is because I, a second generation Asian American woman who grew up believing in the American Dream, have come to know who I am through understanding the nature of my mother's experience; I have come to see connections in our lives as well as the lives of many women like us, and through her I have become more sensitive to the needs of Third World women throughout the world. We need not repeat our past histories; my daughters and I need not merely survive with strength and determination. We can, through collective struggle, live fuller and richer lives. My politics as a woman are deeply rooted in my immigrant parent's and my own past.

Not long ago at one of my readings a woman in the audience said she was deeply moved by my "beautifully tragic but not bitter camp poems which were apparently written long ago,"[1] but she was distressed to hear my poem "To A Lady." "Why are you, at this late date, so angry, and why are you taking it so personally?" she said. "We need to look to the future and stop wallowing in the past so much." I responded that this poem *is not* at all about the past. I am talking about what is happening to us right now, about our nonsupport of each other, about our noncaring about each other, about not seeing connections between racism and sexism in our lives. As a child of immigrant parents, as a woman of color in a white society and as a woman in a patriarchical society, what is personal to me *is* political.

These are the connections we expected our white sisters to see. It should not be too difficult, we feel, for them to see why being a feminist activist is more dangerous for women of color. They should be able to see that political views held by women of color are often misconstrued as being personal rather than ideological. Views critical of the system held by a person in an "out group" are often seen as expressions of personal angers against the dominant society. (If they hate it so much here, why don't they go back?) Many lesbians I know have felt the same kind of frustration when they supported unpopular causes regarded by their critics as vindictive expressions to "get back" at the patriarchical system. They too know the disappointments of having their intentions misinterpreted.

In the 1960's when my family and I belonged to a neighborhood church, I became active in promoting the Fair Housing Bill, and one of my church friends said to me, "Why are you doing this to us? Haven't you and your family been happy with us in our church? Haven't we treated you well?" I knew then that I was not really part of the church at all in the eyes of this person, but only a guest who was being told I should have the good manners to behave like one.

Remembering the blatant acts of selective racism in the past three decades in our country, our white sisters should be able to see how tenuous our position in this country is. Many of us are now third and fourth generation Americans, but this makes no difference; periodic conflicts involving Third World peoples can abruptly change white American's attitudes towards us. This was clearly demonstrated in 1941 to the Japanese Americans who were in hot pursuit of the great American Dream, who went around saying, "Of course I don't eat Japanese food, I'm an American." We found our status as true-blooded Americans was only an illusion in 1942 when we were singled out to be imprisoned for the duration of the war by our own government. The recent outcry against Iranians because of the holding of American hostages tells me that the situation has not changed since 1941. When I hear my students say "We're not against the Iranians here who are minding their own business. We're just against those ungrateful ones who overstep our hospitality by demonstrating and badmouthing our government," I know they speak about me.

Asian Pacific American women will not speak out to say what we have on our minds until we feel secure within ourselves that this is our home too; and until our white sisters indicate by their actions that they want to join us in our struggle because it is theirs also. This means a commitment to a truly communal education where we learn from each other because we want to learn from each other, the kind of commitment we do not seem to have at the present time. I am still hopeful that the women of color in our country will be the link to Third World women throughout the world, and that we can help each other broaden our visions.

[1981]

NOTE

1. *Camp Notes and Other Poems* by Mitsuye Yamada (San Francisco: Shameless Hussy Press) 1976.

 63

The Unhappy Marriage of Marxism and Feminism: Towards a More Progressive Union

HEIDI HARTMANN

The "marriage" of marxism and feminism has been like the marriage of husband and wife depicted in English common law: marxism and feminism are one, and that one is marxism.[1] Recent attempts to integrate marxism and feminism are unsatisfactory to us as feminists because they subsume the feminist struggle into the "larger" struggle against capital. To continue our simile further, either we need a healthier marriage or we need a divorce.

The inequalities in this marriage, like most social phenomena, are no accident. Many marxists typically argue that feminism is at best less important than class conflict and at worst divisive of the working class. This political stance produces an analysis that absorbs feminism into the class struggle. Moreover, the analytic power of marxism with respect to capital has obscured its limitations with respect to sexism. We will argue here that while marxist analysis provides essential insight into the laws of historical development, and those of capital in particular, the categories of marxism are sex-blind. Only a specifically feminist analysis reveals the systemic character of relations between men and women. Yet feminist analysis by itself is inadequate because it has been blind to history and insufficiently materialist. Both marxist analysis, particularly its historical and materialist method, and feminist analysis, especially the identification of patriarchy as a social and historical structure, must be drawn upon if we are to understand the development of western capitalist societies and the predicament of women within them. In this essay we suggest a new direction for marxist feminist analysis.

· · ·

1. MARXISM AND THE WOMAN QUESTION

The woman question has never been the "feminist question." The feminist question is directed at the causes of sexual inequality between women and men, of male dominance over women. Most marxist analyses of women's position take as their question the relationship of women to the economic system, rather than that of women to men, apparently assuming the latter will be explained in their discussion of the former. Marxist analysis of the woman question has taken three main forms. All see women's oppression in our connection (or lack of it) to production. Defining women as part of the working class, these analyses consistently subsume women's relation to men under workers' relation to capital. First, early marxists, including Marx, Engels, Kautsky, and Lenin, saw capitalism drawing all women into the wage labor force, and saw this process destroying the sexual division of labor. Second, contemporary marxists have incorporated women into an analysis of everyday life in capitalism. In this view, all aspects of our lives are seen to reproduce the capitalist system and we are all workers in the system. And third, marxist feminists have focussed on housework and its relation to capital, some arguing that housework produces surplus value and that houseworkers work directly for capitalists. . . .

⋅ ⋅ ⋅

While the approach of the early marxists ignored housework and stressed women's labor force participation, the two more recent approaches emphasize housework to such an extent they ignore women's current role in the labor market. Nevertheless, all three attempt to include women in the category working class and to understand women's oppression as another aspect of class oppression. In doing so all give short shrift to the object of feminist analysis, the relations between women and men. While our "problems" have been elegantly analyzed, they have been misunderstood. The focus of marxist analysis has been class relations; the object of marxist analysis has been understanding the laws of motion of capitalist society. While we believe marxist methodology *can* be used to formulate feminist strategy, these marxist feminist approaches discussed above clearly do not do so; their marxism clearly dominates their feminism.

⋅ ⋅ ⋅

Marxism enables us to understand many aspects of capitalist societies: the structure of production, the generation of a particular occupational structure, and the nature of the dominant ideology. Marx's theory of the development of capitalism is a theory of the development of "empty places." Marx predicted, for example, the growth of the proletariat and the demise of the petit bourgeoisie. More precisely and in more detail, Braverman among others has explained the creation of the "places" clerical worker and service worker in advanced capitalist societies.[2] Just as capital creates these places indifferent to the individuals who fill them, the categories of marxist analysis, class, reserve army of labor, wage-laborer, do not explain why particular people fill particular places. They give no clues about why *women* are subordinate to *men* inside and outside the family and why it is not the other way around. *Marxist categories, like capital itself, are sex-blind.* The categories of marxism cannot tell us who will fill the empty places. Marxist analysis of the woman question has suffered from this basic problem.

⋅ ⋅ ⋅

II. RADICAL FEMINISM AND PATRIARCHY

The great thrust of radical feminist writing has been directed to the documentation of the slogan "the personal is political." Women's discontent, radical feminists argued, is not the neurotic lament of the maladjusted, but a response to a social structure in which women are systematically dominated, exploited, and oppressed. Women's inferior position in the labor market, the male-centered emotional structure of middle class marriage, the use of women in advertising, the so-called understanding of women's psyche as neurotic—popularized by academic and clinical psychology—aspect after aspect of women's lives in advanced capitalist society was researched and analyzed. . . .

⋅ ⋅ ⋅

Radical feminist analysis has greatest strength in its insights into the present. Its greatest weakness is a focus on the psychological which blinds it to history. The reason for this lies not only in radical feminist method, but also in the nature of patriarchy itself, for patriarchy is a strikingly resilient form of social organization. Radical feminists use patriarchy to refer to a social system characterized by male domination over women. Kate Millett's definition is classic:

> our society . . . is a patriarchy. The fact is evident at once if one recalls that the military, industry, technology, universities, science, political offices, finances—in short, every avenue of power within the society, including the coercive force of the police, is entirely in male hands.[3]

This radical feminist definition of patriarchy applies to most societies we know of and cannot distinguish among them. The use of history by radical feminists is typically limited to providing examples of the existence of patriarchy in all times and places.[4] For both marxist and mainstream social scientists before the women's movement, patriarchy referred to a system of relations between men, which formed the political and economic outlines of feudal and some pre-feudal societies, in which hierarchy followed ascribed characteristics. Capitalist societies are understood as meritocratic, bureaucratic, and impersonal by bourgeois social scientists; marxists see capitalist societies as systems of class domination. For both kinds of social scientists neither the historical patriarchal societies nor today's western capitalist societies are understood as systems of relations between men that enable them to dominate women.

Towards a Definition of Patriarchy

We can usefully define patriarchy as a set of social relations between men, which have a material base, and which, though hierarchical, establish or create interdependence and solidarity among men that enable them to dominate women. Though patriarchy is hierarchical and men of different classes, races, or ethnic groups have different places in the patriarchy, they also are united in their shared relationship of dominance over their women; they are dependent on each other to maintain that domination. Hierarchies "work" at least in part because they create vested interests in the status quo. Those at the higher levels can "buy off" those at the lower levels by offering them power over those still lower. In the hierarchy of patriarchy, all men, whatever their rank in the patriarchy, are bought off by being able to control at least some women. There is some evidence to suggest that when patriarchy was first in-stitutionalized in state societies, the ascending rulers literally made men the heads of their families (enforcing their control over their wives and children) in exchange for the men's ceding some of their tribal resources to the new rulers.[5] Men are dependent on one another (despite their hierarchical ordering) to maintain their control over women.

The material base upon which patriarchy rests lies most fundamentally in men's control over women's labor power. Men maintain this control by excluding women from access to some essential productive resources (in capitalist societies, for example, jobs that pay living wages) and by restricting women's sexuality. Monogamous heterosexual marriage is one relatively recent and efficient form that seems to allow men to control both these areas. Controlling women's access to resources and their sexuality, in turn, allows men to control women's labor power, both for the purpose of serving men in many personal and sexual ways and for the purpose of rearing children. The services women render men, and which exonerate men from having to perform many unpleasant tasks (like cleaning toilets) occur outside as well as inside the family setting. Examples outside the family include the harrassment of women workers and students by male bosses and professors as well as the common use of secretaries to run personal errands, make coffee, and provide "sexy" surroundings. Rearing children, whether or not the children's labor power is of immediate benefit to their fathers, is nevertheless a crucial task in perpetuating patriarchy as a system. Just as class society must be reproduced by schools, work places, consumption norms, etc., so must patriarchal social relations. In our society children are generally reared by women at home, women socially defined and recognized as inferior to men, while men appear in the domestic picture only rarely. Children raised in this way generally learn their places in the gender hierarchy well. Central to this process, however, are the areas outside the home where patriarchal behaviors are taught and the inferior position of women enforced and reinforced: churches, schools, sports, clubs, unions, armies, factories, offices, health centers, the media, etc.

The material base of patriarchy, then, does not rest solely on childrearing in the family, but on all the social structures that enable men to control women's labor. The aspects of social structures that perpetuate patriarchy are theoretically identifiable, hence separable from their other aspects. Gayle Rubin has increased our ability to identify the patriarchal element of these social structures enormously by identifying "sex/gender systems":

> a "sex/gender system" is the set of arrangements by which a society transforms biological sexuality into products of human activity, and in which these transformed sexual needs are satisfied.[6]

We are born female and male, biological sexes, but we are created woman and man, socially recognized genders. *How* we are so created is that second aspect of the *mode* of production of which Engels spoke, "the production of human beings themselves, the propagation of the species."

How people propagate the species is socially determined. If, biologically, people are sexually polymorphous, and society were organized in such a way that all forms of sexual expression were equally permissible, reproduction would result only from some sexual encounters, the heterosexual ones. The strict division of labor by sex, a social invention common to all known societies, creates two very separate genders and a need for men and women to get together for economic reasons. It thus helps to direct their sexual needs toward heterosexual fulfillment, and helps to ensure biological reproduction. In more imaginative societies, biological reproduction might be ensured by other techniques, but the division of labor by sex appears to be the universal solution to date. Although it is theoretically possible that a sexual division of labor not imply inequality between the sexes, in most known societies, the socially acceptable division of labor by sex is one which accords lower status to women's work. The sexual division of labor is also the underpinning of sexual subcultures in which men and women experience life differently; it is the material base of male power which is exercised (in our society) not just in not doing housework and in securing superior employment, but psychologically as well.

How people meet their sexual needs, how they reproduce, how they inculcate social norms in new generations, how they learn gender, how it feels to be a man or a woman—all occur in the realm Rubin labels the sex/gender system. Rubin emphasizes the influence of kinship (which tells you with whom you can satisfy sexual needs) and the development of gender specific personalities via childrearing and the "oedipal machine." In addition, however, we can use the concept of the sex/gender system to examine all other social institutions for the roles they play in defining and reinforcing gender hierarchies. Rubin notes that theoretically a sex/gender system could be female dominant, male dominant, or egalitarian, but declines to label various known sex/gender systems or to periodize history accordingly. We choose to label our present sex/gender system patriarchy, because it appropriately captures the notion of hierarchy and male dominance which we see as central to the present system.

Economic production (what marxists are used to referring to as *the* mode of production) and the production of people in the sex/gender sphere both determine "the social organization under which the people of a particular historical epoch and a particular country live," according to Engels. The whole of society, then, can be understood by looking at both these types of production and reproduction, people and things.[7] There is no such thing as "pure capitalism," nor does "pure patriarchy" exist, for they must of necessity coexist. What exists is patriarchal capitalism, or patriarchal feudalism, or egalitarian hunting/gathering societies, or matriarchal horticultural societies, or patriarchal horticultural societies, and so on. There appears to be no necessary connection between *changes* in the one aspect of production and changes in the other. A society could undergo transition from capitalism to socialism, for example, and remain patriarchal. Common sense, history, and our experience tell us, however, that these two aspects of production are so closely intertwined, that change in one ordinarily creates movement, tension, or contradiction in the other.

Racial hierarchies can also be understood in this context. Further elaboration may be possible along the lines of defining color/race systems, arenas of social life that take biological color and turn it into a social category, race. Racial hierarchies, like gender hierarchies, are aspects of our social organization, of how people are produced and reproduced. They are not fundamentally ideological; they constitute that second aspect of our mode of production, the production and reproduction of people. It might be most accurate then to refer to our societies not as, for example, simply capitalist, but as patriarchal capitalist white supremacist. In Part III below, we illustrate one case of capitalism adapting to and making use of racial orders and several examples of the interrelations between capitalism and patriarchy.

Capitalist development creates the places for a hierarchy of workers, but traditional marxist categories cannot tell us who will fill which places. Gender and racial hierarchies determine who fills the empty places. *Patriarchy is not simply hierarchical organization,* but hierarchy in which *particular* people fill *particular* places. It is in studying patriarchy that we learn why it is women who are dominated and how. While we believe that most known societies have been patriarchal, we do not view patriarchy as a universal, unchanging phenomenon. Rather patriarchy, the set of interrelations among men that allow men to dominate women, has changed in form and intensity over time. It is crucial that the hierarchy among men, and their differential access to patriarchal benefits, be examined. Surely, class, race, nationality, and even marital status and sexual orientation, as well as the obvious age, come into play here. And women of different class, race, national, marital status, or sexual orientation groups are subjected to different degrees of patriarchal power. Women may themselves exercise class, race, or national power, or even patriarchal power (through their family connections) over men lower in the patriarchal hierarchy than their own male kin.

To recapitulate, we define patriarchy as a set of social relations which has a material base and in which there are hierarchical relations between men and solidarity among them which enable them in turn to dominate women. The material base of patriarchy is men's control over women's labor power. That control is maintained by excluding women from access to necessary economically productive resources and by restricting women's sexuality. Men exercise their control in receiving personal service work from women, in not having to do housework or rear children, in having access to women's bodies for sex, and in feeling powerful and being powerful. The crucial elements of patriarchy as we *currently* experience them are: heterosexual marriage (and consequent homophobia), female childrearing and housework, women's economic dependence on men

(enforced by arrangements in the labor market), the state, and numerous institutions based on social relations among men—clubs, sports, unions, professions, universities, churches, corporations, and armies. All of these elements need to be examined if we are to understand patriarchal capitalism.

Both hierarchy and interdependence among men and the subordination of women are *integral* to the functioning of our society; that is, these relationships are *systemic*. We leave aside the question of the creation of these relations and ask, can we recognize patriarchal relations in capitalist societies? Within capitalist societies we must discover those same bonds between men which both bourgeois and marxist social scientists claim no longer exist or are, at the most, unimportant leftovers. Can we understand how these relations among men are perpetuated in capitalist societies? Can we identify ways in which patriarchy has shaped the course of capitalist development?

III. THE PARTNERSHIP OF PATRIARCHY AND CAPITAL

How are we to recognize patriarchal social relations in capitalist societies? It appears as if each woman is oppressed by her own man alone; her oppression seems a private affair. Relationships among men and among families seem equally fragmented. It is hard to recognize relationships among men, and between men and women, as *systematically* patriarchal. We argue, however, that patriarchy as a system of relations between men and women exists in capitalism, and that in capitalist societies a healthy and strong partnership exists between patriarchy and capital. Yet if one begins with the concept of patriarchy and an understanding of the capitalist mode of production, one recognizes immediately that the partnership of patriarchy and capital was not inevitable; men and capitalists often have conflicting interests, particularly over the use of women's labor power. Here is one way in which this conflict might manifest itself: the vast majority of men might want their women at home to personally service them. A smaller number of men, who are capitalists, might want most women (not their own) to work in the wage labor market. In examining the tensions of this conflict over women's labor power historically, we will be able to identify the material base of patriarchal relations in capitalist societies, as well as the basis for the partnership between capital and patriarchy.

Industrialization and the Development of Family Wages

Marxists made quite logical inferences from a selection of the social phenomena they witnessed in the nineteenth century. But marxists ultimately underestimated the strength of the preexisting patriarchal social forces with which fledgling capital had to contend and the need for capital to adjust to these forces. The industrial revolution was drawing all people into the labor force, including women and children; in fact the first factories used child and female labor almost exclusively. That women and children could earn wages separately from men both undermined authority relations (as discussed in Part I above) and kept wages low for everyone. . . .

• • •

Male workers resisted the wholesale entrance of women and children into the labor force, and sought to exclude them from union membership and the labor force as well. In 1846 the *Ten-Hours' Advocate* stated:

> It is needless for us to say, that all attempts to improve the morals and physical condition of female factory workers will be abortive, unless their hours are materially reduced. Indeed we may go so far as to say, that married females would be much better occupied in performing the domestic duties of the household, than following the never-tiring motion of machinery. We therefore hope the day is not distant, when the husband will be able to provide for his wife and family, without sending the former to endure the drudgery of a cotton mill.[8]

In the United States in 1854 the National Typographical Union resolved not to "encourage by its act the employment of female compositors." Male unionists did not want to afford union protection to women workers; they tried to exclude them instead. In 1879 Adolph Strasser, president of the Cigarmakers International Union, said: "We cannot drive the females out of the trade, but we can restrict their daily quota of labor through factory laws."[9]

While the problem of cheap competition could have been solved by organizing the wage earning women and youths, the problem of disrupted family life could not be. Men reserved union protection for men and argued for protective labor laws for women and children. Protective labor laws, while they may have ameliorated some of the worst abuses of female and child labor, also limited the participation of adult women in many "male" jobs. Men sought to keep high wage jobs for themselves and to raise male wages generally. They argued for wages sufficient for their wage labor alone to support their families. This "family wage" system gradually came to be the norm for stable working class families at the end of the nineteenth century and the beginning of the twentieth. Several observers have declared the non wage-working wife to be part of the standard of living of male workers. Instead of fighting for equal wages for men and women, male workers sought the family wage, wanting to retain their wives' services at home. In the absence of patriarchy a unified working class might have confronted capitalism, but patriarchal social relations divided the working class, allowing one part (men) to be bought off at the expense of the other (women). Both the hierarchy between men and the solidarity among them were crucial in this process of resolution. Family wages may be understood as a resolution of the conflict over women's labor power which was occurring between patriarchal and capitalist interests at that time.

• • •

While the family wage shows that capitalism adjusts to patriarchy, the changing status of children shows that patriarchy adjusts to capital. Children, like women, came to be excluded from wage labor. As children's ability to earn money declined, their legal relationship to their parents changed. At the beginning of the industrial era in the United States, fulfilling children's need for their fathers was thought to be crucial, even primary, to their happy development; fathers had legal priority in cases of contested custody. As children's ability to contribute to the economic well-being of the family declined, mothers came increasingly to be viewed as crucial to the happy development of their children, and gained legal priority in cases of contested custody.[10] Here patriarchy adapted to the changing economic role of children: when children were productive, men claimed them; as children became unproductive, they were given to women.

• • •

The Family and the Family Wage Today

We argued above, that, with respect to capitalism and patriarchy, the adaptation, or mutual accommodation, took the form of the development of the family wage in the early twentieth century. The family wage cemented the partnership between patriarchy and capital. Despite women's increased labor force participation, particularly rapid since World War II, the family wage is still, we argue, the cornerstone of the present sexual division of labor—in which women are primarily responsible for housework and men primarily for wage work. Women's lower wages in the labor market (combined with the need for children to be reared by someone) assure the continued existence of the family as a necessary income pooling unit. The family, supported by the family wage, thus allows the control of women's labor by men both within and without the family.

Though women's increased wage work may cause stress for the family (similar to the stress Kautsky and Engels noted in the nineteenth century), it would be wrong to think that as a consequence, the concepts and the realities of the family and of the sexual division of labor will soon disappear. The sexual division of labor reappears in the labor market, where women work at women's jobs, often the very jobs they used to do only at home—food preparation and service, cleaning of all kinds, caring for people, and so on. As these jobs are low-status and low-paying patriarchal relations remain intact, though their material base shifts somewhat from the family to the wage differential, from family-based to industrially-based patriarchy.[11]

Industrially based patriarchal relations are enforced in a variety of ways. Union contracts which specify lower wages, lesser benefits, and fewer advancement opportunities for women are not just atavistic hangovers—a case of sexist attitudes or male supremacist ideology—they maintain the material base of the patriarchal system. While some would go so far as to argue that patriarchy is already absent from the family (see, for example, Stewart Ewen, *Captains of Consciousness*),[12] we would not. Although the terms of the compromise between capital and patriarchy are changing as additional tasks formerly located in the family are capitalized, and the location of the deployment of women's labor

power shifts, it is nevertheless true, as we have argued above, that the wage differential caused by extreme job segregation in the labor market reinforces the family, and, with it, the domestic division of labor, by encouraging women to marry. The "ideal" of the family wage—that a man can earn enough to support an entire family—may be giving way to a new ideal that both men and women contribute through wage earning to the cash income of the family. The wage differential, then, will become increasingly necessary in perpetuating patriarchy, the male control of women's labor power. The wage differential will aid in *defining* women's work as secondary to men's at the same time it necessitates women's actual continued economic dependence on men. The sexual division of labor in the labor market and elsewhere should be understood as a manifestation of patriarchy which serves to perpetuate it.

Many people have argued that though the partnership between capital and patriarchy exists now, it may *in the long run* prove intolerable to capitalism; capital may eventually destroy both familial relations and patriarchy. The argument proceeds logically that capitalist social relations (of which the family is not an example) tend to become universalized, that women will become increasingly able to earn money and will increasingly refuse to submit to subordination in the family, and that since the family is oppressive particularly to women and children, it will collapse as soon as people can support themselves outside it.

We do not think that the patriarchal relations embodied in the family can be destroyed so easily by capital, and we see little evidence that the family system is presently disintegrating. Although the increasing labor force participation of women has made divorce more feasible, the incentives to divorce are not overwhelming for women. Women's wages allow very few women to support themselves and their children independently and adequately. . . .

The argument that capital destroys the family also overlooks the social forces which make family life appealing. Despite critiques of nuclear families as psychologically destructive, in a competitive society the family still meets real needs for many people. This is true not only of long-term monogamy, but even more so for raising children. Single parents bear both financial and psychic burdens. For working class women, in particular, these burdens make the "independence" of labor force participation illusory. Single parent families have recently been seen by policy analysts as transitional family formations which become two-parent families upon remarriage.[13]

It could be that the effects of women's increasing labor force participation are found in a declining sexual division of labor within the family, rather than in more frequent divorce, but evidence for this is also lacking. Statistics on who does housework, even in families with wage-earning wives, show little change in recent years; women still do most of it.[14] The double day is a reality for wage-working women. This is hardly surprising since the sexual division of labor outside the family, in the labor market, keeps women financially dependent on men—even when they earn a wage themselves. The future of patriarchy does not, however, rest solely on the future of familial relations. For patriarchy, like capital, can be surprisingly flexible and adaptable.

Whether or not the patriarchal division of labor, inside the family and elsewhere, is "ultimately" intolerable to capital, it is shaping capitalism now. [P]atriarchy both legitimates capitalist control and delegitimates certain forms of struggle against capital.

. . .

IV. TOWARDS A MORE PROGRESSIVE UNION

Many problems remain for us to explore. Patriarchy as we have used it here remains more a descriptive term than an analytic one. If we think marxism alone inadequate, and radical feminism itself insufficient, then we need to develop new categories. What makes our task a difficult one is that the same features, such as the division of labor, often reinforce both patriarchy and capitalism, and in a thoroughly patriarchal capitalist society, it is hard to isolate the mechanisms of patriarchy. Nevertheless, this is what we must do. We have pointed to some starting places: looking at who benefits from women's labor power, uncovering the material base of patriarchy, investigating the mechanisms of hierarchy and solidarity among men. The questions we must ask are endless.

Can we speak of the laws of motion of a patriarchal system? How does patriarchy generate feminist struggle? What kinds of sexual politics and struggle between the sexes can we see in societies other than advanced capitalist ones? What are the contradictions of the patriarchal system and what is their relation to the contradictions of capitalism? We know that patriarchal relations gave rise to the feminist movement, and that capital generates class struggle—but how has the relation of feminism to class struggle been played out in historical contexts? In this section we attempt to provide an answer to this last question.

Feminism and the Class Struggle

Historically and in the present, the relation of feminism and class struggle has been either that of fully separate paths ("bourgeois" feminism on one hand, class struggle on the other), or, within the left, the dominance of feminism by marxism. With respect to the latter, this has been a consequence both of the analytic power of marxism, and of the power of men within the left. These have produced both open struggles on the left, and a contradictory position for marxist feminists.

Most feminists who also see themselves as radicals (antisystem, anti-capitalist, anti-imperialist, socialist, communist, marxist, whatever) agree that the radical wing of the women's movement has lost momentum while the liberal sector seems to have seized the time and forged ahead. Our movement is no longer in that exciting, energetic period when no matter what we did, it worked—to raise consciousness, to bring more women (more even than could be easily incorporated) into the movement, to increase the visibility of women's issues in the society, often in ways fundamentally challenging to both the capitalist and patriarchal relations in society. Now we sense parts of the movement are being coopted and "feminism" is being used against women—for example, in court cases when judges argue that women coming out of long-term marriages in which they were housewives don't need alimony because we all know women are liberated now. The failure to date to secure the passage of the Equal Rights Amendment in the United States indicates the presence of legitimate fears among many women that feminism will continue to be used against women, and it indicates a real need for us to reassess our movement, to analyze why it has been coopted in this way. It is logical for us to turn to marxism for help in that reassessment because it is a developed theory of social change. Marxist theory is well developed compared to feminist theory, and in our attempt to use it, we have sometimes been sidetracked from feminist objectives.

The left has always been ambivalent about the women's movement, often viewing it as dangerous to the cause of socialist revolution. When left women espouse feminism, it may be personally threatening to left men. And of course many left organizations benefit from the labor of women. Therefore, many left analyses (both in progressive and traditional forms) are self-serving, both theoretically and politically. They seek to influence women to abandon attempts to develop an independent understanding of women's situation and to adopt the "left's" analyses of the situation. As for our response to this pressure, it is natural that, as we ourselves have turned to marxist analysis, we would try to join the "fraternity" using this paradigm, and we may end up trying to justify our struggle to the fraternity rather than trying to analyze the situation of women to improve our political practice. Finally, many marxists are satisfied with the traditional marxist analysis of the women question. They see class as the correct framework with which to understand women's position. Women should be understood as part of the working class; the working class's struggle against capitalism should take precedence over any conflict between men and women. Sex conflict must not be allowed to interfere wth class solidarity.

• • •

The struggle against capital and patriarchy cannot be successful if the study and practice of the issues of feminism is abandoned. A struggle aimed only at capitalist relations of oppression will fail, since their underlying supports in patriarchal relations of oppression will be overlooked. And the analysis of patriarchy is essential to a definition of the kind of socialism useful to women. While men and women share a need to overthrow capitalism they retain interests particular to their gender group. It is not clear—from our sketch, from history, or from male socialists—that the socialism being

struggled for is the same for both men and women. For a humane socialism would require not only consensus on what the new society should look like and what a healthy person should look like, but more concretely, it would require that men relinquish their privilege.

As women we must not allow ourselves to be talked out of the urgency and importance of our tasks, as we have so many times in the past. We must fight the attempted coercion, both subtle and not so subtle, to abandon feminist objectives.

This suggests two strategic considerations. First, a struggle to establish socialism must be a struggle in which groups with different interests form an alliance. Women should not trust men to liberate them after the revolution, in part, because there is no reason to think they would know how; in part, because there is no necessity for them to do so. In fact their immediate self-interest lies in our continued oppression. Instead we must have our own organizations and our own power base. Second, we think the sexual division of labor within capitalism has given women a practice in which we have learned to understand what human interdependence and needs are. While men have long struggled *against* capital, women know what to struggle *for*.[15] As a general rule, men's position in patriarchy and capitalism prevents them from recognizing both human needs for nurturance, sharing, and growth, and the potential for meeting those needs in a nonhierarchical, nonpatriarchal society. But even if we raise their consciousness, they might assess the potential gains against the potential losses and choose the status quo. Men have more to lose than their chains.

As feminist socialists, we must organize a practice which addresses both the struggle against patriarchy and the struggle against capitalism. We must insist that the society we want to create is a society in which recognition of interdependence is liberation rather than shame, nurturance is a universal, not an oppressive practice, and in which women do not continue to support the false as well as the concrete freedoms of men.

[1981]

NOTES

1. Often paraphrased as "the husband and wife are one and that one is the husband," English law held the "by mar-

riage, the husband and wife are one person in law: that is, the very being or legal existence of the women is suspended during the marriage, or at least is incorporated and consolidated into that of the Husband," I. Blackstone, *Commentaries*, 1965, pp. 442–445, cited in Kenneth M. Davidson, Ruth B. Ginsburg, and Herma H. Kay, *Sex Based Discrimination* (St. Paul, Minn.: West Publishing Co., 1974), p. 117.

2. Harry Braverman, *Labor and Monopoly Capital* (New York: Monthly Review Press, 1975).

3. Kate Millett, *Sexual Politics* (New York: Avon Books, 1971), p. 25.

4. One example of this type of radical feminist history is Susan Brownmiller's *Against Our Will, Men, Women, and Rape* (New York: Simon & Shuster, 1975).

5. See Viana Muller, "The Formation of the State and the Oppression of Women: Some Theoretical Considerations and a Case Study in England and Wales," *Review of Radical Political Economics*, Vol. 9, no. 3 (Fall 1977), pp. 7–21.

6. Gayle Rubin, "The Traffic in Women," in *Anthropology of Women*, ed. Reiter, p. 159.

7. Himmelweit and Mohun point out that both aspects of production (people and things) are logically necessary to describe a mode of production because by definition a mode of production must be capable of reproducing itself. Either aspect alone is not self-sufficient. To put it simply the production of things requires people, and the production of people requires things. Marx, though recognizing capitalism's need for people did not concern himself with how they were produced or what the connections between the two aspects of production were. See Himmelweit and Mohun, "Domestic Labour and Capital," *Cambridge Journal of Economics*, Vol. 1, no. 1 (March 1977), pp. 15–31.

8. Cited in Neil Smelser, *Social Change and the Industrial Revolution* (Chicago: University of Chicago Press, 1959), p. 301.

9. These examples are from Heidi I. Hartmann, "Capitalism, Patriarchy, and Job Segregation by Sex," *Signs: Journal of Women in Culture and Society*, Vol. 1, no. 3, pt. 2 (Spring 1976), pp. 162–163.

10. Carol Brown, "Patriarchial Capitalism and the Female-Headed Family," *Social Scientist* (India); no. 40–41 (November–December 1975), pp. 28–39.

11. Carol Brown, in "Patriarchal Capitalism," argues, for example, that we are moving from "family based" to "industrially-based" patriarchy within capitalism.

12. Stewart Ewen, *Captains of Consciousness* (New York: Random House, 1976).

13. Heather L. Ross and Isabel B. Sawhill, *Time of Transition: The Growth of Families Headed by Women* (Washington, D.C.: The Urban Institute, 1975).

14. See Kathryn E. Walker and Margaret E. Woods, *Time Use: A Measure of Household Production of Family Goods and Services* (Washington D.C.: American Home Economics Association, 1976; and Heidi I. Hartmann, "The Family as the Locus of Gender, Class, and Political Struggle: The Example of Housework," *Signs: Journal of Women in Culture and Society*, Vol. 6, no. 3 (Spring 1981).

15. Lise Vogel, "The Earthly Family." *Radical America*, Vol. 7, no. 4–5 (July–October 1973), pp. 9–50.

 # 64

From In a Different Voice

CAROL GILLIGAN

CONCEPTS OF SELF AND MORALITY

. . .

In order to go beyond the question, "How much like men do women think, how capable are they of engaging in the abstract and hypothetical construction of reality?" it is necessary to identify and define developmental criteria that encompass the categories of women's thought. [Norma] Haan [1975] points out the necessity to derive such criteria from the resolution of the "more frequently occurring, real-life moral dilemmas of interpersonal, empathic, fellow-feeling concerns" (p. 34) which have long been the center of women's moral concern. But to derive developmental criteria from the language of women's moral discourse, it is necessary first to see whether women's construction of the moral domain relies on a language different from that of men and one that deserves equal credence in the definition of development. This in turn requires finding places where women have the power to choose and thus are willing to speak in their own voice.

When birth control and abortion provide women with effective means for controlling their fertility, the dilemma of choice enters a central arena of women's lives. Then the relationships that have traditionally defined women's identities and framed their moral judgments no longer flow inevitably from their reproductive capacity but become matters of decision over which they have control. Released from the passivity and reticence of a sexuality that binds them in dependence, women can question with Freud what it is that they want and can assert their own answers to that question. However, while society may affirm publicly the woman's right to choose for herself, the exercise of such choice brings her privately into conflict with the conventions of femininity, particularly the moral equation of goodness with self-sacrifice. Although independent assertion in judgment and action is considered to be the hallmark of adulthood, it is rather in their care and concern for others that women have both judged themselves and been judged.

The conflict between self and other thus constitutes the central moral problem for women, posing a dilemma whose resolution requires a reconciliation between femininity and adulthood. In the absence of such a reconciliation, the moral problem cannot be resolved. The "good woman" masks assertion in evasion, denying responsibility by claiming only to meet the needs of others, while the "bad woman" forgoes or renounces the commitments that bind her in self-deception and betrayal. It is precisely this dilemma—the conflict between compassion and autonomy, between virtue and power—which the feminine voice struggles to resolve in its effort to reclaim the self and to solve the moral problem in such a way that no one is hurt.

When a woman considers whether to continue or abort a pregnancy, she contemplates a decision that affects both self and others and engages directly the critical moral issue of hurting. Since the choice is ultimately hers and therefore one for which she is responsible, it raises precisely those questions of judgment that have been most problematic for women. Now she is asked whether she wishes to interrupt that stream of life which for centuries has immersed her in the passivity of dependence while at the same time imposing on her the responsibility for care. Thus the abortion decision brings to the core of feminine apprehension, to what Joan Didion (1972) calls "the irreconcilable difference of it—that sense of living one's deepest life underwater, that dark involvement with blood and birth and death" (p. 14), the adult questions of responsibility and choice.

. . .

Women's constructions of the abortion dilemma in particular reveal the existence of a distinct moral language whose evolution traces a sequence of development. This is the language of selfishness and responsibility, which defines the moral problem as one of obligation to exercise care and avoid hurt. The inflicting of hurt is considered selfish and immoral in its reflection of unconcern, while the expression of care is seen as the fulfillment of moral responsibility. The reiterative use by the women of the words *selfish* and *responsible* in talking about moral conflict and choice, given the underlying moral orientation that this language reflects, sets the women apart from the men whom Kohlberg studied and points toward a different understanding of moral development.

The three moral perspectives revealed by the abortion decision study denote a sequence in the development of the ethic of care. These different views of care and the transitions between them emerged from an analysis of the ways in which the women used moral language—words such as *should, ought, better, right, good,* and *bad,* by the changes and shifts that appeared in their thinking, and by the way in which they reflected on and judged their thought. In this sequence, an initial focus on caring for the self in order to ensure survival is followed by a transitional phase in which this judgment is criticized as selfish. The criticism signals a new understanding of the connection between self and others which is articulated by the concept of responsibility. The elaboration of this concept of responsibility and its fusion with a maternal morality that seeks to ensure care for the dependent and unequal characterizes the second perspective. At this point, the good is equated with caring for others. However, when only others are legitimized as the recipients of the woman's care, the exclusion of herself gives rise to problems in relationships, creating a disequilibrium that initiates the second transition. The equation of conformity with care, in its conventional definition, and the illogic of the inequality between other and self, lead to a reconsideration of relationships in an effort to sort out the confusion between self-sacrifice and care inherent in the conventions of feminine goodness. The third perspective focuses on the dynamics of relationships and dissipates the tension between selfishness and responsibility through a new understanding of the interconnection between other and self. Care becomes the self-chosen principle of a judgment that remains psychological in its concern with relationships and response but becomes universal in its condemnation of exploitation and hurt. Thus a progressively more adequate understanding of the psychology of human relationships—an increasing differentiation of self and other and a growing comprehension of the dynamics of social interaction—informs the development of an ethic of care. This ethic, which reflects a cumulative knowledge of human relationships, evolves around a central insight, that self and other are interdependent. The different ways of thinking about this connection or the different modes of its apprehension mark the three perspectives and their transitional phases. In this sequence, the fact of interconnection informs the central, recurring recognition that just as the incidence of violence is in the end destructive to all, so the activity of care enhances both others and self.

• • •

To admit the truth of the women's perspective to the conception of moral development is to recognize for both sexes the importance throughout life of the connection between self and other, the universality of the need for compassion and care. The concept of the separate self and of moral principles uncompromised by the constraints of reality is an adolescent ideal, the elaborately wrought philosophy of a Stephen Daedalus whose flight we know to be in jeopardy. Erikson (1964), in contrasting the ideological morality of the adolescent with the adult ethic of taking care, attempts to grapple with this problem of integration. But when he charts a developmental path where the sole precursor to the intimacy of adult love and the generativity of adult work and relationships is the trust established in infancy, and where all intervening experience is marked as steps toward autonomy and independence, then separation itself becomes the model and the measure of growth. Though Erikson observes that, for women, identity has as much to do with intimacy as with separation, this observation is not integrated into his developmental chart.

The morality of responsibility that women describe stands, like their concept of self, apart from the path marked to maturity. The progress to moral maturity is depicted as leading through the adolescent questioning of conventional morality to the discovery of individual rights. The generalization of this discovery into a principled conception of justice is illustrated by the definition of morality given by Ned, a senior in the college student study:

Morality is a prescription, a thing to follow, and the idea of having a concept of morality is to try to figure out what it is that people can do in order to make life with each other livable, make for a kind of balance, a kind of equilibrium, a harmony in which everybody feels he has a place and an equal share in

things. Doing that is kind of contributing to a state of affairs that goes beyond the individual, in the absence of which the individual has no chance for self-fulfillment of any kind. Fairness, morality, is kind of essential, it seems to me, for creating the kind of environment, interaction between people, that is prerequisite to the fulfillment of most individual goals. If you want other people not to interfere with your pursuit of whatever you are into, you have to play the game.

In contrast, Diane, a woman in her late twenties, defines a morality not of rights but of responsibility, when explaining what makes an issue moral:

Some sense of trying to uncover a right path in which to live, and always in my mind is that the world is full of real and recognizable trouble, and it is heading for some sort of doom, and is it right to bring children into this world when we currently have an overpopulation problem, and is it right to spend money on a pair of shoes when I have a pair of shoes and other people are shoeless? It is part of a self-critical view, part of saying, "How am I spending my time and in what sense am I working?" I think I have a real drive, a real maternal drive, to take care of someone—to take care of my mother, to take care of children, to take care of other people's children, to take care of my own children, to take care of the world. When I am dealing with moral issues, I am sort of saying to myself constantly, "Are you taking care of all the things that you think are important, and in what ways are you wasting yourself and wasting those issues?"

While the postconventional nature of Diane's perspective seems clear, her judgment of moral dilemmas does not meet the criteria for principled thinking in the justice orientation. This judgment, however, reflects a different moral conception in which moral judgment is oriented toward issues of responsibility and care. The way in which the responsibility orientation guides moral decision at the postconventional level is illustrated by Sharon, a woman in her thirties when questioned about the right way to make moral decisions:

The only way I know is to try to be as awake as possible, to try to know the range of what you feel, to try to consider all that's involved, to be as aware as you can be of what's going on, as conscious as you can of where you're walking. (*Are there principles that guide you?*) The principle would have something to do with responsibility, responsibility and caring about yourself and others. But it's not that on the one hand you choose to be responsible and on the other hand you choose to be irresponsible. Both ways you can be responsible. That's why there's not just a principle that once you take hold of you settle. The principle put into practice here is still going to leave you with conflict.

The moral imperative that emerges repeatedly in interviews with women is an injunction to care, a responsibility to discern and alleviate the "real and recognizable trouble" of this world. For men, the moral imperative appears rather as an injunction to respect the rights of others and thus to protect from interference the rights to life and self-fulfillment. Women's insistence on care is at first self-critical rather than self-protective, while men initially conceive obligation to others negatively in terms of non-interference. Development for both sexes would therefore seem to entail an integration of rights and responsibilities through the discovery of the complementarity of these disparate views. For women, the integration of rights and responsibilities takes place through an understanding of the psychological logic of relationships. This understanding tempers the self-destructive potential of a self-critical morality by asserting the need of all persons for care. For men, recognition through experience of the need for more active responsibility in taking care corrects the potential indifference of a morality of noninterference and turns attention from the logic to the consequences of choice (Gilligan and Murphy, 1979; Gilligan, 1981). In the development of a postconventional ethical understanding, women come to see the violence inherent in inequality, while men come to see the limitations of a conception of justice blinded to the differences in human life.

Hypothetical dilemmas, in the abstraction of their presentation, divest moral actors from the history and psychology of their individual lives and separate the moral problem from the social contingencies of its possible occurrence. In doing so, these dilemmas are useful for the distillation and refinement of objective principles of justice and for measuring the formal logic of equality and reciprocity. However, the reconstruction of the dilemma in its contextual particularity allows the understanding of cause and consequence which engages the compassion and tolerance repeatedly noted to distinguish the moral judgments of women. Only when substance is given to the skeletal lives of hypothetical people is it possible to consider the social injustice that their moral problems may reflect and to imagine the individual suffering their occurrence may signify or their resolution engender.

The proclivity of women to reconstruct hypothetical dilemmas in terms of the real, to request or to supply missing information about the nature of the people and the places where they live, shifts their judgment away from the hierarchical ordering of principles and the formal procedures of decision making. This insistence on the particular signifies an orientation to the dilemma and to moral problems in general that differs from any current developmental stage descriptions. Consequently, though several of the women in the abortion study clearly articulate a postconventional metaethical position, none of them are considered principled in their normative moral judgments of Kohlberg's hypothetical dilemmas. Instead, the women's judgments point toward an identification of the violence inherent in the dilemma itself, which is seen to compromise the justice of any of its possible resolutions. This construction of the dilemma leads the women to recast the moral judgment from a consideration of the good to a choice between evils.

· · ·

The abortion study suggests that women impose a distinctive construction on moral problems, seeing moral dilemmas in terms of conflicting responsibilities. This construction was traced through a sequence of three perspectives, each perspective representing a more complex understanding of the relationship between self and other and each transition involving a critical reinterpretation of the conflict between selfishness and responsibility. The sequence of women's moral judgment proceeds from an initial concern with survival to a focus on goodness and finally to a reflective understanding of care as the most adequate guide to the resolution of conflicts in human relationships. The abortion study demonstrates the centrality of the concepts of responsibility and care in women's constructions of the moral domain, the close tie in women's thinking between conceptions of the self and of morality, and ultimately the need for an expanded developmental theory that includes, rather than rules out from consideration, the differences in the feminine voice. Such an inclusion seems essential, not only for explaining the development of women but also for understanding in both sexes the characteristics and precursors of an adult moral conception.

[1982]

REFERENCES

Didion, Joan. "The Women's Movement." *New York Times Book Review,* July 30, 1972, pp. 1–2, 14.

Erikson, Erik H. *Insight and Responsibility.* New York: W. W. Norton, 1964.

Gilligan, Carol. "Moral Development in the College Years." In A. Chickering, ed., *The Modern American College.* San Francisco: Jossey-Bass, 1981.

Gilligan, Carol, and Murphy, John Michael. "Development from Adolescence to Adulthood: The Philosopher and the 'Dilemma of the Fact.'" In D. Kuhn, ed., *Intellectual Development Beyond Childhood.* New Directions for Child Development, no. 5. San Francisco: Jossey-Bass, 1979.

Haan, Norma. "Hypothetical and Actual Moral Reasoning in a Situation of Civil Disobedience." *Journal of Personality and Social Psychology* 32 (1975): 255–270.

 65

Is the Gaze Male?

E. ANN KAPLAN

• • •

Using psychoanalysis to deconstruct Hollywood films enables us to see clearly the patriarchal myths through which we have been positioned as Other (enigma, mystery), and as eternal and unchanging. We can also see how the family melodrama, as a genre geared specifically to women, functions both to expose the constraints and limitations that the capitalist nuclear family imposes on women and, at the same time, to "educate" women to accept those constraints as "natural," inevitable—as "given." For part of what defines melodrama as a form is its concern explicitly with Oedipal issues—illicit love relationships (overtly or incipiently incestuous), mother–child relationships, husband–wife relationships, father–son relationships: these are the staple fare of melodrama as surely as they are largely excluded from the dominant Hollywood genres, the

western and the gangster film, that melodrama compensates for.

Using the framework developed by Peter Brooks, we might say that the western and gangster genres aim to duplicate the functions that tragedy once fulfilled, in the sense of placing man within the larger cosmic scene. But Brooks points out that we are now in a period when "mythmaking [can] only be personal and individual" since we lack "a clear transcendent value to be reconciled to;" so that even these genres, broadly speaking, fall into melodrama. All Hollywood films, taking this large view, require what Brooks considers essential to melodrama, namely "a social order to be purged, a set of ethical imperatives to be made clear."[1]

It is important that women are excluded from the central role in the main, highly respected Hollywood genres; women, and female issues, are only central in the family melodrama (which we can see as an offshoot of other melodramatic forms). Here Brooks's definition of the way characters in melodrama "assume primary psychic roles, Father, Mother, Child, and express basic psychic conditions"[2] seems particularly relevant, as is also his explicit linking of psychoanalysis and melodrama at the end of the book. Psychoanalytic processes themselves, he notes, reveal the "melodrama aesthetic" (we will see in chapter 11 that the directors of a recent feminist film, *Sigmund Freud's Dora,* also view psychoanalysis as melodrama); but important for our purposes here is his comment that the melodramatic form deals with "the processes of repression and the status of repressed content." Brooks concludes that "the structure of ego, superego and id suggests the subjacent manichaeism of melodramatic persons."[3]

Laura Mulvey (the British filmmaker and critic whose theories are central to new developments) also views melodrama as concerned with Oedipal issues, but she sees it primarily as a female form, acting as a corrective to the main genres that celebrate male action. The family melodrama is important, she says, in "probing pent-up emotion, bitterness and disillusion well known to women." For Mulvey, melodrama serves a useful function for women who lack any coherent culture of oppression. "The simple fact of recognition has aesthetic importance," she notes; "there is a dizzy satisfaction in witnessing the way that sexual difference under patriarchy is fraught, explosive and erupts dramatically into violence within its own private stomping ground, the family."[4] But Mulvey concludes that if melodrama is important in bringing ideological contradictions to the surface, and in being made for a female audience, events are never reconciled at the end in ways beneficial to women.

So why is it that women are drawn to melodrama? Why do we find our objectification and surrender pleasurable? This is precisely an issue that psychoanalysis can help to explain: for such pleasure is not surprising if we consider the shape of the girl's Oedipal crisis. Following Lacan for a moment, we see that the girl is forced to turn away from the illusory unity with the Mother in the prelinguistic realm and has to enter the symbolic world which involves subject and object. Assigned the place of object (lack), she is the recipient of male desire, passively appearing rather than acting. Her sexual pleasure in this position can thus be constructed only around her own objectification. Furthermore, given the male structuring around sadism, the girl may adopt a corresponding masochism.[5]

In practice, this masochism is rarely reflected in more than a tendency for women to be passive in sexual relations; but in the realm of myth, masochism is often prominent. We could say that in locating herself in fantasy in the erotic, the woman places herself as either passive recipient of male desire or, at one remove, as *watching* a woman who is passive recipient of male desires and sexual actions. Although the evidence we have to go on is slim, it does seem that women's sexual fantasies would confirm the predominance of these positionings. (We will look shortly at some corresponding male fantasies.)

Nancy Friday's volumes provide discourses on the level of dream and, however questionable as "scientific" evidence, show narratives in which the woman speaker largely arranges events for her sexual pleasure so that things are done to her, or in which she is the object of men's lascivious gaze.[6] Often, there is pleasure in anonymity, or in a strange man approaching her when she is with her husband. Rarely does the dreamer initiate the sexual activity, and the man's large erect penis usually is central in the fantasy. Nearly all the fantasies have the dominance–submission pattern, with the woman in the latter place.

It is significant that in the lesbian fantasies that Friday has collected, women occupy *both* positions, the dreamer excited either by dominating another woman, forcing her to have sex, or enjoying being so dominated. These fantasies suggest either that the female positioning is not as monolithic as critics often imply or that women occupy the "male" position when they become dominant.[7] Whichever the case may be (and I will say more about this in a moment), the prevalence of the dominance–submission pattern as a sexual turn-on is clear. At a discussion about pornography organized by Julia LeSage at the Conference on Feminist Film Criticism (Northwestern University, 1980), both gay and straight women admitted their pleasure (in both fantasy and actuality) in being "forced" or "forcing" someone else. Some women claimed that this was a result of growing up in Victorian-style households where all sexuality was repressed, but others denied that it had anything to do with patriarchy. Women wanted, rightly, to accept themselves sexually, whatever the turn-on mechanism.[8] But simply to celebrate whatever gives us sexual pleasure seems to me both too easy and too problematic: we need to analyze *how it is* that certain things turn us on, how sexuality has been constructed in patriarchy to produce pleasure in the dominance–submission forms, before we *advocate* these modes.[9]

It was predictable that many of the male fantasies in Friday's book *Men in Love* show the speaker constructing events so that he is in control: again, the "I" of identity remains central, as it is not in the female narrations. Many male fantasies focus on the man's excitement in arranging for his woman to expose herself (or even give herself) to other men, while he watches.[10]

The difference between this male voyeurism and the female form is striking. For the woman does not own the desire, even when she watches; her watching is to place responsibility for sexuality at yet one more remove, *to distance herself from sex*. The man, on the other hand, *owns the desire and the woman*, and gets pleasure from exchanging the woman, as in Lévi-Strauss's kinship system.[11]

Yet, some of the fantasies in Friday's book show men's wish to be taken over by an aggressive woman, who would force them to become helpless, like the little boy in his mother's hands. A tour of Times Square in 1980 (the organization Women Against Pornography runs them regularly) corroborated this. After a slide show that focused totally on male sadism and violent sexual exploitation of women, we were taken to sex shops that by no means stressed male domination. We saw literature and films expressing as many fantasies of male as of female submission. The situations were the predictable ones: young boys (but sometimes men) seduced by women in a form of authority—governesses, nursemaids, nurses, schoolteachers, stepmothers, etc. (Of course, it is significant that the corresponding dominance–submission fantasies of women have men in authority positions that carry much more status—professors, doctors, policemen, executives: these men seduce the innocent girls or young wives who cross their paths.)

Two interesting things emerge here. One is that dominance–submission patterns are apparently a crucial part of both male and female sexuality as constructed in western civilization. The other is that men have a far wider range of positions available: more readily both dominant and submissive, they vacillate between supreme control and supreme abandonment. Women, meanwhile, are more consistently submissive, but not excessively abandoned. In their own fantasies, women do not position themselves as exchanging men, although a *man* might find being exchanged an exciting fantasy.[12]

The passivity revealed in women's sexual fantasies is reinforced by the way women are positioned in film. In an interesting paper on "The 'woman's film': possession and address," Mary Ann Doane has shown that in the one film genre (i.e. melodrama) that, as we have seen, constructs a female spectator, the spectator is made to participate in what is essentially a masochistic fantasy. Doane notes that in the major classical genres, the female body *is* sexuality, providing the erotic object for the male spectator. In the woman's film, the gaze must be de-eroticized (since the spectator is now assumed to be female), but in doing this the films effectively disembody their spectator. The repeated, masochistic scenarios effectively immobilize the female viewer. She is refused pleasure in that imaginary identification which, as Mulvey has shown, repeats

for men the experience of the mirror phase. The idealized male screen heroes give back to the male spectator his more perfect mirror self, together with a sense of mastery and control. In contrast, the female is given only powerless, victimized figures who, far from perfect, reinforce the basic sense of worthlessness that already exists.[13]

Later on in her paper, Doane shows that Freud's "A child is being beaten" is important in distinguishing the way a common masochistic fantasy works out for boys and for girls. In the male fantasy, "sexuality remains on the surface" and the man "retains his own role and his own gratification in the context of the scenario. The 'I' of identity remains." But the female fantasy is first desexualized and second, "necessitates the woman's assumption of the position of spectator, outside of the event." In this way, the girl manages, as Freud says, "to escape from the demands of the erotic side of her life altogether."[14]

But the important question remains: when women are in the dominant position, are they in the *masculine* position? Can we envisage a female dominant position that would differ qualitatively from the male form of dominance? Or is there merely the possibility of both sex genders occupying the positions we now know as "masculine" and "feminine?"

The experience of films of the 1970s and 1980s would support the latter possibility, and explain why many feminists have not been excited by the so-called "liberated" woman on the screen, or by the fact that some male stars have recently been made the object of the "female" gaze. Traditionally male stars did not necessarily (or even primarily) derive their "glamor" from their looks or their sexuality but from the power they were able to wield within the filmic world in which they functioned (e.g. John Wayne); these men, as Laura Mulvey has shown, became ego-ideals for the men in the audience, corresponding to the image in the mirror, who was more in control of motor coordination than the young child looking in. "The male figure," Mulvey notes, "is free to command the stage . . . of spatial illusion in which he articulates the look and creates the action."[15]

Recent films have begun to change this pattern: stars like John Travolta (*Saturday Night Fever, Urban Cowboy, Moment by Moment*) have been rendered object of woman's gaze and in some of the films (e.g. *Moment by Moment*) placed explicitly as a sexual object to a woman who controlled the film's action. Robert Redford likewise has begun to be used as object of "female" desire (e.g. in *Electric Horseman*). But it is significant that in all these films, when the man steps out of his traditional role as the one who controls the whole action, and when he is set up as sex object, the woman then takes on the "masculine" role as bearer of the gaze and initiator of the action. She nearly always loses her traditionally feminine characteristics in so doing—not those of attractiveness, but rather of kindness, humaneness, motherliness. She is now often cold, driving, ambitious, manipulating, just like the men whose position she has usurped.

Even in a supposedly "feminist" film like *My Brilliant Career,* the same processes are at work. The film is interesting because it foregrounds the independently minded heroine's dilemma in a clearly patriarchal culture: in love with a wealthy neighbor, the heroine makes him the object of her gaze, but the problem is that, as female, her desire has no power. Men's desire naturally carries power with it, so that when the hero finally concedes his love for her, he comes to get her. However, being able to conceive of "love" only as "submission," an end to autonomy and to her life as a creative writer, the heroine now refuses him. The film thus plays with established positions, but is unable to work through them to something else.

What we can conclude from the discussion so far is that our culture is deeply committed to myths of demarcated sex differences, called "masculine" and "feminine," which in turn revolve first on a complex gaze apparatus and second on dominance–submission patterns. This positioning of the two sex genders in representation clearly privileges the male (through the mechanisms of voyeurism and fetishism, which are male operations, and because his desire carries power/action where woman's usually does not). However, as a result of the recent women's movement, women have been permitted in representation to assume (step into) the position defined as "masculine," as long as the man then steps into *her* position, thus keeping the whole structure intact.

It is significant, of course, that while this substitution is made to happen relatively easily in the cinema, in real life any such "swapping" is fraught with immense psychological difficulties that only psychoanalysis can unravel. In any case, such "exchanges" do not do much for either sex, since nothing has essentially changed: the roles remain locked into their static boundaries. Showing images of mere reversal may in fact provide a safety valve for the social tensions that the women's movement has created by demanding a more dominant role for women.

We have thus arrived at a point where we must question the necessity for the dominance–submission structure. The gaze is not necessarily male (literally), but to own and activate the gaze, given our language and the structure of the unconscious, is to be in the "masculine" position. It is this persistent presentation of the masculine position that feminist film critics have demonstrated in their analysis of Hollywood films. Dominant, Hollywood cinema, they show, is constructed according to the unconscious of patriarchy; film narratives are organized by means of a male-based language and discourse which parallels the language of the unconscious. Women in film thus do not function as signifiers for a signified (a real woman), as sociological critics have assumed, but signifier and signified have been elided into a sign that represents something in the male unconscious.

Two basic Freudian concepts—voyeurism and fetishism—have been used to explain what exactly woman represents and the mechanisms that come into play for the male spectator watching a female screen image. (Or, to put it rather differently, voyeurism and fetishism are mechanisms the dominant cinema uses to *construct* the male spectator in accordance with the needs of his unconscious.) The first, voyeurism, is linked to the scopophilic instinct (i.e. the male pleasure in his own sexual organ transferred to pleasure in watching other people having sex). Critics argue that the cinema relies on this instinct, making the spectator essentially a voyeur. The drive that causes little boys to peek through keyholes of parental bedrooms to learn about their sexual activities (or to get sexual gratification by thinking about these activities) comes into play when the male adult watches films, sitting in a dark room. The original eye of the camera, controlling and limiting what can be seen, is reproduced by the projector aperture which lights up one frame at a time; and both processes (camera and projector) duplicate the eye at the keyhole, whose gaze is confined by the keyhole "frame." The spectator is obviously in the voyeur position when there are sex scenes on the screen, but screen images of women are sexualized no matter what the women are doing literally or what kind of plot may be involved.

According to Laura Mulvey, this eroticization of women on the screen comes about through the way the cinema is structured around three explicitly male looks or gazes: there is the look of the camera in the situation being filmed (called the pro-filmic event); while technically neutral, this look, as we've seen, is inherently voyeuristic and usually "male" in the sense that a man is generally doing the filming; there is the look of the men within the narrative, which is structured so as to make women objects of their gaze; and finally there is the look of the male spectator (discussed above) which imitates (or is necessarily in the same position as) the first two looks.[16]

But if women were simply eroticized and objectified, matters might not be too bad, since objectification, as I have already shown, may be an inherent component of both male and female eroticism as constructed in western culture. But two further elements suggest themselves. To begin with, men do not simply look; their gaze carries with it the power of action and of possession which is lacking in the female gaze. Women receive and return a gaze, but cannot act upon it. Second, the sexualization and objectification of women is not simply for the purposes of eroticism; from a psychoanalytic point of view, it is designed to annihilate the threat that woman (as castrated and possessing a sinister genital organ) poses. In her article "The dread of women" (1932) Karen Horney goes to literature to show that "Men have never tired of fashioning expressions for the violent force by which man feels himself drawn to the woman, and side by side with his longing, the dread that through her he might die and be undone."[17] Horney goes on to conjecture that even man's glorification of women "has its

source not only in his cravings for love, but also in his desire to conceal his dread. A similar relief, however, is also sought and found in the disparagement of women that men often display ostentatiously in their attitudes."[18] Horney then explores the basis of the dread of women not only in castration (more related to the father) but in fear of the vagina.

But psychoanalysts agree that, for whatever reason—fear of castration (Freud) or in an attempt to deny the existence of the sinister female genital (Horney), men endeavor to find the penis in women. Feminist film critics have seen this phenomenon (clinically known as fetishism[19]) operating in the cinema; the camera (unconsciously) fetishizes the female form, rendering it phallus-like so as to mitigate woman's threat. Men, that is, turn "the represented figure itself into a fetish so that it becomes reassuring rather than dangerous (hence overvaluation, the cult of the female star)."[20]

The apparently contradictory attitudes of glorification and disparagement pointed out by Horney thus turn out to be a reflection of the same ultimate need to annihilate the dread that woman inspires. In the cinema, the twin mechanisms of fetishism and of voyeurism represent two different ways of handling this dread. As Mulvey points out, fetishism "builds up the physical beauty of the object, turning it into something satisfying in itself," while voyeurism, linked to disparagement, has a sadistic side, and is involved with pleasure through control or domination and with punishing the woman (guilty for being castrated).[21] For Claire Johnston, both mechanisms result in woman not being presented qua *woman* at all. Extending the *Cahiers du Cinéma* analysis of *Morocco*, Johnston argues that Von Sternberg represses "the idea of woman as a social and sexual being," thus replacing the opposition man–woman with male–non-male.[22]

With this look at feminist film theories and at the issues around the problem of the gaze and of the female spectator that psychoanalysis illuminates, we can begin to see the larger theoretical issues the psychoanalytic methodology involves,[23] particularly in relation to possibilities for change. It is this aspect of the new theoretical approaches that has begun to polarize the feminist film community.[24] For example, in a round-table discussion in 1978, some women voiced their displeasure with theories that were themselves originally devised by men, and with women's preoccupation with how we have been seen/placed/positioned by the dominant male order. Julia LeSage, for instance, argued that the use of Lacanian criticism has been destructive in reifying women "in a childlike position that patriarchy has wanted to see them in"; for LeSage, the Lacanian framework establishes "a discourse which is totally male."[25] And Ruby Rich objected to theories that rest with the apparent elimination of women from both screen and audience. She asked how we can move beyond our placing, rather than just analyzing it.[26]

As if in response to Rich's request, some feminist film critics have begun to take up the challenge to move beyond the preoccupation with how women have been constructed in patriarchal cinema. Judith Mayne, for example, in a useful summary of issues in recent feminist film criticism, argues that the context for discussion of women's cinema needs to be "opened up" to include the film spectator: "The task of criticism," she says, "is to examine the processes that determine how films evoke responses and how spectators produce them."[27] A little later on, Mayne suggests that the proper place for the feminist critic may well be close to the machine that is the agency for the propulsion of images onto the screen, i.e. the projector. By forcing our gaze to dwell on the images by slowing down or stopping the projection that creates patriarchal voyeurism, we may be able to provide a "reading against the grain" that will give us information about our positioning as spectators.

If Mayne's, LeSage's, and Rich's objections lead in a fruitful direction, those of Lucy Arbuthnot and Gail Seneca are problematic, but useful here for the purposes of illustration. In a paper on *Gentlemen Prefer Blondes* Arbuthnot and Seneca attempt to appropriate for themselves some of the images hitherto defined as repressive. They begin by expressing their dissatisfactions not only with current feminist film theory as outlined above, but also with the new theoretical feminist films, which, they say, "focus more on denying men their cathexis with women as erotic objects than in connecting women with each other." In addition, these films by "destroying the narrative and the possibility for viewer identification

with the characters, destroy both the male viewer's pleasure and our pleasure."[28] Asserting their need for identification with strong, female screen images, they argue that Hollywood films offer many examples of pleasurable identification; in a clever analysis, the relationship between Marilyn Monroe and Jane Russell in *Gentlemen Prefer Blondes* is offered as an example of strong women, who care for one another, providing a model we need.

However, looking at the construction of the film as a whole, rather than simply isolating certain shots, it is clear that Monroe and Russell are positioned, and position themselves, as objects for a specifically male gaze. The men's weakness does not mitigate their narrative power, and the women are left merely with the limited control they can wield through their sexuality. The film constructs them as "to-be-looked-at," and their manipulations end up as merely comic, since "capturing" the men involves their "being captured." The images of Monroe show her fetishized placement, aimed at reducing her sexual threat,[29] while Russell's stance becomes a parody of the male position. The result is that the two women repeat, in exaggerated form, dominant gender stereotypes.

The weakness of Arbuthnot and Seneca's analysis is that it ignores the way that all dominant images are basically male constructs. Recognizing this has led Julia Kristeva and others to say that it is impossible to know what the "feminine" might be, outside of male constructs. Kristeva says that while we must reserve the category "women" for social demands and publicity, by the word "woman" she means "that which is not represented, that which is unspoken, that which is left out of meanings and ideologies."[30] For similar reasons, Sandy Flitterman and Judith Barry have argued that feminist artists must avoid claiming a specific female power residing in the body of women and representing "an inherent feminine artistic essence which could find expression if allowed to be explored freely."[31] The impulse toward this kind of art is understandable in a culture that denies satisfaction in being a woman, but it results in Motherhood being redefined as the seat of female creativity, while women "are proposed as the bearers of culture, albeit an alternative one."[32]

Flitterman and Barry argue that this form of feminist art, along with some others that they outline, is dangerous in not taking into account "the social contradictions involved in 'femininity'." They suggest that "A radical feminist art would include an understanding of how women are constituted through social practices in culture" and argue for "an aesthetics designed to subvert the production of 'woman' as commodity," much as Claire Johnston and Laura Mulvey had earlier stated that to be feminist a cinema had to be a counter-cinema.

But the problem with this notion of a counter-cinema hinges on the issue of pleasure. Aware that a feminist counter-cinema would almost by definition deny pleasure, Mulvey argued that this denial was a necessary prerequisite for freedom but did not go into the problems involved. In introducing the notion of pleasure, Arbuthnot and Seneca have located a central and little-discussed issue, namely our need for feminist films that at once construct woman as spectator without offering the repressive identifications of Hollywood films and that satisfy our craving for *pleasure*.[33] They have pinpointed a paradox in which feminist film critics have been caught without realizing it, namely our fascination with Hollywood films, rather than with, say, avant-garde films, because they bring us pleasure; but we have (rightly) been wary of admitting the degree to which the pleasure comes from identification with objectification. Our positioning as "to-be-looked-at," as object of the (male) gaze, has come to be sexually pleasurable.

However, it will not do simply to enjoy our oppression unproblematically; to appropriate Hollywood images to ourselves, taking them out of the context of the total structure in which they appear, will not get us very far. As I suggested above, in order fully to understand *how it is* that women take pleasure in objectification one has to have recourse to psychoanalysis.

Christian Metz, Stephen Heath, and others have shown that the processes of cinema mimic in many ways those of the unconscious.[34] The mechanisms Freud distinguishes in relation to dream and the unconscious have been likened to the mechanism of film. In this analysis, film narratives, like dreams, symbolize a latent, repressed content, except that now the "content" refers not to an individual unconscious but to that of patriarchy in general. If psychoanalysis is a tool that will unlock the meaning of dreams, it should also unlock that of films.

The psychoanalytic methodology is thus justified as an essential first step in the feminist project of understanding our socialization in patriarchy. My analyses of Hollywood films amply demonstrate the ways in which patriarchal myths function to position women as silent, absent, and marginal. But, once we have fully understood our placing and the way that both language and psychoanalytic processes, inherent in our particular form of nuclear family, have constructed it, we have to think about strategies for changing discourse, since these changes would, in turn, affect the structuring of our lives in society.

· · ·

[1982]

NOTES

1. Peter Brooks (1976) *The Melodramatic Imagination.* New Haven and London. Yale University Press, p. 17.
2. Ibid., p. 15.
3. Ibid., p. 201.
4. Laura Mulvey (1976–1977) "Notes on Sirk and melodrama," *Movie,* Nos 25–26. p. 54.
5. Freud's work is, of course, central to any discussion of sadism and masochism, especially his "Beyond the pleasure principle," *Standard Edition,* Vol. 17, pp. 3–44. "A child is being beaten," *Standard Edition,* Vol. 17, pp. 175–204, and "The economic problem in masochism," *Standard Edition,* Vol. 19, pp. 157ff. Since I wrote this, the issues have been taken up in Kaja Silverman (1981) "Masochism and subjectivity." *Framework,* No. 12, pp. 2–9, and (in terms of case histories) in Joel Kovel (1981) *The Age of Desire: Reflections of a Radical Psychoanalyst,* New York. Pantheon.
6. Nancy Friday (1974) *My Secret Garden: Women's Sexual Fantasies,* New York, Pocket Books, pp. 100–109.
7. Ibid., pp. 80–90. There is obviously a problem with assuming that to be in the dominant position is to be in the "male" position; when critics talk in this way, it seems to me that they are using the term metaphorically (i.e. in this culture, the dominant position has been associated with the male gender). Clearly, in any new construction of society, gender connotations would be fundamentally changed to avoid any such identifications.
8. Unpublished transcript of a discussion, organized by Julia LeSage, at the Conference on Feminist Film Criticism, Northwestern University, Nov. 1980. See also, for discussion of dominance–submission patterns, Pat Califa (1981) "Feminism and sadomasochism," *Heresies,* Vol. 3, No. 4, pp. 30–34, and Robert Stoller (1975) *Perversions: The Erotic Form of Hatred,* New York, Pantheon.
9. Since I wrote this, the whole issue of sadomasochism has exploded in feminist circles; Pat Califa's article (1979) "Unraveling the sexual fringe: a secret side of lesbian sexuality," *The Advocate,* 27 Dec., pp. 19–23, had inserted a position that was highly controversial, and in-

creasing tension over women's sexual choices finally culminated in the heated debate about the Barnard Women Scholars Conference on Sexuality in April 1982. The resulting booklet, *Diary of a Conference on Sexuality.* New York, Faculty Press, 1982, describes the debates about sexuality that took place among the co-ordinators, and in the process many crucial issues are raised.

10. Nancy Friday (1980) *Men in Love.* New York, Dell Publishing.

11. Claude Lévi-Strauss (1969) *The Elementary Structures of Kinship,* London, Eyre & Spottiswoode.

12. Kaja Silverman's article ("Masochism and subjectivity") is important in underscoring some of Freud's observations about masochism and sadism. She stresses that both male and female subjects are attracted to passivity and masochism, to negativity and loss. It is this lure toward what has been defined as the "feminine" position that male subjects must resist and repress, since to recognize it would be to admit insufficiency, castration.

13. See Mary Ann Doane, "The woman's film: possession and address," paper delivered at the Conference on Cinema History, Asilomar, Monterey, May 1981, pp. 3–8, forthcoming in P. Mellencamp, L. Williams, and M. A. Doane (eds) *Re-Visions: Feminist Essays in Film Analysis,* Los Angeles, American Film Institute.

14. Ibid., p. 17.

15. Laura Mulvey (1975) "Visual pleasure and narrative cinema," *Screen,* Vol. 16, No. 3, pp. 12–13.

16. Ibid., pp. 6–18.

17. Karen Horney (1932) "The dread of woman," reprinted in Harold Kelman (ed.) (1967) *Feminine Psychology,* New York, Norton, p. 134.

18. Ibid., p. 136.

19. For a useful discussion of fetishism, see Otto Fenichel (1945) *The Psychoanalytic Theory of Neurosis,* New York, Norton, pp. 341–345.

20. Mulvey, "Visual pleasure," p. 14.

21. Ibid.

22. Claire Johnston (1973) "Woman's cinema as counter-cinema," in Claire Johnston (ed.) *Notes on Women's Cinema,* London, Society for Education in Film and Television, p. 26.

23. For a full discussion of this, see chapter 9 of Kaplan, Women and Film.

24. This has been evident in feminist film sessions at conferences, but was particularly clear at the Lolita Rodgers Memorial Conference on Feminist Film Criticism, held at Northwestern University, Nov. 1980. For a report of some differences, see Barbara Klinger (1981) "Conference report," *Camera Obscura,* No. 7, pp. 137–143.

25. In "Women and film: a discussion of feminist aesthetics," *New German Critique,* No. 13 (1978), p. 93.

26. Ibid., p. 87.

27. Judith Mayne (1981) "The woman at the keyhole: women's cinema and feminist criticism," *New German Critique,* No. 23, pp. 27–43.

28. Lucy Arbuthnot and Gail Seneca, "Pre-text and text in *Gentlemen Prefer Blondes,*" paper delivered at the Conference on Feminist Film Criticism, Northwestern University, Nov. 1980, and published in *Film Reader,* No. 5 (1982), p. 14.

29. See Maureen Turim (1979) "Gentlemen consume blondes," *Wide Angle,* Vol. 1, No. 1, pp. 52–59. Carol Rowe also (if somewhat mockingly) shows Monroe's phallicism in her film *Grand Delusion* (1977).

30. Julia Kristeva (1980) "Woman can never be defined," trans. of "La Femme, ce n'est jamais ça" by Marilyn A. August, in Isabelle de Courtivron and Elaine Marks (eds) *New French Feminisms,* Amherst, Mass., University of Massachusetts Press, pp. 137–138.

31. Judith Barry and Sandy Flitterman (1980) "Textual strategies: the politics of artmaking," *Screen,* Vol. 21. No. 2, p. 37.

32. Ibid.

33. Mulvey, "Visual pleasure," pp. 7–8, 18. It is true that "Women whose image has continually been stolen and used for this end (i.e., satisfaction, pleasure, etc.) cannot view the decline of the traditional film form with anything much more than sentimental regret," but the question remains as to what the pleasure in cinema will be replaced *with.*

34. See, for example, the essays in *Edinburgh Magazine,* No. 1 (1976), especially those by Rosalind Coward, "Lacan and signification: an introduction," pp. 6–20; Christian Metz, "History/discourse: notes on two voyeurisms," pp. 21–25; Stephen Heath, "Screen images, film memory," pp. 33–42; Claire Johnston, "Towards a feminist film practice: some theses," pp. 50–59. Cf. also issue of *Screen* devoted to "Psychoanalysis and cinema," Vol. 16, No. 2 (1975), in which articles of particular interest are Christian Metz, "The imaginary signifier," pp. 14–76, and Stephen Heath, "Film and system: terms of analysis, Part II," pp. 91–113.

 66

The Fear That Feminism Will Free Men First

DEIRDRE ENGLISH

For feminists, the most difficult aspect of the 1980s' backlash against women's abortion rights, and other emancipatory new rights and attitudes related to sex, is the fact that a large part of the anti-choice ("pro-life") movement is made up of women. What we have for the past ten years grown accustomed to calling the "women's movement" claimed to represent the collective good of all women: the opposition was expected to be male. But now we are faced with an opposing women's movement, and one that also claims to stand for the best interests of all women. It is as confusing, as frustrating, as if, at the height of the civil rights movement, a large percentage of blacks had suddenly organized to say: "Wait a minute. We don't want equal rights. We like things just the way they are."

The very existence of such a movement represents a deep crisis in the community of women, and a profound challenge to the analytical and synthetical powers of feminist theory. Before proceeding, an old feminist touchstone is a good reminder: though we may be in conflict with them, other women rarely prove to be our real enemies. Even in opposing the politics of the anti-feminist women, we must begin by recognizing and honoring her experiences, her prospects, her hopes and fears.

To do that, it is essential to separate the motivations of those men who organize against women's rights and the women who do so, even when they are found holding the same credo in the same organizations. For while men in the anti-abortion movement stand to increase the measure of male control over women, the women can gain nothing but greater sexual submission. Now that is a suspicious thing in itself, because any people asking only to give in to a more powerful group must be well convinced that their survival is at stake. After all, the anti-feminist woman is neither stupid nor incompetent, whatever she may wish her male leaders to believe. Legitimately enough, she has her own self-interest in mind, in a world in which she did not create the options.

THE OTHER WOMAN

Clearly, the anti-choice activist is not primarily concerned with refusing an abortion for herself; that she has the power to do no matter what the laws are. (By contrast, women in the pro-choice movement are almost invariably women who feel, at some level, a personal need for abortion rights.) But no one is taking away another person's right to bear children, no feminist is circumscribing individual ethical or religious beliefs that would prohibit abortion. What is solely at question to the anti-choice activist is the *other* woman's right to make this decision herself; her objective is to refuse social legitimation for abortion decisions that are not her own.

The anti-abortionists are, as they have been accused, seeking to impose their morality on society. But that is part of the very definition of moralism: a *moralist* is "one concerned with regulating the mor-

als of others." The anti-abortion movement is a perfect example of a moralistic movement, and it demonstrates some interesting things about the functions of moral systems.

In opposing the Right-to-Lifers, pro-choice advocates most frequently argue that a woman has an absolute right to control her own body. The insistence on individual rights is at the foundation of the feminist position. A woman's right to control her own body encompasses endless new meanings in feminism: from the right to refuse sex (as in marital rape) to the right to a freely chosen sexuality; from the right to be protected from sexual violence to the right to plan one's own reproductivity. The complete realization of those rights alone would mark a new era for women. For now, the recognition of woman's body as the *terra firma* of female liberation must be counted as one of the great political accomplishments of our day. But it is far from enough.

After all, this is a society: we are interdependent; individual actions have repercussions. The struggle is not and can never be only over the actual act of abortion. The struggle is necessarily over a larger sexual morality—and moral systems do have a bearing on virtually everybody's behavior. The anti-abortion people have tried to insist on single-issue politics partly because it is much easier for them to attack the keystone of abortion than to defend the system of morality that is tied to compulsory motherhood. It falls to us to identify the moral system they are upholding and, at the same time, to define our own.

The anti-feminist woman is right about one crucial thing: the other woman's right to have an abortion does affect her. It does something very simple and, to many women, very upsetting: it takes away their ability *not* to choose. Where abortion is available, the birth of every baby becomes a willed choice, a purposeful act. And that new factor destroys the set of basic assumptions on which many traditional marriages have been based. It breaks the rules and wrecks the game.

THE SEX CONTRACT

Remember the rules of the old game? They began with this: men did not get to have sex with women (at least not women of their own class or higher) unless they married them. Then men were morally obligated to provide for the children they had helped to conceive. In other words, sex was supposed to incur a major responsibility for men—as it did for women. Only thirty years ago, the average marrying age in the United States was twenty for women and twenty-two for men, and hundreds of thousands of brides have been pregnant on their wedding day.

Men always complained about this sexual bargain. "Nature kidded us," said a young Irish Catholic father of two in a short story by Frank O'Connor. "We had our freedom and we didn't value it. Now our lives are run for us by women." But men's regrets, however deeply felt, were still the complaints of the relatively more powerful party. It was women who, for physical and financial reasons, really *needed* marriage.

In a society that effectively condoned widespread male sexual violence and severely restricted economic opportunities for women outside of marriage, the deck was heavily stacked. If men did not "value their freedom," women had little freedom to value. The one short-lived power women had was withholding sex; and even that was only good until marriage—possibly periodically thereafter, with the more tolerant husbands. But in general, women had to earn their keep not only with sex, but with submissiveness, and acceptance of the male not as an equal partner but as a superior. Seen in these terms, the marriage contract seems a little more like extortion under the threat of abandonment.

But to point this out is not the way to play the game. The essential thing about the system—like moral systems in general—is that everyone must play by the same rules. In the past, the community of women has often been hard on those who "give away" for free—or for money—what the rest trade for love and marriage. Then came birth control, the sexual revolution, and legalized abortion.

THE ESCAPE CLAUSE

It was the availability of relatively reliable contraception that provided the first escape clause to the old marital Russian roulette, both for men and women. The "99 percent effective" pill sparked the sexual revolution in the 1960s and 1970s and permitted women for the first time in history to decisively separate intercourse from reproduction. (Only after that historic schism could the modern woman's new fascination with discovering her own sexuality begin to emerge.)

For the most part, women of all classes and religions enthusiastically welcomed the advent of reliable contraception. True, it did have the effect of releasing men from some responsibility for their sexual acts, but the gains for women seemed much greater. Sexual liberation and birth control brought women new-found sexual pleasure, began to erode the double standard, allowed women to plan their pregnancies—and therefore participate in the work world on new terms—and in general seemed to tend to equalize the sexes. Other things, unfortunately, did not change so fast. Especially not the economy.

CATCH 22

Most women who want to have children still cannot make it, financially, without a man. In an era in which an increasingly larger number of people are spending significant parts of their lives outside of the marriage coupling, the socioeconomic differences between men and women become increasingly, painfully obvious. According to 1978 Bureau of Labor statistics, only some 7 percent of women make more than $15,000 per year, while more than 46 percent of men do. Marriage is still the major means of economic stability—even survival—for women.

In this sense, men have reaped more than their share of benefits from women's liberation. If women hold jobs, no matter how poorly paid, men may more easily renounce any responsibility for the economic support of women and children. Thus woman's meager new economic independence, and her greater sexual freedom outside the bounds of marriage, have allowed men to garner great new freedoms. Because there is no "trick of nature" to make the link between sex and fatherhood, and little social stigma on he who loves and leaves, a woman faces the abdication of any male responsibility for pregnancy—let alone for any ensuing children. If a woman gets pregnant, the man who twenty years ago might have married her may feel today that he is gallant if he splits the cost of an abortion. The man who might have remained in a dead-end marriage out of a sense of duty finds increasingly that he faces no great social disapproval if he walks out on his family, even while his kids are still in diapers.

Divorce leaves women putting a higher percentage of both their incomes and their time into child care. According to the U.S. Census, the number of one-parent families headed by divorced women jumped almost 200 percent in one decade—from 956,000 in 1970 to 2.7 million in 1981. During the same period, the number of single-parent families headed by men actually declined. (Nationally, there are more youthful products of divorce cared for by relatives other than a parent than by their fathers alone.)

It is also worth noting the difference in the economic impact of divorce on fathers versus mothers. Roughly 40 percent of absent fathers contribute *no* money for child support after divorce, and the other 60 percent average a contribution of less than $2,000 per year. A recent study of 3,000 divorces showed, shockingly, that men improved their standard of living an average of 42 percent in the first year following divorce, while women with children saw their living standard decline by 73 percent. Under these circumstances, the fear has risen that feminism will free men first—and might never get around to freeing women.

All this is not to imply that either men or women *should* stay in loveless, unhappy marriages out of some sense of duty. Rather, both sexes need the right to change their circumstances. So far, our progress, like all progress, has been ragged: men, more independent to begin with, have been able to profit from women's new independence sometimes more fully than women themselves.

It seems revealing that the anti-feminist backlash, as well as the anti-sexual-liberation backlash, took so long to develop the momentum that it has today. It is the period of unremitting economic decline that has brought it on, the nightfall of economic prospects for women. It is as though the country reserved judgment during ten or fifteen years of experimentation with sexual politics, as long as economic conditions permitted it. In a climate of affluence, women had more hope of successfully freeing themselves from male-dominant relationships. But today, a greater number of working women are perceiving that the feminist revolution may not rapidly succeed in actually equalizing the material opportunities of the sexes. When working-class men no longer hold their own against unemployment, union-management rollbacks, or even inflation, what hope is there for women to close the economic gap between the male and female worker?

Giving up marriage and children for an interesting career may be one thing (although this is an either/or choice that men rarely face), but it may not be a decent trade for a dead-end job in the pink-collar ghetto. If men can no longer support families on a single paycheck, most women certainly cannot. The media presents us with the image of successful management-level women, but in fact even these women are almost always contained in middle-management positions, at under $20,000 a year. For the less-than-fervent feminist who is not prepared to pay any price at all for independence, the future looks bleak.

FEAR AND REACTION

It begins to seem clearer that the anti-feminist woman, like other women, is grappling with the terms of her survival. She is responding to social circumstances—a worsening economy, a lack of support and commitment from men—that feminists did not create and from which feminists also suffer the consequences. The conditions she faces face all women.

The differences lie in our strategies for dealing with all this. The anti-feminist woman's strategy is defensive: reactionary in the sense of reacting to change, with the desire to return to the supposedly simple solutions of the past. Like other patriotic or fundamentalist solutions, like going to war or being "born again," the longed-for return to the old feminine style seems to promise an end to complexity, compromise, and ambivalence. For many of the advocates of the anti-choice movement, the ideal is ready-made and well polished. It is the American family of the 1950s: dad in the den with his pipe, mom in her sunny kitchen with cafe curtains, the girls dressed in pink and the boys in blue. It could be called nostalgic utopianism—the glorification of a lost past rather than an undiscovered future. What has not been accepted is that the road to that ideal is as impossible to find—and to many people, as little desired—as the road back to childhood.

To feminists, the only response to the dilemma of the present lies in pressing onward. We must continue to show how a complete feminist sexual and reproductive politics could lead to the transformation of all society, without curtailing the freedom of any individual. True reproductive freedom, for example, would inevitably require fair opportunities for financial equality, so that women could bear children without facing either dependency or impoverishment. There would be practical child-care support for working parents of both sexes and an equal affirmation by men of their responsibility for parenthood. Yet, the individual's right to choose whether to bear a child would remain at the heart of the feminist position.

Today, the individual decision to have an abortion remains a sobering one; it puts a woman face-to-face with her dreams and her prospects and with the frequently startling fact that she is choosing not to be a passive victim, but rather an active shaper of her existence. The difficulties she will encounter as she continues to try to create her own destiny will repeatedly call for that same strength of will. In demonstrating it, she is already helping to bring about a new order of sexual equality, a world more worthy of the next generation. Few who have clearly seen the vision of that new world will want to turn back.

[1983]

 67

Under Western Eyes: Feminist Scholarship and Colonial Discourses

CHANDRA TALPADE MOHANTY

Any discussion of the intellectual and political construction of "third world feminisms" must address itself to two simultaneous projects: the internal critique of hegemonic "Western" feminisms, and the formulation of autonomous, geographically, historically, and culturally grounded feminist concerns and strategies. The first project is one of deconstructing and dismantling; the second, one of building and constructing. While these projects appear to be contradictory, the one working negatively and the other positively, unless these two tasks are addressed simultaneously, "third world" feminisms run the

risk of marginalization or ghettoization from both mainstream (right and left) and Western feminist discourses.

It is to the first project that I address myself. What I wish to analyze is specifically the production of the "third world woman" as a singular monolithic subject in some recent (Western) feminist texts. The definition of colonization I wish to invoke here is a predominantly *discursive* one, focusing on a certain mode of appropriation and codification of "scholarship" and "knowledge" about women in the third world by particular analytic categories employed in specific writings on the subject which take as their referent feminist interests as they have been articulated in the U.S. and Western Europe. If one of the tasks of formulating and understanding the locus of "third world feminisms" is delineating the way in which it resists and *works against* what I am referring to as "Western feminist discourse," an analysis of the discursive construction of "third world women" in Western feminism is an important first step.

Clearly Western feminist discourse and political practice is neither singular nor homogeneous in its goals, interests, or analyses. However, it is possible to trace a coherence of *effects* resulting from the implicit assumption of "the West" (in all its complexities and contradictions) as the primary referent in theory and praxis. My reference is "Western feminism" is by no means intended to imply that it is a monolith. Rather, I am attempting to draw attention to the similar effects of various textual strategies used by writers which codify Others as non-Western and hence themselves as (implicitly) Western. It is in this sense that I use the term *Western feminist.* Similar arguments can be made in terms of middle-class urban African or Asian scholars producing scholarship on or about their rural or working-class sisters which assumes their own middle-class cultures as the norm, and codifies working-class histories and cultures as Other. Thus, while this essay focuses specifically on what I refer to as "Western feminist" discourse on women in the third world, the critiques I offer also pertain to third world scholars writing about their own cultures, which employ identical analytic strategies.

It ought to be of some political significance, at least, that the term *colonization* has come to denote a variety of phenomena in recent feminist and left writings in general. From its analytic value as a category of exploitative economic exchange in both traditional and contemporary Marxisms (cf. particularly contemporary theorists such as Baran 1962, Amin 1977, and Gunder-Frank 1967) to its use by feminist women of color in the U.S. to describe the appropriation of their experiences and struggles by hegemonic white women's movements (cf. especially Moraga and Anzaldúa 1983, Smith 1983, Joseph and Lewis 1981, and Moraga 1984), colonization has been used to characterize everything from the most evident economic and political hierarchies to the production of a particular cultural discourse about what is called the "third world."[1] However sophisticated or problematical its use as an explanatory construct, colonization almost invariably implies a relation of structural domination, and a suppression—often violent—of the heterogeneity of the subject(s) in question.

My concern about such writings derives from my own implication and investment in contemporary debates in feminist theory, and the urgent political necessity (especially in the age of Reagan/Bush) of forming strategic coalitions across class, race, and national boundaries. The analytic principles discussed below serve to distort Western feminist political practices, and limit the possibility of coalitions among (usually white) Western feminists and working-class feminists and feminists of color around the world. These limitations are evident in the construction of the (implicitly consensual) priority of issues around which apparently *all* women are expected to organize. The necessary and integral connection between feminist scholarship and feminist political practice and organizing determines the significance and status of Western feminist writings on women in the third world, for feminist scholarship, like most other kinds of scholarship, is not the mere production of knowledge about a certain subject. It is a directly political and discursive *practice* in that it is purposeful and ideological. It is best seen as a mode of intervention into particular hegemonic discourses (for example, traditional anthropology, sociology, literary criticism, etc.); it is a political praxis which counters and resists the totalizing imperative of age-old "legitimate" and "scientific" bodies of knowledge. Thus, feminist scholarly practices (whether reading, writing, critical, or textual) are inscribed in

relations of power—relations which they counter, resist, or even perhaps implicitly support. There can, of course, be no apolitical scholarship.

The relationship between "Woman"—a cultural and ideological composite Other constructed through diverse representational discourses (scientific, literary, juridical, linguistic, cinematic, etc.)—and "women"—real, material subjects of their collective histories—is one of the central questions the practice of feminist scholarship seeks to address. This connection between women as historical subjects and the re-presentation of Woman produced by hegemonic discourses is not a relation of direct identity, or a relation of correspondence or simple implication.[2] It is an arbitrary relation set up by particular cultures. I would like to suggest that the feminist writings I analyze here discursively colonize the material and historical heterogeneities of the lives of women in the third world, thereby producing/re-presenting a composite, singular "third world woman"—an image which appears arbitrarily constructed, but nevertheless carries with it the authorizing signature of Western humanist discourse.[3]

I argue that assumptions of privilege and ethnocentric universality, on the one hand, and inadequate self-consciousness about the effect of Western scholarship on the "third world" in the context of a world system dominated by the West, on the other, characterize a sizable extent of Western feminist work on women in the third world. An analysis of "sexual difference" in the form of a cross-culturally singular, monolithic notion of patriarchy or male dominance leads to the construction of a similarly reductive and homogeneous notion of what I call the "third world difference"—that stable, ahistorical something that apparently oppresses most if not all the women in these countries. And it is in the production of this "third world difference" that Western feminisms appropriate and "colonize" the constitutive complexities which characterize the lives of women in these countries. It is in this process of discursive homogenization and systematization of the oppression of women in the third world that power is exercised in much of recent Western feminist discourse, and this power needs to be defined and named.

• • •

The first analytic presupposition I focus on is involved in the strategic location of the category "women" vis-à-vis the context of analysis. The assumption of women as an already constituted, coherent group with identical interests and desires, regardless of class, ethnic or racial location, or contradictions, implies a notion of gender or sexual difference or even patriarchy which can be applied universally and cross-culturally. (The context of analysis can be anything from kinship structures and the organization of labor to media representations.) The second analytical presupposition is evident on the methodological level, in the uncritical way "proof" of universality and cross-cultural validity are provided. The third is a more specifically political presupposition underlying the methodologies and the analytic strategies, i.e., the model of power and struggle they imply and suggest. I argue that as a result of the two modes—or, rather, frames—of analysis described above, a homogeneous notion of the oppression of women as a group is assumed, which, in turn, produces the image of an "average third world woman." This average third world woman leads an essentially truncated life based on her feminine gender (read: sexually constrained) and her being "third world" (read: ignorant, poor, uneducated, tradition-bound, domestic, family-oriented, victimized, etc.). This, I suggest, is in contrast to the (implicit) self-representation of Western women as educated, as modern, as having control over their own bodies and sexualities, and the freedom to make their own decisions.

The distinction between Western feminist representation of women in the third world and Western feminist self-presentation is a distinction of the same order as that made by some Marxists between the "maintenance" function of the housewife and real "productive" role of wage labor, or the characterization by developmentalists of the third world as being engaged in the lesser production of "raw materials" in contrast to the "real" productive activity of the first world. These distinctions are made on the basis of the privileging of a particular group as the norm or referent. Men involved in wage labor, first world producers, and, I suggest, Western feminists who sometimes cast third world women in terms of "ourselves undressed" (Michelle Rosaldo's [1980] term), all construct themselves as the normative referent in such a binary analytic.

"WOMEN" AS CATEGORY OF ANALYSIS, OR: WE ARE ALL SISTERS IN STRUGGLE

By women as a category of analysis, I am referring to the crucial assumption that all of us of the same gender, across classes and cultures, are somehow socially constituted as a homogeneous group identified prior to the process of analysis. This is an assumption which characterizes much feminist discourse. The homogeneity of women as a group is produced not on the basis of biological essentials but rather on the basis of secondary sociological and anthropological universals. Thus, for instance, in any given piece of feminist analysis, women are characterized as a singular group on the basis of a shared oppression. What binds women together is a sociological notion of the "sameness" of their oppression. It is at this point that an elision takes place between "women" as a discursively constructed group and "women" as material subjects of their own history. Thus, the discursively consensual homogeneity of "women" as a group is mistaken for the historically specific material reality of groups of women. This results in an assumption of women as an always already constituted group, one which has been labeled "powerless," "exploited," "sexually harassed," etc., by feminist scientific, economic, legal, and sociological discourses. (Notice that this is quite similar to sexist discourse labeling women weak, emotional, having math anxiety, etc.) This focus is not on uncovering the material and ideological specificities that constitute a particular group of women as "powerless" in a particular context. It is, rather, on finding a variety of cases of "powerless" groups of women to prove the general point that women as a group are powerless.

. . .

WOMEN AND RELIGIOUS IDEOLOGIES

. . .

What is problematical about this kind of use of "women" as a group, as a stable category of analysis, is that it assumes an ahistorical, universal unity between women based on a generalized notion of their subordination. Instead of analytically *demonstrating* the production of women as socioeconomic political groups within particular local contexts, this analytical move limits the definition of the female subject to gender identity, completely bypassing social class and ethnic identities. What characterizes women as a group is their gender (sociologically, not necessarily biologically, defined) over and above everything else, indicating a monolithic notion of sexual difference. Because women are thus constituted as a coherent group, sexual difference becomes coterminous with female subordination, and power is automatically defined in binary terms: people who have it (read: men), and people who do not (read: women). Men exploit, women are exploited. Such simplistic formulations are historically reductive; they are also ineffectual in designing strategies to combat oppressions. All they do is reinforce binary divisions between men and women.

What would an analysis which did not do this look like? Maria Mies's work illustrates the strength of Western feminist work on women in the third world which does not fall into the traps discussed above. Mies's study of the lace makers of Narsapur, India (1982), attempts to carefully analyze a substantial household industry in which "housewives" produce lace doilies for consumption in the world market. Through a detailed analysis of the structure of the lace industry, production and reproduction relations, the sexual division of labor, profits and exploitation, and the overall consequences of defining women as "non-working housewives" and their work as "leisure-time activity." Mies demonstrates the levels of exploitation in this industry and the impact of this production system on the work and living conditions of the women involved in it. In addition, she is able to analyze the "ideology of the housewife," the notion of a woman sitting in the house, as providing the necessary subjective and sociocultural element for the creation and maintenance of a production system that contributes to the increasing pauperization of women, and keeps them totally atomized and disorganized as workers. Mies's analysis shows the effect of a certain historically and culturally specific mode of patriarchal organization, an organization constructed on the basis of the definition of the lace makers as "non-working housewives" at familial, local, regional, statewide, and international levels. The intricacies and the effects of particular power networks not only are emphasized, but they form the basis of Mies's analysis of how this particular group of women is situated at the center of a hegemonic, exploitative world market.

This is a good example of what careful, politically focused, local analyses can accomplish. It illustrates how the category of women is constructed in a variety of political contexts that often exist simultaneously and overlaid on top of one another. There is no easy generalization in the direction of "women" in India, or "women in the third world"; nor is there a reduction of the political construction of the exploitation of the lace makers to cultural explanations about the passivity or obedience that might characterize these women and their situation. Finally, this mode of local, political analysis which generates theoretical categories from within the situation and context being analyzed, also suggests corresponding effective strategies for organizing against the exploitation faced by the lace makers. Narsapur women are not mere victims of the production process, because they resist, challenge, and subvert the process at various junctures. Here is one instance of how Mies delineates the connections between the housewife ideology, the self-consciousness of the lace makers, and their interrelationships as contributing to the latent resistances she perceives among the women:

> The persistence of the housewife ideology, the self-perception of the lace makers as petty commodity producers rather than as workers, is not only upheld by the structure of the industry as such but also by the deliberate propagation and reinforcement of reactionary patriarchal norms and institutions. Thus, most of the lace makers voiced the same opinion about the rules of *purdah* and seclusion in their communities which were also propagated by the lace exporters. In particular, the *Kapu* women said that they had never gone out of their houses, that women of their community could not do any other work than housework and lace work etc. but in spite of the face that most of them still subscribed fully to the patriarchal norms of the *gosha* women, there were also contradictory elements in their consciousness. Thus, although they looked down with contempt upon women who were able to work outside the house—like the untouchable *Mala* and *Madiga* women or women of other lower castes, they could not ignore the fact that these women were earning more money precisely because they were *not* respectable housewives but workers. At one discussion, they even admitted that it would be better if they could also go out and do

coolie work. And when they were asked whether they would be ready to come out of their houses and work in one place in some sort of a factory, they said they would do that. This shows that the *purdah* and housewife ideology, although still fully internalized, already had some cracks, because it has been confronted with several contradictory realities. (157)

It is only by understanding the *contradictions* inherent in women's location within various structures that effective political action and challenges can be devised. Mies's study goes a long way toward offering such analysis. While there are now an increasing number of Western feminist writings in this tradition, there is also, unfortunately, a large block of writing which succumbs to the cultural reductionism discussed earlier.

METHODOLOGICAL UNIVERSALISMS, OR: WOMEN'S OPPRESSION IS A GLOBAL PHENOMENON

Western feminist writings on women in the third world subscribe to a variety of methodologies to demonstrate the universal cross-cultural operation of male dominance and female exploitation. I summarize and critique three such methods below, moving from the simplest to the most complex.

First, proof of universalism is provided through the use of an arithmetic method. The argument goes like this: the greater the number of women who wear the veil, the more universal is the sexual segregation and control of women (Deardon 1975, 4–5). Similarly, a large number of different, fragmented examples from a variety of countries also apparently add up to a universal fact. For instance, Muslim women in Saudi Arabia, Iran, Pakistan, India, and Egypt all wear some sort of a veil. Hence, this indicates that the sexual control of women is a universal fact in those countries in which the women are veiled (Deardon 1975, 7, 10). Fran Hosken writes, "Rape, forced prostitution, polygamy, genital mutilation, pornography, the beating of girls and women, purdah (segregation of women) are all violations of basic human rights" (1981, 15). By equating purdah with rape, domestic violence, and forced prostitution, Hosken asserts its "sexual control" function as the primary explanation for purdah, whatever the context. Institutions of purdah are thus

denied any cultural and historical specificity, and contradictions and potentially subversive aspects are totally ruled out.

In both these examples, the problem is not in asserting that the practice of wearing a veil is widespread. This assertion can be made on the basis of numbers. It is a descriptive generalization. However, it is the analytic leap from the practice of veiling to an assertion of its general significance in controlling women that must be questioned. While there may be a physical similarity in the veils worn by women in Saudi Arabia and Iran, the specific meaning attached to this practice varies according to the cultural and ideological context. In addition, the symbolic space occupied by the practice of purdah may be similar in certain contexts, but this does not automatically indicate that the practices themselves have identical significance in the social realm. For example, as is well known, Iranian middle-class women veiled themselves during the 1979 revolution to indicate solidarity with their veiled working-class sisters, while in contemporary Iran, mandatory Islamic laws dictate that all Iranian women wear veils. While in both these instances, similar reasons might be offered for the veil (opposition to the Shah and Western cultural colonization in the first case, and the true Islamicization of Iran in the second), the concrete *meanings* attached to Iranian women wearing the veil are clearly different in both historical contexts. In the first case, wearing the veil is both an oppositional and a revolutionary gesture on the part of Iranian middle-class women; in the second case, it is a coercive, institutional mandate (see Tabari 1980 for detailed discussion). It is on the basis of such context-specific differentiated analysis that effective political strategies can be generated. To assume that the mere practice of veiling women in a number of Muslim countries indicates the universal oppression of women through sexual segregation not only is analytically reductive, but also proves quite useless when it comes to the elaboration of oppositional political strategy.

Second, concepts such as reproduction, the sexual division of labor, the family, marriage, household, patriarchy, etc., are often used without their specification in local cultural and historical contexts. Feminists use these concepts in providing explanations for women's subordination, apparently assuming their universal applicability. For instance, how is it possible to refer to "the" sexual division of labor when the *content* of this division changes radically from one environment to the next, and from one historical juncture to another? At its most abstract level, it is the fact of the differential assignation of tasks according to sex that is significant; however, this is quite different from the *meaning* or *value* that the content of this sexual division of labor assumes in different contexts. In most cases the assigning of tasks on the basis of sex has an ideological origin. There is no question that a claim such as "women are concentrated in service-oriented occupations in a large number of countries around the world" is descriptively valid. Descriptively, then, perhaps the existence of a similar sexual division of labor (where women work in service occupations such as nursing, social work, etc., and men in other kinds of occupations) in a variety of different countries can be asserted. However, the concept of the "sexual division of labor" is more than just a descriptive category. It indicates the differential *value* placed on "men's work" versus "women's work."

• • •

To summarize: I have discussed three methodological moves identifiable in feminist (and other academic) cross-cultural work which seeks to uncover a universality in women's subordinate position in society. The next and final section pulls together the previous sections, attempting to outline the political effects of the analytical strategies in the context of Western feminist writing on women in the third world. These arguments are not against generalization as much as they are for careful, historically specific generalizations responsive to complex realities. Nor do these arguments deny the necessity of forming strategic political identities and affinities. Thus, while Indian women of different religions, castes, and classes might forge a political unity on the basis of organizing against police brutality toward women (see Kishwar and Vanita 1984), an *analysis* of police brutality must be contextual. Strategic coalitions which construct oppositional political identities for themselves are based on generalization and provisional unities, but the analysis of these group identities cannot be based on universalistic, ahistorical categories.

• • •

THE SUBJECT(S) OF POWER
• • •

What happens when this assumption of "women as an oppressed group" is situated in the context of Western feminist writing about third world women? It is here that I locate the colonialist move. By contrasting the representation of women in the third world with what I referred to earlier as Western feminisms' self-presentation in the same context, we see how Western feminists alone become the true "subjects" of this counterhistory. Third world women, on the other hand, never rise above the debilitating generality of their "object" status.

While radical and liberal feminist assumptions of women as a sex class might elucidate (however inadequately) the autonomy of particular women's struggles in the West, the application of the notion of women as a homogeneous category to women in the third world colonizes and appropriates the pluralities of the simultaneous location of different groups of women in social class and ethnic frameworks; in doing so it ultimately robs them of their historical and political *agency*. Similarly, many Zed Press authors who ground themselves in the basic analytic strategies of traditional Marxism also implicitly create a "unity" of women by substituting "women's activity" for "labor" as the primary theoretical determinant of women's situation. Here again, women are constituted as a coherent group not on the basis of "natural" qualities or needs but on the basis of the sociological "unity" of their role in domestic production and wage labor (see Haraway 1985, esp. p. 76). In other words, Western feminist discourse, by assuming women as a coherent, already constituted group which is placed in kinship, legal, and other structures, defines third world women as subjects *outside* social relations, instead of looking at the way women are constituted *through* these very structures.

Legal, economic, religious, and familial structures are treated as phenomena to be judged by Western standards. It is here that ethnocentric universality comes into play. When these structures are defined as "underdeveloped" or "developing" and women are placed within them, an implicit image of the "average third world woman" is produced. This is the transformation of the (implicitly Western) "oppressed woman" into the "oppressed third world woman." While the category of "oppressed woman" is generated through an exclusive focus on gender difference, "the oppressed third world woman" category has an additional attribute—the "third world difference!" The "third world difference" includes a paternalistic attitude toward women in the third world. Since discussions of the various themes I identified earlier (kinship, education, religion, etc.) are conducted in the context of the relative "underdevelopment" of the third world (which is nothing less than unjustifiably confusing development with the separate path taken by the West in its development, as well as ignoring the directionality of the first-third world power relationship), third world women as a group or category are automatically and necessarily defined as religious (read "not progressive"), family-oriented (read "traditional"), legal minors (read "they-are-still-not-conscious-of-their-rights"), illiterate (read "ignorant"), domestic (read "backward"), and sometimes revolutionary (read "their-country-is-in-a-state-of-war; they-must-fight!"). This is how the "third world difference" is produced.

When the category of "sexually oppressed women" is located within particular systems in the third world which are defined on a scale which is normed through Eurocentric assumptions, not only are third world women defined in a particular way prior to their entry into social relations, but since no connections are made between first and third world power shifts, the assumption is reinforced that the third world just has not evolved to the extent that the West has. This mode of feminist analysis, by homogenizing and systematizing the experiences of different groups of women in these countries, erases all marginal and resistant modes and experiences. It is significant that none of the texts I reviewed in the Zed Press series focuses on lesbian politics or the politics of ethnic and religious marginal organizations in third world women's groups. Resistance can thus be defined only as cumulatively reactive, not as something inherent in the operation of power. If power, as Michel Foucault has argued recently, can really be understood only in the context of resistance,[4] this misconceptualization is both analytically and strategically problematical. It limits theoretical analysis as well as reinforces Western cultural imperialism. For in the context of a first/third world

balance of power, feminist analyses which perpetrate and sustain the hegemony of the idea of the superiority of the West produce a corresponding set of universal images of the "third world woman," images such as the veiled woman, the powerful mother, the chaste virgin, the obedient wife, etc. These images exist in universal, ahistorical splendor, setting in motion a colonialist discourse which exercises a very specific power in defining, coding, and maintaining existing first/third world connections.

To conclude, then, let me suggest some disconcerting similarities between the typically authorizing signature of such Western feminist writings on women in the third world, and the authorizing signature of the project of humanism in general—humanism as a Western ideological and political project which involves the necessary recuperation of the "East" and "Woman" as Others.

. . .

As discussed earlier, a comparison between Western feminist self-presentation and Western feminist re-presentation of women in the third world yields significant results. Universal images of "the third world woman" (the veiled woman, chaste virgin, etc.), images constructed from adding the "third world difference" to "sexual difference," are predicated upon (and hence obviously bring into sharper focus) assumptions about Western women as secular, liberated, and having control over their own lives. This is not to suggest that Western women *are* secular, liberated, and in control of their own lives. I am referring to a *discursive* self-presentation, not necessarily to material reality. If this were a material reality, there would be no need for political movements in the West. Similarly, only from the vantage point of the West is it possible to define the "third world" as underdeveloped and economically dependent. Without the overdetermined discourse that creates the *third* world, there would be no (singular and privileged) first world. Without the "third world woman," the particular self-presentation of Western women mentioned above would be problematical. I am suggesting, then, that the one enables and sustains the other. This is not to say that the signature of Western feminist writings on the third world has the same authority as the project of Western humanism. However, in the context of the hegemony of the Western scholarly establishment in the production and dissemination of texts, and in the context of the legitimating imperative of humanistic and scientific discourse, the definition of "the third world woman" as a monolith might well tie into the larger economic and ideological praxis of "disinterested" scientific inquiry and pluralism which are the surface manifestations of a latent economic and cultural colonization of the "non-Western" world. It is time to move beyond the Marx who found it possible to say: They cannot represent themselves; they must be represented.

[1984/1991]

NOTES

1. Terms such as *third* and *first world* are very problematical both in suggesting oversimplified similarities between and among countries labeled thus, and in implicitly reinforcing existing economic, cultural, and ideological hierarchies which are conjured up in using such terminology. I use the term *"third world"* with full awareness of its problems, only because this is the terminology available to us at the moment. The use of quotation marks is meant to suggest a continuous questioning of the designation. Even when I do not use quotation marks, I mean to use the term critically.
2. I am indebted to Teresa de Lauretis for this particular formulation of the project of feminist theorizing. See especially her introduction in de Lauretis, *Alice Doesn't: Feminism, Semiotics, Cinema* (Bloomington: Indiana University Press, 1984); see also Sylvia Wynter, "The Politics of Domination," unpublished manuscript.
3. This argument is similar to Homi Bhabha's definition of colonial discourse as strategically creating a space for a subject people through the production of knowledges and the exercise of power. The full quote reads: "[colonial discourse is] an apparatus of power. . . . an apparatus that turns on the recognition and disavowal of racial/cultural/historical differences. Its predominant strategic function is the creation of a space for a subject people through the production of knowledges in terms of which surveillance is exercised and a complex form of pleasure/unpleasure is incited. It (i.e. colonial discourse) seeks authorization for its strategies by the production of knowledges by coloniser and colonised which are stereotypical but antithetically evaluated" (1983, 23).
4. This is one of M. Foucault's (1978, 1980) central points in his reconceptualization of the strategies and workings of power networks.

REFERENCES

Amin, Samir. 1977. *Imperialism and Unequal Development.* New York: Monthly Review Press.
Baran, Paul A. 1962. *The Political Economy of Growth.* New York: Monthly Review Press.
Deardon, Ann, ed. 1975. *Arab Women.* London: Minority Rights Group Report no. 27.
Foucault, Michel. 1978. *History of Sexuality: Volume One.* New York: Random House.
———. 1980. *Power/Knowledge.* New York: Pantheon.
Gunder-Frank, Audre. 1967. *Capitalism and Underdevelopment in Latin America.* New York: Monthly Review Press.
Haraway, Donna. 1985. "A Manifesto for Cyborgs: Science, Technology and Socialist Feminism in the 1980s." *Socialist Review* 80 (March/April):65–108.
Hosken, Fran. 1981. "Female Genital Mutilation and Human Rights." *Feminist Issues* 1, no. 3.
Joseph, Gloria, and Jill Lewis. 1981. *Common Differences: Conflicts in Black and White Feminist Perspectives.* Boston: Beacon Press.
Kishwar, Madhu, and Ruth Vanita. 1984. *In Search of Answers: Indian Women's Voices from Manushi.* London: Zed Press.
Mies, Maria. 1982. *The Lace Makers of Narsapur: Indian Housewives Produce for the World Market.* London: Zed Press.
Moraga, Cherrie. 1984. *Loving in the War Years.* Boston: South End Press.
Moraga, Cherríe, and Gloria Anzaldúa, eds. 1983. *This Bridge Called My Back: Writings by Radical Women of Color.* New York: Kitchen Table Press.
Rosaldo, M. A. 1980. "The Use and Abuse of Anthropology: Reflections on Feminism and Cross-Cultural Understanding." *Signs* 53:389–417.
Smith, Barbara, ed. 1983. *Home Girls: A Black Feminist Anthology.* New York: Kitchen Table Press.
Tabari, Azar. 1980. "The Enigma of the Veiled Iranian Women." *Feminist Review* 5:19–32.

 68

From Maternal Thinking

SARA RUDDICK

· · ·

THINKING AND PRACTICE

· · ·

Truth is perspectival, relative to the practices in which it is made. To say that true statements are relative in this sense does not mean that their truth is a matter of the opinion of communities of speakers. The statement that Mount Baldy is ten feet high is false, whatever any like-minded group of people may think. The point is that it is possible to make the false statement (and the alternative true one) because some people have identified mountains and invented a vocabulary of measurement. To speak, name, and measure means to act in social contexts in which geography and height matter to us. It is true that Margaret Thatcher was reelected prime minister of Great Britain, no matter how much a group of her opponents might wish otherwise, but that truth is dependent on a whole set of institutions in which the meaning of "elect" and "prime minister" have been constituted.

It is only within a practice that thinkers judge which questions are sensible, which answers are appropriate to them, and which criteria distinguish between better and worse answers. . . .

In sum, any discipline will distinguish true from false, will take some matters on faith, others on evidence, will judge evidence inadequate or faith misplaced. The practicalist's point is that the criteria for truth and falsity, the nature of evidence, and the role of faith will vary with the practice, whether the practice be religious, scientific, critical—or maternal.

MATERNAL PRACTICE

Maternal practice begins in a response to the reality of a biological child in a particular social world. To be a "mother" is to take upon oneself the responsibility of child care, making its work a regular and substantial part of one's working life.

Mothers, as individuals, engage in all sorts of other activities, from farming to deep sea diving, from astrophysics to elephant training. Mothers as individuals are not defined by their work; they are lovers and friends; they watch baseball, ballet, or the soaps; they run marathons, play chess, organize church bazaars and rent strikes. Mothers are as diverse as any other humans and are equally shaped by the social milieu in which they work. In my terminology they are "mothers" just because and to the degree that they are committed to meeting demands that define maternal work.

Both her child and the social world in which a mother works make these demands. "Demands" is an artificial term. Children demand all sorts of things—to eat ice cream before dinner, stay up all night, take the subway alone, watch the latest horror show on TV. A mother's social group demands of her all sorts of behavior—that she learn to sew or get a high school degree, hold her tongue or speak wittily in public, pay her taxes or go to jail for refusing to do so, sit ladylike in a restaurant or sit in at a lunch counter. A mother will decide in her own way which of these demands she will meet.

But in my discussion of maternal practice, I mean by "demands" those requirements that are imposed on anyone doing maternal work, in the way respect for experiment is imposed on scientists and racing past the finish line is imposed on jockeys. In this sense of demand, children "demand" that their lives be preserved and their growth fostered. In addition, the primary social groups with which a mother is identified, whether by force, kinship, or choice, demand that she raise her children in a manner acceptable to them. These three demands—for *preservation, growth,* and *social acceptability*—constitute maternal work; to be a mother is to be committed to meeting these demands by works of preservative love, nurturance, and training.

Conceptually and historically, the preeminent of these demands is that of preservation. As a species, human children share prolonged physical fragility and therefore prolonged dependence on adults for their safety and well-being. In all societies, children need protective care, though the causes and types of fragility and the means of protection vary widely. This universal need of human children creates and defines a category of human work. A mother who callously endangers her child's well-being is simply not doing maternal work. (This does not mean that she is a bad person. She may sacrifice maternal work out of desperation or in a noble cause.)

The demand for protection is both epistemological and practical. Meeting the demand presupposes a minimal attentiveness to children and an awareness that their survival depends upon protective care. Imaginatively grasping the significance of children's biological vulnerability is necessary but not sufficient for responding to them. The perception that someone is in need of care may lead to caring; but then again it may lead to running away. In the settings where I first encountered polliwogs and goldfish (usually in jars and bowls where I'd managed to put them), they were exceedingly vulnerable. When I was young, I saw that these little creatures were vulnerable and I cared for them. Much later, when I was dealing with my children's attachment to them, I found the vulnerability and total unpredictability of goldfish merely an annoyance. I cared for them because I cared for my children but, given the total inadequacy of our caring, I would have been delighted if my children had forgotten them altogether. Now I almost never think about goldfish and never want to care for one the rest of my life.

Given the passions that we have for children, comparing them to goldfish may seem frivolous. When you *see* children as demanding care, the reality of their vulnerability and the necessity of a caring response seem unshakable. But I deliberately stress the optional character first of perceiving "vulnerability" and then of responding with care. Maternal responses are complicated acts that social beings make to biological beings whose existence is inseparable from social interpretations. Maternal practice begins with a double vision—seeing the fact of biological vulnerability as socially signficant and as demanding care. Neither birth nor the actual presence of a vulnerable infant guarantees care. In the most desperate circumstances mothers are more apt to feed their babies than to let them sicken and starve. Yet when infants were dependent solely on mothers' milk, biological mothers could refuse the food their children needed, for example, sending them away to wet-nurses, although this was known to have a high risk of illness and even death. To be committed to meeting children's demand for preservation does not require enthusiasm or even love; it simply means to see vulnerability and to respond to it with care rather than abuse, indifference, or flight. Preserving the lives of children is the central constitutive, invariant aim of maternal practice; the commitment to achieving that aim is the constitutive maternal act.

The demand to preserve a child's life is quickly supplemented by the second demand, to nurture its emotional and intellectual growth. Children grow in complex ways, undergoing radical qualitative as well as quantitative change from childhood to adulthood. They experience intense emotions and varieties of changing, complex sexual desire. As they grow they develop more or less useful ways of coping with other people and their own feelings—adaptive strategies and defenses against anxiety, fear, shame, and guilt. Children's minds also develop gradually, their cognitive capacities and uses of memory becoming different in kind as they move from early childhood through adolescence. In one sense, children grow "naturally," provided favorable conditions for growing. On the other hand, each child grows in her or his distinctive, often peculiar way. Children's de-

sires, defenses, and goals can be hurtful to others and to themselves; their cognitive and emotional development is easily distorted or inhibited. They "demand" nurturance.

This demand to foster children's growth appears to be historically and culturally specific to a degree that the demand for preservation is not. To be aware of children's need for nurturance depends on a belief, prevalent in my social milieu, that children have complicated lives, that their minds and psyches need attending. But even in social groups I know firsthand, some people—in my experience more often men—claim that if children are protected and trained, growth takes care of itself. On the other hand, it is difficult to judge what mothers themselves really believe about the conditions of growth. Some mothers who say that children simply grow and need little nurturance nonetheless act in ways that indicate they believe their children are complex and needy beings.

To say that the demand to foster growth is culturally and historically specific does not mean that the complexity of children's lives is primarily a cultural creation. In cultures dramatically different from middle-class North American culture—where, for example, there are no notions of "adolescence" or "cognitive development"—children's growth is still complex. Only some cultures, and some people within a culture, may believe, as I do, that children's spiritual and intellectual growth requires nurturance. But what I believe, I believe about all children. When others claim that children are simple, naturally growing beings whose growth does not require attentive nurturance, we disagree in our beliefs about *all* children's needs. To believe that only the children of one's own or similar cultures are complex—that their complexity is essentially a cultural creation—is a familiar form of racism. Certainly, some children exist in conditions in which they can do no better than "simply" survive. It seems grotesque to speak of the complex psychological needs of children who are dying of famine. Yet those children, in my view, are as complicated and demanding of nurturance as any others. Where terror or deprivation reduces children to the most basic need for simple survival, they are nonetheless fragile, complicated human creatures who have been so reduced.

In the urban middle-class cultures I know best, mothers who believe that children's development is sufficiently complex to require nurturance shoulder a considerable burden. Many people other than mothers are interested in children's growth—fathers, lovers, teachers, doctors, therapists, coaches. But typically a mother assumes the primary task of maintaining conditions of growth: it is a mother who considers herself and is considered by others to be primarily responsible for arrested or defective growth. The demand to nurture children's growth is not as ineluctable as the demand to ensure their survival. Mothers often find themselves unable to deal with the complexities of their children's experience because they are overwhelmed simply tending to their children's survival or are preoccupied by their own projects or are simply exhausted and confused. Children survive nonetheless.

The third demand on which maternal practice is based is made not by children's needs but by the social groups of which a mother is a member. Social groups require that mothers shape their children's growth in "acceptable" ways. What counts as acceptable varies enormously within and among groups and cultures. The demand for acceptability, however, does not vary, nor does there seem to be much dissent from the belief that children cannot "naturally" develop in socially correct ways but must be "trained." I use the neutral, though somewhat harsh, term "training" to underline a mother's active aims to make her children "acceptable." Her training strategies may be persuasive, manipulative, educative, abusive, seductive, or respectful and are typically a mix of most of these.

A mother's group is that set of people with whom she identifies to the degree that she would count failure to meet their criteria of acceptability as her failure. The criteria of acceptability consist of the group values that a mother has internalized as well as the values of group members whom she feels she must please. Acceptability is not merely a demand imposed on a mother by her group. Indeed, mothers themselves as part of the larger social group formulate its ideals and are usually governed by an especially stringent form of acceptability that nonmothers in the group may not necessarily adhere to. Mothers want their children to grow into people whom they themselves and those closest to

them can delightedly appreciate. This demand gives an urgency—sometimes exhilarating, sometimes painful—to mothers' daily lives.

In training their children, mature and socially powerful mothers find opportunities to express their own values as well as to challenge and invigorate dominant creeds. Often, however, a mother is ambivalent about her group's values and feels alienated or harassed by the group's demands on her and her children. Mothers are usually women, and women typically, though to varying degrees, have less power than men of their group. Many mothers are, at least at the beginning of their work, young women. Although they consider failing the group as their own failure, this assessment may be less motivated by moral self-definition than by fear or a need for social survival. If a group demands acceptable behavior that, in a mother's eyes, contradicts her children's need for protection and nurturance, then the mother will be caught in painful and self-fragmenting conflict. Nonetheless, however alienated they feel, mothers seem to recognize the demand to train their children as an ineluctable demand made on them as mothers.

In addition to preservation, growth, and social acceptability there may well be other demands that constitute maternal practices. Certainly there are other ways to categorize maternal commitment. But without any claim to exhaustiveness, I take the goals of preservation, growth, and social acceptability as constitutive of maternal practice.

Although in my view all social groups demand training, all mothers recognize their children's demand to be protected, and all children require some kind of nurturance, it may well be that some cultures do not recognize "children" and "mothers" in my sense of the terms. The concept of "mother" depends on that of "child," a creature considered to be of value and in need of protection. Only in societies that recognize children as creatures who demand protection, nurturance, and training is there a maternal practice that meets those demands. Social historians tell us that in many cultures, it was a normal practice to exploit, neglect, or abuse children. What I call "maternal practice" is probably not ubiquitous, even though what I call "children" exist everywhere.

In any culture, maternal commitment is far more voluntary than people like to believe. Women as well as men may refuse to be aware of or to respond to the demands of children; some women abuse or abandon creatures who are, in all cultures, dependent and vulnerable. All mothers sometimes turn away, refuse to listen, stop caring. Both maternal work and the thinking that is provoked by it are decisively shaped by the possibility that any mother may refuse to see creatures as children or to respond to them as complicated, fragile, and needy.

Among those cultures who do recognize children, perceptions of their fragility and adult responses to it vary enormously and may be difficult for outsiders to understand. As anyone knows who listens to mothers, commonality of childhood demands does not preclude sharp disagreement about children's "nature" and appropriate maternal responses to it. Comparing and contrasting differing strategies of maternal work goes on among mothers all the time. When it is generous and thoughtful, this collective, self-reflective activity is a source of critical and creative maternal thinking.

To protect, nurture, and train—however abstract the schema, the story is simple. A child leans out of a high-rise window to drop a balloon full of water on a passerby. She must be hauled in from the window (preservation) and taught not to endanger innocent people (training), and the method used must not endanger her self-respect or confidence (nurturance). In any mother's day, the demands of preservation, growth, and acceptability are intertwined. Yet a reflective mother can separately identify each demand, partly because they are often in conflict. If a child wants to walk to the store alone, do you worry about her safety or applaud her developing capacity to take care of herself? If you overhear your son hurling insults at a neighbor's child, do you rush to instill decency and compassion in him, or do you let him act on his own impulses in his need to overcome shyness? If your older child, in her competitive zeal, pushes ahead of your younger, smaller child while climbing a high slide, do you inhibit her competitive pleasure or allow an aggressiveness you cannot appreciate? Should her younger brother learn to fight back? And if he doesn't, is he bowing too easily to greater strength? Most urgently, whatever you do, is somebody going to get hurt? Love may make these questions painful; it does not provide the answers. Mothers must *think*.

MATERNAL THINKING

Daily, mothers think out strategies of protection, nurturance, and training. Frequently conflicts between strategies or between fundamental demands provoke mothers to think about the meaning and relative weight of preservation, growth, and acceptability. In quieter moments, mothers reflect on their practice as a whole. As in any group of thinkers, some mothers are more ambitiously reflective than others, either out of temperamental thoughtfulness, moral and political concerns, or, most often, because they have serious problems with their children. However, maternal thinking is no rarity. Maternal work itself demands that mothers think; out of this need for thoughtfulness, a distinctive discipline emerges.

I speak about a mother's thought—the intellectual capacities she develops, the judgments she makes, the metaphysical attitudes she assumes, the values she affirms. Like a scientist writing up her experiment, a critic working over a text, or a historian assessing documents, a mother caring for children engages in a discipline. She asks certain questions—those relevant to her aims—rather than others; she accepts certain criteria for the truth, adequacy, and relevance of proposed answers; and she cares about the findings she makes and can act on. The discipline of maternal thought, like other disciplines, establishes criteria for determining failure and success, sets priorities, and identifies virtues that the discipline requires. Like any other work, mothering is prey to characteristic temptations that it must identify. To describe the capacities, judgments, metaphysical attitudes, and values of maternal thought presumes not maternal achievement, but a *conception* of achievement.

Maternal thinking is one kind of disciplined reflection among many, each with identifying questions, methods, and aims. Some disciplines overlap. A mother who is also a critic may learn something about "reading" a child's behavior from reading texts or learn something about reading itself from her child. A believer's prayer or a historian's sense of causal narrative or a scientist's clear-eyed scrutiny may enliven maternal attentiveness, which in its turn may prepare a mother for prayer, historical insight, or experiment. Disciplines may, on the other hand, be undertaken quite separately without conflicting. An engineer may find the particular kind of reasoning required by engineering almost entirely different from that required by mothering, and each may provide welcome relief from the other. Even though people's behavior is limited by the disciplines they engage in, no one need be limited to a single discipline. No person because she is a woman, no woman or man because they are mothers, should be denied any intellectual activities that attract them. A scientist cannot disregard evidence for the sake of beauty, but she may care differently at different times about both. If a mother is called on to decide an appropriate punishment for a child's misbehavior or to weigh the possible success of a medical treatment against its serious pain, she cannot compose a sonata in response. There is a time for composing and a time for maternal thinking and, on happy days, time for both.

Mothers meeting together at their jobs, in playgrounds, or over coffee can be heard thinking. This does not necessarily mean that they can be heard being good. Mothers are not any more or less wonderful than other people—they are not especially sensible or foolish, noble or ignoble, courageous or cowardly. Mothers, like gardeners or historians, identify virtues appropriate to their work. But to identify a virtue is not to possess it. When mothers speak of virtues they speak as often of failure as of success. Almost always they reflect on the *struggles* that revolve around the temptations to which they are prey in their work. What they share is not virtuous characteristics but rather an identification and a discourse about the strengths required by their ongoing commitments to protect, nurture, and train.

Identifying virtues within maternal thinking should not be confused with evaluating the virtue of maternal thinking itself. Though no less thoughtful, no less a discipline than other kinds of thinking, maternal thinking is also not free from flaws. For example, as I will show later, in training children, mothers often value destructive ways of thinking and misidentify virtues. This means that mothers not only fail but in certain respects mischaracterize what counts as success and failure.

If thinking arises in and is tested by practice, who is qualified to judge the intellectual strength and moral character of a practice as a whole? It is some-

times said that only those who participate in a practice can criticize its thinking. Accordingly, it might be argued that it is not possible to evaluate maternal thinking without practicing maternal work or living closely and sympathetically with those who do. When mothers engage in self-criticism, their judgments presuppose a knowledge of the efforts required to respond to children's demands that those unpracticed in tending to children do not have. Maternal criticisms are best left to those who know what it means to attempt to protect, nurture, and train, just as criticism of scientific or—to use a controversial example—psychoanalytic thinking should be left to those who have engaged in these practices.

There are moral grounds for critical restraint. People who have not engaged in a practice or who have not lived closely with a practitioner have no right to criticize. Although any group might make this claim, the point is particularly apt for maternal thinkers. Mothers have been a powerless group whose thinking, when it has been acknowledged at all, has most often been recognized by people interested in interpreting and controlling rather than in listening. Philosophically minded mothers have only begun to articulate the precepts of a thought whose existence other philosophers do not recognize. Surely, they should have time to think among and for themselves.

• • •

. . . I, for example, hope that maternal thinkers will be affected by my claims that certain concepts of maternal thinking that arise from training are inconsistent with other maternal concepts and that preservative love is at least *prima facie* incompatible with maternal militarism. But although my respect for consistency is not connected to mothering, my particular identification of contradictions within maternal thinking arises from my experience of maternal practice, and the effect of my criticism can be measured only by mothers' responses.

One should not, however, conflate epistemological restraint with critical silence. The practical origins of reason do not preclude radical self-criticism. Indeed, developing vocabularies and standards of self-criticism is a central intellectual activity in most practices. More important, although all criticism arises from some practice or other, interpractice criticism is both possible and necessary for change. It is common sense epistemologically that alternative perspectives offer distinctive critical advantages. A historian, medical ethicist, and peace activist—especially if they themselves were conversant with science—might claim to have a better sense than a scientist not only of the limits but also of the character of scientific discipline. Militarists criticize maternal thinkers for insufficient respect for abstract causes, while peacemakers criticize them for the parochial character of maternal commitment.

Interpractice criticism is possible and often desirable; yet there is no privileged practice capable of judging all other practices. To criticize is to act on one's practical commitments, not to stand above them. Maternal thinking is one discipline among others, capable of criticizing and being criticized. It does not offer nor can it be judged from a standpoint uncontaminated by practical struggle and passion.

[1985]

PART VI

1985–1995

1985–1995: Introduction

Toward the end of the 1980s, feminism and women's studies could reasonably be said to have made a substantial impact inside and outside the academy. Women could mark real increases in their access to most areas of education and employment. A large percentage of colleges and universities had women's studies programs and some had begun to establish graduate degrees in the field. Most disciplines showed the significant impact of feminist thought. In addition, work in women's studies and other ethnic studies had helped to catalyze a serious conversation about interdisciplinary knowledge across the academy.

On the other hand, the latter part of the 1980s, after eight years of Republican presidencies and Reaganomics, were times of confronting backlash and dealing with an organized academic and political right. The academic right used the rhetoric of "political correctness" and the funding of right-wing political organizations to attack women's studies programs; curriculum transformation projects; feminist, gay, and lesbian scholars and scholarship; as well as funding agencies that supported such activities. At the same time, this was the height of antichoice politics, expressed in clinic blockades, bombings, and assaults on and killing of doctors and other medical personnel providing reproductive services.

The shift in feminist theory in this period may be charted by reference to the 1985 publication of Donna Haraway's "Manifesto for Cyborgs." It argues for epistemologies that resist such dualisms as nature/culture and are more interested in boundaries, partiality, and coalition than in hierarchies, organic wholes, and coherent identities. The trajectories that Haraway's argument suggests are played out both in Diana Fuss's exploration of the interconnectedness of essentialism and social construction, as well as in the explorations of epistemologies of Gloria Anzaldua and Pat Hill Collins. Feminist theory's other major engagements in this period are with post-modernism, represented here in essays by Linda Alcoff and Joan Scott; with science and its assumption of objectivity, seen in the essays by Sandra Harding and Evelyn Fox Keller; and with queer theory, engaged by Judith Butler.

The globalization of economies, markets, technologies, and the workforce make feminists increasingly aware of the need for a theory and practice appropriate to this "new world order." The war in the Persian Gulf, the conflict in the former Yugoslavia, the disintegration of the U.S.S.R. and communist Eastern Europe, and the integration of Europe all signal global realignments of power. These developments challenge U.S. feminists to work in coalition with women throughout the world and to think from multiple perspectives. The 1995 U.N. Conference in Beijing and NGO Forum in Huairou were perhaps the most productive of these conferences, due both to the synergy between technologies of dissemination of knowledge and to a renewed emphasis on women's rights as human rights.

We have yet to see where feminism will go in response to the challenges of the latter part of this period. "Third Wave" feminism and self-described "girls" or grrls" challenge the articulations of their feminist predecessors. The new technologies and practices of networks, webs, on-line services, chat rooms, and listserves offer new possibilities and yet seem to be forms of commodification of information and knowledge. Even as these new areas open, we are still debating questions that have been with us for more than a hundred years. However these entangled threads play out in the next decades, feminist theory has far from met its demise. On the contrary, it has traced out a field of inquiry that has quite thoroughly permeated both **what** we know and **how** we know it.

69

A Cyborg Manifesto: Science, Technology, and Socialist-Feminism in the Late Twentieth Century

DONNA HARAWAY

AN IRONIC DREAM OF A COMMON LANGUAGE FOR WOMEN IN THE INTEGRATED CIRCUIT

This chapter is an effort to build an ironic political myth faithful to feminism, socialism, and materialism. Perhaps more faithful as blasphemy is faithful, than as reverent worship and identification. Blasphemy has always seemed to require taking things very seriously. I know no better stance to adopt from within the secular-religious, evangelical traditions of United States politics, including the politics of socialist-feminism. Blasphemy protects one from the moral majority within, while still insisting on the need for community. Blasphemy is not apostasy. Irony is about contradictions that do not resolve into larger wholes, even dialectically, about the tension of holding incompatible things together because both or all are necessary and true. Irony is about humour and serious play. It is also a rhetorical strategy and a political method, one I would like to see more honoured within socialist-feminism. At the centre of my ironic faith, my blasphemy, is the image of the cyborg.

A cyborg is a cybernetic organism, a hybrid of machine and organism, a creature of social reality as well as a creature of fiction. Social reality is lived social relations, our most important political construction, a world-changing fiction. The international women's movements have constructed 'women's experience', as well as uncovered or discovered this crucial collective object. This experience is a fiction and fact of the most crucial, political kind. Liberation rests on the construction of the consciousness, the imaginative apprehension, of oppression, and so of possibility. The cyborg is a matter of fiction and lived experience that changes what counts as women's experience in the late twentieth century. This is a struggle over life and death, but the boundary between science fiction and social reality is an optical illusion.

Contemporary science fiction is full of cyborgs—creatures simultaneously animal and machine, who populate worlds ambiguously natural and crafted. Modern medicine is also full of cyborgs, of couplings between organism and machine, each conceived as coded devices, in an intimacy and with a power that was not generated in the history of sexuality. Cyborg 'sex' restores some of the lovely replicative baroque of ferns and invertebrates (such nice organic prophylactics against heterosexism). Cyborg replication is uncoupled from organic reproduction. Modern production seems like a dream of cyborg colonization work, a dream that makes the nightmare of Taylorism seem idyllic. And modern war is a cyborg orgy, coded by C^3I, command-control-communication-intelligence, an $84 billion item in 1984's US defence budget. I am making an argument for the cyborg as a fiction mapping our social and bodily reality and as an imaginative resource suggesting some very fruitful couplings. Michael Foucault's biopolitics is a flaccid premonition of cyborg politics, a very open field.

By the late twentieth century, our time, a mythic time, we are all chimeras, theorized and fabricated hybrids of machine and organism; in short, we are cyborgs. The cyborg is our ontology; it gives us our politics. The cyborg is a condensed image of both imagination and material reality, the two joined centres structuring any possibility of historical transformation. In the traditions of 'Western' science and politics—the tradition of racist, male-dominant capitalism; the tradition of progress; the tradition of the appropriation of nature as resource for the productions of culture; the tradition of reproduction of the self from the reflections of the other—the relation between organism and machine has been a border war. The stakes in the border war have been the territories of production, reproduction, and imagination. This chapter is an argument for *pleasure* in the confusion of boundaries and for *responsibility* in their construction. It is also an effort to contribute to socialist-feminist culture and theory in a postmodernist, non-naturalist mode and in the utopian tradition of imagining a world without gender, which is perhaps a world without genesis, but maybe also a world without end. The cyborg incarnation is outside salvation history. Nor does it mark time on an oedipal calendar, attempting to heal the terrible cleavages of gender in an oral symbiotic utopia or post-oedipal apocalypse. As Zoe Sofoulis argues in her unpublished manuscript on Jacques Lacan, Melanie Klein, and nuclear culture, *Lacklein,* the most terrible and perhaps the most promising monsters in cyborg worlds are embodied in non-oedipal narratives with a different logic of repression, which we need to understand for our survival.

The cyborg is a creature in post-gender world; it has no truck with bisexuality, pre-oedipal symbiosis, unalienated labour, or other seductions to organic wholeness through a final appropriation of all the powers of the parts into a higher unity. In a sense, the cyborg has no origin story in the Western sense—a 'final' irony since the cyborg is also the awful apocalyptic *telos* of the 'West's' escalating dominations of abstract individuation, an ultimate self untied at last from all dependency, a man in space. An origin story in the 'Western', humanist sense depends on the myth of original unity, fullness, bliss and terror, represented by the phallic mother from whom all humans must separate, the task of individual development and of history, the twin potent myths inscribed most powerfully for us in psychoanalysis and Marxism. Hilary Klein has argued that both Marxism and psychoanalysis, in their concepts of labour and of individuation and gender formation, depend on the plot of original unity out of which difference must be produced and enlisted in a drama of escalating domination of woman/nature. The cyborg skips the step of original unity, of identification with nature in the Western sense. This is its illegitimate promise that might lead to subversion of its teleology as star wars.

The cyborg is resolutely committed to partiality, irony, intimacy, and perversity. It is oppositional, utopian, and completely without innocence. No longer structured by the polarity of public and private, the cyborg defines a technological polis based partly on a revolution of social relations in the *oikos,* the household. Nature and culture are reworked; the one can no longer be the resource for appropriation or incorporation by the other. The relationships for forming wholes from parts, including those of polarity and hierarchical domination, are at issue in the cyborg world. Unlike the hopes of Frankenstein's monster, the cyborg does not expect its father to save it through a restoration of the garden; that is, through the fabrication of a heterosexual mate, through its completion in a finished whole, a city and cosmos. The cyborg does not dream of community on the model of the organic family, this time without the oedipal project. The cyborg would not recognize the Garden of Eden; it is not made of mud and cannot dream of returning to dust. Perhaps that is why I want to see if cyborgs can subvert the apocalypse of returning to nuclear dust in the manic compulsion to name the Enemy. Cyborgs are not reverent; they do not re-member the cosmos. They are wary of holism, but needy for connection—they seem to have a natural feel for united front politics, but without the vanguard party. The main trouble with cyborgs, of course, is that they are the illegitimate offspring of militarism and patriarchal capitalism, not to mention state socialism. But illegitimate offspring are often exceedingly unfaithful to their origins. Their fathers, after all, are inessential.

• • •

So my cyborg myth is about transgressed boundaries, potent fusions, and dangerous possibilities which progressive people might explore as one part of needed political work. One of my premises is that most American socialists and feminists see deepened dualisms of mind and body, animal and machine, idealism and materialism in the social practices, symbolic formulations, and physical artefacts associated with 'high technology' and scientific culture. From *One-Dimensional Man* (Marcuse, 1964) to *The Death of Nature* (Merchant, 1980), the analytic resources developed by progressives have insisted on the necessary domination of technics and recalled us to an imagined organic body to integrate our resistance. Another of my premises is that the need for unity of people trying to resist world-wide intensification of domination has never been more acute. But a slightly perverse shift of perspective might better enable us to contest for meanings, as well as for other forms of power and pleasure in technologically mediated societies.

From one perspective, a cyborg world is about the final imposition of a grid of control on the planet, about the final abstraction embodied in a Star Wars apocalypse waged in the name of defence, about the final appropriation of women's bodies in a masculinist orgy of war (Sofia, 1984). From another perspective, a cyborg world might be about lived social and bodily realities in which people are not afraid of their joint kinship with animals and machines, not afraid of permanently partial identities and contradictory standpoints. The political struggle is to see from both perspectives at once because each reveals both dominations and possibilities unimaginable from the other vantage point. Single vision produces worse illusions than double vision or many-headed monsters. Cyborg unities are monstrous and illegitimate; in our present political circumstances, we could hardly hope for more potent myths for resistance and recoupling. I like to imagine LAG, the Livermore Action Group, as a kind of cyborg society, dedicated to realistically converting the laboratories that most fiercely embody and spew out the tools of technological apocalypse, and committed to building a political form that actually manages to hold together witches, engineers, elders, perverts, Christians, mothers, and Leninists long enough to disarm the state. Fission Impossible is the name of the affinity group in my town. (Affinity: related not by blood but by choice, the appeal of one chemical nuclear group for another, avidity.)

• • •

THE INFORMATICS OF DOMINATION

In this attempt at an epistemological and political position, I would like to sketch a picture of possible unity, a picture indebted to socialist and feminist principles of design. The frame for my sketch is set by the extent and importance of rearrangements in world-wide social relations tied to science and technology. I argue for a politics rooted in claims about fundamental changes in the nature of class, race, and gender in an emerging system of world order analogous in its novelty and scope to that created by industrial capitalism; we are living through a movement from an organic, industrial society to a polymorphous, information system—from all work to all play, a deadly game. Simultaneously material and ideological, the dichotomies may be expressed in the following chart of transitions from the comfortable old hierarchical dominations to the scary new networks I have called the informatics of domination:

Representation	Simulation
Bourgeois novel, realism	Science fiction, postmodernism
Organism	Biotic component
Depth, integrity	Surface, boundary
Heat	Noise
Biology as clinical practice	Biology as inscription
Physiology	Communications engineering
Small group	Subsystem
Perfection	Optimization
Eugenics	Population Control
Decadence, *Magic Mountain*	Obsolescence, *Future Shock*
Hygiene	Stress Management
Microbiology, tuberculosis	Immunology, AIDS
Organic division of labour	Ergonomics/ cybernetics of labour
Functional specialization	Modular construction
Reproduction	Replication
Organic sex role specialization	Optimal genetic strategies
Biological determinism	Evolutionary inertia, constraints
Community ecology	Ecosystem
Racial chain of being	Neo-imperialism, United Nations humanism
Scientific management in home/factory	Global factory/ Electronic cottage
Family/Market/Factory	Women in the Integrated Circuit
Family wage	Comparable worth
Public/Private	Cyborg citizenship
Nature/Culture	Fields of difference
Co-operation	Communications enhancement
Freud	Lacan
Sex	Genetic engineering
Labour	Robotics
Mind	Artificial Intelligence
Second World War	Star Wars
White Capitalist Patriarchy	Informatics of Domination

This list suggests several interesting things. First, the objects on the right-hand side cannot be coded as 'natural', a realization that subverts naturalistic coding for the left-hand side as well. We cannot go back ideologically or materially. It's not just that 'god' is dead; so is the 'goddess'. Or both are revivified in the worlds charged with microelectronic and biotechnological politics. In relation to objects like biotic components, one must think not in terms of essential properties, but in terms of design, boundary constraints, rates of flows, systems logics, costs of lowering constraints. Sexual reproduction is one kind of reproductive strategy among many, with costs and benefits as a function of the system environment. Ideologies of sexual reproduction can no longer reasonably call on notions of sex and sex role as organic aspects in natural objects like organisms and families. Such reasoning will be unmasked as irrational, and ironically corporate executives reading *Playboy* and anti-porn radical feminists will make strange bedfellows in jointly unmasking the irrationalism.

Likewise for race, ideologies about human diversity have to be formulated in terms of frequencies of parameters, like blood groups or intelligence scores. It is 'irrational' to invoke concepts like primitive and civilized. For liberals and radicals, the search for integrated social systems gives way to a new practice called 'experimental ethnography' in which an organic object dissipates in attention to the play of writing. At the level of ideology, we see translations of racism and colonialism into languages of development and under-development, rates and constraints of modernization. Any objects or persons can be reasonably thought of in terms of disassembly and reassembly; no 'natural' architectures constrain system design. The financial districts in all the world's cities, as well as the export-processing and free-trade zones, proclaim this elementary fact of 'late capitalism'. The entire universe of objects that can be known scientifically must be formulated as problems in communications engineering (for the managers) or theories of the text (for those who would resist). Both are cyborg semiologies.

One should expect control strategies to concentrate on boundary conditions and interfaces, on rates of flow across boundaries—and not on the integrity of natural objects. 'Integrity' or 'sincerity' of the Western self gives way to decision procedures and expert systems. For example, control strategies applied to women's capacities to give birth to new human beings will be developed in the languages of population control and maximization of goal achievement for individual decision-makers. Control strategies will be formulated in terms of rates, costs of constraints, degrees of freedom. Human beings, like any other component or subsystem, must be localized in a system architecture whose basic modes of operation are probabilistic, statistical. No objects, spaces, or bodies are sacred in themselves; any component can be interfaced with any other if the proper standard, the proper code, can be constructed for processing signals in a common language. Exchange in this world transcends the universal translation effected by capitalist markets that Marx analysed so well. The privileged pathology affecting all kinds of components in this universe is stress—communications breakdown (Hogness, 1983). The cyborg is not subject to Foucault's biopolitics; the cyborg simulates politics, a much more potent field of operations.

This kind of analysis of scientific and cultural objects of knowledge which have appeared historically since the Second World War prepares us to notice some important inadequacies in feminist analysis which has proceeded as if the organic, hierarchical dualisms ordering discourse in 'the West' since Aristotle still ruled. They have been cannibalized, or as Zoe Sofia (Sofoulis) might put it, they have been 'techno-digested'. The dichotomies between mind and body, animal and human, organism and machine, public and private, nature and culture, men and women, primitive and civilized are all in question ideologically. The actual situation of women is their integration/exploitation into a world system of production/reproduction and communication called the informatics of domination. The home, workplace, market, public arena, the body itself—all can be dispersed and interfaced in nearly infinite, polymorphous ways, with large consequences for women and others—consequences that themselves are very different for different people and which make potent oppositional international movements difficult to imagine and essential for survival. One important route for reconstructing socialist-feminist politics is through theory and practice addressed to the social relations of science and technology, including crucially the systems of myth and meanings structuring our imaginations. The cyborg is a kind of disassembled and reassembled, postmodern collective and personal self. This is the self feminists must code.

Communications technologies and biotechnologies are the crucial tools recrafting our bodies. These tools embody and enforce new social relations for women world-wide. Technologies and scientific discourses can be partially understood as formalizations, i.e., as frozen moments, of the fluid social interactions constituting them, but they should also be viewed as instruments for enforcing meanings. The boundary is permeable between tool and myth, instrument and concept, historical systems of social relations and historical anatomies of possible bodies, including objects of knowledge. Indeed, myth and tool mutually constitute each other.

Furthermore, communications sciences and modern biologies are constructed by a common move—*the translation of the world into a problem of coding*, a search for a common language in which all resistance to instrumental control disappears and all heterogeneity can be submitted to disassembly, reassembly, investment, and exchange.

In communications sciences, the translation of the world into a problem in coding can be illustrated by looking at cybernetic (feedback-controlled) systems theories applied to telephone technology, computer design, weapons deployment, or data base construction and maintenance. In each case, solution to the key questions rests on theory of language and control; the key operation is determining the rates, directions, and probabilities of flow of a quantity called information. The world is subdivided by boundaries differentially permeable to information. Information is just that kind of quantifiable element (unit, basis of unity) which allows universal translation, and so unhindered instrumental power (called effective communication). The biggest threat to such power is interruption of communication. Any system breakdown is a function of stress. The fundamentals of this technology can be condensed into the metaphor C^3I, command-control-communication-intelligence, the military's symbol for its operations theory.

In modern biologies, the translation of the world into a problem in coding can be illustrated by molecular genetics, ecology, sociobiological evolutionary theory, and immunobiology. The organism has been translated into problems of genetic coding and read-out. Biotechnology, a writing technology, informs research broadly. In a sense, organisms have ceased to exist as objects of knowledge, giving way to biotic components, i.e., special kinds of information-processing devices. The analogous moves in ecology could be examined by probing the history and utility of the concept of the ecosystem. Immunobiology and associated medical practices are rich exemplars of the privilege of coding and recognition systems as objects of knowledge, as constructions of bodily reality for us. Biology here is a kind of cryptography. Research is necessarily a kind of intelligence activity. Ironies abound. A stressed system goes awry, its communication processes break down; it fails to recognize the difference between self and other. Human babies with baboon hearts evoke national ethical perplexity—for animal rights activists at least as much as for the guardians of human purity. In the US gay men and intravenous drug users are the 'privileged' victims of an awful immune system disease that marks (inscribes on the body) confusion of boundaries and moral pollution (Treichler, 1987).

But these excursions into communications sciences and biology have been at a rarefied level; there is a mundane, largely economic reality to support my claim that these sciences and technologies indicate fundamental transformations in the structure of the world for us. Communications technologies depend on electronics. Modern states, multinational corporations, military power, welfare state apparatuses, satellite systems, political processes, fabrication of our imaginations, labour-control systems, medical constructions of our bodies, commercial pornography, the international division of labour, and religious evangelism depend intimately upon electronics. Microelectronics is the technical basis of simulacra; that is, of copies without originals.

Microelectronics mediates the translations of labour into robotics and word processing, sex into genetic engineering and reproductive technologies, and mind into artificial intelligence and decision procedures. The new biotechnologies concern more than human reproduction. Biology as a powerful engineering science for redesigning materials and processes has revolutionary implications for industry, perhaps most obvious today in areas of fermentation, agriculture, and energy. Communications sciences and biology are constructions of natural-technical objects of knowledge in which the difference between machine and organism is thoroughly blurred; mind, body, and tool are on very intimate terms. The 'multinational' material organization of the production and reproduction of daily life and the symbolic organization of the production and reproduction of culture and imagination seem equally implicated. The boundary-maintaining images of base and superstructure, public and private, or material and ideal never seemed more feeble.

I have used Rachel Grossman's (1980) image of women in the integrated circuit to name the situation of women in a world so intimately restructured through the social relations of science and technology. I used the odd circumlocution, 'the social relations of science and technology', to indicate that we are not dealing with a technological determinism, but with a historical system depending upon structured relations among people. But the phrase should also indicate that science and technology provide fresh sources of power, that we need fresh sources of analysis and political action (Latour, 1984). Some of the rearrangements of race, sex, and class rooted in high-tech-facilitated social relations can make socialist-feminism more relevant to effective progressive politics.

· · ·

WOMEN IN THE INTEGRATED CIRCUIT

Let me summarize the picture of women's historical locations in advanced industrial societies, as these positions have been restructured partly through the social relations of science and technology. If it was ever possible ideologically to characterize women's lives by the distinction of public and private domains—suggested by images of the division of working-class life into factory and home, of bourgeois life into market and home, and of gender existence into personal and political realms—it is

now a totally misleading ideology, even to show how both terms of these dichotomies construct each other in practice and in theory. I prefer a network ideological image, suggesting the profusion of spaces and identities and the permeability of boundaries in the personal body and in the body politic. 'Networking' is both a feminist practice and a multinational corporate strategy—weaving is for oppositional cyborgs.

So let me return to the earlier image of the informatics of domination and trace one vision of women's 'place' in the integrated circuit, touching only a few idealized social locations seen primarily from the point of view of advanced capitalist societies: Home, Market, Paid Work Place, State, School, Clinic-Hospital, and Church. Each of these idealized spaces is logically and practically implied in every other locus, perhaps analogous to a holographic photograph. I want to suggest the impact of the social relations mediated and enforced by the new technologies in order to help formulate needed analysis and practical work. However, there is no 'place' for women in these networks, only geometrics of difference and contradiction crucial to women's cyborg identities. If we learn how to read these webs of power and social life, we might learn new couplings, new coalitions. There is no way to read the following list from a standpoint of 'identification', of a unitary self. The issue is dispersion. The task is to survive in the diaspora.

Home: Women-headed households, serial monogamy, flight of men, old women alone, technology of domestic work, paid homework, reemergence of home sweat-shops, home-based businesses and telecommuting, electronic cottage, urban homelessness, migration, module architecture, reinforced (simulated) nuclear family, intense domestic violence.

Market: Women's continuing consumption work, newly targeted to buy the profusion of new production from the new technologies (especially as the competitive race among industrialized and industrializing nations to avoid dangerous mass unemployment necessitates finding ever bigger new markets for ever less clearly needed commodities); bimodal buying power, coupled with advertising targeting of the numerous affluent groups and neglect of the previous mass markets; growing importance of informal markets in labour and commodities parallel to high-tech, affluent market structures; surveillance systems through electronic funds transfer; intensified market abstraction (commodification) of experience, resulting in ineffective utopian or equivalent cynical theories of community; extreme mobility (abstraction) of marketing/financing systems; interpretation of sexual and labour markets; intensified sexualization of abstracted and alienated consumption.

Paid Work Place: Continued intense sexual and racial division of labour, but considerable growth of membership in privileged occupational categories for many white women and people of colour; impact of new technologies on women's work in clerical, service, manufacturing (especially textiles), agriculture, electronics; international restructuring of the working classes; development of new time arrangements to facilitate the homework economy (flex time, part time, over time, no time); homework and out work; increased pressures for two-tiered wage structures; significant numbers of people in cash-dependent populations world-wide with no experience or no further hope of stable employment; most labour 'marginal' or 'feminized'.

State: Continued erosion of the welfare state; decentralizations with increased surveillance and control; citizenship by telematics; imperialism and political power broadly in the form of information rich/information poor differentiation; increased high-tech militarization increasingly opposed by many social groups; reduction of civil service jobs as a result of the growing capital intensification of office work, with implications for occupational mobility for women of colour; growing privatization material and ideological life and culture; close integration of privatization and militarization, the high-tech forms of bourgeois capitalist personal and public life; invisibility of different social groups to each other, linked to psychological mechanisms of belief in abstract enemies.

School: Deepening coupling of high-tech capital needs and public education at all levels, differentiated by race, class, and gender; managerial classes involved in educational reform and refunding at the cost of remaining progressive educational democratic structures for children and teachers; education for mass ignorance and repression in technocratic and militarized culture; growing anti-science mystery cults in dissenting and radical political movements;

continued relative scientific illiteracy among white women and people of colour; growing industrial direction of education (especially higher education) by science-based multinationals (particularly in electronics- and biotechnology-dependent companies); highly educated, numerous élites in a progressively bimodal society.

Clinic-hospital: Intensified machine–body relations; renegotiations of public metaphors which channel personal experience of the body, particularly in relation to reproduction, immune system functions, and 'stress' phenomena; intensification of reproductive politics in response to world historical implications of women's unrealized, potential control of their relation to reproduction; emergence of new, historically specific diseases; struggles over meanings and means of health in environments pervaded by high technology products and processes; continuing feminization of health work; intensified struggle over state responsibility for health; continued ideological role of popular health movements as a major form of American politics.

Church: Electronic fundamentalist 'super-saver' preachers solemnizing the union of electronic capital and automated fetish gods; intensified importance of churches in resisting the militarized state; central struggle over women's meanings and authority in religion; continued relevance of spirituality, intertwined with sex and health, in political struggle.

The only way to characterize the informatics of domination is as a massive intensification of insecurity and cultural impoverishment, with common failure of subsistence networks for the most vulnerable. Since much of this picture interweaves with the social relations of science and technology, the urgency of a socialist-feminist politics addressed to science and technology is plain. There is much now being done, and the grounds for political work are rich. For example, the efforts to develop forms of collective struggle for women in paid work, like SEIU's District 925 (Service Employees International Union's office workers' organization in the U.S.) should be a high priority for all of us. These efforts are profoundly tied to technical restructuring of labour processes and reformations of working classes. These efforts also are providing understanding of a more comprehensive kind of labour organization, involving community, sexuality, and family issues never privileged in the largely white male industrial unions.

The structural rearrangements related to the social relations of science and technology evoke strong ambivalence. But it is not necessary to be ultimately depressed by the implications of late twentieth-century women's relation to all aspects of work, culture, production of knowledge, sexuality, and reproduction. For excellent reasons, most Marxisms see domination best and have trouble understanding what can only look like false consciousness and people's complicity in their own domination in late capitalism. It is crucial to remember that what is lost, perhaps especially from women's points of view, is often virulent forms of oppression, nostalgically naturalized in the face of current violation. Ambivalence towards the disrupted unities mediated by high-tech culture requires not sorting conscious-ess into categories of 'clear-sighted critique grounding a solid political epistemology' versus 'manipulated false consciousness', but subtle understanding of emerging pleasures, experiences, and powers with serious potential for changing the rules of the game.

There are grounds for hope in the emerging bases for new kinds of unity across race, gender, and class, as these elementary units of socialist-feminist analysis themselves suffer protein transformations. Intensifications of hardship experienced worldwide in connection with the social relations of science and technology are severe. But what people are experiencing is not transparently clear, and we lack sufficiently subtle connections for collectively building effective theories of experience. Present efforts—Marxist, psychoanalytic, feminist, anthropological—to clarify even 'our' experience are rudimentary.

I am conscious of the odd perspective provided by my historical position—a PhD in biology for an Irish Catholic girl was made possible by Sputnik's impact on US national science-education policy. I have a body and mind as much constructed by the post-Second World War arms race and cold war as by the women's movements. There are more grounds for hope in focusing on the contradictory effects of politics designed to produce loyal American technocrats, which also produced large num-

bers of dissidents, than in focusing on the present defeats.

The permanent partiality of feminist points of view has consequences for our expectations of forms of political organization and participation. We do not need a totality in order to work well. The feminist dream of a common language, like all dreams for a perfectly true language, of perfectly faithful naming of experience, is a totalizing and imperialist one. In that sense, dialectics too is a dream language, longing to resolve contradiction. Perhaps, ironically, we can learn from our fusions with animals and machines how not to be Man, the embodiment of Western logos. From the point of view of pleasure in these potent and taboo fusions, made inevitable by the social relations of science and technology, there might indeed be a feminist science.

CYBORGS: A MYTH OF POLITICAL IDENTITY

. . .

Writing is pre-eminently the technology of cyborgs, etched surfaces of the late twentieth century. Cyborg politics is the struggle for language and the struggle against perfect communication, against the one code that translates all meaning perfectly, the central dogma of phallogocentrism. That is why cyborg politics insist on noise and advocate pollution, rejoicing in the illegitimate fusions of animal and machine. These are the couplings which make Man and Woman so problematic, subverting the structure of desire, the force imagined to generate language and gender, and so subverting the structure and modes of reproduction of 'Western' identity, of nature and culture, of mirror and eye, slave and master, body and mind. 'We' did not originally choose to be cyborgs, but choice grounds a liberal politics and epistemology that imagines the reproduction of individuals before the wider replications of 'texts'.

From the perspective of cyborgs, freed of the need to ground politics in 'our' privileged position of the oppression that incorporates all other dominations, the innocence of the merely violated, the ground of those closer to nature, we can see powerful possibilities. Feminisms and Marxisms have run argound on Western epistemological imperatives to construct a revolutionary subject from the perspective of a hierarchy of oppressions and/or a latent position of moral superiority, innocence, and greater closeness to nature. With no available original dream of a common language or original symbiosis promising protection from hostile 'masculine' separation, but written into the play of a text that has no finally privileged reading or salvation history, to recognize 'oneself' as fully implicated in the world, frees us of the need to root politics in identification, vanguard parties, purity, and mothering. Stripped of identity, the bastard race teaches about the power of the margins and the importance of a mother like Malinche. Women of colour have transformed her from the evil mother of masculinist fear into the originally literate mother who teaches survival.

This is not just literary deconstruction, but liminal transformation. Every story that begins with original innocence and privileges the return to wholeness imagines the drama of life to be individuation, separation, the birth of the self, the tragedy of autonomy, the fall into writing, alienation; that is, war, tempered by imaginary respite in the bosom of the Other. These plots are ruled by a reproductive politics—rebirth without flaw, perfection, abstraction. In this plot women are imagined either better or worse off, but all agree they have less selfhood, weaker individuation, more fusion to the oral, to Mother, less at stake in masculine autonomy. But there is another route to having less at stake in masculine autonomy, a route that does not pass through Woman, Primitive, Zero, the Mirror Stage and its imaginary. It passes through women and other present-tense, illegitimate cyborgs, not of Woman born, who refuse the ideological resources of victimization so as to have a real life. These cyborgs are the people who refuse to disappear on cue, no matter how many times a 'Western' commentator remarks on the sad passing of another primitive, another organic group done in by 'Western' technology, by writing. These real-life cyborgs (for example, the Southeast Asian village women workers in Japanese and US electronics firms described by Aihwa Ong) are actively rewriting the texts of their bodies and societies. Survival is the stakes in this play of readings.

To recapitulate, certain dualisms have been persistent in Western traditions; they have all been systemic to the logics and practices of domination of women, people of colour, nature, workers, animals—in short, domination of all constituted as others, whose task is to mirror the self. Chief among these troubling dualisms are self/other, mind/body, culture/nature, male/female, civilized/primitive, reality/appearance, whole/part, agent/resource, maker/made, active/passive, right/wrong, truth/illusion, total/partial, God/man. The self is the One who is not dominated, who knows that by the service of the other, the other is the one who holds the future, who knows that by the experience of domination, which gives the lie to the autonomy of the self. To be One is to be autonomous, to be powerful, to be God; but to be One is to be an illusion, and so to be involved in a dialectic of apocalypse with the other. Yet to be other is to be multiple, without clear boundary, frayed, insubstantial. One is too few, but two are too many.

High-tech culture challenges these dualisms in intriguing ways. It is not clear who makes and who is made in the relation between human and machine. It is not clear what is mind and what body in machines that resolve into coding practices. In so far as we know ourselves in both formal discourse (for example, biology) and in daily practice (for example, the homework economy in the integrated circuit), we find ourselves to be cyborgs, hybrids, mosaics, chimeras. Biological organisms have become biotic systems, communications devices like others. There is no fundamental, ontological separation in our formal knowledge of machine and organism, of technical and organic. The replicant Rachel in the Ridley Scott film *Blade Runner* stands as the image of a cyborg culture's fear, love, and confusion.

One consequence is that our sense of connection to our tools is heightened. The trance state experienced by many computer users has become a staple of science-fiction film and cultural jokes. Perhaps paraplegics and other severely handicapped people can (and sometimes do) have the most intense experiences of complex hybridization with other communication devices. Anne McCaffrey's pre-feminist *The Ship Who Sang* (1969) explored the consciousness of a cyborg, hybrid of girl's brain and complex machinery, formed after the birth of a severely handicapped child. Gender, sexuality, embodiment, skill: all were reconstituted in the story. Why should our bodies end at the skin, or include at best other beings encapsulated by skin? From the seventeenth century till now, machines could be animated—given ghostly souls to make them speak or move or to account for their orderly development and mental capacities. Or organisms could be mechanized—reduced to body understood as resource of mind. These machine/organism relationships are obsolete, unnecessary. For us, in imagination and in other practice, machines can be prosthetic devices, intimate components, friendly selves. We don't need organic holism to give impermeable wholeness, the total woman and her feminist variants (mutants?). Let me conclude this point by a very partial reading of the logic of the cyborg monsters of my second group of texts, feminist science fiction.

· · ·

Monsters have always defined the limits of community in Western imaginations. The Centaurs and Amazons of ancient Greece established the limits of the centred polis of the Greek male human by their disruption of marriage and boundary pollutions of the warrior with animality and woman. Unseparated twins and hermaphrodites were the confused human material in early modern France who grounded discourse on the natural and supernatural, medical and legal, portents and diseases—all crucial to establishing modern identity. The evolutionary and behavioural sciences of monkeys and apes have marked the multiple boundaries of late twentieth-century industrial identities. Cyborg monsters in feminist science fiction define quite different political possibilities and limits from those proposed by the mundane fiction of Man and Woman.

There are several consequences to taking seriously the imagery of cyborgs as other than our enemies. Our bodies, ourselves; bodies are maps of power and identity. Cyborgs are no exception. A cyborg body is not innocent; it was not born in a garden; it does not seek unitary identity and so generate antagonistic dualisms without end (or until the world ends); it takes irony for granted. One is too few, and two is only one possibility. Intense pleasure in skill, machine skill, ceases to be a sin, but an aspect of embodiment. The machine is not an *it* to be animated, worshipped, and dominated. The ma-

chine is us, our processes, an aspect of our embodiment. We can be responsible for machines; *they* do not dominate or threaten us. We are responsible for boundaries; we are they. Up till now (once upon a time), female embodiment seemed to be given, organic, necessary; and female embodiment seemed to mean skill in mothering and its metaphoric extensions. Only by being out of place could we take intense pleasure in machines, and then with excuses that this was organic activity after all, appropriate to females. Cyborgs might consider more seriously the partial, fluid, sometimes aspect of sex and sexual embodiment. Gender might not be global identity after all, even if it has profound historical breadth and depth.

The ideologically charged question of what counts as daily activity, as experience, can be approached by exploiting the cyborg image. Feminists have recently claimed that women are given to dailiness, that women more than men somehow sustain daily life, and so have a privileged epistemological position potentially. There is a compelling aspect to this claim, one that makes visible unvalued female activity and names it as the ground of life. But *the* ground of life? What about all the ignorance of women, all the exclusions and failures of knowledge and skill? What about men's access to daily competence, to knowing how to build things, to take them apart, to play? What about other embodiments? Cyborg gender is a local possibility taking a global vengeance. Race, gender, and capital require a cyborg theory of wholes and parts. There is no drive in cyborgs to produce total theory, but there is an intimate experience of boundaries, their construction and deconstruction. There is a myth system waiting to become a political language to ground one way of looking at science and technology and challenging the informatics of domination—in order to act potently.

One last image: organisms and organismic, holistic politics depend on metaphors of rebirth and invariably call on the resources of reproductive sex. I would suggest that cyborgs have more to do with regeneration and are suspicious of the reproductive matrix and of most birthing. For salamanders, regeneration after injury, such as the loss of a limb, involves regrowth of structure and restoration of function with the constant possibility of twinning or other odd topographical productions at the site of former injury. The regrown limb can be monstrous, duplicated, potent. We have all been injured, profoundly. We require regeneration, not rebirth, and the possibilities for our reconstitution include the utopian dream of the hope for a monstrous world without gender.

Cyborg imagery can help express two crucial arguments in this essay: first, the production of universal, totalizing theory is a major mistake that misses most of reality, probably always, but certainly now; and second, taking responsibility for the social relations of science and technology means refusing an anti-science metaphysics, a demonology of technology, and so means embracing the skilful task of reconstructing the boundaries of daily life, in partial connection with others, in communication with all of our parts. It is not just that science and technology are possible means of great human satisfaction, as well as a matrix of complex dominations. Cyborg imagery can suggest a way out of the maze of dualisms in which we have explained our bodies and our tools to ourselves. This is a dream not of a common language, but of a powerful infidel heteroglossia. It is an imagination of a feminist speaking in tongues to strike fear into the circuits of the super-savers of the new right. It means both building and destroying machines, identities, categories, relationships, space stories. Though both are bound in the spiral dance, I would rather be a cyborg than a goddess.

[1985]

REFERENCES

Grossman, Rachel (1980) 'Women's place in the integrated circuit', *Radical America* 14(1): 29–50.

Hogness, E. Rusten (1983) 'Why stress? A look at the making of stress, 1936–56', unpublished paper available from the author, 4437 Mill Creek Rd, Healdsburg, CA 95448.

Klein, Hilary (1989) 'Marxism, psychoanalysis, and mother nature', *Feminist Studies* 15(2): 255–278.

Latour, Bruno (1984) *Les microbes, guerre et paix, suivi des irréductions*. Paris: Métailié.

McCaffrey, Anne (1969) *The Ship Who Sang*. New York: Ballantine.

Marcuse, Herbert (1964) *One-Dimensional Man: Studies in the Ideology of Advanced Industrial Society*. Boston: Beacon.

Merchant, Carolyn (1980) *The Death of Nature: Women, Ecology, and the Scientific Revolution*. New York: Harper & Row.

Ong, Aihwa (1987) *Spirits of Resistance and Capitalist Discipline: Factory Workers in Malaysia*. Albany: State University of New York Press.

Sofia, Zoe (also Zoe Sofoulis) (1984) 'Exterminating fetuses: abortion, disarmament, and the sexo-semiotics of extra-terrestrialism', *Diacritics* 14(2): 47–59.

Sofoulis, Zoe (1987) 'Lacklein', University of California at Santa Cruz, unpublished essay.

Treichler, Paula (1987) 'AIDS, homophobia, and biomedical discourse: an epidemic of signification', *October* 43: 31–70.

 70

Kochinnenako in Academe: Three Approaches to Interpreting a Keres Indian Tale

PAULA GUNN ALLEN

I became engaged in studying feminist thought and theory when I was first studying and teaching American Indian literature in the early 1970s. Over the ensuing fifteen years, my own stances toward both feminist and American Indian life and thought have intertwined as they have unfolded. I have always included feminist content and perspectives in my teaching of American Indian subjects, though at first the mating was uneasy at best. My determination that both areas were interdependent and mutually significant to a balanced pedagogy of American Indian studies led me to grow into an approach to both that is best described as tribal-feminism, or feminist-tribalism. Both terms are applicable: if I am dealing with feminism, I approach it from a strongly tribal posture, and when I am dealing with American Indian literature, history, culture, or philosophy I approach it from a strongly feminist one.

A feminist approach to the study and teaching of American Indian life and thought is essential because the area has been dominated by paternalistic, male-dominant modes of consciousness since the first writings about American Indians in the fifteenth century. This male bias has seriously skewed our understanding of tribal life and philosophy, distorting it in ways that are sometimes obvious but are most often invisible.

Often what appears to be a misinterpretation caused by racial differences is a distortion based on sexual politics. When the patriarchal paradigm that characterizes western thinking is applied to gyne-centric tribal modes, it transforms the ideas, significances, and raw data into something that is not only unrecognizable to the tribes but entirely incongruent with their philosophies and theories. We know that materials and interpretations amassed by the white intellectual establishment are in error, but we have not pinpointed the major sources of that error. I believe that a fundamental source has been male bias and that feminist theory, when judiciously applied to the field, makes the error correctible, freeing the data for reinterpretation that is at least congruent with a tribal perceptual mode.

To demonstrate the interconnections between tribal and feminist approaches as I use them in my work, I have developed an analysis of a traditional Kochinnenako, or Yellow Woman, story of the Laguna-Acoma Keres, as recast by my mother's uncle John M. Gunn in his book *Schat Chen*.[1] My analysis utilizes three approaches and demonstrates the relationship of context to meaning, illuminating three consciousness styles and providing students with a traditionally tribal, nonracist, feminist understanding of traditional and contemporary American Indian life.

SOME THEORETICAL CONSIDERATIONS

Analyzing tribal cultural systems from a mainstream feminist point of view allows an otherwise overlooked insight into the complex interplay of factors that have led to the systematic loosening of tribal ties, the disruption of tribal cohesion and complexity, and the growing disequilibrium of cultures that were anciently based on a belief in balance, relationship, and the centrality of women, particularly elder women. A feminist approach reveals not only the exploitation and oppression of the tribes by whites and white government but also areas of oppression within the tribes and the sources and nature of that oppression. To a large extent, such an analysis can provide strategies for ameliorating the effects of patriarchal colonialism, enabling many of the tribes to reclaim their ancient gynarchical, egalitarian, and sacred traditions.

At the present time, American Indians in general are not comfortable with feminist analysis or action

within the reservation or urban Indian enclaves. Many Indian women are uncomfortable with feminism because they perceive it (correctly) as white-dominated. They (not so correctly) believe it is concerned with issues that have little bearing on their own lives. They are also uncomfortable with it because they have been reared in an anglophobic world that views white society with fear and hostility. But because of their fear of and bitterness toward whites and their consequent unwillingness to examine the dynamics of white socialization, American Indian women often overlook the central areas of damage done to tribal tradition by white Christian and secular patriarchal dominance. Militant and "progressive" American Indian men are even more likely to quarrel with feminism; they have benefited in certain ways from white male-centeredness, and while those benefits are of real danger to the tribes, the individual rewards are compelling.

It is within the context of growing violence against women and the concominant lowering of our status among Native Americans that I teach and write. Certainly I could not locate the mechanisms of colonization that have led to the virulent rise of woman-hating among American Indian men (and, to a certain extent, among many of the women) without a secure and determined feminism. Just as certainly, feminist theory applied to my literary studies clarifies a number of issues for me, including the patriarchal bias that has been systematically imposed on traditional literary materials and the mechanism by which that bias has affected contemporary American Indian life, thought, and culture.

The oral tradition is more than a record of a people's culture. It is the creative source of their collective and individual selves. When that wellspring of identity is tampered with, the sense of self is also tampered with; and when that tampering includes the sexist and classist assumptions of the white world within the body of an Indian tradition, serious consequences necessarily ensue.

The oral tradition is a living body. It is in continuous flux, which enables it to accommodate itself to the real circumstances of a people's lives. That is its strength, but it is also its weakness, for when a people finds itself living within a racist, classist, and sexist reality, the oral tradition will reflect those values and will thus shape the people's consciousness to include and accept racism, classism, and sexism, and they will incorporate that change, hardly noticing the shift. If the oral tradition is altered in certain subtle, fundamental ways, if elements alien to it are introduced so that its internal coherence is disturbed, it becomes the major instrument of colonization and oppression.

. . .

John Gunn received the story I am using here from a Keres-speaking informant and translated it himself. The story, which he titles "Sh-ah-cock and Miochin or the Battle of the Seasons," is in reality a narrative version of a ritual. The ritual brings about the change of season and of moiety among the Keres. Gunn doesn't mention this, perhaps because he was interested in stories and not in religion or perhaps because his informant did not mention the connection to him.

What is interesting about his rendering is his use of European, classist, conflict-centered patriarchal assumptions as plotting devices. These interpolations dislocate the significance of the tale and subtly alter the ideational context of woman-centered, largely pacifist people whose ritual story this is. I have developed three critiques of the tale as it appears is his book, using feminist and tribal understandings to discuss the various meanings of the story when it is read from three different perspectives.

In the first reading, I apply tribal understanding to the story. In the second, I apply the sort of feminist perspective I applied to traditional stories, historical events, traditional culture, and contemporary literature when I began developing a feminist perspective. The third reading applies what I call a feminist-tribal perspective. Each analysis is somewhat less detailed than it might be; but as I am interested in describing modes of perception and their impact on our understanding of cultural artifacts (and by extension our understanding of people who come from different cultural contexts than our own) rather than critiquing a story, they are adequate.

YELLOW WOMAN STORIES

The Keres of Laguna and Acoma Pueblos in New Mexico have stories that are called Yellow Woman stories. The themes and to a large extent the motifs of these stories are always female-centered, always told from Yellow Woman's point of view. Some older recorded versions of Yellow Woman tales (as in Gunn) make Yellow Woman the daughter of the hocheni. Gunn translates *hocheni* as "ruler." But Keres notions of the hocheni's function and position are as cacique or Mother Chief, which differ greatly from Anglo-European ideas of rulership. However, for Gunn to render *hocheni* as "ruler" is congruent with the European folktale tradition.

Kochinnenako, Yellow Woman, is in some sense a name that means Woman-Woman because among the Keres, yellow is the color for women (as pink and red are among Anglo-European Americans), and it is the color ascribed to the Northwest. Keres women paint their faces yellow on certain ceremonial occasions and are so painted at death so that the guardian at the gate of the spirit world, Naiya Iyatiku (Mother Corn Woman), will recognize that the newly arrived person is a woman. It is also the name of a particular Irriaku, Corn Mother (sacred corn-ear bundle), and Yellow Woman stories in their original form detail rituals in which the Irriaku figures prominently.

Yellow Woman stories are about all sorts of things—abduction, meeting with happy powerful spirits, birth of twins, getting power from the spirit worlds and returning it to the people, refusing to marry, weaving, grinding corn, getting water, outsmarting witches, eluding or escaping from malintentioned spirits, and more. Yellow Woman's sisters are often in the stories (Blue, White, and Red Corn) as is Grandmother Spider and her helper Spider Boy, the Sun God or one of his aspects, Yellow Woman's twin sons, witches, magicians, gamblers, and mothers-in-law.

Many Yellow Woman tales highlight her alienation from the people: she lives with her grandmother at the edge of the village, for example, or she is in some way atypical, maybe a woman who refuses to marry, one who is known for some particular special talent, or one who is very quick-witted and resourceful. In many ways Kochinnenako is a role model, though she possesses some behaviors that are not likely to occur in many of the women who hear her stories. She is, one might say, the Spirit of Woman.

The stories do not necessarily imply that difference is punishable; on the contrary, it is often her very difference that makes her special adventures possible, and these adventures often have happy outcomes for Kochinnenako and for her people. This is significant among a people who value conformity and propriety above almost anything. It suggests that the behavior of women, at least at certain times or under certain circumstances, must be improper or nonconformist for the greater good of the whole. Not that all the stories are graced with a happy ending. Some come to a tragic conclusion, sometimes resulting from someone's inability to follow the rules or perform a ritual in the proper way.

Other Kochinnenako stories are about her centrality to the harmony, balance, and prosperity of the tribe. "Sh-ah-cock and Miochin" is one of these stories. John Gunn prefaces the narrative with the comment that while the story is about a battle, war stories are rarely told by the Keres because they are not "a war like people" and "very rarely refer to their exploits in war."

SH-AH-COCK AND MIOCHIN
OR THE BATTLE OF THE SEASONS

In the Kush-kut-ret-u-nah-tit (white village of the north) was once a ruler by the name of Hut-cha-mun Ki-uk (the broken prayer stick), one of whose daughters, Ko-chin-ne-nako, became the bride of Sh-ah-cock (the spirit of winter), a person of very violent temper. He always manifested his presence by blizzards of snow or sleet or by freezing cold, and on account of his alliance with the ruler's daughter, he was most of the time in the vicinity of Kush-kut-ret, and as these manifestations continued from month to month and year to year, the people of Kush-kut-ret found that their crops would not mature, and finally they were compelled to subsist on the leaves of the cactus.

On one occasion Ko-chin-ne-nako had wandered a long way from home in search of the cactus and had gathered quite a bundle and was preparing to carry them home by singeing off the thorns, when on looking up she found herself confronted by a very bold but handsome young man. His attire attracted her gaze at once. He wore a shirt of yellow woven from the silks of corn, a belt made from the broad green blades of the same plant, a tall pointed hat made from the same kind of material and from the top which waved a yellow corn tassel. He wore green leggings woven from kow-e-nuh, the green

stringy moss that forms in springs and ponds. His moccasins were beautifully embroidered with flowers and butterflies. In his hand he carried an ear of green corn.

His whole appearance proclaimed him a stranger and as Ko-chin-ne-nako gaped in wonder, he spoke to her in a very pleasing voice asking her what she was doing. She told him that on account of the cold and drouth [*sic*], the people of Kush-kut-ret were forced to eat the leaves of the cactus to keep from starving.

"Here," said the young man, handing her the ear of green corn. "Eat this and I will go and bring more that you may take home with you."

He left her and soon disappeared going towards the south. In a short time he returned bringing with him a big load of green corn. Ko-chin-ne-nako asked him where he had gathered corn and if it grew near by. "No," he replied, "it is from my home far away to the south, where the corn grows and the flowers bloom all the year around. Would you not like to accompany me back to my country?" Ko-chin-ne-nako replied that his home must be very beautiful, but that she could not go with him because she was the wife of Sh-ah-cock. And then she told him of her alliance with the Spirit of Winter, and admitted that her husband was very cold and disagreeable and that she did not love him. The strange young man urged her to go with him to the warm land of the south, saying that he did not fear Sh-ah-cock. But Ko-chin-ne-nako would not consent. So the stranger directed her to return to her home with the corn he had brought and cautioned her not to throw away any of the husks out of the door. Upon leaving he said to her, "you must meet me at this place tomorrow. I will bring more corn for you."

Ko-chin-ne-nako had not proceeded far on her homeward way ere she met her sisters who, having become uneasy because of her long absence, had come in search of her. They were greatly surprised at seeing her with an armful of corn instead of cactus. Ko-chin-ne-nako told them the whole story of how she had obtained it, and thereby only added wonderment to their surprise. They helped her to carry the corn home; and there she again had to tell her story to her father and mother.

When she had described the stranger even from his peaked hat to his butterfly moccasins, and had told them that she was to meet him again on the day following, Hut-cha-mun Ki-uk, the father, exclaimed:

"It is Mi-o-chin!"

"It is Mi-o-chin! It is Mi-o-chin!," echoed the mother. "Tomorrow you must bring him home with you."

The next day Ko-chin-ne-nako went again to the spot where she had met Mi-o-chin, for it was indeed Mi-o-chin, the Spirit of Summer. He was already there, awaiting her coming. With him he had brought a huge bundle of corn.

Ko-chin-ne-nako pressed upon him the invitation of her parents to accompany her home, so together they carried the corn to Kush-kut-ret. When it had been distributed there was sufficient to feed all the people of the city. Amid great rejoicing and thanksgiving, Mi-o-chin was welcomed at the Hotchin's (ruler's) house.

In the evening, as was his custom, Sh-ah-cock, the Spirit of the Winter, returned to his home. He came in a blinding storm of snow and hail and sleet, for he was in a boisterous mood. On approaching the city, he felt within his bones that Mi-o-chin was there, so he called in a loud and blustering voice:

"Ha! Mi-o-chin, are you here?"

For answer, Mi-o-chin advanced to meet him.

Then Sh-ah-cock, beholding him, called again,

"Ha! Mi-o-chin, I will destroy you."

"Ha! Sh-ah-cock, I will destroy you," replied Mi-o-chin, still advancing.

Sh-ah-cock paused, irresolute. He was covered from head to foot with frost (skah). Icycles [*sic*] (ya-pet-tu-ne) draped him round. The fierce, cold wind proceeded from his nostrils.

As Mi-o-chin drew near, the wintry wind changed to a warm summer breeze. The frost and icycles melted and displayed beneath them, the dry, bleached bulrushes (ska-ra-ru-ka) in which Sh-ah-cock was clad.

Seeing that he was doomed to defeat, Sh-ah-cock cried out:

"I will not fight you now, for we cannot try our powers. We will make ready, and in four days from this time, we will meet here and fight for supremacy. The victor shall claim Ko-chin-ne-nako for his wife."

With this, Sh-ah-cock withdrew in rage. The wind again roared and shook the very houses; but the people were warm within them, for Mi-o-chin was with them.

The next day Mi-o-chin left Kush Kutret for his home in the south. Arriving there, he began to make his preparations to meet Sh-ah-cock in battle.

First he sent an eagle as a messenger to his friend, Ya-chun-ne-ne-moot (kind of shaley rock that becomes very hot in the fire), who lived in the west, requesting him to come and help to battle Sh-ah-cock. Then he called together the birds and the four legged animals—all those that live in sunny climes. For his advance guard and shield he selected the bat (pickikke), as its tough skin would best resist the sleet and hail that Sh-ah-cock would hurl at him.

Meantime Sh-ah-cock had gone to his home in the north to make his preparations for battle. To his aid he called all the winter birds and all of the four legged animals of the wintry climates. For his advance guard and shield he selected Shro-ak-ah (a magpie).

When these formidable forces had been mustered by the rivals, they advanced, Mi-o-chin from the south and Sh-ah-cock from the north, in battle array.

Ya-chun-ne-ne-moot kindled his fires and piled great heaps of resinous fuel upon them until volumes of steam and smoke ascended, forming enormous clouds that hurried forward toward Kush-kut-ret and the battle ground. Upon these clouds rode Mi-o-chin, the Spirit of Summer, and his vast army. All the animals of the army, encountering the smoke from Ya-chun-ne-ne-moot's fires, were colored by the smoke so that, from that day, the animals from the south have been black or brown in color.

Sh-ah-cock and his army came out of the north in a howling blizzard and borne forward on black storm clouds driven by a freezing wintry wind. As he came on, the lakes and rivers over which he passed were frozen and the air was filled with blinding sleet.

When the combatants drew near to Kush-kut-ret, they advanced with fearful rapidity. Their arrival upon the field was marked by fierce and terrific strife.

Flashes of lightning darted from Mi-o-chin's clouds. Striking the animals of Sh-ah-cock, they singed the hair upon them, and turned it white, so that, from that day, the animals from the north have worn a covering of white or have white markings upon them.

From the south, the black clouds still rolled upward, the thunder spoke again and again. Clouds of smoke and vapor rushed onward, melting the snow and ice weapons of Sh-ah-cock and compelling him, at length, to retire from the field. Mi-o-chin, assured of victory, pursued him. To save himself from total defeat and destruction, Sh-ah-cock called for armistice.

This being granted on the part of Mi-o-chin, the rivals met at Kush-kut-ret to arrange the terms of the treaty. Sh-ah-cock acknowledged himself defeated. He consented to give up Ko-chin-ne-nako to Mi-o-chin. This concession was received with rejoicing by Ko-chin-ne-nako and all the people of Kush-kut-ret.

It was then agreed between the late combatants that, for all time thereafter, Mi-o-chin was to rule at Kush-kut-ret during one-half of the year, and Sh-ah-cock was to rule during the remaining half, and that neither should molest the other.[2]

John Gunn's version has a formal plot structure that makes the account seem to be a narrative. But had he translated it directly from the Keres, even in "narrative" form, as in a storytelling session, its ritual nature would have been clearer.

I can only surmise about how the account might go if it were done that way, basing my ideas on renderings of Keres rituals in narrative forms I am acquainted with. But a direct translation from the Keres would have sounded more like the following than like Gunn's rendition of it:

> Long ago. Eh. There in the North. Yellow Woman. Up northward she went. Then she picked burrs and cactus. Then here went Summer. From the south he came. Above there he arrived. Thus spoke Summer. "Are you here? How is it going?" said Summer. "Did you come here?" thus said Yellow Woman. Then answered Yellow Woman. "I pick these poor things because I am hungry." "Why do you not eat corn and melons?" asked Summer. Then he gave her some corn and melons. "Take it!" Then thus spoke Yellow Woman, "It is good. Let us go. To my house I take you." "Is not your husband there?" "No. He went hunting deer. Today at night he will come back."
>
> Then in the north they arrived. In the west they went down. Arrived then they in the east. "Are you here?" Remembering Prayer Sticks said. "Yes" Summer said. "How is it going?" Summer said. Then he said, "Your daughter Yellow Woman, she brought me here." "Eh. That is good." Thus spoke Remembering Prayer Sticks.

The Story would continue, with many of the elements contained in Gunn's version but organized along the axis of directions, movement of the participants, their maternal relationships to each other (daughter, mother, mother chief, etc.), and events

sketched in only as they pertained to directions and the division of the year into its ritual/ceremonial segments, one belonging to the Kurena (summer supernaturals or powers who are connected to the summer people or clans) and the other belonging to the Kashare, perhaps in conjunction with the Kopishtaya, the Spirits.

Summer, Miochin, is the Shiwana who lives on the south mountain, and Sh-ah-cock is the Shiwana who lives on the north mountain. It is interesting to note that the Kurena wear three eagle feathers and ctc'otika' feathers (white striped) on their heads, bells, and woman's dress and carry a reed flute, which perhaps is connected with Iyatiku's sister, Istoakoa, Reed Woman.

A Keres Interpretation

When a traditional Keres reads the tale of Kochinnenako, she listens with certain information about her people in mind: she knows, for example, that Hutchamun Kiuk (properly it means Remembering Prayer Sticks, though Gunn translates it as Broken Prayer Sticks)[3] refers to the ritual (sacred) identity of the cacique and that the story is a narrative version of a ceremony related to the planting of corn. She knows that Lagunas and Acomas don't have rulers in the Anglo-European sense of monarchs, lords, and such (though they do, in recent times, have elected governors, but that's another matter), and that a person's social status is determined by her mother's clan and position in it rather than by her relationship to the cacique as his daughter. (Actually, in various accounts, the *cacique* refers to Yellow Woman as his mother, so the designation of her as his daughter is troublesome unless one is aware that relationships in the context of their ritual significance are being delineated here.)

In any case, our hypothetical Keres reader also knows that the story is about a ritual that takes place every year and that the battle imagery refers to events that take place during the ritual; she is also aware that Kochinnenako's will, as expressed in her attraction to Miochin, is a central element of the ritual. She knows further that the ritual is partly about the coming of summer and partly about the ritual relationship and exchange of primacy between the two divisions of the tribe, that the ritual described in the narrative is enacted by men, dressed as Miochin and Sh-ah-cock, and that Yellow Woman in her Corn Mother aspect is the center of this and other sacred rites of the Kurena, though in this ritual she may also be danced by a Kurena mask dancer. (Gunn includes a drawing of this figure, made by a Laguna, and titled "Ko-chin-ne-nako— In the Mask Dances.")

. . .

A Keres is of course aware that balance and harmony are two primary assumptions of Keres society and will not approach the narrative wondering whether the handsome Miochin will win the hand of the unhappy wife and triumph over the enemy, thereby heroically saving the people from disaster. The triumph of handsome youth over ugly age or of virile liberality over withered tyranny doesn't make sense in a Keres context because such views contradict central Keres values.

A traditional Keres is satisfied by the story because it reaffirms a Keres sense of rightness, of propriety. It is a tale that affirms ritual understandings, and the Keres reader can visualize the ritual itself when reading Gunn's story. Such a reader is likely to be puzzled by the references of rulers and by the tone of heroic romance but will be reasonably satisfied by the account because in spite of its westernized changes, it still ends happily with the orderly transfer of focality between the moieties and seasons accomplished in seasonal splendor as winter in New Mexico blusters and sleets its way north and summer sings and warms its way home. In the end, the primary Keres values of harmony, balance, and the centrality of woman to maintain them have been validated, and the fundamental Keres principal of proper order is celebrated and affirmed once again.

A Modern Feminist Interpretation

A non-Keres feminist, reading this tale, is likely to wrongly suppose that this narrative is about the importance of men and the use of a passive female figure as a pawn in their bid for power. And, given the way Gunn renders the story, a modern feminist would have good reason to make such an inference. As Gunn recounts it, the story opens in classic patriarchal style and implies certain patriarchal complications: that Kochinnenako has married a man who is violent and destructive. She is the ruler's daughter, which might suggest that the traditional

Keres are concerned with the abuses of power of the wealthy. This in turn suggests that the traditional Keres social system, like the traditional Anglo-European ones, suffer from oppressive class structures in which the rich and powerful bring misery to the people, who in the tale are reduced to bare subsistence seemingly as a result of Kochinnenako's unfortunate alliance. A reader making the usual assumptions western readers make when enjoying folktales will think she is reading a sort of Robin Hood story, replete with a lovely maid Marian, an evil Sheriff, and a green-clad agent of social justice with the Indian name Miochin.

Given the usual assumptions that underlie European folktales, the Western romantic view of the Indian, and the usual antipatriarchal bias that characterizes feminist analysis, a feminist reader might assume that Kochinnenako has been compelled to make an unhappy match by her father the ruler, who must be gaining some power from the alliance. Besides, his name is given as Broken Prayer Stick, which might be taken to mean that he is an unholy man, remiss in his religious duties and weak spiritually.

Gunn's tale does not clarify these issues. Instead it proceeds in a way best calculated to confirm a feminist's interpretation of the tale as only another example of the low status of women in tribal cultures. In accordance with this entrenched American myth, Gunn makes it clear that Kochinnenako is not happy in her marriage; she thinks Sh-ah-cock is "cold and disagreeable, and she cannot love him." Certainly, contemporary American women will read that to mean that Sh-ah-cock is an emotionally uncaring, perhaps cruel husband and that Kochinnenako is forced to accept a life bereft of warmth and love. A feminist reader might imagine that Kochinnenako, like many women, has been socialized into submission. So obedient is she, it seems, so lacking in spirit and independence, that she doesn't seize her chance to escape a bad situation, preferring instead to remain obedient to the patriarchal institution of marriage. As it turns out (in Gunn's tale), Kochinnenako is delivered from the clutches of her violent and unwanted mate by the timely intervention of a much more pleasant man, the hero.

A radical feminist is likely to read the story for its content vis à vis racism and resistance to oppression. From a radical perspective, it seems politically significant that Sh-ah-cock is white. That is, winter is white. Snow is white. Blizzards are white. Clearly, while the story does not give much support to concepts of a people's struggles, it could be construed to mean that the oppressor is designated white in the story because the Keres are engaged in serious combat with white colonial power and, given the significance of storytelling in tribal cultures, are chronicling that struggle in this tale. Read this way, it would seem to acknowledge the right and duty of the people in overthrowing the hated white dictator, who by this account possesses the power of life and death over them.

· · ·

A radical lesbian separatist might find herself uncomfortable with the story even though it is so clearly correct in identifying the enemy as white and violent. But the overthrow of the tyrant is placed squarely in the hands of another male figure, Miochin. This rescue is likely to be viewed with a jaundiced eye by many feminists (though more romantic women might be satisfied with it, since it's a story about an Indian woman of long ago), as Kochinnenako has to await the coming of a handsome stranger for her salvation, and her fate is decided by her father and the more salutary suitor Miochin. No one asks Kochinnenako what she wants to do; the reader is informed that her marriage is not to her liking when she admits to Miochin that she is unhappy. Nevertheless, Kochinnenako acts like any passive, dependent woman who is exploited by the males in her life, who get what they want regardless of her own needs or desires.

Some readers (like myself) might find themselves wondering hopefully whether Miochin isn't really female, disguised by males as one of them in order to buttress their position of relative power. After all, this figure is dressed in yellow and green, the colors of corn, a plant always associated with Woman. Kochinnenako and her sisters are all Corn Women and her mother is, presumably, the head of the Corn Clan; and the Earth Mother of the Keres, Iyatiku, is Corn Woman herself. Alas, I haven't yet found evidence to support such a wishful notion, except that the mask dancer who impersonates Kochinnenako is male, dressed female, which is sort of the obverse side of the wish.

A Feminist-Tribal Interpretation

The feminist interpretation I have sketched—which is a fair representation of one of my early readings from what I took to be a feminist perspective—proceeds from two unspoken assumptions: that women are essentially powerless and that conflict is basic to human existence. The first is a fundamental position, while the second is basic to Anglo-European thought; neither, however, is characteristic of Keres thought. To a modern feminist, marriage is an institution developed to establish and maintain male supremacy; because she is the ruler's daughter, Kochinnenako's choice of a husband determines which male will hold power over the people and who will inherit the throne.[4]

When Western assumptions are applied to tribal narratives, they become mildly confusing and moderately annoying from any perspective. Western assumptions about the nature of human society (and thus of literature) when contextualizing a tribal story or ritual must necessarily leave certain elements unclear. If the battle between Summer Spirit and Winter Spirit is about the triumph of warmth, generosity, and kindness over coldness, miserliness, and cruelty, supremacy of the good over the bad, why does the hero grant his antagonist rights over the village and Kochinnenako for half of each year?

The contexts of Anglo-European and Keres Indian life differ so greatly in virtually every assumption about the nature of reality, society, ethics, female roles, and the sacred importance of seasonal change that simply telling a Keres tale within an Anglo-European narrative context creates a dizzying series of false impressions and unanswerable (perhaps even unposable) questions.

· · ·

Agency is Kochinnenako's ritual role here; it is through her ritual agency that the orderly, harmonious transfer of primacy between the Summer and Winter people is accomplished. This transfer takes place at the time of the year that Winter goes north and Summer comes to the pueblo from the south, the time when the sun moves north along the line it makes with the edge of the sun's house as ascertained by the hocheni calendar keeper who determines the proper solar and astronomical times for various ceremonies. Thus, in the proper time, Kochinnenako empowers Summer to enter the village.

Kochinnenako's careful observance of the ritual requirements together with the proper conduct of her sisters, her mother, the priests (symbolized by the title Hutchamun Kiuk, whom Gunn identifies as the ruler and Yellow Woman's father, though he could as properly—more properly, actually—be called her mother), the animals and birds, the weather, and the people at last brings summer to the village, ending the winter and the famine that accompanies winter's end.

A feminist who is conscious of tribal thought and practice will know that the real story of Sh-ah-cock and Miochin underscores the central role that woman plays in the orderly life of the people. Reading Gunn's version, she will be aware of the vast gulf between the Lagunas and John Gunn in their understanding of the role of women in a traditional gynecentric society such as that of the western Keres. Knowing that the central role of woman is harmonizing spiritual relationships between the people and the rest of the universe by empowering ritual activities, she will be able to read the story for its western colonial content, aware that Gunn's version reveals more about American consciousness when it meets tribal thought than it reveals about the tribe. When the story is analyzed within the context to which it rightly belongs, its feminist content becomes clear, as do the various purposes to which industrialized patriarchal people can put a tribal story.

· · ·

The net effect of Gunn's rendition of the story is the unhappy wedding of the woman-centered tradition of the western Keres to patriarchal Anglo-European tradition and thus the dislocation of the central position of Keres women by their assumption under the rule of the men. When one understands that the hocheni is the person who tells the time and prays for all the people, even the white people, and that the Hutchamun Kiuk is the ruler only in the sense that the Constitution of the United States is the ruler of the citizens and government of the United States, then the Keres organization of women, men, spirit folk, equinoxes, seasons, and clouds into a balanced and integral dynamic will be seen reflected in the narrative. Knowing this, a feminist will also be able to see how the interpolations of patriarchal thinking distort all the relationships in the story and, by extension, how such impositions

of patriarchy on gynocracy disorder harmonious social and spiritual relationships.

A careful feminist-tribal analysis of Gunn's rendition of a story that would be better titled "The Transfer of Ianyi (ritual power, sacred power) from Winter to Summer" will provide a tribally conscious feminist with an interesting example of how colonization works, however consciously or unconsciously to misinform both the colonized and the colonizer. She will be able to note the process by which the victim of the translation process, the Keres woman who reads the tale, is misinformed because she reads Gunn's book. Even though she knows that something odd is happening in the tale, she is not likely to apply sophisticated feminist analysis to the rendition; in the absence of real knowledge of the colonizing process of story-changing, she is all too likely to find bits of the Gunn tale sticking in her mind and subtly altering her perception of herself, her role in her society, and her relationship to the larger world.

The hazard to male Keres readers is, of course, equally great. They are likely to imagine that the proper relationship of women to men is subservience. And it is because of such a shockingly untraditional modern interpretation, brought on as much by reading Gunn as by other, perhaps more obvious societal mechanisms, that the relationships between men and women are so severely disordered at Laguna that wife-abuse, rape, and battery of women there has reached frightening levels in recent years.

· · ·

TRIBAL NARRATIVES AND WOMEN'S LIVES

Reading American Indian traditional stories and songs is not an easy task. Adequate comprehension requires that the reader be aware that Indians never think like whites and that any typeset version of traditional materials is distorting.

In many ways, literary conventions, as well as the conventions of literacy, militate against an understanding of traditional tribal materials. Western technological-industrialized minds cannot adequately interpret tribal materials because they are generally trained to perceive their entire world in ways that are alien to tribal understandings.

This problem is not exclusive to tribal literature. It is one that all ethnic writers who write out of a tribal or folk tradition face, and one that is also shared by women writers, who, after all, inhabit a separate folk tradition. Much of women's culture bears marked resemblance to tribal culture. The perceptual modes that women, even those of us who are literate, industrialized, and reared within masculinist academic traditions, habitually engage in more closely resemble inclusive-field perception than excluding foreground-background perceptions.

Women's traditional occupations, their arts and crafts, and their literature and philosophies are more often accretive than linear, more achronological than chronological, and more dependent on harmonious relationships of all elements within a field of perception than western culture in general is thought to be. Indeed, the patchwork quilt is the best material example I can think of to describe the plot and process of a traditional tribal narrative, and quilting is a non-Indian woman's art, one that Indian women have taken to avidly and that they display in their ceremonies, rituals, and social gatherings as well as in their homes.

It is the nature of woman's existence to be and to create background. This fact, viewed with unhappiness by many feminists, is of ultimate importance in a tribal context. Certainly no art object is bereft of background. Certainly the contents and tone of one's background will largely determine the direction and meaning of one's life and, therefore, the meaning and effect of one's performance in any given sphere of activity.

Westerners have for a long time discounted the importance of background. The earth herself, which is our most inclusive background, is dealt with summarily as a source of food, metals, water, and profit, while the fact that she is the fundamental agent of all planetary life is blithely ignored. Similarly, women's activities—cooking, planting, harvesting, preservation, storage, homebuilding, decorating, maintaining, doctoring, nursing, soothing, and healing, along with the bearing, nurturing, and rearing of children—are devalued as blithely. An anti-background bias is bound to have social costs that have so far remained unexplored, but elite attitudes toward workers, nonwhite races, and women are all part of the price we pay for overvaluing the foreground.

In the western mind, shadows highlight the foreground. In contrast, in the tribal view the mutual relationships among shadows and light in all their varying degrees of intensity create a living web of definition and depth, and significance arises from their interplay. Traditional and contemporary tribal arts and crafts testify powerfully to the importance of balance among all elements in tribal perception, aesthetics, and social systems.

Traditional peoples perceive their world in a unified-field fashion that is very different from the single-focus perception that generally characterizes western masculinist, monotheistic modes of perception. Because of this, tribal cultures are consistently misperceived and misrepresented by nontribal folklorists, ethnographers, artists, writers, and social workers. A number of scholars have recently addressed this issue, but they have had little success because the demands of type and of analysis are, after all, linear and fixed, while the requirements of tribal literatures are accretive and fluid. The one is unidimensional, monolithic, excluding, and chronological while the other is multidimensional, achronological, and including.

How one teaches or writes about the one perspective in terms of the other is problematic. This essay itself is a pale representation of a tribal understanding of the Kochinnenako tale. I am acutely aware that much of what I have said is likely to be understood in ways I did not intend, and I am also aware of how much I did not say that probably needed to be said if the real story of the transfer of responsibility from one segment of the tribe to the other is to be made clear.

In the end, the tale I have analyzed is not about Kochinnenako or Sh-ah-cock and Miochin. It is about the change of seasons and it is about the centrality of woman as agent and empowerer of that change. It is about how a people engage themselves as a people within the spiritual cosmos and in an ordered and proper way that bestows the dignity of each upon all with careful respect, folkish humor, and ceremonial delight. It is about how everyone is part of the background that shapes the meaning and value of each person's life. It is about propriety, mutuality, and the dynamics of socioenvironmental change.

[1986]

NOTES

1. John M. Gunn, *Schat Chen: History, Traditions and Narratives of the Queres Indians of Laguna and Acoma* (Albuquerque, N. Mex.: Albright and Anderson, 1917; reprint,

New York: AMS, 1977). Gunn, my mother's uncle, lived among the Lagunas all his adult life. He spoke Laguna (Keres) and gathered information in somewhat informal ways while sitting in the sun visiting with older people. He married Meta Atseye, my great-grandmother, years after her husband (John Gunn's brother) died and may have taken much of his information from her stories or explanations of Laguna ceremonial events. She had a way of "translating" terms and concepts from Keres into English and from a Laguna conceptual framework into an American one, as she understood it. For example, she used to refer to the Navajo people as "gypsies," probably because they traveled in covered wagons and the women wear long, full skirts and head scarves and both men and women wear a great deal of jewelry.

2.   Gunn, *Schat Chen*, pp. 217–222.

3.   Boas, *Keresan Texts*, p. 288. Boas says he made the same mistake at first, having misheard the word they used.

4.   For a detailed exposition of what this dynamic consists of, see Adrienne Rich, "Compulsory Heterosexuality and Lesbian Existence," *Signs: Journal of Women in Culture and Society,* vol. 5, no. 4 (Summer 1980). Reprinted in 1982 as a pamphlet with an updated foreward, Antelope Publications, 1612 St. Paul, Denver, CO 80206.

 71

Jewish Memory From a Feminist Perspective

JUDITH PLASKOW

There is perhaps no verse in the Torah more disturbing to the feminist than Moses' warning to his people in Exodus 19:15, "Be ready for the third day; do not go near a woman." For here, at the very moment that the Jewish people stand at Mount Sinai ready to enter into the covenant—not now the covenant with the individual patriarchs but presumably with the people as a whole—Moses addresses the community only as men. The specific issue is ritual impurity: an emission of semen renders both a man and his female partner temporarily unfit to approach the sacred (Leviticus 15:16–18). But Moses does not say, "Men and women do not go near each other." At the central moment of Jewish history, women are invisible. It was not their experience that interested the chronicler or that informed and shaped the text.

This verse sets forth a pattern recapitulated again and again in Jewish sources. Women's invisibility at the moment of entry into the covenant is reflected in the content of the covenant which, in both grammar and substance, addresses the community as male heads of household. It is perpetuated by the later tradition that in its comments and codifications takes women as objects of concern or legislation but rarely sees them as shapers of tradition and actors in their own right.

It is not just a historical injustice that is at stake in this verse, however. There is another dimension to the problem of the Sinai passage essential for understanding the task of Jewish feminism today. Were this passage simply the record of a historical event long in the past, the exclusion of women at this critical juncture would be troubling, but also comprehensible for its time. The Torah is not just history, however, but also living memory. The Torah reading, as a central part of the Sabbath and holiday liturgy, calls to mind and recreates the past for succeeding generations. When the story of Sinai is recited as part of the annual cycle of Torah readings or as a special reading for Shavuot, women each time hear ourselves thrust aside anew, eavesdropping on a conversation among men and between man and God.[1]

Significant and disturbing as this passage is, however, equally significant is the tension between it and the reality of the Jewish woman who hears or reads it. The passage affronts because of a contradiction between the holes in the text and many women's felt experience. If Moses' words shock and anger, it is because women have always known or assumed our presence at Sinai; the passage is painful because it seems to deny what we have always taken for granted. On the one hand, of course we were there; on the other, how is it then that the text could imply we were not there?

This contradiction seems to me crucial, for construed a certain way, it is a potential bridge to a new relationship with the tradition. On the one hand, women can choose to accept our absence from Sinai, in which case we allow the male text to define us and our relationship to the tradition. On the other hand, we can stand on the ground of our experience, on the certainty of our membership in our own people. To do this, however, is to be forced to re-member and recreate its history. It is to move from anger at the tradition, through anger to empowerment. It is to begin the journey toward the creation of a feminist Judaism.

GIVE US OUR HISTORY

The notion that a feminist Judaism must reclaim Jewish history requires some explication, for it is by no means generally accepted. There are many Jewish feminists who feel that women can take on positions of authority, create new liturgy, and do what we need to do to create a community responsive to our needs in the present without dredging around in a history that can only cause us pain. What we need to do, according to this view, is to acknowledge and accept the patriarchal nature of the Jewish past and then get on with issues of contemporary change.

But while the notion of accepting women's past subordination and attending to the present has some attractiveness, it strikes me as in the end untenable. If it is possible within any historical, textual tradition to create a present in dramatic discontinuity with the past—and I doubt that it is—it certainly seems impossible within Judaism. For as I have already suggested, the central events of the Jewish past are not simply history but living, active memory that continues to shape Jewish identity and self-understanding. In Judaism, memory is not simply a given but a religious obligation.[2] "We Jews are a community based on memory," says Martin Buber. "The spiritual life of the Jews is part and parcel of their memory."[3] It is in retelling the story of our past as Jews that we learn who we truly are in the present.

While the Passover Seder is perhaps the most vivid example of the importance of memory in Judaism, the rabbinic reconstruction of Jewish history after the destruction of the second Temple provides an example of remembrance that is also recreation. So deeply is the Jewish present rooted in Jewish history that, after 70 C.E., when the rabbis profoundly transformed Jewish life, the changes they wrought in Jewish reality were also read back into the past so that they could be read out of the past as a foundation for the present. Again and again in rabbinic interpretations, we find contemporary practice projected back into earlier periods so that the chain of tradition can remain unbroken. In Genesis, for example, Abraham greets his three angelic visitors by killing a calf and serving it to them with milk (18:7–8),

clearly a violation of the laws of kashrut which forbid eating milk and meat together. As later rabbinic sources read the passage, however, Abraham first served his visitors milk and only then meat, a practice permitted by rabbinic law.[4] The links between past and present were felt so passionately that any important change in the present had to entail a new understanding of history.

This has an important moral for Jewish feminists. We too cannot redefine Judaism in the present without redefining our past because our present grows out of our history. The Jewish need to reconstruct the past in light of the present converges with the feminist need to recover women's history within Judaism. Knowing that women are active members of the Jewish community in the present, we know that we were always part of the community, not simply as objects of male purposes but as subjects and shapers of tradition. To accept androcentric texts and contemporary androcentric histories as the whole of Jewish history is to enter into a secret collusion with those who would exclude us from full membership in the Jewish community. It is to accept the idea that men were the only significant agents in Jewish history when we would never accept this (still current) account of contemporary Jewish life. The Jewish community today is a community of women and men, and it has never been otherwise. It is time, therefore, to recover our history as the history of women and men, a task that will both restore our own history to women and provide a fuller Jewish history for the Jewish community as a whole.[5]

HISTORY, HISTORIOGRAPHY, AND TORAH

It is one thing to see the importance of recovering women's history, however, and another to accomplish this task in a meaningful way. First of all, as historian, the Jewish feminist faces all the same problems as any feminist historian trying to recover women's experience: both her sources and the historians who have gone before her record male activities and male deeds in accounts ordered by male values. What we know of women's past are those things men considered significant to remember, seen and interpreted through a value system that places men at the center.[6] But, as if this were not enough, the Jewish feminist faces additional problems raised by working with religious sources. The primary Jewish sources available to her for historical reconstruction are not simply collections of historical materials but also Torah. As Torah, as Jewish teaching, they are understood by the tradition to represent divine revelation, patterns of living adequate for all time. In seeking to restore the history of Jewish women, the Jewish feminist historian is not "simply" trying to revolutionize the writing of history but is also implicitly or explicitly acting as theologian, claiming to amplify Torah, and thus questioning the finality of the Torah we have. It is important, therefore, in placing the recovery of women's history in the context of a feminist Judaism to confront the view of Torah that this implies.

I understand Torah, both in the narrow sense of the five books of Moses and in the broader sense of Jewish teaching, to be the partial record of the "Godwrestling" of part of the Jewish people.[7] Again and again in the course of its existence, the Jewish people has felt itself called by and held accountable to a power not of its own making, a power that seemed to direct its destiny and give meaning to its life. In both ordinary and extraordinary moments, it has found itself guided by a reality that both propelled and sustained it and to which gratitude and obedience seemed the only fitting response.

The term "Godwrestling" seems appropriate to me to describe the written residue of these experiences, for I do not imagine them à la Cecil B. DeMille as the booming of a clear (male) voice or the flashing of tongues of flame, publicly visible, publicly verifiable, needing only to be transcribed. Rather, they were moments of profound experience, sometimes of ilumination but also of mystery, moments when some who had eyes to see understood the meaning of events that all had undergone. Such illumination might be hard-won, or sudden experiences of clarity or presence that come unexpected as precious gifts. But they would need to be interpreted and applied, struggled with and puzzled over, passed down and lived out before they came to us as the Torah of God.

I call this record partial, for moments of intense religious experience cannot be pinned down and reproduced; they can only be suggested and pointed to so that readers or listeners may, from time to time, catch for themselves the deeper reality vibrating behind the text. Moreover, while moments of revelation may lead to abandonment of important presuppositions and openness to ideas and experiences that are genuinely new, they also occur within cultural frameworks that can never be escaped entirely, so that the more radical implications of a new understanding may not even be seen. I call Torah the record of part of the Jewish people because the experience and wrestling found there are for the most part those of men. The experience of being summoned and saved by a single power, the experience of human likeness to the creator God, the experiences of liberation and God's passion for justice were sustained within a patriarchal framework that the interpretation of divine revelation served to consolidate rather than shatter.[8]

There is a strand in the tradition that acknowledges this partiality of Torah and thus indirectly allows us to see what is at stake in the recovery of women's past. According to many ancient Jewish sources, the Torah pre-existed the creation of the world. It was the first of God's works, identified with the divine wisdom in Proverbs 8. It was written with black fire on white fire and rested on the knee of God. It was the architectural plan God consulted in creating the universe.[9] For the Kabbalists, this pre-existent or primordial Torah is God's wisdom and essence; it expresses the immensity of God's being and power. The written Torah of ink and parchment is only the "outer garments," a limited interpretation of what lies hidden, a document that the initiate must penetrate more and more deeply to gain momentary glimpses of what lies behind. A later development of the idea of a secret Torah asserted that each of the 600,000 souls that stood at Sinai had its own special portion of Torah that only that soul could understand.[10] Obviously, no account of revelatory experience by men or women can describe or exhaust the depths of divine reality. But this image of the relation between hidden and manifest Torah reminds us that half the souls of Israel have not left for us the Torah they have seen. Insofar as we can begin to recover the God-wrestling of women, insofar as we can restore a part of their vision and experience, we have more of the primordial Torah, the divine fullness, of which the present Torah of Israel is only a fragment and a sign.

The recovery of primordial Torah is a large task, however, to ask "history" to perform. And in fact, in the foregoing discussion, I have been slipping back and forth between different meanings and levels of the term "history." The rabbinic reconstruction of history, which I used as an example of rewriting Jewish history, by no means involved "doing history" in our modern sense. On the contrary, it was anachronistic and ahistorical. Taking for granted the historical factuality of the momentous events at Sinai, the rabbis turned their attention to mining their eternal significance. Reshaping Jewish memory did not involve discovering what "really happened," but projecting later developments back onto the eternal present of Sinai.[11]

Recovering women's history through modern historiography, a second meaning of history that I have used implicitly, is not just different from rabbinic modes of thinking, it is in conflict with them. It assumes precisely that the original revelation, at least as we have it, is not sufficient, that there are enormous gaps both in tradition and in the scriptural record, that to recapture women's experiences we need to go behind our records and *add* to Torah, acknowledging that that is what we are doing.[12]

But while the tensions between feminist and traditional approaches to Jewish history are significant and real, there is one important thing they have in common. The feminist too is not simply interested in acquiring more knowledge about the past but in incorporating women's history as part of the living memory of the Jewish people. Information about women's past may be instructive and even stirring, but it is not transformative until it becomes part of the community's collective memory, part of what Jews call to mind in remembering Jewish history. While historiographical research may be crucial to recovering women's history, it is not sufficient to make that history live. The Jewish feminist reshaping of Jewish history must therefore proceed on several levels at once. Feminist historiography can open up new questions to be brought to the past and new perspectives to be gleaned from it. It must be combined, however, with feminist midrash, or storytelling, and feminist liturgy before it becomes part of a living feminist Judaism.

RESHAPING JEWISH MEMORY

Feminist historiography as a starting point for the feminist reconstruction of Jewish memory challenges the traditional androcentric view of Jewish history and opens up our understanding of the Jewish past. In the last two decades, feminist historians have demanded and effected a far-reaching reorientation of the presuppositions and methods of historical writing. Questioning the assumption that men have made history while women have stayed home and had babies, they have insisted that women and men have lived and shaped history together. Any account of a period or civilization that does not look at the roles of both women and men, their relation and interaction, is "men's history" rather than the universal history it generally claims to be.[13]

Any number of examples might show how the insights and methods of feminist historians have been applied to Jewish women's history. Archeologist Carol Meyers, for instance, has begun to reconstruct the roles of women in ancient Israel through a combination of biblical and archeological evidence. She asks important new questions about the changing roles of women in biblical society, questions that point to the social construction of gender in biblical culture. In the period of early settlement, she argues, when women's biological and agricultural contributions would have been crucial, their status was likely higher than in the different cultural context of the monarchy. Restrictions on women's roles that were initially practical only later became the basis for "ideologies of female inferiority and subordination."[14] New Testament scholar Bernadette Brooten, working on the inscriptional evidence for women's leadership in the ancient synagogue, shows that during the Roman and Byzantine periods, women took on important synagogue functions in a number of corners of the Jewish world.[15] Her research on the inscriptions, and also on Jewish women's exercise of the right to divorce,[16] sheds light on the wider social world in which the Mishnah (a second century code of Jewish law) emerged, clarifying and questioning the extent of its authority. Chava Weissler's work on the *tekhines*, the petitionary prayers of Eastern European Jewish women, provides us with sources that come in part from women's hands, giving us an intimate view of women's perceptions. While these sources have often been dismissed as "women's literature" or relegated to casual reading, they give us important glimpses of women's religious experiences. They also make us aware of the subtle interplay between the ways women have found to express themselves and the influence of patriarchal religion.[17]

While none of this women's history alters the fundamentally androcentric perspective of "normative" texts or proves that Judaism is really egalitarian, it does reveal another world around and underneath the textual tradition, a world in which women are historical agents struggling within and against a patriarchal culture. In the light of women's history, we cannot see the Tanakh (the Bible) or the Mishnah or any Jewish text simply as given, as having emerged organically from an eternal, unambiguous, uncontested religious vision. Indeed, feminist historians have come to recognize that religious, literary, and philosophical works setting forth women's nature or tasks are often prescriptive rather than descriptive of reality. So far from giving us the world "as it is," "normative" texts may reflect the tensions within patriarchal culture, seeking to maintain a particular view of the world over against social, political, or religious change.[18] "Normative" texts reflect the views of the historical winners, winners whose victories were often achieved at the expense of women and of religious forms that allowed women some power and scope.[19] Insofar as women's religious and social self-expression and empowerment are values we bring to these texts, the texts are relativized, their normative status shaken. We see them against the background of alternative religious possibilities, alternatives that must now be taken seriously because without them, we have only the Judaism of a male elite and not the Judaism of all Jews.

Recovering Jewish women's history, then, extends the realm of the potentially usable Jewish past. Women's experiences expand the domain of Jewish resources on which we can drawn in recreating Judaism in the present. In writing women into Jewish history, we ground a contemporary Jewish community that can be a community of women and men. But historiography by itself cannot reshape Jewish memory. The gaps in the historical record alone would prompt us to seek other ways of remembering. However sensitively we read between the lines of mainstream texts seeking to recapture the reality of women's lives, however carefully we mine nonliterary and non-Jewish materials using them to challenge "normative" sources, many of our constructions will remain speculations and many of our questions will go unanswered.

Moreover, even if it were not the case that the sources are sparse and unconcerned with our most urgent questions, feminist historiography would still provide only a fragile grounding for Jewish feminist memory. For historiography recalls events that memory does not recognize.[20] It challenges memory, ties to dethrone it; it calls it partial and distorted. History provides a more and more complex and nuanced picture of the past; memory is selective. How do we recover the parts of Jewish women's history that are forgotten, and how do we then ensure that they will be *remembered*—incorporated into our communal sense of self?

The answer to these questions is partly connected to the wider reconstruction of Jewish life. We turn to the past with new questions because of present commitments, but we also remember more deeply what a changed present requires us to know. Yet Jewish feminists are already entering into a new relationship with history based not simply on historiography but also on more traditional strategies for Jewish remembrance. The rabbinic reconstruction of Jewish history, after all, was not historiographical but midrashic. Assuming the infinite meaningfulness of biblical texts, the rabbis took passages that were sketchy or troubling and wrote them forward. They brought to the Bible their own questions and found answers that showed the eternal relevance of biblical truth. Why was Abraham chosen to be the father of a people? What was the status of the law before the Torah was given? Who was Adam's first wife? Why was Dinah raped? These were not questions for historical investigation but imaginative exegesis and literary amplification.

The open-ended process of writing midrash, simultaneously serious and playful, imaginative, metaphoric, has easily lent itself to feminist use. While feminist midrash—like all midrash—is a reflection of contemporary beliefs and experiences, its root conviction is utterly traditional. It stands on the rabbinic insistence that the Bible can be made to speak to the present day. If the Torah is our text, it can and must answer our questions and share our values; if we wrestle with it, it will yield meaning.

Together and individually then, orally and in writing, women are exploring and telling stories that connect our history with present experience. Ellen Umansky, for example, retelling the story of the sacrifice of Isaac from Sarah's perspective, explores the dilemma of a woman in patriarchal culture trying to hold onto her sense of self. Isaac was God's gift to Sarah in her old age. She has no power to prevent Abraham's journey to Moriah; she can only wait wailing and trembling for him to return. But she is angry; she knows that God does not require such sacrifices. Abraham cannot deprive her of her own religious understanding, whatever demands he may make upon her as his wife.[21]

While midrash can float entirely free from historiography, as it does in this example, the latter can also feed the former so that midrash plays with historical clues but extends them beyond the boundaries of the fragmentary evidence. In her midrash on the verse, "And Dinah . . . went out to see the daughters of the land" (Genesis 34:1), Lynn Gottlieb explores the possible relations between Dinah and Canaanite women based on the presumption of Israelite women's historical attachment to many gods and goddesses.[22] A group of my students once used the same historical theme to write their own midrash on the sacrifice of Isaac as experienced by Sarah. In their version, Sarah, finding Abraham and Isaac absent, calls to Yahweh all day without avail. Finally, almost in despair, she takes out her Asherah and prays to it, only to see her husband and son over the horizon wending their way home.

Moving from history into midrash, Jewish feminists cross a boundary to be both honored and ignored. Certainly, there is a difference between an ancient Aramaic divorce document written by a woman and a modern midrash on Miriam and Sarah. The former confronts and challenges; it invites us to find a framework for understanding the past broad enough to include data at odds with selective memory. The latter is more fully an expression of our own convictions, a creative imagining based on our own experience. Yet in the realm of Jewish religious expression, imagination is permitted and even encouraged. Midrash is not a violation of historical canons but an enactment of commitment to the fruitfulness and relevance of biblical texts. It is partly through midrash that the figurine or document, potentially integrable into memory but still on the periphery, is transformed into narrative the religious ear can hear. The discovery of women in our history can feed the impulse to create midrash; midrash can seize on history and make it religiously meaningful. Remembering and inventing together help recover the hidden half of Torah, reshaping Jewish memory to let women speak.

There is also a third mode of recovery: speaking/acting. Historically, the primary vehicle for transmission of Jewish memory has been prayer and ritual, the liturgical reenactment and celebration of formative events. Midrash can instruct, amuse, edify, but the cycles of the week and year have been the most potent reminders of central Jewish experience and values. The entry of the High Priest into the Holy of Holies on the Day of Atonement, the Exodus of Israel from Egypt every Passover: these are remembered not just verbally but through the body and thus doubly imprinted on Jewish consciousness.

Liturgy and ritual, therefore, have been particularly important areas for Jewish feminist inventiveness. Feminists have been writing liturgy and ritual that flow from and incorporate women's experience, in the process drawing on history and midrash but also allowing them to emerge from concrete forms. One of the earliest and most tenacious feminist rituals, for example, is the celebration of Rosh Hodesh, the new moon, as a woman's holiday. The numerous Rosh Hodesh groups that have sprung up around the country in the last decade have experimented with new spiritual forms within the framework of a traditional women's observance that had been largely forgotten. The association of women with the moon at the heart of the original ceremony provides a starting point for exploration of women's symbols within Judaism and cross-culturally. At the same time, the simplicity of the traditional ritual leaves ample space for invention.[23] Feminist haggadot, on the other hand, seek to inject women's presence into an already established ritual, building on the theme of liberation to make women's experience and struggle an issue for the Seder. Drawing on history, poetry, and midrash, they seek to integrate women's experiences into the central Jewish story and central ritual enactment of the Jewish year.[24]

These two areas have provided basic structures around which a great deal of varied experimentation has taken place. But from reinterpretations of mikveh, to a major reworking of Sabbath blessings, to simple inclusion of the *imahot* (matriarchs) in daily and Sabbath liturgies—which, however minimally, says, "We too had a covenant; we too were there"—women are seeking to transform Jewish ritual so that it acknowledges our existence and experience.[25] In the ritual moment, women's history is made present.

We have then an interweaving of forms that borrow from and give life to each other. Women's history challenges us to confront the incompleteness of what has been called "Jewish history," to attend to the hidden and hitherto marginal, to attempt a true Jewish history which is a history of women and men. It restores to us some of women's voices in and out of the "normative" tradition, sometimes in accommodation and sometimes in struggle, but the voices of Jews defining their own Jewishness as they participate in the communal life. Midrash expands and burrows, invents the forgotten and prods the memory, takes from history and asks for more. It gives us the inner life history cannot follow, building links between the stories of our foremothers and our own joy and pain. Ritual asserts women's presence in the present. Borrowing from history and midrash, it transforms them into living memory. Creating new forms, it offers them to be remembered.

Thus, through diverse paths, we re-member ourselves. Moses' injunction at Sinai—"Do not go near a woman"—though no less painful, is only part of a story expanded and reinvigorated as women enter into the shaping of Torah. If in Jewish terms history provides a basis for identity, then out of our new sense of identity we are also claiming our past. Beginning with the conviction of our presence both at Sinai and now, we rediscover and invent ourselves in the Jewish communal past and present, continuing the age-old process of reshaping Jewish memory as we reshape the community today.

[1986]

NOTES

1. Rachel Adler, "'I've Had Nothing Yet So I Can't Take More,'" *Moment* 8 (Sept. 1983): 22–23.
2. Yosef Hayim Yerushalmi, *Zakhor: Jewish History and Jewish Memory* (Seattle, WA: University of Washington Press, 1982), 9.
3. Martin Buber, *Israel and the World: Essays in a Time of Crisis* (New York: Schocken Books, 1963), 146.
4. Louis Ginsberg, *The Legends of the Jews,* 7 vols. (Philadelphia: Jewish Publication Society, 1909), 5:235, n. 140.
5. Elisabeth Schüssler Fiorenza, *In Memory of Her: A Feminist Theological Reconstruction of Christian Origins* (New York: Crossroad, 1983), 14–20. I am indebted to Schüssler Fiorenza for this whole paragraph and, indeed, much of my approach to the recovery of Jewish women's history.
6. Gerda Lerner, *The Majority Finds Its Past: Placing Women in History* (New York: Oxford University Press, 1979), 160, 168–169.
7. The term "Godwrestling" comes from Arthur Waskow, *Godwrestling* (New York: Schocken Books, 1978).
8. See Norman K. Gottwald, *The Tribes of Yahweh* (Maryknoll, NY: Orbis Books, 1979), 685.
9. Ginsberg, *The Legends of the Jews,* 1:3–4.
10. Gershom G. Scholem, *On the Kabbalah and Its Symbolism* (New York: Schocken Books, 1965), 37–65.
11. Gershom G. Scholem, "Tradition and Commentary as Religious Categories in Judaism," *Judaism* 15 (Winter 1966): 26.
12. See Yerushalmi, *Zakhor,* 94.
13. Lerner, *The Majority Finds Its Past,* chaps. 10–12, especially pp. 168, 180.
14. Carol Meyers, "The Roots of Restriction: Women in Early Israel," *Biblical Archeologist* 41 (Sept. 1978): 101. See the whole article (pp. 91–103) and also her "Procreation, Production, and Protection: Male-Female Balance in Early Israel," *Journal of the American Academy of Religion* 51 (December 1983): 569–593.
15. Bernadette J. Brooten, *Women Leaders in the Ancient Synagogue: Inscriptional Evidence and Background Issues* (Chico, CA: Scholars Press, 1982).
16. Bernadette J. Brooten, "Could Women Initiate Divorce in Ancient Judaism? The Implications for Mark 10:11–12 and I Corinthians 7:10–11" (The Ernest Cadman Colwell Lecture, School of Theology at Claremont, CA, April 14, 1981).
17. Chava Weissler, "Voices From the Heart: Women's Devotional Prayers," in *The Jewish Almanac,* ed. Richard Siegel and Carl Rheins (New York: Bantam Books, 1980), 541–545.
18. Lerner, *The Majority Finds Its Past,* 149. Schüssler Fiorenza makes this point repeatedly. See, for example, *In Memory of Her,* 60.
19. Sheila Collins, *A Different Heaven and Earth* (Valley Forge, PA: Judson Press), chap. 4; Carol P. Christ, "Heretics and Outsiders: The Struggle Over Female Power in Western Religion," *Soundings* 61 (Fall 1978): 260–280.
20. Yerushalmi, *Zakhor,* 94.
21. Ellen M. Umansky, "Creating a Jewish Feminist Theology: Possibilities and Problems," *Anima* 10 (Spring Equinox 1984): 133–134.
22. Presentation at the First National Havurah Summer Institute, West Hartford, CT, 1980.

23. Arlene Agus, "This Month is for You: Observing Rosh Hodesh as a Woman's Holiday," in *The Jewish Woman: New Perspectives,* ed. Elizabeth Koltun (New York: Schocken Books, 1976), 84–93; Penina Adelman, *Miriam's Well: Rituals for Jewish Women Around the Year* (Fresh Meadows, NY: Biblio Press, 1986).

24. See, for example, Esther Broner, "Honor and Ceremony in Women's Rituals," in *The Politcs of Women's Spirituality: Essays on the Rise of Spiritual Power Within the Feminist Movement,* ed. Charlene Spretnak (Garden City, NY: Doubleday, Anchor Press, 1982), 237–241; Aviva Cantor Zuckoff (now Cantor), "Jewish Women's Haggadah," in *The Jewish Women,* ed. Koltun, 94–102. There are numerous *haggadot* circulating privately.

25. Rachel Adler, "Tumah and Taharah; Ends and Beginnings," in *The Jewish Woman,* ed. Koltun, 63–71; Marcia Falk, "What About God?" *Moment* 10 (March 1985): 32–36, and her essay in *Weaving the Vision: New Patterns in Feminist Spirituality* (San Francisco: Harper, 1989).

 72

From the Woman Question in Science to the Science Question in Feminism

SANDRA HARDING

Feminist scholars have studied women, men, and social relations between the genders within, across, and insistently against the conceptual frameworks of the disciplines. In each area we have come to understand that what we took to be humanly inclusive problematics, concepts, theories, objective methodologies, and transcendental truths are in fact far less than that. Instead, these products of thought bear the mark of their collective and individual creators, and the creators in turn have been distinctively marked as to gender, class, race, and culture.[1] We can now discern the effects of these cultural markings in the discrepancies between the methods of knowing and the interpretations of the world provided by the creators of modern Western culture and those characteristic of the rest of us. Western culture's favored beliefs mirror in sometimes clear and sometimes distorting ways not the world as it is or as we might want it to be, but the social projects of their historically identifiable creators.

The natural sciences are a comparatively recent subject of feminist scrutiny. The critiques excite immense anticipation—or fear—yet they remain far more fragmented and less clearly conceptualized than feminist analyses in other disciplines.

The anticipation and fear are based in the recognition that we are a scientific culture, that scientific rationality has permeated not only the modes of thinking and acting of our public institutions but even the ways we think about the most intimate details of our private lives. Widely read manuals and magazine articles on child rearing and sexual relations gain their authority and popularity by appealing to science. And during the last century, the social use of science has shifted: formerly an occasional assistant, it has become the direct generator of economic, political, and social accumulation and control. Now we can see that the hope to "dominate nature" for the betterment of the species has become the effort to gain unequal access to nature's resources for purposes of social domination. No longer is the scientist—if he ever was—an eccentric and socially marginal genius spending private funds and often private time on whatever purely intellectual pursuits happen to interest him. Only very rarely does his research have no foreseeable social uses. Instead, he (or, more recently, she) is part of a vast work force, is trained from elementary school on to enter academic, industrial, and governmental laboratories where 99+ percent of the research is expected to be immediately applicable to social projects. If these vast industrialized empires, devoted—whether intentionally or not—to material accumulation and social control, cannot be shown to serve the best interests of social progress by appeal to objective, dispassionate, impartial, rational knowledge-seeking, then in our culture they cannot be legitimated at all. Neither God nor tradition is privileged with the same credibility as scientific rationality in modern cultures.

Of course, feminists are not the first group to scrutinize modern science in this way. Struggles against racism, colonialism, capitalism, and homophobia, as well as the counter culture movement of the 1960s and the contemporary ecology and antimilitarism movements, have all produced pointed analyses of the uses and abuses of science. But the feminist criticisms appear to touch especially raw nerves. For one thing, at their best they incorporate the key insights of these other movements while challenging the low priority that specifically feminist concerns have been assigned in such agendas for social reform. For another, they question the division of labor by gender—a social aspect of the organization of human relations that has been deeply obscured by our perceptions of what is "natural" and what is social. Perhaps most disturbingly, they challenge our sense of personal identity at its most prerational level, at the core. They challenge the desirability of the gendered aspects of our personalities and the expression of gender in social practices, which for most men and women have provided deeply satisfying parts of self-identity.

Finally, as a symbol system, gender difference is the most ancient, most universal, and most powerful origin of many morally valued conceptualizations of everything else in the world around us. Cultures assign a gender to such nonhuman entities as hurricanes and mountains, ships and nations. As far back in history as we can see, we have organized our social and natural worlds in terms of gender meanings within which historically specific racial, class, and cultural institutions and meanings have been constructed. Once we begin to theorize gender—to define gender as an analytic category within which humans think about and organize their social activity rather than as a natural consequence of sex difference, or even merely as a social variable assigned to individual people in different ways from culture to culture—we can begin to appreciate the extent to which gender meanings have suffused our belief systems, institutions, and even such apparently gender-free phenomena as our architecture and urban planning. When feminist thinking about science is adequately theorized, we will have a clearer grasp of how scientific activity is and is not gendered in this sense.

Now it is certainly true that racism, classism, and cultural imperialism often more deeply restrict the life opportunities of individuals than does sexism. We can easily see this if we compare the different life opportunities available to women of the same race but in different classes, or of the same class but in different races, in the United States today or at any other time and place in history. Consequently, it is understandable why working-class people and victims of racism and imperialism often place feminist projects low on their political agendas. Further-

more, gender appears only in culturally specific forms. . . . [G]endered social life is produced through three distinct processes: it is the result of assigning dualistic gender metaphors to various perceived dichotomies that rarely have anything to do with sex differences; it is the consequence of appealing to these gender dualisms to organize social activity, of dividing necessary social activities between different groups of humans; it is a form of socially constructed individual identity only imperfectly correlated with either the "reality" or the perception of sex differences. I shall be referring to these three aspects of gender as *gender symbolism* (or, borrowing a term from anthropology, "gender totemism"), *gender structure* (or the division of labor by gender), and *individual gender*. The referents for all three meanings of masculinity and femininity differ from culture to culture, though within any culture the three forms of gender are related to each other. Probably few, if any, symbolic, institutional, or individual identity or behavioral expressions of masculinity and femininity can be observed in all cultures or at all times in history.

But the fact that there are class, race, and cultural differences between women and between men is not, as some have thought, a reason to find gender difference either theoretically unimportant or politically irrelevant. In virtually every culture, gender difference is a pivotal way in which humans identify themselves as persons, organize social relations, and symbolize meaningful natural and social events and processes. And in virtually all cultures, whatever is thought of as manly is more highly valued than what is thought of as womanly. Moreover, we need to recognize that in cultures stratified by both gender and race, gender is always also a racial category and race a gender category. That is, sexist public policies are different for people of the same gender but different race, and racist policies are different for women and men within the same race. One commentator has proposed that we think of these policies as, respectively, racist sexism and sexist racism.[2]

Finally, we shall later examine the important role to be played in emancipatory epistemologies and politics by open recognition of gender differences within racial groups and racial and cultural differences within gender groups. "Difference" can be a slippery and dangerous rallying point for inquiry projects and for politics, but each emancipatory struggle needs to recognize the agendas of other struggles as integral parts of its own in order to succeed. (After all, people of color come in at least two genders, and women are of many colors.) For each struggle, epistemologies and politics grounded in solidarities could replace the problematic ones that appeal to essentialized identities, which are, perhaps, spurious.

For all these reasons, feminist critiques claiming that science, too, is gendered appear deeply threatening to the social order, even in societies such as ours where racism, classism, and imperialism also direct all our lives. Obviously, the different forms of domination use one another as resources and support one another in complex ways. If we find it difficult to imagine the day-to-day details of living in a world no longer structured by racism and classism, most of us do not even know how to start imagining a world in which gender difference, in its equation of masculinity with authority and value, no longer constrains the ways we think, feel, and act. And the day-to-day world we live in is so permeated by scientific rationality as well as gender that to nonfeminists and perhaps even some feminists, the very idea of a feminist critique of scientific rationality appears closer to blasphemy than to social-criticism-as-usual.

Feminists in other fields of inquiry have begun to formulate clear and coherent challenges to the conceptual frameworks of their disciplines. By putting women's perspective on gender symbolism, gender structure, and individual gender at the center of their thinking, they have been able to reconceive the purposes of research programs in anthropology, history, literary criticism, and so forth.[3] They have begun to retheorize the proper subject matters of the understandings these disciplines could provide. But I think the proper subject matters and purposes of a feminist critique of science have, thus far, eluded the firm grip and the clear conceptualizations that are becoming evident in much of this other research. The voice of feminist science criticism alternates among five different kinds of projects, each with its own audience, subject matter, ideas of what science is and what gender is, and set of remedies for androcentrism. In certain respects, the assumptions guiding these analyses directly con-

flict. It is not at all clear how their authors conceive of the theoretical connections between them, nor, therefore, what a comprehensive strategy for eliminating androcentrism from science would look like. This is particularly troublesome because clarity about so fundamental a component of our culture can have powerful effects elsewhere in feminist struggles.

One problem may be that we have been so preoccupied with responding to the sins of contemporary science in the same terms our culture uses to justify these sins that we have not yet given adequate attention to envisioning truly emancipatory knowledge-seeking. We have not yet found the space to step back and image up the whole picture of what science might be in the future. In our culture, reflecting on an appropriate model of rationality may well seem a luxury for the few, but it is a project with immense potential consequences: it could produce a politics of knowledge-seeking that would show us the conditions necessary to transfer control from the "haves" to the "have-nots."

What kind of understanding of science would we have if we began not with the categories we now use to grasp its inequities, misuses, falsities, and obscurities but with those of the biologist protagonist imagined by Marge Piercy in *Woman on the Edge of Time*, who can shift her/his sex at will and who lives in a culture that does not institutionalize (i.e., does not have) gender? or with the assumptions of a world where such categories as machine, human, and animal are no longer either distinct or of cultural interest, as in Anne McCaffrey's *The Ship Who Sang*?[4] Perhaps we should turn to our novelists and poets for a better intuitive grasp of the theory we need. Though often leaders in the political struggles for a more just and caring culture, they are professionally less conditioned than we to respond point by point to a culture's defenses of its ways of being in the world.

FIVE RESEARCH PROGRAMS

To draw attention to the lack of a developed feminist theory for the critique of the natural sciences is not to overlook the contributions these young but flourishing lines of inquiry have made. In a very short period of time, we have derived a far clearer picture of the extent to which science, too, is gendered.

Now we can begin to understand the economic, political, and psychological mechanisms that keep science sexist and that must be eliminated if the nature, uses, and valuations of knowledge-seeking are to become humanly inclusive ones. Each of these lines of inquiry raises intriguing political and conceptual issues, not only for the practices of science and the ways these practices are legitimated but also for each other. Details of these research programs are discussed in following chapters; I emphasize here the problems they raise primarily to indicate the undertheorization of the whole field.

First of all, equity studies have documented the massive historical resistance to women's getting the education, credentials, and jobs available to similarly talented men;[5] they have also identified the psychological and social mechanisms through which discrimination is informally maintained even when the formal barriers have been eliminated. Motivation studies have shown why boys and men more often want to excel at science, engineering, and math than do girls and women.[6] But should women want to become "just like men" in science, as many of these studies assume? That is, should feminism set such a low goal as mere equality with men? And to which men in science should women want to be equal—to underpaid and exploited lab technicians as well as Nobel Prize winners? Moreover, should women want to contribute to scientific projects that have sexist, racist, and classist problematics and outcomes? Should they want to be military researchers? Furthermore, what has been the effect of women's naiveté about the depth and extent of masculine resistance—that is, would women have struggled to enter science if they had understood how little equity would be produced by eliminating the formal barriers against women's participation?[7] Finally, does the increased presence of women in science have any effect at all on the nature of scientific problematics and outcomes?

Second, studies of the uses and abuses of biology, the social sciences, and their technologies have revealed the ways science is used in the service of sexist, racist, homophobic, and classist social projects. Oppressive reproductive policies; white men's management of all women's domestic labor; the stigmatization of, discrimination against, and medical "cure" of homosexuals; gender discrimination in workplaces—all these have been justified on the basis of sexist research and maintained through technologies, developed out of this research, that move control of women's lives from women to men of the dominant group.[8] Despite the importance of these studies, critics of the sexist uses of science often make two problematic assumptions: that there is a value-free, pure scientific research which can be distinguished from the social uses of science; and that there are proper uses of science with which we can contrast its improper uses. Can we really make these distinctions? Is it possible to isolate a value-neutral core from the uses of science and its technologies? And what distinguishes improper from proper uses? Furthermore, each misuse and abuse has been racist and classist as well as oppressive to women. This becomes clear when we note that there are different reproductive policies, forms of domestic labor, and forms of workplace discrimination mandated for women of different classes and races even within U.S. culture at any single moment in history. (Think, for instance, of the current attempt to restrict the availability of abortion and contraceptive information for some social groups at the same time that sterilization is forced on others. Think of the resuscitation of scientifically supported sentimental images of motherhood and nuclear forms of family life for some at the same time that social supports for mothers and nonnuclear families are systematically withdrawn for others.) Must not feminism take on as a central project of its own the struggle to eliminate class society and racism, homophobia and imperialism, in order to eliminate the sexist uses of science?

Third, in the critiques of biology and the social sciences, two kinds of challenges have been raised not just to the actual but to the possible existence of any pure science at all.[9] The selection and definition of problematics—deciding what phenomena in the world need explanation, and defining what is problematic about them—have clearly been skewed toward men's perception of what they find puzzling. Surely it is "bad science" to assume that men's problems are everyone's problems, thereby leaving unexplained many things that women find problematic, and to assume that men's explanations of what they find problematic are undistorted by their gender needs and desires. But is this merely—or, perhaps, even—an example of bad science? Will not the selection and definition of problems always bear the social fingerprints of the dominant groups in a culture? With these questions we glimpse the fundamental value-ladenness of knowledge-seeking and thus the impossibility of distinguishing between bad science and science-as-usual. Furthermore, the design and interpretation of research again and again has proceeded in masculine-biased ways. But if problems are necessarily value-laden, if theories are constructed to explain problems, if methodologies are always theory-laden, and if observations are methodology-laden, can there be value-neutral design and interpretation of research? This line of reasoning leads us to ask whether it is possible that some kinds of value-laden research are nevertheless maximally objective. For example, are overtly antisexist research designs inherently more objective than overtly sexist or, more important, "sex-blind" (i.e., gender-blind) ones? And are antisexist inquiries that are also self-consciously antiracist more objective than those that are not? There are precedents in the history of science for preferring the distinction between objectivity-increasing and objectivity-decreasing social values to the distinction between value-free and value-laden research. A different problem is raised by asking what implications these criticisms of biology and social science have for areas such as physics and chemistry, where the subject matter purportedly is physical nature rather than social beings ("purportedly" because, as we shall see, we must be skeptical about being able to make any clear distinctions between the physical and the nonphysical). What implications could these findings and this kind of reasoning about objectivity have for our understanding of the scientific world view more generally?

Fourth, the related techniques of literary criticism, historical interpretation, and psychoanalysis have been used to "read science as a text" in order to reveal the social meanings—the hidden symbolic and structural agendas—of purportedly value-neutral claims and practices.[10] In textual criticism, metaphors of gender politics in the writings of the fathers of modern science, as well as in the claims made by the defenders of the scientific world view today, are no longer read as individual idiosyncrasies or as irrelevant to the meanings science has for

its enthusiasts. Furthermore, the concern to define and maintain a series of rigid dichotomies in science and epistemology no longer appears to be a reflection of the progressive character of scientific inquiry; rather, it is inextricably connected with specifically masculine—and perhaps uniquely Western and bourgeois—needs and desires. Objectivity vs. subjectivity, the scientist as knowing subject vs. the objects of his inquiry, reason vs. the emotions, mind vs. body—in each case the former has been associated with masculinity and the latter with femininity. In each case it has been claimed that human progress requires the former to achieve domination of the latter.[11]

Valuable as these textual criticisms have been, they raise many questions. What relevance do the writings of the fathers of modern science have to contemporary scientific practice? What theory would justify regarding these metaphors as fundamental components of scientific explanations? How can metaphors of gender politics continue to shape the cognitive form and content of scientific theories and practices even when they are no longer overtly expressed? And can we imagine what a scientific mode of knowledge-seeking would look like that was not concerned to distinguish between objectivity and subjectivity, reason and the emotions?

Fifth, a series of epistemological inquiries has laid the basis for an alternative understanding of how beliefs are grounded in social experiences, and of what kind of experience should ground the beliefs we honor as knowledge.[12] These feminist epistemologies imply a relation between knowing and being, between epistemology and metaphysics, that is an alternative to the dominant epistemologies developed to justify science's modes of knowledge-seeking and ways of being in the world. It is the conflicts between these epistemologies that generate the major themes of this study.

A GUIDE TO FEMINIST EPISTEMOLOGIES

The epistemological problem for feminism is to explain an apparently paradoxical situation. Feminism is a political movement for social change. But many claims, clearly motivated by feminist concerns, made by researchers and theorists in the social sciences, in biology, and in the social studies of the natural sciences appear more plausible—more likely to be confirmed by evidence—than the beliefs they would replace. How can such politicized research be increasing the objectivity of inquiry? On what grounds should these feminist claims be justified?

We can usefully divide the main feminist responses to this apparent paradox into two relatively well-developed solutions and one agenda for a solution. I will refer to these three responses as *feminist empiricism,* the *feminist standpoint,* and *feminist postmodernism.*

Feminist empiricism argues that sexism and androcentrism are social biases correctable by stricter adherence to the existing methodological norms of scientific inquiry. Movements for social liberation "make it possible for people to see the world in an enlarged perspective because they remove the covers and blinders that obscure knowledge and observation."[13] The women's movement produces not only the opportunity for such an enlarged perspective but more women scientists, and they are more likely than men to notice androcentric bias.

This solution to the epistemological paradox is appealing for a number of reasons, not the least because it appears to leave unchallenged the existing methodological norms of science. It is easier to gain acceptance of feminist claims through this kind of argument, for it identifies only bad science as the problem, not science-as-usual.

Its considerable strategic advantage, however, often leads its defenders to overlook the fact that the feminist empiricist solution in fact deeply subverts empiricism. The social identity of the inquirer is supposed to be irrelevant to the "goodness" of the results of research. Scientific method is supposed to be capable of eliminating any biases due to the fact that individual researchers are white or black, Chinese or French, men or women. But feminist empiricism argues that women (or feminists, whether men or women) *as a group* are more likely to produce unbiased and objective results than are men (or nonfeminists) as a group.

Moreover, though empiricism holds that scientific method is sufficent to account for historical increases in the objectivity of the picture of the world that science presents, one can argue that history shows otherwise. It is movements for social liberation that have most increased the objectivity of science, not the norms of science as they have in fact

been practiced, or as philosophers have rationally reconstructed them. Think, for instance, of the effects of the bourgeois revolution of the fifteenth to seventeenth centuries, which produced modern science itself; or of the effects of the proletarian revolution of the nineteenth and early twentieth centuries. Think of the effects on scientific objectivity of the twentieth-century deconstruction of colonialism.

We shall also see that a key origin of androcentric bias can be found in the selection of problems for inquiry, and in the definition of what is problematic about these phenomena. But empiricism insists that its methodological norms are meant to apply only to the "context of justification"—to the testing of hypotheses and interpretation of evidence—not to the "context of discovery" where problems are identified and defined. Thus a powerful source of social bias appears completely to escape the control of science's methodological norms. Finally, it appears that following the norms of inquiry is exactly what often results in androcentric results.

Thus, feminist attempts to reform what is perceived as bad science bring to our attention deep logical incoherences and what, paradoxically, we can call empirical inadequacies in empiricist epistemologies.

The feminist standpoint originates in Hegel's thinking about the relationship between the master and the slave and in the elaboration of this analysis in the writings of Marx, Engels, and the Hungarian Marxist theorist, G. Lukacs. Briefly, this proposal argues that men's dominating position in social life results in partial and perverse understandings, whereas women's subjugated position provides the possibility of more complete and less perverse understandings. Feminism and the women's movement provide the theory and motivation for inquiry and political struggle that can transform the perspective of women into a "standpoint"—a morally and scientifically preferable grounding for our interpretations and explanations of nature and social life. The feminist critiques of social and natural science, whether expressed by women or by men, are grounded in the universal features of women's experience as understood from the perspective of feminism.[14]

While this attempted solution to the epistemological paradox avoids the problems that beset feminist empiricism, it generates its own tensions. First of all, those wedded to empiricism will be loath to commit themselves to the belief that the social identity of the observer can be an important variable in the potential objectivity of research results. Strategically, this is a less convincing explanation for the greater adequacy of feminist claims for all but the already convinced; it is particularly unlikely to appear plausible to natural scientists or natural science enthusiasts.

Considered on its own terms, the feminist standpoint response raises two further questions. Can there be *a* feminist standpoint if women's (or feminists') social experience is divided by class, race, and culture? Must there be Black and white, working-class and professional-class, American and Nigerian feminist standpoints? This kind of consideration leads to the postmodernist skepticism: "Perhaps 'reality' can have 'a' structure only from the falsely universalizing perspective of the master. That is, only to the extent that one person or group can dominate the whole, can 'reality' appear to be governed by one set of rules or be constituted by one privileged set of social relations."[15] Is the feminist standpoint project still too firmly grounded in the historically disastrous alliance between knowledge and power characteristic of the modern epoch? Is it too firmly rooted in a problematic politics of essentialized identities?

Before turning briefly to the feminist postmodernism from which this last criticism emerges, we should note that both of the preceding epistemological approaches appear to assert that objectivity never has been and could not be increased by value-neutrality. Instead, it is commitments to antiauthoritarian, antielitist, participatory, and emancipatory values and projects that increase the objectivity of science. Furthermore, the reader will need to avoid the temptation to leap to relativist understandings of feminist claims. In the first place, feminist inquirers are never saying that sexist and antisexist claims are equally plausible—that it is equally plausible to regard women's situation as primarily biological *and* as primarily social, or to regard "the human" both as identical *and* nonidentical with "the masculine." The *evidence* for feminist vs. nonfeminist claims may be inconclusive in some cases, and many feminist claims that today appear evidentially secure will no doubt be abandoned as additional evidence is gathered and better hypotheses and concepts are constructed. Indeed, there should be no doubt that these normal conditions of research hold for many feminist claims. But agnosticism and recognition of the hypothetical character of all scientific claims are quite different epistemological stances from relativism. Moreover, whether or not feminists take a relativist stance, it is hard to imagine a coherent defense of cognitive relativism when one thinks of the conflicting claims.

Feminist postmodernism challenges the assumptions upon which feminist empiricism and the feminist standpoint are based, although strains of postmodernist skepticism appear in the thought of these theorists, too. Along with such mainstream thinkers as Nietzsche, Derrida, Foucault, Lacan, Rorty, Cavell, Feyerabend, Gadamer, Wittgenstein, and Unger, and such intellectual movements as semiotics, deconstruction, psychoanalysis, structuralism, archeology/genealogy, and nihilism, feminists "share a profound skepticism regarding universal (or universalizing) claims about the existence, nature and powers of reason, progress, science, language and the 'subject/self.'"[16]

This approach requires embracing as a fruitful grounding for inquiry the fractured identities modern life creates: Black-feminist, socialist-feminist, women-of-color, and so on. It requires seeking a solidarity in our oppositions to the dangerous fiction of the naturalized, essentialized, uniquely "human" (read "manly") and to the distortion and exploitation perpetrated on behalf of this fiction. It may require rejecting fantasized returns to the primal wholeness of infancy, preclass societies, or pregender "unitary" consciousnesses of the species—all of which have motivated standpoint epistemologies. From this perspective, feminist claims are more plausible and less distorting only insofar as they are grounded in a solidarity between these modern fractured identities and between the politics they create.

Feminist postmodernism creates its own tensions. In what ways does it, like the empiricist and standpoint epistemologies, reveal incoherences in its parental mainstream discourse? Can we afford to give up the necessity of trying to provide "one, true, feminist story of reality" in the face of the deep alliances between science and sexist, racist, classist, and imperialist social projects?

Clearly, there are contradictory tendencies among the feminist epistemological discourses, and each has its own set of problems. The contradictions and problems do not originate in the feminist discourses, however, but reflect the disarray in mainstream epistemologies and philosophies of science since the mid-1960s. They also reflect shifting configurations of gender, race, and class—both the analytic categories and the lived realities. New social groups—such as feminists who are seeking to bridge a gap between their own social experience and the available theoretical frameworks—are more likely to hone in on "subjugated knowledge" about the world than are groups whose experience more comfortably fits familiar conceptual schemes. Most likely, the feminist entrance into these disputes should be seen as making significant contributions to clarifying the nature and implications of paradoxical tendencies in contemporary intellectual and social life.

The feminist criticisms of science have produced an array of conceptual questions that threaten both our cultural identity as a democratic and socially progressive society and our core personal identities as gender-distinct individuals. I do not mean to overwhelm these illuminating lines of inquiry with criticisms so early in my study—to suggest that they are not really feminist or that they have not advanced our understanding. On the contrary, each has greatly enhanced our ability to grasp the extent of androcentrism in science. Collectively, they have made it possible for us to formulate new questions about science.

It is a virtue of these critiques that they quickly bring to our attention the socially damaging incoherences in all the nonfeminist discourses. Considered in the sequence described in this chapter, they move us from the Woman Question in science to the more radical Science Question in feminism. Where the first three kinds of criticism primarily ask how women can be more equitably treated within and by science, the last two ask how a science apparently so deeply involved in distinctively masculine projects can possibly be used for emancipatory ends. Where the Woman Question critiques still conceptualize the scientific enterprise we have as redeemable, as reformable, the Science Question critiques appear skeptical that we can locate anything morally and politically worth redeeming or reforming in the sci-

entific world view, its underlying epistemology, or the practices these legitimate.

[1986]

NOTES

1. I make a sharp distinction between "sex" and "gender" (even though this is a dichotomy I shall later problematize); thus I refer to "gender roles" rather than "sex roles," etc., retaining only a few terms such as "sexism," where the substitution seems more distracting than useful. Otherwise (except in direct quotations), I use "sex" only when it is, indeed, biology that is at issue. There are two reasons for this policy. First, in spite of feminist insistence for decades, perhaps centuries, that women's and men's "natures" and activities are primarily shaped by social relations, not by immutable biological determinants, many people still do not grasp this point or are unwilling to commit themselves to its full implications (the current fascination with sociobiology is just one evidence of this problem). Second, the very thought of sex exerts its own fatal attraction for many otherwise well-intentioned people: such phrases as "sexual politics," "the battle between the sexes," and "male chauvinism" make the continuation of gender hostilities sound far more exciting than feminism should desire.
2. Boch (1983). See also Caulfield (1974); Davis (1971). (Works cited in my notes by author and year of publication receive full citation in the bibliography, which lists the sources I have found most useful for this study. Additional references appear in full in the footnotes.)
3. McIntosh (1983).
4. Marge Piercy, *Woman on the Edge of Time* (New York: Fawcett, 1981); Anne McCaffrey, *The Ship Who Sang* (New York: Ballantine, 1976). Donna Haraway (1985) discusses the potentialities that McCaffrey's kind of antidualism opens up for feminist theorizing.
5. See, e.g., Rossiter (1982b); Walsh (1977).
6. See Aldrich (1978).
7. Rossiter (1982b) makes this point.
8. See Tobach and Rosoff (1978; 1979; 1981; 1984); Brighton Women and Science Group (1980); Ehrenreich and English (1979); Rothschild (1983); Zimmerman (1983); Arditti, Duelli-Klein, and Minden (1984).
9. The literature here is immense. For examples of these criticisms, see Longino and Doell (1983); Hubbard, Henifin, and Fried (1982); Gross and Averill (1983); Tobach and Rosoff (1978; 1979; 1981; 1984); Millman and Kanter (1975); Andersen (1983); Westkott (1979).
10. Good examples are Keller (1984); Merchant (1980); Griffin (1978); Flax (1983); Jordanova (1980); Bloch and Bloch (1980); Harding (1980).
11. The key "object-relations" theorists among these textual critics are Dinnerstein (1976); Chodorow (1978); Flax (1983). See also Balbus (1982).
12. See Flax (1983); Rose (1983); Hartsock (1983b); Smith (1974; 1977; 1979; 1981); Harding (1983b); Fee (1981). Haraway (1985) proposes a somewhat different epistemology for feminism.
13. Millman and Kanter (1975, vii).
14. Flax (1983), Rose (1983), Hartsock (1983b), and Smith (1974; 1977; 1979; 1981) all develop this standpoint approach.

15. Flax (1986, 17). Strains of postmodernism appear in all of the standpoint thinking. Of this group, Flax has most overtly articulated also the postmodernist epistemological issues.

16. Flax (1986, 3). This is Flax's list of the mainstream postmodernist thinkers and movements. See Haraway (1985), Marks and de Courtivron (1980), and *Signs* (1981) for discussion of the feminist postmodernist issues.

REFERENCES

Aldrich, Michele L. 1978. "Women in Science." *Signs: Journal of Women in Culture and Society* 4(no. 1).

Andersen, Margaret. 1983. *Thinking about Women*. New York: Macmillan.

Arditti, Rita, Renate Duelli-Klein, and Shelly Minden, eds. 1984. *Test-Tube Women: What Future for Motherhood?* Boston: Pandora Press.

Balbus, Isaac. 1982. *Marxism and Domination*. Princeton, N.J.: Princeton University Press.

Bloch, Maurice, and Jean Bloch. 1980. "Women and the Dialectics of Nature in Eighteenth Century French Thought." In *Nature, Culture and Gender*, ed. C. MacCormack and M. Strathern. Cambridge: Cambridge University Press.

Boch, Gisela. 1983. "Racism and Sexism in Nazi Germany: Motherhood, Compulsory Sterilization, and the State." *Signs: Journal of Women in Culture and Society* 8(no. 3).

Brighton Women and Science Group. 1980. *Alice through the Microscope*. London: Virago Press.

Caulfield, Mina Davis. 1974. "Imperialism, the Family, and Cultures of Resistance." *Socialist Revolution* 4(no. 2).

Chodorow, Nancy. 1978. *The Reproduction of Mothering*. Berkeley: University of California Press.

Davis, Angela. 1971. "The Black Woman's Role in the Community of Slaves." *Black Scholar* 2.

Dinnerstein, Dorothy. 1976. *The Mermaid and the Minotaur: Sexual Arrangements and Human Malaise*. New York: Harper & Row.

Ehrenreich, Barbara, and Deirdre English. 1979. *For Her Own Good: 150 Years of Experts' Advice to Women*. New York: Doubleday.

Fee, Elizabeth. 1981. "Women's Nature and Scientific Objectivity." In *Woman's Nature: Rationalizations of Inequality*, ed. M. Lowe and R. Hubbard. New York: Pergamon Press. Originally appeared as "Is Feminism a Threat to Scientific Objectivity?" in *International Journal of Women's Studies* 4(no. 4).

Flax, Jane. 1983. "Political Philosophy and the Patriarchal Unconscious: A Psychoanalytic Perspective on Epistemology and Metaphysics." In *Discovering Reality: Feminist Perspectives on Epistemology, Metaphysics, Methodology and Philosophy of Science*, ed. S. Harding and M. Hintikka. Dordrecht: Reidel.

———. 1986. "Gender as a Social Problem: In and For Feminist Theory." *American Studies/Amerika Studien*, journal of the German Association for American Studies.

Griffin, Susan. 1978. *Woman and Nature: The Roaring inside Her*. New York: Harper & Row.

Gross, Michael, and Mary Beth Averill. 1983. "Evolution and Patriarchal Myths of Scarcity and Competition." In *Discovering Reality: Feminist Perspectives on Epistemology,*

Metaphysics, Methodology and Philosophy of Science, ed. S. Harding and M. Hintikka. Dordrecht: Reidel.

Haraway, Donna. 1985. "A Manifesto for Cyborgs: Science, Technology, and Socialist Feminism in the 1980's." *Socialist Review* 80.

Harding, Sandra. 1980. "The Norms of Social Inquiry and Masculine Experience." In *PSA 1980*, vol. 2, ed. P. D. Asquith and R. N. Giere. East Lansing, Mich.: Philosophy of Science Association.

———. 1983. "Why Has the Sex-Gender System Become Visible Only Now?" In *Discovering Reality: Feminist Perspectives on Epistemology, Metaphysics, Methodology and Philosophy of Science*, ed. S. Harding and M. Hintikka. Dordrecht: Reidel.

Hartsock, Nancy. 1983. "The Feminist Standpoint: Developing the Ground for a Specifically Feminist Historical Materialism." In *Discovering Reality: Feminist Perspectives on Epistemology, Metaphysics, Methodology and Philosophy of Science*, ed. S. Harding and M. Hintikka. Dordrecht: Reidel.

Hubbard, Ruth, M. S. Henifin, and Barbara Fried, eds. 1982. *Biological Woman: The Convenient Myth*. Cambridge, Mass.: Schenkman. Earlier version published 1979 under the title *Women Look at Biology Looking at Women*.

Jordanova, L. J. 1980. "Natural Facts: A Historical Perspective on Science and Sexuality." In *Nature, Culture and Gender,* ed. C. MacCormack and M. Strathern. New York: Cambridge University Press.

Keller, Evelyn Fox. 1984. *Reflections on Gender and Science*. New Haven, Conn.: Yale University Press.

Longino, Helen, and Ruth Doell. 1983. "Body, Bias, and Behavior: A Comparative Analysis of Reasoning in Two Areas of Biological Science." *Signs: Journal of Women in Culture and Society* 9(no. 2).

McIntosh, Peggy. 1983. "Interactive Phases of Curricular Revision: A Feminist Perspective." Working paper no. 124. Wellesley, Mass.: Wellesley College Center for Research on Women.

Marks, Elaine, and Isabelle de Courtivron, eds. 1980. *New French Feminisms*. Amherst: University of Massachusetts Press.

Merchant, Carolyn. 1980. *The Death of Nature: Women, Ecology and the Scientific Revolution*. New York: Harper & Row.

Millman, Marcia, and Rosabeth Moss Kanter, eds. 1975. *Another Voice: Feminist Perspectives on Social Life and Social Science*. New York: Anchor Books.

Rose, Hilary, and Steven Rose, eds. 1976. *Ideology of/in the Natural Sciences*. Cambridge, Mass.: Schenkman.

Rossiter, Margaret. 1982a. "Fair Enough?" *Isis* 72.

———. 1982b. *Women Scientists in America: Struggles and Strategies to 1940*. Baltimore, Md.: Johns Hopkins University Press.

Rothschild, Joan. 1983. *Machina ex Dea: Feminist Perspectives on Technology*. New York: Pergamon Press.

Signs: Journal of Women in Culture and Society. 1981. Special issue on French feminism, 7(no. 1).

Smith, Dorothy. 1974. "Women's Perspective as a Radical Critique of Sociology." *Sociological Inquiry* 44.

———. 1977. "Some Implications of a Sociology for Women." In *Woman in a Man-Made World: A Socioeconomic Handbook,* ed. N. Glazer and H. Waehrer. Chicago: Rand-McNally.

———. 1979. "A Sociology For Women." In *The Prism of Sex: Essays in the Sociology of Knowledge,* ed. J. Sherman and E. T. Beck. Madison: University of Wisconsin Press.

———. 1981. "The Experienced World as Problematic: A Feminist Method." Sorokin Lecture no. 12. Saskatoon: University of Saskatchewan.

Tobach, Ethel, and Betty Rosoff, eds. 1978, 1979, 1981, 1984. *Genes and Gender,* vols. 1–4. New York: Gordian Press.

Westkott, Marcia. 1979. "Feminist Criticism of the Social Sciences." *Harvard Educational Review* 49.

Zimmerman, Jan, ed. 1983. *The Technological Woman: Interfacing with Tomorrow.* New York: Praeger.

 73

La Conciencia de la Mestiza: Towards a New Consciousness

GLORIA ANZALDÚA

*Por la mujer de mi raza
hablará el espíritu.*[1]

Jose Vasconcelos, Mexican philosopher, envisaged *una raza mestiza, una mezcla de razas afines, una raza de color—la primera raza síntesis del globo.* He called it a cosmis race, *la raza cosmica,* a fifth race embracing the four major races of the world.[2] Opposite to the theory of the pure Aryan, and to the policy of racial purity that white America practices, his theory is one of inclusivity. At the confluence of two or more genetic streams, with chromosomes constantly "crossing over," this mixture of races, rather than resulting in an inferior being, provides hybrid progeny, a mutable, more malleable species with a rich gene pool. From this racial, ideological, cultural and biological cross-pollinization, an "alien" consciousness is presently in the making—a new *mestiza* consciousness, *una conciencia de mujer.* It is a consciousness of the Borderlands.

Una lucha de fronteras/
A Struggle of Borders

Because I, a *mestiza,*
continually walk out of one culture
and into another,
because I am in all cultures at the same time,
*alma entre dos mundos, tres, cuatro,
me zumba la cabeza con lo contradictorio.*

Estoy norteada por todas las voces que me hablan simultáneamente.

The ambivalence from the clash of voices results in mental and emotional states of perplexity. Internal strife results in insecurity and indecisivenes. The *mestiza*'s dual or multiple personality is plagued by psychic restlessness.

In a constant state of mental nepantilism, an Aztec word meaning torn between ways, *la mestiza* is a product of the transfer of the cultural and spiritual values of one group to another. Being tricultural, monolingual, bilingual or multilingual, speaking a patois, and in a state of perpetual transition, the *mestiza* faces the dilemma of the mixed breed: which collectivity does the daughter of a darkskinned mother listen to?

El choque de un alma atrapado entre el mundo del espíritu y el mundo de la ténica a veces la deja entullada. Cradled in one culture, sandwiched between two cultures, straddling all three cultures and their value systems, *la mestiza* undergoes a struggle of flesh, a struggle of borders, an inner war. Like all people, we perceive the version of reality that our culture communicates. Like other having or living in more than one culture, we get multiple, often opposing messages. The coming together of two self-consistent but habitually incompatible frames of reference[3] causes *un choque,* a cultural collision.

Within us and within *la cultura chicana,* commonly held beliefs of the white culture attack commonly held beliefs of the Mexican culture, and both attack commonly held beliefs of the indigenous culture. Subconsciously, we see an attack on ourselves and our beliefs as a threat and we attempt to block with a counterstance.

But it is not enough to stand on the opposite river bank, shouting questions, challenging patriarchical, white conventions. A counterstance locks one into a duel of oppressor and oppressed; locked in mortal combat, like the cop and the criminal, both are reduced to a common denominator of violence. The counterstance refutes the dominant culture's views and beliefs, and, for this, it is proudly defiant. All reaction is limited by, and dependent on, what it is reacting against. Because the counterstance stems from a problem with authority—outer as well as inner—it's a step towards liberation from cultural domination. But it is not a way of life. At some point, on our way to a new consciousness, we will have to leave the opposite bank, the split between the two mortal combatants somehow healed so that we are on both shores at once and, at once, see through serpent and eagle eyes. Or perhaps we will decide to disengage from the dominant culture, write it off altogether as a lost cause, and cross the border into a wholly new and separate territory. Or we might go another route. The possibilities are numerous once we decide to act and not react.

A TOLERANCE FOR AMBIGUITY

These numerous possibilities leave *la mestiza* floundering in uncharted seas. In perceiving conflicting information and points of view, she is subjected to a swamping of her psychological borders. She has discovered that she can't hold concepts or ideas in rigid boundaries. The borders and walls that are supposed to keep the undesirable ideas out are entrenched habits and patterns of behavior; these habits and patterns are the enemy within. Rigidity means death. Only by remaining flexible is she able to stretch the psyche horizontally and vertically. *La mestiza* constantly has to shift out of habitual formations; from convergent thinking, analytical reasoning that tends to use rationality to move toward a single goal (a Western mode), to divergent thinking,[4] characterized by movement away from set patterns and goals and toward a more whole perspective, one that includes rather than excludes.

The new *mestiza* copes by developing a tolerance for contradictions, a tolerance for ambiguity. She learns to be an Indian in Mexican culture, to be Mexican from an Anglo point of view. She learns to juggle cultures. She has a plural personality, she operates in a pluralistic mode—nothing is thrust out, the good, the bad and the ugly, nothing rejected, nothing abandoned. Not only does she sustain contradictions, she turns the ambivalence into something else.

She can be jarred out of ambivalence by an intense, and often painful, emotional event which inverts or resolves the ambivalence. I'm not sure exactly how. The work takes place underground—subconsciously. It is work that the soul performs. That focal point or fulcrum, that juncture where the *mestiza* stands, is where phenomena tend to collide. It is where the possibility of uniting all that is separate occurs. This assembly is not one where severed or separated pieces merely come together. Nor is it a balancing of opposing powers. In attempting to work out a synthesis, the self has added a third element which is greater than the sum of its severed parts. That third element is a new consciousness—a *mestiza* consciousness—and though it is a source of intense pain, its energy comes from a continual creative motion that keeps breaking down the unitary aspect of each new paradigm.

En unas pocas centurias, the future will belong to the *mestiza.* Because the future depends on the breaking down of paradigms, it depends on the straddling of two or more cultures. By creating a new mythos—that is, a change in the way we perceive reality, the way we see ourselves and the ways we behave—*la mestiza* creates a new consciousness.

The work of *mestiza* consciousness is to break down the subject-object duality that keeps her a prisoner and to show in the flesh and through the images in her work how duality is transcended. The answer to the problem between the white race and the colored, between males and females, lies in healing the split that originates in the very foundation of our lives, our culture, our languages, our thoughts. A massive uprooting of dualistic thinking in the individual and collective consciousness is the beginning of a long struggle, but one that could, in our best hopes, bring us to the end of rape, of violence, of war.

La encrucijada/*The Crossroads*

A chicken is being sacrificed
 at a crossroads, a simple mound of earth
a mud shrine for *Eshu,*
 Yoruba god of indeterminacy,
who blesses her choice of path.
 She begins her journey.

Su cuerpo es una bocacalle. La mestiza has gone from being the sacrificial goat to becoming the officiating priestess at the crossroads.

As a *mestiza* I have no country, my homeland cast me out; yet all countries are mine because I am every woman's sister or potential lover. (As a lesbian

I have no race, my own people disclaim me; but I am all races because there is the queer of me in all races.) I am cultureless because, as a feminist, I challenge the collective cultural/religious male-derived beliefs of Indo-Hispanics and Anglos; yet I am cultured because I am participating in the creation of yet another culture, a new story to explain the world and our participation in it, a new value system with images and symbols that connect us to each other and to the planet. *Soy un amasamiento,* I am an act of kneading, of uniting and joining that not only has produced both a creature of darkness and a creature of light, but also a creature that questions the definitions of light and dark and gives them new meanings.

We are the people who leap in the dark, we are the people on the knees of the gods. In our flesh, (r)evolution works out the clash of cultures. It makes us crazy constantly, but if the center holds, we've made some kind of evolutionary step forward. *Nuestra alma el trabajo,* the opus, the great alchemical work; spiritual *mestizaje,* a "morphogenesis,"[5] an inevitable unfolding. We have become the quickening serpent movement.

· · ·

El camino de la mestiza/*The* Mestiza *Way*

Caught between the sudden contraction, the breath sucked in and the endless space, the brown woman stands still, looks at the sky. She decides to go down, digging her way along the roots of trees. Sifting through the bones, she shakes them to see if there is any marrow in them. Then, touching the dirt to her forehead, to her tongue, she takes a few bones, leaves the rest in their burial place.

She goes through her backpack, keeps her journal and address book, throws away the muni-bart metromaps. The coins are heavy and they go next, then the greenbacks flutter through the air. She keeps her knife, can opener and eyebrow pencil. She puts bones, pieces of bark, *hierbas,* eagle feather, snakeskin, tape recorder, the rattle and drum in her pack and she sets out to become the complete *tolteca.*

Her first step is to take inventory. *Despojando, desgranando, quitando paja.* Just what did she inherit from her ancestors? This weight on her back—which is the baggage from the Indian mother, which the baggage from the Spanish father, which the baggage from the Anglo?

Pero es difícil differentiating between *lo heredado, lo adquirido, lo impuesto.* She puts history through a sieve, winnows out the lies, looks at the forces that we as a race, as women, have been a part of. *Luego bota lo que no vale, los desmientos, los desencuentros, el embrutecimiento. Aguarda el juicio, hondo y enraízado, de la gente antigua.* This step is a conscious rupture with all oppressive traditions of all cultures and religions. She communicates that rupture, documents the struggle. She reinterprets history and, using new symbols, she shapes new myths. She adopts new perspectives toward the darkskinned, women and queers. She strengthens her tolerance (and intolerance) for ambiguity. She is willing to share, to make herself vulnerable to foreign ways of seeing and thinking. She surrenders all notions of safety, of the familiar. Deconstruct, construct. She becomes a *nahual,* able to transform herself into a tree, a coyote, into another person. She learns to transform the small "I" into the total Self. *Se hace moldeadora de su alma. Según la concepción que tiene de sí misma, así será.*

Que no se nos olvide los hombres

"Tú no sirves pa' nada—
you're good for nothing.
Eres pura vieja."

"You're nothing but a woman" means you are defective. Its opposite is to be *un macho.* The modern meaning of the word "machismo," as well as the concept, is actually an Anglo invention. For men like my father, being "macho" meant being strong enough to protect and support my mother and us, yet being able to show love. Today's macho has doubts about his ability to feed and protect his family. His "machismo" is an adaptation to oppression and poverty and low self-esteem. It is the result of hierarchical male dominance. The Anglo, feeling inadequate and inferior and powerless, displaces or transfers these feeling to the Chicano by shaming him. In the Gringo world, the Chicano suffers from excessive humility and self-effacement, shame of self and self-deprecation. Around Latinos he suffers from a sense of language inadequacy and its accompanying discomfort; with Native Americans he suffers from a racial amnesia which ignores our common blood, and from guilt because the Spanish part of him took their land and oppressed them. He has an excessive compensatory hubris when around Mexicans from the other side. It overlays a deep sense of racial shame.

The loss of a sense of dignity and respect in the macho breeds a false machismo which leads him to put down women and even to brutalize them. Co-existing with his sexist behavior is a love for the mother which takes precedence over that of all others. Devoted son, macho pig. To wash down the shame of his acts, of his very being, and to handle the brute in the mirror, he takes to the bottle, the snort, the needle and the fist.

Though we "understand" the root causes of male hatred and fear, and the subsequent wounding of women, we do not excuse, we do not condone and we will not longer put up with it. From the men of our race, we demand the admission/acknowledgment/ disclosure/testimony that they wound us, violate us, are afraid of us and of our power. We need them to say they will begin to eliminate their hurtful put-down ways. But more than the words, we demand acts. We say to them: we will develop equal power with you and those who have shamed us.

It is imperative that *mestizas* support each other in changing the sexist elements in the Mexican-Indian culture. As long as woman is put down, the Indian and the Black in all of us is put down. The struggle of the *mestiza* is above all a feminist one. As long as *los hombres* think they have to *chingar mujeres* and each other to be men, as long as men are taught that they are superior and therefore culturally favored over *la mujer,* as long as to be a *vieja* is a thing of derision, there can be no real healing of our psyches. We're halfway there—we have such love of the Mother, the good mother. The first step is to unlearn the *puta/virgen* dichotomy and to see *Coatlapopeuh*—*Coatlicue* in the Mother, *Guadalupe.*

Tenderness, a sign of vulnerability, is so feared that it is showered on women with verbal abuse and blows. Men, even more than women, are fettered to gender roles. Women at least have had the guts to break out of bondage. Only gay men have had the courage to expose themselves to the woman inside them and to challenge the current masculinity. I've encountered a few scattered and isolated gentle straight men, the beginnings of a new breed, but they are confused, and entangled with sexist behaviors that they have not been able to eradicate. We need a new masculinity and the new man needs a movement.

Lumping the males who deviate from the general norm with man, the oppressor, is a gross injustice. *Asombra pensar que nos hemos quedado en ese pozo oscuro donde el mundo encierra a las lesbianas. Asombra pensar que hemos, como femenistas y lesbianas, cerrado nuestros corazónes a los hombres, a nuestros hermanos los jotos, desheredados y marginales como nosotros.* Being the supreme crossers of cultures, homosexuals have strong bonds with the queer white, Black, Asian, Native American, Latino and with the queer in Italy, Australia and the rest of the planet. We come from all colors, all classes, all races, all time periods. Our role is to link people with each other—the Blacks with Jews with Indians with Asians with whites with extraterrestrials. It is to transfer ideas and information from one culture to another. Colored homosexuals have more knowledge of other cultures; have always been at the forefront (although sometimes in the closet) of all liberation struggles in this country; have suffered more injustices and have survived them despite all odds. Chicanos need to acknowledge the political and artistic contributions of their queer. People, listen to what your *jotería* is saying.

The *mestizo* and the queer exist at this time and point on the evolutionary continuum for a purpose. We are a blending that proves that all blood is intricately woven together, and that we are spawned out of similar souls.

· · ·

El día de la Chicana

I will not be shamed again
Nor will I shame myself.

I am possessed by a vision: that we Chicanas and Chicanos have taken back or uncovered our true faces, our dignity and self-respect. It's a validation vision.

Seeing the Chicana anew in light of her history. I seek an exoneration, a seeing through the fictions of white supremacy, a seeing of ourselves in our true guises and not as the false racial personality that has been given to us and that we have given to ourselves. I seek our woman's face, our true features, the positive and the negative seen clearly, free of the tainted biases of male dominance. I seek new images of identity, new beliefs about ourselves, our humanity and worth no longer in question.

Estamos viviendo en la noche de la Raza, un tiempo cuando el trabajo se hace a lo quieto, en el oscuro. El día cuando aceptamos tal y como somos y para en donde vamos y porque—ese día será el día de la Raza. Yo tengo el conpromiso de expresar mi visión, mi sensibilidad, mi percepción de la revalidación de la gente mexicana, su mérito, estimación, honra, aprecio y validez.

On December 2nd when my sun goes into my first house, I celebrate *el día de la Chicana y el Chicano.* On that day I clean my altars, light my *Coatlalopeuh* candle, burn sage and copal, take *el baño para espantar basura,* sweep my house. On that day I bare my soul, make myself vulnerable to friends and family by expressing my feelings. On that day I affirm who we are.

On that day I look inside our conflicts and our basic introverted racial temperament. I identify our needs, voice them. I acknowledge that the self and the race have been wounded. I recognize the need to take care of our personhood, of our racial self. On that day I gather the splintered and disowned parts of *la gente mexicana* and hold them in my arms. *Todas las partes de nostros valen.*

On that day I say, "Yes, all you people wound us when you reject us. Rejection strips us of self-worth; our vulnerability exposes us to shame. It is our innate identity you find wanting. We are ashamed that we need your good opinion, that we need your acceptance. We can no longer camouflage our needs, can no longer let defenses and fences sprout around us. We can no longer withdraw. To rage and look upon you with contempt is to rage and be contemptuous of ourselves. We can no longer blame you, nor disown the white parts, the male parts, the pathological parts, the queer parts, the vulnerable parts. Here we are weaponless with open arms, with only our magic. Let's try it our way, the *mestiza* way, the Chicana way, the woman way.

On that day, I search for our essential dignity as a people, a people with a sense of purpose—to belong and contribute to something greater than our *pueblo.* On that day I seek to recover and reshape my spiritual identity. *¡Animate! Raza, a celebrar el día de la Chicana.*

El retorno

All movements are accomplished in six stages,
and the seventh brings return.
                                        —I CHING[6]

Tanto tiempo sin verte casa mía,
mi cuna, mi hondo nido de la huerta.
                                        —"SOLEDAD"[7]

I stand at the river, watch the curving, twisting serpent, a serpent nailed to the fence where the mouth of the Rio Grande empties into the Gulf.

I have come back. *Tanto dolor me costó el alejamiento.* I shade my eyes and look up. The bone beak of a hawk slowly circling over me, checking me out as potential carrion. In its wake a little bird flickering its wings, swimming sporadically like a fish. In the distance the expressway and the slough of traffic like an irritated sow. The sudden pull in my gut, *la tierra, los aguaceros.* My land, *el viento soplando la arena, el lagartijo debajo de un nopalito. Me acuerdo como era antes. Una región desértica de vasta llanuras, costeras de baja altura, de escasa lluvia, de chaparrales formados por mesquites y huizaches.* If I look real hard I can almost see the Spanish fathers who were called "the cavalry of Christ" enter this valley riding their burros, see the clash of cultures commence.

Tierra natal. This is home, the small towns in the Valley, *los pueblitos* with chicken pens and goats picketed to mesquite shrubs. *En las colonias* on the other side of the tracks, junk cars line the front yards of hot pink and lavender-trimmed houses—Chicano architecture we call it, self-consciously. I have missed the TV shows where hosts speak in half and half, and where awards are given in the category of Tex-Mex music. I have missed the Mexican cemeteries blooming with artificial flowers, the fields of aloe vera and red pepper, rows of sugar cane, of corn hanging on the stalks, the cloud of *polvareda* in the dirt roads behind a speeding truck, *el sabor de tamales de rez y venado.* I have missed *la yegua colorada* gnawing the wooden gate of her stall, the smell of horse flesh from Carito's corrals. *He hecho menos las noches calientes sin aire, noches de linternas y lechuzas* making holes in the night.

I still feel the old despair when I look at the unpainted, dilapidated, scrap lumber houses consisting mostly of corrugated aluminum. Some of the poorest people in the U.S. live in the Lower Rio Grande Valley, an arid and semi-arid land of irrigated farming, intense sunlight and heat, citrus groves next to chaparral and cactus. I walk through the elementary school I attended so long ago, that remained segregated until recently. I remember how the white teachers used to punish us for being Mexican.

How I love this tragic valley of South Texas, as Ricardo Sánchez calls it; this borderland between the Nueces and the Rio Grande. This land has survived possession and ill-use by five countries: Spain, Mexico, the Republic of Texas, the Confederacy, and the U.S. again. It has survived Anglo-Mexican blood feuds, lynchings, burnings, rapes, pillage.

· · ·

I walk out to the back yard, stare at *los rosales de mamá*. She wants me to help her prune the rose bushes, dig out the carpet grass that is choking them. *Mamagrande Ramona también tenía rosales.* Here every Mexican grows flowers. If they don't have a piece of dirt, they use car tires, jars, cans, shoe boxes. Roses are the Mexican's favorite flower. I think, how symbolic—thorns and all.

Yes, the Chicano and Chicana have always taken care of growing things and the land. Again I see the four of us kids getting off the school bus, changing into our work clothes, walking into the field with Papí and Mamí, all six of us bending to the ground. Below our feet, under the earth lie the watermelon seeds. We cover them with paper plates, putting *terremotes* on top of the plates to keep them from being blown away by the wind. The paper plates keep the freeze away. Next day or the next, we remove the plates, bare the tiny green shoots to the elements. They survive and grow, give fruit hundreds of times the size of the seed. We water them and hoe them. We harvest them. The vines dry, rot, are plowed under. Growth, death, decay, birth. The soil prepared again and again, impregnated, worked on. A constant changing of forms, *renacimientos de la tierra madre.*

This land was Mexican once
  was Indian always
    and is.
      And will be again.

[1987]

NOTES

1. This is my own "take-off" on Jose Vasconcelos' idea. Jose Vasconcelos, *La Raza Cósmica: Missión de la Raza Ibero-Americana* (México: Aguilar S.A. de Ediciones, 1961).
2. Vasconcelos.
3. Arthur Koestler termed this "bisociation." Albert Rothenberg, *The Creative Process in Art, Science, and Other Fields* (Chicago, IL: University of Chicago Press, 1979), 12.
4. In part, I derive my definitions for "convergent" and "divergent" thinking from Rothenberg, 12–13.
5. To borrow chemist Ilya Prigogine's theory of "dissipative structures." Prigogine discovered that substances interact not in predictable ways as it was taught in science, but in different and fluctuating ways to produce new and more complex structures, a kind of birth he called "morphogenesis," which created unpredictable innovations. See Harold Gilliam, "Searching for a New World View," *This World* (January, 1981), 23.
6. Richard Wilhelm, *The I Ching or Book of Changes*, trans. Cary F. Baynes (Princeton, NJ: Princeton University Press, 1950), 98.
7. "*Soledad*" is sung by the group Haciendo Punto en Otro Son.

 74

Cultural Feminism Versus Post-Structuralism: The Identity Crisis in Feminist Theory

LINDA ALCOFF

For many contemporary feminist theorists, the concept of woman is a problem. It is a problem of primary significance because the concept of woman is the central concept for feminist theory and yet it is a concept that is impossible to formulate precisely for feminists. It is the central concept for feminists because the concept and category of woman is the necessary point of departure for any feminist theory and feminist politics, predicated as these are on the transformation of women's lived experience in contemporary culture and the reevaluation of social theory and practice from women's point of view. But as a concept it is radically problematic precisely for feminists because it is crowded with the overdeterminations of male supremacy, invoking in every formulation the limit, contrasting Other, or mediated self-reflection of a culture built on the control of females. In attempting to speak for women, feminism often seems to presuppose that it knows what women truly are, but such an assumption is foolhardy given that every source of knowledge about women has been contaminated with misogyny and sexism. No matter where we turn—to historical documents, philosophical constructions, social scientific statistics, introspection, or daily practices—the mediation of female bodies into constructions of woman is dominated by misogynist discourse. For feminists, who must transcend this discourse, it appears we have nowhere to turn.

Thus the dilemma facing feminist theorists today is that our very self-definition is grounded in a concept that we must deconstruct and de-essentialize in all of its aspects. Man has said that woman can be defined, delineated, captured—understood, explained, and diagnosed—to a level of determination never accorded to man himself, who is conceived as a rational animal with free will. Where man's behavior is underdetermined, free to construct its own future along the course of its rational choice, woman's nature has overdetermined her behavior, the limits of her intellectual endeavors, and the inevitabilities of her emotional journey through life. Whether she is construed as essentially immoral and irrational (à la Schopenhauer) or essentially kind and benevolent (à la Kant), she is always construed as an essential *something* inevitably accessible to direct intuited apprehension by males. Despite the variety of ways in which man has construed her essential characteristics, she is always the Object, a conglomeration of attributes to be predicted and controlled along with other natural phenomena. The place of the free-willed subject who can transcend nature's mandates is reserved exclusively for men.

Feminist thinkers have articulated two major responses to this situation over the last ten years. The first response is to claim that feminists have the exclusive right to describe and evaluate woman. Thus cultural feminists argue that the problem of male supremacist culture is the problem of a process in which women are defined by men, that is, by a group who has a contrasting point of view and set of interests from women, not to mention a possible fear and hatred of women. The result of this has been a distortion and de-

valuation of feminine characteristics, which now can be corrected by a more accurate feminist description and appraisal. Thus the cultural feminist reappraisal construes woman's passivity as her peacefulness, her sentimentality as her proclivity to nurture, her subjectiveness as her advanced self-awareness, and so forth. Cultural feminists have not challenged the defining of woman but only that definition given by men.

The second major response has been to reject the possibility of defining woman as such at all. Feminists who take this tactic go about the business of deconstructing all concepts of woman and argue that both feminist and misogynist attempts to define woman are politically reactionary and ontologically mistaken. Replacing woman-as-housewife with woman-as-supermom (or earth mother or super professional) is no advance. Using French poststructuralist theory these feminists argue that such errors occur because we are in fundamental ways duplicating misogynist strategies when we try to define women, characterize women, or speak for women, even though allowing for a range of differences within the gender. The politics of gender or sexual difference must be replaced with a plurality of difference where gender loses its position of significance.

Briefly put, then, the cultural feminist response to Simone de Beauvoir's question, "Are there women?" is to answer yes and to define women by their activities and attributes in the present culture. The post-structuralist response is to answer no and attack the category and the concept of woman through problematizing subjectivity. Each response has serious limitations, and it is becoming increasingly obvious that transcending these limitations while retaining the theoretical framework from which they emerge is impossible. As a result, a few brave souls are now rejecting these choices and attempting to map out a new course, a course that will avoid the major problems of the earlier responses. In this paper I will discuss some of the pioneer work being done to develop a new concept of woman and offer my own contribution toward it. But first, I must spell out more clearly the inadequacies of the first two responses to the problem of woman and explain why I believe these inadequacies are inherent.

CULTURAL FEMINISM

Cultural feminism is the ideology of a female nature or female essence reappropriated by feminists themselves in an effort to revalidate undervalued female attributes. For cultural feminists, the enemy of women is not merely a social system or economic institution or set of backward beliefs but masculinity itself and in some cases male biology. Cultural feminist politics revolve around creating and maintaining a healthy environment—free of masculinist values and all their offshoots such as pornography—for the female principle. Feminist theory, the explanation of sexism, and the justification of feminist demands can all be grounded securely and unambiguously on the concept of the essential female.

Mary Daly and Adrienne Rich have been influential proponents of this position. Breaking from the trend toward androgyny and the minimizing of gender differences that was popular among feminists in the early seventies, both Daly and Rich argue for a returned focus on femaleness.

For Daly, male barrenness leads to parasitism on female energy, which flows from our life-affirming, life-creating biological condition: "Since female energy is essentially biophilic, the female spirit/body is the primary target in this perpetual war of aggression against life. Gyn/Ecology is the re-claiming of life-loving female energy."[1] Despite Daly's warnings against biological reductionism,[2] her own analysis of sexism uses gender-specific biological traits to explain male hatred for women. The childless state of "all males" leads to a dependency on women, which in turn leads men to "deeply identify with 'unwanted fetal tissue.'"[3] Given their state of fear and insecurity it becomes almost understandable, then, that men would desire to dominate and control that which is so vitally necessary to them: the life-energy of women. Female energy, conceived by Daly as a natural essence, needs to be freed from its male parasites, released for creative expression and recharged through bonding with other women. In this free space women's "natural" attributes of love, creativity, and the ability to nurture can thrive.

Women's identification as female is their defining essence for Daly, their haecceity, overriding any other way in which they may be defined or may define themselves. Thus Daly states: "Women who ac-

cept false inclusion among the fathers and the sons are easily polarized against other women on the basis of ethnic, national, class, religious and other *male-defined differences,* applauding the defeat of 'enemy' women."[4] These differences are apparent rather than real, inessential rather than essential. The only real difference, the only difference that can change a person's ontological placement on Daly's dichotomous map, is sex difference. Our essence is defined here, in our sex, from which flow all the facts about us: who are our potential allies, who is our enemy, what are our objective interests, what is our true nature. Thus, Daly defines women again and her definition is strongly linked to female biology.

Many of Rich's writings have exhibited surprising similarities to Daly's position described above, surprising given their difference in style and temperament. Rich defines a "female consciousness"[5] that has a great deal to do with the female body.

> I have come to believe . . . that female biology—the diffuse, intense sensuality radiating out from clitoris, breasts, uterus, vagina; the lunar cycles of menstruation; the gestation and fruition of life which can take place in the female body—has far more radical implications than we have yet to appreciate. Patriarchal thought has limited female biology to its own narrow specifications. The feminist vision has recoiled from female biology for these reasons; it will, I believe, come to view our physicality as a resource, rather than a destiny. . . . We must touch the unity and resonance of our physicality, our bond with the natural order, the corporeal ground for our intelligence.[6]

Thus Rich argues that we should not reject the importance of female biology simply because patriarchy has used it to subjugate us. Rich believes that "our biological grounding, the miracle and paradox of the female body and its spiritual and political meanings" holds the key to our rejuvenation and our reconnection with our specific female attributes, which she lists as "our great mental capacities . . . ; our highly developed tactile sense; our genius for close observation; our complicated, pain-enduring, multi-pleasured physicality."[7]

Rich further echoes Daly in her explanation of misogyny: "The ancient, continuing envy, awe and dread of the male for the female capacity to create life has repeatedly taken the form of hatred for every other female aspect of creativity."[8] Thus Rich, like Daly, identifies a female essence, defines patriarchy as the subjugation and colonization of this essence out of male envy and need, and then promotes a solution that revolves around rediscovering our essence and bonding with other women. Neither Rich nor Daly espouse biological reductionism, but this is because they reject the oppositional dichotomy of mind and body that such a reductionism presupposes. The female essence for Daly and Rich is not simply spiritual or simply biological—it is both. Yet the key point remains that it is our specifically female anatomy that is the primary constituent of our identity and the source of our female essence. Rich prophesies that "the repossession by women of our bodies will bring far more essential change to human society than the seizing of the means of production by workers. . . . In such a world women will truly create new life, bringing forth not only children (if and as we choose) but the visions, and the thinking, necessary to sustain, console and alter human existence—a new relationship to the universe. Sexuality, politics, intelligence, power, motherhood, work, community, intimacy will develop new meanings; thinking itself will be transformed."[9]

. . .

Interestingly, I have not included any feminist writings from women of oppressed nationalities and races in the category of cultural feminism, nor does [Alice] Echols. I have heard it argued that the emphasis placed on cultural identity by such writers as Cherríe Moraga and Audre Lorde reveals a tendency toward essentialism also. However, in my view their work has consistently rejected essentialist conceptions of gender. Consider the following passage from Moraga: "When you start to talk about sexism, the world becomes increasingly complex. The power no longer breaks down into neat little hierarchical categories, but becomes a series of starts and detours. Since the categories are not easy to arrive at, the enemy is not easy to name. It is all so difficult to unravel."[10] Moraga goes on to assert that "some men oppress the very women they love," implying that we need new categories and new concepts to describe such complex and contradictory relations of oppression. In this problematic understanding of sexism, Moraga seems to me light-years

ahead of Daly's manichean ontology or Rich's romanticized conception of the female. The simultaneity of oppressions experienced by women such as Moraga resists essentialist conclusions. Universalist conceptions of female or male experiences and attributes are not plausible in the context of such a complex network of relations, and without an ability to universalize, the essentialist argument is difficult if not impossible to make. White women cannot be all good or all bad; neither can men from oppressed groups. I have simply not found writings by feminists who are oppressed also by race and/or class that place or position maleness wholly as Other. Reflected in their problematized understanding of masculinity is a richer and likewise problematized concept of woman.

Even if cultural feminism is the product of white feminists, it is not homogeneous. . . . The biological accounts of sexism given by Daly and Brownmiller, for example, are not embraced by Rush or Dworkin. But the key link between these feminists is their tendency toward invoking universalizing conceptions of woman and mother in an essentialist way. Therefore, despite the lack of complete homogeneity within the category, it seems still justifiable and important to identify (and criticize) within these sometimes disparate works their tendency to offer an essentialist response to misogyny and sexism through adopting a homogeneous, unproblematized, and ahistorical conception of woman.

One does not have to be influenced by French post-structuralism to disagree with essentialism. It is well documented that the innateness of gender differences in personality and character is at this point factually and philosophically indefensible. . . . Our gender categories are positively constitutive and not mere hindsight descriptions of previous activities. There is a self-perpetuating circularity between defining woman as essentially peaceful and nurturing and the observations and judgments we shall make of future women and the practices we shall engage in as women in the future. Do feminists want to buy another ticket for women of the world on the merry-go-round of feminine constructions? Don't we want rather to get off the merry-go-round and run away?

This should not imply that the political effects of cultural feminism have all been negative. The insistence on viewing traditional feminine characteristics from a different point of view, to use a "looking glass" perspective, as a means of engendering a gestalt switch on the body of data we all currently share about women, has had positive effect. After a decade of hearing liberal feminists advising us to wear business suits and enter the male world, it is a helpful corrective to have cultural feminists argue instead that women's world is full of superior virtues and values, to be credited and learned from rather than despised. Herein lies the positive impact of cultural feminism. And surely much of their point is well taken, that it was our mothers who made our families survive, that women's handiwork is truly artistic, that women's care-giving really is superior in value to male competitivness.

Unfortunately, however, the cultural feminist championing of a redefined "womanhood" cannot provide a useful long-range program for a feminist movement and, in fact, places obstacles in the way of developing one. Under conditions of oppression and restrictions on freedom of movement, women, like other oppressed groups, have developed strengths and attributes that should be correctly credited, valued, and promoted. What we should not promote, however, are the restrictive conditions that gave rise to those attributes: forced parenting, lack of physical autonomy, dependency for survival on mediation skills, for instance. What conditions for women do we want to promote? A freedom of movement such that we can compete in the capitalist world alongside men? A continued restriction to child-centered activities? To the extent cultural feminism merely valorizes genuinely positive attributes developed under oppression, it cannot map our future long-range course. To the extent that it reinforces essentialist explanations of these attributes, it is in danger of solidifying an important bulwark for sexist oppression: the belief in an innate "womanhood" to which we must all adhere lest we be deemed either inferior or not "true" women.

POST-STRUCTURALISM

For many feminists, the problem with the cultural feminist response to sexism is that it does not criticize the fundamental mechanism of oppressive power used to perpetuate sexism and in fact reinvokes that mechanism in its supposed solution. The mechanism of power referred to here is the construction of the subject by a discourse that weaves knowledge and power into a coercive structure that "forces the individual back on himself and ties him to his own identity in a constraining way."[11] On this view, essentialist formulations of womanhood, even when made by feminists, "tie" the individual to her identity as a woman and thus cannot represent a solution to sexism.

This articulation of the problem has been borrowed by feminists from a number of recently influential French thinkers who are sometimes called post-structuralist but who also might be called post-humanist and post-essentialist. Lacan, Derrida, and Foucault are the front-runners in this group. Disparate as these writers are, their (one) common theme is that the self-contained, authentic subject conceived by humanism to be discoverable below a veneer of cultural and ideological overlay is in reality a construct of that very humanist discourse. The subject is not a locus of authorial intentions or natural attributes or even a privileged, separate consciousness. Lacan uses psychoanalysis, Derrida uses grammar, and Foucault uses the history of discourses all to attack and "deconstruct" our concept of the subject as having an essential identity and an authentic core that has been repressed by society. There is no essential core "natural" to us, and so there is no repression in the humanist sense.

There is an interesting sort of neodeterminism in this view. The subject or self is never determined by biology in such a way that human history is predictable or even explainable, and there is no unilinear direction of a determinist arrow pointing from some fairly static, "natural" phenomena to human experience. On the other hand, this rejection of biological determinism is not grounded in the belief that human subjects are underdetermined but, rather, in the belief that we are overdetermined (i.e., constructed) by a social discourse and/or cultural practice. The idea here is that we individuals really have little choice in the matter of who we are, for as Derrida and Foucault like to remind us, individual motivations and intentions count for nil or almost nil in the scheme of social reality. We are constructs—that is, our experience of our very subjectivity is a construct mediated by and/or grounded on a social discourse beyond (way beyond) individual control. As

Foucault puts it, we are bodies "totally imprinted by history."[12] Thus, subjective experiences are determined in some sense by macro forces. . . .

Post-structuralists unite with Marx in asserting the social dimension of individual traits and intentions. Thus, they say we cannot understand society as the conglomerate of individual intentions but, rather, must understand individual intentions as constructed within a social reality. To the extent post-structuralists emphasize social explanations of individual practices and experiences I find their work illuminating and persuasive. My disagreement occurs, however, when they seem totally to erase any room for maneuver by the individual within a social discourse or set of institutions. It is that totalization of history's imprint that I reject. In their defense of a total construction of the subject, post-structuralists deny the subject's ability to reflect on the social discourse and challenge its determinations.

Applied to the concept of woman the post-structuralist's view results in what I shall call nominalism: the idea that the category "woman" is a fiction and that feminist efforts must be directed toward dismantling this fiction. "Perhaps . . . 'woman' is not a determinable identity. Perhaps woman is not some thing which announces itself from a distance, at a distance from some other thing. . . . Perhaps woman—a non-identity, non-figure, a simulacrum—is distance's very chasm, the out-distancing of distance, the interval's cadence, distance itself."[13] Derrida's interest in feminism stems from his belief, expressed above, that woman may represent the rupture in the functional discourse of what he calls logocentrism, an essentialist discourse that entails hierarchies of difference and a Kantian ontology. Because woman has in a sense been excluded from this discourse, it is possible to hope that she might provide a real source of resistance. But her resistance will not be at all effective if she continues to use the mechanism of logocentrism to redefine woman: she can be an effective resister only if she drifts and dodges all attempts to capture her. Then, Derrida hopes, the following futuristic picture will come true: "Out of the depths, endless and unfathomable, she engulfs and distorts all vestige of essentiality, of identity, of property. And the philosophical discourse, blinded, founders on these shoals and is hurled down these depths to its ruin."[14] For Derrida, women have always been defined as a subjugated difference within a binary opposition: man/woman, culture/nature, positive/negative, analytical/intuitive. To assert an essential gender difference as cultural feminists do is to reinvoke this oppositional structure. The only way to break out of this structure, and in fact to subvert the structure itself, is to assert total difference, to be that which cannot be pinned down or subjugated within a dichotomous hierarchy. Paradoxically, it is to be what is not. Thus feminists cannot demarcate a definitive category of "woman" without eliminating all possibility for the defeat of logocentrism and its oppressive power.

Foucault similarly rejects all constructions of oppositional subjects—whether the "proletariat," "woman," or "the oppressed"—as mirror images that merely recreate and sustain the discourse of power. As Biddy Martin points out, "The point from which Foucault deconstructs is off-center, out of line, apparently unaligned. It is not the point of an imagined absolute otherness, but an 'alterity' which understands itself as an internal exclusion."[15]

Following Foucault and Derrida, an effective feminism could only be a wholly negative feminism, deconstructing everything and refusing to construct anything. This is the position Julia Kristeva adopts, herself an influential French post-structuralist. She says: "A woman cannot be; it is something which does not even belong in the order of being. *It follows that a feminist practice can only be negative,* at odds with what already exists so that we may say 'that's not it' and 'that's still not it.'"[16] The problematic character of subjectivity does not mean, then, that there can be no political struggle, as one might surmise from the fact that post-structuralism deconstructs the position of the revolutionary in the same breath as it deconstructs the position of the reactionary. But the political struggle can have only a "negative function," rejecting "everything finite, definite, structured, loaded with meaning, in the existing state of society."[17]

The attraction of the post-structuralist critique of subjectivity for feminists is two-fold. First, it seems to hold out the promise of an increased freedom for women, the "free play" of a plurality of differences, unhampered by any predetermined gender identity as formulated by either patriarchy or cultural feminism. Second, it moves decisively beyond cultural feminism and liberal feminism in further theorizing what they leave untouched: the construction of subjectivity. We can learn a great deal here about the mechanisms of sexist oppression and the construction of specific gender categories by relating these to social discourse and by conceiving of the subject as a cultural product. Certainly, too, this analysis can help us understand right-wing women, the reproduction of ideology, and the mechanisms that block social progress. However, adopting nominalism creates significant problems for feminism. How can we seriously adopt Kristeva's plan for only negative struggle? As the Left should by now have learned, you cannot mobilize a movement that is only and always against: you must have a positive alternative, a vision of a better future that can motivate people to sacrifice their time and energy toward its realization. Moreover, a feminist adoption of nominalism will be confronted with the same problem theories of ideology have, that is, Why is a right-wing woman's consciousness constructed via social discourse but a feminist's consciousness not? Post-structuralist critiques of subjectivity pertain to the construction of all subjects or they pertain to none. And here is precisely the dilemma for feminists: How can we ground a feminist politics that deconstructs the female subject? Nominalism threatens to wipe out feminism itself.

. . .

A nominalist position on subjectivity has the deleterious effect of de-gendering our analysis, of in effect making gender invisible once again. Foucault's ontology includes only bodies and pleasures, and he is notorious for not including gender as a category of analysis. If gender is simply a social construct, the need and even the possibility of a feminist politics becomes immediately problematic. What can we demand in the name of women if "women" do not exist and demands in their name simply reinforce the myth that they do? How can we speak out against sexism as detrimental to the interests of women if the category is a fiction? How can we demand legal abortions, adequate child care, or wages based on comparable worth without invoking a concept of "woman"?

Post-structuralism undercuts our ability to oppose the dominant trend (and, one might argue, the dominant danger) in mainstream Western intellectual thought, that is, the insistence on a universal, neutral, perspectiveless epistemology, metaphysics, and ethics. . . . For the post-structuralist, race, class, and gender are constructs and, therefore, incapable of decisively validating conceptions of justice and truth because underneath there lies no natural core to build on or liberate or maximize. Hence, once again, underneath we are all the same.) It is, in fact, a desire to topple this commitment to the possibility of a worldview—purported in fact as the best of all possible worldviews—grounded in a generic human, that motivates much of the cultural feminist glorification of femininity as a valid specificity legitimately grounding feminist theory.

The preceding characterizations of cultural feminism and post-structuralist feminism will anger many feminists by assuming too much homogeneity and by blithely pigeonholing large and complex theories. However, I believe the tendencies I have outlined toward essentialism and toward nominalism represent the main, current responses by feminist theory to the task of reconceptualizing "woman." Both responses have significant advantages and serious shortcomings. Cultural feminism has provided a useful corrective to the "generic human" thesis of classical liberalism and has promoted community and self-affirmation, but it cannot provide a long-range future course of action for feminist theory or practice, and it is founded on a claim of essentialism that we are far from having the evidence to justify. The feminist appropriation of post-structuralism has provided suggestive insights on the construction of female and male subjectivity and has issued a crucial warning against creating a feminism that reinvokes the mechanisms of oppressive power. Nonetheless, it limits feminism to the negative tactics of reaction and deconstruction and endangers the attack against classical liberalism by discrediting the notion of an epistemologically significant, specific subjectivity. What's a feminist to do?

We cannot simply embrace the paradox. In order to avoid the serious disadvantages of cultural feminism and post-structuralism, feminism needs to transcend the dilemma by developing a third course, an alternative theory of the subject that avoids both essentialism and nominalism. This new alternative might share the post-structuralist insight that the category "woman" needs to be theorized through an exploration of the experience of subjectivity, as opposed to a description of current attributes, but it need not concede that such an exploration will necessarily result in a nominalist position on gender, or an erasure of it. Feminists need to explore the possibility of a theory of the gendered subject that does not slide into essentialism. In the following two sections I will discuss recent work* that makes a contribution to the development of such a theory, or so I shall argue, and in the final section I will develop my own contribution in the form of a concept of gendered identity as positionality.

TERESA DE LAURETIS

Lauretis's influential book, *Alice Doesn't,* is a series of essays organized around an exploration of the problem of conceptualizing woman as subject. This problem is formulated in her work as arising out of the conflict between "woman" as a "fictional construct" and "women" as "real historical beings."[18] She says: "The relation between women as historical subjects and the notion of woman as it is produced by hegemonic discourses is neither a direct relation of identity, a one-to-one correspondence, nor a relation of simple implication. Like all other relations expressed in language, it is an arbitrary and symbolic one, that is to say, culturally set up. The manner and effects of that set-up are what the book intends to explore."[19] The strength of Lauretis's approach is that she never loses sight of the political imperative of feminist theory and, thus, never forgets that we must seek not only to describe this relation in which women's subjectivity is grounded but also to change it. And yet, given her view that we are constructed via a semiotic discourse, this political mandate becomes a crucial problem. As she puts it, "Paradoxically, the only way to position oneself outside of that discourse is to displace oneself within it—to refuse the question as formulated, or to answer deviously (though in its words), even to

quote (but against the grain). The limit posed but not worked through in this book is thus the contradiction of feminist theory itself, at once excluded from discourse and imprisoned within it."[20] As with feminist theory, so, too, is the female subject "at once excluded from discourse and imprisoned within it." Constructing a theory of the subject that both concedes these truths and yet allows for the possibility of feminism is the problem Lauretis tackles throughout *Alice Doesn't.* To concede the construction of the subject via discourse entails that the feminist project cannot be simply "how to make visible the invisible" as if the essence of gender were out there waiting to be recognized by the dominant discourse. Yet Lauretis does not give up on the possibility of producing "the conditions of visibility for a different social subject."[21] In her view, a nominalist position on subjectivity can be avoided by linking subjectivity to a Peircean notion of practices and a further theorized notion of experience.[22] I shall look briefly at her discussion of this latter claim.

Lauretis's main thesis is that subjectivity, that is, what one "perceives and comprehends as subjective," is constructed through a continuous process, an ongoing constant renewal based on an interaction with the world, which she defines as experience: "And thus [subjectivity] is produced not by external ideas, values, or material causes, but by one's personal, subjective engagement in the practices, discourses, and institutions that lend significance (value, meaning, and affect) to the events of the world."[23] . . . For all her insistence on a subjectivity constructed through practices, Lauretis is clear that *that* conception of subjectivity is not what she wishes to propose. A subjectivity that is fundamentally shaped by gender appears to lead irrevocably to essentialism, the posing of a male/female opposition as universal and ahistorical. A subjectivity that is not fundamentally shaped by gender appears to lead to the conception of a generic human subject, as if we could peel away our "cultural" layers and get to the real root of human nature, which turns out to be genderless. Are these really our only choices?

In *Alice Doesn't* Lauretis develops the beginnings of a new conception of subjectivity. She argues that subjectivity is neither (over)determined by biology nor by "free, rational, intentionality" but, rather, by experience, which she defines (via Lacan, Eco, and

---

*[Editor's Note: In the discussion that follows Alcoff examines the work of both Teresa de Lauretis and Denise Riley. Only the first of these two discussions is included here.]

Peirce) as "a complex of habits resulting from the semiotic interaction of 'outer world' and 'inner world,' the continuous engagement of a self or subject in social reality."[24] Given this definition, the question obviously becomes, Can we ascertain a "female experience"? This is the question Lauretis prompts us to consider, more specifically, to analyze "that complex of habits, dispositions, associations and perceptions, which en-genders one as female."[25] Lauretis ends her book with an insightful observation that can serve as a critical starting point:

> This is where the specificity of a feminist theory may be sought: not in femininity as a privileged nearness to nature, the body, or the unconscious, an essence which inheres in women but to which males too now lay a claim; not in female tradition simply understood as private, marginal, and yet intact, outside of history but fully there to be discovered or recovered; not, finally, in the chinks and cracks of masculinity, the fissures of male identity or the repressed of phallic discourse; *but rather in that political, theoretical, self-analyzing practice* by which the relations of the subject in social reality can be rearticulated from the historical experience of women. Much, very much, is still to be done.[26]

Thus Lauretis asserts that the way out of the totalizing imprint of history and discourse is through our "political, theoretical self-analyzing practice." This should not be taken to imply that only intellectual articles in academic journals represent a free space or ground for maneuver but, rather, that all women can (and do) think about, criticize, and alter discourse and, thus, that subjectivity can be reconstructed through the process of reflective practice. The key component of Lauretis's formulation is the dynamic she poses at the heart of subjectivity: a fluid interaction in constant motion and open to alteration by self-analyzing practice.

Recently, Lauretis has taken off from this point and developed further her conception of subjectivity. In the introductory essay for her latest book, *Feminist Studies/Critical Studies*, Lauretis claims that an individual's identity is constituted with a historical process of consciousness, a process in which one's history "is interpreted or reconstructed by each of us within the horizon of meanings and knowledges available in the culture at given historical moments, a horizon that also includes modes of

political commitment and struggle. . . . Consciousness, therefore, is never fixed, never attained once and for all because discursive boundaries change with historical conditions."[27] Here Lauretis guides our way out of the dilemma she articulated for us in *Alice Doesn't*. The agency of the subject is made possible through this process of political interpretation. And what emerges is multiple and shifting, neither "prefigured . . . in an unchangeable symbolic order" nor merely "fragmented, or intermittent."[28] Lauretis formulates a subjectivity that gives agency to the individual while at the same time placing her within "particular discursive configurations" and, moreover, conceives of the process of consciousness as a strategy. Subjectivity may thus become imbued with race, class, and gender without being subjected to an overdetermination that erases agency.

• • •

A CONCEPT OF POSITIONALITY

• • •

[I]t seems important to use Teresa de Lauretis's conception of experience as a way to begin to describe the features of human subjectivity. Lauretis starts with no given biological or psychological features and thus avoids assuming an essential characterization of subjectivity, but she also avoids the idealism that can follow from a rejection of materialist analyses by basing her conception on real practices and events. The importance of this focus on practices is, in part, Lauretis's shift away from the belief in the totalization of language or textuality to which most antiessentialist analyses become wedded. Lauretis wants to argue that language is not the sole source and locus of meaning, that habits and practices are crucial in the construction of meaning, and that through self-analyzing practices we can rearticulate female subjectivity. Gender is not a point to start from in the sense of being a given thing but is, instead, a posit or construct, formalizable in a nonarbitrary way through a matrix of habits, practices, and discourses. Further, it is an interpretation of our history within a particular discursive constellation, a history in which we are both subjects of and subjected to social construction.

The advantage of such an analysis is its ability to articulate a concept of gendered subjectivity without pinning it down one way or another for all time.

Given this and given the danger that essentialist conceptions of the subject pose specifically for women, it seems both possible and desirable to construe a gendered subjectivity in relation to concrete habits, practices, and discourses while at the same time recognizing the fluidity of these.

As . . . Lacan . . . remind[s] us, we must continually emphasize within any account of subjectivity the historical dimension.[29] This will waylay the tendency to produce general, universal, or essential accounts by making all our conclusions contingent and revisable. Thus, through a conception of human subjectivity as an emergent property of a historicized experience, we can say "feminine subjectivity is construed here and now in such and such a way" without this ever entailing a universalizable maxim about the "feminine."

It seems to me equally important to add to this approach an "identity politics," a concept that developed from the Combahee River Collective's "A Black Feminist Statement."[30] The idea here is that one's identity is taken (and defined) as a political point of departure, as a motivation for action, and as a delineation of one's politics. Lauretis and the authors of *Yours in Struggle* are clear about the problematic nature of one's identity, one's subject-ness, and yet argue that the concept of identity politics is useful because identity is a posit that is politically paramount. Their suggestion is to recognize one's identity as always a construction yet also a necessary point of departure.

. . .

Identity politics provides a decisive rejoinder to the generic human thesis and the mainstream methodology of Western political theory. According to the latter, the approach to political theory must be through a "veil of ignorance" where the theorist's personal interests and needs are hypothetically set aside. The goal is a theory of universal scope to which all ideally rational, disinterested agents would acquiesce if given sufficient information. Stripped of their particularities, these rational agents are considered to be potentially equally persuadable. Identity politics provides a materialist response to this and, in so doing, sides with Marxist class analysis. The best political theory will not be one ascertained through a veil of ignorance, a veil that is impossible to construct. Rather, political theory must base itself

on the initial premise that all persons, including the theorist, have a fleshy, material identity that will influence and pass judgment on all political claims. Indeed, the best political theory for the theorist herself will be one that acknowledges this fact. As I see it, the concept of identity politics does not presuppose a prepackaged set of objective needs or political implications but problematizes the connection of identity and politics and introduces identity as a factor in any political analysis.

If we combine the concept of identity politics with a conception of the subject as positionality, we can conceive of the subject as nonessentialized and emergent from a historical experience and yet retain our political ability to take gender as an important point of departure. Thus we can say at one and the same time that gender is not natural, biological, universal, ahistorical, or essential and yet still claim that gender is relevant because we are taking gender as a position from which to act politically. What does position mean here?

When the concept "woman" is defined not by a particular set of attributes but by a particular position, the internal characteristics of the person thus identified are not denoted so much as the external context within which that person is situated. The external situation determines the person's relative position, just as the position of a pawn on a chessboard is considered safe or dangerous, powerful or weak, according to its relation to the other chess pieces. The essentialist definition of woman makes her identity independent of her external situation: since her nurturing and peaceful traits are innate they are ontologically autonomous of her position with respect to others or to the external historical and social conditions generally. The positional definition, on the other hand, makes her identity relative to a constantly shifting context, to a situation that includes a network of elements involving others, the objective economic conditions, cultural and political institutions and ideologies, and so on. If it is possible to identify women by their position within this network of relations, then it becomes possible to ground a feminist argument for women, not on a claim that their innate capacities are being stunted, but that their position within the network lacks power and mobility and requires radical change. The position of women is relative and not innate, and yet neither is it "undecidable." Through social critique and analysis we can identify women via their position relative to an existing cultural and social network.

It may sound all too familiar to say that the oppression of women involves their relative position within a society; but my claim goes further than this. I assert that the very subjectivity (or subjective experience of being a woman) and the very identity of women is constituted by women's position. However, this view should not imply that the concept of "woman" is determined solely by external elements and that the woman herself is merely a passive recipient of an identity created by these forces. Rather, she herself is part of the historicized, fluid movement, and she therefore actively contributes to the context within which her position can be delineated. I would include Lauretis's point here, that the identity of a woman is the product of her own interpretation and reconstruction of her history, as mediated through the cultural discursive context to which she has access.[31] Therefore, the concept of positionality includes two points: first, as already stated, that the concept of woman is a relational term identifiable only within a (constantly moving) context; but, second, that the position that women find themselves in can be actively utilized (rather than transcended) as a location for the construction of meaning, a place from where meaning is constructed, rather than simply the place where a meaning can be *discovered* (the meaning of femaleness). The concept of woman as positionality shows how women use their positional perspective as a place from which values are interpreted and constructed rather than as a locus of an already determined set of values. When women become feminists the crucial thing that has occurred is not that they have learned any new facts about the world but that they come to view those facts from a different position, from their own position as subjects. When colonial subjects begin to be critical of the formerly imitative attitude they had toward the colonists, what is happening is that they begin to identify with the colonized rather than the colonizers.[32] This difference in positional perspective does not necessitate a change in what are taken to be facts, although new facts may come into view from the new position, but it does necessitate a political

change in perspective since the point of departure, the point from which all things are measured, has changed.

In this analysis, then, the concept of positionality allows for a determinate though fluid identity of woman that does not fall into essentialism: woman is a position from which a feminist politics can emerge rather than a set of attributes that are "objectively identifiable." Seen in this way, being a "woman" is to take up a position within a moving historical context and to be able to choose what we make of this position and how we alter this context. From the perspective of that fairly determinate though fluid and mutable position, women can themselves articulate a set of interests and ground a feminist politics.

• • •

[1988]

NOTES

1. Mary Daly, *Gyn/Ecology* (Boston: Beacon, 1978), 355.
2. Ibid., 60.
3. Ibid., 59.
4. Ibid., 365 (my emphasis).
5. Adrienne Rich, *On Lies, Secrets, and Silence* (New York: Norton, 1979), 18.
6. Adrienne Rich, *Of Woman Born* (New York: Bantam, 1977), 21.
7. Ibid., 290.
8. Ibid., 21.
9. Ibid., 292.
10. Cherríe Moraga, "From a Long Line of Vendidas: Chicanas and Feminism," in *Feminist Studies/Critical Studies,* ed. Teresa de Lauretis (Bloomington: Indiana University Press, 1986), 180.
11. Michel Foucault, "Why Study Power: The Question of the Subject," in *Beyond Structuralism and Hermeneutics: Michel Foucault,* ed. Hubert L. Dreyfus and Paul Rabinow, 2d ed. (Chicago: University of Chicago Press, 1983), 212.
12. Michel Foucault, "Nietzsche, Genealogy, History," in *The Foucault Reader,* ed. Paul Rabinow (New York: Pantheon, 1984), 83.
13. Jacques Derrida, *Spurs,* trans. Barbara Harlow (Chicago: University of Chicago Press, 1978), 49.
14. Ibid., 51.
15. Biddy Martin, "Feminism, Criticism, and Foucault," *New German Critique* 27 (1982): 11.
16. Julia Kristeva, "Woman Can Never Be Defined," in *New French Feminisms,* ed. Elaine Marks and Isabelle de Courtivron (New York: Schocken, 1981), 137 (my italics).
17. Julia Kristeva, "Oscillation between Power and Denial," in Marks and Courtivron, eds., 166.
18. Teresa de Lauretis, *Alice Doesn't* (Bloomington: Indiana University Press, 1984), 5.
19. Ibid., 5–6.

20. Ibid., 7.
21. Ibid., 8–9.
22. Ibid., 11.
23. Ibid., 159.
24. Ibid., 182. The principal texts Lauretis relies on in her exposition of Lacan, Eco, and Peirce are Jacques Lacan, *Ecrits* (Paris: Seuil, 1966); Umberto Eco, *A Theory of Semiotics* (Bloomington: Indiana University Press, 1976), and *The Role of the Reader: Explorations in the Semiotic of Texts* (Bloomington: Indiana University Press, 1979); and Charles Sanders Peirce, *Collected Papers*, vols. 1–8 (Cambridge, Mass.: Harvard University Press, 1931–58).
25. Lauretis, *Alice Doesn't* (n. 18 above), 182.
26. Ibid., 186 (my italics).
27. Lauretis, ed. (n. 10 above), 8.
28. Ibid., 9.
29. See Juliet Mitchell, "Introduction I," in Mitchell and Rose, eds., 4–5.
30. This was suggested to me by Teresa de Lauretis in an informal talk she gave at the Pembroke Center, 1984–85.
31. See Teresa de Lauretis, "Feminist Studies/Critical Studies: Issues, Terms, Contexts," in Lauretis, ed. (n. 10 above), 8–9.
32. This point is brought out by Homi Bhabba in his "Of Mimicry and Man: The Ambivalence of Colonial Discourse," *October* 28 (1984): 125–33; and by Abdur Rahman in his *Intellectual Colonisation* (New Delhi: Vikas, 1983).

❧ 75

Deconstructing Equality-Versus-Difference: or, The Uses of Poststructuralist Theory for Feminism

JOAN W. SCOTT

That feminism needs theory goes without saying (perhaps because it has been said so often). What is not always clear is what that theory will do, although there are certain common assumptions I think we can find in a wide range of feminist writings. We need theory that can analyze the workings of patriarchy in all its manifestations—ideological, institutional, organizational, subjective—accounting not only for continuities but also for change over time. We need theory that will let us think in terms of pluralities and diversities rather than of unities and universals. We need theory that will break the con-

ceptual hold, at least, of those long traditions of (Western) philosophy that have systematically and repeatedly construed the world hierarchically in terms of masculine universals and feminine specificities. We need theory that will enable us to articulate alternative ways of thinking about (and thus acting upon) gender without either simply reversing the old hierarchies or confirming them. And we need theory that will be useful and relevant for political practice.

It seems to me that the body of theory referred to as poststructuralism best meets all these requirements. It is not by any means the only theory nor are its positions and formulations unique. In my own case, however, it was reading poststructuralist theory and arguing with literary scholars that provided the elements of clarification for which I was looking. I found a new way of analyzing constructions of meaning and relationships of power that called unitary, universal categories into question and historicized concepts otherwise treated as natural (such as man/woman) or absolute (such as equality or justice). In addition, what attracted me was the historical connection between the two movements. Poststructuralism and contemporary feminism are late-twentieth-century movements that share a certain self-conscious critical relationship to established philosophical and political traditions. It thus seemed worthwhile for feminist scholars to exploit that relationship for their own ends.[1]

This article will not discuss the history of these various "exploitations" or elaborate on all the reasons a historian might look to this theory to organize her inquiry.[2] What seems most useful here is to give a short list of some major theoretical points and then devote most of my effort to a specific illustration. The first part of this article is a brief discussion of concepts used by poststructuralists that are also useful for feminists. The second part applies some of these concepts to one of the hotly contested issues among contemporary (U.S.) feminists—the "equality-versus-difference" debate.

Among the useful terms feminists have appropriated from poststructuralism are language, discourse, difference, and deconstruction.

Language. Following the work of structuralist linguistics and anthropology, the term is used to mean not simply words or even a vocabulary and set of grammatical rules but, rather, a meaning-constituting system: that is, any system—strictly verbal or other—through which meaning is constructed and cultural practices organized and by which, accordingly, people represent and understand their world, including who they are and how they relate to others. "Language," so conceived, is a central focus of poststructuralist analysis.

Language is not assumed to be a representation of ideas that either cause material relations or from which such relations follow; indeed, the idealist/materialist opposition is a false one to impose on this approach. Rather, the analysis of language provides a crucial point of entry, a starting point for understanding how social relations are conceived, and therefore—because understanding how they are conceived means understanding how they work—how institutions are organized, how relations of production are experienced, and how collective identity is established. Without attention to language and the processes by which meanings and categories are constituted, one only imposes oversimplified models on the world, models that perpetuate conventional understandings rather than open up new interpretive possibilities.

The point is to find ways to analyze specific "texts"—not only books and documents but also utterances of any kind and in any medium including cultural practices—in terms of specific historical and contextual meanings. Poststructuralists insist that words and texts have no fixed or intrinsic meanings, that there is no transparent or self-evident relationship between them and either ideas or things, no basic or ultimate correspondence between language and the world. The questions that must be answered in such an analysis, then, are how, in what specific contexts, among which specific communities of people, and by what textual and social processes has meaning been acquired? More generally, the questions are: How do meanings change? How have some meanings emerged as normative and others have been eclipsed or disappeared? What do these processes reveal about how power is constituted and operates?

Discourse. Some of the answers to these questions are offered in the concept of discourse, especially as it has been developed in the work of Michel Foucault. A discourse is not a language or a text but a historically, socially, and institutionally specific structure of statements, terms, categories, and beliefs. Foucault suggests that the elaboration of meaning involves conflict and power, that meanings are locally contested within discursive "fields of force," that (at least since the Enlightenment) the power to control a particular field resides in claims to (scientific) knowledge embodied not only in writing but also in disciplinary and professional organizations, in institutions (hospitals, prisons, schools, factories), and in social relationships (doctor/patient, teacher/student, employer/worker, parent/child, husband/wife). Discourse is thus contained or expressed in organizations and institutions as well as in words; all of these constitute texts or documents to be read.[3]

Discursive fields overlap, influence, and compete with one another; they appeal to one another's "truths" for authority and legitimation. These truths are assumed to be outside human invention, either already known and self-evident or discoverable through scientific inquiry. Precisely because they are assigned the status of objective knowledge, they seem to be beyond dispute and thus serve a powerful legitimating function. Darwinian theories of natural selection are one example of such legitimating truths; biological theories about sexual difference are another. The power of these "truths" comes from the way they function as givens or first premises for both sides in an argument, so that conflicts within discursive fields are framed to follow from rather than question them. The brilliance of so much of Foucault's work has been to illuminate the shared assumptions of what seemed to be sharply different arguments, thus exposing the limits of radical criticism and the extent of the power of dominant ideologies or epistemologies.

In addition, Foucault has shown how badly even challenges to fundamental assumptions often fared. They have been marginalized or silenced, forced to underplay their most radical claims in order to win a short-term goal, or completely absorbed into an existing framework. Yet the fact of change is crucial to Foucault's notion of "archaeology," to the way in which he uses contrasts from different historical periods to present his arguments. Exactly how the process happens is not spelled out to the satisfaction of many historians, some of whom want a more explicit causal model. But when causal theories are highly general, we are often drawn into the assumptions of the very discourse we ought to question. (If we are to question those assumptions, it may be necessary to forgo existing standards of historical inquiry.) Although some have read Foucault as an argument about the futility of human agency in the struggle for social change, I think that he is more appropriately taken as warning against simple solutions to difficult problems, as advising human actors to think strategically and more self-consciously about the philosophical and political implications and meanings of the programs they endorse. From this perspective, Foucault's work provides an important way of thinking differently (and perhaps more creatively) about the politics of the contextual construction of social meanings, about such organizing principles for political action as "equality" and "difference."

Difference. An important dimension of post-structuralist analyses of language has to do with the concept of difference, the notion (following Ferdinand de Saussure's structuralist linguistics) that meaning is made through implicit or explicit contrast, that a positive definition rests on the negation or repression of something represented as antithetical to it. Thus, any unitary concept in fact contains repressed or negated material; it is established in explicit opposition to another term. Any analysis of meaning involves teasing out these negations and oppositions, figuring out how (and whether) they are operating in specific contexts. Oppositions rest on metaphors and cross-references, and often in patriarchal discourse, sexual difference (the contrast masculine/feminine) serves to encode or establish meanings that are literally unrelated to gender or the body. In that way, the meanings of gender become tied to many kinds of cultural representations, and these in turn establish terms by which relations between women and men are organized and understood. The possibilities of this kind of analysis have, for obvious reasons, drawn the interest and attention of feminist scholars.

Fixed oppositions conceal the extent to which things presented as oppositional are, in fact, interdependent—that is, they derive their meaning from a particularly established contrast rather than from some inherent or pure antithesis. Furthermore, according to Jacques Derrida, the interdependence is hierarchical with one term dominant or prior, the opposite term subordinate and secondary. The Western philosophical tradition, he argues, rests on binary oppositions: unity/diversity, identity/difference, presence/absence, and universality/specificity. The leading terms are accorded primacy; their partners are represented as weaker or derivative. Yet the first terms depend on and derive their meaning from the second to such an extent that the secondary terms can be seen as generative of the definition of the first terms. If binary oppositions provide insight into the way meaning is constructed, and if they operate as Derrida suggests, then analyses or meaning cannot take binary oppositions at face value but rather must "deconstruct" them for the processes they embody.

Deconstruction. Although this term is used loosely among scholars—often to refer to a dismantling or destructive enterprise—it also has a precise definition in the work of Derrida and his followers. Deconstruction involves analyzing the operations of difference in texts, the ways in which meanings are made to work. The method consists of two related steps: the reversal and displacement of binary oppositions. This double process reveals the interdependence of seemingly dichotomous terms and their meaning relative to a particular history. It shows them to be not natural but constructed oppositions, constructed for particular purposes in particular contexts. The literary critic Barbara Johnson describes deconstruction as crucially dependent on difference.

> The starting point is often a binary difference that is subsequently shown to be an illusion created by the working of differences much harder to pin down. The differences *between* entities . . . are shown to be based on a repression of differences *within* entities, ways in which an entity differs from itself. . . . The "deconstruction" of a binary opposition is thus not an annihilation of all values or differences; it is an attempt to follow the subtle, powerful effects of differences already at work within the illusion of a binary opposition.[4]

Deconstruction is, then, an important exercise, for it allows us to be critical of the way in which ideas we want to use are ordinarily expressed, exhibited in patterns of meaning that may undercut the ends we seek to attain. A case in point—of meaning expressed in a politically self-defeating way—is the "equality-versus-difference" debate among feminists. Here a binary opposition has been created to offer a choice to feminists, of either endorsing "equality" or its presumed antithesis "difference." In fact, the antithesis itself hides the interdependence of the two terms, for equality is not the elimination of difference, and difference does not preclude equality.

In the past few years, " equality-versus-difference" has been used as a shorthand to characterize conflicting feminist positions and political strategies.[5] Those who argue that sexual difference ought to be an irrelevant consideration in schools, employment, the courts, and the legislature are put in the equality category. Those who insist that appeals on behalf of women ought to be made in terms of the needs, interests, and characteristics common to women as a group are placed in the difference category. In the clashes over the superiority of one or another of these strategies, feminists have invoked history, philosophy, and morality and have devised new classificatory labels: cultural feminism, liberal feminism, feminist separatism, and so on. Most recently, the debate about equality and difference has been used to analyze the Sears case, the sex discrimination suit brought against the retailing giant by the Equal Employment Opportunities Commission (EEOC) in 1984, in which historians Alice Kessler-Harris and Rosalind Rosenberg testified on opposite sides.

There have been many articles written on the Sears case, among them a recent one by Ruth Milkman. Milkman insists that we attend to the political context of seemingly timeless principles: "We ignore the political dimensions of the equality-versus-difference debate at our peril, especially in a period of conservative resurgence like the present." She concludes:

> As long as this is the political context in which we find ourselves, feminist scholars must be aware of the real danger that arguments about "difference" or "women's culture" will be put to uses other than those for which they were originally developed. That does not mean we must abandon these arguments or the intellectual terrain they have opened up; it does mean that we must be self-conscious in our formulations, keeping firmly in view the ways in which our work can be exploited politically.[6]

Milkman's carefully nuanced formulation implies that equality is our safest course, but she is also reluctant to reject difference entirely. She feels a need to choose a side, but which side is the problem. Milkman's ambivalence is an example of what the legal theorist Martha Minow has labeled in another context "the difference dilemma." Ignoring difference in the case of subordinated groups, Minow points out, "leaves in place a faulty neutrality," but focusing on difference can underscore the stigma of deviance. "Both focusing on and ignoring difference risk recreating it. This is the dilemma of difference."[7] What is required, Minow suggests, is a new way of thinking about difference, and this involves rejecting the idea that equality-versus-difference constitutes an opposition. Instead of framing analyses and strategies as if such binary pairs were timeless and true, we need to ask how the dichotomous pairing of equality and difference itself works. Instead of remaining with the terms of existing political discourse, we need to subject those terms to critical examination. Until we understand how the concepts work to constrain and construct specific meanings, we cannot make them work for us.

A close look at the evidence in the Sears case suggests that equality-versus-difference may not accurately depict the opposing sides in the Sears case. During testimony, most of the arguments against equality and for difference were, in fact, made by the Sears lawyers or by Rosalind Rosenberg. They constructed an opponent against whom they asserted that women and men differed, that "fundamental differences"—the result of culture on long-standing patterns of socialization—led to women's presumed lack of interest in commission sales jobs. In order to make their own claim that sexual difference and not discrimination could explain the hiring patterns of Sears, the Sears defense attributed to EEOC an assumption that no one had made in those terms—that women and men had identical interests. Alice Kessler-Harris did not argue that women were the same as men; instead, she used a variety of strategies to challenge Rosenberg's assertions. First, she argued that historical evidence suggested far more variety in the jobs women actually took than Rosenberg assumed. Second, she maintained that economic considerations usually offset the effects of socialization in women's attitudes to employment. And, third, she pointed out that, historically, job segregation by sex was the consequence of employer preferences, not employee choices. The question of women's choices could not be resolved, Kessler-Harris maintained, when the hiring process itself predetermined the outcome, imposing generalized gendered criteria that were not necessarily relevant to the work at hand. The debate joined then not around equality-versus-difference but around the relevance of general ideas of sexual difference in a specific context.[8]

To make the case for employer discrimination, EEOC lawyers cited obviously biased job applicant questionnaires and statements by personnel officers, but they had no individuals to testify that they had experienced discrimination. Kessler-Harris referred to past patterns of sexual segregation in the job market as the product of employer choices, but mostly she invoked history to break down Rosenberg's contention that women as a group differed consistently in the details of their behavior from men, instead insisting that variety characterized female job choices (as it did male job choices), that it made no sense in this case to talk about women as a uniform group. She defined equality to mean a presumption that women and men might have an equal interest in sales commission jobs. She did not claim that women and men, by definition, had such an equal interest. Rather, Kessler-Harris and the EEOC called into question the relevance for hiring decisions of generalizations about the necessarily antithetical behaviors of women and men. EEOC argued that Sears's hiring practices reflected inaccurate and inapplicable notions of sexual difference; Sears argued that "fundamental" differences between the sexes (and not its own actions) explained the gender imbalances in its labor force.

The Sears case was complicated by the fact that almost all the evidence offered was statistical. The testimony of the historians, therefore, could only be inferential at best. Each of them sought to explain small statistical disparities by reference to gross generalizations about the entire history of working women; furthermore, neither historian had much information about what had actually happened at Sears. They were forced, instead, to swear to the truth or falsehood of interpretive generalizations developed for purposes other than legal contestation, and they were forced to treat their interpretive premises as matters of fact. Reading the cross-examination of Kessler-Harris is revealing in this respect. Each of her carefully nuanced explanations of women's work history was forced into a reductive assertion by the Sears lawyers' insistence that she answer questions only by saying yes or no. Similarly, Rosalind Rosenberg's rebuttal to Alice Kessler-Harris eschewed the historian's subtle contextual reading of evidence and sought instead to impose a test of absolute consistency. She juxtaposed Kessler-Harris's testimony in the trial to her earlier published work (in which Kessler-Harris stressed differences between female and male workers in their approaches to work, arguing that women were more domestically oriented and less individualistic than men) in an effort to show that Kessler-Harris had misled the court.[9] Outside the courtroom, however, the disparities of the Kessler-Harris argument could also be explained in other ways. In relationship to a labor history that had typically excluded women, it might make sense to overgeneralize about women's experience, emphasizing difference in order to demonstrate that the universal term "worker" was really a male reference that could not account for all aspects of women's job experiences. In relationship to an employer who sought to justify discrimination by reference to sexual difference, it made more sense to deny the totalizing effects of difference by stressing instead the diversity and complexity of women's behavior and motivation. In the first case, difference served a positive function, unveiling the inequity hidden in a presumably neutral term; in the second case, difference served a negative purpose, justifying what Kessler-Harris believed to be unequal treatment. Although the inconsistency might have been avoided with a more self-conscious analysis of the "difference dilemma," Kessler-Harris's different positions were quite legitimately different emphases for different contexts; only in a courtroom could they be taken as proof of bad faith.[10]

The exacting demands of the courtroom for consistency and "truth" also point out the profound difficulties of arguing about difference. Although the testimony of the historians had to explain only a relatively small statistical disparity in the numbers of women and men hired for full-time commission sales jobs, the explanations that were preferred were totalizing and categorical.[11] In cross-examination, Kessler-Harris's multiple interpretations were found to be contradictory and confusing, although the judge praised Rosenberg for her coherence and lucidity.[12] In part, that was because Rosenberg held to a tight model that unproblematically linked socialization to individual choice; in part it was because her descriptions of gender differences accorded with prevailing normative views. In contrast, Kessler-Harris had trouble finding a simple model that would at once acknowledge difference *and* refuse it as an acceptable explanation for the employment pattern of Sears. So she fell into great difficulty maintaining her case in the face of hostile questioning. On the one hand, she was accused of assuming that economic opportunism equally affected women and men (and thus of believing that women and men were the same). How, then, could she explain the differences her own work had identified? On the other hand, she was tarred (by Rosenberg) with the brush of subversion, for implying that all employers might have some interest in sex typing the labor force, for deducing from her own (presumably Marxist) theory, a "conspiratorial" conclusion about the behavior of Sears.[13] If the patterns of discrimination that Kessler-Harris alluded to were real, after all, one of their effects might well be the kind of difference Rosenberg pointed out. Caught within the framework of Rosenberg's use of historical evidence, Kessler-Harris and her lawyers relied on an essentially negative strategy, offering details designed to complicate and undercut Rosenberg's assertions. Kessler-Harris did not directly challenge the theoretical shortcomings of Rosenberg's socialization model, nor did she offer an alternative model of her own. That would have required, I think, either fully developing the case for employer discrimination or insisting more completely on the "differences" line of argument by exposing the "equality-versus-difference" formulation as an illusion.

In the end, the most nuanced arguments of Kessler-Harris were rejected as contradictory or inapplicable, and the judge decided in Sears's favor, repeating the defense argument that an assumption of equal interest was "unfounded" because of the differences between women and men.[14] Not only was EEOC's position rejected, but the hiring poli-

cies of Sears were implicitly endorsed. According to the judge, because difference was real and fundamental, it could explain statistical variations in Sears's hiring. Discrimination was redefined as simply the recognition of "natural" difference (however culturally or historically produced), fitting in nicely with the logic of Reagan conservatism. Difference was substituted for inequality, the appropriate antithesis of equality, becoming inequality's explanation and legitimation. The judge's decision illustrates a process literary scholar Naomi Schor has described in another context: it "essentializes difference and naturalizes social inequity."[15]

The Sears case offers a sobering lesson in the operation of a discursive, that is a political field. Analysis of language here provides insight not only into the manipulation of concepts and definitions but also into the implementation and justification of institutional and political power. References to categorical differences between women and men set the terms within which Sears defended its policies *and* EEOC challenged them. Equality-versus-difference was the intellectual trap within which historians argued not about tiny disparities in Sears's employment practices, but about the normative behaviors of women and men. Although we might conclude that the balance of power was against EEOC by the time the case was heard and that, therefore, its outcome was inevitable (part of the Reagan plan to reverse affirmative action programs of the 1970s), we still need to articulate a critique of what happened that can inform the next round of political encounter. How should that position be conceptualized?

When equality and difference are paired dichotomously, they structure an impossible choice. If one opts for equality, one is forced to accept the notion that difference is antithetical to it. If one opts for difference, one admits that equality is unattainable. That, in a sense, is the dilemma apparent in Milkman's conclusion cited above. Feminists cannot give up "difference"; it has been our most creative analytic tool. We cannot give up equality, at least as long as we want to speak to the principles and values of our political system. But it makes no sense for the feminist movement to let its arguments be forced into preexisting categories and its political disputes to be characterized by a dichotomy we did not invent. How then do we recognize and use notions of sexual difference and yet make arguments for equality? The only response is a double one: the unmasking of the power relationship constructed by posing equality as the antithesis of difference and the refusal of its consequent dichotomous construction of political choices.

Equality-versus-difference cannot structure choices for feminist politics; the oppositional pairing misrepresents the relationship of both terms. Equality, in the political theory of rights that lies behind the claims of excluded groups for justice, means the ignoring of differences between individuals for a particular purpose or in a particular context. Michael Walzer puts it this way: "The root meaning of equality is negative; egalitarianism in its origins is an abolitionist politics. It aims at eliminating not all differences, but a particular set of differences, and a different set in differet times and places."[16] This presumes a social agreement to consider obviously different people as equivalent (not identical) for a stated purpose. In this usage, the opposite of equality is inequality or inequivalence, the noncommensurability of individuals or groups in certain circumstances, for certain purposes. Thus, for purposes of democratic citizenship, the measure of equivalence has been, at different times, independence or ownership of property or race or sex. The political notion of equality thus includes, indeed depends on, an acknowledgment of the existence of difference. Demands for equality have rested on implicit and usually unrecognized arguments from difference; if individuals or groups were identical or the same there would be no need to ask for equality. Equality might well be defined as deliberate indifference to specified differences.

The antithesis of difference in most usages is sameness or identity. But even here the contrast and the context must be specified. There is nothing self-evident or transcendent about difference, even if the fact of difference—sexual difference, for example—seems apparent to the naked eye. The questions always ought to be, What qualities or aspects are being compared? What is the nature of the comparison? How is the meaning of difference being constructed? Yet in the Sears testimony and in some debates among feminists (sexual) difference is assumed to be an immutable fact, its meaning inherent in the categories female and male. The lawyers

for Sears put it this way: "The reasonableness of the EEOC's *a priori* assumptions of male/female sameness with respect to preferences, interests, and qualifications is . . . the crux of the issue."[17] The point of the EEOC challenge, however, was never sameness but the irrelevance of categorical differences.

The opposition men/women, as Rosenberg employed it, asserted the incomparability of the sexes, and although history and socialization were the explanatory factors, these resonated with categorical distinctions inferred from the facts of bodily difference. When the opposition men/women is invoked, as it was in the Sears case, it refers a specific issue (the small statistical discrepancy between women and men hired for commission sales jobs) back to a general principle (the "fundamental" differences between women and men). The differences within each group that might apply to this particular situation—the fact, for example, that some women might choose "aggressive" or "risk-taking" jobs or that some women might prefer high- to low-paying positions—were excluded by definition in the antithesis between the groups. The irony is, of course, that the statistical case required only a small percentage of women's behaviors to be explained. Yet the historical testimony argued categorically about "women." It thus became impossible to argue (as EEOC and Kessler-Harris tried to) that within the female category, women typically exhibit and participate in all sorts of "male" behaviors, that socialization is a complex process that does not yield uniform choices. To make the argument would have required a direct attack on categorical thinking about gender. For the generalized opposition male/female serves to obscure the differences among women in behavior, character, desire, subjectivity, sexuality, gender identification, and historical experience. In the light of Rosenberg's insistence on the primacy of sexual difference, Kessler-Harris's insistence on the specificity (and historically variable aspect) of women's actions could be dismissed as an unreasonable and trivial claim.

The alternative to the binary construction of sexual difference is not sameness, identity, or androgyny. By subsuming women into a general "human" identity, we lose the specificity of female diversity and women's experiences; we are back, in other words, to the days when "Man's" story was supposed to be everyone's story, when women were "hidden from history," when the feminine served as the negative counterpoint, the "Other," for the construction of positive masculine identity. It is not sameness *or* identity between women and men that we want to claim but a more complicated historically variable diversity than is permitted by the opposition male/female, a diversity that is also differently expressed for different purposes in different contexts. In effect, the duality this opposition creates draws one line of difference, invests it with biological explanations, and then treats each side of the opposition as a unitary phenomenon. Everything in each category (male/female) is assumed to be the same; hence, differences within either category are suppressed. In contrast, our goal is to see not only differences between the sexes but also the way these work to repress differences within gender groups. The sameness constructed on each side of the binary opposition hides the multiple play of differences and maintains their irrelevance and invisibility.

Placing equality and difference in antithetical relationship has, then, a double effect. It denies the way in which difference has long figured in political notions of equality and it suggests that sameness is the only ground on which equality can be claimed. It thus puts feminists in an impossible position, for as long as we argue within the terms of a discourse set up by this opposition we grant the current conservative premise that because women cannot be identical to men in all respects, we cannot expect to be equal to them. The only alternative, it seems to me, is to refuse to oppose equality to difference and insist continually on differences—differences as the condition of individual and collective identities, differences as the constant challenge to the fixing of those identities, history as the repeated illustration of the play of differences, differences as the very meaning of equality itself.

Alice Kessler-Harris's experience in the Sears case shows, however, that the assertion of differences in the face of gender categories is not a sufficient strategy. What is required in addition is an analysis of fixed gender categories as normative statements that organize cultural understandings of sexual difference. This means that we must open to scrutiny the terms women and men as they are used

to define one another in particular contexts—workplaces, for example. The history of women's work needs to be retold from this perspective as part of the story of the creation of a gendered workforce. In the nineteenth century, for example, certain concepts of male skill rested on a contrast with female labor (by definition unskilled). The organization and reorganization of work processes was accomplished by reference to the gender attributes of workers, rather than to issues of training, education, or social class. And wage differentials between the sexes were attributed to fundamentally different family roles that preceded (rather than followed from) employment arrangements. In all these processes the meaning of "worker" was established through a contrast between the presumably natural qualities of women and men. If we write the history of women's work by gathering data that describes the activities, needs, interests, and culture of "women workers," we leave in place the naturalized contrast and reify a fixed categorical difference between women and men. We start the story, in other words, too late, by uncritically accepting a gendered category (the "woman worker") that itself needs investigation because its meaning is relative to its history.

If in our histories we relativize the categories woman and man, it means, of course, that we must also recognize the contingent and specific nature of our political claims. Political strategies then will rest on analyses of the utility of certain arguments in certain discursive contexts, without, however, invoking absolute qualities for women or men. There are moments when it makes sense for mothers to demand consideration for their social role, and contexts within which motherhood is irrelevant to women's behavior; but to maintain that womanhood is motherhood is to obscure the differences that make choice possible. There are moments when it makes sense to demand a reevaluation of the status of what has been socially constructed as women's work ("comparable worth" strategies are the current example) and contexts within which it makes much more sense to prepare women for entry into "nontraditional" jobs. But to maintain that feminity predisposes women to certain (nurturing) jobs or (collaborative) styles of work is to naturalize complex economic and social processes and, once again, to obscure the differences that have characterized women's occupational histories. An insistence on differences undercuts the tendency to abolutist, and in the case of sexual difference, essentialist categories. It does not deny the existence of gender difference, but it does suggest that its meanings are always relative to particular constructions in specified contexts. In contrast, absolutist categorizations of difference end up always enforcing normative rules.

It is surely not easy to formulate a "deconstructive" political strategy in the face of powerful tendencies that construct the world in binary terms. Yet there seems to me no other choice. Perhaps as we learn to think this way solutions will become more readily apparent. Perhaps the theoretical and historical work we do can prepare the ground. Certainly we can take heart from the history of feminism, which is full of illustrations of refusals of simple dichotomies and attempts instead to demonstrate that equality requires the recognition and inclusion of differences. Indeed, one way historians could contribute to a genuine rethinking of these concepts, is to stop writing the history of feminisms as a story of oscillations between demands for equality and affirmations of difference. This approach inadvertently strengthens the hold of the binary construction, establishing it as inevitable by giving it a long history. When looked at closely, in fact, the historical arguments of feminists do not usually fall into these neat compartments; they are instead attempts to reconcile theories of equal rights with cultural concepts of sexual difference, to question the validity of normative constructions of gender in the light of the existence of behaviors and qualities that contradict the rules, to point up rather than resolve conditions of contradiction, to articulate a political identity for women without conforming to existing stereotypes about them.

In histories of feminism and in feminist political strategies there needs to be at once attention to the operations of difference and an insistence on differences, but not a simple substitution of multiple for binary difference for it is not a happy pluralism we ought to invoke. The resolution of the "difference dilemma" comes neither from ignoring nor embracing difference as it is normatively constituted. Instead, it seems to me that the critical feminist position must always involve *two* moves. The first is the systematic criticism of the operations of categorical difference, the exposure of the kinds of exclusions and inclusions —the hierarchies—it constructs, and a refusal of their ultimate "truth." A refusal, however, not in the name of an equality that implies sameness or identity, but rather (and this is the second move) in the name of an equality that rests on differences—differences that confound, disrupt, and render ambiguous the meaning of any fixed binary opposition. To do anything else is to buy into the political argument that sameness is a requirement for equality, an untenable position for feminists (and historians) who know that power is constructed on and so must be challenged from the ground of difference.

[1988]

NOTES

1. On the problem of appropriating poststructuralism for feminism, see Biddy Martin, "Feminism, Criticism, Foucault," *New German Critique* 27 (Fall 1982): 3–30.
2. Joan W. Scott, "Gender: A Useful Category of Historical Analysis," *American Historical Review* 91 (December 1986); 1053–75; Donna Haraway, "A Manifesto for Cyborgs: Science, Technology, and Socialist Feminism in the 1980s," *Socialist Review* 15 (March-April 1985): 65–107.
3. Examples of Michel Foucault's work include *The Archaeology of Knowledge* (New York: Harper & Row, 1976), *The History of Sexuality*, vol. 1, *An Introduction* (New York: Vintage, 1980), and *Power/Knowledge: Selected Interviews and Other Writings, 1972–1977* (New York: Pantheon, 1980). See also Hubert L. Dreyfus and Paul Rabinow, *Michel Foucault: Beyond Structuralism and Hermeneutics* (Chicago: University of Chicago Press, 1983).
4. Barbara Johnson, *The Critical Difference: Essays in the Contemporary Rhetoric of Reading* (Baltimore: Johns Hopkins University Press, 1980): x–xi.
5. Most recently, attention has been focused on the issue of pregnancy benefits. See, for example, Lucina M. Finley, "Transcending Equality Theory: A Way Out of the Maternity and the Workplace Debate," *Columbia Law Review* 86 (October 1986): 1118–83. See Sylvia A. Law, "Rethinking Sex and the Constitution," *University of Pennsylvania Law Review* 132 (June 1984): 955–1040.
6. Ruth Milkman, "Women's History and the Sears Case," *Feminist Studies* 12 (Summer 1986): 394–95. In my discussion of the Sears case, I have drawn heavily on this careful and intelligent article, the best so far of the many that have been written on the subject.
7. Martha Minow, "Learning to Live with the Dilemma of Difference: Bilingual and Special Education," *Law and Contemporary Problems* 48, no. 2 (1984): 157–211; quotation is from p. 160; see also pp. 202–6.
8. Rosenberg's "Offer of Proof" and Kessler-Harris's "Written Testimony" appeared in *Signs* 11 (Summer 1986): 757–79. The "Written Rebuttal Testimony of Dr. Rosalind Rosenberg" is part of the official transcript of the case. U.S. District Court for the Northern District of Illinois, Eastern Division, *EEOC vs Sears*, Civil Action No. 79-C-4373. (I am grateful to Sanford Levinson for sharing the trial documents with me and for our many conversations about them.)

9. Appendix to the "Written Rebuttal Testimony of Dr. Rosalind Rosenberg," 1–12.

10. On the limits imposed by courtrooms and the pitfalls expert witnesses may encounter, see Nadine Taub, "Thinking about Testifying," *Perspectives* (American Historical Association Newsletter) 24 (November 1986): 10–11.

11. On this point, Taub asks a useful question: "Is there a danger in discrimination cases that historical or other expert testimony not grounded in the particular facts of the case will reinforce the idea that it is acceptable to make generalizations about particular groups?" (p. 11).

12. See the cross-examination of Kessler-Harris, *EEOC vs Sears,* 16376–619.

13. The Rosenberg "Rebuttal" is particularly vehement on this question: "This assumption that all employers discriminate is prominent in her (Kessler-Harris's) work. . . . In a 1979 article, she wrote hopefully that women harbor values, attitudes, and behavior patterns potentially subversive to capitalism" (p. 11). "There are, of course, documented instances of employers limiting the opportunities of women. But the fact that some employers have discriminated does not prove that all do" (p. 19). The rebuttal raises another issue about the political and ideological limits of a courtroom or, perhaps it is better to say, about the way the courtroom reproduces dominant ideologies. The general notion that employers discriminate was unacceptable (but the general notion that women prefer certain jobs was not). This unacceptability was underscored by linking it to subversion and Marxism, positions intolerable in U.S. political discourse. Rosenberg's innuendos attempted to discredit Kessler-Harris on two counts—first, by suggesting she was making a ridiculous generalization and, second, by suggesting that only people outside acceptable politics could even entertain that generalization.

14. Milkman, 391.

15. Naomi Schor, "Reading Double: Sand's Difference," in *The Poetics of Gender,* ed. Nancy K. Miller (New York: Columbia University Press, 1986), 256.

16. Michael Walzer, *Spheres of Justice: A Defense of Pluralism and Equality* (New York: Basic Books, 1983), xii. See also Minow, 202–3.

17. Milkman, 384.

 76

The "Risk" of Essence

DIANA FUSS

One of the prime motivations behind the production of this book is the desire to break or in some way to weaken the hold which the essentialist/constructionist binarism has on feminist theory. It is my conviction that the deadlock created by the longstanding controversy over the issue of human essences (essential femininity, essential blackness, essential gayness . . .) has, on the one hand, encouraged more careful attention to cultural and historical specificities where perhaps we have hitherto been too quick to universalize but, on the other hand, foreclosed more ambitious investigations of specificity and difference by fostering a certain paranoia around the perceived threat of essentialism. It could be said that the tension produced by the essentialist/constructionist debate is responsible for some of feminist theory's greatest insights, that is, the very tension is constitutive of the field of feminist theory. But it can also be maintained that this same dispute has created the current impasse in feminism, an impasse predicated on the difficulty of theorizing the social in relation to the natural, or the theoretical in relation to the political. The very confusion over whether or not the essentialist/constructionist tension is beneficial or detrimental to the health of feminism is itself overdetermined and constrained by the terms of the opposition in question.

One needs, therefore, to tread cautiously when mapping the boundaries of this important structuring debate for feminism. This chapter will begin by identifying the two key positions which are largely responsible for the current deadlock, and it will discuss some of the strengths and weaknesses of each position. One of the main contentions of this book is that essentialism, when held most under suspicion by constructionists, is often effectively doing its work elsewhere, under other guises, and sometimes laying the groundwork for its own critique. The bulk of the chapter will therefore address the way in which essentialism is *essential* to social constructionism, a point that powerfully throws into question the stability and impermeability of the essentialist/constructionist binarism. To this end I will look closely at currently two of the most important and influential theories of anti-essentialism, Lacanian psychoanalysis and Derridean deconstruction. In both cases I intend to demonstrate the way in which the logic of essentialism can be shown to be irreducible even in those discourses most explicitly concerned with repudiating it.

Essentialism vs. Constructionism

Essentialism is classically defined as a belief in true essence—that which is most irreducible, unchanging, and therefore constitutive of a given person or thing. This definition represents the traditional Aristotelian understanding of essence, the definition with the greatest amount of currency in the history of Western metaphysics.[1] In feminist theory, essentialism articulates itself in a variety of ways and subtends a number of related assumptions. Most obviously, essentialism can be located in appeals to a pure or original femininity, a female essence, outside the boundaries of the social and thereby untainted (though perhaps repressed) by a patriarchal order. It can also be read in the accounts of universal female oppression, the assumption of a totalizing symbolic system which subjugates all women everywhere, throughout history and across cultures. Further, essentialism underwrites claims for the autonomy of a female voice and the potentiality of a feminine language (notions which find their most sophisticated expression in the much discussed concept of *écriture féminine*).[2] Essentialism emerges perhaps most strongly within the very discourse of feminism, a discourse which presumes upon the unity of its object of inquiry (women) *even* when it is at pains to demonstrate the differences within this admittedly generalizing and imprecise category.

Constructionism, articulated in opposition to essentialism and concerned with its philosophical refutation, insists that essence is itself a historical construction. Constructionists take the refusal of essence as the inaugural moment of their own projects and proceed to demonstrate the way previously assumed self-evident kinds (like "man" or "woman") are in fact the effects of complicated discursive practices. Anti-essentialists are engaged in interrogating the intricate and interlacing processes which work together to produce all seemingly "natural" or "given" objects. What is at stake for a constructionist are systems of representations, social and material practices, laws of discourses, and ideological effects. In short, constructionists are concerned above all with the *production* and *organization* of differences, and they therefore reject the idea that any essential or natural givens precede the processes of social determination.

Essentialists and constructionists are most polarized around the issue of the relation between the social and the natural. For the essentialist, the natural provides the raw material and determinative starting point for the practices and laws of the social. For example, sexual difference (the division into "male" and "female") is taken as prior to social differences which are presumed to be mapped on to, *a posteriori,* the biological subject. For the constructionist, the natural is itself posited as a construction of the social. In this view, sexual difference is discursively produced, elaborated as an effect of the social rather than its *tabula rasa,* its prior object. Thus while the essentialist holds that the natural is *repressed* by the social, the constructionist maintains that the natural is *produced* by the social. The difference in philosophical positions can be summed up by Ernest Jones's question: "Is woman born or made?" For an essentialist like Jones, woman is born not made; for an anti-essentialist like Simone de Beauvoir, woman is made not born.

Each of these positions, essentialism and constructionism, has demonstrated in the range of its deployment certain analytical strengths and weaknesses. The problems with essentialism are perhaps better known. Essentialist arguments frequently make recourse to an ontology which stands outside the sphere of cultural influence and historical change. "Man" and "woman," to take one example, are assumed to be ontologically stable objects, coherent signs which derive their coherency from their unchangeability and predictability (there have *always* been men and women it is argued). No allowance is made for the historical production of these categories which would necessitate a recognition that what the classical Greeks understood by "man" and "woman" is radically different from what the Renaissance French understood them to signify or even what the contemporary postindustrial, postmodernist, poststructuralist theoretician is likely to understand by these terms. "Man" and "woman" are not stable or universal categories, nor do they have the explanatory power they are routinely invested with. Essentialist arguments are not necessarily ahistorical, but they frequently theorize history as an unbroken continuum that transports, across cultures and through time, categories such as "man" and "woman" without in any way (re)defining or indeed (re)constituting them. History itself is theorized as essential, and thus unchanging; its essence is to generate change but not itself to *be* changed.

Constructionists, too, though they might make recourse to historicity as a way to challenge essentialism, nonetheless often work with uncomplicated or essentializing notions of history. While a constructionist might recognize that "man" and "woman" are produced across a spectrum of discourses, the categories "man" and "woman" still remain constant. Some minimal point of commonality and continuity necessitates at least the linguistic retention of these particular terms. The same problem emerges with the sign "history" itself, for while a constructionist might insist that we can only speak of *histories* (just as we can only speak of feminisms or deconstructionisms) the question that remains unanswered is what motivates or dictates the continued semantic use of the term "histories"? This is just one of many instances which suggest that essentialism is more entrenched in constructionism than we previously thought. In my mind, it is difficult to see how constructionism can *be* constructionism without a fundamental dependency upon essentialism.

It is common practice in social constructionist argumentation to shift from the singular to the plural in order to privilege heterogeneity and to highlight important cultural and social differences. Thus, woman becomes women, history becomes histories, feminism becomes feminisms, and so on. While this maneuver does mark a break with unitary conceptual categories (eternal woman, totalizing history, monolithic feminism), the hasty attempts to pluralize do not operate as sufficient defenses or safeguards against essentialism. The plural category "women," for instance, though conceptually signaling heterogeneity nonetheless semantically marks a collectivity; constructed or not, "women" still occupies the space of a linguistic unity. It is for this reason that a statement like "American women are 'x'" is no less essentializing than its formulation in the singular, "*The* American woman is 'x.'" The essentialism at stake is not countered so much as *displaced*.

If essentialism is more entrenched in constructionist logic than we previously acknowledged, if indeed there is no sure way to bracket off and to contain essentialist maneuvers in anti-essentialist arguments, then we must also simultaneously acknowledge that there is no essence to essentialism, that essence *as* irreducible has been *constructed* to be irreducible. Furthermore, if we can never securely displace essentialism, then it becomes useful for analytical purposes to distinguish between *kinds* of essentialisms, as John Locke has done with his theory

of "real" versus "nominal" essence. Real essence connotes the Aristotelian understanding of essence as that which is most irreducible and unchanging about a thing; nominal essence signifies for Locke a view of essence as merely a linguistic convenience, a classifactory fiction we need to categorize and to label. Real essences are discovered by close empirical observation; nominal essences are not "discovered" so much as assigned or produced—produced specifically by language. This specific distinction between real and nominal essence corresponds roughly to the broader oppositional categories of essentialism and constructionism: an essentialist assumes that innate or given essences sort objects naturally into species or kinds, whereas a constructionist assumes that it is language, the names arbitrarily affixed to objects, which establishes their existence in the mind. To clarify, a rose by any other name would still be a rose—for an essentialist; for a constructionist, a rose by any other name would not be a rose, it would be something altogether rather different.

· · ·

My point here . . . is that social constructionists do not definitively escape the pull of essentialism, that indeed essentialism subtends the very idea of constructionism. Let me take another example, one often cited as the exemplary problem which separates the essentialist from the constructionist: the question of "the body." For the essentialist, the body occupies a pure, pre-social, pre-discursive space. The body is "real," accessible, and transparent; it is always *there* and directly interpretable through the senses. For the constructionist, the body is never simply there, rather it is composed of a network of effects continually subject to sociopolitical determination. The body is "always already" culturally mapped; it never exists in a pure or uncoded state. Now the strength of the constructionist position is its rigorous insistence on the production of social categories like "the body" and its attention to systems of representation. But this strength is not built on the grounds of essentialism's demise, rather it works its power by strategically deferring the encounter with essence, displacing it, in this case, onto the concept of sociality.

To say that the body is always already deeply embedded in the social is not by any sure means to preclude essentialism. Essentialism is embedded in the idea of the social and lodged in the problem of social determination (and even, as I will later argue, directly implicated in the deconstructionist turn of phrase "always already"). Too often, constructionists presume that the category of the social automatically escapes essentialism, in contradistinction to the way the category of the natural is presupposed to be inevitably entrapped within it. But there is no compelling reason to assume that the natural is in essence, essentialist and that the social is, in essence, constructionist. If we are to intervene effectively in the impasse created by the essentialist/constructionist divide, it might be necessary to begin questioning the *constructionist* assumption that nature and fixity go together (naturally) just as sociality and change go together (naturally). In other words, it may be time to ask whether essences can change and whether constructions can be normative.

Lacanian Psychoanalysis

It has often been remarked that biological determinism and social determinism are simply two sides of the same coin: both posit an utterly passive subject subordinated to the shaping influence of either nature or culture, and both disregard the unsettling effects of the psyche. There is a sense in which social constructionism can be unveiled as merely a form of sociological essentialism, a position predicated on the assumption that the subject is, in essence, a social construction. It may well be that at this particular historical moment it has become imperative to retrieve the subject from a total subordination to social determination. Perhaps that is why so many feminist theorists have turned to psychoanalysis as a more compelling, less essentializing account of the constructionist process. Psychoanalysis is in many ways the anti-essentialist discourse *par excellence* in that sexual difference is taken as something to be *explained* rather than assumed. But even psychoanalysis cannot do its work without making recourse to certain essentialist assumptions.

. . .

Lacan's contribution to constructionism emerges out of his revision of some key Freudian concepts. For Freud, the Oedipus complex is the fundamental structure responsible for the formation of sexual identity in the child. But Lacan insists that while oedipal relations and the complicated processes of identification and desire they engender are crucial to the child's psychical development, the Oedipus complex is not a given but rather itself a problem to be elucidated through psychoanalytic inquiry. According to Lacan, Freud "falsifies the conception of the Oedipus complex from the start, by making it define as natural, rather than normative, the predominance of the paternal figure" ("Intervention on Transference," Mitchell and Rose 1982, 69). For Lacan the Oedipus complex is not biologically framed but symbolically cast; in fact, it is a product of that order which Lacan labels "the Symbolic." More specifically, the Symbolic represents the order of language which permits the child entry into subjectivity, into the realm of speech, law, and sociality. The Imaginary signifies the mother-child dyad which the Symbolic interrupts through the agency of the paternal function—the "Name-of-the-Father," rather than the biological father *per se*. Through this important shift from the father to the Name-of-the-Father, Lacan denaturalizes the Oedipal structure which Freud takes as universal, de-essentializes Freud's theory of subject constitution by opening it up to the play of language, symbol, and metaphor.

A second important point of revision which further positions Lacan as more "truly" anti-essentialist than Freud pertains to the role of the phallus in sexual differentiation. Here, too, Lacan faults his predecessor for failing to make the crucial distinction between anatomical organ (the penis) and representational symbol (the phallus). Freud repeatedly collapses the two, leaving himself vulnerable to charges of biologism and essentialism. Lacan is more careful to separate them, insisting that the phallus is not a fantasy, not an object, and most especially not an organ (the penis or the clitoris) ("The Meaning of the Phallus," Mitchell and Rose 1982, 79). The phallus is instead a *signifier,* a privileged signifier of the Symbolic order which may point to the penis as the most visible mark of sexual difference but nevertheless cannot be reduced to it. This non-coincidence of phallus and penis is important because "the relation of the subject to the phallus is set up regardless of the anatomical difference between the sexes" ("The Meaning of the Phallus," 76). In a sense, the phallus is *prior* to the penis; it is the privileged mark through which both sexes accede to sexual identity by a recognition and acceptance of castration.

There are a number of problems with Lacan's penis/phallus distinction. . . . To the extent that the phallus risks continually conjuring up images of the penis, that is, to the extent that the bar between these two terms cannot be rigidly sustained, Lacan is never very far from the essentialism he so vigorously disclaims. It is true that the phallus is *not* the penis in any simple way; as a signifier it operates as a sign in a signifying chain, a symbolic metaphor and not a natural fact of difference. But it is also true that this metaphor derives its power from the very object it symbolizes; the phallus is pre-eminently a metaphor but it is also metonymically close to the penis and derives much of its signifying importance from this by no means arbitrary relation. It is precisely because a woman does not have a penis that her relation to the phallus, the signifying order, the order of language and the law, is so complicated and fraught with difficulties. The privileging of the phallus as "transcendental signifier" (the signifier without a signified) has led to charges that Lacan is endorsing the phallocentrism he purports to critique. . . .

While Lacan strategically employs linguistics to clean Freud's house of biologism, essentialism quietly returns to poststructuralist psychoanalysis through the back door carried on the soles of Lacan's theory of signification. Lacan is careful to specify that when he says the subject is constituted in language, language does *not* signify for him mere social discourse. Lacan is here following Ferdinand de Saussure's description of language as a system of relational signs, where meaning is a product of differences between signs and not an essential property of any fixed sign. Sassure makes a well-known distinction between "speech" and "language" in which speech (the individual communication act) is "accidental" and language (the communal system of rules and codes which govern speech) is "essential" (1915, 14). Lacan, recognizing the inseparability of one from the other, sees both language and speech as "essential" to the founding of the human subject. . . . What is irreducible to the discourse of psychoanalysis ("the talking cure") is speech. And, within the terms of this discourse, what is universal to psychoanalysis is the production of the subject

in the Symbolic. From its institutional beginnings, psychoanalysis has relied upon "the function and field of speech and language" as its essential deessentializing mechanisms of subject constitution, and (in Lacan's own words) it has taken as "selfevident fact that it deals solely with words" ("Intervention on Transference," Mitchell and Rose 1982, 63).

This brings us to the essentialism within Lacan's overall aim to return the institution of psychoanalysis to its authentic Freudian roots. Lacan's mission is to restore psychoanalysis to its essential truths, to what is most radical and irreducible about it. I must disagree with those commentators on Lacan who interpret his notion of a "return to Freud" as "merely a slogan." Lacan's goal is to reinstate the truth of psychoanalysis, to recapture "the Freudian experience along authentic lines" ("Agency of the Letter in the Unconscious or Reason Since Freud" 1977, 171). . . . The "return to Freud" cannot be easily divorced from the notions of authenticity, recuperation, and truth-discourse which it repeatedly invokes. Perhaps it is this indissociability of the idea of return from the ideology of humanism which compels Lacan to acknowledge, at the end of the English selection of *Ecrits,* that it is humanism which marks the return of the repressed in his own work: "I must admit that I am partial to a certain form of humanism, a humanism that . . . has a certain quality of candour about it: 'When the miner comes home, his wife rubs him down . . .' I am left defenceless against such things" ("The Subversion of the Subject and the Dialectic of Desire in the Freudian Unconscious" 1977, 324).

The choice of a working-class couple (a wife attending to the material bodily needs of her minerhusband) to signal his "defencelessness" in the face of lived experience is an unusual example for Lacan, who generally makes few references in his work to class positions or material relations. This tendency points to an important vestige of essentialism in Lacan's theory of subjectivity: the assumption that the subject is raceless and classless. The Lacanian subject is a sexed subject first and last; few allowances are made for the way in which other modes of difference might complicate or even facilitate the account of identity formation Lacan outlines along the axis of sex alone. Within the specific realm of sexual differentiation, essentialism emerges most strongly in Lacan's very attempts to displace the essence of "woman." Of real material women, such as the miner's wife, Lacan has nothing to say, readily admits his knowing ignorance. But of "woman" as sign Lacan has everything to say (especially since women, as we shall see, cannot say "it" themselves).

In Seminar XX, devoted to the enigma of woman and the riddle of femininity, Lacan tells us that woman, as such, does not exist:

> when any speaking being whatever lines up under the banner of women it is by being constituted as not all that they are placed within the phallic function. It is this that defines the . . . the what?—the woman precisely, except that *The* woman can only be written with *The* crossed through. There is no such thing as *The* woman, where the definite article stands for the universal. ("God and the *Jouissance* of ~~The~~ Woman," Mitchell and Rose 1982, 144)

On the surface, Lacan's erasure of the "The" in "The woman" is a calculated effort to de-essentialize woman. Eternal Woman, the myth of Woman, Transcendental Woman—all are false universals for Lacan, held in place only by the dubious efforts of the "signifier which cannot signify anything"—the definite article "the" ("God and the *Jouissance* of ~~The~~ Woman," 144). But is Lacan's mathematical "woman" (in "Seminar of 21 January 1975" he describes woman as an "empty set") any less universalizing than the metaphysical notion of woman he seeks to challenge? Essence quickly reappears as a "risk" Lacan cannot resist taking: "There is no such thing as *The* woman since of her essence—having already risked the term, why think twice about it?—of her essence, she is not all" ("God and the *Jouissance* of ~~The~~ Woman," 144). The project to de-essentialize "woman" is activated on the grounds of simultaneously re-essentializing her. The "risk" lies in the double gesture, the very process of transgressing the essentialist/constructionist divide.

In defining the essence of woman as "not all," the penis/phallus distinction once again comes into play, but this time as a way to keep essentialism in place. "It is through the phallic function that man takes up his inscription as all," Lacan explains in "A Love Letter" (Mitchell and Rose 1982, 150). All speaking beings are allowed to place themselves on the side of the not all, on the side of woman. Woman's supplementary *jouissance,* a *jouissance* "beyond the phallus," is "proper" to biological women but not exclusive to them. Men (specifically male mystics for Lacan) can also occupy the subject-position "woman"; in fact, "there are men who are just as good as women. It does happen" ("God and the *Jouissance* of ~~The~~ Woman," 147). But, importantly, the converse is not true for Lacan: not all speaking beings are allowed to inscribe themselves on the side of the all since only men have penises which give them more direct access to "the phallic function." Exclusion from *total* access to the Symbolic's privileged transcendental signifier has certain implications for the already castrated woman, not the least of which is a highly problematized relation to speech and language. . . .

[T]hrough the evasive and elliptical style which is his trademark, Lacan attempts to bring woman to the point of speech by approximating the vanishing point in his own speech. In his theory of woman as "not all," Lacan posits the essence of woman as an enigmatic excess or remainder. In this regard, woman remains for Lacan the enigma she was for Freud. In fact, essence operates in Lacan as a leftover classical component which reemerges in his theory of woman precisely because it is woman who escapes complete subjection to the Symbolic and its formative operations. In her inscription as not all (as Truth, lack, Other, *objet a,* God) woman becomes for Lacan the very repository of essence.

Derridean Deconstruction

And what of Derrida's theory of essence? Does Derrida "transcend" essentialism more successfully than Lacan, and if not, where is it inscribed and what implications might it hold for the most rigorous anti-essentialist discourse of all: deconstruction? My position here is that the possibility of any radical constructionism can only be built on the foundations of a hidden essentialism. Derrida would, of course, be quick to agree that despite the dislocating effects of deconstruction's strategies of reversal/displacement we can never get beyond metaphysics, and therefore, since all of Western metaphysics is predicated upon Aristotle's essence/

accident distinction, we can never truly get beyond essentialism. This is why we should not be surprised to see certain metaphysical holds operative in Derrida's own work, supporting even his relentless pursuit of binary oppositions and phenomenological essences. My interest in exploring what Derrida calls "fringes of irreducibility" (1972b, 67) as they operate in deconstruction itself is motivated not by a desire to demonstrate that Derrida is a *failed* constructionist (this would be a pointless exercise, given the terms of my argument) but by an interest in uncovering the ways in which deconstruction deploys essentialism against itself, leans heavily on essence in its determination to displace essence. Derrida's theory of woman is one place to start, though as I hope to show, essentialism works its logic through a number of important "Derrideanisms," including the emphasis upon undecidability and the related notions of contradiction and heterogeneity.

Woman and undecidability are, in fact, rather closely linked in Derrida's work. This intimate association is most evident in *Spurs* (1978) where Derrida attempts to come to grips with the question "What is woman?" through a sustained reading of the inscription of woman in Nietzsche's philosophy. Woman occupies for Nietzsche the site of a contradiction: she represents both truth and non-truth, distance and proximity, wisdom and deceit, authenticity and simulation. But Derrida points out that woman can be none of these things, in essence, since "there is no such thing as a woman, as a truth in itself of woman in itself" (101). Like Lacan, Derrida's project is to displace the essence of woman, but also like Lacan, Derrida is actively engaged in the redeployment of essentialism elsewhere. For Derrida, woman operates as the very figure of undecidability. It is woman as undecidable variable who displaces the rigid dualisms of Western metaphysics: "The question of the woman suspends the decidable opposition of true and nontrue and inaugurates the epochal regime of quotation marks which is to be enforced for every concept belonging to the system of philosophical decidability" (107). Woman, in short, is yet another figure for *différance,* the mechanism which undoes and disables "ontological decidability" (111). But more than this, she is the non-place which centers deconstruction's own

marginal status in philosophical discourse. When Gayatri Spivak identifies the phenomenon of woman's "double displacement" in deconstruction, she is referring to the tendency of deconstruction to announce its own displacement by situating woman as a figure of displacement (see Spivak 1983 and Spivak 1984). While there may be nothing essentialistic about this maneuver *per se,* one at least has to recognize that positing woman as a figure of displacement risks, in its effects, continually displacing real material women.

"Choreographies" (1982) extends Derrida's critique of the essence of woman by warning against the dangers of seeking to locate and to identify "woman's place": "in my view there is no one place for woman. It is without a doubt risky to say that there is no place for woman, but this idea is not antifeminist . . ." (68). There is an interesting slippage here from the claim that "there is no one place for woman" to the claim that "there is no place for woman"—two rather different statements indeed. But Derrida's point seems to be simply that a "woman's place," a single place, must necessarily be essentializing. This is doubtless true, but we need to ask whether positing multiple places for women is necessarily any *less* essentializing. Does "woman's *places*" effectively challenge the unitary, metaphysical notion of the subject/woman who presumably fills these particular places and not others? Derrida also makes the claim in "Choreographies" that there is no essence of woman, at least no "essence which is rigorously or properly identifiable" (72). Here one sees more clearly the opening for essentialism's re-entry onto the stage of deconstruction, for in the end Derrida does not so much challenge that woman has an essence as insist that we can never "rigorously" or "properly" identify it. Woman's essence is simply "undecidable," a position which frequently inverts itself in deconstruction to the suggestion that it is the essence of woman to *be* the undecidable. To say that woman's essence is to be the undecidable is different from claiming that woman's essence is undecidable and different still from claiming that it is undecidable whether woman has an essence at all. Derrida's theory of essence moves between and among these contradictory positions, playing upon the undecidability and

ambiguity which underwrites his own deconstructionist maneuvers.

. . .

. . . Essence manifests itself in deconstruction in that
most pervasive, most recognizable of Derridean
phrases, "always already" (*toujours déjà*).³ This
phrase marks a phenomenological carryover in Derrida's work, a point of refuge for essentialism which
otherwise, in deconstruction, comes so consistently
under attack. It is my belief that "always already"
frequently appears at those points where Derrida
wishes to put the brakes on the analysis in progress
and to make a turn in another direction. Occur-
rences of "always already" (or sometimes its abbre-
viated form "always") function as stop signs that alert
us to some of Derrida's central assumptions. . . .

. . .

A danger implicit in the ready application of the
logic of *toujours déjà* is the temptation to rely upon
the "always already" self-evident "nature" of "always already." The fact that "always already" is a
phrase that has been so readily appropriated (and on
occasion parodied) in academic circles immediately
casts suspicion on its efficacy. At the present moment,
"always already" has such wide currency amongst
poststructuralists and non-poststructuralists alike
that it has lost much of the rhetorical power and
energy which characterizes its appearances in Derrida's work. . . .

In Derrida's work "always already" operates as
something of a contradiction: it arrests analysis at a
crucial stage, but it also shifts analytical gears and
moves us along in another direction. . . . It is a technique which deliberately frustrates closure and
keeps meaning in play; but it is also a technique that
relies upon the self-evidence of contradiction and
heterogeneity. . . . Derrida holds a mirror up to his
detractors and reflects their charges of "monolithic
thinking" and "homogeneity" back to them, unwilling to recognize any possible contradictions within
his own discourse, willing only (in surprisingly
unDerridean fashion) to treat contradiction on a
thematic level and not on a deeper textual level.

"The risk of essence may have to be taken"
Despite the uncertainty and confusion surrounding
the sign "essence," more than one influential theorist has advocated that perhaps we cannot do with-

out recourse to irreducibilities. One thinks of Stephen Heath's by now famous suggestion, "the risk
of essence may have to be taken" ("Difference"
1978, 99). It is poststructuralist feminists who seem
most intrigued by this call to risk essence. Alice Jardine, for example, finds Stephen Heath's procla-
mation (later echoed by Gayatri Spivak) to be "one
of the most thought-provoking statements of recent
date" ("Men in Feminism: Odor di Uomo Or Com-
pagnons de Route?" in Jardine and Smith 1987,
58). . . .

But the call to risk essence is not merely an "impatient reaction" to deconstruction (though it might
indeed be this in certain specific instances); it can
also operate as a deconstructionist strategy. "Is not
strategy itself the real risk?" Derrida asks in his
seminar on feminism ("Women in the Beehive," in
Jardine and Smith 1987, 192). To the deconstructionist, strategy of any kind is a risk because its effects, its outcome, are always unpredictable and
undecidable. Depending on the historical moment
and the cultural context, a strategy can be "radically
revolutionary or deconstructive" or it can be "dangerously reactive" (193). What is risky is giving up
the security—and the fantasy—of occupying a
single subject-position and instead occupying two
places at once. . . .

It must be pointed out here that the constructionist strategy of specifying more precisely these
sub-categories or "woman" does not necessarily
preclude essentialism. "French bourgeois woman"
or "Anglo-American lesbian," while crucially emphasizing in their very specificity that "woman" is
by no means a monolithic category, nonetheless
reinscribe an essentialist logic at the very level of
historicism. Historicism is not always an effective
counter to essentialism if it succeeds only in fragmenting the subject into multiple identities, each
with its own self-contained, self-referential essence.
The constructionist impulse to specify, rather than
definitively counteracting essentialism, often simply redeploys it through the very strategy of histo-
ricization, rerouting and dispersing it through a
number of micropolitical units or sub-categorical
classifications, each presupposing its own unique
interior composition or metaphysical core.

There is an important distinction to be made, I
would submit, between "deploying" or "activating"

essentialism and "falling into" or "lapsing into" essentialism. "Falling into" or "lapsing into" implies that essentialism is inherently reactionary—inevitably and inescapably a problem or a mistake. "Deploying" or "activating," on the other hand, implies that essentialism may have some strategic or interventionary value. What I am suggesting is that the political investments of the sign "essence" are predicated on the subject's complex positioning in a particular social field, and that the appraisal of this investment depends not on any interior values intrinsic to the sign itself but rather on the shifting and determinative discursive relations which produced it. As subsequent chapters will more forcefully suggest, the radicality or conservatism of essentialism depends, to a significant degree, on *who* is utilizing it, *how* it is deployed, and *where* its effects are concentrated.

It is important not to forget that essence is a sign, and as such historically contingent and constantly subject to change and to redefinition. Historically, we have never been very confident of the definition of essence, nor have we been very certain that the definition of essence is to *be* the definitional. Even the essence/accident distinction, the inaugural moment of Western metaphysics, is by no means a stable or secure binarism. The entire history of metaphysics can be read as an interminable pursuit of the essence of essence, motivated by the anxiety that essence may well be accidental, changing and unknowable. Essentialism is not, and has rarely been, monolithically coded. Certainly it is difficult to identify a single philosopher whose work does not attempt to account for the question of essentialism in some way; the repeated attempts by these philosophers to fix or to define essence suggest that essence is a slippery and elusive category, and that the sign itself does not remain stationary or uniform.

The deconstruction of essentialism, rather than putting essence to rest, simply raises the discussion to a more sophisticated level, leaps the analysis up to another higher register, above all, keeps the sign of essence in play, even if (indeed *because*) it is continually held under erasure. Constructionists, then, need to be wary of too quickly crying "essentialism." Perhaps the most dangerous problem for anti-essentialists is to see the category of essence as "al-

ways already" knowable, as immediately apparent and naturally transparent. Similarly, we need to beware of the tendency to "naturalize" the category of the natural, to see this category, too, as obvious and immediately perceptible *as such*. Essentialism may be at once more intractable and more irrecuperable than we thought; it may be essential to our thinking while at the same time there is nothing "quintessential" about it. To insist that essentialism is always and everywhere reactionary is, for the constructionist, to buy into essentialism in the very act of making the charge; *it is to act as if essentialism has an essence.*

[1989]

NOTES

1. A comprehensive discussion of the essence/accident distinction is elaborated in Book Z of Aristotle's *Metaphysics*. For a history of the philosophical concept of essentialism, readers might wish to consult DeGrood (1976) or Rorty (1979).
2. See, for example, Hélène Cixous's contribution to *The Newly Born Woman* (1986).
3. Though we have come to associate this phrase with Derrida, it has, in fact, a more extended philosophical history. One can detect its recurrence in the works of such disparate theorists as Husserl, Heidegger, Althusser, and Lacan. For Derrida's discussion of Heidegger's use of "always already," see "The Ends of Man," 1972b, 124–25.

REFERENCES

Benvenuto, Bice and Roger Kennedy. 1986. *The Works of Jacques Lacan*. New York: St. Martin's Press.

Cixous, Hélène and Catherine Clément. 1975. *La jeune neé*. Paris: Union Générale d'Editions. Trans. Betsy Wing (1986). *The Newly Born Woman*. Minneapolis: University of Minnesota Press.

DeGrood, David H. 1976. *Philosophies of Essence: An Examination of the Category of Essence*. Amsterdam: B. R. Gruner Publishing Company.

Derrida, Jacques. 1962. Translation and Introduction to Edmund Husserl, *L'Origine de la géométrie*. Paris: Presses Universitaires de France. Trans. John Leavey (1978). *Edmund Husserl's 'Origin of Geometry': An Introduction*. Pittsburgh: Duquesne University Press.

Derrida, Jacques. 1967c. *L'Ecriture et la différence*. Paris: Seuil. Trans. Alan Bass (1978). *Writing and Difference*. Chicago: University of Chicago Press.

Derrida, Jacques, 1972a. *Marges de la philosophie*. Paris: Minuit. Trans. Alan Bass (1982). *Margins of Philosophy*. Chicago: University of Chicago Press.

Derrida, Jacques, 1972b. *Positions*. Paris: Minuit. Trans. Alan Bass (1981). *Positions*. Chicago: University of Chicago Press.

Derrida, Jacques. 1978. *Eperons: Les styles de Nietzsche*. Paris: Flammarion. Trans. Barbara Harlow. 1979. *Spurs: Nietzsche's Styles*. Chicago: University of Chicago Press.

Derrida, Jacques. 1980. *La carte postale.* Trans. Alan Bass (1987). *The Post Card.* Chicago: University of Chicago Press.

Derrida, Jacques. 1982a. "Choreographies." Interview with Christie V. McDonald. *Diacritics* 12:2 (Summer): 66–76.

Heath, Stephen. 1978. "Difference." *Screen* 19:3 (Autumn): 50–112.

Irigaray, Luce. 1977a. *Ce Sexe qui n'en est pas un.* Trans. Catherine Porter with Carolyn Burke (1985). *This Sex Which Is Not One.* Ithaca: Cornell University Press.

Jardine, Alice and Paul Smith (eds). 1987. *Men in Feminism.* New York and London: Methuen.

Kaplan, E. Ann. 1987. "Feminist Criticism and Television." In Robert C. Allen (ed). *Channels of Discourse: Television and Contemporary Criticism.* Chapel Hill and London: University of North Carolina Press.

Lacan, Jacques. 1977. *Écrits.* Trans. Alan Sheridan. New York: W. W. Norton & Company.

Locke, John. 1690. *An Essay Concerning Human Understanding.* London: Printed by Elizabeth Holt for Thomas Bassett.

MacCannell, Juliet Flower. 1986. *Figuring Lacan: Criticism and the Cultural Unconscious.* Lincoln: University of Nebraska Press.

Mitchell, Juliet and Jacqueline Rose. 1982. *Feminine Sexuality: Jacques Lacan and the école freudienne.* New York: W. W. Norton and Company.

Moi, Toril. 1985. *Sexual/Textual Politics: Feminist Literary Theory.* New York: Methuen.

Ragland-Sullivan, Ellie. 1986. *Jacques Lacan and the Philosophy of Psychoanalysis.* Urbana and Chicago: University of Illinois Press.

Rorty, Richard. 1979. *Philosophy and the Mirror of Nature.* Princeton: Princeton University Press.

Smith, Paul. 1988. *Discerning the Subject.* Minneapolis: University of Minnesota Press.

Spivak, Gayatri Chakravorty. 1983. "Displacement and the Discourse of Woman." In Mark Krupnick, (ed). *Displacement: Derrida and After.* Bloomington: Indiana University Press, 169–95.

Spivak, Gayatri Chakravorty. 1984. "Love Me, Love My Ombre, Elle." *Diacritics* (Winter): 19–36.

 77

Feminism: A Transformational Politic

b e l l h o o k s

We live in a world of crisis—a world governed by politics of domination, one in which the belief in a notion of superior and inferior, and its concomitant ideology—that the superior should rule over the inferior—effects the lives of all people everywhere, whether poor or privileged, literate or illiterate. Systematic dehumanization, worldwide famine, ecological devastation, industrial contamination, and the possibility of nuclear destruction are realities which remind us daily that we are in crisis. Contemporary feminist thinkers often cite sexual politics as the origin of this crisis. They point to the insistence on difference as that factor which becomes the occasion for separation and domination and suggest that differentiation of status between females and males globally is an indication that patriarchal domination of the planet is the root of the problem. Such an assumption has fostered the notion that elimination of sexist oppression would necessarily lead to the eradication of all forms of domination. It is an argument that has led influential Western white women to feel that feminist movement should be *the* central political agenda for females globally. Ideologically, thinking in this direction enables Western women, especially privileged white women, to suggest that racism and class exploitation are merely the offspring of the parent system: patriarchy. Within feminist movement in the West, this has led to the assumption that resisting patriarchal domination is a more legitimate feminist action that resisting racism and other forms of domination. Such thinking prevails despite radical critiques made by black women and other women of color who question this proposition. To speculate that an oppositional division between men and women existed in early human communities is to impose on the past, on these non-white groups, a world view that fits all too neatly within contemporary feminist paradigms that name man as the enemy and woman as the victim.

Clearly, differentiation between strong and weak, powerful and powerless, has been a central defining aspect of gender globally, carrying with it the assumption that men should have greater authority than women, and should rule over them. As significant and important as this fact is, it should not obscure the reality that women can and do participate in politics of domination, as perpetrators as well as victims—that we dominate, that we are dominated. If focus on patriarchal domination masks this reality or becomes the means by which women deflect attention from the real conditions and circumstances of our lives, then women cooperate in suppressing and promoting false consciousness, inhibiting our capacity to assume responsibility for transforming ourselves and society.

Thinking speculatively about early human social arrangement, about women and men struggling to survive in small communities, it is likely that the parent-child relationship with its very real imposed survival structure of dependency, of strong and weak, of powerful and powerless, was a site for the construction of a paradigm of domination. While this circumstance of dependency is not necessarily one that leads to domination, it lends itself to the enactment of a social drama wherein domination could easily occur as a means of exercising and maintaining control. This speculation does not place women outside the practice of domination, in the exclusive role of victim. It centrally names women as agents of domination, as potential theoreticians, and creators of a paradigm for social relationships wherein those groups of individuals designated as "strong" exercise power both benevolently and coercively over those designated as "weak."

Emphasizing paradigms of domination that call attention to woman's capacity to dominate is one way to deconstruct and challenge the simplistic notion that man is the enemy, woman the victim; the notion that men have always been the oppressors. Such thinking enables us to examine our role as women in the perpetuation and maintenance of systems of domination. To understand domination, we must understand that our capacity as women and men to be either dominated or dominating is a point of connection, of commonality. Even though I speak from the particular experience of living as a black woman in the United States, a white-supremacist, capitalist, patriarchal society, where small numbers of white men (and honorary "white men") constitute ruling groups, I understand that in many places in the world oppressed and oppressor share the same color. I understand that right here in this room, oppressed and oppressor share the same gender. Right now as I speak, a man who is himself victimized, wounded, hurt by racism and class exploitation is actively dominating a woman in his

life—that even as I speak, women who are ourselves exploited, victimized, are dominating children. It is necessary for us to remember, as we think critically about domination, that we all have the capacity to act in ways that oppress, dominate, wound (whether or not that power is institutionalized). It is necessary to remember that it is first the potential oppressor within that we must resist—the potential victim within that we must rescue—otherwise we cannot hope for an end to domination, for liberation.

This knowledge seems especially important at this historical moment when black women and other women of color have worked to create awareness of the ways in which racism empowers white women to act as exploiters and oppressors. Increasingly this fact is considered a reason we should not support feminist struggle even though sexism and sexist oppression is a real issue in our lives as black women (see, for example, Vivian Gordon's *Black Women, Feminism, Black Liberation: Which Way?*). It becomes necessary for us to speak continually about the convictions that inform our continued advocacy of feminist struggle. By calling attention to interlocking systems of domination—sex, race, and class—black women and many other groups of women acknowledge the diversity and complexity of female experience, of our relationship to power and domination. The intent is not to dissuade people of color from becoming engaged in feminist movement. Feminist struggle to end patriarchal domination should be of primary importance to women and men globally not because it is the foundation of all other oppressive structures but because it is that form of domination we are most likely to encounter in an ongoing way in everyday life.

Unlike other forms of domination, sexism directly shapes and determines relations of power in our private lives, in familiar social spaces, in that most intimate context—home—and in that most intimate sphere of relations—family. Usually, it is within the family that we witness coercive domination and learn to accept it, whether it be domination of parent over child, or male over female. Even though family relations may be, and most often are, informed by acceptance of a politic of domination, they are simultaneously relations of care and connection. It is this convergence of two contradictory impulses—the urge to promote growth and the urge to inhibit growth—that provides a practical setting for feminist critique, resistance, and transformation.

Growing up in a black, working-class, father-dominated household, I experienced coercive adult male authority as more immediately threatening, as more likely to cause immediate pain than racist oppression or class exploitation. It was equally clear that experiencing exploitation and oppression in the home made one feel all the more powerless when encountering dominating forces outside the home. This is true for many people. If we are unable to resist and end domination in relations where there is care, it seems totally unimaginable that we can resist and end it in other institutionalized relations of power. If we cannot convince the mothers and/or fathers who care not to humiliate and degrade us, how can we imagine convincing or resisting an employer, a lover, a stranger who systematically humiliates and degrades?

Feminist effort to end patriarchal domination should be of primary concern precisely because it insists on the eradication of exploitation and oppression in the family context and in all other intimate relationships. It is that political movement which most radically addresses the person—the personal—citing the need for transformation of self, of relationships, so that we might be better able to act in a revolutionary manner, challenging and resisting domination, transforming the world outside the self. Strategically, feminist movement should be a central component of all other liberation struggles because it challenges each of us to alter our person, our personal engagement (either as victims or perpetrators or both) in a system of domination.

Feminism, as liberation struggle, must exist apart from and as a part of the larger struggle to eradicate domination in all its forms. We must understand that patriarchal domination shares an ideological foundation with racism and other forms of group oppression, that there is no hope that it can be eradicated while these systems remain intact. This knowledge should consistently inform the direction of feminist theory and practice. Unfortunately, racism and class elitism among women has frequently led to the suppression and distortion of this connection so that it is now necessary for feminist thinkers

to critique and revise much feminist theory and the direction of feminist movement. This effort at revision is perhaps most evident in the current widespread acknowledgement that sexism, racism, and class exploitation constitute interlocking systems of domination—that sex, race, and class, and not sex alone, determine the nature of any female's identity, status, and circumstance, the degree to which she will or will not be dominated, the extent to which she will have the power to dominate.

While acknowledgement of the complex nature of woman's status (which has been most impressed upon everyone's consciousness by radical women of color) is a significant corrective, it is only a starting point. It provides a frame of reference which must serve as the basis for thoroughly altering and revising feminist theory and practice. It challenges and calls us to re-think popular assumptions about the nature of feminism that have had the deepest impact on a large majority of women, on mass consciousness. It radically calls into question the notion of a fundamentally common female experience which has been seen as the prerequisite for our coming together, for political unity. Recognition of the interconnectedness of sex, race, and class highlights the diversity of experience, compelling redefinition of the terms for unity. If women do not share "common oppression," what then can serve as a basis for our coming together?

Unlike many feminist comrades, I believe women and men must share a common understanding—a basic knowledge of what feminism is—if it is ever to be a powerful mass-based political movement. In *Feminist Theory: from margin to center,* I suggest that defining feminism broadly as "a movement to end sexism and sexist oppression" would enable us to have a common political goal. We would then have a basis on which to build solidarity. Multiple and contradictory definitions of feminism create confusion and undermine the effort to construct feminist movement so that it addresses everyone. Sharing a common goal does not imply that women and men will not have radically divergent perspectives on how that goal might be reached. Because each individual starts the process of engagement in feminist struggle at a unique level of awareness, very real differences in experience, perspective, and knowledge make developing varied strategies for participation and transformation a necessary agenda.

Feminist thinkers engaged in radically revisioning central tenets of feminist thought must continually emphasize the importance of sex, race and class as factors which *together* determine the social construction of femaleness, as it has been so deeply ingrained in the consciousness of many women active in feminist movement that gender is the sole factor determining destiny. However, the work of education for critical consciousness (usually called consciousness-raising) cannot end there. Much feminist consciousness-raising has in the past focussed on identifying the particular ways men oppress and exploit women. Using the paradigm of sex, race, and class means that the focus does not begin with men and what they do to women, but rather with women working to identify both individually and collectively the specific character of our social identity.

Imagine a group of women from diverse backgrounds coming together to talk about feminism. First they concentrate on working out their status in terms of sex, race, and class using this as the standpoint from which they begin discussing patriarchy or their particular relations with individual men. Within the old frame of reference, a discussion might consist solely of talk about their experiences as victims in relationship to male oppressors. Two women—one poor, the other quite wealthy—might describe the process by which they have suffered physical abuse by male partners and find certain commonalities which might serve as a basis for bonding. Yet if these same two women engaged in a discussion of class, not only would the social construction and expression of femaleness differ, so too would their ideas about how to confront and change their circumstances. Broadening the discussion to include an analysis of race and class would expose many additional differences even as commonalities emerged.

Clearly the process of bonding would be more complex, yet this broader discussion might enable the sharing of perspectives and strategies for change that would enrich rather than diminish our understanding of gender. While feminists have increasingly given "lip service" to the idea of diversity, we have not developed strategies of communication

and inclusion that allow for the successful enactment of this feminist vision.

Small groups are no longer the central place for feminist consciousness-raising. Much feminist education for critical consciousness takes place in Women's Studies classes or at conferences which focus on gender. Books are a primary source of education which means that already masses of people who do not read have no access. The separation of grassroots ways of sharing feminist thinking across kitchen tables from the spheres where much of that thinking is generated, the academy, undermines feminist movement. It would further feminist movement if new feminist thinking could be once again shared in small group contexts, integrating critical analysis with discussion of personal experience. It would be useful to promote anew the small group setting as an arena for education for critical consciousness, so that women and men might come together in neighborhoods and communities to discuss feminist concerns.

Small groups remain an important place for education for critical consciousness for several reasons. An especially important aspect of the small group setting is the emphasis on communicating feminist thinking, feminist theory, in a manner that can be easily understood. In small groups, individuals do not need to be equally literate or literate at all because the information is primarily shared through conversation, in dialogue which is necessarily a liberatory expression. (Literacy should be a goal for feminists even as we ensure that it not become a requirement for participation in feminist education.) Reforming small groups would subvert the appropriation of feminist thinking by a select group of academic women and men, usually white, usually from privileged class backgrounds.

Small groups of people coming together to engage in feminist discussion, in dialectical struggle make a space where the "personal is political" as a starting point for education for critical consciousness can be extended to include politicization of the self that focuses on creating understanding of the ways, sex, race, and class together determine our individual lot and our collective experience. It would further feminist movement if many well known feminist thinkers would participate in small groups, critically re-examining ways their works might be changed by incorporating broader perspectives. All efforts at self-transformation challenge us to engage in ongoing, critical self-examination and reflection about feminist practice, about how we live in the world. This individual commitment, when coupled with engagement in collective discussion, provides a space for critical feedback which strengthens our efforts to change and make ourselves new. It is in this commitment to feminist principles in our words and deeds that the hope of feminist revolution lies.

Working collectively to confront difference, to expand our awareness of sex, race, and class as interlocking systems of domination, of the ways we reinforce and perpetuate these structures, is the context in which we learn the true meaning of solidarity. It is this work that must be the foundation of feminist movement. Without it, we cannot effectively resist patriarchal domination; without it, we remain estranged and alienated from one another. Fear of painful confrontation often leads women and men active in feminist movement to avoid rigorous critical encounter, yet if we cannot engage dialectically in a committed, rigorous, humanizing manner, we cannot hope to change the world. True politicization—coming to critical consciousness—is a difficult, "trying" process, one that demands that we give up set ways of thinking and being, that we shift our paradigms, that we open ourselves to the unknown, the unfamiliar. Undergoing this process, we learn what it means to struggle and in this effort we experience the dignity and integrity of being that comes with revolutionary change. If we do not change our consciousness, we cannot change our actions or demand change from others.

Our renewed commitment to a rigorous process of education for critical consciousness will determine the shape and direction of future feminist movement. Until new perspectives are created, we cannot be living symbols of the power of feminist thinking. Given the privileged lot of many leading feminist thinkers, both in terms of status, class, and race, it is harder these days to convince women of the primacy of this process of politicization. More and more, we seem to form select interest groups composed of individuals who share similar perspectives. This limits our capacity to engage in critical discussion. It is difficult to involve women in new processes of feminist politicization because so many of us think that identifying men as the enemy, resisting male domination, gaining equal access to power and privilege is the end of feminist movement. Not only is it not the end, it is not even the place we want revitalized feminist movement to begin. We want to begin as women seriously addressing ourselves, not solely in relation to men, but in relation to an entire structure of domination of which patriarchy is one part. While the struggle to eradicate sexism and sexist oppression is and should be the primary thrust of feminist movement, to prepare ourselves politically for this effort we must first learn how to be in solidarity, how to struggle with one another.

Only when we confront the realities of sex, race, and class, the ways they divide us, make us different, stand us in opposition, and work to reconcile and resolve these issues will we be able to participate in the making of feminist revolution, in the transformation of the world. Feminism, as Charlotte Bunch emphasizes again and again in *Passionate Politics,* is a transformational politics, a struggle against domination wherein the effort is to change ourselves as well as structures. Speaking about the struggle to confront difference, Bunch asserts:

> A crucial point of the process is understanding that reality does not look the same from different people's perspective. It is not surprising that one way feminists have come to understand about differences has been through the love of a person from another culture or race. It takes persistence and motivation—which love often engenders—to get beyond one's ethnocentric assumptions and really learn about other perspectives. In this process and while seeking to eliminate oppression, we also discover new possibilities and insights that come from the experience and survival of other peoples.

Embedded in the commitment to feminist revolution is the challenge to love. Love can be and is an important source of empowerment when we struggle to confront issues of sex, race, and class. Working together to identify and face our differences—to face the ways we dominate and are dominated—to change our actions, we need a mediating force that can sustain us so that we are not broken in this process, so that we do not despair.

Not enough feminist work has focussed on documenting and sharing ways individuals confront differences constructively and successfully. Women and men need to know what is on the other side of the pain experienced in politicization. We need detailed accounts of the ways our lives are fuller and richer as we change and grow politically, as we learn to live each moment as committed feminists, as comrades working to end domination. In reconceptualizing and reformulating strategies for future feminist movement, we need to concentrate on the politicization of love, not just in the context of talking about victimization in intimate relationships, but in a critical discussion where love can be understood as a powerful force that challenges and resists domination. As we work to be loving, to create a culture that celebrates life, that makes love possible, we move against dehumanization, against domination. In *Pedagogy of the Oppressed*, Paulo Freire evokes this power of love, declaring:

> I am more and more convinced that true revolutionaries must perceive the revolution, because of its creative and liberating nature, as an act of love. For me, the revolution, which is not possible without a theory of revolution—and therefore science—is not irreconcilable with love. . . . The distortion imposed on the word "love" by the capitalist world cannot prevent the revolution from being essentially loving in character, nor can it prevent the revolutionaries from affirming their love of life.

That aspect of feminist revolution that calls women to love womanness, that calls men to resist dehumanizing concepts of masculinity, is an essential part of our struggle. It is the process by which we move from seeing ourselves as objects to acting as subjects. When women and men understand that working to eradicate patriarchal domination is a struggle rooted in the longing to make a world where everyone can live fully and freely, then we know our work to be a gesture of love. Let us draw upon that love to heighten our awareness, deepen our compassion, intensify our courage, and strengthen our commitment.

[1989]

REFERENCES

Bunch, Charlotte, *Passionate Politics*, New York: St Martin's Press, 1987.
Freire, Paulo, *Pedagogy of the Oppressed*, New York: Herder and Herden, 1970.
Gordon, Vivian. *Black Women, Feminism and Black Liberation—Which Way?* Third World Press, 1991.

 78

Sexuality

CATHARINE A. MACKINNON

then she says (and this is what I live through over
    and over)—she says: *I do not know*
    if sex is an illusion

I do not know
who I was when I did those things
or who I said I was
or whether I willed to feel
what I had read about
or who in fact was there with me
or whether I knew, even then
that there was doubt about these things
    —Adrienne Rich, "Dialogue"

I had always been fond of her in the most innocent, asexual way. It was as if her body was always entirely hidden behind her radiant mind, the modesty of her behavior, and her taste in dress. She had never offered me the slightest chink through which to view the glow of her nakedness. And now suddenly the butcher knife of fear had slit her open. She was as open to me as the carcass of a heifer slit down the middle and hanging on a hook. There we were . . . and suddenly I felt a violent desire to make love to her. Or to be more exact, a violent desire to rape her.
—Milan Kundera, *The Book of Laughter and Forgetting*

She had thought of something, something about the body, about the passions which it was unfitting for her as a woman to say. Men, her reason told her, would be shocked. . . . Telling the truth about my own experiences as a body, I do not think I solved. I doubt that any woman has solved it yet. The obstacles against her are still immensely powerful—and yet they are very difficult to define.

    —Virginia Woolf, "Professions for Women"

What is it about woman's experience that produces a distinctive perspective on social reality? How is an angle of vision and an interpretive hermeneutics of social life created in the group women? What happens to women to give them a particular interest in social arrangements, something to have a consciousness *of*? How are the qualities we know as male and female socially created and enforced on an everyday level? Sexual objectification of women—

first in the world, then in the head, first in visual appropriation, then in forced sex, finally in sexual murder—provides answers.[1]

Male dominance is sexual. Meaning: men in particular, if not men alone, sexualize hierarchy; gender is one. As much a sexual theory of gender as a gendered theory of sex, this is the theory of sexuality that has grown out of consciousness raising in the women's movement. Recent feminist work, both interpretive and empirical—on rape, battery, sexual harassment, sexual abuse of children, prostitution, and pornography—supports it. These practices, taken together, express and actualize the distinctive power of men over women in society; their effective permissibility confirms and extends it. If one believes women's accounts of sexual use and abuse by men; if the pervasiveness of male sexual violence against women substantiated in these studies is not denied, minimized, or excepted as deviant[2] or episodic; if the fact that only 7.8 percent of women in the United States are not sexually assaulted or harassed in their lifetimes[3] is considered not ignorable or inconsequential; if the women to whom it happens are not considered expendable; if violation of women is understood as sexualized on some level— then sexuality itself can no longer be regarded as unimplicated. The meaning of practices of sexual violence cannot be categorized away as violence, not sex, either. The male sexual role, this work taken together suggests, centers on aggressive intrusion on those with less power. Such acts of dominance are experienced as sexually arousing, as sex itself.[4] They therefore are. The evidence on the sexual violation of women by men thus frames an inquiry into the place of sexuality in gender and of gender in sexuality.

A feminist theory of sexuality would locate sexuality within a theory of gender inequality, meaning the social hierarchy of men over women. To make a theory feminist, it is not enough that it be authored by a biological female. Nor that it describe female sexuality as different from (if equal to) male sexuality, or as if sexuality in women ineluctably exists in some realm beyond, beneath, above, behind—in any event, fundamentally untouched and unmoved by—an unequal social order. A theory of sexuality becomes feminist to the extent it treats sexuality as a social construct of male power: defined by men,

forced on women, and constitutive in the meaning of gender. Such an approach centers feminism on the perspective of the subordination of women to men as it identifies sex—that is, the sexuality of dominance and submission—as crucial, as a fundamental, as on some level definitive, in that process. Feminist theory becomes a project of analyzing that situation in order to face it for what it is, in order to change it.

Focusing on gender inequality without a sexual account of its dynamics, as most work has, one could criticize the sexism of existing theories of sexuality and emerge knowing that men author scripts to their own advantage, women and men act them out; that men set conditions, women and men have their behavior conditioned; that men develop developmental categories through which men develop, and that women develop or not; that men are socially allowed selves hence identities with personalities into which sexuality is or is not well integrated, women being that which is or is not integrated, that through the alterity of which a self experiences itself as having an identity; that men have object relations, women are objects of those relations, and so on. Following such critique, one could attempt to invert or correct the premises or applications of these theories to make them gender neutral, even if the reality to which they refer looks more like the theories— once their gender specificity is revealed—than it looks gender neutral. Or, one could attempt to enshrine a distinctive "women's reality" as if it really were permitted to exist as something more than one dimension of women's response to a condition of powerlessness. Such exercises would be revealing and instructive, even deconstructive, but to limit feminism to correcting sex bias by acting in theory as if male power did not exist in fact, including by valorizing in writing what women have had little choice but to be limited to becoming in life, is to limit feminist theory the way sexism limits women's lives: to a response to terms men set.

A distinctively feminist theory conceptualizes social reality, including sexual reality, on its own terms. The question is, What are they? If women have been substantially deprived not only of their own experience but of terms of their own in which to view it, then a feminist theory of sexuality that seeks to understand women's situation in order to change it, must first identify and criticize the construct "sexuality" as a construct that has circumscribed and defined experience as well as theory. This requires capturing it *in the world,* in its situated social meanings, as it is being constructed in life on a daily basis. It must be studied in its experienced empirical existence, not just in the texts of history (as Foucault), in the social psyche (as Lacan) or in language (as Derrida). Sexual meaning is not made only, or even primarily, by words and in texts. In feminist terms, the fact that male power has power means that the interests of male sexuality construct what sexuality as such means in life, including the standard way it is allowed and recognized to be felt and expressed and experienced, in a way that determines women's biographies, including sexual ones. Existing theories, until they grasp this, will not only misattribute what they call female sexuality to women as such, as if it is not imposed on women daily, they will participate in enforcing the hegemony of the social construct "desire," hence its product, "sexuality," hence its construct "woman," on the world.

The gender issue thus becomes the issue of what is taken to be "sexuality": what sex means and what is meant by sex, when, how, and with whom and with what consequences to whom. Such questions are almost never systematically confronted, even in discourses that purport feminist awareness. What sex is—how it comes to be attached and attributed to what it is, embodied and practiced as it is, contextualized in the ways it is, signifying and referring to what it does—is taken as a baseline, a given, except when explaining what happened when it is thought to have gone wrong. It is as if "erotic," for example, can be taken as having an understood referent, although it is never defined. Except to imply that it is universal yet individual, ultimately variable and plastic. Essentially indefinable but overwhelmingly positive. "Desire," the vicissitudes of which are endlessly extolled and philosophized in culture high and low, is not seen as fundamentally problematic or calling for explanation on the concrete, interpersonal operative level, unless (again) it is supposed to be there and is not. To list and analyze what seem to be the essential elements for male sexual arousal, what has to be there for the penis to work, seems faintly blasphemous, like a pornographer doing market research. Sex is supposed both too individual and too universally transcendent for that. To suggest that the sexual might be continuous with something other than sex itself—something like politics—is seldom done, is treated as detumescent, even by feminists. It is as if sexuality comes from the stork.

Sexuality, in feminist light, is not a discrete sphere of interaction or feeling or sensation or behavior in which preexisting social divisions may or may not be played out. It is a pervasive dimension throughout the whole of social life, a dimension along which gender pervasively occurs and through which gender is socially constituted; in this culture, it is a dimension along which other social divisions, like race and class, partly play themselves out. Dominance eroticized defines the imperatives of its masculinity, submission eroticized defines its femininity. So many distinctive features of women's status as second class—the restriction and constraint and contortion, the servility and the display, the self-mutilation and requisite presentation of self as a beautiful thing, the enforced passivity, the humiliation—are made into the content of sex for women. Being a thing for sexual use is fundamental to it. This identifies not just a sexuality that is shaped under conditions of gender inequality but this sexuality itself as the dynamic of the inequality of the sexes. It is to argue that the excitement at reduction of a person to a thing, to less than a human being, as socially defined, is its fundamental motive force. It is to argue sexual difference as a function of sexual dominance. It is to argue a sexual theory of the distribution of social power by gender, in which this sexuality that is sexuality is substantially what makes the gender division be what it is, which is male dominant, wherever it is, which is nearly everywhere.

Across cultures, from this perspective, sexuality is whatever a given culture defines it as. The next questions concern its relation to gender asymmetry and to gender as a division of power. Male dominance appears to exist cross-culturally, if in locally particular forms. Is whatever defines women as "different" the same as whatever defines women as "inferior" the same as whatever defines women's "sexuality"? Is that which defines gender inequality as merely the sex difference also the content of the erotic, cross-culturally? In this view, the feminist theory of sexuality is its theory of politics, its distinctive contribution to social and political explanation. To explain gender inequality in terms of "sexual politics"[5] is to advance not only a political theory of the sexual that defines gender but also a sexual theory of the political to which gender is fundamental.

In this approach, male power takes the social form of what men as a gender want sexually, which centers on power itself, as socially defined. Masculinity is having it; femininity is not having it. Masculinity precedes male as femininity precedes female and male sexual desire defines both. Specifically, "woman" is defined by what male desire requires for arousal and satisfaction and is socially tautologous with "female sexuality" and "the female sex." In the permissible ways a woman can be treated, the ways that are socially considered not violations but appropriate to her nature, one finds the particulars of male sexual interests and requirements. In the concomitant sexual paradigm, the ruling norms of sexual attraction and expressions are fused with gender identity formation and affirmation, such that sexuality equals heterosexuality equals the sexuality of (male) dominance and (female) submission.

Post-Lacan, actually post-Foucault,[6] it has become customary to affirm that sexuality is socially constructed. Seldom specified is what, socially, it is constructed of, far less who does the constructing or how, when, or where. When capitalism is the favored social construct, sexuality is shaped and controlled and exploited and repressed by capitalism; not, capitalism creates sexuality as we know it. When sexuality is a construct of discourses of power, gender is never one of them; force is central to its deployment but only through repressing it, not through constituting it; speech is not concretely investigated for its participation in this construction process. "Constructed" seems to mean influenced by, directed, channeled, like a highway constructs traffic patterns. Not: Why cars? Who's driving? Where's everybody going? What makes mobility matter? Who can own a car? Are all these accidents not very accidental? Although there are partial exceptions (but disclaimers notwithstanding), the typical model of sexuality that is tacitly accepted remains deeply Freudian and essentialist: sexuality is an innate primary natural prepolitical uncondi-

tioned drive divided along the biological gender line, centering on heterosexual intercourse, that is, penile intromission, full actualization of which is repressed by civilization. Even if the sublimation aspect of this theory is rejected, or the reasons for the repression are seen to vary (for the survival of civilization or to maintain fascist control or to keep capitalism moving), sexual expression is implicitly seen as the expression of something that is to a significant extent presocial and is socially denied its full force. Sexuality remains precultural and universally invariant to some extent, social only in that it needs society to take what are always to some extent socially specific forms. The impetus itself is a hunger, an appetite founded on a biological need; what it is specifically hungry for and how it is satisfied is then open to endless cultural and individual variance, like cuisine, like cooking.

Allowed/not-allowed are this sexuality's basic ideological axes. The fact that sexuality is ideologically bounded is known. That there are its axes, central to the way its "drive" is driven, and that this is fundamental to the gender difference, is not.[7] Its basic normative assumption is that whatever is considered sexuality should be allowed to be "expressed." Whatever is called sex is attributed a normatively positive valence, an affirmative valuation. This ex cathedra assumption, affirmation of which appears indispensable to one's credibility on any subject that gets near the sexual, means that sex as such (whatever it is) is good—natural, healthy, positive, appropriate, pleasurable, wholesome, fine, one's own, and to be approved and expressed. This, sometimes characterized as "sex-positive," is, rather, obviously, a value judgment.

• • •

While intending the opposite, some feminists have encouraged and participated in this type of analysis by conceiving rape as violence not sex. While this approach gave needed emphasis to rape's previously effaced elements of power and dominance, it obscured its elements of sex. Aside from failing to answer the rather obvious question, if it's violence not sex why didn't he just hit her, this approach made it impossible to see that violence is sex when it is practiced as sex. This is obvious once what sexuality is, is understood as a matter of what it means, of how it is interpreted. To say rape is violence not sex preserves the "sex is good" norm by simply distinguishing forced sex as "not sex," whether it means sex to the perpetrator or even, later, to the victim, who has difficulty experiencing sex without reexperiencing the rape. Whatever is sex, cannot be violent; whatever is violent, cannot be sex. This analytic wish-fulfillment makes it possible for rape to be opposed by those who would save sexuality from the rapists while leaving the sexual fundamentals of male dominance intact.

While much prior work on rape has analyzed it as a problem of inequality between the sexes but not as a problem of unequal sexuality on the basis of gender,[8] other contemporary explorations of sexuality that purport to be feminist lack comprehension either of gender as a form of social power or of the realities of sexual violence. For instance, the editors of *Powers of Desire* take sex "as a central form of expression, one that defines identity and is seen as a primary source of energy and pleasure."[9] This may be how it "is seen" but it is also how they, operatively, see it. As if women choose sexuality as definitive of identity. As if it is as much a form of women's "expression" as it is men's. As if violation and abuse are not equally central to sexuality as women live it.

The *Diary* of the Barnard conference on sexuality pervasively equates sexuality with 'pleasure.' "Perhaps the overall question we need to ask is: How do women . . . negotiate sexual pleasure?"[10] As if women under male supremacy have power to. As if "negotiation" is a form of freedom. As if pleasure and how to get it, rather than dominance and how to end it, is the "overall" issue sexuality presents feminism. As if women do just need a good fuck. In these texts, taboos are treated as real restrictions—as things that really are not allowed—instead of as guises under which hierarchy is eroticized. The domain of the sexual is divided into "restriction, repression and danger" on the one hand and "exploration, pleasure and agency" on the other.[11] This division parallels the ideological forms through which dominance and submission are eroticized, variously socially coded as heterosexuality's male/female, lesbian culture's butch/femme, and sadomasochism's top/bottom.[12] Speaking in role terms, the one who pleasures in the illusion of freedom and security within the reality of danger is the "girl"; the one who pleasures in the reality of freedom and se-

curity within the illusion of danger is the "boy." That is, the *Diary* uncritically adopts as an analytical tool the central dynamic of the phenomenon it purports to be analyzing. Presumably, one is to have a sexual experience of the text.

The terms of these discourses preclude or evade crucial feminist questions. What do sexuality and gender inequality have to do with each other? How do dominance and submission become sexualized, or, why is hierarchy sexy? How does it get attached to male and female? Why does sexuality center on intercourse, the reproductive act by physical design? Is masculinity the enjoyment of violation, femininity the enjoyment of being violated? Is that the central meaning of intercourse? Why do "men love death"?[13] What is the etiology of heterosexuality in women? Is its pleasure women's stake in subordination?

Taken together and taken seriously, feminist inquiries into the realities or rape, battery, sexual harassment, incest, child sexual abuse, prostitution, and pornography answer these questions by suggesting a theory of the sexual mechanism. Its script, learning, conditioning, developmental logos, imprinting of the microdot, its deus ex machina, whatever sexual process term defines sexual arousal itself, is force, power's expression. Force is sex, not just sexualized; force is the desire dynamic, not just a response to the desired object when desire's expression is frustrated. Pressure, gender socialization, withholding benefits, extending indulgences, the how-to books, the sex therapy are the soft end; the fuck, the fist, the street, the chains, the poverty are the hard end. Hostility and contempt, or arousal of master to slave, together with awe and vulnerability, or arousal of slave to master—these are the emotions of this sexuality's excitement. "Sadomasochism is to sex what war is to civil life: the magnificent experience," writes Susan Sontag.[14] "It is hostility—the desire, overt or hidden, to harm another person—that generates and enhances sexual excitement," writes Robert Stoller.[15] Harriet Jacobs, a slave, speaking of her systematic rape by her master, writes, "It seems less demeaning to give one's self, than to submit to compulsion."[16] Looking at the data, the force in sex and the sex in force is a matter of simple empirical description—unless one accepts the force in sex is not force anymore, it is just sex; or, if whenever a woman is forced it is what she really wants or it or she does not matter; or, unless prior aversion or sentimentality substitutes what one wants sex to be, or will condone or countenance as sex, for what is actually happening.

To be clear: what is sexual is what gives a man an erection. Whatever it takes to make a penis shudder and stiffen with the experience of its potency is what sexuality means culturally. Whatever else does, fear does, hostility does, hatred does, the helplessness of a child or a student or an infantilized or restrained or vulnerable woman does, revulsion does, death does. Hierarchy, a constant creation of person/thing, top/bottom, dominance/subordination relations does. What is understood as violation, conventionally penetration and intercourse, defines the paradigmatic sexual encounter. The scenario of sexual abuse is: you do what I say. These textualities become sexuality. All this suggests that that which is called sexuality is the dynamic of control by which male dominance—in forms that range from intimate to institutional, from a look to a rape—eroticizes as man and woman, as identity and pleasure. It is also that which maintains and defines male supremacy as a political system. Male sexual desire is thereby simultaneously created and serviced, never satisfied once and for all, while male force is romanticized, even sacralized, potentiated, and naturalized, by being submerged into sex itself.

In contemporary philosophical terms, nothing is "indeterminate" in the poststructuralist sense here; it is all too determinate.[17] Nor does its reality provide just one perspective on a relativistic interpersonal world that could mean anything or its opposite.[18] The reality of pervasive sexual abuse and its erotization does not shift relative to perspective, although whether or not one will see it or accord it significance may. Interpretation varies relative to place in sexual abuse, certainly; but the fact that women are sexually abused as women, in a social matrix of sexualized subordination does not go away because it is often ignored or authoritatively disbelieved or interpreted out of existence. Indeed, some ideological supports for its persistence rely precisely upon techniques of social indeterminacy: no language but the obscene to describe the unspeakable; denial by the powerful casting doubt on the facticity of the injuries; actually driving its victims insane. Indeterminacy is a neo-Cartesian mind

game that undermines the actual social meaning of words by raising acontextualized interpretive possibilities that have no real social meaning or real possibility of any, dissolving the ability to criticize actual meanings without making space for new ones. The feminist point is simple. Men are women's material conditions. If it happens to women, it happens.

Women often find ways to resist male supremacy and to expand their spheres of action. But they are never free of it. Women also embrace the standards of women's place in this regime as "our own" to varying degrees and in varying voices—as affirmation of identity and right to pleasure, in order to be loved and approved and paid, in order just to make it through another day. This, not inert passivity, is the meaning of being a victim. The term is not moral: who is to blame or to be pitied or condemned or held responsible. It is not prescriptive: what we should do next. It is not strategic: how to construe the situation so it can be changed. It is not emotional: what one feels better thinking. It is descriptive: who does what to whom and gets away with it?

• • •

Pornography is a means through which sexuality is socially constructed, a site of construction, a domain of exercise. It constructs women as things for sexual use and constructs its consumers to desperately want women to desperately want possession and cruelty and dehumanization. Inequality itself, subjection itself, hierarchy itself, objectification itself, with self-determination ecstatically relinquished, is the apparent content of women's sexual desire and desirability. "The major theme of pornography as a genre," writes Andrea Dworkin, "is male power."[19] Women are in pornography to be violated and taken, men to violate and take them, either on screen or by camera or pen, on behalf of the viewer. Not that sexuality in life or in media never expresses love and affection; only that love and affection are not what is sexualized in this society's actual sexual paradigm, as pornography testifies to it. Violation of the powerless, intrusion on women, is. The milder forms, possession and use, the mildest of which is visual objectification, are. The sexuality of observation, visual intrusion and access, of entertainment, makes sex largely a spectator sport for its participants.

If pornography has not become sex to and from the male point of view, it is hard to explain why the pornography industry makes a known ten billion dollars a year selling it as sex mostly to men; why it is used to teach sex to child prostitutes, recalcitrant wives and girlfriends and daughters, and to medical students, and to sex offenders; why it is nearly universally classified as a subdivision of "erotic literature"; why it is protected and defended as if it were sex itself.[20] And why a prominent sexologist fears that enforcing the views of feminists against pornography in society would make men "erotically inert wimps." No pornography, no male sexuality.

A feminist critique of sexuality in this sense is advanced in Andrea Dworkin's *Pornography: Men Possessing Women*. Building on her earlier identification of gender inequality as a system of social meaning,[21] an ideology lacking basis in anything other than the social reality its power constructs and maintains, she argues that sexuality is a construct of that power, given meaning by, through, and in pornography. In this perspective, pornography is not harmless fantasy or a corrupt and confused misrepresentation of otherwise natural healthy sex, nor is it fundamentally a distortion, reflection, projection, expression, representation, fantasy, or symbol of it.[22] Through pornography, among other practices, gender inequality becomes both sexual and socially real. Pornography "reveals that male pleasure is inextricably tied to victimizing, hurting, exploiting."[23] "Dominance in the male system is pleasure."[24] Rape is "the defining paradigm of sexuality,"[25] to avoid which boys choose manhood and homophobia.[26]

Women, who are not given a choice, are objectified, or, rather, "the object is allowed to desire, if she desires to be an object."[27] Psychology sets the proper bounds of this objectification by terming its improper excesses "fetishism,"[28] distinguishing the uses from the abuses of women. Dworkin shows how the process and content of women's definition as women, an underclass, are the process and content of their sexualization as objects for male sexual use. The mechanism is (again) force, imbued with meaning because it is the means to death[29] and death is the ultimate sexual act, the ultimate making of a person into a thing.

· · ·

To be sexually objectified means having a social meaning imposed on your being that defines you as to be sexually used, according to your desired uses, and then using you that way. Doing this is sex in the male system. Pornography is a sexual practice of this because it exists in a social system in which sex in life is no less mediated than it is in representation. There is no irreducible essence, no "just sex." If sex is a social construct of sexism, men have sex with their image of a woman. Pornography creates an accessible sexual object, the possession and consumption of which is male sexuality, to be possessed and consumed as which is female sexuality. This is not because pornography depicts objectified sex but because it creates the experience of a sexuality which is itself objectified. The appearance of choice or consent, with their attribution to inherent nature, are crucial in concealing the reality of force. Love of violation, variously termed female masochism and consent, comes to define female sexuality, legitimizing this political system by concealing the force on which it is based.

In this system, a victim, usually female, always feminized, is "never forced, only actualized."[30] Women whose attributes particularly fixate men— such as women with large breasts—are seen as full of sexual desire. Women men want, want men. Women fake vaginal orgasms, the only 'mature' sexuality, because men demand that they enjoy vaginal penetration.[31] Raped women are seen as asking for it: if a man wanted her, she must have wanted him. Men force women to become sexual objects, "that thing which causes erection, then hold themselves helpless and powerless when aroused by her."[32] Men who sexually harass, say women sexually harass them. They mean they are aroused by women who turn them down. This elaborate projective system of demand characteristics—taken to pinnacles like fantasizing a clitoris in women's throats so that men can enjoy forced fellatio in real life assured that women do too—is surely a delusional and projective structure deserving of serious psychological study. Instead, it is women who resist it that are studied, seen as in need of explanation and adjustment, stigmatized as inhibited and repressed and asexual. The assumption that, in matters sexual, women really want what men want from women makes male force against women in sex invisible. It makes rape sex. Women's sexual "reluctance, dislike, and frigidity," women's puritanism and prudery in the face of this sex, is the "silent rebellion of women against the force of the penis . . . an ineffective rebellion, but a rebellion nonetheless."[33]

Nor is homosexuality without stake in this gendered sexual system. Putting to one side the obviously gendered content of expressly adopted roles, clothing, and sexual mimicry, to the extent the gender of a sexual object is crucial to arousal, the structure of social power that stands behind and defines gender is hardly irrelevant, even if it is rearranged. Some have argued that lesbian sexuality—meaning here simply women having sex with women not men—solves the problem of gender by eliminating men from women's voluntary sexual encounters.[34] Yet women's sexuality remains constructed under conditions of male supremacy; women remain socially defined as women in relation to men; the definition of women as men's inferiors remains sexual even if not heterosexual, whether men are present at the time or not. To the extent gay men choose men because they are men, the meaning of masculinity is affirmed as well as undermined. It may also be that sexuality is so gender marked that it carries dominance and submission with it, no matter the gender of its participants

. . .

As pornography connects sexuality with gender in social reality, the feminist critique of pornography connects feminist work on violence against women with its inquiry into women's consciousness and gender roles. It is not only that women are the principal targets of rape, which by conservative definition happens to almost half of all women at least once in their lives. It is not only that over a third of all women are sexually molested by older trusted male family members or friends or authority figures as an early, perhaps initiatory, interpersonal sexual encounter. It is not only that at least the same percentage as adult women are battered in homes by male intimates. It is not only that about a fifth of American women have been or are known to be prostitutes, and most cannot get out of it. It is not only that 85 percent of working women will be sexually harassed on the job, many physically, at some point in their working lives.[35] All this documents the extent and terrain of abuse and the effectively unrestrained and systematic sexual aggression of one-half of the population against the other half. It suggests that it is basically allowed.

It does not by itself show that availablity for this treatment defines the identity attributed to that other half of the population; or, that such treatment, all this torment and debasement, is socially considered not only rightful but enjoyable, and is in fact enjoyed by the dominant half; or, that the ability to engage in such behaviors defines the identity of that half. And not only of that half. Now consider the content of gender roles. All the social requirements for male sexual arousal and satisfaction are identical to the gender definition of "female." All the essentials of the male gender role are also the qualities sexualized as 'male' in male dominant sexuality. If gender is a social construct, and sexuality is a social construct, and the question is, of what is each constructed, the fact that their contents are identical—not to mention that the word 'sex' refers to both—might be more than a coincidence.

As to gender, what is sexual about pornography is what is unequal about social life. To say that pornography sexualizes gender and genders sexuality means that it provides a concrete social process through which gender and sexuality become functions of each other. Gender and sexuality, in this view, become two different shapes taken by the single social equation of male with dominance and female with submission. Being this as identity, acting it as role, inhabiting and presenting it as self, is the domain of gender. Enjoying it as the erotic, centering upon when it elicits genital arousal, is the domain of sexuality. Inequality is what is sexualized through pornography; it is what is sexual about it. The more unequal, the more sexual. The violence against women in pornography is an expression of gender hierarchy, the extremity of the hierarchy expressed and created through the extremity of the abuse, producing the extremity of the male sexual response. Pornography's multiple variations on and departures from the male dominant/female submissive sexual/gender theme are not exceptions to these gender regularities. They affirm them. The capacity of gender reversals (dominatrixes) and inversions (homosexuality) to stimulate sexual excitement is derived precisely from their mimicry or parody or negation or reversal of the standard arrangement. This affirms rather than undermines or qualifies the standard sexual arrangement as the standard sexual arrangement, the definition of sex, the standard from which all else is defined, that in which sexuality as such inheres.

Such formal data as exist on the relationship between pornography and male sexual arousal tend to substantiate this connection between gender hierarchy and male sexuality. 'Normal' men viewing pornography over time in laboratory settings become more aroused to scenes of rape than to scenes of explicit but not expressly violent sex, even if (especially if?) the woman is shown as hating it.[36] As sustained exposure perceptually inures subjects to the violent component in expressly violent sexual material, its sexual arousal value remains or increases. "On the first day, when they see women being raped and aggressed against, it bothers them. By day five, it does not bother them at all, in fact, they enjoy it."[37] Sexual material that is seen as nonviolent, by contrast, is less arousing to begin with, becomes even less arousing over time,[38] after which exposure to sexual violence is sexually arousing.[39] Viewing sexual material containing express aggression against women makes normal men more willing to aggress against women.[40] It also makes them see a woman rape victim as less human, more object-like, less worthy, less injured, and more to blame for the rape. Sexually explicit material that is not seen as expressly violent but presents women as hysterically responsive to male sexual demands, in which women are verbally abused, dominated and degraded, and treated as sexual things, makes men twice as likely to report willingness to sexually aggress against women than they were before exposure. So-called nonviolent materials like these make men see women as less than human, as good only for sex, as objects, as worthless and blameworthy when raped, and as really wanting to be raped and as unequal to men.[41] As to material showing violence only, it might be expected that rapists would be sexually aroused to scenes of violence against women, and they are.[42] But many normal male subjects, too, when seeing a woman being aggressed against by a man, perceive the interaction to be sexual even if no sex is shown.[43]

Male sexuality is apparently activated by violence against women and expresses itself in violence against women to a significant extent. If violence is seen as occupying the most fully achieved end of a dehumanization continuum on which objectification occupies the least express end, one question that is raised is whether some form of hierarchy—the dynamic of the continuum—is currently essential for male sexuality to experience itself. If so, and gender is understood to be a hierarchy, perhaps the sexes are unequal so that men can be sexually aroused. To put it another way, perhaps gender must be maintained as a social hierarchy so that men will be able to get erections; or, part of the male interest in keeping women down lies in the fact that it gets men up. Maybe feminists are considered castrating because equality is not sexy.

Recent inquiries into rape support such suspicions. Men often rape women, it turns out, because they want to and enjoy it. The act, including the dominance, is sexually arousing, sexually affirming, and supportive of the perpetrator's masculinity. Many unreported rapists report an increase in self-esteem as a result of the rape.[44] Indications are that reported rapists perceive that getting caught accounts for most of the unpleasant effects of raping.[45] About a third of all men say they would rape a woman if they knew they wouldn't get caught.[46] That the low conviction rate[47] may give them confidence is supported by the prevalence rate.[48] Some convicted rapists see rape as an "exciting" form of interpersonal sex, a recreational activity or "adventure," or as a means of revenge or punishment on all women or some subgroup of women or an individual woman. Even some of those who did the act out of bad feelings make it clear that raping made them feel better. "Men rape because it is rewarding to do so."[49] If rapists experience rape as sex, does that mean there can be nothing wrong with it?

• • •

Compare victims' reports of rape with women's reports of sex. They look a lot alike.[50] Compare victims' reports of rape with what pornography says is sex. They look a lot alike.[51] In this light, the major distinction between intercourse (normal) and rape (abnormal) is that the normal happens so often that one cannot get anyone to see anything wrong with it. Which also means that anything sexual that happens often and one cannot get anyone to consider wrong is intercourse not rape, no matter what was done. The distinctions that purport to divide this territory look more like the ideological supports for normalizing the usual male use and abuse of women as "sexuality" through authoritatively pretending that whatever is exposed of it is deviant. This may have something to do with the conviction rate in rape cases (making all those unconvicted men into normal men, and all those acts into sex). It may have something to do with the fact that most convicted rapists, and many observers, find rape convictions incomprehensible.[52] And the fact that marital rape is considered by many to be a contradiction in terms. ("But if you can't rape your wife, who can you rape?")[53] And the fact that so many rape victims have trouble with sex afterward.[54]

What effect does the pervasive reality of sexual abuse of women by men have on what are deemed the more ordinary forms of sexual interaction? How do these material experiences create interest and point of view? Consider women. Recall that over a third of all girls experience sex, perhaps are sexually initiated, under conditions that even this society recognizes are forced or at least unequal. Perhaps they learn this process of sexualized dominance as sex. Top-down relations feel sexual. Is sexuality throughout life then ever not on some level a reenactment of, a response to, that backdrop? Rape, adding more women to the list, can produce similar resonance. Sexually abused women—most women—seem to become either sexually disinclined or compulsively promiscuous or both in series, trying to avoid the painful events, and/or repeating them over and over almost addictively, in an attempt to reacquire a sense of control or to make them come out right. Too, women widely experience sexuality as a means to male approval; male approval translates into nearly all social goods. Violation can be sustained, even sought out, to this end. Sex can, then, be a means of trying to feel alive by redoing what has made one feel dead, of expressing a denigrated self-image seeking its own reflection in self-action in order to feel fulfilled, or of keeping up one's stock with the powerful.

· · ·

If the existing social model and reality of sexuality centers on male force, and if that sex is socially learned and ideologically considered positive and is rewarded, what is surprising is that not all women eroticize dominance, not all love pornography, and many resent rape. As Valerie Heller has said of her experience with incest and use in pornography both as a child and as an adult, "I believed I existed only after I was turned on, like a light switch by another

person. When I needed to be nurtured I thought I wanted to be used. . . . Marks and bruises and being used was the way I measured my self worth. You must remember that I was taught that because men were fucking my body and using it for their needs it meant I was loved."[55] Given the pervasiveness of such experiences, the truly interesting question becomes why and how sexuality in women is ever other than masochistic.

All women live in sexual objectification like fish live in water. Given the statistical realities, all women live all the time under the shadow of the threat of sexual abuse. The question is, what can life as a woman mean, what can sex mean to targeted survivors in a rape culture? Given the statistical realities, much of women's sexual lives will occur under post-traumatic stress. Being surrounded by pornography—which is not only socially ubiquitous but often directly used as part of sex[56]—makes this a relatively constant condition. Women cope with objectification through trying to meet the male standard, and measure their self-worth by the degree to which they succeed. Women seem to cope with sexual abuse principally through denial or fear. On the denial side, immense energy goes into defending sexuality as just fine and getting better all the time, and into trying to make sexuality feel all right, like it is supposed to feel. Women who are compromised, cajoled, pressured, tricked, blackmailed, or outright forced into sex (or pornography) often respond to the unspeakable humiliation, coupled with the sense of having lost some irreplaceable integrity by claiming that sexuality as their own. Faced with no alternatives, the strategy to acquire self-respect and pride is: I chose it.

Consider the conditions under which this is done. This is a culture in which women are socially expected—and themselves necessarily expect and want—to be able to distinguish the socially, epistemologically, indistinguishable. Rape and intercourse are not authoritatively separated by any difference between the physical acts or amount of force involved but only legally, by a standard that revolves around the man's interpretation of the encounter. Thus, although raped women, that is, most women, are supposed to be able to feel every day and every night that they have some meaningful determining part in having their sex life—their life, period—not be a series of rapes, the most they provide is the raw data for the man to see as he sees it. And he has been seeing pornography. Similarly, "consent" is supposed the crucial line between rape and intercourse, but the legal standard for it is so passive, so acquiescent, that a woman can be dead and have consented under it. The mind fuck of all of this makes the complicitous collapse into "I chose it" feel like a strategy for sanity. It certainly makes a woman at one with the world.

· · ·

So long as sexual inequality remains unequal and sexual, attempts to value sexuality as women's, possessive as if women possess it, will remain part of limiting women to it, to what women are now defined as being. Outside of truly rare and contrapuntal glimpses (which almost everyone thinks they live almost their entire sex life within), to seek an equal sexuality, to seek sexual equality, without political transformation is to seek equality under conditions of inequality. Rejecting this, and rejecting the glorification of settling for the best inequality has to offer or has stimulated the resourceful to invent, are what Ti-Grace Atkinson meant to reject when she said, "I do not know any feminist worthy of that name who, if forced to choose between freedom and sex, would choose sex. She'd choose freedom every time."[57]

· · ·

[1989]

NOTES

1. See Jane Caputi, *The Age of Sex Crime* (Bowling Green, Ohio: Bowling Green State University Popular Press, 1987); Deborah Cameron and Elizabeth Frazer, *The Lust to Kill: A Feminist Investigation of Sexual Murder* (New York: New York University Press, 1987).
2. E. Schur, *Labeling Women Deviant: Gender, Stigma and Social Control* (New York: Random House, 1983) (a superb review urging a "continuum" rather than a "deviance" approach to issues of sex inequality).
3. Diana Russell produced this figure at my request from the random sample data base of 930 San Francisco households discussed in her *The Secret Trauma: Incest in the Lives of Girls and Women*, pp. 20–37, and *Rape in Marriage*, pp. 27–41. The figure includes all the forms of rape or other sexual abuse or harassment surveyed, noncontact as well as contact, from gang rape by strangers and marital rape to obscene phone calls, unwanted sexual advances on the street, unwelcome requests to pose for pornography, and subjection to peeping toms and sexual exhibitionists (flashers).
4. S. D. Smithyman, "The Undetected Rapist" (Ph.D. diss., Claremont Graduate School, 1978); N. Groth, *Men Who Rape: The Psychology of the Offender* (New York: St. Martin's, 1982); D. Scully and J. Marolla, " 'Riding the Bull at Gilley's: Convicted Rapists Describe the Rewards of Rape," *Social Problems* 32 (1985): 251. (The manuscript version of this paper was subtitled "Convicted Rapists Describe the Pleasure of Raping.")
5. K. Millett, *Sexual Politics* (New York: Doubleday, 1970).
6. J. Lacan, *Feminine Sexuality*, trans. J. Rose (New York: Norton, 1982); M. Foucault, *The History of Sexuality*, vol. 1, *An Introduction* (New York: Random House, 1980), and *Power/Knowledge*, ed. C. Gordon (New York: Pantheon, 1980).
7. The contributions and limitations of Foucault in such an analysis are discussed illuminatingly in Frigga Haug, ed., *Female Sexualization*, trans. Erica Carter (London: Verso, 1987), pp. 190–98.
8. Brownmiller did analyze rape as something men do to women, hence as a problem of gender, even if her concept of gender is biologically based (see, e.g., her pp. 4, 6, and discussion in chap. 3). An exception is Clark and Lewis.
9. A. Snitow, C. Stansell, and S. Thompson, introduction to *Powers of Desire: The Politics of Sexuality*, ed. A. Snitow, C. Stansell, and S. Thompson (New York: Monthly Review Press, 1983), p. 9.
10. C. Vance, "Concept Paper: Toward a Politics of Sexuality," in H. Alderfer, B. Jaker, and M. Nelson, eds., *Diary of a Conference on Sexuality*, record of the planning committee of the Conference, the Scholar and the Feminist IX: Toward a Politics of Sexuality, April 24, 1982, p. 27: to address "women's sexual pleasure, choice, and autonomy, acknowledging that sexuality is simultaneously a domain of restriction, repression and danger as well as a domain of exploration, pleasure and agency." Parts of the *Diary*, with the conference papers, were later published. C. Vance, ed., *Pleasure and Danger: Exploring Female Sexuality* (London: Routledge & Kegan Paul, 1984).
11. Vance, "Concept Paper," p. 38.
12. For examples, see A. Hollibaugh and C. Moraga, "What We're Rolling around in Bed with: Sexual Silences in Feminism," in Snitow, Stansell, and Thompson, eds., pp. 394–405, esp. 398; Samois, *Coming to Power* (Berkeley, Calif.: Samois, 1983).
13. A. Dworkin, "Why So-called Radical Men Love and Need Pornography," in Lederer, ed., p. 48.
14. S. Sonta, "Fascinating Fascism," in her *Under the Sign of Saturn* (New York: Farrar, Straus & Giroux, 1975), p. 103.
15. R. Stoller, *Sexual Excitement: Dynamics of Erotic Life* (New York: Pantheon, 1979), p. 6.
16. Harriet Jacobs, quoted by Rennie Simson, "The Afro-American Female: The Historical Context of the Construction of Sexual Identity," in Snitow, Stansell, and Thompson, eds., p. 231. Jacobs subsequently resisted by hiding in an attic cubbyhole "almost deprived of light and air, and with no space to move my limbs, for nearly seven years" to avoid him.
17. A similar rejection of indeterminancy can be found in Linda Alcoff, "Cultural Feminism versus Post-Structuralism: The Identity Crisis in Feminist Theory," *Signs: Journal of Women in Culture and Society* 13 (1988): 419–20. The article otherwise misdiagnoses the division in feminism as that between so-called cultural feminists and post-structuralism, when the division is between those who

take sexual misogyny seriously as a mainspring to gender hierarchy and those who wish, liberal-fashion, to affirm "differences" without seeing that sameness/difference is a dichotomy of exactly the sort post-structuralism purports to deconstruct.

18. See Sandra Harding, "Introduction: Is There a Feminist Methodology?" in *Feminism and Methodology*, ed. Sandra Harding (Bloomington: Indiana University Press, 1987).

19. Dworkin, *Pornography*, p. 24.

20. J. Cook, "The X-rated Economy," *Forbes* (1978), p. 18; Langelan (see Appendix), p. 5; *Public Hearings on Ordinances to Add Pornography as Discrimination against Women*, Minneapolis, Minnesota: December 12, and 13, 1983 (hereafter cited as *Public Hearings*); F. Schauer, "Response: Pornography and the First Amendment," *University of Pittsburgh Law Review* 40 (1979): 616.

21. A. Dworkin, "The Root Cause," in *Our Blood: Prophesies and Discourses on Sexual Politics* (New York: Harper & Row, 1976), pp. 96–111.

22. See MacKinnon, *Toward a Feminist Theory of the State* (Cambridge, Mass.: Harvard University Press, 1989), chap. 12 for further discussion.

23. Dworkin, *Pornography* (Appendix), p. 69.

24. Ibid., p. 136.

25. Ibid., p. 69.

26. Ibid., chap. 2, "Men and Boys."

27. Ibid., p. 109.

28. Ibid., pp. 113–28.

29. Ibid., p. 174.

30. Ibid., p. 146.

31. A. Koedt, "The Myth of the Vaginal Orgasm," *Notes from the Second Year: Women's Liberation*, vol. 2 (1970): Ti-Grace Atkinson, *Amazon Odyssey* (New York: Link Books, 1974); Phelps.

32. Dworkin, *Pornography*, p. 22.

33. Dworkin, "The Root Cause," p. 56.

34. A prominent if dated example is Jill Johnston, *Lesbian Nation* (New York: Simon & Schuster, 1974).

35. Kathleen Barry defines "female sexual slavery" as a condition of prostitution that one cannot get out of.

36. E. Donnerstein, testimony, *Public Hearings* (see n. 20 above), pp. 35–36. The relationship between consenting and nonconsenting depictions and sexual arousal among men with varying self-reported propensities to rape are examined in the following studies: N. Malamuth, "Rape Fantasies as a Function of Exposure to Violent-Sexual Stimuli," *Archives of Sexual Behavior* 6 (1977): 33–47; N. Malamuth and J. Check, "Penile Tumescence and Perceptual Responses to Rape as a Function of Victim's Perceived Reactions," *Journal of Applied Social Psychology* 10 (1980): 528–47; N. Malamuth, M. Heim, and S. Feshbach, "The Sexual Responsiveness of College Students to Rape Depictions: Inhibitory and Disinhibitory Effects," *Journal of Personality and Social Psychology* 38 (1980): 399–408; N. Malamuth and J. Check, "Sexual Arousal to Rape and Consenting Depictions: The Importance of the Woman's Arousal," *Journal of Abnormal Psychology* 39 (1980): 763–66; N. Malamuth, "Rape Proclivity among Males," *Journal of Social Issues* 37 (1981): 138–57; E. Donnerstein and L. Berkowitz, "Victim Reactions in Aggressive Erotic Films as a Factor in Violence against Women," *Journal of Personality and Social Psychology* 41 (1981): 710–24; J. Check and T.

Guloien, "Reported Proclivity for Coercive Sex Following Repeated Exposure to Sexually Violent Pornography, Nonviolent Dehumanizing Pornography, and Erotica," in *Pornography: Recent Research, Interpretations, and Policy Considerations*, ed. D. Zillman and J. Bryant (Hillside, N.J.: Erlbaum, in press).

37. Donnerstein, testimony, *Public Hearings*, p. 36.

38. The soporific effects of explicit sex depicted without express violence are apparent in the *Report of the President's Commission on Obscenity and Pornography* (Washington, D.C.: Government Printing Office, 1971).

39. Donnerstein, testimony, *Public Hearings*, p. 36.

40. Donnerstein and Berkowitz (see n. 36 above): E. Donnerstein, "Pornography: Its Effect on Violence against Women," in Malamuth and Donnerstein, eds. (*Aggression: Theoretical and Empirical Reviews* [New York: Academic, 1985]). This conclusion is the cumulative result of years of experimental research showing that "if you can measure sexual arousal to sexual images and measure people's attitudes about rape you can predict aggressive behavior with women" (Donnerstein, testimony, *Public Hearings*, p. 29). Some of the more prominent supporting experimental work, in addition to citations previously referenced here, include E. Donnerstein and J. Hallam, "The Facilitating Effects of Erotica on Aggression toward Females," *Journal of Personality and Social Psychology* 36 (1978): 1270–77; R. G. Green, D. Stonner, and G. L. Shope, "The Facilitation of Aggression by Aggression: Evidence against the Catharsis Hypothesis," *Journal of Personality and Social Psychology* 31 (1975): 721–26; D. Zillman, J. Hoyt, and K. Day, "Strength and Duration of the Effects of Aggressive, Violent, and Erotic Communications on Subsequent Aggressive Behavior," *Communications Research* 1 (1974): 286–306; B. Sapolsky and D. Zillman, "The Effect of Soft-core and Hard-core Erotica on Provoked and Unprovoked Hostile Behavior," *Journal of Sex Research* 17 (1981): 319–43; D. L. Mosher, "Pornographic Films, Male Verbal Aggression against Women, and Guilt," in *Technical Report of the Commission on Obscenity and Pornography* (Washington, D.C.: Government Printing Office, 1971), vol. 8. See also E. Summers and J. Check, "An Empirical Investigation of the Role of Pornography in the Verbal and Physical Abuse of Women," *Violence and Victims* 2 (1987): 189–209; and P. Harmon, "The Role of Pornography in Women Abuse" (Ph.D. diss., York University, 1987). These experiments establish that the relationship between expressly violent sexual material and subsequent aggression against women is causal, not correlational.

41. Key research is summarized and reported in Check and Galoien (see n. 36 above); see also D. Zillman, "Effects of Repeated Exposure to Nonviolent Pornography," presented to U.S. Attorney General's Commission on Pornography, Houston, Texas (June 1986). Donnerstein's most recent experiments, as reported in *Public Hearings* and his book edited with Malamuth (see n. 40 above), clarify, culminate, and extend years of experimental research by many. See, e.g., D. Mosher, "Sex Callousness toward Women," in *Technical Report of the Commission on Obscenity and Pornography*, vol. 8; N. Malamuth and J. Check, "The Effects of Mass Media Exposure on Acceptance of Violence against Women: A Field Experiment," *Journal of Research in Personality* 15

(1981): 436–46. The studies are tending to confirm women's reports and feminist analyses of the consequences of exposure to pornography on attitudes and behaviors toward women. See J. Check and N. Malamuth ("An Empirical Assessment of Some Feminist Hypotheses About Rape." *International Journal of Women's Studies* 8 (1985): 414–23.).

42. G. G. Abel, D. H. Barlow, E. Blanchard, and D. Guild, "The Components of Rapists' Sexual Arousal," *Archives of General Psychiatry* 34 (1977): 395–403; G. G. Abel, J. V. Becker, and I. J. Skinner, "Aggressive Behavior and Sex," *Psychiatric Clinics of North America* 3 (1980): 133–55; G. G. Abel, E. B. Blanchard, J. V. Becker, and A. Djenderedjian, "Differentiating Sexual Aggressiveness with Penile Measures," *Criminal Justice and Behavior* 2 (1978): 315–32.

43. Donnerstein, testimony, *Public Hearings,* p. 31.

44. Smithyman (n. 4 above).

45. Scully and Marolla (n. 4 above).

46. In addition to previous citations to Malamuth, "Rape Proclivity among Males" (see n. 36 above); and Malamuth and Check, "Sexual Arousal to Rape and Consenting Depictions" (see n. 36 above); see T. Tieger, "Self-Reported Likelihood of Raping and the Social Perception of Rape," *Journal of Research in Personality* 15 (1981): 147–58; and N. Malamuth, S. Haber, and S. Feshbach, "Testing Hypotheses Regarding Rape: Exposure to Sexual Violence, Sex Differences, and the 'Normality' of Rape," *Journal of Research in Personality* 14 (1980): 121–37.

47. M. Burt and R. Albin, "Rape Myths, Rape Definitions and Probability of Conviction," *Journal of Applied Social Psychology,* vol. 11 (1981); G. D. LaFree, "The Effect of Sexual Stratification by Race on Official Reactions to Rape," *American Sociological Review* 4–5 (1984): 842–54, esp. 850; J. Galvin and K. Polk, "Attribution in Case Processing: Is Rape Unique?" *Journal of Research in Crime and Delinquency* 20 (1983): 126–54. The latter work seems not to understand that rape can be institutionally treated in a way that is sex-specific even if comparable statistics are generated by crimes against the other sex. Further, this study assumes that 53 percent of rapes are reported, when the real figure is closer to 10 percent (Russell, *Sexual Exploitation*).

48. Russell, "The Prevalence and Incidence of Forcible Rape and Attempted Rape of Females," pp. 1–4.

49. Scully and Marolla, p. 2.

50. Compare, e.g., Hite (*The Hite Report: A Nationwide Survey of Female Sexuality* [New York: Macmillan, 1976]) with Russell, *The Politics of Rape* (New York: Stein & Day, 1975).

51. This is truly obvious from looking at the pornography. A fair amount of pornography actually calls the acts it celebrates "rape." Too, "In depictions of sexual behavior [in pornography] there is typically evidence of a difference of power between the participants" (L. Baron and M. A. Straus, "Conceptual and Ethical Problems in Research on Pornography" [paper presented at the annual meeting of the Society for the Study of Social Problems, 1983], p. 6)." Given that this characterizes the reality, consider the content attributed to "sex itself" in the following methodologically liberal quotations on the subject: "Only if one thinks of *sex itself* as a degrading act can one believe that all pornography degrades and

harms women" (P. Califia, "Among Us, against Us—the New Puritans," *Advocate* [April 17, 1980], p. 14 [emphasis added]). Given the realization that violence against women *is* sexual, consider the content of the "sexual" in the following criticism: "The only form in which a politics opposed to violence against women is being expressed is anti-sexual" (English, Hollibaugh, and Rubin, "Talking Sex: A Conversation on Sexuality and Feminism," *Socialist Review,* vol. 11 [1981], p. 51). And "the feminist anti-pornography movement has become deeply erotophobic and anti-sexual" (A Hollibaugh, "The Erotophobic Voice of Women," *New York Native* [1983], p. 34).

52. J. Wolfe and V. Baker, "Characteristics of Imprisoned Rapists and Circumstances of the Rape," in *Rape and Sexual Assault,* ed. C. G. Warner (Germantown, Md.: Aspen Systems Co., 1980).

53. This statement was widely attributed to California State Senator Bob Wilson; see Joanne Schulman, "The Material Rape Exemption in the Criminal Law," *Clearinghouse Review,* vol. 14 [1980]) on the Rideout marital rape case. He has equally widely denied that comment was seriously intended. I consider it by now apocryphal as well as stunningly revelatory, whether or not humorously intended, on the topic of the indistinguishability of rape from intercourse from the male point of view.

54. Carolyn Craven, "No More Victims: Carolyn Craven Talks about Rape, and What Women and Men Can Do to Stop It," ed. Alison Wells (Berkeley, Calif., 1978, mimeographed) p. 2; Russell, *The Politics of Rape* (New York: Stein & Day, 1975), pp. 84–85, 105, 114, 135, 147, 185, 196, and 205; P. Bart, "Rape Doesn't End with a Kiss," *Viva* 11 (1975): 39–41 and 100–101; J. Becker, L. Skinner, G. Abel, R. Axelrod, and J. Cichon, "Sexual Problems of Sexual Assault Survivors," *Women and Health* 9 (1984): 5–20.

55. March for Women's Dignity, New York City, May 1984.

56. *Public Hearings* (n. 20 above); M. Atwood, *Bodily Harm* (Toronto: McClelland & Stewart, 1983), pp. 207–12.

57. Ti-Grace Atkinson, "Why I'm Against S/M Liberation," in *Against Sadomasochism: A Radical Feminist Analysis,* ed. R. Linden, D. Pagano, D. Russell, and S. Star (East Palo Alto, Calif.: Frog in the Well, 1982), p. 91.

 79

From Transforming Knowledge

ELIZABETH MINNICH

BACK TO BASICS

. . .

There is a *root problem* at the base of the dominant meaning system that informs our curricula—a tangle that results from taking the few to be the inclusive term, the norm, and the ideal for all. That problem, which can be considered in part as one of *faulty generalization*, even universalization, is compounded by the (not surprising) consequence of privileging central *singular* terms, notably "man" and "mankind," which lead directly to such singular abstract notions—and ideals—as "the citizen," "the philosopher," "the poet." Such singularity makes thinking of plurality, let alone diversity, very difficult indeed, and, in its idealizing aspects, promotes circular meaning. Together, faulty universalization, an emphasis on singularity, and circularity tend strongly and stubbornly to make considerations of time and space, of history and place, difficult to include in knowledge and meaning constructions: the universal, singular, normative Man appears to have no particular contexts at all. Thus, Man, with other foundational concepts, is *mystified*, made to appear what it is not, and whole systems of knowledge built around such concepts come to appear to have neither contexts nor consequences that should be considered to be central (rather than peripheral) to their truth and meaning. The result is *partial knowledge* masquerading as general, even universal.

Again, what we know reveals itself to contain errors of (1) faulty generalization (generalizing too far from too few without recognizing it), and (2) circularity of reasoning (drawing on definitions, principles, standards derived from faulty generalizations to explain and justify the continuing exclusion and devaluation of all that was held out of the initial inquiry). The confusions that result underlie and perpetuate the creation of (3) mystified concepts (in which the partial origins of the hierarchically invidious tradition are hidden but continue to have effect), so that (4) partial modes of knowing and knowledge systems, considered without analysis that reveals their contexts and consequences, produce ways of thinking about knowledge that, rather than providing perspective on those modes and systems, perpetuate and justify the original exclusions.

Furthermore, because the few not only were taken to be the inclusive term, the norm, and the ideal, but were defined and came to know themselves *in contradistinction* to all others, deuniversalizing everything in our knowledge and meaning systems is not, by itself, enough.

If we did no more than particularize what has been considered general, or even universal, the hegemonic few would then appear as one set of particulars among others—as if all we needed to do were to add "and she" to all references to "he," and/or give the few their 'markers' by saying, for example, "the privileged Euro-American male heterosexual philosopher," or, more startlingly in today's virulently homophobic society, "the great male Athenian homosexual philosopher, Plato." (Using the latter 'marker' would open up another huge tangle in the dominant tradition, which includes in its canon of Great Books many by men who would today be labeled, and very likely persecuted as, "homosexuals," as they would not have been earlier.) It is indeed helpful to particularize, but while undoing universals derived from faulty abstractions does clear the space and unblock the light we need to see those who are present mostly as absences, or Others, lesser beings, or victims, we must also recognize *how* the dominant few have been particular. Their particularity has been and is different from that of other groups: they have been only one group among many, but they have been so as a defining, power-wielding few. They have been particular in the mode of false universality; of being the definers for others who were the defined; of being the subjects who 'knew' the others as their objects, claiming that only their own standpoints transcended 'mere' subjectivity. They have been, in many senses, the colonizers.

As we work to particularize this group without mystifying it yet again by overlooking the fact that it has been "more equal than others" (to borrow Orwell's classic phrase), we need also to work with the observation that the defined were for the most part not positively but, rather, negatively defined. We cannot, with a few qualifiers added after the fact, arrive at equalized plurality. Many of us have been present only as absences, as that from which 'real' people separated and distinguished themselves. That is why democratic pluralism, on the face of it a fine position, cannot be espoused in today's world as if all we had to do was *choose* it. To achieve a truly egalitarian pluralism conceptually and politically, it is necessary for all groups to achieve self-knowledge, developed from within rather than imposed from without; for that knowledge to be fully and equally taken into account in any general concepts, theories, laws, principles, organizations, polities; and for provision to be made for the long transition period we face before the hierarchically invidious monism that is expressed in almost all dominant structures is truly transformed.

When people say to me, "But isn't the point to be able to speak of *humankind*? Shouldn't we drop all the emphasis on women, on different groups of women, on all the 'kinds' of men, and get on with learning about and caring for *humans*?" I say, "That may be a goal, but if we act now as if we have already achieved it, as if all we need do is assert our gender-, race-, or class-blindness, the awful weight of an old, fully developed, very powerful meaning and power system will ensure that in critical ways 'human' will continue to be conflated with 'man,' and 'man' with a particular group of males. *Saying* we are now inclusive cannot make it so. It will take a while to transform what has been developing for millennia."

Those who like to pretend that the fragile transitional measures and protections we have just barely established are instances of "reverse discrimination" are trying to have it both ways. They want Man to continue to be universal so they can pretend that their privilege comes from a neutral, disinterested assessment of their own personal merit, but when tiny pockets of consideration are designed to compensate others for the inequities of that mystified hegemonic status, they rush to proclaim themselves just one group among many and hence entitled to the 'special' provisions too. We cannot pretend *either* that we are able to think well about humans *or* that giving us all equally particular prefixes or group identifications fixes the problem.

Furthermore, the self-knowledge of all nonuniversalized groups must also take into account the ways in which those primarily defined in contradistinction to the hegemonic few have also been defined against each other. There has been a hierarchy among Others, too; Black women and white women have been defined-against as well as defined-with each other as white women have participated in race and (often associated) class privileges denied Black women. Some Black men have claimed the rights due their 'manhood' not only from white men but in opposition to the equal rights (personal as well as political) of Black women.

We are aided, not impeded, in holding onto these simple/complex realizations by the fact that we stumble into them almost every time we open our mouths, and we can hardly complete a statement without rediscovering just how used we are to the singular, universal "he," the long string of prefixes carried by all who do not belong to the single group that is itself rarely if ever prefixed. Such utterly nontrivial language difficulties confront us with the magnitude of our task; we cannot even speak to each other in the course of our daily affairs without encountering it, nor can we avoid it at the highest levels of abstraction.

To repeat: we cannot just tack on discrepant ideas; we cannot add the idea that the earth is round to the idea that it is flat. In our case, (1) we cannot add ourselves to a part that has claimed to be the whole, nor (2) can we reduce the hegemonic part to one-among-others by simple intellectual fiat. We must deal directly, stubbornly, consistently, at all levels with the realization that there is one part that has claimed to be the whole, the norm, and the ideal—and has held the power necessary to enforce that contradictory status. It is certainly not crystalline clarity, nor consistency, nor avoidance of contradictions that has held the dominant system in its place for so long; power, exercised and suffered directly through acts of exclusion, internalized in a sense of entitlement in some, in a sense of vulnerability or inadequacy in many others, is at play here.

But let us be clear: our goal is not necessarily to undo all universals and the very idea of universals. It is to particularize accurately, to demystify the functions of power and hierarchy. It is not, after all, universalization itself, or abstraction itself, that is necessarily harmful; it is *false* universals, faulty and mystified abstractions, that concern us. And they concern us precisely because they mask the possibility of approaching, at least, visions and concepts and commitments that could inspire us all.[1]

We are by no means concerned only with destruction, as I have noted, nor do we adopt a purely "us against them" position when we undertake the work of transforming the dominant tradition. We admit our participation (to varying degrees that must be honestly recognized) in that which we are struggling to change, recognizing that the errors are so complex and all-pervasive that few are utterly free of their effects, and that changed thinking does not begin, or create, *de novo*. And that is not all bad; there are moments of great inspiration as well as examples of a rich diversity and of liberatory thinking within the dominant tradition. We can find much that is of help to us, much that can inspire our work in the tradition as well as outside it when we stop ignoring or blithely explaining away its errors and exclusions. Thus, in the classroom, we invite students to join us in approaching what has come down to us in a spirit of inquiry that will help us all think well and freely about what they will, in turn, critique, create, pass on. We try to inform quests for knowledge, explorations of modes of knowing, with a sense of responsibility for the human world. We admit, then, that it *matters* that Aristotle's modes of thinking allowed him to support his culture's justifications of slavery and the subordination of women. Having done so, we can also then notice and take very seriously the fact that Plato's method took him on occasion beyond his times, as when he observed that sex is not an appropriate criterion in the selection of philosopher–leaders. We can then begin to locate and focus on other striking instances of liberatory thinking within the tradition itself. After all, what is more fascinating and more important than discovering how even the privileged have on occasion thought themselves free? We do not pay the dominant tradition a compliment when we think we must pass quickly over or excuse its errors—quite the contrary. In doing so we risk trivializing some of its moments of lasting greatness, and the lessons we can learn from them.

At the same time, we need to explore a much richer range of materials, lives, voices, visions, and achievements, to learn the stories and modes of thought and creation of others. As we do so, we engage students by recognizing their diverse as well as common connections to our shared world, working with them to approach an education that might be, in the rich meaning of the terms, both humane and liberal in the sense of liberatory, compatible with freedom.

Thought and Action

. . .

Here there is a recognition of the responsibility of the quest for knowledge to be open to all humankind in a way that might make possible an approach to (never an arrival at) communication that is *both* intimate *and* universal. To insist on both intimacy and universality, understood as regulative ideals rather than possible achievements, is to insist on openness to the individual, to the particular, as well as to the general, the universal. Intimacy is a mode of relation that refuses generalizations: to be intimate means to break through *what* someone is in order to become open to *who* s/he is, to experience *this* person as she is herself, not as she seems to be when filtered through pre-judgments about the category Woman. Great literature gives us such moments of comprehension and, in so doing, suggests that the intimate and the universal are not opposites after all. Universality is a creation of thought that moves through all limitations, all particular definition, in recognition of profound connectedness. It need not come only or primarily or most convincingly through an abstraction that creates utterly context-free symbols such as numbers. It can emerge from immersion in the particular, the individual, as well (as in stories). Between these ideas that call us to commune with each thing, each person, each moment, with full attentiveness, and to reach, also, for visions of connections within a whole beyond any particular, lie the richly complex social and political realms in which we struggle to live with each other. The intimate and the universal both remove us temporarily from the tension of the plural, active public realm, but we need always to return to it as well.

Arendt wrote, "We are all the same, that is, human, in such a way that nobody is ever the same as anyone who ever lived, lives or will live."[2] She insisted on our sameness in the apparently paradoxical mode of uniqueness (which makes the old errors impossible, if we can succeed in understanding and honoring it) in the context of discussing action, the political. "Plurality," which is uniqueness recognized in public, where we can see and experience that we are each unique, "is the condition of human action."[3] Plurality is also a result, a gift, of action. Without action in a public realm held open to all by guarantees of equality, it is all too easy to think of uniqueness as a special quality of the privileged few—there are the individuals who appear before us, revealing themselves through what they say and do, and then there are "the masses," "the common people." To be denied freedom of action, to be denied equality, is to be denied the opportunity to reveal and experience one's uniqueness, the opportunity to recognize that we are *all* unique.

Undoing *false* universals that have given only a few the privilege of being both unique and universal is not the same as undoing the idea of universality itself. "We are all the same" can be a highly ethical and politically sensitive claim, one that calls on us to remember human connectedness, and to value it. It is dangerous when we misconstrue sameness, as I have noted before, but that does not mean that we must or should give up our belief in our deepest connections. "The brotherhood of mankind" may be a notion we wish to undo, but that is because it is cast in partial terms, and false universals divide us; they do not connect us. In fact, they make it impossible to think universally because they have universalized falsely, inflated a part into the whole.

I am suggesting that, in addition to our conceptual critique, we can learn to see the partiality of past universals when we stop severing the quest for knowledge from genuine experience of action. The life of the mind and the life of action may be two different modes of human life, but that does not mean they are radically discontinuous. Both were restricted for too long to privileged men; the meanings of both have been misconstrued as a result. Consider: you have heard of "the man of action." Have you ever heard of "the woman of action"? Or, even more strikingly: news commentators and political pundits like to speak of "the man in the street." But the only parallel for women is "a woman of the streets." Man, outside in public, is political; Woman in the same place is sexual. Our understandings of action and of politics are as skewed as our understanding of the life of the mind, and for the same reasons.

What we need to comprehend is and will be related to what we need to do; what we need to do is related to what we need to comprehend. Knowledge, untransformed, is irrelevant to citizenship, to action, not because it is about 'higher' things than politics, not because knowledge is 'purer' than action, but because what we have known and the modes of knowing behind it are locked into universals derived from partial, faulty, hierarchically arranged abstractions that cannot be found in or illuminate real, existent, particulars, or develop a feeling of universal egalitarian connectedness, or help us learn to think in the place of many others. A transforming vision of knowledge expresses our realization that humans are natal as well as mortal, that the human condition of plurality is made visible in a free public life, that we *need* that plurality for knowledge that approaches comprehensiveness, and hence that knowing is related to acting as knowledge is related to politics.

• • •

Another View of Beginnings

In the realm of thinking, as in that of action, nothing is ever finally settled. Whenever thinking seems to reach a conclusion, another thought, another question, another voice, emerges. There is always another way to turn an idea, another perspective on a phenomenon, a different conceptual approach to explore, a fresh and startlingly suggestive example to be taken into account. What seems settled one moment is unsettled again the next. I presume, then, that if you have been thinking with me and all the others whose voices I have invited into our conversation, you have at least as many unsettled questions now as you did at the beginning. Perhaps you even have more.

If so, I am pleased. While others are doing the invaluable work of detailed research that answers important specific questions, I want to join in thinking about what those questions and findings might mean for us. And while still others, more systematically minded, work to explore, re-create, and create theoretical frameworks to give conceptual contexts for facts, descriptions, interpretations, explanations, I cannot help stepping back and trying to think about those theories, too. I do not want there to be one "feminist theory," or "theory of feminism." I want there to be many, so that, on that level too, we are called back into thought by the multiplicity of possible ways of knowing. All of this work is important; there can be no sound theories without careful research to uncover and to create facts, facts require theory to help us make sense of them, and facts and theories should, I believe, be constantly considered to see what they *mean*, what difference they make. To act aimlessly and always only in response to the immediate situation because there is no theoretical framework is a problem for action, as is the turning of theory into rigid ideology. The adoption of a theory can be a critical turning point for action, for good and for ill. It matters.

And when we ask ourselves, What does this *mean*? we are calling on our ability to think alone and together in a way that prepares us to make judgments, to make choices, to take responsibility in the world of action we share with others.

I say all this to bring my book to a close with the recognition that I have not dealt with strategies for change, but I hope I have joined many others in helping to prepare the ground for a whole different set of conversations that are directed expressly at action informed by the on-going effort of conceptual critique and reflexive thinking. I am aware that the open-endedness of thinking and the 'negativity' of critique seem, to some, to make action more difficult. Over the years I have been asked many times if I do not think some kind of utopian vision, rather than critique, is necessary for real change, and why I do not get on with envisioning alternatives. I have several responses. First, there are others whose gifts lie in imagining alternatives.[4] We could not do without them, and there is no reason why I should try to do what they do so well. Second, I worry about 'new' visions emerging without an on-going critique, since I have a great respect for the power of unanalyzed assumptions and error to continue to affect us without our wishing them to. Third, I find a great deal of positive and creative vision within critique. To begin to uncover what is wrong is to begin to be able to see what could be right, and to do so by concentrating on what *is,* not what *ought to be.* It sometimes seems to me that we are more likely to be able to change what is if we understand it very well than if we turn from it, imagine something quite different, and then have to begin afresh to figure out how to get there from here. Furthermore, I am always worried by efforts to 'get there from here' when the 'there' toward which we act is too clear to us, too developed. Such visions turn far too easily into prescriptive ends, in view of which present pressing realities—and too often real people—turn into no more than means.

And, finally, I believe, as I have said, that thinking reflexively is one of the grounds of human freedom,

in part because it reveals to us that we are always both subject and object of our own knowing, of our culture, of our world. We are not just products, objects, of our world, nor are we just subjects existing in a void. We are free subjects whose freedom is conditioned—not determined—by a world not of our making but in many ways open to the effects of our actions. If nothing else, then, I believe in the educational importance of thinking and of critique as preparations for a kind of action that engages with others, and with the world, rather than submitting to it or trying to 'master' it.

• • •

[1989]

NOTES

1. I am grateful here for an exchange of letters with Carl Schorske following the "History And . . ." Conference at Scripps College in the spring of 1988, which led me to think further about the role and importance of universals.
2. Arendt, *The Human Condition,* p. 8.
3. Ibid., p. 8.
4. See, for example, works by Ursula K. LeGuin, Marge Piercy, and Charlotte Perkins Gilman.

 80

Birth Pangs: Conceptive Technologies and the Threat to Motherhood

MICHELLE STANWORTH

INTRODUCTION

Louise Brown celebrates her twelfth birthday in 1990; the world's first "test-tube baby" is not a baby any more. In the years since her birth, reproductive technologies that initially seemed bizarre have come to acquire a sense of the routine. Terms such as in vitro fertilization or surrogate motherhood have gained the status of household words. More and more people turn to the new reproductive technologies not as a last "desperate" pioneering option, but as a predictable stage in a reproductive career. If we judge by the number of women and men seeking their use, or by the flimsy evidence from opinion polls, reproductive technologies are increasingly popular. Yet within the feminist community, opposition to these technologies has become more coherent and more intense. In this essay, I would like to explore the reception of the new conceptive technologies, particularly in vitro fertilization and related techniques and, to a lesser extent, surrogacy.[1]

One basis for feminist hostility to the conceptive technologies is a powerful theoretical critique which sees in these new techniques a means for men to wrest "not only control of reproduction, but reproduction itself" from women.[2] It has been suggested that men's alienation from reproduction—men's sense of disconnection from their seed during the process of conception, pregnancy, and birth—has underpinned through the ages a relentless male desire to master nature, and to construct social institutions and cultural patterns that will not only subdue the waywardness of women but also give men an illusion of procreative power. New reproductive technologies are the vehicle that will turn men's illusions of reproductive control into a reality. By manipulating eggs and embryos, scientists will determine the sort of children who are born—will make themselves the fathers of humankind. By removing eggs and embryos from some women and implanting them in others, medical practitioners will gain unprecedented control over motherhood itself. Motherhood as a unified biological process will be effectively deconstructed: in place of "mother," there will be ovarian mothers who supply eggs, uterine mothers who give birth to children, and, presumably, social mothers who raise them. Through the eventual development of artificial wombs, the capacity may arise to make biological motherhood redundant. Whether or not women are reduced by this process to the level of "reproductive prostitutes," the object and the effect of the emergent technologies is to deconstruct motherhood and to destroy the claim to reproduction that is the foundation of women's identity.

While this theoretical account of the new technologies may be in some ways extremely radical, in other respects it ironically tends to echo positions that feminists have been keen to challenge. In the first place, this analysis entails an exaggerated view of the power of science and medicine, a mirror image of that which scientists and medical practitioners often try themselves to promote. Science may well be, as Emily Martin argues, a hegemonic system; but as she shows, that system does not go unchallenged.[3] The vigorous critique of science in this account needs to be tempered with a deeper understanding of the constraints within which science and medicine operate, and of the way these can be shaped for the greater protection of women and men. Second, in the urgent concern to protect infertile women from the sometimes unscrupulous attentions of medical science, infertile women are all too often portrayed as "desperate people," rendered incapable by pronatal pressures of making rational and ethical decisions.[4] This view of infertile women (and by implication, of all women) comes uncomfortably close to that espoused by some members of the medical profession. Third, this theoretical account sometimes seems to suggest that anything "less" than a natural process, from conception through to birth, represents the degradation of motherhood itself. But motherhood means different things to different women, and to identify motherhood so exclusively with nature, with the absence of technology, and indeed, with pregnancy and childbirth runs the risk of blunting the cutting edge of feminist critique.

THE CASE AGAINST REPRODUCTIVE TECHNOLOGY

Feminist opposition to conceptive technologies, like all oppositions, has a history. In the mid-1960s, I and many of my classmates at the University of British Columbia had no difficulty believing that we were emancipated because we had access to "the pill." The significance of the fact that the pill had to be obtained illegally, with fake identification that suggested we were married, seemed to escape us—technology was freedom, however sordidly obtained.

Today the honeymoon with technology is decisively over. Decades of involvement with technologies of fertility control, as well as with those directed at the "management" of labor and childbirth, have left most women somewhat sadder and a great deal wiser. The health risks and the side-effects of existing means of contraception, and the fact that we weren't informed of these dangers beforehand; the escalating use of aggressive medical intervention in childbirth; the tendency to relegate maternal welfare in the broadest sense to third place, after the safety of the fetus and the convenience of medical personnel; the linking of reproductive technology to medical models in which menstruation is seen as failed production and pregnancy as a pathological state; and, finally, the management of reproductive technologies in such a way that access depends powerfully on women's age, ethnicity, social class, sexual orientation, and physical abilities—so that black women, for example, have even less control over the experience of birthing than white women, or so that access to safe abortion depends on ability to pay: all these and more contribute to healthy skepticism among women about the potential effects of new forms of reproductive technology.[5]

This skepticism goes far beyond the simple dictum that medicine makes mistakes. After all, we all (even feminists) make mistakes. Instead, it has been recognized that far from being neutral artefacts or neutral ways of doing things that are independent of the societies they inhabit, reproductive technologies —like all technologies—bear the hallmark of the cultural context in which they emerge. Prevailing social relations are reflected in the nature of technologies, their particular strengths and weaknesses, the possibilities they open up, and the avenues they foreclose.[6] So, for example, the failure to develop safer and more acceptable means of birth control is not simply a technical problem; in part, it reflects the low priority given to women's health, and a tendency to disregard issues and symptoms that women themselves think are important.[7] Or, for instance, the fact that most obstetricians and gynecologists are male goes some way to account for the extensive use of technologies such as ultrasound which help to establish that medical practitioners "know more" about pregnancy and women's bodies than women do themselves.[8]

Against this background, it is not surprising that the detailed case against conceptive technologies, so forcefully and frequently articulated by feminist critics, has found a ready hearing within the feminist community. With the aid of Bryan Jennett's criteria for the evaluation of high-technology medicine (and the addition of a few of my own), I have organized the charges laid against the major conceptive technologies into seven discrete categories.[9] Conceptive technologies are accused of being:

Unsuccessful: Whatever the image of in vitro fertilization with embryo transfer, or of GIFT, as miracle cures for infertility, the miracle works in remarkably few cases.[10]

Unsafe: Risks are associated with the hormonal drugs used to stimulate ovulation for ivf patients, and those used to regulate cycles in some types of surrogacy. Where several embryos are transferred, infant and maternal health may suffer because of the frequency of multiple births. Women undergoing conceptive treatments are subject even more frequently than other women to procedures (e.g., ultrasound, caesarian deliveries) the routine use of which has been challenged by the women's health movement.[11]

Unkind: Whether treatment is "successful" or not, the pressure, emotional upheaval, disruption, and indignities involved do incommensurable damage to a woman's quality of life. The very existence of conceptive technologies makes it difficult for women to reconcile themselves to childlessness.[12]

Unnecessary: Infertility is a social condition, the seriousness of which depends entirely on the social evaluations attached to childlessness. Infertility does not require in vitro fertilization, or surrogacy, or any medical solution at all. If there were less hype about conceptive technologies, and if infertile people were less obsessed with securing their own biological child, then infertility might be resolved by the more satisfactory strategy of adoption.[13]

Unwanted: Women who expose their bodies to conceptive technologies or submit themselves as "surrogate" mothers have been coerced (1) by pressure from male partners, (2) by the limited economic opportunities for women and restricted avenues of self-esteem, which mean (especially in the case of "surrogate" mothers) that the "choice" isn't really a choice, (3) by pronatalist values and practices, which ensure that women who fail to bear children face constant reminders of the extent to which they fall short of hegemonic ideals. As Grundberg and Dowrick so clearly put it, none of us is free in our choices until it is possible to say aloud without fear of censure, "I don't wish to have children," (4) by unscrupulous and authoritarian doctors, who mislead them about the risks, intimidate them into "consent," or whose clinics offer "counseling into treatment" rather than counseling about treatment.[14]

Unsisterly: Women who use conceptive technologies harm other women, including women who don't (1) by seeking medical solutions to infertility, and thereby reinforcing the illusion that childbearing is a necessary component of femininity, (2) by providing doctors with experimental data and material to further their knowledge of the reproductive process and thus, by contributing to the expansion of a medical empire, the power of which is inimicable to women, (3) by taking advantage of a "surrogate" mother's poverty and powerlessness (or altruism) for their own benefit; this exploitation is potentially racist or imperialist, since women from subordinate ethnic communities and from poorer countries might be extensively used as "surrogate" mothers by privileged Western women in the future.[15]

Unwise: The low success rate of conceptive technologies as well as their many disadvantages make them an unwise focus for resources. Greater benefits would be derived if the resources currently being absorbed by in vitro fertilization and associated techniques were redeployed to fund research into the causes of infertility, or into preventative measures.[16]

The above charges constitute a powerful analysis of the impact of conceptive technologies, an analysis that goes beyond the unacceptably narrow terms of conventional medical assessment. But the strength of the feminist position we ultimately evolve depends upon the care with which these accusations are deployed and upon the implications for action that are drawn from them. Take, for example, the accusations that conceptive technologies are both *unwanted and unsisterly.* Underlying these charges is a telling critique of coercive pronatalism and of the place of medical practice in relation to it. But even this extremely useful analysis raises a number of questions.

While challenging the ways that coercive pronatalism shapes women's motivations to mother, we must be very clear that "shaped" is not the same as "determined." The battery of sanctions and rewards designed to entice women into motherhood indicates, not that conformity is guaranteed, but that childlessness is a genuine option, which efforts are made to contain. The most effective analyses of pronatalism are scrupulous about recognizing that even the pain of infertility does not prevent infertile women from making rational decisions about motherhood, and that the rejection of childbearing, while a difficult option for many women, is not necessarily a more authentic one.

As well as exposing pronatalist ideologies, we need also to articulate more convincing rationales for childlessness. For instance, in recent critiques of pronatalism (perhaps reacting against the fragile compromise involved in "having it all"?) it sometimes seems as if eschewing motherhood depends upon the compensation provided by a career. As one article says about protagonists in the Baby M surrogacy case:[17]

> the Sterns are not free either. . . . The Sterns, two people deeply committed to challenging professional careers, still feel the cultural imperative to "have" a child.

But why is it relevant to such a compulsion that people are committed to challenging professional careers? If it is assumed that a career can and should displace the wish for a child, then what type of economism does that bespeak? And what are we to make of the implied contrast: that professional women might be expected to have their minds on higher things, but that motherhood is the sensible course for women without rewarding careers? These interpretations may well not be what the authors of the above remarks on the Sterns had in mind, but they do signal how difficult it is for us to deal with the question of voluntary childlessness in a theoretically adequate way. To the extent that our discussions of pronatalism inadvertently justify childlessness in terms of career commitment, we run the risk of leaving no justification for childlessness—no refuge against pronatalist pressures—for the majority of women.

Finally, indignation at coercive pronatalism needs to be matched by an equally resolute opposition to the invidious distinctions that target some women as mothers and label others, on grounds that have little to do with their capacity to nurture a child, as unfit.

As all participants in the debate are aware, pro-motherhood propaganda is not uniformly disseminated;[18] it coexists with disincentives and obstacles to motherhood for women from disempowered groups. According to ideologies of motherhood, all women want children; but single women and teenagers, women from ethnic minorities and those on state support, lesbian women and women with disabilities are often urged to forgo mothering "in the interests of the child." Do some feminists unintentionally endorse a similar pattern of invidious distinctions when it seems to be suggested that infertile women should not be mothers, or that their desire for children (and only theirs) is selfish, misguided, and potentially dangerous?

It seems to me that our critique of pronatalism and of reproductive technologies will be all the more persuasive when it ceases to distinguish so categorically between fertile women and infertile. The pressures which propel women into motherhood—the cultural imperative to have a child, the expectations of male partners, and the limited sources for women of fulfillment, security, and self-esteem—enter into the decision of any woman to be a mother, regardless of her fertility. There is no particular reason to challenge the authenticity of the desire for motherhood of women who are infertile. Nor is there any good reason to identify infertile women in particular as unsisterly for reinforcing the illusion that motherhood is inevitable; any desired pregnancy, presumably, could have that effect (just as any pregnancy *may* be interpreted as a rebuke to women who are childless). And is it only infertile women whose attendance at medical clinics validates medical power, or is this an unintended side-effect of the use of many contraceptive or abortion or birthing technologies as well as of conceptive ones? And if the latter, can we be justified in asking only infertile women to turn their backs on medical treatment—or should we be seeking ways of containing medical power that are more consistent across different groups of women? That doctors pressure women into treatment, for example, and fail to provide the data necessary for informed consent, is a problem against which we must make a stand, but it is a problem by no means confined to infertility treatment.[19]

One of the most politically sensitive elements of the case against conceptive technologies is the claim that these are *"unnecessary"*—that infertility does not dictate a medical solution, and that the condition of involuntary childlessness can be resolved satisfactorily by adoption. For some infertile women (and I count myself among them) this happy ending is indeed possible. But it is a long and implausible leap from there to the conclusion that conceptive technologies are in general unnecessary.

For one thing, the description of infertility as a social condition of involuntary childlessness doesn't hold for all women. For some women, pregnancy and childbirth are not only a route to a child, but a desired end in itself.[20] Our passionate concern as feminists to defend the integrity of the experience of childbirth (against intrusive obstetricians, for example) would sit uneasily with the view that the attachment to giving birth of some infertile women reflects a misguided commitment to biological motherhood.

For another, it would be naive to regard the adoption process as necessarily free of the drawbacks and risks that characterize medically assisted conception. Adoption and fostering are often subject to strict surveillance and regulation and that surveillance and regulation is not necessarily benign to women. Adoption agencies in many countries are (rightly) rigorous about who may exercise parental rights: but their policies and criteria of assessment are framed against a conventional notion of parenting—and particularly, of motherhood—which will deter many would-be mothers. Adoption agencies in Britain may (and often do) refuse single women or those aged over thirty; may (and usually do) refuse those who are not heterosexual, whether married or not; may (and sometimes do) refuse women who have jobs, women who have had psychiatric referrals, women with disabilities, women whose unconventional life-styles cast doubt—for the social workers at least—on their suitability as mothers. They are also likely to refuse, in spite of the long and uncertain waiting period for adoption, women who intend to continue trying to achieve a pregnancy. For many would-be mothers, particularly those who want their relationship with a child to begin while it is still in infancy or toddlerhood, the conceptive technologies are not so much about biological motherhood as about having a child at all. The tensions surrounding the adoption process, the raising and dashing of hopes, the rejection by adoption agencies of prospective mothers who would have endured no question about their fitness had they been fertile—all of these mean that adoption may, like the conceptive technologies, sometimes be "unsuccessful," sometimes "unsafe" and often "unkind."

And there is, of course, another complication when we consider the adoption process from the point of view of the birthmother. To the same extent that surrogacy can be seen as "*unsisterly*"—as involving the exploitation of birthmothers by infertile women—adoption can be seen as unsisterly too. The pressures that lead some women to surrender their babies for adoption are very like those condemned in the case of surrogate mothers, right down to the possibility of exploitation of women from subordinate ethnic communities or from poorer nations. Indeed, in Britain, the potential for exploitation has been an element in a largely successful campaign to eliminate "trans-racial" adoptions of black children by white parents. It is ironic that while adoption is often presented in a positive light as a solution to infertility, the sometimes painful experiences of women who have surrendered their children to adoption are also involved to demonstrate the dangers of surrogacy.[21]

In highlighting the difficulties of adoption, I am not arguing for an end to adoption, nor am I identifying it as an unsatisfactory practice. On the contrary, I think adoption is to be encouraged; it is often the basis for strong and joyful mother-child relationships, and it enables many birthmothers to find a secure and loving home for children whom they decide not to mother.[22] What I would like to emphasize is that the impact of adoption on women (like that of surrogacy or other conceptive technologies) depends upon the conditions we create for these practices. We cannot ensure that a birthmother's decision to surrender her child for adoption will be painless (any more than we can make abortion decisions easy). But what we can and must do is to try to create conditions—crucially, about freedom from restriction during pregnancy and about custody—that will preserve her autonomy and help to ensure that the decision is hers,[23] and we can commit ourselves with renewed vigor to efforts to secure forms of economic and social support for all mothers so

that fewer such decisions are coerced by poverty and need.

The exaggerated and untruthful promises made by many infertility clinics in the 1980s for conceptive technologies as a safe and simple "cure" for infertility have been ruthlessly and rigorously exposed by feminist researchers. They have demonstrated beyond a doubt that while in vitro fertilization may be the only route to pregnancy for some women, it is by no means a certain route or a kind one. Because of the dearth of studies that compare treated and untreated women who are similar in terms of age, fertility problems, and so forth, lack of safety is harder to establish; but what is clear is that evidence of safety has not been a priority for clinicians, and that in the absence of such evidence, we are right to maintain a skeptical stance.

Feminist attempts to document the charges that conceptive technologies are *unsuccessful, unsafe, and unkind* have received a wide circulation. In Europe, for example, these views were prominently represented at the first WHO debate on reproductive technologies,[24] and have been influential in shaping policies within the Green movement. The success of this feminist critique is also reflected in its makeup in medical circles; articles sharply critical of current practice with regard to in vitro fertilization have recently appeared in major medical journals in several countries.[25]

But what is still at issue is the best way for feminists to respond to the data that has been so painstakingly brought to light. For it is a hallmark of critical discussion of science and medicine that technical knowledge (about efficacy, or safety, or anything else) should inform the choices we make, rather than dictate decisions.[26] It is important to remember this, because among other things the calculus of risks and benefits for reproductive technologies is different for different social groups, according to their circumstances and the resources they can command. For instance, it makes excellent sense for women to refuse contraceptives that carry health risks when they have better contraceptive options, or access to safe abortion, or are able to refuse intercourse; for women in less enviable circumstances the availability of such contraceptives can sometimes mean the difference between life and death. Before we reject technologies that are relatively unsuccessful, unsafe, or unkind, we need always to remind ourselves that the rejection of reproductive technology can sometimes be a luxury that only relatively privileged women can realistically afford.[27]

With conceptive technologies, the central issue is slightly different. Before setting our minds against conceptive technologies, we have to consider whether this is really the best way to protect women who have sought (and will continue to seek) their use. An implacable opposition to conceptive technologies could mean that any chance of exerting pressure on those who organize infertility services—for example, pressure for better research and for disclosure of information; for more stringent conditions of consent; for means of access for poorer women, who are likely to be the majority of those with infertility problems—would be lost. Would it be wise to abandon infertile women to the untender mercies of infertility specialists, when a campaign, say, to limit the number of embryos that may be implanted (and thereby to reduce multiple pregnancies, pressures for selective reduction and so forth), or to regulate the use of hormonal stimulation, might do a great deal to reduce the possible risks to women and to their infants?[28]

Perhaps in the light of these reflections, we might reconsider the claim that these technologies are *"unwise"*—that it would be better to divert resources to fund research into causes of infertility. Better for whom? Infertility services are often the poor cousin of health services—poorly funded, badly organized, extremely unequally distributed, and run in an authoritarian and insensitive fashion.[29] Do we really want to argue that resources be removed from the already inadequate provision for infertile people, and redeployed for the protection of those who are currently fertile? Surely this kind of divisive strategy runs counter to the feminist concern to improve health care provisions for all women, and to be sensitive to the needs of the infertile. On the other hand, a feminist campaign for a better range of services around infertility (research into causes, independent woman-staffed counseling services, and a range of treatments, high-tech and low) would make common cause with infertile women and men, who are often themselves very critical of the quality of help they are offered and the terms on which it is available.

TENSIONS AROUND MOTHERHOOD

The depth of feeling among feminists about conceptive technologies has partly to do with their links, not to medical technology, but to the difficult terrain of motherhood. In some accounts, conceptive technologies have been used to delineate a boundary between "good" motherhood and "bad." On one side of the boundary is empowering motherhood, the motherhood that represents a positive counterpole to masculinity. On the other side of the boundary, where creating or sustaining a pregnancy depends upon medical assistance, lies coercive motherhood that locks women into subordination.

The starkness of this contrast between "good" motherhood and "bad" may reflect the difficulty of juggling positive and negative interpretations of women as mothers, in the face of the paradox that motherhood is simultaneously women's weakness and women's strength.[30] On the one hand, maternal practices are increasingly acknowledged as a source of alternative values—as generating, in Sara Ruddick's terms, a discipline that orients mothers to distinctive themes and commitments, virtues and standards of achievement some of which stand in hopeful opposition to oppressive forms of thought.[31] On the other hand, feminists also recognize the pivotal role of motherhood in the subordination of women. The material and social disadvantages that follow from childcare; the cultural associations with birth that condemn women to an inferior place in symbolic systems; the psychological effects on future adults of asymmetrical mothercare: all suggest that motherhood locks women into institutional and psychological structures of dependency and powerlessness, which render them vulnerable to men. In a sense, the debates around conceptive technologies are a way of talking about different cultural conceptions of motherhood—a way of expressing both a commitment to the positive experience of motherhood and an opposition to its sometimes debilitating effects on women.

These competing conceptions of motherhood resonate with tensions at the level of personal politics and over the difficult individual decision whether or not to have children. Political and economic developments in the past fifteen years (for example, the new right's vociferous insistence on self-sufficiency, and the growing view of children as a personal indulgence; the changing opportunity structure for women; or the failure to establish a rationale for childlessness, even among feminists, that can challenge the near-hegemonic appeal of maternity) have tended to sharpen the divisions between women with young children and those without. But the positive feminist understanding of motherhood makes it more difficult to challenge maternity, and as a result this conflict is rarely addressed. A focus on the degrading impact of conceptive technologies is attractive, perhaps, because it seems to make possible the impossible: to attack the coercive aspects of maternity, the way that motherhood makes victims of women—and to do so in the name of motherhood itself.

But beyond this, an apocalyptic reading of the impact of conceptive technologies speaks to our sense that motherhood is today endangered. Discussions of surrogacy and of in vitro fertilization ring with references to the commercialization of motherhood, to the potential to turn babies and motherhood itself into a commodity like any other, to the replacement of maternal love with the cold harsh flare of clinical lights. This makes me wonder whether it is not motherhood per se that we feel the need to preserve, but whether we are afraid instead (as Linda Gordon once said in a different context) "of a loss of mothering, in the symbolic sense"—of a society in which tenderness and caring are displaced by the ruthless pursuit of individual advantage.[32] As more and more women grapple with the endless pressure involved in combining commitments to career with children, this fear speaks to feelings that many feminist mothers have about their lives—that all too often there is less time for tenderness, less chance for closeness, than we might wish. The "eye of love" may be steadfast on our children but it often has not the time to be "patient"—and indeed there is less time than we need to mother even ourselves. The urgency of the "dangers to motherhood" we apprehend in the new conceptive technologies has something to do, I suspect, with our own sense of loss, our sense that in current circumstances some aspects of mothering are escaping our grasp.

And we feel motherhood to be threatened, too, in another respect. The escalating rate of divorce over recent decades, and the rapid rate of formation of stepfamilies or reconstituted families, signify a markedly greater uncertainty in the 1980s and 1990s (compared with say the 1950s) about the ties that bind individual parents to individual children. Legal battles over custody and access are only part of the story: alongside these run uncounted numbers of households in which uncontested custody or access arrangements are nevertheless a source of anxiety, in which one parent or both must be more self-conscious about the basis of their claims upon the child. And this experience is not confined to parents: grandmothers and grandfathers, uncles and aunts, friends or lovers who have shared in the upbringing of a child, discover in times of break-up new difficulties in negotiating a secure relationship with children whom they love. It seems to me that the concern about genetic and biological parenthood that has greeted the arrival of new technologies—the attention of commissions of inquiry to issues of inheritance and paternity, the huge public interest in court cases concerned with the custody not only of children born of surrogacy arrangements, but also of embryos—reflects in part these pre-existing uncertainties about claims on relationships to children. In the face of divorce and rising rates of remarriage, the pressure to rethink the moral and legal basis of claims upon children is clearly intense.

But if anxiety about claims on children has a wide purchase, it is particularly poignant for women. It is women who make the largest investment in children, in terms of daily, weekly, yearly care and commitment; and it is women who are held (and hold themselves) most responsible when something goes wrong. Women's worries are fueled by a political context where women are, indeed, at particular risk in the judicial process; where mothers' prerogatives over children are often represented as selfish and unjust; and where fathers and children "are increasingly depicted as the losers [of a judicial preference for mother custody] in emotional and material terms."[33] Thus women are, and know themselves to be, vulnerable as mothers;[34] the urge to protect biological motherhood stems partly from the desperate need to find a secure and defensible basis on which to reassert mothers' claims.

But while the anxiety and the vulnerability that triggers it is real, we need to address that vulnerability in the most effective way. While men cannot bear children, every child does have a "biological" father; and trends towards enhancing the legal rights that flow from biological parenthood, as opposed to purposive parental commitment and care, could work decisively to the detriment of women.[35] One of our concerns must be that, in the search for a secure incontestable basis for claims to children, the anxieties that conceptive technologies crystallize do not lead us to give even greater legal priority to biological claims.[36]

The fears generated by conceptive technologies may be a way not only for women to articulate perceived threats to motherhood, but also to keep those threats at bay, by projecting them onto one particular group of women (the infertile) who aren't "really" mothers anyway. But however appealing this solution, and whatever conclusions we come to in the final analysis about the impact of conceptive technologies, the tendency to foreground technology is risky not so much because of what it says as because of what it ignores.

It ignores, first, the strenuous and partly successful efforts of the women's movement to transcend the identification of women with nature. Conception, pregnancy, and childbirth (as we are forever reminding members of the medical profession) are not merely the biological rite of passage that signifies a woman's entry into motherhood. The thrust of feminist analysis since the mid-1970s has been to rescue childbearing from the status of the "natural," to insist more and more confidently upon seeing pregnancy and childbirth as part of a sphere of significant action as meaningful and as civilized as any of the accomplishments of men. But the attempt to reclaim motherhood as a female accomplishment need not mean giving the natural priority over the technological—that pregnancy is natural and good, technology unnatural and bad. As I have argued elsewhere, it is not at all clear what a "natural" relationship to our fertility, our reproductive capacity, would look like—and it is even less clear that it

would be desirable.[37] The defense of motherhood that we ultimately construct will be stronger if we resist the temptation to use nature as a territory on which to stake our claims.[38]

Moreover, an emphasis upon conceptive technologies is problematic insofar as it overshadows a concern with other dimensions of the social context of motherhood. How important is medical intervention in conception compared with the institutional structures, for example, that make childcare for many women isolating and exhausting, rather than enriching? That give fathers control without responsibility over children they conceive? That burden mothers with expectations dictated by "experts," but fail to provide them with the resources necessary to meet those standards? How much space do we leave for a concern with the legal system that, for example, denies many lesbians custody of their children, or sends mothers to prison for refusing access to violent or abusive fathers? With the material conditions that force some women to choose between health care for themselves or medicine for their children? With the fundamental question of whether the woman who becomes pregnant by "natural" means wishes to be a mother or not?

We know now (or ought to know) that the balance of positive and negative elements in motherhood is historically and culturally specific—that the nature of motherhood and its impact, as well as the qualities evinced by those who mother, is not the same in any two societies; nor is the experience of motherhood identical across different groups of women within the same society.[39] Many feminists in the West can strongly identify with *Balancing Acts,* Katherine Gieve's collection of candid accounts of contemporary British women's often wistful relinquishment of fantasies of the "perfect mother," and of their struggles to combine politics, careers, and relationships with children.[40] But what a world of difference between these mothers and Toni Morrison's Baby Suggs, who had three children stolen from her by the slavemasters and who "could not or would not" love the rest.[41] Or between the European mothers in Jacklyn Cock's compelling study of South Africa, and the African nannies who look after the European children but are rarely enabled to spend time with their own daughters and sons.[42] While motherhood exacts sacrifices from most women and provides joy, only the blandest generalities are true in any universal sense. Attempts to understand and to influence the nature of motherhood must, it seems to me, come to terms with the range of conditions—social, legal, political, and economic, as well as medical—that sustain these differences. Only in this context will conceptive technology, and the impact of technology more generally, be allowed its proper place.

[1990]

NOTES

I would like to thank David Held, Marianne Hirsch and Evelyn Fox Keller for their encouragement and advice.

1. By in vitro fertilization I generally mean ivf with embryo transfer; related techniques include insemination, embryo transfer without ivf, lavage, and gamete intra-fallopian transfer or GIFT. For descriptions of these techniques, see the glossary of Patricia Spallone, *Beyond Conception* (London: Macmillan, 1989).

2. Janice Raymond, "Preface," p. 12, in Gena Corea et al., eds,. *Man-Made Women* (London, Hutchinson, 1985). This critique is associated with FINRRAGE, the Feminist International Network of Resistance to Genetic and Reproductive Engineering, whose views are elaborated in a number of books, including Jocelynne Scutt, ed., *The Baby Machine: the Commercialization of Motherhood* (Carlton, Australia: McCulloch Publishing, 1988).

3. Emily Martin, *The Woman in the Body* (Milton Keynes: Open U. Press, 1989). Feminists have been responsible for broadcasting alternative views of women and health, while the women's health movement has campaigned vigorously for the extension of health services and for their transformation, to make them more accountable to women and more responsive to women's needs.

4. Infertile women are far from being passive victims of medical technology, not only in the sense that they actively seek out infertility treatments (as Gerson rightly points out) but also (as Pfeffer argues) in the sense that they question those treatments, stop them, reject them in favor of others, or never present for treatment at all. Deborah Gerson, "Infertility and the construction of desperation," *Socialist Review*, vol. 19, no. 3 (July–September 1989) and Naomi Pfeffer, "Artificial insemination, in-vitro fertilization and the stigma of infertility," in Michelle Stanworth, ed., *Reproductive Technologies: Gender, Motherhood, and Medicine* (Minneapolis: U. Of Minnesota Press, 1988).

5. Boston Women's Health Book Collective, *The New Our Bodies Ourselves*, 3rd edn (New York: Simon and Schuster, 1985); Ann Oakley, *The Captured Womb* (Oxford: Basil Blackwell, 1985); Lesley Doyal, *The Political Economy of Health* (London: Pluto Press, 1979); Janet Gallagher, "Eggs, embryos and foetuses: anxiety and the law," in Michelle Stanworth, ed., *Reproductive Technologies;* Rosalind Pollack Petchesky, *Abortion and Woman's Choice* (Boston: Northeastern U. Press, 1986); Ruth Hubbard, "Personal courage is not enough: some hazards of childbearing in the 1980s," in Rita Arditti et al., eds., *Test-Tube Women* (London and Boston: Pandora Press, 1984); Jennifer Terry, "The body invaded: medical surveillance of women as reproducers," *Socialist Review*, vol. 19, no. 3 (July–September 1989), pp. 13–43.

6. Donald MacKenzie and Judy Wajcman, eds., *The Social Shaping of Technology* (Milton Keynes: Open U. Press, 1985); Judy Wajcman, *Women and Technology* (Cambridge: Polity Press, forthcoming, 1991).

7. Scarlett Pollock, "Refusing to take women seriously," in Rita Arditti et al., eds., *Test-Tube Women.*

8. Ann Oakley, "From walking wombs to test-tube babies"; Rosalind Pollack Petchesky, "Foetal images: the power of visual culture in the politics of reproduction"; both in Michelle Stanworth, ed., *Reproductive Technologies.*

9. Jennett's original five criteria were: unnecessary, unsuccessful, unsafe, unkind, unwise. Scambler suggested the addition of 'unwanted' in his discussion of childbirth. Bryan Jennett, *High Technology Medicine: Benefits and Burdens* (Oxford: Oxford U. Press, 1986), p. 174. Graham Scambler, "Habermas and the power of medical expertise," in Scambler, ed., *Sociological Theory and Medical Sociology* (London: Tavistock, 1987).

10. E.g., Gena Corea and Susan Ince, "Report of a survey of IVF clinics in the USA," in Patricia Spallone and Deborah Steinberg, eds., *Made to Order: the Myth of Reproductive and Genetic Progress* (Oxford: Pergamon Press, 1987).

11. E.g., Renate Duelli Klein and Robyn Rowland, "Women as test-sites for fertility drugs," *Reproductive and Genetic Engineering* vol. 1, no. 3 (1988), pp. 251–273.

12. E.g., Christine Crowe, "Bearing the consequences—women experiencing IVF," in Jocelynne Scutt, ed., *The Baby Machine.*

13. This has been argued most elegantly by Deborah Gerson, "Infertility and the construction of desperation"; also Mary Sue Henifin, "Introduction" to Elaine Hoffman Baruch et al. eds., *Embryos, Ethics and Women's Rights* (New York and London: Harrington Park Press, 1988).

14. E.g., Judith Lorber, "In vitro fertilization and gender politics," in Elaine Hoffman Baruch et al., eds., *Embryos, Ethics and Women's Rights,* for a very thoughtful analysis of the dominance of male partners in reproductive decisions. The restricted "choice" of women with regard to reproductive technologies is argued eloquently by Andrea Dworkin, *Right-Wing Women* (London: The Women's Press, 1983), pp. 181–182; and by various contributors to Renate Duellie Klein, ed., *Infertility: Women Speak Out* (London: Pandora Press, 1989), who also offer vivid illustration of the power of pronatalism. For the way that clinics may manipulate women into treatment, see e.g. Gena Corea, *The Mother Machine* (New York: Harper and Row, 1985). Stephanie Dowrick and Sibyl Grundberg's sensitive discussion of pronatalism is in their edited collection, *Why Children?* (London: The Women's Press, 1980).

15. E.g., Sultana Kamal, "Seizure of reproductive rights? A discussion on population control in the third world and the emergence of new reproductive technologies in the west," in Patricia Spallone and Deborah Steinberg, eds., *Made to Order.* In her extended discussion of surrogacy contracts, Carole Pateman makes the pertinent observation that the view of surrogacy as involving women in

helping or exploiting other women conveniently obscures the part of men in surrogacy arrangements; Carole Pateman, *The Sexual Contract* (Cambridge: Polity
Press, 1988).

16. E.g., Mary Sue Henifin, "Introduction: women's health
and the new reproductive technologies," in Elaine Hoff-
man Baruch et al., eds., *Embryos, Ethics and Women's
Rights;* or Marion Brown, Kay Fielden, and Jocelynne
Scutt, "New frontiers or old recycled?" in Jocelynne
Scutt, ed., *The Baby Machine.*

17. Janice Doane and Devon Hodges, "Risky business: familial ideology and the case of Baby M," *differences,* vol.
1, no. 1 (Winter 1989), pp. 67–81.

18. Linda Singer, "Bodies—pleasures—powers," *differences,* vol. 1, no. 1 (Winter 1989), pp. 45–65, writes
tellingly of the "differential strategies" by which motherhood is currently marketed to particular segments of the
female population.

19. For example, it was recently reported that 46% of medical students in the U.K. "gained their first experience of
vaginal examinations on unconscious patients, some of
whom may not have given their consent"; from "Shock
survey sparks curb on medical tests," *Cambridge Evening
News,* February 3, 1989. More generally, see Carolyn
Faulder, *Whose Body is It?* (London: Virago, 1985).

20. Naomi Pfeffer and Anne Woollett, *The Experience of Infertility* (London: Virago, 1983).

21. Betty Jean Lifton urges us to consider also the psychological effects of surrogacy on children, in the light of
the experiences of some adopted children; "Brave new
baby in the brave new world," in Elaine Hoffman Baruch
et al., eds., *Embryos, Ethics and Women's Rights.*

22. Feminist support for adoption rests, among other things,
on the recognition that motherhood is not a unitary experience, to which all women have the same relationship
(or to which any woman necessarily has the same relationship throughout her life). Different orientations to
pregnancy and childbirth are discussed in, for example,
Emily Martin, *The Woman in the Body,* pp. 104–105;
Kristin Luker, *Abortion and the Politics of Motherhood*
(Berkeley and London: U. of California Press, 1984);
see esp. Sara Ruddick, *Maternal Thinking: Toward a Politics of Peace* (Boston: Beacon Press, 1989).

23. There have been encouraging calls in recent articles for
the risks to be shared more equally by all parties to a
surrogacy contract, rather than being all taken by the
mother; this might entail no restrictions on behavior, diet,
health, or even abortion during pregnancy, and full rights
to change her mind for a period of time after the birth.
Janice Doane and Devon Hodges, "Risky business: familial ideology and the case of Baby M," pp. 77–79; and
Linda Singer, "Bodies—pleasures—powers," p. 63.

24. Margaret Stacey, "The manipulation of the birth process," paper prepared for the February 1988 meeting of
the European Advisory Committee for Health Research,
World Health Organization.

25. E.g., Marsden G. Wagner and Patricia St. Clair, "Are
in-vitro fertilisation and embryo transfer of benefit to
all?," *The Lancet* (October 28, 1989), pp. 1027–1030;
F. J. Stanley, "In vitro fertilization: a gift for the infertile
or a cycle of despair?" *Medical Journal of Australia,* no.
148 (1988) pp. 425–426.

26. Hilary Rose, "Victorian values in the test-tube," in
Michelle Stanworth, ed., *Reproductive Technologies.*

27. Rebecca Sarah, "Power, certainty and the fear of death,"
in Elaine Hoffman Baruch et al., eds., *Embryos, Ethics
and Women's Rights.*

28. These are merely off-the-cuff examples of campaigns
that might benefit women using infertility services; but
it is the principle of feminist intervention to improve
safety standards that interests me, and I am by no means
committed to these particular campaigns.

29. Lesley Doyal, "Infertility—a life sentence? Women and
the National Health Service," in Michelle Stanworth,
ed., *Reproductive Technologies;* Naomi Pfeffer and Alison
Quick, *Infertility Services: A Desperate Case* (London:
GLACH, 1988); David Mathieson, *Infertility Services in
the NHS—What's Going On?* Report prepared for Frank
Dobson, M.P., Shadow Minister of Health, 1986.

30. Ann Oakley, "The woman's place," *New Society* (March
6, 1987) pp. 14–16; Ann Ferguson makes a similar point
in *Blood at the Root: Motherhood, Sexuality and Male
Dominance* (London: Pandora, 1989), pp. 171–172, but
she also emphasizes that the impact of motherhood depends on the social context in which it takes place.

31. Sara Ruddick, "Maternal thinking," in Barrie Thorne
and Marilyn Yalom, eds., *Rethinking the Family* (New
York and London: Longman, 1982).

32. Linda Gordon makes this point in relation to opponents
of abortion, in "Why nineteenth century feminists did
not support birth control and twentieth century feminists do," in Barrie Thorne and Marilyn Yalom, eds.,
Rethinking the Family.

33. Carol Smart and Selma Sevenhuijsen, eds., *Child
Custody and the Politics of Gender* (London: Routledge, 1989); the quotation is from the editors' preface,
p. xvi.

34. Susan Suleiman's "On maternal splitting" is a stimulat-
ing discussion of the effect of mothers' vulnerability on
their reluctance to relinquish the fantasy of the perfect
mother. She locates surrogacy, alongside divorce and
custody disputes, as one of the "causes" of mothers' vulnerability; I'm locating reactions to surrogacy and other
conceptive technologies as part of the "effect." Suleiman, "On maternal splitting: a propos of Mary Gordon's *Men and Angels,*" *Signs,* vol. 14, no. 1 (Autumn
1988), pp. 25–41.

35. Carol Smart and Selma Sevenhuijsen, eds., *Child Custody and the Politics of Gender.*

36. "As a result of legislation on reproductive technology the
legal concept of paternity could be extended" argues
Juliette Zipper, in "What else is new? Reproductive
technologies and custody politics," in Carol Smart and
Selma Sevenhuijsen, *ibid.,* p. 266.

37. Michelle Stanworth, "Reproductive technologies and
the deconstruction of motherhood," in Stanworth, ed.,
Reproductive Technologies, pp. 32–35.

38. The excellent and extensive literature on this issue includes: Rosalind Coward, *The Whole Truth: The Myth of
Alternative Health* (London: Faber, 1989); Carol
MacCormack and Marilyn Strathern, eds., *Nature, Culture and Gender* (Cambridge: Cambridge U. Press,
1980); Maureen McNeil, "Introduction" to her edited
collection, *Gender and Expertise* (London: Free Association Books, 1987).

39. Henrietta Moore, *Feminism and Anthropology* (Minneapolis: U. of Minnesota Press, 1986); Felicity Edholm,
"The unnatural family," in Elizabeth Whitelegg et al.,

eds., *The Changing Experience of Women* (Milton Keynes: Open U. Press, 1982).

40. Katherine Gieve, *Balancing Acts: On Being a Mother* (London: Virago, 1989).

41. From the novel *Beloved* by Toni Morrison (London: Picador, 1988). The experience of "Baby Suggs" is described on page 23.

42. Jacklyn Cock, *Maids and Madams: Domestic Workers under Apartheid* (London: The Women's Press, rev. edn 1989).

 81

From Gender Trouble: Feminism and the Subversion of Identity

JUDITH BUTLER

BODILY INSCRIPTIONS, PERFORMATIVE SUBVERSIONS

"Garbo 'got in drag' whenever she took some heavy glamour part, whenever she melted in or out of a man's arms, whenever she simply let that heavenly-flexed neck . . . bear the weight of her thrown-back head. . . . How resplendent seems the art of acting! It is all impersonation, whether the sex underneath is true or not."

—Parker Tyler, "The Garbo Image," quoted in
Esther Newton, *Mother Camp*

Categories of true sex, discrete gender, and specific sexuality have constituted the stable point of reference for a great deal of feminist theory and politics. These constructs of identity serve as the points of epistemic departure from which theory emerges and politics itself is shaped. In the case of feminism, politics is ostensibly shaped to express the interests, the perspectives, of "women." But is there a political shape to "women," as it were, that precedes and prefigures the political elaboration of their interests and epistemic point of view? How is that identity shaped, and is it a political shaping that takes the very morphology and boundary of the sexed body as the ground, surface, or site of cultural inscription? What circumscribes that site as "the female body"? Is "the body" or "the sexed body" the firm foundation on which gender and systems of compulsory sexuality operate? Or is "the body" itself shaped by political forces with strategic interests in keeping that body bounded and constituted by the markers of sex?

The sex/gender distinction and the category of sex itself appear to presuppose a generalization of "the body" that preexists the acquisition of its sexed significance. This "body" often appears to be a passive medium that is signified by an inscription from a cultural source figured as "external" to that body. Any theory of the culturally constructed body, however, ought to question "the body" as a construct of suspect generality when it is figured as passive and prior to discourse. There are Christian and Cartesian precedents to such views which, prior to the emergence of vitalistic biologies in the nineteenth century, understand "the body" as so much inert matter, signifying nothing or, more specifically, signifying a profane void, the fallen state: deception, sin, the premonitional metaphorics of hell and the eternal feminine. There are many occasions in both Sartre's and Beauvoir's work where "the body" is figured as a mute facticity, anticipating some meaning that can be attributed only by a transcendent consciousness, understood in Cartesian terms as radically immaterial. But what establishes this dualism for us? What separates off "the body" as indifferent to signification, and signification itself as the act of a radically disembodied consciousness or, rather, the act that radically disembodies that consciousness? To what extent is that Cartesian dualism presupposed in phenomenology adapted to the structuralist frame in which mind/body is redescribed as culture/nature? With respect to gender discourse, to what extent do these problematic dualisms still operate within the very descriptions that are supposed to lead us out of that binarism and its implicit hierarchy? How are the contours of the body clearly marked as the taken-for-granted ground or surface upon which gender significations are inscribed, a mere facticity devoid of value, prior to significance?

Wittig suggests that a culturally specific epistemic *a priori* establishes the naturalness of "sex." But by what enigmatic means has "the body" been accepted as a *prima facie* given that admits of no genealogy? Even within Foucault's essay on the very theme of genealogy, the body is figured as a surface and the scene of a cultural inscription: "the body is the inscribed surface of events."[1] The task of genealogy, he claims, is "to expose a body totally imprinted by history." His sentence continues, however, by referring to the goal of "history"—here clearly understood on the model of Freud's "civilization"—as the "destruction of the body" (148). Forces and impulses with multiple directionalities are precisely that which history both destroys and preserves through the *entstehung* (historical event) of inscription. As "a volume in perpetual disintegration" (148), the body is always under siege, suffering destruction by the very terms of history. And history is the creation of values and meanings by a signifying practice that requires the subjection of the body. This corporeal destruction is necessary to produce the speaking subject and its significations. This is a body, described through the language of surface and force, weakened through a "single drama" of domination, inscription, and creation (150). This is not the *modus vivendi* of one kind of history rather than another, but is, for Foucault, "history" (148) in its essential and repressive gesture.

Although Foucault writes, "Nothing in man [*sic*]—not even his body—is sufficiently stable to serve as the basis for self-recognition or for understanding other men [*sic*]" (153), he nevertheless points to the constancy of cultural inscription as a "single drama" that acts on the body. If the creation of values, that historical mode of signification, requires the destruction of the body, much as the instrument of torture in Kafka's *In the Penal Colony* destroys the body on which it writes, then there must be a body prior to that inscription, stable and self-identical, subject to that sacrificial destruction. In a sense, for Foucault, as for Nietzsche, cultural values emerge as the result of an inscription on the body, understood as a medium, indeed, a blank page; in order for this inscription to signify, however, that medium must itself be destroyed—that is, fully transvaluated into a sublimated domain of values. Within the metaphorics of this notion of cultural values is the figure of history as a relentless writing instrument, and the body as the medium which must be destroyed and transfigured in order for "culture" to emerge.

By maintaining a body prior to its cultural inscription, Foucault appears to assume a materiality prior to signification and form. Because this distinction operates as essential to the task of genealogy as

he defines it, the distinction itself is precluded as an object of genealogical investigation. Occasionally in his analysis of Herculine, Foucault subscribes to a prediscursive multiplicity of bodily forces that break through the surface of the body to disrupt the regulating practices of cultural coherence imposed upon that body by a power regime, understood as a vicissitude of "history." If the presumption of some kind of precategorical source of disruption is refused, is it still possible to give a genealogical account of the demarcation of the body as such as a signifying practice? This demarcation is not initiated by a reified history or by a subject. This marking is the result of a diffuse and active structuring of the social field. This signifying practice effects a social space for and of the body within certain regulatory grids of intelligibility.

Mary Douglas' *Purity and Danger* suggests that the very contours of "the body" are established through markings that seek to establish specific codes of cultural coherence. Any discourse that establishes the boundaries of the body serves the purpose of instating and naturalizing certain taboos regarding the appropriate limits, postures, and modes of exchange that define what it is that constitutes bodies:

> ideas about separating, purifying, demarcating and punishing transgressions have as their main function to impose system on an inherently untidy experience. It is only by exaggerating the difference between within and without, above and below, male and female, with and against, that a semblance of order is created.[2]

Although Douglas clearly subscribes to a structuralist distinction between an inherently unruly nature and an order imposed by cultural means, the "untidiness" to which she refers can be redescribed as a region of *cultural* unruliness and disorder. Assuming the inevitably binary structure of the nature/culture distinction, Douglas cannot point toward an alternative configuration of culture in which such distinctions become malleable or proliferate beyond the binary frame. Her analysis, however, provides a possible point of departure for understanding the relationship by which social taboos institute and maintain the boundaries of the body as such. Her analysis suggests that what constitutes the limit of the body is never merely material, but that the surface, the skin, is systemically signified by taboos and anticipated transgressions; indeed, the boundaries of the body become, within her analysis, the limits of the social *per se*. A poststructuralist appropriation of her view might well understand the boundaries of the body as the limits of the socially *hegemonic*. In a variety of cultures, she maintains, there are

> pollution powers which inhere in the structure of ideas itself and which punish a symbolic breaking of that which should be joined or joining of that which should be separate. It follows from this that pollution is a type of danger which is not likely to occur except where the lines of structure, cosmic or social, are clearly defined.
>
> A polluting person is always in the wrong. He [*sic*] has developed some wrong condition or simply crossed over some line which should not have been crossed and this displacement unleashes danger for someone.[3]

In a sense, Simon Watney has identified the contemporary construction of "the polluting person" as the person with AIDS in his *Policing Desire: AIDS, Pornography, and the Media*.[4] Not only is the illness figured as the "gay disease," but throughout the media's hysterical and homophobic response to the illness there is a tactical construction of a continuity between the polluted status of the homosexual by virtue of the boundary-trespass that *is* homosexuality and the disease as a specific modality of homosexual pollution. That the disease is transmitted through the exchange of bodily fluids suggests within the sensationalist graphics of homophobic signifying systems the dangers that permeable bodily boundaries present to the social order as such. Douglas remarks that "the body is a model that can stand for any bounded system. Its boundaries can represent any boundaries which are threatened or precarious."[5] And she asks a question which one might have expected to read in Foucault: "Why should bodily margins be thought to be specifically invested with power and danger?[6]

Douglas suggests that all social systems are vulnerable at their margins, and that all margins are accordingly considered dangerous. If the body is synecdochal for the social system *per se* or a site in which open systems converge, then any kind of unregulated permeability constitutes a site of pollution

and endangerment. Since anal and oral sex among men clearly establishes certain kinds of bodily permeabilities unsanctioned by the hegemonic order, male homosexuality would, within such a hegemonic point of view, constitute a site of danger and pollution, prior to and regardless of the cultural presence of AIDS. Similarly, the "polluted" status of lesbians, regardless of their low-risk status with respect to AIDS, brings into relief the dangers of their bodily exchanges. Significantly, being "outside" the hegemonic order does not signify being "in" a state of filthy and untidy nature. Paradoxically, homosexuality is almost always conceived within the homophobic signifying economy as *both* uncivilized and unnatural.

The construction of stable bodily contours relies upon fixed sites of corporeal permeability and impermeability. Those sexual practices in both homosexual and heterosexual contexts that open surfaces and orifices to erotic signification or close down others effectively reinscribe the boundaries of the body along new cultural lines. Anal sex among men is an example, as is the radical re-membering of the body in Wittig's *The Lesbian Body*. Douglas alludes to "a kind of sex pollution which expresses a desire to keep the body (physical and social) intact,"[7] suggesting that the naturalized notion of "the" body is itself a consequence of taboos that render that body discrete by virtue of its stable boundaries. Further, the rites of passage that govern various bodily orifices presuppose a heterosexual construction of gendered exchange, positions, and erotic possibilities. The deregulation of such exchanges accordingly disrupts the very boundaries that determine what it is to be a body at all. Indeed, the critical inquiry that traces the regulatory practices within which bodily contours are constructed constitutes precisely the genealogy of "the body" in its discreteness that might further radicalize Foucault's theory.[8]

Significantly, Kristeva's discussion of abjection in *The Powers of Horror* begins to suggest the uses of this structuralist notion of a boundary-constituting taboo for the purposes of constructing a discrete subject through exclusion.[9] The "abject" designates that which has been expelled from the body, discharged as excrement, literally rendered "Other." This appears as an expulsion of alien elements, but the alien is effectively established through this expulsion. The construction of the "not-me" as the abject establishes the boundaries of the body which are also the first contours of the subject. Kristeva writes:

> *nausea* makes me balk at that milk cream, separates me from the mother and father who proffer it. "I" want none of that element, sign of their desire; "I" do not want to listen, "I" do not assimilate it, "I" expel it. But since the food is not an "other" for "me," who am only in their desire, I expel *myself*, I spit *myself* out, I abject *myself* within the same motion through which "I" claim to establish myself.[10]

The boundary of the body as well as the distinction between internal and external is established through the ejection and transvaluation of something originally part of identity into a defiling otherness. As Iris Young has suggested in her use of Kristeva to understand sexism, homophobia, and racism, the repudiation of bodies for their sex, sexuality, and/or color is an "expulsion" followed by a "repulsion" that founds and consolidates culturally hegemonic identities along sex/race/sexuality axes of differentiation.[11] Young's appropriation of Kristeva shows how the operation of repulsion can consolidate "identities" founded on the instituting of the "Other" or a set of Others through exclusion and domination. What constitutes through division the "inner" and "outer" worlds of the subject is a border and boundary tenuously maintained for the purposes of social regulation and control. The boundary between the inner and outer is confounded by those excremental passages in which the inner effectively becomes outer, and this excreting function becomes, as it were, the model by which other forms of identity-differentiation are accomplished. In effect, this is the mode by which Others become shit. For inner and outer worlds to remain utterly distinct, the entire surface of the body would have to achieve an impossible impermeability. This sealing of its surfaces would constitute the seamless boundary of the subject; but this enclosure would invariably be exploded by precisely that excremental filth that it fears.

Regardless of the compelling metaphors of the spatial distinctions of inner and outer, they remain linguistic terms that facilitate and articulate a set of fantasies, feared and desired. "Inner" and "outer" make sense only with reference to a mediating

boundary that strives for stability. And this stability, this coherence, is determined in large part by cultural orders that sanction the subject and compel its differentiation from the abject. Hence, "inner" and "outer" constitute a binary distinction that stabilizes and consolidates the coherent subject. When that subject is challenged, the meaning and necessity of the terms are subject to displacement. If the "inner world" no longer designates a topos, then the internal fixity of the self and, indeed, the internal locale of gender identity, become similarly suspect. The critical question is not *how* did that identity become *internalized*? as if internalization were a process or a mechanism that might be descriptively reconstructed. Rather, the question is: From what strategic position in public discourse and for what reasons has the trope of interiority and the disjunctive binary of inner/outer taken hold? In what language is "inner space" figured? What kind of figuration is it, and through what figure of the body is it signified? How does a body figure on its surface the very invisibility of its hidden depth?

FROM INTERIORITY TO GENDER PERFORMATIVES

In *Discipline and Punish* Foucault challenges the language of internalization as it operates in the service of the disciplinary regime of the subjection and subjectivation of criminals.[12] Although Foucault objected to what he understood to be the psychoanalytic belief in the "inner" truth of sex in *The History of Sexuality*, he turns to a criticism of the doctrine of internalization for separate purposes in the context of his history of criminology. In a sense, *Discipline and Punish* can be read as Foucault's effort to rewrite Nietzsche's doctrine of internalization in *On the Genealogy of Morals* on the model of *inscription*. In the context of prisoners, Foucault writes, the strategy has been not to enforce a repression of their desires, but to compel their bodies to signify the prohibitive law as their very essence, style, and necessity. That law is not literally internalized, but incorporated, with the consequence that bodies are produced which signify that law on and through the body; there the law is manifest as the essence of their selves, the meaning of their soul, their conscience, the law of their desire. In effect, the law is at once fully manifest and fully latent, for it never appears as external to the bodies it subjects and subjectivates. Foucault writes:

> It would be wrong to say that the soul is an illusion, or an ideological effect. On the contrary, it exists, it has a reality, it is produced permanently *around, on, within,* the body by the functioning of a power that is exercised on those that are punished (my emphasis).[13]

The figure of the interior soul understood as "within" the body is signified through its inscription *on* the body, even though its primary mode of signification is through its very absence, its potent invisibility. The effect of a structuring inner space is produced through the signification of a body as a vital and sacred enclosure. The soul is precisely what the body lacks; hence, the body presents itself as a signifying lack. That lack which *is* the body signifies the soul as that which cannot show. In this sense, then, the soul is a surface signification that contests and displaces the inner/outer distinction itself, a figure of interior psychic space inscribed *on* the body as a social signification that perpetually renounces itself as such. In Foucault's terms, the soul is not imprisoned by or within the body, as some Christian imagery would suggest, but "the soul is the prison of the body."[14]

The redescription of intrapsychic processes in terms of the surface politics of the body implies a corollary redescription of gender as the disciplinary production of the figures of fantasy through the play of presence and absence on the body's surface, the construction of the gendered body through a series of exclusions and denials, signifying absences. But what determines the manifest and latent text of the body politic? What is the prohibitive law that generates the corporeal stylization of gender, the fantasied and fantastic figuration of the body? We have already considered the incest taboo and the prior taboo against homosexuality as the generative moments of gender identity, the prohibitions that produce identity along the culturally intelligible grids of an idealized and compulsory heterosexuality. That disciplinary production of gender effects a false stabilization of gender in the interests of the heterosexual construction and regulation of sexuality within the reproductive domain. The construction of coherence conceals the gender discontinuities that run rampant within heterosexual, bisexual, and gay and lesbian contexts in which gender does not necessarily follow from sex, and desire, or sexuality generally, does not seem to follow from gender—indeed, where none of these dimensions of significant corporeality express or reflect one another. When the disorganization and disaggregation of the field of bodies disrupt the regulatory fiction of heterosexual coherence, it seems that the expressive model loses its descriptive force. That regulatory ideal is then exposed as a norm and a fiction that disguises itself as a developmental law regulating the sexual field that it purports to describe.

According to the understanding of identification as an enacted fantasy or incorporation, however, it is clear that coherence is desired, wished for, idealized, and that this idealization is an effect of a corporeal signification. In other words, acts, gestures, and desire produce the effect of an internal core or substance, but produce this *on the surface* of the body, through the play of signifying absences that suggest, but never reveal, the organizing principle of identity as a cause. Such acts, gestures, enactments, generally construed, are *performative* in the sense that the essence or identity that they otherwise purport to express are *fabrications* manufactured and sustained through corporeal signs and other discursive means. That the gendered body is performative suggests that it has no ontological status apart from the various acts which constitute its reality. This also suggests that if that reality is fabricated as an interior essence, that very interiority is an effect and function of a decidedly public and social discourse, the public regulation of fantasy through the surface politics of the body, the gender border control that differentiates inner from outer, and so institutes the "integrity" of the subject. In other words, acts and gestures, articulated and enacted desires create the illusion of an interior and organizing gender core, an illusion discursively maintained for the purposes of the regulation of sexuality within the obligatory frame of reproductive heterosexuality. If the "cause" of desire, gesture, and act can be localized within the "self" of the actor, then the political regulations and disciplinary practices which produce that ostensibly coherent gender are effectively displaced from view. The displacement of a political and discursive origin of gender identity onto a psychological "core" precludes an analysis of the political constitution of the gendered subject and its fabricated notions about the ineffable interiority of its sex or of its true identity.

If the inner truth of gender is a fabrication and if a true gender is a fantasy instituted and inscribed on the surface of bodies, then it seems that genders can be neither true nor false, but are only produced as the truth effects of a discourse of primary and stable identity. In *Mother Camp: Female Impersonators in America,* anthropologist Esther Newton suggests that the structure of impersonation reveals one of the key fabricating mechanisms through which the social construction of gender takes place.[15] I would suggest as well that drag fully subverts the distinction between inner and outer psychic space and effectively mocks both the expressive model of gender and the notion of a true gender identity. Newton writes:

> At its most complex, [drag] is a double inversion that says, "appearance is an illusion." Drag says [Newton's curious personification] "my 'outside' appearance is feminine, but my essence 'inside' [the body] is masculine." At the same time it symbolizes the opposite inversion; "my appearance 'outside' [my body, my gender] is masculine but my essence 'inside' [myself] is feminine."[16]

Both claims to truth contradict one another and so displace the entire enactment of gender significations from the discourse of truth and falsity.

The notion of an original or primary gender identity is often parodied within the cultural practices of drag, cross-dressing, and the sexual stylization of butch/femme identities. Within feminist theory, such parodic identities have been understood to be either degrading to women, in the case of drag and cross-dressing, or an uncritical appropriation of sex-role stereotyping from within the practice of heterosexuality, especially in the case of butch/femme lesbian identities. But the relation between the "imitation" and the "original" is, I think, more complicated than that critique generally allows. Moreover, it gives us a clue to the way in which the relationship between primary identification—that is, the original meanings accorded to gender—and subsequent gender experience might be reframed. The performance of drag plays upon the distinction between the anatomy of the performer and the gender that is being performed. But we are actually in the presence of three contingent

dimensions of significant corporeality: anatomical sex, gender identity, and gender performance. If the anatomy of the performer is already distinct from the gender of the performer, and both of those are distinct from the gender of the performance, then the performance suggests a dissonance not only between sex and performance, but sex and gender, and gender and performance. As much as drag creates a unified picture of "woman" (what its critics often oppose), it also reveals the distinctness of those aspects of gendered experience which are falsely naturalized as a unity through the regulatory fiction of heterosexual coherence. *In imitating gender, drag implicitly reveals the imitative structure of gender itself—as well as its contingency.* Indeed, part of the pleasure, the giddiness of the performance is in the recognition of a radical contingency in the relation between sex and gender in the face of cultural configurations of causal unities that are regularly assumed to be natural and necessary. In the place of the law of heterosexual coherence, we see sex and gender denaturalized by means of a performance which avows their distinctness and dramatizes the cultural mechanism of their fabricated unity.

The notion of gender parody defended here does not assume that there is an original which such parodic identities imitate. Indeed, the parody is *of* the very notion of an original; just as the psychoanalytic notion of gender identification is constituted by a fantasy of a fantasy, the transfiguration of an Other who is always already a "figure" in that double sense, so gender parody reveals that the original identity after which gender fashions itself is an imitation without an origin. To be more precise, it is a production which, in effect—that is, in its effect—postures as an imitation. This perpetual displacement constitutes a fluidity of identities that suggests an openness to resignification and recontextualization; parodic proliferation deprives hegemonic culture and its critics of the claim to naturalized or essentialist gender identities. Although the gender meanings taken up in these parodic styles are clearly part of hegemonic, misogynist culture, they are nevertheless denaturalized and mobilized through their parodic recontextualization. As imitations which effectively displace the meaning of the original, they imitate the myth of originality itself. In the place of an original identification which serves as a determining cause, gender identity might be reconceived as a personal/cultural history of received meanings subject to a set of imitative practices which refer laterally to other imitations and which, jointly, construct the illusion of a primary and interior gendered self or parody the mechanism of that construction.

According to Fredric Jameson's "Postmodernism and Consumer Society," the imitation that mocks the notion of an original is characteristic of pastiche rather than parody:

> Pastiche is, like parody, the imitation of a peculiar or unique style, the wearing of a stylistic mask, speech in a dead language: but it is a neutral practice of mimicry, without parody's ulterior motive, without the satirical impulse, without laughter, without that still latent feeling that there exists something *normal* compared to which what is being imitated is rather comic. Pastiche is blank parody, parody that has lost its humor.[17]

The loss of the sense of "the normal," however, can be its own occasion for laughter, especially when "the normal," "the original" is revealed to be a copy, and an inevitably failed one, an ideal that no one *can* embody. In this sense, laughter emerges in the realization that all along the original was derived.

Parody by itself is not subversive, and there must be a way to understand what makes certain kinds of parodic repetitions effectively disruptive, truly troubling, and which repetitions become domesticated and recirculated as instruments of cultural hegemony. A typology of actions would clearly not suffice, for parodic displacement, indeed, parodic laughter, depends on a context and reception in which subversive confusions can be fostered. What performance where will invert the inner/outer distinction and compel a radical rethinking of the psychological presuppositions of gender identity and sexuality? What performance where will compel a reconsideration of the *place* and stability of the masculine and the feminine? And what kind of gender performance will enact and reveal the performativity of gender itself in a way that destabilizes the naturalized categories of identity and desire.

If the body is not a "being," but a variable boundary, a surface whose permeability is politically regulated, a signifying practice within a cultural field of gender hierarchy and compulsory heterosexuality, then what language is left for understanding this corporeal enactment, gender, that constitutes its "interior" signification on its surface? Sartre would perhaps have called this act "a style of being," Foucault, "a stylistics of existence." And in my earlier reading of Beauvoir, I suggest that gendered bodies are so many "styles of the flesh." These styles all never fully self-styled, for styles have a history, and those histories condition and limit the possibilities. Consider gender, for instance, as *a corporeal style,* an "act," as it were, which is both intentional and performative, where "*performative*" suggests a dramatic and contingent construction of meaning.

Wittig understands gender as the workings of "sex," where "sex" is an obligatory injunction for the body to become a cultural sign, to materialize itself in obedience to a historically delimited possibility, and to do this, not once or twice, but as a sustained and repeated corporeal project. The notion of a "project," however, suggests the originating force of a radical will, and because gender is a project which has cultural survival as its end, the term *strategy* better suggests the situation of duress under which gender performance always and variously occurs. Hence, as a strategy of survival within compulsory systems, gender is a performance with clearly punitive consequences. Discrete genders are part of what "humanizes" individuals within contemporary culture; indeed, we regularly punish those who fail to do their gender right. Because there is neither an "essence" that gender expresses or externalizes nor an objective ideal to which gender aspires, and because gender is not a fact, the various acts of gender create the idea of gender, and without those acts, there would be no gender at all. Gender is, thus, a construction that regularly conceals its genesis; the tacit collective agreement to perform, produce, and sustain discrete and polar genders as cultural fictions is obscured by the credibility of those productions—and the punishments that attend not agreeing to believe in them; the construction "compels" our belief in its necessity and naturalness. The historical possibilities materialized through various corporeal styles are nothing other than those punitively regulated cultural fictions alternately embodied and deflected under duress.

Consider that a sedimentation of gender norms produces the peculiar phenomenon of a "natural sex" or a "real woman" or any number of prevalent and compelling social fictions, and that this is a sedimentation that over time has produced a set of corporeal styles which, in reified form, appear as the natural configuration of bodies into sexes existing in a binary relation to one another. If these styles are enacted, and if they produce the coherent gendered subjects who pose as their originators, what kind of performance might reveal this ostensible "cause" to be an "effect"?

In what senses, then, is gender an act? As in other ritual social dramas, the action of gender requires a performance that is *repeated*. This repetition is at once a reenactment and reexperiencing of a set of meanings already socially established; and it is the mundane and ritualized form of their legitimation.[18] Although there are individual bodies that enact these significations by becoming stylized into gendered modes, this "action" is a public action. There are temporal and collective dimensions to these actions, and their public character is not inconsequential; indeed, the performance is effected with the strategic aim of maintaining gender within its binary frame—an aim that cannot be attributed to a subject, but, rather, must be understood to found and consolidate the subject.

Gender ought not to be construed as a stable identity or locus of agency from which various acts follow; rather, gender is an identity tenuously constituted in time, instituted in an exterior space through a *stylized repetition of acts*. The effect of gender is produced through the stylization of the body and, hence, must be understood as the mundane way in which bodily gestures, movements, and styles of various kinds constitute the illusion of an abiding gendered self. This formulation moves the conception of gender off the ground of a substantial model of identity to one that requires a conception of gender as a constituted *social temporality*. Significantly, if gender is instituted through acts which are internally discontinuous, then the *appearance of substance* is precisely that, a constructed identity, a performative accomplishment which the mundane social audience, including the actors themselves, come to believe and to perform in the mode of belief. Gender is also a norm that can never be fully internalized; "the internal" is a surface signification, and gender norms are finally phantasmatic, impos-

sible to embody. If the ground of gender identity is the stylized repetition of acts through time and not a seemingly seamless identity, then the spatial metaphor of a "ground" will be displaced and revealed as a stylized configuration, indeed, a gendered corporealization of time. The abiding gendered self will then be shown to be structured by repeated acts that seek to approximate the ideal of a substantial ground of identity, but which, in their occasional *dis*continuity, reveal the temporal and contingent groundlessness of this "ground." The possibilities of gender transformation are to be found precisely in the arbitrary relation between such acts, in the possibility of a failure to repeat, a de-formity, or a parodic repetition that exposes the phantasmatic effect of abiding identity as a politically tenuous construction.

If gender attributes, however, are not expressive but performative, then these attributes effectively constitute the identity they are said to express or reveal. The distinction between expression and performativeness is crucial. If gender attributes and acts, the various ways in which a body shows or produces its cultural signification, are performative, then there is no preexisting identity by which an act or attribute might be measured; there would be no true or false, real or distorted acts of gender, and the postulation of a true gender identity would be revealed as a regulatory fiction. That gender reality is created through sustained social performances means that the very notions of an essential sex and a true or abiding masculinity or feminity are also constituted as part of the strategy that conceals gender's performative character and the performative possibilities for proliferating gender configurations outside the restricting frames of masculinist domination and compulsory heterosexuality.

Genders can be neither true nor false, neither real nor apparent, neither original nor derived. As credible bearers of those attributes, however, genders can also be rendered thoroughly and radically *incredible*.

[1990]

NOTES

1. Michel Foucault, "Nietzsche, Genealogy, History," in *Language, Counter-Memory, Practice: Selected Essays and Interviews by Michel Foucault*, trans. Donald F. Bouchard

and Sherry Simon, ed. Donald F. Bouchard (Ithaca: Cornell University Press, 1977), p. 148. References in the text are to this essay.

2. Mary Douglas, *Purity and Danger* (London, Boston, and Henley: Routledge and Kegan Paul, 1969), p. 4.

3. Ibid., p. 113.

4. Simon Watney, *Policing Desire: AIDS, Pornography, and the Media* (Minneapolis: University of Minnesota Press, 1988).

5. Douglas, *Purity and Danger,* p. 115.

6. Ibid., p. 121.

7. Ibid., p. 140.

8. Foucault's essay "A Preface to Transgression" (in *Language, Counter-Memory, Practice*) does provide an interesting juxtaposition with Douglas' notion of body boundaries constituted by incest taboos. Originally written in honor of Georges Bataille, this essay explores in part the metaphorical "dirt" of transgressive pleasures and the association of the forbidden orifice with the dirt-covered tomb. See pp. 46–48.

9. Kristeva discusses Mary Douglas work in a short section of *The Powers of Horror: An Essay on Abjection,* trans. Leon Roudiez (New York: Columbia University Press, 1982), originally published as *Pouvoirs de l'horreur* (Paris: Éditions de Seuil, 1980). Assimilating Douglas' insights to her own reformulation of Lacan, Kristeva writes, "Defilement is what is jettisoned from the *symbolic system.* It is what escapes that social rationality, that logical order on which a social aggregate is based, which then becomes differentiated from a temporary agglomeration of individuals and, in short, constitutes a *classification system* or *a structure*" (p. 65).

10. Ibid., p. 3.

11. Iris Marion Young, "Abjection and Oppression: Unconscious Dynamics of Racism, Sexism, and Homophobia," paper presented at the Society of Phenomenology and Existential Philosophy Meetings, Northwestern University, 1988. The paper will be published in the proceedings of the 1988 meetings by the State University of New York Press. It will also be included as part of a larger chapter in her forthcoming *The Politics of Difference.*

12. Parts of the following discussion were published in two different contexts, in my "Gender Trouble, Feminist Theory, and Psychoanalytic Discourse," in *Feminism/Postmodernism,* ed. Linda J. Nicholson (New York: Routledge, 1989) and "Performative Acts and Gender Constitution: An Essay in Phenomenology and Feminist Theory," *Theatre Journal,* Vol. 20, No. 3, Winter 1988.

13. Michel Foucault, *Discipline and Punish: the Birth of the Prison,* trans. Alan Sheridan (New York: Vintage, 1979), p. 29.

14. Ibid., p. 30.

15. See the chapter "Role Models" in Esther Newton, *Mother Camp: Female Impersonators in America* (Chicago: University of Chicago Press, 1972).

16. Ibid., p. 103.

17. Fredric Jameson, "Postmodernism and Consumer Society," in *The Anti-Aesthetic: Essays on Postmodern Culture,* ed. Hal Foster (Port Townsend, WA.: Bay Press, 1983), p. 114.

18. See Victor Turner, *Dramas, Fields and Metaphors* (Ithaca: Cornell University Press, 1974). See also Clifford Geertz, "Blurred Genres: The Refiguration of Thought," in *Local Knowledge, Further Essays in Interpretive Anthropology* (New York: Basic Books, 1983).

 82

From Black Feminist Thought: Knowledge, Consciousness, and the Politics of Empowerment

PAT HILL COLLINS

KNOWLEDGE, CONSCIOUSNESS, AND THE POLITICS OF EMPOWERMENT

Black feminist thought demonstrates Black women's emerging power as agents of knowledge. By portraying African-American women as self-defined, self-reliant individuals confronting race, gender, and class oppression, Afrocentric feminist thought speaks to the importance that knowledge plays in empowering oppressed people. One distinguishing feature of Black feminist thought is its insistence that both the changed consciousness of individuals and the social transformation of political and economic institutions constitute essential ingredients for social change. New knowledge is important for both dimensions of change.

. . .

Epistemological Shifts: Dialogue, Empathy, and Truth

Black Women as Agents of Knowledge   Living life as an African-American woman is a necessary prerequisite for producing Black feminist thought because within Black women's communities thought is validated and produced with reference to a particular set of historical, material, and epistemological conditions. African-American women who adhere to the idea that claims about Black women must be substantiated by Black women's sense of our own experiences and who anchor our knowledge claims in an Afrocentric epistemology have produced a rich tradition of Black feminist thought.

Traditionally such women were blues singers, poets, autobiographers, storytellers, and orators validated by everyday Black women as experts on a Black women's standpoint. Only a few unusual African-American feminist scholars have been able to defy Eurocentric masculinist epistemologies and explicitly embrace an Afrocentric feminist epistemology. Consider Alice Walker's description of Zora Neale Hurston:

> In my mind, Zora Neale Hurston, Billie Holiday, and Bessie Smith form a sort of unholy trinity. Zora *belongs* in the tradition of black women singers, rather than among "the literati." . . . Like Billie and Bessie she followed her own road, believed in her own gods, pursued her own dreams, and refused to separate herself from "common" people. (Walker 1977, xvii–xviii)

Zora Neale Hurston is an exception for prior to 1950, few African-American women earned advanced degrees and most of those who did complied with Eurocentric masculinist epistemologies. Although these women worked on behalf of Black women, they did so within the confines of pervasive race and gender oppression. Black women scholars were in a position to see the exclusion of African-American women from scholarly discourse, and the thematic content of their work often reflected their interest in examining a Black women's standpoint. However, their tenuous status in academic institutions led them to adhere to Eurocentric masculinist epistemologies so that their work would be accepted as scholarly. As a result, while they produced Black feminist thought, those African-American women most likely to gain academic credentials were often least likely to produce Black feminist thought that used an Afrocentric feminist epistemology.

An ongoing tension exists for Black women as agents of knowledge, a tension rooted in the sometimes conflicting demands of Afrocentricity and feminism. Those Black women who are feminists are critical of how Black culture and many of its traditions oppress women. For example, the strong pronatal beliefs in African-American communities that foster early motherhood among adolescent girls, the lack of self-actualization that can accompany the double-day of paid employment and work in the home, and the emotional and physical abuse that many Black women experience from their fathers, lovers, and husbands all reflect practices opposed by African-American women who are feminists. But these same women may have a parallel desire as members of an oppressed racial group to affirm the value of that same culture and traditions (Narayan 1989). Thus strong Black mothers appear in Black women's literature, Black women's economic contributions to families is lauded, and a curious silence exists concerning domestic abuse.

As more African-American women earn advanced degrees, the range of Black feminist scholarship is expanding. Increasing numbers of African-American women scholars are explicitly choosing to ground their work in Black women's experiences, and, by doing so, they implicitly adhere to an Afrocentric feminist epistemology. Rather than being restrained by their both/and status of marginality, these women make creative use of their outsider-within status and produce innovative Afrocentric feminist thought. The difficulties these women face lie less in demonstrating that they have mastered white male epistemologies than in resisting the hegemonic nature of these patterns of thought in order to see, value, and use existing alternative Afrocentric feminist ways of knowing.

In establishing the legitimacy of their knowledge claims, Black women scholars who want to develop Afrocentric feminist thought may encounter the often conflicting standards of three key groups. First, Black feminist thought must be validated by ordinary African-American women who, in the words of Hannah Nelson, grow to womanhood "in a world where the saner you are, the madder you are made to appear" (Gwaltney 1980, 7). To be credible in the eyes of this group, scholars must be personal advocates for their material, be accountable for the consequences of their work, have lived or experienced their material in some fashion, and be willing to engage in dialogues about their findings with ordinary, everyday people. Second, Black feminist thought also must be accepted by the community of Black women scholars. These scholars place varying amounts of importance on rearticulating a Black women's standpoint using an Afrocentric feminist epistemology. Third, Afrocentric feminist thought within academia must be prepared to confront Eurocentric masculinist political and epistemological requirements.

The dilemma facing Black women scholars engaged in creating Black feminist thought is that a knowledge claim that meets the criteria of adequacy for one group and thus is judged to be an acceptable knowledge claim may not be translatable into the terms of a different group. Using the example of Black English, June Jordan illustrates the difficulty of moving among epistemologies:

> You cannot "translate" instances of Standard English preoccupied with abstraction or with nothing/nobody evidently alive into Black English. That would warp the language into uses antithetical to the guiding perspective of its community of users. Rather you must first change those Standard English sentences, themselves, into ideas consistent with the person-centered assumptions of Black English. (Jordan 1985, 130)

Although both worldviews share a common vocabulary, the ideas themselves defy direct translation.

For Black women who are agents of knowledge, the marginality that accompanies outsider-within status can be the source of both frustration and creativity. In an attempt to minimize the differences between the cultural context of African-American communities and the expectations of social institutions, some women dichotomize their behavior and become two different people. Over time, the strain of doing this can be enormous. Others reject their cultural context and work against their own best interests by enforcing the dominant group's specialized thought. Still others manage to inhabit both contexts but do so critically, using their outsider-within perspectives as a source of insights and ideas. But while outsiders within can make substantial contributions as agents of knowledge, they rarely do so without substantial personal cost. "Eventually it comes to you," observes Lorraine Hansberry, "the thing that makes you exceptional, if you are at all, is inevitably that which must also make you lonely" (1969, 148).

Once Black feminist scholars face the notion that, on certain dimensions of a Black women's standpoint, it may be fruitless to try and translate ideas from an Afrocentric feminist epistemology into a Eurocentric masculinist framework, then other choices emerge. Rather than trying to uncover universal knowledge claims that can withstand the translation from one epistemology to another (initially, at least), Black women intellectuals might find efforts to rearticulate a Black women's standpoint especially fruitful. Rearticulating a Black women's standpoint refashions the concrete and reveals the more universal human dimensions of Black women's everyday lives. "I date all my work," notes Nikki Giovanni, "because I think poetry, or any writing, is but a reflection of the moment. The universal comes from the particular" (1988, 57). Bell Hooks maintains, "my goal as a feminist thinker and theorist is to take that abstraction and articulate it in a language that renders it accessible—not less complex or rigorous—but simply more accessible" (1989, 39). The complexity exists; interpreting it remains the unfulfilled challenge for Black women intellectuals.

Situated Knowledge, Subjugated Knowledge, and Partial Perspectives   "My life seems to be an increasing revelation of the intimate face of universal struggle," claims June Jordan:

> You begin with your family and the kids on the block, and next you open your eyes to what you call your people and that leads you into land reform into Black English into Angola leads you back to your own bed where you lie by yourself, wondering if you deserve to be peaceful, or trusted or desired or left to the freedom of your own unfaltering heart. And the scale shrinks to the size of a skull: your own interior cage. (Jordan 1981, xi)

Lorraine Hansberry expresses a similar idea: "I believe that one of the most sound ideas in dramatic writing is that in order to create the universal, you must pay very great attention to the specific. Universality, I think, emerges from the truthful identity of what is" (1969, 128). Jordan and Hansberry's insights that universal struggle and truth may wear a particularistic, intimate face suggest a new epistemological stance concerning how we negotiate competing knowledge claims and identify "truth."

The context in which African-American women's ideas are nurtured or suppressed matters. Understanding the content and epistemology of Black women's ideas as specialized knowledge requires attending to the context from which those ideas emerge. While produced by individuals, Black feminist thought as situated knowledge is embedded in the communities in which African-American women find ourselves (Haraway 1988).

A Black women's standpoint and those of other oppressed groups is not only embedded in a context but exists in a situation characterized by domination. Because Black women's ideas have been suppressed, this suppression has stimulated African-American women to create knowledge that empowers people to resist domination. Thus Afrocentric feminist thought represents a subjugated knowledge (Foucault 1980). A Black women's standpoint may provide a preferred stance from which to view the matrix of domination because, in principle, Black feminist thought as specialized thought is less likely than the specialized knowledge produced by dominant groups to deny the connection between ideas and the vested interests of their creators. However, Black feminist thought as subjugated knowledge is not exempt from critical analysis, because subjugation is not grounds for an epistemology (Haraway 1988).

Despite African-American women's potential power to reveal new insights about the matrix of domination, a Black women's standpoint is only one angle of vision. Thus Black feminist thought represents a partial perspective. The overarching matrix of domination houses multiple groups, each with varying experiences with penalty and privilege that produce corresponding partial perspectives, situated knowledges, and, for clearly identifiable subordinate groups, subjugated knowledges. No one group has a clear angle of vision. No one group possesses the theory of methodology that allows it to discover the absolute "truth" or, worse yet, proclaim its theories and methodologies as the universal norm evaluating other groups' experiences. Given that groups are unequal in power in making themselves heard, dominant groups have a vested interest in suppressing the knowledge produced by subordinate groups. Given the existence of multiple and competing knowledge claims to "truth" produced by groups with partial perspectives, what epistemological approach offers the most promise?

Dialogue and Empathy   Western social and political thought contains two alternative approaches to ascertaining "truth." The first, reflected in positivist science, has long claimed that absolute truths exist and that the task of scholarship is to develop objective, unbiased tools of science to measure these truths. But Afrocentric, feminist, and other bodies of critical theory have unmasked the concepts and epistemology of this version of science as representing the vested interests of elite white men and therefore as being less valid when applied to experiences of other groups and, more recently, to white male recounting of their own exploits. Earlier versions of standpoint theories, themselves rooted in a Marxist positivism, essentially reversed positivist science's assumptions concerning whose truth would prevail. These approaches suggest that the oppressed allegedly have a clearer view of "truth" than their oppressors because they lack the blinders created by the dominant group's ideology. But this version of standpoint theory basically duplicates the positivist belief in one "true" interpretation of reality and, like positivist science, comes with its own set of problems.

Relativism, the second approach, has been forwarded as the antithesis of and inevitable outcome of rejecting a positivist science. From a relativist perspective all groups produce specialized thought and each group's thought is equally valid. No group can claim to have a better interpretation of the "truth" than another. In a sense, relativism represents the opposite of scientific ideologies of objectivity. As epistemological stances, both positivist science and relativism minimize the importance of specific location in influencing a group's knowledge claims, the power inequities among groups that produce subjugated knowledges, and the strengths and limitations of partial perspective (Haraway 1988).

The existence of Black feminist thought suggests another alternative to the ostensibly objective norms of science and to relativism's claims that groups with competing knowledge claims are equal. In this volume I placed Black women's subjectivity in the center of analysis and examined the interdependence of the everyday, taken-for-granted knowledge shared by African-American women as a group, the more specialized knowledge produced by Black women intellectuals, and the social conditions shaping both types of thought. This approach allowed me to describe the creative tension linking how sociological conditions influenced a Black women's standpoint and how the power of the ideas themselves gave many African-American women the strength to shape those same sociological conditions. I approached Afrocentric feminist thought as situated in a context of domination and not as a system of ideas divorced from political and economic reality. Moreover, I presented Black feminist thought as subjugated knowledge in that African-American women have long struggled to find alternative locations and techniques for articulating our own standpoint. In brief, I examined the situated, subjugated standpoint of African-American women in order to understand Black feminist thought as a partial perspective on domination.

This approach to Afrocentric feminist thought allows African-American women to bring a Black women's standpoint to larger epistemological dialogues concerning the nature of the matrix of domination. Eventually such dialogues may get us to a point at which, claims Elsa Barkley Brown, "all people can learn to center in another experience, validate it, and judge it by its own standards without need of comparison or need to adopt that framework as their own" (1989, 922). In such dialogues, "one has no need to 'decenter' anyone in order to center someone else; one has only to constantly, appropriately, 'pivot the center'" (p. 922).

Those ideas that are validated as true by African-American women, African-American men, Latina lesbians, Asian-American women, Puerto Rican men, and other groups with distinctive standpoints, with each group using the epistemological approaches growing from its unique standpoint, thus become the most "objective" truths. Each group speaks from its own standpoint and shares its own partial, situated knowledge. But because each group perceives its own truth as partial, its knowledge is unfinished. Each group becomes better able to consider other groups' standpoints without relinquishing the uniqueness of its own standpoint or suppressing other groups' partial perspectives. "What is always needed in the appreciation of art, or life," maintains Alice Walker, "is the larger perspective. Connections made, or at least attempted, where none existed before, the straining to encompass in one's glance at the varied world the common thread, the unifying theme through immense diversity" (1983, 5). Partiality and not universality is the condition of being heard; individuals and groups forwarding knowledge claims without owning their position are deemed less credible than those who do.

Dialogue is critical to the success of this epistemological approach, the type of dialogue long extant in the Afrocentric call-and-response tradition whereby power dynamics are fluid, everyone has a voice, but everyone must listen and respond to other voices in order to be allowed to remain in the community. Sharing a common cause fosters dialogue and encourages groups to transcend their differences.

Existing power inequities among groups must be addressed before an alternative epistemology such as that described by Elsa Barkley Brown or Alice Walker can be utilized. The presence of subjugated knowledges means that groups are not equal in making their standpoints known to themselves and others. "Decentering" the dominant group is essential, and relinquishing privilege of this magnitude is unlikely to occur without struggle. But still the vision exists, one encompassing "coming to believe in the possibility of a variety of experiences, a variety of ways of understanding the world, a variety of frameworks of operation, without imposing consciously or unconsciously a notion of the norm" (Brown 1989, 921).

· · ·

[1990]

REFERENCES

Brown, Elsa Barkely. 1986. *Hearing Our Mothers' Lives*. Atlanta: Fifteenth Anniversary of African-American and African Studies, Emory University. (unpublished)

————. 1989. "African-American Women's Quilting: A Framework for Conceptualizing and Teaching African-American Women's History." *Signs* 14(4): 921–29.

Foucault, Michel. 1980. *Power/Knowledge: Selected Interviews and Other Writings 1972–1977*, edited by Colin Gordon. New York: Pantheon.

Giovanni, Nikki. 1988. *Sacred Cows . . . and Other Edibles*. New York: Quill/William Morrow.

Gwaltney, John Langston. 1980. *Drylongso, A Self-Portrait of Black America*. New York: Vintage.

Hansberry, Lorraine. 1969. *To Be Young, Gifted and Black*. New York: Signet.

Haraway, Donna. 1988. "Situated Knowledges: The Science Question in Feminism and the Privilege of Partial Perspective." *Feminist Studies* 14(3): 575–99.

Hooks, Bell. 1989. *Talking Back: Thinking Feminist, Thinking Black*. Boston: South End Press.

Jordan, June. 1985. *On Call*. Boston: South End Press.

Narayan, Uma. 1989. "The Project of Feminist Epistemology: Perspectives from a Nonwestern Feminist." In *Gender/Body/Knowledge: Feminist Reconstructions of Being and Knowing*, edited by Alison M. Jaggar and Susan R. Bordo, 256–69. New Brunswick, NJ: Rutgers University Press.

Walker, Alice. 1977. "Zora Neale Hurston: A Cautionary Tale and a Partisan View." Foreward to *Zora Neale Hurston: A Literary Biography,* by Robert Hemenway, xi–xviii. Urbana: University of Illinois Press.

———. 1983. *In Search of Our Mothers' Gardens.* New York: Harcourt Brace Jovanovich.

 83

Outcast Mothers and Surrogates: Racism and Reproductive Politics in the Nineties

ANGELA Y. DAVIS

The historical construction of women's reproductive role, which is largely synonymous with the historical failure to acknowledge the possibility of reproductive self-determination, has been informed by a peculiar constellation of racist and misogynist assumptions. These assumptions have undergone mutations even as they remain tethered to their historical origins. To explore the politics of reproduction in a contemporary context is to recognize the growing intervention of technology into the most intimate spaces of human life: from computerized bombings in the Persian Gulf, that have taken life from thousands of children and adults as if they were nothing more than the abstract statistics of a video game, to the complex technologies awaiting women who wish to transcend biological, or socially induced infertility. I do not mean to suggest that technology is inherently oppressive. Rather, the socioeconomic conditions within which reproductive technologies are being developed, applied, and rendered accessible or inaccessible maneuver them in directions that most often maintain or deepen misogynist, anti-working class, and racist marginalization.

To the extent that fatherhood is denied as a socially significant moment in the process of biological reproduction, the politics of reproduction hinge on the social construction of motherhood. The new developments in reproductive technology have encouraged the contemporary emergence of popular attitudes—at least among the middle classes—that bear a remarkable resemblance to the nineteenth-century cult of motherhood, including the moral, legal, and political taboos it developed against abortion. While the rise of industrial capitalism led to the historical obsolescence of the domestic economy and the ideological imprisonment of (white and middle-class) women within a privatized home sphere, the late twentieth-century breakthroughs in reproductive technology are resuscitating that ideology in bizarre and contradictory ways. Women who can afford to take advantage of the new technology—who are often career women for whom motherhood is no longer a primary or exclusive vocation—now encounter a mystification of maternity emanating from the possibility of transcending biological (and socially defined) reproductive incapacity. It is as if the recognition of infertility is now a catalyst—among some groups of women—for a motherhood quest that has become more compulsive and more openly ideological than during the nineteenth century. Considering the anti-abortion campaign, it is not difficult to envision this contemporary ideological mystification of motherhood as central to the efforts to deny all women the legal rights that would help shift the politics of reproduction toward a recognition of our autonomy with respect to the biological functions of our bodies.

In the United States, the nineteenth-century cult of motherhood was complicated by a number of class- and race-based contradictions. Women who had recently immigrated from Europe were cast, like their male counterparts, into the industrial proletariat, and were therefore compelled to play economic roles that contradicted the increasing representation of women as wives/mothers. Moreover, in conflating slave motherhood and the reproduction of its labor force, the moribund slave economy effectively denied motherhood to vast numbers of African women. My female ancestors were not led to believe that, as women, their primary vocation was motherhood. Yet slave women were imprisoned within their reproductive role as well. The same socio-historical reasons for the ideological location of European women in an increasingly obsolete domestic economy as the producers, nurturers, and rearers of children caused slave women to be valued in accordance with their role as breeders. Of course, both motherhood, as it was ideologically constructed, and breederhood, as it historically unfolded, were contingent upon the biological birth process. However, the one presumed to capture the moral essence of womaness, while the other denied, on the basis of racist presumptions and economic necessity, the very possibility of morality and thus also participation in this motherhood cult.

During the first half of the nineteenth century, when the industrial demand for cotton led to the obsessive expansion of slavery at a time when the importation of Africans was no longer legal, the "slaveocracy" demanded of African women that they bear as many children as they were biologically capable of bearing. Thus, many women had 14, 15, 16, 17, 18, 19, 20 children. My own grandmother, whose parents were slaves, was one of 13 children.

At the same time, therefore, that nineteenth-century white women were being ideologically incarcerated within their biological reproductive role, essentialized as mothers, African women were forced to bear children, not as evidence of their role as mothers, but for the purpose of expanding the human property held by slave owners. The reproductive role imposed upon African slave women bore no relationship to a subjective project of motherhood. In fact, as Toni Morrison's novel, *Beloved,* indicates—inspired as it is by an actual historical case of a woman killing her daughter—some slave women committed infanticide as a means of resisting the enslavement of their progeny.

Slave women were *birth mothers* or *genetic mothers*—to employ terms rendered possible by the new reproductive technologies—but they possessed no legal rights as mothers of any kind. Considering the commodification of their children—and indeed, of their own persons—their status was similar to that of the contemporary *surrogate mother.* I am suggesting that the term *surrogate mother* might be invoked as a retroactive description of their status because the economic appropriation of their reproductive capacity reflected the inability of the slave economy to produce and reproduce its own laborers—a limitation with respect to the forces of economic production that is being transformed in this era of advanced capitalism by the increasing computerization and robotization of the economy.

The children of slave mothers could be sold away by their owners for business reasons or as a result of a strategy of repression. They could also be forced to give birth to children fathered by their masters, knowing full well that the white fathers would never recognize their Black children as offspring. As a consequence of the socially constructed invisibility of the white father—a pretended invisibility strangely respected by the white and Black community alike—Black children would grow up in an intimate relation to their white half-brothers and sisters, except that their biological kinship, often revealed by a visible physical resemblance, would remain shrouded in silence. That feature of slave motherhood was something about which no one could speak. Slave women who had been compelled—or had, for their own reasons, agreed—to engage in sexual intercourse with their masters would be committing the equivalent of a crime if they publicly revealed the fathers of their children.[1] These women knew that it was quite likely that their children might also be sold or brutalized or beaten by their own fathers, brothers, uncles, or nephews.

If I have lingered over what I see as some of the salient reproductive issues in African-American women's history, it is because they seem to shed light on the ideological context of contemporary technological intervention in the realm of reproduction. Within the contemporary feminist discourse about the new reproductive technologies—in vitro fertilization, surrogacy, embryo transfer, etc.—concern has been expressed about what is sometimes described as the "deconstruction of motherhood"[2] as a unified biological process. While the new technological developments have rendered the fragmentation of maternity more obvious, the economic system of slavery fundamentally relied upon alienated and fragmented maternities, as women were forced to bear children, whom masters claimed as potentially profitable labor machines. Birth mothers could not therefore expect to be mothers in the legal sense. Legally these children were chattel and therefore motherless. Slave states passed laws to the effect that children of slave women no more belonged to their biological mothers than the young of animals belonged to the females that birthed them.[3]

At the same time, slave women and particularly those who were house slaves were expected to nur-

ture and rear and mother the children of their owners. It was not uncommon for white children of the
slave-owning class to have relationships of a far
greater emotional intensity with the slave women
who were their "mammies" than with their own
white biological mothers. We might even question
the meaning of this conception of "biological motherhood" in light of the fact that the Black nurturers
of these white children were frequently "wet nurses"
as well. They nourished the babies in their care with
the milk produced by their own hormones. It seems,
therefore, that Black women were not only treated
as surrogates with respect to the reproduction of
slave labor, they also served as surrogate mothers
for the white children of the slave-owners.

. . .

The economic history of African-American
women—from slavery to the present—like the economic history of immigrant women, both from Europe and colonized or formerly colonized nations,
reveals the persisting theme of work as household
servants. Mexican women and Irish women, West
Indian women and Chinese women have been compelled, by virtue of their economic standing, to
function as servants for the wealthy. They have
cleaned their houses and—our present concern—
they have nurtured and reared their employers' babies. They have functioned as surrogate mothers.
Considering this previous history, is it not possible
to imagine the possibility that poor women—especially poor women of color—might be transformed
into a special caste of hired pregnancy carriers?
Certainly such fears are not simply the product of
an itinerant imagination. In any event, whether or
not such a caste of women baby-bearers eventually
makes its way into history, these historical experiences constitute a socio-historical backdrop for the
present debate around the new reproductive technologies. The very fact that the discussion over surrogacy tends to coincide, by virtue of corporate
involvement and intervention in the new technologies, with the debate over surrogacy for profit,
makes it necessary to acknowledge historical economic precedents for surrogate motherhood. Those
patterns are more or less likely to persist under the
impact of the technology in its market context. The
commodification of reproductive technologies, and,
in particular, the labor services of pregnant surro-

gate mothers, means that money is being made and
that, therefore, someone is being exploited.

Once upon a time—and this is still the case
outside the technologically advanced capitalist
societies—a woman who discovered that she was
infertile would have to reconcile herself to the impossibility of giving birth to her own biological offspring. She would therefore either try to create a life
for herself that did not absolutely require the presence of children, or she chose to enter into a mothering relationship in other ways. There was the
possibility of foster motherhood, adoptive motherhood, or play motherhood.[4] This last possibility is
deeply rooted in the Black community tradition of
extended families and relationships based both on
biological kinship—though not necessarily biological motherhood—and on personal history, which is
often as binding as biological kinship. But even
within the biological network itself, relationships between, for example, an aunt and niece or nephew, in
the African-American and other family traditions,
might be as strong or stronger than those between a
mother and daughter or son.

My own mother grew up in a family of foster
parents with no siblings. Her best friend had no sisters and brothers either, so they invented a sister
relation between them. Though many years passed
before I became aware that they were not "really"
sisters, this knowledge had no significant impact on
me: I considered my Aunt Elizabeth no less my aunt
later than during the earlier years of my childhood.
Because she herself had no children, her relation to
me, my sister, and two brothers was one of a second
mother.

If she were alive and in her childbearing years
today, I wonder whether she would bemoan the fact
that she lacked the financial resources to employ all
the various technological means available to women
who wish to reverse their infertility. I wonder if she
would feel a greater compulsion to fulfill a female
vocation of motherhood. While working-class
women are not often in the position to explore the
new technology, infertile women—or the wives/
partners of infertile men—who are financially able
to do so are increasingly expected to try everything.
They are expected to try in vitro fertilization, embryo transplants, surrogacy. The availability of the
technology further mythologizes motherhood as the

true vocation of women. In fact, the new reproductive medicine sends out a message to those who are capable of receiving it: motherhood lies just beyond the next technology. The consequence is an ideological compulsion toward a palpable goal: a child one creates either via one's own reproductive activity or via someone else's.

Those who opt to employ a surrogate mother will participate in the economic as well as ideological exploitation of her services. And the woman who becomes a surrogate mother earns relatively low wages. A few years ago, the going rate was twenty thousand dollars. Considering the fact that pregnancy is a 24-hour-a-day job, what might seem like a substantial sum of money is actually not even a minimum wage. This commodification of motherhood is quite frightening in the sense that it comes forth as permission to allow women and their partners to participate in a program that is generative of life. However, it seems that what is really generated is sexism and profits.

The economic model evoked by the relationship between the surrogate mother and the woman [or man] who makes use of her services is the feudalistic bond between servant and her employer. Because domestic work has been primarily performed in the United States by women of color, native-born as well as recent immigrants (and immigrant women of European descent), elements of racism and class bias adhere to the concept of surrogate motherhood as potential historical features, even in the contemporary absence of large numbers of surrogate mothers of color.

If the emerging debate around the new reproductive technologies is presently anchored to the socioeconomic conditions of relatively affluent families, the reproductive issues most frequently associated with poor and working-class women of color revolve around the apparent proliferation of young single parents, especially in the African-American community. For the last decade or so, teenage pregnancy has been ideologically represented as one of the greatest obstacles to social progress in the most impoverished sectors of the Black community. In actuality, the *rate* of teenage pregnancy in the Black community—like that among white teenagers—has been waning for quite a number of years. According to a National Research

Council study, fertility rates in 1960 were 156 births per 1,000 Black women aged 15 to 19, and 97 in 1985.[5] What distinguishes teenage pregnancy in the Black community today from its historical counterpart is the decreasing likelihood of teenage marriages. There is a constellation of reasons for the failure of young teenagers to consolidate traditional two-parent families. The most obvious one is that it rarely makes economic sense for an unemployed young woman to marry an unemployed young man. As a consequence of shop closures in industries previously accessible to young Black male workers—and the overarching deindustrialization of the economy—young men capable of contributing to the support of their children are becoming increasingly scarce. For a young woman whose pregnancy results from a relationship with an unemployed youth, it makes little sense to enter into a marriage that will probably bring in an extra adult as well as a child to be supported by her own mother/father/grandmother, etc.

The rise of single motherhood cannot be construed, however, as synonymous with the "fall" of the nuclear family within the Black community—if only because it is an extremely questionable proposition that there was such an uncontested structure as the nuclear family to begin with. Historically, family relationships within the Black community have rarely coincided with the traditional nuclear model. The nuclear family, in fact, is a relatively recent configuration, integrally connected with the development of industrial capitalism. It is a family configuration that is rapidly losing its previous, if limited, historical viability: presently, the majority of U.S. families, regardless of membership in a particular cultural or ethnic group, cannot be characterized as "nuclear" in the traditional sense. Considering the gender-based division of labor at the core of the nuclear model, even those families that consist of the mother-father-children nucleus—often popularly referred to as "nuclear families"—do not, rigorously speaking, conform to the nuclear model. The increasingly widespread phenomenon of the "working mother," as opposed to the wife/mother whose economic responsibilities are confined to the household and the children, thoroughly contradicts and renders anachronistic the nuclear family model. Not too many mothers stay at home

[margin note: families in Black community]

by choice anymore; not too many mothers can afford to stay at home, unless, of course, they benefit from the class privileges that accrue to the wealthy. In other words, even for those whose historical realities were the basis of the emergence of this nuclear family model, the model is rapidly losing its ability to contain and be responsive to contemporary social/economic/psychic realities.

It angers me that such a simplistic interpretation of the material and spiritual impoverishment of the African-American community as being largely rooted in teenage pregnancy is so widely accepted. This is not to imply that teenage pregnancy is unproblematic. It is extremely problematic, but I cannot assent to the representation of teenage pregnancy as "the problem." There are reasons why young Black women become pregnant and/or desire pregnancy. I do not think I am far off-target when I point out that few young women who choose pregnancy are offered an alternative range of opportunities for self-expression and development. Are those Black teenage girls with the potential for higher education offered scholarships permitting them to study at colleges and universities like Le Moyne? Are teenagers who choose pregnancy offered even a vision of well-paying and creative jobs?

Is it really so hard to grasp why so many young women would choose motherhood? Isn't this path toward adulthood still thrust upon them by the old but persisting ideological constructions of femaleness? Doesn't motherhood still equal adult womanhood in the popular imagination? Don't the new reproductive technologies further develop this equation of womanhood and motherhood? I would venture to say that many young women make conscious decisions to bear children in order to convince themselves that they are alive and creative human beings. As a consequence of this choice, they are also characterized as immoral for not marrying the fathers of their children.

I have chosen to evoke the reproductive issues of single motherhood among teenagers in order to highlight the absurdity of locating motherhood in a transcendent space—as the anti-abortion theorists and activists do—in which involuntary motherhood is as sacred as voluntary motherhood. In this context, there is a glaring exception: motherhood among Black and Latina teens is constructed as a moral and social evil—but even so, they are denied accessible and affordable abortions. Moreover, teen mothers are ideologically assaulted because of their premature and impoverished entrance into the realm of motherhood while older, whiter, and wealthier women are coaxed to buy the technology to assist them in achieving an utterly commodified motherhood.

Further contradictions in the contemporary social compulsion toward motherhood—contradictions rooted in race and class—can be found in the persisting problem of sterilization abuse. While poor women in many states have effectively lost access to abortion, they may be sterilized with the full financial support of the government. While the "right" to opt for surgical sterilization is an important feature of women's control over the reproductive functions of their bodies, the imbalance between the difficulty of access to abortions and the ease of access to sterilization reveals the continued and tenacious insinuation of racism into the politics of reproduction. The astoundingly high—and continually mounting—statistics regarding the sterilization of Puerto Rican women expose one of the most dramatic ways in which women's bodies bear the evidence of colonization. Likewise, the bodies of vast numbers of sterilized indigenous women within the presumed borders of the U.S. bear the traces of a 500-year-old tradition of genocide. While there is as yet no evidence of large-scale sterilization of African-American and Latina teenage girls, there is documented evidence of the federal government's promotion and funding of sterilization operations for young Black girls during the 1960s and 70s. This historical precedent convinces me that it is not inappropriate to speculate about such a future possibility of preventing teenage pregnancy. Or—to engage in further speculation—of recruiting healthy young poor women, a disproportionate number of whom would probably be Black, Latina, Native American, Asian, or from the Pacific Islands, to serve as pregnancy carriers for women who can afford to purchase their services.

• • •

The process through which a significant portion of the population of young Black, Latina, Native American, Asian, and Pacific women are criminalized, along with the poor European women, who, by their association with women of color are deemed criminal, hinges on a manipulation of a certain ideological representation of motherhood. A poor teenage Black or Latina girl who is a single mother is suspected of criminality simply by virtue of the fact that she is poor and has had a child "out of wedlock." This process of criminalization affects the young men in a different way—not as fathers, but rather by virtue of a more all-embracing racialization. Any young Black man can be potentially labeled as criminal: a shabby appearance is equated with drug addiction, yet an elegant and expensive self-presentation is interpreted as drug dealing. While it may appear that this process of criminalization is unrelated to the construction of the politics of reproduction, there are significant implications here for the expansion of single motherhood in Black and Latino communities. The 25 percent of African-American men in jails and prisons,[6] for example, naturally find it difficult, even in a vicarious sense, to engage in any significant parenting projects.

In pursuing a few of the ways in which racism—and class bias—inform the contemporary politics of reproduction, I am suggesting that there are numerous unexplored vantage points from which we can reconceptualize reproductive issues. It is no longer acceptable to ground an analysis of the politics of reproduction in a conceptual construction of "woman" as a sex. It is not enough to assume that female beings whose bodies are distinguished by vaginas, ovarian tubes, uteri, and other biological features related to reproduction should be able to claim such "rights" to exercise control over the processes of these organs, as the right to abortion. The social/economic/political circumstances that oppress and marginalize women of various racial, ethnic, and class backgrounds, and thus alter the impact of ideological conceptions of motherhood, cannot be ignored without affirming the same structures of domination that have led to such different—but related—politics of reproduction in the first place.

In conclusion, I will point to some of the strategic constellations that should be taken into consideration in reconceiving an agenda of reproductive rights. I do not present the following points as an exhaustive list of such goals, but rather I am trying to allude to a few of the contemporary issues requiring further theoretical examination and practical/political action. While the multiple arenas in which women's legal abortion rights are presently being assaulted and eroded can account for the foregrounding of this struggle, the failure to regard economic accessibility of birth control and abortion has equally important results in the inevitable marginalization of poor women's reproductive rights. With respect to a related issue, the "right" and access to sterilization is important, but again, it is equally important to look at those economic and ideological conditions that track some women toward sterilization, thus denying them the possibility of bearing and rearing children in numbers they themselves choose.

Although the new reproductive technologies cannot be construed as inherently affirmative or violative of women's reproductive rights, the anchoring of the technologies to the profit schemes of their producers and distributors results in a commodification of motherhood that complicates and deepens power relationships based on class and race. Yet, beneath this marriage of technology, profit, and the assertion of a historically obsolete bourgeois individualism lies the critical issue of the right to determine the character of one's family. The assault on this "right"—a term I have used throughout, which is not, however, unproblematic—is implicated in the ideological offensive against single motherhood as well as in the homophobic refusal to recognize lesbian and gay family configurations—and especially in the persisting denial of custody (even though some changes have occurred) to lesbians with children from previous heterosexual marriages. This is one of the many ways in which the present-day ideological compulsion toward motherhood that I have attempted to weave into all of my arguments further resonates. Moreover, this ideology of motherhood is wedded to an obdurate denial of the very social services women require in order to make meaningful choices to bear or not to bear children. Such services include health care—from the prenatal period to old age—child care, housing, education, jobs, and all the basic services human beings require to lead decent lives. The privatization of family responsibilities—particularly during an era when so many new family configurations are being invented that the definition of family stretches beyond its own borders—takes on increasingly reactionary implications. This is why I want to close with a point of departure: the reconceptualization of family and of reproductive rights in terms that move from the private to the public, from the individual to the social.

[1991]

NOTES

1. See Harriet A. Jacobs. *Incidents in the Life of a Slave Girl.* Edited and Introduction by Jean Fagan Yellin. Cambridge, Mass.: Harvard University Press, p. 1087.
2. See Michelle Stanworth, ed. *Reproductive Technologies: Gender, Motherhood and Medicine.* Minneapolis: University of Minnesota Press, 1987.
3. See Paula Giddings. *When and Where I Enter: The Impact of Black Women on Race and Sex in America.* New York: William Morrow, 1984.
4. The tradition of Black women acting as "play mothers" is still a vital means of inventing kinship relations unrelated to biological origin.
5. Gerald David Jaynes and Robin M. Williams, Jr., ed. *A Common Destiny: Blacks and American Society,* Washington, D.C.: National Academy Press, 1989, p. 515.
6. See Marc Mauer, "Young Black Men and the Criminal Justice System: A Growing National Problem." A Report by the Sentencing Project, 918 F Street, N.W. Suite 501, Washington, D.C. 20004, February 1990.

 84

Making Gender Visible in the Pursuit of Nature's Secrets

EVELYN FOX KELLER

In teaching us to see gender as a socially constructed and culturally transmitted organizer of our inner and outer worlds, in, as it were, making gender visible, feminist theory has provided us with an instrument of immense subversive power. And along with this provision comes a commitment: nothing less than the deconstruction and reconstitution of conventional knowledge. Necessarily, such a venture requires close textual reading of all attributions of gender, wherever they occur. My own work, for example, has focused on the implications for science and, accordingly, for all of us, of the uses of gender in modern constructions of mind, nature, and the relation between the two.[1] Ultimately, what we are most interested in is clarification of the space of alternative possibilities. If meaning depends on gender, we want to know what changes in meaning, in science as elsewhere, would accrue from shifting meanings or uses of gender—even from abandoning gender altogether—in our construction and de(con)struction of nature.

This method of feminist analysis is unquestionably powerful, but it is not always unproblematic. Two difficulties come to mind immediately: one arises from the obvious fact that images of male and female evoke different responses in different people, and the second arises from the fact that people are not necessarily consistent. Although labels of masculine and feminine are almost always used to designate polarities (or dichotomies), sometimes the two poles are distinguished in one way, sometimes in another. Consider, for example, discussions of brain lateralization: sometimes the right brain is said to be feminine, sometimes the left brain.[2] True, whichever is assumed to be better is sure to be seen as masculine. But my point is that however eager we seem to be to divide the world of personal attributes into categories of male and female, we are not always sure which is which.

So it is, as well, when we try to explore the function of gender in the world of archetypal myths and abstract categories. Sometimes the ambiguity of gender can itself be functional and indeed can be read as a map of another kind of structure. Nature, for instance, although almost always female in Western prescientific and scientific traditions, is not always so. As I have tried to show in examining the differences in imagery between Plato and Bacon, a great deal can be learned about the range of impulses and aims underlying the pursuit of scientific knowledge by exploring the differences of meaning that accrue as the gender of nature shifts.[3]

In this paper, I want to address—and even to take issue with—a reading of gender associations that has become familiar in recent feminist literary criticism. Christine Froula, for one, writes of "the archetypal association of maleness with invisibility, and of femaleness with visibility."[4] She cites Freud for rooting the evolution from immediate sense perception to abstract thinking (what Freud himself calls the "triumph of invisibility," "a victory of spirituality over the senses") in "the turning from the mother to the father." The basis for this presumed archetypal association, Freud tells us, is the fact that "maternity is proved by the senses whereas paternity is a surmise."[5]

For anyone who has thought about the psychology of gender, this claim must seem at least a little surprising, and to someone like myself, used to thinking about the function of gender metaphors in science, it is deeply startling. More reasonably, it might seem, the rise of modern science could be called the "triumph of the visible," its principal goal being clarity, elucidation, enlightenment, the elimination of opacity, and the vanquishing of darkness. The scientific text is, ideally, an open book, and the scientific society an open community—both constructed on a principled intolerance of secrets. Does that suggest that science should be seen as a returning from the father to the mother? Clearly not. Rather, it reminds us of how necessary to our understanding of these archetypal associations it is that we ask: visibility of what, and to whom? An absence of which secrets, and from whom? Even a superficial inspection of scientific discourse, and indeed of much of ordinary language, suggests, at the very least, the need for a higher dimensional typology. At the very least, the link Froula (like Freud) intuits between masculinity and invisibility must, as I will try to show, be seen as mediated by a prior link between power and invisibility.

There is, in fact, a long historical tradition in which femaleness is most typically associated not with visibility but with obscurity: visible, to be sure, on the surface, but invisible in its (or her) interior, in her innermost and most vital parts. Prior to the advent of science, nature as female is dark, secretive, and opaque. In more immediate human experience, paternity may demand surmise from a father, but in principle, if not in practice, it can be clear enough to the mother: she remains the ultimate arbiter of doubt. Pregnancy, on the other hand, though visible to all the world in its outward signs, is—be it distressingly or miraculously—invisible in its internal dynamics. It is, in fact, the ultimate secret of life, knowable if not visible to the mother, but absolutely inaccessible to the father.

Well-kept secrets pose a predictable challenge to those who are not privy. Secrets function to articulate a boundary: an interior not visible to outsiders, the demarcation of a separate domain, a sphere of autonomous power. And indeed, the secrets of women, like the secrets of nature, are and have traditionally been seen by men as potentially threatening—or if not threatening, then alluring—in that they articulate a boundary that excludes them, and so invite exposure or require finding out. Nobel laureate Richard Feynman once said, perhaps by way of explaining the extraordinary facility for lock picking that had won him so much fame as a young physicist at Los Alamos: "One of my diseases, one of my things in life, is that anything that is secret, I try to undo."[6]

In Western culture, the threat of the allure presented by nature's secrets has met with a definitive response. Modern science has invented a strategy for dealing with this threat, for asserting power over nature's potentially autonomous sphere. That strategy is, of course, precisely a *method* for the "undoing" of nature's secrets; for the rendering of what was previously opaque, transparent, and of what was previously invisible, visible—to the mind's eye, if not to the physical eye. However, the representation of the book of nature as a transparent text is a move with consequences that are anything but transparent.

The ferreting out of nature's secrets, understood as the illumination of a female interior, or the tearing of nature's veil, may be seen as expressing one of the most unembarrassedly stereotypic impulses of the scientific project. In this interpretation, the task of scientific enlightenment—the illumination of the reality behind appearances—is an inversion of surface and interior, an interchange between visible and invisible, that effectively routs the last vestiges of archaic, subterranean female power. Like the deceptive solidity of Eddington's table, the visible surface dissolves into transparent unreality. Scientific enlightenment is in this sense a drama between visibility and invisibility, light and dark, a drama in need of constant reenactment at ever-receding recesses of nature's secrets.

In the remarks that follow, I want to give two examples, or rather one example and one counter-example, which together serve to inform each other in their apparent contradiction. The example is a particularly vivid reenactment of that "drama" which can be seen in the story of the rise of molecular biology—a drama that was, in fact, quite explicitly cast in the language of "light and life,"[7] the quest for the secret of life, and then, once that secret was claimed to have been found, ended with the ultimate banishment of the very language of secrets, mystery, and darkness from biological discourse.

As it is usually told, in its classical format, the story of the rise of molecular biology is a drama between science and nature. It begins with the claim of a few physicists—most notably Erwin Schroedinger, Max Delbruck, and Leo Szilard—that the time was ripe to extend the promise of physics for clear and precise knowledge to the last frontier: the problem of of life. Emboldened by their example, two especially brave young scientific adventurers, namely, James Watson and Francis Crick, took up the challenge and did, in fact, succeed in vanquishing nature's ultimate and definitive stronghold. As if in direct refutation of the earlier, more circumspect suggestion of Niels Bohr that what quantum mechanics taught us was that "the minimal freedom we must allow the organism will be just large enough to permit it, so to say, to hide its ultimate secrets from us,"[8] Watson and Crick succeeded in showing "that areas apparently too mysterious to be explained by physics and chemistry could in fact be so explained."[9] In short, they found the secret of life.

There is another story here, however, one that takes place in the realm of science itself—a drama not between science and nature but between competing motifs in science, indeed among competing visions of what a biological science should look like. When Watson and Crick embarked on a quest that they themselves described as a "calculated assault on the secret of life," they were employing a language that was, at the same time, not only grandiose and provocatively unfashionable but, as Donald

Fleming has pointed out, "in total defiance of contemporary standards of good taste in biological discourse."[10] The story of real interest to historians of science, I suggest, is in the redefinition of what a scientific biology meant; the story of the transformation of biology from a science in which the language of mystery had a place not only legitimate but highly functional, to a science that tolerated no secrets, a science more like physics, predicated on the conviction that the mysteries of life were there to be unraveled. In this retelling, our focus inevitably shifts from the accomplishments of molecular biology to the representation of those accomplishments.

The subplot is in effect a story of cognitive politics. It is a story of the growing authority of physics, and physicists; of an authority that drew directly from the momentous achievements of quantum mechanics early in the century and indirectly from the very fresh acclaim accruing to physicists for their role in winning the Second World War. Told in this way, we can begin to make sense of the puzzle that has long plagued historians of contemporary biology. Despite initial claims and hopes, molecular biology gave no new laws of physics and revealed no paradoxes. What, then, did the physicists, described as having led the revolution of molecular biology, actually provide?

Leo Szilard said it quite clearly: it was "not any skills acquired in physics, but rather an attitude: the conviction which few biologists had at the time, that mysteries can be solved."[11] He went on to say, "If secrets exist, they must be explainable. You see, this is something which modern biologists brought into biology, something which the classical biologists did not have. . . . They lacked the faith that things are explainable—and it is this faith . . . which leads to major advances in biology."

And indeed, he was right. This attitude, this conviction that life's secrets could be found, this view of themselves (especially Watson and Crick) as conquistadores who could and would find it—a stance that drew directly and vigorously on the authority of physicists for its license—proved to be extraordinarily productive. It permitted the conviction, and just a few years later the sharing of that conviction, that life's secret *had* been found. As Max Delbruck said in his Nobel address in 1970:

Molecular genetics has taught us to spell out the connectivity of life in such palpable detail that we may say in plain words, "The riddle of life has been solved."[12]

In shifting our focus from the successes of molecular biology to the representation of those successes, this retelling inevitably raises the question, What difference does such a representation make?

Much has been written about the race to the double helix—about why Rosalind Franklin, or even Erwin Chargaff, did not see it, about how long it would have taken Franklin if Watson and Crick had not beaten her to it, etc. And I've always thought that that was an essentially boring discussion. It was relevant, of course, to matters of credit, but it had no bearing, I thought, on the course of science. I now think differently. If Rosalind Franklin *had* found the structure of DNA, as she surely would have, she would also, almost equally surely, have seen in that structure a mechanism for genetic replication. *What she would not in all likelihood have seen in it was the secret of life.* Or, as Chargaff himself has written:

> If Rosalind Franklin and I could have collaborated, we might have come up with something of the sort in one or two years. I doubt, however, that we could ever have elevated the double helix into "the mighty symbol that has replaced the cross as the signature of the biological alphabet."[13]

The representation of the mechanism of genetic replication as the secret of life was a move that neither Rosalind Franklin, nor Chargaff, nor any number of others could have made, for the simple reason that the traditions from which they came would not have permitted such a linguistic and ideological sweep. That Watson and Crick *were* able to make it was a direct consequence of the existence of a small but significant culture of like-minded "new thinkers" in biology that had grown up around them, in response to the same forces that had influenced them.

I also want to suggest that this description of the mechanism of genetic replication as the secret of life—or, conversely, this representation of the secret of life as the mechanism of genetic replication—had decisive consequences for the future course of biology. It permitted a more complete vindication of a set of beliefs than would otherwise have been possible:

beliefs in the absolute adequacy of mechanism, in the incontrovertible value of simplicity, and in the decisive power of a particular conception of biology. No doubt the triumph of the double helix would have been major no matter how it had been described, but its particular representation allowed molecular biologists an assumption of scientific hegemony theretofore unfamiliar in biology. Having solved the problem of life "in principle if not in all details," as Jacques Monod put it,[14] there was no longer room for doubt, for uncertainty, for questions unanswerable within that framework, even for data that would not fit, or for another conception of biology. A science that had historically been characterized by diversity—perhaps like the life it presumed to study—became if not quite monolithic, then very close to it. Certainly in their own minds, molecular biology had become synonymous with scientific biology.

The representation of the secret of life as the mechanism of genetic replication led, once that mechanism had been illuminated, to the conclusion that life itself was not complex, as had been thought earlier, but simple; simple, indeed, beyond our wildest dreams. The only secret of nature was that there were no secrets, and now that secret was out. Henceforth, the very language of biological discourse was to be cleansed of any reference to mystery. Words such as *complexity* and *mystery,* words with a long-standing tradition in biology, soon became disreputable and manifestly unscientific.

Barbara McClintock, finally rewarded in 1983 with the Nobel prize, was for many years discounted, in part because of her blatant indifference to the new credo. If she continues to be described as "unscientific," it is for the same reason: mystery, for her, remained, and continues to remain, a positive value.[15] And if McClintock is revealed as a relic of a bygone era by her regard for mystery, Erwin Chargaff is revealed as not only old but also bitter and jealous. *Only* a bitter old man would say, in 1978, as he did,

> It would seem that man cannot live without mysteries. One could say, the great biologists worked in the very light of darkness. We have been deprived of this fertile light. . . . What will have to go next?[16]

Finally, it was not only language that changed. The very conception of what counted as a legitimate question also changed. Questions without clear and definitive answers not only were not worth asking, they were not asked. Similarly, the meaning of explanation was correspondingly circumscribed. Biological explanations were now limited to "how things worked." The proof of understanding was to be provided by a mechanism. That which mechanism failed to illuminate, rapidly fell from consciousness.

It is important to note, at this juncture, the great irony of the fact that in the end, it was the very pursuit of molecular mechanisms that ultimately created the conditions enabling the retelling of its own story. That is, the story of the representation of the successes of molecular biology can be told today precisely because of all the research that has emerged, from molecular biology itself, to challenge that representation.[17] Because of this work, we are granted *scientific* authority to look at the underside of the successes of molecular biology, to look at some of the costs that were incurred by embracing the metaphoric quest of nature as an open book or a transparent text harboring no secrets, having no interior, and science as a clear and apparent (although not transparent) reflection of that text. This quest is one in which both science and nature are collapsed into two-dimensional surfaces. Both are self-evident texts in which nothing is hidden; there is, apparently, nothing behind the text. But while it may or may not be true that nothing lies behind the book of nature, it is certainly the case that behind the scientific text lies its author—his invisibility and unassailability now secured by the very self-evidence of his text. Science thus becomes less of a mirror and more of a one-way glass, transparent to the scientist, but impenetrable to anyone or anything outside.

To return to my opening remarks, I think Freud was right when he argued that the invisibility of Moses' divine patriarch permitted believers "a much more grandiose idea of their God" (p. 143). But I suggest that Freud's crucial insight has more to do with the relationship between invisibility and power than with the relationship between invisibility and masculinity. That is to say, the invisibility of nature's interiority, like the invisibility of women's interiority, is threatening precisely because it threatens the balance of power between man and nature, and be-

tween men and women. To this problem, the culture of modern science has found a truly effective solution, indeed a far more effective solution than those that had gone before. Instead of banishing the Furies underground, out of sight, as did the Greeks, modern science has sought to expose female interiority, to bring it into the light, and thus to dissolve its threat entirely.

In a parallel assertion of power, the secrets of God are also put to the light: where the secrets of nature are *visible,* the laws of nature are *knowable,* that is to say, visible to the mind's eye. In this new ontology, invisibility is sanctioned in only one place: ideally, the scientific text has no signature. The author of the modern scientific text, or the authority of modern science, is simultaneously everywhere and nowhere; on the one hand, it is manifest, self-evident, the archenemy of secrets and secrecy, and on the other, anonymous, uninterpretable, and unidentifiable. There for all to see, eschewing all constraints, barriers, and walls, the scientific text denies the very possibility of decoding by its insistent visibility, and all the while remains, in its own interior, as invisible as Moses' patriarch.

That is the predominant mythology in its normal form. Powerful, formative, it shapes the very meaning of science. But before concluding, I want to put before you an apparent counterexample; in fact, an example illustrating what can happen to this mythic structure when its fundamental condition of openness is not met. As it happens, perhaps not accidentally, this example is drawn from the very events that served so conspicuously to bolster the authority of science in our own time, and, more specifically, to bolster the authority of physics at just the time when molecular biology was coming into existence.

Many people have written about the severe problems that the demands of military secrecy posed for the physicists of the Manhattan Project. The very nature of their enterprise, Oppenheimer claimed, demanded the free and open exchange of ideas and information—free and open amongst the physicists themselves, that is. Oppenheimer won enough concessions from General Groves to permit the physicists to proceed, but the larger demand for secrecy was, of course, never relaxed. The making of the bomb was perhaps the biggest and best-kept secret that science has ever harbored. It was a secret kept from the Germans and the Japanese, from the American public, and indeed from the wives of the very men who produced the bomb. Several of the Los Alamos wives have remarked that Alamogordo was the first they knew of what their husbands were doing, and indeed of what their entire community—a community fully dependent on intimacy and mutual dependency for its survival—was working toward.

The Manhattan Project was a project in which the most privileged secret belonged not to the women but to the men. It was a scientific venture predicated not on openness but on its opposite, on absolute secrecy. Hardly an open book that anyone could read, Los Alamos had an interior. And what was produced out of this interiority was (shall we say, with pregnant irony?) "Oppenheimer's baby." As Brian Easlea has amply documented, the metaphor of pregnancy and birth in fact became the prevailing metaphor surrounding the production and the testing of first the atomic bomb and later the hydrogen bomb.[18] It was used not only as a precautionary code but as a mode of description that was fully embraced by the physicists at Los Alamos, by the government, and ultimately by the public at large.

As early as December 1942, physicists at Chicago received acknowledgment for their work on plutonium with a telegram from Ernest Lawrence that read, "Congratulations to the parents. Can hardly wait to see the new arrival."[19] In point of fact, they had to wait another two and a half years. Finally, in July 1945, Richard Feynman was summoned back to Los Alamos with a wire announcing the day on which the birth of the "baby" was expected. Robert Oppenheimer may have been the father of the A-bomb, but Kistiakowsky tells us that "the bomb, after all, was the baby of the Laboratory, and there was little the Security Office could do to dampen parental interests."[20]

Two days after the Alamogordo test, Secretary of War Henry Stimpson received a cable in Potsdam which read:

> Doctor has just returned most enthusiastic and confident that the little boy is as husky as his big brother. The light in his eyes discernible from here to Highhold and I could have heard his screams from here to my farm.[21]

And, as the whole world was to learn just three weeks later, the "little boy" was indeed as husky as his brother.

In this inversion of the traditional metaphor, this veritable backfiring, more monstrous in its reality than any fantasies of anal birth explored by psychoanalysts, nature's veil is rent, maternal procreativity is effectively coopted, but the secret of life has become the secret of death. When the bomb exploded, Oppenheimer was reminded of the lines from the Bhagavad-Gita: If the radiance of a thousand suns / were to burst into the sky, / that would be like / the splendor of the Mighty One. / But as the cloud rose up in the distance, he also recalled, I am become Death, the shatterer of worlds.[22]

It is perhaps not surprising if, after that, some physicists sought to retreat to the safer ground of biology. Here they could reassert a more traditional quest, now (merely!) the secret of life. But in this turn, or return, they brought with them a new authority, grounded in a vastly more terrible prowess.

[1993]

NOTES

1. Evelyn Fox Keller, "Feminism and Science," *Signs: Journal of Women in Culture and Society* 7, no. 3 (1982): 589–602; and *Reflections on Gender and Science* (New Haven: Yale University Press, 1985). For other work dedicated to the same venture, see Brian Easlea, *Science and Sexual Oppression* (London: Weidenfeld and Nicolson, 1981); Elizabeth Fee, "Is Feminism a Threat to Scientific Objectivity?" *International Journal of Women's Studies* 4 (1981): 378–92; Sandra Harding, "Is Gender a Variable in Conceptions of Rationality?" *Dialectica* 36, no. 2–3 (1982): 225–42; Carolyn Merchant, *The Death of Nature* (San Francisco: Harper and Row, 1980); Hilary Rose, "Hand, Brain, and Heart: A Feminist Epistemology for the Natural Sciences," *Signs* 9, no. 1 (1983): 73–90.
2. For an excellent review of this subject, see Ruth Bleier, *Science and Gender* (New York: Pergamon, 1984).
3. See Keller, *Reflections*, chaps. 1, 2, and 3.
4. Christine Froula, "When Eve Reads Milton: Undoing the Canonical Economy," *Critical Inquiry* 10 (December 1983): 321–47.
5. Sigmund Freud, *Moses and Monotheism*, trans. Katherine Jones (New York, 1967), pp. 145–6, quoted by Froula, p. 133.
6. Richard Feynman, "Los Alamos from Below," *Engineering and Science* 39, no. 2 (1976):19.
7. See Niels Bohr, "Light and Life," in *Atomic Physics and Human Knowledge* (New York: John Wiley and Sons, 1958).
8. *Ibid.*, p. 9.

9. Letter from Crick to Olby, in Robert Olby, "Francis Crick, DNA, and the Central Dogma," *Daedalus* (Fall 1970), pp. 938–87.

10. Donald Fleming, "Emigré Physicists and the Biological Revolution," *Perspectives in American History*, vol. 2 (Cambridge, Mass.: Harvard University Press, 1960), p. 155.

11. *Ibid.*, p. 161.

12. Max Delbruck, "A Physicist's Renewed Look at Biology: Twenty Years Later," *Science* 168 (1970): 1312.

13. Erwin Chargaff, *Heraclitean Fire* (New York: Rockefeller University Press, 1978), p. 103.

14. Quoted in Horace Freeland Judson, *The Eighth Day of Creation* (New York: Simon and Schuster, 1979), p. 216.

15. See Evelyn Fox Keller, *A Feeling for the Organism: The Life and Work of Barbara McClintock* (New York: W. H. Freeman, 1983).

16. Chargaff, *Heraclitean Fire*, p. 109.

17. See, e.g., Keller, *A Feeling*.

18. Brian Easlea, *Fathering the Unthinkable: Masculinity, Scientists, and the Nuclear Arms Race* (London: Pluto Press, 1983).

19. *Ibid.*, p. 107.

20. *Ibid.*, p. 203.

21. *Ibid.*, p. 90.

22. Robert Jungk, *Brighter Than a Thousand Suns* (New York: Grove Press, 1958), p. 201.

 85

Speaking From the Margin: Uninvited Discourse on Sexuality and Power

EMMA PÉREZ

Don't remain within the psychoanalytic closure. Take a look, then cut through.
　　　　　—Hélène Cixous, "The Laugh of the Medusa"

My socialist-feminist position has pushed me toward a psychoanalytic end, if only momentarily. When I was a budding graduate student in Chicana/o history and women's history, I tried stubbornly to show that a class-based movement subsumed gender. While Chicano scholars argue that race must be integrated into a class-based revolution, many Chicana scholars defend the premise that the secondary status given to women's issues in a race- and class-based revolution cheats the revolution.

The "unhappy marriage" between Marxism and feminism, however, remains the chosen marriage,

because the alternative for feminists is capitalism—a deadly, destructive husband.[1] As socialist feminists, we opt for the man who, as our mothers point out, "sí toma hija, pero no te golpea" (yes, he drinks, but he doesn't batter you). He is far from perfect, but we tenaciously hitch ourselves to the man we are desperate to change in order to improve the marriage. This "husband" has potential if he abandons the ego-driven anxiety that defines his world on his terms. With him, at least, there is a potential for equality and freedom. With the capitalist, we are battered, raped, and left to die in factories, fields, bedrooms, and boardrooms. The Marxist tells us that "women are oppressed," as he gathers with his male cohorts, then yells to you, "Oye corazón, are you finished typing my manuscript?" Lip service is worth something, whether it's in the boardroom or the bedroom, but it is not a revolution.

I want to take us beyond the antiquated Marxist-feminist debate, assuming we agree that class struggle is unavoidable and that race/gender analysis and sexual autonomy must be the vanguard of a victorious revolution. The question is: How are we going to achieve such a revolution given the strength and persistence of the patriarchy—a political, social, and economic system that has bound women historically to an inferior status? I analyze the patriarchy by invoking Freud, Jacques Lacan, and Michel Foucault, if only briefly, in terms of the French feminist analysis of Luce Irigaray, which deconstructs male-centered psychoanalysis. Admittedly, deconstructing white European feminism in order to reconstruct Chicana feminism is inorganic, but no more so than taking from Marx—the quintessential white, middle-class, German man—to explain the exploitation of a Chicana in the cotton fields of Texas. Consciousness—whether of race, class, gender, or sexuality—is born from one's intimate awareness of one's oppression. Theoretical models provide shortcuts to dissect exploitation. Just as Marx provided a general paradigm for grasping the relationship between worker and capitalist, I claim that Luce Irigaray suggests models that interpret social and sexual relationships and hierarchical structures between and among heterosexuals, lesbians, and gay men beyond the borders of France.

But where do culture, race, and colonization fit into these paradigms? Marx's theories on colonization were ethnocentric and male-centered; and Freud, Lacan, and Irigaray do not even mention colonization and its consequences for people of color. I hope to raise questions about how sexuality is expressed for colonized people, especially women. How do we, as women of color, analyze the intersection of sexism with racism in order to deconstruct the pervasive ideology based on them? How do we liberate ourselves from the sexism, heterosexism, and homophobia in our Chicano community while we combat the insipid racism in Anglo society, given that men of color experience racial oppression and displace their frustration onto women of color? I cannot answer these rhetorical questions, but I articulate them in order to acknowledge the complexities we face as women of color and to place the argument back upon sexuality, because sexuality remains an obscure controversy in our Chicana/o academic community.

As a historian trained in the Western European tradition, I ardently question white male ideology and white women's assumptions about women of color. Hence, I turn to European feminists with ambivalence and criticism. Theirs is not my language or my history, imbued as theirs is with conquest and colonization. Indeed, Europeans acted their history as conquerors and colonizers. French feminist discourse deconstructs white male language; but one of the pitfalls of deconstruction is that the method builds upon what it calls into question.[2] These feminists argue for women's method and culture yet ignore racial memory. Some, however, rebel against that which I as a Chicana historical materialist also resist—the male symbolic order. The way the French school dismembers male dominion is what intrigues me. By scrutinizing their offerings, I attempt to supplement an analysis for Chicanas that chiefly summons sexuality and embraces sexuality's relationship to race, class, and gender within our culture.

EXALTING MALE BEHAVIOR: FREUD, LACAN, AND FOUCAULT

Men must cease to be theoretical imbeciles.
        Marguerite Duras, in *New French Feminisms*

To address sexuality, discourse, and power, I digress briefly to Freud, Lucan, and Foucault, the male theoreticians who, I believe, best define, classify, and—whether deliberately or not—exalt male behavior.[3] But where women are concerned, these men deserve to be labeled "theoretical imbeciles."

Let me begin with Freud, the omnipotent father. The Oedipal moment is basic to his discourse: the moment when a boy realizes he cannot have his first love object, his mother, because she belongs to his powerful father. His fear of this man, whose penis looms larger than his, increases when he realizes that his mother does not have one at all and that he, too, could lack one. Hence, castration anxiety is linked to a dread of women. Although the son repudiates the mother and allies himself with the father because they both have penises, he still competes with this powerful figure, spending his life proving that his is "bigger" and "more powerful" than any symbolic father's.[4]

He also persists in simultaneously renouncing and searching for his mother. In Luce Irigaray's words, "The little boy will never cease to desire his mother."[5] His Oedipus complex is never resolved; therefore, he acts out against women through his fear and anxiety, making a society where the laws, ideas, and customs permit him to reenact the Oedipus complex. All he has to do, he believes, is give up his desire for one woman: "Thus the—fictional—disappearance of the Oedipus complex would resolve itself into the individual's ability to make capital out of ideals and [thereby also] out of mothers, wives-mothers, laws, gazes. . . . Oedipus will have all the mothers he wants, all laws in his favor, and the right to look at anything . . . all, or most, mothers, laws, views (or at any rate points of view). Oedipus will be rich and have no complexes about it. All he has given up is the desire for a woman, for a woman's sex/organ because in any case *that had no value*."[6]

Irigaray links capital to the Oedipus complex. Men must reify their desire for their mothers in rules, laws, and social constructs that deny women their existence. Pornography, which results from a man's "gaze," helps him swear that he no longer suffers from Oedipal anxiety. Women become his idea—castrated, passive, and eternally feminine in his eyes, in his gaze. As long as he can "gaze," as long as his "love of looking is satisfied, his domination is secure."[7]

Lacan employs Freudian theory to explain the "symbolic law of the father" entrenched in language.[8] Language, he argues, is imbued with symbols that dictate patriarchal power. But in his discussion, he, like Freud, dismisses women's subjectivity and exalts the phallus, again because women do not have one.

The French feminists argue that Freud and Lacan place woman "outside the Symbolic," outside language, the law, culture, and society, because she "does not enjoy what orders masculinity—the castration complex."[9] To French feminists, patriarchy is a law of death, of destruction, of violence. Maleness is socially constructed to be competitive, maniacal, and violent—all qualities rooted in the castration complex and evident in war, violence against women and children, the violent conquest of Third World people, rape, battering, sexual molestation, sexual harassment, and nuclear weapons shaped like penises that ejaculate death. Femaleness, on the other hand, is socially constructed to be collective, intuitive, creative, life-affirming—the other. But women who accept the symbolic law of the father perpetuate it and, in essence, are male-identified women denying a bond with women and affirming men's superiority.[10] Even when women accept the law of the father, however, they do not rape, batter, and sexually molest children in the horrendous numbers that men do. The symbolic phallus, the tool of oppression, reified in guns and bombs, reduces men to dangerous imbeciles attesting to their death drive.

Foucault transcribes historical documents to ventilate "the power of discourse." He argues that "through discourse power/knowledge is realized."[11] Language, after all, is power. Third World people know that to learn the colonizer's language gives one access to power and privilege—albeit controlled, qualified power. As a historian, I have explored Foucault's writings because he surveys the history of discourse on sexuality. I read the first volume of *The History of Sexuality* with curiosity but soon discovered that Foucault, like Freud and Lacan, speaks to men, about men, and for men in male language. In a single paragraph, Foucault "thrust," "penetrated," "rigidified," and "extended" power.[12] By the end of the page, I felt violated. The imagery of "seminal" ideas "ejaculated" onto paper made reading painful at first and then comically apparent. Are these male theoreticians so pained with castration anxiety that they must spurt on paper at every opportunity? It is precisely this kind of male writing and language that rapes, numbs, and dismisses female experience at every stage.

Because Foucault limits his study to the history of male discourse, he restricts himself to male-defined arenas, where women are either absent or silenced. When he argues that the discourse changes through the centuries, I am suspicious, because he reveals how men's language about sexuality and power has changed without acknowledging his bias. Like Freud and Lacan, he would have women indulge in patriarchal interpretations, at the expense of women's sanity, to reconfirm male notions of hysteria. As the other, not the subject, women remain objectified in Foucault's discourse.

I am most impatient with Foucault, however, because of what he neglects to say in this volume. In the last chapter, he discusses power and its relationship to sexuality, but he overlooks the obvious. Like male theoreticians who build abstractions to mask the simple, he does not say: men, especially white men from the middle and upper classes, hold political, social, racial, and sexual power over women, but especially women of color, and these men have used that power throughout history to control women and to sustain patriarchal power. *Punto.* Is this premise transhistorical? Is it cross-cultural? Yes and no. Every aberration of sexual abuse against women and children of all races and against men of color has its historical antecedents. This, I believe, is a point of departure for women historians. But Chicana historians must begin with what Foucault neglects to say.

Why can't Foucault declare the obvious? Because he is blinded by his privilege, his male prerogative? Surely it's not that simple. I cannot spurn Foucault so easily. As a historian, I appreciate his historical specificity, because within his constructs he forces me to ask whether patriarchal power is indeed transhistorical and whether the Oedipus complex is transhistorical and transcultural. Is an understanding of the Oedipus complex useful to Chicanas writing our history, which is inextricably enmeshed with conquest and colonization?

"EL CHINGÓN": OCTAVIO PAZ AND THE OEDIPAL-CONQUEST COMPLEX

The worst kind of betrayal lies in making us believe that the Indian woman in us is the betrayer.
                  Gloria Anzaldúa, *Borderlands (La Frontera)*

Perhaps Lacan is for French feminists what Octavio Paz is for Chicanas. Inevitably, we invoke Paz's *Labyrinth of Solitude,* where he unites us metaphorically with La Chingada, or La Malinche.[13] We react, we respond repeatedly to his misogyny. But misogyny alone is not what we contest. We dispute a historically specific moment that denigrates us, immortalizes us as "the betrayer" for all time, eternally stuck in an image, *la puta* (the whore). Long before the arrival of the Virgen de Guadalupe, we were La Chingada. The metaphor cuts to the core of each Chicana; each *mestiza* is flouted as *la india*/whore. Worse yet is that *la india* is our mother, and Paz slashes away at her beauty. He subordinates our first love object by violently raping her in historical text, in male language.

To Paz, the Aztec princess Malintzín, also called Malinche, "gave" herself to Hernán Cortés, the symbol of the Spanish Conquest; therefore, Paz charges her with the downfall of Mexico. In Paz, we have the symbolic son, the *mestizo,* repudiating the symbolic father, Cortés. The Oedipal triangle is completed by *la india,* whom they raped and tamed, literally and metaphorically. Malintzín, the "other," the inferior, disdained female, was not worthy of marrying, so Cortés passed her down to a soldier. With the soldier Jaramaillo, Malinche bore the first *mestizos.* For Paz, *la india* personifies the passive whore who acquiesced to the Spaniard, the conqueror, his symbolic father—the father he despises for choosing an inferior woman who begat an inferior race and the father he fears for his powerful phallus.

Paz's essay reveals more about his own castration complex than about Malinche. Obsessed with *chingar,* he expounds a theory to explain the inferiority complex of *mestizos/as.* But self-hate, the internalized racism with which Paz must contend, emanates from his text. After all, the mighty Cortés was the white Western European male conqueror, the symbol of power that Paz was a step away from, not just as the son but, more important, as the bastard Mex-

icano. Paz exhibits his own internalized racial inferiority. He is far less powerful than his symbolic white father, the conquistador. On the other hand, his hatred of *las chingadas* (women) and all that is female symbolically begins with this Oedipal-conquest triangle. Here the sexual, political, social, and psychological violence against *la india*—the core of the Chicana—is born. This core has been plundered through conquest and colonization. We reclaim the core for our women-tempered *sitios y lenguas* (spaces and languages).

Lacan's symbolic order of "language and meaning"[14] is epitomized in the Oedipal-conquest triangle when the *mestizo* enters the pained moment of castration anxiety; for the *mestizo* male, the entry into the symbolic order is even more confusing, because he does not know the white father's language. He cannot even guess at the meaning of symbols between himself and his conquering/colonizing father. Cultural differences divided *el español y el indio,* who were thrown together at the moment of Spanish Conquest and who misunderstood each other's symbols and language.

Mestizos/as master the conqueror's language as the language of survival, but it never completely belongs to the conquered. People whose language has been swindled twice, first the native tongue, then the appropriated tongue, are forced to stumble over colonizer language. As an adult, the Chicano male is perceived as the powerless son of the white Oedipal father who makes laws in his language. An African-American man called "boy" by white men and women is reduced to this symbolic son, but African-American history of conquest and enslavement is unlike ours, and I am in no position to conjecture about this similarity. In a racist society, the *mestizo* male is a castrated man in relation to the white male colonizer-father. His anxiety encompasses not only the fear of castration but also the fear that his power will never match the supreme power of the white man. Whereas the white son has the promise of becoming the father, the *mestizo,* even when he becomes the father, is set apart by his skin color and by a lack of language, the dominant language of the colonizer. Moreover, he must repudiate *la india y la mestiza* for fear that he also could be a weak, castrated betrayer of his people. He colludes with the white colonizer-father as they both condemn the Chicana.

The Oedipal-conquest triangle dictates the sexual politics of miscegenation in the twentieth century. Although Chicanos are usually incensed when Chicanas marry the "enemy," white men, they exercise male prerogative by marrying white women to both defy and collaborate with the white father. In having half-white children, they move their sons a step closer to the nexus of power—the white colonizer-father. The Chicana who marries a white male, by contrast, embraces the white Oedipal-colonizer ambivalently, because—although theoretically she gains access to power—realistically she is still perceived as *la india* by a white dominant culture that disapproves of miscegenation. She is not her half-white children, nor will she ever be; her half-white sons will always have more social, political, and sexual power than she could imagine. (Certainly, the same principle applies to the Chicano with a white wife, but his male privilege has already granted him rank that a Chicana cannot earn.) The daughter of a white male and a Chicana has the father's white name to carry her through racist institutions, placing her closer to power relations in society.

Paz's phallocratic discourse reflects the Oedipal-conquest triangle, which symbolizes social-sexual-racial relations between Chicanos and Chicanas and among the white women and white men who oversee the dilemma. It is a metaphor that dictates social-sexual-racial relations. That the Oedipal moment is historically or culturally inaccurate is not the issue. The point is that it is a symbol unconsciously perceived by Paz, who imposed the psychodrama of conquest upon the Chicano, who in turn inflicts misogyny in the image of La Malinche upon Chicanas/Mexicanas. Paz cannot be held responsible for the conquest; he merely interprets history from a masculinist ideology.

The law of the white colonizer-father conditions our world in the late twentieth century. Our challenge is to rebel against the symbol of the white father and affirm our separation from the destructive ideology to create life-affirming *sitios*. But before defying the law of the father, we must understand why we are so struck and so addicted to the perpetrator of destruction. Why do we uphold the law of the white European colonizer-father when we know the extent of damage and pain for Chicanas and Chicanos? Chicanos who absorb the white colonizer-father's ways hierarchically impose them on Chicanas, becoming caricatures of the white colonizer-father. One has only to look at any institution where Chicanos have been integrated to see how they emulate the white father to exclude women, especially women of color.

BREAKING THE ADDICTIVE/DEPENDENT CYCLE OF POWER

He has no desire for woman to upset him in his sexual habits . . . his rather suspect respect for law and order. He does not want her to be anything but his daughter, whose gratifying fantasies of seduction it is his task to interpret, and who must be initiated into, and curbed by, the "reasonable" discourse of his [sexual] law. Or else he wants her to be his mother, whose erotic reveries he would finally gain access to. Unless again some very "unconscious" homosexual transference is tied in there, sotto voce.
—Luce Irigaray, *Speculum of the Other Woman*

In his theater production *Corridos*, Luis Valdez reenacts a provocative *corrido* about father-daughter incest.[15] Both Valdez's choice and his presentation of the *corrido* intrigue me. He seems titillated by and almost condones the arrangement. Valdez's "Delgadina" provides insight into the patriarchy, revealing the dynamic between perpetrators and victims who create an addictive cycle of dependence between the powerful and the powerless.[16] Like the preceding works by male centralist theorists, the production exposes Valdez's castration anxiety through his "gaze," his male definition and interpretation of what is feminine.

I use the *corrido* to critique Freud's "Electra complex," the inverse of the Oedipus complex. Freud hypothesized the Electra complex to explain a daughter's recognition that she cannot have her father. But he cannot establish just how a daughter transfers desire for her mother as her first love object to the father, so that she can embrace heterosexuality. I believe, like many feminists, that he invokes patriarchal law to put an end to the daughter's wavering transference, thereby rationalizing his own desire for the daughter to transfer her desire from the mother to the father.

Patriarchal law dictates the tacit language and behavior of incest, which place fear in the daughter's psyche. At some point, she unconsciously recognizes the supreme phallus's potential to harm her psyche. Freud does not speculate that the remotest possibility of incest victimizes the daughter. According to Freud, the questions to ask about a daughter are: Does she repudiate her mother to embrace the father and to be impregnated by him, producing a baby as a substitute for the penis she was not born with? Does she turn to the father to embrace "normal" femininity? Freud, however, refuses to ask whether the daughter can remain attached to her first love object, her mother. If so, the questions change: Wouldn't a daughter's attachment to her mother lead to a woman-loving culture? Or to lesbianism? Wouldn't the mother-daughter relationship press heterosexual women to examine their bisexual ambivalence—their occasional desire for women even while gripping the law of the father?[17]

The "Delgadina" *corrido* represents a daughter's painful entrance into the law of the father. The first part of her name—*De,* meaning "belonging to," "a man's possession"—is worth noting.

Briefly, the *corrido* tells the story of a beautiful young woman whose father watches her dance by moonlight, craves her, and then decides to pounce. As they walk home from church one day, he commands her to be his lover. When she refuses, he jails her in a tower (phallic), waiting for her to succumb. While in the tower, she is denied food and water as punishment for disobeying her father. She begs her mother, her brother, and her sister for food, water, and release. Each one fears violating the father's orders, his sexual laws; so each ostracizes Delgadina. Her mother and her sister, who are "an integral part of a phallic masculine economy," betray her.[18] And yet, what is their alternative? For women need a moment, a specific moment of consciousness, when they can separate from the law of the father into their own space and language. Delgadina has nowhere to turn and eventually dies from hunger for nourishment, for freedom. Her father, a broken

man, is left with the memory of never having consummated sex with the young, alluring love object—his daughter.

Unlike La Malinche, Delgadina does not succumb. Indeed, she dies a virgin. A patriarchal society betrays her by blinding itself and keeping a secret in disbelief that the father could rape his daughter or desire to rape her. But behavior and language are basic to sexual molestation. A sign, a word, a gesture can be as damaging as penetration by the penis. But patriarchal laws ignore behavior and language in cases of molestation. According to these male-defined laws, the penis must penetrate; otherwise, these laws will not consider that harm was done. For Delgadina, a patriarch's peremptory laws penetrate "only" her psyche.

Valdez chose to tell us this story to peer into the "secret" of a father's sexual arousal by his daughter. This is voyeurism, the male gaze asserted. Like Hollywood's pornographic filmmakers, Valdez eroticizes women's victimization to appeal to his male audience. All this is not beside the point. To eroticize the father-daughter incestuous relationship implicitly grants permission to older men who seek young women as lovers and marriage partners. The relationship asserts male sexual power over a younger woman who could very likely be a daughter. Patriarchal society condones the older man–young woman relationship; in fact, it envies the man who successfully catches a young woman. Such a woman, after all, gives complete adoration—at first. Indeed, there are historical roots to arrangements between older men and younger women. In colonial California, the Catholic church and the Spanish-Mexican settlers colluded when the church condoned marriages between older men and young women, often nieces, to keep property within the family. Older Spanish-Mexican soldiers also married young women to be assured that the women were virgins.[19]

But there is another implicit message in the *corrido.* That is, although the *corrido* warns against incest, it also communicates the danger to a young woman when she challenges the sexual law of the father. She cannot break that law, happy and free to join women who believe her or a community who will allow her to be herself. There is no such community. Instead, a male-centered society with male-identified women cannot even hear her language, her pain. They only know that they cannot defy the father.

But Delgadina does not have an opportunity to resist her father, because—even before he commands her to be his lover—he has already employed incestuous language and behavior. The "molestation" parodied in his behavior creates her "memory of molestation," which by social definition has not taken place because physical touch and penetration by the penis never occur. But in her memory, it did take place. The behavior, inappropriate for a father, to say the least, is not confronted by her mother, her sister, or her brother. Not by anyone.

The addictive/dependent cycle has begun for both of them. When she tries to break from it, however, she finds no support. Like Delgadina, women live in a cycle of addiction/dependency to the patriarchy that has ruled them since the precise historical moment in which they became aware that women's bodies are sexually desired and/or overpowered by the penis. A young girl fears its power and tries to tame it, manipulate it, adore it, loathe it, or ignore it. She may feel any variety of emotions toward the tool of oppression, but envy is not one of them. Why should she envy that which symbolically destroys?

This reminder, this memory of molestation, a memory of origin, haunts the young girl through womanhood. Indeed, the memories of sexual molestation dictate sexual desire. Either women repudiate the molester/perpetrator or they embrace him. This pattern persists throughout their relationships until the addictive/dependent cycle is broken. Not until victims resist perpetrators and have the courage to abandon the pattern, not until women and men stop assigning the perpetrators power, can women and men abandon phallocratic law and order.

When will those of us making a revolution expunge the capitalist patriarchal tradition of sexual law and order that dictates the perpetrator-victim dynamic? When will we embrace the real, yet ideal, beliefs of the collective, to work together for the common good? Within capitalist patriarchal ideology, the sensitive human being who is willing to transform the world is disregarded; Marxist patriarchs are also guilty. Our personal revolutions—

each member of the collective taking responsibility for her/his contradictions within the collective—are belittled in our movements. Are we willing to grapple with questions like "Am I exploiting anyone, and if I am, how can I change?" If we do not challenge our own contradictions, then we only pretend to make a revolution.

Both women and men are addicted to that which destroys them—the patriarchy within capitalist constructs in the late twentieth century. The social-sexual-racial relations between men and women condoned by the patriarchy are inherently unhealthy and destructive most of the time. The dynamic begins, I argue, in the collective memories of Western European conquerors and people of color, who are subdued by the memory of the Oedipal-conquest triangle.

How do we achieve a successful revolution/movement given the strength and persistence of the patriarchy? In one respect, the answer lies in rejecting the addictive pattern. We begin by shedding internalized sexist, homophobic, elitist, and racist behaviors. We change destructive patterns today, immediately, with the hope of raising children and teaching students who do not have to appropriate society's addictive capitalist patriarchal discourse to survive. The individual is responsible to the collective, after all. When one heals oneself within the collective, the collective is healed. But that is only one small integral step. There is much more to do.

[1993]

NOTES

1. See "The Unhappy Marriage of Marxism and Feminism: Towards a More Progressive Union," in *Women and Revolution,* ed. Lydia Sargent (Boston: South End Press, 1981), pp. 2–41.
2. G. C. Spivak quotes Jacques Derrida, "The enterprise of deconstruction always in a certain way falls prey to its own work" (see Spivak, "Feminism and Deconstruction, Again," in *Between Feminism and Psychoanalysis,* ed. Teresa Brennan [New York: Routledge, 1989], p. 213).
3. I use the definition of discourse put forth by the editors Elaine Marks and Isabelle de Courtivron in *New French Feminisms* (Amherst: University of Massachusetts Press, 1980), p. 3.
4. This is gross oversimplification, but it suits my needs. For Freud's own words, see Sigmund Freud, *Sexuality and the Psychology of Love,* ed. Philip Rieff (New York: Macmillan, 1963), pp. 176–182.
5. Luce Irigaray, *Speculum of the Other Woman,* trans. Gillian G. Gill (Ithaca, N.Y.: Cornell University Press, 1985), p. 81.

6. Ibid.

7. [S]ee Toril Moi, *Sexual/Textual Politics* (New York: Routledge, 1985), p. 134. Also see Irigaray, *Speculum*, p. 47.

8. Jacques Lacan, *Écrits: A Selection*, trans. Alan Sheridan (New York: Norton, 1977).

9. Hélène Cixous, "Castration or Decapitation?" *Signs* 7, no. 1 (Autumn 1981): 46.

10. Xaviere Gauthier, "Is There Such a Thing as Women's Writing?" in *New French Feminisms*, p. 162.

11. Jeffrey Weeks, *Sex, Politics and Society: The Regulation of Sexuality since 1800* (London: Longman, 1981), p. 7.

12. Michel Foucault, *The History of Sexuality*, vol. 1: *An Introduction*, trans. Robert Hurley (New York: Pantheon Books, 1978), p. 48.

13. Octavio Paz, *The Labyrinth of Solitude*, trans. Lysander Kemp (New York: Grove Press, 1961), pp. 65–88.

14. On Lacan, see Weeks, *Sex, Politics and Society*, pp. 3–4.

15. For more on Valdez, see Yolanda Broyles-González, "What Price Mainstream? Luis Valdez's *Corridos* on Stage and Film," *Cultural Studies* 4, no. 3 (October 1990): 281–293.

16. I am indebted to Helen Bauer, executive director of the Ephpheta Counseling Center in Ontario, California, for her ideas about the addiction/dependency cycle. I developed my analysis of the cycle's relationship to the patriarchy from her concept.

17. Irigaray, *Speculum*, p. 72. She discusses "the girl's turning to the father" to embrace "normal" femininity and "renounce phallic activity."

18. Antoinette Fouque, in *New French Feminisms*, p. 117.

19. Castañeda, "Presidarias y Pobladoras," chap. 5.

 86

Femmenism

JEANNINE DELOMBARD

Waves—which, by definition, curve alternately in opposite directions—embody contradiction. For me femmenism is where the third wave of Western feminism and the third wave of American lesbianism intersect. Femmenism is the riptide that drags nature and nurture, essentialism and constructivism, and all other binary oppositions out to sea. Femmenism is nothing if not contradictory. Femmenism is looking like a straight woman and living like a dyke. Femmenism is being attracted to someone of the same sex who is very much your opposite. Femmenism is calling yourself a girly-girl and insisting that others call you a woman. Femmenism is playing up your femininity even when you know it can and will be used against you. Femmenism is using the master's tools to dismantle the master's house. Femmenism is political but not correct.

MEMOIRS OF AN OUT-OF-SYNC GIRLHOOD

I can still remember the day I learned what the word *lesbian* meant. I was in the third grade and had just kissed my best friend Erica on the lips. Suddenly everyone in my homeroom was screaming "Eeee-yew! Lezzies!" and making gagging noises. I didn't know what "lezzy" meant, but I could tell it wasn't good. When I discovered later that "lezzy" was short for "lesbian" and what *that* meant, I was more confused than ever. Despite the ugly way I learned it, I thought "lesbian" was the most beautiful word I had ever heard. Not even the image it conjured up, just the sound the vowels and the consonants made together. And when I did consider its meaning, I thought the word even more beautiful. For me, as a child, beautiful meant feminine, and what could be more feminine than two women making love?

The irony, of course, is that I was thinking all this in 1975, when the second wave of feminism was cresting, and many women (especially lesbians) were challenging traditional notions of femininity. Although she was no feminist activist, my mother considered herself a liberated woman and, looking back, I realize I must have driven her slightly crazy with my girliness. Not only did I embrace all things feminine, but I hated everything that I perceived as tainted with masculinity. I would only wear pants under duress and absolutely refused to wear jeans under any circumstances, although my mother and almost every other woman I knew wore them every day. Needless to say, I hated boys, and I hated it even more when some friend of my parents would chuckle knowingly and say that *that* would change soon enough.

I clearly recall the battles my mother and I would have over "appropriate" clothing and toys. I wanted to wear pouffy pastel party dresses and Mary Janes every day of the week; she bought me corduroys and hiking boots. I routinely begged for—and was just as routinely denied—what I saw as the staples of girlhood: Barbies, a nurse kit, and Tinker Bell play makeup. Instead, I received entire clans of politically correct dolls (the Sunshine Family was white and the Happy Family was black, but their hair and facial features were the same). Even my literary heroes were wrong. I aspired to be just like clever, stylish Nancy Drew, whom my mother dismissed as prissy and dependent; she thought Laura Ingalls, the boisterous tomboy from the "Little House on the Prairie" TV series, a much better role model.

I grew up in a home where gender roles were anything but strict, and breaking out of them was strictly encouraged. Fresh out of the hospital, my mother, attempting to diaper a very small, squirmy baby with a very large, pointy diaper pin, passed out cold. My father, the oldest of seven children, finished the job neatly. I know this story not because it is a rare example of active parenting on my father's part, but because it illustrates how labor was divided in our household—on the basis of ability as much as gender. It was my father who stayed home with me (he was a student at the time) while my mother went off to work as a teacher in the local elementary school. (Later, when my father also began to work out of the home, a photograph of Divine—in her trademark teal blue eyeshadow and body-hugging tulle dress—always hung above his desk.)

By a strange twist of sociocultural fate, my mother and I were in a similar situation: both of us would have gotten much of what we wanted as children if we only had been born boys. In the fifties, my mother's affinity for masculine clothing and activities was considered unnatural: in the seventies, my desire for ultra-feminine toys and accessories was perceived much the same way. Listening to "William Wants a Doll" on my Free to Be You and Me record, I understood that for a boy to plead for a baby doll was daring and original, while for a girl to do so would be old-fashioned and unimaginative. I have no doubt that, had I been born a boy, my parents would have tried to interest me in tea sets and Betty Crocker ovens in an effort to steer me away from G.I. Joes and Hot Wheels. Dominated by a new kind of double standard, my childhood taught me that avoiding gender roles can be every bit as frustrating, limiting, and ridiculous as adhering to them.

DROWNING IN THE SECOND WAVE

I came out in 1985, when I was a freshman at Vassar and political correctness was sweeping American campuses. Three years earlier at a Barnard women's

studies conference, sex activists like Joan Nestle, Pat Califia, and Amber Hollibaugh had battled it out with hard-line feminists opposed to pornography, S/M, and butch-femme. These pivotal "lesbian sex wars" marked an end to old-style lesbian feminism with all its rigidity and uniformity, ushering in an era of sexual experimentation, diversity, and inclusiveness. Located just two hours up the Hudson from Barnard, Vassar's lesbian community remained blissfully unaware of these changes, thus avoiding the difficult challenges the conflict would have posed to our identities, our politics, and, last but most assuredly not least, our sex.

At Vassar and, I suspect, other college campuses of the time, the political often superseded the personal. For many of us, coming out didn't mean sleeping with a woman or even having a crush on one; it meant walking that longest mile every Thursday evening to the Gold Parlor, where LFL (the Lesbian Feminist League) met.

LFL is where I first heard about butch-femme— as an antiquated relic from the dark ages of lesbian herstory. While LFL's facilitator admitted that some poor misguided souls still engaged in such "role playing," the message was that butch-femme would soon be a thing of the past and not a minute too soon. When the topic came up again a couple years later, one woman, a histrionic British exchange student, told (complete with tears and supportive back-rubbing) of her traumatic experience as a femme— a cautionary tale for those of us tempted to enter into such an oppressive relationship.

Not that our own politically correct unions were particularly liberating. Like most other LFLers, I was in "a long-term, committed monogamous relationship" with a woman whom I resembled in thought, action, and dress. We shared our clothing (oversized men's shirts, bulky knee-length Greek fisherman's sweaters, and baggy Indonesian pants) and our politics (protesting the KKK in Philly, celebrating gay pride in New York, and marching for choice in D.C.). We even went to therapy together. Monogamy was no problem for me; having been date-raped at the age of fourteen by a man at least twice my age and cowed into sexual intercourse by numerous other males since, I approached *all* sex with more than a little trepidation. Our intimate, passionless relationship seemed to confirm the

"Dear Abby" stereotype that women prefer snuggling to sex.

I had come to college with all my junior femme accessories in tow: trunks of kitschy 1950s prom dresses; countless fishnet stockings; black velvet pumps with four-inch heels; and, for everyday wear, skin-tight mini-skirts in a variety of colors. But after a year at Vassar, I was being chased out of women's rest rooms because with my buzzed hair, ripped jeans, leather jacket, clunky black shoes, and six-foot frame I looked like a man. By the time I graduated, I had not only entirely new political convictions (and a wardrobe to match), but a severe eating disorder and impenetrable (so to speak) sexual anxieties.

Looking back on all this now, I can't help but think that, for many of us, certain aspects of lesbian feminism were *enabling* (to use a term popular in the twelve-stepping eighties) rather that *empowering* (to use another). While even an ardent femmenist like myself is hesitant to add to the already considerable amount of time, energy, and paper that has been spent debating lesbians' sartorial preferences, I think it's worth pointing out that the standard dyke or lesbian feminist uniform—baggy, rumpled clothes, Birkenstocks, no makeup, unstyled hair— may have contributed to the negative body images many of us had (and may still have).

Studiously indifferent to our appearance, swaddled in loose, drab clothing, we were not androgynous, just asexual. For me, and, I suspect, for numerous others, the dyke aesthetic was economically as well as politically expedient: with a few minor adjustments, the same outfit could camouflage my body as it passed from anorexic scrawniness to bulimic bloat and back again.

Outwardly proud of our bravery and daring as lovers of women, we concealed our awkward bodies and unspoken anxieties under yards of fabric. Choosing not to wear makeup or "do" our hair not only articulated our rejection of patriarchal notions of femininity, but saved us from having to face ourselves in the mirror every day.

RENAISSANCE WOMAN

Two years after leaving college, in my second year of graduate school, I carried on a long-distance affair with a bartender I had met when I finally got up the nerve to go alone to Hepburn's, Philadelphia's only women's bar. Our relationship was a homecoming for me in many ways. This woman introduced me to a gay demimonde of drag queens, moving parties, leather bars, and after-hours clubs. In this new, glamorous, and sexually charged environment, I felt suddenly free—free to shed the formerly de rigueur, frumpy dyke uniform and don the slinky Spandex mini-dresses I'd been longing to wear. To my delight, this woman and her gay male friends not only refrained from doing an in-depth political analysis of my internalized heterosexism, but actually rewarded me by treating me like the prom queen I'd always dreamed of being. Finally, I felt like I had found the real me. I had come out years before as a lesbian, but I didn't really come to terms with my sexuality until I came out as a femme.

Apparently, I'm not alone. As Karen Everett and historian Lillian Faderman have pointed out, the lesbian community is in the throes of a butch-femme renaissance. And as it turns out, I am a typical renaissance woman: a middle-class academic. But it's more than my class status and bookishness that set me apart from my pre-Stonewall predecessors, who were predominantly working-class bar dykes. On the one hand, I have benefited—often in ways I am not even aware of—from more than two decades of feminism and gay rights activism.

On the other hand, however, I feel a little like a freak in my own community, renaissance or not. During American lesbianism's first wave, young or newly out lesbians could count on being initiated into the mysteries of butch-femme courtship, dress, manners, and sex by a more experienced mentor. Today, although I know a lot of women I would describe as butch, and countless "lipstick lesbians," I know of only one self-identified butch-femme couple. (And the last time I saw them, the butch hit on me and the femme gave me laundry tips.) As a rule, my lesbian friends' response to butch-femme ranges from polite dismissal to scornful ridicule. To them, butch-femme is a label, it's role playing, and they want no part of it.

Not that I can blame them. Anyone who's had a pleasant walk with her lover spoiled by some jerk yelling, "Which one of you is the man?" knows the frustration of having one's lesbianism taken for a cheap imitation of heterosexuality. Likewise, anyone who's been called "sir," or worse yet, "little boy," simply because she has short hair, a flat chest, or unpierced ears knows how alienating *that* can be. But butch-femme is not about aping traditional notions of masculinity and femininity any more than it is about mimicking heterosexuality.

Nor has it ever been. From the late 1930s to the early 1960s, bar dykes implicitly understood butch and femme as two distinct lesbian-specific genders. Then, as now, you'll occasionally hear butch women jokingly call their evenings together "boys' night out." But unlike gay male culture, where drag queens and gay men often refer to each other as "she," both butches and femmes use the female pronoun when speaking of themselves and other lesbians.

I remember a conversation I had a couple of years ago with a friend who had just come back from a lesbian cruise. She said that you had to identify as either butch or femme to participate in the on-deck games. She refused to play at all and was angry because, as she put it, "I didn't pay $7,000 to have someone tell me I have to choose between butch and fuckin' femme." Although I am no more anxious than the next dyke to return to the days when butch and femme were the only options open to lesbians, I do wish that they could be accepted as two legitimate choices among many.

A year ago I expressed this wish in a review of Joan Nestle's groundbreaking anthology, *The Persistent Desire: A Femme-Butch Reader.* About a month later a woman wrote a letter to the editor of the alternative newspaper in which the review appeared, calling my article "dangerous" and accusing me of "proudly broadcasting restrictive, insulting, and oversimplified terms for behavior (Butch & Femme) without including some of the subtle intricacies, the complexities that truly make up a [lesbian] relationship." Ironically, the point I was trying to make in that essay is that butch-femme is nothing if not intricate, subtle, and highly complex, despite the fact that it is often oversimplified as a monolithic set of prescribed, restrictive behaviors by straight people and lesbians alike.

If lesbians see butch-femme as a capitulation to heterosexual norms, most of the straight world believes that butch-femme lurks at the core of *every* lesbian relationship, while the rest see it as a kinky, exotic sex game, better left in the bedroom closet along with the strap-on dildo, the handcuffs, and the edible underwear. Like pornography, everyone has an opinion about butch-femme, but no one seems very clear about what exactly it is.

My lover and I are no exception to the rule. Although we laughingly refer to *The Persistent Desire* as "the manual," we both have the sense that we are making up what it means to be butch and femme as we go along.

For me, being a femme means that I take pride in wearing just the right shade of lipstick, drawing the perfect black line above my eyelashes, keeping my legs smooth, and smelling good. Being a femmenist means knowing I am just as attractive when I don't wear makeup, shave, or put on perfume.

Being a femme also means that I want to be with a woman who appreciates it when I do these things—not silently, but openly and enthusiastically. A woman who sends me flowers; helps me out of cars; and knows how to take care of all the details, like choosing the right wine, tipping the bartender, and calling a cab. Being a femmenist means both making sure that I know how to do all these things myself *and* getting an erotic charge of having them done for me.

Being a femme does *not* mean that I would rather be with a man, nor does it mean that I am attracted to masculine women. Unlike most of my friends, I prefer curvy, voluptuous women to buff, hard-bodied ones. But that doesn't mean I want to kiss a lipsticked mouth or caress a stockinged knee. Although I enjoy playing up my own femininity, I like to be with a woman who keeps hers under wraps, a gift for me alone to open and enjoy.

If butch women aren't masculine or even (in lesbian-feminist parlance) male-identified, what are they? To me a butch woman is one who exudes confidence, authority, independence, and a certain sexual cockiness. These may be considered masculine qualities, but I only find them attractive in women.

I remember one night my bartender girlfriend made a call from a pay phone at 3 A.M. Six feet tall, she was wearing heavy work shoes, black jeans, and a bomber jacket, her long blond hair hidden in her wool cap. As she was dialing, she tensed as a tough-looking young man approached, only to relax when he greeted her with, "Evening, officer." The man, making an assumption about her authority, not her gender, was responding to her butchness, not her "masculinity."

The same thing happens when my lover and I go out to dinner: no matter how we are dressed, invariably the server will take my order first, have my girlfriend taste the wine, and present her with the bill (even when I have requested it, credit card in hand).

According to the old dyke saying, there are more butches on the streets than between the sheets, which is just fine with me. What I love most about the woman I have been living with for the past two years is that underneath her crisp, starched shirts, behind her precise, controlled gestures is someone who is not only considerate, gentle, and patient, but beautifully, undeniably female. Far from simplifying our relationship, butch-femme layers it with a tantalizing intricacy and a highly erotic contradictoriness. If my girlfriend and I choose to split up our household chores fairly evenly, the division of labor in our bedroom is more complex. Suffice to say that when the sight of my lover's nude body makes me as hormonal as a thirteen-year-old boy, I feel perfectly free to act like one.

Life as a femme on the streets is seldom as pleasant or as safe as it is between the sheets. On the one hand, being a femme increases exponentially my much-publicized invisibility as a lesbian. Almost every day, and usually several times a day, all sorts of heterosexual men strike up conversations with me, comment on my appearance, or shout lewd remarks at me. Since to them I don't look like a dyke or even a liberated woman, they automatically assume that I look the way I do to provoke male attention and approval. For me, being a femme in public means constantly weighing my personal comfort against my personal safety. On the other hand, my lesbian invisibility is suddenly, dangerously, stripped away when I am with my lover. We found this out the hard way one night on vacation in France, when we were returning to our Left Bank hotel from a bar in the Marais, Paris, gay district. Conscious of the late hour, we resisted the temptation to stroll arm-in-arm or even touch hands. As we were walking in front of Nortre Dame, a man passing in the opposite direction jammed his hand be-

tween my legs and roughly grabbed my crotch. Before I could get any words out, he was walking—not running—away, clearly unafraid of what my lover or myself might do to him.

I am convinced that the man attacked me because my girlfriend and I were so obviously lovers, not just because we were "unaccompanied" women. With that one gesture he challenged my lover's right to my body as much as he violated my right to myself. And it worked. For a few days, whenever my girlfriend touched me, all I could feel was that hand.

As a femme, I know that this kind of attack can and will happen again; as a femmenist, I am both willing to do everything I can to ensure that it doesn't and capable of understanding what's at stake when it does anyway.

RIDING THE THIRD WAVE

For years people gay and otherwise have tried to determine whether sexuality is a product of biology or environment. Like many gay men and lesbians, I realize this is a moot point. Perhaps I would not have become a lesbian had I been born in a different era, culture, or even family, but I certainly would not be who I am without some very—shall we say—basic instincts.

Likewise, my femmenism. Although my early girly tendencies felt very instinctive to me, perhaps I would not have become a femme if my parents and the feminist movement had not pushed me so hard in the opposite direction. Perhaps being a femme is my way of rebelling against my parents; maybe it's just part of the current antifeminist backlash.

But I don't think so. I owe a lot to my first-wave foremothers: the turn of the century cultural feminists who based their politics on their femininity as well as the bar dykes of the forties and fifties who developed butch-femme into an art form. But I owe even more to my second-wave sisters: the feminists of the 1960s and '70s who separated gender from sex and sex from sexuality, and their lesbian counterparts who recognized in their homosexuality a source of pride, not shame.

This, it seems to me, is what femmenism is all about. Unlike my first- and second-wave predecessors, no one force-fed me femininity. Quite the contrary: I had to fight for it tooth and nail. I'm not claiming to have grown up in a vacuum: certainly, feminism or no feminism, there was still a lot of social pressure for me to get with the age-old restrictive feminine program. And I don't doubt that some of my femme identity comes from that pressure. But also unlike my lesbian/feminist predecessors, my female socialization was countered by feminism, a critical apparatus that enabled me, indeed forced me, to question every step I made along the long and winding road of gender-role identification. Having grown up in such an environment, I realize that my femmenism has not only been carefully nurtured, it is also perfectly natural.

This essay is dedicated in loving memory to Emily Polachek.

[1995]

 87

The Unbearable Autonomy of Being

PATRICIA J. WILLIAMS

None of the secrets of success will work unless you do.
  —Fortune cookie received with the author's dinner
  during the 1992 Republican National Convention

One of the least laughable consequences of Dan Quayle's *Murphy Brown* remarks was the breadth of their impact. The vice presidency is, for all the ribbing, among the most powerful offices in the world. The deference given power is notoriously indiscriminate: when the king takes up the fish knife with which to carve his meat, not only do the subjects follow, but they are likely to start a trend. When the smart set takes up fox hunting, foxes have reason to run for their lives. When the vice president of the United States of America took aim at single mothers, then open season was declared.

Living life as the pornographic target of another's fantasies is always a nightmare, even when the fantasy is one of idealized desire—never mind when the fantasy is one of disdainful vilification. Life as a bull's-eye has nothing to do with who you really are, or the statistical realities of the group you represent. The fact that 90 percent of women on welfare have only two children, and that most welfare recipients are white, means nothing to those who indulge in their masturbatory mulling about black welfare queens who purportedly reproduce like rabbits. The fact that AFDC provides virtually no money, never mind incentive, for having additional children on welfare does not alter the common perception that poor women have child after child for the supposed "extra benefits" upon which they will be able to lounge in consummate indolence. The fact that the poor pay proportionally more taxes than anyone else in America does nothing to alter the cynical perceptions of middle- and upper-class policymakers who remain convinced that *they* are the "real" taxpayers upon whose largesse the ungrateful, noncontributory poor feed insatiably. And if Hillary Clinton is an unfit wife and mother, then the black single mother—beyond hope of ever being within the protective grace of "wife," good, bad, or otherwise—becomes presumptively symbolic of she who has just emerged from a simultaneous roll in the hay and a snort at the crackhouse.

I adopted my son exactly one week after Dan Quayle made his *Murphy Brown* speech. My child, in other words, was guided into the world not by the stork or the stars but by the flaring political runway that culminated in the 1992 Republican National Convention. I remember it particularly because family values was the buzzword of the day, and amid all the excitement and joy of the baby's arrival I remained vaguely aware that in some sectors of this nation my use of the word "family" might be seen as purloined. I am so many of the things that many people seemed to think were antifamily—"unwed," "black," "single," everything but "teenage." Add "mother" and it began to sound like a curse. Stand at the mirror and say it to *your*self a few times: I am an (over-the-hill) black single mother.

It bears emphasizing that I am an especially privileged mother—whether single or not. I am a lawyer, pretty well established in my career, and my employer permitted me to take off a few months when the baby arrived. My life is such that I have time enough to sit down and muse about single motherhood in print, and I am well aware of how uncommon a luxury that is.

But what is striking to me is how much social resistance I have encountered despite the tremendous privilege of my shining lawyerly middle-classness. If things are this hard for someone like me who has everything, they have got to be unbearably difficult for women who have much less.

• • •

All this is, again, the description of a very privileged option, but I wonder if it need be so. Increasing numbers of corporations have experimented with on-site daycare facilities with great success and enhanced productivity of workers. It could be cost-efficient and emotionally reassuring for both parents and children. Yet in a rapidly downscaling economy, I fear that such measures are denied to all but a few management-level employees. "A woman's place is in the home," seems to be the solution of choice, as though women's liberation were responsible for the global economy.

During the Great Depression, "spinsters," widows, and single mothers were allowed more of a certain kind of deference—albeit a condescending, pitying deference—as secretaries, as school-teachers—than in today's business world; by contrast, married women (then the overwhelming majority) were ignored, routinely denied jobs so that "men with families" could be employed. In today's recession/depression, in some inverted reiteration of that old formula, it is increasingly "women with families" who have been most severely penalized, for not aligning themselves more economically under the heading of men's dependents.

This shift in public perception of who deserves what slice of dwindling resources has been accompanied and fed by a growing assumption that single mothers ruin their children. It is an interesting notion, since, at least in some of its aspects, it is quite a new one. The Horatio Alger myth, after all, was about captains of industry who came up the hard but noble way, the proud products of struggling widows, urban single mothers. And peaking in the 1930s there was a whole genre of Depression-inspired literature in which single mothers and their resolute sons plowed the fields and wrassled coyotes, milked their bone-dry cows with faith and patience, and told each other stories. Then a miracle would happen and they'd be graced with just the right amounts of rain, hay, and milk.

Somehow the years have eroded this mythology; single mothers, who now bear a greater responsibil-

ity than at any time in our history for raising the children of this society, are demonized as never before. Complex economic forces and social migrations are only part of what has contributed to the fragmentation of civic, political, and extended-family systems, not only in this country but around the world. For all the nostalgia for the nuclear family of the 1950s, the notion of nuclear family was itself only the idealized side of what was even by then the loss of settled extended family in an increasingly mobile, industrialized society. The cruel mother-in-law jokes so popular in vaudeville have vastly diminished in popularity, not I would guess because of the women's movement, but because mothers-in-law are so rarely a constant feature of anyone's family life today. Those with a live-in mother-in-law are more often seen as richly blessed with a reliable, tax-free babysitter.

Telling single women to get married in the face of decades of demographic and economic tumult is the silliest, most simplistic of antidotes. Nor does it treat as real the social factors that so often isolate couples as well as single parents. I think that if the children of single women are suffering disproportionately from the effects of poverty, we should be examining the continuing ghettoization of women in the workplace, the continuing disparity between women's and men's salaries, and the direct links between these inequalities and the fact that women fall below the poverty level in greater numbers than men.

Nor should we forget to consider lost jobs, declining standards of living, and poverty as contributing to the breakdown of marital relations. We should be asking not what happened to the two-parent household but what happened to our kinship circles. A friend of mine from Ghana could not even fathom what single motherhood meant: "If a girl has a child, she always has her family to turn to, yes?" No, I answered. "Her tribe?" I shook my head. "Her language group . . . ?" he persisted with diminished conviction. "Yeah, sure," I said in my best American idiom.

An important part of what has happened since the Great Depression is that the politics of single motherhood has been racialized. Horatio Alger has turned into Willie Horton, and his regal hard-working mother who always gets her just deserts in the end has turned into a shiftless welfare queen who always

welfare queens

gets more than she deserves. This powerful ideological myth has somehow trumped every bit of empirical reality, even in the minds of well-educated policymakers. Most Americans still believe that blacks are having more than their fair share of babies, that blacks account for most welfare recipients, and that women on welfare are "addicted" (as Dan Quayle implied) not just to drugs but to being on welfare—as though welfare were the latest fad in euphoric "high."

Yet, again, the facts are that most welfare recipients are white women, many of whom have come out of bad marriages with bad settlements, and that welfare in New York, for an example of a state that has long been considered "too generous," pays only two dollars a week more in benefits for a new child—a dead loss, and certainly not an incentive. Contrary to public opinion, births among black women have been decreasing since the 1960s; infant mortality rates are scandalously high (higher in Harlem than in Bangladesh); and shortened life expectancy, unattended medical conditions, and lack of health care are such serious problems among blacks that, once women enter their twenties, complication from pregnancy becomes a serious health risk. In other words, it makes biological sense, if not normative social sense, to have one's children while in one's teens under such circumstances.

And while I am all for population control, I'm curious as to the eugenic implications of that concept as it is applied to blacks exclusively, while simultaneously a major industry in fertility has grown up for a principally white clientele, providing more eggs, more motility, more births. I have no problem trying to curb the population explosion—or not—but I think constitutional notions of equality demand evenhandedness no less as to class than as to race if we are to make judgments about who deserves to be a parent and who does not.

I am fascinated by the power of such mythology: it has visited me on occasion, and I am taken aback by the cruelty, condescension, arrogance, and just plain in-your-face-ness I have encountered. When my son was one month old, I engaged in a spirited public debate about the upcoming presidential election. At the end, one of my opponents stood up, shook the hand of the woman on the other side of me and said, "Thank you for being so polite. It's

obvious *you* come from a two-parent household." When my son was five months old, I called him "sweetheart" in the presence of a neighbor. My neighbor snapped: "You'd better stop talking to him like that unless you want to see him putting Nair on his legs by the time he's seventeen." When my son was eight months old, a young white male law student chided me publicly for not caring about "young black males" because I had adopted him as a "black single mother."

I cite the personal litany not because of how all this makes me feel—wretched!—but because it seems so prevalent as a political force, and so misguided in terms of its sense of cause and effect. Some people act as though single mothers both are vacuum-sealed in a world without men and live in a perpetual state of sexual overindulgence. No role models, just pimps. While I am not a great fan of idealization of any sort, I have begun to long for just a touch of counter-mythology. Say, the mythic black single mother educates her young'uns against all the odds, wrassles urban coyotes, and all while stretching that two-dollar welfare check over twenty-one meals 'til Sunday.

At some level, all of this is about sex, sin, and what lives are worth living. It is also about disguising the class problems of our supposedly classless society, primarily by filtering them through certain kinds of discussions about race and the shiftless, undeserving, unemployable black "underclass." (Which is most emphatically not to say that we shouldn't be talking about the great power of racism in this society: what I mean to say is that welfare is not primarily a black problem, yet the impression that it is functions to avoid discussion of how broad the scar of poverty truly is.) What results is a powerful schema of thought justifying significant intrusions into the lives of black and white women, but poor young black women in particular. (The intrusions into the lives of poor young black men, of course, deserve a book—a long, tragic book—of their own.)

The wholesale demonization of "the black single mother" is quite focused on black patterns of sexual behavior as deviant from larger social norms. I would like to see this voguish literature concentrate a little less on black women's reproductive and man troubles and more on encounters with those who guard the borders of their isolation—employers, schoolteachers, hospital workers, police officers—the lived encounters that make it hard for them to raise a family at all. I would like to see the high rates of black teenage pregnancy framed less by moralistic attributions of black "social disorganization" and more by comparative patterns of the widespread sexual activity among all teens (or for that matter among all politicians, to name a random population whose social indiscretions might take volumes to describe); I would like to see direct, rather than quite subtly implied, links made between pregnancy rates and the availability of health education and reliable birth control as economic resources. Otherwise, one is left with the impression that the rights to children, intimacy, and privacy are the rewards of wealth; one is left with an image in which mainstream society's punitive and oppressive desire to literally make poor blacks disappear wins acceptance when re-expressed as *their* uncontrolled desire for babies *they* can't afford.

In this sense, much of today's demonization of single motherhood conforms to the kind of theorizing first associated with the anthropologist Oscar Lewis—the assumption of a "culture of poverty" that creates destructive intergenerational behavioral archetypes. The frequent use of these purportedly self-perpetuating archetypes to mask the larger society's perpetuation of its own *stereo*types makes this form of sociology the subject of heated debate.

I have to think that some of this is an unconscious ordering, and quite old in our history. My great-great-grandmother, whom my mother's family called Mammy Sophie, was a twelve-year-old slave when she was impregnated by her master. Sophie bore him a daughter, my great-grandmother Mattie. Her master's white wife, Mary, raised the slave daughter Mattie to be "moral," "Christian," and contemptuous of her mother. My mother, Mattie's granddaughter, grew up thinking of Sophie as immoral because she had been raped by this man starting at the age of eleven. My mother says she grew up resenting Sophie the way his white wife must have resented Sophie—as wild, godless, and disruptive. An embarrassment to "the family," although I wonder just whose. Mary raised the light-skinned black Mattie to be tame, Episcopalian, and a palliative racial mediator. Mattie was married at the age

of seventeen to a man named Morgan, also light-skinned and thoroughly bred, and together they were given the task of setting up a black Episcopal church, so that they could intercede like oil upon the waters and spread the word of God to the heathen. Mr. Morgan died of consumption at a very young age, and Mattie was married again, to my great-grandfather, a French-Canadian-Cherokee, a man whom I grew up hearing about only as "the dignified Mr. Ross."

My mother told of the time a neighbor and black contemporary of Mattie's died, having contracted consumption from his white family, like so many servants-who-were-also-family. At the wake, Mammy Sophie said to the widow: "My condolences; I know just how you feel." The widow rose up and said, "I was legally married to a husband. You have no idea how I feel." Then Mattie rose up and spoke against her own mother: "And I've had two legal husbands; you can't possibly know what it's like."

My mother grew up with that as a cautionary tale about how awful Sophie was—how loose and irredeemable, how she produced children without mothering them. My mother, in her turn, taught me that black teenage motherhood was deplorable. It was not until I started writing about it, my mother says, that she started rethinking the valuations embedded in this ordering of the account.

History is filled with mirrors in whose stark reflections we must find the lessons for change. Recently I have been haunted by the story of a twelve-year-old girl who gave birth alone in a corridor of her Brooklyn project house, and threw the newborn down a trash chute. The building's maintenance men heard cries just as they were about to activate the trash compactor, and the baby was saved. According to all the papers, no one knew the girl was pregnant—not her mother, not the neighbors, not the teacher of her sixth-grade slow-learner class. It turned out the father of the baby was her twenty-two-year-old uncle. He was being prosecuted for statutory rape. The prosecutor's office announced its intention to prosecute the twelve-year-old girl for attempted murder.

I think that the current insistence on blaming single mothers for the troubles of this country is a concerted way of not seeing the fiscal, racial, and political catastrophes that so beg for our attention. Poverty and disfunction among single mothers and their children are a symptom, not a cause. The vicious stereotypes with which my son and I have been greeted by significant numbers of random strangers—whether the assumption is that unless I am earning the equivalent of Oprah Winfrey's salary my child will inevitably grow up asking society for handouts and stealing for a living, or that even if I were making Oprah's salary I would still sabotage and "feminize" my son's mythic warrior spirit—are things that have nothing to do with me or my son, who is the most delightful, intelligent young man in the world. These stereotypes, so commonly misunderstood as the "difficulty" with single motherhood, are more accurately seen as part of the daily battle that all parents must wage with the world in order to create the space in which our children may grow into gentle, wise, and loving adults with the emotional resources to do bigger battle than street war. And this is a daily struggle that we all—black, white, female, male, parents or not—ought to be engaged in anyway, whether on behalf of our children or ourselves.

It is time to stop demonizing single mothers or anyone else who makes family where there was none before. Children, in their happy irrationality and complete dependence, are perpetual reminders that we are all members of a larger community, that we can never quite attain the atomistic nuclear status to which the sweet nostalgia of *Happy Days* sometimes tempts us. Raising children, even for black single mothers on welfare, is dependent on the very wonderful belief that community is possible; that there is family not only within but beyond the walls of one's home; that there is regeneration for oneself and a life for one's child in the world at large. This belief is what makes me such a tenacious, annoying, finger-shaking communitarian moralist ("Socialist!" sighs my sister); but perhaps if we could just see that family not only is about individuals acting autonomously within some private sphere but also is communally inspired and socially dependent—if we could just refrain from penalizing the nonformulaic (and unduly deferring to the nuclear formula even when domestic abuse rules the roost)—if we could but act on all this in even modest fashion, then we might begin to imagine communities in which

no "single" mother need ever be alone, and no child raised in this supposed "man's world" should be without dozens of good men to look to for protection. Cultivating the extraordinary richness of what children offer us depends neither on a mother nor on a father alone, but is a responsibility that extends to grandparents, friends, neighbors, and civic community—across fences, across religion, across class, and across town.

[1995]

 88

The Beijing Declaration and Platform for Action

BEIJING DECLARATION

1. We, the Governments participating in the Fourth World Conference on Women,

2. Gathered here in Beijing in September 1995, the year of the fiftieth anniversary of the founding of the United Nations,

3. Determined to advance the goals of equality, development and peace for all women everywhere in the interest of all humanity,

4. Acknowledging the voices of all women everywhere and taking note of the diversity of women and their roles and circumstances, honouring the women who paved the way and inspired by the hope present in the world's youth,

5. Recognize that the status of women has advanced in some important respects in the past decade but that progress has been uneven, inequalities between women and men have persisted and major obstacles remain, with serious consequences for the well-being of all people,

6. Also recognize that this situation is exacerbated by the increasing poverty that is affecting the lives of the majority of the world's people, in particular women and children, with origins in both the national and international domains,

7. Dedicate ourselves unreservedly to addressing these constraints and obstacles and thus enhancing further the advancement and empowerment of women all over the world, and agree that this re-

quires urgent action in the spirit of determination, hope, cooperation and solidarity, now and to carry us forward into the next century.

We reaffirm our commitment to:

8. The equal rights and inherent human dignity of women and men and other purposes and principles enshrined in the Charter of the United Nations, to the Universal Declaration of Human Rights and other international human rights instruments, in particular the Convention on the Elimination of All Forms of Discrimination against Women and the Convention on the Rights of the Child, as well as the Declaration on the Elimination of Violence against Women and the Declaration on the Right to Development;

9. Ensure the full implementation of the human rights of women and of the girl child as an inalienable, integral and indivisible part of all human rights and fundamental freedoms;

10. Build on consensus and progress made at previous United Nations conferences and summits—on women in Nairobi in 1985, on children in New York in 1990, on environment and development in Rio de Janeiro in 1992, on human rights in Vienna in 1993, on population and development in Cairo in 1994 and on social development in Copenhagen in 1995 with the objective of achieving equality, development and peace;

11. Achieve the full and effective implementation of the Nairobi Forward-looking Strategies for the Advancement of Women;

12. The empowerment and advancement of women, including the right to freedom of thought, conscience, religion and belief, thus contributing to the moral, ethical, spiritual and intellectual needs of women and men, individually or in community with others and thereby guaranteeing them the possibility of realizing their full potential in society and shaping their lives in accordance with their own aspirations.

We are convinced that:

13. Women's empowerment and their full participation on the basis of equality in all spheres of society, including participation in the decision-making process and access to power, are fundamental for the achievement of equality, development and peace;

14. Women's rights are human rights;

15. Equal rights, opportunities and access to resources, equal sharing of responsibilities for the family by men and women, and a harmonious partnership between them are critical to their well-being and that of their families as well as to the consolidation of democracy;

16. Eradication of poverty based on sustained economic growth, social development, environmental protection and social justice requires the involvement of women in economic and social development, equal opportunities and the full and equal participation of women and men as agents and beneficiaries of people-centered sustainable development;

17. The explicit recognition and reaffirmation of the right of all women to control all aspects of their health, in particular their own fertility, is basic to their empowerment;

18. Local, national, regional and global peace is attainable and is inextricably linked with the advancement of women, who are a fundamental force for leadership, conflict resolution and the promotion of lasting peace at all levels;

19. It is essential to design, implement and monitor, with the full participation of women, effective, efficient and mutually reinforcing gender-sensitive policies and programmes, including development policies and programmes, at all levels that will foster the empowerment and advancement of women;

20. The participation and contribution of all actors of civil society, particularly women's groups and networks and other non-governmental organizations and community-based organizations, with full respect for their autonomy, in cooperation with Governments, are important to the effective implementation and follow-up of the Platform for Action;

21. The implementation of the Platform for Action requires commitment from Governments and the international community. By making national and international commitments for action, including those made at the Conference, Governments and the international community recognize the need to take priority action for the empowerment and advancement of women.

We are determined to:

22. Intensify efforts and actions to achieve the goals of the Nairobi Forward-looking Strategies for the Advancement of Women by the end of this century;

23. Ensure the full enjoyment by women and the girl child of all human rights and fundamental freedoms and take effective action against violations of these rights and freedoms;

24. Take all necessary measures to eliminate all forms of discrimination against women and the girl child and remove all obstacles to gender equality and the advancement and empowerment of women;

25. Encourage men to participate fully in all actions towards equality;

26. Promote women's economic independence, including employment, and eradicate the persistent and increasing burden of poverty on women by addressing the structural causes of poverty through changes in economic structures, ensuring equal access for all women, including those in rural areas, as vital development agents, to productive resources, opportunities and public services;

27. Promote people-centred sustainable development, including sustained economic growth, through the provision of basic education, lifelong education, literacy and training, and primary health care for girls and women;

28. Take positive steps to ensure peace for the advancement of women and, recognizing the leading role that women have played in the peace movement, work actively towards general and complete disarmament under strict and effective international control, and support negotiations on the conclusion, without delay, of a universal and multilaterally and effectively verifiable comprehensive nculear-test-ban treaty which contributes to nuclear disarmament and the prevention of the proliferation of nuclear weapons in all its aspects;

29. Prevent and eliminate all forms of violence against women and girls;

30. Ensure equal access to and equal treatment of women and men in education and health care and enhance women's sexual and reproductive health as well as education;

31. Promote and protect all human rights of women and girls;

32. Intensify efforts to ensure equal enjoyment of all human rights and fundamental freedoms for all women and girls who face multiple barriers to their empowerment and advancement because of such factors as their race, age, language, ethnicity, culture, religion, or disability, or because they are indigenous people;

33. Ensure respect for international law, including humanitarian law, in order to protect women and girls in particular;

34. Develop the fullest potential of girls and women of all ages, ensure their full and equal participation in building a better world for all and enhance their role in the development process.

We are determined to:

35. Ensure women's equal access to economic resources, including land, credit, science and technology, vocational training, information, communication and markets, as a means to further the advancement and empowerment of women and girls, including through the enhancement of their capacities to enjoy the benefits of equal access to these resources, *inter alia,* by means of international cooperation;

36. Ensure the success of the Platform for Action, which will require a strong commitment on the part of Governments, international organizations and institutions at all levels. We are deeply convinced that economic development, social development and environmental protection are interdependent and mutually reinforcing components of sustainable development, which is the framework for our efforts to achieve a higher quality of life for all people. Equitable social development that recognizes empowering the poor, particularly women living in poverty, to utilize environmental resources sustainably is a necessary foundation for sustainable development. We also recognize that broad-based and sustained economic growth in the context of sustainable development is necessary to sustain social development and social justice. The success of the Platform for Action will also require adequate mobilization of resources at the national and international levels as well as new and additional resources to the developing countries from all available funding mechanisms, including multilateral, bilateral and private sources for the advancement of women; financial resources to strengthen the capacity of national, subregional, regional and international institutions; a commitment to equal rights, equal responsibilities and equal opportunities and to the equal participation of women and men in all national, regional and international bodies and policy-making processes;

and the establishment or strengthening of mechanisms at all levels for accountability to the world's women;

37. Ensure also the success of the Platform for Action in countries with economies in transition, which will require continued international cooperation and assistance;

38. We hereby adopt and commit ourselves as Governments to implement the following Platform for Action, ensuring that a gender perspective is reflected in all our policies and programmes. We urge the United Nations system, regional and international financial institutions, other relevant regional and international institutions and all women and men, as well as non-governmental organizations, with full respect for their autonomy, and all sectors of civil society, in cooperation with Governments, to fully commit themselves and contribute to the implementation of this Platform for Action.

· · ·

Critical Areas of Concern

41. The advancement of women and the achievement of equality between women and men are a matter of human rights and a condition for social justice and should not be seen in isolation as a women's issue. They are the only way to build a sustainable, just and developed society. Empowerment of women and equality between women and men are prerequisites for achieving political, social, economic, cultural and environmental security among all peoples.

42. Most of the goals set out in the Nairobi Forward-looking Strategies for the Advancement of Women have not been achieved. Barriers to women's empowerment remain, despite the efforts of Governments, as well as non-governmental organizations and women and men everywhere. Vast political, economic and ecological crises persist in many parts of the world. Among them are wars of aggression, armed conflicts, colonial or other forms of alien domination or foreign occupation, civil wars and terrorism. These situations, combined with systematic or de facto discrimination, violations of and failure to protect all human rights and fundamental freedoms of all women, and their civil, cultural, economic, political and social rights, including the right to development and ingrained prejudicial atti-

tudes towards women and girls are but a few of the impediments encountered since the World Conference to Review and Appraise the Achievements of the United Nations Decade for Women: Equality, Development and Peace, in 1985.

43. A review of progress since the Nairobi Conference highlights special concerns—areas of particular urgency that stand out as priorities for action. All actors should focus action and resources on the strategic objectives relating to the critical areas of concern which are, necessarily, interrelated, interdependent and of high priority. There is a need for these actors to develop and implement mechanisms of accountability for all the areas of concern.

44. To this end, Governments, the international community and civil society, including non-governmental organizations and the private sector, are called upon to take strategic action in the following critical areas of concern:

- The persistent and increasing burden of poverty on women
- Inequalities and inadequacies in and unequal access to education and training
- Inequalities and inadequacies in and unequal access to health care and related services
- Violence against women
- The effects of armed or other kinds of conflict on women, including those living under foreign occupation
- Inequality in economic structures and policies, in all forms of productive activities and in access to resources
- Inequality between men and women in the sharing of power and decision-making at all levels
- Insufficient mechanisms at all levels to promote the advancement of women
- Lack of respect for and inadequate promotion and protection of the human rights of women
- Stereotyping of women and inequality in women's access to and participation in all communication systems, especially in the media
- Gender inequalities in the management of natural resources and in the safeguarding of the environment
- Persistent discrimination against and violation of the rights of the girl-child

[1995]

Bibliography

1792–1920

Addams, Jane. (1910). *Twenty Years at Hull House*. New York: Macmillan.

Anthony, Susan B., Elizabeth Cady Stanton, and Matilda Joslyn Gage. (1922). *A History of Woman Suffrage*. New York: Fowler and Wells. (Original work published 1881)

Bebel, August. (1910). *Woman and Socialism* (Meta Stern, Trans.). New York: Socialist Literature. (Original work published 1885)

Butler, Josephine. (1868). *The Education and Employment of Women*. London: Macmillan.

———. (1869). *Woman's Work and Woman's Culture: A Series of Essays*. London: Macmillan.

Catt, Carrie Chapman. (1897). *The Ballot and the Bullet*. Philadelphia: A. J. Ferris.

Cobbe, Frances Power. (1881). *The Duties of Women: A Course of Lectures*. London: Williams and Norgate.

———. (1863). *Essays on the Pursuits of Women*. London: E. Faithful.

Eastman, Crystal. (1978). *Crystal Eastman: On Women and Revolution*. Blanche Wiesen Cook (Ed.). New York: Oxford University Press.

Fawcett, Millicent Garrett. (1871). *Electoral Diabilities of Women*. London: Tavistock.

———. (1868). "The Uses of Higher Education for Women." *The Fortnightly Review, 4,* 554–557.

———. (1891). "The Emancipation of Women." *Fortnightly Review, NS 50,* 672–685.

Freud, Sigmund. (1963). *Dora: An Analysis of a Case of Hysteria. Collected Papers of Sigmund Freud*. New York: Collier.

Fuller, Margaret. (1845). *Woman in the Nineteenth Century*. London: Clarke.

Gage, Matilda Joslyn. (1893). *Woman, Church, and State: The Original Exposé of Male Collaboration Against the Female Sex*. Chicago: C. H. Kerr.

Gilman, Charlotte Perkins. (1979). *Herland*. New York: Pantheon. (Original work published 1979)

Goldman, Emma. (1910). *Anarchism and Other Essays*. New York: Mother Earth.

Jacobs, Harriet Brent. (1973). *Incidents in the Life of a Slave Girl*. New York: Harcourt Brace. (Original work published 1861)

Key, Ellen. (1976). *The Woman Movement*. (Mamah Bouton Borthwick, Trans.). Westport, CT: Hyperion. (Original work published 1912)

Kollontai, Alexandra. (1920). *Communism and the Family*. New York: Contemporary.

Martineau, Harriet. (1832). *Illustrations of Political Economy*. London: Charles Fox.

Nightingale, Florence. (1979). *Cassandra*. Old Westbury, NY: The Feminist Press. (Original work published 1852–59)

Pankhurst, Cristabel. (1913). *The Great Scourge and How to End It*. London: E. Pankhurst.

Pankhurst, Emmeline. (1914). *My Own Story*. London: John Day.

Schreiner, Olive. (1987). *An Olive Schreiner Reader: Writings on Women and South Africa*. London: Pandora.

Simcox, E. J. (1877). *Natural Law, An Essay In Ethics*. London: Trubner.

Stewart, Maria W. (1987). *America's First Black Woman Political Writer: Essays and Speeches*. [1820s and 30s]. Bloomington, IN: Indiana University Press.

Stopes, Marie. (1918). *Married Love: A New Contribution to the Solution of Sex Difficulties*. London: Putnam.

Wells, Ida B. (1970). *Crusade for Justice: The Autobiography of Ida B. Wells*. Alfreda Duster (Ed.). Chicago: University of Chicago Press.

————. (1969). *On Lynchings: Southern Horrors; A Red Record; Mob Rule in New Orleans*. New York: Arno. (Original work published 1892, 1895, 1900)

Wollstonecraft, Mary. (1787). *Thought on the Education of Daughters*. London: Johnson.

————. (1798). *Maria, or the Wrongs of Woman*. London: Johnson.

Woodhull, Victoria, and Tennessee Claflin. (1870). *Woodhull and Claflin's Weekly*.

Wright, Frances. (1821). *Views on Society and Manners in America*. New York: Bliss and White.

1920–1963

Addams, Jane. (1922). *Peace and Bread in Time of War*. New York: Macmillan.

Beard, Mary Ritter. (1953). *The Force of Women in Japanese History*. Washington, DC: Public Affairs Press.

————. (1931). *On Understanding Women*. New York: Longmans.

Beauvoir, Simone de. (1959). *Memoirs of a Dutiful Daughter*. Cleveland, OH: World.

Catt, Carrie Chapman, and Nettie Rogers Shuler. (1923). *Woman Suffrage and Politics: The Inner Story of the Suffrage Movement*. New York: Scribner.

Deutsch, Helene. (1944). *Psychology of Women: A Psychoanalytic Interpretation*. New York: Grune and Stratton.

Diner, Helen. (1965). *Mothers and Amazons: The First Feminine History of Culture*. (John Philip Lundin, Trans.). New York: Julian Press.

Freud, Sigmund. (1933). "Femininity" *Standard Edition*. London: Hogarth Press.

Horney, Karen. (1932). *Feminine Psychology*. New York: Norton.

Klein, Melanie. (1949). *The Psychoanalysis of Children*. (Alix Strachey, Trans.). London: Hogarth Press.

Klein, Viola. (1946). *The Feminine Character: History of an Ideology*. London: K. Paul, Trench & Trubner.

Komarovsky, Mirra. (1953). *Women in the Modern World: Their Education and Dilemmas*. Boston: Little Brown.

Lafollette, Suzanne. (1926). *Concerning Women*. New York: A. C. Boni.

Mead, Margaret. (1928). *Coming of Age in Samoa*. New York: Morrow.

————. (1949). *Male and Female: A Study of the Sexes in a Changing World*. New York: Dell.

Roosevelt, Eleanor. (1995). *What I Hope to Leave Behind: The Essential Essays of Eleanor Roosevelt*. Allida Black (Ed.). New York: Carlson.

Russell, Dora. (1983). *The Dora Russell Reader: 57 Years of Writing and Journalism, 1925–1982*. London: Routledge.

Sand, George. (1929). *The Intimate Journals of George Sand*. (Marie Howe, Trans.). New York: John Day.

Sanger, Margaret. (1970). *The New Motherhood*. Elmsford, NY: Maxwell. (Original work published 1922)

Terrell, Mary Church. (1940). *A Colored Woman in a White World*. Washington, DC: Ransdell.

Webb, Beatrice. (1926). *My Apprenticeship*. London: Longmans.

————, with Sidney Webb. (1923). *The Decay of Capitalist Civilization*. New York: Harcourt Brace.

Winnicott, D. W. (1958). *Collected Papers: Through Pediatrics to Psychoanalysis*. London: Tavistock.

Woolf, Virginia. (1938). *Three Guineas*. London: Hogarth Press.

Zetkin, Clara. (1984). *Selected Writings*. Philip Foner (Ed.). New York: International.

1963–1975

Bernard, Jessie. (1972). *The Future of Marriage*. New York: World.

————. (1974). *The Future of Motherhood*. New York: Penguin.

Bird, Caroline. (1968). *Born Female: The High Cost of Keeping Women Down*. New York: D. Mckay.

Boserup, Esther. (1970). *Women and Economic Development*. New York: St. Martin's.

Boston Women's Health Book Collective. (1973). *Our Bodies, Our Selves.* New York: Simon and Schuster.

Bunch, Charlotte, and Nancy Myron. (1975). *Lesbianism and the Women's Movement.* Baltimore, MD: Diana.

Burris, Betty. (1973). "Fourth World Manifesto." In Ann Koedt et al. (Eds.). *Radical Feminism.* New York: Quadrangle.

Chesler, Phyllis. (1972). *Women and Madness.* New York: Doubleday.

Daly, Mary. (1968). *The Church and the Second Sex.* New York: Harper and Row.

———. (1973). *Beyond God the Father.* Boston: Beacon Press.

Douglas, Mary. (1975). *Implicit Meanings: Essays in Anthropology.* London: Routledge.

Dworkin, Andrea. (1974). *Woman Hating.* New York: Dutton.

Ellman, Mary. (1968). *Thinking About Women.* New York: Harcourt Brace.

Gornick, Vivian, and Barbara Moran (Eds.). (1971). *Women in Sexist Society.* New York: Basic Books.

Greer, Germaine. (1970). *The Female Eunuch.* London: McGibbon Kaye.

Johnston, Jill. (1974). *Lesbian Nation: The Feminist Solution.* New York: Simon and Schuster.

Joreen. (1970). "The Bitch Manifesto." Pittsburgh, PA: KNOW, Inc.

Koedt, Ann. (1973). "The Myth of the Vaginal Orgasm." In Ann Koedt et al. (Eds.). *Radical Feminism.* New York: Quadrangle.

Kristeva, Julia. (1977). *About Chinese Women.* (Anita Barrows, Trans.). London: Boyars.

Lacan, Jacques. (1977). "The Signification of the Phallus." In *Ecrits: A Selection.* (Alan Sheridan, Trans.). New York: Norton. (Original work published 1966)

Lerner, Gerda (Ed.). (1972). *Black Women in White America.* New York: Pantheon.

Mitchell, Juliet. (1974). *Psychoanalysis and Feminism.* Harmondsworth, UK: Penguin.

———. (1973). *Woman's Estate.* Harmondsworth, UK: Penguin.

Morgan, Robin. (1970). *Sisterhood Is Powerful.* New York: Vintage.

Nochlin, Linda. (1971). "Why Have There Been No Great Women Artists?" In Vivian Gornick and Barbara Moran (Eds.). *Women in Sexist Society.* New York: Basic Books.

Oakley, Ann. (1974). *Women's Work: The Housewife Past and Present.* Totowa, NJ: Roman and Allenheld.

Reed, Evelyn. (1975) *Women's Evolution: From Matriarchal Clan to Patriarchal Family.* New York: Pathfinder.

Reuther, Rosemary. (1970). *Religion and Sexism.* New York: Simon and Schuster.

Rosaldo, Michelle, and Louise Lamphere (Eds.). (1974). *Woman, Culture and Society.* Stanford, CA: Stanford University Press.

Rossi, Alice. (1970). *The Feminist Papers: From Adams to de Beauvoir.* New York: Bantam.

Rowbotham, Sheila. (1973). *Women's Consciousness, Man's World.* Harmondsworth, UK: Penguin.

Smith, Dorothy. (1974). "Women's Perspective as a Radical Critique of Sociology." *Sociological Inquiry* 44(1), 7–13.

Thorne, Barrie, and Nancy Henley (Eds.). (1975). *Language and Sex: Difference and Dominance.* Rowley, MA: Newbury House.

1975–1985

Barrett, Michelle. (1980). *Women's Oppression Today: Problems in Marxist Feminist Analysis.* London: Verso.

Beck, Evelyn Torten. (1984). *Nice Jewish Girls: A Lesbian Anthology.* Trumansburg, NY: Crossing Press.

Bleier, Ruth. (1984). *Science and Gender: A Critique of Biology and its Theories on Women.* New York: Pergamon.

Bowles, Gloria, and Renate Duelli Klein (Eds.). (1983). *Theories of Women's Studies.* London: Routledge.

Brownmiller, Susan. (1984). *Femininity.* New York: Simon and Schuster.

Bulkin, Ellie et al. (1984). *Yours in Struggle: Three Feminist Perspectives on Anti-Semitism and Racism.* New York: Longhaul.

Bunch, Charlotte. (1987). "Not for Lesbians Only." In *Passionate Politics: Feminist Theory in Action.* New York: St. Martins. (Original work published 1975)

———. (1987). "Lesbians in Revolt." In *Passionate Politics: Feminist Theory in Action.* New York: St. Martins. (Original work published 1972)

Christ, Carol, and Judith Plaskow (Eds.). (1979). *Womanspirit Rising.* San Francisco: Harper and Row.

Cixous, Hélène. (1986). *The Newly Born Woman.* (Betsy Wing, Trans.). Minneapolis: University of Minnesota Press. (Original work published 1975)

Corea, Gena. (1977). *The Hidden Malpractice: How American Medicine Treats Women as Patients and Professionals.* New York: Morrow.

Cott, Nancy. (1977). *The Bonds of Womanhood: Woman's Sphere in New England 1780–1835.* New Haven: Yale University Press.

Chruikshank, Margaret. (1982). *Lesbian Studies: Present and Future.* Old Westbury, NY: Feminist Press.

Coward, Rosalind. (1983). *Patriarchal Precedents: Sexuality and Social Relations.* London: Routledge.

Culley, Margo, and Catherine Portugues. (1985). *Gendered Subjects.* London: Routledge.

Daly, Mary. (1978). *Gyn/Ecology: The Metaethics of Radical Feminism.* Boston: Beacon.

Delphy, Christine. (1975). *Close to Home: A Materialist Analysis of Women's Oppression.* London: Hutchinson.

Davis, Angela. (1980). *Women, Race and Class.* New York: Random House.

de Lauretis, Teresa. (1984). *Alice Doesn't: Sexuality, Semiotics, Cinema.* Bloomington: Indiana University Press.

Dinnerstein, Dorothy. (1977). *The Mermaid and the Minotaur: Sexual Arrangements and Human Malaise.* New York: Harper.

Claudia Dreifus, (Ed.). (1977). *Seizing Our Bodies: The Politics of Women's Health.* New York: Vintage.

Dworkin, Andrea. (1983). *Right-Wing Women.* New York: Putnam.

Eisenstein, Zillah. (1979). *Capitalist Patriarchy and the Case for Socialist Feminism.* New York: Monthly Review Press.

———. (1981). *The Radical Future of Liberal Feminism.* Boston: G. K. Hall.

Ehrenreich, Barbara and Dierdre English. (1978). *For Her Own Good: 150 Years of the Experts' Advice to Women.* New York: Anchor.

Eisenstein, Hester, and Alice Jardine, (Eds.). (1980). *The Future of Difference.* Boston: G. K. Hall.

Enloe, Cynthia. (1983). *Does Khaki Become Her?: The Militarization of Women's Lives.* Boston: South End Press.

Faderman, Lillian. (1981). *Surpassing the Love of Men: Romantic Friendship and Love Between Women From the Renaissance to the Present.* New York: Morrow.

Flax, Jane. (1983). "Political Philosophy and the Patriarchal Unconscious: A Psychoanalytic Perspective on Philosophy and Metaphysics." In Merrill Hintikka and Sandra Harding (Eds.). *Discovering Reality.* Boston: D. Reidel.

Freedman, Estelle. (1985). *The Lesbian Issue: Essays From Signs.* Chicago: University of Chicago Press.

French, Marilyn. (1983). *Beyond Power: On Women, Men and Morals.* London: Cape.

Frye, Marilyn. (1983). *The Politics of Reality.* Trumansburg, NY: Crossing.

Fuentes, Annette, and Barbara Ehrenreich. (1983). *Women in the Global Factory.* Boston: South End Press.

Gallop, Jane. (1982). *The Daughter's Seduction: Feminism and Psychoanalysis.* Ithaca, NY: Cornell.

Gilbert, Sandra, and Susan Gubar. (1977). *The Madwoman in the Attic: The Woman Writer and the Nineteenth-Century Literary Imagination.* New Haven: Yale University Press.

Griffin, Susan. (1981). *Pornography and Silence: Culture's Revenge Against Nature.* New York: Harper.

———. (1978). *Woman and Nature: The Roaring Inside Her.* New York: Harper.

Harding, Sandra and Merrill B. Hintikka (Eds.). (1983). *Discovering Reality: Feminist Perspectives on Epistemology, Metaphysics, Methodology, and Philosophy of Science.* Boston: D. Reidel.

Hartmann, Heidi. (1976). "Capitalism, Patriarchy and Job Segregation by Sex." *Signs 1,* (3), 137–169.

Hartsock, Nancy. (1983). *Money, Sex and Power: Toward a Feminist Historical Materialism.* New York: Longman.

hooks, bell. (1984). *Feminist Theory: From Margin to Center.* Boston: South End.

Howe, Florence. (1984). *Myths of Coeducation: Selected Essays, 1963–84.* Bloomington, IN: Indiana University Press.

Hubbard, Ruth, and Marion Lowe. (1983). *Woman's Nature: Rationalizations of Inequality.* New York: Pergamon.

Hull, Gloria, Patricia Bell Scott, and Barbara Smith. (1982). *All the Women Are White, All the Blacks Are Men, But Some of Us Are Brave.* Old Westbury, NY: Feminist Press.

Irigaray, Luce. (1985). *This Sex Which Is Not One.* (Catherine Porter, Trans.). Ithaca, NY: Cornell. (Original work published 1977)

———. (1985). *Speculum of the Other Woman.* (Gillian Gill, Trans.). Ithaca, NY: Cornell. (Original work published 1974).

Jaggar, Alison. (1983). *Feminist Politics and Human Nature.* Totowa, NJ: Roman and Allenheld.

Jardine, Alice. (1985). *Gynesis: Configurations of Women and Modernity.* Ithaca, NY: Cornell.

Jehlen, Myra. (1981). "Archimedes and the Paradox of Feminist Criticism." *Signs,* 6(4), 575–601.

Joseph, Gloria, and Jill Lewis. (1981). *Common Differences: Conflicts in Black and White Feminist Perspectives.* Garden City, NY: Anchor.

Kaplan, Cora. (1983). *Sea Changes: Culture and Feminism.* London: Verso.

Kaplan, E. Ann. (1983). *Women and Film: Both Sides of the Camera.* New York: Routledge.

Keller, Evelyn Fox. (1978). "Gender and Science." *Psychoanalysis and Contemporary Thought,* 6, 409–433.

Kelly-Gadol, Joan. (1984). *Women, History and Theory.* Chicago: University of Chicago Press.

Kolodny, Annette. (1980, Spring). "Dancing through the Minefield: Some Observations on Theory, Practice and Politics of Feminist Literary Criticism." *Feminist Studies,* 6(1), 1–25.

Kristeva, Julia. (1980). *Desire in Language: A Semiotic Approach to Literature and Art.* 1969/1977. Leon S. Roudiez (Ed.). (Thomas Gora, Alice Jardine, and Leon S. Roudiez, Trans.). New York: Columbia. (Original work published 1969, 1977)

———. (1981). "Woman's Time." (Alice Jardine and Harry Blake, Trans.) *Signs,* 7, 13–35.

Lerner, Gerda. (1986). *The Creation of Patriarchy.* Oxford: Oxford University Press.

Lloyd, Genevieve. (1984). *The Man of Reason: "Male" and "Female" in Western Philosophy.* Minneapolis: University of Minnesota Press.

Lorde, Audre. (1984). *Sister Outsider: Essays and Speeches.* Trumansburg, NY: Crossing.

———. (1982). *Zami, A New Spelling of My Name.* Trumansburg, NY: Crossing.

MacKinnon, Catharine. (1982). "Feminism, Marxism Method and the State: A Agenda for Theory." *Signs,* 7(3), 515–544.

Marks, Elaine, and Isabel de Courtivron. (1980). *New French Feminisms.* New York: Schocken.

Merchant, Carolyn. (1980). *The Death of Nature: Women, Ecology and the Scientific Revolution.* San Francisco: Harper and Row.

Miller, Jean Baker. (1976). *Toward a New Psychology of Women.* Boston: Beacon.

Moi, Toril. (1985). *Sexual/Textual Politics.* London: Methuen.

Moraga, Cherrie, and Gloria Anzaldúa. (1983). *This Bridge Called My Back: Writings by Radical Women of Color.* New York: Kitchen Table: Women of Color Press.

Olsen, Tillie. (1978). *Silences*. New York: Delacorte.

Pagels, Elaine. (1979). *The Gnostic Gospels*. New York: Random House.

Radway, Janice. (1984). *Reading the Romance: Women, Patriarchy and Popular Literature*. Chapel Hill, NC: University of North Carolina Press.

Rich, Adrienne. (1986). "Notes Toward a Politics of Location." In *Blood, Bread and Poetry: Selected Prose, 1979–1985*. New York: Norton.

———. (1976). *Of Woman Born: Motherhood as Experience and Institution*. New York: Norton.

———. (1979). *On Lies, Secrets, and Silence: Selected Prose, 1966–1978*. New York: Norton.

Sanday, Peggy. (1981). *Female Power and Male Dominance*. Cambridge: Cambridge University Press.

Showalter, Elaine. (1979). "Towards a Feminist Poetics." In *Women Writing and Writing About Women*. Mary Jacobus (Ed.). London: Croom Helm.

Smith, Barbara. (1977). "Toward a Black Feminist Criticism" *All the Women Are White, All the Blacks Are Men, But Some of Us Are Brave: Black Women's Studies*. Old Westbury, NY: Feminist Press.

Smith-Rosenberg, Carroll. (1986). *Disorderly Conduct: Visions of Gender in Victorian America*. New York: Knopf.

Snitow, Ann, Christine Stansell, and Sharon Thompson. (1983). *Powers of Desire: The Politics of Sexuality*. New York: Monthly Review Press.

Spender, Dale. (1980). *Man-Made Language*. New York: Pergamon.

Stanley, Liz, and Sue Wise. (1983). *Breaking Out: Feminist Consciousness and Feminist Research*. London: Routledge.

Starhawk. (1982). *Dreaming the Dark*. Boston: Beacon.

Trebilcot, Joyce. (1983). *Mothering: Essays in Feminist Theory*. Totowa, NJ: Roman and Allenheld.

Vance, Carole (Ed.). (1984). *Pleasure and Danger: Exploring Female Sexuality*. Boston: Routledge.

Walker, Alice. (1983). *In Search of Our Mother's Gardens*. New York: Harcourt Brace.

Wittig, Monique. (1981). "One Is Not Born a Woman." *Feminist Issues, 1* (2), 47–54.

1985–1995

Alcoff, Linda and Elizabeth Potter (Eds.). (1993). *Feminist Epistemologies*. New York: Routledge.

Allen, Jeffner (Ed.). (1990). *Lesbian Philosophies and Cultures*. Albany, NY: SUNY Press.

Allen, Paula Gunn. (1986). *The Sacred Hoop: Recovering the Feminine in American Indian Traditions*. Boston: Beacon.

Anzaldúa, Gloria. (1987). *Borderlands/LaFrontera: The New Mestiza*. San Francisco: Spinsters/Aunt Lute.

———. (Ed.). (1990). *Making Face, Making Soul: Haciendo Caras: Creative and Critical Perspective by Women of Color*. San Francisco: Aunt Lute.

Belenky, Mary Field. (1986). *Women's Ways of Knowing: The Development of Self, Voice and Mind*. New York: Basic Books.

Benhabib, Seyla, and Drucilla Cornell. (1987). *Feminism as Critique: Essays on the Politics of Gender in Late-Capitalist Societies*. Cambridge, UK: Polity.

Bordo, Susan. (1993). *Unbearable Weight: Feminism, Western Culture and the Body*. Berkeley: University of California Press.

Braidotti, Rosi. (1994). *Nomadic Subjects: Embodiment and Sexual Difference in Contemporary Feminist Theory*. New York: Columbia.

Butler, Judith. (1993). *Bodies That Matter*. New York: Routledge.

——— and Joan W. Scott (Eds.). (1992). *Feminists Theorize the Political*. New York: Routledge.

———. *Gender Trouble: Feminism and the Subversion of Identity*. New York: Routledge.

Chodorow, Nancy. (1994). *Femininities, Masculinities, Sexualities: Freud and Beyond*. Lexington: University Press of Kentucky.

Chow, Rey. (1989). "'It's You and Not Me: Domination and 'Othering' in Theorizing the 'Third World'." In Elizabeth Weed (Ed.), *Coming to Terms*. New York: Routledge.

————. (1993). *Writing Diaspora*. Bloomington: Indiana University Press.

Christian, Barbara. (1989). "The Race for Theory." In Linda Kauffman (Ed.). *Gender and Theory: Dialogues in Feminist Criticism*. Oxford: Blackwell.

Corea, Gena et al. (Eds.) (1985). *Man-Made Woman: How New Reproductive Technologies Affect Women*. London: Hutchinson.

Cott, Nancy. (1987). *The Grounding of Modern Feminism*. New Haven: Yale University Press.

————. (1990). "Historical Perspectives: The Equal Rights Amendment Conflict in the 1920s." In Evelyn Fox Keller and Marianne Hirsch (Eds.). *Conflicts in Feminism*. New York: Routledge.

Daly, Mary. (1987). *Webster's First New Intergalactic Wickedary of the English Language*. Boston: Beacon.

de Lauretis, Teresa. (1991). "Upping the Anti (sic) in Feminist Theory." In Evelyn Fox Keller and Marianne Hirsch (Eds.). *Conflicts in Feminism*. New York: Routledge.

Delmar, Rosalyn. (1986). "What Is Feminism?" In Juliet Mitchell and Ann Oakley (Eds.). *What Is Feminism*. Oxford: Blackwell.

Dworkin, Andrea. (1987). *Intercourse*. New York: Free Press.

Echols, Alice. (1989). *Daring to Be Bad: Radical Feminism in America 1967–1975*. Minneapolis: University of Minnesota Press.

Enloe, Cynthia. (1989). *Bananas, Beaches and Bases: Making Feminist Sense of International Politics*. London: Pandora.

Flax, Jane. (1993). *Disputed Subjects: Essays on Psychoanalysis, Politics and Philosophy*. New York: Routledge.

Fraser, Nancy. (1989). *Unruly Practices: Power, Discourse and Gender in Contemporary Social Thought*. Minneapolis: University of Minnesota Press.

Frye, Marilyn. (1992). *Willful Virgin: Essays in Feminism*. Trumansburg. NY: Crossing.

Fuss, Diana. (1991). *Inside/out: Lesbian Theories, Gay Theories*. New York: Routledge.

Gilligan, Carol (Ed.). (1988). *Mapping the Moral Domain: A Contribution of Women's Thinking to Psychological Theory and Education*. Cambridge, MA: Center for the Study of Gender, Education and Human Development, Harvard University.

Grant, Judith. (1993). *Fundamental Feminisms: Contesting the Core Concepts of Feminist Theory*. New York: Routledge.

Grosz, Elizabeth. (1994). *Volatile Bodies: Toward a Corporeal Feminism*. Bloomington: Indiana University Press.

Haraway, Donna. (1991). *Simians, Cyborgs, and Women: The Reinvention of Nature*. New York: Routledge.

————. (1989). *Primate Visions: Gender, Race, and Nature in the World of Modern Science*. New York: Routledge.

Harding, Sandra (Ed.). (1993). *The "Racial" Economy of Science: Toward a Democratic Future*. Bloomington: Indiana University Press.

————. (1991). *Whose Science? Whose Knowledge?: Thinking from Women's Lives*. Ithaca, NY: Cornell.

Hartsock, Nancy. (1987). "The Feminist Standpoint: Developing the Ground for a Specifically Feminist Historical Materialism." In Sandra Harding (Ed.). *Feminism and Methodology*. Bloomington: Indiana University Press.

Heilbrun, Caroline. (1989). *Writing a Woman's Life*. New York: Norton.

Hirsch, Marianne, and Evelyn Fox Keller (Eds.). (1992). *Conflicts in Feminism*. New York: Routledge.

hooks, bell. (1989). *Talking Back: Thinking Feminist, Thinking Black*. Boston: South End.

————. (1994). *Teaching to Transgress: Education as the Practice of Freedom*. New York: Routledge.

————. (1990). *Yearning: Race, Gender and Cultural Politics*. Boston: South End.

Hubbard, Ruth. (1993). *The Politics of Women's Biology*. New York: Routledge.

Irigaray, Luce. (1993). *An Ethics of Sexual Difference*. (Carolyn Burke and Gillian Gill, Trans.). Ithaca, NY: Cornell.

James, Stanlie, and Abenia Busia. (1993). *Theorizing Black Feminisms*. New York: Routledge.

Jardine, Alice, and Paul Smith. (1987). *Men in Feminism*. London: Methuen.

Kaplan, E. Ann. (1992). *Motherhood and Representation: The Mother in Popular Culture and Melodrama*. New York: Routledge.

King, Ynestra. (Ed.) with Adrienne Harris. (1989). *Rocking the Ship of State: Toward a Feminist Peace Politics*. Boulder, CO: Westview.

MacKinnon, Catharine. (1987). *Feminism Unmodified: Discourses on Life and Law*. Cambridge, MA: Harvard.

———. (1989). *Toward a Feminist Theory of the State*. Cambridge, MA: Harvard.

Martin, Emily. (1987). *The Woman in the Body: A Cultural Analysis of Reproduction*. Boston: Beacon.

McClintock, Ann. (1995). *Imperial Leather: Race, Gender and Sexuality in the Imperial Conquest*. New York: Routledge.

Mies, Maria. (1986). *Patriarchy and Accumulation on a World Scale*. London: Zed Books.

———, and Vandan Shiva. (1993). *Ecofeminism*. London: Zed Books.

Modleski, Tanya. (1991). *Feminism Without Women: Culture and Criticism in a "Postfeminist" Age*. New York: Routledge.

Morrison, Toni. (1992). *Playing in the Dark: Whiteness and the Literary Imagination*. New York: Vintage.

Nicholson, Linda. (1990). *Feminism/Postmodernism*. New York: Routledge.

Petchesky, Rosalind. (1986). *Abortion and Woman's Choice*. London: Verso.

Phelan, Shane. (1991). *Identity Politics: Lesbian Feminism and the Limits of Community*. Philadelphia: Temple.

Plaskow, Judith. (1990). *Standing Again at Sinai: Judaism From a Feminist Perspective*. New York: Harper and Row.

———, and Carol P. Christ (Eds.). (1989). Weaving the Visions: New Patterns in Feminist Spirituality. San Francisco: Harper and Row.

Pollock, Griselda. (1988). *Vision and Difference: Feminity, Feminism and Histories of Art*. London: Routledge.

Riley, Denise. (1988). *"Am I that Name?": Feminism and the Category of "Women" in History*. London: Macmillan.

Roof, Judith. (1991). *A Lure of Knowledge: Lesbian Sexuality and Theory*. New York: Columbia.

Sandoval, Chela. (1995). "US Third World Feminism: The Theory and Method of Oppositional Consciousness in the Postmodern World." In Judith Kegan Gardiner (Ed.). *Provoking Agents: Gender and Agency in Theory and Practice*. Urbana: University of Illinois Press.

Sayers, Janet, et al. (Eds.). (1987). *Engels Revisited: New Feminist Essays*. London: Tavistock.

Schor, Naomi, and Elizabeth Weed (Eds.). (1994). *The Essential Difference*. New York: Routledge.

Scott, Joan Wallach. (1988). *Gender and the Politics of History*. New York: Columbia.

Sedgwick, Eve. (1991). *Epistemology of the Closet*. Berkeley: University of California Press.

Showalter, Elaine. (1990). *Sexual Anarchy: Gender and Culture at the Fin de Siecle*. New York: Viking.

Silverman, Kaja. (1988). *The Acoustic Mirror: Female Voice in Psychoanalysis and Cinema*. Bloomington: Indiana University Press.

Smith, Dorothy. (1988). *The Everyday World as Problematic*. Boston: Northeastern.

Spelman, Elizabeth. (1987). *Inessential Woman*. Boston: Beacon.

Spivak, Gayatri. (1986). *In Other Worlds: Essays in Cultural Politics*. London: Methuen.

Stanworth, Michelle. (Ed.). (1987). *Reproductive Technologies: Gender, Motherhood, and Medicine*. Minneapolis: University of Minnesota Press.

Suleiman, Susan. (1986). *The Female Body in Western Culture*. Cambridge, MA: Harvard.

Trinh, T. Minh Ha. (1989). *Woman/Native/Other: Writing Postcoloniality and Feminism.* Bloomington: Indiana University Press.

Williams, Patricia. (1991). *Alchemy of Race and Rights.* Cambridge, MA: Harvard.

Young, Iris Marion. (1990). *Throwing Like a Girl and Other Essays in Feminist Philosophy and Social Theory.* Princeton, NJ: Princeton.

Zimmerman, Bonnie. (1991). *The Safe Sea of Women: Lesbian Fiction 1969–1989.* Boston: Beacon.

FURTHER READING OUTSIDE THE READER

Bodies

Mary Douglas. (1991). *Purity and Danger: An Analysis of Concepts of Pollution and Taboo.* New York: Routledge. (Original work published 1966)

Jacques Lacan. (1977). "The Signification of the Phallus." *Ecrits: A Selection.* Trans. Alan Sheridan. New York: Norton. (Original work published 1966)

Boston Women's Health Collective. (1971). *Our Bodies, Our Selves.* New York: Simon and Schuster.

Laura Mulvey. (1975). "Visual Pleasure and Narrative Cinema." *Screen.* Rptd. (1989) in *Visual and Other Pleasures.* Bloomington, IN: Indiana University Press.

Adrienne Rich. (1976). *Of Woman Born: Motherhood as Institution and Experience.* New York: Norton.

Claudia Dreifus (Ed.). (1977). *Seizing Our Bodies: The Politics of Women's Health.* New York: Vintage.

Susan Griffin. (1978). *Woman and Nature: The Roaring Inside Her.* New York: Harper.

Angela Davis. "Rape, Racism and the Myth of the Black Rapist." *Women, Race and Class.* New York: Random House.

Alice Walker. (1983). "Beauty: When the Other Dancer Is the Self." Walker, Alice. *In Search of Our Mother's Gardens.* New York: Harcourt Brace.

Audre Lorde. (1984). "The Uses of the Erotic" from *Sister/Outsider.* Trumansburg, NY: Crossing.

Evelyn Hammonds. (1986). "Missing Persons: African American Women, AIDS, and the History of Disease." *Radical America* 20, No. 6, 7–23.

Susan Suleiman. (1986). *The Female Body in Western Culture.* Cambridge, MA: Harvard.

Donna Haraway. (1989). "The Biopolitics of the Post Modern Body."

Emily Martin. (1991). *The Woman in the Body: A Cultural Analysis of Reproduction.* Boston: Beacon.

Nancy Cott. (1990). "Historical Perspectives: The Equal Rights Amendment Conflict in the 1920s." Evelyn Fox Keller and Marianne Hirsch (Eds). In *Conflicts in Feminism.* New York: Routledge.

Ruth Hubbard. (1990). *The Politics of Women's Biology.* New York: Routledge.

Iris Marion Young. (1990). *Throwing Like a Girl and Other Essays.* Princeton, NJ: Princeton.

Susan Bordo. (1993). *Unbearable Weight: Feminism, Western Culture and the Body.* Berkeley, CA: University of California Press.

Judith Butler. (1993). *Bodies That Matter.* Berkeley, New York: Routledge.

Epistemologies

Audre Lorde. (1984). "The Master's Tools Will Never Dismantle the Master's House." Rptd. (1979) in *Sister/Outsider.* Trumansburg, NY: Crossing.

Myra Jehlen. (1981). "Archimedes and the Paradox of Feminist Criticism." *Signs* 6: 4.

Sandra Harding and Merrill B. Hintikka (Eds.). (1983). *Discovering Reality: Feminist Perspectives on Epistemology, Metaphysics, Methodology, and Philosophy of Science.* Boston: D. Reidel.

Nancy Hartsock. (1983). "The Feminist Standpoiont: Developing the Ground of a Specifically Feminist Historical Materialism." *Money, Sex and Power: Toward a Feminist Historical Materialism.*

Alison Jaggar (Ed.). (1983). *Feminist Politics and Human Nature.* Totowa, NJ: Roman and Allenheld.

bell hooks. (1984). *Feminist Theory: From Margin to Center.* Boston: South End.

Adrienne Rich. (1986). "Notes Toward a Politics of Location." *Blood, Bread and Poetry: Selected Prose, 1979–1985.* New York: Norton. (Original essay published 1984)

Mary Field Belenky *et. al.* (Eds.). (1986). *Women's Ways of Knowing: The Development of Self, Voice, and Mind.* New York: Basic Books.

Rey Chow. (1989). "'It's You and Not Me: Domination and 'Othering' in Theorizing the 'Third World.'" In Elizabeth Weed (Ed.). *Coming to Terms.* New York: Routledge.

Uma Narayan. (1989). "The Project of Feminist Epistemology: Perspectives Form a Non-Western Feminist." In Alison M. Jaggar and Susan Bordo (Eds.). *Gender/Body/Knowledge: Feminist Reconstructions of Being and Knowing.* New Brunswick: Rutgers University Press.

Norma Alarcon. (1990). "The Theoretical Subjects of *This Bridge Called My Back* and Anglo-American Feminism." *Making Face/Making Soul.* San Francisco: Aunt Lute.

Donna Haraway. (1991). "Situated Knowledge: The Science Question in Feminism and the Privilege of Partial Perspective." *Simians, Cyborgs and Women.* New York: Routledge.

Linda Alcoff (Ed.). (1993). *Feminist Epistemologies.* New York: Routledge.

Essentialism/Social Construction/Difference

Florence Nightingale. (1979). *Cassandra.* New York: Feminist Press. (Original work published 1852–1859)

Mary Daly. (1978). *Gyn/Ecology: A Metaethics of Radical Feminism.* Boston: Beacon.

bell hooks. (1984). *Feminist Theory: From Margin to Center.* Boston: South End.

Gayatri Spivak. (1993). Interview Sara Danius and Stefan Jonsson. *Boundary 2.*

———. (1987). *In Other Worlds: Essays in Cultural Politics.* London: Methuen.

Denise Riley. (1988). *'Am I that Name?': Feminism and the Category of 'Women' in History.* London: Macmillan.

Elizabeth V. Spelman. (1988). *Inessential Woman: Problems of Exclusion in Feminist Thought.* Boston: Beacon.

Rosi Braidotti. (1989). "The Politics of Ontological Difference." In Teresa Brennan (Ed.). *Between Psychoanalysis and Feminism.* New York: Routledge.

Ruth Hubbard. (1990). *The Politics of Women's Biology.* New York: Routledge.

Judith P. Butler. (1993). *Bodies That Matter: On the Discursive Limits of 'Sex.'* New York: Routledge.

Naomi Schor and Elizabeth Weed (Eds.). (1994). *The Essential Difference.* New York: Routledge.

Teresa de Lauretis. (1991). "Upping the Anti (sic) in Feminist Theory." In Evelyn Fox Keller and Marianne Hirsch (Eds.). *Conflicts in Feminism.* New York: Routledge.

Intersections of Race, Class, and Gender

Charlotte Bunch. (1987). "Not for Lesbians Only." Rptd. in *Passionate Politics.* New York: St. Martin's. (Original work published 1975)

Barbara Smith. (Oct. 1977). "Toward a Black Feminist Criticism." *Conditions: Two,* 1, no. 2.

Audre Lorde. (1984). "The Master's Tools Will Never Dismantle the Master's House." Rptd. (1979) in *Sister/Outsider.* Trumansburg, NY: Crossing.

Gloria Hull, Patricia Bell Scott, and Barbara Smith. (1982). *All the Women Are White, All the Blacks Are Men, but Some of Us Are Brave.* Old Westbury, NY: Feminist Press.

Bonnie Dill. (1983, Spring). "Race, Class and Gender: Prospects for an All-Inclusive Sisterhood." *Feminist Studies.* Vol. 9, 131–150.

Cherrie Moraga and Gloria Anzaldúa. (1983). *This Bridge Called My Back: Writing by Radical Women of Color.* Kitchen Table: Women of Color Press.

Adrienne Rich. (1986). "Notes Toward a Politics of Location." *Blood, Bread, and Poetry: Selected Prose, 1979–1985.* (Original work published 1984)

bell hooks. (1984). *Feminist Theory: From Margin to Center.* Boston: South End.

Deborah King. (Autumn 1988). "Multiple Jeopardy, Multiple Consciousness: The Context of Black Feminist Ideology." *Signs: Journal of Women in Culture and Society.* Vol. 14, no. 1, 42–72.

Teresa Amott and Julie Matthei. (1991). *Race, Gender and Work: A Multicultural Economic History of Women in the United States.*

Sandra Harding. (1991). "Thinking from the Perspective of Lesbian Lives." *Whose Science? Whose Knowledge?*

Shirley Geok-lin Lim. (1993). "Feminist and Ethnic Theories in Asian American Literature." *Feminist Studies.*

Zillah Eisenstein. (1994). *The Color of Gender: Reimagining Democracy.* Berkeley: University of California Press.

Beverly Guy-Sheftall. (1995). *Words of Fire.* New York: New Press.

Language

Julia Kristeva. (1980). *Desire in Language.* Ed. Leon S. Roudiez. Trans. Thomas Gora, Alice Jardine, and Leon S. Roudiez. New York: Columbia. (Original work published 1969)

Adrienne Rich. (1971). "When Dead Awaken: Writing as Revision." *On Lies, Secrets and Silence.* New York: Norton.

Mary Daly. (1973). *Beyond God the Father.* Boston: Beacon.

Nancy Henley and Barrie Thorne. (1975). *Language and Sex: Difference and Dominance.* Rowley, MA: Newbury House.

Robin Lakoff. (1975). *Language and Woman's Place.* New York: Harper & Row.

Lillian Robinson. (1983, Spring). "Treason Our Text: Feminist Challenges to the Literary Canon." *Tulsa Studies in Women's Literature.* Vol. 2, no. 1.

Tillie Olsen. (1978). *Silences.* New York: Delacorte.

Annette Kolodny. (1980, Spring). "Dancing Through the Minefield: Some Observations on the Theory, Practice, and Politics of a Feminist Literary Criticism." *Feminist Studies.* Vol. 6, no. 1, 1–25.

Dale Spender. (1980). *Man Made Language.* New York: Pergamon.

Ann Rosalind Jones. (1981, Summer). "Writing the Body: Toward an Understanding of L'Ecriture Feminine." *Feminist Studies.* Vol. 7, no. 2, 247–263.

Rosemary Radford Ruether. (1983). *Sexism and God-Talk: Toward a Feminist Theology.* Boston: Beacon.

Toril Moi. (1985). *Sexual/Textual Politics.* London: Routledge.

Deborah Cameron. (1985). *Feminism and Linguistic Theory.* London: Macmillan.

Mary Daly. (1987). *Webster's First New Intergalactic Wickedary of the English Language.* Boston: Beacon.

Deborah Cameron. (1990). *The Feminist Critique of Language.* New York: Routledge.

Elizabeth Wright (Ed.). (1992). *Feminism and Psychoanalysis: A Critical Dictionary.* London: Blackwell.

Sexual Division of Labor

Alexandra Kollontai. (1908). *The Social Basis of the Woman Question.*

———. (1920). *Communism and the Family.* Cleveland: Hera Press.

Juliet Mitchell. (1971). *Woman's Estate.* Harmondsworth, UK: Penguin.

Sheila Rowbowthan. (1973). *Women's Consciousness, Man's World.* Harmondsworth, UK: Penguin.

Christine Delphy. (1975). *Close to Home: A Materialist Analysis of Women's Oppression.* London: Hutchinson.

Zillah Eisenstein. (1979). *Capitalist Patriarchy and the Case for Socialist Feminism.* Monthly Review P.

Michelle Barrett. (1980). *Women's Oppression Today.* London: Verso.

Angela Davis. (1981). *Women, Race and Class.* New York: Random House.

Nancy Hartsock. (1981). *Money, Sex and Power: Toward a Feminist Historical Materialism.* New York: Longman.

Lourdes Beneria. (1982). *Women and Development.* New York: Praeger.

Annette Fuentes and Barbara Ehrenreich. (1983). *Women in the Global Factory.* Boston: South End Press.

Maria Mies. (1986). *Patriarchy and Accumulation on a World Scale.* London: Zed Books.

Jane Humphries. (1987). "Origins of the Family, Born Out of Scarcity Not Wealth." In Janet Sayers *et al.* (Eds.). *Engels Revisited: New Feminist Essays.* London: Routledge.

Janet Henshall Momsen, Vivian Kinnaird (Eds.). (1993). *Different Places, Different Voices: Gender and Development in Africa, Asia, and Latin America.* New York: Routledge.

Sexualities

Ann Koedt. (1973). "The Myth of the Vaginal Orgasm." In Ann Koedt and Ellen Levine (Eds.). *Radical Feminism.* New York: Quadrangle.

Michel Foucault. (1989). *History of Sexuality.* Trans. Robert Hurley. New York: Vintage.

Judith Walkowitz. (1980). *Prostitution and Victorian Society: Women, Class and the State.* Cambridge: Cambridge University Press.

Monique Witting. (1981). "One Is Not Born a Woman." *Feminist Issues.* Vol. 1, no. 2, 47–54.

Carole Vance. (1984). *Pleasure and Danger: Exploring Female Sexuality.* New York: Routledge.

Ti-Grace Atkinson. (1984). *Amazon Odyssey.* New York: Links.

Sheila Jeffrey. (1985). *The Spinster and Her Enemies: Feminism and Sexuality 1880–1930.* London: Pandora.

Charlotte Bunch. (1987). *Passionate Politics.* New York: St. Martin's.

Andrea Dworkin. (1987). *Intercourse.* New York: Free Press.

Dorchen Leidholdt and Janice Raymond. (1990). *The Sexual Liberals and the Attack on Feminism.* New York: Pergamon.

Eve Sedgwick. (1991). *Epistemology of the Closet.* Berkeley: Unviersity of California Press.

Leslie Feinberg. (1993). *Stone Butch Blues.* Ithaca, NY: Firebrand Books.

Cheryl Clarke. (1983). "Lesbianism: An Act of Resistance." In Cherrie Moraga and Gloria Anzaldúa. (Eds.). *This Bridge Called My Back: Writing by Radical Women of Color.* Kitchen Table: Women of Color Press.

bell hooks. (1994). *Outlaw Culture: Resisting Representations.* New York: Routledge.

"Third World"/Global Feminism

Robin Morgan (Ed.). (1984). *Sisterhood Is Global: The International Women's Movement Anthology.* Garden City: Doubleday.

Eleanor Leacock and Safa. (1986). *Women's Work: Development and the Division of Labor by Gender.* South Hadley, MA: Bergin and Garvey.

Maria Mies. (1986). *Patriarchy and Accumulation on a World Scale.* London: Zed Books.

Gayatri Spivak. (1987). *In Other Worlds: Essays in Cultural Politics.* London: Methuen.

Aihwa Ong. (1988). "Colonialism and Modernity: Feminist Re-presentations of Women in Non-Western Societies." *Inscriptions.* Vol. 3. no. 4, 79–93.

Charlotte Bunch. (1987). "Bringing the Global Home": "Prospects for Global Feminism" "Reflections on Global Feminism after Nairobi." *Passionate Politics.* New York: St. Martin's.

Cynthia Enloe. (1989). *Bananas, Beaches and Bases: Making Feminist Sense of International Politics.* Berkeley: University of California Press.

Rey Chow. (1993). *Writing Diaspora.* Bloomington, IN: Indiana University Press.
Rosi Braidotti *et al.* (Eds.). (1994). *Women, the Environment and Sustainable Development: Towards a Theoretical Synthesis.* London: Zed Books.
Ann McClintock. (1995). *Imperial Leather: Race, Gender and Sexuality in the Imperial Context.* New York: Routledge.

Credits

Cornell University Press. Used by permission of the publisher.

HEIDI HARTMANN, "The Unhappy Marriage of Marxism and Feminism: Towards a More Progressive Union" by Heidi Hartmann 1981. Reprinted by permission of South End Press.

CAROLYN HEILBRUN, from *Toward a Recognition of Androgyny.* Copyright © 1973 W. W. Norton & Co. Reprinted by permission of the publisher.

BELL HOOKS, "Feminism: A Transformational Politic" from *Talking Back: Thinking Black, Thinking Feminist* by bell hooks. Reprinted by permission of South End Press.

BELL HOOKS, "Theory as Liberatory Practice." From *Teaching to Transgress* by bell hooks. Copyright © 1994 Gloria Watkins. Reproduced by permission of Routledge, Inc.

KAREN HORNEY, from *Feminine Mystique.* Copyright © 1967 by W. W. Norton & Company, Inc. Reprinted by permission of W. W. Norton & Company, Inc.

LUCE IRIGARAY, from *This Sex Which Is Not One.* Copyright © 1977 by Editions de Minuit. English translation reprinted from Elaine Marks and Isabelle de Courtivron's, eds., *New French Feminisms: An Anthology,* Amherst: University of Massachusetts Press, 1980. Copyright © 1980 by the University of Massachusetts Press.

E. ANN KAPLAN, "Is the Gaze Male?" from *Women & Film: Both Sides of the Camera* by E. Ann Kaplan. Copyright © 1983 E. Ann Kaplan. Reprinted by permission of Routledge, Inc.

EVELYN FOX KELLER, from *Feminist Studies, Critical Studies,* edited by Tere De Lauretis. Reprinted by permission of Indiana University Press.

FLORYNCE KENNEDY, "A Comparative Study: Accentuating the Similarities of the Societal Position of Women and Negroes," from *Color Me Flo: My Hard Life and Good Times.* Copyright © 1976 by Florynce R. Kennedy. Reprinted with permission of Simon & Schuster.

YNESTRA KING, "Feminism and the Revolt of Nature" from *Heresies,* no. 13, 1981. Reprinted with permission from the author.

CHERIS KRAMARAE, PAULA TREICHLER, from *The Feminist Dictionary,* 1985 with permission from the authors.

AUDRE LORDE, Reprinted with permission from "Poetry Is Not a Luxury" in *Sister/Outsider: Essays and Speeches.* Copyright © 1984 The Crossing Press. With permission from the publisher.

AUDRE LORDE, Reprinted with permission from "Age, Race, Class, and Sex: Women Redefining Difference" in *Sister/Outsider: Essays and Speeches.* Copyright © 1984 The Crossing Press. With permission from the publisher.

MARIA C. LUGONES, ELIZABETH V. SPELMAN, "Have We Got a Theory for You! Feminist Theory, Cultural Imperialism and the Demand for 'The Woman's Voice'" from *Women's Studies International Forum,* No. 6, pp. 573–581, 1983. Reprinted with permission from Elsevier Science.

CATHARINE M. MACKINNON, "Sexuality" as appeared in *Feminist Theory of the State* (1989). Reprinted by permission of the author.

MARGARET MEAD, from *Sex and Temperament in Three Primitive Societies* by Margaret Mead. Copyright © 1935, 1950, 1963 by Margaret Mead. Reprinted by permission of William Morrow & Company, Inc.

FATIMA MERNISSI, from *Beyond the Veil: Male-Female Dynamics in Modern Muslim Society.* Reprinted by permission of Indiana University Press.

CASEY MILLER, KATE SWIFT, "Semantic Polarization" from *Words and Women, Updated*-HarperCollins 1991 (Anchor Press/Doubleday, 1976). Reprinted by permission of the authors.

KATE MILLETT, *Sexual Politics.* Copyright © 1969, 1970, 1990 by Kate Millett. Reprinted by permission of Georges Borchardt, Inc. for the author.

ELIZABETH MINNICH, from "Chapter V: Back to Basics" included in *Transforming Knowledge* by Elizabeth Minnich. Copyright © 1990 by Temple University Press. All Rights Reserved. With Permission from the publisher.

CHANDRA TALPADE MOHANTY, "Under Western Eyes: Feminist Scholarship and Colonial Discourses" by Chandra Talpade Mohanty from *Third World Women and the Politics of Feminism,* edited by Chandra Talpade Mohanty, Ann Russo, and Lourdes Torres, Indiana University Press, 1991. Reprinted by permission of the author.

PAULI MURRAY, "The Liberation of Black Women." Copyright © 1970 by Pauli Murray. Reprinted by permission of The Charlotte Sheedy Literary Agency, Inc.

NATIONAL ORGANIZATION FOR WOMEN, INC., Reprinted by permission of the National Organization for Women. This is a historical document (1966) and does not reflect the current language or priorities of the organization.

OLDER WOMEN'S LEAGUE, "Why Owl?" reprinted by permission.

SHERRY B. ORTNER, from *Woman, Culture, and Society* edited by Michelle Zimbalist Rosaldo and Louise Lamphere with permission of the publishers, Stanford University Press. Copyright © 1974 by the Board of Trustees of the Leland Stanford Junior University.

ELAINE H. PAGELS, "What Became of God the Mother? Conflicting Images of God in Early Christianity" from *The Signs Reader.* Reprinted by permission of The University of Chicago Press and the author.

EMMA PÉREZ, "Speaking from the Margin: Uninvited Discourse on Sexuality and Power" from *Building With Our Hands: New Directions in Chicana Studies.* Copyright © 1993 The Regents of the University of California. Reprinted by permission of The University of California Press and the author.

JUDITH PLASKOW, "Jewish Memory From a Feminist Perspective" reprinted from *Tikkun* Magazine, a bi-monthly Jewish Critique of Politics, Culture, and Society. Information and subscriptions are available from Tikkun, 26 Fell Street, San Francisco, CA 94102.